Writing
the
Range

Writing the Range

Race, Class, and Culture in the Women's West

Edited and with Introductions by
Elizabeth Jameson and Susan Armitage

University of Oklahoma Press : Norman and London

The following articles were first published, in slightly different versions, as follows, and are reprinted in this volume by permission of the authors and the publishers. "Race, Gender, and Intercultural Relations," by Peggy Pascoe; "Dead Ends or Gold Mines?," by Vicki Ruiz; and "Desperately Seeking 'Deirdre,'" by Valerie Matsumoto, *Frontiers* 12, no. 1 (1991): 5–18, 33–56, 19–32. "Mexican American Women Grassroots Community Activists," by Mary Pardo, *Frontiers* 11, no. 1 (1990): 1–7. "The Women of Lincoln County, 1860–1900," by Darlis A. Miller, in *New Mexico Women: Intercultural Perspectives,* ed. Joan M. Jensen and Darlis A. Miller (Albuquerque: University of New Mexico Press, 1986), 169–200. "'I See What I Have Done,'" by Coll-Peter Thrush and Robert H. Keller, Jr., *Western Historical Quarterly* 26, no. 2 (Summer 1995): 169–83. "'Yo Sola Aprendi,'" by Genaro Padilla, in *Revealing Lives: Autobiography, Biography, and Gender,* ed. Susan G. Bell and Marilyn Yalom (Albany: State University of New York Press, 1990), 115–29. Copyright by the publisher. "Beyond the Stereotypes," by Annette White-Parks, in *Women and the Journey: The Female Travel Experience,* ed. Bonnie Frederick and Susan H. McLeod (Pullman: Washington State University Press, 1993), 100–16. "'We Are Women Irish,'" by Laurie Mercier, *Montana The Magazine of Western History* 44, no. 1 (Winter 1994): 28–41. "Lifting As We Climb," by Lynda F. Dickson, *Essays in Colorado History,* no. 13 (1992), 69–98. "Introduction to *Quiet Odyssey,*" by Sucheng Chan, in Mary Paik Lee, *Quiet Odyssey: A Pioneer Korean Woman in America,* ed. Sucheng Chan (Seattle: University of Washington Press, 1990), xxi–lx, 179–201). "Tsugiki, a Grafting," by Gail M. Nomura, in *Women in Pacific Northwest History,* ed. Karen Blair (Seattle: University of Washington Press, 1988), 207–29. Cherríe Moraga's poem "The Welder," which appears in "Empowering 'The Welder,'" by Marian Perales, is reprinted by permission of the poet and Kitchen Table/Women of Color Press.

Library of Congress Cataloging-in-Publication Data

Writing the range: race, class, and culture in the women's West/edited with
   introductions by Elizabeth Jameson and Susan Armitage.
      p.   cm.
   Includes bibliographical references (p.) and index.
   1. Women—West (U.S.)—History.   2. Minority women—West (U.S.)—History.
3. Frontier and pioneer life—West (U.S.)—History.   4. West (U.S.)—Race relations—
History.   5. West (U.S.)—Ethnic relations—History.   I. Jameson, Elizabeth.
II. Armitage, Susan H. (Susan Hodge).
HQ1410.W73   1997
305.4'0978—dc21   96-39163
ISBN 0–8061–2929–8 (cloth)   CIP
ISBN 0–8061–2952–2 (paper)

The paper in this book meets the guidelines for permanence and durability of the Committee on Production Guidelines for Book Longevity of the Council on Library Resources, Inc. ∞

1 2 3 4 5 6 7 8 9 10

Dedication

For Our Children, E.V., Amy, Julia, Peter, and Daniel

Contents

Illustrations

Acknowledgments

This book represents the work and energy of many authors of the new ethnic, women's, and western histories. We are grateful to everyone who has helped stimulate the ferment of new ideas in which we have been fortunate to work and from whose work and criticism we have benefited. We especially want to thank our talented, outspoken, and inquisitive graduate students for their part in our shared discussions.

We owe a special debt to the authors in this volume and to the colleagues who introduced us to them, especially Dick Etulain, Estelle Freedman, Mary Murphy, and Vicki Ruiz. Quintard Taylor generously shared his own research with us. Sucheng Chan kindly acceded to our late request for an edited article; her administrative assistant, Sally Foxen, was especially helpful in managing the details. Joan Jensen, Beverly Guy-Sheftall, Patricia Albers, Sarah Deutsch, Gail Nomura, and several anonymous reviewers provided helpful comments on articles and introductions at various stages of the editing process. The University of New Mexico Press, University of Washington Press, Washington State University Press, State University of New York Press, *Western Historical Quarterly*, *Essays in Colorado History*, *Montana, The Magazine of Western History*, and *Frontiers: A Journal of Women Studies* generously allowed us to reprint articles. Cherríe Moraga and Kitchen Table/Women of Color Press granted permission to use Moraga's poem, "The Welder." We are grateful to them all.

We were fortunate to have the assistance of Leslie Downs at the beginning of this project and of Evelyn Schlatter, Dedra McDonald, Juneal Leversee, and Tom Gentry as we wound up the last ragged ends. Mary Ann Holland and Cindy Tyson cheerfully sent endless faxes. Barbara Radziemski and Loretta Hayoz faxed, phoned, kept track of details, and provided daily cheer. We are also grateful to Cathy Imboden and Alice Stanton at the University of Oklahoma Press and to Ursula Smith, copyeditor extraordinaire, for their attention to details.

We owe particular thanks to two individuals. Vicki Ruiz has, throughout our work, been unfailingly generous with advice, support, suggestions, and criticism. Our editor, John Drayton, encouraged us to undertake this project, remained supportive through its long gestation, facilitated the extensive review process we requested, and retained his patience and good humor even when the book took longer and got bigger than any of us expected. So, John, thanks. "Godzilla" is done.

Writing
the
Range

Editors' Introduction

This book grew from our commitment to an inclusive history that is yet to be written. We, like many other western women's historians, have opposed a national history told from the limited perspectives of the urban East, of public politics and power, of white Americans, and of men. We wanted western history to reflect the diverse cultures, genders, and races of the region; we wanted women's history to include women of all regions, races, and classes.

In our earlier anthology, *The Women's West*, we wrote that "western women's history must be inclusive. It should offer a multicultural economic perspective that includes all races and classes, in addition to both sexes."[1] That commitment, it turns out, is easier said than done.

BEYOND HISLAND

Susan Armitage opened the first Women's West Conference in 1983 with a description of "Hisland"—a mythic place perpetuated in western history texts and survey courses, where seldom was heard a discouraging word, and never a woman's voice. She evoked a historical landscape where, "under perpetually cloudless western skies, a cast of heroic characters engage in dramatic combat, sometimes with nature, sometimes with each other. Occupationally these heroes are diverse: they are mountain men, cowboys, Indians, soldiers, farmers, miners, and desperadoes, but they share one distinguishing characteristic—they are all men."[2]

They were also, except for the Indians, overwhelmingly white.

If women entered this landscape at all, they were either brief diversions in a saloon or brothel, or they were hazy supporting figures far in the background, stoically oppressed or angelically supportive, and certainly voiceless and passive. They were mostly all white, too.

If persons of color entered the scene, they were most likely Plains Indians on the far horizon, swooping down to be slaughtered, or, perhaps, an Indian Princess, like Sacagawea, who functioned as a prop in a Euro-American story of westward expansion, important only because she helped the whites achieve the inevitable triumphs of Manifest Destiny and European civilization.[3]

A great deal has changed since we published *The Women's West* in 1987. New western women's and ethnic histories have begun to change the historical landscape of Hisland. The West has become less heroic, less pastoral, the

3

cast of characters more diverse, the meanings of the drama more equivocal as historians hotly debate the elements of the story and its significance. The skies are often cloudy, we sometimes focus on what happens inside the home on the range, and we have certainly heard many a discouraging word.

The first step toward an inclusive history was to begin to imagine it. The second was to document the lives of the many peoples who have lived in what is now the western United States, an effort that has generated an exciting variety of new histories of women and people of color.[4] Ethnic history, women's history, and environmental history have all nourished a new western history, its focus considerably broader than the nineteenth-century Euro-American frontier, its actors considerably more diverse than the white male rugged individuals who were the sole inhabitants of Hisland. Recent works by new western historians emphasize diversities of race, ethnicity, class, and gender; conflicts among groups; struggles to control resources; social adaptation and cultural change; and relationships of power and dependency. The land itself, once portrayed as empty and virginal, is now seen to include the people who lived there and left their marks.[5]

The next steps toward inclusive histories are harder. We once suggested that the first steps we needed to take in western women's history were to see the West through women's eyes and to listen to women's words. Putting men's and women's perspectives together, we thought, would lead to a more accurate and fully dimensional history.[6] We have recovered unrecorded lives of many women, but it is less easy to put them all together. As we have moved from Hisland toward more realistic western histories, our historical landscape has become much richer—and much more complicated. There are many, many perspectives to be brought into common focus.

That task becomes more complex when we recognize the countless combinations of race, ethnicity, class, gender, age, religion, and many other factors that have helped shape cultures, communities, and identities in the West. Imagine all the women and men of all the hundreds of American Indian cultures, the Spanish Mexicans who settled the northern frontiers of New Spain, the French and British fur traders of the Upper Plains and Pacific Northwest. Imagine the new métis and mestizo peoples born to Indian mothers and French, Spanish, or British fathers. Now imagine all the successive waves of people who migrated to the West—Irish, Cornish, Welsh, Chinese, Japanese, Norwegians, Swedes, Germans from Russia, Russian and Polish and German Jews, Koreans, Filipinos, Finns, Italians, African Americans, Vietnamese, Cambodians, Laotians, and many others. The nineteenth-century West of Euro-American pioneer history was in fact the most culturally diverse section of the country. From 1860 to 1900 between a third and a fourth of all people living in the West had been born in another country.[7] When this immigrant population is added to second-generation immigrant children, and to native-born Indians and Mexican Americans, native-born Euro-Americans become a distinct minority. Now remember that for all these diverse people, there were also differences of class and gender and age and religion.

If we try, then, to imagine the West "through women's eyes," we must imagine how a common historical space appeared from many different lines of sight. Seen from all these perspectives, incorporating all these voices, western history becomes an incredibly dynamic story. The frameworks of older histories cannot hold all this diversity. To begin to hear the past in new ways, we must think of it as a series of conversations, not a monologue narrating the lives of individuals or of nation-states. The next steps, we believe, are to develop inclusive historical frameworks and to imagine historical narratives from many perspectives. This book is an effort in that direction—toward "writing the range," the full range of all the stories and of all the actors, into a common western history.

PREMISES AND DEFINITIONS: POWER, RACE, ETHNICITY, CLASS, AND GENDER

Inclusive history is essential because all people are historical actors. We say this because our basic premise is that most history begins with daily acts of ordinary people. Those acts create and maintain human social relations. As people change their behavior, they transform their relationships with other people. When men start changing diapers, or women leave abusive marriages, parenting and family relationships change. All people, then, are historical actors, and half of the actors are women. Among the most basic social interactions are those between men and women, parents and children. They create and re-create families, homes, and communities. In the process, people negotiate who will do what work and what behaviors are appropriate for each. That process of daily negotiation is something we have all experienced. It occurs as children lobby for later bedtimes, as family members discuss whose job it is to wash the dishes or take out the garbage. The mundane process of personal negotiation is fundamental to how people change their social roles and possibilities.

In the American West, as different people occupied the region, struggles to control the land and its resources engendered a series of conflicts among people of different races and ethnicities. The outcomes of those conflicts determined that people of particular races and ethnicities had greater power than others. The conquerors tended to think that their superior power was "natural," that different races possessed different qualities and abilities, that winners were obviously and naturally better than losers. But in fact, in the history of the American West, the racial power rankings have changed again and again. Countless territorial rivalries among Indian peoples preceded European colonization and continued after the Europeans shifted territorial boundaries. During the sixteenth century, Spanish colonizers conquered the native peoples of present-day New Mexico; in 1680 the Pueblos revolted and forced the Spanish Mexican colonists south for twelve years. Spanish colonial power, reestablished in 1692, ended with Mexican independence in 1821. Mexican control ended in turn in 1846 when the United States occupied New Mexico and California in the Mexican-American War. Farther north, in lands that later became parts of Canada and the United

States, the French, British, and finally Americans struggled with one another and with many native peoples in their quests to control the fur trade. Each of these public conquests brought new social relations among the conquerors and the conquered, including private encounters among women and men of different races. Their children, new peoples of mixed heritage, changed previous systems of race and ethnicity.

As these examples suggest, westerners of different heritages constantly redefined race and ethnicity in their relationships with one another. This process occurred at all social levels: in large arenas of political power, in the more immediate realms of access to jobs and skills, and in the personal choices of friends, neighbors, and sexual partners. An accurate western history therefore involves all the actors in these relationships, including women and men of all races, ethnicities, and classes.

Before we go further, some definitions seem in order. Like many historians, we think that race, ethnicity, class, and gender are not "natural" categories but, rather, are socially and historically constructed. One way to understand race and ethnicity as historical categories is to look at how labels change over time. Racial and ethnic categories established by governments or by people asserting their superiority over others often ignore internal distinctions that are important to the people they describe. Thus, people from many African tribes were combined into the category of "blacks" in the United States, just as many different indigenous Americans became "Indians"; as Dakota and Lakota became "Sioux"; as Chinese, Japanese, Vietnamese, and Filipinos all became "Asians"; and as people from England, Ireland, Germany, and Austria all became "Europeans" or "whites."

The various ways that people label race tells us a great deal about how race and ethnicity function in different cultures. In the Spanish colonies, an intricate system of ethnic designation connected class and race. Among the "Spanish Mexican" colonizers were people of Spanish, Indian, and African ancestries. Their colonial system recognized a variety of racial ethnic categories, including a variety of mixed-race categories that testified to the intermingling of all these groups: *mestizos* (persons descended from Spaniards and Mexican Indians), *coyotes* (Spanish and New Mexican Indian), *mulatos* (usually African and Spanish, but sometimes Spanish and Indian), *lobos* (a racial mixture), *color quebrado* (a racial mixture, possibly any combination of white, Indian, and African descent), and *genízaros* (detribalized Indians).[8] In the Spanish colonial system, moreover, these categories did not necessarily signify biological heritage; they could also denote class, so that a powerful person could acquire the top status of "Hispano," regardless of biological parentage. While the Spanish terms codified a system of status and the legacies of colonial sexual encounters, they also reduced the variety of Pueblo peoples (e.g., Acoma, Cochiti, Hopi, Taos) to "indios" and gave particular pueblos Spanish saints' names (Santo Domingo, San Felipe, Santa Clara). As these complex naming systems demonstrate, cultural changes occurred in interlocking systems of race, class, gender, and religion. What we call ourselves and what others call us is part of the continual historical process of creating social power and social relationships.[9]

Most Americans recognize the historical power of race and color. We know the significance of black and white, expressed in slavery and its historical legacy. "Black" and "white" were both invented social categories and included people with very different roots, cultures, and heritages. In the American West the color power systems were even more intricate and complicated. "Whiteness" still collapsed enormous differences of ethnic culture, religion, class, sexual orientation, and historical experience into a single identity that served mostly to exclude other peoples. Who was "white" and who was not determined access to jobs, schools, and public accommodations. Nonwhites were not allowed to marry whites, to eat with them in restaurants, swim with them in municipal swimming pools, or sit with them in theaters. But the racial boundaries were drawn differently throughout the West. In some circumstances, Mexican Americans were "white"; in others, they were not. The phrase "a white man's camp" was common in western mining towns, but maintaining a white man's camp could, in different areas, mean keeping out Indians, Chinese, Japanese, Mexican Americans, Italians, or Greeks. In some white men's camps Chinese were excluded, but not African Americans. "Whiteness" defined who was excluded. Whiteness was also important, however, for the differences it glossed over, like historical legacies that had divided Cornish Methodists, Irish Catholics, Ulster Protestants, German Lutherans, German Catholics, and German Jews. The notion that such disparate people shared a common identity was linked to the belief that assimilation was a desirable goal—for "whites" at least. White Americans might retain some ethnic identity but still forge a common bond with one another that superseded their ethnic roots.

The language of race and ethnicity, if used precisely, gets enormously complicated and often sounds awkward. In this volume we discuss women of many different races and ethnicities. Race and ethnicity are not the same thing, of course; one can be simultaneously Caucasian and Irish, German, Italian, Spanish, or Mexican American. In the United States, we have frequently collapsed ethnic distinctions into racial categories for purposes of establishing legal and social power relationships, so that people of different national and cultural heritages are lumped together as white, Asian, Indian, or black. As a shorthand for historically constructed and changing definitions of race and ethnicity, we have borrowed Evelyn Nakano Glenn's term "racial ethnic" to connote what are actually complex systems of identity and discrimination.[10]

The differences between racial ethnic categories and individual identities brings us to the slippery concept of ethnic culture. The concept of ethnic difference occurs when we label a group of people as somehow different from "us," whoever we think "we" are. The ethnic categories created by the majority are often based on prejudiced stereotypes and are part of a system of racial discrimination. Ethnic stereotypes reflect popular beliefs about ethnic traits, cultures, and traditions. Those images, and the ethnic labels themselves, may have very little to do with either group or individual identities. Ethnic cultures are not molds into which people of common backgrounds fit themselves. Some Italians serve fish on Christmas Eve, others eat turkey or ravioli; some Christians open Christmas presents on Christmas Eve, some on Christmas morning; some Jews keep kosher, others do not. Ethnic cultures are a broad range of shared mental resources from which we choose and which change over time. They are not static. They do not rigidly determine behavior. They provide a range of observances, values, and behaviors from which people draw their identities. Families are one primary place we learn culture and transform it through daily practice. In the interplay among heritage, ethnic labels, and individual identity, we each continually redefine the meanings of our own ethnic heritages and our understandings of race and ethnicity.[11]

Gender as a social category is equally complex. Whether one is male or female is, for the most part, a matter of biology. But the roles, values, and behaviors different people assign to that natural fact are enormously varied. "Gender" is the term we use to distinguish the many social and historical meanings associated with being physically male or female from biological sex itself. Gender is fundamentally a concept of relationship, since it occurs in relationships between the sexes. It involves different systems of family and kinship and how men and women operate within these structures; it defines acceptable sexual behavior, appropriate work roles, and differential access to authority and power for women and men. Like race and ethnicity, it is also constantly reevaluated and changed.

Of all the basic social categories, class is probably the one we see most easily as historically constructed, though in other times and cultures it seemed an unchanging fact of parentage and birth. It is not easy, however, to integrate class as a concept with other social categories like race, ethnicity, and gender. From women's perspectives, class is more complex than who controls the means of production and who works for wages. What is the class of a woman secretary who is married to a man who owns a factory? A professional nurse married to a carpenter? These two examples illustrate how gender relationships complicate class. They also suggest another connection among class, race, and gender—that all work, public and private, paid and unpaid, is generally allocated not only by class but by race and gender as well. Does the secretary do her own housework, or does she hire another woman to clean for her? Housework is generally assigned by gender (women do it), but it means different things depending on whether one delegates domestic work to servants or does one's own after putting in a full day cleaning someone else's house.

Class in the West reflects how particular relations of race and gender function in particular regional economies. Chinese men and Mexican American women, for instance, have both done domestic work in the West that in other times and regions was more commonly performed by Irish or African American women.

Finally, for each of us, our gender, racial ethnic identity, economic class, religion, and many other factors interact as we form our individual and group identities. If we understand how all our social experiences *together* construct our identities, we cannot assume that racial ethnic background *alone*, sex *alone*, religion *alone*, or class *alone* forge common bonds and common histories. We all have multiple sources of identity. If we are asked what is most important to how we see ourselves—our sex, our sexual orientation, our race, our ethnic heritage, our religion, our job, our class, our family—it's a little like being asked what's more a part of you, your right hand or your left foot. Our identities are not that separate. And the identities that concern us most here—race, ethnicity, gender, class—affect us all. Men's options and identities are influenced by gender relations. White people's positions are affected by relationships among races; rich people's options are embedded in class relations. Our common legacy is the history of those relationships.

CONCEIVING AN INCLUSIVE HISTORY

How then, in all this historical variety, do we find common lenses through which to view diverse experiences? Frameworks for inclusive history come from the things that bring diverse people into relationships with one another—migrations that bring us to the same place, economies that link us in unequal work relationships, systems of marriage and kinship that link us in intimate and reproductive relationships, the changing systems of racial privilege that linked us and separated our possibilities in the West. The West we inherit was, in the words of historian Peggy Pascoe, a cultural crossroads.[12] It was formed through exchanges among many different people, in which gender was always significant. In these contexts, we can look at the experiences of women of different racial ethnic groups through such lenses as work, intimate relationships, sexuality, reproduction, and access to power.

We begin this volume with a section that examines some of the ways older scholarship distorted racial ethnic women's lives and reviews efforts to write new histories from their perspectives. We examine the development of multicultural western women's histories and some of the conceptual issues that scholarship raises.

The rest of the book is roughly chronological in format. Conceptually, the image that governs its organization is succeeding waves of migrants who encounter people already living in the West. In each time period we introduce new arrivals; suggest some of the ways that women and gender changed as newcomers adapted to new places, possibilities, and constraints, and explore how cultural exchanges between the persisters and the newcomers affected previous racial ethnic gender relations and existing systems of social power. We begin our chronology with a section on colonial frontiers that examines how work, property, and sexuality all changed for the women of the northern Spanish colonies—Spanish Mexican, mestizo, and American Indian alike. The next section covers the period of roughly the mid-to-late nineteenth century. Here we see some of what happened to Spanish Mexican women after Mexicans won independence from Spain in 1821 and then after the U.S. victory in the Mexican-American war transferred northern Mexico to the United States in 1848. Now Mexican Americans, these women were part of a conquered minority whose own understandings of class and gender differed from the Euro-American newcomers'. As the United States expanded westward, it developed its own Indian policies, including programs designed to "civilize" Indians by settling them on family farms and efforts to teach "proper" Euro-American gender roles. We examine some of these experiments and the ways that various Indian women resisted and accommodated the new government regulations.

Next, in the section that covers the late nineteenth and early twentieth centuries, we introduce a variety of newcomers to the West, including the relatively few Chinese women who were allowed to emigrate to the United States and some of the Europeans who settled in the West. Three articles in this section explore the experiences of women of many different European origins, including Basques, Irish, Serbs, Croats, and Hungarians. They also force us to confront the immense ethnic diversity packed into the racial category "white."

Traditional Euro-American frontier history examined the period when women were most isolated. Preoccupied with establishing farms and families, they were often homebound by heavy workloads and constant childbearing. This narrow focus on the early years of settlement obscured subsequent efforts by women of all races to create community institutions like schools and churches and to organize on their own behalf for suffrage, married women's property laws, or protection of women from domestic abuse. Our next section examines some of the ways racial ethnic women organized for empowerment and for social and political reform. Race, class, and gender all shaped their agendas and their strategies. When we look at the issues that moved racial ethnic women to organize, we recognize that white women's organizing is only one piece of the history of western feminism. Similarly, histories of movements for racial equality are incomplete without accounts of racial ethnic women's organizing and their daily resistance to racial and gender discrimination.

Popular culture has been enormously powerful in constructing stereotypes and images that distort women of color. Yet culture, as we have noted, is constantly reconstructed. Thus the ways that popular culture affects group identity depend partly on its power to teach demeaning stereotypes and partly on the ways that people use cultural symbols for their own purposes. Our next section examines some of the ways mass culture manipulated and distorted the images of racial ethnic women and how the women in turn used older cultural forms and symbols as well as newer "American" models to build new identities for themselves.

In our final section we turn to the urban West that was the destination of many twentieth-century immigrants. We explore how World War II, long seen as an important turning point in western history, affected African American and Navajo women, both drawn to jobs in western war-related industries. After 1945, the West experienced social trends that affected the rest of the nation. Racial ethnic people were more concentrated in urban centers; women of all races increasingly worked for wages outside the home. We examine how urban life affected new movements for social justice through an organization of Mexican American mothers in East Los Angeles and explore the changing gender relationships of some of the newest western immigrants—the Cambodian, Laotian, and Vietnamese women who came to western cities, fleeing, for many reasons, the aftermaths of the Vietnam War. The book ends with an article that emphasizes the complex and changing meanings of race and gender through the history of the Brackettville Seminoles, a people of African American and Seminole heritage, whose already complex identities were changed by the African American civil rights movement and the promise of urban possibilities for rural Brackettville Seminole young people.

As different groups contested the right to control the West and its resources, they were linked in relationships of social inequality. Their encounters with one another left no one unchanged. As different people adapted to new western environments and social circumstances, and as they negotiated power and possibility, they changed prior understandings of race and gender. The articles in this volume focus on these key exchanges in western history.

Racial ethnic women have been, thus far, most visible in "mainstream" history texts when they came in contact with whites, and particularly with white men. It is important to recognize their significant roles in cross-cultural exchanges, particularly on the frontiers of the older history, where their importance was seldom acknowledged. But it is equally important to recognize that for most women the most common experiences and exchanges occurred with people of their own racial ethnic communities. A first step in rejecting the privileged position white experience has held in American history is to begin to see women of color as subjects of their own histories and not merely as supporting players in a Euro-American story.

A CHANGING WESTERN HISTORY

How then, does western history change if we include women of different races and cultures? We don't entirely know yet. But we do know that through the experiences of racial ethnic women, we see more clearly how power is distributed in relationships of race and class and gender. Social power, for instance, involves control of reproduction and sexuality. An obvious example is white power in the antebellum South, which depended on slave owners' ability to control African American women's sexuality and the children they bore. In the West, Europeans and Euro Americans tried to convert various Indian peoples to their standards of sexuality, family, and male authority. Part of Euro-American efforts to control Chinese and Japanese men in the West involved immigration regulations and laws to bar Chinese and Japanese women and thus restrict the men's marriage options.[13] And, as we have noted, the particular wage work available to racial ethnic women in different parts of the West depended on local economies and understandings about which jobs were appropriate for women and men and for people of different races. This does not mean that western women's history is all about victimization. It is also about sources of support and identity, daily acts of resistance, and organized movements that redefined relationships of race, gender, and social power.

We talked in *The Women's West* about expanding our historical vision. As this brief summary suggests, the histories of racial ethnic women enlarge our understanding of what is historically significant. We see families and sexuality as central to social identity and to systems of social control. We see both race and gender as ever-changing—and changeable—social experiences. And we begin to see more clearly how gender and race influence all the actors in western history, from the racially diverse prostitutes of mining and cattle towns to the miners, cowboys, and soldiers of traditional western lore. The Marlboro Man would not be the same without his masculinity and his whiteness.

As we rethink western history from many different perspectives, we will probably rethink standard historical periods. Expanding the cast in western history also expands the time frame. If we could truly reconstruct the history of the region, it would begin long before Europeans, Africans, and Asians arrived—and hence we would need new names for a period we call "precolonial" and rarely explore beyond that. "Precolonial" in this sense is also "prehistorical" and carries the unstated assumption that the important history began when the Europeans arrived. As Elliott West has commented, "One wonders how the Nez Perce and Navajos survived the boredom of long centuries waiting for invaders from the East to show up."[14]

We will need not only to expand our time frame but to look for more inclusive ways to separate time into periods that are meaningful for all the participants. Some historians, for instance, have called the period in U.S. history from roughly 1820 to 1850 "the age of the common man," a name that makes little sense for women or slaves. The period that U.S. history texts have called "the Progressive Era" is known in African American history as "the nadir," because during that time the South enacted repressive Jim Crow laws and lynchings occurred with horrifying frequency. Similarly, in the West, the promise of frontier opportunity is not a meaningful concept for most Indians. We will need to rethink how to divide our history into time periods that are meaningful for different "westerners."

Periodization is part of the larger task of considering which stories are most important to record and tell. That is one of the hardest leaps to make. The story of intrepid pioneers coming west, persevering, and overcoming hardship and obstacles to tame a difficult land and win a better future is highly seductive—unless, of course, you are one of the "obstacles" the pioneers "overcame." Part of what we are discovering is that the history we learn in school is pretty powerful. The versions of western history many of us inherited are very hard to get out of our minds. They subtly tell us that the actors we read about were important and the people who are missing were insignificant. For many people those stories established the standard of what was historically important. They separated private life from "history." So, sometimes "ordinary" people tried to shape the versions of their lives they presented to fit the histories they inherited. Part of seeing the past more inclusively is imagining new stories rather than fitting diverse lives into the partial and restricted plots of national expansion and conquest.

Reconceived from these perspectives, the histories of racial ethnic women shift the ways we see women, the West, and ultimately our national history. We look not just at the promise of western opportunities but at where people came from and how prior possibilities shaped their own measures of the successes, failures, and promise of the West. The time lines and periods change. The colonial period begins not with Jamestown and Plymouth but with St. Augustine and Santa Fe; the history of "westward" movements probably starts with the first migrations across the Bering land bridge. Our concepts of race change from the black/white dichotomy of southern history to a more complex set of shifting racial categories and hierarchies of racial ethnic privilege. Euro-Americans from the eastern United States are no longer the "norm," but one group in a more complex cast of historical actors. The westward migrations inspired by the United States's commitment to Manifest Destiny become only another chapter in a series of migrations to a contested territory. And we begin to see just how many different ways people interpreted what it meant to be female or male, how many malleable and variable customs knit gender in work, kinship, sexuality, and family, in relationships of power and privilege. We must consider how various women and men redefined manhood and womanhood and what the West, from their perspectives, promised for the textures of daily life.

These are enormous historical agendas. They will engage us for some time to come, and we expect to move very far from some of the starting points in this volume. The histories in this book, and other histories of race and gender in the West, will transform our collective pasts. But that is not the only reason, or even the most important reason, to make them available. The main reason to recover the lives of racial ethnic women is the same reason any people seek their past—to provide a sense of social ancestry that empowers us individually and collectively, because our histories are part of who we are and what we may become.

Our collective history is vitally important to us all. History must be inclusive because it is one of the fundamental ways we come to know ourselves and one another. It has become trendy to talk about inclusive history as simply "politically correct" and thus to dismiss much of the new history as the ideological ramblings of people with particular political agendas. We think, however, that inclusiveness is the only way to correct incomplete histories and the relationships of power they reflect. We cannot understand how social institutions are created, cultural values transmitted, or public power enacted without understanding the daily private experiences of work and family or the struggles over resources and policies in which losers as well as winners were part of the action. Accurate histories must include the relationships among all the actors.

A FINAL WORD

This brings us to some related issues of authorship and inclusiveness. We believe very strongly that inclusive histories can only be achieved by inclusive historians. Access to education, historical sources, and publishers determines who records the past and the pasts we have recorded. When we first decided to undertake this project, we were aware that as white women with particular sexual orientations, religious backgrounds, and ethnic, generational, and class experiences, we would bring our own perspectives to a book about women of many racial and ethnic cultures. We are not suggesting that historians can or should write only about their own personal heritages. But beyond simple issues of equity, we believe that particular experiences of race, class, gender, and culture suggest categories of analysis that enrich historical inquiry. Women historians, for instance, did not know what domestic work or childbearing was like in nineteenth-century America, but we did know these were important areas to explore in histories of nineteenth-century women. As more women became historians, our daily conversations opened up new areas of research and new ways to think about gender and history. A racially and culturally inclusive profession would extend our conversations to new ways to think about race, class, and culture in history.

We believe that inclusive history is a collective responsibility and that it requires a long-term commitment. No single volume can present more than a sampling of the enormous racial ethnic diversity of the West or document all the forms of racism, gender inequality, and class privilege that are part of our common legacy. There is a lot still to do to record those histories and to imagine historical frameworks to connect and interpret them. We are not experts in the histories of all the people in this volume. No one can be, which is why history must be a collective and collaborative enterprise. We saw this book as one step to make more materials available on the histories of racial ethnic women, so that we might imagine new ways to see the past.

We want to underline our personal beliefs about doing inclusive history, to stress that, however fashionable it may be to speak of multicultural history, the actual practice is difficult and demanding. It requires a substantial time commitment and an even greater commitment of the imagination. It demands a wide range of sources, collecting oral histories, and immersing oneself in different cultures and different systems of class and gender relationships. This work must be accompanied by the imaginative effort to recognize our own unconscious cultural values, to transcend the assumptions and frameworks of our own experience and of the histories we have inherited.

We have found that this process of historical revision is sometimes scary, because it requires us to question older frameworks that have explained our world and because the power relationships of race, class, and gender we confront in the process may raise feelings of pain or anger. We hope that this book stimulates a process of critical imagination for readers who want to think about the past in new and more inclusive ways and that it stimulates further conversations about the historical relationships that link us and the important tasks that engage us. The commitment to inclusiveness is a necessary step to end one historical legacy, the denial of our common past. The authors in this book take us farther on a journey toward an accurate history, created in the heat of daily struggles, affirmations, and resistance, a history that acknowledges power, pain, privilege, and the agency of all the players. They chronicle the lives of women who make it increasingly inconceivable to imagine a Hisland or an all-white West.

Notes

1. Susan Armitage and Elizabeth Jameson, eds., *The Women's West* (Norman: University of Oklahoma Press, 1987), 5.

2. Susan Armitage, "Through Women's Eyes: A New View of the West," in *Women's West*, 9–18; quote, 9. Western women's history as a separate field of historical study may be dated from two conferences—the Women's West Conference in Sun Valley, Idaho, 10–13 August 1983, and the "Western Women: Their Land, Their Lives" conference in Tucson, Arizona, 12–15 January 1984. Armitage's article was the opening keynote at the Women's West Conference. Anthologies published from these conferences are Armitage and Jameson, *The Women's West*, and Lillian Schlissel, Vicki Ruiz, and Janice Monk, eds., *Western Women: Their Land, Their Lives* (Albuquerque: University of New Mexico Press, 1988).

3. The Indian Princess was generally modeled on Pocahontas. For the folkloric roots of the Pocahontas figure and other stereotypes of Indian women, see Rayna Green, "The Pocahontas Perplex: The Image of Indian Women in American Culture," *Massachusetts Review* 16, no. 4 (1976): 698–714.

4. For histories of racial ethnic women, see Elizabeth Jameson, "Toward a Multicultural History of Women in the Western United States," *Signs* 13, no. 4 (Summer 1988): 761–91; Rayna Green, *Native American Women: A Contextual Bibliography* (Bloomington: Indiana University Press, 1983); Lyle Koehler, "Native American Women of the Americas: A Bibliography," *Frontiers* 6, no. 3 (Fall 1981): 73–101; Catherine Loeb, "La Chicana: A Bibliographic Survey," *Frontiers* 5, no. 2 (Summer 1980): 59–74; Lillian Castillo-Speed, "Chicana Studies: A Selected List of Materials since 1980," *Frontiers* 11, no. 1 (1990): 66–84; Lenwood G. Davis, *The Black Woman in American Society: A Selected Annotated Bibliography* (Boston: G. K. Hall, 1975); Lawrence B. De Graaf, "Race, Sex, and Region: Black Women in the American West, 1850–1920," *Pacific Historical Review* 49, no. 2 (May 1980): 285–314; Susan H. Armitage and Deborah Gallacci Wilbert, "Black Women in the Pacific Northwest: A Survey and Research Prospectus," in *Women in Pacific Northwest History: An Anthology*, ed. Karen J. Blair (Seattle: University of Washington Press, 1988), 136–51; Gail M. Nomura, "Significant Lives: Asia and Asian Americans in the History of the U.S. West," *Western Historical Quarterly* 25, no. 1 (Spring 1994): 69–88. Two useful anthologies are Sucheng Chan, Douglas Henry Daniels, Mario T. García, and Terry P. Wilson, eds., *Peoples of Color in the American West* (Lexington, Mass.: D. C. Heath, 1994); and Vicki L. Ruiz and Ellen Carol DuBois, eds., *Unequal Sisters: A Multicultural Reader in U.S. Women's History*, 2d ed. (New York: Routledge, 1994), which includes extensive bibliographies.

5. The new western history is a large, diverse, and vital field, which includes numerous topics, approaches, and considerable disagreement and debate. For a few representative works, see Patricia Nelson Limerick, *The Legacy of Conquest: The Unbroken Past of the American West* (New York: W. W. Norton, 1987); Richard White, *It's Your Misfortune and None of My Own: A New History of the American West* (Norman: University of Oklahoma Press, 1991); Patricia Nelson Limerick, Clyde A. Milner II, and Charles Rankin, eds., *Trails: Toward a New Western History* (Lawrence: University Press of Kansas, 1991); William Cronon, George Miles, and Jay Gitlin, eds., *Under an Open Sky* (New York: W. W. Norton, 1992); William Cronon, *Nature's Metropolis* (New York: Hill and Wang, 1983); Donald Worster, *Rivers of Empire: Water, Aridity, and the Growth of the American West* (New York: Pantheon, 1985); and Richard White, *The Roots of Dependency: Subsistence, Environment, and Social Change among the Choctaw, Pawnees, and Navajos* (Lincoln: University of Nebraska Press, 1983).

6. See Armitage, "Through Women's Eyes," and Elizabeth Jameson, "Women as Workers, Women as Civilizers: True Womanhood in the American West," in *Women's West*, 145–64.

7. Calculated from *Report on Population of the United States at the Eleventh Census: 1890*, pt. 1 (Washington, D.C.: U.S. Government Printing Office, 1895), 398–99; *Twelfth Census of the United States: 1900*, pt. 1 (Washington, D.C.: U.S. Census Office, 1901), 575–608, 736–95.

8. Virginia L. Olmsted, introduction to the 1790 Spanish colonial census of the Province of New Mexico, together with the 1823 and 1845; Fray Angelico Chávez, *Archives of the Archdiocese of Santa Fe, 1678–1900* (Washington, D.C.: Academy of American Franciscan History, 1957), 201.

9. Throughout this volume, the racial ethnic categories we use are chosen with historical and political contexts in mind. Thus, for example, people of Spanish and Mexican ancestry are called "Spanish Mexican" if they colonized the seventeenth-century northern Spanish frontier and "Mexican American" if they lived in the United States after 1848. "Chicano/a" is used here to connote the contemporary activist identity.

10. Evelyn Nakano Glenn, "Racial Ethnic Women's Labor: The Intersection of Race, Gender and Class Oppression," *Review of Radical Political Economics* 17, no. 3 (Fall 1985): 86–108.

11. This is an admittedly condensed discussion of a complex body of theory. For debated theories of culture, see Clifford Geertz, *The Interpretation of Culture* (New York: Basic Books, 1973), and James Clifford, *The Predicament of Culture: Twentieth Century Ethnography, Literature and Art* (Cambridge, Mass.: Harvard University Press, 1988). This discussion draws particularly on Micaela di Leonardo, *The Varieties of Ethnic Experience: Kinship, Class, and Gender among California Italian-Americans* (Ithaca, N.Y.: Cornell University Press, 1984), esp. 22–24, 215–17.

12. Peggy Pascoe, "Western Women at the Cultural Crossroads," in *Trails*, 40–58.

13. See Sucheng Chan, ed., *Entry Denied* (Philadelphia: Temple University Press, 1991), esp. chap. 4, Chan, "The Exclusion of Chinese Women, 1870–1943," 94–146; and Yuji Ichioka, *"Amerika Nadeshiko:* Japanese Immigrant Women in the United States, 1900–1924," *Pacific Historical Review* 49, no. 2 (1980): 339–57.

14. Elliott West, "A Longer, Grimmer, but More Interesting Story," in *Trails*, 103–117, esp. 107.

PART ONE

Perspectives

A major purpose of this volume is to provide model articles that illustrate different ways to explore the complex linkages of race and class and gender in historical studies. As a preface to the case studies in subsequent sections, this section is devoted to exploring some theoretical perspectives that have been used in comparative studies.

Before we do that, a brief sketch of the steps toward multiculturalism in western women's history may provide some useful background. In the 1970s, as the topic of western women was just beginning to be explored, both women's and ethnic historians found a common target in the limited and demeaning stereotypes of women in the "Hisland" version of western history described in the Editors' Introduction. Early work challenged the stereotypes of American Indian women as princesses and squaws; Asian American women as dolls and oppressed wives; African American women as victims and matriarchs; Mexican American women as Spanish señoritas and Mexican prostitutes; and Euro-American women as civilizers and helpmates, hell-raisers and "bad" women.[1]

In general, however, divergent scholarly approaches dominated the early period of western women's history. Historians of color were interested in the experiences of indigenous people before and after Euro-American conquest and in the cultures that racial ethnic immigrants created for themselves within a dominant, hostile society. Many drew inspiration from third-world anticolonial scholarship. In thinking about the history of the U.S. West, racial ethnic scholars found two theoretical ideas especially useful: internal colonialism and international labor migration. Chicano/a scholars used the notion of internal colonialism, first proposed by Latin American scholars, to explore how a small number of white invaders developed and maintained control over the larger indigenous and mixed-race population of what became (after 1848) the American Southwest. Both Chicano/a and Asian American historians linked capitalism to imperialism by noting that successive migrations to the West were prompted by the search for a cheap labor supply from those parts of the world that were the targets of American economic imperialism (in particular, east Asia, the Philippines, and Mexico). Both theories had the advantage of locating the experiences of racial ethnic groups in a broad international perspective rather than an exclusively American one. They therefore challenged the basic framework of western history, namely, the emphasis on the Euro-American "westward movement" of the nineteenth century. The earliest works by ethnic studies scholars paid scant attention to gender, but as Marian Perales's article in this section shows, female ethnic studies scholars were quick to challenge the male bias of their colleagues.[2]

On the other hand, most white women's historians did not at first question the customary Euro-American focus of western history. Working within the framework of the nineteenth-century "westward movement," women's historians focused largely on the gender differences in work and values between white pioneer women and men. Race was rarely mentioned in these works, and cross-cultural contacts between women were generally presented in benign terms as examples of a mutual desire for universal sisterhood that crossed racial boundaries.[3]

In 1980, Joan Jensen and Darlis Miller published their influential bibliographic essay, "The Gentle Tamers Revisited," in which they challenged the Euro-American focus of western history and demonstrated the rich variety of sources for women of many racial and ethnic groups. Their multi-culturalism was an important influence on much subsequent scholarship, but as Antonia Castañeda tellingly pointed out, most Anglo scholars treated it as an "add-on."[4] That is, western history still began at the point of European contact, and the experiences of women of color were considered only in comparison with those of whites. One exception to this approach was Elizabeth Jameson's 1988 review article, "Toward a Multicultural History of Women in the Western United States," in which she attempted to consider women of different racial ethnic groups (including Euro-Americans) in their own cultural contexts and critiqued the underlying racism of most cross-cultural frameworks.[5] Today, as the articles in this volume and elsewhere indicate, historical studies of racial ethnic women are increasingly conducted on their own terms.[6]

Although we now have multiple perspectives on western women's history, comparative studies that offer a genuinely intercultural perspective are still rare. One reason for this has been lack of adequate theory. Most historians have been trained to be suspicious of theory, but it seems to us essential for multicultural work. We must have organizing concepts to understand the range and diversity of women's experiences and how they have changed over time. There is, however, the problem of finding theories that are adequately inclusive.[7] The articles in this section suggest some issues that such theories must consider.

First, we must look for sorting and organizing concepts that are genuinely inclusive. This has turned out to be extremely difficult, but the principle is still valid: An adequate comparative theory must incorporate concepts *that are equally appropriate to all women. Many people are suspicious of general theories, fearing that they lead to homogenization that obliterates cultural, racial, or individual particularities. There certainly are aspects of the lives of women of different cultures and races that are distinctive. But while acknowledging the importance of difference, we need to continue the search for theory that seeks to be adequately inclusive.*

Second, a multicultural theory must respect the distinctive characteristics of women of all racial ethnic groups without stereotyping them. It has been difficult for both Euro-American and historians of color to escape from the effects of damaging stereotypes of racial ethnic women. Because the power relationships embedded in the old stereotypes have not been examined and transformed, the result has been flawed scholarship and troubled personal and professional relationships. We believe that it will not be possible to do truly cooperative and comparative work until we confront these power relationships and act to change them.

Finally, important as theory is, we need to treat it cautiously. We concur with the reservations Peggy Pascoe expresses in her article in this section. She is worried about some abstract cultural studies approaches that ignore the crucial issues of individual identity and agency. Recent studies in this volume and elsewhere regard racial ethnic women as agents with the power to make their own life choices and self-definitions. Such an approach in no way denies the possibility that racial ethnic women may be forced to interact with oppressors on unfavorable terms or may make choices that seem to be contrary to their own self-interest. Rather, the emphasis on agency is a vital concept that allows us to see how women understood and organized the complex linkages of race, class, and gender in their own lives. We cannot regard anyone as a historical actor if we deny that person agency in her or his own life.

The implications of such an approach to history are enormous. Speaking specifically of early American history, but with insight useful to us all, Joyce Appleby noted:

It is important to note that multiculturalism does not share the postmodernist stance. Its passions are political; its assumptions empirical; its conception of identities visceral. For it, there is no doubting that history is something that happened and that those happenings have left their mark within our collective consciousness. History for multiculturalists is not a succession of dissolving texts, but a dense tangle of past actions that have reshaped the landscape, distributed the nation's wealth, established boundaries, engendered prejudices, and unleashed energies. To look at those aspects of the American past that do not fit into a one-sidedly celebratory account of the nation's origins will require more, not less, rigorous standards of proof, a greater commitment to research, and a superior capacity for analytical persuasion.[8]

This clear-eyed challenge is one that we hope historians committed to writing inclusive histories of women and the West will want to meet.

Notes

1. Antonia Castañeda, "Women of Color and the Rewriting of Western History: The Discourse, Politics, and Decolonization of History," *Pacific Historical Review*, Special Issue: Western Women's History Revisited, 61, no. 4 (November 1992): 514–19; Beverly Stoeltje, "'A Helpmate for Man Indeed': The Image of the Frontier Woman," *Journal of American Folklore* 88, no. 347 (January–March 1975): 25–41; Elizabeth Jameson, "Toward a Multicultural History of Women in the Western United States," *Signs* 13, no. 4 (1988): 762.

2. An example of the theory of internal colonialism is Mario Barrera, *Race and Class in the Southwest: A Theory of Racial Inequality* (Notre Dame, Ind.: University of Notre Dame Press, 1979); of international labor migration, Lucie Cheng and Edna Bonacich, eds., *Labor Immigration under Capitalism: Asian Immigrant Workers in the U.S. before World War II* (Berkeley: University of California Press, 1984).

3. Examples of this early work, pathbreaking at the time, are Julie Jeffrey, *Frontier Women: The Trans-Mississippi West, 1840–1880* (New York: Hill and Wang, 1979), and Lillian Schlissel, *Women's Diaries of the Westward Journey* (New York: Schocken, 1982).

4. Joan Jensen and Darlis Miller, "The Gentle Tamers Revisited: New Approaches to the History of Women in the American West," *Pacific Historical Review*, 49 (1980): 173–213, and Castañeda, "Women of Color," 508–512.

5. Jameson, "Toward a Multicultural History," 761–91.

6. Influential examples of work by racial ethnic scholars of women have appeared in the collection edited by Vicki Ruiz and Ellen DuBois, *Unequal Sisters: A Multicultural Reader in U.S. Women's History*, 2d ed. (New York: Routledge, 1994), and in anthologies such as Patricia Albers and Beatrice Medicine, eds., *The Hidden Half: Studies of Plains Indian Women* (Washington, D.C.: University Press of America, 1983); Adela de la Torre and Beatríz M. Pesquera, eds., *Building with Our Hands: New Directions in Chicana Studies* (Berkeley: University of California Press, 1993); Asian Women United of California, eds., *Making Waves: An Anthology of Writings by and about Asian American Women* (Boston: Beacon Press, 1989); Shirley Geok-lin Lim, Mayumi Tsutakawa, and Margarita Donnelly, eds., *The Forbidden Stitch: An Asian American Women's Anthology* (Corvallis, Ore.: Calyx, 1980).

7. See, for example, the different perspectives among the four articles in the 1992 special western women's history issue of the *Pacific Historical Review*, cited in note 1.

8. Joyce Appleby, "Recovering America's Historic Diversity: Beyond Exceptionalism," *Journal of American History* 79, no. 2 (September 1992): 430–31.

1.
_____

Empowering "The Welder": A Historical Survey of Women of Color in the West

MARIAN PERALES

In this useful review essay, Marian Perales shows how the histories of racial ethnic women have moved from the margins to the center of western women's history. She does this not by tracing western women's scholarship alone but by examining wider challenges to racial bias in U.S. women's history. Within this fascinating story of the growing realization that difference, not uniformity, is the key issue, Perales finds some important regional differences. Southern historians insisted on the importance of race but proposed a white/black biracial model that was simply inadequate to explain the multicultural history of the U.S. West. Thus it has been historians of racial ethnic women in the West who have taken the lead in developing multicultural (as opposed to biracial) perspectives. As this volume attests, today multiculturalism is at the heart of western women's history.

I am a welder.
Not an alchemist.
I am interested in the blend
of common elements to make
a common thing.

No magic here.
Only the heat of my desire to fuse
what I already know
exists. Is possible.

We plead to each other,
we all come from the same rock
we all come from the same rock
ignoring the fact that we bend
at different temperatures
that each of us is malleable
up to a point.

Yes, fusion *is* possible
but only if things get hot enough—
all else is

temporary adhesion,
patching up.

It is the intimacy of steel melting
into steel, the fire of our individual
passion to take hold of ourselves
that makes sculpture of our lives,
builds buildings.

And I am not talking about skyscrapers,
merely structures that can support us
without fear
of trembling.

For too long a time
the heat of my heavy hands
has been smoldering
in the pockets of other people's business—
they need oxygen to make fire.

I am now
coming up for air.
yes, I *am*
picking up the torch.

I am the welder.
I understand the capacity of heat
to change the shape of things.
I am suited to work
within the realm of sparks
out of control.

I am the welder.
I am taking the power
into my own hands.[1]

CHALLENGING ELITE HISTORY
AND UNIVERSAL SISTERHOOD

Cherríe Moraga's eloquent poem provides us with an especially apt metaphor
for how historical scholarship on women of color has been transformed.
Responding to the challenge that Moraga's poem expresses, western women's
history has begun to employ a multicultural perspective. My purpose in
this article is not to provide an exhaustive survey of the literature, but to
trace the larger contours that have shaped western women's history. Themes
like immigration, cross-cultural marriage, labor force participation, and
imagery illustrate the way in which the experiences of women of color moved
"from margin to center."[2] Examining some of the recent scholarship on

women of color in the West reveals that originally muted objects became empowered multivocal subjects yearning to "talk back."[3]

Multicultural western women's history requires the adoption of new models and approaches. To achieve a multicultural history of women in the western United States we must recognize women's heterogenous experiences and challenge distorted historical models that emphasize the contributions of great men, political history, and the experiences of elite eastern women. The public-private split engendered by elite eastern experiences needs to be reevaluated, as does the biracial paradigm that focuses exclusively on white and black women's experiences. Finally, we must challenge ethnic stereotypes perpetuated through the lenses of the dominant culture.

The multicultural emphasis of western women's history developed partly in response to the frameworks of the new women's history, including tendencies to universalize categories of analysis that were appropriate only to other regions or to social elites. Emulating traditional approaches that focused on "great men" (i.e., Euro-American politicians), women's historians in the early 1970s developed paradigms that emphasized women's universal experience. The first school of thought emphasized a compensatory approach. Attempting to "compensate" for the way in which traditional history excluded women's experiences, women's historians highlighted presidential wives and "women worthies" in compendiums like *Notable American Women*. Next, women's historians turned to the ideological construction of gender roles like the nineteenth-century "cult of true womanhood." As important as pioneering research into gender roles was, the roles of Euro-American and middle-class women did not apply to working women and other women of color. Instead of highlighting women's differences, pioneering women historians homed in on shared oppression and conflated "women" to "middle-class Euro-American." An ideology of "separate spheres" in which men were largely public and women largely private reduced women's experiences to those of nineteenth-century elite eastern women. Women's experiences were homogenized and limited to the constraints of "women's sphere," the home. Women's experiences were essentialized to those of middle-class New England Euro-American women.[4]

In the early 1980s, western women's historians, among others, began to challenge the "separate spheres" paradigm. Robert Griswold argued that the "cult of true womanhood" should be reevaluated as an ever-evolving "cultural system," because a "cult" suggests rigidity and prescription, whereas "culture" suggests the malleable meanings domesticity could carry for women of different races and classes. Euro-American westering women were able to wield power, albeit limited, by serving as the moral custodians sanctioning their husbands' behavior. Or, as Griswold put it, "Domesticity empowered women to demand of men respect, consideration, emotional commitment, and even a measure of deference to their better moral judgment."[5]

As Griswold emphasized, histories based on eastern Euro-American women's experiences distorted western women. Eastern elite women and western frontier women worked in diverse regional economies and racial ethnic systems. Nonetheless, women's historians generally continued throughout the 1980s to focus upon white women's experiences. Barbara Christian accurately characterized the feminist theorists during this period when she stated, "[O]ften as a way of clearing themselves they do acknowledge women of color exist, yet they then proceed to do what they were doing with little relevance to us."[6] Christian, Bonnie Thornton Dill, and Maria Lugones and Elizabeth Spellman likewise criticized the "universal woman" paradigm for its essentialist nature. Dill argued that "universal sisterhood" excluded women of color.[7] Class as well as race must be addressed in feminist theory. Feminist theorists, according to Lugones and Spellman, had failed to develop a theory that applied to Latinas. They offered the following suggestions in the hope of achieving an inclusive feminist theory: "[I]f white/Anglo women are to understand our voices they must understand our communities and us in them. . . . Only then can we engage in a mutual dialogue that does not reduce each of us to instances of the abstraction called 'woman' "[8]

Cherríe Moraga and Gloria Anzaldúa's *This Bridge Called My Back* dramatically altered the historiography of women of color. The pathbreaking anthology of poetry and prose illustrated diverse experiences of feminists of color. As Moraga alludes to in "The Welder," as a woman of color she began to "take the power into my own hands." Instead of allowing others to convey their histories, women of color began to tell their own stories. Moraga and Anzaldúa's anthology became a point of departure because, instead of marginalizing women of color, it challenged women's historians to center the experiences of the "racial ethnic" woman.

Rosalinda Méndez González was one of the first women of color to argue that economic class distinguished women of all races. She pointed out that "if one looks at history through the eyes of the majority of women, the poor and the laboring classes, a very different picture of society emerges. The picture is far more complete, for elite eyes take *their* world as the standard and assume that all society exists, or should exist, in their image."[9] Women of color, González argued, were largely unaffected by the private-public dichotomy.

Just as women of color historians rejected models of universal oppression and the universal sisterhood of all women, by the late 1970s and early 1980s the challenge, likewise, was regional. Western women's historians rejected western histories derived from men's experiences, eastern women's histories, white/black racial systems, and narrow time frames limited to the nineteenth century. In 1980, Darlis Miller and Joan Jensen's "Gentle Tamers Revisited: New Approaches to the History of Women in the American West," challenged women's historians to expand their focus to include a wide range of multicultural experiences.[10] Early western women's histories were based on stereotypes of women as gentle tamers, sunbonneted helpmates, hell-raisers, and bad women.[11] Yet these distorted images refer exclusively to frontier Euro-American women.[12]

Responding to Jensen and Miller's call, during the early 1980s two western women's history conferences addressed the need to examine diverse experiences and generated anthologies that began to define western women's history. Susan Armitage and Elizabeth Jameson's *The Women's West* was based on papers presented at the 1983 Women's West Conference in Sun Valley, Idaho. Armitage and Jameson contended that western history had been distorted by the exclusion of women. Their anthology also demonstrated that western women did not fit the New England construct of womanhood, thereby debunking the theory of the universality of womanhood. Finally, they recognized that western women's history must be inclusive: Since the history of the West began with the establishment of indigenous communities, western women's history needed to recenter indigenous experiences.[13]

Lillian Schlissel, Vicki Ruiz and Janice Monk's *Western Women: Their Land, Their Lives*, based on papers given at the 1984 "Western Women: Their Land, Their Lives" conference in Tucson, Arizona, also recognized that western history must be perceived through a cross-cultural lens. They argued that it was important to study marginalized groups, and even more important to study the interactions among disparate cultures.[14] To comprehend the significance of women's multi-faceted experiences, relationships among diverse women must be emphasized.

Finally, Jensen and Miller compiled *New Mexico Women: Intercultural Perspectives*, which highlighted cross-cultural experiences among women. Drawing on a variety of methodologies, including anthropology, history, and literature, *New Mexico Women* documented a variety of women's experiences in New Mexico. Similarly, in *Women on the U.S.–Mexican Border: Responses to Change*, Vicki Ruiz and Susan Tiano illustrated that, although women in the borderland region endured economic exploitation, they remained active participants in shaping their own personal histories and that of the region.[15]

Reviewing the first wave of western women's history, Elizabeth Jameson's "Toward a Multicultural History of Women in the Western United States" explored how western women's history had been shaped by western history, women's history, and ethnic histories. Jameson argued that much of the research on western women's experiences highlighted Euro-American women, and she reviewed scholarship on women of color in the West and on cross-cultural experiences. Summing up the changes, Jameson argued that "Western women's history has populated the almost exclusively male environment of traditional western history with women and children, and it has replaced images of rugged individuals with families and communities."[16] Though somewhat flawed, all of these early attempts at multiculturalism recognized that a biracial approach was unsuited to the historical circumstances of the U.S. West.

Ellen DuBois and Vicki Ruiz's *Unequal Sisters: A Multicultural Reader in U.S. Women's History* became a point of departure in women's history since it incorporated a diversity of experiences that considered class, race, ethnicity, and culture. Evaluating a variety of experiences such as familial relations, work, politics, and sexuality, DuBois and Ruiz asserted that women's experiences should be perceived as dialectical relationships rather than segregated experiences.[17] In other words, we must recognize the ways in which the complexities of women's experiences are interrelated. Although the articles in this anthology addressed a wide range of experiences, from stereotypes of Indian women to "Americanization and the Mexican Immigrant," DuBois and Ruiz provided a multicultural and multiregional framework and assumed a common theme of empowering women.

Most recently, Antonia Castañeda assessed the shortcomings of these early attempts at multiculturalism in the decades following Jensen and Miller's "Gentle Tamers Revisited." She criticized them for not accurately presenting conflicts among diverse cultures. According to Castañeda, Jensen and Miller merely paid lip service to multiculturalism since notions like "gentle tamers" applied only to Euro-American women. Moreover, as the female counterpart to the male "tamer of the West," these Euro-Americans sought to colonize indigenous lands and peoples. Castañeda argued that while Jensen and Miller explored gender issues, they failed to "examine the ideology and politics of race, culture and class, and expansionism that produced and maintained stereotypic images of white women and women of color."[18]

ADOPTING OLD PARADIGMS

Women of color historians are beginning to recenter the histories of women of color by illuminating their agency and adaptation. Early studies of western women of color emulated the older models that emphasized "significant" historical accomplishments and women's oppression. Although these studies attempted to cast ethnic women as historical actors, they ultimately misrepresented these experiences. In *Diosa y Hembra: The History and Heritage of Chicanas in the U.S.*, Martha Cotera surveyed the experiences of Mexicanas and Chicanas from the pre-Columbian period to the contemporary era. Her research represented a major breakthrough in Chicana history, even though she employed the problematic compensatory approach. She included numerous accounts of "notable" Mexican American women yet failed to adequately develop them. Finally, in her discussion of Chicanas during the contemporary era, she failed to explore the subordination of Chicana activists in the Chicano movement.[19]

Many scholars of women of color initially interpreted women from a passive victim perspective. In "Amerika Nadeshiko: Japanese Immigrant Women in the United States, 1900–1924," Yuji Ichioka depicted the experiences of Japanese picture brides in the United States, whom he perceived as victims of their husbands' ploys.[20] Some disillusioned picture brides deserted their husbands. Ichioka construed marital estrangement as the catalyst for desertion, yet instead of seeing desertion as an attempt to gain autonomy, Ichioka portrayed it as a tragedy. Ultimately, the tragedy of "Amerika Nadeshiko" was that women were viewed as one-dimensional victims.

Similarly, Alfredo Mirandé and Evangelina Enríquez interpreted Mexican American women as victims of tripartite oppression. Like other women, Mexican Americans endured sexist oppression. Like all Mexican Americans, they endured the racist oppression that the dominant society inflicted upon marginalized groups. Finally, they experienced internal oppression "by a cultural heritage that tends to be dominated by males and exaggerates male domination over women."[21] From this "blaming the victim" perspective, Mirandé and Enríquez explored cultural heritage, family roles, education, work, images in literature, and feminism. Unfortunately, much like Ichioka, Mirande and Enriquez denied women's agency by perceiving them as passive victims.

BEYOND BIRACIAL MODELS AND STEREOTYPES

In an attempt to recognize diverse experiences, women's historians first adopted a biracial model. Numerous studies investigated relationships between white slave owners and African American slave women.[22] Although the biracial approach to women's history empowered African American women by allowing their voices to be heard, it simultaneously caused women of color to compete for the coveted "other" position.[23] Western women's historians challenged the biracial approach when they began to explore immigration to the West. Asian immigrant women's experience did not conform to models based on Euro-American or African American experiences, and they dramatically altered the perspective from which we might view a "westward" journey. Historians began to examine immigration from the perspectives of immigrant women.[24] In " 'A Bowlful of Tears': Chinese Immigrants on Angel Island," Judy Yung examined the arrival of Chinese immigrant women at Angel Island from 1910 to 1941. Drawing on oral histories and scraps of poetry scratched on the walls of detention cells, Yung paints a vivid picture of the isolation and fear Chinese women experienced as they waited for the harsh interrogation they had to undergo before they were allowed to enter the United States.[25]

Further attempts to transcend biracial models involved challenging Euro-American racial stereotypes, part of a lengthy process to abandon the perspectives and paradigms of Euro-American women. At first, western women's historians simply documented white stereotypes of women of color, among them stereotypical depictions of Native American women. In "The Pocahontas Perplex: The Image of Indian Women in American Culture," Rayna Green traced the history of both the "Pocahontas Princess" and the "depraved Squaw" in popular literature and ballads. The light-skinned princess was lauded for her ability to assist John Smith, while her counterpart, the dark-skinned squaw, was denigrated because she represented a lusty, promiscuous woman. To achieve a more accurate account of Native American experiences, Green admonished that we must look "outside the boundaries of the stories, songs and pictures given us in tradition," to find "a more humane truth."[26] Similarly, Glenda Riley explored stereotypes of Native American women that popular American literature promulgated during the nineteenth century.[27] Patricia Albers and William James examined stereotypes in southwestern postcards. Exploring the changing imagery of Native American women, Albers and James observed that unidimensional portrayals of Native American women as princesses "reinforce and play to popular notions of Indian people as spectacle and objects."[28] These (literally) cardboard caricatures failed to represent Native Americans historically or in the present.

For the stereotypes of women of Asian descent, Renee Tajima challenged the stereotypical cinematic portrayals of Asian women in "Lotus Blossoms Don't Bleed: Images of Asian Women." Tajima explored two common stereotypes: the "Lotus Blossom Baby" who is often an American man's "gift" and the devious "Dragon Lady." A good woman was connected with passivity (Lotus Blossom) and a bad woman with deception (Dragon Lady). Tajima further argued that taboo interracial marriages were often conveniently terminated when an Asian woman became the victim of a "fatal disease." Tajima hoped that Asian American filmmakers who challenge these negative stereotypes of Asian women "may soon constitute a critical mass out of which we will see a body of work that gives us a new image, our own image."[29]

Beverly Trulio argued that Euro-American men developed stereotypes of New Mexican women based on Victorian New England values. Since Mexican women did not wear the constricting clothing that New England women adopted, but instead wore loose, breathable clothing, Euro-American men concluded that the Mexican women must have been promiscuous. Euro-Americans often inaccurately interpreted Mexican women's hospitality as inviting sexual relationships.[30] Similarly, Susan Shelby Magoffin, writing in 1846, described the women as "truly shocking."[31] A second interpretive step involved challenging these stereotypes. In "The Independent Women of Hispanic New Mexico, 1821–1846" Janet Lecompte contended that despite the misguided depictions of New Mexico women offered by Euro-Americans, Mexican American women wielded a considerable power that was sanctioned by alcalde courts. Lecompte suggested that Mexican Americans conformed to a strict moral code and that the stereotypes distorted the actual lived experiences of New Mexican women.[32] A Eurocentric gauge measured Mexican women on the basis of the societal expectations for New England women. In addition, we must recognize that these stereotypes were generally perpetuated by Euro-American men.

Most recently, Deena González examined shrewd New Mexican entrepreneur Gertrudis Barceló. Dubbed "La Tules" by her neighbors, Barceló, an unorthodox woman, defied societal expectations deemed appropriate for New Mexican women. Her reputation suffered greatly since her image was filtered through a distorted Anglo lens that emphasized her extraordinary wealth and "promiscuity." She defied Euro-American perceptions of appropriate womanhood and was labeled a "Spanish Mexican degenerate." Her saloon provided Euro-American men with a window to the Spanish Mexican society. Within the confines of her saloon, the men learned about Mexican music, customs, and humor. Despite racist stereotypes that depicted Barceló as a rabble-rousing "female of very loose habits," González aptly concluded that she "exemplified contact and conflict between independent female Catholics and westering male Protestants."[33] Lecompte's and González's research suggests that relying solely upon Euro-American accounts yields inaccurate depictions that ignore the complexity of Mexican American women's lives.

EXPANDING THE OLD MODELS

Challenging racial stereotypes enabled historians of women of color, like historians of white women, to recognize women as active survivors and to illuminate the ways in which women adapted to new situations. The theme of cultural adaptation transcended older models that focused on victimization, oppression, and liberation. Women actively transformed their roles in many arenas, most notably family and work. Anthropologists Micaela di Leonardo and Patricia Zavella challenged the widely held assumption that "traditional" cultures, namely, Italian and Mexican, shaped women's lives. Di Leonardo, in her study of California Italian American women, contended that these women had "varieties of ethnic experience."[34] For example, kinship patterns varied from extended family households to nuclear families. Di Leonardo's study redefined cultures not as static constructs but rather as "the living result of the intersection of all members of a particular group."[35] In "The Impact of 'Sun Belt Industrialization' on Chicanas," Zavella disputed the stereotypical portrayal of the "passive Chicana mother." Employing a sociological survey, Zavella suggested that we must look beyond cultural determinist arguments and recognize that family needs and regional economies influenced women's work decisions. Like di Leonardo, Zavella recognized that Chicana experiences were not based solely on "traditional culture."[36]

Valerie Matsumoto's research on Japanese American internment during World War II similarly stressed how women adapted. Family dynamics were transformed when Japanese American women achieved autonomy by assuming jobs, rejecting arranged marriages, and, in some cases, attending college.[37] Matsumoto's research underscored the shift from interpreting women as passive victims to recognizing them as survivors and adapters.

Historian George Sánchez suggested that Mexican women selectively acculturated yet ultimately retained their traditional cultures. In " 'Go After the Women': Americanization and the Mexican Immigrant Woman, 1915–1929," Sánchez contended that the advent of World War I created a xenophobic climate in the United States that caused the State of California to establish an Americanization program to assimilate Mexican immigrants. The program focused its assimilation tactics on Mexican mothers, since they shaped Mexican society. Despite attempts to inculcate American ideology, Sánchez concluded that these Americanization programs failed to create a "new American woman."[38]

Theda Perdue explored how older practices and Euro-American politics together affected Cherokee women who became active participants in nineteenth-century politics. According to Perdue, Cherokee women always played an integral role in land transactions. In 1817, a cohort of Cherokee women voiced their concern regarding further land cessions to Euro-Americans. By the mid-1820s, the political role that Cherokee women had assumed had diminished, since the newly ratified Cherokee constitution (modeled on the U.S. Constitution) provided voting rights only to "free male citizens." In 1838, the Cherokee were forcibly removed from their land. Cherokee women's political participation remained largely unchanged after removal. Perdue concluded that "the tragedy of the Trail of Tears lies not only in the suffering and death which the Cherokees experienced but also in the failure of many Cherokees to look critically at the political system which they had adopted—a political system dominated by wealth, highly acculturated men, and supported by an ideology that made women subordinate."[39]

Both Emma Gee, in her study of Japanese immigrant women, and Margarita Melville, who researched Mexican American women, illustrated women's adaptation and "selective acculturation." According to Gee, Issei women were not victims, but survivors of new situations. Immigrant women were primarily picture brides who quickly learned to adapt to rural settings and shared living quarters. Gee asserted that "by looking only for the dramatic and heroic moments in history, we tend to forget the small struggles and little victories of human beings."[40] Countering the compensatory approach that previous studies employed, Margarita Melville examined Mexican American women who became active agents defining their destiny. The aim of her *Twice a Minority* was to "modify the stereotypes of Mexican-American women as passive sufferers." Mexican American women "selectively acculturated" to mainstream society, Melville asserted, while simultaneously maintaining their own cultural identities.[41]

Heeding Gee's call, historians began to recognize women's extraordinary everyday experiences. In their quest to dispel the myopic "domestic sphere," historians of women of color focused increasingly upon women's labor force participation.[52] Unlike the conclusions reached by Barbara Welter two decades earlier, studies on women's labor force participation elucidated the shortcomings of the "cult of true womanhood" and its emphasis on domesticity and passivity. Studies such as Evelyn Nakano Glenn's *Issei, Nisei, War Bride: Three Generations of Japanese-American Women in Domestic Service* and Vicki Ruiz's *Cannery Women, Cannery Lives: Mexican Women, Unionization, and the California Food Processing Industry, 1930–1950*, take us far beyond Welter's "domestic ideology."

In her pathbreaking research on Japanese and Japanese American domestic workers, Evelyn Nakano Glenn argued that these women should not be perceived as passive sufferers. Despite the demeaning work that domestic workers performed, they achieved degrees of self-satisfaction by contributing to the family economy. Although Nakano Glenn focused primarily on Japanese and Japanese American women, she also shed light on institutional racism that the labor market inflicted upon all racial ethnic women. Examining Issei (first generation), Nisei (second generation), and war brides (post–World War II immigrants), Nakano Glenn concluded that "the very difficulty of their circumstances forced them into a struggle for survival, a struggle that developed in them a corresponding strength and tenacity." Nakano Glenn's pioneering research on Japanese and Japanese American domestic workers paved the way for future studies in this area. She adopted a dialectical approach to class, race, and gender to illustrate the ways in which both the power of the dominant groups and the active resistance of subordinate groups "carved out areas of autonomy and power" and argued that Japanese American women became victims of tripartite oppression: economic subjugation, institutional racism, and internal sexism within the Japanese patriarchal culture. Despite their oppression, these domestic workers did not remain passive but gained autonomy by such tactics as establishing their own hours.[43]

Patricia Albers and Terry Reynolds explored Native American women's labor force participation. Both studies demonstrated the way in which Native American participation in the economic arena underwent radical changes in the twentieth century. Rising mechanization in the Devil's Lake (North Dakota) area during the 1940s caused Sioux families to rely upon women's wages for subsistence. By adapting their domestic skills to the economic arena, they successfully undermined federally instituted capitalism. "What is especially ironic is that the very program that the federal government has established to make the Sioux dependent on the capitalist production process has created, simultaneously, the basis of their relative autonomy."[44] Similarly, according to Reynolds, adapting their domestic skills to a money economy, Acoma women likewise achieved autonomy. Utilizing their skills at pottery enabled Acoma women to contribute to the family economy.[45]

Turning to organized labor, Vicki Ruiz's *Cannery Women, Cannery Lives* examined how Mexican American women assumed active leadership roles in unionizing efforts despite cultural traditions that encouraged passivity. Ruiz's research focused extensively on the United Cannery, Agricultural, Packing and Allied Workers of America (UCAPAWA) from 1930 to 1950. The networks of support that women established at the packing plants paved the way for unionizing and strikes.[46]

CROSS CULTURAL PERSPECTIVES

To explore both cultural difference and power relationships, historians of women of color have examined cross-cultural marriages. In her examination of Mexican American women in San Antonio, Texas, Jane Dysart found that assimilation occurred when upper-class Mexican women married Euro-American men. Instead of retaining their culture, subsequent generations of Mexican Americans became Americanized.[47] In "Cross Cultural Marriages in the Southwest: The New Mexico Experience, 1846–1900," Darlis Miller explored intermarriages, which occurred frequently in New Mexico because Euro-American men typically migrated to New Mexico without wives or families. Unlike Dysart, Miller concluded that assimilation varied significantly among Mexicanas: "Some wives adopted an

Anglo mode of living but retained Spanish customs, becoming bicultural in the process."[48] While second-generation marriages offer clues to the degree to which assimilation occurred, Miller argued, no significant patterns emerged.

Susan Johnson investigated cross-cultural relationships in "Sharing Bed and Board: Cohabitation and Cultural Difference in Central Arizona Mining Towns, 1863-1873." Tracing the cohabitation patterns of Mexican women and Euro-American women, Johnson argued that this practice seemed to be more accepted in Mexican communities. Although Johnson found few cases of Euro-American cohabitation, she suggested that Euro-American women in those relationships appeared to defy societal expectations of womanhood. Euro-American women who lived with men outside the confines of marriage were harshly condemned by their communities. Johnson concluded that "the nature, meaning, and consequence of cohabitation differed according to a woman's ethnicity and that of her companion. For Mexican women, informal union existed as a cultural category in a way that it did not for Anglo women."[49]

In her insightful research on the fur trade in western Canada, Sylvia Van Kirk shed light on native women, most notably Crees, Ojibwas, and Chipewyans, who played a significant role as the liaison between British and French trappers and traders and native peoples. Since a paucity of European women resided in western Canada, many traders established unions with native women. According to Van Kirk, the indigenous peoples perceived "marriage in an integrated social and economic context; marital alliances created reciprocal social ties, which served to consolidate their economic relationships with the incoming strangers." Additionally, the trapper reaped positive benefits since his wife assisted his efforts. Van Kirk's research demonstrated the ways in which the native women helped to forge strong alliances between Europeans and native people but were ultimately replaced by second-generation métis daughters and then by Euro-American women, French, and Native Americans.[50]

Some studies that employed an intercultural model explored the relationships forged by Euro-American missionaries and women of color. Sarah Deutsch in *No Separate Refuge: Culture, Class, and Gender on an Anglo Hispanic Frontier in the American Southwest, 1880-1940*, argued that while the goal of missionary women was to achieve successful conversion to Protestantism, generally a dialectical relationship developed between missionaries and Mexicanas. Though Mexican women accepted material items such as language and technology, they refused to accept the prevailing American ideology. Deutsch noted that "they selected those elements of an evolving Anglo culture best suited to their own evolving culture, and refused, for the most part, to receive the message in exactly the spirit it was given." The Euro-American missionary women adopted some Mexican traditions, especially family-centered activities.[51] It was not uncommon for an Anglo missionary woman to become a *curandera*, who served as the primary medical practioner in the Mexican village. The Mexican traditions co-opted by Euro-American missionaries became a part of a syncretic western frontier. This example illustrates the weakness of interpreting the frontier only through a Eurocentric lens; we should look for and expect to find many more instances of syncretic process.

Similarly, in *Relations of Rescue: The Search for Female Moral Authority in the American West, 1874–1939,* Peggy Pascoe contended that while the goal of the rescue missions was to inculcate Chinese women with both the tenets of Protestantism and the ideology of Victorian womanhood, Chinese women selectively adopted the ideals of the Christian rescue homes and became involved in a nexus of complex relationships. These "rescued women" overwhelmingly converted to Protestantism yet still retained Chinese traditions. Though missionaries espoused the "universality of women," they perceived themselves as racially superior to the Chinese women. Thus, Chinese women could never achieve full autonomy because the missionaries would not allow them to transcend their positions as native helpers. On the other hand, when these "reformed" Chinese women interacted with Chinese men, they were deemed "bad women" because they had adopted values of self-respect and independence. Some Chinese men who ran prostitution rings criticized the rescue missions because they hurt their business, while other Chinese men criticized these "rescued women" because they threatened the traditional patriarchal power structure. Ultimately, Chinese women were faced with an ongoing dilemma that pitted newly achieved autonomy against traditional Chinese deference.[52]

As a number of articles in this volume demonstrate, the need to reevaluate power relations among women is a strong theme in the most recent scholarship on women of color.[53] As Pascoe has written, "[I]t was the points at which two or more cultures came into contact that seemed significant, for it was at such cultural crossroads that the power relations between groups were most apparent."[54]

RACIAL ETHNIC WOMEN AT THE HISTORICAL CENTER

Although these cross-cultural studies are pathbreaking challenges to preconceived notions of frontier and culture, they also suggest a need to reexamine relationships among women of color without Euro-American experiences as the referential experience. Patricia Albers and Beatrice Medicine's *The Hidden Half: Studies of Plains Indian Women* became a point of departure in Native American scholarship because it moved women of color to the center of historical scholarship. Their compilation of essays reevaluated the role and status of Plains Indian women who enacted variations of traditional gender behavior and norms. Echoing the ideology of other feminists of color, Albers and Medicine suggested a shift away from "an emphasis on uniformity of female experiences cross-culturally" to recognition that women's experiences were in a constant state of flux. Though the central focus of *The Hidden Half* was Plains Indian women, the editors pointed out that "introducing a new awareness about Indian women also expands our understanding of women as a whole."[55]

A common theme uniting *The Hidden Half* is the need to reevaluate misguided interpretations of Native American gender roles. Medicine argued that rigid cultural constructs developed largely by Euro-American ethnographers created a false picture of a male-dominated warrior society that incorporated a rigid system of gender stratification.[56] Rather, Medicine concluded gender roles were not rigidly defined in this society since numerous women warriors and male *berdaches* existed. In another article, Raymond DeMallie contended that the desire to perceive Lakota society as male-dominated was engendered by Euro-American biases. Examining the system of warfare based on honoring and protecting women, DeMallie stressed that "in a culturally real sense it was men who subordinated themselves to women."[57] DeMallie concluded that we must reexamine Lakotas through an accurate gender lens.

Other studies of sexuality and gender demonstrate the need to reconsider dichotomous (male/female) gender systems and heterosexist assumptions.[58] Evelyn Blackwood examined Native American cross-gender roles in "Sexuality and Gender in Certain Native American Tribes: The Case of Cross-Gender Females." There she challenged assumptions that all societies adhere to dichotomous gender systems. Native American ideology in some tribes separated sexual behavior from gender roles since "traditional females" who married "cross-gender" females were not considered lesbians. Blackwood argued that "it is imperative to develop an analysis of variant gender roles based on the historical conditions that faced particular tribes since gender systems vary in different cultures and change as modes of production change," a point that Ramona Ford's article in this volume elaborates.[59]

Other scholars of sexuality focused on ethnic communities or specific geographical regions. Scholars have recently begun to explore Asian American lesbian communities.[60] Pamela H. argued that a lesbian often has difficulty "coming out" since she has been socialized in a stringently heterosexual society. To many of Asian-descent groups, homosexuality is interpreted as "losing touch with one's Asian heritage, of becoming too assimilated."[61] Additionally, in "Differences and Identities: Feminism and the Albuquerque Lesbian Community," Trisha Franzen explored the development of an Albuquerque lesbian network between 1965 and 1980. Franzen suggested that a bar culture had emerged in Albuquerque during that time and argued that although there were two lesbian cultures, one closeted and one bolstered by the bar culture, the two groups constantly interacted. She concluded, "Only now is the diversity of lesbian voices being heard, and it has taken time for lesbians to research and reveal the history needed to build theory and examine how race and class differences are entwined with sexuality and issues of trust and power."[62]

TOWARD A MULTICULTURAL FEMINIST HISTORY

Histories of women of color force us to reevaluate feminism and movements for racial empowerment. Alma Garcia explored the treatment of women in the Chicano movement and concluded that instead of addressing the needs of Chicanas, the movement elevated race as the primary concern.[63] Consequently, while the Chicano movement focused its attention upon racial oppression, Chicana feminists focused upon the internal sexism that the movement underscored. Similarly, African American and Asian American women reported sexism and racism within their political communities.[64] For example, Esther Ngan-Ling Chow investigated the mainstream feminist movement's inability to accommodate women of color. She identified factors such as patriarchy and the absence of support networks as impeding Asian American women's political activism. Since many Asian American women were of the working class, they had fewer opportunities for political activism. Advocating Asian American women's political activism, Ngan-Ling Chow concluded, "[P]olitical activism is the first step toward becoming visible, eradicating the stereotype of passivity. . . . [P]olitical participation is necessary to overcome voicelessness as Asian American women."[65] The efforts to overturn the historical "voicelessness" of women of color are also political. In their important interdisciplinary anthology, *Building with Our Hands: New Directions in Chicana Studies*, Adela de la Torre and Beatríz Pesquera and their colleagues speak frankly about the politics of the universities within which they work and struggle: "Within these contradictions of barriers and success, acceptance and disdain, recognition and indifference, our scholarship will be produced— and in time, we hope, will flourish."[66]

This examination of the recent scholarship of women of color in the West shows the transformation that has occurred in women's history in general. A universal notion of "woman" ignored the rich cultural experiences that women of color offered. Even though women's historians attempted to incorporate the varying perspectives of women of color, ultimately these diverse cultural experiences became marginalized. Instead of recognizing a diversity of experiences, mainstream women's historians recognized either "white" women or "black" women. Unfortunately, this biracial model caused women of color to compete for the coveted "other" position.

The advent of scholarship that advocated multiculturalism represented a significant point of departure in western women's history. Now the voices of women of color can clearly be distinguished. Now the once-marginalized woman becomes an active agent delineating her history. Now the oppressed woman of color proclaims, "Yes, I *am* a survivor." As the intercultural approach replaces the limited biracial model, interactions between diverse cultures are highlighted. Instead of perceiving cultures as static, historians are now recognizing the way in which cultural borders blend and merge together. As Moraga's poem suggests, as women of color historians we have become "the welder"; we are "picking up the torch . . . [and] taking the power into [our] own hands."

Notes

I would like to thank Vicki Ruiz for providing me with helpful comments on an earlier draft of this paper. I appreciate Sham Duckworth's unflagging support and encouragement. Special thanks to editors Elizabeth Jameson and Susan Armitage, who shared insightful comments and suggestions on several drafts of this paper.

1. Cherríe Moraga, "The Welder," in *This Bridge Called My Back: Writings by Radical Women of Color*, ed. Cherríe Moraga and Gloria Anzaldúa (New York: Kitchen Table/Women of Color Press, 1983). Moraga's final stanzas are the most compelling since they recognize the necessity to reshape women's history "within the realm of sparks out of control" and to empower women of color to "take the power into [their] own hands."

2. The phrase "from margin to center" refers to bell hooks's *Feminist Theory: From margin to center* (Boston: South End Press, 1984). hooks, an African American feminist scholar, recognized the need to redefine the feminist perspective since it only represented the experiences of white middle-class women. hooks asserts, "[W]hile it is evident that many women suffer from sexist tyranny, there is little indication that this forges 'a common bond among all women.' There is much evidence substantiating the reality that race and class identity creates differences in quality of life, social status, and lifestyle that take precedence over the common women-shared differences which are rarely transcended." hooks, *Feminist Theory*, 4.

3. I refer here to bell hooks's insightful *Talking Back: Thinking Feminist, Thinking Black* (Boston: South End Press, 1989). The concept of "talking back" is especially apt when referring to the emergence of scholars of color. hooks writes, "In the world of the southern black community I grew up in, 'back talk' and 'talking back' meant speaking as an equal to an authority figure. It meant daring to disagree and sometimes it just meant having an opinion." hooks, *Talking Back*, 5.

4. Barbara Welter, "The Cult of True Womenhood: 1820–1860," *American Quarterly* 18 (Summer 1966): 151–74. In *Up from the Pedestal*, Aileen Kraditor compiled primary documents that explored the notion of "separate spheres." The rise of the Industrial Revolution bolstered separate spheres since immigrants primarily became factory workers. Aileen Kraditor, ed., *Up from the Pedestal: Selected Writings in the History of American Feminism* (Chicago: Quadrangle Books, 1968). In the mid-1970s, Carroll Smith-Rosenberg reinterpreted "separate spheres" as a positive paradigm. Smith-Rosenberg argued that the woman's separate world fostered relationships between women that created a distinctive women's culture. Carroll Smith-Rosenberg, "The Female World of Love and Ritual: Relations between Women in Nineteenth Century America," *Signs* 1 (Autumn 1975): 1–29. In "The Lady and the Mill Girl" Gerda Lerner argued that the early 1800s marked the birth of the leisured "lady" and the immigrant "workinggirl." Separate spheres became a symbol of status since working-class women could not be confined solely to the domestic arena. See Gerda Lerner, "The Lady and the Mill Girl: Changes in the Status of Women in the Age of Jackson," *Midcontinent American Studies Journal* 10 (Spring 1969): 5–15. For an insightful article exploring the debates regarding separate spheres, see Linda Kerber, "Separate Spheres, Female Worlds, Woman's Place: The Rhetoric of Women's History," *Journal of American History* 75 (June 1988): 1, 9–39.

5. For example, see Robert Griswold, "Anglo Women and Domestic Ideology in the American West in the Nineteenth and Early Twentieth Centuries," in *Western Women: Their Land, Their Lives*, ed. Lillian Schlissel, Vicki Ruiz, and Janice Monk (Albuquerque: University of New Mexico Press, 1988), 15–29; Elizabeth Jameson, "Women as Workers, Women as Civilizers: True Womanhood in the American West," in *The Women's West*, ed. Susan Armitage and Elizabeth Jameson (Norman: University of Oklahoma Press, 1987), 237–51. See Griswold, "Anglo Women," 28.

6. Barbara Christian, "The Race for Theory," *Feminist Studies* 14 (Spring 1988): 75.

7. Bonnie Thornton Dill, "Race, Class, and Gender: Prospects for an All-Inclusive Sisterhood," *Feminist Studies* 1 (Spring 1987): 131–49. For example, the Declaration of Sentiments drafted at the 1848 Seneca Falls Convention reflected the desires and concerns exclusively of white middle-class women.

8. Maria Lugones and Elizabeth Spellman, "Have We Got a Theory for You! Feminist Theory, Cultural Imperialism, and the Demand for the Woman's Voice," *Women's Studies International Forum* 6, no. 6 (1983): 581.

9. Rosalinda Méndez González, "Distinctions in Western Women's Experience: Ethnicity, Class, and Social Change," in *Women's West*, 240.

10. Joan Jensen and Darlis Miller, "The Gentle Tamers Revisited: New Approaches to the History of Women in the American West," *Pacific Historical Review* 49 (1980): 173–213.

11. Beverly Stoeltje identified these early stereotypes of western women. See Stoeltje, " 'A Helpmate for Man Indeed': The Image of the Frontier Woman," *Journal of American Folklore* 88 (1975): 27–31.

12. For example, Glenda Riley's *Women and Indians* implied that the "women" represented a homogenous group and "Indians" signified male Native Americans. See Riley, *Women and Indians on the Frontier: 1825–1915* (Albuquerque: University of New Mexico Press, 1984).

13. Armitage and Jameson, *Women's West.*

14. Schlissel, Ruiz, and Monk, eds., *Western Women.*

15. Joan Jensen and Darlis Miller, *New Mexico Women: Intercultural Perspectives* (Albuqerque: University of New Mexico, 1986). Also, for recent scholarship on African American women in New Mexico, see Charlotte Mock, *Bridges: New Mexican Black Women, 1900–1950* (Albuquerque: New Mexico Commission on the Study of Women, 1985); Vicki Ruiz and Susan Tiano, *Women on the U.S.–Mexican Border: Responses to Change* (Westminster, Mass.: Allen and Unwin, 1987).

16. Elizabeth Jameson, "Toward a Multicultural History of Women in the Western United States," *Signs* 13, no. 4 (1988): 791.

17. Ellen DuBois and Vicki Ruiz, eds., *Unequal Sisters: A Multicultural Reader in U.S. Women's History* (New York: Routledge, 1990), xiii.

18. Antonia Castañeda, "Women of Color and the Rewriting of Western History: The Discourse, Politics, and Decolonization of History," *Pacific Historical Review* 61, no. 4 (1992): 501–533, esp. 520–21, 516–17.

19. Martha Cotera, *Diosa y Hembra: The History and Heritage of Chicanas in the U.S.* (Austin, Tex.: Information Systems Development, 1977). Instead of illuminating the experiences of ordinary yet important Chicanas, Cotera highlights women like Malíntzin Tenépal who became Hernán Cortés's concubine and eventual interpreter. Ongoing debates have emerged that challenge the perception of Malíntzin as "La Chingada." For research on Malíntzin, see Cordelia Candelaria, "La Malinche, Feminist Prototype," *Frontiers* 5, no. 2 (1980): 1–6; and Adelaída del Castillo, "Malíntzin Tenépal: A Preliminary Look into a New Perspective" in *Essays on La Mujer*, ed. Rosaura Sánchez and Rosa Martinez Cruz (Los Angeles: UCLA Chicano Studies Center, 1977), 124–49.

20. For more details on picture bride marriages, see Yuji Ichioka "Amerika Nadeshiko," *Pacific Historical Review* 48, no. 2 (May 1980): 339–57. Also see Ichihasshi Yamamoto, *Japanese in the United States* (Stanford, Calif.: Stanford University Press, 1969). After the couple married through the mail, the new bride would journey to meet her prospective husband. Often to her dismay, her husband was not as attractive or as young as he appeared in his photograph, since men sent altered pictures that often flattered their appearance. Similar to the Japanese, Korean women migrated to the United States as picture brides. See, for example, Sun Bin Yim, "Korean Immigrant Women in Early Twentieth Century America," in *Making Waves: An Anthology of Writings by and about Asian American Women*, ed. Asian Women United of California (Boston: Beacon Press, 1989), 50–60. *Making Waves* is an important contribution to scholarship on Japanese American, Korean American, Filipino American, Chinese American, and Southeast Asian American women. The entries vary from poetry and short stories to historical essays that seek to dispel stereotypical portrayals of these diverse women. For recent research on Korean picture brides, see Alice Yun Chai, "Picture Brides: Feminist Analysis of Life Histories of Hawai'i's Early Immigrant Women from Japan, Okinawa and Korea," in *Seeking Common Ground: Multidisciplinary Studies of Immigrant Women in the United States*, ed. Donna Gabaccia (Westport, Conn.: Greenwood Press, 1992), 123–38.

21. Alfredo Mirandé and Evangelina Enríquez, *La Chicana: The Mexican-American Woman* (Chicago: University of Chicago Press, 1979), 12–13. Additionally, Mirandé, a sociologist, and Enríquez, a professor of literature, falsely assumed that the Chicano family could be equated with the Aztec family. This ahistorical approach obfuscated the significance of the Chicano family.

22. See, for example, Elizabeth Fox-Genovese, *Within the Plantation Household: Black and White Women of the Old South* (Chapel Hill: University of North Carolina Press, 1988); Jacqueline Jones, *Labor of Love, Labor of Sorrow: Black Women, Work and the Family from Slavery to the Present* (New York: Basic Books, 1985); and Deborah Gray White, *Ar'nt I a Woman? Female Slaves in the Plantation South* (New York: W. W. Norton, 1985).

23. Many women's historians privileged African American women as the most "important" minority.

24. For information on Chinese immigration experiences, see Judy Yung, *Chinese Women of America: A Pictorial History* (Seattle: University of Washington Press for the Chinese Culture Foundation of San Francisco, 1986); Lucie Cheng Hirata, "Chinese Immigrant Women in Nineteenth Century California," in *Women in America, A History*, ed. Carol Ruth Berkin and Mary Beth Norton (Boston: Houghton Mifflin, 1979), 224–44; Ludy Cheng Hirata, "Free, Indentured, Enslaved: Chinese Prostitutes in Nineteenth Century America," *Signs* 5, no. 1 (Autumn 1979): 3–29. Also in *Relations of Rescue: The Search for Female Moral Authority in the American West, 1874–1939* (New York: Oxford University Press, 1990), Peggy Pascoe suggests that Protestant mission homes became refuges for Chinese women who sought to escape Chinese patriarchy and prostitution rings. For additional information on Japanese immigration experiences, see Yuji Ichioka, *The Issei: The World of First Generation Japanese Immigrants, 1885–1924* (New York: Free Press, 1988), and Valerie Matsumoto, *Farming the Home Place: A Japanese American Community in California, 1919–1982* (Ithaca, N.Y.: Cornell University Press, 1993). Also see Ronald Takaki, *Strangers from a Different Shore: A History of Asian Americans* (New York: Penguin Books, 1989). For twentieth-century Chinese immigration, see Sue Fawn Chung's "Gue Gim Wah: Pioneering Chinese American Woman of Nevada," in *History of Humanities: Essays in Honor of Wilbur Shepperson*, ed. Francis Hartigan (Reno: University of Nevada Press, 1989), 45–73.

25. Judy Yung, " 'A Bowlful of Tears': Chinese Women Immigrants on Angel Island," *Frontiers* 2, no. 2 (Summer 1977): 52–55. See also Sucheng Chan, *This Bittersweet Soil: The Chinese in California Agriculture, 1860–1910* (Berkeley: University of California Press, 1986).

26. Rayna Green, "The Pocahontas Perplex: The Image of Indian Women in American Culture," in *Unequal Sisters*, 1st ed. (1990), 21. See also Rebecca Tsosie, "Changing Woman: The Crosscurrents of American Indian Feminine Identity," *Unequal Sisters*, 2nd ed. (1994), 508–30.

27. Riley, *Women and Indians*, 21–35.

28. Patricia Albers and William James, "Illusion and Illumination: Visual Images of American Indian Women in the West," in *Women's West*, 48–49.

29. Renee Tajima, "Lotus Blossoms Don't Bleed: Images of Asian Women," in *Making Waves*, 309, 317.

30. Beverly Trulio, "Anglo American Attitudes toward New Mexican Women," *Journal of the West* 12, no. 2 (1973); 229–39.

31. Susan Shelby Magoffin, *Down the Santa Fe Trail*, ed. Stella Drum (reprint, New Haven, Conn.: Yale University Press, 1975).

32. Janet Lecompte, "The Independent Women of New Mexico, 1821–1846," in *New Mexico Women*, 71–93. Lecompte emphasized the way in which Mexican Americans retained legal rights until the advent of U.S. encroachment. She relied on rich archival sources to counter the inaccurate depictions offered by Euro-American diarists. For further research on Anglo attitudes toward Mexican women, see Magoffin's diary, *Down the Santa Fe Trail*.

33. Deena Gonázlez, "La Tules of Image and Reality: Euro-American Attitudes and Legend Formation on a Spanish-Mexican Frontier," in *Unequal Sisters*, (2nd ed., 1994) 60–61, 64, 66.

34. For further information on Italian American experiences, see Micaela di Leonardo, *The Varieties of Ethnic Experience: Kinship, Class and Gender among Italian-Americans in Northern California* (Ithaca, N.Y.: Cornell University Press, 1984).

35. Micaela di Leonardo, "The Myth of the Urban Village: Women, Work and Family among Italian-Americans in Twentieth Century California," in *Women's West*, 208.

36. Patricia Zavella, "The Impact of 'Sun Belt Industrialization' on Chicanas," in *Women's West*, 291–304.

37. Valerie Matsumoto, "Japanese-American Women during World War II," in *Unequal Sisters*, 1st ed. (1990), 373–86.

38. George Sánchez, " 'Go After the Women,' " in *Unequal Sisters*, 2d. ed. (1994), 284–97.

39. Theda Perdue, "Cherokee Women and the Trail of Tears," in *Unequal Sisters*, 2d ed. (1994), 37, 41. Similarly, Judy Yung explores Chinese women's political participation in "The Social Awakening of Chinese-American Women as Reported in Chung Sai Yat Po, 1900–1911," in *Unequal Sisters*, 1st ed. (1990), 195–207.

40. Emma Gee, "Issei: The First Women," in *Asian American Women* (Berkeley: University of California Press, 1971), 15.

41. Margarita Melville, *Twice a Minority: Mexican American Women* (St. Louis: C. V. Mosby, 1980), 1, 8. In her sociological approach, Melville compiled essays that explored gender roles and cross-cultural relationships.

42. For recent scholarship on women's labor force participation see articles by Evelyn Nakano Glenn and Vicki Ruiz in *Unequal Sisters*, 2d ed. (1994), 405–435, and 1st ed. (1990), 264–74; Evelyn Nakano Glenn, "The Dialectics of Wage Work: Japanese-American Women and Domestic Service, 1905–1940," *Feminist Studies* 6 (Fall 1980) 432–71; Gail Nomura, "Issei Working Women in Hawaii," in *Making Waves*, 135–48; Vicki Ruiz, "By the Day or the Week: Mexicana Domestic Workers in El Paso," in *Women on the U.S.-Mexican Border*, 61–76, and Ruiz, "And Miles to Go . . . : Mexican Women and Work, 1930–1985," in *Western Women*, 117–36; Patricia Zavella, *Women's Work and Chicano Families: Cannery Workers of Santa Clara Valley* (Ithaca, N.Y.: Cornell University Press, 1988), and Zavella, "Impact of 'Sun Belt Industrialization,' " in *Women's West*, 291–304; and Joan Jensen, " 'I've Worked, I'm Not Afraid of Work': Farm Women in New Mexico, 1920–1940," in *New Mexico Women*, 227–35.

43. Evelyn Nakano Glenn, *Issei, Nisei, War Bride: Three Generations of Japanese-American Women in Domestic Service*, (Philadelphia: Temple University Press, 1986), xi, xii, 162. See also Patricia Zavella's "Impact of 'Sun Belt Industrialization,' " in *Women's West*, 291–304. Zavella sought to dispel the stereotype of the passive Chicana in her research on Chicanas in the Albuquerque industrial sector. Burgeoning sunbelt industrialization significantly affected Chicanas since they became the major labor pool. Although the Albuquerque Chicanas Zavella studied were generally compelled to work out of economic necessity, many learned to value their new autonomy.

44. Patricia Albers, "Sioux Women in Transition: A Study of Their Changing Status in a Domestic and Capitalist Sector of Production," in *The Hidden Half: Studies of Plains Indian Women*, ed. Patricia Albers and Beatrice Medicine, (Washington, D.C.: University Press of America, 1983), 220. For more on Sioux women, see Marla Powers, *Oglala Women: Myth, Ritual and Reality* (Chicago: University of Chicago Press, 1986).

45. Terry Reynolds, "Women, Pottery and Economics at Acoma Pueblo," in *New Mexico Women*, 290.

46. Vicki Ruiz, *Cannery Women, Cannery Lives* (Albuquerque: University of New Mexico Press, 1987). Children became fledgling protesters, conducting strikes at the home of the Shapiros. According to Ruiz, "These youngsters carried signs with such slogans as 'Shapiro is starving my Mama,' and 'I'm underfed because my Mama is underpaid,' " 76. Besides work, generational change provided another framework to explore transforming gender relationships. See, for example, *Apache Mothers and Daughters* (Norman: University of Oklahoma Press, 1992) in which Ruth Boyer and Narcissus Gayton use oral history to examine the lives of four generations of Apache women.

For other research on Chicana union participation, see Melissa Hield, "Union Minded: Women in Texas ILGWU, 1933–1950," *Frontiers* 4, no. 2 (Summer 1979): 59–70; Margaret Rose, "Women in the United Farm Workers: A Study of Chicana and Mexicana Participation in a Labor Union, 1950–1980" (Ph.D. dissertation, University of California Los Angeles, 1988); and Magdalena

Mora and Adelaída del Castillo, *Mexican Women in the United States: Struggles Past and Present* (Los Angeles: UCLA Chicano Studies Research Center Publications, 1980).

47. Jane Dysart, "Mexican Women in San Antonio, 1830–1860," *Western Historical Quarterly*, 7, no. 4 (October 1976): 372. According to Dysart, a powerful alliance took place when the daughter of a wealthy Mexican married a politically influential Euro-American. Subsequent generations of Mexicanas followed suit by marrying Euro-American men.

48. Darlis Miller, "Cross Cultural Marriages in the Southwest: The New Mexico Experience, 1846–1900," in *New Mexico Women*, 110.

49. Susan Johnson, "Sharing Bed and Board: Cohabitation and Cultural Difference in Central Arizona Mining Towns, 1863–1873," in *Women's West*, 77–91.

50. Sylvia Van Kirk, "The Role of Native Women in the Creation of Fur Trade Society in Western Canada, 1670–1830," in *Women's West*, 53–62. See also Sylvia Van Kirk, *Many Tender Ties: Women in Fur-Trade Society, 1670–1870* (Norman: University of Oklahoma Press, 1983).

51. Sarah Deutsch, *No Separate Refuge: Culture, Class, and Gender on an Anglo Hispanic Frontier in the American Southwest, 1880–1940* (New York: Oxford University Press, 1987), 81–86; quote, 86.

52. Peggy Pascoe, *Relations of Rescue: The Search for Female Moral Authority in the American West, 1874–1939* (New York: Oxford University Press, 1990), esp. 114–45. Pascoe showed that these "rescued Chinese women" eventually became the rank-and-file Chinese middle-class population. She also pointed out that, while racial hierarchies were quite common within the confines of the mission homes, gender hierarchies dominated the Chinese community.

53. See especially Peggy Pascoe, "Race, Gender, and Intercultural Relations: The Case of Interracial Marriage"; Valerie Matsumoto, "Desperately Seeking 'Deirdre': Gender Roles, Multicultural Relations, and Nisei Women Writers of the 1930s"; and Vicki Ruiz, "Dead Ends or Gold Mines? Using Records in Mexican American Women's History," in this anthology. For other recent scholarship that employs an intercultural approach, see Antonia Castañeda, "Gender, Race, and Culture: Spanish-Mexican Women in the Historiography of Frontier California," *Frontiers* 11 (1990): 8–20; Sánchez, " 'Go After the Women,' " in *Unequal Sisters*, 1st ed. (1990), 250–63; and Pascoe, *Relations of Rescue*. The benefactors of the moral rescue missions advocated the "cult of true womanhood," with specific emphasis on piety and purity. Ultimately, their goal was to rescue "fallen women" from vices like prostitution.

54. Peggy Pascoe, "At the Crossroads of Culture," *Women's Review of Books* 7 (February 1990): 5.

55. Albers and Medicine, *Hidden Half*, 13, 15.

56. Beatrice Medicine, "Warrior Women: Sex Role Alternatives for Plains Indian Women," in *Hidden Half*, 276.

57. Raymond DeMallie, "Male and Female in Traditional Lakota Culture," in *Hidden Half*, 261.

58. For example, see Alicia Gaspar de Alba, "Tortillerismo: Work by Chicana Lesbians," *Signs* 18, no. 4 (Summer 1993): 956–63. For more on lesbian and gay Native American scholarship, see work by Paula Gunn Allen and Will Roscoe. For example, in "How the West Was Really Won" Allen argues that gays and lesbians have always occupied an important position in Native American societies. See Allen in *The Sacred Hoop: Recovering the Feminine in American Indian Traditions* (Boston: Beacon Press, 1984), 194–298, and Allen, "Beloved Women: Lesbians in American Indian Culture," *Conditions* 7 (1981): 67–87. Will Roscoe explores the Zuni *berdache* tradition in *The Zuni Man-Woman* (Albuquerque: University of New Mexico Press, 1991). Also see Roscoe's anthology of lesbian and gay Native American history entitled *Living the Spirit: A Gay American Indian Anthology* (New York: St. Martin's Press, 1986).

59. Evelyn Blackwood, "Sexuality and Gender in Certain Native American Tribes: The Case of Cross-Gender Females," *Signs* 10, no. 1 (Autumn 1984): 28–29, 35, 42. Despite the negative portrayals of cross-gender Native Americans that outsiders have perpetuated, Blackwood attempted to shed light on the role of cross-gender women in Native American communities. Some Native American girls became socialized as little boys; hence they became "cross-gender" females. As

a cross-gender female reached puberty, instead of becoming "marriageable property," she began to search for her own wife.

60. See Pamela H., "Asian American Lesbians: An Emerging Voice in the Asian Community," in *Making Waves*, 282–90, and Alice Hom, "Family Matters: A Historical Study of the Asian Pacific Lesbian Network" (master's thesis, University of California Los Angeles, 1992).

61. Pamela H., "Asian American Lesbians," 284.

62. Trisha Franzen, "Differences and Identities: Feminism and the Albuquerque Lesbian Community," *Signs* 18, no. 4 (Summer 1993): 895, 903. The bars provided lesbians with a safe arena for social interaction. Franzen's conclusions are similar to those that Elizabeth Kennedy and Madeline Davis drew in *Boots of Leather, Slippers of Gold* (New York: Routledge, 1993), a study of the Buffalo (New York) lesbian bar culture during the 1940s and 1950s.

63. Alma Garcia, "The Development of Chicana Feminist Discourse, 1970–1980," in *Unequal Sisters*, 1st ed. (1990), 418–31. Chicanas often criticized the notion of preserving cultural pride since this ideology failed to recognize the "need to alter male-female relations within Chicano communities." For more on Chicana feminism, see Ramón Gutiérrez's insightful "Community, Patriarchy and Individualism: The Politics of Chicano History and the Dream of Equality," *American Quarterly* 45, no. 1 (March 1993):44–72; also see Denise Segura and Beatríz Pesquera, "Beyond Indifference and Apathy: The Chicana Movement and Chicana Feminist Discourse," *Aztlán* 19, no. 2 (1988–1990): 69–92.

64. For African American woman's struggles against African American cultural nationalism, see Frances White, "Listening to the Voices of Black Feminism," *Radical America* 18: 7–25. For scholarship addressing the issue of African American exclusion in the woman suffrage movement, see Angela Davis, *Women, Race and Class* (New York: Random House, 1981), and Paula Giddings, *When and Where I Enter: The Impact of Black Women on Race and Sex in America* (New York: William Morrow, 1984). Also, for Asian American women's encounters of sexism in their communities, see Esther Ngan-Ling Chow, "The Development of Feminist Consciousness among Asian-American Women," *Gender and Society* 1: 284–99.

65. Esther Ngan-Ling Chow, "The Feminist Movement: Where Are All the Asian Women?" in *Making Waves*, 369, 372, 375. See also both Moraga and Anzaldúa's *This Bridge Called My Back* and hooks's *From Margin to Center*, which likewise illuminate the shortcomings of the mainstream women's movement. For more on the experiences of Asian American women and feminist politics, see Alice Yun Chai, "Toward A Holistic Paradigm for Asian-American Women's Studies: A Synthesis of Feminist Scholarship and Women of Color's Feminist Politics," *Women's Studies International Forum* 8, no. 1 (1985):59–66; King-Kok Cheung, "The Woman Warrior versus the Chinaman Pacific: Must a Chinese American Critic Choose between Feminism and Heroism?" in *Conflicts in Feminism*, ed. Marianne Hirsch and Evelyn Fox Keller (New York: Routledge, 1990), 234–51; and Susie Ling, "The Mountain Movers: Asian American Women's Movement in Los Angeles," *Amerasia* 15, no. 1 (1989): 51–67.

66. Adela de la Torre and Beatríz Pesquera, eds., *Building with Our Hands: New Directions in Chicana Studies* (Berkeley: University of California Press, 1993), 232.

2.
_____

Native American Women: Changing Statuses, Changing Interpretations

RAMONA FORD

This article about American Indian women is a good introduction to the challenge of studying gender difference. Most nineteenth-century white observers (male and female) viewed American Indian women through the lens of Euro-American culture and were shocked by deviations from their own gender roles. Recently, as white women's historians tried to understand Indian women "in their own terms," they were hindered by lack of familiarity with the culture and customs of specific American Indian peoples. Consequently, some of the first books about American Indian women lumped them all together as generic "Indians" and failed to recognize the importance of cultural differences.

Ramona Ford's article provides a structure within which to think about gender difference. She does what anthropologists do best: She takes the concept of status apart, identifies the various components encompassed by the term, and provides many examples of the variety of ways in which the statuses of women were constructed in different American Indian cultures. Then she shows how these statuses were historically changed by Euro-American conquest. She is refreshingly at ease with complex explanations, drawing on three different analytic theories (because no single one is adequate) and firmly insisting that "social positions are really plural, composed of a number of statuses." The result is an eye-opening article that quietly makes the point that American Indian concepts of gender were much more complex, subtle, and varied than most Euro-Americans have imagined.

We will not be defeated until the hearts of our women are on the ground.

—TRADITIONAL SAYING OF SEVERAL TRIBES

Our ancestors considered it a great offence to reject the counsels of their women, particularly female governesses. They were esteemed the mistresses of the soil. Who, said they, bring us into being? Who cultivates our land, kindles our fires [or administers food to the hungry], but our women?

—DOMINE PATER, SENECA/CAYUGA
TO GOVERNOR CLINTON OF NEW YORK, 1788

I knew they were going to say, "You can't run [for governor] because it is against tribal tradition.'' My thinking has always been, "Hey, we didn't have a constitution. We didn't even have a governor until the Spaniards came up." So where do we draw the line with tradition? We didn't have a governor. We had a whole religious structure. We had a hierarchy with our religious elders that ran the tribe, and many of them were women. Clan mothers had a big say. We're matrilineal. We belong to our mother's clan. So where did the story change here?

—GOVERNOR VERNA WILLIAMSON, ISLETA PUEBLO
INTERVIEW, 12 JULY 1990

Now, you understand that the women in [my] family carried with them, and carry with us to this very day, the very strong matrilineal and matrilocal tradition of our people. The women are extraordinarily strong. Males who have come into our family follow us. It's matrilocal. Where we go, our men go. We are the lightbulb around which the male moths pivot. That's not an ugly thing, because if you work it well and in a humane fashion, you have have symbiosis so that the bee and the flower need each other and both are quite handsome creatures of the Great Spirit.

—DR. SHIRLEY HILL WITT, AKWESASNE MOHAWK
INTERVIEW, 4 AUGUST 1990

Euro-American women's history and changing gender roles do not prepare us to understand the histories of other women in the United States. Native American women's history forces us to rethink what is "normative" or possible in women's roles. Today there are occasional comments in the mass media regarding the variety of leadership roles Indian women are taking in their communities. For example, in the mid-1990s 20 percent of the heads of tribal councils and boards were women. Neither the Pocahontas nor the squaw-drudge stereotype of Native American women explains such active community orientation. Women who are in these leadership positions are often quoted as saying that it was not unusual for women in their group to have an important role in decision making "in the old days." Clearly a more accurate picture of women's roles in Indian societies is needed.[1] Despite problems with the validity, reliability, and sparseness of the data on Native American women, researchers from anthropology, history, sociology, and other disciplines are now reexamining old documents with new questions and interpretations. New ethnographies and oral histories are also providing further understanding of past and present women's roles. These attempts to sort out the verifiable data that have been overlooked are a valuable resource for our society.[2]

Two major approaches to material on the changing statuses of women in Native American societies are commonly used, and a third, a newer approach, has been called for to alert researchers to the dynamics of microlevel social interaction.[3]

1. *Historical materialism* stresses access to and control of production and resources in native social systems and the ways in which these relationships

Verna Williamson, former
governor of Isleta Pueblo.
(Courtesy Southwest Texas
State University.)

changed over time, given the types of contact with the market system and
ideologies of the dominant Euro-American society.

2. *Social/cultural constructionism* emphasizes the native cultural value
systems that justified their social organization and placed responsibility and
esteem on categories of people for doing various activities necessary for
group survival. These values are expressed either symbolically or explicitly
in creation myths in which female deities are important, in rituals, and in
traditional practices such as kinship organization and gender roles. For
example, one might ask if women in a particular group had personal
autonomy in such areas as marriage, divorce, reproduction, and work. Were
they responsible for the support and betterment of their kinship group and
community in rituals, healing, defense, provision of goods for giveaways
or potlatches and gift exchanges between families in marriage ceremonials?
Were they considered endowed with supernatural powers or consulted as
wise women in their old age? Did people have flexibility in their gender
roles and activities? If the belief system supported active community roles
for women, how were beliefs and practices affected by the dominant society's
influence? Are native societies today using traditional cultural demands for
women's responsibilities, or are they increasingly acculturated into the
dominant society's structure and its cultural commands for gender roles?

Dr. Shirley Hill Witt, founding
member of the National Indian
Youth Council. (Photo from
author's collection.)

3. *Processual analysis/community interaction* research, fostered by Jo-
Anne Fiske and Robert Lynch, pays attention to local-level interaction and
considers how individual women and their voluntary groups and kinship
networks operate in face-to-face encounters today within both local and
dominant society power structures and cultural formations. Women's goals
for themselves, their kinship groups, communities, and tribes and the means
of achieving these goals may run counter to entrenched comprador native
elites and to dominant society social structures, bureaucracies, and cultural
norms. A current example can be drawn from the grassroots mobilization
on many reservations to block the dumping of toxic and radioactive wastes
on Indian lands. Contracts that had been quietly signed between tribal
councils and waste management companies have been negated or stymied
by organized popular demand, thanks in large part to women's efforts.

GENDER AND SOCIAL STATUS
IN PREINDUSTRIAL SOCIETIES

While it is possible to say that in some Native American societies the overall
position of women was more independent or esteemed than in others, a

point now emphasized in cross-cultural comparison of preindustrial societies is that social positions are really plural, composed of a number of statuses.[4] Women in a society may control the use of rights to land yet not control distribution of the products. They may have some political influence and organization but may not have much participation in religious rites. Some Plains hunting groups had female ownership of all domestic goods, including dwellings; some did not. Some tribes allowed similar standards of sexual conduct for males and females; a few had a double standard by the time of recorded data. The permutations of possibilities seem endless.

When individual societies are studied, it seems natural to attribute a causal relationship between women's importance in one category and their importance in another. For example, the often-cited case of political influence of Iroquois women's clans has been attributed to their control of the use of land, tools, and products.[5] While this may be legitimate for the Iroquois, it is not safe to generalize this to any other group until an examination is made of the specific society's values and social organization. Patricia Albers points out that the failure to take such a holistic, inclusive view of women's statuses has produced conflicting accounts of whether women's status rose or fell in a particular group during contact.[6]

Cross-cultural statistical comparisons, such as Martin Whyte's worldwide study of ninety-three preindustrial societies on fifty-two variables relating to the relative position of women, also indicate that there is no one key variable that will predict the status of women on the other variables. Testing eighteen hypotheses commonly found in the literature on women's status, Whyte failed to support almost all of them with his particular data set. He did find modest, but significant, correlations in three areas of interest in our discussion of Native American women's statuses:

1. Matrilineal descent and matrilocal residence are somewhat associated with benefits in certain areas—especially property rights.

2. The existence of individual private property is associated with some forms of male advantage—such as the low value placed on the labor of women.

3. Societal complexity in preindustrial societies is associated with the statuses of women, with simpler, less stratified societies in general allowing more equality.[7]

It could be argued that Whyte's findings support a historical materialism approach, that is, that control of economic resources is important, that private property has been associated historically with patriarchy, and that the formation of complex stratified societies and the garnering of their surplus value have not been conducive to women's equality in preindustrial societies. Somehow this does not seem entirely satisfying in that preindustrial groups seem to confer status in other areas besides economic production, which forces us back to the questions raised by cultural constructionism and its processes. What were the statuses of women in different lineal systems and culture complexes and how did people deal with or resist change in cross-cultural contact?

MATRILINEAL, BILATERAL,
AND PATRILINEAL SOCIETIES

Ethnographies of various societies usually include data on lineal descent and residence, although ethnographers sometimes disagree on a group's classification. Descent and inheritance can be through the mother's clan or lineage (matrilineal), the father's group (patrilineal), or through both parents (bilateral). Residence of the newly married couple can be with the bride's people (matrilocal or uxorilocal); with the groom's people (patrilocal or virilocal); with either of the couple's people, depending on their choice (ambilocal); with the bride's mother's brother (avunculocal); or with nonrelated groups (neolocal).

A few writers have focused specifically on the effects of lineality and residence on women's statuses.[8] The findings by Whyte and the other researchers that women's statuses made some general gains in matrilineal and/or matrilocal societies are especially interesting in light of the surprising number of such societies among Native American groups, shown in Table 2.1. Only 15 percent of the 563 cultures in G. P. Murdock's world ethnographic sample are matrilineal, and these are predominantly horticultural groups located in Africa, the Pacific Islands, and North and South America.[9] Valerie Mathes, however, estimates that one-quarter of the aboriginal groups in what is now the United States were matrilineal and these include some of the more populous groups.[10] Also, matrilocal societies are especially numerous in North and South America and this tends to increase the possibility of women's higher statuses.[11] Whyte points out that matrilineality "disappears" with the introduction of the plow, the expansion of market economies, the spread of patriarchal ideology and law, and the increasing complexity of social organization. In groups that have not acculturated completely or that have become bicultural, perhaps vestiges of matrilineality and other cultural values continue to influence gender roles in new ways.[12]

In addition to those groups cited by name as matrilineal in Table 2.1, there were also matrilineal groups among the Northwest Coast Indians, the eastern Algonquian-speaking groups (such as those in the Powhattan Confederacy and other confederacies of the mid-Hudson, Chesapeake Bay, and Massachusetts Bay areas), the Caddoan-speaking groups of the Mississippi Valley, and the Siouan-speaking groups of the Piedmont area.[13] For some groups there is a question as to whether they were bilateral, patrilineal, or matrilineal; these have been indicated with an asterisk in the table.[14]

Wherever horticulture was the dominant mode of subsistence among early Native Americans, the social organization was likely, but not guaranteed, to be matrilineal with matrilocal residence. (The Shawnee and Pima, among others, remind us that not all horticultural groups were matrilineal. Note that Pima men were in charge of irrigated agriculture while women gathered. Complex irrigation systems began to put groups into higher technology, which pulled them toward patrilineality.) Groups on the eastern seaboard and in the Southeast, some groups around the Great Lakes and in the

Table 2.1. Matrilineal, Bilateral, and Patrilineal Native American Societies

Matrilineal	Bilateral	Patrilineal
Arikara	Arapaho* (matrilocal)	Assiniboine
Athapaskan-speakers	Athapaskan (matrilocal)	Blackfoot*
Ahtna	Bearlake	Gros Ventre/Atsina
Carrier	Beaver	Illinois
Han	Chilcotin	Kaskaskia
Kaska	Chipewyan	Peoria
Koyukon	Dogrib	Iowa
Kutchin	Hare	Kansa
Navajo	Ingalik	Menominee
Tahltan	Mountain	Missouri*
Tanaina	Sarsi	Ojibwa (Chippewa)
Tanana	Sekani	Omaha
Tutchone	Slave*	Osage
Western Apache	Chiricahua Apache	Oto*
Cherokee	Jicarilla Apache	Papago
Chickasaw	Lipan Apache	Pima
Choctaw	Mescalero Apache	Ponca
Creek	Cheyenne (matrilocal)	Pueblo
Crow	Comanche	Nambe
Haida	Paiute	Picuris
Haisla	Northern*	San Ildefonso
Hidatsa	Southern	San Juan
Hopi	Plains Cree	Santa Clara
Huron	Salish	Taos
Iroquois	Shoshone	Tesuque
Cayuga	Teton Lakota*	Zia
Mohawk	Ute (matrilocal)	Shawnee
Oneida		Winnebago
Onondaga		Yakima
Seneca		
Tuscarora		
Mandan		
Natchez		
Pawnee		
Pueblo		
Acoma		
Cochiti		
Isleta		
Jemez		
Laguna		
San Felipe		
Sandia		
Santa Ana		
Santo Domingo		
Zuni		
Seminole		
Tlingit (avunculocal)		
Tonkawa		
Tsimshian		
Wichita		
Wyandot		

*There is some question as to how descent is traced in the group, whether it is matrilineal, patrilineal, or bilateral. The group is placed in the most probable category. See note 14.

Sources for this table are listed in note 15.

Upper Missouri area, and tribes in the Southwest were predominantly horticultural and matrilineal, and usually matrilocal. The matrilineal groups that were partly horticultural and partly hunters on the plains during some of the year and the matrilineal Crow—horticulturalists who became full-time hunters—are particularly interesting, since the effects of the incoming horse and hide complex can be compared with the effects on the non-matrilineal nomadic Plains groups. The bilateral/patrilineal groups have also been the subject of some debate as to their original social organization. Anthropologists have archaeological evidence of the movement of groups from eastern areas just prior to the reintroduction of horses to the Americas. Horses became a store of private wealth, and a new system of social organization and priorities began to evolve. Some of these differences in response to social change will be noted in the discussion of Plains groups below.

In the Southwest, Navajo, Hopi, and western Pueblos and some other Pueblo women controlled their own property, which they bequeathed to their children. Matrons of the women's clans made ultimate decisions in economic and domestic matters in their kinship-based societies. With the coming of the Spaniards, who would deal only with male representatives, women's "public" roles were overlooked by the outsiders and their formal powers began to recede. Informally, however, clan mothers continued to hold their ritual significance and private power among those who maintained traditional ties within their communities.

Among the matrilineal, matrilocal Seneca of the Iroquois in the Northeast, women nominated and recalled chiefs in the council of elders, had control of the group's store of wealth, influenced decisions in the timing of warfare and long-distance hunting, controlled agricultural land and tools, farmed in women's cooperative groups, arranged marriages and determined when men were no longer welcome in the longhouse of the wife's clan, presided over feasts celebrating women's food providing and fertility in the ceremonial cycle, and adopted captives into the tribe to replace manpower lost in war.[16] In the Southeast, Cherokee women had councils that deliberated with the men's councils on war and peace and other matters of diplomacy. They controlled their own property, sexuality, and reproduction.

Tlingit women in the Pacific Northwest were held responsible for the wealth (or lack of it) in their families, as men were known to be "foolish with money."[17] This is reported to have given women a strong role in family affairs and in trade. Diaries and logs of foreign traders note that women preferred to do the trading and that if a husband made a fur trade that the wife thought was too disadvantageous she brought him right back to renegotiate. These women drove a hard bargain, it was said.

Bilateral societies such as the Salish, some Apache groups, and the Arapaho allowed women a certain latitude in roles as traders, warriors, and shamans. Women held their own property, controlled their own sexuality, and sometimes spoke in council.[18] Among the Apache the girls' puberty rite is still the most important event in the ceremonial calendar.

Women in the patrilineal Plains groups—such as the Iowa, Oto, Missouri, Omaha, Ponca, Osage, and Kansa—began to lose some power with the coming of the horse and hide trade. Although "hell came with horses" according to some women's testimony, it was also true that women could have the position of favored "sit-beside-him-wife" or "favored-child," which allowed some degree of independence. Among the Lakota, women gained status through participation in the Buffalo ceremony and Virgin Fire ritual. Many groups also reserved a high position for the holy women who could sponsor the Sun Dance.[19] Plains women made ceremonial objects and elaborate arts and crafts through which they gained status.[20] Women of the Blackfoot, Dakota and Lakota, Arapaho, and Cheyenne formed craft guilds (which gave prizes for designs that were passed to heirs with a sort of patent on use) and claimed coups according to the number of robes they produced.[21] The failure to notice these things earlier has been attributed to the bias of the western male observers.[21]

Even on the reservations, set up to be male-dominated by the Bureau of Indian Affairs (BIA), women maintained control over what they produced in the garden or the crafts they sold.[23] Cross-gender, warrior, and chieftain roles were open to the few who wished to pursue male activities, and the Blackfoot woman could eventually improve her status and independence through the "manly hearted woman" role.

THE ROLES OF THE "MANLY-HEARTED WOMAN" AND THE CROSS-GENDER/*BERDACHE* AMONG WESTERN GROUPS

Among the Plains and other western groups two roles have been mentioned that deserve further explanation since they indicate a certain flexibility for women and men within many traditional societies. These two roles, those of the "manly-hearted woman" and the cross-gender/*berdache*, allowed Native American women to pursue what would have ordinarily been regarded as male personality characteristics or roles in their particular societies.

The manly-hearted women, as described by Oscar Lewis, on the North Piegan (Blackfoot) Brocket Reserve in Canada were not transvestites, homosexuals, or warriors, but were demonstrating a personality type.[24] This term was applied only to older (but not necessarily postmenopausal) propertied women who had been married. These women (14 of the 109 married or formerly married women on the reserve) were recognized as "manly-hearted" because they were independent, outspoken, and assertive in public. Six of the women Lewis studied were medicine women. Manly-hearted women ran their own households and, if they were still married, also ran their husbands—a phenomenon noted by a trader in 1794. They participated in religion by sponsoring Sun Dances, were considered to be sexually active and experimental, were more mature, and were wealthier from inheritance and their own endeavors. In fact, only wealthy women of high social position were eligible for this designation; poor women who showed the same traits were derided as presumptuous.

Some of these women had been rather independent all their lives, having been "favored-child" or "sit-beside" wife. Others had grown into independence with age, experience, and wealth. One thing these women had in common was that they would not put up with abuse from their spouses. Those who had been beaten by earlier husbands, a not-uncommon practice among the Piegan during the recent historical period, had fought back with weapons or with shaming their husbands in public; if all else failed, they left the abusive spouse. This semi-institutionalized role was feared and criticized and admired. Manly-hearted widows, who were women of wealth, social position, and presumed sexual abilities, were much sought after by younger men. Some women seemed to see the role as one of protest in a male-dominated society, and many women aspired to achieve this status, according to Lewis.

Berdache, a term originally used for males but now also applied to females, is currently being replaced by a more neutral term—"the cross-gender role." The cross-gender role was more complicated than that of the manly-hearted personality; it indicated that the individual had chosen to temporarily or permanently take on some aspect of the role of the other gender in tasks, rituals, and sometimes dress and hairstyle.[24] This category included those who *wanted* to adopt the other gender role; it excluded men who had been forced to dress like women—a shaming device used among some Plains groups for those who had shown cowardice in battle.

Cross-gender role status might include those born with indeterminate genitals, those with homosexual preferences, or those whose preferences and/or socialization had inclined them to cross-gender roles. The preference often surfaced in visions or dreams. Some groups said these visions came while in the womb. In the case of biological uncertainty, the parents might allow the individual to choose which way to go by observing what toys the child preferred. Among the Kaska, parents without sons might deliberately pick a daughter with the most assertive qualities to socialize into the male role; at the age of five a bag containing bear ovaries was tied around the girl child's neck or to her belt and her male training began.[25] Sue-Ellen Jacobs found documentation for two societies in which a particularly handsome boy might be raised as a girl, but no societies have been cited as raising a girl as a boy because she was homely.[26] The story of Sitting-in-the-Water-Grizzly/Bowdash (Kutenai), however, provides us with the possibility that her powerful physique caused a rejection by Native American males and led her to a cross-gender role that she eventually fulfilled rather well as a guide, prophet, and warrior—after a slow start with a bad temper that moved her to wife-beating.[27]

Homosexuality does not appear to have been the major reason for cross-gender or *berdache* roles, since reports indicate that homosexuality was practiced by those who were not *berdaches* in their communities.[28] The early Spanish writers, for example, thought they found male homosexual practices all over the Americas, but the practices were not limited to the institutionalized, more permanent *berdache* role where women's duties were included. Among some groups *berdaches* were bisexual or heterosexual. Navajos, for example, can often point to a *berdache* (*nadle*) grandfather or great-grandfather. A Navajo cross-gender-role person was considered in a third gender category. A *nadle*'s legal status, however, was that of a woman. For example, the blood payment for murdering a *nadle* was the same as for killing a woman, higher than that for killing a man. The legal status was determined by the type of work performed, rather than by biology.[29]

If homosexuality was not the basis for selecting the cross-gender role, other possibilities have to be considered: (1) an individual's preference for the tasks of the opposite sex, (2) belief in visions and dreams from the Spirit World, and (3) expediency. In the latter instance, women sometimes became hunters and warriors to feed and protect their families. One such example was Woman Chief, a Gros Ventre adopted by the Crow and a favorite child who took over the raising of her siblings when her adopted parents died. Hunting and raiding were time-consuming activities and it was eventually necessary for her to take four wives to do the women's tasks.[30] Running Eagle (Piegan Blackfoot) may present a similar situation; she too found it necessary to support her siblings. Lozen (Chiricahua Apache), Buffalo Calf Road (Northern Cheyenne), and others might not have become warriors in more pacific times.[31] These particular cases do not imply homosexuality but economic or defensive necessity and a proclivity for male tasks. Table 2.2 shows documented cases of female cross-gender roles; not included are cases in which women in various tribes temporarily served as warriors.

It is difficult to speculate from this distance what motivations predominated in each of the time periods in various societies or even individual documented cases of gender-role deviation. Several factors should be considered further.

Table 2.2. Native American Tribes with Documentation of Female Cross-Gender Roles

Subartic	Northwest	California/Oregon	Southwest	Great Basin	Plains
Carrier	Bella Coola	Achomawi	Apache	Northern	Blackfoot
Ingalik	Haisla	Atsugewi	Cocopa	Paiute	Crow
Kaska	Lillooet	Hupa	Maricopa	Shoshoni	Kutenai (Plateau)
	Nootka	Kalekau	Mohave	Southern	Ojibwa
	Okanagon	Kato	Navajo	Paiute	
	, Queets	Klamath	Papago	Southern	
	Quinalt	Lassik	Pima	Ute	
		Northern	Yuma	Ute	
		Pomo	Zuni	Washoe	
		Shasta			
		Tipai			
		Tubatulabal			
		Wintu			
		Wiyot			
		Yokuts			
		Youki			

Sources for this table are listed in note 32.

First, those taking up cross-gender roles were sometimes held in reverence. The visions and dreams in which these persons were directed to take on the "role of the other" meant that they were touched by and in contact with the Great Spirit. If the gods had willed it, so be it. In some societies these persons were sought out and paid for giving children magical secret names (Teton), for performing ceremonies involving the dead (California Indians), or for divination in locating lost objects or predicting the time and direction of the approach of enemies. Sue-Ellen Jacobs found few societies in which the *berdache* was not a respected community member until long-term contact with whites intervened and the role became a shameful one.[32] Although cross-gender roles lost much overt community support, they did not completely disappear, and today they have a respected spiritual role among traditional members of their societies.[33]

Second, these persons often were exceedingly good providers. Male *berdaches* were known for their high productivity in crafts (which brought top price in trade) and their fine tipis. According to Ralph Linton, "It was the highest compliment if a woman was told that her work was as good as a berdache's."[34] Some male *berdaches* became the wealthiest persons in their group, as reports from the Zuni, Crow, and California Yurok indicate. Navajos considered themselves fortunate to have a *berdache* in the extended household, because it would ensure wealth. This prestige and wealth were possible because in most groups women retained control over their own property and craft production. Women in cross-gender roles were known as exceptional producers and hunters. (Recall that Woman Chief needed four wives to keep up with her hunting ability.) The suggestion that they had to "try harder" to prove themselves in an unusual role is not without merit. Men were not reluctant to take male *berdache* second wives, nor apparently were women reluctant to have female *berdache* husbands. Spouses of cross-gender-role persons were not considered homosexual, but heterosexual persons fulfilling their normal gender roles. In sum, cross-gender-role persons were usually good economic providers. Speculatively, perhaps they were also sometimes psychologically sympathetic to their same-sex partners—a point not mentioned in the literature but worthy of thought.

Anglo observers of societies with cross-gender roles (Ruth Benedict, Paul Radin, Robert Lowie, Ralph Linton, for example) tended to stress psycho logical causes. While the locals said cross-gender-role persons were "born thus," were directed by a vision, or preferred opposite-gender tasks, anthropologists generally referred to the pressures of society or fear of failure in the male role, sometimes even labeling them "psychiatric cases."[35]

Cross-gender roles, whether permanent or temporary, as in the case of some warrior women, were more accepted in many Native American societies than by the incoming Europeans. What documentation is available indicates that the practice may have been more widespread for men than for women (although early observers were European males talking mostly to Native American males) and that cross-gender roles declined with European contact—or went underground and informants refused to discuss it. Charles Callendar and Lee Kochems list 113 Native American societies in which male *berdaches* have been documented, together with citations to the original reports for each group.[36] So far data have been found for only forty-four societies—mostly west of the Mississippi—with females in cross-gender roles. (See Table 2.2) The larger number of cases found in the Southwest may be due to later, more intrusive contact with whites, by which time anthropologists were on hand to ask leading questions.[37] (One must bear in mind the fact that their judgmental positions might not have elicited open answers.)

There were many comments from the early Spanish (in Florida, the U.S. Southwest, and Latin America) and French (more concentrated in the Northeast) explorers and missionaries about native male *berdache* customs, but on women in institutionalized cross-gender roles they are strangely silent. The mention of temporary women warriors among eastern groups—the Iroquois, Cherokee, and others—could mean that we are overlooking something in the data and/or the data are forever incomplete on this point. While it does seem surprising that so little documentation would have been made of such a phenomenon if it existed in eastern seaboard groups, still the Spanish, who were busy trying to stamp out "male sodomy," which they apparently found quite common, missed the fact that women had cross-gender roles in some of these groups with which they had contact. Why were women's roles underreported and was this true in other regions of early European contact?

In sum, gender-role identity was not equated in Native American thinking with biology alone, and an individual was accepted for whatever gender work and ritual roles the person assumed. The choice might have been made by deliberate or less deliberate socialization (for example, the case of the favorite girl child who is allowed to participate in men's activities); through personality, ability, and preference for occupations of the other sex; by direction of supernatural forces; or by expediency as male roles needed to be filled. The key is that "women as well as men could step outside the boundaries of traditional sex role assignments and, as individuals, make group-respected choices."[38] This choice was precluded in Euro-American ideologies, which expected people to adhere to more narrow biological and gender-role classifications.

EURO-AMERICAN CONTACT
AND WOMEN'S STATUSES

Native American women had a variety of statuses, rights, and responsibilities at the time of European contact, but it is apparent that in some respects their positions subsequently declined in varying degrees. How did this happen? Despite the differences in tribal social organization and the variance in time, place, and nature of foreign contact, a few comparisons can be made. Five broad interactive categories of change factors are used here to obtain an overview.

1. *The fur (or other early) trade and disease:* Trade and accompanying diseases were early factors in the contact between incoming groups and

Native American societies. It is thought that the Danes, possibly Chinese, and others arrived prior to the 1500s, before the Russians, Dutch, Swedes, French, Spanish, and English did. These explorers and fur traders introduced several things—diseases foreign to the genetic immunities of the American inhabitants (both the peoples and the animals they hunted), trade goods, new means of subsistence, and new social roles.

The early trade established a felt need among many Native Americans for the trade goods—metal tools, cloth, beads (which held ritual significance for some groups), new foods, and so forth. Women in the Northwest, for example, were much taken with these goods and actively pursued trade, both personally and through their menfolk. Some women formed trade networks with kin and supplied knowledge of local customs and politics that eased the path of their white or native trader-husbands. There is an indication that this may have increased their options and wealth—either as agents themselves or as wives of traders and hunters. Research indicates a particularly independent position for women in the Northwest.

Entrepreneurial high-status matrons of Salish clans provided young women-for-hire for the traders from among the female captive slaves and the young women of the tribe who were allowed this latitude before "settling down" as married women.[39] This point is interesting to note, since some writers argue that women lose the right to control their sexuality with the first signs of accumulated wealth and social stratification in a society. The Salish had both a highly stratified society and a similar sexual standard for women and men—at least before marriage.

While some indigenous women's crafts, such as the making of rain hats (Northwest), baskets (Paiute), pottery (Pueblo), and rugs or blankets (Navajo), were encouraged by trade, the more common effect was to produce a lessening of local domestic production in favor of gaining substitute foreign goods—similar to colonized third world countries elsewhere where homemade goods have been devalued in favor of foreign-manufactured, high-status products. Women did, however, sell their garden produce and sometimes pelts to the fur-trading forts and were able to supply some of the new luxuries for their families by their production.

In the Great Lakes and northern Missouri River regions, women in matrilineal groups are known to have traded their garden produce and shared the trade goods from the sale of hides they processed, which were usually traded by the men. Some women complained that they did not get their fair share, but traders were careful to stock goods that women might be likely to select.[40]

Women in patrilineal or more male-dominated Plains groups—the Blackfoot, for example—seemed to have become more dependent on men as the usual more egalitarian means of subsistence declined and women became processors of goods over which they had no control. Among bilateral Plains groups, women's status appears to have held up much better, even into the reservation period where women continued craft production and women's societies. These examples appear to support the concept that women's institutionalized control over their production and their societies helped them maintain some control over their status. The fur or hide trade of the plains will be further discussed below with that "new technology," the horse.

The fur trade also introduced wage work for women who performed domestic and gardening work on the trading posts or who worked in the fish canneries in coastal trading posts. While these types of occupations may have helped to support the families, we do not have a clear picture of how the women themselves viewed the effect on their lives—an emic view. From an etic, or an outsider's, view, women do not appear to gain, in general, if they lack control over what they produce and wages are minimal.

One of the outcomes of unions between French and British traders or trappers and Native American women was the creation of a mixed-blood group. In Canada the French-Indian mixed-bloods (métis) form a group considered as separate from either Indian or white. In the United States, mixed-bloods were considered Indian but were more likely to have received Euro-American education and to have become part of an elite "comprador" group who often worked more closely with whites and the Bureau of Indian Affairs.

While the Spanish, and later Mexicans, in the Southwest were not seeking furs and trade as much as precious metals and outposts to defend their northern frontier, they too produced offspring who became either Indian or Hispanic, depending on the culture in which they remained. In this region the mix of Hispano, Native American, and more recently Anglo heritage can be very complex. Descendants of elite Spanish Anglo persons in New Mexico have been able to retain some status, but the majority of men and women in the mixed-blood category in the Southwest have been limited in their opportunities.

2. *Warfare:* Native Americans had their own factions and warfare before the advent of whites. For some groups, raiding their neighbors was a common practice; other societies were philosophically opposed to war unless attacked. The schisms among the British, French, and Spanish (and later, the Civil War) increased warfare for Native Americans, as each European group enlisted its Indian trading partners to fight with them against other European powers and their Indian allies. Native groups also fought each other for territory as they were forced westward by settlers and the scarcity of game.

One might assume that with increased warfare the position of men would rise. This is reported to have been the case for nonmatrilineal Plains groups. Martin Whyte, however, warned of a lack of correlation in his statistical data of warfare and women's positions in preindustrial societies.[41] The positions of women were not as strictly defined in Native American groups as Euro-Americans presumed. Women could and did have alternative roles. The warrior role for women was an increasing option during times of faction and warfare, and examples of this in groups all across the country have been cited. In addition, women in some matrilineal societies in the eighteenth and nineteenth centuries might initiate or end conflict through their women's councils, Pretty Women societies, or Beloved Woman (diviner/strategist) statuses, or just by supplying or withholding provisions necessary for long-distance raids. Artist Rudolph Kurz reported that in his travels on the plains he observed the matrilineal Crow to be very orderly. He speculated that this was probably because women joined the councils and made men "listen to reason," something he had not seen in other groups.[42] Since women in these societies had a say in war and peace and in adoption of captives into the tribe to replace lost kin, their positions may not have declined initially. This relationship, or lack of relationship, of women and warfare needs closer analysis since we have seen that under certain social conditions Native American women in some groups may have made some gains while others may have had losses. The long-range effects of warfare on women and men were to be loss of land and traditional subsistence patterns, eventual exhaustion and defeat, and confinement to reservations for survivors.

More recently, World War II had a profound impact on many in Indian country. Over twenty-four thousand Native American women and men served in the military and an estimated forty thousand migrated to participate in defense work in urban areas. Many individuals and families who had remained fairly isolated were suddenly immersed in the dominant culture. The disorientation of returning soldiers has been a frequent theme in Native American literature.

3. *Ideological assault:* Christian missionaries, schools, and ideology are all aspects of the thought-change process required in conquering a people culturally. The incoming patriarchal ideology from Europe was somewhat accepted—often begrudgingly—in the wake of disease, war, and the introduction of new goods and technology. Before the introduction of the horse to the Plains cultures, an exaggerated form of male dominance probably did not exist for Native Americans. Kinship-based social organization, cultural values, and the importance of women's production and reproduction allowed native women in North America a great deal of influence, either directly or indirectly.

All of this was affected by the major new ideas brought by missionaries, schoolteachers, and others, such as:

- Patrilineal, father-dominated families with women dependent on husbands for maintenance
- Private property held in the name of the male head of household
- Female chastity and a double sexual standard (note that a few Plains groups had already developed a milder form of the double standard)
- An education system that reinforced limited gender roles, that is, women working in the home and men serving as breadwinners

Because Native American women played an important part in traditional horticultural or gathering production, the Euro-American system meant some loss of economic and political status. For men it was also a wrenching change from hunting, raiding, and warfare to farming, a role formerly associated with women in most horticultural groups. For matrilineal horticultural groups it meant the transfer of traditional land-use rights from the female clans to land titles in severalty (individual ownership) in men's names.⁴³ With these disruptions the power of matrilineal clans was diminished and other aspects of the dominant patriarchal culture became more difficult to resist.

The new ideology also meant that a double standard in sexual conduct was introduced into those groups whose traditional female autonomy so shocked the missionaries.⁴⁴ It meant the loss of women's control over their reproduction, as native means of birth control were discouraged or forgotten. Cherokee women, for example, previously had the right to limit offspring through infanticide, while for men infanticide was forbidden.⁴⁵ Educational programs were initiated to spread the "cult of true womanhood"—the nineteenth-century Victorian ideology that women were submissive, delicate, chaste (if not asexual), and bound to the house.⁴⁶ This meshed with the English common law idea that women, children, and women's property and earnings were the property of their husbands. Quaker and reformist policy would continue to influence the government's programs, laws, and educational practice in the direction of domesticity for women and agriculture for men as heads-of-house. Bureau of Indian Affairs schools, which perpetuated this philosophy, were educating 80 percent of those Indian children who were in school at the turn of the century. Educators often complained, however, that many of their promising pupils returned to the reservation and went "back to the blanket." Some women today refer to their parents or grandparents as "sacrifice generations" who lost some of the language and customs through long stays at BIA schools or life away from their own reservations, through mixed-tribal marriages or employment with the BIA on other Indian agencies.

In sum, as Euro-Americans overwhelmed native systems by disease and conquest, European ideas of proper gender roles became more difficult to resist. Native American women often lost their economic base, their formal political rights as clan matrons (although in more isolated traditional groups some informal power has been retained), their sexual freedom, their reproductive rights, and their right to be cross-gender or different in their roles when they chose.⁴⁷

4. *New technology:* By mid-eighteenth century, the Plains Indians had adopted the horse, which had been reintroduced by the Spanish, and were developing a new equestrian culture that changed the roles and statuses of the Plains woman, mostly adversely according to later accounts by Plains women themselves. From horseback the hunt became a more individualized male activity, instead of a mixed-group activity of impoundment or cliff drives. In addition, horses became private property and differences in wealth and status increased. Male sodalities began to replace the kinship group in political decision making, except for the matrilineal Crow whose social organization and cultural beliefs seem to have upheld the position of women.⁴⁸ As the hide trade grew from the late eighteenth to mid-nineteenth centuries and guns became more common, the race was on to kill far more buffalo and other animals than were needed for subsistence. Women in non-matrilineal groups appear to have receded into the role of processors of whatever men brought home. Polygyny became more necessary for the

successful hunter. (Also, because warfare, hunting, and raiding had taken their toll on men, some groups had twice as many women as men, and surviving men were often obligated to become guardians of widows of deceased relatives.) Processing in itself is not necessarily detrimental to the status of women, and sororal polygyny may have given sisters some united clout with their husbands. Still, being one of the processors valued basically for her labors does suggest a diminution of status if the finished product is controlled by someone else.

New technology was not rejected out of hand by traditional women. Seneca and Cherokee women took advantage of spinning wheels and looms and that powerful new tool—literacy.[49] When the plow was introduced as new technology, its effects were complicated by the fact that it came with the European ideology that men should use it as the principal providers and landowners. If it had been introduced in some other manner, or if men had been able to continue hunting or to have some alternative means of livelihood, the plow might not have become such a symbol of male dominance. Women can and do plow behind teams of horses or oxen the world over. Since it was introduced to Native Americans, however, with the ideological and legal baggage that only men should farm and own land held in severalty, the plow was not an improvement in the traditional status of the Native American woman horticulturalist. The new land tenure system separated women onto individual farms and broke down their cooperative work groups, social solidarity, and political organization. This happened not only in the case of the Iroquois and Cherokee, but for other groups as well.

In the Southwest, Navajo matrilineal clans adopted the new Spanish technology of raising domesticated stock, especially sheep and goats. By mid-twentieth century government policy had forced stock reduction, and the means of wealth began to shift to cattle owned by men and wage work that favored male workers. The statuses of women declined, except for those who temporarily maintained outfits in the back-country or pursued higher education or adopted male crafts, since such crafts pay more per hour invested than do women's crafts (e.g., silversmithing and painting versus weaving and pottery).[50] More recently, changes in technology and the economy have favored women in terms of getting a job, but this has not generally brought them adequate wages.

A study of the purchasing records from 1909–1912 on the Yakima Reservation indicates that women of these patrilineal tribes in the Northwest Plateau region made a majority of the purchases. Women bought 53 percent of the horses, 57 percent of the cattle, 81 percent of household goods (including roofing and repair materials), 62 percent of buggies and wagons, 40 percent of horse collars and work harnesses, and 47 percent of farm equipment.[51] Where the money came from and who used the new technology were not recorded. Women were obviously engaged in acquiring and undoubtedly in using new technology.

5. *Settlers, corporations, government agents, and federal policies:* Those who wanted Native American land and resources were, and continue to

be for tribes with natural resources, the major instruments of change in the lives and statuses of indigenous peoples. If the object of foreign intrusion had remained at the early fur trade or missionary levels, statuses would not have been so severely affected. But native groups were eventually surrounded by settlers, defeated by the military, forced to sign treaties, and removed to ever-smaller plots of land called reservations. Under the General Allotment (Dawes) Act of 1887, 90 million of the 140 million acres once deeded to native peoples were lost by shady means until land alienation was stopped by the 1934 Indian Reorganization Act. On the reservation many government Indian agents operated like princes of small kingdoms, and even in recent years they have been able to subvert reform movements.[52] The massive intrusion changed the means of economic subsistence for most native groups. For Native Americans who took up agriculture in severalty, we saw that this meant a loss of status for women who had traditionally been the agricultural producers. For those women who took up wage work, it often meant more dependence on men, unless, as in the case of the Navajo sheepherders, women could find some means (temporary, in this case) to accumulate wealth and status on their own.

The post–World War II era has seen an increasing alienation of resources from Indian lands, with renewed conflict as traditional Native Americans have resisted this exploitation both physically and in the courts. Some have called this ongoing conflict the "second Indian wars."[53] Women have been active in the protest in sit-ins and demonstrations, in legal battles in the courts as lawyers and testimony givers, and in increased participation in tribal politics, sometimes challenging the male comprador elites who have been entrenched since the 1934 Indian Reorganization Act installed tribal councils to deal with the Bureau of Indian Affairs.

Official policy has, in general, followed the needs of Euro-American lobbyists and bureaucrats, not the needs of traditional Indians. Treaties, laws and judicial decisions, wars, removals, tribal status termination, and education toward acculturation into dominant group values and norms have been used to gain Native American resources and to induce the indigenous peoples to disappear quietly, often in terms of "their own good." Notable in government policy have been the various treaties confining groups to reserves; the 1830 Indian Removal Act; the Indian wars culminating in the post–Civil War expansion across the Midwest; the 1885 Seven Major Crimes Act; the 1887 General Allotment (Dawes) Act and 1898 Curtis Act that divided many reservations (leaving Oklahoma with only one small Osage reservation); BIA boarding schools to promote the dominant ideology; water and other resource policies, especially after discovery of fossil fuels; the 1934 Indian Reorganization (Wheeler-Howard) Act, which saddled tribes with tribal councils and definite factions; and the 1950s removal and termination laws and programs aimed at urbanization and detribalization.[54] More recent policies have allowed varying degrees of tribal self-determination, which has opened an avenue for women's individual and collective actions.

THE ONGOING STRUGGLE

With the civil rights movement and a revival of cultural pride have come more favorable federal policies, increased education in terms of both years attained and availability of bicultural materials, the intervention of native women and men lawyers on behalf of individuals and tribes, more aggressive Native American organizations at the grassroots and pantribal national levels, and the support of environmentalists and others on the behalf of Native American groups. Beginning with the 1964 Equal Opportunity Act, some tribes gained federal grants and began operating their own community action programs in human services and economic development.[55] There has been some movement on the part of the U.S. government to allow limited "tribal sovereignty"—for example, the 1975 Indian Self-Determination and Educational Assistance Act. Tribes now control twenty-nine community colleges, which have ties to state-controlled four-year schools to ease the transition to baccalaureate degrees, and there has been some improvement of the economic base on a few reservations. Some of these economic enterprises are tribally or individually Indian-owned craft and other businesses, while others are owned by multinational corporations. Gambling syndicate control over gaming palaces in Indian territory is a large question mark involving big dollars. Critics are quick to point out how limited tribes really are under these policies, but it must be granted that the last three decades have brought a marked improvement from what went before.[56]

None of these activities has yet served to restore completely the earlier statuses of Native American women, as we are now coming to understand them. Increased education, political involvement, and networking may eventually be means to improving the statuses of women and of their communities. It has been said that "Indian women today are in the process of redefining identities long-obscured by the stereotypes and misconceptions of others."[57] They are tribal council members, chiefs and governors, clerical workers, technicians, social service and health care providers (including some traditional healers) and administrators, educators (both of tribal language and traditions and the curriculum supplied by the state), counselors (spiritual and/or certified by secular outside agencies), environmental activists, preservers of traditional arts and culture, writers and musicians, businesswomen, lawyers and judges, and community organizers and volunteers.[58]

In interviews with twenty-four women leaders from eleven tribes, this author was impressed with the women's determination to see that their tribeswomen learn as much as they can about their own traditional cultures and the dominant culture in order to become mentally, physically, and spiritually healthy and to serve their communities well. Many of these leaders stressed the importance of maintaining an Indian sense of humor and the idea of humans as just one small part of creation in order to keep one's sense of harmony and balance. They are proud of their traditional roots, which give them motivation and the ability to cope with the stresses of being minority women living in two worlds. And they are putting their skills to work for their communities which, they say, is what Indian women have always done, recalling the many ancient stories that tell of female deities creating the earth (often with the help of a sea-diving creature who brings up mud) and agricultural products from their bodies; of Thought Woman of the Pueblo, who created everything from thinking it into being and then charged all created things with cocreating by their own subsequent thinking; of the women who brought the sun, as in the Spider Grandmother stories from the Cherokee, or the moon.

The power of women to produce and reproduce is highly regarded in both creation stories and in practice. Women were historically responsible for the welfare of their communities. These responsibilities have been pursued as pressures from the policies and culture of the dominant society have been eased in recent years to allow women to participate more formally. We shall see what such motivated women can do.

Notes

Initial historical research was made possible through a National Endowment for the Humanities Summer Seminar grant in 1988 to attend the New Directions in Native American History course directed by Dr. Roger Nichols of the Department of History at the University of Arizona. A Research Enhancement travel grant from Southwest Texas State University enabled the videotaping of interviews with twenty-four women leaders from eleven tribes between 1990 and 1992.

1. While women of the West are the subject of this volume, some examples of women of eastern tribes are recounted here because of instructive documentation on Euro-American contact with native matrilineal social organization before many of these tribes were forced westward. This also offers a comparative view with what was to come later for western matrilineal and nonmatrilineal groups.

2. Until recently most documents—diaries, letters, government reports, journalistic and scientific accounts—were written by male explorers, travelers, traders, missionaries, military personnel, Indian agents, and anthropologists working with mostly male informants. These views were filtered through the ideas of the observers' times and cultures. See Alice B. Kehoe, "The Shackles of Tradition," in *The Hidden Half: Studies of Plains Indian Women*, ed. Patricia Albers and Beatrice Medicine (Washington, D.C.: University Press of America, 1983), 53–73, on biases in early ethnography. Sleuthing the lives of specific earlier historical women or gender roles in a particular group is a challenge. See E. G. Chuinard, "The Actual Role of the Bird Woman," *Montana The Magazine of Western History* 26, no. 3 (July 1976): 18–29, on Sacagawea; Rosemary Agonito and Joseph Agonito, "Resurrecting History's Forgotten Women: A Case Study from the Cheyenne Indians," *Frontiers* 6, no. 3 (Fall 1981): 8–16, on Buffalo Calf Road; Christine St. Peter, " 'Woman's Truth' and the Native Tradition: Anne Cameron's 'Daughters of Copper Woman,' " *Feminist Studies* 15, no. 4 (Fall 1989): 499–523, on Vancouver Island women in myth and oral history.

Life histories add texture to understanding women's experiences and their views. For a discussion of types of life histories and an annotated bibliography, see Gretchen M. Bataille and Kathleen Mullen Sands, *American Indian Women: Telling Their Lives* (Lincoln: University of Nebraska Press, 1984). Tribal communities also read these stories. For examples of issues this may raise, see Margaret B. Blackman, "Returning Home: Life Histories and the Native Community," *Journal of Narrative and Life History* 2, no. 1 (1992): 49–59.

3. For more discussion of theories see, for example, Peggy Reeves Sanday, *Female Power and Male Dominance: On the Origins of Sexual Inequality* (Cambridge, Eng.: Cambridge University Press, 1981); Patricia Albers, "From Illusion to Illumination: Anthropological Studies of American Indian Women," in *Gender and Anthropology: Critical Reviews for Research and Teaching*, ed. Sandra Morgen (Washington, D.C.: American Anthropological Association, 1989), 132–70;

Jo-Anne Fiske, "Gender and Politics in a Carrier Indian Community" (Ph.D. dissertation, University of British Columbia, 1989); Robert N. Lynch, "Women in Northern Paiute Politics," *Signs* 11, no. 2 (Winter 1986): 352–66; Nancy Shoemaker, "Introduction," in her edited work *Negotiators of Change: Historical Perspectives on Native American Women* (New York: Routledge, 1995), 1–25.

4. Martha C. Knack, "Contemporary Southern Paiute Women and the Measurement of Women's Economic and Political Status," *Ethnology* 28 (July 1989): 233–48; Carol C. Mukhopadhyay and Patricia J. Higgins, "Anthropological Studies of Women's Status Revisited: 1977–1987," *Annual Review of Anthropology* 17 (1988): 461–95; Naomi Quinn, "Anthropological Studies on Women's Status," *Annual Review of Anthropology* 6 (1977): 181–225.

5. Judith Brown, "Economic Organization and the Position of Women among the Iroquois," *Ethnohistory* 17, no. 3–4 (Summer-Fall 1970): 151–67; Judith Brown, "A Note on the Division of Labor by Sex," *American Anthropologist* 72, no. 5 (October 1970): 1073–78.

6. Patricia Albers, "Sioux Women in Transition: A Study of Their Changing Status in Domestic and Capitalist Sectors of Production," in *Hidden Half*, 175–234.

7. Martin King Whyte, *The Status of Women in Preindustrial Societies* (Princeton: Princeton University Press, 1978), 171–73.

8. Melvin Ember and Carol R. Ember, "The Conditions Favoring Matrilocal versus Patrilocal Residence," *American Anthropologist* 73, no. 3 (June 1971): 571–94; Roger M. Keesing, *Kin Groups and Social Structure* (New York: Holt, Rinehart and Winston, 1975); Eleanor Leacock, "Women's Status in Egalitarian Society: Implications for Social Evolution," *Current Anthropology* 19, no. 2 (June 1978): 247–75; Richard J. Perry, "Matrilineal Descent in a Hunting Context: The Athapaskan Case," *Ethnology: An International Journal of Cultural and Social Anthropology* 28, no. 1 (January 1989): 33–51; Alice Schlegel, *Male Dominance and Female Autonomy: Domestic Authority in Matrilineal Societies* (n.p.: HRAF Press, 1972); David M. Schneider and Kathleen Gough, eds., *Matrilineal Kinship* (Berkeley: University of California Press, 1961).

9. George Peter Murdock, *Atlas of World Cultures* (Pittsburgh: University of Pittsburgh Press, 1981), 134.

10. Valerie Sherer Mathes, "A New Look at the Role of Women in Indian Society," *American Indian Quarterly* 2, no. 2 (Summer 1975): 131–39.

11. David F. Aberle, "Matrilineal Descent in Cross-Cultural Perspective," in *Matrilineal Kinship*, ed. David M. Schneider and Kathleen Gough (Berkeley: University of California Press, 1961), 655–727.

12. Whyte, *Status of Women*, 156–84.

13. Harold E. Driver, *Indians of North America*, 2d ed. rev. (Chicago: University of Chicago Press, 1969), 247 and maps 31 and 32; Robert Steven Grumet, "Sunksquaws, Shamans, and Tradeswomen: Middle Atlantic Coastal Algonkian Women during the 17th and 18th Centuries," in *Women and Colonization*, ed. Mona Etienne and Eleanor Leacock (New York: Praeger, 1980), 43–62; Robert Lowie, "The Matrilineal Complex," *American Archaeology and Ethnology* (U-CA) 16, no. 2 (29 March 1919): 29–45; Robert Lowie, *Indians of the Plains* (New York: American Museum of Natural History, 1954); John Upton Terrell and Donna M. Terrell, *Indian Women of the Western Morning: Their Life in Early America* (Garden City, N.Y.: Doubleday, 1974), 24.

14. For example, the Teton (Western Lakota) are often popularly thought of as patrilineal. Evidence suggests they might have been matrilineal before migrating onto the plains and are often classified now as bilateral with matrilineal carryovers, hence, the asterisk in Table 2.1. See Shirley R. Bysiewicz and Ruth E. Van de Mark, "The Legal Status of the Dakota Indian Woman," *American Indian Law Review* 3 (1977): 255–312; Robert F. Spencer and Jesse D. Jennings et al., *The Native Americans: Ethnology and Backgrounds of the North American Indians*, 2d ed. (New York: Harper & Row, 1977), 328, 341. Culture complexes do not fit neatly into categories.

15. Sources for Table 2.1 are as follows: Daniel L. Boxberger, ed., *Native North Americans: An Ethnohistorical Approach* (Dubuque, Iowa: Kendall/Hunt, 1990) 244; Shirley R. Bysiewicz and Ruth E. Van de Mark, "The Legal Status of the Dakota Indian Woman," *American Indian Law Review* 3 (1977): 266, 296; Harold E. Driver, *Indians of North America*, 2d ed. rev. (Chicago: University of Chicago Press, 1969), 238–72; Bertha P. Dutton, *American Indians of the Southwest*

(Albuquerque: University of New Mexico Press, 1983); James H. Howard, *Shawnee! The Ceremonialism of a Native Indian Tribe and Its Cultural Background* (Athens: Ohio University Press, 1981); Marie Jaimes, "Toward a New Image of American Indians: The Renewing Power of Feminism," *Journal of American Indian Education* 22, no. 1 (October 1982): 20; Margot Liberty, "Hell Came with Horses: Plains Indian Women in the Equestrian Era," *Montana The Magazine of Western History* 32, no. 3 (Summer 1982): 14; Robert Lowie, "The Matrilineal Complex," *American Archaeology and Ethnology* (U-CA) 16, no. 2 (29 March 1919): 21; Robert Lowie, *Indians of the Plains* (New York: American Museum of Natural History, 1954); Ann Patton Malone, *Women on the Texas Frontier: A Cross-Cultural Perspective* (El Paso: Texas Western Press, 1983), 3; Valerie Sherer Mathes, "A New Look at the Role of Women in Indian Society," *American Indian Quarterly* 2, no. 2 (Summer 1975): 131–39; Beatrice Medicine, "American Indian Family: Cultural Change and Adaptive Strategies," *Journal of Ethnic Studies* 8 (December 1981): 15–16; W. W. Newcomb, Jr., *The Indians of Texas: From Prehistoric to Modern Times* (Austin: University of Texas Press, 1961), 141–42; Richard J. Perry, "Matrilineal Descent in a Hunting Context: The Athapaskan Case," *Ethnology: An International Journal of Cultural and Social Anthropology* 23, no. 1 (January 1989): 35; Robert F. Spencer, Jesse D. Jennings et al., *The Native Americans: Ethnology and Backgrounds of the North American Indians*, 2d ed. (New York: Harper & Row, 1977), 579; John Upton Terrell and Donna M. Terrell, *Indian Women of the Western Morning: Their Life in Early America* (Garden City, N.Y.: Doubleday, 1974), 20–24.

16. Brown, "Economic Organization," and "A Note"; A. A. Goldenweiser, "Functions of Women in Iroquois Society," *American Anthropologist* 17 (1915): 376–77; Joan M. Jensen, "Native American Women and Agriculture: A Seneca Case Study," *Sex Roles* 3, no. 5 (1977): 423–41; Kay M. Martin and Barbara Voorheis, *Female of the Species* (New York: Columbia University Press, 1975), 225–29; Carolyn Niethammer, *Daughters of the Earth: The Lives and Legends of American Indian Women* (New York: Collier, 1977), 139–40; Cara E. Richards, "Onondaga Women: Among the Liberated," in *Many Sisters: Women in Cross-Cultural Perspective*, ed. Carolyn J. Matthiasson (New York: Free Press, 1974), 401–419; Diane Rothenberg, "Erosion of Power: An Economic Basis for the Selective Conservatism of Seneca Women in the Nineteenth Century," *Western Canadian Journal of Anthropology* 6, no. 3 (1976): 106–122; Diane Rothenberg, "The Mothers of the Nation: Seneca Resistance to Quaker Intervention," in *Women and Colonization*, 63–87; Anthony F. C. Wallace, "Handsome Lake and the Decline of the Illinois Matriarchate," in *Kinship and Culture*, ed. Francis L. K. Hsu (Chicago: Aldine, 1971), 367–76.

17. Laura F. Klein, "Contending with Colonization: Tlingit Men and Women in Change," in *Women and Colonization*, 88–108.

18. Eve Ball, *In the Days of Victorio: Recollections of a Warm Springs Apache (James Kaywaykla)* (Tucson: University of Arizona Press, 1970); Regina Flannery, "The Position of Women among the Mescalero Apache," *Primitive Man (Anthropological Quarterly)* 5 (1932): 26–32; Niethammer, *Daughters of the Earth*; Mary C. Wright, "Economic Development and Native American Women in the Early 19th Century," *American Indian Quarterly* 33, no. 5 (Winter 1981): 525–36.

19. Liberty, "Hell Came with Horses," 10–17; Frank Bird Linderman, *Pretty-Shield, Medicine Woman of the Crows* (New York: John Day, 1960), originally published as *Red Mother* (1932).

20. Marsha Clift Bol, "Lakota Women's Artistic Strategies in Support of the Social Structure," *American Indian Culture and Research Journal* 9, no. 1 (1985): 33–51; Mary Jane Schneider, "Women's Work: An Examination of Women's Roles in Plains Indian Arts and Crafts," in *Hidden Half*, 101–121.

21. Liberty, "Hell Came with Horses," 18.

22. Kehoe, "Shackles of Tradition," 70.

23. Albers, "Sioux Women in Transition," 182–223.

24. Oscar Lewis, "Manly-Hearted Women among the North Piegan," *American Anthropologist* 43, no. 2 (1941): 173–87.

25. Evelyn Blackwood, "Sexuality and Gender in Certain Native American Tribes: The Case of Cross-Gender Females," *Signs*, 10 (Autumn 1984): 30; Williams, *Spirit and the Flesh*, 235.

26. Sue-Ellen Jacobs, "Berdache: A Brief Review of the Literature," *Colorado Anthropologist* 1 (1968): 28.

27. Claude E. Schaeffer, "The Kutenai Female Berdache: Courier, Guide, Prophetess, and Warrior," *Ethnohistory* 12, no. 3 (Summer 1965), 193–236.

28. Harriet Whitehead, "The Bow and the Burden Strap: A New Look at Institutionalized Homosexuality in Native North America," in *Sexual Meanings: The Cultural Construction of Gender and Sexuality*, ed. Sherry B. Ortner and Harriet Whitehead (Cambridge, Eng.: Cambridge University Press, 1981), 95–97.

29. Jacobs, "Berdache," 30.

30. Blackwood, "Sexuality and Gender," 37–38.

31. Mary Ann (Adams) Maverick said in her diary regarding her eyewitness view of the 1840 Council House fight in San Antonio between Comanches and Texians ("Texian" designates persons in the Republic of Texas, 1836–45): "The Indian women dressed and fought like the men, and could not be told apart." Quoted in Jo Ella Powell Exley, *Texas Tears and Texas Sunshine: Voices of Frontier Women* (College Station: Texas A&M University Press, 1985), 97. Pretty-Shield recounted the bravery in the battle of the Rosebud in 1876 of The-Other-Magpie and Finds-Them-And-Kills-Them, two Crow women employed as scouts by the cavalry under General Crook (Linderman, *Pretty-Shield*, 227–31). She describes them as "a woman and neither a man nor a woman . . . a half-woman." The first was bad, brave, and pretty, with no man of her own, avenging the death of her brother at the hands of the Lakota, armed with only a powerful coup stick. The half-woman looked like a man, carried a gun, wore woman's clothing, had the heart of a woman, and did woman's work—not as strong as a man but wiser than a woman. Williams (*Spirit and Flesh*, 179) notes a Crow male *berdache* by this name during this time period. Could this have been the same person viewed differently by informants of different cultures?

32. Sources for Table 2.2 are as follows: Paula Gunn Allen, *The Sacred Hoop: Recovering the Feminine in American Indian Traditions* (Boston: Beacon Press, 1986); Beryl Lieff Benderly, "Men and/or Women," *Psychology Today* 21, no. 4 (April 1987): 74–75; Blackwood, "Sexuality and Gender," 27–42; Priscilla K. Buffalohead, "Farmers, Warriors, Traders: A Fresh Look at Ojibway Women," *Minnesota History* 48 (Summer 1983): 236–44; Charles Callendar and Lee M. Kochems, "North American Berdache," *Current Anthropology* 24 (1983): 443–56; Raymond DeMallie, "Male and Female in Traditional Lakota Culture," in *Hidden Half*, 237–65; Jacobs, "Berdache," 25–40; Jay Miller, "People, Berdaches, and Left-Handed Bears: Human Variation in Native America," *Journal of Anthropological Research* 38, no. 3 (Fall 1982): 274–87; Schaeffer, "The Kutenai Female Berdache," 193–236; Whitehead, "The Bow and the Burden Strap," 80–115; Walter L. Williams, *The Spirit and the Flesh: Sexual Diversity in American Indian Culture* (Boston: Beacon Press, 1987).

33. Jacobs, "Berdache," 30–32.

34. Williams, *Spirit and Flesh*, 170–71, 180–229, 249–51.

35. Jacobs, "Berdache," 30, quoting Linton.

36. Ibid., 28; Williams, *Spirit and Flesh*, 184–85.

37. Callendar and Kochems, "North American Berdache," 445.

38. Blackwood, "Sexuality and Gender," 38.

39. Buffalohead, "Farmers, Warriors, Traders," 38.

40. Sylvia Van Kirk, *Many Tender Ties: Women in Fur-Trade Society, 1670–1870* (Norman: University of Oklahoma Press, 1980); Wright, "Economic Development."

41. Katherine M. Weist, "Beasts of Burden and Menial Slaves: 19th Century Observations of Northern Plains Women," in *Hidden Half*, 42–43; Martha Harroun Foster, "Of Baggage and Bondage: Gender and Status among Hidatsa and Crow Women," *American Indian Culture and Research Journal* 17, no. 2 (Spring 1993): 121–52.

42. Whyte, *Status of Women*, 129–30.

43. Foster, "Of Baggage and Bondage," 131–32.

44. Theda Perdue, "Cherokee Women and the Trail of Tears," *Journal of Women's History* 1, no. 1 (Spring 1989): 14–30; John A. Price, "North American Indian Families," in *Ethnic Families*

in America: Patterns and Variations, 2d ed., ed. Charles H. Mindel and Robert W. Habenstein (New York: Elsevier, 1981), 250–54.

45. In historic times a wide range of degrees of sexual freedom for Native American women existed among the various groups. Among the Cherokee, premarital chastity was not of major importance and divorce was easily obtained by either party who wanted to change partners. Iroquois groups were egalitarian along these lines, and men who were not acceptable as husbands were removed from the women's longhouses. On the other hand, the Cheyenne were quite circumspect about female chastity; the Blackfoot sometimes disfigured adulterous women. Other Plains groups varied, often not overtly punishing sexual wanderings but rather denying these women the high status of the virtuous who could sponsor the Sun Dance. Erring Navajo husbands might return to find their personal belongings outside the hogan door, which meant that they had been divorced and must move on. The Pacific Northwest Salish expected marital chastity but tolerated premarital experimentation. While marriage in matrilineal societies seems particularly brittle, it has been suggested that marriage was not a major factor in family status for most groups, which allowed more individual autonomy than Euro-Americans had until recently. See Albers, "From Illusion to Illumination," in *Gender and Anthropology*, 137. Among a number of groups, such as the Creek, divorce became less common after the birth of a child. See Kathryn E. Holland Braund, "Guardians of Tradition and Handmaidens to Change: Women's Roles in Creek Economic and Social Life during the Eighteenth Century," *American Indian Quarterly* 14, no. 3 (Summer 1990): 239–58.

Eleanor Leacock ("Women's Status," 272) reports an example of the influence of missionaries on women's marital autonomy among the Montagnais in Canada. Jesuit Father Paul Le Jeune in a report of an incident in 1692 noted the egalitarian nature of the society and the success he was having in civilizing them, i.e., getting men to obey priestly authority and women to obey men. A woman who had left her husband was caught by a group of Christian native men and was tied up and threatened. "Some Pagan young men, observing this violence,—of which the Savages have a horror, and which is more remote from their customs than Heaven is from Earth,—made use of threats, declaring they would kill any one who laid a hand on the woman." The woman saw a fight was about to happen, promised to return to her husband and be more obedient, and Christianity and women's subservience under threat of violence won the day. The priest was relieved that his teachings were having such a civilizing effect. Given their natural independence, it was a miracle that these people were learning authority and obedience, he concluded.

46. Virginia Elizabeth Milam, "Cherokee Women," in *Women in Oklahoma: A Century of Change*, ed. Melvena K. Thurman (Oklahoma City: Oklahoma Historical Society, 1983), 48.

47. Helen M. Bannan, " 'True Womanhood' on the Reservation: Field Matrons in the United States Indian Service," Working Paper no. 18 (Tucson: University of Arizona, Southwest Institute for Research on Women, 1984); Marla N. Powers, *Oglala Women: Myth, Ritual, and Reality* (Chicago: University of Chicago Press, 1986); Margaret Connell Szasz, *Education and the American Indian* (Albuquerque: University of New Mexico Press, 1977); Margaret Connell Szasz, "Listening to the Native Voice: American Indian Schooling in the Twentieth Century," *Montana The Magazine of Western History* 39, no. 3 (Summer 1989): 42–53; Robert A. Trennert, "Education of Indian Girls at Nonreservation Boarding Schools, 1878–1920," *Western Historical Quarterly* 13 (July 1982): 271–90; Robert A. Trennert, "Victorian Morality and the Supervision of Indian Women Working in Phoenix, 1906–1930," *Journal of Social History* 22, no. 1 (Fall 1988): 113–28. For interesting commentary by and about the thirty-four Native American women who served in the government's field matron corps (about 13 percent of the total between 1895 and 1927), see Lisa E. Emmerich, " 'Right in the Midst of My Own People': Native American Women and the Field Matron Program," *American Indian Quarterly* 15, no. 2 (Spring 1991): 201–216.

48. An example from the late nineteenth century is the story of Sahaykwisa, whose cross-gender role ran afoul of the changing norms of some of the acculturating men of the Mohave group. After much physical and emotional abuse, she gave up her male role and her wife but was still killed as a witch. Blackwood, "Sexuality and Gender," 40. The reports of such cases had virtually disappeared by the late nineteenth century, but Williams (*Spirit and Flesh*) suggests that these practices went underground and are still supported by those with traditional values. Contact with urban

gay/lesbian communities has created some confusion between those with traditional norms and today's youth, as Native American *berdaches* had to fulfill spiritual roles not found in the dominant culture.

49. Alan M. Klein, "The Plains Truth: The Impact of Colonialism on Indian Women," *Dialectical Anthropology* 7, no. 4 (February 1983): 299–313; Alan Klein, "The Political Economy of Gender: A 19th Century Plains Indian Case Study," in *Hidden Half*, 143–73; Foster, "Of Baggage and Bondage," 121–52.

50. Milam, "Cherokee Women"; Rothenberg, "Erosion of Power," and "Mothers of the Nation"; Mary E. Young, "Women, Civilization, and the Indian Question," in *Clio Was a Woman: Studies in the History of American Women*, ed. Mabel E. Deutrich and Virginia C. Purdy (Washington, D.C.: Howard University Press, 1980).

51. Christine Conte, "Ladies, Livestock, Land, and Lucre: Women's Networks and Social Status on the Western Navajo Reservation," *American Indian Quarterly* 6, no. 1–2 (Spring-Summer 1982): 125–48; James F. Downs, "The Cowboy and the Lady: Models as a Determinant of the Rate of Acculturation among the Piñon Navajo," in *Native Americans Today: Sociological Perspectives*, ed. Howard M. Bahr, Bruce A. Chadwick, and Robert C. Day (New York: Harper & Row, 1972), 275–91; Laila Shukry Hamamsy, "The Roles of Women in a Changing Navajo Society," *American Anthropologist* 59, no. 1 (1957): 101–111; Evelyn S. Kessler, *Women, an Anthropological View* (New York: Holt, Rinehart and Winston, 1976); Jerrold E. Levy, Eric B. Henderson, and Tracy J. Andrews, "The Effects of Regional Variation and Temporal Change on Matrilineal Elements of Navajo Social Organization," *Journal of Anthropological Research* 45, no. 4 (Winter 1989): 173–87; Mary Shepardson, "The Status of Navajo Women," *American Indian Quarterly* 6 (Spring 1982): 149–69.

52. Clifford E. Trafzer, "Horses and Cattle, Buggies and Hacks," in *Negotiators of Change*, 176–92.

53. Lynch in "Women in Northern Paiute Politics" presents an interesting example.

54. Ward Churchill and Jim Vander Wall, *Agents of Repression: The FBI's Secret Wars against the Black Panther Party and the American Indian Movement* (Boston: South End Press, 1988); Joseph G. Jorgensen, "A Century of Political Economic Effects on American Indian Society," *Journal of Ethnic Studies* 6, no. 3 (Fall 1978): 1–82, and Jorgensen with the assistance of Sally Swenson, eds., *Native Americans and Energy Development II* (Boston: Anthropology Resource Center and the Seventh Generation Fund, 1984); Alvin M. Josephy, Jr., *Now That the Buffalo's Gone: A Study of Today's American Indians* (Norman: University of Oklahoma Press, 1984); Winona LaDuke, "They Always Come Back," in *A Gathering of Spirit*, ed. Beth Brant (n.p.: Sinister Wisdom Books, 1984); Rex Weyler, *Blood of the Land: The Government and Corporate War against the American Indian Movement* (New York: Random House, 1982), and articles in M. Annette Jaimes, ed., *The State of Native America: Genocide, Colonization, and Resistance* (Boston: South End Press, 1992).

55. See Vine Deloria, Jr., and Clifford M. Lytle, *The Nations Within: The Past and Future of American Indian Sovereignty* (New York: Pantheon, 1984), and Jorgensen, "A Century of Political Economic Effects," for detailed discussions of the effects of U.S. government policy over the years. In addition to the negative effects of stock reduction, strip mining, uranium radiation, timber clear-cutting, abrogation of fishing treaties, and urban removal, water policy decisions have affected western tribes in particular. See Raul Fernandez, "Evaluating the Loss of Kinship Structures: A Case Study of North American Indians," *Human Organization* 46, no. 1 (Spring 1987): 1–9, for an account of the loss of kinship structures and disruption of life of the Soboba Indians of California because of U.S. water policy from the 1920s through the 1940s. Some recent U.S. government activities, apparently aimed at clearing the way for use of reservation resources by non-Indian corporations, are documented in Weyler's *Blood of the Land*, Churchill and Vander Wall's *Agents of Repression*, and Jaimes's *State of Native America*.

56. Paivi H. Hoikkala, "Mothers and Community Builders: Salt River Pima and Maricopa Women in Community Action," in *Negotiators of Change*, 213–34.

57. See critiques of current tribal sovereignty by various authors in Jaimes's *State of Native America*. On the other hand, attorney Susan Williams (Sisseton-Wahpeton Sioux/Chippewa) told

me how the traditional river-culture stories and rituals were returning to the tribes from the elders on the Wind River Reservation after their water rights were restored. The sacred river had been diverted every summer for use by non-Indian farmers since around 1916. Williams successfully defended the tribes' case before the U.S. Supreme Court in the late 1980s. On the day we discussed this, 16 July 1990, the Department of Interior had called to say they would back the reservation's case if the State of Wyoming tried to reopen it in court. Williams said that in the early twentieth century the great-great-grandmother who had ridden with Sitting Bull and Crazy Horse had told her father, as he was being dragged off to a BIA boarding school, "In the old days we fought our wars with bows and arrows and through fighting, but if we want to preserve our people, the war really is in obtaining an education to learn how the oppressive system operates."

58. Teresa D. LaFromboise, Anneliese M. Heyle, and Emily J. Ozer, "Changing and Diverse Roles of Women in American Indian Cultures," *Sex Roles* 22, no. 7/8 (1990): 455–76; quote, 471.

59. Owanah Anderson, *Ohoyo One Thousand: A Resource Guide of American Indian/Alaska Native Women, 1982* (Washington, D.C.: U.S. Department of Education, Women's Educational Equity Act, 1982); Supplement, 1983.

3.

Race, Gender and Intercultural Relations: The Case of Interracial Marriage

PEGGY PASCOE

Peggy Pascoe has the unusual ability to untangle the knotted strands of complex ideas. She translates the often-convoluted formulations of cultural theory into words the rest of us speak—and then she makes sure that we really do understand their precise meaning. In this essay, first published in 1991, Pascoe uses interracial marriage as a place where we can see precisely how the concept of the "social construction" of gender and race operates. Her analysis continues with a deceptively simple dissection of changing uses of the term "culture," which is immensely valuable in clarifying a much-used and much-muddied term. Finally, she lays bare the central tension between feminist scholarship and cultural studies: the difficulty of viewing women as active agents while simultaneously attending to larger power relationships that determine the historical context within which they operate. As the essays throughout this volume make clear, the major requirement for thinking about gender is to resist the urge to simplify the complexity of its many links with race and class. Pascoe's clear vision helps to clarify that complexity for us.

For scholars interested in the social construction of race, gender, and culture, few subjects are as potentially revealing as the history of interracial marriage. Clearly, the phenomenon of interracial marriage involves the making and remaking of notions of race, gender, and culture in individual lives as well as at the level of social and political policy. Yet the potential of the subject has barely been tapped. The vast majority of studies have been carried out by social scientists who search for laws of social behavior that might either predict or account for the incidence of interracial marriage.[1] The handful of historians who have taken up the topic use their insight into change over time to expose flaws in nearly every theory the social scientists have proposed. But whether historians focus on the actual patterns of intermarriage or on the enactment of laws against it, they tend to accept the social-scientific assumption that race and sex themselves are immutable categories, the "givens" of historical analysis; they stop short of investigating historical changes in notions of race and gender.[2]

Assumptions like these are distinctly at odds with the work of both the vast majority of feminist scholars, who see gender as a social construction, and a growing group of ethnic studies scholars, who challenge the notion that race should be conceived of as a biological category. When I started to think about writing a history of interracial marriage, I found the gap between these two sets of assumptions at first puzzling, then intriguing. Now I think it is a vital clue to the way a study of interracial marriage might address three central conceptual challenges faced by women's historians seeking to write multicultural history:

1. The challenge of exploring the interconnections between gender and race relations

2. The challenge of learning to see race, as well as gender, as a social construction

3. The challenge of choosing a definition of culture suitable for writing intercultural history

In this rather speculative essay, I will use my preliminary research on the history of interracial marriage in the U.S. West to offer some thoughts on each of these challenges.

First, however, a little background is in order. Probably the most intriguing aspect of the history of interracial marriage in the United States is that, although such marriages were infrequent throughout most of U.S. history, an enormous amount of time and energy was spent trying to prevent them from taking place.

From the colonial period clear through the mid-twentieth century, state legislators made it their business to pass laws designed to prohibit what they came by the 1860s to call "miscegenation," a term that means mixture of the races. The laws were enacted first—and abandoned last—in the South, but it was in the West, not the South, that the laws became most elaborate. In the late nineteenth century, western legislators built a labyrinthine system of prohibitions on marriages between whites and Chinese, Japanese, Filipinos, Hawaiians, Hindus, and Native Americans, as well as on marriages between whites and blacks. Legislators targeted both interracial sex and interracial marriage, but the latter drew the strongest prohibitions and the most litigation, largely, I think, because marriage involved property obligations. Although most northern states repealed their prohibitions after the Civil War, in the South and the West, laws against interracial marriage remained in force through much of the twentieth century. Many were erased from the books only after the Supreme Court declared them unconstitutional in 1967.[3]

Interracial marriage has been studied far more often by social scientists than by historians, but both groups have seen it primarily as an issue of race relations. Yet, as any historian of women would suspect, interracial marriage is also an issue of gender relations, in obvious and not-so-obvious ways. The first challenge in writing its history is to learn to see interracial marriage as a matter of both gender and race relations.

To begin with the obvious, the campaign to prohibit interracial marriage reflects U.S. gender hierarchies as well as racial hierarchies. One of the very first prohibitions on interracial marriage, passed in Maryland in 1664, was straightforwardly sex-specific: It prohibited marriages between "freeborn[e] English women" and "Negro slaves."[4] Although most other colonies and states framed their laws in more generic terms, New Mexico followed the Maryland model as late as 1857, prohibiting marriage between, to use the language of the law, "any woman of the white race" and any "free negro or mulatto."[5] In conjunction with laws that defined the children of slave women as slaves and laws that denied legal legitimacy to slave marriages, miscegenation statutes contributed to a context in which white women's sexuality was firmly controlled even as white men were allowed a great deal of informal sexual access to black women.[6]

As it turns out, sex-specific miscegenation laws, unusual as they were, provide clues to the gender hierarchies structured by the majority of miscegenation laws, which were technically gender-blind.[7] In the United States, these laws were most likely to pass when legislators proposed them in the wake of scandals over white women's participation in interracial relationships. My research indicates that the laws were applied most stringently to groups like the Chinese, Japanese, and Filipinos, whose men were thought likely to marry white women. They were applied least stringently to groups like the Native Americans (who were inconsistently mentioned in the laws) and Hispanics (who were not mentioned at all), groups whose women were historically likely to marry white men.

Another side of these gender and race hierarchies can be seen in the miscegenation cases that ended up in appeals courts. Until the mid-twentieth century, only a few of these cases were brought by either interracial couples seeking the right to marry or law enforcement officials trying to prevent them from doing so. Most of the cases were ex post facto attempts to invalidate interracial marriages that had already lasted for a long time. Such cases were brought by relatives or by the state after the death of one spouse, most often a white man. The lawsuits were designed with a specific purpose in mind: to take property or inheritances away from the surviving spouse, most often a woman of color.

This is what happened, for example, in the 1921 Oregon case, *In re Paquet's Estate*.[8] In this case, decided after the death of Fred Paquet (a white man), Ophelia Paquet (his Native American wife) lost control of her husband's estate to her late husband's brother John (a white man), who challenged her for its control. The language of Oregon's miscegenation law was broad: It declared null and void marriages between "any white person" and "any negro, Chinese, or any person having one fourth or more negro, Chinese, or Kanaka blood, or any person having more than one half Indian blood."[9] Under the provisions of this law, the Oregon Supreme Court declared the Paquets' thirty-year marriage invalid. To do so, the court dismissed Ophelia Paquet's claim that the miscegenation statute denied Native Americans the same rights as whites. Echoing state courts all over the country, the Oregon court held that the statute did not discriminate against Native Americans because, as the judge said, "It applies alike to all persons, either white, negroes, Chinese, Kanakas, or Indians."[10]

The elements of this decision—the primacy of the issue of property, the tug-of-war between women of color and their white opponents for control of white men's estates, and the willingness of courts to invalidate long-term marriages in proceedings not directly related to the marriages themselves—were quite standard in miscegenation case law. The only unusual note in this decision was that, having deprived Ophelia Paquet of her inheritance, the court went out of its way to express its sympathy for her, suggesting to the victorious John Paquet that because Ophelia had been "a good and faithful wife" to his brother "for more than 30 years," he should consider offering her "a fair and reasonable settlement."[11]

This intertwining of gender and racial hierarchies is the most obvious aspect of gender relations in interracial marriage, but it is not the only aspect. A different kind of story, one as much about social construction as about hierarchy, can be seen in interviews conducted with participants in interracial marriages. There is an abundance of such interviews because, beginning in the early twentieth century, social scientists who studied race relations grew fascinated with interracial marriage, which they saw as a prime index of assimilation. Perhaps the best known of these interview projects is the survey of race relations carried out by University of Chicago sociologist Robert Park. The survey, conducted up and down the Pacific Coast in the 1920s, resulted in several hundred interviews, including many with participants in interracial marriages.[12] A host of somewhat-lesser-known sociologists and anthropologists, from Romanzo Adams in Hawaii to Manuel Gamio in the Southwest, shared Park's fascination with interracial marriage and also conducted interviews with participants.

Like most researchers after them, these early-twentieth-century social scientists saw interracial marriage primarily as a matter of race relations. What is, however, most interesting to me as I look at the interviews is that individual men's and women's decisions to cross racial boundary lines were often rooted in conceptions of gender relations. Consider, for example, the Hawaiian woman who told Romanzo Adams why so many Hawaiian women married non-Hawaiian men. "The Hawaiian men," she said, "are not steady workers and good providers. The Chinese men are good to provide, but they are stingy. The white men are good providers and they give their wives more money."[13] Her comment, of course, expresses race and class hierarchies, but both of these hierarchies are rooted in comparative definitions of manhood: Note that she emphasized above all the desire to marry men who fit the role of the "good provider." In choosing men they hoped would fit this role over men who may not even have aspired to do so, Hawaiian women shaped gender relations by promoting a particular definition of manhood. Much the same might be said of the post–World War II white soldiers who married Japanese women because, they said, Japanese women were more "feminine" than white women.[14]

These examples of the social construction of gender are specific to the history of interracial marriage, but the general concept of the social construction of gender is a familiar one to historians of women, who have long distinguished between the notion of sex (a biological category) and gender (a social construction). Although a vanguard of feminist theorists have recently begun to argue that the distinction is an artificial one, it is significant that they make the case that both sex and gender are social constructions; in this sense, their arguments demonstrate that, within feminist history, the notion that gender is a social construction is now considered so obvious as to be beyond dispute.

Unfortunately, the same point cannot yet be made about race. Consequently, the second conceptual challenge of writing a history of interracial marriage is to apply the same sophistication that women's historians use in tracing reformulations of gender to the analysis of reformulations of race.

Perhaps the most surprising thing I've learned by studying interracial marriage is how reluctant historians are to see race as a social construction. On one level, of course, any historian knows that race is, as Barbara J. Fields argues, a social category without real content; that is, social attitudes and institutions, not biological difference, sustain white dominance.[15] Yet, at the same time, most histories of racial groups—and most considerations of the role of race in women's history—tend to treat race as if it were a fixed biological marker, a reliable index to an unchanging history of social hierarchy.

So, in the late twentieth century, at a time when biologists themselves maintain that racial categories are so arbitrary as to carry no useful meaning at all, historians continue to refer to "race" as a factor in history, to speak of peoples of different "races," and to regard "racism" as a sort of prejudice rooted as much in individual psychological needs as in social history. Historians have tended to view race relations as a superstructure built on a biological base. Because their viewpoint has prevented them from seeing that race, like gender, is a social construction (the contours of which have undergone significant changes over time), a reassessment is needed.

Part of the problem, I think, is the lack of a term for "race" that functions in the same way as does the term "gender," that is, to signal a social construction distinct from biological classification. In the absence of such a term, historians tend to use the term "race" to refer to both biological categories and social relations, conflating the two in a way that makes it difficult to see race as a social construction. In an attempt to avoid this problem, scholars in other disciplines have begun to experiment with new terminology. Literary critic Henry Gates, Jr., puts the word "race" in quotation marks whenever he uses it; ethnic studies experts Michael Omi and Howard Winant speak of "racial formations"; poststructuralists refer to ideas of "racial difference" as analogous to ideas of "sexual difference."[16]

If the lack of a term for race analogous to "gender" is one roadblock to understanding the social construction of race, another is the historians' tendency to think of race relations primarily in terms of the African American experience. When we look at race relations through a multicultural lens, historical shifts in the meaning of the term "race" rise to the surface. Late-nineteenth-century miscegenation laws in the West are a case in point; they provide a virtual road map of the changing legal definition of race and offer clues to a major reformulation of the notion of racial difference that emerged in the late 1800s and solidified in the first half of the twentieth century.

During this period, western state legislators significantly expanded the original southern prohibitions on marriages between blacks and whites by

adding new groups—first Native Americans and then Asian Americans—
to the list of those prohibited from marrying whites. The banning of Asian
Americans took various forms. In the 1860s, it was common for lawmakers
to single out the Chinese, the first Asian group to immigrate to the United
States in large numbers, for mention in miscegenation laws.[17] As Chinese
immigrants were followed by Japanese immigrants, some states enacted
miscegenation laws that made use of the catchall term "Mongolians,"
intended to cover both groups.[18] Even this expansion, however, did not satisfy
legislators for long.

In 1933, for example, a California judge was presented with the issue
of whether a Filipino man who wanted to marry a white woman should
be classified as a member of the "Mongolian race" or the "Malay race."[19]
After a lengthy discussion of racial classifications, the judge held that
Filipinos could not be classified as "Mongolians" and so must be considered
"Malays." Under California miscegenation law, "Mongolians" were
prohibited from marrying whites, but "Malays" were not mentioned;
therefore, the judge's decision paved the way for the couple in question to
marry. The California legislature, however, promptly subverted the decision
by passing a new law that added "Malays" to the list of those already
forbidden to marry whites.[20]

This expansion of the definition of race in miscegenation law in the late
nineteenth and early twentieth centuries contrasts sharply with late-twentieth-
century developments, so much so that we can, I think, speak of another
reformulation of the notion of racial difference in our own time. In 1967,
after years of intermittent pressure, the U.S. Supreme Court declared
miscegenation laws unconstitutional.[21] The decision in *Loving v. Virginia*
marked a substantial shift in the social construction of race: By Supreme
Court ruling, biological race is no longer a significant category in U.S.
marriage law.

This recent shift may mark a point in U.S. history at which race proves
to be an even more malleable social construction than gender for, at the
same time that the notion of biological race was being removed from marriage
law, the notion of biological sex was becoming more deeply embedded in
it. In Utah, for example, the state legislature repealed its ban on interracial
marriages in 1963; then, in 1977, it passed a ban on same-sex marriages.[22]
In this case, Utah turns out to be more typical than exceptional. Fifteen
of the nineteen states whose laws I have surveyed had, since their territorial
periods, defined marriage as a contract between "parties," gender
unspecified. Between 1970 and 1980, nine of these same states enacted a
new definition, one that used sex-specific language, usually declaring that
marriage was a contract between "a man and a woman."[23] To add insult
to injury, sex-specific definitions of marriage were frequently passed as
parts of bills intended to erase gender differences in marriage law. They
were usually included in legislation designed to eliminate the difference
in legal ages between men and women and to replace the generic pronoun
"he" with "he and she." But that is, perhaps, another story.

For the moment, all I want to suggest is that the history of interracial marriage provides rich evidence of the formulation and reformulation of race and gender and of the connections between the two. With those points in mind, I will turn to the last of the three challenges I want to discuss, one that I might call the problem of the paradigm.

For a history of interracial marriage set in a multicultural arena and seen as a problem in intercultural relations, culture is as important a category of analysis as are race and gender. Writing multicultural history requires a working definition of the term "culture." Yet, at the present time, to study culture is to enter one of the most amorphous areas of historical research. There is no shortage of possibilities. Although definitions of culture remain elusive, the concept of culture has become ubiquitous. Just think for a moment of some of the categories of culture currently used by U.S. historians. There are, to begin with, the racial and ethnic categories: African American culture, Hispanic culture, Asian American culture, and so on. There are also economic categories: corporate culture, work culture, working-class culture, consumer culture. There are chronological categories: traditional culture, Victorian culture, modernist culture. There are even hierarchical categories: high culture and popular culture. And I could go on, from women's culture to political culture to "the new cultural history."[24]

Scholars in a variety of disciplines are trying to make sense of this embarrassment of cultural riches. As I survey their work, it seems to me that we are witnessing a major shift in the reigning paradigm of culture. The direction of change seems reasonably clear—it leads away from a paradigm of culture as a unified system of values and beliefs toward a paradigm of culture as a series of conflicts over meaning played out along such dividing lines as race, class, and gender.

The older paradigm, in which culture is seen as a relatively unified system of values and beliefs, was rooted in the kind of cultural anthropology usually identified with Clifford Geertz. For a couple of decades now, social historians have adopted this model of culture with enthusiasm. They use it to emphasize the community strength, collective consciousness, and active agency of people in the various cultures they study. In the most common work of this kind, social historians attach the term "culture" to one of the categories of race, class, or gender. When they do this, they end up with topics such as women's culture, working-class culture, or slave culture, all of which have become popular subjects in U.S. social history. The great strength of this kind of work is its "thick descriptions" of the central values and beliefs within each of these cultures. The great weakness is that its practitioners tend to encapsulate each culture, isolating it from its historical and social context. Power relations within each culture are deemphasized, and power relations between cultures are ignored.[25]

The newer approach to studying culture, now rapidly becoming paradigmatic, focuses directly on power and conflict, though it more often highlights conflict within a given culture than conflict between cultures. This newer approach is most closely associated with the critical wing of the emerging discipline of cultural studies, those academics who call themselves "cultural critics."[26] Their approach has roots in critical theory, poststructuralist literary criticism, and postmodern anthropology. From the cultural critical perspective, culture is not, as many social historians would have it, the embodiment of community consciousness. Instead, culture is a site of conflict in which various groups struggle to control symbols and meanings.

Cultural critics take on the task of uncovering power relations in every aspect of life, from social institutions to the forms of knowledge to language itself. In the process, they emphasize the forces that limit human agency, they challenge the notion that identity is a unified phenomenon, and they assert that experience (a favorite category of social historians, feminists, and ethnic studies scholars) is not what it seems. The critics drive home their point by describing peoples' consciousness as, to use one of their favorite phrases, "always already" shaped by forces outside their control.[27]

The distance between the "old" and "new" paradigms of culture can be traced in a variety of disciplines. In anthropology, it is the distance between Clifford Geertz's "interpretation" of culture and James Clifford's critique of the "predicament" of culture. In history, it is the distance between social histories of working-class, slave, or women's cultures on the one hand and, on the other, Thomas Bender's call for the study of a "public culture" in which workers, slaves, and women are considered "parts" of a much larger cultural "whole." In feminist studies, it is the distance between Barbara Smith's call for a black feminist literary criticism and Gayatri Spivak's reflections on *whether* subaltern women can speak *at all*.[28]

For a history of interracial marriage, neither of these paradigms is completely sufficient. If I accepted the social historical model, my study of intermarriage could find no room to grow. Social historians keep relationships between cultures on the margins (or perhaps I should say in the introductions, footnotes, or conclusions) of their studies. If, on the other hand, I framed my work according to the cultural critical model, my history of interracial marriage would emphasize large shaping forces and deemphasize people as active agents. To adopt for a moment the language of cultural critics, my study would become the story of the cultural production of hegemonic definitions of racial and sexual difference embedded in legal discourse.[29]

The cultural critical model is becoming enormously popular among literary critics and postmodern anthropologists, but most social historians retain their dedication to unearthing the viewpoint of subordinate groups and their attachment to the triad of agency, identity, and experience that cultural critics attack so fiercely. Historians of women are, I think, positioned right in the middle of the two groups and therefore are exceptionally well placed to see the strengths and the weaknesses of the cultural critical paradigm.[30]

The great strength of cultural criticism is its attention to power relations within given cultures. Historians of women certainly understand the need to analyze these power relations; in fact, feminist scholars were instrumental in exposing the gender divisions that exploded the rather romantic social historical depictions of supposedly unified working-class, ethnic, and racial cultures.

But historians of women have also developed the notion of a powerful, albeit sometimes idealized, "women's culture," which has in some respects provided an affirming vision for subordinate groups.[31] Thus, historians of women should be especially alert to the dangers of adopting a critical cultural paradigm that builds its case by attacking the concepts of human identity, experience, and agency.

In trying to build a model that acknowledges the constraining power of structures over peoples' lives, cultural critics have created a paradigm that itself imposes significant constraints on our ability to understand peoples' active participation in building and challenging social structures. To return to my example for a moment, because a cultural critical study of interracial marriage would emphasize shaping forces, it would deemphasize a central part of the story I want to tell: the active agency of the participants in interracial marriages. It would, in other words, limit my ability to understand participants' involvement in the reformulation of race and gender relations.

Such a paradigm is problematic no matter whom it is applied to, but it is especially troubling that cultural critics are deconstructing concepts of individual and community agency just at the point when feminist historians are extending their accounts of female agency from white middle-class women to women of color.[32] It might even be said, I think, that because cultural critics doubt that scholars can ever comprehend powerless groups, they have created something of a crisis among those who want to write the histories of subordinate peoples. The problem can most easily be seen by once again comparing the cultural critics with their social history predecessors. In essence, adopting the cultural critical approach means replacing the old social history project of reclaiming the voices of powerless peoples with a different project—that of critiquing dominant peoples' depictions of subaltern "others."

And there is another, related aspect of critical cultural studies that historians of women should worry about: the growing tendency to use the term "cultural" in the generic singular instead of in the plural.[33] Partly because of their doubts about the ability of scholars to understand subordinate groups, cultural critics are a particularly inward-looking group. When they do go as far as to critique power relations between cultures, they do so from a vantage point located (however ambivalently) within the dominant culture.

For a historian interested in writing a history of interracial marriage—or in developing a multicultural history of women—this simply won't do. If, as cultural critics would suggest, culture is a site from which to begin analysis, it makes a considerable difference which site we choose to begin from. To keep a firm eye on the tension between the power of the dominant on the one hand and the agency of the oppressed on the other, we must choose sites in which multiple cultures are present, and we must focus on the problem of recovering the perspectives of the powerless as well as of the powerful. And here we come back to the U.S. West for, with its remarkable history of cultural diversity, no area offers a better location for considering the theoretical questions of race, gender, and intercultural relations that are at the heart of the history of interracial marriage.

Notes

This paper was originally presented at the Eighth Berkshire Conference on the History of Women at Douglass College, Rutgers University, 1990, and thereafter published in *Frontiers* 12, no. 1 (1991).

1. For a thorough review of these studies, see Paul R. Spickard, *Mixed Blood: Intermarriage and Ethnic Identity in Twentieth-Century America* (Madison: University of Wisconsin Press, 1989), 6–17.

2. On the patterns of interracial marriage, see Spickard, *Mixed Blood*; Joel Williamson, *New People: Miscegenation and Mulattoes in the United States* (New York: Free Press, 1980); Rebecca McDowell Craver, *The Impact of Intimacy: Mexican-Anglo Intermarriage in New Mexico, 1821–1846*, Southwestern Studies #66 (El Paso: Texas Western Press, 1982); Darlis A. Miller, "Cross-Cultural Marriages in the Southwest: The New Mexico Experience, 1846–1900," *New Mexico Historical Review* 57 (October 1982): 335–59; Tanis C. Thorne, "People of the River: Mixed-Blood Families on the Lower Missouri," (Ph.D. dissertation, University of California, Los Angeles, 1987); Sylvia Van Kirk, *Many Tender Ties: Women in Fur-Trade Society, 1670–1870* (Norman: University of Oklahoma Press, 1980); Jennifer Brown, *Strangers in Blood: Fur Trade Company Families in Indian Country* (Vancouver: University of British Columbia, 1980); Jacqueline Peterson and Jennifer Brown, eds., *The New Peoples: Being and Becoming Métis in North America* (Lincoln: University of Nebraska Press, 1985); Jacqueline Peterson, "Women Dreaming: The Religiopsychology of Indian-White Marriage and the Rise of Métis Culture," in *Western Women: Their Land, Their Lives*, ed. Lillian Schlissel, Vicki L. Ruiz, and Janice Monk (Albuquerque: University of New Mexico Press, 1988), 49–68; and John Faragher, "The Custom of the Country: Cross-Cultural Marriage in the Far Western Fur Trade," in *Western Women*, 199–226. On miscegenation law, see Robert J. Sickels, *Race, Marriage, and the Law* (Albuquerque: University of New Mexico Press, 1972); Byron Curti Martyn, "Racism in the United States: A History of the Anti-Miscegenation Legislation and Litigation," (Ph.D. dissertation, University of Southern California, 1979); David H. Fowler, *Northern Attitudes towards Interracial Marriage: Legislation and Public Opinion in the Middle Atlantic and the States of the Old Northwest, 1780–1930* (1963; New York: Garland, 1987); Megumi Dick Osumi, "Asians and California's Anti-Miscegenation Laws," in *Asian and Pacific American Experiences: Women's Perspectives*, ed. John Nobuya Tsuchida (Minneapolis: University of Minnesota, Asian/Pacific American Learning Resource Center, 1982), 2–8; Roger D. Hardaway, "Prohibiting Interracial Marriage: Miscegenation Law in Wyoming," *Annals of Wyoming* 52 (Spring 1980): 55–60; and Roger D. Hardaway, "Unlawful Love: A History of Arizona's Miscegenation Law," *Journal of Arizona History* 27 (Winter 1986): 377–90.

3. *Loving v. Virginia*, 388 US 1, 18 L ed 2d 1010, 87 S Ct 1817 (1967).

4. William H. Browne, ed., *Archives of Maryland* I, 533–34, cited in *Northern Attitudes*, 381. For interpretations of these early laws, see A. Leon Higginbotham, Jr., and Barbara K. Kopytoff, "Racial Purity and Interracial Sex in the Law of Colonial and Antebellum Virginia," *Georgetown Law Journal* 77 (August 1989): 1967–2029; George Fredrickson, *The Arrogance of Race: Historical Perspectives on Slavery, Racism, and Social Inequality* (Middletown, Conn.: Wesleyan University Press, 1988), 195–96; and Barbara J. Fields, "Slavery, Race and Ideology in the United States of America," *New Left Review* 181 (May–June 1990): 95–119. As Fields points out (p. 107), the fact that the Maryland law of 1664 referred to "Freeborne English women" rather than "white" women suggests that the law does not so much reflect racial categories as it shows "society in the act of inventing race."

5. *New Mexico Terr. Laws*, chap. 20, secs. 3 and 4, cited in Martyn, "Racism in the United States," 459.

6. John D'Emilio and Estelle B. Freedman, *Intimate Matters: A History of Sexuality in America* (New York: Harper & Row, 1989), 92–97, 100–104; Jacquelyn Dowd Hall, " 'The Mind That Burns

in Each Body': Women, Rape, and Racial Violence," in *Powers of Desire: The Politics of Sexuality*, ed. Ann Snitow et al. (New York: Monthly Review Press, 1983), 328–49; Thelma Jennings, " 'Us Colored Women Had to Go through a Plenty': Sexual Exploitation of African-American Slave Women," *Journal of Women's History 1* (Winter 1990): 45–74.

7. On this point, see esp. Higginbotham and Kopytoff, "Racial Purity."

8. *In re Paquet's Estate*, 200 P. 911.

9. *Oregon Code*, 1887, sec. 1927. "Kanaka" refers to native Hawaiians.

10. *In re Paquet's Estate*, 200 P. 911, 913.

11. Ibid., 200 P. 911, 914.

12. Park's Survey of Race Relations is housed in the Hoover Institution Archives at Stanford University.

13. Romanzo Adams, *Interracial Marriage in Hawaii: A Study of the Mutually Conditioned Processes of Acculturation and Amalgamation* (New York: Macmillan, 1937), 48.

14. On white soldiers who married Japanese women, see Spickard, *Mixed Blood*, chap. 5, 123–57.

15. Barbara J. Fields, "Ideology and Race in American History," in *Region, Race, and Reconstruction: Essays in Honor of C. Vann Woodward*, ed. J. Morgan Kousser and James M. McPherson (New York: Oxford University Press, 1982), 143–78, esp. 151. See also Fields, "Slavery, Race and Ideology."

16. Henry Louis Gates, Jr., *"Race," Writing, and Difference* (Chicago: University of Chicago Press, 1986); Michael Omi and Howard Winant, *Racial Formation in the United States: From the 1960s to the 1980s* (Boston: Routledge & Kegan Paul, 1986). For examples of poststructuralist discourse, see Homi K. Bhabha, "The Other Question . . . Homi K. Bhabha Reconsiders the Stereotype and Colonial Discourse," *Screen* 24 (1983): 18–36, and Joan Wallach Scott's definition of gender as "knowledge about sexual difference" in *Gender and the Politics of History* (New York: Columbia University Press, 1988), 2. A useful recent collection of articles on the social construction of "racisms" is David Theo Goldberg, ed., *Anatomy of Racism* (Minneapolis: University of Minnesota Press, 1990).

17. "Chinese" were mentioned in the miscegenation laws of Nevada (1861–1912), Idaho (1864–87), Oregon (1866–1951), Montana (1909–53), and Nebraska (1913–63).

18. "Mongolians" were mentioned in the miscegenation laws of Arizona (1865–1962), Wyoming (1869–82 and 1913–65), California (1880–1959), Utah (1888–1963), Oregon (1893–1951), Nevada (1912–59), South Dakota (1913–57), and Idaho (1921–59).

19. *Roldan v. Los Angeles County*, 129 Cal. App. 267 (1933).

20. *Statutes of California*, 1933, 561. Five other states also prohibited whites from marrying "Malays": Nevada (1912–59), South Dakota (1913–57), Wyoming (1913–65), Arizona (1931–62), and Utah (1939–63).

21. *Loving v. Virginia*, 388 US 1, 18 L ed 2d 1010, 87 S Ct 1817 (1967). The major precedent for Supreme Court action was a 1948 case, *Perez v. Sharp*, in which the California Supreme Court had declared its state miscegenation statute unconstitutional. *Perez v. Sharp*, 32 Cal. 2d 711, 198 P. 2d 17 (1948). In the years between the *Perez* and the *Loving* decisions, most western state legislatures repealed their miscegenation laws: Oregon (1951), Montana (1953), North Dakota (1955), Colorado (1957), South Dakota (1957), California (1959), Idaho (1959), Nevada (1959), Arizona (1962), Nebraska (1963), Utah (1963), and Wyoming (1965). Miscegenation legislation in two western states (Oklahoma and Texas) and a number of southern states remained in force until the *Loving* decision.

22. *Utah Laws*, 1963, p. 163; *Utah Laws*, 1977, 1st S S, p. 2.

23. The states that defined marriage in terms of "parties" or "persons" were Arizona, California, Colorado, Idaho, Kansas, Montana, Nebraska, Nevada, New Mexico, North Dakota, Oklahoma, Oregon, South Dakota, Texas, and Wyoming. Those (besides Utah) that adopted sex-specific definitions were Colorado (1973), Montana (1973), Texas (1973), Nevada (1975), North Dakota (1975), California (1977), Wyoming (1977), and Kansas (1980). Only two states, Washington (1970) and Alaska (1983), moved in the opposite direction, replacing definitions of marriage that originally spoke of "males and females" with definitions that spoke of "persons." These changes, however, offered same-sex couples little protection. In *Singer v. Hara*, a 1974 case, the Washington State

Court of Appeals refused to allow a same-sex couple access to a marriage license, ruling that the introduction of the word "persons" in the state's new definition of marriage had been intended only to eliminate different age requirements by sex. *Singer v. Hara*, 11 Wash. App. 247 (1974).

24. On this last, see esp. Lynn Hunt, ed., *The New Cultural History* (Berkeley: University of California Press, 1989).

25. For analyses, see Thomas Bender, "Wholes and Parts: The Need for Synthesis in American History," *Journal of American History* 73 (June 1986): 127–32, and Peggy Pascoe, *Relations of Rescue: The Search for Female Moral Authority in the American West, 1874–1939* (New York: Oxford University Press, 1990), 208–212.

26. See Richard Johnson, "What Is Cultural Studies Anyway?" *Social Text 16* (Winter 1986–87): 38–80; Lawrence Grossberg, "Formations of Cultural Studies: An American in Birmingham," *Strategies* 2 (1989): 114–48; Victor Burgin, "Cultural Studies in Britain: Two Paradigms," *Center for Cultural Studies Newsletter* (University of California, Santa Cruz), Spring 1990; and Scott Heller, "Cultural Studies: Eclectic and Controversial Mix of Research Sparks a Growing Movement," *Chronicle of Higher Education*, 31 January 1990.

27. For a fine critique of deconstructionist use of the phrase "always already," see Diana Fuss, *Essentially Speaking: Feminism, Nature, and Difference* (New York: Routledge, 1989), 17.

28. Clifford Geertz, *The Interpretation of Cultures* (New York: Basic Books, 1973); James Clifford, *The Predicament of Culture: Twentieth-Century Ethnography, Literature, and Art* (Cambridge, Mass.: Harvard University Press, 1988); Bender, "Wholes and Parts"; Barbara Smith, "Toward a Black Feminist Criticism," *Conditions: Two* 1 (October 1977), reprinted in *The New Feminist Criticism: Essays on Women, Literature, and Theory*, ed. Elaine Showalter (New York: Pantheon, 1985), 168–85; Gayatri Chakravorty Spivak, "Can the Subaltern Speak?" in *Marxism and the Interpretation of Culture*, ed. Gary Nelson and Lawrence Grossberg (Urbana: University of Illinois Press, 1988), 271–313.

29. For an example of this approach, see Eva Saks, "Representing Miscegenation Law," *Raritan* 8 (Fall 1988): 39–69.

30. For a parallel argument about the significance of intellectual history, see John Toews, "Intellectual History after the Linguistic Turn: The Autonomy of Meaning and the Irreducibility of Experience," *American Historical Review* 92 (October 1987): 879–907.

31. On the concept of women's culture in women's history, see Ellen DuBois, Mari Jo Buhle, Temma Kaplan, Gerda Lerner, and Carroll Smith-Rosenberg, "Politics and Culture in Women's History: A Symposium," *Feminist Studies* 6 (Spring 1980): 65–75; Nancy Hewitt, "Beyond the Search for Sisterhood: American Women's History in the 1980s," *Social History* 10 (October 1985): 299–321; Linda Kerber, "Separate Spheres, Female Worlds, Woman's Place: The Rhetoric of Women's History," *Journal of American History* 75 (June 1988): 9–39; Cecile Dauphin et al., "Women's Culture and Women's Power: An Attempt at Historiography," *Journal of Women's History* 1 (Spring 1989): 63–102.

32. For a parallel argument on this point, see Nancy Hartsock, "Foucault on Power: A Theory for Women?" in *Feminism/Postmodernism*, ed. Linda J. Nicholson (New York: Routledge, 1990), 163–64.

33. Note, for example, that Thomas Bender reserves the use of the term "culture" for his discussions of U.S. "public culture," thereby demoting all the cultures social historians have unearthed—women's culture, slave culture, and so forth—to the status of groups within the larger public culture. For an argument for the need to resuscitate the notion of a national culture (but one that retains the concept of multiple cultures within U.S. society), see Elizabeth Fox-Genovese, "Between Individualism and Fragmentation: American Culture and the New Literary Studies of Race and Gender," *American Quarterly* 42 (March 1990): 7–34.

PART TWO

Frontiers

The perspectives of racial ethnic women alter western history in fundamental ways. We begin with American Indian women, not the Europeans who "discovered" them. Western history is no longer the story of people who landed at Jamestown and Plymouth and progressively claimed the continent, but the story of indigenous peoples and their relationships with newcomers.

Those encounters redefine the frontier, one of the most enduring concepts in western history. The superintendent of the U.S. census defined the frontier in 1890 as an unbroken line of settlement with two or fewer people per square mile, by which criterion he determined that the frontier no longer existed. Western historians subsequently defined frontiers as the edges of Euro-American settlement. Different frontiers were typically characterized by male economic endeavors—the Indian trader's frontier, the rancher's frontier, the soldier's frontier, the miner's frontier, and so on—but not, for instance, the poultry frontier or the schoolteacher's frontier. Equating frontiers with economic opportunities and access to land, some historians argued that frontier opportunity extended well into the twentieth century. Others replaced the concept of "frontier" with "conquest," changing the story of westward expansion into a virgin wilderness to a tale of conflicts among peoples to control already inhabited territory.[1]

If, however, we think of our history not as the history of the United States but as the history of its peoples, then frontiers are not just the edges of territorial claims or national conquest, but the places where people of different cultures met. We have just begun to think about what frontiers were for women and how gender changed in frontier encounters. For Indian women of diverse cultures, frontier histories began long before Europeans arrived. We can never recover the stories of all the frontier contacts different Indian peoples had with one another. But one step toward an inclusive history is the awareness that the first frontierswomen were Indian women. On colonial frontiers, Indian women of many cultures negotiated relationships with an

81

assortment of Europeans, including fur traders, explorers, missionaries, farmers, and soldiers. In all these diverse circumstances, one social fact connected most frontiers—the newcomers were overwhelmingly male. When European and Euro-American men joined indigenous women and men, the women were outnumbered. The unbalanced numbers of men and women increased demands for women's domestic skills and sexual companionship and profoundly affected their options. As domestic workers and domestic partners, Indian women's contacts with European men ranged from demeaning and violent relationships to emotional intimacy.

In part, these relationships varied with the aspirations that brought Europeans to America—to trade, to settle, to establish Christian missions, to conquer territory. A number of nations established colonial settlements in western North America, while the English, French, and Dutch settled the East. From the founding of the Hudson's Bay Company in 1670, French and English fur traders established families and trading partnerships with Canadian Indian peoples; in 1713 the French established a trading post on the Red River in present-day North Dakota. Russia established the first permanent European settlement in Alaska in 1784 and built Fort Ross north of San Francisco in 1812 to supply its colony. The first significant colonial settlement in what is now the U.S. West occurred on the northern frontiers of Spanish Mexican settlement in New Mexico, California, and Texas.

The conquest of the West began when Hernán Cortés landed at Tabasco in 1519 and began his two-year campaign to conquer the Aztecs. The history of gender relationships on the European/American frontier is often dated from Cortés's relationship with Malíntzin Tenépal, his interpreter and companion. Malíntzin Tenépal and their son, Don Martín Cortés Tenépal, demonstrate the human costs exacted from people caught between cultures on intimate frontiers. The Spaniards accused Don Martín of treason and tortured and killed him. Malíntzin Tenépal, derogatorily called "La Malinche," was long portrayed as a woman who betrayed her people by helping the invaders and sleeping with the enemy. More recently, feminist historians have interpreted her as a survivor and as the mother of a new mestizo people, descended from Spaniards and Indians.[2]

The figure of La Malinche demonstrates the vulnerable positions of women outnumbered by men on most frontiers. For women, being a numerical minority meant many things, including increased demands for their sexuality, their domestic labor, and their assistance, sometimes voluntary and sometimes coerced, as cultural mediators. For Indian and European women alike, gender systems changed as a result of contact. Native women welcomed some changes, like access to new trade goods such as needles and iron pots and to new economic resources like sheep. Europeans in turn learned about native foods and about clothing and housing suited to the environment. But these cultural exchanges, for most women on all sides, occurred in contexts of dependency. Indian women's lives were disrupted by disease, by loss of land and resources, and by forced attempts to change their religions, family systems, work roles, and sexual behaviors. Women colonizers were often isolated, outnumbered, and dependent on men for protection and support.

Spanish Mexicans expanded northward into New Mexico in the sixteenth century, and then into Texas and California to establish Catholic missions during the 1700s. Don Juan de Oñate established the first permanent settlement on the northern Spanish Mexican frontier in 1598 in present-day New Mexico. His band of 158 colonizers included 29 women, who were outnumbered both by Spanish Mexican men and by the indigenous Indian peoples. All the people on Spain's colonial frontiers—Spanish Mexican priests and colonists and the indigenous peoples they came to conquer and convert—viewed one another's gender systems as strange, unnatural, or immoral. Pueblo women's work as mothers, cooks, and manufacturers of textiles and clothing all fit Spanish concepts, but other women's tasks jarred Spanish understandings of gender, like the fact that Pueblo women built, plastered, and owned their homes. The Spaniards ultimately accepted this "strange" practice, and missionaries employed Pueblo women as laborers to help build mission churches. However, not all exchanges were so benign. The Spanish demand for blankets for tribute placed severe burdens on Pueblo women's labor. Spanish priests tried to eradicate sexual behaviors that they did not understand but that were at the heart of Pueblo spiritual practice. For the Pueblo women of New Mexico, the pressure to change their personal and social behavior occurred as their people were devastated by warfare and disease. By the end of the seventeenth century, the Pueblo population of New Mexico had shrunk from an estimated fifty thousand to sixteen thousand; only nineteen pueblos survived of the ninety that had existed at contact.

Such human and cultural loss sparked active resistance. Spanish efforts to control the Pueblos' land and labor, and to change their systems of religion, kinship, and sexuality led ultimately to the successful Pueblo Revolt of 1680. In the aftermath of the Pueblo victory, the Spanish Mexicans fled south to a site near present-day El Paso, among them large numbers of women and children. When the soldiers left the settlement on reconquest expeditions, the Spanish Mexican women, as heads of households, labored to keep the refugees alive. After twelve years of wretched impoverishment, they helped reconquer New Mexico in 1692. Women's perspectives shift well-known frontier stories of warfare and conquest such as the Pueblo Revolt. They lead us to focus on the intimate invasions that sparked resistance and on the daily work of survival that maintained Spanish colonial authority.[3]

Colonial encounters reverberated in the lives of women far removed from direct colonization and conquest. The horses that Cortés brought to New Spain had reached the northern plains by the eighteenth century. Within another century, a new horse and hide trade dramatically intensified the work of Plains Indian women, who spent more and more time processing the hides men acquired with the guns and horses Europeans introduced. The increased demand for women's labor to process buffalo hides narrowed the variety of roles to which they had access and led to a rise in polygamy.[4] *Similarly, in the Southwest, Navajo women learned agriculture and weaving from Pueblos who fled the Spanish reconquest. The Navajo acquired sheep from the Spaniards but may have modeled female ownership and management of livestock on the Pueblo women, who cared for domesticated turkeys.*[5] *As these examples show, colonial encounters rippled throughout the West to change the economies and the gender systems of people who had little direct contact with Europeans and who lived far from the Spanish Mexican frontier.*

These brief sketches only hint at new ways to see frontiers as we place racial ethnic women at the center of our histories. From their perspectives we see how new systems of economic and social relationships were forged, what they offered and what they cost.

Reclaiming these stories is not easy. It is hard to tease out the histories of women—Indian and European alike—from records largely produced by European men. It takes great imagination to look past the record keepers' cultural and gender assumptions and to envision the encounters from the other side. It takes greater imagination to ask what is missing from the records and to respect the silences and the omissions we cannot recover. The authors in this section make resourceful use of Spanish colonial mission records, wills, censuses, settlement records, and estate inventories. They build from previous scholarship, using histories that were not primarily concerned with gender, anthropologists' accounts of Indian cultures, and social theory. Through careful use of filtered sources and filtered scholarship, they reconstruct women's experiences and the relationships of gender and power on colonial frontiers.

Notes

1. *Extra Census Bulletin*, No. 2, 20 April 1892; Frederick Jackson Turner, "The Significance of the Frontier in American History," in *Annual Report of the American Historical Association for the Year 1893* (Washington, D.C.: U.S. Government Printing Office, 1894); Patricia Nelson Limerick, "What on Earth Is the New Western History?" in *Trails: Toward a New Western History*, ed. Patricia Nelson Limerick, Clyde A. Milner II, and Charles E. Rankin (Lawrence: University Press of Kansas, 1991), 81–87; and Patricia Nelson Limerick, *Legacy of Conquest: The Unbroken Past of the American West* (New York: W. W. Norton, 1987).

2. Cordelia Candelaria, "La Malinche, Feminist Prototype," *Frontiers* 5, no. 2 (Summer 1980): 1–6; Adelaída R. del Castillo, "Malíntzin Tenépal: A Preliminary Look into a New Perspective," in *Essays on La Mujer*, ed. Rosaura Sánchez and Rosa Martínez Cruz (Los Angeles: UCLA Chicano Studies Center Publications, 1977), 24–49.

3. See Salomé Hernández, *"Nueva Mexicanas* as Refugees and Reconquest Settlers, 1680–1696," in *New Mexico Women: Intercultural Perspectives*, ed. Joan M. Jensen and Darlis A. Miller (Albuquerque: University of New Mexico Press, 1986), 41–70; Cheryl J. Foote and Sandra K. Schackel, "Indian Women of New Mexico, 1535–1680," in *New Mexico Women*, 17–40, esp. 20; Salomé Hernández, "The United States Southwest: Female Participation in Official Spanish Settlement Expeditions" (Ph.D. dissertation, University of New Mexico, 1987); Ramón Gutiérrez, *When Jesus Came, the Corn Mothers Went Away: Marriage, Sexuality, and Power in New Mexico, 1500–1846* (Stanford, Calif.: Stanford University Press, 1991).

4. Alan M. Klein, "The Political-Economy of Gender: A Nineteenth-Century Plains Indian Case Study," in *The Hidden Half: Studies of Plains Indian Women*, ed. Patricia Albers and Beatrice Medicine (Washington, D.C.: University Press of America, 1983), 143–75; Evelyn Blackwood, "Sexuality and Gender in Certain Native American Tribes: The Case of Cross-Gender Females," *Signs* 10, no. 1 (Autumn 1984): 27–42.

5. Foote and Schackel, "Indian Women," 31–33.

4.

"A Poor Widow Burdened with Children": Widows and Land in Colonial New Mexico

YOLANDA CHÁVEZ LEYVA

Widowhood, a common experience, provides a window into women's status by allowing us to look at what resources women had to support themselves after their husbands died. In this article, Yolanda Leyva uses widowhood to analyze women's options in Spanish colonial New Mexico. Spanish Mexican women controlled property they brought into a marriage and generally received half of a couple's property when their husbands died. Widows established some autonomy for themselves and for other women through their access to land and to marital property and through their right to bequeath their property. These property rights exceed those accorded women in the English colonies, where widows generally were guaranteed only the use of a "widow's third" of a couple's holdings, a difference that might suggest a higher status for Spanish Mexican women.

Yet Leyva's analysis cautions against such simple comparisons of different legal systems by demonstrating the complexity of women's status. Spanish Mexican women occupied an ambiguous position. They were the guardians of their families and were themselves the wards of men and of the government. Their ability to achieve a degree of autonomy depended on using their status as "protected protectors" to carve out their own survival strategies. Leyva's careful analysis of scattered colonial documents demonstrates how important it is to get past debates about which women were more liberated or more oppressed and to look instead at the specific strategies women used to adapt in particular circumstances.

In 1769, the widow María Martín of Santa Fe, New Mexico, lay dying. Her final testament provides us a small window through which we may catch a glimpse of her life and of her final thoughts. Although much of her will employs the standard wording of countless other colonial Mexican wills, it still reflects traces of the individual woman who, faced with her own mortality, attempted to put her life in order. Her last testament reads, in part, "It is my will that my house and the adjacent piece of land be given to my daughter, María, because she is a woman and because she is poor and for accompanying me during my life, never having left me helpless."[1]

This simple yet eloquent statement of affection, gratitude, and reciprocity expresses more than the personal; it also reveals something about the economic and social conditions of women on Mexico's northern frontier.

This single sentence hints at the vulnerability of women trying to survive alone but also at the strategies that women used in order to survive. Women alone—whether single, widowed, abandoned, or separated—experienced problems and opportunities very different from those of their married counterparts.[2]

Widowhood, universal in its presence across many cultures and across time, is also shaped by the individual. The ability of a woman to navigate the often rough course of her widowhood depends on factors ranging from her specific circumstances to the expectations and resources of the larger society. Using a variety of colonial New Mexican archival documents, this investigation broadens our understanding of widowhood on Mexico's northern frontier by exploring these women's survival strategies.[3] Wills in particular form the foundation of the research for it is in these documents that we see the final outcomes of these women's lives. The documents reveal that women, although constrained in many ways by societal norms, both used and, in fact, often reinforced a system that provided them some measure of governmental and familial protection in return for their behaving within the boundaries of those norms and expectations. In the case of widows, women claimed an identity as a group worthy of protection constructed largely upon the basis of their poverty and their obligations.

Widows held a unique legal position among women in colonial Spanish America. Women were legally covered by the concept of *patria postestad*; that is, they were subject to their fathers' will and control until they reached the age of twenty-five or were married. Once she was married, a woman's husband took over the role of protector and the law required his consent for any legal transaction. Widowhood severed the legal restrictions that placed women under male guardianship. Widows acquired half the wealth accumulated by the couple during their marriage as well as any existing dowry. Frequently, they gained the right to administer the inheritance of any minor children until the children reached adulthood.[4] This increased independence, however, came with a price. In an impoverished frontier society such as New Mexico, the obligations attached to widowhood could far outweigh the benefits.

Both the church and the state in Spain and Spanish America believed it vital to their own interests to protect marriage and the family. This preservation of marriage and family required the protection of certain vulnerable groups within society, particularly women and children. Both men and women expected that socially acceptable women would have access to a minimum level of protection in dangerous situations, including widowhood. As historian Asunción Lavrin has written, this protection took different forms: governmental, institutional, religious, and personal. Women, according to Lavrin, "became the guarded guardians, the protected protectors, of marriage and family."[5] The duality of "protected protector" followed women into widowhood. In fact, widowhood strengthened it.

This dual identity is much in evidence among widows, who were seen both as more vulnerable than women under the direct protection of husbands or fathers and as shouldering a heavier burden in parenting their children alone. This duality played itself out time and time again within the arena of land ownership and tenure. Women found ways to use their status as a protected group in order to gain and maintain ownership of land. In turn, they used their land and the inheritance system to ensure their daughters' and granddaughters' survival.

Because land formed the very foundation of colonial New Mexico's agriculturally based economy, its significance to women cannot be over-emphasized. There are frequent references to widows' involvement in land transactions during the colonial period. Land provided widows with income in a number of ways—from sale, exchange, subsistence farming, or ranching. For example, in 1707 the widow Isabel Jorge sold to the widow Micaela Velasco a piece of land she had received as a *merced* (land grant) several years earlier. In exchange for the house and land she received another house and land as well as an additional 80 pesos. By 1708, the widow Velasco had, in turn, sold the land to José Blas for 170 pesos.[6] These types of transactions were not uncommon. Sale and exchange, along with the inheritance system, reshaped New Mexico's landholding patterns every generation.

Land became essential to widows who had little access to other occupations. Information on women's work is difficult to secure, although there is evidence that women were employed as servants and in some commercial ventures. The 1790 New Mexico census indicates that 90 percent of the heads of households with no listed occupation were widows. Yet the documents often allude to women's work. In a 1762 document, for example, the heirs of the widow Tomasa Benavides stated that "she was always poor and she supported herself during the time of her widowhood through her diligence and work." In 1785, Josefa Mestas echoed this sentiment when she declared that "with the goods left to me I have supported myself during my widowhood."[7] In an agricultural economy, access to land was vital to women seeking to support themselves and their families.

Although archival materials more often than not document small or modest landholdings, some widows obtained far more extensive properties. The widow Juana Lujan, one of the largest landowners in the jurisdiction of Santa Cruz de la Cañada in the early eighteenth century, acquired land both legally and illegally over a number of decades. Her Rancho de San Antonio, a twenty-four-room house with a stable, a garden, and a fruit orchard, was composed of land acquired through purchase as well as encroachment on Pueblo Indian land. The encroachment by Lujan and her children continued for more than fifty years. Following her death in the summer of 1762, litigation over the land persisted for twenty years. Lujan, although an exceptional case, represents an example of an extremely successful widow whose acquisition of land provided for the economic and social welfare of her family.[8]

Although upper-class widows such as Juana Lujan found ways in which to use the legal system to their own benefit, overall the relationship between the legal system and poor widows was an ambivalent one. Provincial officials, such as alcaldes, determined how Hispanic law would be carried out locally.

Most alcaldes did not use a strictly formal code of laws since few had either law books or legal training. The existence of a rather informal, frontier legal system had great implications for women. Officials passed judgments based on a number of elements injurious to widows' interests, including the personal gain of the official, animosity toward the individual widow, and the prevailing customs of the community. The flexibility of this informal system, however, could also provide widows with opportunities to claim protection and assistance.[9]

Widows both praised and criticized this legal system when forced to appeal to it for their protection. Women's control of property was often threatened from a number of fronts. Governmental officials, neighbors, and even relatives could lay claim to a widow's land. In 1781, Teodora Ortiz petitioned the court to provide her a copy of her husband's will, claiming that he had fraudulently listed her possessions among his. "No one can dispossess me of the just rights I have towards the property that I brought into the marriage . . . nor of half the property we acquired during our marriage," Ortiz declared. Furthermore, she added, the fact that judges "lacked intelligence" did not detract from her rights. Wills, she concluded, caused more confusion and arguments than understanding. The majority of wills, said Ortiz, ignored women's rights.[10]

Despite these obstacles, however, women were not hesitant to call on the legal system for protection when threatened. In 1810, for example, the widow María Márquez of Pojoaque complained that her deceased son, Mariano Trujillo, had illegally sold her house and land in order to pay off his debts prior to his death. Márquez offered to return the purchase price to the buyer in return for her land. Márquez pleaded with the alcalde mayor to assist her, calling him the "father of children and the refuge of the helpless."[11] In doing so, she was appealing to a deeply held belief among many widows— that the government could act on their behalf, that the system could indeed provide them a refuge.

The Márquez case took a number of unusual turns revolving around the issue of her competency, including a fascinating discussion of whether she could be ruled "legally dead," although in reality still alive. After almost a year, the parties came to a resolution. The alcalde ruled against Márquez but reasoned that charity demanded that she receive some sort of protection, particularly since her son was dead. The widow Márquez agreed to forfeit her claim to the land in return for help with her future burial expenses plus an additional fifty pesos.[12] Although Márquez received some remuneration, her vulnerability at the hands of the governmental official is clear.

In another case, María Micaela Maese of Bado accused an alcalde mayor of depriving her of her land. Maese testified that her husband, Martin Padilla, had been granted the land in 1816, subsequently "pulling up weeds, throwing sticks, pulling down tree branches and performing other ceremonies and acts of possession." The following year, her husband died. This, in conjunction with the appointment of a new local official in charge of land distribution, had grave consequences for Maese. The new judge, Vicente Villanueva, deprived her of her lands. The final outcome of the case is not known; documentation is incomplete, but again, it points to the vulnerability of women within their own communities.[13]

Widows also found neighbors to be a threat to their control over land. In 1733, the widow Isabel Jorge, along with two neighbors, filed a complaint against another neighbor, Cristoval García, who sought to build an irrigation canal through their land. García's defense rested largely on his contention that Jorge's two neighbors, both male, were manipulating the widow into filing the complaint. After all, testified García, "Isabel Jorge is a seventy-year-old woman and moreover, poor because she has neither a cow nor a sheep nor a horse nor anything else that could be harmed . . . [yet] they have involved her in this dispute." Jorge quickly refuted García's attempts to use her vulnerability for his own defense. She retorted, "[T]he fact that I do not own cattle or sheep or horses is beside the point and proves nothing." While portraying herself as a strong woman capable of independent judgment in order to assert control over her land, she downplayed the issue of her vulnerability.[14]

In 1696, however, a much younger Jorge had described herself as a "poor widow" in need of assistance. Attempting to acquire control of a pre-Revolt land grant, Jorge claimed privilege as the granddaughter of a conqueror but also protection as a poor widow with children. As an impoverished seventy-year-old, however, the image of "poor widow" did not benefit her. Although she could use this identity to her own advantage, she was not willing to allow others to use it against her.[15]

Poverty was a common element in many widows' lives. Even the wealthiest woman had no guarantees. Both the inheritance system and familial politics could undermine any woman's economic security. Josefa Bustamante was the richest woman in New Mexico at the time of her husband's death in 1769. Her husband, Nicolas Ortiz III, a politically and economically powerful man, had extensive landholdings and was involved in numerous commercial ventures. Ortiz had several children with his first wife, Gertrudis Hurtado. Upon his death, his eldest son, Antonio José Ortiz, inherited much of his father's estate. In 1784, Josefa mortgaged her landholding at Pojoaque and sold her Santa Fe lands to her stepson (who coincidentally was also her brother-in-law), Antonio José. He foreclosed on her only two years later because of her inability to pay the mortgage. By 1790, the once-wealthy widow was broke. Family connections and wealth could not ensure that she would escape the poverty faced by so many of her contemporaries.[16]

As historian Silvia Arrom concludes in her study of women in colonial Mexico City, "the feminization of poverty that U.S. journalists so suddenly discovered in the 1970s is far from a new phenomenon."[17] Evidence of the bleak economic conditions faced by widows comes down to us not only in the wills of these women but in popular culture as well. A New Mexican *romance* collected by folklorist Aurelio Espinosa at the turn of this century illustrates this point. Entitled "Las Dos Hermanas," the words reflect the despair and the hopelessness of many widows' situations: "The widow is left very sad and tormented. Her children ask her for bread, she has none. Her neighbors ask her what does she have. She answers them, I have nothing."[18] This is a far different picture from the merry widow of another *romance* who says, "I no longer think of my husband. . . . What a pretty widow am I!"[19] Instead, the tragic image of the poor widow in "Las Dos Hermanas" appears again and again in the documents and in the women's own descriptions of themselves.

The inventories listed in widows' wills frequently disclose few material goods and even fewer luxury items. In her 1714 will, for example, the widow Antonia Barela de Loszada listed the goods acquired by herself and her late husband, Antonio Lucero de Godoy, during their marriage: a house and land, a pair of oxen, forty goats, an axe, a firearm, a griddle, and an iron pot. The couple, refugees from the 1680 Pueblo Revolt, had returned to New Mexico as reconquest settlers. Twenty-one years after their return, their material goods were still minimal.[20]

The 1815 will of Doña Feliciana Ortiz y Bustamante attests to the fact that conditions remained much the same, even after the passage of more than a century. Ortiz's will listed a house and land and basic household items such as sheets and kitchenware as well as several religious items. Geographic isolation and a scarcity of currency resulted in the scarcity of many items. Furniture, for example, was limited; even kitchen goods were often made of wood because of the paucity of iron on the frontier. These harsh conditions created a hardship for much of New Mexico's population; widowed women, often impoverished and raising children, found the hardship even greater.[21]

Again and again, women cited their poverty and their obligation to support their children as defining factors in their lives and their decisions. In 1761, the *viuda* Ursula Guillen petitioned the head of the municipal government of Santa Cruz to annul the will of her deceased mother-in-law and to replace it instead with the will of her deceased father-in-law. Her efforts to acquire a larger share of the estate were necessary, Guillen explained, because she was "burdened with children from my deceased husband." In 1699, Isabel Jorge, widow and reconquest settler, petitioned the *gobernador* for a revalidation of her land grant. Hers was the cause, she stated, of a "poor widow burdened with children."[22] In conflict with the stereotype of the silent, long-suffering Mexican mother, these women were anything but silent in speaking out about their difficult situations. The care and survival of their children was burdensome, a source of anxiety and a cause of concern.

Other family members often recognized the heavy obligations placed on widows raising children. In 1765, Santa Fe resident Felipe de Sandoval Fernandez de la Pedrera, for example, renounced his maternal inheritance rights on behalf of his sisters. The document gave his mother the right to use his inheritance until the time that it passed on to his sisters and brothers, stating that he made his decision "considering that his share of his mother's scanty goods would be small . . . and [considering] that his mother finds herself burdened with children . . . he renounces the property which belongs to him [through his inheritance]."[23] The obligations of raising children laid heavily on the lives of many New Mexican widows. Unfortunately, not all women had family members willing or able to renounce their share of the inheritance in order to assist them.

Women's rights to bequeath were well established in Hispanic law. The system of partible inheritance in which all or several of the children received a share of the estate allowed the development of family survival strategies based on maternal inheritance. Although this group of widows bequeathed land to both male and female descendants, maternal inheritance appears to have emerged as one way both to reward daughters for their proper behavior and to ensure their economic survival on the frontier. Although many of the widows appear particularly sensitive to the economic vulnerability of their daughters as women, there is more to their actions than the recognition of vulnerability.

Widows frequently bequeathed land to their daughters and granddaughters in return for their support and assistance. Women's wills do not use the same wording of reciprocity in bequeathing land to their sons or grandsons. Although their wording discloses a sincere concern for their daughters' and other female relatives' well-being, there is also an unwritten dictate at play here. Daughters, in essence, earned their inheritance through their behavior as "good" daughters, living with and taking care of their mothers during their widowhood. This system of reciprocity provided widows with an important degree of control over their daughters and granddaughters.[24]

Women used their status as "good" women and "good" daughters to ensure their survival. For example, when Tomasa Benavides of Santa Fe died intestate in 1762, her widowed daughter-in-law, Manuela de Urioste, found herself potentially homeless. Urioste's case illustrates the various ways in which women attempted to gain protection, using their identity as "good" women. Urioste and her husband, Alejandro Valdez, had lived with his mother, Benavides, prior to his death thirteen years earlier. Since that time, Urioste had continued to live with her mother-in-law. At her mother-in-law's death, however, Urioste no longer had any legal right to stay in the house she had lived in for so many years. Valdez and Urioste had no children; therefore, she could not claim the house on their behalf. The alcalde mayor ruled that Benavides's only heir was her own mother, the very elderly widow Juana Ojeda.[25]

Urioste argued her claim to half of her mother-in-law's house using several strategies. Declaring that she had nowhere else to go, she added that "it is true that she [her mother-in-law] was poor and did not have much more than the little house in which she lived, but she had always told Alejandro that the house was to be his." By implication, as his heir, she hoped to retain part of the house. She went on to characterize her relationship with her mother-in-law as one of mother and daughter, not simply in-laws. Urioste added that, at her husband's death, she had given half his goods to his mother. Furthermore, before his death, her husband had taken care of his mother; after his death, she had followed in his footsteps, taking care of her mother-in-law. Her arguments rested largely on the idea that she had helped Benavides during her lifetime, acting as a good daughter would. Therefore she deserved some reward in return, in this case, half of her mother-in-law's house. It was an expectation of reciprocity that appears time and time again in women's wills.[26]

The alcalde concluded that she would be allowed to continue living in part of the house, although she was not technically an heir of her mother-in-law. Despite Urioste's attempts to claim the reciprocal relationship of a daughter to her mother, the alcalde agreed to rule in her favor, not because she had acted as a "good" daughter, but because she had come into the marriage as a "good" woman. The document reads that Urioste was given this consideration because "she had come under Alejandro's authority with her virginity." The case illustrates how women could successfully claim their identity as "good" women in order to achieve protection by the legal system.[27]

Just as Manuela de Urioste used her claim that she had acted as a good daughter to her mother-in-law to ensure herself a place to live, women like Feliciana Ortiz y Bustamante rewarded their own daughters for helping them. In her 1815 will, Ortiz y Bustamante ordered that her house and its furnishing be given to her three daughters upon her death, "in consideration of their being women and for having served me and accompanied me without giving me cause for grief." Although she ordered two other pieces of land to be divided equally among her four sons and one grandson, her will betrays a note of worry. "I order my male children to comply with this and execute it in this way. For my consolation . . . I hope they do not impede its execution."[28]

Other documents also reveal this same sense of anxiety. When Juana Cisneros composed her last testament, she stated that her only two children had died at a very young age but that she had raised Juana María Cisneros since she was very little and "I have thought of her as my own daughter." Cisneros indicated that she wished for her adoptive daughter to continue living on her land, declaring that "it is my will that no one should try to deter or impede her from living in said house as her own."[29] The threats to women's control of land were real. Women attempted to protect their female relatives, both biological and fictive, by recognizing these threats in their wills.

The extension of this system of reciprocity to fictive kin and to female relatives other than daughters is significant. It allowed women without daughters, or whose daughters had died, to reward women upon whose help they had depended. Their rights to bequeath and the flexibility of the frontier legal system made this possible. The cases of Juana Roybal and Tomasa Benavides, both of Santa Fe, illustrate this point. Roybal's will ordered that her house and land should be divided among the children of her niece because she "had raised them." When the alcalde mayor of Santa Fe ruled in the division of the estate of Tomasa Benavides, he also allocated part of her estate to her "adopted" daughters. "I know that she would view these other poor women with charity because she raised them and they served her."[30] In like manner, in 1766, Isabel Lujan donated a piece of land to her granddaughter, Juana de la Cruz Sans de Garvizu, "because [her grand-daughter] has assisted and helped her in whatever her needs have been and she has always done it sincerely."[31] In the 1740s, Juanotilla, a *coyota* from Cochití, ordered that her two granddaughters, Ysabel and Regina, inherit equally with her children because "they had helped her and kept her company."[32] Again and again, reciprocity between mothers and daughters and other female relatives comes across in the documents.

Land provided an important source of economic survival for widows in colonial New Mexico, and they actively worked to gain access to land through land grant, purchase, and inheritance. As is evidenced through widows' wills, women used their identity as a protected group to gain both governmental and familial protection. In order to maintain this identity, however, they had to continue acting within the norms that defined them as "good" women or "good" daughters. Widows found both benefits and limitations within this identity of the "protected protector."

In her important study of Mexican women in Santa Fe, historian Deena González writes that, prior to the 1870s, women tended to give their property to other women. As occupational and political displacement progressed following the U.S. takeover, more and more women began to pass on their land to their husbands and sons. This transformation decreased their independence, according to González.[33] It also changed the survival strategies that had emerged during the colonial period. We can only guess how the change affected women, both as testators and as heirs.

Certainly the imposition of a different legal system in the nineteenth century decreased women's rights in New Mexico. It would be unfortunate, however, to characterize the earlier survival strategy of maternal inheritance wholly as an indicator of women's independence. Through their words and deeds, across the centuries, we receive a more ambiguous picture of women's lives in colonial New Mexico. As the "protected protectors," widows struggled both to survive and to ensure their children's survival using diverse strategies, including an identity based on their increased vulnerability. Widows' poverty and their obligations to children often defined their lives, giving credence to their claims of heightened vulnerability. Ironically, their claims of vulnerability and the protection it often afforded them also gave them an added measure of control over their land and over their children. During the colonial period, New Mexican widows both benefited from and were constrained by a system that sought to incorporate these women without men into a society based on men's guardianship of women.

Notes

I am grateful to a number of people who shared their expertise and suggestions during the course of this research. Thanks to Cheryl Martin for introducing me to the fascinating study of colonial Mexico and for guiding me in exploring the richness of its documents, to Sherry Smith and Kathleen Staudt for helping me work out some ideas early on, and to Oscar Martínez and Maureen Fitzgerald who continue to challenge and inspire me through the example of their own work.

There are two microfilm collections titled Spanish Archives of New Mexico in the State Records Center, Santa Fe. The 1967 filming will be referred to as SANM. The 1982 filming will be referred to as SANM I. Frame numbers refer to the first page of the document(s) cited. Also, the spelling of names has been standardized in the text in order to facilitate reading.

1. The will of María Martin, SANM I, reel 3, frame 1200.

2. The majority of women investigated in this study defined themselves as *viudas* (widows) and the names of their deceased husbands were included in many of the documents. It is important to note, however, that a woman who called herself a widow may actually have been separated, abandoned, or even single. Censuses in particular may overcount the number of widows since women, especially unmarried women with children, might call themselves widows in order to obscure the truth.

It is difficult to identify changes in widows' status and options over time using only wills and other related documents. Further investigations might profit from looking at changing definitions of the rights and responsibilities of widowhood as reflected in the legal system. In isolated areas like New Mexico, however, the status and options available to widows were often affected more directly by local custom and local understanding of the law rather than by the actual laws themselves. What is remarkable about the wills over the two centuries covered in this essay are not the changes they reflect but instead the consistency over time regarding women's concern for their daughters, their willingness to reward good behavior, and their appeals to the government for assistance.

3. Although we have much to learn about the lives of colonial Mexican women, in recent years scholars have produced some important works on women living on the northern frontier of colonial Mexico. See, for example, Antonia I. Castañeda, "Comparative Frontiers: The Migration of Women to Alta California and New Zealand," in *Western Women: Their Land, Their Lives*, ed. Lillian Schlissel, Vicki L. Ruiz, and Janice Monk (Albuquerque: University of New Mexico Press, 1988), 283–300; Myra Ellen Jenkins, "Some Eighteenth-Century New Mexico Women of Property," in *Hispanic Arts and Ethnohistory*, ed. Marta Weigle, Claudia Larcombe, and Samel Larcombe (Santa Fe: Ancient City Press, 1983), 335–45; Salomé Hernández, "The U.S. Southwest: Female Participation in Official Spanish Settlements: Specific Case Studies in the Sixteenth, Seventeenth, and Eighteenth Centuries" (Ph.D. dissertation, University of New Mexico, 1987); Ramón Gutiérrez, *When Jesus Came, the Corn Mothers Went Away: Marriage, Sexuality, and Power in New Mexico, 1500–1846* (Stanford, Calif.: Stanford University Press, 1991); Rosalind Rock, " 'Pido y Suplico': Women and the Law in Spanish New Mexico," *New Mexico Historical Review*, 65, no. 2 (April 1990): 145–59; Angelina F. Veyna, " 'It Is My Last Wish That . . . ': A Look at Colonial Nuevo Mexicanas through Their Testaments," in Adela de la Torre and Beatríz M. Pesquera, *Building with Our Hands: New Directions in Chicana Studies* (Berkeley: University of California Press, 1993).

For works that explore the lives of New Mexicans in the nineteenth century, see Deena J. González, "The Spanish-Mexican Women of Santa Fe: Patterns of Resistance and Accommodation, 1820–1880" (Ph.D. dissertation, University of California, Berkeley, 1985); Janet Lecompte, "The Independent Women of Hispanic New Mexico, 1821–1846," *Western Historical Quarterly* 12, no. 1 (January 1981): 17–33; and Deena J. González, "The Widowed Women of Santa Fe: Assessments on the Lives of an Unmarried Population, 1850–1880," in *On Their Own: Widows and Widowhood in the American Southwest, 1848–1939*, ed. Arlene Scandron (Urbana: University of Illinois Press, 1988), 65–90.

For a significant early essay that explores the use of women's wills, see Asunción Lavrin and Edith Couturier, "Dowries and Wills: A View of Women's Socioeconomic Role in Colonial Guadalajara and Puebla, 1640–1790," *Hispanic American Historical Review* 59, no. 2 (1979): 280–304.

4. Asunción Lavrin, "In Search of the Colonial Woman in Mexico: The Seventeenth and Eighteenth Centuries," in *Latin American Women, Historical Perspectives*, ed. Asunción Lavrin (Westport, Conn.: Greenwood Press, 1978), 41.

5. Ibid., 39, 48.

6. SANM I, reel 3, frame 165; SANM I, reel 3, frame 162.

7. Alicia V. Tjarks, "Demographic, Ethnic and Occupational Structure of New Mexico, 1790," *The Americas* 35, no. 1 (July 1978): 85; Janie Louise Aragon, "The People of Santa Fe in the 1790s," *Aztlán* 12, no. 3 (Fall 1976): 408–410; SANM I, reel 1, frame 776; the will of Josefa Mestas, SANM I, reel 3, frame 1279.

8. Jenkins, "Some Eighteenth-Century New Mexico Women," 339; Richard Eighme Ahlborn, "The Will of a Woman in 1762," *New Mexico Historical Review* 65, no. 3 (July 1990): 319–55; Myra Ellen Jenkins, "Spanish Land Grants in the Tewa Area," *New Mexico Historical Review* 47, no. 2 (1972), 113–34.

9. Marc Simmons, *Spanish Government in New Mexico* (Albuquerque: University of New Mexico Press, 1968), 170–80.

10. SANM, reel 11, frame 354.

11. SANM I, reel 3, frame 1472.

12. Ibid. It is important to note that the man against whom Márquez had filed employed the brother of the alcalde to represent him in court. Personal connections and familial relationships proved important in many of these situations.

13. SANM I, reel 3, frame 1371.

14. SANM, reel 9, frame 1.

15. SANM, reel 9, frame 1; SANM I, reel 3, frame 158.

16. Jenkins, "Some Eighteenth-Century New Mexico Women," 343–44. For the study of the interfamily rivalry within another influential New Mexican colonial family, revolving again around land, see Richard E. Greenleaf, "Atrisco and Las Ciruelas, 1772–1769," *New Mexico Historical Review* 42, no. 1 (1967): 5–25.

17. Silvia Arrom, *The Women of Mexico City, 1790–1857* (Stanford, Calif.: Stanford University Press, 1985), 200–201.

18. Aurelio Macedonio Espinosa, *Romancero de Nuevo Mejico* (Madrid: Consejo Superior de Investigaciones Cientificas, 1953), 79. A *romance* is a lyrical ballad, descended from anonymous Spanish folk songs. Variations of "Las Dos Hermanas" are found in Spain as well as New Mexico. See Angelina F. Veyna, " 'It Is My Last Wish That . . .': A Look at Colonial Nuevo Mexicanas through Their Testaments," in *Building with Our Hands*, 91–108, for an essay that downplays the poverty of women during this period. Veyna writes that colonial New Mexican women "were neither poor, dependent, nor passive" (91).

19. Espinosa, *Romancero*, 31.

20. The will of Antonia Barela de Losada, SANM I, reel 3, frame 252; Fray Angelico Chávez, *Origins of New Mexico Families* (Santa Fe: The Historical Society of New Mexico, 1954), 209. The Pueblo Revolt began in August 1680, a result of Native American discontent and frustration with Spanish rule. Almost two thousand Spaniards, Native Americans, and mestizos fled New Mexico when the revolt began, most of them settling in the El Paso del Norte area (now El Paso, Texas/Juárez, Chihuahua). The refugees remained in the El Paso area for fourteen years until New Mexico again came under the control of Spain. The term "reconquest settler" refers to anyone residing in New Mexico following the successful reconquest of the province in 1694 by Diego de Vargas. Many of the reconquest settlers had been refugees from the Pueblo Revolt of 1680. Others were new recruits from other areas in colonial Mexico.

21. The will of Doña Feliciana Ortiz y Bustamante, SANM I, reel 4, frame 413; Oakah L. Jones, *Los Paisanos* (Norman: University of Oklahoma Press, 1979), 159. See also Carmen Espinosa, *Shawls, Crinolines, Filigree (The Dress and Adornment of the Women of New Mexico, 1739–1900)* (El Paso: Texas Western Press, 1970), 9–24.

22. SANM, reel 9, frame 352; SANM I, reel 3, frame 158.

23. SANM, reel 9, frame 694.

24. Alida Metcalf has documented a similar development of matrilineal transfer of land as a survival strategy in colonial Brazil. See Metcalf, "Inheritance in a Colonial Brazilian Township," *Hispanic American Historical Review* 66, no. 3 (1986): 455–84.

25. SANM, reel 1, frame 776.

26. Ibid.

27. Ibid. For a discussion of women as sexual beings and their eligibility for protection, see Arrom, *Women of Mexico City*, 71.

28. The will of Feliciana Ortiz y Bustamante, SANM I, reel 4, frame 413. Also see the will of Juana de los Reyes, SANM I, reel 2, frame 928.

29. The will of Juana Cisneros, SANM I, reel 5, frame 66.

30. The will of Juana Roybal, SANM I, reel 4, frame 1236; SANM I, reel 1, frame 776. Fictive kin could be as important as blood relatives. Fictive kin, individuals whose relationship incorporated the qualities of blood relations (including obligations, responsibilities, and respect) included children raised by individuals who were not related to them biologically and were, therefore, adopted informally. The system of fictive kin also included relationships established by the Catholic Church, such as the relationship between a godparent and a godchild or between a child's parents and godparents. Such relationships did not require the individuals to be biologically related.

31. SANM I, reel 5, frame 130. See Louis H. Warner, "Conveyance of Property, the Spanish and Mexican Way," *New Mexico Historical Review* 6, no. 4 (1931): 353, for a discussion of mothers transferring land to their children where the documents clearly record the payment of love and affection.

32. The will of Juanotilla, SANM I, reel 1, frame 1332. In colonial times *coyota/e* referred to someone of mixed ancestry. Although it could specifically refer to someone of Native American and African heritage, it could also be used more generally to mean any mestiza/o. In contemporary times, the term is often used in New Mexico to mean an individual of Mexican American and Anglo American heritage.

33. González, "Spanish-Mexican Women of Santa Fe," 225–26.

5.
_____

"This Evil Extends Especially to the Feminine Sex": Captivity and Identity in New Mexico, 1700–1846

JAMES F. BROOKS

"Cultural exchanges" along the colonial borders of Spanish Mexico included exchanges of human beings who were captured, ransomed, and sold by numerous Indian peoples and Spanish Mexican colonists. This trade began with existing traditions of captive-taking among indigenous Indians and intensified as Spanish Mexicans "redeemed" captives to baptize and acculturate as colonial subjects. In this subtle article, James Brooks examines the trade in captives during the Spanish and Mexican occupations of New Mexico, a system of human exchange in which women were particularly valued "commodities." He examines how women moved from abject powerlessness at the moment of capture to find many ways to gain more secure futures for themselves and their children. Brooks suggests that, working within the constraints set by various captors, women often carved out measures of security for themselves and for their children.

Captive women's children were generally accepted as full members of their fathers' cultures. Their assigned racial and cultural status underscores the fact that race, ethnicity, and other social categories are not simple matters of biology or nature. They also underline the importance of sexuality and reproduction in forging new social relationships. The fact that most women who were captured remained with their captors alerts us to the importance of sexual and maternal ties in women's choices.

Brooks skillfully infers captives' experiences from partial and filtered sources. He gleans the stories of relatively powerless people who left few records of their own but who, acting in constrained circumstances and choosing from limited options, forged new social relationships in the Borderlands.

Late in the summer of 1760, a large Comanche raiding party besieged the fortified *placita* of Pablo Villalpando in the village of Ranchos de Taos, New Mexico. After a day-long fight, the Comanches breached the walls and killed most of the male defenders. They then seized fifty-seven women and children, among whom was twenty-one-year-old María Rosa Villalpando, Pablo's second daughter, and carried them into captivity on the Great Plains. María's young husband, Juan José Xacques, was slain in the assault, but her infant son, José Juliano Xacques, somehow escaped both death and captivity.

The Comanches apparently traded María shortly thereafter to the Pawnees, for by 1767 she was living in a Pawnee village on the Platte River and had borne another son, who would come to be known as Antoine. In that year, the French trader and cofounder of St. Louis, Jean Salé dit Leroie visited the Pawnees and began cohabiting with María. About a year later, she bore Salé a son, whom they named Lambert. This arrangement apparently suited Salé's trading goals, for it wasn't until 1770 that he ended María's Indian captivity and brought her to St. Louis, where they married.

Jean and María (now Marie Rose Salé) had three more children before, for reasons unknown, Jean returned to France, where he remained the rest of his life. María stayed in St. Louis to become the matriarch of an increasingly prominent family. She died at the home of her daughter Helene in 1830, at well over ninety years of age. For María Rosa, captivity had yielded a painful, yet ultimately successful, passage across cultures into security and longevity.[1]

This chapter explores the role captive women like María Rosa played in promoting conflict and accommodation between colonial Spanish (and later Mexican) society and the indigenous people of greater New Mexico. During the Spanish and Mexican occupation of the region, thousands of Indian and hundreds of Spanish women and children "crossed cultures" through the workings of a captive-exchange system that knit diverse communities into vital, and violent, webs of interdependence. These captives, whether of Spanish origin or Native Americans "ransomed" by the Spanish at *rescates* (trade fairs), prove crucial to a borderlands political economy that utilized human beings in far-reaching social and economic exchange.

Developing in the wake of Spanish slave raids and Indian reprisals, over time this commerce in captives provided the basis for a gradual convergence of cultural interests and identities at the village level, emerging in borderlands communities of interest by the middle years of the nineteenth century. Seen as both the most valuable "commodities" in intersocietal trade *and* as key transcultural actors in their own right, captive women and children participated in a terrifying, yet at times fortuitous, colonial dialectic between exploitation and negotiation. Until now, their histories have lain in the shadows of borderlands historiography.[2] An examination of their lives may alter our understanding of colonial processes in New Mexico and elsewhere in North America.

Whatever the large-scale antagonisms between European colonists and Native Americans, at the local level problems of day-to-day survival required methods of cross-cultural negotiation. Prolonged, intensive interaction between New Mexican *pobladores* (village settlers) and nomadic-pastoral Indian societies required some mutually intelligible symbols through which cultural values, interests, and needs could be defined. Horses, guns, and animal hides spring immediately to mind as traditional symbols of exchange, but women and children proved even more valuable—and valorized—as agents—and objects—of cultural negotiation. In New Mexico, as elsewhere in North America, the exchange of women through systems of captivity, adoption, and marriage provided European and native men with mutually understood symbols of power with which to bridge cultural barriers.[3]

Rival men had exchanged women and seized captives long before European colonialism in North America. The exogamous exchange of women between "precapitalist" societies appears to represent a phenomenon by which mutual obligations of reciprocity are established between kindreds, bands, and societies, serving both to reinforce male dominance and to extend the reproductive (social and biological) vigor of communities.[4] The capture and integration of women and children seems the most violent expression along a continuum of such exchange traditions. This patriarchal subordination of women and children, it has been argued, served as a foundation upon which other structures of power and inequality were erected. Gerda Lerner contends that the assertion of male control over captive women's sexual and reproductive services provided a model for patriarchal ownership of women in "monogamous" marriages by which patrilineal bloodlines remained "pure." From this sense of proprietorship grew other notions of property, including the enslavement of human beings as chattels.[5]

In New Spain, under the *Recopilación* of 1680 Spanish subjects had been encouraged to redeem indigenous captives from their captors, baptize them into the Catholic faith, and acculturate them as new "detribalized" colonial subjects.[6] These redemptions occurred in roughly two forms: either through formal "ransoming" at annual trade fairs (*ferias* or *rescates*) or through small-scale bartering (*cambalaches*) in local villages or at trading places on the Great Plains. Trade fairs at Taos, Pecos, and Picuris Pueblos had long fostered the exchange of bison meat for corn, beans, and squash between Plains Indians and the Río Grande Pueblos and had probably included some exchanges of people as well.[7]

These seasonal events continued after the Spanish conquest. Throughout the eighteenth century, Spanish church and secular authorities vied to gain control of this trade, variously blaming each other or local alcaldes for "the saddest of this commerce." In 1761 Fray Pedro Serrano chided the Spanish governors, who "when the fleet was in" scrambled to gather as many horses, axes, hoes, wedges, picks, bridles, and knives as possible in order to "gorge themselves on the great multitude of both sexes offered for sale."[8] Fifteen years later, Fray Atanasio Domínguez reported that the Comanches brought to Taos for sale "pagan Indians, of both sexes, whom they capture from other nations." The going rate of exchange, which seems to have held quite steady until the mid-nineteenth century, was "two good horses and some trifles" for an "Indian girl twelve to twenty years old." Captive boys usually brought a "she mule" or one horse and a "poor bridle . . . garnished with red rags." The general atmosphere, according to Domínguez, resembled a "second hand market in Mexico, the way people mill about."[9]

After 1800 formal *rescates* seem to decline, replaced with smaller, more frequent on-the-spot bartering. This seems to be due to several factors—

Table 5.1. Baptisms of Selected Non-Pueblo Indians, 1700–1850

Tribe	1700–1750	1750–1800	1800–1850	Total
Apaches	632	260	87	979
Pawnees	18	2	3	23
Aas (Crows)	8	62	20	80
Kiowas	17	18	32	67
Comanches	14	179	33	226
Utes	11	63	551	625
Navajos	211	124	422	757
Total	911	708	1148	2757

Adapted from David M. Brugge, *Navajos in the Catholic Church Records of New Mexico, 1694–1875* (Tsaile, Ariz.: Navajo Community College Press: 1985), 22–23.

Plains Indians' wishing to avoid possible exposure to Euro-American disease, a desire on the part of New Mexican villagers to escape taxation of their trade, and a geographical expansion of the borderlands economy. By the 1850s local traders like José Lucero and Powler Sandoval would purchase Mexican captives from Comanches at Plains outposts like Quitaque in Floyd County, Texas, giving, for example, "one mare, one rifle, one shirt, one pair of drawers, thirty small packages of powder, some bullets, and one buffalo robe" in exchange for ten-year-old Teodoro Martel of Saltillo, Mexico.[10]

Judging from extant New Mexican parochial registers (Table 5.1), between 1700 and 1850, nearly three thousand members of nomadic or pastoral Indian groups entered New Mexican society as *indios de rescate, indios genízaros, criados,* or *huérfanos,* primarily through the artifice of "ransom" by colonial purchasers.[11] Ostensibly, the cost of ransom would be retired by ten to twenty years of service to the redeemers, after which time these individuals would become *vecinos* (tithes-paying citizens.) In practice, these people experienced their bondage on a continuum that ranged from near-slavery to familial incorporation, an issue that will be addressed at length in this chapter.

Ransomed captives constituted an important component in colonial society, averaging some 10 to 15 percent of the colonial population. In the peripheral villages, they may have represented as much as 40 percent of the "Spanish" residents.[12] Girls and boys under the age of fifteen composed approximately two-thirds of these captives, and some two-thirds of all captives were women "of serviceable age," or prepubescent girls.[13]

This commerce in women and children was more than a one-way traffic, however. Throughout the period under consideration, nomadic groups like the Comanches and Navajos made regular raids on the scattered *poblaciones,* at times seizing as many as fifty women and children.[14] In 1780, Spanish authorities estimated that the *Naciones del Norte* alone held more than 150 colonial subjects captive, and by 1830 the figure for the Comanches alone may have exceeded 500.[15] Among the Navajos, as late as 1883 Agent Dennis M. Riordan estimated that there were "300 slaves in the hands of the tribe," many of whom were "Mexicans captured in infancy."[16] Like their Indian counterparts, these women and children found themselves most often incorporated into their host society, apparently through indigenous systems of adoption. As fictive kin, they too experienced a range of treatment. It is impossible to arrive at precise numbers of New Mexican captives in Indian societies, but their representation becomes increasingly significant in a discussion of the workings of the captive system and of the personal experiences of captives themselves.

Although the captive-exchange system seems overwhelmingly complex when examined through particular cases, certain overall patterns seem consistent. First, captive taking and trading represented the most violent and exploitative component of a long-term pattern of militarized socioeconomic exchange between Indian and Spanish society. Second, it seems that New Mexican captives and *indios de rescate* generally remained in their "host" societies throughout their lifetimes. Third, female captives often established families within the host society, and their descendants usually became full culture-group members. Male captives, on the other hand, suffered either a quick retributive death or, if young, grew to become semiautonomous auxiliary warriors within their new society. Finally, it appears that many captives found ways to transcend their subordinate status by exercising skills developed during their "cross-cultural" experience. In doing so, they negotiated profound changes in the cultural identity of the societies within which they resided, changes that continue to reverberate in the borderlands today.

THE CAPTIVE EXPERIENCE

Torn from their natal societies in "slave" raids, treated like *piezas* (coins) in a volatile system of intercultural exchange, and finally the "property" of strangers, captive and ransomed women seem unlikely subjects as historical actors. But their experiences show them negotiating narrow fields of agency with noteworthy skill. From positions of virtual powerlessness, captive women learned quickly the range of movement allowed by the host culture, especially in regard to adoption and *compadrazgo* (godparenthood) practices. This first phase of integration gave them "kin" to whom they could turn for protection and guidance. But this security remained limited, and many faced coercive conjugal relationships, if not outright sexual exploitation by their new masters.

Whether of Spanish or Indian origin, two factors seem essential to understanding the lives of captives. First, captive status and treatment within the host society established the "structures of constraint" within which individuals might pursue their goals.[17] Second, sheer luck and the individual captive's personal resources determined the actual lived experience, ranging from terror and exploitation to a few remarkable cases of deft negotiation and good fortune, into which María Rosa Villalpando's story certainly falls. Overall, the interplay of structural constraints, contingency, and skills can be seen in most captives' lives. Another *Nueva Mexicana*, Juana Hurtado Galván, proved so adept at the cross-cultural enterprise that her story exemplifies successful adaptation.

Early in the summer of 1680, shortly before the conflagrations of the Pueblo Revolt, a band of *Apaches del Nabajo* swept down upon the rancho of Captain Andrés Hurtado and took captive his seven-year-old daughter, Juana.[18] For the next twelve years, her life among the Navajos lies concealed, a blank in the historical record that can only be reconstructed by inference and imagination. But those years of captivity seem to hold the key to understanding much of Juana's subsequent life, a long and controversial career that ended in 1753. When she died, Juana owned a rancho with three houses and extensive herds and flocks, and her illegitimate son Juan Galván served as the *teniente* (assistant magistrate) of the Zia district.[19] Nativity had given Juana linkages to both Spanish and Pueblo society, and in her captivity she developed linguistic and kinship ties with the Navajos. Throughout her life, her experience as a captive woman would afford her special negotiating skills with which she pursued security for her lineage.

Juana's mother had come from the pueblo of Zia, probably as a *criada* (domestic servant) of the *encomendero* Hurtado, but we know little more about her life.[20] No doubt sexually used by the *español*, she bore a daughter in 1673, just one among hundreds of such *coyotas* (children of mixed Spanish-Indian parentage) resulting from the Spanish colonization of New Mexico. The mother's connection with Zia Pueblo, however, remained central to her daughter's story. After Juana's half-brother Martín, a soldier in the Spanish *reconquista* of 1692, ransomed Juana from captivity, the young woman petitioned for and received a private *merced* (land grant) at the northwest corner of the Zia Pueblo lands, near the village known today as San Ysidro.[21] This rancho proved a key locus of trade between Navajos, Pueblos, and Spanish *pobladores* for the next half-century—and the source of Juana's wealth and influence.[22]

Although restored to colonial society, Juana never severed connections with her onetime captors. Frequent visits by Navajos to her rancho suggest that she had experienced adoption into a Navajo clan. She may even have married in captivity; she never formalized any future conjugal relationship. Kinship aside, her trilingual skills and cultural intermediacy facilitated economic exchanges between potential enemies. Her affinity with Navajos remained so close that Fray Miguel de Menchero commended her usefulness in assisting proselytization efforts: "They had kept her for so long [that] the Indians of said Nation make friendly visits to her, and in this way the father of the said mission has been able to instruct some of them."[23]

Juana's conduct, however, also attracted criticism from church authorities. Throughout her life, she persisted in maintaining a long-term liaison with a married man of Zia, presumably named Galván. By 1727, this

New Mexico, circa 1847

relationship had resulted in four children and charges of scandalous behavior leveled against her by the padres. When authorities sought to place Juana in stocks, however, the people of Zia "threatened that the whole pueblo would move to the mesa tops, rather than have her mistreated."[24] Like the Navajos, the people of Zia saw tangible benefits in the presence of this kinswoman on their borders. Defining kinship more broadly than did the Spanish, they seemed willing to provoke conflict in defense of their relationship with someone who provided a bridge across three cultures. Drawing upon her qualities and talents as a negotiator, Juana "La Galvana" utilized her experience as a captive to carve out an intermediate niche in the complex power relations of colonial New Mexico.

Juana's intermediacy was accentuated by her mixed-blood status, and her paternal linkage to a Spanish *encomendero* probably allowed her the opportunity to occupy a privileged niche compared with many captives. Since one aspect of the captive system originates in indigenous, precontact exogamous exchange traditions, we need to look at gender and social hierarchies within native societies to begin to understand the structures of constraint that Juana and other captives might have experienced. Although they display variation, women's and captives' status within Indian societies of the Borderlands (Navajo, Apache, Ute, and Comanche) may be generally described as subordinate to that of men and holders of the "cultural franchise" but enhanced by traditions of matrilineality and social mobility.[25]

Navajo patterns of gender and social hierarchies show a blending of Athabascan traditions and cultural adaptations to Spanish colonialism near their homelands. Navajo women owned the flocks of sheep and wove the textiles that formed the core of their pastoral economy. Matrilineal descent, therefore, conferred important productive resources as well as kin-reckoning through women. Navajo men, however, prevailed in "public" decisions involving warfare and diplomacy.[26]

Captives taken in warfare with other tribes or the Spanish again experienced a range of treatment. If not killed in vengeance satisfaction, the captive invariably suffered a period of harsh and terrifying treatment. This "taming" process probably formed the first phase in adoption ritual.[27] After taming, most captives were inducted into the clan of their captor, or of the "rich man" who purchased them from the successful warrior. Once a clan member, it seems few barriers stood in the way of social advancement. The New Mexican captive Nakai Na'dis Saal, raised in a clan on Black Mesa, "became a singer of the Nightway," an important Navajo ceremony.[28] The Sonoran captive Jesús Arviso, taken by Chiricahua Apaches in 1850 as a boy and traded to the Navajo Kla clan, served as the principal interpreter for his host society throughout the Fort Sumner–Long Walk era. Marrying into the Nanasht'ezhii clan, he chose to remain a Navajo, welcoming a congressional delegation to Fort Defiance in 1919 and living at Cubero until his death in 1932.[29]

Captive women usually became clan members and married exogamously. Even if not inducted into clan membership, their children by

Navajo men were considered members of the father's clan.[30] Although we can only speculate, these clan and kin affiliations probably provided Juana Hurtado with the networks that allowed her to act as an intermediary between Zia Pueblo and Spanish society. Indeed, Juana seems noteworthy among captives for having chosen to return to her birthright, for some sources indicate that many captives when "set free . . . immediately took the shortest trail back to the hogans of their masters."[31]

Captives seem to have fared less well among the Jicarilla Apaches, a semisedentary people who practiced a seasonal economy that balanced hunting and collecting with extensive horticulture. Apache women, however, benefited from matrilineality and ownership of fields and crops that "were planted, weeded, and harvested by the joint labors of the entire family." This gender-integrated labor diverged when men hunted or raided and women engaged in the life-cycle labor of family reproduction. While subordinate to men, women made important ritual contributions to the success of hunters: "[A] man and his wife pray together and smoke ceremonially before the husband leaves for the hunt. After his departure the woman continues a series of ritual duties." Likewise, before men departed for warfare or raiding, "a woman [was] chosen to represent each man to serve as proxy in group decisions, [and she] obeyed many restrictions in matters of dress, food, and behavior to ensure his safe return."[32]

Warfare among the Jicarillas often involved the seizure of captives, either for vengeance satisfaction or cultural integration. Adult male captives "were tied to posts and slain by women with lances," but captive women and children found themselves incorporated into the band. A captive woman "could not be molested until she had been brought back and a ceremony . . . performed over her," probably some form of adoption that established her subordination within the Apachean levirate. Even with this adoption, captive women "were not considered fit wives. They were sexually used, and sent from camp to camp to do the heavy work. Their children by Apache men, however, were recognized as Jicarilla" and "accepted into Apache life."[33] We shall see that this second-generation integration appears nearly universal among the indigenous groups in question, and proves an important factor in captive women's decisions to remain within the host society even when offered their "freedom."

These patterns of gender and social subordination, mitigated by adoption and generational enfranchisement, are reiterated in an examination of Comanche society. Jane Collier has argued that women's status in Comanche society, as reflected through the dynamics of bridewealth marriage, "may best be understood in the context of relations between men."[34] Certainly the Comanches represent the most noteworthy case of Plains Indian individualism and status competition between men, where wife stealing often served as an intraband expression of a general cultural pattern.[35] E. A. Hoebel pointed out earlier, however, that although "before the law, [the] Comanche woman was a quasi-chattel," social custom allowed women a considerable degree of choice in extralegal activity.[36]

Both Collier and Hoebel overlooked evidence of women-centered status competition, a stretching of patriarchal structures of constraint. In half of the marital disputes Hoebel recorded, women had left their husbands for other men, often joining their lovers on war parties. In one case, the couple stayed away from the band for two years, and when they returned, the woman had fifteen horses in her personal string.[37] Women could also obtain horses (next to captives the most prestigious "commodity" in Comanche society) through the institution of the Shakedown Dance, whereby successful raiders were shamed into giving a part of their herd to young, unmarried women.[38] Status and prestige also accrued to women through the matrilineal transfer of medicine powers, as in the case of Sanapia, a Comanche Eagle Doctor.[39] These examples suggest that within male-defined structures of constraint, Comanche women exploited opportunities for competitive mobility and status enhancement. Captives, although initially lower in status, appear to have negotiated similar avenues of social mobility.

No other Plains society engaged in captive raiding as vigorously as did the Comanches. This seems a result of both individual status competition and the need to replace a population ravaged by warfare and epidemic disease.[40] Comanche society offered several social locations into which captives could be integrated, ranging from chattels to kinsmen and kinswomen.[41] Ralph Linton suggests that the prestige value of captives reflected their "importance in the social and economic life of the tribe. Mostly Mexican, they tended the horse herds and practiced most of the specialized industries such as gun repairing and saddle-making." The honored position of center-pole cutter in the Comanche Sun Dance went to either a "virtuous Comanche woman, a virtuous captive woman, [or] a captive man who had a number of war-deeds to his credit."[42] Among the Kiowas, a Plains group closely allied with the Comanches after 1805, captives like Loki-Mokeen, a Mexican mulatto, could become officers of the Sun Dance and protectors of the sacred Taimé Bundle.[43] Andrés Martínez, called by the Kiowa "Andali," was seized from his family's pastures near Las Vegas, New Mexico, and grew to adulthood as a Kiowa warrior. In 1889 he converted to Methodism and told his story to the Reverend J. J. Methven.[44] Likewise, the "captive-friend" who fought alongside his Comanche warrior-brother, appears prominently as a type in Hoebel's ethnography.[45]

Captive women often found themselves under the protection of Comanche women. Rosita Rodrígues, writing in 1846, reported she "remained a prisoner among the Comanche Indians about one year, during which time I was obliged to work very hard, but was not otherwise badly treated as I became the property of an old squaw who became much attached to me."[46] Similarly, Sarah Ann Horn, taken captive in 1837, reported that she was taken in "by an old widow woman . . . a merciful exception to the general character of these merciless beings." Although she was "set to work to dress buffalo hides," she did not suffer sexual abuse.[47] It appears that at least some captive women were informally adopted by older women, by which action they received the protection of the Comanche incest taboo.[48]

Rodrígues and Horn are among the very few women who, when repatriated, wrote of their experiences among the Comanche. Most captive women seem to have remained with their captors, marrying and establishing families in the host society.[49] Rodrígues herself had left a son behind among the Comanche, reporting that "I heard from him a short time ago—he is well and hearty but he is pure Indian now."[50] Josiah Gregg noted the presence of Mexican women among the Comanches when he began traveling the Santa Fe Trail in the 1830s. He remarked with surprise that some of these "preferred remaining with [their captors], rather than encounter the horrible ordeal of ill-natured remarks on being restored to civilized life." One woman refused to return even after the offer of one thousand dollars for her ransom. She sent word that the Comanches "had disfigured her by tattooing; that she was married, and perhaps *enceinte* [pregnant], and she would be more unhappy returning . . . under these circumstances than remaining where she was."[51]

These women had good reason to fear social opprobrium if they returned to Spanish society. When authorities introduced an alms-gathering plan in 1780 to raise funds for the ransom of Spanish captives, Teodoro de Croix declared with alarm that "this evil extends especially . . . to the feminine sex . . . on account of the lascivious vice of sensuality in which they are now afforded the greatest liberty to indulge themselves."[52] This may have been a rhetorical flourish to heighten interest in the plan, but it suggests that the conjugal arrangements of Comanche women might entail certain attractions to captive Spanish women as well.

CULTURAL AND SOCIAL ACCOMMODATION IN CAPTIVITY

Spanish concerns about the influence of Indian lifeways on their subjects went beyond anxieties about the behavior of "their" women in captivity. The very fact that thousands of Indian captives and their descendants now resided in Spanish society stimulated a growing polemic of caste-conscious distancing by elite *españoles* from the culturally mixed village people. Ramón Gutiérrez has argued that eighteenth-century New Mexico developed as a "timocracy," where "differences between aristocrats and landed peasants were of degree rather than kind. Spaniards, whatever their estate, were men of honor in comparison to the vanquished Indians." Gutiérrez contends that the *genízaro* caste, formed from the mass of *indios de rescate* obtained by the Spanish through ransom, constituted a "dishonored" status against which all Spanish, regardless of economic position, could define their own *calidad* (status).[53]

While Gutiérrez offers strong evidence for this honor/dishonor distinction among elite *españoles*, his use of prescriptive sources generated by these elites tends to leave on-the-ground relations between mestizo *pobladores* and their *genízaro* neighbors somewhat obscure. As we will see, by the end of the eighteenth century, Spanish ecclesiastics and administrators spoke of their colonial villagers in terms usually associated with *los indios bárbaros,* often referring to them as "indolent," "rude," "independent," and "lewd." Captive exchange lay at the heart of this blurring of cultural boundaries.

New Mexico seems similar to other cultural borderlands, where patterns of cultural accommodation appear beneath colonial structures of conflict, as the exigencies of day-to-day survival promote periods of relatively peaceful coexistence.[54] Always uncertain, and often punctuated by violent exchanges, *poblador* (village settler) and nomadic/pastoral Indian relations seem to have begun to converge in regionally defined communities of interest by late in the eighteenth century, especially after formal negotiations of Spanish, Comanche, Ute, and Navajo peace treaties during 1786. This movement, however, distanced the village people of New Mexico from their colonial administrators, a trend that would lead to internal conflict by the nineteenth century.

Foreshadowing this turmoil, in 1794 Don Fernando de la Concha complained to incoming Governor Don Fernando Chacón that the village people of the province seemed "indolent": "They love distance which makes them independent; and if they recognize the advantages of union, they pretend not to understand them, in order to adopt the liberty and slovenliness they see . . . in their neighbors, the wild Indians."[55]

Concern on the part of Spanish administrators had increased throughout the preceding decades. In 1776 Antonio Bonilla had found the "settlements of the Spaniards . . . scattered and badly defended," protecting neither themselves nor "contributing to the defense of the province."[56] Two years later, Fray Augustín de Morfi attributed this situation to the fact that the "*pobladores* liked to live apart, far from the prying eyes of neighbors and the restraining influence of authorities," where they could "commit with impunity all manner of immoral and criminal acts, and . . . were not ashamed to go about nude so that lewdness was seen here more than in the brutes."[57]

Like Morfi, Concha felt that social intercourse with the *indios bárbaros* lay at the heart of this problem. Life in the villages, he told his successor, had become so distanced from colonial control that he recommended "the removal of more than two thousand [villagers]," whose "bad upbringing results from . . . the proximity and trade of the barbarous tribes." This trade appears to have become increasingly a part of the borderlands economy in New Mexico, and one which villagers sought to conceal from colonial control. Concha complained that the villagers, "under a simulated appearance of ignorance or rusticity . . . conceal the most refined malice."[58]

A decade later, Chacón would note that the villagers were "little dedicated to farming," surviving instead on a vigorous trade with nomadic Indians. In exchange for the *pobladores'* manufactured goods and agricultural products, nomads like the Comanches gave them "Indian captives of both sexes, mules, moccasins, colts, mustangs, all kinds of hides and buffalo meat."[59] As the Bourbon reforms brought efforts to incorporate New Mexico within the economic sphere of New Spain, especially in a developing sheep and textile industry, the informal economic autonomy of villagers seemed a barrier to progress.[60]

Tensions between administrators in Santa Fe and their backcountry subjects exploded in August 1837. The villagers of Río Arriba descended upon the villa and seized the government, executing Governor Albino Pérez in the process.[61] Infuriated by rumored direct taxation under Santa Ana's *centralismo* of 1835, which threatened to interfere with their autonomous indigenous trade, the rebels identified themselves "with the savage tribes . . . making the same cause and their same interests."[62] Mexico restored central authority by 1838, but the "community of interest" between New Mexican villagers and their native neighbors persisted. In 1847 the villages again rose in rebellion, this time against the American military government of occupation. Pueblo Indians and *pobladores* killed Governor Charles Bent in Taos, while Manuel Cortés of Mora joined with Apache and Cheyenne allies to raid U.S. military and commercial supply lines on the eastern frontier.[63] This ability to build strategic linkages across cultural boundaries was a consequence of long experience in economic and human exchange.

The seeds of these linkages were both cultural and biological, as revealed in a village-level intermingling of status groups. In Ranchos de Taos, for example, the Colonial Census of 1750 reported nine Spanish households of fifty-seven persons, six *coyote* households of fifty-five persons, and eight *genízaro* households of twenty-five persons. Even the Spanish households showed a blurring of caste category: the house of Antonio Atiensa included his *coyota* wife, María Romero; their son, Domingo Romero (*castizo*); and the widow Juana with her daughter Manuela, no doubt *criadas*. Likewise, the house of Juan Rosalio Villapando, an important *español*, included his wife, María Valdes, and their six children, all of whom are termed *coyote*, suggesting that María may have been an *india de rescate*. Pablo Francisco Villalpando's household, from which María Rosa would be seized ten years later, contained three female and two male *sirvientes*, two of whom carried the family name. Mixing may have crossed class as well as caste lines in some village families.[64]

The fact that the census arranged households by caste category reveals a conscious concern about *casticidad* on the part of Spanish administrators, but the data also demonstrate how informally these categories might be arranged at the village level. Census findings from a cluster of plazas at Belén show a somewhat different, yet consistent, pattern. In 1790 the third plaza, Nuestra Señora de los Dolores de los Genízaros, contained thirty-three households, all designated as *genízaro*, a strong indication that in some cases true communities developed among some *indios de rescate*. But the adjacent second plaza of Jarales held thirty Spanish, twelve mestizo, four *coyote*, and two *genízaro* households. The marriage patterns from these communities reveal little caste-anxious endogamy; of the twenty-eight unions, only one is *español-española*. Six marriages involved *genízaro-genízara*, and five mestizo-mestiza. The remaining sixteen show a crossing of caste lines. In most of these, hypogamy seems the rule, with women marrying men of "lower" status. Children of these unions, for example, *genízaro-coyota*, seem to follow the father's status and are later enumerated as *genízaros*.[65]

By the late eighteenth century, however, this designation for children born of captive Indian women may not have carried the strictly "dishonored" quality that Gutiérrez proposes. Instead, it may imply a movement toward identity formation on the part of the *genízaros* themselves. As early as 1744, sources report that *genízaro* men played an important role as military auxiliaries for the Spanish.[66] By 1780, a group of thirty-three *genízaros* negotiated with Spanish authorities from a position of some power, threatening that if their lands in the Barrio de Analco in Sante Fe were not protected, they might go "in search of relief to our lands and nation."[67] An official *Tropa de Genízaros* was organized in 1808 to patrol the eastern frontier of New Mexico in response to Zebulon Pike's adventurism of the previous year.[68] And in 1837, following the Río Arriba rebellion noted earlier, the revolutionary *canton* elected as their new governor José Gonzales, a *poblador* and *cibolero* from Taos who may have been a *genízaro*.[69] As subordinate yet militarily skilled members of New Mexican society, *genízaro* men found themselves valued in a colony always in need of men-at-arms. Once established on the outer marches of the province, they managed to assert an intermediate negotiatory identity.

Gradual movement toward borderlands communities of interest emerged as a consequence of the presence of captive Indian women in colonial New Mexico. Initially little more than pawns in a distinctive slave trade, these *indias de rescate* established families within the host society whose members eventually owned land, served in the military, and even led major rebellions. In their case, maternity provided avenues of agency, especially as they manipulated structural constraints to establish increasing security for their offspring and, consequently, for themselves.

Two structures of constraint apply particularly to women in colonial New Mexico; marriage and *compadrazgo* (godparent) relations. For Spanish women, and for mixed-blood or captive women who had internalized their conversion to Christianity, the dictates of the Catholic Church constrained their agency within marriage. Gutiérrez has shown how caste-endogamous marriages served to "purify" the bloodlines of New Mexico's ruling elite.[70] The gender hierarchy of the church also firmly established women's subordination as dependents under the patriarchal authority of husbands and the church, with preservation of family honor through legitimate offspring their principal social role. Unlike women in the English colonies, however, Spanish women maintained separate property throughout their marriage(s) and could bequeath their estates independent of their husbands' wills.[71]

Spanish women's "property" often included *indias de rescate*, who found themselves transferred to daughters as servants or "emancipated" with the condition that they continue to "watch over and assist my daughter as if she were her mother."[72] Others received clear title to parcels of land "in appreciation of years of service to me without salary."[73] When José Riano contested the will of Gregoria Gongora in 1739, he explicitly excepted from the disputed property "a piece of land for the *india* who raised my youngest and other children."[74]

Although these cases suggest a familial quality to the relations between Spanish and Indian women, few masters or mistresses actually formalized this quality in godparent relations. Of the 3,294 "slave" baptisms in New Mexico between 1693 and 1849, only 14 percent featured "owners" as *padrinos*, and the vast majority (65 percent) showed "no apparent relationship," involving simply members of the local Spanish community. Gutiérrez argues that these figures reflect the internal contradictions between the benign character of *compadrazgo* and the exploitative character of master-slave relations.[75]

An alternative explanation might see these baptismal data as representative of mutually supportive relationships between the *pobladores* of New Mexico and *indios de rescate*, a variation upon traditions of adoption that we have seen as ubiquitous in nomadic-pastoral Indian society. Frances Quintana argues that in New Mexico, *compadrazgo* relations show two patterns, an "old world" tradition that "intensified existing kin relationships" among colonial elites and a "new world" innovation that "helped to stabilize relationships between native Indian populations and Spanish and mestizo groups."[76]

In addition to the baptisms of *indios de rescate* noted above, during the same period we see the baptism of 1,984 "illegitimate" children born of the women of the *genízaro* caste. In fact, Gutiérrez has recorded only twenty church-sanctioned marriages among members of this group and suggests that this reveals the continuing control by masters over the sexual services of "slave" women.[77] Certain of his cases support Gutiérrez's conclusion, but we should also recognize that refusal to "consecrate" a conjugal union also served as an act of resistance among both Pueblo and nomadic Indian groups.[78] At Zia Pueblo, and among the Navajos, a refusal to name the parents of "illegitimate" children continually frustrated Spanish authorities.[79] It seems reasonable to conclude here a mixed pattern of sexual exploitation of *indias de rescate* by Spanish masters and a collective strategy of identity maintenance that, by refusing Catholic structures, retained the offspring of those and voluntary unions with Indian men as members of the cultural community.

Although conceived in grossly unequal relationships, the children born of unions with captors often served to strengthen the status of captive women. As full culture-group members of either Indian or *genízaro* communities, these daughters and sons provided social access and security to their mothers. As Marietta Morrissey has found for slave women in the Caribbean, concubinage with dominant men often involved a painful balancing of shame and hope. If they acceded to sexual relations with masters, their children were born free and in a position to assist in the dream of manumission.[80] In some cases as well, real bonds of affection and respect developed between sugar planters and slave women, a factor that seems likely in some of the New Mexican examples.

Although the creation of kinship seems the primary avenue by which captive women sought security and identity, we may also discern other facets of their lives from within the historical record. In addition to the life-cycle labor of family reproduction, these women engaged in subsistence and market production. The eighteenth and nineteenth centuries saw dramatic shifts in the status and work of Plains Indian women as peoples like the Comanches, Kiowas, and Cheyennes began participating in the European fur and hide trade. With the horse and gun, one Indian man could procure fifty to sixty buffalo hides per season, twice as many as one Indian woman could tan for use or exchange. An increase in polygyny, and in raiding for captive women, served to counteract this labor shortage.[81] The captivity narratives quoted earlier make it clear that captive women were "set to work to tan hides" almost immediately. The appearance of polygynous households probably made this work more efficient, for "co-wives" might process hides while the "first-wife" performed higher-status production and distribution like cooking, clothing manufacture, and ceremonial activities.

In New Mexico, *indias de rescate* appear most often as household servants, but to consider their work entirely "domestic" is probably misleading. Since both Apache and Navajo captive women came from societies in which women were the principal horticulturalists, they may have found themselves gardening and even tending flocks. We are only beginning to develop an understanding of women's economic life in colonial New Mexico, but Angelina Veyna's work with women's wills suggests that both Spanish and Indian women may have been more involved in farming than previously thought. The fact that women owned *rejas* (ploughshares) and willed them not to their sons but to their daughters suggests either a farming orientation or a means of attracting potential husbands.[82]

Navajo and Apache women also worked as weavers, both of basketry and textiles. H. P. Mera has described the nineteenth-century Slave Blanket as a crossover style between Navajo and New Mexican techniques, using New Mexican yarns and designs but produced on the distinctive upright looms of Navajo women.[83] These early New Mexican serapes were important trade items at *rescates*, given in exchange for buffalo hides and dried pemmican. Although today in villages like Chimayo men weave the distinctive Rio Grande blankets, this seems the result of a concerted effort early in the nineteenth century to develop a commercial textile industry.[84]

Captive women and children played important roles in one last area, that of Spanish-Indian diplomacy. Their cross-cultural experience made them valuable as interpreters, translators, and envoys for Spanish military leaders. By 1750 the Comanches had obtained French guns, and Governor Vélez declared that unless a peace was negotiated the Comanches might prove "the ruin of this province."[85] In order to communicate with several Comanche hostages held in Santa Fe, Vélez utilized the interpretive services of a Kiowa woman who had been captured by the Comanches, lost to the Utes in a raid, then purchased as a *criada* by Antonio Martín. This negotiation resulted in a temporary truce, sealed by the exchange of several prisoners.[86]

When the peace collapsed in 1760, captive women again served in a diplomatic capacity, this time as emissaries. Unable to find the appropriate Comanche leaders with whom to bargain, Vélez "dispatched six Comanche women prisoners as ambassadors to their nation." Within a month, four of the women had returned, along with nine Comanche captives, and another truce was affirmed by the return to the Comanches of "thirty-one women and children, among whom, fortunately, were their relatives."[87] Likewise, when Governor Juan Bautista de Anza and Ecueracapa negotiated the Spanish-Comanche Peace of 1786, which lasted until 1846, they sealed their agreement by exchanging a Comanche boy, "José Chiquito," for Alejandro Martín, "eleven years a captive among the band of Captain Tosapoy."[88]

CAPTIVITY AND IDENTITY IN NEW MEXICO

Often deemed invisible commodities in the "slave trade" of the Spanish Borderlands, the captive women and children discussed here emerge as human actors engaged in a deeply ambivalent dialectic between exploitation and negotiation. Their stories begin in a moment of abject powerlessness, where subordination serves as a substitute for violent death. But from that moment forward, we see them taking tentative steps toward autonomy and security. Captive women worked within the limits set by their captors, yet through the creation of kinship, their daily labors, and their diplomatic usefulness, they managed to carve out a future for themselves and their lineages. Although fewer in number, captive boys became men who utilized their military skills to attain status and limited autonomy.

Beginning in an indigenous tradition of captive taking, and intensified by Spanish military and economic exploitation, the captive-exchange system developed as the high-stakes component of a borderlands political economy that produced conflict *and* coexistence. Maria Mies has conceptualized the interlinkage of men's militarism and the forcible exchange of women as a universal "predatory mode of appropriation," a paradigm for "all exploitative relations between human beings."[89] In New Mexico, Spanish and Indian men found that even more than horses, guns, or hides, their counterparts valued women and children, and they established a nominal agreement that these would serve as objects and agents of intersocietal exchange. Conflict and accommodation patterns, therefore, between these rival societies may represent attempts by differing forms of patriarchal power to achieve external economic and military objectives while reinforcing the stability of internal social and gender hierarchies.

Yet, despite the exploitative quality of the captive-exchange system, its victims found ways to exercise agency and achieve some measure of security and comfort for themselves and their descendants. Within the structures of constraint lay some opportunity, at times more opportunity than that available in their natal societies. María Rosa Villalpando of Taos found herself traded to the Pawnees, married there, then remarried to become the "matriarch" of a French fur-trading enterprise in St. Louis. When her New Mexican son, José Juliano, visited her there in 1802 and attempted to establish a claim as heir, she paid him off with two hundred pesos and sent him packing. José Juliano took a long route home, for by 1809 New Mexican authorities contacted administrators in San Antonio, Texas, and suggested José be forcibly sent home, for he had a wife and children "without support" in the village of Ojo Caliente.[90] Juana Hurtado received the support of the Zias and Navajos in her role as cultural centerperson. Likewise, a Crow woman might be sold at a *rescate* by the Comanches, escape to find her way homeward, and end up leading a French trading expedition back to New Mexico.[96] Finally, a Pawnee woman in Santa Fe could discover that her master had settled land upon her in his will, for the consideration that she continue to serve as *criada* to his son.[92]

In time, the mixed-blood descendants of captive women and children exhibited new collective interests that influenced their choice of cultural identification. Although this essay is only a preliminary examination, it seems reasonable to suggest that the collective interests of second- and subsequent-generation descendants blurred the boundaries between New Mexican *pobladores* and their Indian neighbors. Plains Indian societies became increasingly militarized and market-oriented during this period, and New Mexican villagers increasingly mobile. By the 1830s, New Mexican *ciboleros* (bison hunters) and *comancheros* (traders and raiders) appeared regularly in travel accounts.[93] Plains societies displayed new forms of collective action, and villagers rose in radically democratic rebellions.

Although the American conquest of 1846–48 resulted in the erosion of shared values and interests between New Mexicans and southwestern Indians, vestiges of the borderlands community of interest still survive. Miguel Montoya, historian of the village of Mora, defines the historical identity of his neighbors in this way: "We were Spanish by law, but Indian by thought-world and custom. We respected *los viejos* [the elders], who looked after our spiritual health. We have relatives in the Pueblos, and out there, in Oklahoma [pointing east, to the reservations of the Comanches and Southern Cheyennes].[94]

Notes

1. Jack B. Tykal, "Taos to St. Louis, the Journey of Maria Rosa Villalpando," *New Mexico Historical Review* 65, no. 3 (April 1990): 161–74.

2. Treatments of "slavery" in New Mexico are L. R. Bailey's *The Indian Slave Trade in the Southwest* (Los Angeles: Western Lore Press, 1966), which contains no analysis of gender differentiation nor captivity among Indian groups; David M. Brugge's *Navajos in the Catholic Church Records of New Mexico, 1694–1875* (Tsaile, Ariz.: Navajo Community College Press, 1985), an important piece of documentary research upon which this essay relies heavily but which does not attempt a unifying analytical framework; and the recent work of Ramón Gutiérrez, *When Jesus Came, the Corn Mothers Went Away: Marriage, Sexuality and Power in New Mexico, 1500–1846* (Stanford, Calif.: Stanford University Press, 1991), whose analysis relies on an exploitation paradigm drawn from chattel slavery in the southern United States. Gutiérrez does not consider the experience of Spanish captives in Indian societies.

3. For an in-depth treatment of this question, see the author's "Captives and Cousins: Bondage and Identity in New Mexico, 1700–1837" (master's thesis, University of California, Davis, 1991), and Ph.D. dissertation, "Captives and Cousins: Violence, Kinship, and Community in the New Mexico Borderlands 1680–1880" (University of California, Davis, 1995).

4. Friederich Engels, *The Origin of the Family, Private Property, and the State* (1884, New York: Pathfinder Press, 1972); Gerda Lerner, *The Creation of Patriarchy* (Oxford: Oxford University Press, 1986); Claude Levi-Strauss, *The Elementary Structures of Kinship* (1949, Boston: Beacon Press, 1969); Gayle Rubin, "The Traffic in Women: Notes on the 'Political Economy' of Sex," in *Toward an Anthropology of Women*, ed. Rayna Reiter (New York: Monthly Review Press, 1975); Verena Martínez-Alier (Stolke), *Marriage, Class, and Colour in Nineteenth Century Cuba* (Cambridge, Eng.: Cambridge University Press, 1974); Jane Fishburne Collier, *Marriage and Inequality in Classless Societies* (Stanford, Calif.: Stanford University Press, 1988).

5. Lerner, *Creation of Patriarchy*; Martínez-Alier (Stolke), *Marriage, Class, and Colour*, applies this argument to nineteenth-century Cuba. Claude Meillasoux makes the case for the patrimony-to-property transition in his synthesis of indigenous-domestic African slave systems in *The Anthropology of Slavery: The Womb of Iron and Gold* (Chicago: University of Chicago Press, 1991).

6. While reiterating the ban on Indian slavery first set forth in 1542, the *Recopilación* reinforced the "just war" doctrine, whereby hostile Indians might be enslaved if taken in conflict. *Indios de rescate* (ransomed Indians), on the other hand, were "saved" from slavery among their captors and owed their redeemers loyalty and service. See Silvio Zavala, *Los Esclavos Indios en Nueva España* (Mexico City: Edician de Colegio Nacional Luis Gonzáles Obregón, 1967) for a complete treatment of these policies.

7. For theoretical and empirical cases, see the essays in Katherine Spielmann, ed., *Farmers, Hunters, and Colonists: Interaction between the Southwest and the Southern Plains* (Tucson: University of Arizona Press, 1991).

8. Report of the Reverend Father Provincial, Fray Pedro Serrano . . . to the Marquis de Cruillas . . . 1761, in Charles Wilson Hackett, trans. and ed., *Historical Documents Relating to New Mexico, Nueva Vizcaya, and Approaches Thereto, to 1773*, vol. III (Washington, D.C.: Smithsonian Institution, 1937), 486–87.

9. Eleanor B. Adams and Fray Angélico Chávez, trans. and eds., *The Missions of New Mexico, 1776: A Description by Fray Francisco Atanasio Domínguez* (Albuquerque: University of New Mexico Press for Cultural Properties Review Committee, 1956), 252. See also Amando Represa, "Las Ferias Hispano-Indias del Nuevo México," in *La España Ilustrada en el Lejano Oeste* (Valladolid: Junta de Castillay León, Consejería de Cultura y Bienestan Social, 1990), 119–25.

10. James S. Calhoun to Commissioner Brown, 31 March 1850, in Annie Heloise Abel, ed., *The Official Correspondence of James S. Calhoun, Indian Agent at Santa Fe* (Washington, D.C.:

U.S. Government Printing Office, 1915), 181–83. For the archaeology of *comanchero* sites on the plains, see Frances Levine, "Economic Perspectives on the Comanchero Trade," in *Farmers, Hunters, and Colonists*, 155–69.

11. Since only some 75 percent of baptismal registers still exist, the actual figures are probably somewhat higher. Brugge, *Navajos in Catholic Church Records*, 2.

12. Analysis of the Spanish Colonial Census of 1750, New Mexico State Records Center, indicates a rural village population of 1,052, of whom 447 are recorded as having some Indian blood. In the "urban" areas of Santa Fe and Albuquerque, a total population of 2,757 contained only 400 individuals similarly designated.

13. Brugge, *Navajos in Catholic Church Records*, 116, estimates a 60-40 female-male ratio for the Navajo captives he studied. Working again with the Spanish Colonial Census of 1750, where individuals are designated either by proper name or by a gendered noun (*criada/o, genízara/o, india/o*), I find that women total 153 of 282 individuals, or 54 percent. Since some bondwomen, for example, are designated simply "cinco indias criadas y ocho coyotitos" (*Spanish Archives of New Mexico* [hereafter SANM] I, roll 4, frame 1175, State Record Center, Santa Fe), we cannot determine a precise gender breakdown. Nineteenth-century figures demonstrate continuity: Lafayette Head's 1865 census of Indian captives held in Costilla and Conejos Counties, Colorado Territory, shows females numbering 99 of 148 captives (67 percent), with children under age fifteen 96 of those 148 (65 percent), *National Archives, New Mexico Superintendency* Microcopy 234, roll 553. In 1770, Don Augustín Flores de Vergara donated "for the sermon of the day" at the Chapel of San Miguel in Santa Fe "one Indian girl of serviceable age valued at 80 pesos." See "Certified copy of the Expenditures made by Captain Don Augustín Flores de Vargara for the Chapel of Glorious San Miguel," Crawford Buel Collection, New Mexico State Records Center, Santa Fe.

14. In 1760, a Comanche band attacked what is now Ranchos de Taos and carried fifty-six women and children into captivity. See "Bishop Tamarón's Visitation of New Mexico, 1760," Eleanor B. Adams, ed. and trans., *Historical Society and New Mexico Publications in History*, vol. 15 (1954), 58. In a raid on Abiquiu in 1747, twenty-three women and children were carried off, as documented in "An Account of Conditions in New Mexico, written by Fray Juan Sanz de Lezuan, in the year 1760," in Hackett, *Historical Documents*, vol. III, 477.

15. "*Bando* of Don Phelipe de Neve, governor and commandant-general of the Interior Provinces of New Spain, May 8, 1784," in the Bexar Archives, Barker History Center, University of Texas, Austin. For the 1830s estimate, see Jean Luis Berlandier in *The Indians of Texas in 1830*, ed. John C. Ewers (Washington, D.C.: Smithsonian Institution Press, 1969), 119. The 1933 Comanche Ethnographic Field School out of Santa Fe estimated that 70 percent of Comanche society at that time were mixed-bloods of primarily Mexican Comanche descent; see E. Adamson Hoebel, "The Political Organization and Law Ways of the Comanche Indians," *Memoirs of the American Anthropological Association*, no. 54 (Menasha, Wisc.: 1940).

16. Riordan to Commissioner, 14 August 1883, *Annual Report of the Commissioner of Indian Affairs for the Year 1883* (U.S. Department of the Interior, Washington, D.C.); it should be noted that here, twenty years after the Emancipation Proclamation, U.S. officials were still attempting to extinguish Indian slavery in New Mexico.

17. Nancy Folbre defines "structures of constraint" as "sets of assets, rules, norms, and preferences that shape the interests and identities of individuals or social groups." In doing so, the structures "define the limits and rewards to individual choice." This conceptualization allows us to recognize the *simultaneity* of exploitation and agency, a key element in this essay. Nancy Folbre, *Who Pays for the Kids? Gender and the Structure of Constraint* (New York: Routledge, 1994).

18. See Fray Angélico Chávez, *Origins of New Mexico Families* (1954, Santa Fe: Museum of New Mexico Press, 1992), 49–50, for reference to Hurtado's *encomienda* holdings, including Santa Ana Pueblo.

19. "Inventory and settlement of the estate of Juana Galvana, *genízara* of Zia Pueblo, 1753," SANM I, no. 193. I thank Frances Quintana for suggesting Juana Hurtado as a case study in

captivity and for sharing her notes with me. Her essay, "They Settled by Little Bubbling Springs," *El Palacio* 84, no. 3 (1978): 19–49, treats the history of the Santísima Trinidad Grant at Los Ojitos Hervidores.

20. SANM II, no. 367, reel 6, frames 1010–023.

21. The journal of Don Diego de Vargas records Martín's ransom of Juana at the Zuni Pueblo of Halona, along with her fourteen-year-old daughter, María Naranjo as well as a younger daughter and a son "about three years old." This raises some confusion as to Juana's age at her capture in 1680 and suggests that at least one and probably two of her children were born to her during her captivity. As we will see, if true, this would have given Juana and her "Navajo" children membership in a Navajo clan and may help explain her long-term good relations with Navajos in the years to come. See J. Manuel Espinosa, trans. and ed., *First Expedition of Vargas into New Mexico, 1692* (Albuquerque: Quivira Society, 1940), 237.

22. Archdiocesan Archives of Santa Fe (hereafter AASF), Burials, reel 43, frame 371; SANM II, no. 406.

23. "Declaration of Fray Miguel de Menchero, Santa Bárbara, May 10, 1744," in Hackett, *Historical Documents*, vol. III, 404–405.

24. Abandonment of the pueblo for defensible mesa-top positions often preceded Pueblo-Spanish conflict. Quintana, "They Settled." See SANM II, no. 345, for details of the incident. For a treatment in broader historical context, see Frances Leon Swadesh, "The Structure of Hispanic-Indian Relations in New Mexico," in *The Survival of Spanish American Villages*, ed. Paul M. Kutsche (Colorado Springs: Colorado College Press, 1979), 53–61.

25. See Morris E. Opler, "The Kinship Systems of the Southern Athabaskan-Speaking Tribes," *American Anthropologist* 38 (1936): 622–33; M. E. Opler, "Cause and Effect in Apachean Agriculture, Division of Labor, Residence Patterns, and Girl's Puberty Rites," *American Anthropologist* 74 (1972): 1133–46; Harold E. Driver, "Reply to Opler . . . ," *American Anthropologist* 74 (1972): 1147–51; Collier, *Marriage and Inequality*.

26. See W. W. Hill, "Some Navaho Culture Changes during Two Centuries, with a Translation of the Early Eighteenth Century Rabal Manuscript," in *Smithsonian Miscellaneous Collections*, vol. 100 (1939), 395–415. For Navajo kinship and marriage systems, see Gary Witherspoon, *Navajo Kinship and Marriage* (Chicago: University of Chicago Press, 1975).

27. See Arnold Van Gennep, *The Rites of Passage* (1909, Chicago: University of Chicago Press, 1960), for a treatment of the common attributes of integration rituals.

28. Brugge, *Navajos in Catholic Church Records*, 138, citing a conversation with Bruce Yazzi, a son of Nakai Na'dis Saal.

29. Ibid., app. B, 175; David M. Brugge, "Story of Interpreter for Treaty of 1868," *Navajo Times*, 21 August 1968.

30. Brugge, *Navajos in Catholic Church Records*, 139. This seems an anomaly in the matrilineal reckoning of kin by Navajo clans, but given the nonkin status of an unadopted captive, it would be the only method of integrating her progeny.

31. "Agent Bowman to the Commissioner of Indian Affairs, Sept. 3, 1884," in *Annual Report of the Commissioners of Indian Affairs for the Year 1884*, quoted with extensive corroborative evidence in Brugge, *Navajos in Catholic Church Records*, 142.

32. Morris E. Opler, "A Summary of Jicarilla Apache Culture," *American Anthropologist* 38 (1936): 206, 208, 209.

33. Ibid., 213. This information, gathered by Opler in the 1930s, may reflect an intensification of social stratification following the American conquest of the 1850s.

34. Collier, *Marriage and Inequality*, 23.

35. Hoebel, "Political Organization," 49 ff.

36. Ibid., 49.

37. Ibid., 51, 62. Absconding cases constituted twenty-two of the forty-five marital disputes recorded by Hoebel.

38. See Ernest Wallace and E. Adamson Hoebel, *The Comanche: Lords of the Southern Plains* (Norman: University of Oklahoma Press, 1952), 72.

39. David E. Jones, *Sanapia: Comanche Medicine Woman* (Prospect Heights, Ill.: Waveland Press, 1984 [1972]). Sanapia received her medicine powers through her mother and maternal uncle, consistent with the Shoshonean levirate. Her powers became fully developed only after she experienced menopause.

40. Stanley Noyes, *Los Comanches: The Horse People* (Albuquerque: University of New Mexico Press, 1993); Brooks, "Captives and Cousins" (Ph.D. diss.), 133–35; Dan Flores, "Bison Ecology and Bison Diplomacy: The Southern Plains from 1800 to 1850," *Journal of American History* 78, no. 2 (September 1991): 465–85.

41. Wallace and Hoebel, *Comanche*, 241–42.

42. Ralph Linton, "The Comanche Sun Dance," *American Anthropologist* 37 (1935): 420–28; quotes, 421. For a detailed description of captives in the Sun Dance, see J. J. Methven, *Andele, or the Mexican-Kiowa Captive: A Story of Real Life among the Indians*, ed. James F. Brooks (1899, Albuquerque: University of New Mexico Press, 1996), 58–69.

43. For Loki-Mokeen's story and others, see Maurice Boyd, "The Southern Plains: Captives and Warfare," in *Kiowa Voices: Myths, Legends, and Folktales*, vol. II, ed. Maurice Boyd (Forth Worth: Texas Christian University Press, 1983), 155–82.

44. For Martínez's life story, see James F. Brooks, ed., *Andele: The Mexican-Kiowa Captive* (1899; Albuquerque: University of New Mexico Press, 1996).

45. Hoebel, "Political Organization," 68.

46. "Rosita Rodrígues to Don Miguel Rodrígues, January 13, 1846," letter in the Bexar Archives, Barker History Center, University of Texas, Austin.

47. "A Narrative of the Captivity of Mrs. Horn and Her Two Children" (St. Louis, 1839) reprinted in C. C. Rister, *Comanche Bondage* (Glendale, Calif.: Western Lore Press, 1955), 157.

48. On the incest taboo, see Hoebel, "Political Organization," 108. I am indebted to Tressa Berman for suggesting the association between captive women's low incidence of sexual abuse and the adoptive incest taboo. For similar examples among other Indian groups, see James Axtell, "The White Indians of Colonial America," in *Colonial America* (New York: W. W. Norton, 1983), 16–47, esp. 27.

49. Cynthia Ann Parker, the mother of Quanah Parker, the last Comanche war chief, is the most famous example. See Margaret Schmidt Hacker, *Cynthia Ann Parker* (El Paso: University of Texas at El Paso Press, 1990). Parker lived thirty-four years among the Comanches and died "of heartbreak" shortly after her "rescue."

50. Rodrígues letter, 13 January 1846.

51. Josiah Gregg, *The Commerce of the Prairies*, ed. Milo Milton Quaife (1844, Lincoln: University of Nebraska Press, 1967), 208.

52. "*Expediente* of de Croix, June 6, 1780; Bonilla's Certification of June 15, 1780," in the Bexar Archives, Barker History Center, University of Texas, Austin.

53. Gutiérrez, *When Jesus Came*, 190, 206. The *genízaros* remain the center of scholarly debate as to their true status in New Mexican society. This focuses on whether they constituted a caste category, defined from without, or if in time they developed as an "ethnogenetic" identity group. See Tibo Chavez, *El Rio Abajo*, chap. X, "The *Genízaro*," (Albuquerque: Pampa Print Shop, date unknown); Fray Angélico Chávez, "*Genízaros*," in *The Handbook of North American Indians*, vol. 9 (Washington, D.C.: Smithsonian Institution Press, 1980), 198–200; Robert Archibald, "Acculturation and Assimilation in Colonial New Mexico," *New Mexico Historical Review* 53, no. 3 (July 1978): 205–217; Stephen M. Horvath, "The *Genízaro* of Eighteenth Century New Mexico: A Re-examination," in *Discovery* (Santa Fe: School of American Research, 1977), 25–40; Russell M. Magnaghi, "Plains Indians in New Mexico: The *Genízaro* Experience," *Great Plains Quarterly* 10 (Spring 1990): 86–95.

54. See Richard White's *The Middle Ground: Indians, Empires, and Republics in the Great Lakes Region, 1640–1820* (Cambridge, Eng.: Cambridge University Press, 1991), and Gregory Evans Dowd, *Spirited Resistance: The North American Indian Struggle for Unity, 1745–1815* (Baltimore: Johns Hopkins Press, 1991), for new, though divergent, conceptualizations of these relationships. Other authors preceded White and Dowd in stressing the importance of intermarriage

in promoting these patterns of accommodation, principally Sylvia Van Kirk in her *Many Tender Ties: Women in Fur-Trade Society in Western Canada, 1670-1870* (Norman: University of Oklahoma Press, 1980) and Jennifer S. H. Brown in *Strangers in Blood: Fur Trade Company Families in Indian Country* (Vancouver: University of British Columbia Press, 1980).

55. "Don Fernando de la Concha to Lieutenant Colonel Don Fernando Chacón, Advice on Governing New Mexico, 1794," Donald E. Worcester, trans., *New Mexico Historical Review* 24, no. 3 (1949): 236–54; quote, 250.

56. Alfred B. Thomas, ed. and trans., "Antonio de Bonilla and the Spanish Plans for the Defense of New Mexico, 1777–1778," in *New Spain and the West*, vol. 1 (Lancaster, Penn.: Lancaster Press, 1932), 196.

57. Fray Juan Agustín de Morfi, Desórdenes que se advierten en el Nuevo Mexico, 1780, *Archivo General de la Nación (AGN)*, Historia, 25.

58. "Don Fernando de la Concha," 251.

59. Marc Simmons, ed. and trans., "The Chacón Economic Report of 1803," *New Mexico Historical Review* 60, no. 1 (1985): 81–83; quotes, 83, 87.

60. The economic "modernization" of New Mexico has usually been attributed to the influence of the St. Louis–Santa Fe–Chihuahua trade that began in 1821. For a much earlier emergence, see Ross H. Frank, "From Settler to Citizen: Economic Development and Cultural Change in Late Colonial New Mexico, 1750–1820" (Ph.D. dissertation, University of California, Berkeley, 1992); for this aspect in the sheep commerce, see John O. Baxter, *Las Carneradas: Sheep Trade in New Mexico, 1700–1860* (Albuquerque: University of New Mexico Press, 1987).

61. Janet Lecompte has collected and interpreted most of the primary source material on this revolt, in *Rebellion in Río Arriba, 1837* (Albuquerque: University of New Mexico Press, 1985). Her class interpretation stresses tensions between *ricos* and *pobres* and neglects to consider the obvious cultural issues at work.

62. Governor Manuel Armijo, "Diario del Gobierno de la República Mexicana, Vol. 9. No. 45, Nov. 30, 1837," trans. in Lecompte, *Rebellion*, 139.

63. For the extensiveness of the 1847 Taos revolt, see *Insurrection against the Military Government in New Mexico and California, 1847 and 1848* (U.S. Senate, 56th Congress, First Session, Document No. 442, 1901); Michael McNierney, ed. and trans., *Taos 1847: The Revolt in Contemporary Accounts* (Boulder: University of Colorado Press, 1980); James W. Goodrich, "Revolt at Mora, 1847," *New Mexico Historical Review* 47, no. 1 (1972): 49–60.

64. See the Spanish Colonial Census of 1750, New Mexico State Records Center, Santa Fe, 47–48.

65. Analysis drawn from Stephen M. Horvath, "The Genízaro of Eighteenth Century New Mexico: A Re-examination," in *Discovery* (Santa Fe: School of American Research, 1977), 25–40.

66. Fray Miguel de Menchero claimed in 1744 that the "*genízaro* Indians . . . engage in agriculture and are under obligation to go out and explore the country in pursuit of the enemy, which they are doing with great bravery and zeal." See Declaration of Menchero, in Hackett, *Historical Documents*, vol. III, 401.

67. See "Appeal of Bentura Bustamante, Lieutenant of Genízaro Indians," 20 June 1780, SANM I, no. 1229, roll 6, frames 323–35.

68. "José Manrique, draft of a Report for Nemesio Salcedo y Salcedo, Nov. 26, 1808," in the Pinart Collection, Bancroft Library, University of California, Berkeley.

69. Lecompte, *Rebellion*, 36–40, n. 54.

70. Gutiérrez, *When Jesus Came*, 7–9.

71. Angelina F. Veyna, "Hago, dispongo, y ordeno mi testamento: Reflections of Colonial New Mexican Women," paper presented at the annual meeting of the Western History Association, October 1991, in possession of author.

72. SANM I, no. 344, cited in Veyna, "Hago, dispongo, y ordeno."

73. "Testament of Don Santiago Roibal, 1762," fragment in New Mexico State Records Center, Santa Fe.

74. SANM II, no. 427, roll 7, frames 1023–25.

75. Gutiérrez, *When Jesus Came*, 182.

76. Frances Quintana, *Pobladores: Hispanic Americans of the Ute Frontier* (South Bend, Ind.: University of Notre Dame Press, 1974; reprint, Aztec, N.M.: privately published, 1991), 206–210.

77. Gutiérrez. *When Jesus Came*, 252.

78. As early as 1714, Spanish authorities were ordering "married" couples in the Río Grande pueblos to establish neolocal households rather than reside with their parents, a clear attempt to break matrilocal residence patterns and assert colonial control over the institution of marriage. (See SANM II, reel 4, frame 1014, as an example.)

79. Swadesh, "They Settled," 44.

80. Marietta Morrissey, *Slave Women in the New World: Gender Stratification in the Caribbean* (Lawrence: University of Kansas Press, 1989), 13–15. The ambiguous benefits of maternity to women held captive in patrilineal societies is borne out by looking at women under indigenous African systems of captivity and slavery. Among the Margi of Nigeria, for example, social integration of captive-descended children could result in the elevation of mothers, if those children achieved social prominence in trade or warfare. See James H. Vaughan, "*Mafakur*: A Limbic Institution of the Margi," in *Slavery in Africa*, eds. Suzanne Miers and Igor Kopytoff, (Wisconsin: University of Wisconsin Press, 1977), 85–102.

81. Alan M. Klein, "The Political Economy of Gender: A Nineteenth Century Plains Indian Case Study," in *The Hidden Half: Studies of Plains Indian Women*, ed. Patricia Albers and Beatrice Medicine (Washington, D.C.: University Press of America, 1983), 143–74; for a study of the Bison economy, see Flores, "Bison Ecology."

82. Veyna, "Hago, dispongo, y ordeno," 9. Veyna also notes that "when tools were distributed to the settlers of Santa Cruz de la Cañada in 1712, only women were allotted *rejas*."

83. H. P. Mera, *The Slave Blanket*, General Series Bulletin No. 5, Laboratory of Anthropology, Santa Fe, 1938.

84. See Lansing Bloom, "Early Weaving in New Mexico," *New Mexico Historical Review* 2 (1927): 228–38; Baxter, *Las Carneradas*, 60. See also Suzanne Baizerman, "Textile Traditions and Tourist Art: Hispanic Weaving in New Mexico" (Ph.D. dissertation, University of Minnesota, St. Paul, 1987), esp. 76–79, 130–31.

85. "General Campaign: Report of Governor Vélez Cachupín to Conde de Revilla Gigedo, Nov. 27, 1751," in A. B. Thomas, *The Plains Indians and New Mexico, 1751–1778* (Norman: University of Oklahoma Press, 1940), 74.

86. "Juan José Lobato to Vélez, August 28, 1752," in Thomas, *Plains Indians*, 114–15.

87. "Report of Vélez to Marqués de Cruillas, 1762," in Thomas, *Plains Indians*, 152–53.

88. "Abstract of report offered by de Anza, as written by Pedro Garrido y Durran, Chihuahua, December 21, 1786," in Alfred B. Thomas, *Forgotten Frontiers: A Study of the Spanish Indian Policy of Don Juan Bautista de Anza, Governor of New Mexico, 1777–1787* (Norman: University of Oklahoma Press, 1932) 296; Elizabeth A. John, *Storms Brewed in Other Men's Worlds* (Lincoln: University of Nebraska Press, 1975), p. 732.

89. Maria Mies, "Social Origins of the Sexual Division of Labor," in *Women: The Last Colony*, ed. Mies, Veronika Bennholdt-Thomsen, and Claudia Von Werlhof (London: Zed Books, 1988), 67–95; quote, 87.

90. Tykal, "From Taos to St. Louis"; "Report of Governor Vélez to Marqués de Cruillas . . . 1762," in Thomas, *Plains Indians*, 151. Vélez had asked the Comanche leader Nimiricante of the whereabouts of the women and children seized at Ranchos de Taos in 1760. Nimiricante replied that "they might have died, or been traded to the French and Jumanos." For José Juliano's problems in San Antonio, see Salcedo to Manrique, July 27, 1809, SANM II, no. 2239.

91. The French traders Jean Chapuis and Luis Fueilli were guided to Santa Fe in 1752 by "an Indian woman of the Aa tribe, who had fled to the house of her master [in Santa Fe] four months before and was following the road to her country." See "Vélez to Revilla Gigedo, Sept. 18, 1752," in Thomas, *Plains Indians*, 109.

92. See SANM I, no. 657, "Demanda puesta por Lucia Ortega contra Roque Lovato sobre una Donacion—Ano del 1769."

93. See Gregg, *Commerce of the Prairies*, 86, 208, 219.

94. Author's interview with Miguel Montoya, Las Vegas, N.M., 17 August 1990.

6.

When Strangers Met:
Sex and Gender on Three Frontiers

ALBERT L. HURTADO

Albert Hurtado shifts our focus from women's survival strategies to the systems of constraint that often endangered their survival. He does this by exploring the most intimate of "cross-cultural exchanges," sexual relationships. Sex, like other basic activities such as eating and sleeping, might appear to be one constant of human relationships, and thus outside the range of history. Hurtado demonstrates that sex, too, is a social and historical category by showing how understandings of sexuality differed vastly among Spaniards, Euro-Americans, and various Indian peoples. In particular, Spanish Mexican and American gender systems had no equivalent for a variety of Indian cross-gender roles, which allowed some people to assume the roles of the other sex. In some cultures, they were actually understood to be the other sex; in others they constituted a third gender, neither traditionally male nor female. Men who adopted cross-gender roles, often called berdache, *could only be understood as homosexuals by Europeans, who likewise misinterpreted Indian women's sexuality in many instances. Hurtado explores how these differences, coupled with vastly unequal power relationships, affected Indian women on three frontiers—in California under the Spanish mission system and later during the gold rush and in the Upper Missouri during the fur trade.*

The evidence is grim. Indian women, Hurtado suggests, were subject to enormous abuse, including rape, venereal disease, and slavery. His research paints a picture vastly different from that suggested by histories of Indian-white relationships in other circumstances, particularly the marriages "according to the custom of the country" among European men and Indian women during the early Canadian fur trade.[1] We need to consider differences in the Europeans' enterprises, economies, and social expectations on various frontiers, as well as variations in Indian cultures, as we untangle what "intimacy" meant in different circumstances.

In the meanwhile, Hurtado offers an important caution. In our desire to recognize the historical agency of women and racial ethnic peoples, we must not ignore the realities of exploitation and abuse or the very limited options many people confronted. Systems of social constraint could sometimes be very constraining indeed. And, as Hurtado reminds us, in order to be able to exercise historical agency, one must first survive.

The West of the eighteenth and nineteenth centuries was a cosmopolitan place—a meeting ground for people of disparate cultures and conflicting motives. Equipped with widely different ideas about correct social behavior, Indians, Hispanos, Anglos, and others frequently misunderstood and mistrusted each other. Yet these people who met as strangers came to live in close association for decades and often entered into sexual relationships—marriage, long-term cohabitation, and briefer connections as well. In some cases these intimate relationships softened the racial friction and violence that so often characterized the frontier. Especially in the fur trade Indian women joined with white men to make families that were the backbone of the trade and frontier society. These relationships produced mixed-blood (métis) children who populated the Great Lakes and Canadian frontiers.[2] In what is now the southwestern United States, the Spanish American frontier assumed a racially and culturally mixed character that in many ways resembled that of Mexico. Marriages and informal alliances between Indians, Spaniards, and others produced a mixed race, or "mestizo," population that dominated the Hispanic settlements of the region.[3] Such unions were, as Richard White has said of the Great Lakes region, "a bridge to the middle ground, an adjustment to interracial sex in the fur trade where the initial conceptions of sexual conduct held by each side were reconciled in a new customary relation."[4]

The bridge provided some Indian women with new, albeit sometimes fleeting, survival routes in a changing world. Yet not all Indians could or would cross that bridge, and some of those who did found that the path was very rough going. This essay will compare several very different people, places, and circumstances—the Franciscan missions, Upper Missouri fur trade, California gold rush, Indians and whites from various nations. It focuses particularly on the experiences of Indian women and to a lesser extent on the *berdache*, a class of morphological males who dressed and acted as women.[5] The *berdache* and the women in these stories probably represent a minority example in the range of Indian experiences, yet they serve to emphasize a major theme of this essay. Changes in social and economic relations put some people at risk— notably the *berdache* and women who were particularly vulnerable. At the same time that some couples built lasting relationships that benefited both parties, interracial sexuality exacerbated Indian-white conflict and violence. While some newcomers welcomed the seemingly open sexual possibilities of the frontier, they usually condemned—at least in public— behavior that challenged conventional European ideas about gender. The intimate experiences of Indians and whites that are presented here are not merely idiosyncratic episodes that are unconnected to the main currents of American history.[6] On the contrary, their sexual histories illustrate how broad-based historical change affected personal life.

Concepts about sex and gender are at the heart of this matter. Sexuality, as John D'Emilio and Estelle Freedman have argued, "has been continually reshaped by the changing nature of the economy, the family, and politics."[7] Sexuality is a part of gender relations, a social construction that varies according to time and circumstances.[8] The historical analysis of gender, feminist scholar Carroll Smith-Rosenberg asserts, "forces us to reconsider our understanding of the most fundamental ordering of social relations, institutions of social relations, institutions and power arrangements within the society we study."[9] Thus, this essay, which is focused on a particular aspect of gender relations, illuminates some of the challenges to Indian societies that were in contact with unusual new cultures in North America. In addition, it explains some of the results—whether intended or not—of the colonization of Indian resources and society.

Needless to say, it is a difficult task to disclose the private lives of any group, much less people who did not leave a personal record of their innermost thoughts and feelings. Moreover, much of what we know of Indian history comes from the writings of white men, most of whom had ethnocentric biases as well as the preoccupations of their gender.[10] Still, the perspective of ethnohistory permits the cautious use of these sources to unravel some of the complex mysteries of sex and gender in the multiethnic American West of more than a century ago.

To begin to understand what happened, we must first know something of Indian, Hispanic, and Anglo ideas about sex and gender. Though sexual norms varied from tribe to tribe, it is fair to generalize that Indians had different ideas about sexuality than did Europeans. The Blackfeet, for example, considered it a disgrace for a young girl to become pregnant before marriage, yet anthropologist John C. Ewers reports that "chastity before marriage was more an ideal than a reality." Blackfeet men bragged of their conquests of single and married women alike.[11] Plains Indians generally tolerated premarital and extramarital sex among men but sought to maintain the virtue of women. A girl's reputation for chastity, or lack of it, affected her chances of marrying well. Nevertheless, love affairs, adultery, and elopements occurred among Plains Indians.[12] Serial monogamy was the usual marital pattern, but polygyny was also accepted, especially for chiefs, shamans, and other powerful people.[13] Divorce was usually easily effected if one partner wanted it. Public ceremonial sexual practices were also known in some tribes, particularly the northern Plains Indians with their buffalo-calling ceremony. Women took lovers, but at their own risk, for their husbands might punish them if they found out. On the other hand, husbands might lend their wives to visitors or trade their sexual services for goods. However, these arrangements were thought of as gift-giving, part of the endless round of reciprocity that marked Indian life. True prostitution—sex as a purely commercial transaction—was rare among Indians before the arrival of Europeans, if it existed at all.

California poses special difficulties in describing sexual behavior and gender roles before European contact. There were more than one hundred distinct groups within the current state boundaries, each with its own language and customs. Nevertheless, patterns emerge from the anthropological literature on the tribes that inhabited the regions that came under mission influence. As with other Indian tribes, it was important for children to marry well. With most tribes premarital sex did not seem to be a matter of great importance. After marriage, however, fidelity was expected and husbands had the authority to punish their errant wives. The Chumash, who lived in the Santa Barbara Channel region, permitted husbands to whip their adulterous wives. To the north, not far from Monterey Bay, a wronged Esselin husband could demand an indemnity payment from his wife's lover. In the Los Angeles region, a Gabrielino cuckold could claim the wife of his wife's lover. Yet the women in these unions possessed some power of their own over their sexual lives. They could divorce husbands who were cruel or who were otherwise not to their liking. As with the Plains tribes serial monogamy was a common marital pattern and polygyny was one of the privileges that came with wealth, power, and high status.[14]

Many tribes on the plains and in California also tolerated—perhaps even respected—the *berdache*, although this is a matter of current debate. It is not altogether clear that the *berdache* engaged in homosexual acts in all tribes, but in some cases they did. More importantly, a *berdache* was not viewed as a deviant male, but as an embodiment of male and female characteristics. In some tribes the *berdache* were regarded as a third gender, endowed with special spiritual attributes and other qualities. When they were so regarded, or when they were regarded sexually as women, their sexual unions with men were not understood as homosexual. Often chiefs would take a *berdache* as a second wife. Unmarried *berdache* often took serial lovers who were regarded as perfectly normal men.[15] In some tribes women also cross-dressed and took on male roles.[16] Such behavior struck Europeans as unnatural, lascivious, and wanton, even though native people regulated sexuality according to their own customs.

Indian sexuality reflected Indian gender roles that differed radically from European norms. Fertility and birth made the power of Indian women palpable to tribesmen. Many Indian societies were matrilineal. In some California tribes women could be shamans and chiefs. Women engaged in other activities that Europeans regarded as men's work, e.g., farming, skinning, butchering. In some tribes, women had considerable control over their sexual lives.[17] Nevertheless, marriage was an important arrangement that established kinship between families, and while women usually could refuse an unwanted union, their families applied pressure to secure especially valuable alliances. The widespread practice of giving the prospective bride's family a gift (sometimes called a "bride price") emphasized reciprocal exchange between families rather than the outright purchase of the woman. While husbands in some tribes—especially on the northern plains—gave or gambled away their wives' sexual service, the wives were not free to dispense favors on their own and risked severe punishment if they did.[18]

Indians' sex and gender customs differed from the sexual ideology of Christian Europeans in many respects. Protestants and Catholics alike condemned extramarital sex, homosexuality, and polygamy. Divorce was difficult or impossible to obtain, and—ideally—the brides and grooms who approached the marriage altar were virgins. Ideas about sexual desire in women changed markedly from the eighteenth to the nineteenth century. In the mid-1700s the notion that women enjoyed sex found wide support, but sex was for procreation and not pleasure alone.[19] In the following century, however, a new idea took root. Women, according to some physicians and social ideologues, were frail, nervous, and uninterested in sex except as an act necessary to procreation. Women's challenges to male authority and the uncertainties of modernizing America inspired these theories that seemed to consign women to child rearing and household chores.[20] These theories about women's sexual nature fit well with the cult of true womanhood, which required them to be pure, pious, and domestic. Moreover, women were thought to exert a civilizing influence on men who had naturally coarse instincts.

Despite—or perhaps because of—the strictures that society placed on sexual behavior, illicit sex flourished in eastern cities even though prostitution seemed to be at odds with prevailing moral standards. Society tolerated the institution in part because it was believed that men were virile and aggressive, while women seldom wanted or enjoyed sex. This belief drove single and married men to brothels to satisfy their animal urges, while women remained at home in blissful ignorance, or perhaps grateful that they did not have to submit to their spouses' base instincts.[21]

A comparison of Anglo and Hispanic sexual attitudes and practices shows similarities and differences. Ideally, Hispanic women were secluded, except when closely chaperoned, to protect their chastity and the honor of their male relatives. In practice women had greater latitude of action than the ideal permitted, especially in frontier regions. Hispanic ideas about female sexuality also differed from Anglo theories. According to Anglo standards, normal women were sexually anesthetic, but in Hispanic lore, Latinas were easily seduced, partly because they were physically weaker than men and partly because women were incapable of mastering their own strong sexual impulses. Hispanic sexual life was further complicated because men acquired honor and status by seducing other men's wives and daughters. At the same time, the Catholic Church decreed that sex should be limited to the marriage bed for the sole purpose of procreation, which should be achieved through the so-called missionary position. All other sexual practices were sinful and prohibited.[22] Spaniards did not always follow the sexual ideology that the church prescribed in their relations with Indians. While Crown and church permitted Spaniards to marry native people, informal sexual relationships also occurred with great regularity and resulted in a large mixed-race mestizo population.[23]

In California's Franciscan missions, Spanish ideas about sex and gender contrasted sharply with local Indian traditions. Missions were supposed to inculcate Catholic and Spanish values in the Indians and prepare them for life as ordinary citizens. Guided by Catholic teachings, missionaries were determined to eradicate sinful behavior, including common Indian practices like extramarital sex, easy divorce, homo-sexuality, and polygyny.[24] Thus, during confession, the friars took care to closely question neophytes about their sexual behavior.[25]

Religious and lay Spaniards alike, who considered homosexuality an execrable sin against nature, one to be extirpated at all costs, had no other sexual framework within which to understand Indians' cross-gender roles. Much to the dismay of Spaniards, *berdache* Indians were ubiqui-tous in California. Captain Pedro Fages in 1775 reported that the Chumash were "addicted to the unspeakable vice of sinning against nature," maintaining that each ranchería had a transvestite "for common use." Fages apologized for even obliquely mentioning homosexuality because it was "an excess so criminal that it seems even forbidden to speak its name."[26] The missionary Pedro Font was more candid. He reported "sodomites addicted to nefarious practices" among the Yuma Indians and concluded that "there will be much to do when the Holy Faith and the Christian religion are established among them."[27]

Other priests were as disturbed by *berdache* behavior as Font was. Father Francisco Palóu reported an incident at Mission San Antonio where a transvestite and another man were discovered "in an unspeakably sinful act." A priest, and two soldiers "punished them," Palóu revealed, "although not as much as they deserved." The horrified priest tried to explain to the Indians how terrible was their sin against nature only to be told that the two men were married. Palóu's reaction to this news was not recorded, but it is doubtful that he accepted it with equanimity. After a severe scolding, the couple left the mission vicinity. Palóu hoped that "these accursed persons will decrease, and such an abominable vice will be eradicated," as the Catholic faith increases "for the greater Glory of God and the good of those pitiful, ignorant people."[28]

Civil and church officials agreed on the need to eradicate homosexuality as an affront to God and Spanish men alike. At Mission Santa Clara the fathers noticed an unconverted Indian who, though dressed like a woman and working among women, did not seem to have breasts, an observation that was made easier because Indian women traditionally wore only necklaces above the waist. The curious friars conspired with the corporal of the guard to take this questionable person into custody where he was completely disrobed, confirming that he was indeed a man. The poor fellow was "more embarrassed than if he had been a woman," according to one friar. For three days the soldiers kept him nude—stripped of his sexual identity—and made him sweep the plaza near the guardhouse—woman's work. He remained "sad and ashamed" until he was released under orders to abjure feminine clothes and stay out of women's company. Instead he fled from the mission to take up residence and a new trans-vestite life among gentiles.[29]

The revulsion and violence that customary Indian sexual relations inspired in the newcomers must have puzzled and frightened native people. Formerly accepted as an ordinary part of social life, the *berdache* faced persecution at the hands of friars and soldiers. To the colonizers, *berdache* were homosexuals and homosexual behavior was loathsome, one of many traits that convinced ethnocentric priests that California Indians were a backward race. In a word, they were "incomprehensible" to Father Geronimo Boscana. The "affirmative with them, is negative," he claimed "and the negative, the affirmative," a perversity that was clearly reflected in homosexuality. In frustration Boscana compared the California Indians with "a species of monkey."[30]

Indian sexuality confounded Spaniards, but friars fretted over the sexual habits not only of neophytes. Some civilians and soldiers brought to California sexual attitudes and behavior that were at odds with Catholic and Indian values alike. Rape was a special concern of friars who condemned Spanish deviant sexual behavior in California.[31] As early as 1772 Father Luís Jayme complained about some of the soldiers who deserved to be hanged for "continuous outrages" on the Diegueño women near the mission.[32] Father Jayme worried that wanton soldiers would turn the Diegueños against the missions. "Many times," he asserted, the Indians were on the verge of attacking the mission because "some soldiers went there and raped their women." The situation was so bad that when the fathers approached the rancherías the Indians would flee, even risking hunger "so the soldiers will not rape their women as they have already done so many times in the past."

San Diego was not unique. Father Jayme complained that rapes had occurred at every mission. Junípero Serra, founder and father-president of the California missions, agreed with Jayme. Serra singled out Spanish muleteers who traveled between the missions as the worst perpetrators of sexual assaults. Rape, Serra believed, ultimately would alienate the Indians and imperil the mission system. The Indians, "until now as gentle as sheep," Serra wrote, "will turn on us like tigers."[33]

Serra was a prophet. In 1775 eight hundred neophyte and gentile Diegueños, fed up with sexual assaults and chafing under missionary supervision, attacked Mission San Diego. They burned the mission and killed three Spaniards, including Father Jayme, beating his face beyond recognition.[34] As Jayme and Serra had predicted, sexual abuse made California a perilous place. Still, the revolt did not dissuade some Spaniards from sexual involvement with Indian women. In 1779 Serra was still criticizing the government for "unconcern in the matter of shameful conduct between the soldiers and Indian women," a complaint that may have included mutual as well as rapacious liaisons.[35]

To reform Indian sexuality and protect unmarried female neophytes from Spanish assaults, friars closely watched their charges by day and kept them under lock and key at night. Unmarried men and women slept in separate quarters, although sexual segregation seems to have done little to halt illicit sexual behavior. Sherburne F. Cook, the foremost California Indian demographer, claimed that restrictions on sexuality may have induced neophytes to flee to the gentile tribes with whom they could enjoy life without unwanted sexual restrictions.[36] The 1824 Chumash rebellion is an illustrative case. During the revolt several hundred Santa Barbara

Monjerios, or girls' dormitories, like this reconstructed one at Mission La Purísima (California), were meant to keep young unmarried women from having voluntary sexual liaisons and to protect them from rape. Women were locked in such buildings every night. Unfortunately, the structures were unsanitary and poorly ventilated and contributed to the spread of diseases, which exacerbated the high death rates for women at the missions. (Courtesy *California History.*)

neophytes fled to the interior, where they exchanged women with Yokuts gentiles and abandoned other Catholic restrictions as well.[37]

Even within the missions, the Franciscans' most stringent efforts did not stop determined neophytes from having forbidden sexual relations. In 1813 a Spanish government official sent a questionnaire to the missionaries inquiring about various aspects of mission Indian life. When asked about the vices most prevalent at each mission, the friars almost universally gave answers such as "impurity," "unchastity," "fornication," and "lust."[38] No doubt the friars had some individual successes in reforming Indian sexual behavior in the forty-four years that missions had existed, but according to their own reports, the missionaries had failed to inculcate Catholic sexual values in the neophytes.

But Spanish colonization had changed Indian sexual behavior in other ways. At the very least, sexual liaisons that were once accepted were now forbidden and had to be enjoyed furtively. There were other changes as well. Before Spaniards had arrived, true prostitution does not seem to have been customary in California, but during the mission era it became common.[39] A report of Father Jayme suggests how prostitution may have begun. In 1772 four soldiers raped two women at a ranchería known as El Corral. After the assault the soldiers tried to convert the act from rape to prostitution by paying the women with some ribbon and a few tortillas. They also paid a neophyte man who had witnessed the assault and warned him not to divulge the incident. Insulted and angry, the Indians were not overawed by the rapists' threats and told Jayme. In retaliation the soldiers locked the neophyte man in the stocks, an injustice that outraged Jayme who personally released him.[40] These rapists had embarked on a program of sexual education. Food and gifts, they taught, could be had in exchange for sex.

Whether or not prostitution evolved from rapes, Spanish demands for sexual service led to the widespread sale of sex. Perhaps the adoption of prostitution was an Indian attempt to reduce the incidence of rape and exert some control over their sexual encounters with Spaniards. In any case, Indian men became involved as procurers. In 1780 Father Serra complained about a neophyte who procured women for the soldiers at Mission San Gabriel.[41] A few years later a Spanish naturalist observed that the Chumash men had "become pimps, even for their own wives, for any miserable profit."[42] So it would appear that the advent of prostitution was another unintended sexual result of the establishment of the California missions.

From a Catholic perspective the missions were failures as institutions of sexual reform, although they resulted in changes in Indian sexual life. From an Indian viewpoint the missionaries' intentions were not benign, but involved radical changes in all phases of Indian life. Franciscans railed bitterly against rape, prostitution, and other sexual practices that the Catholic Church condemned. Nevertheless, some Spaniards persisted in assaults and purchased sexual favors. Since many of these men were young unmarried soldiers, the existence of rape and prostitution in frontier California is not especially surprising. It is worth pointing out, however, that missions and presidios advanced together on the Spanish American frontier. Soldiers protected priests' lives and mission property. Without them the missions could not have endured. Thus, even though missionaries decried sexual brutality, their very presence promoted it. Spiritual, military, and sexual conquest went hand in glove on the California frontier.

Fur traders represented a far different aspect of European and American imperialism than did Franciscan missionaries. These expectant capitalists, as a historian has termed the traders, had material rather than spiritual goals in mind and pursued their vocation with hardly a shadow of humanitarian concern for their Indian clients.[43] Traders were not celibate by inclination or priestly vows. Because their business compelled them to live for extended periods among Indians, many traders married Indian women.[44]

The Mandan and Hidatsa villages on the bluffs of the upper Missouri provide a commanding view of sex and gender at work in the fur trade. These Indians had been farmers and traders for generations before the first whites arrived at their villages in 1738. Strategically located where the expanding horse and gun frontiers met, Mandan and Hidatsa traders were an important force on the upper Missouri in the eighteenth and early nineteenth centuries.[45]

Indian women were one of the prime attractions of the Missouri villages. In 1798 David Thompson, a North West Company trader, reported that his companions wanted to go to the Mandan communities chiefly for women. Thompson—like many other white visitors—remarked on the practice of providing "a bedfellow" to a traveler, adding, "if he has any property."[46] Since traders often gave the women and their husbands presents, whites frequently equated the practice of wife lending with prostitution, but the Missouri tribes and other Plains Indians were involved in a far more complicated sexual enterprise than that. For them, the provision of a sexual partner was a matter of hospitality that cemented friendships and trading relationships. Moreover, they believed that coitus transferred power from one man to another, using the woman as a kind of transmission line. The Mandan institutionalized this principle in the buffalo-calling ceremony, a famous rite where old, respected hunters copulated with the wives of younger men who sought to invoke the elders' spiritual aid. These acts also symbolized intercourse with life-giving buffalo, ensured fertility, and drew nigh the bison herds. Other tribes of the northern plains also practiced ritual intercourse.[47]

The Indians who celebrated these rites no doubt considered their participation to be a sacred obligation, but when whites arrived on the scene the situation became confused. Mandans regarded fur traders as powerful persons, so whites were welcomed into the buffalo-calling ceremony, much to the carnal delight of the members of the Lewis and Clark expedition. As Pierre-Antoine Tabeau drolly remarked, the men of Lewis and Clark were "untiringly zealous in attracting the cow."[48]

Public sexual rites and the frank solicitations of Indian men and their wives were not the only erotic attractions of the Missouri villages. They were also slave marts where fur traders could purchase women. Slave women were captives from enemy tribes, often Shoshone, Sioux, and Arikara. Sacagawea, a Shoshone woman, was one of them. Her husband, Toussaint Charbonneau, purchased her and another young woman from Hidatsa traders sometime between 1800 and 1804.[49] The purchase of slave women for wives was not a romantic arrangement. Expedience and price were the main considerations of Francis A. Chardon who bought an Arikara woman at Fort Clark in 1838. His diary entry shows how casually such purchases were made. Tired of living alone, Chardon concluded "to buy myself a Wife, a young Virgin of 15—which cost $150." A month later Chardon received a present. An Arikara, or perhaps a Gros Ventre man, gave him a twelve-year-old Assiniboine girl, one of eight female captives taken during a fight that killed sixty-four of their kin.[50]

Sacagawea, it is fair to say, is the best known of the luckless slaves who passed through the Missouri villages, but much about her life remains shrouded after her service with Lewis and Clark. Needless to say, we know far less about the uncounted anonymous women who shared her fate. The story of one of them, an extraordinary woman known only as the "flying beauty," suggests how fortunate was Sacagawea. Her story comes to us through Charles McKenzie, a North West Company trader who visited the Mandans in 1805. A Mandan chief called him to his lodge and told him about a young Shoshone woman whom he had recently captured. The Mandan claimed that she was the greatest beauty of all the tribes and that he had saved her for McKenzie, knowing that he would pay a good price for her. He explained that he had "used her kindly," whatever that may have meant. She was all the more interesting because she been captured twice before, only to escape. Unfortunately for her Mandan captor, she had fled again, taking a horse and some weapons, leaving only memories of her uncommon beauty behind. "None of our women equal her," the chief said, "we know the white men would love her."[51]

Perhaps tired of hearing about the qualities of the escaped slave, an old blind woman interrupted. "I wish you had killed the B---h," she said. Not only had the Shoshone absconded, she had stolen the old woman's favorite knife. Encouraged by the outburst, a young girl added, "[T]he bad Slave has stolen my knife also—I wish she was dead!" Inspired by sentiments like these, four young Mandan men pursued the Shoshone, following the trail she made by digging camus roots for food. But the trail vanished at the foot of the Rocky Mountains, and the Mandans wandered aimlessly in unfamiliar territory. Meanwhile, the resourceful flying beauty had killed a buffalo, built a shelter in a mountain valley, and commenced smoking meat for her journey home. She no doubt thought she had eluded her pursuers, but bad luck overtook her. The lost Mandans happened into the valley, killed her with lances, and carried her head back to the Missouri—a trophy on the end of a pole.[52]

It is difficult to know if the experiences of Sacagawea or her kinswoman, the flying beauty, were typical or exceptional examples of Indian slave life. There are no statistical sources that tell how many enslaved Indians were sold to white traders or to Indians. There is no way to know how many women escaped or were killed in trying. Nor do we know how many may have been adopted and married into the tribes of their captors, a common practice.[53] Slave women who were useful and compliant might well have found a valued place among the people who kidnapped them, but that was not their choice. It is fair to say, however, that fortune played a part in the ultimate fate of captive women whose lives were at the disposal of others. Charbonneau did not put Sacagawea's head on a stick, but that was her good luck. No one would have stopped him. The flying beauty was clever and attractive, but she met a sorry end that shows how risky and dangerous the world of the fur trade could be for slave women.

The Mandans continued to capture and sell women until smallpox devastated their villages in 1837. This epidemic nearly wiped out the tribe. Some survivors fled to the Arikaras, but a few remained in the nearly deserted Missouri River village near Fort Clark. Neither group fared well. The Arikaras stole the women of their Mandan guests, a powerless minority unable to stop these assaults. Tiring of this treatment, some moved on to other tribes where they hoped to find a more hospitable and compassionate reception.[54]

In December 1838 the Mandans finally abandoned their village near Fort Clark, leaving behind a sickly old woman who soon died. In January 1839 their old enemies the Sioux burned the deserted town. As a parting gesture, they took the scalp from the Mandan woman's corpse and carried it to their camp. It was a suitable trophy. The Sioux were the rising power of the plains, and their women would no longer be subject to the assaults of Mandans.[55] The women of the Mandans, former masters of the trade in Indian slave women, were now at the mercy of more powerful tribes.

A decade after the Mandan village was reduced to ashes, James Marshall and some Indian workers found gold in California and set off the gold rush. The social and ethnic milieu of the gold rush was far more cosmopolitan than those of the missions and the fur trade, and the added complexity had ramifications for women and men according to their culture and skin color. The mass migration that inundated the Sierra Nevada foothills included people from all over the world, but regardless of origin, young men vastly outnumbered women. Tribes in the gold region were one hundred miles or more from the Spanish and Mexican settlements and had not been directly affected by them. During the Mexican era, however, American and Hudson's Bay Company traders and trappers had scoured the California interior. In 1839 John Sutter established New Helvetia, an outpost in the Sacramento Valley that became a focus for sparse Anglo-American settlement that was nominally under Mexican control. Like Hispanic rancheros on the coast, Sutter and his fellow frontiersmen employed Indian labor to work their herds and fields. Some of these Indian workers were free, others were peons, and some were slaves. After gold was discovered, Anglos and Hispanos alike used Indian hands in the mines until free white labor drove them out.[56]

Though far removed from the mines, the gold rush affected Indians who lived along the overland trail as some immigrants sought sexual gratification on their journey. These sexual liaisons are poorly documented, but two examples suffice to demonstrate activities that were probably widely known but seldom recorded. In 1849 Howard Stansbury reported that "a company of unprincipalled emigrants" committed "a gross and unprincipalled outrage" on some Shoshone women and killed the Indians who attempted to rescue them.[57]

Another recorded sexual incident happened three years later after tens of thousands of overlanders had passed through Shoshone country and sharply depleted Indian food resources. Travelers thoughtlessly killed game and overfished the streams, and their draft animals overgrazed the range and fouled watercourses. By 1852 Shoshones near the trail were suffering. In July John Hudson Wayman, an Indiana physician, passed through Shoshone territory near the present-day Utah-Nevada border. Wayman was obviously unhappy to have Indians in his camp, upset as he was by the "d----d Indians sneaking around beging [sic]." Meanwhile, two of his companions "were conjureing around the Squaws," evidently hoping for sexual favors. Eventually the two men gave an Indian woman "some victuals" with "care & solicitude without receiving any thing in return in sight." The woman led the men away from the wagon train and returned later "without any explanation," a suggestive chain of events of which Wayman disapproved.[58]

This casual assignation represents more than the lust of two men on the long trip to California. It illustrates the poverty of Shoshones who panhandled wagon trains and acquiesced to travelers' sexual solicitations in return for food. Moreover, the gold rush was not the beginning of the Shoshone sexual experience with whites. Shoshone women had been objects in the fur trade of the Upper Missouri for one hundred years. The advent of overland immigration and its sexual component was part of a long chain of events that impinged on the intimate lives of Indian women.

In California the booming gold-rush economy spawned a growing prostitute population that included Indians and other women of color. In 1852, Henry B. Sheldon, a Protestant missionary, described San Francisco prostitutes as the "aristocracy" of San Francisco and estimated that there were about one thousand of them. Courtesans rode in "the most splendid *carriages*, and on the most showy studs," which they often raced near the old Franciscan mission on the Sabbath. "Who can find a virtuous woman?" Sheldon asked rhetorically, adding with unintended irony that if one could be found her price would be far above rubies. The ratio of harlots to honest women was so great that the latter class had to "conduct themselves with the strictest propriety or be cast from the pale of good society," such as it was. San Francisco was not unique. As Sheldon noted, there were "no villages of any size" without prostitutes.[59]

Despite Sheldon's description of the San Francisco high life, most prostitutes lived desperate lives that were shadowed by violence, disease, alcoholism, and crime.[60] Prostitutes in the mining camps worked in much drearier circumstances than the ones that Sheldon described in the city. Warren Saddler's brief sketch of a Sunday morning in the mines conveys how bleak prostitution in the mining districts could be. "We got up early—went to the pit—Then over to Gold-run, to look about, found nothing very flattering. We passed by the Grave-Yard—saw some persons digging graves—several at work digging gold and hundreds at work gambling—all in sight—and a party holding a sort of funeral and so it goes—You can imagine what else there is—a house just below where there are several Kanackers or Sandwich Island girls—there 'aint much of a crowd down there,'" he added wryly. Saddler portrayed the tedium of the mining districts where men waited their turn to have sex with a Hawaiian woman. The view from the bordello must have been just as monotonous. There is little romance in this vision of gold-rush prostitution.[61]

Not surprisingly, California Indians were among the first prostitutes in the mining districts. Like other women of color, they were believed by most Anglo miners to be racially inferior and acceptable only for temporary sexual gratification. Prostitution was not a usual part of California Indian society, but native women took it up in the most desperate circumstances. Starvation, Indian wars, and sexual assaults shaped their sexual lives.[62] The low prices that they received for their services demonstrated their desperation. Moreover, Indian prostitutes ran risks in their own communities, as an 1851 incident in southern Oregon shows. After a young, one-eyed Indian woman had intercourse with a miner for some food, her husband appeared and threatened her. The next day another Indian came to the camp and begged the whites to leave the women alone. He added that among his people the penalty for adultery was the loss of an eye.[63] Far from being part of an aristocracy, as Brother Sheldon had put it, Indian prostitutes were victims of racism and violence who were caught between two worlds with conflicting sexual values.

Rapes of Indian women were widespread in gold-rush California. Whites invaded rancherías and kidnapped tribeswomen. Even on a federal Indian reservation the agents responsible for the Indian inmates raped women "before the very eyes of their husbands and daughters," a newspaper reported, "and they dare not resent the insult, or even complain of the hideous outrage."[64] Some observers blamed sexual assaults for Indian warfare in northern California.[65]

Often Indians attacked white men who had assaulted native women, as in the case of Big Tom, a miner who met his end after abducting a Nisenan woman in 1855.[66] But some infuriated Indian men inflicted violence on tribeswomen who were the victims of white assailants. In 1859 a man named Abbott attempted to kidnap a Honcut Indian woman, and her husband killed her to keep her from the kidnapper. Subsequently Abbott wounded the husband with a pistol. Then the rest of the Indians badly beat Abbott, a fate that some whites believed was well deserved. The local newspaper expressed indignation that a "squaw man" like Abbott could endanger the countryside by inciting the Indians in this way.[67] There were many similar incidents in California in the 1850s.[68]

The gold rush was a deadly period for California Indians, male and female alike. During the 1850s their population declined from about 150,000 to 30,000, but Indian women evidently died at a more rapid rate than men, a circumstance that limited the ability of Indian society to recover demographic losses.[69] The deficit of Indian women intensified competition for potential wives in some Indian communities. In the mid-1850s John Sutter reported that fights over women were a special source of tension among the Nisenans who lived at his Hok Farm near Marysville. Sutter, who had lived among these Indians since 1839, reported that during drunken brawls Nisenan men assaulted women. One suitor murdered a woman who had resisted his importunities.[70] While perhaps not typical, these incidents show the horrific possibilities in a society with a rapidly declining population and few women.

One can hardly imagine more disparate places than the Franciscan missions, Upper Missouri fur posts, and California mines. Missionaries endeavored to change Indian sexual behavior with sharp limitations on old California customs—homosexuality, cross-gender sexuality, polygyny, and extramarital sex. Ultimately, they hoped to incorporate Indians into

Spanish society as part of Indian and mixed families where sanctioned conjugal relations could occur. What happened was a classic example of unintended results. Interracial rape became all too common and prostitution proliferated. Even mission Indian behavior was far from the Catholic standards that the Franciscans imposed. Moreover, while priests recorded thousands of Catholic marriages among Indians, there were disappointingly few mixed-race unions. The mission marriage records indicate that Hispanic Californians—whatever their racial origins—preferred to marry other Hispanos.[71] Sexual relations did not bring substantial numbers of Indian and Hispanic Californians together in stable families.

Fur traders, on the other hand, adapted some Indian sexual conventions. Circumstances compelled some of them to marry the women of their customers while others purchased slave women for conjugal pleasure, companionship, and the convenience of domestic service. Whites uniformly misunderstood the ceremonial significance of ritual intercourse and the ramifications for the transmission of power. Instead, traders emphasized sexual relations as an occasion for an exchange of goods rather than an exchange of strong medicine. Sexual services and female slaves became products for sale in the fur-trading marketplace as well as a reciprocal exchange that assured kinship alliances.[72]

During the gold rush Anglo-Americans forced their sexual needs on native women with no regard for Indian sexual customs. As the white population overwhelmed California, they also engulfed Indian society, impoverished native communities, and forced destitute women to prostitute themselves. Part of the invading population was imbued with a conquest mentality, fear and hatred of Indians that in their minds justified the rape of Indian women. The mining districts became an arena for assaults on women that further debilitated a population already in decline and suffering from a variety of infectious diseases.[73]

The mission, the fur trade, and the gold rush imperiled women and menaced Indian society, although we will never know with precision the extent of these adverse repercussions or how to compare them with other, more positive outcomes. However, there was one physiological result of Indian and white sexual relations that seems to have been nearly universal. From the banks of the wide Missouri to the shores of the rolling Pacific witnesses reported syphilis. This disease probably originated in the Western Hemisphere before Columbus, but Europeans carried the disease far and wide to populations that had not previously been exposed. So rapidly did syphilis spread in the mission region that in 1792 a Spanish naturalist traveling in California believed the disease was endemic among the Chumash.[74] Twenty years later the friars recorded it as the most prevalent and destructive disease in the missions.[75]

Syphilis and perhaps other sexually transmitted diseases were also common among the Missouri tribes. Lewis and Clark reported it among the Mandan.[76] The comments of the trader Tabeau suggested that syphilis was particularly virulent in the Upper Missouri region. "The venereal disease makes terrible ravages here and, from the moment it attacks a man, it makes more progress in eight days than elsewhere in five or six weeks," he claimed. The Indians had no cure for this disease but resorted to shamanistic treatment.[77] In the California gold fields syphilis was particularly loathsome and deadly among the Indians. In 1853 an Indian Office employee reported that many native women were forced into "open and disgusting acts of prostitution" from which they contracted syphilis. In one ranchería alone he saw nine women who were "so far advanced with this disease that they were unable to walk."[78]

Syphilis was much more than a temporary inconvenience for the infected victims. Sherburne Cook, a physiologist and demographer on the Berkeley faculty, reported that some infected mission Indians died outright from the immediate effects of the disease, while others were so enfeebled that they succumbed to other infectious diseases.[79] Other scholars also suggest that syphilis had a dramatic impact on Indian demographic decline: Syphilitic women tend to miscarry, and fetuses carried to term may be stillborn; live babies may be born with syphilis and not survive to adulthood; and untreated, the disease may lead to general debility, madness, and premature death.[80] Sexual contact let loose these profoundly negative biological consequences among western Indians who were already declining from other causes. The impact of syphilis and other sexually transmitted diseases needs particular attention. Medical research on the relationship between syphilis and HIV, or the AIDS virus, reveals much about the complexity and destructiveness of syphilis in combination with other diseases that should inform further historical inquiry.[81]

The history of Indian and white sexuality provides a sobering view of events that have too often been celebrated without due regard for the Indians who paid the price of conquest. Interracial sexuality provided a way to incorporate strangers in tribal life and created kinship ties with newcomers, yet it also put women at risk, subverted traditional gender roles, infected reciprocity with marketplace ethics, aggravated population decline, and thus weakened tribal society. This grim assessment should be taken into account as historians integrate Indian history with western women's history. Sacagawea may yet prove to be an enduring symbol for all of those unnamed other Indians who met with strangers in a time of dramatic upheavals and historic change. For them, crossing the bridge to the middle ground was fraught with possibilities and perils that ranged from the familiar comforts of family life to violent death. They sometimes crossed by force and other times by choice, but all of them went without assurances.

Notes

1. See Sylvia Van Kirk, *Many Tender Ties: Women in Fur-Trade Society, 1670–1870* (Norman: University of Oklahoma Press, 1980).

2. See especially Jennifer S. H. Brown, *Strangers in Blood: Fur Trade Company Families in Indian Country* (Vancouver, B.C.: University of British Columbia Press, 1980); Van Kirk, *Many Tender Ties*; Jacqueline Peterson and Jennifer S. H. Brown, eds., *The New Peoples: Being and*

Becoming Métis in North America (Lincoln: University of Nebraska Press, 1985); Gary Clayton Anderson, *Kinsmen of a Different Kind: Dakota-White in the Upper Mississippi Valley, 1650–1852* (Lincoln: University of Nebraska Press, 1984).

3. Mestizos did not always constitute a majority of frontier populations and they often claimed to be entirely Spanish, regardless of their ethnic and genetic background. Demographic studies of various locales in the Southwest clearly show the racially mixed quality of the populations, although the details varied substantially from place to place. David Weber, *The Spanish Frontier in North America* (New Haven, Conn.: Yale University Press, 1992), 8; Manuel Patricio Servín, "California's Hispanic Heritage: A View into the Spanish Myth," in *New Spain's Far Northern Frontier: Essays on Spain in the American West, 1540–1821,* ed. David J. Weber (Albuquerque: University of New Mexico Press, 1979), 117–33; Alicia Vidaurreta Tjarks, "Comparative Demographic Analysis of Texas, 1777–1793," in *New Spain's Far Northern Frontier,* 135–69; Ramón Gutiérrez, *When Jesus Came, the Corn Mothers Went Away: Marriage, Sexuality, and Power in New Mexico, 1500–1846* (Stanford, Calif.: Stanford University Press, 1991), table 5.3; Henry Dobyns, *Spanish Colonial Tucson: A Demographic History* (Tucson: University of Arizona Press, 1976).

4. Richard White, *The Middle Ground: Indians, Empires, and Republics in the Great Lakes Region, 1650–1815* (Cambridge, Eng.: Cambridge University Press, 1991), 65.

5. The word *berdache* is the most common term associated with Indian men's cross-gender roles. Europeans originally applied it to Indian men who assumed female roles, and thus they reduced numerous cross-gender roles to a single term. It comes from the Arabic *berdaj,* meaning a boy slave kept for sexual purposes. See Evelyn Blackwood, "Sexuality and Gender in Certain Native American Tribes: The Case of Cross-Gender Females," *Signs* 10, no. 1 (1984): 27–42, esp. 27.

6. For a historical overview of sexuality in the United States, see John D'Emilio and Estelle B. Freedman, *Intimate Matters: A History of Sexuality in America* (New York: Harper & Row, 1988), especially chap. 5 on race and sex. For other aspects of sex and gender, see also Richard Slotkin, *Regeneration through Violence: The Mythology of the American Frontier, 1600–1860* (Middletown, Conn.: Wesleyan University Press, 1973); Richard Slotkin, *The Fatal Environment: The Myth of the Frontier in the Age of Industrialization* (Middletown, Conn.: Wesleyan University Press, 1985); Ronald T. Takaki, *Iron Cages: Race and Culture in Nineteenth-Century America* (Seattle: University of Washington Press, 1979); Annette Kolodny, *The Lay of the Land: Metaphor as Experience and History in American Life and Letters* (Chapel Hill: University of North Carolina Press, 1975). Prostitution is perhaps the best-known aspect of western sexuality. See, for example, Anne Butler, *Daughters of Joy, Sisters of Misery: Prostitutes in the American West* (Urbana: University of Illinois Press, 1985); Marion S. Goldman, *Gold Diggers and Silver Miners: Prostitution and Social Life on the Comstock Lode* (Ann Arbor: University of Michigan Press, 1981); Sandra L. Myres, *Westering Women and the Frontier Experience, 1800–1915* (Albuquerque: University of New Mexico Press, 1982), 254–56; Julie Roy Jeffrey, *Frontier Women: The Trans-Mississippi West, 1840–1880* (New York: Hill and Wang, 1979), 107–46. Patricia Nelson Limerick has suggested that the history of western prostitutes can tell us something about gender relations, which in turn can help to illuminate Manifest Destiny. Limerick, *Legacy of Conquest: The Unbroken Past of the American West* (New York: W. W. Norton, 1987), 51. Demographers seldom speak explicitly about sexual behavior, but fertility is certainly reflective of sexuality. Walter Nugent, *Structures of American Social History* (Bloomington: Indiana University Press, 1981); Richard A. Easterlin, "Population Change and Farm Settlement in the Northern United States," *Journal of Economic History* 36 (1976): 45–75; Richard A. Easterlin, "Factors in the Decline of Farm Family Fertility in the United States: Some Preliminary Research Results," *Journal of American History* 63 (1976): 600–614; Jack Eblen, "An Analysis of Nineteenth-Century Frontier Populations," *Demography* 2 (1965): 399–413.

7. D'Emilio and Freedman, *Intimate Matters,* xii. For insights on how sexuality as a social construction changes through time, see Michel Foucault, *The History of Sexuality,* vol. 1, *An Introduction,* trans. Robert Hurley (New York: Pantheon, 1978); Michel Foucault, *The History*

of Sexuality, vol. 2, *The Use of Pleasure*, trans. Robert Hurley (New York: Pantheon, 1985). For a concise introduction to sexuality and its recent literature, see Jeffrey Weeks, *Sexuality* (New York: Ellis Horwood and Tavistock, 1986).

8. Joan Wallach Scott, "Gender: A Useful Category of Historical Analysis," in *Gender and the Politics of History*, ed. Joan Wallach Scott (New York: Columbia University Press, 1988), 28–50.

9. Carroll Smith-Rosenberg, *Disorderly Conduct: Visions of Gender in Victorian America* (New York: Oxford University Press, 1985), 19.

10. On the problems of reading biased sources, see Katherine Weist, "Beasts of Burden and Menial Slaves: Nineteenth Century Observations of Northern Plains Indian Women," in *The Hidden Half: Studies of Plains Indian Women*, ed. Patricia Albers and Beatrice Medicine (Washington, D.C.: University Press of America, 1983), 29–52. See also Rayna Green, *Native American Women: A Contextual Bibliography* (Bloomington: Indiana University Press, 1983); Gretchen M. Bataille and Kathleen Mullen Sands, *American Indian Women: Telling Their Lives* (Lincoln: University of Nebraska Press, 1984); James Axtell, *The Indian Peoples of Eastern America: A Documentary History of the Sexes* (New York: Oxford University Press, 1981).

11. John C. Ewers, *The Blackfeet: Raiders on the Northwestern Plains* (Norman: University of Oklahoma Press, 1958), 98.

12. Robert H. Lowie, *Indians of the Plains* (Lincoln: University of Nebraska Press, 1954; reprint ed., 1982), 78–79.

13. Ibid., 79–80; Ewers, *Blackfeet*, 99–100; Weist, "Beasts of Burden," 43–44.

14. Robert F. Heizer, "The California Indians: Archaeology, Varieties of Culture, Arts of Life," *California Historical Society Quarterly* 41 (March 1962): 5–6, 10–12; Nona C. Willoughby, "Division of Labor among the Indians of California," in *California Indians*, vol. 2, Garland American Indian Ethnohistory Series (New York: Garland, 1974), 60–68; Robert F. Heizer, ed., *Handbook of North American Indians*, vol. 8, *California* (Washington, D.C.: Smithsonian Institution, 1978), 498, 502, 511, 523, 544–45, 556, 566, 602, 684–85; Thomas Blackburn, ed., *December's Child: A Book of Chumash Oral Narratives* (Berkeley: University of California Press, 1975), 56–58, 137–38, 154–55.

15. For accounts that present the *berdache* as respected and important members of their societies, see Walter L. Williams, *The Spirit and the Flesh: Sexual Diversity in American Indian Culture* (Boston: Beacon Press, 1986); Will Roscoe, *The Zuni Man-Woman* (Albuquerque: University of New Mexico Press, 1991). Scholars who depict a more problematic role for the *berdache* are Raymond DeMallie, "Male and Female in Traditional Lakota Culture," in *Hidden Half*, 243–50; Ramón Gutiérrez, "Must We Deracinate Indians to Find Gay Roots?" *Out/Look* (Winter 1989): 61–67; Gutiérrez, *When Jesus Came*, 33–35.

16. Blackwood, "Sexuality and Gender."

17. Weist, "Beasts of Burden," 45.

18. Harold E. Driver, *Indians of North America*, 2d ed. (Chicago: University of Chicago Press, 1969), 222–41; David Smits, "The 'Squaw Drudge': A Prime Index of Savagism," *Ethnohistory* 29 (1982): 281–306; Axtell, *Indian Peoples*. For an observation on the husband's control over his wife's sexual services, see Francois-Antoine Larocque, "Journal of an Excursion of Discovery to the Rocky Mountains by M. Larocque in the Year 1805 from the 2d of June to the 18th of October," in *Early Fur Trade on the Northern Plains: Canadian Traders and the Mandan and Hidatsa Indians, 1738-1818*, ed. W. Raymond Wood and Thomas D. Thiessen (Norman: University of Oklahoma Press, 1985), 208. On the evolution of kinship after the fur trade, see Anderson, *Kinsmen of Another Kind*.

19. D'Emilio and Freedman, *Intimate Matters*, 19–20.

20. Carroll Smith-Rosenberg and Charles Rosenberg, "The Female Animal: Medical and Biological Views of Woman and Her Role in Nineteenth-Century America," *Journal of American History* 60 (September 1973): 332–56.

21. There is evidence that this interpretation of sexuality was at variance with sexual behavior. At least some Victorian women enjoyed sex, and some men exhibited a range of emotions that

transcended mere lust. Peter Gay, *The Bourgeois Experience: Victoria to Freud*, vol. 1, *Education of the Senses* (New York: Oxford University Press, 1984), 109–68; Carl N. Degler, *At Odds: Women and the Family in America from the Revolution to the Present* (New York: Oxford University Press, 1980), 249–78; Barbara Welter, "The Cult of True Womanhood, 1820–1860," *American Quarterly* 18 (Summer 1966): 151–74; and Carroll Smith-Rosenberg, "The Female World of Love and Ritual: Relations between Women in Nineteenth Century America," *Signs* 1 (Autumn 1975): 1–29.

22. Ann Twinam, "Honor, Sexuality, and Illegitimacy in Colonial Spanish America," in *Sexuality and Marriage in Colonial Latin America*, ed. Asunción Lavrin (Lincoln: University of Nebraska Press, 1989), 118–55; Janet Lecompte, "The Independent Women of New Mexico, 1821–1846," *Western Historical Quarterly* 11 (1981): 17–35; Gutiérrez, *When Jesus Came*; Elizabeth Kuzenoff and Robert Oppenheimer, "The Family and Society in Nineteenth-Century Latin America: An Historiographical Introduction," *Journal of Family History* 10 (Fall 1985): 215–34; Patricia Seed, "The Church and the Patriarchal Family: Marriage Conflicts in Sixteenth- and Seventeenth-Century New Spain," *Journal of Family History* 10 (Fall 1985): 284–93; Ramón A. Gutiérrez, "Honor, Ideology, Marriage Negotiation, and Class-Gender Domination in New Mexico, 1690–1846," *Latin American Perspectives* 12 (Winter 1985): 81–104; Ramón A. Gutiérrez, "From Honor to Love: Transformations of the Meaning of Sexuality in Colonial New Mexico," in *Kinship Ideology and Practice in Latin America*, ed. Raymond T. Smith (Chapel Hill: University of North Carolina Press, 1984), 238–63.

23. Gutiérrez, *When Jesus Came*, 176–240; Guillermo Céspedes, *Latin America: The Early Years* (New York: Alfred A. Knopf, 1974), 55–56; Asunción Lavrin, "Sexuality in Colonial Mexico: A Church Dilemma," in *Sexuality and Marriage*, 57–58.

24. Kjerstie Nelson, *Marriage and Divorce Practices in Native California* (Berkeley, Calif.: Archaeological Research Facility, Department of Anthropology, 1975).

25. Albert L. Hurtado, "Sexuality in California's Franciscan Missions: Cultural Perceptions and Sad Realities," *California History* 71 (Fall 1992): 370–85, 451–53. For surviving California confessional dialogues containing questions about sexuality, see Harry Kelsey, ed., *The Doctrina and Confesionario of Juan Cortés* (Altadena, Calif.: Howling Coyote Press, 1979), 107–23; Madison S. Beeler, ed., *The Ventureño Confesionario of José Señan, O.F.M.*, University of California Publications in Linguistics, vol. 47 (Berkeley: University of California Press, 1967).

26. Pedro Fages, *A Historical, Political, and Natural Description of California by Pedro Fages*, trans. Herbert Ingram Priestly (1937; reprint ed. Ramona, Calif.: Ballena Press, 1972), 48, 33.

27. Font quoted in Herbert E. Bolton, ed. and trans., *Font's Complete Diary: A Chronicle of the Founding of San Francisco* (Berkeley: University of California Press, 1931), 105.

28. Francisco Palóu, *Palóu's Life of Fray Junípero Serra*, trans and ed. Maynard J. Geiger, O.F.M. (Washington, D.C.: American Academy of Franciscan History, 1945), 198, 199.

29. Ibid.

30. Geronimo Boscana, *Chingichnich: A Historical Account* (New York: Wiley & Putnam, 1846), 282, 334–35. Boscana also noted transvestism and homosexual marriage, which he regarded as a "horrible custom," 283–84.

31. Daniel J. Garr, "Rare and Desolate Land: Population and Race in Hispanic California," *Western Historical Quarterly* 6 (April 1975): 135–37.

32. Jayme in Maynard J. Geiger, O.F.M., *Letter of Luís Jayme, O.F.M., San Diego, October 17, 1772* (Los Angeles: Dawson's Book Shop, 1970), 38, 39.

33. Serra to Antonio María de Bucareli y Ursua, 22 April 1773, in Serra, *Writings of Junípero Serra*, vol. 1, ed. Antonine Tibesar (Washington, D.C.: Academy of American Franciscan History, 1955–1966), 341. Serra's missionary work is currently a matter of hot debate. See James Sandos, "Junípero Serra's Canonization and the Historical Record," *American Historical Review* 93 (December 1988): 1253–69; Rupert Costo and Jeannette Henry Costo, *The Missions of California: A Legacy of Genocide* (San Francisco: Indian Historian Press, 1987).

34. Hubert Howe Bancroft, *History of California*, vol. 1 (San Francisco: The History Company, 1886–90), 249–54. Franciscan historian Maynard J. Geiger attributes rape as a principal cause of the San Diego revolt in Geiger, ed., *Letter of Luís Jayme*, xxx.

35. Serra to Rafael Verger, 8 August 1779, in Serra, *Writings*, vol. 3, 349–51.

36. Sherburne Cook, "The Indian versus the Spanish Mission," *Ibero-Americana* 21 (1943): 107, 108.

37. See the responses of Indian rebels Leopoldo, Senen, and Fernando Huiliaset, 1 June 1824, in Sherburne F. Cook, ed., "Expeditions to the Interior of California: Central Valley, 1820–1840," *University of California Anthropological Records* 20, no. 5 (1962): 153–54; James A. Sandos, "Levantamiento!: The 1824 Chumash Uprising Reconsidered," *Southern California Quarterly* 67 (Summer 1985): 109–133; Albert L. Hurtado, *Indian Survival on the California Frontier* (New Haven, Conn.: Yale University Press, 1988), 37–39.

38. Maynard Geiger, O.F.M., trans., and Clement W. Meighan, ed., *As the Padres Saw Them: California Indian Life and Customs as Reported by the Franciscan Missionaries, 1813–1815* (Santa Barbara, Calif.: Santa Barbara Mission Archives, 1976), 105–6.

39. Heizer, ed., *Handbook of North American Indians*, vol. 8, 502, reports only one tribe (the Salinan) that practiced prostitution. It is difficult to know if the apparent rarity of prostitution reflects precontact reality or points to defects in modern reporting.

40. Jayme, *Letter of Luís Jayme*, 44–46.

41. Serra to Felipe de Neve, 7 January 1780, in Serra, *Writings*, vol. 3, 409–13.

42. José Longinos, *Journal of José Longinos Martínez: Notes and Observations of the Naturalist of the Botanical Expedition in Old and New California and the South Coast, 1791–1792* (San Francisco: n.p., 1961), 55.

43. William H. Goetzmann, "The Mountain Man as Jacksonian Man," *American Quarterly* 15 (1963): 402–415; Wilbur R. Jacobs, "Frontiersmen, Fur Traders, and Other Varmints: An Ecological Appraisal of the Frontier in American History," *American Historical Association Newsletter* 8 (November 1970): 5–11; David J. Wishart, *The Fur Trade of the American West, 1807–1840* (Lincoln: University of Nebraska Press, 1979). For traders' attitudes toward Indians, see Lewis O. Saum, *The Fur Trader and the Indian* (Seattle: University of Washington Press, 1965).

44. William Swagerty, "Marriage and Settlement Patterns of the Rocky Mountain Trappers and Traders," *Western Historical Quarterly* 11 (1980): 159–80; Brown, *Strangers in Blood*, 73–74, 111–30, 199–230; Van Kirk, *Many Tender Ties*, 28–52, 231–42.

45. Roy W. Meyer, *The Village Indians of the Upper Missouri* (Lincoln: University of Nebraska Press, 1977); Raymond W. Wood, and Thomas D. Thiessen, eds., *Early Fur Trade on the Northern Plains: Canadian Traders among the Mandan and Hidatsa Indians, 1738–1818. The Narratives of John Macdonnell, David Thompson, Francois-Antoine Larocque, and Charles McKenzie* (Norman: University of Oklahoma Press, 1985), 3–8; Edward M. Bruner, "Mandan," in *Perspectives in American Indian Culture Change*, ed. Edward M. Spicer (Chicago: University of Chicago Press, 1961), 187–277.

46. David Thompson quoted in Bruner, "Mandan,", 69.

47. Alice B. Kehoe, "The Function of Ceremonial Sexual Intercourse among the Northern Plains Indians," *Plains Anthropologist* 15 (May 1970): 99–103.

48. Annie Heloise Abel, *Tabeau's Narrative of Loisel's Expedition to the Upper Missouri*, trans. Rose Abel Wright (Norman: University of Oklahoma Press, 1939), 197. James Ronda discusses the buffalo-calling ceremony in *Lewis and Clark among the Indians* (Lincoln: University of Nebraska Press, 1984), 107, 131–32.

49. Ronda, *Lewis and Clark*, 256–59.

50. Annie Heloise Abel, ed., *Chardon's Journal at Fort Clark, 1834–1839* (Pierre: Department of History, State of South Dakota, 1932), 164, 168.

51. Charles McKenzie, "Some Account of the Missouri Indians in the Years 1804, 5, 6, & 7," in *Early Fur Trade*, 263–64.

52. Ibid., 264–65.

53. Weist, "Beasts of Burden," 44.

54. Abel, ed., *Chardon's Journal*, 165.

55. Ibid., 181.

56. Albert L. Hurtado, "'Hardly a Farm House—A Kitchen without Them': Indian and White Households on the California Borderland Frontier in 1860," *Western Historical Quarterly* 13 (1982): 245–70; Hurtado, *Indian Survival*, 39–71.

57. Brigham D. Madsen, *The Shoshone Frontier and the Bear River Massacre* (Salt Lake City: University of Utah Press, 1985), 33.

58. John Wayman, *A Doctor on the California Trail: The Diary of Dr. John Hudson Wayman from Cambridge City, Indiana, to the Gold Fields in 1852*, ed. Edgely Woodman Todd (Denver: Old West Publishing, 1971), 70.

59. H. B. Sheldon to Dear Friends, 25 June 1852, H. B. Sheldon Papers, California Room, State Library, Sacramento.

60. Butler, *Daughters of Joy*.

61. Warren Saddler, undated entry [1849 or 1850], MS Journal, vol. 2, Bancroft Library, University of California, Berkeley.

62. Hurtado, *Indian Survival*, 169–92.

63. Herman Francis Reinhart, *The Golden Frontier: The Recollections of Herman Francis Reinhart, 1851–1865* (Austin: University of Texas Press, 1962), 45.

64. San Francisco Bulletin, 13 September 1856, quoted in Robert F. Heizer, ed., *The Destruction of the California Indians* (Santa Barbara, Calif.: Peregrine Smith, 1974), 278.

65. Sacramento *Union*, 1 October 1858, quoted in Heizer, ed., *Destruction of California Indians*, 279–80.

66. Sacramento *Daily Democratic State Journal*, 1 September 1855, quoted in Robert F. Heizer, ed., *They Were Only Diggers: A Collection of Articles from California Newspapers, 1851–1866, on Indian and White Relations* (Ramona, Calif.: Ballena Press, 1974), 29.

67. Butte *Democrat*, 24 September 1859.

68. See, for example, newspaper articles reprinted in Heizer, ed., *Destruction of California Indians*, 278–83.

69. Hurtado, *Indian Survival*, 169–92.

70. Sutter to Thomas J. Henley, 9 February 1856, Letters Received, Office of Indian Affairs, California Superintendency, 1849–1880, National Archives, RG 75, microfilm publication M234, reel 35; Albert L. Hurtado, "Indians in Town and Country: The Nisenan Indians' Changing Economy and Society as Shown in John A. Sutter's 1856 Correspondence," *American Indian Culture and Research Journal* 12, no. 2 (1988): 31–51.

71. Sherburne F. Cook and Woodrow Borah, *Essays in Population History: Mexico and California* (Berkeley: University of California Press, 1979), 278–310.

72. Anderson, *Kinsmen of Another Kind*, xi–xii, 58–76, 226–260.

73. Hurtado, *Indian Survival*, 169–92.

74. Longinos, *Journal*, 44.

75. Geiger and Meighan, eds., *As the Padres Saw Them*, 71–80.

76. Donald Jackson, ed., *Letters of the Lewis and Clark Expedition with Related Documents*, 2d ed., vol. 2 (Urbana: University of Illinois Press, 1978), 506, 521.

77. Abel, *Tabeau's Narrative*, 183.

78. E. A. Stevenson to Thomas J. Henley, 31 December 1853, quoted in Heizer, ed., *Destruction of California Indians*, 13–16.

79. Cook, "Indian versus the Spanish Mission," 28, 101–13.

80. Geiger and Meighan, eds., *As the Padres Saw Them*, 7; Brenda J. Baker and George J. Armelagos, "The Origin and Antiquity of Syphilis: Paleopathological Diagnosis and Interpretation," *Current Anthropology* 29 (1988): 703–37.

81. Edward W. Hook III, "Syphilis and HIV Infection," *The Journal of Infectious Diseases* 160 (September 1989): 530–34.

PART THREE

Resisting Conquest

Conquered people, we used to believe, were passive victims, robbed of everything, bereft of strength and will to fight back. Now that we are beginning to understand the continuing resources of agency and identity within each person and every culture, we must revise our ideas about the invaded peoples of North America.[1]

This task is all the more necessary if, as Patricia Limerick has argued, conquest and its consequences are defining characteristics of western history. When viewed through the eyes of racial ethnic women, conquest turns out to be quite complicated.[2]

The first and most common understanding of conquest is military. Because of the way most western history used to be written, we think first of violent conflict—the Indian and Mexican-American wars, in particular—and of the rapid Euro-American occupation in the nineteenth century. But military "victory" and "defeat" are often inadequate to describe the subsequent relationships among different peoples. What happens after the battle is equally important. Crucial cultural and territorial changes followed military victory, and the violence hardly ended on the battlefield.

In the largest cultural terms, the American Indian and Spanish Mexican inhabitants of the land were denied their identities. As the result of the Mexican-American War (1845–48) and of the succession of Indian wars that continued through the 1880s, they became conquered peoples whom the Euro-Americans redefined in their own terms. Euro-Americans thought of these different conquered peoples in large, generic racial terms that grouped diverse indigenous peoples into the category "Indian," collapsed the complex racial and ethnic population of the Spanish northern frontier (described in the Editors' Introduction) into the category "Mexican," and denied completely a distinct cultural identity to mestizos, mulattos, and métis.

One consequence of this racial labeling was segregation. American Indians were confined to reservations or forcibly removed to Indian Territory (the *present state of Oklahoma). In the region that became known as the American Southwest, Mexicans long remained a numerical majority but, with the exception of a small group of elites, were segregated by a dual labor system into poorly paid, low-status jobs that were considered appropriate for their "race." Summing up these changes, Richard White noted, "The conquests created vanquished peoples who have remained distinct, unassimilated, and largely in place."*[3]

Nor was this the end of conquest. The articles in this section demonstrate that the continuing struggles over control of land and resources were always cultural struggles that involved women on both sides.

Frederick Jackson Turner's frontier thesis will forever be associated with the most celebrated process in western history. According to Turner, each new frontier in turn marked the dividing line between "savagery" and "civilization," and each followed the same stages of settlement. Successively, the trapper, the cattleman, the miner, and the farmer used the land for his own purposes. Turner never doubted that these successive occupations represented the inevitable march of progress. Nor did he question the idea that the progression of each stage to the next led to the improvement of the "savage" people who lay on the other side of the frontier line.[4]

Seen through the eyes of conquered racial ethnic women, however, the movement from "savagery" to "civilization" was simply a slower form of conquest. As Darlis Miller shows in her article in this section, in the early period of Euro-American settlement in the Southwest, women often took the lead in developing cooperative, interethnic strategies for survival. Incoming Euro-American women, unfamiliar with the land, depended on the knowledge and help of women of other races who were already there. Many diaries and reminiscences by Euro-American women throughout the West described friendly initial contacts with American Indian or Mexican women. But these encounters occurred within a larger context. As the Euro-American population grew in numbers and political power, cooperation became less common. Indeed, we could argue that "civilization" was achieved when Euro-American control was complete and such cooperation was no longer necessary. The same general point could be made about intercultural marriage. Euro-American men at first benefited from the domestic support and the kin and trade networks they gained by marrying indigenous women. Inevitably, however, as Coll-Peter Thrush and Robert Keller show, Indian and métis women married to white men were scorned and mistreated by whites. They could not return to the traditional life of native communities that had been eroded by white settlement.

Even more complicated struggles occurred on American Indian reservations following passage of the Dawes Act in 1887. That act, which remained the cornerstone of U.S. Indian policy until the New Deal, decreed that tribal lands were to be divided into private parcels and farmed by individual nuclear families. This policy, from the government's perspective, had two benefits. It would open up large parts of the remaining tribal lands to white homesteaders and railroads, and it would "raise" American Indians up the "ladder of civilization" by turning nomadic peoples into sedentary *farmers. In other words, it would destroy their autonomy and force them to assimilate. The Dawes Act imposed Euro-American ideas about marriage, gender roles, and private property upon reservation Indians. They resisted not just because of different ideas about the land but because the allotment process threatened traditional gender relationships.*

Some of the complexities of conquest were acted out in the activities of Euro-American women reformers, who were rarely aware of the harm they did while seeking to do good. The encounters between women reformers and their clients have been explored most extensively by historian Peggy Pascoe, who charted middle-class white women's efforts to gain social authority by exercising deeply held moral commitments to help other women who did not necessarily share their values and assumptions.[5] Euro-American women organized settlement houses, rescue missions, schools, and outreach programs to ameliorate poverty for women of other races, classes, and cultures and to rescue them from the moral transgressions of men. Like Annie Bidwell, whom Margaret Jacobs considers in her article, they often acted from assumptions about the desirability of "more civilized" Christian values and Euro-American gender roles. Generally well intentioned, many reform programs were also ethnocentric and class-biased. The reformers condemned customs and practices that were deeply significant for the women they sought to help. However, as Wendy Wall's article also shows, Indian women did not necessarily accept the superior merit of white middle-class values. Although few racial ethnic women had the resources to organize for themselves, they were active participants in these cultural exchanges, selecting what was useful to them from the help they were offered and rejecting or only partially assimilating the moral agendas of their middle-class rescuers.

It is also well to remember, as Genaro Padilla reminds us, that the losers in western conquests did not take their defeat quietly. That we do not already know about their protests is not because they were silent but because until recently we have overlooked their accounts in building a smooth narrative of conquest. Furthermore, the male bias that still lingers in western history has prevented us from appreciating the full spectrum of resistance activities. Seen through the resister's eyes, the act of becoming pregnant as a strategy for getting expelled from a hated Bureau of Indian Affairs boarding school was as courageous as facing the guns of the U.S. Army at Wounded Knee.

Understanding the choices faced by women of both conquering and conquered groups can inform every aspect of conquest. Their stories are often deeply painful: Many people and much cultural heritage were irreparably lost. But the stories also tell us much about cultural survival and adaptation and thus give us a way to think specifically and deeply about that continuous process of change that everyone, "winners" and "losers," experienced in the settlement of the West.

Notes

1. See, for example, Oscar Handlin's classic account of immigration, *The Uprooted* (Boston: Little, Brown, 1951) and Stanley Elkins's 1959 portrait of African slaves stripped of their African heritage, *Slavery: A Problem in American Institutional and Intellectual Life* (Chicago: University of Chicago Press, 1959). Both of these influential studies have now been superseded by more complex and nuanced studies.

2. Patricia Nelson Limerick, *Legacy of Conquest: The Unbroken Past of the American West* (New York: W. W. Norton, 1987).

3. Richard White, "Race Relations in the American West," *American Quarterly* 38, no. 3 (1986): 398.

4. Frederick Jackson Turner, "The Significance of the Frontier in American History," *Annual Report of the American Historical Association for the Year 1893* (Washington, D.C.: U.S. Government Printing Office, 1894).

5. Peggy Pascoe, *Relations of Rescue: The Search for Female Moral Authority in the American West, 1874–1939* (New York: Oxford University Press, 1990). For an international parallel, see Margaret Strobel, *Gender, Sex and Empire*, in Essays on Global and Comparative History Series (Washington, D.C.: American Historical Association, 1993).

7.

The Women of Lincoln County, 1860–1900

DARLIS MILLER

In this essay, Darlis Miller looks at the story beneath the story in one of the West's most notorious places, Lincoln County, New Mexico. The well-known violence of the Lincoln County War of the 1870s has distracted attention from the ongoing story of settlement, which Miller explores by carefully reconstructing the lives of nineteenth-century Hispanic and Anglo women. In so doing, she has followed one of Gerda Lerner's most famous suggestions for doing women's history: "Always ask what did the women do while the men were doing what the textbook tells us was important."[1]

Miller's focus on the women overturns many common assumptions. This mixed community, at first predominantly Hispanic, survived not by the individualism for which the frontier is famous, but by cooperation. Indeed, Miller argues that the crude and dangerous conditions—some of which were created by their own violent men—lessened racial and class differences between women and fostered cooperation. Miller documents the ways in which the work of women of all racial ethnic groups was essential and highly valued not only by their own families but by their communities.

This essay, first published in 1986, was one of the first to illustrate how much information about women can be "mined" from apparently sparse source materials. Miller builds a solid basis for her article by drawing on federal and state censuses, agricultural schedules, probate records and tax rolls. To that she adds evidence from scattered (and usually Anglo) reminiscences and oral histories, newspapers, and the occasional mention of women in county histories.

The article points to a larger issue concerning western history. As Anglo dominance over Hispanos was achieved in Lincoln County, the story of the multicultural cooperation of pioneer women disappeared from the histor-ical record. Only the violent story of the Lincoln County War remained in the history books, even though, as Miller so clearly shows, it is only part of the story of settlement.

From the nearly deserted mining town of White Oaks, twelve miles northeast of Carrizozo, eighty-three-year-old Susan McSween Barber wrote in a letter dated 23 November 1928: "I am now in this place, White

Oaks, still trying to do business and am very old but supple."[2] This perseverance in spite of age and previous misfortune was characteristic of Barber throughout her entire life. One of New Mexico's most successful women ranchers from 1881 to 1902, she was a key figure in the Lincoln County War and witnessed the violence that surrounded the death of her husband, Alexander McSween, during the 1870s. A similar firmness of character helped many other Lincoln County women to survive—and even to flourish—in the crude frontier environment of nineteenth-century southeastern New Mexico.

Settled by Hispanic and Anglo farmers in the 1850s, Lincoln County has become one of the best-known counties in the West, primarily because of the Lincoln County War and other violent episodes that punctuated the county's early history. Modern-day writers have focused on this violence, ignoring topics that would lead to a better understanding of the lives of pioneer families who lived there. To shed light on their experiences, this article will focus on nineteenth-century Lincoln County women, primarily Hispanic and Anglo women, giving special attention to their economic contributions to family and community.

The sources for reconstructing the history of these women are limited. They consist primarily of manuscript census returns, deed books, probate records, a few newspaper accounts, military records, a handful of oral histories, two memoirs written by Anglo women, and secondary accounts authored by Eve Ball and James D. Shinkle. This description of Lincoln County women, therefore, is necessarily incomplete. Nonetheless, by careful analysis of the sources, it has been possible to sketch the central patterns of these women's lives.

At the end of the Civil War, Americans entered an era of exploitation and expansion. Eastern states experienced rapid industrial and urban growth while western states and territories filled with miners, railroad workers, farm and ranch families, and other westward-traveling Americans. New Mexicans migrated internally during these years and established new homes and farms in promising agricultural locations. Some became pioneer settlers in Lincoln County, which was carved out of eastern Socorro County in 1869. The county seat was located at Rio Bonito, also called Las Placitas, but shortly renamed Lincoln. Boundary changes in 1878 enlarged the county so that it stretched across the entire southeast quarter of New Mexico. It is uncertain when the first colonists of European descent found their way to the rich bottomlands of the Bonito, Ruidoso, and Hondo Rivers. Authorities generally agree, however, that permanent settlement became possible after Fort Stanton was established on the Rio Bonito in 1855. Not only did the garrison offer protection against Mescalero Apaches who were resisting encroachment on their lands, but it also provided a market for surplus crops raised by local farmers.[3]

By 1860 276 people resided at Rio Bonito, located nine miles southeast of Fort Stanton. Although sources are not available for a full description of this early settlement, census returns provide information about its composition. This was a mixed community of 193 Hispanos, 66 Anglos, 14 children of Hispanic mothers and Anglo fathers, 1 male and 1 female Indian servant, and 1 six-year-old black girl residing with an Anglo farm family. Living in the community were 77 Hispanic women (7 of whom were married to Anglo men), 6 daughters of mixed marriages, and 19 Anglo women (9 married women and their daughters). All but 7 women were living in some kind of family relationship, either as wife or daughter of a male head of household, whereas at least 68 adult men were living as single men, many working as herders, teamsters, and laborers for more prosperous farm families. Two of the above 7 women, fifty-year-old Nepomucena Silvestre and her twenty-five-year-old daughter Barbara, were living together, supporting themselves as seamstresses. One Hispanic woman, Manuelita Miller, lived alone although she was married to Canadian-born William Miller who was working as a laborer on a nearby ranch. Although women composed only 38 percent of the population, the gender imbalance—a ratio of 17 men to 10 women—was much less than that found in some parts of the West.[4] The ratio of men to women in Colorado in 1860, for example, was 34 to 1; in Arizona in 1870 it was 4 to 1.[5]

The majority of Rio Bonito women, Hispanic and Anglo alike, lived in farm families, their families either owning a farm or the male head of household laboring for other farm owners. The twenty-five farms listed in the 1860 agricultural census ranged in size from sixty-five acres to six hundred acres and in value from two hundred dollars to nine thousand dollars.[6] Some men classified as laborers undoubtedly owned small plots of land on which they raised subsistence crops, although this acreage was not recorded in the agricultural census. The most substantial farm in Rio Bonito was owned by H. M. Beckwith and his Hispanic wife, Refugia, who claimed one hundred acres of improved and five hundred acres of unimproved land valued at nine thousand dollars. In 1860, they owned nine horses, four mules, fifty cows, twenty-eight oxen, sixty beef cattle, and twenty-two hogs. During the preceding year they had harvested sixty bushels of wheat, six hundred bushels of corn, forty bushels of beans, two hundred fifty bushels of Irish potatoes, and fifty tons of hay, and they had manufactured one hundred pounds of butter.[7]

Refugia Beckwith was among the women who soon fled the new settlement. Confederate troops invaded New Mexico in 1861, and shortly thereafter Union soldiers evacuated Fort Stanton, firing the buildings and destroying surplus supplies. Shorn of military protection, Rio Bonito settlers packed their belongings and left for settlements in the valleys of the Rio Grande. Colonel Christopher Carson and the New Mexico volunteers, however, reoccupied the post in the fall of 1862, and their successful campaign against the Mescaleros encouraged settlers to return.[8] By late December, Carson reported that settlements were springing up rapidly on the Bonito and Ruidoso Rivers and that a large quantity of wheat had already been planted. Military officials believed that the country near Fort Stanton contained some of the best grazing and agricultural lands in the territory, and they encouraged settlers to raise more crops in order to reduce the cost of forage and subsistence stores.[9]

Many women who settled along the Bonito and Ruidoso came from the villages of Manzano, San Acacio, and Belen. Among families who migrated from Manzano, a small settlement on the eastern slope of the Manzano Mountains, was that of Geralda and Gregorio Herrera, who moved to Las Placitas (Lincoln) soon after their marriage in 1860. In August of the following year, Geralda gave birth to a daughter, Lorencita. Unfortunately, Gregorio was killed a few days later, and Geralda returned to Manzano where she placed her baby daughter in the care of an aunt, Trinidad Herrera. Sometime later, Geralda, Trinidad, and Lorencita moved back to Las Placitas, where the latter married José D. Miranda in 1877.[10] Among members of the Miranda family who had migrated to Lincoln County from the Rio Grande village of San Acacio, located about fifteen miles north of Socorro, was twelve-year-old Prudencia Miranda, a cousin of José's. Prudencia had crossed the Gallinas Mountains in a wagon drawn by oxen with her parents in 1862. That expedition eventually consisted of fifteen wagons as several other families joined the Miranda party seeking protection against possible Indian attack.[11] Still other Lincoln County women had their origins in the Rio Grande village of Belen. Dolorita Aguilar Carbajal was born in Belen in 1807 and moved by ox-drawn wagon to Lincoln County in 1870 with her husband and several children.[12]

These women were members of families attracted to the fertile agricultural and fine grazing lands along streams flowing out of the White Mountains. By June 1866, three hundred Hispanos and five Anglos were living along the Rio Bonito, where they were cultivating crops of corn, wheat, and beans and herding about five hundred head of sheep, goats, and cattle. Forty Anglos and eighty Hispanos were raising similar crops and herding a small number of cattle along the Ruidoso and Hondo Rivers.[13]

The main factor retarding further agricultural development, however, and further immigration by women, was continued opposition by the Mescalero Apaches. Although the Mescaleros had been forcibly removed to the Bosque Redondo Reservation along the Pecos River early in 1863, they remained under military surveillance only a short time before they quietly slipped away to continue their traditional way of life in the mountains of southeastern New Mexico and northern Mexico.[14] Even during the Bosque Redondo Reservation period, however, about one hundred Mescaleros remained at large, threatening to dislodge white settlers from their newly established homes. In May 1863, a party of Indians raided farmers on the Ruidoso, killing one man, driving off his stock, and then boldly entering Las Placitas and driving off more stock. By September some of the families along the Ruidoso had deserted their farms; others near Fort Stanton were so destitute of food that they were described as being "almost in a starving condition" and the post's commander was authorized to issue them provisions.[15] Three years later, over seventy Rio Bonito men appealed to General James H. Carleton, commander of troops in New Mexico, for protection from Mescalero raiders. The settlers were poorly armed and would have to leave if left unprotected: "Some of us have slings, some have bows without arrows and others who are the best armed have firearms but no ammunition."[16] Carleton gave assurances that he would do all he could to aid settlers in opening the region "to civilization," and the army later established pickets at Nesmith's mill on the Ruidoso and at the junction of the Bonito and Ruidoso Rivers. But the raids continued, and farm families living in unprotected areas became more and more discouraged.[17]

Despite the fact that most settlers in the 1860s lost stock in Indian raids, the fertile countryside continued to attract new residents, and the female population slowly increased.[18] By 1870 the population of Lincoln County was 1,803, including 1,465 Hispanos, 270 Anglos, 54 children of Hispanic mothers and Anglo fathers, and 14 blacks. Women now represented 41 percent of the population, and the sex ratio was 14 men to 10 women. Among the Hispanic population the sex ratio was almost even, for living in the county were 687 Hispanic women (47 percent of the Hispanic population), but only 23 Anglo women (9 percent of the Anglo population). Taking each ethnic group as a unit and excluding daughters of mixed marriages, the ratio of men to women in the Hispanic community was 11 to 10 and that in the Anglo community was 107 to 10. The 23 Anglo women consisted of 13 married women and their daughters. Four Anglo women were soldiers' wives employed as laundresses at Fort Stanton, and 2 others were officers' wives. Approximately 43 Hispanic women were married to Anglo men, representing about 12 percent of the married Hispanic women. Twenty-five daughters of mixed marriages and 5 black women also resided in the county. Anglo women, then, were only 3 percent of the total female population.[19]

Although few Anglo women resided in Lincoln County, most shared with Hispanic women the common experience of living in farm families. Most Hispanic and Anglo women established homes, became mothers, and cared for families on farms. They also were economic producers, contributing to whatever economic success their families attained. Roughly 81 percent of Hispanic and Anglo women lived and worked on one of the 368 farms listed in the Lincoln County 1870 agricultural census. Many of the farms were small affairs; 90 percent contained less than fifty acres, 31 percent less than twenty acres.[20]

Typical of the different types of farms were those of the Flores, the Miranda, and the Baca families. Abrana Flores and her husband, Ramon, owned a small farm near the town of Lincoln. The Floreses farmed 12 improved acres and owned one horse and three hogs. In 1869 they harvested 24 bushels of wheat and 175 bushels of corn, the grain being valued at $300. Thirty-two-year-old Leonarda Miranda and her husband, José, cultivated a more prosperous farm in the same vicinity. They claimed 40 acres of improved land valued at $500. They owned two horses, two milk cows, eight oxen, and seven hogs, and in 1869 they had

Saturnina Baca, Josefa Baca
Corbet, Carlota Baca, and
Sam Corbet. (Courtesy Rio
Grande Historical Collec-
tions, New Mexico State Uni-
versity Library.)

produced 80 bushels of wheat and 500 bushels of corn valued at $1,500.
One of the most successful farm families in the town of Lincoln was that
of Juana and Saturnino Baca, who owned 100 acres of improved and 220
acres of unimproved land valued at $6,000. They owned three horses, one
milk cow, four oxen, and five hogs. During 1869 they produced $1,450
worth of grain—30 bushels of wheat, 500 bushels of corn, 200 bushels
of oats, and 175 bushels of barley. Farms in Lincoln County generally
were larger and more productive than those, say, in Socorro and Santa Fe
Counties, and in only two counties, San Miguel and Taos, did the total
value of all farm production in 1869 exceed that of Lincoln County.[21]
    It is difficult to know just what these farm households of Abrana,
Leonarda, and Juana were like, but primitive living conditions generated
a rough kind of equality among farm families who clearly exhibited social
and economic differences. Some poorer residents lived in jacales, simple
structures made of posts stuck in the ground and plastered with mud.[22]
Most of the farmhouses, however, were flat-roofed adobes with hard-
packed dirt floors. Barbara Jones's first home in the Hondo Valley was
described as a crude hut of logs, poles, and earth, with a blanket covering
the door opening.[23] Ellen Casey's first home near the junction of the
Ruidoso and the Hondo was more spacious if not more elegant: a two
room adobe dwelling, the rooms fourteen by sixteen feet, with dirt floors
and dirt roof.[24] Helena Anne Coe, soon after her marriage, moved into one

of the first houses built in the Ruidoso Valley, consisting of a single room twenty by forty feet, with a dirt floor, flat dirt roof, no windows, and a single door.[25]

Some women remembered a tradition of cooperation among women in the early stages of community building. Looking back on her early years in Lincoln, Lorenzita Miranda recalled that "[People] helped each other with their work. If someone was building a home, neighbors would help build it. If wheat was being cut, everyone would gather to help. . . . Women friends would help their neighbor when they had a bunch of men to feed. . . . Many people that were poor and had small crops, received food in payment when they helped their neighbors."[26] Hispanic residents also welcomed Anglo newcomers, helping them to build homes, fence fields, and construct *acequias* and teaching them methods of irrigation. When Barbara Jones entered her new home at Picacho, ten miles east of the Ruidoso and Bonito junction, she discovered a generous supply of food prepared by women of the village. Hispanic women later taught Jones to prepare chiles and to use a metate and mano to grind corn. The women also exchanged healing lore; the Hispanic women taught Jones to gather herbs and Jones freely shared her medicines. After moving near Fort Stanton, Jones established friendly relations with some Mescalero women. She treated their sick babies and exchanged food for buckskin, from which she made jackets and gloves for her family and neighbors.[27] Women also shared the dangers of childbirth. Sources on this topic for Lincoln County are limited to statements by Anglo women, who expressed fear at being alone at childbirth. The surgeon at Fort Stanton handled some maternity cases, and Barbara Jones served as midwife to Hispanic neighbors. On one occasion, Jones herself gave birth with only her teenage son in attendance. Undoubtedly there were other noted midwives in the small Hispanic communities. Primitive medical knowledge, however, could not prevent tragedies: Barbara Jones's son Sam married in succession two Gordon sisters, and each died in childbirth.[28]

Most of the women were young frontier mothers. The 1870 census demonstrates that the average household in Lincoln County, like any newly settled area, contained very few children. In the precinct that included the town of Lincoln, the majority of Hispanic women who were listed as heads of household (there were twelve) or who lived with husbands, lived in residences containing one child or none. The women with no children living at home included one woman married to a carpenter, one married to a herder, two married to laborers, seven living alone, eight married to miners, and twenty-five married to farmers. The majority of the twenty-five farmwomen were between the ages of seventeen and twenty-five and were married to farmers who were among the least prosperous in Lincoln County. Only a few households in the precinct listed as many as six children living at home. Many factors undoubtedly combined to produce small families, but of major importance was the youthful nature of this precinct. Roughly 65 percent of Hispanic women were under the age of twenty-five and less than 8 percent were forty-five or over.[29]

Lincoln precinct contained several families that were related. Women's kinship networks can be traced through census data and probate records combined. To cite one example, probate records reveal that three farm families residing in adjacent residences—the Farmers, the Montoyas, and the Aguilars—formed the nucleus of an extended family. Sixty-two-year-old Luz Montoya and her seventy-year-old husband, Rafael, lived alone. To one side lived their thirty-six-year-old daughter, María Aguilar, and her husband, Nestor. On the other lived María's twenty-three-year-old daughter, Gabina Farmer; her husband, James; and baby son. A short distance away lived Luz's thirty-three-year-old son, Ramon Montoya, who was living alone with his wife. Still further removed but in the same precinct lived Luz's thirty-two-year-old daughter, Pabla Sylvan, her husband, and five children.[30] In this sparsely populated region where, in 1870, farmland remained relatively easy to acquire, the emphasis may have been for sons and daughters to leave home as soon as possible to establish their own households.

Most women worked hard to maintain families and to assure the success of family enterprises. Although sources describing women's work are more complete for Anglo women than Hispanic women, these accounts make clear that women who migrated to New Mexico in the 1860s acted as partners with their husbands in economic production. Take the case of Ellen Casey. The Casey family bought property on the Hondo, six miles east of the junction of the Bonito and Ruidoso Rivers, which included good farmland and a gristmill. Robert Casey supervised operations of the mill and rented much of the farmland to Hispanic neighbors for half the crops. In addition to the familial tasks of cooking, making clothes, knitting, and taking care of children, Ellen Casey manufactured butter and cheese, raised chickens, harvested a large garden, supervised the gristmill when Robert was away, and provided meals and lodging to travelers. She sold her surplus vegetables, butter, and cheese to the post trader at Fort Stanton.[31] Ellen's daughter Lily learned "to ride, rope, brand, and perform the various functions of a cowboy," and she assumed major responsibility in caring for the Casey cattle.[32] Several daughters of Anglo settlers, in fact, could ride, round up stock, tame broncos, and generally made good cowhands. In addition, Anglo women acquired certain skills needed to survive on the frontier. They learned to shoot and drive teams of oxen, and some traveled alone across the countryside carrying shotguns for protection.[33]

The economic tasks performed by Hispanic women were also essential for the survival of their families. Like Ellen Casey, they cooked, made clothes, took care of children, washed and ironed clothing (using roots of amole for soap), and provided food and lodging to travelers. They also whitewashed houses, hauled wood and water (the latter in ollas balanced on their heads), ground corn and wheat on metates, and gathered herbs for medicines and plants for dyes.[34] It is also likely that Hispanic men of Lincoln County took major responsibility for clearing the fields, digging ditches, and preparing soil for planting and that women and children aided in planting, harvesting, and herding domestic animals.[35] Family histories indicate that in the early twentieth century young girls cared for goats and hogs, milked cows, and helped cut hay and that women made cheese and butter for sale, planted apple trees, and dug ditches for irrigation.[36] One Lincoln County woman recalled that as a young girl prior to 1920 she plowed, planted, brought in stock, and helped cut wood.[37] These women undoubtedly were carrying on a tradition of hard outdoor work that was inherited from their nineteenth-century ancestors. And like Anglo women, Hispanic women learned to ride horses and care for animals. Prudencia Miranda was such a good horsewoman that she participated with men in the sport known as *correr el gallo*, "running the cock," in which competing riders raced to capture a rooster that had been buried alive with only its head remaining above the surface of the ground.[38]

These women who labored on family farms were described in the 1870 census as "keeping house." Only a few Lincoln County women were listed as having other occupations; they included eighteen laundresses, five seamstresses, three domestic servants, two housekeepers, one waitress, and one cook. Eight laundresses—four Anglos and four Hispanas—were employed at Fort Stanton; the three domestic servants were black women also working at Fort Stanton, probably for officers' wives. Mary Emmons was the cook, who with her husband, James, operated a hotel in the Third Precinct. It is not clear from the census how many Lincoln County women had other women working for them. Several women who were married to laborers and described as "keeping house" must have taken in washing and ironing for wealthier women, as Sophie Poe reported happening in the early 1880s.[39]

Violence, the activity for which Lincoln County in the seventies is best remembered, undoubtedly affected all women regardless of class. Men, women, and children shared the danger of living in a region fought over by antagonistic groups: Indians and whites, Hispanos and Texans, cattlemen and cattle rustlers, the Murphy-Dolan and the McSween-Tunstall factions. Part of this lawlessness stemmed from the growth of the cattle industry in Lincoln County; thieves proliferated as quickly as the herds. Texas cattlemen first trailed their cattle into the Pecos area in the mid-1860s to take advantage of markets at Forts Sumner and Stanton. The Pecos Valley and its tributaries had some of the finest grazing in the territory, with natural grasses standing "belly deep to a horse." Attracted by the lush ranges, entrepreneurs like Joseph C. Lea established permanent ranches along the Pecos in the 1870s, contributing to the county's population growth.[40]

The violence that afflicted the county was widespread and not limited to any one area. And although the majority of families survived the decade intact, they experienced the uncertainties associated with living in communities where law and order virtually disappeared. Some families packed their belongings, left crops standing in the fields, and fled the area to escape the terror. Several men and some women lost their lives, others were wounded, and still others were endangered in these deadly encounters.[41] Not only did survivors grieve for murdered spouses and children, but they also experienced economic hardships brought about by the death of family providers.

But Lincoln County women were not passive witnesses to wanton deeds of violence; they fought back and carried on with whatever resources they had. The experiences of Susan McSween, Juana Baca, and a delegation of village women illustrate this point. During the height of the Lincoln County War, Susan McSween chose to remain with her husband and his supporters during the five days that the McSween residence came under heavy gunfire. On the fateful fifth day, she left her burning home in order to appeal to the commanding officer at Fort Stanton to intervene and save lives. Later she unsuccessfully sought revenge in the courts against her husband's enemies and then went on to build a new career for herself as a rancher.[42] Juana Baca, wife of Saturino Baca who had gained the enmity of the McSween faction, was left unprotected when, soon after the killing of Alexander McSween, a military guard was withdrawn from the Baca residence. Juana, however, refused an invitation to move onto the military reservation for protection until after she and the family had cared for crops that were being harvested.[43] Finally, during these dangerous months, two women living in San Patricio were raped by outlaws. A delegation of village women thereafter traveled to Fort Stanton with a petition signed by twenty-seven mothers asking "in the name of God and the Constitution" that soldiers be sent to protect them from further abuse.[44]

Despite the violence, by 1880 Lincoln County had a population of 2,512, an increase of 39 percent over the previous decade.[45] There were now more Anglo women in the population, which included 1,525 Hispanos, 857 Anglos, 66 children of Hispanic mothers and Anglo fathers, 59 blacks, 3 Indians, and 2 Chinese.[56] But in spite of a dramatic increase in the number of Anglo women, women as a whole represented only 38 percent of the population, and the sex imbalance was slightly more pronounced than in 1870, 16 men to 10 women, indicating that men were increasing at a faster rate than women. The female population now consisted of 718 Hispanos, 203 Anglos, 27 daughters of mixed marriages, 11 blacks, and 1 Indian married to an Hispanic man from Mexico. Over 65 percent of Anglo men and women resided in the Fifth Precinct, which encompassed the cattle region bordering the Pecos, and in the new mining districts of White Oaks and Nogal northwest of Lincoln. The majority of Anglo men in the mining districts were living as single men, although several had wives living elsewhere in the United States. As in 1870, the ratio of men to women in the Hispanic population was 11 to 10; the ratio in the Anglo population had dropped to 32 to 10. Only 23 Hispanic women were now married to Anglos, representing about 8 percent of married Hispanic women.[47] This buildup in the Anglo population, from 15 percent of Lincoln County residents in 1870 to 34 percent in 1880, foreshadowed the heavy influx of Anglo families into southeastern New Mexico that occurred around the turn of the century.

The number of black women also increased slightly. Increase in black population was due to the stationing of black soldiers at Fort Stanton. Eight black women resided at or near the post, two employed as laundresses and one as a servant in the commanding officer's household. Kentucky-born Sarah Williams was "keeping house" for her three daughters and sergeant-husband, the only black married couple living in the county. One twenty-seven-year-old black woman, whose occupation was not recorded in the census, lived with Clara McVeigh, a white woman who later in the decade was licensed to sell liquor near the post.[48]

The Hispanic population in Lincoln County experienced little growth in the decade of the seventies, increasing only by thirty-one females and twenty-nine males. Families tended to be slightly larger in 1880 than in 1870 and the population older. In the town of Lincoln, about 41 percent of Hispanic women who were married or heads of household lived in families containing one child or none; about 44 percent lived in families containing two to four children. Only three families listed as many as seven children residing at home. Fifty-six percent of Hispanic women in Lincoln were under the age of twenty-five, and 13 percent were forty-five or over.[49] Families living in Lincoln, San Patricio, Picacho, and other predominantly Hispanic villages probably were becoming more inter related as their children intermarried. One woman recalled that by the early twentieth century almost everyone in San Patricio was related.[50]

Census returns conceal the economic contributions of Anglo and Hispanic women, most of whom continued to live and work in farm and ranching families. Returns also underestimate the total number of farms, thereby giving a misleading picture of agriculture and family life in Lincoln County. The sixty farms listed in the 1880 agricultural census would indicate a precipitous decline in the number of farms as well as in total agricultural production. A decade of lawlessness and intrusion by large cattle herds, as well as the army's inability to consume local grain surpluses, may account for a small decline in local farming.[51] It seems likely, however, that the census taker failed to record many small farms, since in 1890 the census listed 303 farms, only slightly fewer than the 1870 figure. Probate and other county records support this conclusion. The 1882 will of José Alberto Sedillo, for example, indicates that he and his wife Maria owned forty acres of land in Lincoln, on which they probably raised sufficient crops for subsistence, yet he is listed in the 1880 census as a laborer.[52]

The 1880 census returns seem, therefore, to provide information primarily about the more successful farms, such as that owned by Josepha and José Montaño, who also operated a dry goods store in Lincoln. The Montaños owned 319 acres of improved land, on which they raised corn and beans, and 1 acre of vineyards. They also owned five horses, three mules, ten oxen, one hundred beef cattle, ninety sheep, three hogs, forty chickens, and several milk cows. They valued their farm at four thousand dollars, their livestock at four thousand dollars, and their farm production in 1879 at six thousand dollars.[53]

On rare occasions newspaper editors described some aspects of the woman's importance on farms such as these. One of the more successful farming operations in Lincoln County was that operated by Catherine and Charles Fritz on their Spring Ranch eight miles below Lincoln on the Rio Bonito. They claimed ownership of 940 acres, including 400 acres of improved land on which in 1879 they raised 3,900 bushels of corn, 320 bushels of oats, 600 bushels of wheat, and 50 bushels of beans. They owned a variety of domestic animals, including fifteen oxen, fifteen milk cows, three hundred beef cattle, and one hundred chickens. In one twelve-month period, they harvested 250 bushels of apples, manufactured 520 pounds of butter, and collected 1,100 dozen eggs. Their farmland and buildings were valued at fifteen thousand dollars, livestock at five thousand dollars, and farm products at four thousand dollars. When Catherine Fritz died in January 1884, the editor of the Las Cruces *Rio Grande Republican* applauded her industry: "Under her care, [the Fritz] ranch grew to be one of the finest in the county, and she was among the first to establish a dairy and to promote fruitgrowing."[54]

As the century progressed, class distinctions became more noticeable in Lincoln County. By excluding small landowners, the 1880 agricultural census provides a short list of the most prosperous Anglo and Hispanic farm families. Tax assessment and probate records also indicate disparities in wealth among residents. The wealthiest individual taxpayer in San Patricio was José Analla, who in 1898 was assessed $120 in taxes on 320 acres of land, his improvements, and 2,400 sheep and goats. When his estate was probated following his death in 1899, it was revealed that he owned over 10,000 sheep, most of which were rented to others on shares. His wife, Dulces, and his four daughters were among those who inherited this wealth.[55]

Among the few estates of Lincoln County women probated in the nineteenth century was that of Mará Gertrudes Herrera de Chávez, who died at Raventon, northeast of Carrizozo, in 1892. Her property included 160 acres of land valued at $2 an acre, 1,453 sheep, 70 goats, 22 chickens, wearing apparel and gold earrings valued at $200, and a variety of household goods and furnishings. The total estate, valued at $4,313, placed Herrera de Chávez in an economic class above that of most Hispanic women.[56]

Account books of merchants also document disparities in wealth. As one would expect, wealthy women were more likely than poor women to purchase ready-made clothes, canned fruits, perfume, jewelry, and other accessories. Well-to-do Hispanic women in 1890 paid $45 for silk dresses, $8.50 for hats, $3.50 for slippers, $1.75 for corsets, 75¢ for gloves, and 50¢ for bustles. These women also purchased gingham, calico, linen, manta, sateen, silk lace, silk thread, buttons, and ribbons for manufacturing their own clothes. By the end of the century, numerous Lincoln County women owned sewing machines, although the majority continued to lack finances to purchase one.[57]

Daughters of prosperous families attended boarding schools even though public and private schools were available locally. Nearly one year after the death of her mother, twelve-year-old Matilda (Tillie) Fritz entered the Academy of the Visitation conducted by the Sisters of Loretto in Las Cruces. Board and tuition for a ten-month term was two hundred dollars, clearly beyond the means of most Lincoln County families. Instruction in piano, guitar, drawing, and painting cost extra. Midway through the first term, Tillie's father died, and she subsequently enrolled in the academy at Santa Fe, where tuition fees were equally high, to be near a brother who attended St. Michael's College.[58]

Whether rich or poor, Hispanic and Anglo women who were widowed shared the experience of learning to function in society without their husbands. By living in kin-related communities, Hispanic widows—more so than Anglos—could rely upon relatives to cushion the economic and personal shock of widowhood. Among the county's Hispanic population, there were more widows than widowers in 1880. The census listed forty-five Hispanic widows as heads of household, many of whom had children living at home, and twenty-one widows who were residing in other households. In several cases, a widowed daughter lived with her widowed mother; some widows lived alone, including eighty-five-year-old Anna Benavides of Lincoln. The census listed only five Anglo widows as heads of household and four Anglo widows residing in other households.[59]

Widows like Ellen Casey and Bonifacia Brady continued to manage family enterprises after the deaths of their husbands. Robert Casey was shot and killed by a former employee in 1875. "Largely because of the indomitable courage of Ellen E. Casey," one scholar observed, "the family remained a solid working unit."[60] The six Casey children ranged in ages from eighteen months to fifteen years, and Ellen kept the older ones busy planting, herding cattle, and working on the property. She also supervised the Casey store and gristmill, delivering flour as far away as Seven Rivers on the Pecos. During the height of the Lincoln County War, she remained on the ranch, although the older children went to Texas to escape the violence. She tried to remain neutral but, as her daughter noted, "it was hard." The location of their ranch, wrote Lily Casey Klasner, "caused both sides to put up with her as men went back and forth on expeditions and forays. Both sides annoyed her by searching the house and premises for someone hiding."[61] When peaceful times returned in the 1880s, Ellen Casey received final patent to the family homestead, signed at least one government contract to deliver hay at Fort Stanton, and continued to manage the Casey property.[62] Bonifacia Brady, whose husband also died after being shot on the main street of Lincoln during the Lincoln County War, continued to care for her eight children (the oldest was about fifteen years old) and to cultivate the 320-acre family farm, one of the most valuable in Lincoln.[63]

Other widows rented their cattle and sheep on *partido* (shares) to local ranchers. One woman leased eleven head of high-grade cattle for five years, receiving at the termination of the lease double the number of cattle. Another leased her entire stock of cattle (amount unknown), stipulating that at the end of the five-year lease she would receive the original stock plus half the increase.[64]

Still other widows were left in difficult circumstances and relied upon family and community for economic survival. At age sixty-six, newly widowed Margarita Estrada Brown lived in San Patricio with a son who supported her. Because she applied for a Civil War widow's pension, her personal history has been preserved, providing a rare glimpse into the life of a Mexican citizen who migrated to Lincoln County as an adult and subsequently outlived two husbands. Margarita Estrada was born in the state of Chihuahua in 1844; at age twenty-five, still single, she moved to El Paso, Texas, where she supported herself by doing housework. She made subsequent moves to Las Cruces, where she worked in a hotel, and to Tularosa, where she taught school and married her first husband, Juan Torres, who died around 1881. After being widowed a little over a year, she married a Civil War veteran by the name of Henry C. Brown, a widower who was farming along the Ruidoso. They lived together on the "Brown Ranch" for several years until he began seeking medical attention at soldiers' homes. About a year before he died in 1908, he took up residence in the soldiers' home in Los Angeles, sending Margarita a small sum of money every three months. By this date, Margarita was blind and almost totally dependent upon her son.[65]

As one would expect, widows from prosperous families had greater economic security than Margarita Brown. But these widows also experienced economic difficulties when delays occurred in settling estates. One woman, whose husband's property was appraised at ten thousand dollars, went into debt for one year to support herself and child before funds from the estate were made available to her.[66] Much time was consumed in inventorying large estates and in assuring equitable division of property.

New Mexico's inheritance laws in the nineteenth century seemed to have confused and delayed settlement of estates. These laws decreed that upon death of a spouse, one-half of the community property that remained after payment of common debts would be set aside for the surviving husband or wife. From about 1865 until 1884, the law further stipulated that if the decedent died intestate, the decedent's half of the community property as well as his or her personal property (now called the estate) would be divided equally among the decedent's children, except when the estate amounted to more than five thousand dollars; then the surviving spouse would receive one-fourth of the estate, the remainder to be divided equally among the children. In case the decedent left a will, the law was even more complicated and more confusing. In general it appears that from one-fifth to nearly one-half of the decedent's estate would be used to cover legacies, after which division of the estate would follow the same rules as for intestate cases. In 1889, the five thousand dollar provision was dropped and inheritance laws were simplified. The law now stipulated that the decedent's half of the community property and his or her personal property could be disposed of by will, or in absence of will, would be distributed one-fourth to the surviving spouse and the remainder in equal shares to the children.[67]

Delays occurred even in settling small and uncomplicated estates. José Miranda, who lived at Junction Plaza near modern-day Hondo, died intestate in 1880. He and his wife María owned 162 acres of land, valued at about nine hundred dollars. The Rio Bonito flowed through the property, dividing it into two unequal sections. West of the river were 44 acres of good bottomland; east of the river were 36 acres of bottomland and 82 acres of hilly land. The heirs agreed that the two sections, though of unequal size, were of equal value, but final division of the property was not completed until 1890. The widow received one-half of the community property (44 acres west of the river), and Miranda's eight children received equal portions of land east of the river, amounting roughly to 4½ acres of bottomland and 10 acres of hilly land.[68] Occasionally, when only a small amount of land composed the estate, children relinquished their claims and allowed their widowed mother to use the property as long as she lived.

Not only complex laws but complex family patterns could cause difficulty. Schisms appeared in some families when heirs believed that the division of property was unfair. This was especially true when a decedent had children by more than one wife. One rancher in San Patricio who died intestate near the turn of the century left a valuable estate of sheep, cattle, horses, wool, promissory notes, and ranch equipment. His heirs included his third wife, their four children, and six children from two previous marriages. The estate remained unsettled for years, some heirs accusing the estate's administrator—the eldest son of the decedent—of mismanaging the estate and improperly dividing the property.[69]

Sometimes a widow believed that provisions in her husband's will were unjust and rejected its benefits in hopes of obtaining increased benefits from other legal sources. When Charles Fritz died in 1885, leaving a valuable estate in land and personal property, he bequeathed his real estate to his four sons and one daughter to be divided equally among them. He also stipulated in his will that his personal property should be divided equally among his second wife, Amelia, and the above five children. He instructed his sons to give Amelia a good home and provide for her wants as long as she remained single. Amelia, however, surrendered benefits given to her in the will in lieu of her dower right, and she asked that the homestead she occupied at the time of Fritz's death (the valuable Spring Ranch) be included as part of the dower. Under community property laws, the recently married Amelia probably had no claim to the Fritz real estate, since Charles undoubtedly claimed it as his personal property at the time of their marriage. But invoking the common law concept of dower, Amelia hoped for a share of the land, as dower "consisted of a life estate in one-third of all the lands" that the husband possessed during marriage. This was the "interest of the surviving widow" and could not be set aside in the will of the deceased husband. The concept of dower added to the confusion surrounding nineteenth-century inheritance laws and was abolished in New Mexico in 1907. Amelia apparently settled her claim out of court, as the Fritz children subsequently purchased her interest in the estate, formed a corporation to manage Fritz's cattle grazing along the Rio Felix, and divided among themselves the Spring Ranch property on the Rio Bonito.[70]

Amelia Fritz left Spring Ranch and settled in the town of Lincoln, where she first opened a millinery store and later a hotel. Other county women—some probably widows like Amelia—also embarked upon commercial careers during the 1880s. The only record that remains of these female-owned enterprises is a list of business licenses issued to the proprietresses. Six women took out licenses to run hotels, three to retail merchandise, four to retail liquor, one to operate a gaming table, and one—Rosa Esperanza de Emillio—to peddle merchandise from a two-horse wagon. Only one woman—Ellen Casey—had obtained a business license in the previous decade.[71]

The increase in licenses issued to women reflected the county's growth in population, which reached 7,081 in 1890, an increase of 182 percent over the decade. This remarkable growth resulted primarily from increased migration of Anglo families and the expansion of the cattle industry. Many immigrant families came from Texas, which caused one newspaper correspondent to remark: "You cannot go ten miles on any road without seeing the covered wagons [of Texans] with from six to sixteen tow headed children aboard."[72] Texas women brought with them a tradition of hard farmwork. Texas-born Nellie Branum recalled that soon after her family arrived in Lincoln County, her father went to work as a blacksmith at Fort Stanton while her mother and older sister plowed, planted crops, made adobes for the family house, and built a rock fence around the property.[73] Other Texas women recalled similar work experiences.

As population increased throughout New Mexico, farm families such as the Branums brought thousands of acres of land under cultivation. Governor Edmund G. Ross, who described this process in his 1887 annual report, noted that Anglo and Hispanic farmers alike were adopting improved methods of agriculture, discarding "the wooden plow, the sickle, the thrashing stockade, and the winnowing fork" in favor of improved machinery.[74] Family ranches also increased in size. In 1890 Lincoln County officials reported that 126,721 head of cattle and 56,584 head of sheep were grazing on county ranges. Although at this date it is not possible to determine the full extent of female ownership, some of these animals were owned and managed by women. Most women worked as partners with their husbands. Hispanic women in partnership with husbands routinely accepted legal responsibility for livestock taken on shares. A few women entered *partido* arrangements in their own names. Mrs. M. H. Lutz signed a contract with José Analla of San Patricio in 1895 whereby she would receive from Analla 2,000 ewes on shares for five years. She agreed to return the same number of ewes at the end of the contract and to deliver to Analla each October during the life of the contract two pounds of wool for every sheep.[75] Newspapers give tantalizing glimpses of some women who owned cattle. A Mary Sepulver, for example, published a notice in the *New Mexico Interpreter* stating that she was sole owner of certain stock ranging in Lincoln County. Other women who owned cattle published their brands in local newspapers.[76]

Among the most famous of New Mexico's women ranchers was Susan McSween Barber, whose ranching activities deserve much more recognition than they have received by historians. Born in 1845, Susan E. Hummer grew up near Gettysburg, Pennsylvania. She married Alexander A. McSween in Atchison, Kansas, in 1873 and moved to Lincoln two years later where Alexander established a law practice. Her role in the Lincoln County War is vividly portrayed in *Maurice Garland Fulton's History of the Lincoln County War* and need not be recounted here. In this and other secondary accounts, Susan McSween emerges as a strong and courageous woman. Two years after the death of her husband, she was living in Lincoln and managing a 160-acre farm, on which she raised corn and kept an assortment of farm animals.[77]

Susan took her farm property into a second marriage partnership when, on 20 June 1880, she married George B. Barber, a Lincoln County surveyor and later a prominent local attorney.[78] It is obvious from land records that the couple worked in partnership to acquire the land that later became the cornerstone of Susan's cattle enterprise. In fact, the Barbers were typical nineteenth-century entrepreneurs, acquiring land in widely scattered areas that showed potential for economic growth and development: White Oaks, South Spring River near Roswell, and Three Rivers west of the White Mountains. In November 1879, while still a widow, Susan had entered a claim under the Timber Culture Act to 160 acres of land near South Spring River, adjoining property owned by Pitser M. Chisum. In the same area, she subsequently entered a claim to and patented 320 acres under the Desert Land Act and purchased from Sebrian Bates, a former black employee of the McSweens, 160 acres that he had acquired under the Homestead Act. Within ten years, she relinquished the Timber Culture claim and sold for a nice profit the remaining 480 acres.[79]

Rather than developing the South Spring property near the Chisum headquarters, Susan and George Barber established a cattle ranch in the western foothills of Sierra Blanca at Three Rivers, twenty miles north of Tularosa. By 1888 Susan claimed ownership to 1,158 acres of Three Rivers land; this included 400 acres that George patented January 1883 under the Desert Land Act.[80] Susan later said that in 1881 she constructed a dam across Three Rivers (a mere stream) and a half-mile ditch to convey water to her property; apparently these were the first improvements on the ranch.[81] Susan further stated that after the Barbers located their ranch on public domain, and in order "to economize their resources," George returned to Lincoln to open a law office and she took charge of the ranch, having absolute control of its management. "She planned and superintended the construction of all the buildings on the place, designated the location of the fences, corrals, and all the necessary works of this character, at the same time overseeing the cowboys, masons, carpenters and farm lands."[82] While improvements were being made for the cattle ranch, she also had men at work improving another portion of the land for a farm, on which she would raise grain, vegetables, fruit trees, and berries. By the turn of the century, Susan was recognized as one of the most successful fruit growers in Lincoln County.[83]

The cattle ranch prospered under Susan's management and attracted the interest of eastern investors. Indeed, she was building her ranch during the cattle industry's boom period, when many eastern and foreign capitalists were investing in western ranches. In January 1887 Susan sold for an undisclosed sum one-half interest in her Three Rivers property to John Rugee and Emil Durr of Milwaukee, Wisconsin. Although the new partnership never incorporated, it took the name "Three Rivers Land and Cattle Company" and employed Susan as general manager. Five thousand head of cattle soon grazed on the company's ranges. For tax assessment purposes, the company's cattle were valued at forty-nine thousand dollars in 1891.[84]

In writing about Susan's success, a newspaper correspondent declared that she had rendered a valuable service to ranchmen "by demonstrating the fact that cowboys can be gentlemen." He claimed that guns had been "entirely dispensed with" on her ranch and that cowboys working there "wear clean shirts, take off their hats when they come into the house, wash their faces, comb their hair, and put on their coats when they come to the table, and otherwise respect the customs of civilization."[85] By insisting that her employees behave as gentlemen, Susan was conforming to the stereotyped image of western women as the chief civilizing agents who tamed the frontier. In this case, however, it was not the mere presence of a woman that influenced male behavior, as the image makers would have us believe, but rather Susan's power as an employer to hire and fire.

In September 1891, Susan filed for divorce in district court, claiming that George had failed to support her during the marriage and that he had abandoned her the previous March. About the time the divorce became final in 1892, the local press reported that Susan drove between seven hundred and eight hundred head of cattle from her ranch to the railroad at Engle, from which point they were shipped to feedlots in Kansas. Later she traveled east, where she was described in the New York *Commercial Advertiser* as "one of the most remarkable women of this remarkable age." The reporter described with some journalistic license her Three Rivers home: "a low, whitewalled adobe building . . . covered with green vines and fitted out with rich carpets, artistic hangings, books and pictures, exquisite china and silver, and all the dainty belongings with which a refined woman loves to surround herself."[86]

Susan Barber bought back the half interest of Rugee and Durr in 1901 and then sold the ranch and what remained of the cattle—about three hundred head—to Monroe Harper in 1902 for thirty-two thousand dollars. It was Monroe Harper and not Susan Barber, as some authors have claimed, who sold this property in 1915 to Albert B. Fall, a key figure in the Teapot Dome Scandal.[87]

During the years that she managed the cattle ranch, Susan Barber acquired real estate in the communities of Tularosa, Nogal, and White Oaks. The mining camp of White Oaks, in fact, was barely two years old when both she and George secured inexpensive town lots from county officials. Starting in 1887, Susan began purchasing additional lots, undoubtedly for speculation since increased amounts of gold were being extracted from the mines. The Barbers maintained a residence at White Oaks, in addition to the ranch house at Three Rivers, and for a few years George had his law office there. After the divorce, Susan continued to maintain the White Oaks residence and moved there permanently after selling the Three Rivers ranch.[88] By this date the mines had played out, the railroad had bypassed White Oaks, and the once-thriving community had begun its permanent decline. Always the businesswoman, Barber tried late in life to interest oil men in her White Oaks properties but with little success. She died there in 1931—her savings almost depleted—at age eighty-six.[89]

For two decades prior to 1900, White Oaks was a bustling mining community, and its residents considered themselves progressive community builders rather than struggling pioneers. In 1888 White Oaks boasted a population of eight hundred people (making it the largest town in the county), eight mercantile establishments, two weekly newspapers, three hotels, both a public and a private school (whose teachers were frequently young single women from the East), two meat markets, three physicians, three law offices, and a dentist.[90] Although many single men resided there in the early years, the town soon filled with families who would boost civic improvements.

From extant newspapers, it is clear that women played active roles in the community's economic life. Although two of the hotels had male proprietors, their wives prepared the meals and helped maintain the buildings. The barber's wife repaired and cleaned clothes for her husband's customers. The community's principal butter manufacturer was a woman. At least three women established dressmaking and millinery shops, and at least one ran a boardinghouse. The postmaster was Ella G. Timoney, who also sold books and stationery from her stand in the post office building. The White Oaks New Mexico Interpreter in 1891 was edited by Mrs. A. L. McGinnes, who employed another woman as a typesetter. Although the total number of women engaged in these and similar economic activities remained small, residents viewed their work as important to the community and as proper occupations for women.[91]

By 1900, women had achieved a stable and important place in Lincoln County. They now composed 45 percent of the population. Law and order prevailed in most communities, settlers and Indians lived at peace, and the Anglo population equaled that of the Hispanic.[92] Railroads made it convenient for Lincoln County residents to exchange visits with eastern relatives. A few Anglo women had sufficient funds to tour Europe and Japan. Lincoln County women also became active in national movements. Some farmwomen joined local Farmer's Alliances, spoke at meetings, wrote letters to newspaper editors, and served as alliance officers. Several White Oaks women formed a chapter of the Women's Relief Corps, a national organization established in 1882 to assist the Grand Army of the Republic and to aid widows and orphans of Union veterans.[93]

Many women of Lincoln County grew to adulthood during the last four decades of the nineteenth century, coping with frontier conditions that required them to perform hard outdoor farmwork, tasks customarily defined as men's work. They worked as partners with husbands to maintain households and to enlarge family incomes, and their economic roles were valued by their families and communities. And although the women of Lincoln County differed in class and ethnic background, crude and dangerous living conditions fostered cooperation and broke down some of their differences.

Without a doubt, Lincoln County women were productive and hard-working. It is open to question, however, how much their lives were influenced by the nineteenth-century upper-class ideology of "true womanhood," which dictated that proper ladies should be pious, pure, submissive, and domestic, confining their energies to nurturing a family within the privacy of their homes. This ideology presents a passive image of women that does not reflect the behavior of most Lincoln County women. Nevertheless, wealthier women exhibited in their Victorian wearing apparel and household furnishings an awareness of "female propriety." And women like Susan McSween Barber who engaged in male-dominated industries did so in a manner that acknowledged a proper code of conduct for female entrepreneurs. In defending her career as a rancher, Barber once remarked, "I never did anything on that ranch that was uncouth or unbecoming a lady."[94] Women in Lincoln County undoubtedly internalized some Victorian ideals, but most of them lived lives of steady toil, caring for families and farms, doing outdoor labor when necessary, and engaging in other enterprises for economic survival.

Important questions remain unanswered about these pioneer Lincoln County women. Were their daily lives as restricted as those of women living in eastern rural villages? Or did the frontier communities of Lincoln, San Patricio, and White Oaks allow for greater individual freedom and variation? We may never have the correct answers to these questions, but if historians will listen to what the twentieth-century descendants of these women care to tell them, perhaps more precise estimates can be made about the quality of life among nineteenth-century western women.

Notes

This essay first appeared in *New Mexico Women: Intercultural Perspectives*, edited by Joan Jensen and Darlis Miller (Albuquerque: University of New Mexico Press, 1986).

    1. Gerda Lerner, *Teaching Women's History* (Washington, D.C.: American Historical Association, 1981), 16.
    2. Barber to Dilton, 23 November 1928, Old Lincoln County Courthouse, Lincoln, N.M.

3. William A. Keleher, *Violence in Lincoln County, 1869–1881*, (reprint; Albuquerque: University of New Mexico Press, 1982), xxiii; Robert N. Mullin, ed., *Maurice Garland Fulton's History of the Lincoln County War* (Tucson: University of Arizona Press, 1968), 13–15; Cecil Bonney, *Looking over My Shoulder, Seventy-Five Years in the Pecos Valley* (Roswell, N.M.: Hall-Poorbaugh Press, 1971), 57–62.

4. U.S. Department of Commerce, Bureau of the Census, *Eighth Census of the United States, 1860*, Socorro County, N.M., Population Schedules, National Archives (NA), microfilm T-7, roll 158. Hispanos composed 70 percent of Rio Bonito's population, Anglos 24 percent, and children of mixed marriages 5 percent.

5. T. A. Larson, "Women's Role in the American West," *Montana The Magazine of Western History* 24 (Summer 1974): 5.

6. Rio Bonito, Socorro County, N.M., Agricultural Schedules, *Eighth Census of the United States, 1860* (hereafter Agricultural Schedules, 1860), State Records Center and Archives (hereafter SRCA), Santa Fe, N.M. The average size of farms in New Mexico in 1860 was 278 acres; the average value was $532. *Ninth Census of the United States, 1870*, vol. 3 (Washington, D.C.: U.S. Government Printing Office, 1872), 341 (hereafter *Ninth Census, 1870*); U.S., Bureau of the Census, *Historical Statistics of the United States, Colonial Times to 1970*, Bicentennial Edition (Washington, D.C.: U.S. Government Printing Office, 1975), pt. 1, 463 (hereafter *Historical Statistics*).

7. H. M. Beckwith, Socorro County, Agricultural Schedules, 1860.

8. Robert W. Frazer, *Forts of the West* (Norman: University of Oklahoma Press, 1972), 103; Murphy to DeForrest, 11 June 1866, District of New Mexico, Letters Received, Records of the United States Continental Commands, 1821–1920, Record Group 393, NA, microfilm M-1088, roll 3 (hereafter Dist. NM, LR, RG 393, NA, M-1088); Santa Fe *Weekly Gazette*, 27 December 1862.

9. Santa Fe *Weekly Gazette*, 27 December 1862; Carleton to Brady, 27 April 1865, Fort Stanton, Post Records, LR, RG 393, NA, Washington, D.C. (hereafter PR, LR, RG 393, NA).

10. Mrs. Lorencita Miranda, 5 May 1939, WPA Files, SRCA.

11. Elerdo Chávez, 7 July 1939, WPA Files, SRCA.

12. Daniel Carabajal, 23 January 1939, WPA Files, SRCA.

13. Murphy to DeForrest, 11 June 1866, LR, Dist. NM, RG 393, NA, M-1088, roll 3.

14. Robert M. Utley, *Frontiersmen in Blue: The United States Army and the Indian, 1848–1865*, (reprint; Lincoln: University of Nebraska Press, 1981), 236–37, 246.

15. Smith to Cutler, 20 May 1863, 28 August 1863, Fort Stanton, PR, Letters Sent (LS), RG 393, NA; DeForrest to Smith, 5 August 1863, Department of New Mexico, LS, RG 393, NA, microfilm M-1072, roll 3.

16. Romero to Carleton, 18 March 1866, Dist. NM, LR, RG 393, NA, M-1088, roll 4.

17. Carleton to Romero, 8 April 1866, Dist. NM, LS, RG 393, NA, M-1072, roll 3; Santa Fe *Weekly Gazette*, 23 May 1868.

18. Kautz to Townsend, 24 January 1872, Fort Stanton, PR, LS, RG 393, NA.

19. U.S. Department of Commerce, Bureau of the Census, *Ninth Census of the United States, 1870*, Lincoln County, N.M., Population Schedules, NA, M-593, roll 894 (hereafter Lincoln County, Population Schedules, *Ninth Census, 1870*, NA, M-593). In 1870, 81 percent of the Lincoln County population was Hispanic, 15 percent Anglo, 3 percent the children of mixed marriages, and 1 percent black. Approximately 355 Hispanic women were married.

20. Lincoln County, N.M., Agricultural Schedules, *Ninth Census of the United States, 1870* (hereafter Agricultural Schedules, 1870), SRCA. The average size of farms in New Mexico in 1870 was 186 acres; the average value was $404. *Ninth Census, 1870*, vol. 3, 341; *Historical Statistics*, 463.

21. Lincoln County, Agricultural Schedules, 1870; *Ninth Census*, 1870, vol 3, 358, 208–209.

22. Sophie A. Poe, *Buckboard Days* (reprint; Albuquerque: University of New Mexico Press, 1981), 196.

23. Eve Ball, *Ma'am Jones of the Pecos* (Tucson: University of Arizona Press, 1969), 12.

24. Lily Klasner, *My Girlhood among Outlaws*, ed. Eve Ball (Tucson: University of Arizona Press, 1972), 41.

25. Wilbur Coe, *Ranch on the Ruidoso: The Story of a Pioneer Family in New Mexico, 1871–1968* (New York: Alfred A. Knopf, 1968), 71.

26. Interview with Lorenzita [*sic*] Miranda by Nan Boylan, 1953, copy of transcript made available by Nora Henn, Lincoln County Historical Society, and Rio Grande Historical Collections, New Mexico State University (hereafter Lorenzita Miranda interview, 1953).

27. Ball, *Ma'am Jones*, 21–23, 27, 33–35, 41–42, 57. See also Coe, *Ranch on the Ruidoso*, 12.

28. Ball, *Ma'am Jones*, 29, 226; Coe, *Ranch on the Ruidoso*, 72; Poe, *Buckboard Days*, 209–211.

29. Lincoln County, Population Schedules, *Ninth Census, 1870*, NA, M-593, roll 894. Individuals are listed in the 1870 census according to household, but no relationship is recorded for people living in the same household. Women and children are listed beneath a male head of household, and where the surname for a woman has been deleted in preference for a straight line, it is assumed that she carried the same surname as the man and that they were husband and wife. It is not always possible, however, to claim a husband-wife relationship, as sometimes unmarried daughters remained at home to "keep house" for their widowed fathers. Whether one includes or excludes the families where relationships are in doubt, the fact remains that in over half the households where women of marriageable age were living with male heads of household, one child or none lived at home.

30. Lincoln County, Population Schedules, *Ninth Census, 1870*, NA, M-593, roll 894; María de la Luz Torres, Probate Records, Lincoln County Courthouse, Carrizozo, N.M.

31. James D. Shinkle, *Robert Casey and the Ranch on the Rio Hondo* (Roswell, N.M.: Hall-Poorbaugh Press, 1970), 59; Klasner, *My Girlhood*, 45–51.

32. Klasner, *My Girlhood*, 48.

33. Ball, *Ma'am Jones*, 32, 107, 169, 176, 192; Coe, *Ranch on the Ruidoso*, 78, 123; Klasner, *My Girlhood*, 68; Shinkle, *Robert Casey*, 44; Bonney, *Looking over My Shoulder*, 158–61.

34. Poe, *Buckboard Days*, 207–208, 218; Klasner, *My Girlhood*, 43–45; Mrs. Orsemus B. Boyd, *Cavalry Life in Tent and Field* (reprint, Lincoln: University of Nebraska Press, 1982), 172; Ball, *Ma'am Jones*, 42; Lorenzita Miranda interview, 1953.

35. See Frances Leon Swadesh, *Los Primeros Pobladores: Hispanic Americans of the Ute Frontier* (Notre Dame, Ind.: University of Notre Dame Press, 1974), 179.

36. Family history compiled by D. Sanchez, November 1977, New Mexico State University (in possession of the author).

37. Information provided by Lynda A. Sanchez concerning her mother-in-law, in letter to author, 20 June 1983.

38. Lorenzita Miranda interview, 1953; W. W. H. Davis, *El Gringo; or New Mexico and Her People* (reprint, New York: Arno Press, 1973), 188.

39. Lincoln County, Population Schedules, *Ninth Census, 1870*, NA, M-593, roll 894; Poe, *Buckboard Days*, 207–208.

40. See James D. Shinkle, *Fifty Years of Roswell History, 1867–1917* (Roswell, N.M.: Hall-Poorbaugh Press, 1964), 4–8, 18, 26, 40–42.

41. For the Lincoln County War, see Keleher, *Violence in Lincoln County*, and Mullin, ed. *Fulton's History*. For the Horrell war, see P. J. Rasch, "The Horrell War," *New Mexico Historical Review* 31 (July 1956): 223–31. See also Santa Fe *Daily New Mexican*, 30 September 1873, 27 January 1874, 19 January 1875, 4 May 1877; *Grant County Herald* (Silver City), 8 June 1878; Dudley to Devins, 15 August 1878, Dudley to Acting Assistant Adjutant General (AAAG), 28 September 1878, 16 November 1878, 15 February 1879, Fort Stanton, PR, LS, RG 393, NA; Gardner to Dudley, 18 August 1878, Lyon to Post Adjutant, 1 October 1878, Fort Stanton, PR, LR, RG 393, NA.

42. Mullin, ed., *Fulton's History*, 249–69, 303–330, 345–49, 356–67.

43. Mrs. J. Baca to Dudley, 22 August 1878, Fort Stanton, PR, LR, RG 393, NA.

44. Dudley to AAAG, 6 July 1878, 15 February 1879, Fort Stanton, PR, LS, RG 393, NA.

45. U.S. Department of Commerce, Bureau of the Census, *Tenth Census of the United States, 1880*, Lincoln County, N.M., Population Schedules, NA, microfilm T-9, roll 802 (hereafter Lincoln County, Population Schedules, *Tenth Census, 1880*, NA, T-9). The author's count of individuals listed in the 1880 Lincoln County population schedules is one less than the official population listed for Lincoln County, 2,513. See *Tenth Census of the United States, 1880*, vol. 1 (Washington, D.C.: U.S. Government Printing Office, 1883), 72 (hereafter *Tenth Census, 1880*).

46. In 1880, Hispanos composed 61 percent of Lincoln County's population, Anglos 34 percent, children of mixed marriages 3 percent, and blacks 2 percent. The author's count of black residents (59) is one less than the official count (60) listed for Lincoln County. See *Tenth Census, 1880*, vol. 1, 402. Ralph Twitchell in his *Leading Facts of New Mexican History* states that of Lincoln County's 2,513 inhabitants, 2,303 were native to the territory. This is in error. The Census Bureau recorded 2,303 residents as native to the United States, including 1,515 born in the territory. Some historians have used Twitchell's figure to represent the number of Hispanos in Lincoln County. My figure for the Hispanic population includes those individuals born in Mexico as well as those born in New Mexico. Ralph Emerson Twitchell, *The Leading Facts of New Mexican History* (Cedar Rapids, Ia.: The Torch Press, 1917), vol. 3, 129; Tenth Census, 1880, vol. 1, 521.

47. Two hundred sixty-nine married Hispanic women lived in Lincoln County. (This figure excludes widows.)

48. Lincoln County, Population Schedules, *Tenth Census, 1880*, NA, T-9, roll 802.

49. Lincoln County, Population Schedules, *Tenth Census, 1880*, NA, T-9, roll 802.

50. Family history compiled by D. Sanchez, November 1977, New Mexico State University (in possession of the author).

51. Darlis A. Miller, "Civilians and Military Supply in the Southwest," *Journal of Arizona History* 23 (Summer 1982): 132–33.

52. *Eleventh Census of the United States, 1890, Agriculture* (Washington, D.C.: U.S. Government Printing Office, 1895), 166 (hereafter *Eleventh Census, 1890*); *Contracts and Agreements C*, 77, Lincoln County Courthouse, Carrizozo, N.M. The Census Bureau accounted for an apparent reduction in number of farms reported for New Mexico in 1890 by stating there had been a failure "to enumerate a considerable number of small farms belonging to Mexicans." See *Thirteenth Census of the United States, 1910*, vol. 7 (Washington, D.C.: U.S. Government Printing Office, 1913), 148.

53. Lincoln County, N.M., Agricultural Schedules, *Tenth Census of the United States, 1880* (hereafter Agricultural Schedules, *1880*), SRCA. The average size of farms in New Mexico in 1880 was 125 acres; the average value, $1,091. *Tenth Census, 1880*, vol. 3, 25; *Historical Statistics*, 463. The census listed the Montaños as owning three hundred milk cows, but this figure is probably in error. Dairies of this size were seldom found so far from large urban areas.

54. Lincoln County, Agricultural Schedules, *Tenth Census, 1880*; *Rio Grande Republican*, 19 January 1884. In addition to the farmwomen, the 1880 census lists among Lincoln County women one Anglo and eleven Hispanic servants, three Hispanic laundresses, two Hispanic cooks, one Anglo saloonkeeper, and one Anglo actress.

55. Tax Assessment Records, Lincoln County, 1898, SRCA; José Analla, Probate Records, Lincoln County Courthouse, Carrizozo, N.M.

56. María Gertrudes Herrera de Chávez, Probate Records, Lincoln County Courthouse, Carrizozo, N.M.

57. See Account Book, 1890, James J. Dolan Store, Lincoln, N.M. On sewing machines, see *Report of the Governor of New Mexico to the Secretary of the Interior, 1895* (Washington, D.C.: U.S. Government Printing Office, 1895), 18.

58. Charles Fritz, Probate Records, Lincoln County Courthouse, Carrizozo, N.M.; *Rio Grande Republican*, 26 September 1885.

59. Lincoln County, Population Schedules, *Tenth Census, 1880*, NA, T-9, roll 802. There were twenty-six Hispanic widowers, seventeen living as heads of household and nine residing in other households. There were twenty-two Anglo widowers, sixteen listed as heads of household and six residing in other households.

60. Shinkle, *Robert Casey*, 136.

61. Klasner, *My Girlhood*, 173, 188; Shinkle, *Robert Casey*, 88, 112, 123–26.

62. Shinkle, *Robert Casey*, 66–67; Endorsement on Cavenaugh to Chief Quartermaster, 31 October 1884, Dist. NM, LR, RG 393, NA, M 1088, roll 55.

63. Lincoln County, Agricultural Schedules, Tenth Census, 1880, SRCA; Dudley to AAAG, 13 July 1878, Dist. NM, LR, RG 393, NA, M-1088, roll 34.

64. See *Contracts and Agreements C*, 222, 385, Lincoln County Courthouse, Carrizozo, N.M.

65. Henry C. Brown, Pension Application Files, Civil War Series, Records of the Veterans Administration, RG 15, NA.

66. Jefferson D. Grumbles, Probate Records, Lincoln County Courthouse, Carrizozo, N.M.

67. *Compiled Laws of New Mexico, 1884* (Santa Fe: New Mexican Printing Co., 1885), secs. 1410–14; *Compiled Laws of New Mexico, 1897* (Santa Fe: New Mexican Printing Co., 1897), secs. 2030–31.

68. José Miranda, Probate Records, Lincoln County Courthouse, Carrizozo, N.M.

69. José Analla, Probate Records, Lincoln County Courthouse, Carrizozo, N.M.

70. Charles Fritz, Probate Records, Lincoln County Courthouse, Carrizozo, N.M. Similar to dower, the husband held a right in his wife's property known as "curtesy," which constituted "a life estate in all of the wife's lands, provided that a child had been born to the marriage capable of inheriting the land." Arie Poldervaart, *New Mexico Probate Manual* (Albuquerque: University of New Mexico Press, 1961), 82.

71. Records of the Territorial Auditor, Licenses, Lincoln County, Territorial Archives of New Mexico, SRCA, microfilm roll 50.

72. *Eleventh Census, 1890, Population*, pt. 1, 241; *Rio Grande Republican*, August 1885. Eddy and Chaves Counties were carved out of eastern Lincoln County in 1889, but the 1890 census failed to recognize this division, counting their residents as part of Lincoln County.

73. Nellie Branum, [date unclear], WPA Files, SRCA; Lincoln County Pioneer Stories, WPA Files, SRCA.

74. *Report of the Governor of New Mexico to the Secretary of the Interior, 1887* (Washington, D.C.: U.S. Government Printing Office, 1887), 8–9.

75. *Eleventh Census, 1890, Agriculture*, 258, 299; *Contracts and Agreements* D, 18–19, 67–68, 74–75, 136–37, 151–58, 172–73, Lincoln County Courthouse, Carrizozo, N.M.

76. *Nogal Nugget*, 19 July 1888; *New Mexico Interpreter* (White Oaks), 31 July 1891.

77. Mullin, ed., *Fulton's History*, 249–78; *Lincoln County News*, 9 January 1931; Lincoln County, Agricultural Schedules, 1880, SRCA. Documents in the P. J. Rasch Files, Old Lincoln County Courthouse, Lincoln, N.M., indicate that Susan's maiden name was Hummer and not Homer, as stated in her obituary.

78. Susan E. Barber and George B. Barber Divorce Records, SRCA.

79. *Deed Record C*, 175–76, *Deed Record F*, 315–16, *Deed Record I*, 555–57, *Patent Record C*, 60, 178–79, Lincoln County Courthouse, Carrizozo, N.M.; U.S. General Land Office, Registers of Lands in the Office at La Mesilla, Timber Culture, microfilm copy, University of New Mexico, Special Collections.

80. *Patent Record C*, 58, *Deed Record I*, 154–55, *Deed Record K*, 445–46, Lincoln County Courthouse, Carrizozo, N.M.

81. *Water Rights A*, 30, Lincoln County Courthouse, Carrizozo, N.M.

82. *Lincoln County Leader* (White Oaks), 28 July 1888.

83. *Report of the Governor of New Mexico to the Secretary of the Interior, 1900* (Washington, D.C.: U.S. Government Printing Office, 1900), 387.

84. *Deed Record I*, 154–55, Lincoln County Courthouse, Carrizozo, N.M.; Tax Assessment Records, Lincoln and Doña Ana Counties, 1891, SRCA. As a married woman, Susan Barber purchased land in her own name. But when selling land, her husband's signature appears along with her own on the deed of sale.

85. *Lincoln County Leader*, 28 July 1888.

86. Susan E. Barber and George B. Barber Divorce Records, SRCA. Newspaper accounts are found in Keleher, *Violence in Lincoln County*, 160.

87. *Bill of Sales Record D*, 403–404, 446, 448; *Deed Record T*, 215, 218–22, *Deed Record U*, 80–84, Lincoln County Courthouse, Carrizozo, N.M.; *Deed Record 5*, 137–39, Otero County Courthouse, Alamogordo, N.M. A correspondent for the *Roswell Register* (11 July 1902) reported that Barber had sold her ranch for thirty-five thousand dollars.

88. *Deed Record A*, 39–40; *Deed Record H*, 290, 429, 432; *Deed Record J*, 247, 297–98, 306–309, 457–58, Lincoln County Courthouse, Carrizozo, N.M.; *New Mexico Interpreter*, 21 September 1888, 15 November 1889, 2 January 1891, 10 July 1891; *Lincoln Republican* (Lincoln), 8 July 1892.

89. Barber to Fulton, 2 July 1928, 1 August 1930, Maurice Garland Fulton Collection, University of Arizona Library, Tucson, Arizona.

90. *Lincoln County Leader*, 11 August 1888. For a delightful view of early White Oaks residents, see Morris B. Parker's *White Oaks: Life in a New Mexico Gold Camp, 1880–1900* (Tucson: University of Arizona Press, 1971).

91. *Lincoln County Leader*, 2 June 1888, 1 March 1890; *New Mexico Interpreter*, 14 and 21 September 1888, 20 February 1891, 3 and 24 April 1891, 8 May 1891, 31 July 1891, 2 and 30 October 1891; *Contracts and Agreements D*, 33, Lincoln County Courthouse, Carrizozo, N.M.

92. *Report of the Governor of New Mexico to the Secretary of the Interior, 1895* (Washington, D.C.: U.S. Government Printing Office, 1895), 56; *Twelfth Census of the United States, 1900, Population, pt. 1* (Washington, D.C.: U.S. Census Office, 1901), 513.

93. *New Mexico Interpreter*, 3 June 1887, 30 October 1891; *Lincoln County Leader*, 19 May 1888, 1 February 1890, 19 July 1890; *Nogal Nugget*, 1 and 28 June 1888; *Rio Grande Republican*, 1 May 1891. Department commander for all chapters of the Women's Relief Corps in New Mexico was Maggie M. Rudisille of White Oaks, who in 1890 attended the national convention in Boston.

94. Barber to Fulton, 24 March 1926, Maurice Garland Fulton Collection, University of Arizona Library, Tucson, Arizona.

8.
_____

"I See What I Have Done": The Life and Murder Trial of Xwelas, a S'Klallam Woman

COLL-PETER THRUSH AND ROBERT H. KELLER, JR.

This article provides a close-up case study of one aspect of the experience of intercultural cooperation discussed by Darlis Miller in the previous article. The period of cultural interdependence could be short or long, depending on local conditions, but it surely existed on most frontiers. In the Pacific Northwest, one of the most frequent forms of cultural interdependence was intermarriage between white men and Indian women. One such marriage, between Xwelas, a S'Klallam woman, and George Phillips, an immigrant Welsh barrel maker, ended violently when she shot and killed him in 1878. Nevertheless, an all-white male jury acquitted her of murder ten months later. Thrush and Keller use the Phillips murder to explore the realities of intercultural relations in the Pacific Northwest. They skillfully use local history sources, both Euro-American and Indian, to flesh out a very contemporary sounding story about domestic violence and a battered wife pushed past the point of endurance. As important as the local sources is the conceptual framework, informed both by legal history and by current anthropological and historical work questioning rigid gender and racial categories. The result is a fascinating article that seems to confirm the comment apocryphally attributed to Sitting Bull: "The West wasn't wild until the white man got here."

> Bones scatter like the hand of winter, ghost that comes back for the marrow, or evidence.
>
> —GLORIA BIRD, SPOKANE NATION ("BARE BONE WINTER")

Christmas Day, 1878. George Phillips, a Welsh immigrant cooper at the Langdon Lime Works on Orcas Island in Washington Territory, trudges along a forest trail with his teenage stepson, Mason Fitzhugh. Suddenly a gun explodes, lead shot ripping through underbrush beside the path and tearing into Phillips, who staggers backwards and cries to Fitzhugh for help. The boy eases his stepfather to the ground, but within moments Phillips is dead. As Mason Fitzhugh runs for help, he sees the killer standing in the brush along the trail. Shotgun in hand, a baby strapped to her back, the assailant is his mother and Phillips's wife, a woman known as Mary, but whose true name is Xwelas. She had fired the gun; she

172

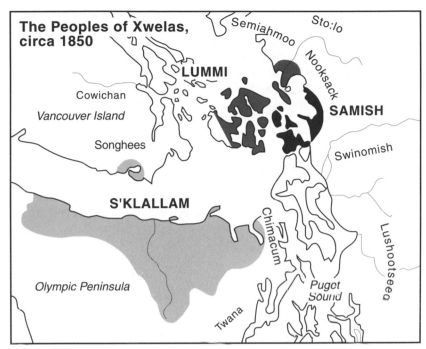

The Peoples of Xwelas,
circa 1850

Semiahmoo

Sto:lo

Nooksack

LUMMI

Cowichan

Vancouver Island

SAMISH

Songhees

Swinomish

S'KLALLAM

Chimacum

Lushootseeq

Olympic Peninsula

Puget
Sound

Twana

Courtesy of David Denton, Western Washington University Media Services

would be indicted for murder and she would eventually be tried and convicted by a court of white men.

Only select histories survive intact. Frequently, these are the histories of war and diplomacy, of the great movers and shakers. In seeking out the other voices—those of mothers, slaves, laborers, natives and others—we often confront the silence and darkness of historical anonymity. When a voice can be traced through echoes reverberating in the records of those around it, that voice can reveal a darker side of our cultural myths. Such is the case in revisionist histories of the American West, in which an emphasis on Indians, women, Asian immigrants, and other "peripheral" voices has challenged and reshaped conventional popular images of the frontier, exposing new stories of accomplishment and survival, exploitation and oppression.[1]

As a nineteenth-century native woman, Xwelas's life was both common and exceptional, and it offers insight into ethnic, gender, and legal relations in the Pacific Northwest. When Xwelas (pronounced hweh-LASS) was born in the 1830s, her people faced sudden and profound changes. She belonged to the S'Klallam, who lived along the northern coast of Washington's Olympic Peninsula, to the southwest of the San Juan Islands. Speakers of the Lkungen dialect of Straits Salish, and relatives of the nearby Lummi and Samish, the S'Klallam in the 1830s were only a few years away from meeting the first large waves of Euro-American settlers. The S'Klallam had first encountered white explorers in July of 1788, when British officer Robert Duffin and his crew explored south from Vancouver Island. Duffin reached the site of today's Port Townsend before being driven away by canoes manned by S'Klallam warriors. Spanish visitors were equally unwelcome during this early period of contact, but when George Vancouver sailed into S'Klallam territory in 1792, the tribe decided to ignore the whites altogether. Vancouver recorded in May of 1790 that the villagers showed "the utmost indifference and unconcern . . . as if such vessels had been familiar to them, and unworthy of their attention."2

A half-century later, new forces gave the S'Klallam, and surrounding native communities, little choice but to pay attention. Diseases such as smallpox began to ravage the coastal peoples, and deadly epidemics— along with a new economy, European trade goods that included alcohol, and massive immigration of white settlers—eroded the North Coast's traditional lifeways. Thus, Xwelas reached adulthood in a period of rapid social change and emotional turmoil. Not only were the S'Klallam forced to contend with the Euro-American settlers, but intertribal raiding and violence in the region may have also increased during the first half of the nineteenth century. Attacks by Vancouver Island tribes and bands from the south, together with the threat of slavery, depopulation due to disease, and the breakdown of traditional ways, could have encouraged a young Indian woman to seek relative refuge in marriage with a white man, miles from her home.3

Xwelas's marriage reveals an important dynamic. Her people and other Northwest native communities did not simply drown under a flood tide of immigrants, merchants, and missionaries. Rather, for several generations after Euro-American settlement, we find extensive cultural interdependence. Newcomers, whether British, Russian, Spanish, American, Hawaiian, or Asian, depended upon native knowledge for survival and for access to resources that fueled the new economies. Likewise, Indians came to depend upon immigrants for trade and protection. Alliances between Indians and whites proved necessary for both parties, one form of alliance being marriage. Before contact with Euro-Americans, different native communities had traditionally intermarried to strengthen bonds and prevent conflict; that practice extended to intermarriage with European and American male settlers after 1840.

One such marriage took place in the 1850s between E-yow-alth and Edmund Clare Fitzhugh. E-yow-alth was herself the daughter of a marriage of alliance between Xwelas's S'Klallam brother, S'ya-whom, and Tsi-swat-oblitsa, a Samish noblewoman. White settlers knew S'ya-whom well enough to apply his anglicized name, Sehome, to a small town on the shores of Bellingham Bay, east of the San Juan Islands. E. C. Fitzhugh resided in Sehome.4

Fitzhugh, a native of Virginia's Stafford County, had served in the Virginia legislature in 1846 and 1847 and had practiced law in California

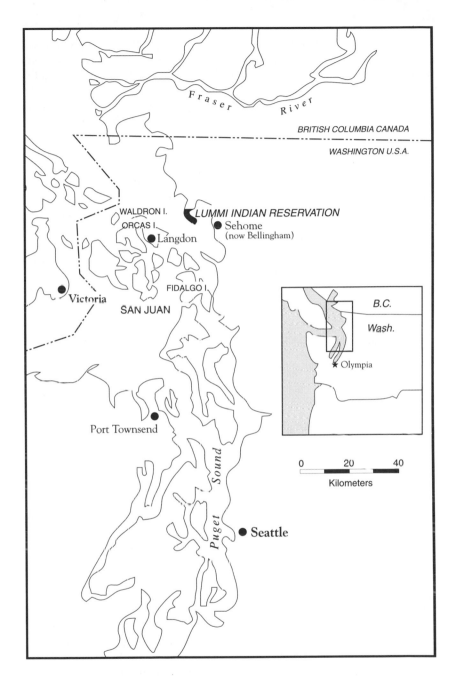

Xwelas's world. Courtesy of David Denton, Western Washington University Media Services.

before coming to the Pacific Northwest in the early 1850s.[5] Although there is no evidence that he was involved in any skirmishes—or that any skirmishes took place at all—Fitzhugh participated as a colonel in the coordination of American troops during the Pig War of 1859, a dispute between Britain and the United States over title to the San Juans.[6] Lottie Roeder Roth, an early popular chronicler of northwest Washington history, described Fitzhugh's years in Sehome as those of the archetypal frontier hero, painting him as "a born fighter, quick to take offense, absolutely without fear, something of a roisterer, imperious and self-willed, following his code of honor without thought of consequences, but withal a man of superior intellect and many kindly impulses. Generous, hospitable, impulsive, self-indulgent, honest and brave; Virginia never sent a more typical example of its chivalry into the Northwest than Edmund Clare Fitzhugh."[7]

Roth's hyperbole aside, Fitzhugh nonetheless was an influential figure during the early years of Sehome. He became, among other things, super-intendent of the Bellingham Bay Coal Company, Indian agent, county auditor, customs inspector, military aide to Governor Isaac I. Stevens, and territorial supreme court justice under President James Buchanan.[8] His busy career did not escape scandal, however. According to one settler's diary, during Fitzhugh's tenure as judge, he allegedly shot and killed a man after a gambling dispute, then promptly tried and acquitted himself of the murder charge.[9]

But perhaps Fitzhugh's most glaring escapades involved his relations with women. Whenever Xwelas or other Indians visited the new white settlements around Bellingham Bay, they did not encounter neatly kept and morally upright communities following an ideal New England or midwestern model. In 1876, Phares B. Harrison, a "home missionary" to Sehome and its sister settlement of New Whatcom, found just the opposite and reacted with revulsion: "We have confronting us here heathenism—enlightened and benighted—civilized and legalized—in its most repulsive forms. . . . Drunkenness with its bloated impurities and crime, is not the most corrupting form of vice among us. Adultery, open, unconcealed, bold, and unblushing, in the cabins of the miners, and in *higher places*, in the Chinese quarters, resists the pure gospel of the Son of God."[10]

Part of this debauchery, in Christian missionary eyes, involved white men's liaisons with native women. In the early Northwest, eligible white brides were few and far between, encouraging the common practice of Caucasian men marrying Indian women, a pact often made for both sexual and economic reasons.[11] In Sehome and surrounding Whatcom County, the Lummi Indians had provided so many brides, or "kloochman," to white settlers that by the time E. C. Fitzhugh sought a partner, Lummi leader Chowitzit protested that too many young women had already married outside the tribe. Chowitzit referred Fitzhugh to the nearby Samish people to the south of Bellingham Bay. There, the Lummi presided over negotiations between Fitzhugh, "the tyee [chief] of Whatcom Falls," and S'ya-whom, the Samish headman. Following the traditions of his culture, in which romantic love played a lesser part in marriage than political diplomacy or social mobility, Chowitzit pointed out the advantages of a marriage alliance, while Fitzhugh spoke of his own wealth and how well he would be able to provide for a wife. In the end, S'ya-whom gave his sixteen-year-old daughter, E-yow-alth, to Fitzhugh, a man more than twenty years her senior. Throughout the nuptial negotiations, E-yow-alth's aunt, Xwelas, watched from the sidelines.[12]

Years later, Xwelas would remember traveling to visit her married niece on Bellingham Bay. The trip required five or six hours by canoe, following the shoreline below the storm-sculpted sandstone cliffs of the Chuckanut Mountains. On arriving for a visit not long after E-yow-alth's wedding, Xwelas learned that all was not well in the white man's household. Fitzhugh had become discontent with E-yow-alth, who had borne him a daughter named Julia, and he now began to entice his young wife's aunt. Eventually, Fitzhugh took Xwelas as his second wife. While multiple marriages would not have raised eyebrows among the Indian population, one might expect it to have done so among white society, particularly when involving a figure as public as Fitzhugh. Suprisingly, however, no recorded condemnation of his bigamy exists. And so Fitzhugh—the "example of chivalry"—took both E-yow-alth and Xwelas, now christened, respectively, Julie and Mary, to form a single family. Xwelas eventually gave birth to two sons named Mason and Julius.[13]

Over time, even with two wives, Fitzhugh found that the appeal of domestic life waned. Sometime in the late 1850s, he suddenly left Sehome for Seattle, taking daughter Julia with him. She disappears from the historical record, but Fitzhugh reappears from time to time. We find him fighting as a Confederate major in the Civil War, representing his home state of Virginia. He formed another family after the war and apparently abandoned them as well, as he would yet a third family in Iowa. Fitzhugh returned briefly to Bellingham Bay in 1874, seeking out his son Mason, now seventeen. Mason, however, gave his father a cold shoulder, and the elder Fitzhugh soon left for San Francisco. On 24 November 1883, his body was found on the floor of a room in that city's What Cheer Hotel.[14] Edmund Clare Fitzhugh's life and death in many ways typify the schism between frontier myth and historical reality: Fondly remembered as a brave pioneer and community leader, he was also an irresponsible, transient womanizer.

While Fitzhugh roamed, E-yow-alth and Xwelas rebuilt their lives. For E-yow-alth, that meant starting again, her daughter having disappeared with Fitzhugh. Eventually, she would marry Henry Barkhousen, yet another county auditor, and would raise a new family on Fidalgo Island.[15] Xwelas also would marry again, this time to a man with a colorful name, but about whom the historical record reveals little: William King Lear.

Lear, an immigrant from Alabama who had profited from the Fraser River gold rush of 1858, settled among the few houses and shops clinging to a spit called Semiahmoo, twenty miles to the north of Bellingham Bay. A land speculator, Lear dispensed titles to lots on the spit and also served his clients as a storekeeper.[16] In the mid-1860s, he married Xwelas, now in her thirties. No details remain of their union, but sometime around 1866, Xwelas gave birth to William Jr., or "Billy." Not long after Billy's arrival, Lear abandoned his family and rushed back to Alabama when he learned that a relative had died. He next appears in 1878, on Wrangell Island in Alaska, where he petitioned to purchase another tract of land.[17] William King Lear did not return to Bellingham Bay for more than twenty years, being finally attracted by the 1889 boom in Sehome and surrounding towns. Whether or not he then made any contact with Xwelas or his son is unknown. Lear's later life is a mystery, but legend has it that he went down with his ship sometime around the turn of the century on another profit-driven passage to Alaska.[18] So, by her early thirties, Xwelas had been twice abandoned by white husbands who pursued their dreams—and their deaths—elsewhere.

According to one report, Xwelas returned to her people near Port Townsend after King Lear left for the East. A single woman with children required support that the extended kinship systems of the S'Klallam community could provide. That she would marry yet a third time comes as no surprise; the S'Klallam allowed and even encouraged individuals to remarry, especially to continue useful alliances.[19] The social standing of Xwelas's third spouse, however, does come as a surprise. Rather than choosing a prominent figure in politics or business such as Fitzhugh or King Lear, she wedded a common laborer. Why? Perhaps, as a forty-year-old woman with three children fathered by two different men, Xwelas may have been considered "used merchandise" by potential white suitors and by tribal leaders looking for strategic marriage alliances. Or perhaps there may have been a romantic attraction between Xwelas and the Welsh cooper. For whatever reasons, Xwelas married George Phillips on 9 February 1873.[20]

As a poor immigrant barrel maker at a lime kiln in the rough-and-ready Orcas Island outpost of Langdon, George Phillips lacked any political or economic standing. Local histories cast him in a much less beneficient light than Xwelas's first two husbands, and by any standard, her marriage to Phillips seems to have been the worst of Xwelas's three marriages. Virtually every account of George Phillips mentions his alcoholism and his penchant for violent rages. His beatings of Xwelas often drew the attention of neighbors, although she was not incapable of defending herself. One account describes an argument between the couple in a canoe, in which Phillips hit Xwelas with a paddle. After a moment of silence, she asked if she could take over the rowing; after taking a few strokes, she then hit him with the oar. Such violence appears to have been a staple of the relationship.[21]

Again, there were children. Two toddlers, young enough to remain unnamed in the records, were playing at the lime works in 1877, when one dropped a lighted match into an open powder keg. The resulting explosion, fire, and deaths may have struck a crippling blow to the already unhealthy marriage of George and Mary Phillips, even though another child named Maggie followed, and Xwelas was pregnant once again at Christmas 1878.[22]

What exactly provoked the Yuletide killing of George Phillips? Some reports claimed that the family—George, the pregnant Xwelas, the infant Maggie, and Xwelas's eldest son, Mason Fitzhugh—had attended a "squaw dance," where Phillips's flirtations with another Indian woman provoked Xwelas's anger. According to this theory, she later ambushed and shot her husband out of jealousy.[23]

Xwelas herself decribed the events of that day during her trial. She and Phillips had gone to the house of a neighbor, William Shattuck, to drink and gamble, she said. She recalled that both she and her husband drank considerably, with Phillips "in very high spirits, laughing & singing songs." Eventually, he became so intoxicated that she asked for help escorting him home after finally persuading him to leave the party:

After we had gone some distance George said, "[W]here were you last night, you old whore you, when I was hunting for you?" After some quarreling I called him a dog & he struck me with the oar on the cheek, then everything became dark and I fell forward. I then rose up & picked up the child when he punched me in the side with the oar. I then called him a dog & said, "don't you know I've got a child in my bowels?" He said he didn't care if he killed me; he'd get another woman, that I was whoring with Siwashes.[24]

According to Xwelas's testimony, her husband repeatedly threatened to kill her after they reached the Langdon settlement and their house in the late afternoon. "George told me to get my things and leave, calling me a slut. He demanded the key to the house & ere I could give it to him, he took the axe & broke open the door." Phillips then grabbed two guns from above the mantle and began loading them. Although Mason Fitzhugh assured her that George would sober up, Xwelas decided to spend the night in the woods. Putting baby Maggie on her back, she took a double-barreled shotgun and walked to a neighbor's root house. As her husband and Mason approached the building along the trail a short time later, Xwelas hid in the nearby brush. Then Maggie cried out "Papa," alerting Phillips:

I raised up from behind the brush. George then rushed forward & grasped the gun by the middle of the barrel. We each tried to pull the gun from the other, & while we were thus struggling the gun went off shooting George. He staggered back calling for Mason. . . . Mason came [and] said to me, "Do you see what you have done?" I answered, "I see what I have done."[25]

The testimony of other witnesses quoted Xwelas as saying that she had feared for her life, but they contradicted her account of self-defense. Especially damaging were descriptions of how buckshot had ripped leaves and branches from the brush along the trail and how no one could have reached the point of firing from the path. To compound the issue,

Phillips's body showed no powder burns, alerting jurors to the fact that he was killed from a distance.

Immediately after Phillips was killed, Mason Fitzhugh, who was near enough that wadding from the shotgun blast flew past him, dragged his stepfather's body into a barnyard and enlisted neighbors to keep the hogs away from the corpse.[26] After a hasty coroner's inquest the next day, Xwelas was indicted for murder. The Orcas Island sheriff immediately took her by boat across the water to Port Townsend, where she awaited a trial that would bring together the two driving personalities in Orcas Island politics and society—Colonel Enoch May and James Francis Tulloch.

Enoch May was no real colonel. The title served merely as a poker-table epithet for this Massachusetts immigrant who led a rough life on Orcas and who had also been present at the Shattuck Christmas party prior to Phillips's death. Although he had been sheriff in Sehome for a few months at the end of the 1850s, locals knew Enoch May better for his criminal exploits in the San Juans, where he smuggled opium, Chinese laborers, and Canadian wool. He once made a bid for the Waldron Island postmaster's job by drafting cronies to sign up as that island's residents when most of them lived elsewhere. May was the San Juan correspondent for at least one newspaper; his letter to the *Puget Sound Argus* first broke the story of George Phillips's death at the hands of Xwelas, whom the editor named "A Disciple of Lucretia Borgia." May used connections with the media to his advantage, once fabricating the story of Lucy Bean, a bogus orphan supposedly living with a missionary family who desperately needed funds to set up schools for Indian children. Thousands of dollars poured in from eastern cities before locals exposed May's scam.[27]

Enoch May had complex relations with the Lummi and other original inhabitants of Orcas. He lived at North Beach where, according to his archrival, James Tulloch, he "had a band of the worst Indian characters always camped under the leadership of an outlaw Indian known as Old Tom to whose credit more than one murder was attributed. Here May posed as King of the Squaw Men, declaring that it was their last ditch [stand] and that he would fight to prevent settlement of the island by white families."[28]

Despite an apparent commitment to maintain Native American dominance on Orcas, May in fact brokered Indian brides to white men. In exchange for fees ranging from twenty-five to fifty dollars depending on age, appearance, health, and social status, May provided women of the Lummi, S'Klallam, Songhees, and other tribal communities to Euro-American settlers. It is quite possible that he sold Xwelas to George Phillips. Men who acquired women through May's service rarely married their mates. In fact, when Superior Court Judge Lewis decreed that white men must either marry their Indian women and assign them one-third of their property or face punishment, a mob of May's men burned the judge in effigy.[29] One wonders at May's motives in preventing white families from settling on Orcas. Was he really an advocate of native control of the island, or was he merely seeking to maintain a clientele of single white men?[30]

Enoch May's role in race relations on Orcas brought him into direct conflict with the island's other major figure who would also testify at Xwelas's trial: James Francis Tulloch. A Methodist preacher's son and a neighbor of George and Mary Phillips, Tulloch had moved to Orcas in 1875 to work at the lime kilns and to farm. He founded and directed the Orcas Island Improvement Association to promote settlement of the island by white Christian families, placing him in direct opposition to May. "[T]he fact was," Tulloch remarked in his diary, "that the half-breed element had always held a grudge against me because they knew I was opposed to miscegenation and had worked hard to get in the white families."[31] May's retinue consisted of Indians, outlaws, miscegenators, and smugglers, while Tulloch enlisted preachers, merchants, and families. Black hat collided with white hat; chaos and debauchery confronted order and purity.

Orcas Island was no simple spaghetti-Western scene, however, and the hats worn by May and Tulloch were of a mixed fabric. On the surface, Tulloch represented an ideal of the pious settler paving the road for civilized progress. At the same time, however, he represented a drive for white racial supremacy in the Northwest. In addition to his negative views of Indians, Tulloch clearly promoted a social order exclusive of other races as well. He founded the Orcas Island Anti-Chinese Association in the 1880s, drafting a constitution and bylaws that would become the model used by similar groups in Sehome, Tacoma, and Olympia.[32]

Despite their personal and political disagreements, testimony from Tulloch and May differed little regarding the death of George Phillips. Both men recalled Phillips's drinking, the fights between him and Xwelas, and the events of Christmas Day. Neighbors Henry Stone and William Shattuck, stepson Mason Fitzhugh, and other witnesses offered only slight variations on the same theme. The major contradiction in testimonies regarded Xwelas's claim that she and Phillips had struggled over the gun; witnesses reported that she had indeed fired from behind a screen of underbrush.[33]

Most of Xwelas's neighbors seemed sympathetic, inclined toward what modern courts would call an insanity defense. Henry Stone, like several other Orcas residents, recalled that

George has at often times told me that the prisoner was not in her right mind. He has often come to my house and told me and my wife that his wife is crazy, and was getting worse every day; and he has told that he was afraid of her. I have seen indications of insanity in her, for instance, she publicly expresses her belief that the death of her two children [at the lime works] was a plot.[34]

Even Xwelas's son, Mason Fitzhugh, testified that his mother would at times act "as if she were not in her right mind and at other times she is all right."[35]

Judge Roger Greene instructed the jurors to weigh whether or not Xwelas understood the consequences of her action and whether or not that action was justified in the light of her husband's violence. Judge Greene also reminded jurors to consider Phillips's character and that he had attacked Xwelas with "the intention of destroying her unborn child."

By common notions of frontier justice, Xwelas should have been hanged. The jury might have doubted whether she was sane or whether her actions were justified, but that she had in fact killed George Phillips was never in question. During this period in the American West, no legal precedents existed that took into account as justification for homicide domestic violence against women.[36] Moreover, one would have expected the bias of white male jurisprudence to prevail over the interests of an Indian woman.

But Xwelas did not hang. When the two-day trial ended on 16 September 1879—almost ten months after the shooting—foreman Rufus Calhoun read the verdict: "We find the defendant guilty of manslaughter and not guilty of murder." The jury recommended Xwelas to the mercy of Judge Greene, who sentenced her to two years in prison, less the ten months spent awaiting trial. In the case of *Washington Territory v. Mary Phillips*, the territorial justice system and Xwelas's neighbors had spent over sixteen hundred dollars to maintain due process of law, to bond witnesses, and to care for Xwelas's children, including the infant Tom, born while she was in the Port Townsend jail.[37] Finally, Xwelas herself was allowed to testify, as was her mixed-blood son Mason. Our conventional wisdom about intercultural relations, about the status of women, about the low value placed on Indian opinion, and about the whimsy of nineteenth-century justice tells us that a jury of white men should have been less forgiving in a case such as this. So why the lenient treatment?

One explanation of the verdict may have been pangs of conscience over convicting a mother with five surviving children, including an infant born in prison. A burgeoning northwest town with eager boosters, prolific newspapers, and a concern for its own image may have found a harsh sentence and the ensuing publicity to its detriment. But other factors emerge as well.

First, many local white men, perhaps even a majority at the time, had married or enjoyed liaisons with Indian women. Even Xwelas's defense attorney had once been a "squaw man."[38] Very possibly some of the jurors had been as well. Thus, while notions of racial and cultural superiority were central to territorial society, white male familiarity with native women could have favored Xwelas in the eyes of the jury.

Second, the presence of Xwelas's S'Klallam kin in the community could have influenced the jury's decision. During the 1870s, Native Americans of the Chimacum, S'Klallam, Lushootseed, Twana, and other tribal groups remained a familiar sight in Port Townsend and other northwest communities. Just as interracial marriages could provide alliances between racial groups, a fair trial and positive outcome for Xwelas could have been important in maintaining stable relations between whites and S'Klallams.[39]

Third, George Phillips's reputation could have prejudiced the jury. Had Xwelas killed Edmund Clare Fitzhugh, William King Lear, or another prominent civic figure, she more likely would have suffered a harsher sentence. But to ambush Phillips, a poor, alcoholic, abusive Welsh laborer, signified no great loss. Social class and national origin could be at least as important as race and gender in ordaining the relative value of human life in the West.

Ultimately, the legal decision probably rested on whether or not Xwelas understood her actions. Unfortunately, the most important psychological evidence, the opinions of doctors called to testify at her trial, has been lost. The foreman's note says nothing on this matter, but it may have been easier to dismiss Xwelas as a crazy Indian woman and to mete out a lesser sentence than to deal with the personal and political consequences of a more severe judgment.

Finally, the murder trial of Xwelas took place during a period in which legal and judicial standards, as they applied to Native Americans, were ill-defined and in a constant state of flux. For example, five years previously, in 1874, a mixed-blood Indian named Henry, or Harry, Fisk stood trial in Olympia for the murder of a Squaxin Indian shaman called Doctor Jackson. Fisk's primary defense for killing Jackson was that the shaman had caused Fisk's wife to become ill and that only Jackson's death could reverse the illness. While nineteenth-century American jurisprudence was not known for allowing shamanic self-defense as a justification for murder, the trial proceedings were marked by an attempt to understand native concepts of justice, and the all-white jury acquitted Fisk after only eight minutes of deliberation.[40] Five years after Xwelas's trial, in 1884, the Sto:lo youth Louie Sam was abducted and lynched by a white mob near Sumas on the Canadian border for the murder of a prominent local shopkeeper named James Bell. According to at least one historian, another white settler named William Osterman was the more likely culprit. Nevertheless, local white thirst for vengeance was slaked when a mob strung up Louie Sam.[41] Considered alongside the trial of Xwelas, in which an Indian woman ironically benefited from a legal system largely created by and for white men, these cases illustrate the kaleidoscopic morass that was the legal status of nineteenth-century Native Americans.

After her conviction, Xwelas virtually disappears from the historical record. Her later life seems to have been removed from crisis or controversy; she lived with sons Billy Lear and Tom Phillips on the Lummi Reservation. She did not marry again, nor did she bear more children, and she seems to have withdrawn from the white world altogether. Sometime near the end of World War I, Mary Sehome Fitzhugh Lear Phillips—Xwelas—died in her tiny home on the reservation.[42]

Xwelas was buried in an unmarked grave at the old Lummi cemetery. Mason Fitzhugh and his family lie in a plot on Orcas Island a few miles from Madrona Point, the traditional Lummi burial ground where the two children killed at the lime works are most likely interred. Other descendants of Xwelas are buried on San Juan Island and near Bellingham Bay. A number of families of the modern Lummi, Samish, Swinomish, and S'Klallam nations are part of her extended lineage.[43]

In his home near the new Lummi cemetery, Gordon Charles keeps a file of yellowed clippings about his ancestors, including Xwelas. One of Charles's grandfathers was Billy Lear and the other Julius Fitzhugh, making him Xwelas's great-grandson on both sides. He brings out photos of William King Lear and family trees penciled on restaurant placemats. He can tell the stories of Xwelas's marriage to E. C. Fitzhugh, of E-yow-alth, and of the negotiations with S'ya-whom. He knows the tale of the murder trial and of King Lear going down with his ship.

Gordon Charles also possesses a photograph of Xwelas. Taken some-time after 1900, it shows a small woman in a gingham dress, her face nearly hidden in shadow by the wide brim of a straw hat. In the background squats the dark, square bulk of a fish cannery; further in the distance are the islands where she spent her years with George Phillips.

Away from Lummi, Xwelas is less well known. On Orcas, only a few people have heard hints of her story; none know her name. Today, the abandoned lime kiln where Xwelas killed her husband is hidden by tangles of bindweed and alder, and the little community called Langdon has disappeared into the forest. Only sixty years after her death, Xwelas is barely a ghost, her voice but a whisper. The evidence of her life is scattered, like the hand of winter.

The story of Xwelas sheds light on the realities of frontier experience in the Northwest, laying bare several assumptions about the region, its history, and its cultural legacy. First, Xwelas's tribal affiliations reveal the fluid nature of Native American societies of the Northwest Coast. Born among the S'Klallam, she lived with the Samish and with whites, returned for a time to the S'Klallam, and then died among the Lummi. In light of her life, we must question the concept of geographically and culturally distinct native tribes existing separate from each other. Instead, complex ties of kinship, political interdependence, and economic alliance wove the native communities together into a regional fabric.[44]

Second, the interdependence of white settlers and Indian residents also becomes clear through her story. Rather than a tide of immigrants erasing the native presence, on many levels—sexual, financial, political—Xwelas's life illustrates the continuing importance of Native Americans long after initial contact. In fact, it may have been the influential political and social presence of her S'Klallam kin that saved Xwelas from a murder conviction.

Finally, Xwelas's relationship to white men helps to shatter the myth that Christian pioneers such as Henry Spalding, Marcus and Narcissa Whit-man, Cushing Eels, and Jason Lee brought civilization and morality to a savage frontier. In many ways, it is the deserter Edmund Clare Fitzhugh, the profiteer William King Lear, the abusive George Phillips, the criminal Enoch May, and the supremacist James Francis Tulloch who represent the savage frontier.

Notes

This essay first appeared in *Western Historical Quarterly* 26, no. 2 (Summer 1995).

The authors are indebted to Sharon Kinley of the Lummi Nation and Northwest Indian College for her genealogical assistance and for introducing them to Gordon Charles. They would also like to thank Francesca Olson for her leads into the history of the San Juans, Steve Kenady for the history and archeology of Langdon, and Lynn and Ann Roberts of the Orcas Island Historical Museum for their invaluable assistance. Ted Hinkley provided information on William King Lear.

1. Leading examples of such history include Patricia Nelson Limerick's *The Legacy of Conquest: The Unbroken Past of the American West* (New York: W. W. Norton, 1987); and Richard White's *"It's Your Misfortune and None of My Own": A History of the American West* (Norman: University of Oklahoma Press, 1991). A superb book using a single life as a window to the past is Laurel Thatcher Ulrich's *A Midwife's Tale: The Life of Martha Ballard, Based on Her Diary, 1785-1812* (New York: Knopf, 1990). For methodological difficulties in studying the lives of nineteenth-century native women, see Rosemary Agonito and Joseph Agonito, "Resurrecting History's Forgotten Women: A Case From the Cheyenne Indians," *Frontiers* 6, no. 3 (1982): 8-16.

2. Edmond S. Meany, ed., *Vancouver's Discovery of Puget Sound* (Portland, Ore.: Binfords & Mort, 1957), 85.

3. The best ethnography of the region is Wayne Suttles, *Coast Salish Essays* (Seattle: University of Washington Press, 1987). On the S'Klallam specifically, consult Erna Gunther, *Klallam Folk Tales*, University of Washington Publications in Anthropology, vol. 1, no. 4 (Seattle, 1925), and *Klallam Ethnography*, University of Washington Publications in Anthropology, vol. 1, no. 5 (Seattle, 1927). For intertribal raiding and violence during this era, see Robert H. Ruby and John A. Brown, *Indian Slavery in the Pacific Northwest* (Spokane: Arthur H. Clark, 1993), chap. 6. For Indian-white relations in the region, see Jerry Gorsline, ed., *Shadows of Our Ancestors: Readings in the History of Klallam-White Relations* (Port Townsend, Wash.: Empty Bowl Press, 1992). Robin Fisher's *Contact and Conflict: Indian-European Relations in British Columbia, 1774-1890* (1977, 2d ed., rev., Vancouver: University of British Columbia Press, 1992) concerns British Columbia but is relevant to the interaction of cultures. Also see Robin Fisher "Indian Warfare and Two Frontiers: A Comparison of British Columbia and Washington Territory during the Early Years of Settlement," *Pacific Historical Review* 50 (February 1981): 31-51. Also refer to Robert H. Keller, Jr., "A Missionary Tour of Washington Territory: T. Dwight Hunt's 1855 Report," *Pacific Northwest Quarterly* 76 (October 1985): 148-55; and Daniel L. Boxberger, *To Fish in Common: The Ethnohistory of Lummi Indian Salmon Fishing* (Lincoln: University of Nebraska Press, 1989).

4. Percival Jeffcoat, "Samish Chief Negotiates with Fitzhugh for Princess," *Bellingham (Wash.) Herald*, 13 October 1968. Although Jeffcoat was a respected local historian, we realize that relying on his undocumented newspaper accounts raises legitimate doubts.

5. *The Virginia General Assembly, July 30 1619 to January 11 1978: A Bicentennial Registry of Members*, comp. Cynthia Miller Leonard (Richmond: Virginia State Library, 1978).

6. See David Richardson, *The Pig War Islands* (Eastsound, Wash.: Orcas Publishing Co., 1971); and Keith A. Murray, *The Pig War*, Pacific Northwest Historical Pamphlet No. 6 (Tacoma: Washington State Historical Society Press, 1968).

7. Lottie Roeder Roth, *History of Whatcom County*, vol. 1 (Seattle: Pioneer Press, 1926), 38.

8. Ibid., 38, 45-46; Percival R. Jeffcoat, "Why Samish Chief's Name Became Sehome," *Bellingham Herald*, 20 October 1968. Fitzhugh's alarm over the plight of the Samish Indians may be found in the Commissioner of Indian Affairs's *Annual Reports, 1856-58*, and in the records of the Bureau of Indian Affairs, Washington Superintendency, for the same years.

9. James F. Tulloch, *The James Francis Tulloch Diary, 1875-1910*, ed. Gordon Keith (Portland, Ore.: Binford & Mort, 1978), 11.

10. From Harrison's November 1876 correspondence with the American Home Mission Society. Correspondence held in the Amistad Research Center, Old U.S. Mint, New Orleans.

Quoted in Robert H. Keller, Jr., "The Gospel Comes to Northwest Washington," *Pacific Northwest Forum* 10 (Winter 1985): 4. Emphasis in text.

11. Gender relations and mores on the frontier were extremely fluid throughout the American and Canadian Wests, continually changing with time and place. Social, economic, political, and personal motives seem to have been as compelling as libido, whether we examine the experiences of the Lewis and Clark expedition or alliances *à la façon du pays* at Fort George, Fort Vancouver, Spokane House, Victoria, or Fort Colville. The life of Xwelas becomes more understandable when we realize that modern categories about racial mixing and generalizations about "marginal people" and "contrived opposites"; about public and private spheres; and about personal, ethnic, and social identity do not necessarily hold up in the context of her life. The authors in the anthology edited by James A. Clifton debunk many of these concepts in *Being and Becoming Indian: Biographical Studies of North American Frontiers* (Chicago: Dorsey Press, 1989), 1–37. Richard White drives home the same point in *The Middle Ground: Indians, Empires, and Republics in the Great Lakes Region, 1650–1815* (Cambridge, Eng.: Cambridge University Press, 1991). For the mixing of trade and personal life as well as the active economic role of native women in the early Northwest, see Sylvia Van Kirk, *Many Tender Ties: Women in Fur-Trade Society, 1670–1870* (Norman: University of Oklahoma Press, 1980); and James P. Ronda, *Lewis and Clark among the Indians* (Lincoln: University of Nebraska Press, 1984). For specific insights into the lives of Xwelas's peers, including her granddaughter Maggie Tom, consult Karen Jones-Lamb, *Native American Wives of San Juan Settlers* (n.p.: Bryn Tirion Publishing, 1994). For discussion of mixed-blood identity, see Jacqueline Peterson and Jennifer S. H. Brown, eds., *The New Peoples: Being and Becoming Métis in North America* (Lincoln: University of Nebraska Press, 1985), especially the contributions of Olive Patricia Dickason and John E. Foster. William E. Unrau examines the issue in *Mixed-Bloods and Tribal Dissolution: Charles Curtis and the Quest for Indian Identity* (Lawrence, Kan.: University of Kansas Press, 1989), 1–21.

12. Jeffcoat, "Samish Chief Negotiates." For more information on S'Klallam and Lummi marriage traditions, see Wayne Suttles, "Central Coast Salish," in *Northwest Coast*, ed. Wayne Suttles, vol. 7 of *Handbook of North American Indians*, ed. William C. Sturtevant (Washington, D.C.: Smithsonian Institution, 1990), 453–75.

13. Jeffcoat, "Why Samish Chief's Name."

14. Jeffcoat, "Why Samish Chief's Name"; Roth, *History*, 38.

15. Percival R. Jeffcoat, "The Last Days of Chief Sehome," *Bellingham Herald*, 3 November 1968.

16. Roth, *History*, 107–8.

17. U. S. Senate, 45th Cong., 3d Sess., *Report of the Committee on Private Land Claims*, S. Rpt. 764, *Serial Set* 1838 (Washington, D.C.: U.S. Government Printing Office, 1879).

18. Jeffcoat, "Last Days"; Roth, *History*, 798; Gordon Charles, interview by Coll-Peter Thrush, Lummi Reservation, 18 May 1993.

19. Suttles, "Central Coast Salish."

20. John D. Carter, ed., *Washington's First Marriages of the 39 Counties* (Spokane: Eastern Washington Genealogical Society, 1980).

21. Pretrial affidavits in *Washington Territory v. Mary Phillips* file, case no. 1070, series 1, box 21, Washington Territorial Case Files, Third Judicial District, Jefferson County, Washington Territory, Washington State Archives: Northwest Region, Western Washington University, Bellingham (hereafter *Wash. Terr. v. Phillips*). We are grateful to Jim Moore, director of the archives, for bringing these records to our attention.

22. Tulloch, *Diary*, 32.

23. *Seattle Weekly Intelligencer*, 4 January 1879.

24. Affidavit of Mary Phillips, Orcas Island, 26 December 1878, *Wash. Terr. v. Phillips*.

25. *Testimony of Mary Phillips, Wash. Terr. v. Phillips*.

26. Pigs are voracious omnivores.

27. Roth, *History*, 35; *Puget Sound Argus* (Port Townsend, Wash.), 2 January 1879; Tulloch, *Diary*, 39–40.

28. Tulloch, *Diary*, 11.

29. Ibid., 11–12.

30. May's position regarding race relations was apparently neutral enough that he was allowed to serve during Xwelas's trial as her interpreter, since she seems to have spoken little or, at best, broken English.

31. Tulloch, *Diary*, 72.

32. Ibid., 71.

33. Testimonies in *Wash. Terr. v. Phillips*.

34. Stone testimony in *Wash. Terr. v. Phillips*.

35. Fitzhugh testimony in *Wash. Terr. v. Phillips*.

36. See Cynthia K. Gillespie, *Justifiable Homicide: Battered Women, Self-Defense, and the Law* (Columbus: Ohio State University Press, 1989), 45.

37. To put this monetary figure in context, consider that in 1880 streetcar operators in New York City earned less than twenty cents an hour, while coal miners earned approximately five hundred dollars a year for working twelve hours a day, six days a week.

38. Tulloch, *Diary*, 36.

39. For an account of nineteenth-century Port Townsend, see Ivan Doig's *Winter Brothers: A Season at the Edge of America* (New York: Harcourt Brace & Jovanovich, 1980).

40. Brad Asher, "The Shaman-Killing Case on Puget Sound, 1873: American Law and Salish Culture," paper presented at the Pacific Northwest History Conference at Western Washington University in Bellingham, 25 March 1994, copy in authors' possession. It is interesting to note that Judge Roger Greene, who presided over Xwelas's trial, also was the judge in the trial of Henry (or Harry) Fisk.

41. Keith Thor Carlson, "The Lynching of Louis Sam: A Story of Cross-Cultural Confusion, Tri-National Relations, and Murder," paper presented at the Pacific Northwest History Conference at Western Washington University in Bellingham, 25 March 1994, copy in authors' possession.

42. Charles interview.

43. Charles interview; Jones-Lamb, *Native American Wives*.

44. Wayne Suttles explores this theme in his essay entitled "The Persistence of Intervillage Ties among the Coast Salish," in *Coast Salish Essays*, 209–30.

9.
___

"Yo Sola Aprendí": Mexican Women's Personal Narratives from Nineteenth-Century California

GENARO PADILLA

In this article, Genaro Padilla shows us some of the ways in which historians can learn from literary critics. In particular, he illustrates the richness of oral history in the hands of a sensitive reader. The oral histories in this article are the testimonies of Spanish Mexican women collected and transcribed by H. H. Bancroft and his assistants in the 1870s. Bancroft wanted narratives for his History of California *that described the daily lives of Californios before the Anglo conquest in 1848. Bancroft got what he wanted but, as Padilla shows, reading the forty women's narratives as personal narrative–autobiography yields information that Bancroft simply did not see. The accounts not only show the personal pain of conquest that Bancroft expected to find but also testify to lives of achievement and self-definition accomplished in spite of the Spanish patriarchal system. This article shows us once again the need to understand women's experience in its complexity: to see how oppression on the one hand and resistance on the other are forged into narratives of self-identity. And it also reminds us that when we bring new questions to even the most one-sided sources, we learn something new.*

Desde muy niñita, ántes de venir de México, me habían enseñado á leer. . . . Ya cuando era mujercita en California, yo sola aprendí á escribir, valiéndome para ello de los libros que veía-imitaba las letras en cualquier papel que lograba conseguir—tales como cajillas de cigarros vacias, ó cualquier papel blanco que hallaba tirado. Así logré aprender bastante para hacerme entender por escrito cuando necesitaba algo.

When I was a very young girl, before coming from Mexico, I had been taught to read. . . . And so when I was a young woman in California, encouraged by the books I saw, I taught myself to write by copying letters of the alphabet on any piece of paper I could find—such as empty cigarette packets, or any blank sheet of paper I found discarded. In that manner I learned enough to make myself understood in writing when I needed something.

So Apolinaria Lorenzana remarks in her "Memorias de la beata" (1878), the account of her life as a nurse and teacher in the mission system of early nineteenth-century California.[1] Doña Lorenzana was one of some forty women whose lives were recorded during the 1870s when Hubert H.

Bancroft was collecting personal testimony for his work on California history. She was in her late seventies at the time she collaborated on her "Memorias"—feeble in body, discouraged because she felt like a burden to the people around her, poor, dispossessed of large tracts of land she had acquired independently during a lifetime of work and service, completely blind. The world she had known was receding into a past as unrecoverable as her sight. Still, during the late winter of 1878 she was scrawling her mark upon history—I say scrawling because at the end of the narrative, transcribed by Thomas Savage, she sealed her life on the last page in a nearly illegible marking of her initials. For an old woman who had lost almost everything, this act of will signified a final utterance of personal identity.

In the 1870s Hubert Howe Bancroft, book-dealer, document collector, and professional historian, solicited scores of personal oral testimonies by "Californios," as the native Hispano-Mexicanos called themselves. These narratives undergird his massive *History of California*, published between 1884 and 1889 in seven volumes, as well as *Pastoral California* (1888), a rather ethnocentric and romanticized history of pre-American California society.[2] As Bancroft himself wrote of the project in *Literary Industries*, he and his field assistants collected some "two hundred volumes of original narrative from memory by as many early Californians, native and pioneers, written by themselves or taken down from their lips . . . the vivid narratives of their experiences."[3] There are, from my count, some 150 Hispano personal narratives, of lengths varying from ten pages to a fair number that are hundreds of pages long. I must confess not only my sense of wonder but my sense of resurrective power at discovering Bancroft's storehouse of California lives; here are scores of disembodied voices, textualized lives stored away for a time when they might be rescued from obscurity: María Inocente Avila, "Cosas de California"; Juan Bernal, "Memoria de un Californio"; Josefa Carrillo de Fitch, "Narración de una Californiana"; Rafael González, "Experiencias de un soldado"; Pío Pico, "Narración histórico"; Vicente Sánchez, "Cartas de un Angelino"; Felipa Osuna de Marron, "Recuerdos del pasado"; Pablo Vejar, "Recuerdos de un viejo."

These personal narratives provide a broad field of information on Hispano Mexicano life before and immediately after the loss of California and much of northern Mexico to the United States in the war of 1846–48.[4] Given the kind of information Bancroft wished to elicit, the narratives generally describe the significant historical, political, and social events of the day; manners, customs, and education; the social economy, and early relations with the native Indian people and the American immigrants. In the act of testimonial compliance, many of the narrators present a picture of an idyllic pre-American California. Nostalgia is especially conspicuous in the recollections of the social elite; however, even those narratives left by members of the lower classes, men who were soldiers and women who worked in the mission system, produce an image of a generally stable, self-sufficient society—at least before the American invasion and subsequent social transformation. The nostalgic tendency of the narratives must be understood, it seems to me, as a direct result of sociocultural loss, especially since almost all are characterized by a general sense of malaise, evident in those narrative stretches that describe political, economic, and cultural rupture. Nostalgia and attendant bitterness is actually the product of testimonial compliance, in which the recollected past is always at counterpoint with the present.

It is the disjuncture between a valorized pre-American life and the profound sense of loss after the invasion that provided the autobiographical moment when past and present could be reconsidered, conjoined, reconciled to some degree. Whereas for Bancroft the collection of these personal narratives was foundational research for his *History of California* project, for the narrators themselves it was the critical and perhaps only occasion for recreating the life of the self, together with the world inhabited by that self. The reconstitution of pre-American society was less an escapist activity than a strategy, only vaguely conscious of its means for sustaining order, sanity, and purpose in the face of economic and political dispossession, spiritual fragmentation, sadness, and longing. An established way of life was disintegrating, being rubbed out, erased—even at the moment the life was being narrated, transcribed, textualized.

I read these narratives as legitimate autobiographical enunciations by individuals whose voices have not been merely forgotten but, like the people themselves, suppressed. Rather than affixing a degree of historical truth-value to their testimony or arguing the merits of their representativeness of Hispano Mexicano culture, my primary concern is to recover the voices of these ghosts. They make their own claim to resurrection simply because, within the confines of oral testimony meant to subordinate their stories to Bancroft's history, these women and men marked their narratives with well-defined personalities. The narratives bequeathed by these individuals may have been used by Bancroft as social history, but it is the ever-present "I" that transforms them from oral history proper into the genre of life-writing we call autobiography. The subtle disclosure of individual experience and the overlay of individual personality upon the description of external sociopolitical realities, as well as the individuating of external events, mark these narratives with distinct autobiographical authority.

As one might expect, of the 150 California narratives in the Bancroft collection, fewer than 40 are by women. When Bancroft was collecting personal narratives, men who held public office, military officials, soldiers, or traders were called upon to record their *recuerdos* more often than were women. Women's narratives, moreover, were considered either supplemental to the men's or as sources of information for what Bancroft referred to as the "woman's sphere."[5]

Typical of men's autobiographies in general, the men's narratives reconstruct the powerful public identities the Californio patriarchs enjoyed before they lost everything to the Americans. Juan Bautista Alvarado, Pío Pico, Antonio Coronel, Mariano and Salvador Vallejo, and

Manuel Castro, along with scores of other once-prominent Californios, collaborated on narratives that reconstituted the period from the late eighteenth to the mid-nineteenth century, an era during which they ruled over a vast expanse of geography and native people as well as their own families. For example, one of the wealthiest and most influential of these patriarchs was Mariano G. Vallejo, whose "Recuerdos históricos y personales tocante a la álta California" (1875) comprises nearly one thousand manuscript pages of personal, familial, social, and cultural history.[6] Aristocratic, socially elitist, manipulative, and exploitative, these men made for themselves and their families a world predicated upon their unquestioned authority as fathers and husbands.

In such a patriarchal world, male authority is seen as giving purpose and coherence to the family as well as to the larger social community. Respect for, obedience to, honor of, and deference toward the patriarch were, for Vallejo, signs of familial and general social well-being before the Americanization; after the displacement of the patriarch, the children fell away from a well-established code of behavior, and the Californio world collapsed upon itself. Once, young men greeted their fathers in the street with respectful address. Young women, once proud of their ability to administer domestic affairs, were in the 1870s interested—according to Vallejo—only in making an impression at the theater and at dances; Vallejo calls them *muñecas incapaces de diriger el manejo de sus casas* (dolls/fashionable mannequins incapable of directing the management of their homes). As he recalls, there were, after the conquest, more *solteronas* (old maids) than ever because men were reluctant to marry, afraid that they would be ruined and dishonored by *mujeres necias y vanidosas* (foolish and vain women).[7]

If, for men like Vallejo, the good old days of patriarchal authority evoke memories of harmonious filial, marital, and social relations, the women's personal narratives provide a markedly different scenario, especially of personal, communal, and gender-related experience. While there is a general affirmation of the Californio way of life, there is also a tendency to expose the constraints placed upon women within the patriarchy. Many of the narratives were composed by women from prominent families whose reminiscences were recorded primarily because of their relationship to certain influential men; yet, although the women may begin their *memorias* speaking about their husbands, fathers, or brothers, almost invariably the men get lost in the narratives. A few of the most memorable narratives were left by working women who claimed for themselves independence and self-sufficiency; men are absent nearly altogether from these stories. My reading suggests that the California women manipulated the interview process whenever they could in order to comment upon gender-related issues, be it tense relations with parents, especially fathers, or with husbands and the patriarchal system in general. In being asked to remember their lives vis-à-vis men, women often subverted the transcription process in order to mark the narratives with their own distinctly gendered autographs.

Aside from the accounts of political intrigues, revolts against various Mexican officials, and the war with the United States that Bancroft wished to elicit from all his informants, from the women he especially wanted "information on manners and customs of the Californians." He prodded the women to remember social events, their favorite dances and songs, their marriages, children's births—in short, their domestic lives as diminutive reflections of the lives of Hispano men. This directive, ironically, meant that memory was pointed back toward women's activities. Providing basic information on the "woman's sphere" created a space in which a woman could remember *herself* and reconstitute her own life. Whenever topical testimony directed by the interviewer gave way to personally significant reminiscence, the narrative becomes genuinely autobiographical. This point of convergence between obligatory testimony and a consciously individuated narrative is also often marked by feminine affiliations— women remember themselves in relation to other women. In each of the narratives I have read, then, a distinct female identity emerges that will not be dismissed.

María de las Angustias de la Guerra's "Ocurrencias en California" (1878) offers a lively account of political intrigues and upper-class relations in pre-American Santa Barbara. Much of the narrative records the revolts against the various governors appointed from Mexico City, the pirate Bouchard's raid on Monterey when Angustias de la Guerra was a girl, social balls and comical scandals, and memories of her politically influential father and brothers. As a representative of the Mexican landholding class and a member of one of the leading California families, Angustias de la Guerra generally ratifies patriarchal concerns over land, wealth, and political and social status. This is as one might expect, since in reaffirming male class prerogatives, she is reaffirming her own privilege. Yet, Angustias de la Guerra is also scathingly critical of the men in power.

When referring to the early incursions of American "adventurers" surveying California, for example, she seizes the moment to issue an unexpected but sustained critique of the Hispano men's handling of the American threat. Referring to events early in the 1840s, she says that it was obvious, at least to the women, that the Americans in the territory were up to no good. When she and other women make their suspicions about a certain Charles Gillespie known to Manuel Castro, a commanding officer, they are chastised. "Castro told us that we were thinking ill of an invalid gentleman, accusing all the women in general of thinking ill of others, much more than the men. We answered that almost always we more often hit the mark."[8] As it turned out, Gillespie was an American agent who was instrumental in staging the Bear Flag uprising in Sonoma (6 June 1846) that led to open warfare between Mexico and the United States.

In a related part of the narrative, Angustias de la Guerra charges that "when the hour came to defend the country against foreign invasion" the military command "performed no more service than the figurehead of a ship." Her sarcastic remarks about the officers are counterpointed by the dramatization of her own part in the struggle against the Americans. She describes an incident (1846) in which a *mexicano*, José Antonio Chavez, who was fleeing for his life from the American troops, was concealed in her home at a time when her husband was away. Although the Americans invade her home, rouse her out of bed—one even points a gun at her—she does not flinch in her resolve to hide Chavez, who is lying under a pile of blankets upon which her infant Carolina is sleeping. In fact, in Angustias de la Guerra's account, it is women alone who are the main saboteurs: María de la Torre, a neighbor; Manuela and Carolina, her daughters; and various maids are all complicit in the concealment of Chavez. Finally, Angustias de la Guerra rather casually mentions that she accomplished all of this after "having given birth to a baby girl a few days before"—this at a time when women were confined to bed for up to forty days after delivery.[9]

The Chavez account, together with her criticism of certain other elements of the patriarchy, constitutes enunciations that mark the narrative with her own name and feminine identity, not those of either of her husbands. Nor is her distinctive personality lost in the a posteriori versions produced by her male editors. Thomas Savage's introductory notes to the narrative he transcribed, as well as those to the 1956 published translation of her memoirs, all but bury her under the weight of men's names and position. Savage wrote, "Mrs. Ord (née Angustias de la Guerra, and whose first husband was Don Manuel Jimeno Casarín, Secretary of State, Senior member of the Assembly, and several times Governor pro tem, of Cal. & c) is well known as a lady of intelligence."[10] The editors of the English translation added, "The historical manuscript, Ord (Angustias de la Guerra), *Ocurrencias en California* was related to Thomas Savage by Mrs. Dr. James L. Ord for the Hubert Howe Bancroft Collection of 1878."[11] María de las Angustias de la Guerra survives only parenthetically in these introductory notes, as well as in much of the solicited narrative, precisely because it was "her connections and position," as Savage noted, that "enabled her to inform herself upon Government affairs"—connections and position vis à vis influential men.[12] Yet, in the entire narrative there is no mention at all of her second husband, Dr. James L. Ord, and only passing remarks on Don Manuel Jimeno Casarín.

Another narrative in which a woman stakes her claim to personal identity other than that of a wife is Eulalia Perez's late-life reminiscence, "Una vieja y sus recuerdos." Perez was reputedly 139 years of age when she related her life as *partera* (midwife), *cocincera principal* (head cook), and *llavera* (keeper of the keys), as well as dueña (supervisor) of various shops at San Gabriel Mission during the first half of the nineteenth century. In recollecting her life history she reenacts the self-empowering process whereby she, some seventy years earlier, had appropriated levels of responsibility within the mission system that, as she makes quite clear in her recollections, granted her authority over numerous men. What presumably begins, for the interviewer at least, as a narrative from which information about the operations of the mission system could be elicited, ends up as a story of a woman, alone with five children, who brought the male-dominated world into conjunction with her own will to be self-sufficient.

Like Angustias de la Guerra, Perez's immediate autobiographical utterance is an act of toponymic self-identification: "Yo Eulalia Perez, nací en el presidio de Loreto en la Baja California."[13] Of her two husbands' names, neither Guillen nor Mariné are noted here or anywhere else in her narrative, except where she concedes her brief marital phases with them; not being present in the text, theirs are names without substance. Eulalia Perez's reappropriation of her given name thus constitutes an act of deliberate self-possession, the willing into textual permanence of her own personal existence. It is as though women like Angustias de la Guerra and Perez realized that their identities were in danger of being submerged and even effaced by the men to whom they were related and by whom they were censored. Their response to the threat of obscurity was to seize the opportunity provided by the Bancroft oral history project to reconstitute their own lives. There are strikingly discernible moments in each of the narratives when, in the process of reciting the customs and manners Bancroft wanted to record, they rediscover areas of long-evaporated personal experience.

Eulalia Perez's location of a distinct identity outside relationships with husbands points to a particularly critical issue in many of the women's narratives. In a word, they reveal no little resentment about marriage expectations. The entire arrangement, from betrothal at an early age to the actual wedding ceremony, was effected almost exclusively between the fathers. The tradition of marrying girls at a young age—between thirteen and fifteen—was a practice that appears especially vexing in many of the women's narratives and is remembered with some bitterness when other momentous life experiences seem forgotten.

María Inocente Pico de Avila, a member of the wealthy and influential Pico family in Los Angeles, defers to her husband's life early in her narrative—"Cosas de California" (1876)—commenting upon his family genealogy, education, military career, and resistance to the American forces. But when remembering their marriage, she suddenly recalls that like other girls she was only beginning to read, write, and do arithmetic when taken from school to begin preparation for her *primary* role in life as a wife. As Pico de Avila remembers:

Muchas niñas no concluían ni esos pocos estudios, porque las quitaban sus madres de la escuela casi siempre para casarlas, porque había la mala costumbre de casar á las niñas muy jovencitas, cuando la pedían. Yo estuve en la escuela solo hasta los 14 años; después me llevó mi madre al rancho para enseñarme a trabajar, y a los 15 años y ocho meses me casé.

Many girls never even finished these few studies, because their mothers nearly always took them from school to marry them off, because there was the bad custom of marrying girls very young, when they were called for. I only stayed in school until my fourteenth year; then my mother took me to the ranch to prepare me to work, and at 15 years and 8 months of age I was married.[14]

In the men's narratives, as one might expect, the primacy of marriage and the shaping of domestic consciousness in women is regarded as central to the maintenance of social order. In his "Notas históricas sobre California" (1874), Salvador Vallejo, brother of Mariano, remembers, "[W]e [the patriarchs, of course, with mothers as the enforcers of male dictates] taught our girls to be good housewives in every branch of their business; our wives and daughters superintended the cooking and every other operation performed in the house, the result of the training was cleanliness, good living and economy."[15] The women's narratives expose such domestic training and early marriages as forms of sexual coercion and social control. Pico de Avila's forceful denunciation of *la mala costumbre de casar a las niñas muy jovencitas* ("mala" here signifying "hateful," "callous," "malign," even "evil") is decisively antipatriarchal. The autobiographical enunciations of the California women, almost without exception, show that they were conscious of the sociosexual function of early marriage, or marriage at any age, for that matter. For women like Pico de Avila, having their schooling abruptly terminated, or being denied a lettered education altogether because of gender, meant having a vital part of the self closed off, stunted.

There were women, of course, who refused to be stunted. Apolinaria Lorenzana, to whom I now return, was one such woman. She had come to Monterey, California, with her mother and a group of orphaned children before she was seven. Lorenzana remembers that the children were distributed among families *como perritos* (like puppies), while she remained with her mother and various other women. Many of the older girls soon married, including her mother, who returned to Mexico with her soldier-husband and died soon thereafter. Over a period of seven years, like the other *perritos*, she was passed between several families, mostly in soldiers' homes. It was during this period, when she was about fourteen, that she taught herself to write on scraps of paper.

Lorenzana looks back to this moment as the beginning of her independent life as a nurse and teacher. She not only proudly describes how she taught herself to write, but how she shared her knowledge with other young women who were eager to learn in a society that discouraged women's intellectual development. But, as she points out, she did not exclude boys from her lessons: "I taught children of either sex to read at the request of their parents."[16]

As for marriage, Apolinaria Lorenzana simply chose spinsterhood. Nowhere in her narrative does she express the least regret that she had no husband or children; never does she complain of having been lonely. On the contrary, she was highly regarded as a result of her teaching and general care of children, enough so that she had nearly two hundred god-children, an honor bestowed much more typically upon men, especially *ricos*, than women, especially *solteronas*. As for not taking a husband, she has this to say: "When I was a girl, there was a young man who often entreated me to marry him. But I did not feel inclined toward matrimony (knowing full well the requirements of that holy institution), and so I refused his offer. He then told me that since I wouldn't marry him, he was leaving for Mexico. So he left."[17]

Lorenzana says no more about the matter. She does, however, have a great deal to say about her work; in fact, much like Eulalia Perez, whom she knew well, she exults in describing various responsibilities in the mission chain. She remembers overland journeys along the coast of the mission. She vividly relates a story told by Doña María de los Angeles, a woman in her care, about an Indian revolt in which her husband was killed and her children kidnapped. Lorenzana's account of this mother's grief is moving: "The miserable mother neither spoke nor cried, for the anguish had crushed her. I tried to console her, and encouraged her to eat, but she was inconsolable . . . and for the rest of her life she suffered terribly, without cheer—at last she died under the weight of her grief."[18]

One notices here and throughout the "Memorias" just how much Lorenzana's narrative is women-centered. She gives substance to women, making their desire to learn, their illnesses, and their griefs real and memorable. Lorenzana often maintained contact with women from their infancy to adulthood through multiple generations; for instance, she recalls: "I had in my charge, caring for her from the time she was two to three years old, a girl, whose mother was my goddaughter in both baptism and marriage and for whose three children I was also godmother. At any rate, that girl, who was my first charge, I taught to read, pray, sew, among other things, and when the time came she married and is now the mother of her own family."[19]

In her late seventies Lorenzana still retains a strong sense of respect from the California community. As Thomas Savage points out in his prefatory remarks to the transcription, "[M]any of the native Californians of both sexes spoke of her in the highest terms of praise . . . as la Beata (the pious)."[20] Yet, there is also a sense of pained resignation at the end of her life. In her own words: "[A]quí me hallo pobre y desvalida, con escasa salud" (Here I find myself poor and destitute, my health broken).[21] Her anguish, however, is not merely the result of age, blindness, and infirmity, for as Savage mentions she "appears to be a good old soul, cheerful," but rather because like many Californios—both women and men—she felt displaced, and hence confused, embittered, resentful toward a nation that had made her a stranger in her own land. Remember, here was a woman who was not only psychologically and socially independent but economically independent as well.

During the many years she worked in the mission, she acquired three separate ranches of her own. Two of these were granted to her by the government, a privilege that was almost never extended to women. The other, situated between the two, she purchased outright. Although Savage notes that she "was loath to speak on this subject, assuring me that she didn't want even to think of it,"[22] she does say enough to convey a strong sense of proprietary interest in her land; she never intended to sell it and is quite clear about the fact that she was swindled out of it, although like many other *mexicanos*, she is not sure precisely how. It is at this point in the narrative, startled by a twenty-five-year-old nightmare, that she says:

Es una história larga y no quiero ni hablar de ella. Los otros dos ranchos me los quitáron de algun modo. Así es que después de haber trabajado tantos años, de haber poseido bienes, de que no me desposeí por vento ni de otro modo, me encuentro de la mayor pobreza, viviendo de favor de Dios y de los que me dan un bocado de comer.

It is a long story and I don't even want to discuss it. The other two ranches they somehow took from me. So, that's the way it turns out that after working so many years, after having acquired an estate, which I certainly didn't dispose of by selling or any other means, here I find myself in the greatest poverty, living only by the grace of God and through the charity of those who give me a mouthful to eat.[23]

Lorenzana discloses no self-pity over her decrepit condition, her loss of sight, nor even her poverty. Evidence of dispiritedness takes the form of sociocultural displacement, present in a majority of the California narratives—in both the women's and the men's. Like nearly all the Californios of her generation, she found herself in the 1870s not only near the end of her life, but at the end of a way of life. With anger and pain apparent in her words, Apolinaria Lorenzana literally inscribes her initials on the final page of her "Memorias" not only as a hedge against her own death, but also, it seems to me, as a gesture of defiance against a form of historical and cultural death.

The women's narratives remind us of just how tenuous existence was in post-1848 society for a people trying to give purpose to the personal life during a time of immense social, political, and cultural upheaval. Life in a stable social world was difficult enough for women. Their narratives make this plain. But what they also make plain is that the American takeover was a trauma that disrupted life for everyone. Bitterness, a profound sense of loss, confusion, and displacement color the women's personal narratives fully as much as the men's. As Lorenzana said over one hundred years ago, the way Mexicanos in the latter part of the nineteenth century were dispossessed of their land and livelihood, often their dignity and their very voice, constitutes a long and troubling story.

Some of the women were so deeply embittered by the events of 1846 that when asked to comment on the war they spoke through clenched teeth. Rosalia Vallejo de Leese, sister to Mariano and Salvador Vallejo, was still so angry three decades after the war that she refused to give more than a brief narrative; what she does remember of the Bear Flag incident of 1846 ends in these words: "[T]hose hated men inspired me with such a large dose of hate against their race, that though twenty-eight years have elapsed since that time, I have not yet forgotten the insults they heaped upon me, and not being desirous of coming in contact with them I have abstained from learning their language."[24] She also forbade her children to speak the language of *los estranjeros* in her presence.

Yes, I know, her words are presented here in English, the language of the enemy, but not of her choice or mine. The document itself was, for some strange reason, transcribed into English even though most of the Californio narratives were given and remain in their native Spanish.[25] Even those few texts that have recently been translated will require careful rereading, since there is evidence of frequent mistranslation. I raise this issue here because it is directly gender-related. To elaborate: Angustias de la Guerra's narrative, one of the handful that have been published in English translation, gives the impression at a crucial juncture that women were not troubled by the American occupation. This happens in Francis Price and William Ellison's translation, *Occurrences in California*, where Angustias de la Guerra is *made* to say that "the conquest of California did not bother the Californians, least of all the women";[26] what she *did* say was "[L]a toma del país no nos gustó nada á los Californios, y menos á las mujeres"—which should be translated as "[T]he taking of the country did not please the Californios one bit, and least of all the women." Contrary to the mistranslation (was it a willed misreading that made for the mistranslation?) of her comments, Angustias de la Guerra's "Ocurrencias" must be read as oppositional narrative. In other words, her narrative as well as those of other California women articulate the fact that they did not welcome the Americans.

Although Bancroft solicited women's personal narratives in order to provide general information on the collective "woman's sphere," the women made the testimonies individually self-reflexive. In each of the narratives I have discussed, a substantive individual identity emerges that warrants autobiographical legitimacy. Apolinaria Lorenzana is distinct from Angustias de la Guerra because both constitute themselves distinctly. Moreover, their narrative lives are contextualized by the sociocultural and gender-related moment that contributed to their historical identities. In that respect, the narratives must be seen as the products of a dialectical process. Since they were collected by men who represented the occupying culture, it is reasonable to assume that Mexican women were engaged in a power struggle within the very interview process. Angustias de la Guerra was sought out for interview because she was related to influential men through whom she had apparently informed "herself upon governmental affairs"; yet by the end of her testimony she had appropriated the narrative process for inscribing her own life. And although at the moment of narration she was "Mrs. Dr. James L. Ord," she did not ratify the American occupation, as perhaps the interviewer had expected. Eulalia Perez was surely approached for interview because she was a curiosity—a woman of 139 years, according to local history; yet she did not relate her life story as a wonder of longevity, but as a story of self-reliance.[27] In each of these narratives there is evidence of evasion, redirection of the past, and reconstitution of a "self" that proceeds beyond interrogatory expectations.

As for the dialectic of gender present in the narratives, while it would be inaccurate to make a generaliding claim that women's narratives roundly criticize the Hispano patriarchal system, they do question masculinist controls within a culture that placed constraints upon their intellectual development, excluded them from the networks of sociopolitical hierarchy, and sought to domesticate their desire for self-sufficiency. Hence, intracultural and gender-related commentary of a critical bent is more manifest in the women's narratives than in the men's, where patriarchal customs are self-servingly remembered. Again and again one reads narratives by women who were articulate, intellectually inquisitive, "self"-conscious, and undoubtedly capable of fully independent lives, as demonstrated by Eulalia Perez and Apolinaria Lorenzana.

Patriarchal and testimonial forms of containment, in fact, often provided the impulse to reconstruct individual identity and personal experience in a genuinely self-empowering manner. María de las Angustias de la Guerra reconstructs her own heroism against the insolent *americano* soldiers and thereby levels a critique at the Californio men; Eulalia Perez marks her consciously planned appropriation of authority in an otherwise male domain; María Inocente Pico gives tribute to her husband but also remembers being yanked out of school to undergo domestic "training" for him; Apolinaria Lorenzana recreates her life not only as nurse and teacher but as property owner who had to contend with swindling Americans. In each of the narratives women push beyond testimonial expectations to discover or invent the narrative space required for reconsidering their lives within a male-controlled domain, for reassessing the social transformation that affected them as much as their male counterparts, and, ultimately, for celebrating their own lives.

Notes

An earlier version of this essay was presented at the Stanford University Conference on Autobiography and Biography: Gender, Text and Context (April 1986); a revised version was published in *Revealing Lives: Autobiography, Biography, and Gender*, edited by Susan G. Bell and Marilyn Yalom (Albany: State University of New York Press, 1990).

I wish to thank Marilyn Yalom of the Stanford Institute for Research on Women and Gender for suggesting changes and expansion. I am also indebted to the encouragement and criticism of Ann Parsons, Josette Price, and Luis Torres.

1. Apolinaria Lorenzana, "Memorias de la beata," 5. This, and each of the personal narratives to which I refer, is housed in the Bancroft Library, University of California, Berkeley. Unless otherwise indicated, references to the manuscripts will be cited by manuscript page. All translations are mine, except those specified in the text.

2. Bancroft's opening comments in *California Pastoral* (San Francisco: The History Co., 1888) should suffice to make my point here: "Before penetrating into the mysteries of our modern lotus-land, or entering upon a description of the golden age of California, if indeed any age characterized by ignorance and laziness can be called golden . . ." (1). The text, comprising some eight hundred pages of ethnographic information on Mexican society before and shortly after 1848, is saturated by this form of ethnocentric consciousness.

3. H. H. Bancroft, *Literary Industries: A Memoir* (San Francisco: The History Co., 1891), 285. It should be pointed out that Bancroft hired numerous assistants to collect the personal narratives. Enrique Cerruti and Thomas Savage were two of the principal collectors who, during a seven-year period from 1863 to 1870, traveled a wide circuit from San Francisco to San Diego transcribing the lives of the Californios. See Savage's "Report on Labors and Archives and Procuring Material for the History of California, 1876–79" and Cerruti's more autobiographical "Ramblings in California" (1874), both in the Manuscript Collection, Bancroft Library, University of California, Berkeley.

4. For useful accounts of the Mexican-American War, as well as the social, political, and cultural transformations that resulted, see Rodolfo Acuña, *Occupied America: A History of Chicanos* (New York: Harper & Row, 1981); Albert Camarillo, *Chicanos in a Changing Society: From Mexican Pueblos to American Barrios in Santa Barbara and Southern California, 1848–1930* (Cambridge, Mass.: Harvard University Press, 1979); Richard Griswold del Castillo, *The Los Angeles Barrio, 1850–1890: A Social History* (Berkeley: University of California Press, 1979); John R. Chávez, *The Lost Land: The Chicano Image in the Southwest* (Albuquerque: University of New Mexico Press, 1984); Leonard Pitt, *The Decline of the Californios: A Social History of the Spanish-Speaking Californians, 1846–1980* (Los Angeles: University of California Press, 1966); Carey McWilliams, *North from Mexico: The Spanish-Speaking People of the United States* (New York: Greenwood, 1968).

5. In *California Pastoral*, Bancroft wishes to appear as a champion of the women, but given his ethnocentric proclivities and his own patriarchal bent, his sentiments are again immediately suspect. For example, chap. 10, "Woman and Her Sphere," opens thus: "Women were not treated with the greatest respect: in Latin and in savage countries they seldom are." (305). The author then adds: "It was a happy day for the California bride whose husband was American, and happier still for the California husband whose bride was Yankee" (312). Later Bancroft delights in comparing Mexican women with their "more beautiful" American sisters, to the merit of neither: "The beauty of women is of shorter duration in Spanish countries than in the United States; but the monster Time behaves differently in the two places. In the states, the sere and yellow leaf of beauty shrivels into scragginess in the extremes of the type; but in Spanish-speaking countries it is not the withering of the gourd of beauty that those have to deplore who sit beneath its shadow with so great delight, but it is the broadening of that shadow. Without altogether endorsing sylph-like forms, it is yet safe to affirm that degrees of beauty in women are not in direct ratio to the degrees of the latitude of their circumference" (324). Otherwise, Bancroft asserts that "among the married women of the common class, there was looseness—not remarkably so, but they were less strict than American women in this respect" (321).

6. The "Recuerdos," unlike the Franklinian autobiographical text that charts the rise of the individual from poverty and obscurity, is a history of the individual's fall from power, loss of wealth, and social displacement. For all its troubling class attitudes and contradictions, it is also a consciously subversive narrative that was, by Vallejo's own reckoning, a staunchly revisionist counterdiscourse. In a letter to his son, Platon, Vallejo writes: "I shall not stop moistening my pen in the blood of our unfounded detractors, certain accursed writers who have insulted us . . . to contradict those who slander 'tis not vengeance, it is regaining a loss." Madie Brown Emparan, *The Vallejos of California* (San Francisco: University of San Francisco Press, 1968), 182.

7. Mariano Vallejo, "Recuerdos," vol. 4, 336–37.

8. María de las Angustias de la Guerra, "Occurencias en California," 140–41.

9. Ibid.

10. Ibid., 1.

11. María de las Angustias de la Guerra Ord, *Occurrences in Hispanic California*, trans. and ed. Francis Price and William Ellison (Washington, D.C.: Academy of American Franciscan History, 1956), foreword.

12. Angustias de la Guerra, "Occurencias," 1.

13. Eulalia Perez, "Una vieja y sus recuerdos," 1.
14. María Inocente Pico de Avila, "Cosas de California," 20.
15. Salvador Vallejo, "Notas historicas sobre California," 99.
16. Lorenzana, "Memorias," 42.
17. Ibid., 43.
18. Ibid., 41.
19. Ibid., 43.
20. Ibid., preface.
21. Ibid., 30.
22. Ibid., preface.
23. Ibid., 30.
24. "History of the Bear Flag Party," Manuscript Collection, Bancroft Library, 5. The Bear Flag rebellion, which initiated the Mexican-American War in California, commenced when a group of Americans took Mariano Vallejo, his brother Salvador, Jacobo Leese, and other Californios prisoner; raised a flag with a bear insignia; and proclaimed their liberation from Mexican rule. Rosalia Vallejo de Leese describes these Americans as "a large group of rough-looking men, some wearing caps made with the skins of coyotes or wolves, some wearing slouched hats full of holes, some wearing straw hats as black as coal. The majority of this marauding band wore buckskin pants . . . several had no shirts, shoes were only to be seen on the feet of the fifteen or twenty among the whole lot." And like Angustias de la Guerra, Vallejo de Leese describes having resisted the Americans, saving a seventeen-year-old girl from being sexually assaulted by John C. Frémont and his officers. She also bitterly remembers being forced to write a letter to a Captain Padilla, who was riding toward Sonoma with troops, requesting him to return to San Jose; she says, "I consented, not for the purpose of saving my life, but being then in the family way I had no right to endanger the life of my unborn baby; moreoever, I judged that a man who had gone so far would not stop at anything (Fremont told me he would burn our houses with us inside them) . . . and being desirous of saving trouble to my countrywomen I wrote the fatal letter."
25. Rosalia Vallejo de Leese's narrative "History of the Bear Flag Party" is only some six pages long. A note in the manuscript vaguely mentions that it was recorded by her daughter Rosalia, but it was probably transcribed by Enrique Cerruti, who was the chief collector in the Sonoma area and whose transcription of Salvador Vallejo's narrative is also recorded in English.
26. Angustias de la Guerra, Occurrences, trans. Price and Ellison, 59.
27. As it turned out, Doña Perez was actually about 104 years old when she narrated her life. Her repute as an "ancient women," however, had circulated sufficiently to make her an item of wide curiosity. In fact, at the very end of the narrative, her daughter, María de Rosario, was worried that a member of the family would try to capitalize on her mother's reputed age: "In June of the year 1876 my sister María Antonia . . . wanted to make some money by capitalizing on my mother for six weeks, exhibiting her in San Francisco for $5,000 in Woodward Gardens, and afterwards taking her to the exposition in Philadelphia. Fortunately, she had already been taken secretly to Los Angeles." Perez "Una vieja," 34.

10

Gender and the "Citizen Indian"

WENDY WALL

Conquest allows the victors to set the rules. U.S. westward expansion in the nineteenth century was based on twin commitments to private property and male-headed nuclear families. These values were legislated in the Homestead Act of 1862, which divided the public domain into parcels of land for individual family settlement. But the same values that were so important to Euro-American settlement had quite different effects on American Indians when they were imposed on them in the Dawes Act of 1887. As described in general terms in the introduction to this section and in specific terms in this article, the Dawes Act forced many changes on Indian reservations.

Various tribes adapted differently to the Dawes Act, sometimes farming collectively for a time, or learning to market women's crafts and domestic products for income. As this article shows, the system of adaptation was complex, and it was not one-sided. Wendy Wall examines government documents and ethnographies from the Round Valley Reservation in California to show the strategies Euro-Americans used to try to teach Indian women "proper" gender roles, and the Indian women's adaptations and resistance. Government policy becomes not just a matter of law, but a series of accommodations and exchanges in which Indian women forged their own survival strategies and government officials adapted their civilizing mission to the resistance they encountered. Wall portrays the active roles of all the women in the process, without losing sight of the power relationships that affected the outcomes.

On 19 November 1910 a fire broke out at the boarding school on the Round Valley Reservation in Mendocino County, California. Before the blaze could be contained, it had destroyed the girls' dormitory, the dining room, the kitchen, and the doctor's residence. Although the cause of the fire was never determined, both the superintendent and students suspected it had been set by several older girls who "hated the school."[1]

The mysterious fire was only the first sign of trouble brewing on the reservation. In ensuing months, the agency's sawmill burned, students ran away, and teenage girls twice tried to torch the remaining buildings. In early 1914, two boys burned the schoolhouse to the ground, while others

Employees and students at the Round Valley Reservation boarding school, circa 1905, Covelo, California. (Collection of the Mendocino County Museum, Willits, California, no. 79-5-4.)

set their dormitory on fire. Meanwhile, adult Indians collected affidavits and circulated petitions calling for the superintendent's removal.

What triggered such overt resistance at the Round Valley Agency between 1910 and 1914? A reconstruction of events at the reservation suggests that the explosion of tensions there resulted largely from attempts by federal officials to meddle in Indians' personal lives. Such meddling stemmed directly from assumptions about gender, family, and sexuality embedded in the policy of "total assimilation" that the federal government pursued from 1887 until the beginning of the New Deal.

As scholars have noted, eighteenth- and nineteenth-century efforts to "civilize" Native Americans often involved attempts to modify Indian gender roles.[2] Missionaries and reformers tried to teach Indian men to farm and women to sew, even as they encouraged both sexes to adopt Euro-American moral standards. The policy launched in 1887 of converting tribal lands to individual ownership—as well as the educational campaigns that buttressed this land allotment program—carried such efforts a step further. In attempting to make citizens of Native Americans, U.S. policymakers envisioned nothing less than, as Theodore Roosevelt put it, the "pulverizing . . . [of] the tribal mass" and the restructuring of

Indian society around patriarchal family units. Indian men would be taught to enter white commercial society as independent farmers and householders, while Indian women would be transformed into the chaste, submissive, and nurturing housewives prescribed by the ideology of Victorian womanhood. These male-headed farm families, reformers believed, would be the vessels that would carry Native Americans into mainstream white society.

The centrality of Euro-American gender norms to the assimilation program—as well as the fierceness with which Native Americans at Round Valley resisted them—highlights the cardinal role played by issues of gender and family in cultural construction and conflict. To the federal officials stationed at Round Valley, legal marriage was a crucial sign of civilization while the boarding school was civilization's cradle. But, because they tampered with personal relationships, it was precisely these institutions that the Indians most resolutely resisted. The Native Americans of Round Valley selectively adopted Euro-American work roles and dress codes that would help them survive in a marketplace dominated by whites. At the same time, they fought off all outside attempts to interfere with their families and their personal lives. This resistance ultimately contributed to the disillusionment of white officials with the innate "equality" of their Indian charges and to the failure of the assimilation campaign.[3]

In the late nineteenth century, American reformers and policymakers saw the idealized Victorian family as the linchpin of civilization. This white, middle-class family ideal revolved around the twin pillars of sexual purity and "separate spheres." The Victorian couple was expected to reserve sexuality for marriage and to remain together until separated by death. The husband would work outside the home, engaging in politics and earning money to support the family. The wife shaped the domestic sphere, nurturing her husband and children and maintaining her home's tranquility and moral character.

However unrealistic this ideal was for many white Americans, it differed dramatically from the conceptions of gender, sexuality, and family held by the various Native American groups overseen by the Round Valley Agency. In 1890, remnants of the Yuki, Concow, Wailaki, Achumawi, and Nomlaki tribes, as well as several bands of Pomo, made their home on the reservation, which was located 150 miles north of San Francisco between the Eel River and what is now the Mendocino National Forest. In the early twentieth century, the agency's purview was extended to encompass hundreds of Indians, mostly Pomo, living in small "rancherías" south of the reservation.[4]

Prior to contact with whites, all of these tribes—like most cultures—distinguished between men's and women's roles; however, their conceptions of those roles differed from one another as well as from the Victorian ideal. All of the Round Valley tribes saw hunting as an exclusively male domain, but women aided in fishing and insect hunts and collected the bulk of the wild plant food on which the Indians subsisted.

Most household duties fell to women; however, men generally performed domestic tasks if their wives were observing menstrual taboos, and Wailaki men fashioned garments. Although mothers played the principal role in child rearing, fathers and other family members also took turns caring for offspring and tribal members were quick to adopt children who had been orphaned or deserted. Most of the tribes had some men who wore female clothing and followed the occupations of women.[5]

The power and privilege reserved for each sex also differed from tribe to tribe. Most of the Round Valley tribes, like Euro-Americans, counted descent through the male line and reserved powerful positions for men. However, two of the tribes most heavily represented at Round Valley—the Yuki and Pomo—accorded women higher status. The Yuki traced descent along maternal lines, and if a Yuki chief left no son, his sister often served until a male successor could be appointed. The Pomo favored both matrilineal descent and matrilocal residence and had some tribelets with female chiefs. Women could become shamans and powerful "bear doctors," and a few were admitted to male societies. A multifamily dwelling and the land surrounding it was said to be owned by the oldest woman. The Pomo often gave their children two names—one conferred by maternal relatives—and naming generally favored the mother's line.[6]

But it was on issues of marriage, divorce, and sexuality where all of the Round Valley Indians differed most dramatically from white middle-class reformers. At Achumawi girls' puberty ceremonies, the celebrants sang bawdy songs and had intercourse in the bushes. Pomos thought of courtship as a time of sexual enjoyment, and none of the tribes barred premarital sex.[7] Girls often married in their early-to-mid teens and were sometimes betrothed even before they reached puberty. Marriage required neither legal nor religious sanction, although family approval was usually necessary. It was accomplished by the couple living together, sometimes followed by an exchange of gifts between families. Although the various tribes held marital fidelity as an ideal, some men took two or more wives and adultery was not always treated seriously. Divorce was common: Either party could leave the other for any reason, and many Indians had two or more partners over the course of a lifetime.[8]

Such cultural patterns were severely tested in the 1850s as gold-seeking white settlers poured into northern California. In the decade following the discovery of gold at Sutter's Fort, the tribes north of San Francisco Bay suffered some of the most brutal treatment of any Native American group on the continent. White miners and other settlers hunted Indian men and raped Indian women, while fortune seekers kidnapped both adults and children and sold them into indentured servitude. Such rampaging on the part of whites prompted the U.S. government to establish the Nome Cult Indian Farm at Round Valley in 1856. Two years later, the farm became the Round Valley Reservation.[9]

By 1890, forty years of contact and conflict with white settlers, soldiers, and missionaries had eroded some native customs, while intertribal marriage and reservation life had blurred some of the distinctions between tribes. Most Round Valley Indians spoke English, wore "white man's clothes," and lived in frame houses rather than slab huts. Nevertheless, they were still far from the "civilized" standards proclaimed by white reformers, policymakers, and bureaucrats. The Round Valley Indians retained their largely communal lifestyle, living in villages and doing a small amount of farming communally. Both men and women supplemented government rations by migrating off the reservation to pick hops for white farmers. With one brief exception, efforts to persuade the Indians to convert to Christianity and marry "legally" had been wholly unsuccessful.[10]

For the federal agents and missionaries trying to "civilize" the Indians before they were overrun by white settlers, time appeared to be running out. White ranchers stole agency cattle and grazed their herds on reservation land. White settlers squatted in the small, fertile valley. In 1887, when the Round Valley agent summoned troops to drive the squatters away, the white settlers persuaded a friendly state court to issue an injunction on their behalf.

Round Valley was not the only reservation facing such difficulties: From the South Dakota badlands to the California coast, white settlements were engulfing Indian reservations and Euro-Americans were clamoring for more land. Independently, many reformers were becoming disillusioned with a reservation system noted mainly for its corruption. Far from helping the Indians, the reservations actually seemed to many whites to be hindering their progress. The solution, reformers concluded, was to do away with reservations entirely and pursue "total assimilation." That meant remaking Indian society—from property values to gender roles—to bring it into line with Euro-American ideals.

The cornerstone of this assimilation program, and of Indian policy for the next half-century, was the General Allotment, or Dawes, Act. Passed in 1887 but implemented over the next several decades, the act established a pathway for bringing Indians into "mainstream" American society by giving the U.S. president the right to divide reservation lands among individual Indians. The federal government would hold these tracts in trust for twenty-five years, at which time Indians would receive full title to the land and could do with it as they wished. When they received their allotments, Indians would also become U.S. citizens. Land that wasn't allotted—reformers and policymakers reasoned that Indians had more than they could possibly manage—would be sold by the government to railroads and settlers. The proceeds would be held by the U.S. Treasury and used to "educate" and "civilize" the tribes.[11]

The Dawes Act temporarily appeased rapacious white westerners by freeing up unallotted Indian land, but it was not simply a cynical land grab. As Frederick Hoxie has shown, it reflected many reformers' deep faith in the great homogenizing power of American institutions, as well as their surprisingly egalitarian assessment of Indians' innate abilities. "The Indian is not unlike his white brother in moral and intellectual endowments and aspirations," J. D. C. Atkins, the commissioner of Indian affairs wrote in 1887. "Any people of whatever race or color would differ little from our Indians" if they lived in tribes, held land communally, and received government rations and clothes. Under such conditions, even "enterprising Yankees" would become "a race of shiftless paupers," Atkins concluded. The Dawes Act would aid the Indians by eliminating such handicaps; it would "dissolve all tribal relations and place each adult Indian upon the broad platform of American citizenship."[12]

But just as American citizenship in the 1880s did not afford equal rights to white men and women, the Dawes Act was informed by the reformers' assumptions about separate and different roles for the Indian sexes. When the Board of Indian Commissioners welcomed the passage of the Dawes Act as the "Indian emancipation day," the commissioners were clearly focusing on male Indians: "The measure gives to the Indian the possibility to become a man instead of remaining a ward of the government. It affords him the opportunity to make for himself and his family a home, and to live among his equals a manly and independent life."[13] As the board's wording suggests, many policymakers and reformers believed that a civilized society was, by definition, one organized around patriarchal family units.

The degree to which this concept of civilization informed the assimilation campaign becomes sharply apparent in the 1892 annual report of the commissioner of Indian affairs. In a section entitled "What Is an Indian?" Commissioner Morgan considered whether a woman who was one-quarter Indian should be denied an allotment because her father was white. Morgan first described the inheritance practices of the U.S. and other "civilized nations": "Under the rule upon which a family is constructed among civilized nations the predominant principle is descent through the father. The father is the head of the family. When a man marries, his wife separates herself from her family and kindred and takes up her abode with her husband, assumes his name, and becomes subordinate, in a sense, to him." That said, Morgan went on to acknowledge that in many North American Indian tribes the line of descent was through the mother, and "in many instances the wife and not the husband is recognized as the head of the family." He concluded that, for purposes of allotment, the law of descent should be loosely construed and take into account Indian practices. However, once Indians became citizens by taking allotments, "the old English common law, which makes the father the controlling factor and determines relationships through him" should apply. In Morgan's schema, patrilineal families were clearly associated with civilization and citizenship; matrilineal families were a sign of savagery. The allotment program would transfer Indians from "primitive" matrilineal to "civilized" patrilineal law.[14]

The implications of this approach soon became apparent on the Round Valley Reservation. In 1894, the agency's Indians finally received their allotments, well ahead of some tribes, but hardly soon enough to satisfy the reservation's agents. Within days of allotment, the new acting agent began moving Indian families out of their villages and onto their allotted tracts of land. By fall, the last of the village houses had been torn down, and soon thereafter all government rations ceased.[15]

As the destruction of the villages suggests, allotment at Round Valley entailed far more than simply giving individual Native Americans tracts of land. Instead, federal officials attempted to break up the Indians' kinship-based communal society and restructure it around patriarchal and patrilineal nuclear families. A circular from the Office of Indian Affairs, for instance, urged Round Valley's agent and school superintendent to "systematically endeavor . . . to have children and wives known by the names of their fathers and husbands." The circular noted that once Indians became citizens, they would be subject to the inheritance laws of the various states. If different family members had different names, the result would be "needless confusion."[16]

Washington's vision of male-headed nuclear families also guided the allotment of land. When the Round Valley Reservation was divided, most Indians received ten acres of valley land; wives got just five acres. Thus, Maggie Hoxie received less land than her husband, her three-year-old son, and even her three-month-old daughter. By contrast, Sallie Haines, who was single, got the full ten acres. So did Martha Doan, a thirty-one-year-old with three children and no husband in sight.[17]

In giving Round Valley wives less land than their husbands and children, federal officials clearly assumed that these women could rely on their husbands for lifelong financial support. But this assumption over-looked the ease and frequency with which the Round Valley Indians divorced.[18] Moreover, the assumption that husbands controlled their wives' property could be used to justify depriving women of full title to their land. In 1912, for instance, departed Round Valley superintendent Horace Johnson recommended against giving Minerva Allen her patent in fee because "I fear her husband would dissipate her property." Allen's husband, Johnson explained, had trouble keeping a job and was rumored to have shown attention to another woman. Johnson recommended that his successor sell Allen's allotment and use the money to buy her a home in the area.[19]

In the long run, however, the most disruptive aspect of this policy was the determination of who constituted a "wife." In 1894 most Indians on the reservation were married only by tribal custom. But the Office of Indian Affairs decreed that all couples cohabiting at the time of allotment would be considered married under state law.[20] This ruling eventually became a major source of tension on the reservation as agents and superintendents tried to prosecute Indians who changed partners without obtaining formal divorce decrees from California courts.

If allotment was the first step in the process of preparing Native Americans for citizenship, education was the second. Reformers from the eighteenth century on had looked to education as a solution to the "Indian problem," but only after the Civil War did the federal government become actively involved. By the 1870s, the Office of Indian Affairs had concluded that only a universal school system could assimilate Native

Americans, and in 1879 it opened the first off-reservation boarding school in Carlisle, Pennsylvania. The philosophy of "full and immediate assimilation" embodied in the Dawes Act gave the federal thrust into Indian education an additional push. "The time has come in our history for us to recognize that the only good Indian is an educated Indian," Commissioner T. J. Morgan told the Indian Rights Association in an 1889 speech. Such education would "enable [the Indians] to compete successfully with the white man on his own ground and with his own methods."[21]

Indian education was designed to teach Native Americans not only reading and writing but also "a love of labor and a habit of working." As several scholars have pointed out, such education revolved around gendered Euro-American ideas of work and morality.[22] Reformers particularly emphasized the education of Indian girls, whom they believed to be the key to "civilized" homes. As one prominent reformer wrote in 1881, "If we educate the girls of to-day, we educate the mothers of tomorrow, and in educating those mothers we prepare the ground for the education of generations to come."[23]

Ironically, although the Victorian ideal revolved around nuclear families, federal officials often believed the first step in instilling this ideal was separating Indian children from their parents. Only in boarding schools, many reformers and policymakers believed, would students be sufficiently isolated from the contaminating influences of their home environments. At Round Valley, agents and superintendents saw a boarding school as crucial to enforcing Euro-American moral and sexual codes.[24]

When the first Indian boarding school opened on the Round Valley Reservation in 1881, Agent Henry Sheldon insisted that the school's teachers maintain sex segregation among the Indian students to prevent sexual contact he deemed immoral. Sheldon was angry when he learned that one instructor had allowed boys and girls to play together when the agent and his wife (a teacher at the school) were absent. He was even angrier when he discovered that the school's missionary had tried to arrange marriages for two Indian girls—ages fourteen and sixteen—whom Sheldon had forbidden to wed. In July 1883 Indian students burned the school to the ground, probably in part because of Sheldon's harsh enforcement of middle-class Euro-American moral codes.[25]

The day school that immediately replaced the burned boarding school continued to teach Indian boys to farm and Indian girls to sew. Nevertheless, the reservation's agents continued to lobby for a new boarding school that would prevent sexual mischief. "The want of a boarding school is seriously felt here," Agent Theodore F. Willsey wrote the commissioner of Indian affairs in 1885. "It is simply impossible to protect the young and half-grown girls from the insults of the young 'bucks' while they are allowed to live in the camps." Two years later, C. H. Yates complained, "The moral training these children receive during [day] school hours is more than offset by the vices of camp life, and I am powerless to prevent this without the aid of a boarding school." In 1890, the returned agent Willsey was blunter still: "Boarding-school buildings should be erected at once for the protection of the young girls. Morality is unknown in Indian camp life. Scarcely a girl reaches the age of 14 without being a mother."[26]

In 1897, three years after the allotment of the Round Valley Reservation, the OIA granted the agents' wish and opened the Round Valley Industrial Boarding School. Just as it enforced Victorian sexual codes, the school taught Indian children Euro-American gender work roles. Although all students spent several hours a day in the classroom, much of their time was devoted to learning practical tasks. The boys worked with the school farmer, gardener, carpenter, stockman, and stableman, while brigades of girls aided the seamstress, laundress, and cook.[27]

At least at the outset, such training seems to have been geared to teaching Indian children to become independent farmers and farmwives. In a report sent to Washington in 1900, Superintendent Harry Liston noted that Indian boys were being taught "such information as is needed to successfully manage a farm in this valley." Meanwhile, in addition to the tasks already noted, girls were being taught to make beds; care for the sick; make butter; and can fruit, jam, jellies, and preserves. These, Liston added, were "all the duties most likely to devolve on a housewife" and thus "everything they will in all probability be called upon to perform in future life."[28]

At the Round Valley school, gifts, games, magazines, and clothes also reinforced gender roles. The school subscribed to *Boys' World* and *Girls' Companion*, as well as to *Cosmopolitan* and the *Ladies' Home Journal*. Teachers taught Indian children "white children's games"—"break bronchos" and marbles for the boys, school and "keep house" for the girls. The school had a marching band and a baseball team, for boys only. Girls received other benefits: In 1905, the school spent $9.60 on five dozen pairs of women's hose.[29]

Despite such amenities, life at the school was frequently harsh. For the older girls, whose work was essential to keeping the school running, chores often left little time for books or play. And discipline was generally strict. In 1902, Liston temporarily suspended the cook after she beat six-year-old Lara Parker for forgetting to put a pitcher of water on the table. Seven years later, U. L. Clardy explained why the laundress would make a good head matron: "Mrs. Tuttle is a woman who understands Indian children and handles them with good results," the agent wrote. "She appears to have little sympathy for the children."[30]

The school could also be a deathtrap. Both the sewage and water systems were in "deplorable condition" when the school opened, and the damp, drafty, overcrowded buildings bred consumption. On a reservation where disease took a heavy toll, the death rate among students was unusually high: Between 1899 and 1905, about 2 percent of the student body died each year, according to the reservation physician. In this, Round Valley was hardly unique. The monthly report forms Washington sent to Indian schools around the country routinely asked how many students had died.[31]

Two Native American girls and a school employee inside a building at the Round Valley Reservation boarding school, circa 1905, Covelo, California. (Collection of the Mendocino County Museum, Willits, California, no. 79-5-5.)

From the beginning, the boarding school stirred distrust and resentment among some Indians. Many older Indians at Round Valley remembered the 1850s and 1860s when rampaging white settlers kidnapped Indian children and sold them into indentured servitude far away from their families. Even many parents who wanted their children educated worried about treatment at the boarding school. But if parents tried to keep their children home, Round Valley officials often sent out the reservation police. Only away from their home environments, the agents and superintendents believed, could girls be protected and children taught their proper roles.[32]

The allotment program and boarding schools were two pillars of the "total assimilation" campaign. But by the early 1890s, the Office of Indian Affairs had begun to worry about a hole in its plans. Adult male Indians had long been instructed in farming techniques by reservation farmers and stockmen, but the Indian woman had been left "to work out as best she could the problem of exchanging a teepee or wigwam for a neat, comfortable and well-ordered home according to civilized standards," one report warned. Unable to observe the practices of civilized white neighbors, she had taken the habits of her outdoor life inside. "Dirt, disease and degradation were the natural consequences," the report concluded.[33]

In the eyes of policymakers and reformers, such dirt and degradation threatened the entire plan to reorganize Indian society around civilized single-family homes. "It is no wonder that Indians sometimes fail to take kindly to civilization presented in such a guise," the commissioner of Indian affairs wrote. He worried that Indians would contrast the "squalid home" to the "freedom, fascination, and quasi-dignity of a roving life." And, though Indian girls learned the habits of housework in school, these practices received no reinforcement and were quickly forgotten.

In 1891, the Office of Indian Affairs developed a program to address this problem. Pressured by female reform groups like the Women's National Indian Association, it dispatched "field matrons" across the country so that "Indian women may be influenced in their home life and duties, and may have done for them in their sphere what farmers and mechanics are supposed to do for Indian men in their sphere." These government-sponsored household missionaries would be the "powerful ally of the schools." They would help put Indian civilization on "the right basis, which is the home basis."[34]

The first Round Valley field matron took up her post in 1897, and over the next two decades at least four other field matrons worked on the reservation or in the district's scattered rancherias and encampments.[35] By visiting Indian women and inviting them into their homes, these middle-class white women instructed their native neighbors in everything from ventilation to virtue. "When Indian women come to my house I treat them like white friends. I do my housework before them and entertain them like any guests," wrote Carrie Moses in November 1897. Eleven years later, Linnian Tindall reported that she tried to encourage marriage and chastity "by kindly talks when visiting."[36]

Through visits, chats, and informal classes, the field matrons instructed Indian women in the principles of "women's work." Over the years, they taught knitting, sewing, ironing, breadmaking, gardening, canning, fancy needlework, and the intricacies of making buttonholes. They handed out recipes, distributed flower seeds and stressed to Indian women "the duty they owe to their families to keep their houses clean." Tindall taught Indian girls the twin principles of grammar and laundry work by having them write compositions on starch making.[37]

At the same time, the field matrons directed much of their attention to the intertwined issues of manners and morals. They promoted church, temperance, and charity and took up the banner of "social purity," the late-nineteenth-century movement that urged both men and women to control their sexuality and confine it to marriage. "I have had much to say to them lately on social purity and try to have them properly married," Moses wrote in 1898. Tindall distributed Bibles and moral literature, organized a women's aid society, and used sewing classes to "talk to [older girls] about their 'future'" and "instill into them the right principles of womanhood."[38]

The field matrons' tone, as reflected in their reports, fluctuated between the moralistic and the practical and humane. This tension became more apparent in the early twentieth century as matrons shifted more of their attention to issues of sanitation and health. "Have called their attention to the disease breeding qualities of refuse," Tindall reported in 1909. "Try to teach them that eating regularly and cooked food is the proper way to live." Tindall campaigned for ventilation, clean underwear, and the widespread use of lime. She passed out sputum cups to consumptives and warned of the dangers of putrified meat. Nevertheless, her frequent use of the word "proper" suggests an underlying cultural agenda: I "tell them that they will be healthier [if they] work and live as white people do," she wrote.[39]

Although the field matrons focused on Indian women and girls, they didn't neglect the male members of the household. The Indian Office encouraged field matrons to "give to the male members of the family kindly admonition as to the 'chores' and heavier kinds of work about the house which in civilized communities [are] generally done by men." While Moses reported that she was doing just that, Tindall went even further. As part of her campaign for marriage and chastity, she urged young boys "to respect their girl companions . . . and lead self-respecting lives." Later, she tried to wipe out "'vulgar' or unseemly talk" by appealing to "the 'manhood' of fathers and brothers."[40]

Charged initially as domestic missionaries, the field matrons soon found they were spending much of their time as nurses and nurturers. Tuberculosis was rampant in the Round Valley district around 1900 and—together with whooping cough, measles, chicken pox and the "grippe"—it took a heavy toll. Moses, Tindall, and Ella S. Brown all cared for the sick and delivered food regularly to elderly and disabled Indians, who had been left deserted and destitute in the new cash-based economy. As Moses wrote in 1898, "The main need here of a Field Matron is to feed the sick and have some heart for the needy."[41]

Confronted daily by sickness and suffering, the field matrons quickly became advocates of increased federal aid. Their monthly and quarterly reports were filled with pleadings for the government to provide land for the landless, medicine for the sick, and food for the old and disabled. "I would have liked to take an Inspector on my walks among the old people. I think the sight would convince him of the great need of a hospital for the helpless," Moses wrote in 1898. By 1914, Emma Alexander had scaled down the request: She wanted two single beds for the room in her quarters that she had converted into an emergency room.[42]

Requests for aid sometimes brought the field matrons into direct conflict with their male supervisors. In November 1908, after months of begging for food and old clothes for elderly and disabled Indians, Linnian Tindall added a note of urgency to her request: "Some of the old ones are apt to freeze or starve if this cannot be done soon." Nevertheless, the Round Valley superintendent, Horace Johnson, recommended that Washington reject the plea. Although he agreed that the government should help the Indian, "this helping hand should not, except in very unusual cases partake of the nature of gratuities, but . . . should be in the nature of assistance that will help him to help himself." Education, field matrons, legal protection, and agricultural advice were acceptable, Johnson concluded. "Subsistence and clothing" were not.[43]

Tindall's aid request may have reflected her growing realization that the idealistic, if ethnocentric, goals of the assimilation program were crashing headlong into both economic reality and Indian resistance. At least initially, both Washington policymakers and Round Valley agents had hoped to turn Indians into independent farmers and farmwives. But this optimistic vision—while revealing an upbeat assessment of Indians' innate ability to assimilate—completely overlooked the realities of their daily lives.

The Dawes Act had called for each Indian head of household to receive 160 acres of farmland, if possible. But Round Valley had little arable land to begin with and large tracts were set aside for agency buildings and sale to whites. Thus, those Indians who received allotments got at most 10 acres of "tillable" land. Some allotments were on steep, rocky hillsides, while others were in swampland or creek beds. Even those Indians who had excellent soil—and who could afford both tools and seed—could hardly run a farm on a 10-acre patch. "Gardening might be very successfully conducted were there any market for garden produce," Superintendent Johnson observed. But the reservation was several days away from the railroad—when the roads were passable at all.[44]

All this meant that even Indians who continued to farm their allotments could rarely make enough to support their families. Many simply leased or abandoned their land, and even those who stayed on the reservation generally migrated off it to work for whites in the area. In this migratory cycle, they were joined by hundreds of ranchería Indians who had never received allotments at all. The men worked as stockmen, sheepshearers, crop pickers and day laborers. The women washed clothes and picked crops too. The field matrons thus often found their work hampered by the striking disparities between what they were trying to teach and the realities of the Indians' daily lives. The gender roles and "civilized" home values dictated by Washington bureaucrats might have been ignored even by the independent farm families those bureaucrats thought they were creating. To the Indians with whom the Round Valley field matrons worked—poor, sometimes landless, migratory laborers—such values were often irrelevant at best.

Field matrons, for instance, were instructed to teach Indian women to "adorn the home, both inside and out, with pictures, curtains, home-made rugs, flowers, grassplots, and trees." But as Linnian Tindall pointed out, the Indians were too poor to afford furnishings, let alone curtains and wallpaper: "They move about so much that it is hard to get them to realize that their homes and yards require ornamentation." Similarly, it made little sense to urge Indians to keep and care for bees and cows, another prescribed task, when they often had no land on which to put the animals.[45]

Land and homes were not the only problems. In September 1908, Tindall explained why she had not been able to teach Indian children "the games and sports of white children" that month: "The children down to eight years worked in the fields. This hard work . . . is really necessary that they may have warm clothing through the winter," she wrote. "So there was no time for play." The following winter, which turned out to be unusually harsh, Tindall added that she had "little to do in the line of food preparation" as "most any food is acceptable."[46]

If the Round Valley Indians quietly ignored some of the field matrons' lessons, they flagrantly flouted other prescriptions of the assimilation campaign. Between 1890 and 1915, no issue caused Round Valley agents and superintendents more consternation than the Indians' failure to obtain marriage licenses, remain with their initial partners, and—when necessary—divorce "legally." In 1897 Agent George Patrick complained that widespread "adultery" made "the task of the officer in charge of preserving order on the reservation difficult and unpleasant." A decade later Thomas Downs estimated that 30 percent of the "younger element" of Indians on the reservation were living in open adultery. "In fact, it is the rottenest state of affairs for the small number of inhabitants that I have ever seen," he lamented.[47]

Some federal officials—seeing in the Native Americans' marital and sexual practices a breakdown of order and a threat to their own authority—tried to coerce Indians into obtaining marriage licenses and marrying legally. Downs, for example, reported that he was "tak[ing] steps to correct the evil and compel those who can legally do so to get married." Downs didn't reveal what steps he planned to take, but a subsequent agent reported that Downs had somehow "persuaded" thirty-two couples to marry![48]

In 1907 Superintendent Horace Johnson consulted the district attorney about cracking down on those Indians whom he saw as setting an immoral example. Told there was little he could do, he eventually looked the other way. The Indians' "state of morality is not particularly high when viewed from a puritanical standpoint, yet I believe it to be not inferior to that of the white people of the same grade of intelligence," Johnson told his Washington superiors in his final report in 1910. Noting that the Indians' labor was "skillful and steady"—and that, by working both on and off the reservation, they were able to support themselves—Johnson recommended closing the agency and relinquishing the Indians' common land. The Office of Indian Affairs ignored his suggestion.[49]

In July 1910, in a move that proved fateful, the Office of Indian Affairs transferred Johnson and appointed Thomas B. Wilson superintendent at Round Valley. Wilson, a fifty-five-year-old Kentucky lawyer who had spent years in the Indian service, immediately set about sorting out the tangled heirship issues on the reservation. Wilson was probably spurred to such activism by a major revision of the Dawes Act that June. The original legislation had barred Indians whose allotments were still held in trust by the federal government from disposing of their land through wills. The 1910 revision lifted this restriction, but made such wills subject to the approval of the secretary of the interior. The act also granted the secretary specific authority to determine the heirs of allotment holders who died intestate. To carry out the legislation, agency superintendents were authorized to help their Indian charges draft wills and to conduct probate hearings. For each will and probate, superintendents were required to forward a case report and recommendations to the interior secretary.[50]

Not surprisingly, Wilson's focus on inheritance issues brought submerged disagreements over marriage and family to a head. From the beginning, marriage and allotment had been so closely tied at Round Valley that one former agent felt compelled to ask the Indian Office if couples who had been allotted together could legally divorce and remarry.[51] The imposition of American heirship law produced additional complications. Who, for instance, was the heir to an Indian who had had several tribal marriages, only the first of which was legally certified by the state? What if the Indian's wives had each entered additional tribal marriages after leaving him? And what if they had remarried legally without bothering to get legally divorced?

In deciding one such case, Horace Johnson sidestepped legal doctrine and relied primarily on common sense.[52] However, Wilson's legal training, combined with new regulations issued by the interior secretary in 1910, led the Round Valley superintendent to a more rigid interpretation of American family law. For instance, Wilson ruled that Jim Halley's wife at the time of allotment, Alice Joe, was Halley's legal heir even though the couple had separated years earlier and both had remarried. Jim's and Alice's subsequent marriages (undertaken under pressure from an earlier agent) had been properly licensed and performed by clergymen. Nevertheless, Wilson held that these later unions were void, since Jim and Alice had never legally divorced. Wilson also ruled against the heirship of Jim's adopted son, Tom Pike, on the grounds that Tom had never been formally adopted.[53]

Although Wilson held dozens of heirship hearings, he constantly complained that the Indians' long-standing patterns of tribal marriage and divorce made his task nearly impossible. "This promiscuous marrying and separating and utter disregard of marital ties on the part of many is the most trying problem of the reservation," Wilson complained bitterly in his 1911 annual report. "Aside from the demoralizing effect on the whole tribe, it renders the task of determining the legal heirs to the property well-nigh impossible."[54]

With encouragement from Washington, Wilson soon took steps to crack down on such relationships. In 1912, the superintendent reported that he had filed criminal complaints, charging adultery, against nine "unmarried" couples and thus persuaded several to procure licenses and marry. But when some couples still refused, Wilson discovered that his legal ground was slippery. Ironically, Wilson used terms like "marital law" and "adultery" carelessly. The district attorney informed him that only individuals who were already legally married could be prosecuted for adultery; California had no law against fornication.[55]

Undiscouraged, Wilson wrote the Office of Indian Affairs about the case of Belle Wilsey, a forty-year-old widow, who was living with Annet Spenser, a twenty-one-year-old man. "Will the office allow such Indians as these to remain on the reservation in defiance of law, order and common decency?" he asked. "As there is no express statute for the punishment of the crime of fornication, then there must be some other way to punish those who commit the act." Although both Indians had allotments on the reservation, Wilson suggested that they be banished because their presence "may be detrimental to the peace and welfare of the Indians."[56]

Wilson seemed even more upset by Wilsey's defiance than by her morality. He reported that Spenser was willing to marry but that Wilsey refused. And when the superintendent sent police to Wilsey's house to collect evidence of wrongdoing, she threatened to shoot them if they ever returned on such business. "She is living in defiance of law and decency and doing so more in contrariness and spite than anything else," Wilson wrote. (Although Wilsey may have defied Wilson out of spite, it is equally possible that she wanted to maintain her legal independence, which would allow her son, rather than Spenser, to inherit her allotment.)

Wilsey was not the only strong-willed woman Wilson tried to rein in. In 1912, Wilson had Minnie Card arrested for adultery after she had been living with George Scott for more than three years. Card's husband, Charles, was serving a forty-year prison sentence for murder, and she had obtained an interlocutory divorce decree. Wilson dropped the case after Card agreed to leave Scott until the divorce was finalized and they could be legally married. But when Card stayed with Scott—and defied Wilson in other ways—the superintendent moved to prevent her divorce. "She is an exceedingly bad character," Wilson explained to his Washington superiors. "George Scott also has a bad reputation and such people as these ought not to be permitted to live together."[57]

Wilson's opinion of Card was shaped in part by a run-in they had that year over the schooling of her daughter. As Wilson recalled the incident, Card had been permitted to remove her daughter, Maude Feliz, from the boarding school one Sunday morning on the condition that the girl return to the school that afternoon. When Maude did not appear, the reservation clerk and policemen visited her house and "Mrs. Card fought vigorously [but unsuccessfully] to keep the girl." Wilson claimed that Card took revenge for the episode by burning hay that belonged to one of the policeman. "She is a disreputable character and not a suitable person to have control of [her] children," Wilson wrote.

In a 1914 affidavit, Minnie Card (known by then as Mrs. Scott) remembered the episode rather differently. She said she had withdrawn her daughter from school because she wanted company while George was away sheepshearing. When the Round Valley clerk, Omar Bates, came to get the girl, Minnie told him she wanted Maude at home at night and that the girl was attending public school in the nearby town of Covelo every day: "Mr. Bates then threatened Mrs. Scott with arrest if she did not comply with his order. A few days later Mr. Bates, accompanied by two police officers—Charles Goodwin and Edward Smith—entered Mrs. Scott's yard and grabbed Mrs. Scott and threw her down and choked her while Charles Goodwin grabbed the girl, Maude Feliz, and dragged her away. Mr. Bates choked Mrs. Scott so severely that his finger marks were left on her throat." The finger marks, Minnie testified, were seen by a local doctor and the justice of the peace.[58]

Although this episode was probably extreme, it reflected a further source of tension between Wilson and the Indians he oversaw. The Round Valley Indians felt it was their privilege to keep their children home from the boarding school when they wanted to, and most agents had allowed this to at least some degree. Wilson, however, took a tough stance. "Because I have not permitted them [to keep their children home], they feel they have been deprived of their liberty, and for this reason have objected very seriously to sending their children to the Government School," Wilson reported. In fact, some Indians in the district had begun petitioning the local school board for the establishment of a public day school on the reservation.[59]

Wilson's frustration with the Indians' resistance strongly colored his verdict on assimilation. "The granting of citizenship has proved a failure," he wrote the Indian Office in 1912. "Citizen Indians are not full-fledged citizens nor wards of the government. The government relinquishes its control and the state refuses to exercise any and they are virtually without restraint." For Wilson, Indian citizenship had come to be defined primarily in terms of control.[60]

Just four months after Wilson assumed office that control began to break down. On 20 November 1910 the superintendent sent an urgent telegram to the commissioner of Indian affairs reporting that a fire the previous night had destroyed the girls' dormitory and several other agency buildings. "The fire started in the girls' clothing room where there was neither fire nor lamp, origin unknown," Wilson reported. He recommended that a new building be erected immediately.[61]

It did not take Wilson long, however, to recognize that trouble was brewing on the reservation. The following spring a "mysterious" fire destroyed the sawmill that was cutting wood for the new dormitory. In November 1911, girls made two attempts to burn the new building, and three of the older girls ran away. Wilson blamed the trouble on a strict head matron and recommended that "for the safety of the school" she be transferred immediately. The Indian Office complied.[62]

The reservation revolt, however, had only begun. In April 1912, two Indians began circulating a petition calling for the superintendent's removal. The Indians charged that Wilson was allowing schoolchildren to be mistreated and not giving them enough to eat. Wilson denied the charges, but a letter from the school's white physician supported the Indians' claims. Dr. Wellstead said Wilson had dismissed his request for a supply of cough medicine, telling him: "Oh, mix up anything and give it to 'em, just so it is medicine; and make it bitter so they won't return for more."[63]

The gathering tensions came to a head in early 1914. On 30 January, a 3 A.M. fire destroyed the schoolhouse and a large quantity of stores. By late that day, two boys, ages twelve and fifteen, had admitted setting the blaze and implicated two more. The young arsonists had previously tried to run away from the boarding school and, as Wilson reported, they thought that if they burned the building "the school would be closed, and they could return home." Instead, the superintendent threw the boys in jail.[64]

That episode proved a turning point on the reservation. A few days later, while Wilson was in San Francisco testifying before the grand jury that indicted the boys, more than 50 Indians met in the home of the local Presbyterian minister to plan a revolt. A traveling white preacher who had been working to set up Indian day schools in the area attended the meeting, and Wilson later charged that this man, the Reverend F. G. Collett, incited the Indians. But the uproar on the reservation can hardly be laid at Collett's feet. Nearly 150 Indians signed the petition calling for Wilson's removal, and scores also petitioned for the removal of clerk Omar Bates. A handful gave money, and some 30 to 40 Native Americans signed affidavits detailing their complaints.[65]

The charges leveled in the petitions, the identity of the revolt's leaders, and the observations of special agents sent out by the Office of Indian Affairs to investigate the controversy all suggest that the uproar resulted from issues long simmering on the reservation. Of the five charges in the petition against Wilson, the first three involved issues of family and heirship. The Indians reiterated their earlier charges that boarding-school students were being mistreated and weren't being given enough to eat. They also complained that Wilson had wrongfully retained money belonging to Indians. As Special Agent C. H. Asbury explained, "Certain heirs thought they should have the money derived from [allotment] leases."[66]

Many of those Indians leading the protest—including several who were former employees of the agency—had had run-ins with Wilson over gender and family issues. The fathers of two of the schoolboys prosecuted by Wilson gave money to press for his ouster. So did George Scott, whose wife Minnie had tangled so unfortunately with Wilson and Bates. Alex Frazier, another vocal opponent of Wilson, was probably hounded by the superintendent because of a "promiscuous" relationship. Beulah E. Smith, who spoke at the initial meeting, had held various posts at the boarding school until Wilson forced her to resign because he suspected she had been seduced by a white employee. In her letter of resignation, Smith complained that she was "being treated and watched like one of the pupils." Wilson, she said, had grilled her about her personal affairs "which I consider of no importance to any one excepting myself."[67]

Ben Neafus, until February the school disciplinarian, spearheaded the effort to collect money and affidavits from the Indians. A one-quarter-blood Indian, Neafus had not long before been recommended by Wilson for promotion. But shortly before the school fire, Wilson forbade Neafus to spend nights with his sick wife, insisting that the disciplinarian was needed at the school. Neafus disobeyed Wilson's orders and was away the night the fire broke out. For this, Wilson had him dismissed.[68]

Two special agents sent out by the Office of Indian Affairs cleared Wilson of wrongdoing, although one criticized the superintendent's lack of patience with the Indians. But Round Valley's Native Americans were to have the final word. On 11 March two twelve-year-old boys tried to burn the boys' dormitory, and a few days later, Wilson sent a lengthy letter urging Washington to abandon the school. Given the recent spate of fires and the unabated hostility of both parents and pupils, it no longer made sense for the government to spend money on a boarding school, Wilson wrote:

These Indians have had the advantage of schools for 43 years . . . and it seems to me that they are about as well prepared to be thrown on their own resources as they ever will be. . . . I recommend that the government say to these Indians, "You have been given every advantage for obtaining an education, have been furnished land and stock and implements to cultivate your land, and from this date you will have to depend on your own resources."

This time the Office of Indian Affairs listened. Later that year, it transferred Wilson, closed the Round Valley boarding school, and opened a day school in its place.[69]

The Indians had won a battle in the assimilation campaign, but had they in fact won the war? Several documents from the Round Valley Agency files suggest the dichotomous results of the assimilation campaign. In September 1914, shortly before he left the reservation for good, Wilson sent Washington a list of student-made articles to be displayed at the Panama-Pacific International Exhibition in San Francisco the following year. The list included a child's white dress, an embroidered pin cushion, and a lawn apron trimmed in ribbon and lace. In a separate missive, Wilson noted that the older Indian women overseen by his agency made baskets only in their spare time. For the most part, he wrote, they did washing for white people, picked hops, and worked as domestics.[70]

In a 1919 inspection report, Special Agent L. A. Dorrington bemoaned what he saw as the rampant immorality of Round Valley Indians. "There are many cases of open adultery," some involving girls under the age of consent, he wrote. "There is no excuse for such conditions as these Indians are largely mixed blood and have lived in close relation with the whites for more than fifty years. . . . They know right from wrong but frequently seem to prefer the latter or rather take to it more readily." The General Allotment Act, Dorrington concluded, "has not been fully received" by the Indians.[71]

Taken together, these documents say much about the ironic outcome of the "total assimilation" campaign. The Indian women and men of Round Valley had indeed learned the gendered skills of Euro-American society, but they were far from being the dutiful housewives and "manly and independent" farmers reformers had once hoped to create. Too poor to sit home and knit doilies, Indian women had survived by putting their skills to work in a marketplace dominated by whites. This put them on a plane more equal to their own men than that Washington had hoped to encourage, but it also deposited them far below the middle-class Euro-American women they served. Instead of embodying the Victorian ideal, the Native American women of Round Valley helped make that ideal possible for others.

At the same time, the Indians of Round Valley fiercely resisted federal efforts to curb their marital freedom or deprive them of control over their children. But this very resistance to attempts at "uplift" disillusioned many white reformers and bureaucrats and contributed to their willingness to abandon their original goals and work instead to slot Indians into American society's lower ranks.[72] As Dorrington wrote in his 1919 report, "Many [whites] feel that [the assimilation campaign] forced a condition upon [the Indians] which they were not prepared to accept."

By 1914, the Office of Indian Affairs had not only accepted but had embraced this inequality. No longer convinced that Indians were inherently equal to Euro-Americans, policymakers and federal bureaucrats had altered their goals. The quarterly reports sent out to field matrons no longer asked about the Indians' adoption of home decorations and white children's games. Instead, the office asked about women's work and what had been done to help "returned students." Ella Brown's answer in December 1914 spoke eloquently about the assimilation program's new direction: "The girls," she wrote, "have all been placed in good homes in domestic science."[73]

Notes

I would like to thank archivist Kathleen M. O'Connor and the rest of the staff at the Pacific Sierra Branch of the National Archives in San Bruno, California. Thanks also to Estelle Freedman, Mary Lou Roberts, and the other members of the Stanford Women's History Workshop for their constructive suggestions.

The following abbreviations will be used in the notes:

CIA   Commissioner of Indian Affairs
LB 1   Letter Book, 14 August 1899 to 13 February 1902
LB 2   Letter Book, 14 February 1902 to 1 April 1904
LB 3   Letter Book, 2 April 1904 to 29 November 1905
LB 4   Letter Book, 2 December 1905 to 11 March 1907
LB 5   Letter Book, 12 March 1907 to 16 February 1908
LB 6   Letter Book, 26 February 1908 to 9 February 1909
LB 7   Letter Book, 16 February 1909 to 26 February 1910
LB 8   Letter Book, 26 March 1910 to 5 January 1911
LB 9   Letter Book, 5 January 1911 to 2 November 1911
LB 10   Letter Book, 2 November 1911 to 21 September 1912
LB 11   Letter Book, 28 September 1912 to 30 June 1913

LB 12   Letter Book, 1 July 1913 to 24 March 1914
LB 13   Letter Book, 27 March 1914 to 30 October 1914
Round Valley Papers   Round Valley Agency, Records of the Bureau of Indian Affairs, Record
      Group 75, Pacific Sierra Branch, National Archives, San Bruno, Calif.
Dorrington Papers   "Investigative Reports of Col. L. A. Dorrington," Records of Col. L. A.
      Dorrington, Special Agent, 1913–1922, Reno Indian Agency, Records of the Bureau of
      Indian Affairs, Record Group 75, Pacific Sierra Branch, National Archives, San
      Bruno, Calif.

1. Elsie Allen, *Pomo Basketmaking: A Supreme Art for the Weaver* (Healdsburg, Calif.: Naturegraph Publishers, 1972), 11. Allen was a student at the school at the time of the fire. Also see telegram from T. B. Wilson to CIA, November. 20, 1910, LB 8, box 2, Round Valley Papers.

2. For discussions of the gender aspects of assimilationist policies and their impact on particular tribes, see Joan Jensen, "Native American Women and Agriculture: A Seneca Case Study," *Sex Roles* 3, no. 5 (1977): 423–41; Mary E. Young, "Women, Civilization and the Indian Question," in *Clio Was a Woman: Studies in the History of American Women* ed. Mabel Deutrich and Virginia C. Purdy (Washington, D.C.: Howard University Press, 1980), 98–110; Theda Perdue, "Southern Indians and the Cult of True Womanhood" in *The Web of Southern Social Relations: Women, Family and Education*, ed. Walter J. Fraser, Jr., R. Frank Saunders, Jr. and Jon L. Wakelyn (Athens: University of Georgia Press, 1985), 35–51; Carolyn Garrett Pool, "Reservation Policy and the Economic Position of Wichita Women," *Great Plains Quarterly* 8, no. 3 (Summer 1988): 158–71; Dolores Janiewski, "Learning to Live 'Just Like White Folks': Gender, Ethnicity, and the State in the Inland Northwest" in *Gendered Domains: Rethinking Public and Private in Women's History*, ed. Dorothy O. Helly and Susan M. Reverby (Ithaca, N.Y.: Cornell University Press, 1992), 167–80; and essays by Theda Perdue and Katherine M.B. Osburn in *Negotiators of Change: Historical Perspectives on Native American Women*, ed. Nancy Shoemaker (New York: Routledge, 1995). Two recent studies of the Dawes Act—Frederick Hoxie's acclaimed *A Final Promise: The Campaign to Assimilate the Indians, 1880–1920* (Lincoln: University of Nebraska Press, 1984) and Janet A. McDonnell's *The Dispossession of the American Indian, 1887–1934* (Bloomington: Indiana University Press, 1991)—ignore gender issues.

3. In general, federal officials heading the Round Valley Agency in the nineteenth century were known as agents, while those who served in the twentieth century bore the title of superintendent. However, there seems to have been a temporary exception to this around 1909. In that year, Thomas Downs first served as the special U.S. Indian agent in charge at Round Valley. He was succeeded briefly by U. L. Clardy, clerk and special disbursing agent, who wrote the agency's 1909 annual report.

4. The rancherías resulted from the unique labor situation in California at the time the territory became a state. By 1850, Anglo and Hispanic ranchers and farmers in California relied heavily on Indian labor. Thus, they were reluctant to have Indians swept wholesale onto the separate reserves and reservations the federal government began establishing in 1851. In 1850, the state assembly passed a bill allowing Indians to remain in "homes and villages" that they had occupied "for a number of years." The white proprietor could apply to have "sufficient" land set aside for the Indians, and they could remain there until "otherwise provided for." Initially, the Round Valley Agency oversaw just the reservation established at Round Valley; however, in the early twentieth century its purview was extended to cover "ranchería" Indians in Mendocino, Sonoma, and Lake Counties. In this paper, I use the term "Round Valley Indians" to refer to all the Indians under the agency's supervision at a given time. For more on the establishment of the rancherías, see Albert L. Hurtado, *Indian Survival on the California Frontier* (New Haven, Conn.: Yale University Press, 1988), 129–30.

5. In general, sources on the gender roles of northern California tribes prior to contact with whites are scattered and scarce: Many tribes—including most of those represented at Round Valley—were decimated during the 1850s, and ethnologists who subsequently studied these tribes primarily interviewed men. The most comprehensive article on the subject is Edith Wallace, "Sexual Status and Role Differences," in *Handbook of North American Indians*, 20 vols., ed.

William C. Sturtevant (Washington, D.C.: Smithsonian Institution, 1978–   ), vol. 8, 683–89. However, Wallace is more interested in generalizing about the region's tribes than in distinguishing between them. Also see articles on the Conkow, Yuki, Wailaki, Achumawi, Nomlaki, and Pomo in that volume. For a further ethnographic discussion of the various tribes, see A. L. Kroeber, *Handbook of the Indians of California, Bureau of American Ethnology Bulletin 78* (Washington D.C.: U.S. Government Printing Office, 1925).

6. In addition to the sources cited in note 5, see Russell Thornton, "History, Structure, and Survival: A Comparison of the Yuki (Ukomno'm) and Tolowa (Hush) Indians of Northern California," *Ethnology* 25, no. 2 (1986): 119–30; and Edwin Loeb, "Pomo Folkways," *University of California Publications in American Archaelogy and Ethnology*, vol. 19, no. 2 (Berkeley: University of California Press, 1926).

The concept of a "Pomo tribe" is itself a social construct invented in the nineteenth century by white ethnographers. For more than a century, the term "Pomo" has been used in anthropological literature to refer to speakers of seven distinct and mutually unintelligible languages in northern California, who nevertheless shared many cultural characteristics. Most of the Indians overseen by the Round Valley Agency probably belonged to the Western and Northeastern Pomo. However, since material on these individual groups is limited—and all of the groups seem to have accorded their women unusually high status—this paper follows the tradition of the ethnographic literature and treats them as one group.

7. See the sources cited in notes 5 and 6, particularly the various articles in the *Handbook of North American Indians*.

8. In 1839, P. Kostromitonov, agent of the Russian American Company at Fort Ross, described the northern California Indians' custom of marrying "without formality whatever" and separating whenever they fought. Although Kostromitonov was clearly ethnocentric and his ethnographic precision must be doubted, he was only the first in a long line of European and Euro-American observers to comment on the "informal" sexual practices of the northern California tribes. See *Ethnographic Observations on the Coast Miwok and Pomo by Contre-Admiral F. P. Von Wrangell and P. Kostromitonov of the Russian Colony Ross, 1839*, trans. Fred Stross (Berkeley: University of California Archaeological Research Facility, 1974), as well as the sources cited in notes 5 and 6 above.

A particularly interesting source on this subject is a set of oral histories conducted around 1940 with three Pomo women who were born in the 1870s and 1880s. All of the women, as well as their mothers, had more than one husband: As the mother of one of the women told an interviewer, "That's the way the Indians do it." The interviews also point up the mixed feelings Indian women had about this practice. Sophie Martinez, who was born at the Round Valley Reservation, was bitter that her father had left her mother and that she had been abandoned by her first three husbands. By contrast, both Ellen Wood and her mother were married to older men when they were quite young to get them away from the sexual advances of relatives. Both later ran away from their first husbands and remarried. "Our way is good—no law. You stay with them as long as you feel like it and then run away and get another man," Wood said. Elizabeth Colson, *Autobiographies of Three Pomo Women* (Berkeley: University of California Archaeological Research Facility, 1974).

Other scholars, including Joan Jensen and Mary Young in the articles cited above, have noted that other Indian groups also followed sexual and marital practices that seemed lax to white observers. However, most historians have paid this only passing attention. Christine Bolt has suggested that "the Indians' free sexual expression from an early age ensured the survival of their numerically small and vulnerable groupings." Albert Hurtado notes that some Plains tribes believed coitus transferred power from one man to another by way of a female intermediary and used sex to establish friendship and trade relations. See Christine Bolt, *American Indian Policy and American Reform: Case Studies of the Campaign to Assimilate the American Indians* (London: Allen & Unwin, 1987), 253; Hurtado, *Indian Survival*, 171.

9. For accounts of the impact of the gold rush on Native Americans in northern California, see Albert Hurtado, *Indian Survival*; Lynwood Carranco and Estle Beard, *Genocide and*

Vendetta: The Round Valley Wars of Northern California (Norman: University of Oklahoma Press, 1981); and Edward Castillo, "The Impact of Euro-American Exploration and Settlement," in *Handbook of North American Indians*, vol. 8, 107–13.

10. In 1874 and 1875, Round Valley agent J. L. Burchard reported a sudden explosion in the number of Indians converting to Christianity and taking Christian vows of marriage. However, this burst of piety proved transient: Apparently the Indians believed that if they joined the church, the government would give them land. For information on this and other developments at Round Valley prior to 1890, see the annual reports filed by the Round Valley agents between 1870 and 1890 and included in the annual *Report of the Commissioner of Indian Affairs*. Also see Todd Benson, "The Consequences of Reservation Life: Native Californians on the Round Valley Reservation, 1871–1884," *Pacific Historical Review* 60 (May 1991): 221–44; Virginia P. Miller, *Ukomno'm: The Yuki Indians of Northern California* (Socorro, N.M.: Ballena Press, 1979); Virginia P. Miller, "The Changing Role of the Chief on a California Indian Reservation," *American Indian Quarterly* 13 (1989), 447–55; and Virginia P. Miller, "The 1870 Ghost Dance and the Methodists: An Unexpected Turn of Events in Round Valley," *Journal of California Anthropology* 3 (Winter 1976): 66–74.

11. Both a copy of the Dawes Act and a discussion of its provisions are included in the 1887 *Report of the Commissioner of Indian Affairs*. The Burke Act of 1906 revised the Dawes Act in three significant ways: (1) It postponed citizenship for future allottees until the end of the trust period; (2) it authorized the president to extend the initial twenty-five-year trust period on allotments (which would further delay citizenship) if conditions so warranted; and (3) it authorized the secretary of the interior to waive the remaining trust period for all Indians judged competent to handle their property independently. Michael L. Lawson, "The Fractionated Estate: The Problem of American Indian Heirship," *South Dakota History* 21, no. 1 (Spring 1991): 14.

12. Hoxie, *Final Promise*, 15. For quotes from Atkins, see the discussion of the Dawes Act in the 1887 *Report of the Commissioner of Indian Affairs*, viii–x.

13. Quoted in S. Lyman Tyler, *A History of Indian Policy* (Washington D.C.: U.S. Department of the Interior, 1973). Ironically, Tyler quotes this passage without making any note of its gender connotations. Similar passages can be found in some of the correspondence of Round Valley agents. For instance, in his 1897 annual report, acting agent George A. Patrick mentions the "manly independence" fostered by the Dawes Act. His report is included in the 1897 *Report of the Commissioner of Indian Affairs*.

14. *Report of the Commissioner of Indian Affairs* for 1892, 31–37. In 1894, the Hopi—another tribe that traced kinship through the maternal line—responded to the commissioner's patrilineal approach with a small lecture on the Hopi way of life. In a remarkable petition addressed to "the Washington Chiefs," the Hopi wrote in part: "The family, the dwelling house and the field are inseparable, because the woman is the heart of these, and they rest with her. Among us the family traces its kin from the mother, hence all its possessions are hers." A copy of the letter can be found in Peter Nabokov, ed., *Native American Testimony: A Chronicle of Indian-White Relations from Prophecy to the Present, 1492–1992* (New York: Viking, 1991), 249–51.

15. See Round Valley agent Thomas Connally's 1894 annual report, included in the *Report of the Commissioner of Indian Affairs*.

16. Circular dated 19 March 1890 from the Office of Indian Affairs, box 30, Round Valley Papers. The ranchería Indians provide an interesting contrast to the federal policy of linking private property ownership to patriarchal nuclear families. One U.S. Indian agent observed in 1912 that the ranchería Indians in the Round Valley district owned tracts of from 5 to 160 acres which they treated as community property: "The title to this land is a sort of community title and it is so assessed, the tax being paid by contribution from the different families, and where they have some agricultural land it is used somewhat in common, or divided into small plots so that each family has the use of same, the houses being grouped in a sort of village." Special Indian Agent to CIA, 13 August 1912, "M1 to 178, July 1, 1912–November 23, 1912" folder, box 24, Round Valley Papers.

17. For general discussions of allotment at Round Valley, see the reservation's annual reports in the *Report of the Commissioner of Indian Affairs* for 1893 and 1894, and Horace Johnson's

discussion of allotment in his letter to the CIA on 19 October 1908, LB 6, box 3, Round Valley Papers. For the amount of land allotted to specific individuals, see "General Land Office Record of Patents for Allotments (1895)" in box 153, Round Valley Papers. This record also shows that some Indians received less than the standard five or ten acres. Most, though not all, of those who received smaller parcels were women.

18. The Dawes Act of 1887 entitled Indian family heads to 160-acre allotments and allowed single adults and orphan minors to qualify for allotments of 40 acres. (In practice, these figures were often prorated.) Alice Fletcher, an anthropologist and allotting agent on the Omaha, Winnebago, and Nez Percé reservations, was among those who noted that this provided little protection for Indian women who were abandoned by their husbands. In response to such pressure, Congress amended the Dawes Act in 1891 to give "80 acres to every man, woman and child, irrespective of age or relation." However, the allotment of the Round Valley Reservation in 1894 shows that this equitable principle was not always followed in practice. Lawson, "Fractionated Estate," 3–4, 8; Janiewski, " 'Learning to Live' " 173–74. For a useful discussion of the problems such gendered assumptions created for divorced Ute women after allotment, see Katherine M. B. Osburn, " 'Dear Friend and Ex-Husband': Marriage, Divorce, and Women's Property Rights on the Southern Ute Reservation, 1887–1930" in *Negotiators of Change*, 157–75.

19. Horace Johnson to T. B. Wilson, 18 June 1912, in "M501-524 (June 10, 1912–June 19, 1912)," box 23, "Incoming Correspondence from Others than the Commissioner, 1903–1914," Round Valley Papers.

20. For example, in a 1911 letter to the CIA, Round Valley superintendent T. B. Wilson noted that "The Office has held that the act of allotment which makes Indians citizens also legalizes the marriage if it were not otherwise legal." See letter dated 6 March 1911, in LB 9, box 4, Round Valley Papers.

21. General T. J. Morgan's speech on "The New Indian School Policy," delivered on 17 December 1889 to the Indian Rights Association in Philadelphia, in box 30, Round Valley Papers. "Supplemental Report on Indian Education" included in the 1889 *Report of the Commissioner of Indian Affairs*.

22. In addition to some of the articles cited in note 2, see Margaret Connell Szasz, " 'Poor Richard' Meets the Native American: Schooling for Young Indian Women in Eighteenth-Century Connecticut," *Pacific Historical Review* 49 (1980): 215–35; Robert A. Trennert, "Victorian Morality and the Supervision of Indian Women Working in Phoenix, 1906–1930," *Journal of Social History* 2, no. 1 (1988): 113–28; and Robert A. Trennert, "Educating Indian Girls at Non-reservation Boarding Schools, 1878–1920," *Western Historical Quarterly* 13, no. 3 (1982): 271–90. Although most scholars have focused on the fact that Native American children were educated to Euro-American gender norms, it should be emphasized these "norms" were in fact middle-class ideals. Christine Stansell has shown that gender ideals among working-class men and women often differed dramatically from those advocated by middle-class reformers. Meanwhile, as Robert Griswold has noted, rising divorce rates in the West during the late nineteenth century suggest that many white middle class couples were also falling short of the domestic ideal. See Christine Stansell, *City of Women: Sex and Class in New York, 1789–1860* (Urbana: University of Illinois Press, 1977), and Robert L. Griswold, *Family and Divorce in California, 1850–1890: Victorian Illusions and Everyday Realities* (Albany: State University of New York Press, 1982).

23. Carl Schurz, "Present Aspects of the Indian Problem," in *Americanizing the American Indians: Writings by the "Friends of the Indian," 1880–1900*, ed. Francis Paul Prucha (Lincoln: University of Nebraska Press, 1973), 20.

24. In 1891 the U.S. Congress passed a law making education—which often meant boarding school—mandatory for Indian children. The commissioner of Indian affairs explained the intent behind the law as follows: "Ordinarily the parent should be regarded as the natural guardian and custodian of his child. . . . When, however, it becomes evident that the parent is unwilling or unable to do this, and that the child, in consequence, is wellnigh certain to grow up idle, vicious, or helpless, a menace or a burden to the public, it becomes not only the right of the Government as a matter of self-protection, but its duty toward the child and toward the community, which is

to be blessed or cursed by the child's activities, to see to it that he shall have in his youth that training that shall save him from vice and fit him for citizenship." 1891 *Report of the Commissioner of Indian Affairs*, 67.

25. Todd Benson describes this episode in "The Consequences of Reservation Life." In the article he does not place this incident in the context of gender concerns or link Sheldon's moral strictness directly to the burning of the school. However, in a subsequent conversation, Benson confirmed that the conclusion drawn here is warranted.

26. See the 1885, 1887, and 1890 annual reports of the Round Valley agent, included in the *Report of the Commissioner of Indian Affairs* for those years.

27. For discussions of the school "curriculum," see, for instance, Harry Liston's letter to the CIA, 26 December 1900, LB 1, box 2, and U. L. Clardy's letter to the CIA, 26 February 1910, LB 7, box 4, Round Valley Papers. The records of the Round Valley school also contain lists of students assigned to various work "brigades" during the 1890s.

28. Harry Liston to the CIA, 26 December 1900, LB 1, box 2, Round Valley Papers.

29. Letters from Horace Johnson to the CIA on 18 March 1905, LB 3, box 2; 15 December 1905 and 26 March 1906, both LB 4, box 3; and 25 January 1909, LB 6, box 3, Round Valley Papers.

30. T. B. Wilson's letter to the CIA, 27 February 1912, LB 10, box 4; Harry Liston's letter to the CIA, 18 December 1902, LB 2, box 2; U. L. Clardy's letter to the CIA, 3 November 1909, LB 7, box 4, Round Valley Papers.

31. Annual report of the Round Valley agent included in the 1897 *Report of the Commissioner of Indian Affairs*; letter from Judson Liftchild, the reservation physician, to CIA on 3 January 1904, LB 2, box 2, Round Valley Papers; letter from Harry Liston to the CIA on 31 August 1899, LB 1, box 2, Round Valley Papers. See also the monthly school report forms found in box 32, Round Valley Papers.

32. Hurtado, in *Indian Survival*, mentions the kidnapping of Indian children in the post–gold rush years. For a first-person account, see Edith V. A. Murphey, "Out of the Past: A True Indian Story Told by Lucy Young of Round Valley Indian Reservation," *California Historical Society Quarterly* 20, no. 4 (1941): 349–64. One indication of the concern Indian parents felt for their children at the boarding school is the number of letters they sent to the Round Valley superintendent inquiring about their offspring. Examples can be found in box 24, Round Valley Papers. Also Superintendent Harry Liston noted that he had met the "opposition of either the father or mother or both in nearly every instance when the child was to be taken any considerable distance from home." Liston to CIA, 10 October 1901, LB 1, box 2, Round Valley Papers.

33. For quotes in this and the following paragraph, see the *Report of the Commissioner of Indian Affairs*, 1893, 54–55.

34. The cover page of each of the Round Valley field matrons' monthly and quarterly reports lists their duties. See also the discussion of field matrons in the *Report of the Commissioner of Indian Affairs*, 1893 and 1894. The role of female reformers and field matrons is discussed in Rebecca Herring, "Their Work Was Never Done: Women Missionaries on the Kiowa-Comanche Reservation," *Chronicles of Oklahoma* 64, no. 1 (1986): 68–83; Martha C. Knack, "Philene T. Hall, Bureau of Indian Affairs Field Matron: Planned Cultural Change of Washakie Shoshone Women," *Prologue* 22, no. 2 (1990): 151–67; Valerie Sherer Mathes, "Nineteenth Century Women and Reform: The Women's National Indian Association," *American Indian Quarterly* 14, no. 1 (1990): 1–18; Lisa E. Emmerich, " 'Right in the Midst of My Own People': Native American Women and the Field Matron Program," *American Indian Quarterly* 15, no. 2 (Spring 1991): 201–216; Lisa E. Emmerich, " 'Civilization' and Transculturation: The Field Matron Program and Crosscultural Contact," *American Indian Culture and Research Journal* 15, no. 4 (1991): 33–41; and Lisa E. Emmerich, "Marguerite LaFlesche Diddock, Office of Indian Affairs Field Matron," *Great Plains Quarterly* 13, no. 3 (1993): 162–71.

35. Five field matrons associated with the Round Valley Agency left some record of their work in the agency papers. Carrie C. Moses, a fifty-one-year-old Wisconsin widow, came to the Round Valley Reservation in 1897 and stayed two years. Linnian Tindall, a married woman in her late

thirties, was based far to the south near Lakeport, California, in 1908 and 1909. Emma J. Alexander was also based near Lakeport in 1914 and 1915. In 1914, Mary E. Tabor worked at the Upper Lake Indian Day School, and Ella S. Brown was affiliated with the Manchester Indian Day School. This paper relies primarily on the reports of Moses and Tindall, since those are the most extensive. For biographical information on the field matrons, see "Record of Employees, 1883–1920," box 147, Round Valley Papers.

36. Carrie Moses, monthly field matron report for November 1897; Linnian Tindall, monthly field matron report for May 1908; both in box 35, Round Valley Papers.

37. Linnian Tindall, monthly field matron reports for February and November 1909, box 35, Round Valley Papers.

38. Carrie Moses, monthly field matron reports for March and April 1898; Linnian Tindall, monthly field matron report for April 1909; both in box 35, Round Valley Papers.

39. Linnian Tindall, monthly field matron reports for May and November 1908, and quarterly field matron report for quarter ending 31 March 1909, box 35, Round Valley Papers.

40. Cover page of all field matron reports, listing duties; Carrie Moses, field matron report for quarter ending 31 December 1897; Linnian Tindall, field matron reports for year ending 30 June 1909 and quarter ending 30 September 1909; all in box 35, Round Valley Papers.

41. Carrie Moses, field matron report for quarter ending 31 March 1898, and report covering 18 June to 30 June 1898, box 35, Round Valley Papers.

42. Carrie Moses, field matron report for quarter ending 30 June 1898, box 35, Round Valley Papers; Emma Alexander, field matron report for quarter ending 30 September 1914, box 41, Round Valley Papers.

43. Linnian Tindall, monthly field matron report for November 1908, box 35, Round Valley Papers; letter from Horace Johnson to CIA, 21 November 1908, LB 6, box 3, Round Valley Papers.

44. Horace Johnson to CIA, 20 October 1903 and 3 November 1903, both in LB 2, box 2, Round Valley Papers. Although the Round Valley Reservation initially contained over 100,000 acres, Congress in 1890 set aside almost two-thirds of that land for sale to whites. Much of the remaining land was not considered tillable, so in 1894, 5,408 acres of valley land were divided among 604 Indians. (All allottees subsequently received between 50 and 70 acres of mountainous land, suitable only for stock raising.) For details on allotment at Round Valley, see the annual reports of the Round Valley agent included in the *Report of the Commissioner of Indian Affairs* for 1893 and 1894, as well as Horace Johnson's discussion of the allotment process in his letter to the CIA on 19 October 1908, LB 6, box 3, Round Valley Papers.

45. Cover page of field matron reports listing their duties; Linnian Tindall, field matron report for quarter ending 30 June 1908, and monthly field matron reports for October and June 1908; all in box 35, Round Valley Papers.

46. Linnian Tindall, monthly field matron reports for September 1908 and January 1909, box 35, Round Valley Papers.

47. Annual report of the Round Valley agent included in the 1897 *Report of the Commissioner of Indian Affairs*; Thomas Downs, special U.S. agent in charge, to the CIA, 16 April 1909, LB 7, box 4, Round Valley Papers.

48. Thomas Downs to CIA, 16 April 1909; U. L. Clardy to CIA, 14 August 1909; both in LB 7, box 4, Round Valley Papers.

49. Horace Johnson to CIA, 1 April 1907, LB 5, box 3, Round Valley Papers, and Horace Johnson to CIA, 11 July 1910, LB 8, box 4, Round Valley Papers. See also Horace Johnson to the CIA, 12 August 1907 and 23 September 1907, both LB 5, box 3, Round Valley Papers.

50. Lawson, "Fractionated Estate," 15–16.

51. Thomas Downs to CIA, 16 April 1909, LB 7, box 4, Round Valley Papers.

52. In this case, an Indian named Jim Henley was legally married to Lucy Moore. They separated—but never secured a divorce—and Henley began living with Lizzie Martin. Henley and Martin also separated, and Martin moved in with another man. However, she and her granddaughter cared for Henley during his final illness and he died in her home. Johnson ruled

that Martin rather than Moore was Henley's heir. Wilson's decisions in similar cases suggests that he would have ruled for Moore, even though Henley and Moore had been separated for more than a decade. See Horace Johnson to CIA, 27 July 1907, LB 5, box 3, Round Valley Papers.

53. Lawson, "Fractionated Estate," 16. T. B. Wilson to CIA, 10 March 1913 and 31 May 1913, both in LB 11, box 5, Round Valley Papers.

54. T. B. Wilson to the CIA, 5 September 1911, LB 9, box 4, Round Valley Papers.

55. T. B. Wilson to CIA, 10 August 1911, LB 9, and 1 July 1912, LB 10, both in box 4, Round Valley Papers. Wilson notes in the first letter that he has been directed by the Office of Indian Affairs "to take vigorous action to break up the practice of Indians living together without being legally married."

56. For the case of Belle Wilsey, see T. B. Wilson to CIA, 11 May 1911, in LB 9, box 4, Round Valley Papers; and T. B. Wilson to CIA, 16 February 1912 and 26 April 1912, both in LB 10, box 4, Round Valley Papers.

57. For Wilson's perspective on the case of Minnie Card Scott, see T. B. Wilson to CIA, 3 September 1912, and 10 September 1912, both in LB 10, box 4, Round Valley Papers; T. B. Wilson to CIA, 26 November 1912, and 17 March 1913, both in LB 11, box 5, Round Valley Papers.

58. Minnie Card Scott's affidavit is quoted in a report filed by the Reverends Frederick G. Collett and Beryl Bishop Collett, who were field secretaries for a California reform group known as the Indian Board of Cooperation. See "Report of Field Secretaries from Jan. 1st to March 20th, 1914," in "Round Valley" folder, box 11, Dorrington Papers.

59. Wilson's 19 March 1914 letter to the Office of Indian Affairs is quoted in Special Agent Colonel L. A. Dorrington's report summarizing his investigation of the Reverend F. G. Collett. The report can be found in "F.G. Collett-2," box 2, Dorrington Papers. Wilson mentions the Indians' attempts to petition for a public school on the reservation in his annual report dated 1 July 1914 contained in LB 13, box 5, Round Valley Papers. Also see folders on the Colletts in box 2 of the Dorrington Papers and folder marked "(School) General" in box 11 of the Dorrington Papers.

60. T. B. Wilson to CIA, 24 April 1912, LB 10, box 4, Round Valley Papers.

61. Telegram from T. B. Wilson to CIA, 20 November 1910, LB 8, box 4, Round Valley Papers. Also see Allen, *Pomo Basketmaking*, 10–11.

62. T. B. Wilson to CIA, 29 May 1911 and 7 July 1911, both in LB 9; and 27 November 1911, LB 10; all in box 4, Round Valley Papers.

63. T. B. Wilson quotes from Dr. Wellstead's letter in his own letter defending himself. Wilson to the CIA, 16 July 1912, LB 10, box 4, Round Valley Papers.

64. Telegram from T. B. Wilson to the CIA, 30 January 1914; letters from T. B. Wilson to the CIA, 30 January 1914, 3 February 1914, and 4 February 1914; all in LB 12, box 5, Round Valley Papers.

65. T. B. Wilson discusses various aspects of the reservation revolt in four letters to the CIA, all found in LB 13, box 5, Round Valley Papers: 18 February 1914; 13 March 1914; 1 August 1914; and 6 August 1914. See also documents contained in the "Round Valley" folder, box 11, Dorrington Papers. Special Agent Colonel L. A. Dorrington describes the episode in some detail in his report on Reverend Collett in "F. G. Collett-2," box 2, Dorrington Papers. Copies of the petitions signed by the Indians and Wilson's response to the report of Special Agent Christie (who also investigated the incident) can be found in "Wilson, T. B." folder, box 52, Round Valley Papers. None of the affidavits could be found in the Round Valley Papers, although they are frequently referred to in the documents above.

66. "Round Valley General Report," filed by C. H. Asbury to the CIA on 1 May 1914, in "Round Valley" folder, box 10, Dorrington Papers. In addition to the three complaints listed in the text, the petitions charged that Wilson leased land to favorites without open and competitive bids and that he permitted the deterioration of cattle and range conditions. However, the special agents sent out to investigate the episode mentioned these complaints only in passing, suggesting that they were secondary.

67. In 1907, Superintendent Horace Johnson consulted the district attorney about taking action against Alex Frazier and the woman with whom he was then living, Frankie Brown. Although

Frazier was widowed, Brown had simply "deserted" her husband of thirteen years. Johnson concluded that he could do little and eventually dropped the case; however, it seems likely that Wilson pursued it as part of his marriage crackdown. See Horace Johnson to CIA, 1 April 1907, LB 5, box 3, Round Valley Papers. Beulah Smith's letter of resignation is in the "Wilson, T. B." folder, box 52, Round Valley Papers. Not all of the Indians who helped spearhead the revolt had tangled with Wilson over gender and family issues; several were former agency employees who had been fired by the superintendent for other reasons. However, the large number of activists who had had such run-ins highlights the salience of these issues.

68. In addition to the documents cited in note 59, see "Report of Indian Employees, 1910–12," box 36, Round Valley Papers; and efficiency report on Neafus in "Round Valley" folder, box 11, Dorrington Papers.

69. Telegrams from T. B. Wilson to CIA, 13 March 1914; letters from Wilson to CIA, 13 March 1914 and 19 March 1914; all in LB 12, box 5, Round Valley Papers. Letters from Wilson to CIA dated 14 May 1914 and 19 June 1914, both in LB 13, box 5, Round Valley Papers.

70. T. B. Wilson to CIA, 9 September 1914 and 14 September 1914, both in LB 13, box 5, Round Valley Papers.

71. "Inspection Report" by L. A. Dorrington dated 11–28 November 1919, in "Round Valley" folder, box 11, Dorrington Papers.

72. In *A Final Promise*, Frederick Hoxie argues convincingly that white reformers and policymakers initially hoped to bring Indian citizens into American society on a plane equal to whites but gradually abandoned this objective in favor of incorporating Indians into society's bottom ranks. However, Hoxie bases his argument entirely on political and ideological changes at the national level. The Round Valley case suggests that Indian resistance at the community level also contributed to the reorientation of the assimilation campaign.

73. Ella S. Brown, field matron report for quarter ended 31 December 1914, box 41, Round Valley Papers.

11.

_____

Resistance to Rescue: The Indians of Bahapki and Mrs. Annie E. K. Bidwell

MARGARET D. JACOBS

Like a zoom lens on a camera, Margaret Jacobs gives us a close-up view of one example of the "civilizing" interaction between Euro-American and American Indian women described by Wendy Wall. Annie Bidwell, whose story is told here, was an exemplar of the nineteenth-century Euro-American female humanitarian reform impulse. She worked diligently to introduce Christianity and domesticity to the Maidu and Bahapki Indians who lived and worked for her husband at Rancho Chico, paying special attention to the women and children. Bidwell had no doubt that her insistence on acculturation was in their best interests. But from the perspective of the Indians, she was a destroyer. Insofar as they could, they resisted her efforts to change their religion, their child-rearing practices, and their family relationships. Margaret Jacobs successfully "reads through" Bidwell's own writings to document the ways in which the Indians Bidwell was trying to "rescue" instead subverted and quietly resisted her efforts.

Jacobs's success in showing us both sides of this interaction changes our understanding of Annie Bidwell. Jacobs does not dispute or disparage Bidwell's humanitarian concern, but by looking at the Indian side of the story, she does clearly show that Bidwell was less effective than she thought. Because Margaret Jacobs begins without assumptions of cultural superiority, she is able to show us how very complex Bidwell's humanitarian "rescue effort" really was.

In the early 1890s, a group of California Indians who lived in a small village on General John Bidwell's ranch in Chico, California, designed and carried out a Fourth of July parade. In an article in *Overland Monthly*, the general's wife, Annie Bidwell, described this event. Leading the procession was a wagon bearing the Goddess of Liberty, portrayed by thirteen-year-old Maggie Lafonso, daughter of Holi Lafonso, headman of the Rancho Chico Indians, and Amanda Wilson, Annie Bidwell's personal maid. Wagons full of other Rancho Chico Indians as well as visiting Indians followed behind the Goddess of Liberty. According to Annie Bidwell, "The brass band, and the marshals on horseback presented a picture never to be forgotten. These very marshals were little unclad savages when my husband first saw them,—now [they were] decorated with silk sashes sent to them by prominent gentlemen of Chico." On seeing this procession, Annie Bidwell, who had labored for more than twenty years to bring these Indians the gospel and civilization, confessed, "This is worth a lifetime of work."[1]

At the end of their parade through town, the Rancho Chico Indians and their visitors retired to a grove where they carried out a program of "prayer, music by band, hymns, patriotic songs, recitations by the children, reading of Declaration of Independence, and an oration by Mr. Dick Phillips, one of the middle-aged men." In addition to the parade and the patriotic exercises, "all day a wonderful exhibit of Indian curios was displayed in the Chapel," and "a foot race with a silver watch from a Chico jeweler for prize, closed the day's sport." The Indians culminated the celebration with an Indian dance in their Dance House that night. But lest her readers think that the Rancho Chico Indians had reverted to heathenism after their day of civility, Annie Bidwell assured them that one of the men explained the dance as an event "to show the old and the new, and the new is better."[2]

From the time she first arrived on Rancho Chico in 1868, Annie Bidwell endeavored to "civilide," Americanize, and Christianize the Indians who labored for her husband. Believing that women represented the key to changing the morals, upbringing, and culture of the Indians, she particularly targeted Indian women in her efforts. From her recounting of these Fourth of July events, it appears that Annie Bidwell had, indeed, triumphed. What better indication that Annie Bidwell had succeeded in her efforts than to show a group of Indians organizing and carrying out their own Fourth of July parade? What event could have provided a better symbol of their adoption of American culture and its rituals? And with a thirteen-year-old Indian girl portraying the Goddess of Liberty, it appeared as if Annie Bidwell had, indeed, brought Indian women "up" to white, middle-class Christian standards.

In keeping with this interpretation, historians have lauded Annie Bidwell's humanitarian efforts to bring civilization and progress to the Rancho Chico Indians. Valerie Mathes concludes that "Annie Bidwell provided a unique example of what personal endeavor and private philanthropy could accomplish in encouraging an Indian village to seek a place in the mainstream of American life."[3] Lamenting the loss of their culture but expressing her approval of the Bidwells' humanitarianism, Dorothy Hill remarks that "had it not been for the Bidwells' interest, the Indians of Chico Rancheria would have experienced a more abrupt, painful, but inevitable change in their lifestyle."[4]

Such a reading leaves unexamined the nature of the interaction between Annie Bidwell and the Indians at Rancho Chico. It fails to examine why Annie Bidwell felt it necessary to undermine native culture and replace it with her own notions of civilization. Hill's and Mathes's interpretations also neglect the ingenious ways in which the Rancho Chico Indians, like other Native Americans, managed to sustain vital aspects of their culture and identity through adaptation and accommodation. In this essay, I aim to place Annie Bidwell in the context of late-nineteenth-century middle-class women's reform movements and to recover the many ways in which Indian women and men at Rancho Chico challenged Annie Bidwell's attempts at acculturation. Such events as the Fourth of July parade illuminate how the Rancho Chico Indians manipulated and appropriated the icons of American acculturation as a means to preserve their culture.

Annie Bidwell came to California by virtue of her marriage to California pioneer John Bidwell, who first ventured west as a member of the Wilkes Expedition in 1841.[5] The land known as Rancho Chico that John Bidwell eventually acquired lay within the territory of the Northwestern Maidu group in the Sacramento Valley of northeastern California.[6] According to Bidwell, he first encountered the Maidu Indians who lived at a village known as Mechoopda in 1847 when he came to survey Rancho Chico and other ranches in northern California.[7] In 1848, Bidwell found gold on the Middle Fork of the Feather River. Faced with a shortage of labor, Bidwell claims he "had to use Indians" to help him clear brush and to mine gold. While Bidwell paid his laborers with beads and clothes, he reportedly mined one hundred thousand dollars worth of gold dust.[8]

In just two years after the discovery of gold, the white population in California increased by more than a hundred thousand. The population of the Sacramento Valley alone surged from a few hundred to twenty or thirty thousand. The pressure the new white miners put on the land had devastating consequences for northern California natives. As they killed deer, duck, rabbit, and other game, the miners deprived Indians of their customary diet. In addition, they upset natural habitats with their mining operations and introduced livestock that devoured the plants, roots, grasses, seeds, and acorns upon which the Indians relied.[9] Before the gold rush, Indians in California numbered about 150,000; by the 1850s, they had suffered an 80 percent decrease in population to 30,000.[10]

In addition to destroying the natural habitat of northern California Indians, incoming miners and settlers also dispossessed them of their land. Those miners who did not find their fortunes in the mines sought to make their living as farmers on plots of land they simply claimed as squatters.[11] Though Bidwell had made a fortune in mining, in 1849 he decided to abandon the industry in favor of purchasing Rancho Chico, a Mexican land grant of more than twenty-two thousand acres that encompassed the Mechoopda village of Maidu Indians.[12] As he had relied on Indians to labor in his surveying and mining operations, Bidwell again turned to Indians to work on Rancho Chico. Because of the encroachments of foreigners on Indian land, John Bidwell found California Indians with few other options for survival but laboring on ranchos.

As whites seized all the most fertile land and robbed the Indians of their customary hunting and gathering grounds, northern California Indians had to either live on nonproductive land or become agricultural laborers or house servants for their invaders.[13] To stave off hunger, some Indians resorted to livestock raiding on white ranches. Whites retaliated with violence, even against Indians who had not taken part in raiding.[14]

Faced with such violence, Indians who lived and worked on John Bidwell's Rancho Chico gained a rare measure of peace and protection. According to Rancho Chico resident Henry Azbill, Bidwell "had a little more concern for the Indian people living on his land," and "to the Indian people who were at that time suffering the many atrocities by the incoming whites, Bidwell did produce some sort of protection for the people living on his place. He saw to it that what he called renegade whites would not bother them, that they had a home of their own, and in this way, they were somewhat protected."[15] In exchange for this protection, Bidwell gained a source of cheap labor to develop his land.

In 1863, conflicts between whites and Indians in Butte County reached their peak when a posse of 500 white men sought to kill or remove every Indian from Butte County, rounding up 461 Indians to be driven to the Round Valley Reservation.[16] As early as February 1864, some Indians left Round Valley and returned to their homes. Some sought refuge at Bidwell's ranch. Representatives from nine other Maidu villages, as well as members of the Yana, Pit River, Nome Lacki, Wintu, and Wailacki tribes, came to reside and work at Rancho Chico, composing the largest nonreservation Indian community in the United States. Though this village had once been called Mechoopda, the older Maidu people came to call this reconstituted community Bahapki, a Maidu word meaning unsifted or mixed, to reflect the combination of cultures it sheltered. Though they had to labor for Bidwell and were often cut off from their ancestral lands, the Indians at Bahapki gained protection and an opportunity to re-create a village, mixing elements from all of their cultures.[17]

Until 1868, when, during his tenure as a U.S. congressman, John Bidwell married Annie Ellicott Kennedy, a member of a prominent Washington, D.C., family, the Indians at Bahapki experienced few efforts to acculturate them to white society. As an adherent to the dominant middle-class ideology of the time that associated men's sphere with business and public affairs and women's realm with religion, morality, and the home, John Bidwell seems to have left much of the job of "civilizing" and Christianizing the Rancho Chico Indians up to his new wife.[18]

When Annie Bidwell arrived at Rancho Chico in 1868, her upbringing had already preconditioned her to believe that it was her Christian and female duty to work for the "uplift" of the "little unclad savages" she found on her husband's ranch. An ardent Presbyterian, a loyal member of the National Woman Suffrage Association (NWSA), and a devout follower of the Woman's Christian Temperance Union (WCTU), Annie Kennedy emerged from a tradition of middle-class Christian women's reform that sought to instill women's perceived moral superiority into the mainstream of American society.[19] Like other women from this tradition, she held deep religious, evangelical convictions. In fact, before she consented to marry General Bidwell in 1868, Kennedy wrote him of her concern that he should be not only a Christian, but a Presbyterian instead of a Methodist.[20] The creation and maintenance of a Christian home composed a key component of the women's moral superiority tradition from which

Annie E. K. Bidwell. (Courtesy Bidwell Mansion State Historic Park and Special Collections, Merriam Library, California State University, Chico.)

Annie Kennedy came. Though middle-class white women were not supposed to invade the male sphere of business and electoral politics, they could exert power within their homes.[21] Apparently, both the general and Annie Kennedy subscribed to this notion, as the general proclaimed, "Annie must be the sole ruler of the domestic circle—she must rule supreme there."[22]

Yet Annie Bidwell and many other middle-class women did venture out of their prescribed sphere in the home, creating a place for themselves in the "public sphere" based on women's identification with morality. Mrs. Bidwell[23] and other middle-class reforming women did not reject their roles as wives and mothers but sought instead to extend "female" values of piety, purity, and the Christian home into the public realm. Rather than challenging male power head-on, these women focused instead on strengthening female moral authority by rescuing women they perceived to be victims.[24] In the late nineteenth century, as reformers increasingly posed assimilation as the key to the so-called Indian problem, women found key roles to play in the campaign to assimilate Native American women.[25]

Mrs. Bidwell's first successful attempt to make contact with Indian women and introduce them to her notions of women's domesticity came seven years after she first arrived at Rancho Chico. Having spent "years of fruitless attempts to become acquainted" with the Indians at Bahapki village, she was not successful until one day when she borrowed a plan from mission work in eastern cities "of giving clothing to those who would make it, provided they would come to the mission school; so by taking the cotton goods to the village and holding it up in a way to excite their curiosity and retain their interest; and by gestures and words, I made them understand that if they would come up to the Mansion (as our home was called), I would show them how to make clothing which they could have for the making." To Mrs. Bidwell's "great joy, the following morning about seven women and a few children appeared, and from that moment we were friends."[26] Evidently, many of the women became quite skilled in Mrs. Bidwell's form of sewing and produced many articles of clothing in the style of which the Bidwells approved.

Hoping to provoke another transformation in the way the Indians lived, Mrs. Bidwell stressed the importance of living in wooden rather than earthen houses. Although she marveled at her first sight of the Indians' earthen-dome dwellings at Bahapki, Mrs. Bidwell took great pleasure when the Indians moved their village in the early 1870s and replaced all but three of their customary homes with wooden houses.[27] In connection with her favorable impression of Indians who built wooden homes, Mrs. Bidwell took pride in Indian women who adopted the middle-class American concern for their homes. On the death of Bahapki Indian Nopanny, the daughter of the headman Luckyan and wife of Billy Preacher, Mrs. Bidwell praised Nopanny as a "devoted wife and excellent housekeeper," whose home was one she always exhibited to visitors.[28]

Not only did Mrs. Bidwell seek to effect outer, material changes in the Indians' clothing and housing, she also tried to transform the Indians' interior souls and minds. Her sewing lessons provided merely a cover for her deeper intentions; once she had ensnared the Indian women in her sewing classes, she began her attempts to teach them and their children English and to convert them to Christianity as well. According to Mrs. Bidwell, "[T]he first half hour [of her classes] was given to devotional exercises; the next, to reading with the women and girls, and the rest of the morning to sewing while the boys had lessons in the rudiments of English."[29] To encourage the Christianization of the Indians, in the late 1870s the Bidwells built a small church for the Indians in their village and later erected a larger one on their own grounds outside the village; eventually they moved this church to the village and enlarged it with a tower and belfry.[30]

In connection with her Christianizing efforts, Mrs. Bidwell desired that the Indians give up their sacred ceremonies and observances. She particularly disapproved of the Bahapki Indians' burial and mourning ceremonies at which they "wailed" for several days and nights and cast beads, baskets, skins, feather belts, and ornaments into the grave alongside the body. To Mrs. Bidwell, not only were the mourning practices a symbol of the Indians' heathenness, but their tradition of burying the dead with valuable objects represented resistance to a culture that prized material accumulation. According to Mrs. Bidwell, her efforts to convince the Indians at Bahapki to abandon their burial practices soon paid off. She asserts that in 1876, only a year after she had started her school, "one of the men . . . said he was going to the white man's God, and he wished to be buried like a white man. He wished our carpenter to make the casket, and ever since caskets have been supplied to all the Indians with the exception of two or three who wished to buy their own."[31]

Predictably, another major point of contention between Mrs. Bidwell and the Indians at Bahapki developed over the Indians' dances. As with Indian burial practices, Mrs. Bidwell opposed the Indian dances for two reasons: They did not conform to Christian religion, and they did not fit with the Indians' new lifestyle as wage laborers on her husband's property. According to her, "The argument I presented against the Indian dance was, that when they had a creek to spring into after the dance, it was a benefit to them, purifying their bodies; but now that they had to sit in the cold wind, it gave them colds and pneumonia. Also that they danced to excess and over-tired their bodies so that the next day they were not in condition of good work."[32]

As Mrs. Bidwell cultivated Christianity while trying to root out the old native ways, she claimed that the Indians at Bahapki gradually gave up their traditional dances. According to Henry Azbill, who grew up in Bahapki, headman Holi Lafonso, under pressure from Mrs. Bidwell, agreed to abandon the old dances but requested that the Indians be allowed to conduct one last complete dance cycle in 1906–07. Lafonso began the cycle in the spring of 1906 with the Acorn or Aki Dance, but before the cycle could be continued and completed, he died that fall. Keeping with their tradition, in February 1907, after the death of their headman, the Indians tore down the Dance House.[33] Thus, in 1907, Mrs. Bidwell could write confidently, "All of these customs have passed away altogether with the Indian Dance, which was a sacred institution."[34]

In Mrs. Bidwell's ardent efforts to enforce Christianity and white American ways at Bahapki, she focused on Indian women. Like most white Protestant women reformers of her time, Mrs. Bidwell believed that Native American men degraded their women. Ethnologists and reformers alike mistook northern California Indian bride-price customs as a form of slavery or prostitution and ignored the complex divisions of labor that accorded native California women status for their agricultural work. Based partly on what they perceived to be the ill and inappropriate treatment of Indian women, they assigned native Californians to the "lowest level of civilization."[35] Entrenched in their own middle-class culture in which white women did not engage in hard physical labor, reformers and researchers assumed that the culture from which they came held women in higher esteem than the Native American cultures they observed.

During her initial interactions with the Indians at Bahapki, Mrs. Bidwell shared this view of Indian women as the degraded slaves of their men. In accordance with her own Victorian gender norms, she never thought it proper to teach men, "especially Indians whom, I thought had less regard for woman than white men."[36] Given this view of Indian women as the drudges of Indian men, Mrs. Bidwell attempted to rescue Indian women from a "heathen" and "uncivilized" life.

Mrs. Bidwell's proselytizing efforts toward women profoundly affected gender relations between Nopanny and Billy Preacher and between Amanda Wilson and her first husband, Holi Lafonso. Mrs. Bidwell described Nopanny as a "remarkable woman. She learned readily to read and sew and was my counselor from the beginning of the mission until her death. We were devoted friends." In contrast to her husband, Billy Preacher, who continued his traditional role in the village as the *kuksu*, or Dance Society instructor, Nopanny Preacher became one of Mrs. Bidwell's disciples in Christianity. Nopanny's conversion generated conflict between her and Billy. The Indian woman evidently asked Mrs. Bidwell for a Bible for her home and kept it wrapped in flannel on her mantle. When Billy disapproved, Nopanny returned the Bible to Mrs. Bidwell, saying, "My husband doesn't believe that Book and I can't keep it." Nopanny mysteriously departed to Sacramento in December of 1881, apparently separating from her husband for some length of time.[37]

Mrs. Bidwell interfered in the domestic disputes rather than in the religious beliefs of Amanda and Holi Lafonso. Though some accounts call Amanda the widow of Holi, Amanda's granddaughter, Thelma Wilson, claims that Amanda and Holi divorced because of Mrs. Bidwell's intervention. Thelma Wilson explains that her grandmother's first marriage

was an unhappy marriage, and she never really told us the details of what happened, but evidently her husband [Holi Lafonso] was most unkind toward her, and I would imagine that that'd probably [be] putting it gently. And so the older woman [Mrs. Bidwell] said to her why we can't let this go on, it's an impossible situation. . . . And of course in those days it wasn't easy just to say, well, all right I'm going to leave you, I can't take this any longer. There has to be somebody to help.[38]

Mrs. Bidwell was the "somebody" who helped Amanda separate from Holi Lafonso and remarry Santa Wilson. As the adopted son of a white family, a bookkeeper, and the eventual minister of the Bidwell's Indian church, Santa Wilson clearly appeared to Mrs. Bidwell as a more suitable mate for a Christian woman than the headman Lafonso.[39] Although Mrs. Bidwell offered Indian women like Amanda Wilson support and protection when faced with male abuse, her intentions went beyond simple assistance in times of distress. Like her sewing classes, Mrs. Bidwell's efforts to rescue women and convert them to her view of womanhood were part of her larger effort to bring Indians into civilization.

Mrs. Bidwell also intervened in the customary socialization process of the Indians at Bahapki by requiring Indian children to attend her school and church. According to Mrs. Bidwell, many younger Indians accepted

Maggie Lafonso. (Courtesy Dorothy Hill Collection and Special Collections, Meriam Library, California State University, Chico.)

baptism and other aspects of Christianity that their parents would not. On the question of baptism, Mrs. Bidwell remarked that "the old Indians have been so determined [not to be baptized] that I have not urged them," but "with the younger Indians this is not so."[40] By intervening early in the socialization of children, Mrs. Bidwell seems to have succeeded in gaining at least a few converts to Christianity. Some of Mrs. Bidwell's students—namely Maggie, Elmer, and Genevieve Lafonso and Burney Wilson—appear to have become committed and zealous Christians. Maggie Lafonso, daughter of headman Holi Lafonso and Amanda Wilson, became the Sunday School teacher at the Indian church in the village until her early death in 1909. Elmer Lafonso, Maggie's brother, made his name as an accomplished hymn singer and traveled around the West in an attempt to spread the gospel to other Indians. Elmer's wife, Genevieve Lafonso, also became an instructor in the Bahapki church and school. Burney Wilson, son of Amanda and Santa Wilson and half-brother to the Lafonsos, tried to pursue a career as a minister.[41]

In the process of attempting to convert younger Indians to Christianity, Mrs. Bidwell appears to have created a division in the Bahapki village between old Indians and young. For example, Burney Wilson wrote Mrs. Bidwell of the conflict with his parents over his attendance at a boarding school in Oregon: "As you know by this time that I left home (while my folks didn't want me to) the latter part of October."[42] These generational conflicts played out not just between individual children and their parents but also in the village as a whole. In 1907, Maggie Lafonso wrote to tell Mrs. Bidwell about the Indians' conflict over the burning ceremony that they conducted each year in honor of their dead. "The Burning is a question which is not yet settled upon. Wish to consult with you on your return home. The young people of the village are trying to banish all Old ways. We have so far great hopes."[43]

In 1907, generational conflicts seem to have led to the destruction of the Dance House. After headman Holi Lafonso's death, the Indians at Bahapki debated whether to tear down the old Dance House and rebuild a new one, according to tradition, or to retain the old one. Apparently, some members of the Bahapki village considered retaining the old house, despite tradition, because no one knew how to dress the center pole.[44] Other sources conclude that older Bahapki Indians feared that the younger Indians would not sustain the Dance Society or rebuild the house and so were reluctant to tear it down. Evidently, in 1907, an adolescent boy decided the issue by riding a horse over the building, breaking the domed roof as well the horse's legs. To some older Indians, this incident proved that the younger people lacked the proper respect toward and desire to continue the Indian dances. Therefore, one Bahapki Indian, George Barber, sold his dance costume to museum collector Stewart Culin on Culin's collecting expedition through northern California in 1907.[45]

Though Mrs. Bidwell presented her interactions with the Indians at Bahapki as subtle and gently persuasive, she and the general actually instituted more coercive measures to control the behavior of the Indians. In his "Proclamation of Rules Made for Rancho Chico Indians" in 1885, General Bidwell asserted that he would allow the Indians to live on his premises as long as they abided by certain conditions. These conditions included that "they drink no whiskey or other liquor"; "that all must be temperate, industrious, and good"; "that all Indians—men, women, and children—must (unless in case of sickness) attend church every Sunday when there is church"; and "that parents must send their children to school when old enough, keep them clean, and teach them to be polite." Thus, though presented as a voluntary choice for the Indians at Bahapki, Mrs. Bidwell's classes and church services were actually mandatory. Not only did the Bidwells require church and school attendance, but they also prohibited the Indians from working off Rancho Chico. General Bidwell proclaimed, "If they go away and work elsewhere, they lose the right to live here; for this place must not be a harbor for tramps or idle or otherwise not useful people."[46]

Using such pressures, it would appear that by the early 1890s, and certainly by 1907, Mrs. Bidwell had accomplished many of her aims. In her mind, or at least according to her writings, the Indians at Bahapki had not only willingly adopted the clothes and wooden houses she promoted, but they had also cheerfully abandoned their old ways in favor of Christianity and middle-class norms of domesticity. But appearances can be deceiving. In order to survive physically, the Indians at Bahapki accommodated to the interests of, and ultimately became dependent upon, the Bidwells. Yet in order to survive culturally and spiritually, they resisted Mrs. Bidwell's civilizing mission in overt as well as subtle ways. Their need for both physical and cultural survival confronted the Bahapki Indians with a dilemma: If they resisted Mrs. Bidwell's efforts, they risked their physical survival as a village. But if they accommodated completely to Mrs. Bidwell's mission, they could lose their cultural identity.

Each individual Indian coped with this dilemma in a different way; no one seems to have accomplished total resistance to Mrs. Bidwell nor to have submitted to total accommodation. When faced with the external, material changes the Bidwells offered to them—the adoption of new material goods and training in sewing and reading—some of the Indians at Bahapki seem to have readily accepted some of these innovations. Though Mrs. Bidwell believed their acceptance of these external changes primed them for adopting deeper internal and religious changes, the Indians at Bahapki did not believe that their selective adoption of certain white material goods and skills meant total acceptance of all white ways. When confronted with the "internal" changes Mrs. Bidwell and her husband sought—abandoning their own religious ways for Christianity—the Bahapki Indians developed a range of strategies for negotiating this assault on their culture.

In some cases, they engaged in outright defiance. The Bidwells tolerated mild infractions of their rules. For example, despite the Bidwells' efforts to ensure that all children attend school, the records from Mrs. Bidwell's industrial school are full of absences of children who had gone off to dances in neighboring Indian communities. And although the Bidwells required the Bahapki Indians to attend church, Mrs. Bidwell's native preachers and teachers would often lament the poor attendance at church.[47]

But the Bidwells did not tolerate more serious forms of outright defiance. Even if desperate, Indians who left Rancho Chico in the 1880s and 1890s in search of other employment could expect to be kicked off Rancho Chico.[48] The Bidwells also threatened with eviction Indians who carried out their traditional dances on the premises. In a series of letters to the secretary of the interior in 1914, Bahapki Indian William Conway asked the U.S. government to buy the Rancho Chico Indians a home in Chico. Apparently the secretary of the interior wrote back to Conway to question why he couldn't work out some arrangement with Mrs. Bidwell. Conway replied that as

far as Mrs. Annie E. K. Bidwell good Friend ship to the Indians is true: I have nothing to say about Mrs. Annie E. K. Bidwell . . . that isn't the question. The question is we have no homes. I will mention why we have no homes. 30th of last December 1913, the Indians gave a social dance: Indians only. Mrs. Bidwell came to the village and told the Indians to get off of her Property: and said this is my Property. We had no Place to go so we still remain where we are now, we might get kick off at any time.

This is why I ask this government for assistance: were we are now located we have no title. We have lived were we are now ever cence 1890.[49]

This passage reveals three important elements of the interaction between Mrs. Bidwell and the Indians who resided at Bahapki. First, if Conway's depiction of this incident is accurate, despite Mrs. Bidwell's claims to the contrary, the Indians had not given up their dances even though they no longer had a Dance House. Secondly, Mrs. Bidwell's representation of herself as "gently" persuading the Indians to come to Christianity and "never interfering" in their ways does not square with Indian accounts. Thirdly, this incident further reveals the debilitating dependence the Indians felt on Mrs. Bidwell. Without title to their own land and the ability to make their own living, the Indians at Bahapki remained dependent on Mrs. Bidwell's good graces. If they defied her openly, they risked, at least, falling out of favor, and at most, their entire village. Thus, this strategy of maintaining cultural integrity through outright defiance could be dangerous.

The Bahapki Indians therefore developed other more subtle and less risky means to preserve their cultural identity in the face of Mrs. Bidwell's pressures. For one, the Indians at Bahapki made sense of and adopted some of the customs Mrs. Bidwell tried to foist on them by accepting them on their own terms. For example, Billy Preacher's eventual acceptance of Christianity came only after he had received a vision that he should do so. Receiving, interpreting, and acting on visions was an integral part of the religion of the Indians at Bahapki. Nopanny, Billy's wife, told Mrs. Bidwell that "My husband died and went to God and God showed him that Book and told him it was His Book, and he must believe it."[50] Thus, Billy Preacher may have accepted Christianity, but he did so on his own terms and via his customary means.

Similarly, when the Bidwells built a church in the Bahapki village, the Indians believed it to be a result of their own visions. As the Indian Tokeeno lay dying in his home, his cousin Nopanny insisted that he be transferred to her home for a Christian service. Nopanny refused to pray in Tokeeno's house because Tokeeno's wife was a "non-believer." As Mrs. Bidwell led the Indians in prayer for Tokeeno in Nopanny's home, Tokeeno made a miraculous recovery. Nopanny then told Mrs. Bidwell that "My cousin says he died and went to God and the good lady prayed and God sent him back to see that church house built, and we want that church house." As a converted Christian, Nopanny may have had ulterior motives in seeing a church house built. Yet her cousin and she legitimated the construction of a church house through traditional Indian spiritual means—a process of visions. In this instance, Mrs. Bidwell accepted the Indians' interpretation of events and the legitimacy of interpreting visions to reveal proper actions. Mrs. Bidwell insisted that the church be built the day after this momentous event, for she felt that "God did send [Tokeeno] to force us to do our duty."[57]

Even those young Indians who appeared to have wholeheartedly adopted Christianity and American ways did so on their own terms and for their own purposes. Elmer Lafonso, for example, used his training in Christianity and hymn singing as a platform from which to launch a vaudeville career. A San Francisco reviewer commented that in addition to his repertoire of Italian operatic arias and popular songs, Elmer Lafonso also "has secured a quiver full of Indian songs, mainly by Charles Cadman, based on the tribal music of Indians." The reviewer noted that Lafonso believed that Indian music could enrich American musical literature. Thus, Elmer Lafonso, the supposedly Christianized Indian who had abandoned his culture, actually had hopes of acting as a kind of missionary, introducing native cultural elements, albeit popularized ones, into the American mainstream.[52]

Elmer's sister, Maggie Lafonso, used her Christian training as a base from which to join Indian efforts to challenge white attitudes and policies toward Indians. Before Maggie died in 1909 at the age of twenty-five, she participated as the only woman in the second annual Zayante Indian conference in 1907 in Mount Hermon, California. Though sponsored by the Northern California Indian Association (NCIA) in order to further the training of young Indians to "uplift" other Indians, the Indians at the conference used the occasion to draw up a list of grievances and policy recommendations. Nineteen Indian men from around northern California and Maggie Lafonso signed a declaration petitioning the state and federal government for land, for protection from liquor traffic, for education, for field physicians, and for legal protection. In her letters to Mrs. Bidwell, Maggie always characterized her Christian commitment as a tool to help her people.[53]

Burney Wilson, too, viewed his Christian mission as an effort to challenge white beliefs about Indians. During his college career, Burney was "called on a mission of the Gospel" many times, because he thought that he "may be of some good in telling of Our Indian Problem." As the only Indian student at Park College in Missouri, Burney felt a special responsibility to prove his worth as an Indian.[54] In essence, these three young Indians negotiated a place for themselves as ambassadors from Bahapki to American culture. Though Mrs. Bidwell and other whites may have seen the Lafonso siblings and Burney Wilson as examples of Indians who had assimilated successfully, these Indians may have defined themselves instead as mediators between two cultures.[55]

In the same way that young Indians made their own uses of the Christian schooling that Mrs. Bidwell provided them, Indian women also interpreted Mrs. Bidwell's domestic teachings and prescribed gender roles in their own manner. Even though Nopanny converted to Christianity, she maintained her faith in the power of visions and revelations. In the case of Amanda Wilson, though she may have accepted Mrs. Bidwell's protection from the cruelty of her first husband, Holi Lafonso, she nevertheless retained her own view of women's roles. For example, unlike white women in the Presbyterian Church who sat passively through the sermon of a male minister, Amanda Wilson felt no inhibition about standing up in church and delivering her own sermon while her second husband, Santa Wilson, led the services.[56] Other researchers have found evidence that Amanda Wilson, as the second in rank in the women's Dance Society, attended the Christian church irregularly and still practiced her native religion.[57] Thus, though Nopanny Preacher and Amanda Wilson may have accepted some of her teachings and assistance, this did not mean that they agreed to all of the conditions Mrs. Bidwell thought accompanied such an acceptance. Rather, they selectively responded to her advances.

In addition to adopting certain aspects of Mrs. Bidwell's offerings on their own terms in order to maintain their cultural integrity, the Indians at Bahapki also practiced a strategy of attempting to define their encounter with Mrs. Bidwell as a two-way rather than a one-way process. For example, according to Mrs. Bidwell, "After the Indians of my mission learned to speak English, I was invited by the women to attend an Indian dance, which I promised to do."[58] This act of sharing an aspect of their culture with Mrs. Bidwell after she had given the Indians knowledge of her own culture provides evidence that Indian women may have imagined their interaction with Bidwell, at least at first, as a cultural exchange. In this, the women at Bahapki may have challenged central aspects of Mrs. Bidwell's ideology. For example, the Indian women's invitation to their dance created conflict between the Bidwells over women's proper roles. When Mrs. Bidwell reported her promise to attend the Indian dance to the general, he replied that it was not a suitable place for her to go. But Mrs. Bidwell defied the general's wishes and attended anyway, albeit with her pastor and some other guests to chaperone her.[59]

Mrs. Bidwell's sustained interaction with the Indians at Bahapki caused her to question gender roles within white society on other occasions as well. For instance, when a group of Bahapki Indians supposedly insisted that she run a church service for them, Mrs. Bidwell agonized over her dilemma. Should she take on an improper role for a woman, that of a minister, and thus give the Indians the wrong idea about how Christian men and women should behave, or should she honor their request because it would bring these Indians closer to God? After God spoke to her, Mrs. Bidwell eventually decided "that it was a question between God and myself and not what others thought, so with many tears, I took charge of the little church. I have often wept all the way from my home to the little church because of my insufficiency and because I did not think it was proper that I, a woman, should teach men, especially Indians whom, I thought had less regard for woman than white men."[60]

Not only did Mrs. Bidwell's experiences on Rancho Chico cause her to challenge her own gender role in American society, but her almost daily contact with the Indians led her to abandon her belief that Indian men "had less regard for woman than white men." Because of her experience in performing church services for both Indian men and women at Bahapki, Mrs. Bidwell concluded, "So ignorant are we . . . the men have stood by me to such an extent as to be the marvel of those who attend the service."[61]

In other instances, although Mrs. Bidwell did not envision her encounter with the Indians as a reciprocal process, she may have subconsciously adopted Indian cultural elements into her own culture. Like the Indians who gave special meaning to their dreams and visions, Mrs. Bidwell too learned to respect and utilize this aspect of Indian spirituality, revealing that God "has helped me on similar lines, without which I would have done [the Indians] a great wrong in rebuking as error what I believed was divine guidance."[62] Thus the Indian strategy of trying to define their interaction with Mrs. Bidwell as a cultural exchange had its advantages. In the process of learning about Bahapki culture, Mrs. Bidwell began to question some of her dearly held assumptions about both her own gender roles and those of the Indians. She also learned to respect certain elements of Indian culture and religion, even to the point of utilizing visions in her own life.[63] Yet this strategy was also unpredictable: Revealing Indian culture to Mrs. Bidwell could produce either greater empathy and understanding on her part or it could serve to underscore her determination to transform the Indians into "civilized" Americans.

Thus, the Indians at Bahapki came to rely on another strategy to cope with Mrs. Bidwell's acculturation efforts. Rather than reject outright Mrs. Bidwell's new rituals and ceremonies, the Indians at Bahapki seem to have, at times, accepted the outer forms of the rituals Mrs. Bidwell offered them while finding an inner meaning that conformed more closely to their own religion. For instance, though Mrs. Bidwell had provided caskets for all the funerals of Indians since 1876, it is not apparent that the Bahapki Indians really used them, at least in the way she intended. Upon the death of Mrs. Nunco, Mrs. Bidwell went to town to get a coffin, but when she returned to Bahapki, the grave was not yet finished. According to Mrs. Bidwell, "The Indians feared I would take cold so insisted on my not remaining but having services before burial, promising to say the Lord's prayer at grace." Before leaving, Mrs. Bidwell noted that Mrs. Nunco was dressed Indian style for her burial.[64] Although we cannot be sure, it appears that the Indians might have hustled Mrs. Bidwell out of Bahapki so that they could perform the burial in their own manner. By outwardly placating Mrs. Bidwell, the Indians may have been able to circumvent some of Mrs. Bidwell's proscriptions.

Some of the Indians at Bahapki may have also used this strategy to continue their traditional dances. Henry Azbill notes that the Indians at Bahapki performed a dance around the time of the winter solstice called the To To to pay homage to the Earth Mother. Eventually, Azbill states, "We termed it Christmas Dance because it comes about that time of the year . . . on the 21st or 22nd of December. In order to get certain people off our backs because we were doing 'heathen' things, and this sort of thing, we just said, 'Well this is a Christmas Dance.' "[65] Azbill's statement is crucial because it clearly shows that the Indians at Bahapki self-consciously manipulated the cultural icons of white Americans to suit their own purposes.

This brings us back to the Fourth of July parade Mrs. Bidwell described as an example of how far the "little unclad savages" had come on their journey to civilization. A more careful reading of Mrs. Bidwell's account of the event brings out some peculiarities. When the procession was ready to start, Mrs. Bidwell noted, the Goddess of Liberty was nowhere to be found. When she finally found the thirteen-year-old Maggie Lafonso standing in her doorway, Mrs. Bidwell asked her why she was not in her place. To Maggie's question as to whether all the people were in the wagon yet, Mrs. Bidwell answered in the affirmative. Hearing that, Maggie said, "I am waiting to be taken." "Just then her father, the Chief [Lafonso] in marshal's garb, arrived," Mrs. Bidwell explained, "and the maiden Maggie stepped off with a grace, dignity, and maturity of manner bewildering to me."[66] The Indians—resident and visiting—paraded through town and gathered with their "white friends" in a grove near their village. There Mrs. Bidwell and the other white guests waited impatiently for nearly an hour for the Fourth of July exercises to begin. Again, the Goddess of Liberty was missing, and the exercises could not go on without her. According to Mrs. Bidwell, "investigation disclosed Maggie still seated on her throne, embowered in trees,—attendants, horses, all gone!" When asked why she would not come down, Maggie replied, "I am waiting to be taken down." Eventually Maggie's uncle approached and "conducted her from her pinnacle to the grand stand, and seated her by her father."[67] Thus, though the Indians engaged in an American Fourth of July parade, they did so in an unusual manner that bewildered even as it pleased Mrs. Bidwell.

In this case, the Indians at Bahapki may have used the Fourth of July in order to conduct a puberty ceremony for thirteen-year-old Maggie Lafonso. It is revealing to compare Mrs. Bidwell's account of the Goddess of Liberty's odd behavior with an account of a puberty ceremony among the Wintu—one of the tribes represented at Bahapki—by early ethnologist Stephen Powers. Powers observed that "when a girl arrives at maturity, about the age of twelve or fourteen, her village friends celebrate the event with a dance in her honor . . . to which all the surrounding villages are invited." For three days the girl isolates herself, after which

The invited tribes now begin to arrive and the dance comes on. As each village or deputation from it arrive on the summit of a hill overlooking the scene, they form in line, two or three abreast or in single file, then dance down the hill and around the village, crooning strange, weird chants. When all the deputations are collected, . . . they unite in a grand dance, passing around the village in solid marching order. . . . In conclusion of the ceremonies the chief takes the maiden by the hand and together they dance down the line, while the company sing songs improvised for the occasion.[68]

Gone from Mrs. Bidwell's account are the songs and "croonings" of Powers' rendering, and instead of dancing in procession, the Indians at Bahapki rode in wagons or on horseback or marched as members of the brass band. And from Mrs. Bidwell's account, we cannot know whether Maggie secluded herself for days before the event. Mrs. Bidwell would not have been privy to such information. Yet the overall picture of the event—Maggie's age, her seclusion before the procession and the exercises, the need for the chief (her father) or her uncle to escort her to the events, the procession itself, and the dance held later that evening—closely parallels Stephen Powers's account. Given that the village of Bahapki included an "unsifted" mixture of Indians from many northern California tribes, it is possible that the Indians there may have developed new customs, mixing the symbols and practices of each other's rites together. And given the pressure Mrs. Bidwell exerted on them to conform to Christian and American ways, it would not be surprising that the Indians devised a means to utilize the Fourth of July for their own purposes, as they did with Christmas.[69]

Thus, faced with Mrs. Bidwell's desire that they become acculturated to white Protestant middle-class American norms, the Indians at Bahapki did not just passively submit to her civilizing mission. Though they may have accepted new skills and adopted material innovations such as wooden houses, the Bahapki Indians nevertheless worked in a number of ways to preserve the heart of their culture. When they could not avoid Mrs. Bidwell or openly defy her, they developed more subtle means to preserve their cultural integrity—adopting aspects of what Mrs. Bidwell offered on their own terms and for their own purposes, defining their interaction with Mrs. Bidwell as a reciprocal rather than a one-way process, and, finally, appearing to accept the rituals of Mrs. Bidwell's culture while attaching a different meaning to them. The Indians adapted their culture both to superficially satisfy Mrs. Bidwell's desire that they acculturate and to fulfill their own needs to maintain cultural identity and affiliation.

After Mrs. Bidwell's death in 1918, the Indians who had lived at Bahapki continued their struggle for cultural integrity and for title to their original land. Mrs. Bidwell bequeathed plots of land to thirty-two Indians, yet because of legal complications, the Indians who had resided at Rancho Chico ended up as wards of the government.[70] In 1957, the federal government terminated the tribal status of the Indians at Bahapki and other Maidu in the state, supposedly signaling the full integration of Native Americans into the mainstream of American society. Yet again we see that the Indians at Bahapki managed to maintain some degree of cultural integrity. For example, despite the dissolution of the village at Bahapki, the Indians who remained in Chico maintained their Indian burial grounds.[71] And through the memories of Bahapki residents, particularly Henry Azbill, the sacred dances that the Bahapki Indians once performed live on. Until his death in 1973, Azbill worked to preserve Maidu culture by teaching both Indians and non-Indians to make dance regalia. This passing on of old ways to the younger generation through the oral tradition allowed for a revival of Maidu dances.[72]

Thus, despite nearly 50 years of Mrs. Bidwell's efforts to "civilize" them, and despite close to 150 years of gradual dispossession and termination at the hands of American society and government, important elements of Bahapki and Maidu culture have survived. This would not have been possible if, as historians have long accepted, Mrs. Bidwell had succeeded in her efforts to wipe out Bahapki customs and identity. Today's revivals pay tribute to the adaptability and innovation of the Indians at Bahapki and to the power of oral tradition.

Notes

I wish to thank the Women's Resource and Referral Center at the University of California at Davis for their financial assistance with the early stages of research for this article. Thanks, too, to Pam Bush of the Merriam Library at California State University, Chico, and the archivists at the California State Library and at the Bancroft Library. A big thank you to Steve Crum for sharing boxes of research materials on the Maidu Indians and on Rancho Chico. I am deeply grateful for the ongoing critical perspective, support, and friendship of Vicki Ruiz. I also wish to acknowledge the community of women—Cherie Barkey, Kathy Cairns, Yolanda Calderon-Wallace, Olivia Martinez-Krippner, Annette Reed-Crum, and Alicia Rodríguez-Estrada—who have offered encouragement and sisterhood throughout this project and others. Finally, special thanks to Tom and Cody Lynch for helping me keep it all in perspective.

    1. Annie Ellicott Kennedy Bidwell, "The Mechoopdas, or Rancho Chico Indians," *Overland Monthly* 27, 2d series (February 1896): 208–209.
    2. Ibid., 209–210.
    3. Valerie Sherer Mathes, "Indian Philanthropy in California: Annie Bidwell and the Mechoopda Indians," *Arizona and the West* 25 (Summer 1983): 166.
    4. Dorothy J. Hill, *The Indians of Chico Rancheria* (Sacramento: California Department of Parks and Recreation, 1978), 88.
    5. Ibid., 10.
    6. For more on Maidu culture prior to contact with Europeans, see Henry Azbill, "They Call Us Conkow," in the pamphlet "Koyo'ngkauwi: We Live in the Open Country" (Davis, Calif.: Hehaka Sapa College, DQ University Indian Education Workshop, Summer 1972); Henry Azbill, "How Death Came to the People," *Indian Historian* 2, no. 2 (Summer 1969): 13–14, 29; Henry Azbill, "World Maker," *Indian Historian* 2, no. 1 (Spring 1969): 20; Annie Bidwell, "Description of Sweat House Ceremonies," part 1, carton 2, Bidwell Papers, Bancroft Library, University of California at Berkeley (hereafter BP, BL); Hill, *Indians of Chico Rancheria*; Marie Potts, *The Northern Maidu* (Happy Camp, Calif.: Naturegraph Publishers, 1977); Richard Simpson, *Ooti: A Maidu Legacy* (Millbrae, Calif.: Celestial Arts, 1977); interview with Thelma Wilson, "A Mechoopda Descendant Relates Her Story," 1972, Northeastern California Oral History Project, California State University, Chico (hereafter NCOHP, CSU); interview with Henry Azbill by Dorothy Hill, undated, NCOHP, CSU.
    7. For a comprehensive discussion of the Spanish and Mexican settlement of California, see Douglas Monroy, *Thrown among Strangers: The Making of Mexican Culture in Frontier California* (Berkeley: University of California Press, 1990). Also see Antonia Castañeda, "Comparative Frontiers: The Migration of Women to Alta California and New Zealand," in *Western Women: Their Land, Their Lives*, ed. Lillian Schlissel, Vicki L. Ruiz, and Janice Monk (Albuquerque: University of New Mexico Press, 1988), 283–300. Regarding California Indians during this period, see Albert Hurtado, *Indian Survival on the California Frontier* (New Haven, Conn.: Yale University Press, 1988); Jack Forbes, *Native Americans of California and Nevada* (Happy Camp, Calif.: Naturegraph Publishers, 1982); Hill, *Indians of Chico Rancheria*; and Potts, *Northern Maidu*.
    8. Annie Bidwell, "California Indians," 1891, box 32, Annie Bidwell Collection, California State Library, Sacramento (hereafter ABC, CSL), 1. This collection includes an interview with

her husband, John. See also Hill, *Indians of Chico Rancheria*, 15, and Donald Jewell, *Indians of the Feather River: Tales and Legends of the Concow Maidu of California* (Menlo Park, Calif.: Ballena Press, 1987), 75. Hill estimates that Bidwell used about twenty Indians to work his mining claim between 1848 and 1849. Jewell claims that Bidwell employed up to three hundred Indians on his mining operation.

9. Hill, *Indians of Chico Rancheria*, 18, 19. See also Azbill, "They Call Us Conkow," 11.

10. Hurtado, *Indian Survival*, 1.

11. Monroy, *Thrown among Strangers*, 180.

12. Anne H. Currie, "Bidwell Rancheria," *California Historical Society Quarterly* 36 (December 1957): 314. According to an article by C. C. Parry in the *Overland Monthly* [11, no. 66, 2d series, (June, 1888): 563], Bidwell's "own personally selected [Mexican land] grant in the lower bottom lands of the Sacramento proved unprofitable" so that after he made a sizable sum of money from his mining operation, Bidwell bought another land grant. Bidwell then faced "tedious legal obstructions" before he could own Rancho Chico outright, but eventually his land claim "was confirmed by the courts in the possession of John Bidwell." An article in the *Chico Record* of 14 April 1935 states that Bidwell did not receive a patent on his land until 1860. Unfortunately, we don't know more about whether Bidwell obtained this grant through unscrupulous means, as so many American settlers did after the Mexican-American War.

13. Forbes, *Native Americans* 79, and Potts, *Northern Maidu*, 8.

14. Hill, *Indians of Chico Rancheria*, 9. In 1851 and 1852, California politicians and the federal government hoped to solve these conflicts by negotiating eighteen treaties with California Indians that would have set aside reservation lands. However, the Senate never ratified the treaties and instead hid them away in Washington, D.C., vaults for about fifty years. For a discussion of the failed treaties of 1851 and 1852, see Hill, *Indians of Chico Rancheria*; Currie, "Bidwell Rancheria"; Forbes, *Native Americans*; and Hurtado, *Indian Survival*.

15. Azbill, "They Call Us Conkow," 7.

16. Hill, *Indians of Chico Rancheria*, 41. See also interview with Thelma Wilson, NCOHP, CSU, 2–4.

17. Henry Azbill, "Bahapki," *Indian Historian* 4, no. 1 (Spring 1971): 57, and Azbill, "They Call Us Conkow," 7. See also Hill, *Indians of Chico Rancheria*, x.

18. Henry Azbill, "Maidu Indians of California: A Historical Note," *Indian Historian* 4, no. 2 (Summer 1971): 21; Will Green, "John Bidwell—A Character Study," *Out West* 19, no. 6 (December 1903): 625–34; Hill, *Indians of Chico Rancheria*; Hurtado, *Indian Survival*, 129–31; and Jewell, *Indians of the Feather River*, 78.

19. For an excellent discussion of Protestant home missionary society women and "women's moral superiority," see Peggy Pascoe's *Relations of Rescue: The Search for Female Moral Authority in the American West, 1874–1939* (New York: Oxford University Press, 1990).

20. Letter from Annie Ellicott Kennedy to John Bidwell, 22 August 1867, part I, box 1, BP, BL.

21. Pascoe, *Relations of Rescue*, 33–37.

22. Letter from John Bidwell to John Reynolds Kennedy, 3 April 1868, part 1, box 1, BP, BL.

23. I have chosen to refer to Annie Ellicott Kennedy Bidwell as Mrs. Bidwell throughout the remainder of the article because this is how the Bahapki Indians referred to her. As this essay is concerned with examining the interaction between Bidwell and the Indians, by using the Indians' title for her, we gain insight into the nature of the relationship between the Bahapki Indians and Annie Bidwell.

24. Pascoe, *Relations of Rescue*, 33–34.

25. On assimilation, see Francis Paul Prucha, *The Great Father: The U.S. Government and the American Indians*, vol. 2 (Lincoln: University of Nebraska Press, 1984); Sandra L. Cadwalader and Vine Deloria Jr., eds., *The Aggressions of Civilization: Federal Indian Policy since the 1880s* (Philadelphia: Temple University Press, 1984); Frederick E. Hoxie, *A Final Promise: The Campaign to Assimilate the Indians, 1880–1920* (Cambridge, Eng.: Cambridge University Press, 1984); and Robert Winston Mardock, *The Reformers and the American Indian*

(Columbia: University of Missouri Press, 1971). On white women's role in Indian reform, see Helen Bannan, " 'True Womanhood' on the Reservation: Field Matrons in the U.S. Indian Service," Southwest Institute for Research on Women, Working Paper #18 (Tucson: Women's Studies, 1984); Lisa Emmerich, " 'To Respect and Love and Seek the Ways of White Women': Field Matrons, the Office of Indian Affairs, and Civilization Policy, 1890-1938" (Ph.D. dissertation, University of Maryland, College Park, 1987); Valerie Mathes, "Nineteenth Century Women and Reform: The Women's National Indian Association," *American Indian Quarterly* 14, no. 1 (1990): 1-18; and Helen M. Wanken, " 'Woman's Sphere' and Indian Reform: The Women's National Indian Association, 1879-1901" (Ph.D. dissertation, Marquette University, 1981).

26. Annie Bidwell, untitled, undated speech, circa 1907, part 1, carton 2, BP, BL, 4. Dorothy Hill has estimated this speech to be from the year 1905, but I place it in 1907 because in it Bidwell remarks that the Indians' dances and burial practices have passed away. The Indians did not stop their dances (publicly) until 1907. Also Bidwell remarks that she has been in association with the Indians for thirty-two years, which, dated from the opening of her school in 1875, would place this speech in 1907.

27. A. Bidwell, circa 1907 speech, BP, BL 5-6.

28. Newspaper clipping, box 32, ABC, CSL.

29. A. Bidwell, circa 1907 speech, BP, BL 5.

30. A. Bidwell, "The Mechoopdas," 208.

31. A. Bidwell, circa 1907 speech, BP, BL 6, 8-9, 13.

32. Ibid., 12. Other accounts corroborate Bidwell's disdain for Indian dances. For example, see interview with Frieda Petersen Knotts by Dorothy Hill, 21 March 1974, NCOHP, CSU, 15.

33. Azbill, "They Call Us Conkow," 9.

34. A. Bidwell, circa 1907 speech, BP, BL 9.

35. For example, see Stephen Powers, "Tribes of California," *Contributions to North American Ethnology* 3 (1877): 270, and Sherburne Cook, "The American Invasion, 1848-1870," *Ibero Americana* 23 (1943): 81, reprinted in Sherburne Cook, *The Conflict between the California Indian and White Civilization* (Berkeley: University of California Press, 1976), 335. In the late nineteenth century, white women missionaries and moral reformers believed that women in all non-Christian societies led lives of drudgery and depravity. See David D. Smits, "The 'Squaw Drudge': A Prime Index of Savagism," *Ethnohistory* 29, no. 4 (1982): 281-306; Bannan, " 'True Womanhood,' " 3; Emmerich, " 'To Respect and Love,' " 13-14, 18-19, 166-67; Pascoe, *Relations of Rescue*, 51-68; Joan Jacobs Brumberg, "Zenanas and Girlless Villages: The Ethnology of American Evangelical Women, 1870-1910," *Journal of American History* 69, no. 2 (September 1982): 347-71; Barbara Welter, "She Hath Done What She Could: Protestant Women's Missionary Careers in the the 19th Century," *American Quarterly* 30 (Winter 1978): 630-31; Marjorie King, "Exporting Femininity, not Feminism: Nineteenth-Century U.S. Missionary Women's Efforts to Emancipate Chinese Women," in *Women's Work for Women: Missionaries and Social Change in Asia*, ed. Leslie Flemming (Boulder, Colo.: Westview Press, 1989), 118-20.

36. A. Bidwell, circa 1907 speech, BP, BL 21.

37. Ibid., 17-19; letter from Nopanny Preacher to Annie Bidwell, n.d., box 32, ABC, CSL; letter from Nopanny [Loppenny] Preacher, Sacramento, to Annie Bidwell, 20 December 1881, folder 19, box 78, ABC, CSL.

38. Interview with Thelma Wilson, NCOHP, CSU, 7.

39. Ibid., 2-8.

40. A. Bidwell, circa 1907 speech, BP, BL 20.

41. Letter from Elmer Lafonso, Chico, to Mrs. Bidwell, 16 November 1900, gives an account of Maggie Lafonso's teaching Sunday school, folder 37, box 77, ABC, CSL; letters from Elmer Lafonso, Pasadena, Calif., to Annie Bidwell, 26 and 29 June 1909, folders 38 and 29, box 77, and from Laguna, N.M., 20 February 1913, folder 50, box 77, ABC, CSL; letter from Burney Wilson, Estes Park, Colo., to Annie Bidwell, 19 June 1913, folder 22, box 81, ABC, CSL.

42. Letter from Burney Wilson, Chemawa, Ore., to Annie Bidwell, 20 November 1910, folder 15, box 81, ABC, CSL.

43. Letter from Maggie Lafonso, Chico, Calif., to Annie Bidwell, Petaluma, Calif., 14 October 1907, folder 11, box 78, ABC, CSL.

44. Cora Du Bois, "The 1870 Ghost Dance," *Anthropological Records* 3, no. 1 (1939): 75; information from conversation between Du Bois and informant Charlie Warthon. Warthon does not mention Lafonso's death but instead says that Lafonso ordered the people to tear down the Dance House because it had a leak.

45. Presentation by Brian Bibby and Craig Bates, "The Mikchopdo Legacy," at the Objects of Myth and Memory Symposium, Oakland Museum, Oakland, Calif., 29 February 1992.

46. John Bidwell, "Proclamation of Rules Made for Rancho Chico Indians," 21 June 1885, part 1, carton 2, BP BL, 2, 3.

47. For example, see entries for 4 January 1876 in Record of Indian School, and undated entry in April, "No school, Indians having gone to Colfax for a dance," in Record of Indian School, 1875–1880, both in box 32, ABC, CSL; also see letter from Maggie Lafonso to Annie Bidwell, 14 April 1903, folder 4, box 78, ABC, CSL.

48. See letter from Nopanny Preacher to Annie Bidwell, 12 June 1887, folder 64, box 78, ABC, CSL. By 1905, the Bidwells appear to have loosened this restriction. See letter from Maggie Lafonso to Annie Bidwell, 15 August 1905, folder 10, box 78, ABC, CSL, for reference to Indians going off the ranch to work, and interview with Thelma Wilson, NCOHP, CSU 1.

49. Letters from William Conway, Chico, Calif., to Secretary of the Interior, 27 February 1914, 23 May 1914, and 29 May 1914, file no. 23841-14, Roseburg, Ore., 310, Record Group (RG) 75, National Archives (hereafter NA). I am extremely grateful to Steven Crum for sharing this set of letters from William Conway to the secretary of the interior with me. The Department of the Interior never granted Conway's request.

50. A. Bidwell, circa 1907 speech, BP, BL, 18.

51. Ibid., 16–17. For a discussion of how métis women were motivated to marry Anglo fur trappers by a process of visions, see Jacqueline Peterson, "Women Dreaming: The Reliopsychology of Indian-White Marriage and the Rise of Métis Culture," in *Western Women*, 49–68.

52. Letters from Elmer Lafonso to Annie Bidwell, 26 August 1910, folder 41, box 77, and 21 March 1912, folder 48, box 77, ABC, CSL; "Indian Melodies to Help Music World," *San Francisco Call*, 28 May 1911, in box 31, ABC, CSL.

53. "Real Needs of our Red Brethren" reprint of article from *San Jose (Calif.) Mercury*, 24 July 1907, box 31, ABC, CSL; see letters from Maggie Lafonso, Capitola, Calif., to Annie Bidwell, 6 and 8 April 1905, folders 7 and 8, box 78, ABC, CSL.

54. Letter from Burney Wilson, Wichita, Kan., to Annie Bidwell, 9 March 1914, folder 23, box 81, and letter from Burney Wilson, Parkville, Mo., to Annie Bidwell, 12 December 1916, box 32, ABC, CSL.

55. For more on Native Americans who acted as cultural mediators, see Margaret Connell Szasz, ed., *Between Indian and White Worlds: The Cultural Broker* (Norman: University of Oklahoma Press, 1994).

56. Interview with Thelma Wilson, NCOHP, CSU, 8.

57. Bates and Bibby, "Mikchopdo Legacy."

58. A. Bidwell, circa 1907 speech, BP, BL, 9; also interview with Frieda Petersen Knotts by Phyllis Knotts, 1978, NCOHP, CSU, 14.

59. A. Bidwell, circa 1907 speech, BP, BL, 9–10.

60. Ibid., 21.

61. Ibid.

62. Ibid., 14.

63. For a fascinating discussion of other instances of "transculturation" in which white women in Navajoland acculturated in varying degrees to Navajo culture, see Helen Bannan, "Newcomers to Navajoland: Transculturation in the Memoirs of Anglo Women, 1900–1945," *New Mexico Historical Review* 59 (April 1984): 165–86.

64. Diary of Annie Bidwell, 22 December 1890, ABC, CSL.

65. Azbill, "They Call us Conkow," 16.

66. A. Bidwell, "The Mechoopdas," 208.

67. Ibid., 209.

68. Powers, "Tribes of California," 235–36.

69. At least one other Indian tribe also used Fourth of July celebrations as a cover for their girls' puberty ceremonies. In her book *Living Life's Circle: Mescalero Apache Cosmovision* (Albuquerque: University of New Mexico Press, 1991), Claire Farrer asserts that at the turn of the century, when the government allowed them only one public gathering a year, the Apaches combined parades and patriotic exercises every Fourth of July with their own girls' puberty ceremonials (133–34).

70. See Currie, "Bidwell Rancheria," for an in-depth discussion of how this occurred.

71. Interview with Thelma Wilson, NCOHP, CSU, 21–22, and interview with Frieda Petersen Knotts, 1978, NCOHP, CSU 14.

72. Bates and Bibby, "Mikchopdo Legacy,", and Potts, *Northern Maidu*, 33.

PART FOUR   Newcomers

Conquest is only a part of the history of the West. "The West," or "El Norte," or "Gum Sam" (the Golden Mountain) was a magnet that drew migrants from all over the world. Immigrants from Asia (first China, later Japan, Korea, and the Philippines) and from many European countries came to the West, joining the American Indians and people of Mexican ancestry whom the dominant Euro-Americans already considered "different." By 1890, the West had the highest proportion of foreign-born residents of any region of the United States. It is doubly ironic, therefore, that the 1890s were also the decade when Frederick Jackson Turner's frontier thesis encouraged American historians to see only the Euro-American westward-moving stream of the international migrations to the American West.

The region's historically multicultural nature has only recently been recognized by western historians. We are just beginning to explore the full implications of such diversity. One thing, however, is already clear. In the West, as elsewhere in the United States, regional economies forced newcomers into distinct occupational niches that were defined by their race or ethnicity. The distinctive western racial ethnic "mix"—in particular, the sizable presence of Mexicans, Asians, and American Indians in some parts of the region—resulted in different and generally more favorable labor options for European ethnic immigrants than existed in the East. Students of ethnicity are beginning to chart those differences for groups as diverse as the Italian immigrants to California in the 1850s and the Irish who dominated hard-rock mining in Butte in the 1880s.[1] Each western study contributes to a new appreciation of diversity in immigration history, a field that has long been dominated by eastern examples. So far, however, few western studies have paid much attention to women immigrants.[2]

Inattention to gender is especially surprising when we realize that control over immigrant women was a key aspect of official policy toward Asian immigrants. A brief survey of policies toward Chinese immigrants helps us untangle this complicated knot of economic, racial, and gender issues.

Even before the importation of thousands of Chinese contract laborers to build the Central Pacific Railroad through the Sierra Mountains in the 1860s, Euro-American racial and economic hostility toward Asians was evident. Special taxes, property restrictions, and outright violence were immediate responses to Chinese miners during the California gold rush, but the most effective method of control struck directly at the possibility of long-term settlement. The Page Act of 1875 and the 1882 Chinese Exclusion Act kept all but a few Chinese women out of the country. Annette White-Parks's article in this section explores the effects of these policies on the handful of Chinese women who managed to immigrate in spite of the restrictions. Subsequent antimiscegenation laws in several western states outlawed intermarriage between Chinese (later Japanese, Koreans, and Filipinos) and Euro-Americans. These immigration and marriage laws remained in force until after World War II, thereby preventing the vast majority of Asian immigrants from building communities with the promise of continuity through the generations. Chinese men opened laundries and restaurants to serve the domestic needs of their bachelor communities. Then Americans reviled them for the very "bachelor society" that U.S. laws had created.[3]

This gendered restriction on Asian immigration lays bare the issue at the heart of all migrations: How do people of a particular race or ethnicity sustain themselves in a new place? How do they maintain and continue their ethnic and racial identity? Phrased this way, the role of women in migration and settlement is obvious: As childbearers, they physically reproduce the next generation; they create and maintain the domestic world in which children are raised; and they share with men the task of passing on their cultural heritage to their descendants. Restrictions on the immigration of Asian women were intended to make permanent settlement and cultural continuity impossible. These efforts did not succeed: Communities were created and maintained, a process that placed special burdens on the few women and children who carried the treasured cultural legacy of largely male communities. Asian American historians of women are currently playing a leading role in explaining how this occurred.[4]

Unlike Asian immigration, there were no restrictions on Europeans until 1924. In the late nineteenth century, vigorous publicity efforts by railroad companies and mining enterprises, among others, drew Europeans from many nations to the West. We still know very little about European immigrations. For this, popular fascination with the Euro-American "westward movement" of the nineteenth century is largely to blame. Large multiethnic mining cities like Butte seemed anomalies, more like Pittsburgh than any "western" city ought to be; similarly, the preponderance of ethnic European homesteaders in North and South Dakota seemed contrary to the image of the all-American pioneer families at home in their little houses on western prairies. In fact, however, there were many distinctive ethnic communities in the West. From the German, German Russian, Norwegian, and Swedish farming communities of the Great Plains to the Italian, Greek and Slavic neighborhoods of coal-mining towns like Price, Utah, and the Finnish lumbering enclaves of the Pacific Northwest, many immigrant men and women built settlements with others from their homelands.[5]

Almost everything we presently know about European ethnic communities in the West concerns the men. This is partly because many European immigrants were employed in the great extractive industries such as mining and lumbering that had largely male workforces. Most histories of these communities concentrate on the most vivid events— namely, the great strikes and the violence that accompanied them. Labor history, like western history, is a field that until recently saw only men.[6]

The dominance of extractive industries in the West had direct consequences for European immigrant women. There were more men than women in mining and lumbering communities. The precise ratio of women to men varied considerably by ethnic group, and these differences directly affected the lives of women. In immigrant groups with highly skewed sex ratios (the number of men per one hundred women), women married at a younger age, their husbands were older, and they bore more children than women in groups where the sex ratio was lower. Although the sex ratio was usually less imbalanced in agricultural communities, the need for family labor was usually great, a factor that caused many young immigrant women to marry young and have many children.[7]

As the linked articles in this section by Dee Garceau, Jeronima Echiverria, and Laurie Mercier show, each European cultural group had its own gender system that directly affected a woman's marriage choices, her work, and her community activities. These articles help us to think about the many different ways in which gender, race, and class interact as people adjust to a new land, a new culture, a new language.

The gender imbalances among immigrants were tied to local economies. Mining and lumbering communities, dominated by their male workforces, offered limited job opportunities for women. Confined largely to domestic and service occupations, European ethnic women in some parts of the West found themselves in competition with Mexican American and American Indian women and Chinese men for laundry work and other domestic jobs.[8] Only at the very beginning of mining booms could cooks and laundresses command high prices. Thereafter, clustering and intercultural competition kept wages low. Thus it was very difficult for any woman in the West, regardless of her race or ethnicity, to aspire to the goal so avidly sought by men, economic independence. That goal remained out of reach for most women except for those who, as Evelyn Schlatter suggests, sought it on male terms.

We are left with many questions: How do the real immigrant women compare with more familiar fictional representations like Ole Rolvaag's

Beret Hansa (in Giants in the Earth*), Willa Cather's Ántonia Shimerda (of*
My Ántonia*), and Sui Sin Far's Mrs. Spring Fragrance?*[9] *How do the lives
of immigrant women to the West differ from those of immigrant woman in
the East? What do their histories tell us about the special characteristics
of the West as a region? We can't fully answer these questions yet, but they
provide substantial food for thought.*

*Migration, settlement, and development have been the great themes of
western history, but they have been thought of primarily in the narrow
Euro-American terms summed up in the phrase, the "westward
movement." We need now to look at other migrations from other places
and to remember that there can be no permanent settlement without
women. Nor can any history of settlement ignore them.*

Notes

1. According to Micaela di Leonardo's pioneering comparative study, Italians in San Francisco differed from immigrants to the East not only in their date of migration and place of origin, but also in the possibilities they found in California. Di Leonardo, *The Varieties of Ethnic Experience: Kinship, Class and Gender among California Italian-Americans* (Ithaca, N.Y.: Cornell University Press, 1984). For Butte, see David Emmons, *The Butte Irish: Class and Ethnicity in an American Mining Town* (Urbana: University of Illinois Press, 1989).

2. Exceptions to this are di Leonardo, *Varieties of Ethnic Experience*; Judy Yung, *Chinese Women of America* (Seattle: University of Washington Press, 1986); Yuji Ichioka, "*Amerika Nadeshiko*: Japanese Immigrant Women in the United States, 1900–1924," *Pacific Historical Review* 48, no. 2 (May 1980): 339–57; George Sánched, *Becoming Mexican American: Ethnicity, Culture, and Identity in Chicano Los Angeles, 1900–1945* (New York: Oxford University Press, 1993); Lucie Cheng Hirata, "Chinese Immigrant Women in Nineteenth Century California," in *Women in America, A History*, ed. Carol Ruth Berkin and Mary Beth Norton (Boston: Houghton Mifflin, 1979); and articles in this volume.

3. Sucheng Chan, *This Bittersweet Soil: The Chinese in California Agriculture 1860–1910* (Berkeley: University of California Press, 1986).

4. Valerie Matsumoto, *Farming the Home Place* (Ithaca, N.Y.: Cornell University Press, 1993); Judy Yung, *Chinese Women of America* (Seattle: University of Washington Press, 1986) and *Unbound Feet: A Social History of Chinese Women in San Francisco* (Berkeley: University of California Press, 1995). See also the articles by Sucheng Chan and Gail Nomura in this volume.

5. Frederick C. Luebke, "Ethnic Group Settlement on the Great Plains," *Western Historical Quarterly* 8, no. 4 (October 1977): 405–430; Gunther Peck, "Padrones and Protest: 'Old Radicals' and New Immigrants in Bingham, Utah, 1905–1912," *Western Historical Quarterly* 24, no. 2 (May 1993): 157–78; Janet Rasmussen, *New Land, New Lives: Scandinavian Immigrants to the Pacific Northwest* (Seattle: University of Washington Press, 1994).

6. Exceptions are Marion Goldman, *Gold Diggers and Silver Miners: Prostitution and Social Life on the Comstock Lode* (Ann Arbor: University of Michigan Press, 1979); Ava Baron, ed *Work Engendered: Toward a New History of American Labor* (Ithaca, N.Y.: Cornell University Press, 1991); Priscilla Long, "The Women of the Colorado Fuel and Iron Strike, 1913–14" in *Women, Work and Protest: A Century of U.S. Women's Labor History* ed. Ruth Milkman, (New York: Routledge and Kegan Paul, 1985); Dana Frank, *Purchasing Power, Consumer Organizing, Gender, and the Seattle Labor Movement, 1919–1929* (New York: Cambridge University Press, 1994); Colleen O'Neil, "Domesticity Deployed: Gender, Race, and the Construction of Class Struggle in the Bisbee Deportations," *Labor History* 34, nos. 2, 3 (Spring/Summer 1993): 256–73; Mary Murphy, "A Place of Greater Opportunity: Irish Women's Search for Home, Family

and Leisure in Butte, Montana," *Journal of the West* 31 (April 1992): 73–78; Mary Murphy, *Mining Cultures: Gender, Work, and Leisure in Butte, 1914–1941* (Urbana: University of Illinois Press, forthcoming); Elizabeth Jameson, "Imperfect Unions: Class and Gender in Cripple Creek 1894–1904," *Frontiers* 1 no. 2 (1976): 89–117; Elizabeth Jameson, *All That Glitters: Class, Culture and Community in Cripple Creek* (Urbana: University of Illinois Press, forthcoming); and the article by Laurie Mercier in this section.

7. In 1930 Kansas, at 101, had the lowest sex ratio of any state west of the Mississippi. Other ratios included Texas 104, Utah 105, Oregon 110, Montana 120, Nevada 139. A balanced sex ratio throughout the West did not occur until midcentury. Calculated from *Bicentennial Edition of the Historical Statistics of the United States, Colonial Times to 1970* (Washington, D.C.: U.S. Department of Commerce, 1970) Series A, 195–209. We are indebted to Heather Kellogg for calculating the statistics.

8. Ronald M. James, Richard D. Adkins, and Rachel J. Hartigan, "Competition and Coexistence in the Laundry: A View of the Comstock," *Western Historical Quarterly* 25, no. 2 (Summer 1994): 164–84.

9. O. E. Rolvaag, *Giants in the Earth* (New York: Harper and Brothers, 1927); Willa Cather, *My Ántonia* (Boston: Houghton Mifflin, 1949); Sui Sin Far, *Mrs. Spring Fragrance and Other Stories*, ed. Amy Ling and Annette White-Parks (Urbana: University of Illinois Press, 1995).

12

Beyond the Stereotypes: Chinese Pioneer Women in the American West

ANNETTE WHITE-PARKS

We have long stereotyped nineteenth-century Chinese immigrant women as prostitutes, and as with all stereotypes, the characterization contains some truth. In the first pathbreaking article on Chinese immigrant women, Lucie Cheng estimated that the proportion of prostitutes among the Chinese female population in San Francisco was 85 percent in 1860 and 71 percent in 1870.[1] These lurid numbers fueled anti-Chinese agitation in California, resulting in enactment of the Page Act of 1875 and the Chinese Exclusion Act of 1882, which excluded most women by portraying them all as prostitutes.

In this article, Annette White-Parks attempts to move beyond stereotypes to a broader understanding of the full range of Chinese women's experience. As she acknowledges, the historical sources are scanty, partly because so few Chinese women came to America and so few of them left records, but also because Chinese immigrant communities did everything they could to hide their personal lives from the scrutiny of hostile Euro-American "barbarians." The Chinese immigrant women White-Parks describes, like the American Indian women of the previous section, fought hard to protect their lives and their culture from reforming Euro-American women.

White-Parks enriches her essay by using the stories of a remarkable Anglo-Chinese woman, Sui Sin Far (Edith Eaton), who made it her literary goal to paint sympathetic pictures of Chinese immigrant women. To sell her articles, Sui Sin Far sugar-coated often bitter stories with a sentimentality and exoticism that seems silly and artificial to us today. But White-Parks shows us that if we take the time to "read through" Sui Sin Far's use of the conventions of nineteenth-century female writing style, we will glimpse an emotional reality that is not accessible through other sources.

When Jone Ho Leong's uncle returned to China in 1940 and complained about how hard he had been made to work in the United States, his niece replied, "OK—you can come back here to stay and send us—the women—over there. We'll see how we can make out in the Golden Mountain."[2] Though her words were spoken almost a century after the California gold rush prompted the first Chinese migrations to North America, Jone Ho Leong spoke for various women who, over the century, were part of those journeys. Though the faces of Chinese pioneer women have been even less visible than those of most women in the American West, they are essential to any accurate picture—not in the passive, simplistic stereotypes of prostitutes and imported wives that texts have customarily shown, but in the details of their individual vitality.

The independent woman who "makes out," as it were, has only recently begun to emerge; she belies traditional stereotypes and forces us to look at Chinese immigrant women, Chinese American culture, and western history from a new angle. It is not the hardships and horrors that Chinese pioneer women have had to endure, then, that tell the final tale, nor how many numbers women totaled in relation to men. It is rather the deeds that individual women performed and the courageous independence with which they responded to circumstances. It is the fight they waged for the survival of themselves, their families, and valued cultural traditions. Here I will look at selected examples of women from China who pioneered the American West, as they are reflected in both history and literature. I will discuss some of the reasons these women left China, what they found when they arrived in the United States, and the ingenious strategies they devised for surviving under often desperate conditions.

Chinese tradition may have dictated that no "decent" woman could travel,[3] yet Judy Yung clearly shows Chinese women immigrating to the western frontier as early as Chinese men. The first recorded of these women, Marie Seise, stepped off a ship named *The Eagle* in San Francisco in 1848 as the servant of a family of traders, the Gillespies of New York. Lest her journey sound trivial, it is worth emphasizing the route Marie traversed before meeting the Gillespies: She ran away from her parents in China to avoid being sold, worked as a servant in Macao, married a Portuguese sailor, and moved as a servant with another family to the Sandwich Islands after the sailor deserted her. Marie Seise was obviously determined, at whatever expense, to chart her own course.[4]

Nor was Seise alone. Another "China Mary"—a generic name, Yung explains, ascribed to many Chinese immigrant women by their new frontier neighbors—ran away from her home in China when she was nine, had made her way to Canada by age thirteen, outlived two husbands, and then moved to Sitka, Alaska, where she survived as a fisherwoman, hunter and prospector, restaurant keeper, nurse, laundress, and official matron of the Sitka federal jail. Yet another, Ah Yuen, similarly outlived three husbands and was said to have been "the toast of her countrymen" in the Wyoming mining and railroad camps where she cooked during Pony Express days. Another notable woman was Mary Tape, who sailed from Shanghai with missionaries at age eleven, then married and lived in California. Mary Tape worked as an interpreter and contractor of labor, taught herself photography and telegraphy, and, when they tried to bar her daughter from public schools, won a case against the San Francisco Board of Education in court.[5]

To appreciate the odds these women faced—independent in the ways they responded to life's experience, despite rules that societies on either side of the Pacific had charted for them—we need to look at the positions traditionally assigned to women in both China and the United States in the mid-nineteenth century. Amy Ling notes that Confucius classified women "with slaves and small humans" and further cites that "a code governing the behavior and training of women, called the Three Obediences and Four Virtues, was promulgated by imperial decree throughout China and remained continuously effective . . . until the early twentieth century."[6] Basically, this code decreed that a woman must "obey her father before marriage, her husband after marriage, and her oldest son after her husband's death"—all roles of subordination sanctioned by conventions so ancient that to defy them was to challenge the sacred. When the injunction is added that no "decent" woman of the Chinese upper or middle class could travel even to a shop in the village without escort and covered face, it becomes obvious that a decision to cross the Pacific would have taken some courage. Once she arrived, the laws of U.S. Chinatowns applied these same restrictions for women of the upper and middle classes. Yet the protection she gained in return for her obedience was often analogous to the "protection" Sojourner Truth expressed for nineteenth-century African American women—none at all. In the words of the narrator in Maxine Hong Kingston's *Woman Warrior*, "girls are maggots in the rice"—if the need arose, they could be sold. Such a transaction forced many Chinese females into journeys of which the old doctrine took no account.[7]

Added to her continued subordination by gender in the American West, the Chinese immigrant woman also faced, on that U.S. side of the waters, hostile immigration laws and dehumanizing stereotypes imposed by the westerners on all Chinese. The writer Sui Sin Far refers to this when she describes being told by an editor, "I cannot reconcile myself to the fact that the Chinese are humans like ourselves; their faces seem so utterly void of expression that I cannot help but doubt."[8] The dehumanization assumed in the editor's remark becomes a mockery when viewed alongside the courageous ingenuity of women such as Marie Seise who were determined to have a voice in their own journeys, whatever the odds. The gap between the editor's stereotype and the complex human details of Chinese pioneer women's everyday lives proves the editor's ignorance.

Equally removed from reality was the stereotype Sui Sin Far confronted when she was advised that "to succeed in literature in America I should dress in Chinese costume, carry a fan in my hand, wear a pair of scarlet beaded slippers, live in New York, and come of high birth."[9] The posed China doll Sui Sin Far was invited to emulate reflected a popular conception of both the Chinese noblewoman and the successful courtesan and harkened back to the days when Chinese women were brought by entrepreneurs and exhibitors to the United States. Like a doll, a woman named Pwan Yekoo was displayed at Barnum's Chinese Museum in 1850, eating with chopsticks, playing Chinese musical instruments, and twinkling her tiny "fairy feet (only two and a half inches long)."[10] But as historian Lucie Cheng Hirata shows, in reality most Chinese immigrant women in the nineteenth century were working-class wage earners and wives. Besides cooking and cleaning and making clothing and shoes for her own family, the immigrant woman—in common with most other pioneer females of America's West—usually worked also at sewing, cooking, and cleaning for others, along with doing laundry and gardening.[11] Quock Jung Mey's mother sailed to Monterey, California, where she gave birth to her daughter in 1859 and worked throughout her life at baiting fishing hooks, processing each day's catch, and gathering seaweed.[12]

The doll-like stereotype, then, ignored the complex dynamics of the Chinese immigrant woman's identity—which included not only race and gender, but also class. Further, like most stereotypes, the "doll" served its purpose—to establish distance between white Americans and their new countrywomen and thus to substitute a fantasy of the "exotic Oriental" for knowledge based on contact with flesh-and-blood Chinese Americans on a personal basis. Ultimately, the racist assumptions about the Chinese as "other" that underlie this stereotype would lead to contentions that the Chinese were unassimilable aliens and help to justify discriminatory legislation.

If the fantasy in fan and beaded slippers had any relevance to actual Chinese immigrant women, it was to the wives of Chinatown merchants who, Hirata points out, customarily enjoyed more luxurious accommodations (if often less freedom) than their working-class sisters.[13] Not unlike other Victorian middle-class women, the well-to-do Chinese merchant's wife often lived in a comfortably furnished apartment, occupied her days with bits of cooking and needlework, and broke the routine with afternoon teas and chats with her friends when, as Sui Sin Far put it in an 1897 article, "there is such a clattering of tongues one would almost think they were American women."[14]

Such lifestyles were rare, however, applying in the late nineteenth century to no more than 1 percent of Chinese American women.[15] In the first years of the gold rush many immigrant Chinese women were brought to North America to serve as slaves and prostitutes for men of every racial descent, on a western frontier where few women of any race existed and where sexual pressure was increased on Chinese male immigrants by miscegenation laws that forbade them to marry or mix sexually with white women. In 1882 the United States government enacted the Chinese Exclusion Act, which stopped all Chinese women, except the wives (or wives-to-be) of Chinese American merchants, from being admitted as legal migrants. The value of the wife of a merchant thus stood very high, by a measure that parallels in some ways, yet differs profoundly from, the value of women prostitutes during the earlier years.[16] Merchants' wives were brought to North America from China to begin raising families, implicitly making possible the establishment of permanent communities in the new world—a threat to the European-based cultures of Canada and the United States that later exclusionary legislation in both countries would attempt to eliminate.[17]

One similarity between prostitutes and merchants' wives as travelers to Golden Mountain, however, is that the decision to migrate was seldom made by the woman herself. The Chinatown wife, too, was often shipped across the Pacific in response to the needs of a male. Moreover, as depicted in the fiction of Sui Sin Far, these wives had their own difficulties.[18] In Sui Sin Far's story "The Americanization of Pau Tsu" (1912), for example, the Chinese woman Pau Tsu is betrothed to Lin Fo before he leaves China, then waits at the home of the parents of her intended to be sent to him "in a few years' time." When Pau Tsu arrives in San Francisco and Lin Fo takes his bride to the Chinatown apartment that he has "furnished in American style," Pau Tsu declares her own preference by bringing out the furnishings she has carried over the Pacific and transforming "the American flat into an Oriental bower." Thus begins a conflict that rages throughout the story, as Lin Fo tells Pau Tsu to eat with a fork and she mourns for her chopsticks, as he buys her elegant Western-style dresses that she refuses to wear. The climax is reached when Pau Tsu gets sick and her husband sends for a male Anglo-American doctor, before whom Pau Tsu's breast is exposed and "the modesty of generations of maternal ancestors was crucified." Determined to maintain her cultural identity, Pau Tsu flees from Lin Fo, moving with her maid, A-Toy, into the home of "a woman learned in herb lore."[19]

The shock of transition between cultures is a constant issue in Sui Sin Far's stories of Chinese immigrant brides. From the moment that Pau Lin, heroine of "The Wisdom of the New" (1912), arrives on a steamer at the San Francisco docks and meets Wou Sankwei, the husband she had wed in China seven years earlier, the distance between the Americanized husband and the wife who stayed behind to care for his aging parents and raise their child yawns wider than geography. Not only does Sankwei have to ask the ship's officer to point out his wife and son before he can recognize her "as his," but he also arrives with two white women, for whom Pau Lin feels "a suspicion natural to one who had come from a land where friendship between a man and woman is almost unknown." These women are customers and informal patrons of Sankwei, who has become a successful Chinatown bookkeeper, but as one of the women sketches the couple's six-year-old son Yen—though Pau Lin decorously "keeps a quiet tongue in the presence of her man"—her resentment simmers inwardly like a bed of banked coals. As her husband increasingly takes their son out, leaving Pau Lin to her housekeeping, the bewildered and lonely new immigrant spends "most of her time in the society of one or the other of the neighboring merchants' wives."[20]

One source of courage for women who travel, especially under pioneering conditions, has always been other women; in this, the Chinese immigrant woman of any class was no exception. On the night that little Yen comes home speaking English, Pau Lin burns the boy's hand in reprisal and, after Sankwei retaliates by taking little Yen out to supper and a show, Pau Lin's frustration is eased by the circle of women that Sui Sin Far gathers around her. "You did perfectly right. . . . Had I again a son to rear, I should see to it that he followed not after the white people," old Sien Lau leans over her balcony to say to Pau Lin. "One needs not be born here to be made a fool of," Pau Tsu adds in the voice of experience. "In this country, she is most happy who has no child," Lae Choo interjects, resting her elbow upon the shoulder of Sien Lau.

Other heroines in Sui Sin Far stories demonstrate that the external reticence of these merchants' wives, whose journeys were undertaken at the decree of their husbands, should never be mistaken for passivity. Beneath their acquiescence to duty a cautiously held rebellion trembles and finds its own outlets, rising to its most intense when their children and the Chinese cultural traditions they value are threatened. In "The Wisdom of the New," the story's climax is foreshadowed on the night Sankwei tells Pau Lin that in the morning Yen will begin attending an American school. At early dawn the father hears a strange noise, goes into Yen's room and finds him dead, poisoned by his mother. If it seems a monstrous act, we must pause and consider Pau Lin's expressed motive: "'He is saved,' smiled she, 'from the Wisdom of the New.'" We have seen the mother's love and despair the night she lifts the sleeping Yen from his bed and rocks him, "crooning and crying." In the aftermath of a second baby's death, she had once held her first son and vowed: "Sooner would I, O heart of my heart, that the light of thine eyes were also quenched, than that thou shouldst be contaminated with the wisdom of the new." And on the eve of Yen's death, she tells the boy that his feet are to his "spirit as the cocoon to the butterfly." Like the black mother in Tony Morrison's *Beloved* who kills her infant daughter to save her from slavery, Pau Lin sacrifices her child's body to save his soul—in her definition, the Chinese heritage that her husband's enthusiasm for Western culture threatens to eradicate.

Rarely is a married woman depicted by Sui Sin Far who is not cradling a baby or child, as she exercises passionate vigilance against forces ever poised to take that treasure from her. The importance of children, suggests Gail Nomura, is that in a situation where all other family have been left behind, a baby is a treasure, a start of the new.[21] Inversely, through the generational lifelines they offer, children are also a link with the past and home culture. In fact, one major reason a man traditionally married before leaving China was in the hope that his wife would bear him a son and thus assure his enduring position in the land he was leaving. Either way the child represents more than itself; it brings cultural continuity.

Sui Sin Far's story "In the Land of the Free" shows the damage that child theft can inflict: not just loss of the child, but, more far-reaching, loss of the child's culture. This story opens with Lae Choo completing her voyage from China back to San Francisco, where her home had already been established with her husband, Hom Hing, before she sailed back to China to give birth and take care of Hom Hing's aging parents. The ship pulls into the dock where her husband is waiting, and Lae Choo presents their son to him. Hom Hing lifts the child up joyously. At this moment a customs officer steps in between, asking for the child's papers. When papers cannot be produced, The Little One is physically confiscated. The couple spend ten months of their life, all of Hom Hing's money, and Lae Choo's family jewels getting him back. Furthermore, when Lae Choo finally walks into the mission nursery to reclaim her baby she finds not The Little One she remembers, but a boy dressed "in blue cotton overalls and white soled shoes," who—when his mother reaches for him—hides "in the folds of the white woman's skirt."[22]

A close look at the story's details shows that Lae Choo had sensed this danger from the beginning and had done everything in her power to prevent it from happening. When the officer first reached out for her child on the docks, Hom Hing was holding him. "No, you not take him; he my son, too," Lae Choo had cried in defiance, grabbing her child back. It is Hom Hing who was persuaded that "Tis the law" and who had convinced his wife to hand him the baby whom he, in turn, "delivered . . . to the first officer." Why did Lae Choo "yield" the boy? Because, the story's narrator reveals, she was "accustomed to obedience." That she was not docile, however, Lae Choo had proved by defying the officer. "You, too," she said to her husband accusingly, as the couple walked to their apartment above Hom Hing's Chinatown grocery.

In Sui Sin Far's stories, the environments in which women travel are dangerous, fraught with restrictive conventions from one culture and hostile laws in the other. Taking a decisive course of action is often not easy for these women, but take action they do, even in the direst of circumstances. Fin Fan, of "The Prize China Baby," experiences the dual position of being both a slave and the wife of the Chinatown merchant, Chung Kee, to whom she is sold. She has a daughter who is her "one gleam of sunshine." Mindful of the fact that Chung Kee does not want the baby because it takes too much of her time from winding tobacco leaves in his factory, Fin Fan gets up very early and goes to bed very late, trying to make as much money as she did before having the baby so Chung Kee will not get rid of it. Hearing one day of a "Chinese baby show" being staged by the Presbyterians, Fin Fan rolls her baby into her shawl and slips out, hoping that if the child wins a prize, its father will value it. While they are away, the father makes arrangements to sell the baby—it may be significant that she is a girl. In one of Sui Sin Far's multilayered ironies, Fin Fan thwarts his plans when she and her daughter are run down by a butcher's cart on the way home and "her head fell back beside the prize baby's—hers forever." Fin Fan does keep her baby, though not in the way she or Sui Sin Far's reading audience might have desired.[23]

Death obviously is not defeat in Pau Lin's or Fin Fan's stories, but a stand that, in the minds of the individuals taking it, seems less horrific than the alternative when pressed to the wall. Sometimes rewards come in the future, bringing resolution from pain. Within context, Pau Lin's act is successful, for, with the death of his son, Sankwei finally comprehends his wife's desperation and returns with her to China, symbolically healing the split in their family and restoring cultural wholeness. In a similar spirit does Lin Fo of "The Americanization of Pau Tsu" locate his wife Pau Tsu, vowing, "I will not care if she never speaks an American word, and I will take her for a trip to China, so that our son may be born in the country that Heaven loves." Both women thus successfully resist the journey into assimilation by white North America, choosing instead to turn back to their cultural roots.

The experience of the enslaved prostitute was the most difficult for the Chinese woman pioneer to overcome, partly because the patriarchal traditions of both Christianity and Confucianism blamed a woman for her own victimization and judged her responsible for a situation over which she often had no control. According to Christianity, if a woman was sexually violated by men, it was because she had been born a temptress and thus somehow "asked for" whatever befell her. By Confucian doctrine, she was the least-valued member in the familial-societal chain and thus subject to use by the rest in times of need. Two incompatible images coalesce in the stereotype of the prostitute: In the one, she wears the scarlet beaded slippers and carries the fan we have seen in the image pressed upon Sui Sin Far; in the other, she is pressed against the bars of a small cage, or "crib," face emptied of hope.[24] The reality of her story is often that she was torn from home soil and enslaved, to lead a fragmentary and short-lived existence helping her captors get rich.

An alternative perspective is suggested by Lucie Cheng Hirata, who regards the first five years of the California gold rush, 1849 to 1854, as a period of "free competition" during which a few Chinese women, in common with prostitutes from other countries, saw the Golden Mountain as opportunity and migrated under individual initiative.[25] The legendary Ah-Choi, also known as A-Toy, came to San Francisco and rose to be belle of the city; she earned enough in two years to open her own brothel, which attracted lines of men a block long who, it was claimed, would pay a full ounce of gold simply to look on her face.[26] Another woman, Lai Chow, started her career as one among two dozen twelve-year-olds, all shipped from China in crates labeled "dishware"; Lai Chow grew up to smuggle in her own "girls."[27]

Hirata cites a best-selling novel in China that interpreted the capitalistic aims of such travelers through the character of a Cantonese prostitute who, after seven years in California where she had gone with her "American paramour," returned to Hong Kong with $16,300, "married a Chinese laborer," and opened an import store.[28] Similarly, in her short story "Lin John," Sui Sin Far portrays a Chinese prostitute who is happy with her lot and resists her brother's efforts to "rescue" her because she prefers the material rewards of her work to his goals of returning her to China for "respectability in marriage."[29]

However, it is important to note that the women discussed above—who worked independently and made money for themselves—were exceptions. Further, the era of free competition was short-lived. By the mid-1850s, entrepreneurs in both China and the United States had caught the rich scent of money and taken over the reins, giving rise to a trade in enslaved Chinese women across the Pacific.[30]

Writer John Gardner once suggested that there are only two plots in literature: A person takes a journey or a stranger comes to town.[31] For the Chinese woman who came up against the horrors of slavery, these two plots were allied—in her case, it was the "stranger" who brought the journey about. In the negotiations that prepared for her trip, a young Chinese female could move from "decent" woman to prostitute in the time it took a procurer to strike a bargain, usually with the girl's parents.[32]

A number of stories are told about such metamorphoses. Sometimes the capture came via coercion, as in the case of Lalu Nathoy who had been her father's "treasure"—his "thousand pieces of gold"—until the moment a bandit threatened the father, threw two bags of soybean seed at his feet as payment, and rode off with the captive Lalu.[33] Sometimes it was managed with sweet talk, as when the mother of Wong Ah So was promised that the $450 she was paid for her daughter would continue to draw dividends through the months ahead, from the earnings Wong Ah So would be sending back "as an entertainer at Chinese banquets."[34] Such ruses became even more devious when the bargainer was a returned immigrant from the family's own village, someone whom they knew well and trusted. Victorian melodrama has nothing on the pathos of some of these actual cases. There was Ah Yee, "a refined, sensitive little creature" of dead father and poor mother, whom the "dashing young adventurer" Jeah Sing Fong married, telling her that her troubles were over. He escorted his new bride to the Golden Gate Hotel on a honeymoon, then turned her over to King Fah, the female brothel keeper who paid the nuptial pair a welcome-home visit and procured Ah Yee as a prostitute.[35]

These stories make it clear that the stereotype categorizing all enslaved females as coming from the lowest socioeconomic classes in China was simply not true. Jean Ying, for example, was the kidnapped "daughter of a well-to-do Canton manufacturer."[36] Nor is it accurate to generalize them as "women"; recalling Lai Chow, who at age twelve was packed in a dish crate along with other stolen girls, we recognize that many were barely adolescents. An even more extreme case is the baby girl brought to the United States by a "grandmother" who had purchased the baby for ten dollars in China and planned to raise her as an investment in future merchandise—for merchandise, in actuality, is what the enslaved female became during the course of her journey.[37]

A method that superficially sounds more legitimate was the "contract," similar to indentured servitude except that the women whose lives were quite literally being laid on the line could neither read nor write. They "signed" not with a name but with a thumbprint affixed at the bottom of the document after the deal had been settled.[38] Simple purchase was frequent. Hirata tells of an old woman servant in California who had been resold four times, the first at age seven when her way of fighting against banishment from home and family was to cry and hide under the bed.[39] If all else failed, there was kidnapping, as in the case of the woman who was invited by a man to tour a steamer anchored at the dock in Shanghai, then found herself sailing across the Pacific in the bottom of the coal bucket he had pushed her into.[40]

The usual attitude in the United States was to fault the Chinese exclusively for this trade in female slavery. But one would have to seek far to find a more mutually cooperative Chinese-American venture in the nineteenth century than the enslavement of these Chinese women. Historian Dorothy Gray describes the dual responsibility: "The system had its roots in the culture of the homeland China where prostitution and slavery were open practices. But in America the slave system of prostitution contravened the most essential aspect of law and was possible only through the continued connivance of American officials who amassed fortunes in graft."[41] This point again illustrates how the immigrating woman was often caught between the repressive aspects of her traditional culture and the unbridled exploitation of the new capitalism.

A normal passage from China to North America's West Coast took one to two months,[42] but the clandestine traveler might find herself diverted through Mexico or Canada. Lai Chow, of Nell Kimball's autobiography, tells of bringing her cargo in through Canadian ports, then on to San Francisco by coach. Sometimes the entry was managed in the same manner used by George Sand to gain access to Parisian streets late at night—through disguise as a man. Sui Sin Far's "Smuggling of Wah To," though not a slave incident, narrates the attempted migration of a young Chinese "male" who jumps into the river to avoid police while crossing the Canadian border. The body, when retrieved, turns out to be female.[43]

On the American side of the border the enslaved woman's immediate destination was customarily San Francisco, where she was held in a kind of underground warehouse termed a "barracoon."[44] There—unless a purchase had been made in advance—she was put up for bid. Her purchaser might be, as in the case of the fictional Fin Fan in Sui Sin Far's "The Prize China Baby," a Chinatown merchant seeking a slave wife. It might be the owner of a local brothel (distinguished by Yung as either "high class" or "inferior den"). It might be, as in the case of Lalu Nathoy (who became Polly Bemis), a saloonkeeper from an Idaho mining camp, a transaction causing her journey to swerve from urban to rural. Although Lalu/Polly personally led a long life, Yung notes that "prostitutes could meet with no worse fate than to be banished to the mining camps, where they led lives as harsh as they were short."[45]

Altogether, evidence indicates that the enslavement of Chinese immigrant women was the most widely known secret in the American West in the mid-nineteenth century. In the same era that Lincoln was signing the Emancipation Proclamation to free black slaves in the Confederacy, Gray estimates that several thousand Chinese females a year were being smuggled through San Francisco's immigrant station to be sold into slavery. Public knowledge of the slave trade was such that, in 1869, the *San Francisco Chronicle* could report the arrival of a ship from China in this manner: "The particular fine portions of the cargo, the fresh and pretty females who come from the interior, are used to fill special orders from wealthy merchants and prosperous tradesmen. A very considerable portion are sent into the interior . . . in answer to demands from well-to-do miners and successful vegetable producers."[46] Well into the twentieth century, newspapers sported headlines such as "Woman Tells of Traffic in Slave Girls," and novels with titles like *Chop Suey Lady* enjoyed popular sales.[47] Epithets of "frail, childlike creatures" with "exotic dress and features" reduced human individuals to romantic figments who could be slipped not only past customs officials but also past the ideals of democracy professed by the United States.[48]

Responses of these Chinese females to their predicaments were as varied as their constrained circumstances permitted. When learning that her role as a San Francisco "entertainer" was a euphemism for prostitution, Wong Ah So turned inward, resigning herself to accept her condition with dutiful recitations of "stories of Chinese children renowned for their piety" and promising her mother to "return to China and become a Buddhist nun" when she had earned enough money.[49] One Idaho China Annie (a generic name like China Mary) chose a more aggressive method—running off with her lover to Boise, where they were married and won out over Annie's former owner in court after he sued her for "stealing herself."[50] Others who broke for freedom took a real risk by going to law enforcement officials, for—from the "Chinatown Specials" to San Francisco's City Hall, according to Richard Dillon—many were on the tong's payroll.[51]

Protestant mission houses, opening on the edges of Chinatowns during the Progressive Era, offered another option for women to escape prostitution. Launching what was as close to an antislavery reform movement as the West would experience, the Christian missions had a historical connection with China. Frank Chin refers to the "almost fifty years of travel books on China written by Chinese missionaries and 'world travelers' who cited missionaries as authorities on China."[52] Missionaries coming from China frequently brought converts back, and those in American Chinatowns, as noted by Yung, "proved to be a vital link" in joining homebound immigrant wives, such as the fictional Pau Lin and Pau Tsu, to a world outside their small flats.[53]

Margaret Culberston, director of the Presbyterian Chinese Mission later to achieve fame as San Francisco's Cameron House, issued a challenge in regard to prostituted immigrant women: "Cannot anyone suggest a plan to remedy this evil?"[54] Writers of purple prose, both in fiction and daily newspapers, were fond of scenes in which runaway women slaves fell at the feet of white policemen, begging for help. The lawmen, if they did not hand the women back to the "highbinders" (the term for men sent to retrieve runaway prostitutes), usually passed them along to the Presbyterian mission. This was especially true after the arrival of Donaldina Cameron, who set about to free enslaved Chinatown women with a fervor causing Dorothy Gray to term her "the most active and daring freedom fighter in the history of the West."[55] Known by the tongs as "the White

Devil," Cameron staged constant raids, using methods that created episodes in the journeys of Chinese immigrant women that resemble the pages of Gothic fiction: "If a word that the White Devil was coming preceded the raid, the slaver would try to smuggle the girl away through the dark, narrow alleys of Chinatown. Sometimes girls were hurried away over the rooftops. But Donaldina was quick in pursuit and in time developed an instinct for where the quarry might emerge and stationed a policeman or assistants from the refuge to watch the possible exit."[56]

Though Cameron is generally credited with being a redeemer, the women she "rescued" did not necessarily see her this way. Wong Ah So, for example, had been told by her owner that Cameron "was in the habit of draining blood from the arteries of newly 'captured' girls and drinking it to keep up her own vitality." Yet because she was "tired" and "sick," the young woman broke through her fears and went to the mission where she subsequently "reformed" and married with the missionaries' blessing. Thus she followed the pattern Peggy Pascoe describes of exchanging "prostitution for marriage," a choice that often replaced one form of servitude for another.[57]

The price of such "rescue work" is frequently dramatized by Sui Sin Far through mission woman characters who continually attempt to lure Chinese children away from their home culture, a fiction grounded in historical records through which Pascoe shows how Christian missionaries brought female children they termed "neglected or abused" into their homes, raising them and gaining control over the next generation by arranging their marriages to Chinese immigrant men who were converted Christians. A twist on this motif appears in the short story "Pat and Pan," in which the mission woman Anna Harrison arranges for a little white boy to be taken away from the Chinese American family with whom the boy's dying mother has left him to be raised and places him with a white American family.[58]

It is interesting to contrast the fate of the city voyager Wong Ah So with that of the rural Lalu Nathoy. Taken from her father in exchange for two bags of soybean seed and bought in San Francisco by an Idaho saloon-keeper, Lalu was later won in a poker game by Charlie Bemis, who gave her freedom. She went on to marry Charlie, eventually to bury him, and finally to inherit the mining claim they had worked together. Thus Lalu Nathoy became Polly Bemis, probably the first Chinese immigrant woman actually to achieve a stake in the Golden Mountain. Should her journey be viewed within the pattern of slave prostitution? of marriage? of legendary Wild West success?

As Lalu Nathoy's life story shows, the experiences of Chinese pioneer women are too complex for rigid prescription. Among the many such women who defied stereotypes, we would have to go far to find one more determined to write her own journey than Sui Sin Far herself, whose mother made her way to North America via missionary training in England and marriage to an English trader in Shanghai. Not only did Sui Sin Far fight for personal survival against racism and invalidism and

The mother of Sui Sin Far was known both as Lotus Blossom and as Grace A. Eaton. Neither of these names is authentic in terms of the woman's personal identity. Her birth name is unknown and virtually impossible to recover. The Victorian dress gives evidence of a vain attempt to disguise Chineseness and assimilate into the Euro-American culture. (Courtesy L. Charles Laferriere, Montreal.)

sexism and poverty, growing up in England and New York and Montreal as one of fourteen siblings. She also battled for her parents and brothers and sisters against the severe prejudices they encountered wherever they roamed.

As an adult, Sui Sin Far continued the struggle: from Montreal to the West Indies, from Seattle to Boston, up and down the U.S. West Coast, working as a stenographer and reporter, writing copy for the railroads to pay for her travels, living wherever she could earn her way to continue writing the stories about Chinese pioneers in North America she had committed her brief lifetime to telling. Arriving in San Francisco "so reduced by another attack of rheumatic fever" that she weighed only eighty-four pounds, Sui Sin Far typed correspondence for a railway agency at five dollars a month, yet remained "hopeful that the sale of a story or newspaper article [might] add" to her income.[59] Viewed with caution by her mother's people because she looked European and could not speak the "mother tongue," scorned by her father's when they learned she was one of "the 'brown people' of the earth," she continued to defend her right simply to *be* in either arena. And somehow she survived, and somehow she kept writing, enriching those of us who want to learn about Chinese immigrant women nearly a century later with accounts of journeys we might otherwise never experience.

This brief survey of the journeys made to the Golden Mountain by women from China belies previous stereotypes of Chinese women as passive, silent, and submissive. In the words of Benson Tong about prostituted women, they "not only survived subjugation but also, in many cases, summoned the strength to change their fate."[60] Moreover, the dynamics of Chinese pioneer women's participation in the American westering experience shifts the shape of the whole. I do not claim that Chinese immigrant women did not suffer oppression or that they were always able to overcome it. It is obvious, first, that they came up against as many difficulties as did other pioneer women and, second, that these difficulties were multiplied because they were of Chinese descent in a racist society during an era of exreme xenophobia. Nevertheless, the above examples clearly demonstrate the courage and independence of Chinese pioneer women and the vital roles they played in the creation of an emerging Chinese American culture. Thus we must view Jone Ho Leong's offer to "see how we [women] make out in the Golden Mountain" in 1940, not as a first or rare undertaking, but in the context of the century of Chinese immigrant women who had "made out" before.[61]

Notes

An earlier version of this essay first appeared in *Women and The Journey: The Female Travel Experience*, edited by Bonnie Frederick and Susan H. McLeod (Pullman: Washington State University Press, 1993).

I would like to thank the members of the Women in Literature Research Collective at Washington State University who have provided hours of support and editing help on this manuscript.

1. Lucie Cheng Hirata, "Free, Indentured, Enslaved: Chinese Prostitutes in Nineteenth-Century America," *Signs* 5, no. 1 (Autumn 1979): 3–29.

2. Jone Ho Leong, *Bitter Melon: Stories from the Last Rural Chinese Town in America*, ed. Jeff Gillenkirk and James Motlow (Seattle: University of Washington Press, 1987), 101.

3. Hirata, "Free, Indentured, Enslaved."

4. Judy Yung, *Chinese Women of America* (Seattle: University of Washington Press, 1986), 14.

5. Ibid., 25, 30.

6. Amy Ling, *Between Worlds: Women Writers of Chinese Ancestry* (New York: Pergamon Press, 1990), 3. Ling further writes that "The authorship of this oppressive code has been attributed to Ban Tso (A.D. 43?–A.D. 115?), a highly educated woman".

7. Maxine Hong Kingston, *The Woman Warrior: Memoirs of a Girlhood among Ghosts* (New York: Alfred A. Knopf, 1977), and Amy Ling, *Between Worlds*, both explore the low status assigned to daughters relative to sons in traditional China.

8. Sui Sin Far, "Leaves from the Mental Portfolio of an Eurasian," *Independent* 66, no. 3138 (21 January 1909): 129.

9. Sui Sin Far, "Leaves," 131.

10. Yung, *Chinese Women*, 4.

11. Lucie Cheng Hirata, "Chinese Immigrant Women in Nineteenth-Century California," *Women of America: A History*, ed. Carol Ruth Berkin and Mary Beth Norton (Boston: Houghton Mifflin, 1979), 222–44.

12. Yung, *Chinese Women*, 15.

13. Hirata, "Chinese Immigrant Women," 238.

14. Sui Sin Far, "Chinese Women in America," *The Land of Sunshine* 6, no. 2 (January 1897): 62.

15. Hirata, "Chinese Immigrant Women," 224–27.

16. In "Free, Indentured, Enslaved," Hirata thoroughly examines this subject.

17. The first major anti-Chinese legislation in the United States was the Exclusion Act of 1882, which excluded all Chinese women, except wives of merchants, from legally entering the country. Discriminatory legislation in Canada took the form of singling out Chinese immigrants to pay "head taxes"; these began in 1896 at ten dollars and were increased regularly until by 1904 they had reached their peak of five hundred dollars.

18. For a study of the relationship between Sui Sin Far's fictional characterizations and Chinese immigrant women's lives, see my book, *Sui Sin Far/Edith Maude Eaton: A Literary Biography* (Champaign: University of Illinois Press, 1995). In the essay here, I look at women from history and literature interchangeably, with the belief that each reflects cultural experience from its own angle.

19. Sui Sin Far, "The Americanization of Pau Tsu," in her collection of short fiction, *Mrs. Spring Fragrance* (Chicago: A. C. McClurg, 1912), 144–61.

20. "The Wisdom of the New," in *Mrs. Spring Fragrance*, 47–84.

21. Interview by the author, Washington State University, Pullman, February 1987.

22. "In the Land of the Free," *Independent* 67, no. 3170 (2 September 1909): 504–8.

23. "The Prize China Baby," in *Mrs. Spring Fragrance*, 214–19.

24. Yung in *Chinese Women*, describes the crib as a "small cubicle." No larger than a small closet, the crib had bars on the windows, from behind which prostitutes "hawked their trade to passersby," 23.

25. This category is from Hirata, "Free, Indentured, Enslaved," which details in depth experiences of prostitutes, both free and enslaved.

26. Yung, *Chinese Women*, 14.

27. Dorothy Gray, *Women of the West* (Millbrae, Calif.: Les Femmes, 1976), 68–69. See also Nell Kimball's autobiography, *The Life of an American Madam* (New York: Macmillan, 1970).

28. Hirata, "Chinese Immigrant Women," 4.

29. *The Land of Sunshine* 10, no. 2 (January 1899): 225–28.

30. Hirata, "Free, Indentured, Enslaved," 8. The precise date set by Hirata for the end of the period of "free competition" is 1853, at which time her designated period of "organized trade" began, lasting until 1925.

31. Mary Morris, "Hers," *New York Times*, 30 April 1987.

32. Benson Tong, *Unsubmissive Women: Chinese Prostitutes in Nineteenth-Century San Francisco* (Norman: University of Oklahoma Press, 1994), examines in detail the context and circumstances in which Chinese women became Chinese American prostitutes. See especially chapter 2.

33. The story of Lalu Nathoy, later known as Polly Bemis, is told by Ruthanne Lum McCunn in *A Thousand Pieces of Gold* (New York: Dell Publishing, 1981).

34. Peggy Pascoe, *Relations of Rescue: The Search for Female Moral Authority in the American West, 1874–1939* (New York: Oxford University Press, 1990).

35. Hirata, "Chinese Immigrant Women," 7, quoted from Charles Shepherd, "Chinese Girl Slavery in America," *Missionary Review* 46 (1923): 893–95.

36. Richard H. Dillon, *The Hatchet Men: The Story of the Tong Wars in San Francisco's Chinatown* (New York: Coward-McCann, 1962), 237.

37. Gray, *Women of the West*, 71.

38. Hirata, "Free, Indentured, Enslaved," 9.

39. Hirata, "Chinese Immigrant Women," 17.

40. Hirata, "Free, Indentured, Enslaved," 12.

41. Gray, *Women of the West*, 72.

42. Yung, *Chinese Women*, 17.

43. "The Smuggling of Wah To," in *Mrs. Spring Fragrance*, 185-93.

44. Hirata, "Free, Indentured, Enslaved," 13.

45. Yung, *Chinese Women*, 19.

46. As cited by Stephen Longstreet, *The Wilder Shore: A Gala Social History of San Francisco's Sinners and Spenders, 1849-1906* (Garden City, N.Y.: Doubleday, 1968), 160-61.

47. William Purviance Fenn, "Ah Sin and His Brethren in American Literature" (Ph.D. dissertation, State University of Iowa, 1932), 109.

48. Gray, *Women of the West*, 71.

49. Pascoe, *Relations of Rescue*, 6.

50. Yung, *Chinese Women*, 19.

51. Gray, *Women of the West*, and Dillon, *Hatchet Men*.

52. Frank Chin et al., eds., *Aiiieeeee!: An Anthology of Asian American Writers* (New York: Anchor Books, 1975), xiii.

53. Yung, *Chinese Women*, 30.

54. Dillon, *Hatchet Men*, 225.

55. Gray, *Women of the West*, 68.

56. Ibid., 70.

57. Pascoe, *Relations of Rescue*, 1, 11.

58. "Pat and Pan," in *Mrs. Spring Fragrance*, 333-44.

59. Sui Sin Far, "Leaves," 130.

60. Tong, *Unsubmissive Women*, xix.

61. Ruthanne Lum McCunn's, *Chinese American Portraits, Personal Histories 1828-1988* (San Francisco: Chronicle Books, 1988) documents many more journeys of Chinese immigrants to North America.

13.

"I Got a Girl Here, Would You Like to Meet Her?": Courtship, Ethnicity, and Community in Sweetwater County, 1900–1925

One of the most common human experiences, marriage, took many forms in the American West. To continue their ethnic cultures, westerners had to marry and have children. But for many of the young, single immigrants of both sexes, finding a marriage partner of one's own ethnic group was no simple matter. Frequently the choice was more a matter of economics than of romance. Many women came to the West to marry men they had never met. The most well-known instances of this practice are Japanese and Korean "picture brides," who were virtually the only possible marriage partners for Japanese and Korean men. However, immigrant bachelors from many nations sought brides from their former homelands. For the women, these marriages could vary from satisfying partnerships to horrifyingly abusive encounters in situations where they were isolated and dependent on strangers. Perhaps the best-known examples are the four strangers who entrusted their futures (and indeed, their lives) to the abusive husband that Mari Sandoz so unsparingly portrays in her family memoir, Old Jules.[1]

In this article, Dee Garceau brings together oral histories, census statistics, and the work of other feminist historians to provide a richly textured account of courtship in southwest Wyoming. As Garceau shows us, immigrant women's options depended on many things: on the support of other women, on the supervision of parents, on the institutions created by ethnic communities, and on the ways that courtship practices changed in the social and physical environments of western farms and mining towns. Garceau helps us see that the common experience of intimacy was as varied, changing, and historically constructed as all other human practices. She also helps us see the enormous cultural variety in the patterns of the daily encounters that wove new western communities.

Studies of courtship in the West have addressed neither the immigrant experience nor the early twentieth century.[2] Historians addressing twentieth-century courtship have focused on changing role prescriptions and behavior among urban women. Initially, these scholars emphasized the decline of Victorian ideology and the emergence of the "New Woman," a harbinger of modern behaviors like unchaperoned dating and sexual expressiveness.[3] More recently, in a study based primarily on eastern and midwestern sources, Ellen Rothman linked the decline of Victorian sexual reticence to the formation of a separate middle-class youth culture.[4]

So too, working-class, immigrant women in the East have been the focus of recent research on courtship. Rather than stressing rejection of Victorian mores, which did not reflect working-class realities, these studies emphasized generational or class conflict and the effects of urban life on family authority. In a study of working-class women and leisure in turn-of-the-century New York City, Kathy Peiss traced the decline of supervised courtships as commercial recreation drew young women and men away from their own ethnic neighborhoods. At dance palaces, movie houses, and amusement parks, working-class youth of different nationalities mixed, unchaperoned by parents, relatives, or neighbors. Single working-class women allowed men to "treat" them to meals, drinks, tickets, rides, and cover charges in exchange for sexual favors. Thus Peiss added an immigrant, "working class variant" to the themes of sexual expressiveness and escape from parental authority in early-twentieth-century courtship.[5]

But what about courtship on the early-twentieth-century western plains? Did the working-class immigrant women who settled mining towns during this period also venture into unchaperoned dating and freer sexual expression? What about their native-born peers in ranching communities? Did they explore New Woman styles of courtship? A case study of Sweetwater County, Wyoming, 1900–1925, suggests that courtship on this ranching and mining frontier did not fit the eastern urban model. Instead, the regional economy and demographics of southwest Wyoming shaped women's courtship behavior in distinctive ways. Census data and oral histories suggest that the ethnic diversity, mobility, and economic instability of mining towns encouraged close supervision of courting couples among first-generation immigrants. In contrast, the relative stability and homogeneity of ranching settlements preserved a Victorian sexual standard while paradoxically allowing young men and women considerable freedom.

In neither case did a modern peer culture hold sway. Rather, courtship expressed community standards, which, in Sweetwater County, still were set by the larger, multigenerational adult community. That is, courtship was not simply about romance, choosing a husband, or degrees of supervision and sexual activity. It was also an expression of shared values that were seen as important to survival on the southwest Wyoming frontier. In mining towns, courtship reflected the high value placed on kin and ethnic ties in a chaotic environment where ethnic community did not exist residentially. In rural areas, courtship underscored a Victorian morality grounded in the homogeneous cultural heritage of agricultural settlers. In each case, courtship highlighted single women's roles in building and sustaining community.

Sweetwater County lies in the southwest corner of Wyoming. It is high-plains desert, bisected by the Green River, running north to south, and the Union Pacific Railroad, running east to west. By the 1880s, white settlements dotted these two transportation routes. Homesteaders from the Mississippi Valley and the East Coast filed claims along the Green River bottomlands, some herding stock on the arid plateaus beyond. Immigrants from Germany and the British Isles established small businesses at Green River City, the central railhead. At the same time, coal camps bloomed along the Union Pacific railway, drawing workers from England, Ireland, Wales, China, and Japan.[6] Mining methods were primitive and dangerous, exacerbating conflicts between British and Asian labor. In 1885, racial tension exploded with the Rock Springs Massacre, in which twenty-eight Chinese miners were killed and several hundred Chinese residents were driven from town. The massacre became a demographic watershed; thereafter, the Union Pacific began recruiting European rather than British or Asian labor. Scandinavian workers took jobs in the mines and by 1900 nearly outnumbered settlers from the British Isles.[7]

Between 1898 and 1910, coal production in Wyoming doubled, and Sweetwater County coal towns expanded. World War I further increased the demand for fuel, pushing the coal boom to the end of the next decade. During this time, Hungarians, Austrians, Slavs, and Italians joined the ranks of miners until, by 1910, almost two-thirds of the population was foreign-born.[8] Southern and eastern Europeans continued to migrate to Union Pacific coal towns in Sweetwater County until the National Origins Act restricted immigration in 1924.[9]

In the outlying rural areas, liberalization of homestead law in 1909 and 1912 and corporate irrigation projects facilitated by the Carey Act brought a second wave of homesteaders that lasted through the early 1920s. Still, between 1880 and 1910, 85.1 percent of the county population clustered in mining towns like Rock Springs, Superior, Reliance, Megeath, and Winton.[10]

Mining towns in Sweetwater County were, on the surface, melting pots, for ethnic neighborhoods never developed.[11] Old photographs of residential areas in Rock Springs show rows of narrow clapboard homes abutting unpaved streets.[12] Had you walked these streets in 1910, you might have heard Italian spoken in one house, Austrian German in the next, Slovenian in the next, and Finnish at the corner.[13] Indeed, two out of every three residents you met would have been first-generation immigrants from Europe. One of every three would have been a woman. Every other man you met would have been unmarried. Finally, had you asked one of the men how long he planned to stay in town, he might have gestured toward the mines and replied, "As long as there is work."

Such were the demographics of coal towns in Sweetwater County. Between 1900 and 1910, 66 percent of town dwellers were foreign-born. By 1921, Rock Springs alone boasted forty-one nationalities. Men outnumbered women, and single men outnumbered single women by about five to one.[14] The possibilities for cross-cultural romance were many.

But the possibilities for settling permanently in town were slim. Transience was the common denominator in this diverse population. Rock Springs, Reliance, Superior, Megeath, and Winton were single-industry towns, where coal mining dominated the economy. Every summer, the coal market flagged, and hundreds of miners were laid off, or found their hours cut back.[15] Some left Wyoming for timber harvests in Oregon and Washington. Others looked for work in Nevada, Arizona, Utah, and Colorado. Even during the "on" season, mining was subject to boom and bust cycles, and layoffs, injuries, or disputes might send miners and their families packing. In short, it was common for miners to move often, following fluctuations in the job market for semiskilled and unskilled labor.[16] The instability of the mining industry, the lack of alternative job opportunities, and the resulting transience of the population worked against development of ethnic neighborhoods.

Single-industry towns in Sweetwater County discouraged formation of ethnic enclaves in one other significant way as well. Coal towns were company towns, owned and operated by the Union Pacific Railroad and Coal Company. The Union Pacific so thoroughly controlled the housing market that after the turn of the century, coal-town settlers "had little choice but to live in company housing." By 1905, for example, only 4 percent of Sweetwater County residents owned their own homes. By 1915, only 8 percent did.[17] Thus, when newcomers arrived from Europe, they settled wherever a vacancy was available in company housing, regardless of what nationality lived next door. Saloon owners worked in cooperation with women who rented rooms, sending newcomers to board with families of the same nationality whenever possible. But their efforts were inevitably limited by the availability of housing.[18] Pronounced ethnic diversity within neighborhoods and the transience of these neighborhoods made for an unpredictable social milieu. Immigration historian John Bodnar observed that when working-class ethnic neighborhoods did form in industrial cities, they could be "secure and friendly places," where neighbors visited on the street, or gathered at each other's flats for communal work and socializing.[19] But in Sweetwater coal towns, where no "urban villages" developed, no such security existed. Instead, immigrants struggled to form ethnic community ties despite their scattered residences.

The example of the southern Slavs is instructive, for east Europeans composed the fastest-growing ethnic population in Sweetwater County between 1900 and 1920. Indeed, by 1910, east Europeans formed the largest segment of the ethnic population.[20] The term "east European" refers to Hungarians, Austrians, and Slavs, the latter including Croatians, Czechs, Poles, Serbs, Slovaks, and Slovenes. Among the east Europeans who settled Sweetwater County, southern Slavs made up the largest group.[21] The term "southern Slav" refers to those ethnic groups once encompassed by Yugoslavia—Slovenes, Croatians, and Serbs.[22] The example of the southern Slavs, then, represents a significant portion of the first-generation immigrant experience in Sweetwater County mining towns.

The most visible example of southern Slavs' efforts to create an ethnic social space was construction of the Slovenski Dom in Rock Springs in

1914. Funded jointly by Croatian and Slovenian fraternal lodges, the Slovenski Dom was a social hall built to serve southern Slavs from Rock Springs, Superior, Reliance, and other mining towns. Slovenski Dom, which means "Slovenian home," became a gathering place for men's and women's groups, family and ethnic celebrations.[23] Less visible, but equally significant, was John Mrak's saloon on K Street in Rock Springs. Mrak's saloon functioned as a social space for southern Slavs in a way that local neighborhoods could not. Men and women stopped in to exchange news and gossip. Weddings and funerals were held upstairs. Women gathered there to set up feasts for holidays. Mine workers socialized downstairs. In many ways, Mrak's saloon served as a clearinghouse for Rock Springs' southern Slav immigrants. Newcomers, for example, went to Mrak to locate relatives, jobs, or housing.[24] Like the Slovenski Dom, John Mrak's saloon functioned like an ethnic neighborhood, as a social space where southern Slavs counted on hearing their language spoken, seeing familiar faces, and sharing cultural tradition with others of similar background.

Outside the parameters of Mrak's saloon or the Slovenski Dom, southern Slavs nurtured informal social ties with others of their own ethnic group whenever possible.[25] Nowhere was this more evident than in matters of courtship. Indeed, southern Slav women courted within a close-knit web of familial and ethnic social networks. Relatives, acquaintances, coworkers, and employers assumed responsibility as matchmakers. Single women without kin sometimes formed quasi-parental relationships with their boardinghouse keepers, and sought advice from them on matters of the heart. Parents chaperoned dates and dances and approved or rejected potential husbands. The degree to which southern Slavs brought family and ethnic ties to bear on courtship suggests that despite the lack of residential cohesion—or perhaps in response to it—their impulse to create ethnic community was strong.

The most well-known matchmaker among southern Slavs in Rock Springs was John Mrak, proprietor of the K Street saloon. Not only did Mrak help newcomers to get established, he also helped single men and women to find marriage partners. As Dorothy Pivik described it, "Let's say if a woman came here, he [Mrak] would find a man [for her] and they'd marry, or vice versa. . . . It's like he mated them. He always found a partner for one or the other."[26]

John Mrak was not the only one alert to possible matches. Older Slovene, Croatian, or Serbian men and women seized casual, through not subtle, opportunities to suggest matches to their young, single acquaintances, neighbors, or employees. Dorothy Pivik described her husband's first marriage in Rock Springs as a match initiated by an older acquaintance:

[T]he way he [Mr. Pivik] met her [his first wife] is through my uncle. My uncle worked for the Rock Springs Commercial Store and he delivered groceries in Quealy [mining camp] and he told my husband—of course at the time he was just a young boy—he said,

"I have a girl picked out for you, and she works for my wife," she was her maid . . .
so he [Dorothy's uncle] brought him [Dorothy's husband, as a young man] in on the
horse and buggy, and he met her and he said they were married soon after.[27]

Mary Jesersek was introduced to her future husband by one of her
employers, an older woman of the same ethnicity whom she helped with
housework: "[T]here was a friend of Suvicks that, the lady had a baby,
and she needed somebody to work for her, so I went to work in her home;
and my [future] husband was working in the butcher shop and he'd deliver
meat, and this lady says, 'I got a girl here, would you like to meet her?' "[28]
Mary and the butcher began their courtship that day and married within
the year. John Mrak's, Dorothy Pivik's and Mary Jesersek's stories suggest
that matchmaking was an accepted practice among southern Slavic
immigrants. These matches were informal; a matchmaker introduced a
young man and woman, then left the outcome to them.

Indeed, single women were free to refuse proposals. Before meeting the
butcher, Mary Jesersek had refused to marry a man with whom she had
been matched. The story behind her decision is revealing, for it also
demonstrates how single women without kin formed alternative support
networks. Mary was a boarder who turned to her boardinghouse keepers,
in lieu of parents, for guidance and encouragement.

Mary Jesersek grew up in a Slovenian village at the turn of the century.
When she was seventeen, one of her neighbors emigrated to Wyoming.
Evidently this neighbor suggested Mary as a potential wife to one of his
Slovenian friends in Rock Springs, for Mary received a written proposal
in the mail from the young hopeful. She agreed to marry the Rock Springs
suitor on the recommendation of her former neighbor. So the Slovenian
miner booked and paid for her passage to America. But when Mary
arrived in Rock Springs and met her fiancé, she found, to her dismay, that
she did not like him: "The first day I was here I stayed with the family
of that fella that I came for . . . and he was boarding down at Number
Four [mine]. Then the next day, there was a dance, Labor Day? And we
went to the dance. . . . I don't know, that fella just didn't appeal to me."[29]

At the dance, another Slovenian woman, Mrs. Luzan, noticed Mary's
unease and questioned her about her plans: "She [Mrs. Luzan] says to me,
'You like that fella? do you want to marry him?' She says, 'You don't have
to get married. I could get you a place to work.'" Mrs. Luzan described
Mary's dilemma to the Suvicks, an older Slovenian couple who kept
boarders. Mary remembered the Suvicks as a lifeline, for they offered her
a way out of marriage to a stranger whom she did not like. "Mr. Suvick,"
Mary recalled, "said, 'Stay with us.'" Mary accepted the Suvick's offer,
and told her fiancé, "That wedding is off. I want to go to work." The next
day, she moved into the Suvicks' boardinghouse, where she cooked and
cleaned for room, board, and ten dollars per month.[30]

Mary felt adamant about repaying her erstwhile fiance for the cost of
her travel: "I don't remember him saying that he wanted money for the
ticket, but I thought, I don't want to be obligated to nobody. . . . I work

until I pay my ticket, it was $105.00." Having discharged that obligation, Mary remained with the Suviks, where she had both a job and a home. By the time she married the butcher, Mary had lived with the Suvicks for two years, and she later remembered them fondly: "They were really nice people."[31] Like surrogate parents, the Suvicks had taken her in, steered her away from a doubtful marriage, and provided a stable home-base. For Mary Jesersek, the Suvicks had supplied social and emotional support in a world where she faced major decisions without benefit of guidance from kin. Her story suggests that southern Slav women without kin sometimes found a supportive "home" boarding with families of the same nationality.

Mary Jesersek's story also illustrates the informality of matchmaking. Indeed, the only commitment Mary felt toward her hapless fiancé was monetary; she reimbursed him for travel. Other than paying that debt, the arrangement carried no obligation.

On the other hand, parents sometimes forbade marriage to a partner independently chosen. Single women who ignored well-meaning match-makers also risked their parents' disapproval. Such was the case with Dorothy Pivik. Pivik grew up in Rock Springs during the 'teens and 'twenties. Independent of matchmakers, she fell in love with a young man whom she met at school. But Dorothy's parents disapproved of the match because the young man in question was not a southern Slav. "Our folks always felt that we should marry the same nationality," she said. "Now this boy that I met, he was English and we were very much in love, but it didn't work out. . . . My parents were against it. And I listened to them." Dorothy complied with her parents' judgment, and ended the relationship. Though she felt some regrets later, at the time, she recalled, "We did listen to our parents, we had to listen to them."[32] In Dorothy Pivik's case, obedience to parental authority foreclosed the option of choosing her own spouse.

Religion figured in this equation, for religion was inseparable from ethnic identity among Slovenes, Croats, and Serbs. Croatian immigrant Ann LeVar Powell remembered her parents' directive to marry a man of the same faith. "The unspoken rule," she said, was "Do marry a Cath-olic."[33] Mary Lou Anselmi Unguren confirmed that southern Slav parents supervised courtship, and that Catholic Croats and Catholic Slovenes urged their daughters to marry within the faith, if not within the same nationality. Unguren's mother, Louise Schuster, had immigrated to Rock Springs from Slovenia with her parents before World War I. When Louise fell in love with Rudy Anselmi, an Italian, her parents initially frowned upon the match. But the fact that Anselmi was Catholic, and that Slovenians who worked with Rudy said he "had a good reputation," moved Louise Schuster's parents to approve the marriage.[34] Family authority carried weight in southern Slav courtships, then, for women like Dorothy Pivik, Ann LeVar Powell, and Louise Schuster needed their parents' approval to continue a relationship. One had to pick a spouse whom one's parents would accept.

Not surprisingly, southern Slav parents kept a close watch on whom their daughters saw. Louise Luzan Leskovec's story typified that of many single southern Slav women whose parents supervised courtship. Louise Luzan grew to womanhood in Rock Springs during the 'teens and early 'twenties. During this time, John Mrak's saloon held dances several times per year. As Louise recalled, "I always went to dances with my mother and father. They wouldn't let us go alone."[35] The Luzans were not unique in this respect. Dances at Mrak's saloon took traditional working-class form. That is, they were intergenerational events, attended by entire families. Usually they were sponsored by a local club or mutual benefit society, or in the case of wedding parties, by the families of the bride and groom. At these dances, young women and men socialized in the constant presence of parents, relatives, and neighbors.[36]

In her study of working-class women's recreation in eastern cities during the same period, Kathy Peiss found a gradual movement among ethnic youth away from traditional working-class dances and into commercialized dance halls. In these large dance palaces, couples enjoyed anonymity, far from the eyes of parents, relatives, and neighbors.[37] Commercialized recreation came to Sweetwater coal towns in the form of the Rialto Amusement Company. By 1914, the company had opened two theaters in Rock Springs, featuring movies, visiting musicals, drama, and vaudeville acts. Rialto did not, however, open any dance halls. As late as 1921, Rock Springs, Superior, Reliance, Megeath, and Green River had no commercialized dance palaces that catered to a separate youth culture, like those found in the metropolitan East.[38] And so ethnic youth in southwest Wyoming coal towns continued to attend traditional working-class dances. There, under the watchful eyes of chaperones, young women and men found circumspect ways to court. Marion Buchan, a single Yugoslavian miner, arrived in Rock Springs in 1910. He described a custom in which if a boy danced the last dance with a girl, it meant he liked her especially.[39] This custom seems a far cry from courtship at the unsupervised, commercial dance halls of large cities, where ethnic, working-class couples were openly sexually expressive.[40]

Dances were not the only form of courtship subject to adult supervision. In an exchange with interviewers Ann Burns and Nancy Cranford, Louise Luzan Leskovec described dating in 1918, when her courtship with Matt Leskovec began:

LL: One year, he [Matt Leskovec] went to a convention with Mr. Plemel, and he sent me a card. When he got back, he called me up for a date, and my mother said that, Yes, I could go.

Int.:   You did have to ask your mother?

LL: Oh, yes. She never let me go on dates by myself.

Int.:   Now, who went with you?

LL: My mother and dad. (Laughter) We went to the show.

Int.:   You all four went to the show?

LL: Yes.[41]

Dorothy Pivik's and Louise Leskovec's accounts of their own courtships and engagements in early-twentieth-century Rock Springs suggest that southern Slav parents played a strong role in their daughters' choice of spouse. Chaperoning dates and dances, as well as granting permission to marry, gave parents considerable influence over daughters' marriage plans.

The purpose of such influence was to encourage daughters to marry a man of the same nationality. And judging from the demographic record, these efforts were successful. The 1910 census sample from Sweetwater County yielded ninety-six foreign-born women who immigrated while single, then married after settling in the United States. Of these, twenty-five were eastern Europeans, all of whom married a man of the same nationality.[42] Choosing a man of the same ethnic background offered the comforts of shared tradition; in particular, the tradition of mutual obligation among family members.[43] Kinship ties formed a crucial community of support in an environment characterized by occupational hazard, economic instability, and lack of residential ethnic enclaves. Indeed, the prospect of marriage without extended kinship support in the new country was bleak. Married daughters often moved far from home as a consequence of their husbands' search for work.[44] If a woman married and moved away to another county or state, she would be beyond the immediate reach of her own kin networks. If she married a man of another nationality, she might not be accepted by his kin.[45] Then who could be sure that she or her children would find the support they needed, in the event of illness, death, or economic disaster? Parents like the Luzans and the Piviks, who encouraged their daughters to marry within their own ethnic group, must have felt keenly the necessity of kinship ties, for these ties functioned like social service networks among first-generation immigrants.

Indeed, one consistent impression about life in the old country that emerged from southern Slav oral history informants was that families expected every able member, even small children, to contribute labor or income to the household. For example, when a family faced poverty, sons and daughters left home as soon as possible, to ease the burden on the household. Away from home, they supported themselves and sent money to parents and siblings left behind.[46] Brothers, sisters, parents, and children thus shared responsibility for family survival. In the new country, this tradition proved invaluable.[47]

Memories of the need for kin ties in the new country were especially poignant among residents of coal towns, where industrial accidents tore at the fabric of family life.[48] Helen Korich Krmpotich's account of her parents' experience shows how kinship networks functioned like a safety net in times of disaster. In 1906, the Koriches, a young Serbian couple, immigrated to Chicago with Helen, then a baby, and her five-year-old sister. Mr. Korich worked in the steel mills; Mrs. Korich ran the household. But the steel mills were dangerous, and before long, injury sidelined Mr. Korich. As Helen described it, Mr. Korich "got burned, all his scalp, in Chicago in the mills. He didn't like that work after that because he was six months in the hospital. So then he heard—my Aunt Pearl lived in Pueblo, Colorado—that she wanted us to move there."[49]

As soon as Mr. Korich was able, the family moved to Colorado, where Pearl helped them to resettle. There Mr. Korich found work in the nearby mines. But the mines in Colorado were no safer than the steel mills in Chicago. By 1912 the Koriches were living in Hastings, Colorado, where gas collected like a time bomb in the mine shafts. Mr. Korich escaped the 1912 Hastings explosion, which killed 350 miners, but it convinced him to move on. The family headed north to Sweetwater County and settled in Superior. After four years there without incident, the Koriches moved on to Megeath, a boomtown prospering on wartime demand for coal. In 1918, the great flu epidemic killed 750 people in Wyoming, among them Helen's mother. At first, Helen, age twelve, quit school to run the household and tend her four brothers and sisters. But this became a tenuous arrangement as Mr. Korich's health deteriorated. Illness forced him to quit the mines, and Helen became the breadwinner. Mr. Korich stayed home with the children, while Helen found work at a boardinghouse, waiting on tables, washing dishes, peeling potatoes, "and whatever there was to help the cook."[50]

In 1920, Mr. Korich died of cancer. Helen, age fourteen, could not both watch the younger children and hold her job: "I had to stay home because my brother was only four years old and we didn't have babysitters like they have today. . . . So my uncle came from Toronto and took over the five of us and he raised us." Mr. Korich's brother moved to Megeath and took over the care of his orphaned nieces and nephews. Helen lived with her uncle and siblings until 1924, when she married.[51]

The Korichs thus relied on family to see them through injury, relocation, illness, and death: Helen's Aunt Pearl helped the family move to Colorado, following her father's accident in the steel mills. Helen ran the household when her mother died, then found income-earning work when her father's illness necessitated quitting the mines. Finally, Helen's uncle took over care of the Korich children when they were orphaned. Aunt, father, daughter, and uncle—all supported the Korich household when family survival was threatened. In an environment fraught with work-related injuries, low wages, and frequent mobility, kinship networks like the Koriches' supported families through transition and misfortune. Given the centrality of this tradition in southern Slav immigrants' lives, it is no wonder that they placed a high value on marriage within their own ethnic group.

The example of southern Slavs, then, suggests several ways that the demography and economics of early-twentieth-century Wyoming coal towns shaped courtship. In these mining towns, ethnically diverse, changing neighborhoods offered a smorgasbord of cross-cultural possibilities for romance. But while heterogeneous neighborhoods would seem to create perfect conditions for the melting pot of legend, southern Slavs instead reinforced ethnic solidarity through marriage, a crucial link in strategies of family survival. Indeed, the vagaries of mining-town life underscored the value of kinship ties, hence marriage within one's ethnic group. And so southern Slav parents and elders steered young women toward their own kind, by supervising courtship, suggesting matches, and approving or vetoing engagements. Indeed, the extent to which familial and ethnic ties played a role in courtship was testament to Croatian, Serb, and Slovenian efforts to build ethnic community—a form of social cohesion whose value was intensified by their lack of residential cohesion. Thus while single immigrant "New Women" in large cities rejected family and neighborhood authority, drawn instead to the anonymity of public amusements, southern Slav immigrant women in Sweetwater mining towns courted within a close-knit web of family and ethnic networks.

In contrast, women and men in rural Sweetwater County courted with far less supervision. Long distances between homesteads discouraged family control of courtship. Because of distance, visits between ranchers took the form of infrequent but extended stays. At the least, visitors stayed overnight; more often they stayed two or three days.[52] During such visits, and during travel between ranches, couples often spent time together unchaperoned. But distance was not the only factor that relaxed rules of courtship. Ranching communities in Sweetwater County were relatively stable and culturally homogeneous; hence parents felt less need to monitor their daughters' social lives.

Rancher Mae Mickelson's account of Elsie Ann Johnson's wooing provides a telling glimpse of rural courtship. Born in Wyoming, Elsie Johnson grew up on a ranch in north Sweetwater County during the 1890s and early 1900s. In 1912, she married Jesse Chase, a neighboring rancher. As Mae Mickelson described it:

Elsie and Jesse knew each other as children. Their families were always friendly.
    . . . [W]hen [Elsie] and Jesse started dating, [they went] . . . to a dance at Lot Haley's on Cottonwood above Big Piney. . . . Everyone in the country came and mixed with everyone. The dance lasted all night which was usual in those days. When daylight came, everyone started wending their way homeward.
    . . . Helen Sargent was a young schoolteacher in the Basin, living at Bonderants, the first time Jesse came to take Elsie for a horseback ride. She said Claire Bonderant stood and watched them ride off and that he was heartbroken! He was in love with Elsie too.
    Ira Dodge, Justice of the Peace, married Jesse and Elsie in Big Piney on the 22nd of March, 1912. The snow was very deep. They had driven a sleigh from Cottonwood.[53]

This account of courtship suggests that young women and men in rural Sweetwater County were trusted with unchaperoned time together. Couples like Elsie and Jesse were free to go horseback riding and to travel long distances, unaccompanied by parents, relatives, or peers. In short, Elsie Ann Johnson enjoyed a less-supervised courtship than did her southern Slav peers in coal towns.[54]

Mickelson's narrative also alludes to the sense of community stability and homogeneity that contributed to more relaxed rules of courtship in rural areas. "Elsie and Jesse knew each other as children," Mrs. Mickelson wrote, "Their families were always friendly." With less turnover in the rural population, those who stayed developed long-term relationships with neighbors and shared a sense of rootedness. Parents like the Johnsons felt comfortable about their daughter spending time with Jesse Chase, a man they had known since his childhood. "Everyone in the country came and mixed with everyone" at the dance, continued Mrs. Mickelson, suggesting that no major cultural differences divided ranch folk in her area. Indeed, nearly three-quarters of rural dwellers in Sweetwater County, 1880–1910, were native-born, and most of these native-born ranchers hailed from the Midwest.[55] Among the 27 percent of foreign-born rural settlers, most came from the English-speaking countries of Great Britain.[56] The relative homogeneity of ranch culture seems to have made parents and daughters alike more trusting of social situations involving single men and women.

Other narratives from rural Wyoming reinforced this impression. Helen Coburn, a single homesteader in Worland from 1905 to 1908, felt safe attending local dances on her own because those present shared her cultural background. Born in Iowa, Helen had moved to Wyoming to homestead with her friend Mary Culbertson. Before leaving Iowa, Helen had promised her father not to attend any ranch dances, because the people might be "crude." But she soon found that other homesteaders in her community "were all people from the middle West, like myself, and were from families of good background." So Helen attended ranch dances and wrote to her father that she "was not breaking her promise, but just taking it back, as he didn't know the true conditions of the West."[57]

Similarly, Eden Valley homesteader Mrs. Nathan Hodson remembered most of the settlers in her area, from 1909 through the 1920s, being from "Kansas, Missouri, Wisconsin, Iowa, Kentucky, and Illinois . . . all were friends and interested in each other's welfare."[58] Helen Coburn's, Mrs. Nathan Hodson's, and Mae Mickelson's narratives suggest that rural ranching populations in Sweetwater County were stable and culturally homogeneous, relative to the mobile and ethnically diverse populations of mining towns. Secure among native-born peers from similar backgrounds, familiar with homesteaders throughout their locale, rural folk were less guarded in their attitude toward courtship.

Despite the trust accorded unchaperoned couples, single ranchwomen were physically and socially vulnerable when they spent time alone with men. If sexual activity occurred, they risked unwed pregnancy and disgrace. Folk songs common to early-twentieth-century ranching communities warned single women to avoid premarital sex. In ballads about cowboy/ranchgirl romances, premarital sex led to abandonment and unwed motherhood. In scenarios involving unchaperoned courtship, cowboys appeared as charming playboys, single women as their willing victims.

"The Wild, Rippling Water" was a popular western folk song based on a British ballad, rewritten to fit ranch life. It tells the story of a "fair maid" who goes "a rambling" alone with a cowboy,

> Just down by the river,
> just down by the spring,
> to see the wild water
> and hear the nightingale sing.

In this song, the "wild, rippling water," a metaphor for sexuality, proves too compelling to resist, and the fair maid winds up pregnant. She asks the cowboy if he will marry her. He declines and rides away. The last verse holds the moral of the story:

> Come all you young ladies, take warning from me
> Never place your affections in a cowboy so free
> He'll go away and leave you as mine left me
> Leave you rocking the cradle, singing "Bye, oh baby"
> Leave you rocking the cradle, singing "Bye, oh baby."[59]

Like "The Wild, Rippling Water," the popular western song "Bucking Broncho" recognized the power of sexual desire and warned single women of its consequences. The narrator of "Bucking Broncho" is a young woman in love with a cowboy who rides the wild broncs. She describes her flirtation with the cowboy, their dances together, and their engagement. She alludes to their sexual relationship as well in a humorous double entendre:

> My love has a gun that has gone to the bad,
> Which makes poor old Jimmy feel pretty damn sad,
> For the gun it shoots high and the gun it shoots low,
> And it wobbles about like a bucking broncho.

In the end, the cowboy lover leaves, reneging on his promise to marry. The song concludes with a warning almost identical to that in "The Wild, Rippling Water":

> Now all you young maidens, where'er you reside,
> Beware of the cowboy who swings the rawhide,
> He'll court you and pet you and leave you and go
> In the spring up the trail on his bucking broncho.[60]

The theme of premarital sex and abandonment is repeated in "I'll Give You My Story." According to folksinger Rosalie Sorrels, this song originated in the West, becoming most popular in Idaho and Utah. "I'll Give You My Story" bemoans the fate of the pregnant, single woman, deserted by her lover:

> I'll give you my story,
> I'm heavy with child;
> You said when we parted
> You'd be but a while.

The vanished lover never returns, and the unwed mother-to-be is left to contemplate her future:

> I grieved when we parted,
> I cried night and day;
> Now all of my sorrows
> Have passed away.[61]

The last two lines are ambiguous, and somewhat ominous; did the narrator abort the baby or has she simply gone numb? Like "The Wild, Rippling Water" and "Bucking Broncho," "I'll Give You My Story" depicts the physical and emotional consequences of premarital sex, that is, the risk of unwed motherhood.

Ranching communities in Sweetwater County reinforced such folk wisdom by emphasizing the social consequences of premarital sex. Single women were admonished to protect their reputations. Indeed, a double standard of sexual morality prevailed, in which the woman was held responsible for a couple's behavior together. "He's as good as the girl he is with" was the saying Jerrine Stewart Wire remembered.[62] This Victorian moral standard took the place of chaperones as a social control. That is, the consequences of flouting this standard were dire. Women who "allowed" sexual activity to happen became outcasts in a tight-knit community where everyone knew everyone else's history.

The double standard encompassed sexual assault as well as consenting sexual relations. Jerrine Stewart Wire's memory of a sexual assault during her teens was telling. Jerrine grew up on a ranch in Burnt Fork, from 1909 through the early 1920s. As a young woman, she was sexually assaulted by a neighbor while fishing alone, several miles from her parents' homestead. Jerrine never told her parents about the incident because she was convinced it would destroy her reputation. Sixty-odd years later, she described what happened:

I went fishing one time and when you fish out here there are streams that move along, they are coming down out of the mountain and they are running along at a pretty good clip. And they make a lot of noise so you can't hear what is going on. . . .

I was sitting there fishing and one of our neighbors came up behind me and took a notion to see what I was made out of. I didn't hear a thing until all of a sudden he had ahold of me and he pulled me over backwards and I lost my fishing rod and my fish and he proceeds to see if he can undo me a little bit, I guess he was wondering what I had underneath my shirt. I started beating and kicking.

Jerrine fought off her attacker and ran home. "My family all said, 'Where is the fish and where is the fishing rod and what's with you?' And I never told them . . . because I knew if I did I would be disgraced."[63]

So powerful was the threat of community judgment and social exclusion that women like Jerrine were afraid to report sexual assault. Jerrine knew that she would be held responsible for her neighbor's sexual attack, and she did not question this attitude. "He's as good as the girl he is with."

Jerrine had learned early, from her mother, that if a single woman and man had sexual contact, the woman became a pariah. This lesson came home through her mother's work as a midwife. As a child, Jerrine knew that her mother, Elinore Stewart, did not discriminate among those she helped in childbirth. As midwife, Elinore attended ranch wives and unwed mothers alike. At home in Jerrine's presence, however, Elinore made a point of snubbing unwed mothers. "She often took a stand in front of me," Jerrine said, "that she would not have taken if I weren't there":

I remember there was a girl in our neighborhood who got herself in trouble. . . . . She was so proud when the baby was born, like all new mothers are, they want everybody to see that pretty thing that they helped to make. . . . [S]he walked about four and a half, maybe five miles [to the Stewart ranch] carrying that big, fat, pretty baby . . . to show my mother . . . and my mother wouldn't even let her in the house.
. . . But she would have, if it had just been the two of them there. . . . She was afraid I might think she gave her stamp of approval . . . I thought it was too bad that girl had walked for hours and then had to walk all the way back.[64]

For Jerrine, the incident was a vivid lesson in the social consequences of unwed motherhood. Elinore Stewart had made it clear to her daughter that the unwed mother was subject to public shaming and exclusion from community. The unwed father was never mentioned. Perhaps Victorian morality was emphasized precisely because premarital sex was an omnipresent reality, as suggested by Jerrine's memory of the discrepancy between her mother's work as a midwife and the lesson she taught her daughter.

Recalling these events sixty years later, it never occurred to Jerrine to hold men responsible for sexually active or sexually aggressive behavior. She attributed no responsibility to her unwed neighbor's partner: The single mother had "got herself in trouble." Nor did she attribute responsibility to her attacker at the fishing stream. Instead, she placed it upon herself—"he took a notion *to see what I was made out of*" [emphasis mine]. Jerrine Stewart Wire's experience suggests that despite the lack of supervision, the ranching community excercised powerful social controls on courtship, holding single women responsible for prevention of premarital sexual activity. Single ranchwomen, then, were both physically and socially vulnerable in unsupervised situations. The stable and homogeneous community that made chaperones unnecessary also held the threat of public shame and social isolation for those who veered from its rules. In rural areas where everyone knew and judged each other by a double moral standard, single women's reputations hung in the balance.

Neither mining nor ranching communities in early-twentieth-century Sweetwater County embraced the courtship style represented by the New Woman. While the New Woman of eastern urban life experimented with freer sexual expression, single ranchwomen observed an older code of behavior: the Victorian notion that women must control male sexuality. While news media in major cities raised concern about parental permissiveness, southern Slav parents in coal towns wielded considerable authority in their daughters' social lives, and ranching mothers emphasized to their daughters the harsh social consequences of unwed motherhood. And while New Women among urban, immigrant, working-classes flocked to unchaperoned public amusements, single southern Slav women in Wyoming courted under the watchful eyes of parents, matchmakers, and sometimes, boardinghouse keepers.

In mining towns, and on ranches, then, courtship highlighted the nature of community in single women's lives. Problems of survival in mining towns heightened the value of supportive kin ties, a cornerstone of southern Slav tradition. At the same time, the unstable, single-industry economy offered the likelihood that a newly married woman would move far from her family of origin. Under these conditions, acceptance within her in-laws' extended kin networks gained importance. Marrying within one's ethnic group promised such acceptance; yet the lack of ethnic neighborhoods created an unpredictable social milieu. In this environment, Croatians, Slovenes, and Serbs created community out of family and ethnic ties whenever possible. Indeed, the involvement of parents and matchmakers in courtship and the high rate of endogamy among first-generation east Europeans reflected their efforts to build and maintain ethnic community in the midst of transient, ethnically mixed neighborhoods.

By contrast, the relative cultural homogeneity and stability of native-born ranching settlements gave rural courtship a different flavor. A shared Anglo heritage and development of long-term relationships between neighbors bred trust among ranching families. In this atmosphere, residents were less anxious to create community, and rural courtships were more casual as a result. Still, casual and unchaperoned did not mean "free." In the isolation of rural settlements, Victorian sexual mores common to ranchers' nineteenth-century, middle-class Anglo heritage persisted. Indeed, the secure sense of community that fostered unsupervised courtship was double-edged, for it also threatened single women with exclusion from community if they violated its standards. The double moral standard was nearly as effective as chaperones in discouraging women from sexual expression.

In closing, this study suggests several ways in which the demography and regional economy of early-twentieth-century southwest Wyoming shaped courtship in ways different from contemporary urban life. Moreover, within Sweetwater County itself, the contrasts between coal-town southern Slav and rural native born courtship further demonstrate the importance of local economy, settlement patterns, and ethnicity in women's lives. That is, courtship was deeply situational: Urban mores were not unknown in these places; they simply did not fit the needs and values of southwest Wyoming mining and ranching communities.

In a larger sense, courtship provides a window on single women's roles within informal social networks that framed and sustained community identity—whether moral or ethnic. Through their charge to maintain sexual control, single ranchwomen bore responsibility for preserving moral consensus. Through their choice of spouse, southern Slav women bore responsibility for expanding networks of reciprocal kin ties. And through their part as advisors to these women, parents and matchmakers played a significant role in promoting mutuality within their own ethnic group. In short, both the ranchers' experience and the southern Slav examples demonstrate that courtship activated informal social networks as important to building community as were more formalized institutions like women's clubs or fraternal lodges. The southern Slavs' influence on choice of spouse, like the ranching community's use of judgment and isolation as social controls on courtship, suggests not only the power and significance of informal social networks in single women's lives but also the significance of single women in the life of the community.

Notes

For encouragment and incisive criticism, I would like to thank Betsy Jameson, David Emmons, Ken Lockridge, Sue Armitage, and Mary Murphy. For their warmth, generosity and regional expertise, I am indebted to A. Dudley Gardner, Marcia Hensley, and the women from Sweetwater County who shared their stories with me. Finally, special thanks to Craig Rayle, who sustained me in more ways than I can name.

1. Mari Sandoz, *Old Jules* (Lincoln: University of Nebraska Press, 1962); for a discussion of domestic violence in this novel and others, see Melody Graulich, "Violence against Women: Power Dynamics in Literature of the Western Family," in *The Women's West*, ed. Susan Armitage and Elizabeth Jameson (Norman: University of Oklahoma Press, 1987), 111–25. See also Rachel Calof and J. Sanford Rikoon, *Rachel Calof's Story: A Jewish Homesteader on the Northern Plains* (Bloomington: Indiana University Press, 1995), for a memoir of a Russian Jewish woman homesteader's arranged marriage.

2. Little is known about frontier courtship among whites outside the parameters of mid- and late-nineteenth-century middle-class Anglo culture. John Faragher, Lillian Schlissel, and Elizabeth Hampsten have defined inquiry about courtship among native-born Anglo settlers in the nineteenth-century West. In an early study, Faragher traced overland emigrants' attitudes about courtship to their rural midwestern origins and found their expectations of marriage rooted in an agricultural version of the mid-nineteenth-century ideology of separate spheres. See Faragher, *Women and Men on the Overland Trail* (New Haven, Conn.: Yale University Press, 1979).

In another study of overland emigrants, Lillian Schlissel touched on courtship as a divisive issue in frontier family life. Within one typical emigrant family, Schlissel documented the middle daughter's impulsive liaison with a cavalryman and the youngest daughter's elopement as examples of a frontier "impulse toward personal independence" that fragmented families. See Schlissel, "Family on the Western Frontier," in *Western Women: Their Land, Their Lives*, ed. Lillian Schlissel, Vicki Ruiz, and Janice Monk (Albuquerque: University of New Mexico Press, 1988), 81–92.

Elizabeth Hampsten analyzed the love letters of a white, native-born, middle-class North Dakota couple who married in 1890. Hampsten found that they used a circumspect language of intimacy based on everyday concerns such as furnishing a home rather than direct erotic expression. Hampsten concluded that the couple was typical of their time and class and "that this language worked . . . for them, and doubtless for many others." See Hampsten, "Lena Olmstead and Oscar Phillips: Love and Marriage," in *Women's West*, 127–42.

In addition, frontier history is peppered with anecdotal narratives about courtship. See Grace Logan Schaedel, "The Story of Ernest and Lizzie Logan—A Frontier Courtship," *Annals of Wyoming* 54, no. 2 (1982): 48–61. Annotated, published letters between sweethearts, often edited by relatives, also provide glimpses into the lives of those who left written record of their courtship. See John Wade Geil, ed., "Babe and Gabriel: An Oregon Courtship," *Oregon Historical Quarterly* 87, no. 2 (Summer 1986): 117–66; and Phyllis Luman Metal, *Cattle King on the Green River: The Family Life and Legends of Abner Luman, A Cowboy King of the Upper Green River Valley* (Wilson, Wyo.: Sunshine Ranch and Friends, 1983). These stories are idiosyncratic and call for analysis within the context of gender and community on the frontier.

3. Early studies include Mary Ryan, "The Projection of a New Womanhood: The Movie Moderns of the 1920s," in *Our American Sisters: Women in American Life and Thought*, ed. Jean Friedman and William Shade (Lexington, Mass.: Heath, 1982), 500–518; James R. McGovern, "The American Woman's Pre-World War I Freedom in Manners and Morals," in *Our American Sisters*, 479–99; Linda Gordon, "Birth Control and Social Revolution," in *A Heritage of Her Own: Toward a New Social History of American Women*, ed. Nancy Cott and Elizabeth Pleck (New York: Simon & Schuster, 1980), 445–75; and Blanche Weisen Cook, "Female Support Networks and Political Activism: Lillian Wald, Crystal Eastman, Emma Goldman," in *Heritage of Her Own*, 412–44.

4. Ellen Rothman, *Hands and Hearts: A History of Courtship in America* (Cambridge, Mass.: Harvard University Press, 1987), 203–95. For discussion of decline in adult supervision, see 205–7; for the pre-World War I bohemian subculture in Greenwich Village, 241–42; for the loosening of sexual mores during World War I, 243–44; for the emergence of a peer-controlled system of social and sexual relationships during the 1920s, 289–95.

5. Kathy Peiss, *Cheap Amusements: Working Women and Leisure in Turn-of-the-Century New York* (Philadelphia: Temple University Press, 1986); see chap. 4, "Dance Madness," 88–114. Elizabeth Ewen echoed the theme of generational conflict over social and sexual mores as immigrant daughters moved into the worlds of wage work and commercialized youth culture in *Immigrant Women in the Land of Dollars: Life and Culture on the Lower East Side, 1890–1925* (New York: Monthly Review Press, 1985).

Analyses of Progressive reform aimed at controlling single working-class women's sexuality also confirm the loosening of family and neighborhood supervision of courtship in large, urban centers. See Elizabeth Perry, " 'The General Motherhood of the Commonwealth': Dance Hall Reform in the Progressive Era," *American Quarterly* 37, no. 5 (1985): 719–33; Elizabeth Lunbeck, " 'A New Generation of Women': Progressive Psychiatrists and the 'Hypersexual' Female," *Feminist Studies* 13, no. 3 (Fall 1987): 513–44; and Nancy Bristow, "Patriots and Prostitutes: Class, Race, and Government Control of Women during World War I," paper delivered at Northwest Women's Studies Association Conference, "Living in the Margins: Race, Class, and Gender," Washington State University, Pullman, 20 April 1991, 1–23.

6. White settlement followed the oppression and removal of Native Americans from the region, primarily the Shoshone, who were sent north to the Wind River Reservation. For information on Indian resistance and the northern plains wars, see Dee Brown, *Bury My Heart at Wounded Knee* (New York: Holt, Rinehart, and Winston, 1970), chap. 4–7, 67–170. See also T. A. Larson, *A History of Wyoming* (Lincoln: University of Nebraska Press, 1965), chap. 2, "The Indians," 12–35.

For accounts of white settlement in coal camps along the Union Pacific Railroad, see *History of the Union Pacific Coal Mines, 1868–1940* (Omaha, Neb.: Colonial Press, 1940) (hereafter *UP History*); Florence Kerr and Margaret Sowers, "Historical Sketch of Sweetwater County," Works Progress Administration Historical Records Survey, Division of Women's and Professional Projects (Cheyenne, Wyo., 1939)(hereafter *WPA County History*), 5–17; and Lola Homsher and Mary Lou Pence, *The Ghost Towns of Wyoming* (New York: Hastings House, 1956), 12–16.

For accounts of ranching settlement in the Green River Valley and its tributaries, see Ora Wright and Lenora Wright, *Our Valley: Eden Valley, Wyoming* (Portland, Ore.: Gann Publishing, 1987); Kerr and Sowers, *WPA County History*, 5–17; Larson, *History of Wyoming*, 163–76; and Dorothy E. Cook, "History of the Sheep Industry in Wyoming," Wyoming Works Progress Administration, 23 April 1941 (Cheyenne: Wyoming State Archives & Historical Dept.) (hereafter WSAHD), MSS-WPA 327.

7. Ethnicity analysis, Sweetwater County census, 1880, 1900. Regarding early mining conditions, see *UP History*, 52. Regarding the Rock Springs Massacre and recruitment of European labor, see Larson, *History of Wyoming*, 141–44; and Kerr and Sowers, *WPA County History*, 16–17.

8. Ethnicity analysis, Sweetwater County census, 1900, 1910. The proportion of foreign-born residents rose from 58.6 percent in 1900 to 62.7 percent in 1910. For figures on coal production, see Larson, *History of Wyoming*, 336, 396–98; for the expansion of coal towns, see *UP History*, 46–55, 138–41, 150–53.

9. For discussion of southern and eastern European immigration to Wyoming and the National Origins Act of 1924, see Earl Stinneford, "Mines and Miners: The Eastern Europeans in Wyoming," in *Peopling the High Plains: Wyoming's European Heritage*, ed. Gordon Olaf Hendrickson (Cheyenne: WSAHD, 1977), 121–48, esp. 124. See also David Kathka, "The Italian Experience in Wyoming," in *Peopling the High Plains*, 68–94, esp. 68, 88. See also Larson, *History of Wyoming*, 412.

10. Residency analysis, Sweetwater County Census, 1880, 1900, 1910. Liberalization of homestead law made the arid plains of Wyoming more attractive to ranchers and dryland farmers: In 1909, the Mondell Revisory bill enlarged claims from 160 to 320 acres if the claim was filed on arid lands. In 1912, Congress reduced the residency requirement on claims from five to three years. And in 1916, grazing homesteads of 640 acres became available. See Larson, *History of Wyoming*, 362, 385.

The Carey Act also spurred agricultural settlement of high-plains desert by encouraging large-scale irrigation projects through donation by the federal government of up to 1 million acres of arid land to each state willing to direct corporate reclamation of such lands. A Carey Act irrigation project was organized in Sweetwater County in 1905 to divert portions of the Big Sandy River into Eden Valley. By 1909, Eden Land and Irrigation Company began attracting homesteaders, and by 1914 the company had completed a reservoir and forty-five miles of canals. See Larson, *History of Wyoming*, 303–6; Wright and Wright, *Our Valley*, 1–9; and "Eden Irrigation Project Is Sold," *Rock Springs Miner*, 13 August 1926.

11. Immigration historians have found a variety of patterns of ethnic settlement throughout the West, from residentially cohesive ethnic enclaves to transient, ethnically mixed neighborhoods. Not surprisingly, there is considerable debate about the significance of ethnic community as a cultural force in immigrants' lives. John Bodnar, for example, suggested a flexible definition of ethnic community in a broad study of urban immigrants from 1830 to 1930. Surveying both eastern and western cities, Bodnar argued against the concept of insulated ethnic ghettos as a given in urban life. Rejecting both cultural and structural determinism, Bodnar presented immigrants as individuals who mediated between ethnic tradition, economic reality, and political opportunity in order to meet "the central requirement in their lives: to secure the welfare and well-being of their familial or household base" (xvii). This led to a variety of strategies for survival and a variety of conflicting interests within ethnic groups. Indeed, Bodnar argued that the family, not the ethnic community, was the locus of support for the individual. See Bodnar, *The Transplanted: A History of Immigrants in Urban America* (Bloomington: Indiana University Press, 1985).

In a study of Italo-American women in northern California, Micaela di Leonardo found that Italian immigrants did not uniformly create "urban villages" in which women replicated their old world roles. Rather, in response to the regional economy and demographics of northern California, Italian women there developed familial patterns and occupational strategies different from those of their eastern metropolitan sisters. See di Leonardo, "The Myth of the Urban

Village: Women, Work and Family among Italian-Americans in Twentieth-Century California," in *Women's West*, 277–89.

Similarly, in a study of Irish immigrants in Butte, Montana, David Emmons demonstrated the significance of regional economy and settlement patterns in shaping ethnic identity and community. While divisions surfaced between Irish mine owners, workers, and managers, class tensions were somewhat mitigated by their shared ethnic identity as well as by the relatively high wage and steady work typical of Butte's copper industry during the late nineteenth century. At the same time, Irish labor developed a strong working-class identity, bonded by the profound physical hazards of subsurface mining. Over time, changes in the copper industry and the arrival of other European immigrants fragmented Butte's "labor aristocracy," and Irish labor lost power. See Emmons, *The Butte Irish: Class and Ethnicity in an American Mining Town* (Urbana: University of Illinois Press, 1989).

For further discussion of ethnic identity and community in the United States, see Henry B. Leonard, "American Immigration: An Historiographical Essay," *Ethnic Forum* (1987): 9–23; and James Barrett, "Americanization from the Bottom Up: Immigration and the Remaking of the Working Class in the United States, 1880–1930," *Journal of American History* 79, no. 3 (December 1992): 996–1020. The only consensus seems to be that ethnic communities, multilayered and sometimes deeply divided, varied in their significance to newcomers as a cultural resource.

12. "Rock Springs, That Grew Into a Great City," *UP History*, 46–55, esp. 46–47.

13. Census manuscripts show the ethnic diversity of working-class neighborhoods. Typically, any street inhabited by miners and their families showed household-by-household variations in ethnicity. Consider Ninth Street in Rock Springs, 1910. The first household was inhabited by Americans, the one beside it by Slovaks, the next two by Slovenes, the next three by British, the next by Americans, and the next by Germans. Sweetwater County census, 1910, "Ninth Street," Rock Springs. The 1900 census shows the same pattern of ethnically mixed neighborhoods in mining towns. For example, in the "Great Flat" area in Rock Springs, 1900, miners and their families lived in rental (company) housing. The first house was inhabited by Italians, the next by Austrians, the next by Norwegians, the next by Finns, the two beside that by Italians, and the three following that by Danes. See Sweetwater County census, 1900, Rock Springs, South Side Precinct, sheet 19, "Great Flat."

14. Residential and ethnicity analysis of adult men and women, Sweetwater County census, 1900, 1910. Out of 654 town dwellers sampled, 432 were foreign-born, or 66.05 percent. "Forty-one nationalities are represented here," boasted the short description of Rock Springs in the *Wyoming State Business Directory* (Denver, Colo.: Gazetteer Publishing Co., 1921), 358. Analysis of sex and marital status for adult residents, Sweetwater County census, 1910.

15. Interview, Louise Luzan Leskovec by Ann Burns and Nancy Cranford, Rock Springs, 15 November 1976 (Cheyenne: WSAHD), OH-557. Interview, Helen Korich Krmpotich by Burns and Cranford, Rock Springs, 16 February 1977 (Cheyenne: WSAHD), OH-555.

16. Interviews, Leskovec and Krmpotich. Interview, Mary Jesersek Taucher by Burns and Cranford, Rock Springs, 4 December 1976 (Cheyenne: WSAHD), OH-570. See also Stinneford, "Mines and Miners," 126–27; and Carlos Schwantes, "The Concept of the Wage Workers' Frontier: A Framework for Future Research," *Western Historical Quarterly* 18 (January 1987): 39–55. "As late as the eve of World War I," wrote Schwantes, "it was common to find . . . miners living in Montana one month and Nevada or Arizona the next" (46). Wyoming was no exception to this rule.

To do a demographic analysis of Sweetwater County, I took a random sample of one hundred households for each census year: 1880, 1900, and 1910. Because the random sample did not always yield the same streets from one census year to the next, I could not check for residential persistence. Nevertheless, evidence from oral histories and secondary works on coal mining in the Intermountain West points consistently to the transience of neighborhoods in Union Pacific coal towns.

17. A. Dudley Gardner and Verla Flores, *Forgotten Frontier: A History of Wyoming Coal Mining* (Boulder, Colo.: Westview Press, 1989), 107. See also Larson, *History of Wyoming*, 109–11, 378–80.

18. Interview, Leskovec; interview, Dorothy Pivik by Burns and Cranford, Rock Springs, 16 February 1977 (Cheyenne: WSAHD). Leskovec noted that company housing encouraged a mix of nationalities in the neighborhoods. Pivik described saloonkeepers' efforts to help newcomers find room and board with a family of the same nationality. See also Stinneford, "Mines and Miners," 125.

19. Bodnar, *Transplanted*, 178.

20. In 1900, east Europeans composed only 12.3 percent of the foreign-born population. British, Germans, and Scandinavians composed the largest ethnic groups at this time. Ethnicity analysis of adult men and women, Sweetwater County census, 1900. However, by 1910, the proportion of east Europeans had more than doubled. At 29.9 percent of the foreign-born population, east Europeans outnumbered immigrants from Great Britain (17.4 percent), the Scandinavian countries (28.9 percent), Germany (28.9 percent), France and Belgium (3.8 percent), Italy (1.5 percent), and a handful of other nationalities. Ethnicity analysis of adult men and women, Sweetwater County census, 1910. Although the proportion of Germans and Scandinavians nearly equaled that of east Europeans in 1910, German and Scandinavian immigration was dropping off, while east European immigration was on the rise. Between 1910 and 1920, Wyoming saw the largest increase in east Europeans ever because of political and military unrest in the Balkans. Indeed, during that decade, immigration from east Europe more than tripled, from 825 in 1910 to 2,671 in 1920. See Stinneford, "Mines and Miners," 124, table 1.

21. Ethnicity analysis, Sweetwater County census, 1900, 1910. East European nationalities appeared on census manuscripts under a variety of labels, some of them invented by the enumerator. Croatians, for example, were occasionally listed as "Austrian Croatians," Slovenes as "Austrian Slovenian," and Hungarians as "Magyar," or "Austrian-Hungarian." I am indebted to Frederick Skinner, professor of Russian and eastern European history at the University of Montana, who helped me to properly identify which ethnic groups were represented by the more puzzling entries.

Between 1910 and 1930, southern Slavs composed the largest group of eastern Europeans in Wyoming. During this period, 2,842 southern Slavs migrated to Wyoming as compared with 1,148 Poles, 1,040 Czechs, and 961 Hungarians. See Stinneford, "Mines and Miners," 124, table 1.

22. In using the term "southern Slav" as shorthand for Serbian, Slovenian, and Croatian, I do not assume that these ethnic groups consistently shared social solidarity, particularly in light of continuing unrest in the region formerly known as Yugoslavia. The evidence from Sweetwater County, however, suggests that in Wyoming mining towns, southern Slavs did share similar values regarding courtship and community. Moreover, it was not uncommon for Serbs, Slovenes, and Croatians to identify somewhat with each other as a common cultural group—southern Slavs—once they had immigrated to the United States. Their common bonds as working-class people meeting the challenges of adaptation to a foreign environment tended to outweigh whatever political or sectarian differences might have divided them in the old country. Finally, in the old country, a certain amount of fraternization and cooperation existed between southern Slav ethnic groups living in mountain villages. That is, as political boundaries changed, extended kin sometimes found themselves separated by new borders over which they crossed back and forth, depending upon the demands of family obligation. Conversations with Istvan Deak, professor of eastern European history, Columbia University, 19 February 1993; and Frederick Skinner, professor of Russian and eastern European history, University of Montana, 25 June 1993.

23. Interview, Leskovec; interview, Elsie Oblock Frolic by Burns and Cranford, Rock Springs, 8 January 1977 (Cheyenne: WSAHD), OH-553. See also Stinneford, "Mines and Miners," 130–31.

24. Interview, Leskovec; interview, Pivik

25. Oral history informants described several examples of valued ethnic social ties: Informal women's networks were activated by special events such as weddings, which called for communal cooking and sewing. Men, too, described informal ethnic networks centered around communal work. Rock Springs resident Henry Kovach recalled, "There would be groups of them [Slovenian men] come and help butcher a hog and they would share. [Then] a different guy would have one,

and they'd all get together and butcher his hog." Interview, Henry Kovach by Todd Horn, Rock Springs, December 1987 (Rock Springs: Archaeological Services of Western Wyoming Community College, hereafter WAS).

Southern Slavs preferred to do business at the Rock Springs Commercial Store, rather than at the Union Pacific Company Store because the Rock Springs Commercial was owned and run by a southern Slav couple. And though southern Slavs in Rock Springs shared a Catholic church with Italians, Slovaks, Czechs, and Irish, they formed their own altar society. See interviews, Krmpotich, Pivik, Leskovec, and Frolic; and interview, Margaret Metelko by Burns and Cranford, Rock Springs, 16 February 1977 (Cheyenne: WSAHD), OH-559.

26. Interview, Pivik.

27. Ibid.

28. Interview, Mary Jesersek Taucher.

29. Ibid.

30. Ibid.

31. Ibid.

32. Interview, Pivik. Louise Luzan Leskovec also remembered dating only those of the same nationality. She described "mixing more" with peers of other nationalities at school but said that even there, she "still had Slovenian boyfriends. I didn't go off with very many others." Interview, Leskovec.

33. Interview, Ann LeVar Powell by Dee Garceau, Rock Springs, 27 May 1994.

34. Interview, Mary Lou Anselmi Unguren by Dee Garceau, Rock Springs, 27 May 1994.

35. Interview, Leskovec. Also interview, Krmpotich. Helen Korich Krmpotich met her future husband when he came to visit her father. "My Dad wouldn't let us go out on dates," she said.

36. Interviews, Pivik, Leskovec, and Frolic. For description of "traditional working class dances," see Peiss, *Cheap Amusements*, 90–92. These dances "took place in an environment controlled . . . by familial supervision and community ties" (91).

37. Ibid., 93–114.

38. Interview, Frolic. See also *Wyoming Business Directory*, Green River, 244–47; Megeath, 315; Reliance, 350; South Superior, 400–401; Superior, 405–6; and Rock Springs, 358–68.

39. Interview, Marion Buchan, by Burns and Cranford, Rock Springs, 15 January 1977 (Cheyenne: WSAHD), OH-551.

40. Peiss, *Cheap Amusements*, 100–14.

41. Interview, Leskovec.

42. Of these twenty-five east European women, every one married a man of the same ethnic group: Slovenes married Slovenes, Croatians chose Croatians, Slovaks married Slovaks, and so forth. Analysis for endogamy, date of immigration, and date of marriage among foreign-born married couples, Sweetwater County census, 1910. Women who married the same year that they immigrated were not included in this sample, since those marriages might have resulted from relationships begun in the old country.

Census data from the early twentieth century indicates that first-generation eastern European immigrant women almost always married within their own ethnic group. In a study of immigrant marriage patterns using a national sample drawn from the 1910 census, Deanna Pagnini and S. Philip Morgan found that "new immigrants" from southern and eastern Europe usually married within their own ethnic group. (Only 6 percent of eastern Europeans and 2 percent of Italians outmarried.) In contrast, exogamy (marriage outside one's ethnic group) was more common among "old immigrant" groups such as the British, Irish, Germans, and Scandinavians (58 percent of British immigrants outmarried, and 36 percent of Germans did so, as did 18 percent of Scandinavians). See Deanna Pagnini and S. Philip Morgan, "Intermarriage and Social Distance among U.S. Immigrants at the Turn of the Century," *American Journal of Sociology* 96 (September 1990): 405–32.

Sweetwater County echoed the national pattern in that the majority of "new immigrant" women married men of the same nationality. Among the ninety-eight foreign-born women who emigrated while single, then married after settling in the United States, eighty, or 81.6 percent, married within their ethnic group. Among the eighteen remaining who outmarried, all were matches between "old immigrants" (e.g., British/German) or between Americans and "old immigrants" (e.g., American/British, American/German). The difference between Pagnini and Morgan's national sample and my Sweetwater County sample lies in interpretation. Pagnini and Morgan hypothesized that endogamy among "new immigrants" was due primarily to residential and occupational segregation and secondarily to xenophobia on the part of "old immigrants" toward those whose language, customs, and appearance differed more dramatically from Anglo culture. In Sweetwater County coal towns, however, there was neither residential nor occupational segregation. Working-class neighborhoods were ethnically mixed; so too was labor in the mines. My interpretation, elaborated in this article, is that endogamy reflected efforts to build and maintain ethnic community in an environment where it did not exist residentially.

For accounts of marriage within one's ethnic group among southern Slavs after 1910, see interviews, Pivik, Leskovec, Krmpotich, and Frolic, and interview, Anna Sulentich by Amy Peterson, Rock Springs, 1977 (Cheyenne: WSAHD), OH-569.

43. Southern Slav oral history informants shared numerous stories of mutual aid among kinfolk. Interviews, Krmpotich, Metelko, Taucher, and Leskovec; interview, Pat Huntley LeFaivre by Dee Garceau, Green River, 26 May 1994. Among historians, the importance of family networks to immigrant survival is widely recognized. For discussion of major works on immigrant women's roles within traditions of mutual aid among relatives, see Stella DeRosa Torgoff, "Immigrant Women, the Family, and Work: 1850-1950," *Trends in History* 2, no. 4 (1980): 31-47. Torgoff observed that "despite differing emphases on continuity or change, there is general agreement among immigrant historians that the family played a crucial role in cushioning the immigrants' first years in the new world" (39). For more recent discussion of this topic, see Bodnar, *Transplanted*, xv-xxi, and Emmons, *Butte Irish*, 27-29.

44. Interview, Krmpotich. A husband's search for work almost always took place within an ethnic network. That is, ethnic workingmen stayed within the ethnic pipeline in their travels; hence endogamous marriage was important to them too. See John Bodnar, *Worker's World: _inship, Community, and Protest in an Industrial Society, 1900-1940* (Baltimore: Johns Hopkins Press, 1982).

45. Elinore Bastalich Tolar recalled that her Croatian grandfather refused to live with his brothers "because they had married English women" when they settled in Wyoming coal towns. Rejection by extended family meant significant loss of informal networks of support. Interview, Elinore Tolar by Glenn Biggs, Reliance, 1988 (Rock Springs: WAS). Also interview, Joe Melinkovich by Percilla Martin, 28 October 1991 (WAS). Melinkovich emphasized that during the 'teens and 'twenties, southern Slavs customarily married within their own nationality.

46. Mary Jesersek Taucher's story is typical. As a child in rural Slovenia, she shared the burden of household support. When Mary was seven years old, a poor harvest left the family impoverished. "So I went from my home to work at this family, at another farm. . . . I worked there for seven years . . . to help my family and myself." Interview, Taucher. Studies of Slavic immigrants in eastern cities during the same period also document the existence of a familial culture of mutual obligation. See Laura Anker, "Women, Work and Family: Polish, Italian, and Eastern European Immigrants in Industrial Connecticut, 1890-1940," *Polish-American Studies* 45, no. 2 (1988): 23-49; and JoAnne Schneider, "Patterns for Getting By: Polish Women's Employment in Delaware County, PA, 1900-1930," *Pennsylvania Magazine of History and Biography* (October 1990): 517-41.

For discussion of the relationship between developing capitalism in Europe and the nature of family reciprocity, see Anker, "Women, Work and Family," 25-29. By the early twentieth century, east European "peasant and artisanal households had been increasingly drawn into a complex nexus of market relationships." As wages became increasingly necessary, both to buy goods no longer produced at home and to pay property taxes, the ethic of family reciprocity increasingly mandated leaving home in search of wage work. In many cases, migration to the United States was an extension of the job search motivated by family obligation.

47. For further discussion of how kin ties linked family members to jobs, housing, nursing, welfare, and emotional support in the new country, see John Bodnar's study of southern Slav mining families in the East, "Family and Community in Pennsylvania's Anthracite Region, 1900–1940," *Pennsylvania Heritage* (Summer 1983): 13–17.

48. In coal mines alone, between 1900 and 1940, 1,748 men were killed in explosions in the Intermountain West, most of them within the first twenty-five years. H. B. Humphrey, *Historical Summary of Coal Mine Explosions in the United States, 1810–1958* (Washington, D.C.: U.S. Government Printing Office, 1960), 17, 22, 38–41.

49. Interview, Krmpotich.

50. Ibid.

51. Interview, Krmpotich.

52. Gladys Spitz narrative, in *Calico Hill: Recalling the Early Years, Good Times, and Hardships of Homesteaders*, ed. The Jolly Dry Farmers Club (Cheyenne: Pioneer Printing, 1973), 44. See also interview, Dorothy Austin Higginson by Dennis Roe, Green River, 12 February 1977 (Cheyenne: WSAHD), OH-543.

53. Mae E. Mickelson, "The Life of a Southwestern Wyoming Cowboy and His Wife," *Bits and Pieces: Your Own Western History Magazine* (October 1969): 13–14.

54. Other narratives from rural Wyoming reinforce this impression. Dorothy Austin Higginson met her future husband when he stayed several days at her family's ranch while trading calves with her father and grandfather. During that stay, she enjoyed unsupervised time with young Higginson, on several occasions for hours at a time. See interview, Higginson.

Similarly, Helen Coburn and Mary Culbertson, single women homesteaders in Worland, Wyoming, 1905–1908, went on day-long buggy trips with their respective boyfriends. See interview, Helen Coburn and Mary Culbertson by L.L.H., 26 June 1936 (Cheyenne: WSAHD), WPA MSS-798. Fern Dumbrill Spencer also recorded unchaperoned time with the young man who courted her during a two-week Christmas house party. See Fern Dumbrill Spencer, "A Woman's Memoirs of Homesteading," appendix to Charles Floyd Spencer, *Wyoming Homestead Heritage* (Hicksville, N.Y.: Exposition Press, 1975), 175–99.

55. From a sample of 136 rural adults, 1880–1910, 72.8 percent were native-born (99 out of 136); 27.2 percent were foreign-born (37 out of 136); and 1.4 percent were Native American (2 out of 136). Among native-born rural residents, 41.4 percent came from the Midwest; 15.2 percent from the Northeast, 14.1 percent from the South; and 29.3 percent from the Far West. Ethnicity analysis of rural men and women over age 15, Sweetwater County census, 1880, 1900, 1910.

56. Of the foreign-born rural residents, 91.99 percent came from Great Britain. Ethnicity analysis, rural adult men and women, Sweetwater County census, 1880, 1900, 1910. English outnumbered Irish settlers in the ranching community by about two to one. All but two of the Irish women were married to American men. None of the homesteaders' narratives mention outbreaks of hostility between English and Irish ranchers, which suggests that within the rural agricultural milieu, assimilation or common economic struggles transcended any residual ethnic conflict.

57. Interview, Helen Coburn Howell by L.L.H., 26 June 1936 (Cheyenne: WSAHD), WPA MSS-798, 9–10.

58. Mrs. Nathan Hodson narrative, in Wright and Wright, *Our Valley*, 143.

59. "The Wild, Rippling Water," author unknown; words and music in Austin Fife, *Cowboy and Western Songs* (Logan: Utah State University, 1967), 7.

60. "Bucking Broncho," author unknown; lyrics in WPA Wyoming Folksong Collection (Cheyenne: WSAHD), WPA MSS-261.

61. "I'll Give You My Story," author unknown. Folksinger Rosalie Sorrels learned this song from Dick Person of Cascade, Idaho. See p. 3, album insert, *Folksongs of Idaho and Utah*, ed. and annot. by Kenneth Goldstein (New York: Folkways Records, 1961).

62. Interview with Jerrine Stewart Wire by Dee Garceau, Croyden, Penn., 23 March 1986.

63. Ibid.

64. Ibid.

14

Euskaldun Andreak: Basque Women As Hard Workers, Hoteleras, and Matriarchs

JERONIMA ECHEVERRIA

To the topics of courtship and marriage discussed in the previous article, Jeronima Echeverria adds the closely related topic of women's work. The Basques, one of the smaller European ethnic groups, found their distinctive occupational niche in the U.S. West in sheepherding, a famously solitary and male activity. But sheepherders depended on a support network in which women's work was vital. Echeverria shows that a key institution, the Basque boardinghouse, functioned as a way to recruit women's labor through marriage. Single Basque immigrant women found suitable marriage partners at the ostatuak *and subsequently performed prodigious amounts of work to keep the boardinghouses and the wider Basque network going. Because of the patriarchal nature of Basque society, most women's work remained invisible and unacknowledged, with the rare exception of the occasional "matriarch" who achieved recognition in this visibly unequal system.*

The distinctiveness of the Basque gender system in comparison with that of other European immigrant ethnic groups reminds us that "Euro-American" is a generic term that we need to use carefully. Equally important is the evidence that Basque women were devoted to maintaining their original culture in the American West, no matter how exploitative it appeared to outside observers. Echeverria's examination of the centrality of women to the Basque boardinghouses offers a valuable gendered perspective on the immigrant experience by clearly showing the links among kinship, work, and culture.

In the spring of 1913, shortly after their marriage, Francisco and Dominica Landa walked to a small hilltop fifteen miles outside of the sleepy little town of Brea, California. There the two Basque immigrants decided to build their home. By the end of the year, they had dug out the cellar by hand, framed and constructed the tiny kitchen and bedroom, put a sheep corral and ramada on the hill, and moved their flocks to the site.[1] Though numerous stories outlived the Landas, one always caught my attention. This tale described Dominica as she tirelessly shoveled, loaded, and carted wheelbarrows full of sheep manure to a pickup truck while Francisco looked on from his favorite siesta spot under the old shaded ramada. Having filled the truckbed, she nodded and waved in Francisco's direction, climbed into the rig, drove to town, sold the manure to local citrus farmers for fertilizer, and returned to prepare the evening meal— only to find Francisco sleeping in the ramada.[2] At this point in the tale, those listening usually chuckled, and, after a pause, the storyteller would nod in my direction, "What a hard worker your grandmother was."

Though Dominica and Francisco would not have recognized it at the time, their individual accounts of immigrating to the United States, as well as the disparity between their workloads, was quite representative of Basques arriving near the turn of the century. Like the majority of other Basques reaching the western United States between 1890 and 1940, Francisco and Dominica were born and raised on rural *baserriak*, or farmsteads, in the Pyrenees Mountains between Spain and France. There they developed a high regard for self-sufficiency and an understanding that those who did not inherit must move on as soon as they reached adolescence or young adulthood. As Dominica Layana reached this point in her life, she considered invitations from siblings in southern California. When her sister Martina expressed interest in joining her, the two asked their father to accompany them from Juarietta, Navarra, to the French frontier. Just over the mountains, they caught a train that took them to the port of Bayonne. Ten years earlier, on an Abaurea Alta farm eight kilometers from Juarietta, young Francisco Landa had made the same decision and had walked the same path over the Pyrenees.

Dominica and Francisco arrived in California during peak migratory years in Basque American history. Though small concentrations of Basques emerged throughout the eleven western states in the nineteenth century, by 1890 more first-, second-, and third-generation *Euskaldunak* lived in Los Angeles than in any other city or town in the United States.[3] When Francisco arrived in 1901, he encountered a thriving "Basque town" in the Alameda and Aliso Street neighborhood of Los Angeles, as did Dominica when she arrived in 1911. From 1880 through the late 1930s, Los Angeles–area Basques gathered in the *ostatuak* (Basque boardinghouses) clustered within that geographically compact district.[4]

A half-century before Francisco and Dominica struck out for Los Angeles, their forefathers who had emigrated to South America and Mexico responded to the magnetic call of California's gold mines. Soundest estimates of Basque immigrants to California between 1849 and 1852 place the number at several hundred. Basque passengers embarking in Valparaiso for San Francisco between 1849 and 1852, for example, tallied 170.[5] While these numbers are small when compared with those of larger immigrant groups, they represent a drastic increase in California's Basque population within a brief three-year period.

Direct participation in gold mining among Basques was relatively short-lived, however. When their luck with the sluice boxes and gold pans failed, they turned to a lucrative ancillary industry and established a chain migration system that would reach into the twentieth century. Since food for hungry miners was often scarce and prices high, a handful of Basques began trailing sheep into the Sierra Nevadas where lambs could be sold for as much as fifteen to twenty dollars per head. Eventually California sheep raising expanded onto cattle lands, gradually surpassing beef production. Additional factors contributed to the growth of California's sheep industry over the next decades, such as the ability of sheep to survive semiarid pasture better than cattle, open grazing on public domain, the improved quality of merino wool, and a ready market for wool products as a consequence of reduced cotton production after the Civil War.[6]

Altogether, opportunities in the California sheep industry could scarcely have been better choreographed for Basques disappointed with their luck in the goldfields. From their experience in the Pampas, they carried with them a knowledge of open-range herding practices that they instituted in California's central corridor and eventually expanded into the eleven western states. By 1890 the basic migratory pattern of Basques within the United States had shifted. Whereas in the 1850s the tide had originated in San Francisco and moved eastward, by the 1890s it had taken on a powerful east-to-west flow.[7]

Recent immigration statistics indicate interesting trends among Basques who arrived in New York in the five-year period from 1897 through 1902. Of the 636 names in the population studied, 86 percent were male and 77 percent were single. Although of varied ages, 65 percent of the men ranged between sixteen and thirty. And 464 of the 636 were Spanish Basque rather than French Basque. A clear pattern emerges: Most Basque immigrants during this period were young unmarried males from Spain.[8]

This pattern was also evident in Marie Pierre Arrizabalaga's comparative study of the censuses of 1900 and 1910. From her data, one can also conclude that Basque Americans have always been and continue to be a relatively small ethnic group. In 1900, when the number of Basques in *Euskal herria* (the Basque region) was 1,084,616, only 986 were living in California, Nevada, Idaho and Wyoming. Ten years later, the Old World Basque population was 1,160,023 while Basques living in the four western states numbered 8,398. Basque Americans in the West represented less than 0.01 percent of the total Basque population in 1900, but had increased ten years later to 0.7 percent, revealing a dramatic surge in Basque migration between 1900 and 1910.[9]

In departing Navarra's Valley of Baztan and arriving in Los Angeles's "Basque town," Francisco Landa and Dominica Layana followed the path of thousands of their compatriots. They also selected the livelihoods that siblings, neighbors, and cousins had described in letters home. Francisco herded sheep until he could buy his own herd; Dominica served as house girl and cleaning woman until they married. And, like so many other *Euskaldunak* before them, they relied upon the Basque boardinghouses to ease their transition and meet prospective mates.

Basque boardinghouses have been closely linked to the expansions and contractions of the sheep industry in the American West. For the single Basque sheepmen who came to earn their fortune before returning to the Basque homeland, and for the single Basque women who came to work in the *ostatuak* as serving girls and maids, the boardinghouse became home away from home. In the absence of a New World family setting, the *ostatuak* became the major social institution of Basques in the American West, for it was in the *ostatuak* that these newly arrived found work; spoke their native *Euskara*; ate familiar foods; stored their bedrolls, Sunday suits and camp gear; received mail; and arranged for interpreters to help them understand "American ways."

It should be noted that other ethnic groups have hosted boardinghouses that, in some cases, share similarities with the *ostatuak*. But because non-Basques were less dependent upon their boardinghouses for arranging jobs, travel assistance, and in-town translation, it could be said that Basque boardinghouses were unique among ethnic boardinghouses. In addition, *hoteleros* clung to a "Basques-only" policy whenever possible, developed strong ties with the Basque-dominated sheep industry, and during peak years actively supported their clients' resistance to "Americanize."

Basque *ostatuak* dotted the western landscape from Montana to New Mexico and then west to the Pacific Ocean. Small communities, such as Yakima, Washington, Jordan Valley, Oregon, and Ogden, Utah, at one time had sufficiently large Basque colonies to host *ostatuak*. Some observers have suggested that a boardinghouse would open about five years after the appearance of the first Basque in a critical sheep-raising town, with two or more to follow within a decade.[10] In the nineteenth and early twentieth century, Basque-owned boardinghouses were rare. Even though their customers thought of them as proprietors, *hoteleros* usually gathered just enough seed money to sign a lease and launch the enterprise.

Whether leasing or owning, the *hoteleros* and their *ostatuak* served important functions for the Basque American family. Wives living on remote ranches would come into town to stay during the last stages of their pregnancies and frequently gave birth there. Not uncommonly, outlying Basque ranchers sent their children to the boardinghouses during the school year. Moreover, special occasions such as marriages, family celebrations, dances, and wakes often took place in the *ostatuak*. And so frequently did Basques meet their future husbands and wives at the *ostatuak* that they have been referred to as "marriage mills."[11]

Nor is it surprising that Francisco Landa and Dominica Layana met at Ignacio Mayo's boardinghouse shortly after her arrival in Los Angeles.[12] Dominica and her sister had been instructed to rent a room at the 610 Alameda *ostatu* and to wait there for their brother to meet them. Since the Mayos hosted a predominantly Navarran Basque clientele, Francisco always stopped in there when he was in town. Because Ignacio and his wife introduced the two Navarrans, and because so many of their Old World neighbors came to the *ostatu*, much of their courtship took place at Mayo's. In April of 1913, the two were married by the Basque priest Father Dominic Zaldivar a few blocks from "Basque town" in the Old Plaza Church.

At Mayo's the Landas met, courted, were engaged, and spent their first two weeks as newlyweds. Just as that boardinghouse was vital to their early days together, so too were *hoteleros* crucial to the success of their *ostatuak*. Hotelkeepers were called upon to represent both Old and New Worlds, serving as interpreters of American culture for the newly arrived while providing a sense of Old World heritage for the New World Basques and their children. In essence, they had to win the trust of the Old World Basques while accommodating the demands of the younger generations as well.

Very rarely was a hotelkeeper alone able to manage an *ostatu*. More often, a husband-and-wife team operated the hotel with the occasional assistance of other family members. Traditionally, he ran the bar from morning until closing while she supervised the preparation of noon and evening meals, the serving girls who waited tables, and the *criadas* (cleaning girls or maids) who maintained the rooms. If business was good and there was ample demand, hotelkeepers hired additional bartenders, serving girls, *criadas*, and cooks. If the couple could not afford additional help, the two did the work themselves.

Generally speaking, an Old World–born Basque male and an American-born Basque female formed the "perfect" hotelkeeping couple. With this combination, the first-generation client could share common Old World concerns with the *hotelero* in their native *Euskara* but turn to the *hotelera* when he needed assistance with New World dilemmas. She was generally the more familiar with "American ways" and could serve as translator, escort, and advisor. Among eleven sets of *hoteleros* interviewed by Jean DeCroos, for example, nine were Old World Basques and a majority had married New World Basques.[13]

A majority of Basque women prearranged living with family members or former neighbors from the *Euskal herria*. Because they were often the old country's disenfranchised or poor, they generally came in need of work and most often found it in the boardinghouses and ranches of the American West. In these settings, the domestic chores of cleaning, cooking, and serving were reminiscent of *Euskal herria* where women rarely worked outside the home. In addition, a convincing majority of newly arrived Basque women met their husbands while working at or attending dances and social functions at local *ostatuak*. In fact, of the 150 Basque subjects I have interviewed, about 85 percent met their spouses in the boardinghouses.[14] Such high "marrying-in" ratios among first- and second-generation Basques can be explained in part by language, for a majority of them spoke *Euskara* exclusively upon arrival.

During their courtship in Los Angeles, Dominica and Francisco became friends with many *hoteleros*. In addition to the Mayos, they often visited with Pierre and Marie Sorcabal who owned the Oyamburu Hotel, as well as with the Urrutys and the Bengocheas on Aliso Street.[15] They would have witnessed a disparity between male and female work distribution in these hotels. As one male resident of "Basque town" reported decades later, "the women who worked in those hotels—like my mother—were slaves."[16] Seventy years later, her octagenarian son angrily recalled details of Marie Sorcabal's arduous and extended daily schedule. For her, work began around five with the preparation of sack lunches and breakfast for schoolchildren and the boarders who worked in town. Between breakfast and the main midday meal, she cleaned rooms, purchased groceries, washed linens, set the tables, ran errands, and prepared a feast for dozens. After lunch, there was the customary cleaning, unfinished chores from the morning, boarders to translate for in town, and dinner to cook. After dinner, there was more cleanup, resetting tables, socializing with friends and customers in the bar, a few dances in front of the Victrola and, on special occasions, a late-night omelette prepared for friends just after closing time.

Of course, many *hoteleras* hired Basque girls to help them cope with this incredible daily routine. If the business could not bear the additional expense, however, she was expected to handle all details related to cleaning, cooking, serving, translating, and caretaking on her own. His responsibility was to orchestrate the barroom, cardroom, and *cancha* (handball) activities. Though the *hotelero*'s networking with clientele could be key to the success of the business enterprise, there is no contesting a disparity in the distribution of physical labor. In the case of the Sorcabals' boardinghouse, for example, Pierre hired an additional bartender years before Marie hired a serving girl.

As in the *ostatuak*, Basque women on ranches also worked extended hours. They prepared and served meals to family and ranchhands, cleaned dishes, darned clothing, raised gardens, tended to children, canned vegetables and foodstuffs in the summer, and made chorizo and blood sausage in the springtime. On more than a few occasions, Basque women conducted these activities from sheep-camp tents—which meant cooking over open fires, baking underground with campfire coals, roasting on spits, and laundering clothes on washboards along riversides.[17] Later, when the herds expanded and their husbands prospered, these women enjoyed the comparative luxury of two- and three-bedroom ranch houses, but they generally continued with strenuous daily tasks nonetheless. Extended work schedules similar to those on ranches and *ostatuak* could be found among Basque women working alongside their husbands in the laundries and bakeries of San Francisco, Bakersfield, and Stockton.

In the spring of 1913, then, as Dominica and Francisco set out to establish their sheep ranch, they were also beginning to re-create work patterns that they had witnessed in Los Angeles and that they would have found developing for Basque men and women throughout the American West. As Gretchen Holbert recognized while interviewing Nevada *hoteleros* and as Paquita Garatea discovered in eastern Oregon, Basque wives often worked longer and tougher hours than their husbands.[18] Nearly forty years after I first heard renditions of Dominica and Francisco's story, I realized that the lighthearted storyteller was masking the unequal distribution of labor between my grandmother and grandfather rather than complimenting my grandmother for her "hard-working" nature.

About 85 percent of my interviews with boardinghouse keepers have been with women. Interestingly, *hoteleras* rarely claim that they worked longer hours or had tougher tasks than their husbands. When asked about division of work in the boardinghouses, these women most often focus on their dedication to the success of their business and their family. When directly asked whether they worked harder than their husbands, many replied, "Well, we were both there the same amount . . . after all, we lived there . . . but I probably did have more to do." Ironically, the sons, friends, and employees of *hoteleras* are more likely to report the disparity in the workloads between the hotelkeeping couple. It is interesting to note that when *hoteleras did* state that they worked harder or longer hours than their husbands, they always asked not to be quoted. Thus, the *hoteleras* have bowed to the stereotypical gender hierarchy found in other families.[19]

In *Open Country, Iowa*, Deborah Fink outlined three modes of women's work relating the household and market.[20] In the first case, women labored on the farm to help sustain the family, perhaps raising crops, milking cows, tending chickens, and preserving food items. In the second, women worked within the house to produce goods—such as cloth, butter, or perserves—in exchange for products outside of the home. In the third, the women toiled outside the home in order to earn money to help support the household. Basque *hoteleras* related to their markets in a combination of all three strategies. They raised crops, hogs, chickens, and cattle for their kitchens; they sewed for their customers and families; and they traded for goods not found in the *ostatuak*. Finally, they lived with their families in their workplace.

Hotelkeeping could be difficult for the families running the boardinghouses. In one interview, a *hotelera* stated that in the hotels "there was no room for weakness" and the daily demands of cleaning, cooking, and serving interfered with family cohesion. Another interviewee stated that during the years she and her husband owned a hotel, they never "got away together." In addition, a child of a hotelkeeper reported angrily that "we kids never wanted to run a hotel when we grew up. . . . [Y]our front room was always a bar."[21]

Rigorous daily schedules and the strains upon family life undoubtedly contributed to hotel operators' relatively brief tenure in business. In fact, *hoteleros* rarely remained in business beyond fifteen or twenty years, if that long.[22] The fatiguing morning-to-night work hours in part explain the short term of hotel ownership. In addition, *ostatuak* rarely passed successfully to second-generation family members. In all but a handful of cases among the eleven western states, the second generation was too far removed from the Old World villages, the sheep camp, and the natal language to continue the family business. Moreover, there are no cases where a Basque woman opened and operated a boardinghouse independently. Some *hoteleras* did so for a few months while their husbands were out on the range, some inherited the enterprise from their parents, and some took over after the deaths of their husbands. But such arrangements were seasonal or short-lived, as they were untenable on a full-time basis. Just as very few female-owned farms appear in studies of rural America, so too do very few female-owned *ostatuak*.[23]

Certainly, *Euskaldun andreak* (Basque women) played a greater role in the survival of early communities than Basque American literature suggests. All too often, such literature features the "lonely Basque shepherd" who roamed the American West with his band of sheep. While it is true that a majority of Basques arriving at the turn of the century intended to herd for a few years and then return to *Euzkadi*, it is not true for all of them. Many remained and married girls from villages in Bizkaia, Gipuzkua, and their home provinces, planting roots in the Great Basin region and other western states, just as Francisco and Dominica did.[24]

The Basque shepherd needed an elaborate support system in order to succeed. As I have stated, the Basque *ostatuak* and the hotel network were critical factors in the newcomer's transition to America.[25] This was especially true in the earliest decades of Basque immigration to the United States, say from 1860 through 1910. Beyond those years, however, we have witnessed the settling of Basque immigrants. Those young Basque bachelors began to find sweethearts, marry, and raise children. But they did not stop herding sheep. Some set up homes and *ostatuak* in town and went out to herd in the mountains on a seasonal basis, as was the case of Dominique and Marie Laxalt. In *Sweet Promised Land* and *The Hotel*, their son described how his mother stepped in to run family business matters, discipline children, operate a small hotel in Carson City, and generally keep things going while his father was away in the sheep camps.[26] His account is reminiscent of another study of women's work in a fishing village in the old country. In that study, Charlotte Crawford describes the responsibilities that wives take on as their fishermen leave for the five-month cod season.[27] In each of these chronicles, Basque women had a great deal of responsibility—if not partnership—with their husbands.

Other authors have suggested an elevated interpretation for Basque women in Old World Basque society. The anthropological and socio-logical studies of Teresa del Valle, Jacqueline Urla, and Roslyn Frank suggest that Basque women play a much more important role in family development, financial matters, and societal development than that with which they have been credited. In so many words, the Old World *andreak* are much more powerful than they seem.[28]

This correction in the record seems accurate for Basque American women as well. In some communities, Basque women in key positions have taken on an almost larger-than-life position. For example, in the Bakersfield Basque colony Graciana (Grace) Elizalde's legacy is enor-mous. At the age of twenty she arrived in Tehachapi, California, to work as a maid in a hotel owned by family friends from her home town of Anhaux.[29] There, at the old Franco-American Hotel, she met Jean Elizalde who had come to California in 1905 under the sponsorship of his uncle Jean Burubeltz. Grace and Jean married, and when they lost their flocks in the crash of 1929, Grace went to work at the Old Commercial Hotel in Tehachapi. After two years there, the Elizaldes moved to Bakersfield where they leased the Noriega Hotel in late 1931.

Bakersfield Basques rarely fail to remember at least one of Grace's kindnesses. In part, the number of "Mama Elizalde" stories may be due to Grace's unusually long forty-two-year stay at the Noriega. But more to the point, her compassionate actions left a legacy for local hotelkeepers. Whether buying a large burial plot in the local cemetery for bachelor herders, tending to the needs of infirm boarders, or making a quiet loan to a local rancher, Grace seems to have touched most Bakersfield Basques. If an elderly boarder needed special care or bathing, Grace would climb the stairs and harass the old-timer until she succeeded in getting him to take care of himself. Oftentimes, she gave or loaned herders suits of clothing to wear on special occasions such as funerals, weddings, and baptisms. Because she never learned to drive but still insisted on helping others whenever needed, her kitchen help and her children knew they needed to be ready at any moment to drop whatever they were doing and drive her on her errands of mercy.

On one occasion, Grace decided to raise funds for one of her serving girls who was expecting her first child. Because Grace loved to gamble, she decided to set up a lottery on the sex of the child. By the time the baby girl was born, Grace had wagered over three hundred dollars, betting that the child would be female. When Grace was proven correct, she collected the money and opened a savings account in the child's name. The account funded an elaborate wedding twenty-five years later.[31]

Despite illness from cancer in her last years, Grace Elizalde managed the Noriega—and the Bakersfield Basque colony—continuously from 1931 until her death in 1974. She is still remembered in even the most casual conversations at picnics, dances, and dinners around Bakersfield. Loved by so many, she became a matriarchal figure in her community. In other Basque communities, other women have filled similar roles. In Fresno, California, for example, retired restauranteur and *hotelera* Lyda Esain enjoys a special position of respect and regard because of her sixty years of service to that Basque community. In earlier years, near my hometown, Juanita Bastanchury enjoyed the role of Orange County's Basque matriarch. In the 1920s and 1930s, her ranch was a favorite place of southern California's Basques: There they congregated, picnicked, played handball, and danced nearly every Sunday afternnon.

Grace Elizalde, Lyda Esain, and Juanita Bastanchury shared some similar characteristics. More than working long hours in an endless workweek, more even than offering invaluable support to their husbands as business partners, they extended themselves to the Basque community and made life easier for those around them. Each became "the one" that Basque men and women would go to first for help in troubled times. All three reached their eighties or beyond, all three were regarded as financially successful, and all three enjoyed extended relationships with Basque families of their areas. They became trusted advisors. In addition, local police, lawyers, politicians, and other non-Basques seeking information or advice on Basque-related issues learned to consult these "Basque senior stateswomen" before making many decisions.

While each Basque community in the West has its leaders, not every one has produced a matriarch. Nor have I yet discovered a male Basque who was trusted over decades to the degree these three women were. Rather than suggesting a lack of male leadership, this underscores the special role reserved for a few exemplary Basque women in the American West.

In a sense, the role of matriarch has been a means for Basque communities to distinguish the role of their women on both small and large scales. Not uncommonly, male and female Basques report reverence for their mothers, overt respect for their power, and confusion when comparing their perceptions of their mothers with perceptions of mothers held by non-Basques—suggesting that Basque Americans have a higher regard for women in their subculture than other Americans have of women.

There may be some cultural evidence from the old country to support such a suggestion. For example, a recent study comparing male-female gender identification between the Basque and American English languages is provocative.[32] In this study, coauthor of the *Basque-English Dictionary* Linda White demonstrates that English as spoken in the United States is much more sexist than is Basque. For example, Basques use the same third-person pronoun for he, she, and it. Depending upon dialect, they use *bera* or *hura*. There is no distinction, no orthographic change to reflect male and female in the third person. In addition, terms like "postman," "chairman," and "milkman" have no direct equivalent in Basque. For example, chairman in Basque is *mahaiburu*. This translates literally to "the head of the table," completely avoiding our American soul-searching over whether a female chair should be called chairwoman, chairperson, or chairman. Nor does Basque assign grammatical gender to nouns as do the romance languages. Those of us studying Basque do not have to agonize over whether a book is feminine or masculine, for example. It is simply *liburua*.

Since languages reflect the cultures that employ them, this less-sexist approach to labeling among Basques is somewhat encouraging. Such comparisons suggest that *Euskara* is at least linguistically less sexist than neighboring French and Spanish and American English. However, this does not mean that Old World society has been egalitarian. To paraphase the lexicographers, Basque is a less-sexist language in a sexist culture.[33]

Primogeniture (rules regarding inheritance) is a second area where Basques have been comparatively less sexist than their Anglo counterparts. In the Basque region, inheritance patterns vary slightly from village to village: The first-born child might inherit the family farmstead in one town, while the first-born son might in the next. Occasionally, the child deemed most able to operate the *baserri* will be selected upon reaching maturity. The fact that women have been deemed worthy to inherit the family farm in some areas marks Basques as relatively egalitarian when compared with other Europeans. On the Echeverria side of my family, for example, my father's oldest sister inherited our *Casa Altamira* in Arrieta, Bizkaia. And, as William Douglass has demonstrated, primogeniture decisions have influenced the settlement patterns of Basques throughout the world, often causing younger, noninheriting Basques like my father to migrate to the New World.[34]

Old World factors, such as language-born biases and primogeniture, combined with New World factors, such as challenging working conditions and the absence of husbands from the home for extended periods, created an environment in which many Basque American women thrived. Though their workloads were often trying and their efforts not always appreciated, a number of Basque American women have been able to exert quite a bit of say in their own family life, and some have held positions of leadership in their communities. My mother, for example, was an American-born Basque who co-owned a sheep ranch with my uncle while owning, operating, and managing a small cafe in town. Despite a few attempts, neither my father nor my uncle were ever able to cancel her vote in business matters. It is possible that Basque American women have enjoyed more say-so within family matters than their American counterparts because Basques have been slow to subscribe to "American ways." This view is carefully qualified, as similar factors are also at play within other American immigrant groups.

To no one's surprise, Basque women do not fit neatly into the three most common stereotypes for women in the West. Of the three offered by Beverly Stoeltje—the "refined lady," "loyal helpmate," and "bad woman"—most Basque women would feel comfortable with the "loyal helpmate." But it is difficult to fit Grace Elizalde into such a subservient-sounding category when she and women like Lyda Esain and Juanita Bastanchury actually created their own categories. And I dare say that only the most foolish Basque husband would label his wife in such a manner.

Though hard-and-fast depictions always have flaws, Basque American immigrants provide ample evidence of an unequal male-female workload near the turn of the century. Many *Euskaldun andreak* responded to greater demands than their husbands with little promise of reward or praise. Only a handful earned acknowledgment, acclaim, and status over time. In addition to working hard, as had their predecessors, these matriarchs enjoyed luck, longevity, and the appreciation of their counterparts. Still, they are representative of *Euskaldun andreak* who remain unacknowledged. Whether she realized it or not, when Dominica Landa took up the shovel to load sheep manure, she was acting out a pattern that repeated itself throughout the American West among Basque women in those peak years of immigration.

Notes

1. Jeronima Echeverria, "Ole Man Landa's Place: A Southern California Sheep Ranch," *Journal of Basque Studies in America* 10 (Summer 1990): 47–56.

2. Lorenzo Echanis and John Yturri, interview by author, Brea, Calif., 12 November 1989.

3. Marie Pierre Arrizabalaga, "A Statistical Study of Basque Immigration into California, Nevada, Idaho, and Wyoming" (master's thesis, University of Nevada, Reno, 1986), 61.

4. Jeronima Echeverria, "California-ko ostatuak: A History of California's Basque Hotels" (Ph.D. dissertation University of North Texas, 1988), 64–94; Karen J. Weitz, "Aliso Street Historical Report for the City of Los Angeles," Office of Environmental Planning, Department of Transportation, Sacramento, Calif., January 1980.

5. William A. Douglass and Jon Bilbao, *Amerikanuak: Basques in the New World* (Reno: University of Nevada Press, 1975), 209, 418–20. Calculations are based upon Santiago de Zarautz's "Pasajeros salidos de Valparaíso para California, años 1849–1852," manuscript, Basque Studies Collection, University of Nevada, Reno.

6. E. N. Wentworth and C. W. Towne, *Shepherd's Empire* (Norman: University of Oklahoma Press, 1945), 166; and Robert Glass Cleland, *Cattle on a Thousand Hills, 1850–1880* (San Marino, Calif.: Huntington Library, 1964), 140–42.

7. Craig Campbell, "The Basque-American Ethnic Area: Geographical Perspectives on Migration, Population, and Settlement," *Journal of Basque Studies* 6 (1985): 83–89.

8. Iban Bilbao and Chantal de Eguilaz, *Diaspora Vasca*, vol. 1: *Vascos llegados al puerto de Nueva York, 1897–1902* (Vitoria: Gasteiz, 1981).

9. Arrizabalaga, "Statistical Study of Basque Immigration," 40.

10. Douglass and Bilbao, *Amerikanuak*, 375. For a further discussion of the role of Basque boardinghouses as an ethnic institution, see Jeronima Echeverria, *Ostatu Amerikanuak: A History of Basque Boardinghouses* (Reno: University of Nevada Press, forthcoming).

11. Ibid., 377.

12. Sofia Landa, interview by author, Brea, Calif., 22 September 1975; and *Los Angeles City Directory 1912* (Los Angeles: Los Angeles Directory Company, 1912), 1050.

13. The "perfect couple" concept is presented in Jean DeCroos, *The Long Journey: Social Integration and Ethnicity among Urban Basques in the San Francisco Bay Region* (Reno: Associated Faculty Press and Basque Studies Program, 1983), 44–47; William A Douglass, "Home Is a Hotel," *American West* 17 (July/August 1980): 31; Douglass and Bilbao, *Amerikanuak*, 379.

14. For further discussion, see Echeverria, "California-ko ostatuak," 186–203.

15. Dominic Sorcabal, interview by author, Huntington Beach, Calif., 1 May 1987.

16. Ibid.

17. Elena Celayeta Talbott, interview by author, Los Banos, Calif., 10 March 1987; and Sodie Arbios, *Memories of My Life: An Oral History of a California Sheepman* (Stockton, Calif.: Techni-Graphics Printing, 1980), 20–33.

18. The Holbert-Osa Oral History Collection, Basque Studies Library, University of Nevada, Reno; private interview collection, Paquita Garatea, Portland, Ore.

19. Deborah Fink, *Open Country, Iowa: Rural Women, Tradition, and Change* (Albany: State University of New York Press, 1986), 234–40; Glenda Riley, *The Female Frontier: A Comparative View of Women on the Prairie and the Plains* (Lawrence: University Press of Kansas, 1988), 14–41; and Deborah Fink, *Agrarian Women: Wives and Mothers in Rural Nebraska, 1880–1940* (Chapel Hill: University of North Carolina Press, 1992), 189–96.

20. Fink, *Open Country*, 3.

21. Anonymous, interview by author.

22. Echeverria, "California-ko ostatuak," 158–60, 196. For example, only three of seventy-one boardinghouses in Stockton, California, lasted over fifteen years. Only one exceeded twenty.

23. Ibid., 238.

24. Bilbao and Equilaz, *Diaspora Vasca*, vol. 1, and Arrizabalaga, "A Statistical Study."

25. Echeverria, "California-ko ostatuak," 186–204.

26. Robert Laxalt, *Sweet Promised Land* (New York: Harper Brothers, 1957); Robert Laxalt, *The Hotel* (Reno: University of Nevada Press, 1989).

27. Charlotte Crawford, "The Position of Women in a Basque Fishing Community," in *Anglo-American Contributions to Basque Studies: Essays in Honor of Jon Bilbao*, ed. William A. Douglass, Richard W. Etulain, and William H. Jacobsen, Jr. (Reno: Desert Research Institute, 1977), 145–52.

28. Teresa del Valle, "The Current Status of the Anthropology of Women: Models and Paradigms," in *Essays in Basque Social Anthropolgy and History,* ed. William A. Douglass (Reno: Basque Studies Program, 1989), 129–48; Jacqueline Urla, "Reinventing Basque Society: Cultural Difference and the Quest for Modernity, 1918–1936," in *Essays in Basque Social Anthropolgy,* 149–76; and Roslyn Frank, "The Religious Role of Women in Basque Culture," in *Anglo-American Contributions*, 153–62.

29. Mary Grace Paquette, *Basques to Bakersfield* (Bakersfield: Kern County Historical Society, 1982), 89.

30. Ibid., 90; Janice Elizalde, interview by author, Bakersfield, Calif., 1 April 1987; and Mayie Maitia, interview by author, Bakersfield, Calif., 2 April 1987.

31. Maitia interview.

32. Linda White, "Feminism and Lexicography: Dealing With Sexist Language in a Bilingual Dictionary," *Frontiers* 10, no. 3 (1989): 61–64. White is coauthor with Gorka Aulestia of *Basque-English Dictionary* (Reno: University of Nevada Press, 1989).

33. White, "Feminism," 62.

34. William A. Douglass, "Rural Exodus in Two Spanish Basque Villages: A Cultural Explanation," *American Anthropologist* 73 (October 1971): 1100–1114; William A. Douglass, *Echalar and Murelaga: Opportunity and Rural Depopulation in Two Spanish Basque Villages* (New York: St. Martin's Press, 1975); and Douglass and Bilbao, *Amerikanuak*, 2–6.

15.

"We Are Women Irish":
Gender, Class, Religious, and Ethnic Identity in Anaconda, Montana

LAURIE MERCIER

This article by Laurie Mercier shows us yet another distinctive linkage among ethnicity, gender, and the occupations of working-class immigrants in the American West. In contrast to the generally isolated rural Basque women described in the previous article, Irish women in the Montana smelter town of Anaconda mobilized as "women Irish" to work for wider community and working-class goals.

Mining, the great extractive industry of the U.S. West, depended on the work of first- and second-generation European ethnic men. Consequently, the structures of work and community in mature mining towns such as Butte and Cripple Creek and smelting towns like Anaconda revolved around workingmen's lives in the mines, miners' union activities, men's fraternal orders, and ethnic associations. Women's wage work, traditionally limited to serving men's domestic needs, was simply not as valued. But, as Mercier shows us, in Anaconda, women's family work was critical not only to the work of the men but to how immigrants transplanted and modified their culture from Ireland to the American West. Oral histories provide Mercier with much of the rich and convincing detail with which she makes her case. There is no better source for documenting the myriad female activities that historians used to think were impossible to document and too unimportant to mention.

Mercier never lets us forget the ways in which this particular Irish ethnic community is embedded in Anaconda's specific class and interethnic circumstances, but neither does she freeze her portrait in time. "Women Irish," she shows us, is a meaningful identity that women themselves have shaped over time.

In 1904 Ellen Mulkerin joined thousands of other single young Irish women and departed her homeland to seek a better life in the United States. Leaving behind parents and customary life in County Galway, twenty-one-year-old Mulkerin headed to Anaconda, Montana, the copper-smelter community where her sister Nora had immigrated earlier. The thriving industrial town twenty-five miles west of Butte offered Irish immigrant women job opportunities and familiar surroundings, for it was, as one commentator complained, dominated by Irish Catholics and "getting to be thoroughly 'Mick.'"[1]

Ellen Mulkerin (left) and Tim Tracy (seated) pose for a wedding portrait in 1906 with Tillie King, maid of honor, and King's brother William, best man. (Courtesy Isabel Tracy McCarthy, Anaconda.)

Mulkerin found work at the Gavin House, the Anaconda Copper Mining Company's large boardinghouse on East Park Street. There she met Tim Tracy, an Irishman from County Waterford. The two soon married and formally adopted Anaconda as their permanent home, becoming U.S. citizens in 1911. Once married, Mulkerin quit her job and raised eight children of her own and seven assorted cousins, nieces, and nephews. She also participated in community institutions that she viewed as essential to her identity and her family's welfare, primarily the Daughters of Erin and St. Peter's Catholic Church. Long after her death in 1943, many of Ellen's children and grandchildren remained in the Anaconda area, an indication that the transplanted Irish had helped mold the kind of community their children and grandchildren wanted to live in.[2]

Ellen Mulkerin's story parallels the experiences of many Irish women who came to Anaconda at the turn of the century. Although at first fewer in numbers and less visible to chroniclers than Irish men, the female Irish cooperated with other Catholic and working-class women and shaped their community through their productive roles, kin and neighbor relationships, preservation of ethnic traditions, and participation in institutions such as the Ancient Order of Hibernians Ladies' Auxiliary and the Catholic Church. As they laid a firm foundation for their "New Ireland," Irish women adapted their cultural heritage to their particular needs in Anaconda, an isolated community dependent on a single industry.

Irish women were unique among the female immigrants who came to the United States in the late nineteenth and early twentieth centuries. Unlike other immigrant women, they composed more than half of the Irish who emigrated, and for the most part they came alone, free to create new lives in a new land. More women than men emigrated during this period because of the American demand for female domestic servants and the new economic realities in postfamine agricultural Ireland that diminished women's economic and social status. Ireland's shift to larger farms and to less domestic manufacturing reduced women's significance in the rural enterprise and left them with fewer marriage opportunities. The United States, on the other hand, offered female immigrants economic and personal opportunities—a chance to earn wages, find a suitable husband, and escape the watchful eyes of parents, priests, and neighbors. Pushed by conditions at home and pulled by letters from relatives abroad, two-thirds of a million Irish women, most unmarried and under thirty-five years of age, immigrated to the United States between 1885 and 1920.[3]

East Coast cities such as New York and Boston were the destinations of most female Irish immigrants, who sought established ethnic communities as well as economic opportunities. Women had fled hardships in Ireland and were not anxious to embrace the challenges of raw, new towns farther west. The 1895 Anaconda census, listing almost twice as many Irish-born men as women, contrasted sharply with general Irish immigration trends and reflected the preponderance of males in mining and industrial communities of the nineteenth-century Rocky Mountain West.[4]

When Irish-born Marcus Daly began building the Anaconda Reduction Works at Warm Springs Creek in 1883 to process the rich copper ores from his Butte mines, immigrants streamed to the new community in search of employment. Within fifteen years Anaconda had one of the largest foreign-born populations in Montana, fully one-half of its total population. Italians, Slavs, and Scandinavians swelled the town's numbers, but the Irish were by far the largest ethnic group. By 1900 more than a quarter of Anaconda's total population of 9,500 had either been born in the Emerald Isle or had Irish-born parents, and the Irish composed 25 percent of the city's foreign-born through the first half of the twentieth century.[5] Their large numbers assured them economic, social, and political security not attainable in most other U.S. cities where they had minority status and where they often faced discrimination.[6]

Most single Irish women migrated to Anaconda at the encouragement of a relative already settled. Others followed siblings to the urban centers of the East and the mining camps of the West where they found employment and often married before eventually moving to Anaconda. Margaret and Edward Kelly, for example, met and married in the mining town of Leadville, Colorado, and fled to Anaconda in 1896 after soldiers repressed a strike at Leadville and threatened their lives. Madeline McKittrick Heaney's Irish parents also met in Leadville and later married in Anaconda. Delia Vaughan left Ireland at age eighteen to join two sisters in Pittsburgh, where she worked until she met and married a countryman who was recruited by the Anaconda Company to work at its Rocky Mountain smelter in 1919.[7]

Although excluded from working at the Anaconda smelter, Irish women found plenty of opportunities in the service economy that housed, fed, and entertained smelter workers. Help wanted ads in the *Anaconda Standard* between the 1880s and 1930 begged for housekeepers, waitresses, chambermaids, seamstresses, laundry girls, and dishwashers. Three Irish sisters, Jessie, Kate, and Mary Crowley, found jobs as chambermaids at the Montana Hotel in 1895. Domestic jobs paid poorly, however, and women often sought opportunities to improve their economic status. Kate Tracy, for example, worked at a boardinghouse when she arrived in Anaconda in 1903 from County Roscommon, but she soon learned how to sew and hired herself out as a seamstress. Some Irish women managed or owned businesses catering to smelter workers. Lydia McCarty advertised laundry services out of her home; Jennie O'Brien owned an inn, the Deer Lodge House; Ellen Fitzpatrick managed the Commercial Hotel; and Maggie Lynch ran the Anaconda Restaurant.[8]

At the turn of the century occupational choices for women depended not only on what services the smelter city required, but also on age, ethnicity, and marital status. Female immigrants soon found the same gender segmentation of labor as they had known in Ireland. Most single young Irish women worked as domestics, and more mature women, particularly widows, often rented rooms in their homes or ran boardinghouses. From the 1880s to the 1920s, Annie McDonald, Annie Lennon, Mary McDaniel, Nellie Mollene, Mary Morris, Ann McGreevey, and other Irish women dominated the boardinghouse business and competed for patrons among Anaconda's transient bachelor population. The businesswomen survived a crowded trade by offering good service at reasonable prices. Ann Walsh, proprietor of the Girton House, advertised to smelter workers "Good Board and Lodging at the Very Lowest Rates." Margaret O'Connor attracted customers to her Vendome House because of her reputation for kindliness, efficiency, and cleanliness, including outfitting her waitresses in freshly laundered, pleated skirts.[9]

For Irish newcomers, the boardinghouse represented a home-away-from-home, where they could reestablish kin and village ties, develop job networks, and satisfy their hunger for Irish talk and food. Boardinghouse proprietors often sustained newcomers until they could find work, and they served as confidants, general contractors, and matchmakers for their immigrant guests. Michael McKeon, who arrived in Anaconda in 1910 from County Monaghan, was unable to find an aunt he had heard lived in Anaconda and so an Irish boardinghouse operator accommodated him until he secured a job at the smelter.[10] Many of Anaconda's unattached women Irish met beaus while scrubbing or cooking at one of the town's many hostels.

Although many women left Ireland unattached, their marriages to countrymen in Anaconda reflected their choices to maintain ethnic traditions and ties. Yet these arrangements also symbolized Irish women's break from the old country, as they met Irish men from unfamiliar counties, independent of parental and parish selections. Immigrant marriages nurtured a growing Irish settlement and ensured a substantial marriageable pool for American-born children, who continued to influence Anaconda's character after immigration diminished in the 1920s. Many Anaconda Irish parents even discouraged "outside" marriage among their American-born children until the 1940s. Virginia Cox Tracy remembered that marrying a non-Irish Catholic American "was a real taboo." The Irish community's emphasis on family life, however, restricted possibilities for Anaconda's single women who chose not to marry. Many who chose not to conform to Irish codes of proper marriage left Anaconda to pursue occupational, educational, and other interests elsewhere.[11]

For those Irish immigrant women who did marry and remain in Anaconda, most abandoned wage work to raise children and grapple with the downswings and hardships of the smelter economy. Domestic and economic spheres overlapped, and Irish working-class women had few "noneconomic" activities, although their work was often uncompensated and unrecognized. Once married and out of the wage-earning economy, women still occupied an integral productive position within their families and community. A smelter worker's income was not sufficient to support a household, and like working-class women in other industrial communities, Anaconda's female Irish found ways to help families survive.

Married women often earned income by housing and feeding bachelor smelter workers. Some constructed and leased small cabins on the tiny lots behind their houses, while others rented rooms despite cramped family living space. Kate Tracy rented her family's only bedroom to bring in needed income. Working-class Irish women also supplemented family earnings by raising chickens and gardens and trading labor for food For twenty-five years, Delia Vaughan helped a neighbor woman do the laundry of the smelter superintendents; in exchange for her help, Vaughan received groceries at a discount from the woman's small store. The frequency of this type of informal production and exchange, as revealed by oral history interviews, underscores its importance to Anaconda's economy. Many Irish women served as general contractors, too, managing their children's labor both inside and outside the home. Girls assisted with babysitting, cleaning, sewing, and cooking, and boys collected bottles, delivered papers, and cleaned schoolhouses and churches. Several Irish Americans recalled their mothers procuring jobs for them and noted the common practice of contributing wages to the general household or paying mothers room and board until leaving home.[12]

Many married women also maintained some economic autonomy by managing family finances. Delia Vaughan, for example, received her husband's paycheck and then gave him an allowance. With just a first-grade education, she taught herself to read and calculate to carefully manage family income and purchases so that they could live more comfortably. Isabel Tracy McCarthy took her husband's paycheck and budgeted money to run the household and pay bills. She noted that her husband never questioned her expenditures. Many women picked up their husband's paychecks from the Anaconda Company pay office to assert their control over family wages and acquisitions.[13]

Before a revitalized International Union of Mine, Mill and Smelter Workers (IUMMSW) Local No. 117 could negotiate better pay and benefits after the 1930s, smelter families faced a steady stream of hardships from smelter shutdowns, pay cuts, and accidents. Workers often died young from consumption, an infirmity afflicting those breathing arsenic, sulphur, and other industrial by-products. The death of the primary breadwinner devastated most families, and widows, although helped by the community, received little compensation from the Anaconda Company. Women had few wage-earning options, especially when burdened with children. Widows had to take "anything they could get" to support themselves by washing, ironing, cleaning houses, or renting rooms. Virginia Cox Tracy remembered that her widowed Irish grandmother divided her house to rent two rooms. The company, meanwhile, provided only "a load of wood from the foundry every month" as compensation for her husband's smelter-related death.[14]

Some Irish widows had special skills or enough money to open small stores or boardinghouses, but their work usually had to be home-based to care for children. Women worked long hours, sacrificing family and social life. Mary McNelis lost two husbands during the 1920s, one from a mining accident and the other from emphysema contracted at the smelter. She worked as a midwife and often could not manage the daily care of her two sons; periodically she placed them in the St. Joseph's Orphanage in Helena. Her son, Mike McNelis, said that her job often kept her away from home for a week or more. "[She'd] cook and wash and take care of the woman who had the baby," McNelis explained, "and no matter how big the family was, that was it. Sometimes she'd walk in where there'd be seven or eight kids and she'd take care of them all and see some off to school and change the [diapers] on the babies."[15] When Mary Jane Walton's father died, her Irish mother supported her children by washing smeltermen's clothes and raising chickens. Walton lost her own husband in the 1920s and cleaned for her family's room and board until she used her husband's $2,000 life insurance payment to open a store. Female friends helped her clean and ready the store, and "she started up and she never looked back," her daughter, Josephine Weiss Casey, recalled. "She knew all the old bachelors around here and you know she was a young woman . . . and opened that store when the shift [street]car went down at 6:00 in the morning and closed it when the last one came up at 11:20 at night, that's the kind of hours [she worked]."[16]

The makeup of the industrial community determined women's economic roles before and after marriage. Generally, Irish immigrant women in the United States were less likely than other immigrant women to hold wage-earning jobs after marriage.[17] But in Anaconda, women of all ethnic backgrounds shared the same employment future. Both custom and the patriarchal, single-industry economy circumscribed women's work lives.

Beginning in the 1920s, Anaconda stores and the Anaconda Company began hiring single female salesclerks and stenographers but still prohibited married women from employment. After graduating from high school, Delia Sweeney found work in the corset and shoe departments of the Copper City Commercial Company, and Margaret Laughlin Kelly worked briefly as a housekeeper and cook until obtaining a job at Stagg's Furniture Store. Margaret and Isabel Tracy worked at Woolworth's during the 1930s until they each married. Although these Irish American daughters welcomed pink-collar opportunities, by 1930 over one-third of Anaconda's workingwomen were still engaged in domestic service and hotel, restaurant, and laundry work. Not until the 1940s, when married women began to work outside their homes in war-related and other jobs, did the proportion of Anaconda women workers increase in clerical, sales, and professional jobs and decrease in traditional domestic and service roles.[18]

Although female Irish immigrants sought to improve their economic status by running boardinghouses, they encouraged their American daughters to pursue teaching as a way up the economic ladder. Delia Sweeney remembered that many women "by hook or by crook" saved enough money to send their daughters to the teacher-training college in Dillon. As a result of her mother's influence, Virginia Cox Tracy taught school in the early 1940s until she married. The district refused to employ married women, so Tracy worked at the J. C. Penney store until she was hired to work at the smelter during the war. By 1960 the school district had abolished its prohibition against married women, and Tracy was rehired to teach.[19]

Like many working-class women throughout the country, Anaconda Irish and Irish American women worked because they had to survive, but they also accepted the responsibility to contribute what they could to their community and to the well-being of their immediate and extended families. Often their contributions came in the form of unpaid time to instruct and encourage children, care for sick neighbors, take in destitute kin, preserve ethnic traditions, or raise money for the church. This "helping out" was essential to their Irish and non-Irish communities, especially given the exigencies of a one-company town. Sister Gilmary Vaughan recalled, for example, how women consistently provided the sustenance to carry people through hard times. If anybody was sick, she said, her mother "always sent over some kind of a dinner. If anyone died . . . dinner was prepared a day before the funeral, so that the family would be able to eat together. And this was a thing that many people did." Margaret Laughlin Kelly's mother regularly helped a young widow with her laundry business and refused to accept payment for her services. Like many other Irish women, Ellen Mulkerin Tracy took in relatives as part of her obligations to her extended family. Isabel Tracy McCarthy recalled that her mother "could never say no. . . . It seemed like we always had such a big family there." Her sister, Margaret Tracy McLean, remembered their mother's penchant for feeding the hungry. "If anybody came by she had to feed them. They used to mark [our house] I think . . . when the hoboes would come they knew where they could get something to eat."[20]

Irish women and their American-born daughters preserved some of their forebearers' customs, adapted others to their new environment, and discarded others that no longer served a useful purpose in a small Montana community. Second-generation Anaconda Irish remembered that many of their parents, particularly mothers, clung to various traditions associated with "old Eire," such as superstitions, fortune-telling, music, and witty toasts. Some Irish women, for example, feared black cats, insisted that guests leave by the door they entered, and never left a hat on a bed. To ward off evil spirits after a family member's death, mothers might pin a small bag of salt on children's clothing. Isabel Tracy McCarthy remembered that she and her friends eagerly visited Irish neighbor women who could tell fortunes from cards or tea leaves. Such reminders of and habits from the Old World were rarely sustained by Anaconda's second-generation Irish. Daughters seemed to view their mothers' traditions as quaint superstitions bearing little relevance to their American lives.[21]

Perhaps the most valued tradition immigrant women sought to preserve was "the Irish get-together." Socializing among friends and family in homes or on picnics was a favorite pastime, and visits sometimes included singing Irish songs and dancing jigs. For the most part, conversations were in English, for few Irish immigrants preserved the Gaelic language in Anaconda. Sister Gilmary Vaughan recalled that her parents, Delia and Martin Vaughan, spoke Gaelic only when other Irish-speaking friends visited in their home. "So we never learned the language," she said. "We knew some of it, we could understand it, and there was always kind of pride [when they spoke Gaelic]," but the children were not encouraged to learn it. Isabel Tracy McCarthy believed that few Irish customs were perpetuated by her family, except for the social visits with other Anaconda Irish families where tea was served, Irish origins discussed, and toasts proposed. Although reminiscing about an Irish past diminished in later years as the numbers of foreign-born decreased, informal visiting among family and friends remained a treasured activity among Anaconda's Irish Americans through the twentieth century.[22]

Much visiting took place within separate gendered spheres. Men met at bars and lodge and union halls, and women gathered more informally at homes and churches. Virginia Cox Tracy remembered her mother's visits with friends after mass where they would serve cake and play Irish songs on the piano.[23] Margaret Laughlin Kelly recalled that her Irish mother and her friends would call on one another during husbands' smelter shifts:

They visited with each other all the time. They took their children with them . . . in the afternoon if they had afternoon shift. As soon as the husband went to work they visited. And it seems that the [neighborhood Irish] men had the same shift, they all worked down in the converters together, this was the Walshs, the Laughlins, and the Meloys. . . . [The women] never played cards or anything like that like they do now, just visited, talked about the old country, and they always had to have their tea and soda bread.[24]

Immigrant groups have been most successful in preserving their foodways long after shedding other aspects of ethnic identity, such as language and even political loyalties to the "old country." The Irish felt right at home in Montana, where cold climate and poor transportation limited most families to a bland cuisine of meat and potatoes. Some eating habits and favorite Irish dishes persisted, even in the most unlikely settings. Stews, for example, were popular picnic fare because the "old-time Irish" did not like cold lunches. Margaret Tracy McLean recalled her mother laboriously preparing a hot stew to deliver to family at the Washoe picnic grounds. Madeline Heaney remembered her mother making Irish soda bread and roasts, and Caithin "Kotch" Gallagher Francisco recalled traditional Christmas fare of fish, white sauce, and boiled potatoes. American-born daughters incorporated new foods into their culinary lexicon, including the popular pasty, the Cornish meat-and-potato pie relished by Butte miners and Anaconda smeltermen, and many switched from drinking their parents' tea to coffee, the more ubiquitous western beverage.[25]

Anaconda Irish women may have intentionally modified some traditions that interfered with their American routines. One such casualty was the Irish wake. Wakes usually were held in the homes of the deceased and often lasted several days and nights. Mourners presumedly distracted the widow from grief by eating, drinking, and eulogizing in her home until the corpse was taken to the church for services and to the Mount Carmel Catholic Cemetery for burial. Luke McKeon remembered the special characteristics of Anaconda Irish wakes: "The Irish funeral was a very long funeral. The body would be brought home and it would be waked in the family home for two or three days . . . and around the clock. The women would be in the . . . parlor or the living room with the wife and widow and the men would all be in the kitchen. The beer and the whiskey and the food would flow rather freely."[26]

Although men fondly recounted the sometimes-raucous tradition, women were less enthusiastic about the vigils. The custom placed a great deal of strain on women who, although stricken with grief, were expected to greet visitors and serve food and drink to men toasting the beloved memory of their kinsman. Lucy McNelis recalled: "You'd have to set the table sometimes fifteen times. Even if it was a big dining room table, you'd set it and set it and set it. They'd be eating from one o'clock until four o'clock in the morning, just keep it up all night long. It was really wearing, too much." One Anaconda writer commented that by the end of a three-day wake, "the immediate family was numb, not from grief alone, but from hard work."[27]

Women may have played a central role in the demise of the wake, preferring not to perpetuate a tradition that taxed their stamina. The Finnegan Funeral Home, which primarily served Catholic families after it opened for business in 1883, gradually expanded its facilities to accommodate wakes. "Tiny" Longfellow, a local undertaker, believed that moving the grieving formalities to the funeral homes greatly relieved women of the emotional and physical burden of having rowdy visitors in their home. By the mid-twentieth century, Anaconda wakes had been transformed into a ceremony where mourners visited the dead at the funeral home and then gathered at widows' homes for a short meal.[28]

Anaconda's working-class women were less successful in modifying another Irish institution, the neighborhood pub. The custom of drinking was certainly not limited to the Irish, and Anaconda's workingmen frequented the bars lining the Third Street streetcar route to the smelter. Escaping the toil of the smelter and responsibilities at home, men found refuge in local bars. Howard Rosenleaf explained that Anaconda's working class "drank because they had to, not because they wanted to. . . . We lived under the fallacy that you work hard, you play hard and you drink hard." Mike McNelis contended that the Irish maintained the saloons' prosperity: "If it weren't for the Irish all them birds would have been 'up spot' a long time ago."[29]

Viewed as harmless socializing by many men, these after-shift stops at taverns were generally seen by women as a perilous drain on family income, especially considering the expensive Anaconda custom of buying drinks for the house. Temperance movements were ineffective, and even during Prohibition, Anaconda's bars were reportedly "wide open" and flourishing. Men stubbornly resisted efforts to restrict their revered drinking customs. To them, bars represented one of the few arenas in which they could release frustrations and relax with compatible company. Women countered by trying to control their husband's paychecks and by sending their children to bars to fetch fathers after shifts ended. Though women failed to curb drinking, they did change the nature of the all-male preserve during the 1940s, when more women began frequenting Anaconda taverns.[30]

Anaconda's Irish community undoubtedly found its greatest ethnic cohesion in local chapters of the Ancient Order of Hibernians (AOH) and the AOH Ladies' Auxiliary. These groups played key roles in the cultural, political, economic, and social affairs of the community. Men and women worked together to support projects of mutual concern to their ethnic group and separately pursued issues of interest to their gender. In 1885, one year after the opening of the Anaconda Reduction Works, Irish men formed a chapter of the Hibernians. The Daughters of Erin formally established its Anaconda association the following year, just two years after the national AOH Ladies' Auxiliary was organized. The *Anaconda Standard* reported that the women's society probably would become the largest in the state with forty-five "enthusiastic" charter members. Women joined the Ladies' Auxiliary for the same reasons men joined the AOH: to promote their Irish heritage and a free Ireland, to "bind closer together Irishmen and Irishwomen," to provide sick and funeral benefits to members, to support the Catholic Church, and to afford a social outlet. The social dimension may have been the most attractive to Anaconda women, who had few formal opportunities to fraternize.[31]

The men's and women's groups often had contrasting agendas. Male Hibernians expressed much more concern about political struggles in Ireland than did their female counterparts, but they also attended to community needs. For example, the Anaconda AOH frequently pledged financial support to widows and orphans, whether they were survivors of executed rebels in the Emerald Isle or of deceased smelter workers in Anaconda.[32] Apparently less fervent nationalists, Anaconda Irish women were beset with their own struggles and appeared more interested in visiting and planning fund-raisers for their association, church, and members in need than in pursuing a liberated Ireland. The AOH Auxiliary's almost single-minded devotion to local concerns reflected its community-building motives and its willful determination to look forward. The women Irish were more eager immigrants and, unlike many of their male comrades, did not view their stay as temporary exile.[33]

The Ladies' Auxiliary and the AOH frequently collaborated on projects, such as sponsoring the annual St. Patrick's Day festivities, installing officers, and attending state conventions together. This cooperation helped mitigate class, gender, and age differences to solidify the ethnic community. Even though men often heaped patronizing praise on their female compatriots, evidence suggests that male Hibernians understood that Irish women's cooperation and contributions were essential to their community. Joint ventures between the two groups indicate that Irish women were not content to create a separate sphere for addressing women's concerns but worked with men to stimulate a vital ethnic community.[34]

Finances were a persistent problem for the female Hibernians who depended on dues and fund-raisers to pay for members' insurance, masses, funerals, AOH Hall rental, meeting refreshments, and gifts to local nuns and community members in need. The Ladies' Auxiliary often had to depend on the largesse of the AOH, an indication of women's economic dependence in public as well as private life. When the AOH in 1920 received one dollar from the women's group for fuel used in the AOH Hall for a card party, they decided to return the dollar to the Auxiliary. And later that year, the AOH bought fifty tickets for an Auxiliary card party, then returned the tickets, a generous offer that not only gave the

Daughters of Erin a chance to profit twice from the same tickets but also symbolized the women's dependence on the men. The Auxiliary, of course, repaid AOH generosity manyfold through its assistance in organizing and preparing for AOH/Auxiliary functions.[35]

St. Patrick's Day festivities marked an important annual observance for Anaconda's Irish community. Beginning in the 1880s and continuing to the present, the unbroken ritual that linked ethnic and religious heritage featured the AOH and Auxiliary procession to St. Paul's or St. Peter's Church, an early morning mass, a parade, an evening entertainment, and a dance. Although the AOH typically financed, publicized, and took credit for the affair, women organized and performed at the events. One woman remembered that St. Patrick's Day in Anaconda had more of a family, historical, and religious focus than later commemorations. As late as the 1940s children wore St. Patrick's medals instead of green and accompanied parents to the church and AOH Hall festivities.[36]

Irish immigration declined in the 1920s when economic conditions improved in Ireland, and the United States lost its appeal because of restrictive immigration legislation and increased competition for jobs.[37] As Anaconda's Irish-born population declined to just 3 percent of the town's population (but still a quarter of Anaconda's total foreign-born) by 1950, St. Patrick's Day lost much of its nationalistic, emotional, and even spiritual content. But the persistence of March 17 observances underscored Anaconda's significant Irish Catholic heritage. By the 1960s, when Anaconda boasted Montana's only AOH chapter, even the more numerous Butte Irish population traveled to the smelter town for St. Patrick's Day activities. No longer a celebration solely for the town's Irish, Anaconda commemorations became communitywide events, signifying among Irish Americans a greater sense of security and eagerness to display ethnic pride.[38]

While middle-class women dominated most Anaconda women's groups, the AOH Auxiliary attracted working-class women. In the early 1920s, most of the organization's 230 members lived east of Main Street in the working-class district frequently referred to as "Goosetown." Although low initiation fees (one dollar until 1990) and dues (fifty cents a month) made it possible for many working-class women to join, many Irish women had neither the time nor the money to participate.[39] Virginia Cox Tracy's widowed grandmother struggled to make a living selling produce, eggs, and butter. "She wasn't really reclusive," Tracy recalled, "but she was too busy just surviving." Mike McNelis recalled the hardships faced by the town's many boardinghouse operators, who regularly worked sixteen- or eighteen-hour days: "By the time you fix seven or eight lunch buckets and you fix breakfast for seven or eight guys, and you cook supper for them guys coming in with an appetite like a horse for supper, why, you didn't have much time for socializing."[40] Maggie Morris McGeever saved every penny to pay for interest and fuel for her boardinghouse and "didn't have money for social things." Margaret Laughlin Kelly believed that most Irish women were "at home people" instead of "joiners," and she believed that most who were active in the AOH Auxiliary participated before they bore children or after their children were grown.[41]

Although the Catholic Church was the most important cultural institution to Anaconda's Irish women, it diluted Irish bonds. Just as the smelter and its working-class neighborhoods were sites of interethnic mingling, so too did different Catholic ethnic groups meet at church and parochial school. Despite the Catholic hierarchy's support of ethnic parishes and Irish domination of the national and Montana clergy, religion and class intersected in Anaconda, and its two parishes split Irish along economic and neighborhood lines.[42]

Because Irish Americans controlled the American Catholic Church, their kin in Anaconda profoundly influenced the smelter community's parishes. At its inauguration in 1888, St. Paul's Catholic Church—St. Patrick's on early town maps—already boasted one thousand communicants. Like larger eastern cities, Anaconda soon supported distinct ethnic parishes. Responding to the Irish domination of St. Paul's Church, Slav immigrants constructed St. Peter's "Austrian" Catholic Church in 1897 on the town's east side. Serbo-Croatian residents were St. Peter's first trustees, and two Slav priests, Fathers Solnce and Pirnat, ministered to the parishioners for many decades. But Anaconda was too small and its working-class housing too limited to segregate ethnic groups for long. Many Irish claimed St. Peter's as theirs, too, illustrating how class arrangements often obscured ethnicity in Anaconda, with the Goosetown church drawing upon its poorer laboring families and St. Paul's catering to the more upwardly mobile "two-bathroom" Irish.[43] Anaconda's Irish leaders tried to blunt class and neighborhood differences among their ethnic community by rotating St. Patrick's Day services between St. Paul's and St. Peter's.

Female parishioners did volunteer work for their churches because they thought them essential to community life. As early as 1888, the Ladies of the Catholic Church were raising money for their new church by selling raffle tickets for a gold watch. That same year organizers and "an enthusiastic corps of lady assistants" hosted the Catholic Church Fair. Women served meals from noon to midnight for four days. By 1906 the event had grown to a ten-day affair, and women were clearly in charge. The parish women planned to use proceeds to pay off the debt on the priest's residence, pay for church repairs, and add an iron fence and cement walk.[44] Irish church women continued to volunteer well into the twentieth century. They sponsored innumerable fund-raising events such as the popular weekly St. Paul's and St. Peter's "aids," or card parties and dances, which often attracted over eight hundred people. Money raised supported projects such as the Maple Street school and convent constructed in 1923.[45]

Just as Irish working-class men found refuge in the town's bars, women found spiritual solace at mass and camaraderie at meetings with other Catholic women. The Irish Catholic custom of church participation, transferred from mother to daughter, and the nature of the smelter community worked together to strengthen the church as an institution among Anaconda's women. Even though the church's patriarchal structure excluded them from the most significant church roles, many Irish Catholic women welcomed the opportunity to escape home and family duties to visit with other women and contribute to the well-being of the larger community. They joined the Women's Catholic Order of Foresters, Ladies of Maccabees, sodalities, and the St. Paul Council of Catholic Women. At first dominated by Irish women, by the 1920s, the organizations included other ethnic women, indicating the growing cooperation among a variety of Catholics. The Ladies' Catholic Benevolent Association, for example, had only Irish or Irish American officers until 1925, when Fredricka Barich, a Slav, became the financial secretary.[46]

The Catholic Church attempted to inculcate narrow gender roles. It affirmed women's authoritative position in the home and celebrated motherhood by sanctioning large families and honoring women's loyalty, duty, and faith. Catholic teachings, however, often contradicted the realities of life in a smelter town. Many Anaconda Irish and Irish American women were primary decision makers on family matters, especially children's work, education, and religious training. With fathers often away working at the smelter, attending union or AOH meetings, or socializing at neighborhood taverns, Irish families relied on mothers for care, fiscal management, guidance, and collective decisions. Because women took their family obligations seriously, they often asserted leadership, authority, and autonomy, hardly the passive stance church imagery projected.[47]

Despite their strict religious training, many Irish American young women rejected rigid roles and built on their mothers' efforts to link domestic duties to broader public purposes. One 1902 graduate of Anaconda's Ursuline Convent delivered a commencement address entitled "Woman's Influence" in which she embraced female essentialism to justify women's reform work. Anna Sullivan assured her audience that "woman's dearest, purest and holiest rights" remained in the domestic sphere, but her subtext outlined women's civic accomplishments. She concluded by instructing her fellow graduates to become active and help make "the world a brighter, happier home, for if [it] is ever to be reclaimed from frivolity, indifference and infidelity . . . that happy reform must be brought about by the gentle hand of a woman."[48]

Just as Irish men supported women's expanded economic and cultural roles within their families and ethnic associations while clinging to confining gender ideologies, the Catholic Church simultaneously preached domesticity and action. Church activities offered Irish women an opportunity to exercise their talents, contribute to their children's spiritual upbringing, and socialize with other women. Despite Catholicism's limited official roles for women, many working-class Irish women supported their parish because of their earnest faith and because it offered a reciprocal relationship. One devout Anacondan noted, "[Women] always could go to the church for whatever they needed. They also supported the church tremendously over the years, and the church was a support to them."[49]

Many working-class Irish women tried, despite hardships, to send their children to parochial schools to receive what they considered a necessary religious education. Margaret Laughlin Kelly, who grew up with great respect for nuns and priests, sent her children to Catholic schools so that they would have a similar positive experience. Many Irish mothers did not want their children to end up at the smelter. They believed education offered an alternative and sacrificed to send their children to school. Josephine Casey recalled that her mother worked fifteen-hour days at her small grocery store like many others who "went without a lot of things to see that their kids got an education." Delia Sweeney recalled her mother saying, "The poor Irish would go without if they thought their son or daughter could amount to something." Isabel Tracy McCarthy sent her twelve children to parochial schools by encouraging them to deliver papers, babysit, and work as school janitors to help pay for tuition and school clothes. Anacondans financed parochial elementary schools and a high school until 1973, when the city's three parish councils decided to close them.[50]

Children of Anaconda's Irish and other ethnic Catholic families intermingled in the parochial schools. By the 1940s, religious education had transformed a unique Irish identity into a special sense of what it meant to be Catholic. In supporting a traditional Irish institution that was also important to the city's Italian and Slav Catholic communities, Anaconda's Irish, in effect, helped erase ethnic differences.

Although the parochial schools eventually diminished Irish distinctiveness, for many years Anaconda Irish urged educators to include Irish history in the curriculum. As late as the 1930s, the AOH persuaded the Ursuline sisters to teach Irish history in exchange for needed schoolbooks. The AOH Irish History Committee offered awards to outstanding Irish students, with Irish American girls often the recipients of the prizes, indicating the ethnic community's pride in its daughters' as well as its sons' educational achievements. Ruth Ann Boyd and Helen Monahan, students at St. Paul's School and winners of the 1934 Irish History Awards, thanked the AOH for "the value of these competitive tests in the making of better men and women."[51]

Irish and Irish American Ursuline, Benedictine, and Dominican sisters and Sisters of Charity were prominent figures in Anaconda society and operated schools, the hospital, and other social services. Father Crawley, in a mass at St. Peter's on St. Patrick's Day in 1926, praised the local sisters and reminded parishioners that "Your teachers are mostly daughters of daughters of Erin, and the hospital staff are nigh all daughters of the Emerald Isle." As educated, independent, and devoted women, nuns were influential role models to many Anaconda girls. Continuing a practice of their Irish forebears, many Anaconda mothers encouraged at least one of their children to enter church service. Sister Gilmary Vaughan, who received her first communion in Anaconda at age five, admired the white habits of the nuns and "just knew from the time I started school, that's where I was going to go."[52]

Anaconda's small size and domination by a single industry presented special challenges to Irish and other immigrants anxious to preserve old-country ways. Anaconda fostered cultural exchange instead of neighborhood enclaves, and residents were more likely to be segregated by class, religion, and occasionally race than ethnicity. Working-class Irish, Italian, Swedish, Croatian, and some Native American and African American residents lived side by side in the densely populated smelter neighborhood on the town's eastern edge. The more fortunate skilled workers, merchants, and professionals, including many Irish, lived farther west and upwind of the smelter. Especially after the 1940s, ethnicity no longer played a central role in Anaconda community life. Irish Americans more frequently married outside their ethnic group. Union contracts supplanted the need for kinship social services, and one's ethnic heritage no longer helped nor hindered one's occupational or class position. Until the smelter shutdown in 1980, when the entire fabric of Anaconda society seemed to unravel, class and religious identity often overshadowed one's Irish heritage.

Working-class Irish women were conscious of the income differences that separated families regardless of ethnicity. One's Irish alliances did not always lead to a good job at the smelter, Virginia Cox Tracy recalled. Her Irish grandfather Patrick Naughton was a union activist and lacked family connections and "had to take one of those kinds of jobs that . . . actually was hazardous to his health." Tracy believed that social snobbery extended to Irish women's circles, creating distinctions between those who "were fairly well off" and those who were not.[53]

Working-class Irish women cooperated with men to champion the work of unions to improve family livelihoods. IUMMSW Local 117 frequently had to resort to strikes to exact concessions from a resistant Anaconda Copper Mining Company. Strikes took a heavy toll on women, for they were more directly involved in caring for families and witnessed the immediate effects of reduced income. While husbands and fathers often left Anaconda in search of other work, wives managed tight budgets and stretched meager food supplies. Still, women usually supported strikers. Isabel Tracy McCarthy noted that "there were times when you had to strike to get your rights. . . . All my family were very union . . . and we went along with it." Sister Gilmary Vaughan recalled Anaconda's strong labor solidarity: "Scabs were doomed for life. . . . Oh man, you just didn't cross that picket line, whether you were going to starve, you didn't cross that picket line. Anybody who did, they were condemned." Madeline Heaney remembered her parents' struggles with an insufficient smelter paycheck and credited the unions for making life more tolerable for Anaconda families. Many Irish women believed that greater economic security ultimately depended on alliances with other working families instead of or in addition to their ethnic community.[54]

Anaconda's Irish women joined with non-Irish women and men to support class, political, or religious interests just as often as they cultivated their ethnic community, experiencing what Sarah Deutsch calls the "multiple relations" that shape identity.[55] In many cases, Irish American women sacrificed ethnic ties to volunteer their limited time to the union auxiliary, local political activities, or the church. Delia Sweeney, for example, was active in the local Democratic Party, where she felt her time was better spent than in the Daughters of Erin or other specifically Irish associations. The Democratic Party, as a political institution that promised to work for the interests of working families, represented another form of identity for many Anacondans. Jerry Hansen remembered being "baptized a Democrat" as well as an Irish Catholic by his grandmother Julia Moran.[56]

Yet Irish ethnic identity persisted in Anaconda long after most Irish in the American West had assimilated into mainstream culture. When many other Hibernian and other ethnic associations in the nation folded in the 1940s, the Anaconda AOH and Auxiliary survived. In fact, as late as the 1980s the Anaconda and San Francisco Irish had the distinction of having the only two orders west of the Mississippi.[57] Anaconda's small size, multiple ethnic groups, and dependence on a single industry would seem to militate against a distinct Irish American culture, making its tenacity even more remarkable. Perhaps the community's isolation and reliance on a single industry contributed to the enduring bonds of kinship and friendship. For those who remained in Anaconda, there were few opportunities for dramatic economic and social mobility, and ethnic ties offered a sense of belonging that softened economic stagnation. Women and men intermingled with other ethnic groups in their workplaces, neighborhoods, churches, and schools, but they retained pride in their parents' and grandparents' heritage. Many Anacondans hung on to their Irish identity, even if only on a periodic basis. Since the smelter shutdown in 1980, interest in Hibernianism has revived. A resurgence in AOH membership and activities may indicate that Anacondans have reclaimed a comforting ethnicity amid economic uncertainties when identity no longer revolves around work, unions, or the Anaconda Company.

Irish immigrant women told plenty of stories about the old country, maintained their contacts with family and village, and hoped that their American-born children would prosper enough to visit the Emerald Isle. But unlike many other immigrant groups, the Irish resigned themselves to their new home, knowing that there were few opportunities for them or their children across the Atlantic. Virginia Cox Tracy's grandmother Naughton told her stories about banshees and her birthplace, "but there was never this idea of making Ireland an exalted place, the only place to be from." Madeline McKittrick Heaney's mother did not talk much about her former home: "My mother just got fed up with Ireland. They worked hard there, and they couldn't get anywhere with English rule, and it was just too hard. They were thankful to get to America." Irish women cherished socializing with countrywomen in their homes, at Auxiliary meetings and family picnics, but their energies for the most part were spent not in longing for old Eire but in making a living, maintaining their religious faith, and securing for their children a better life.[58]

Although enthusiasm for an Irish past has ebbed and flowed through Anaconda's century-long history, pride in Irish roots represents something more durable. The national reawakening of the values of ethnic pluralism in the 1970s and Anaconda's bleak economic picture in the 1980s are not the only keys to understanding its distinct Irish heritage. The uniqueness of Anaconda—with the early domination by the Irish-born and their institutions, the special patterns of life that developed in response to Anaconda Company dictates, and the creative economic, cultural, and community networking among its working-class Irish women—nurtured this persistent ethnic identity. Many Irish immigrant women came to Anaconda individually, but as part of their "New Ireland," they cooperated in family, neighborhood, religious, class, and ethnic associations. These relationships gave Anacondans strength in the face of sometimes unexpected and uncontrollable economic forces, such as the 1980 plant shutdown.

Many Anaconda Irish Americans credit their mothers and grandmothers for instilling in them a sense of being "Irish," even if they cannot articulate precisely what that means. Margaret Laughlin Kelly claimed, "I'm proud to be Irish," although she could not say why. She thought it was the many talents of the Irish, including her mother's constant singing and positive disposition, despite adversity, which she was so pleased to inherit. Thelma Doran, the Irish consul general who visited Anaconda in 1990, agreed that it was "probably the Irish mothers" who communicated Irish pride in their American-born offspring. Alice Clark Finnegan recalled the respect people still had for their Irish roots during the 1950s, a decade generally perceived to emphasize acculturation. As a youngster then, she remembers feeling "left out" because her grandmothers did not speak with an Irish brogue like the grandmothers of many of her friends.[59]

Irish American daughters preserved some of their mothers' and grandmothers' memories, traditions, and activities, and they also pioneered new directions for their families and community. Reflecting a move among other women's auxiliaries across the nation, which were becoming more autonomous organizations in the 1970s and 1980s as a result of the women's movement, the AOH Auxiliary revised its constitution in 1984 and changed its name. The new Ladies AOH maintained its original purpose to promote Christian charity, encourage civic participation, support Irish independence, and perpetuate Irish culture, but it declared that the women's group was now self-governing and no longer subordinate to AOH supervision. In explaining the change, Anaconda's Ladies AOH president Caithin "Kotch" Gallagher Francisco defended the group's independent course, explaining "We're not just helping men; we are women Irish."[60] For over one hundred years, Anaconda's Irish women have fused their ethnic, religious, gender, and class identities to shape new lives, adapt their cultural roots, and leave a distinctive mark on one of the American West's most enduring ethnic communities.

Notes

An earlier version of this essay appeard in *Montana The Magazine of Western History* 44, no. 1 (Winter 1994).

I would like to acknowledge the following: Mary Murphy for inspiring this essay; Anacondans Alice Finnegan, Jerry Hansen, Ed McCarthy, Isabel McCarthy, and Bob McCarthy for their generous assistance; and David Stratton, Louise Wade, Dave Emmons, Richard Brown, Chuck Rankin, and Marilyn Grant for their helpful editorial suggestions.

1. Isabel Tracy McCarthy, Tracy family history, copy in possession of author; quote by Spencer L. Tripp, correspondence to mother in California, 7 February 1892, excerpted in Mary Dolan, *Anaconda Memorabilia 1883–1983* (Missoula: Acme Press, 1983), 35.

2. Margaret Tracy McLean, interview by Ada Ewan, 17 May 1989, Anaconda, Anaconda-Deer Lodge County Historical Society (hereafter AHS).

3. Fifty-two percent of Irish immigrants to the United States were female, as compared with 21 percent of Italian immigrants. Janet Nolan, *Ourselves Alone: Women's Emigration from Ireland, 1885–1920* (Lexington: University Press of Kentucky, 1989), 2, 27, 42, 49, 53; Kerby A. Miller, *Emigrants and Exiles: Ireland and the Irish Exodus to North America* (New York: Oxford University Press, 1985), 406–413; Hasia Diner, *Erin's Daughters in America: Irish Immigrant Women in the 19th Century* (Baltimore: Johns Hopkins Press, 1983), 19–20, 34, 42; Robert E. Kennedy, Jr., *The Irish: Emigration, Marriage, and Fertility* (Berkeley: University of California Press, 1973), 16, 82–85.

4. Ninety percent of Irish immigrants resided in cities in 1920, and two-thirds of these lived on the East Coast. The majority of Irish immigrants in the West lived in California, and men outnumbered women in western cities. Stephan Thernstrom, ed., *Harvard Encyclopedia of American Ethnic Groups* (Cambridge, Mass.: Harvard University Press, 1980), 530. Hasia Diner contends that Irish women were reluctant to leave eastern cities for the West because they relied on established urban female social networks. Diner, *Erin's Daughters*, 65, 126.

Several studies note that Irish men found greater opportunity and acceptance in western cities such as San Francisco than in the East. See, for example, Timothy Sarbaugh, "Exiles of Confidence: The Irish-American Community of San Francisco, 1880–1920," in *From Paddy to Studs: Irish-American Communities in the Turn of the Century Era, 1880–1920*, ed. Timothy J. Meagher (Westport, Conn.: Greenwood Press, 1986), 187. Patrick J. Blessing questions whether the West offered more opportunities for the Irish and posits that higher success rates were due to advanced education levels and longer time in the United States in "Paddy: The Image and Reality of Irish Immigrants in the American Community: A Review Essay," *Journal of American Ethnic History* 9 (Fall 1989): 117. The Irish of Anaconda do not fit the paradigms of either East or West Coast Irish communities. While they did not face the discrimination that many Irish in the East experienced, neither did they have ample opportunities to rise economically, as many of their compatriots did in San Francisco. The smelter town offered few occupational choices for those who remained, regardless of education and time spent in the United States. Deer Lodge County, *1895 Census* (Anaconda, 1895), AHS.

5. Written accounts suggest that the miner-turned-capitalist Marcus Daly encouraged his Irish brethren to migrate to the smokestack community. See, for example, Ruth Meidl and George Wellcome, eds., *Anaconda, Montana, 1883–1983: A Century of History* (Anaconda: n.p., 1983), 3. For a description of Daly's influence among the Irish of Butte and Anaconda, see Thomas B. McCarthy, "From West Cork to Butte: The Irish Immigration to Montana, 1860–1900" (master's thesis, Washington State University, 1987), 93–96. Population summaries from the Bureau of the Census, *Twelfth Census of the United States: Population* (1900) (Washington, D.C.: U.S. Government Printing Office, 1901), vol. 1, table 34, p. 768; *Thirteenth Census* (1910) (Washington, D.C.: U.S. Government Printing Office, 1913), vol. 2, table 3, p. 1159; *Fourteenth Census* (1920) (Washington, D.C.: U.S. Government Printing Office, 1922), vol. 3, table 12, p. 586; *Fifteenth Census* (1930) (Washington, D.C.: U.S. Government Printing Office, 1932), vol. 3, pt. 2, tables 18–19, pp. 32–33; *Sixteenth Census* (1940) (Washington, D.C.: U.S. Government Printing Office,

1943), vol. 2, pt. 4, table 24, p. 56; *Seventeenth Census* (1950) (Washington, D.C.: U.S. Government Printing Office, 1952), vol. 2, pt. 26, table 34a, pp. 26–40, and table 42a, pp. 26–62.

6. Twenty-three percent of smelter employees in 1894 were Irish-born. Scandinavians, at 9 percent of the workforce, composed the next-largest national group. Half of the names on an 1898 roster of Anaconda Company officials are Irish. Oral history interviews with former smelter workers confirm that foremen and superintendents picked fellow Irish for jobs, at least until the union gained clout after 1934. The Irish dominated certain parts of the smelter, such as the converters and reverbatories, and obtained the prestigious crafts positions. Anaconda Mining Company, "Statement of Wages Paid and Employees," September 1894, Anaconda, Montana, Anaconda Copper Mining Company Records (hereafter ACM), MC 169, box 57, folder 40, Montana Historical Society Archives (hereafter MHSA); "1898 ACM Company Officials," "Anaconda Company" vertical file, AHS; Luke McKeon, interview by author, 29 July 1986; Joe Bolkovatz, interview by author, 12 August 1986, and John Phillip, interview by author, November 1981, MHSA. All interviews conducted in Anaconda unless otherwise noted.

David M. Emmons outlines how Irish immigrants in Butte, as the first arrivals and dominant ethnic group, were in a position to build the city and monopolize jobs, in *The Butte Irish: Class and Ethnicity in an American Mining Town, 1875–1925* (Urbana: University of Illinois Press, 1989).

7. Robert Kelly, interview by author, 2 October 1986, MHSA; Madeline McKittrick Heaney, interview by Ada Ewan, 22 May 1989, AHS; Sister Gilmary Vaughan, interview by author, 30 July 1986, MHSA.

8. *Anaconda Standard*, 31 March 1905, 3 April 1905, and 17 March 1926; Deer Lodge County, *1895 Census*; Evans and McMurray, *Anaconda City Directory* (1896); Margaret Tracy Walsh, interview by Ada Ewan, 19 May 1989, AHS.

9. "Earnings of Company Boarding Houses" (for three years ending 30 June 1900), ACM, box 49, folder 7, MHSA; *Anaconda City Directory* (1896); Delia Sweeney, interview by Alice Finnegan, 30 September 1987, AHS.

10. McKeon interview.

11. The relatively balanced sex ratio among Irish immigrants contributed to their national high rate of in-group marriage. As late as 1920, almost 75 percent of the Irish-born were married to other Irish; two-thirds of Irish immigrants who married non-Irish married second-generation or American-born children of Irish immigrants. Thernstrom, ed. *Harvard Encyclopedia*, 532. In the post–Second World War era, Anacondans encouraged matches among Catholics regardless of ethnic background. Virginia Cox Tracy, interview by Alice Finnegan, 31 August 1989, AHS.

12. Mike McNelis, interview by author, 22 November 1982, MHSA; Walsh, Vaughan, and Heaney interviews.

13. Vaughan interview; Isabel Tracy McCarthy, interview by author, 2 October 1986, MHSA.

14. Tracy interview. Several scholars discuss the comparatively greater proportion of female Irish single-headed households and their poverty. Hasia Diner notes the striking contrast in economic status between single Irish immigrant women, who had the possibility to achieve some success, and the poverty of widows, who "could not share in the bounty of American life." Diner, *Erin's Daughters*, 105.

15. McNelis interview. The St. Joseph's Orphanage was a favorite charity of the Anaconda Irish, indicating that it may have served as home for many of the community's children. Anaconda Ancient Order of Hibernian Records, Minutes, 25 October 1933, and 14 November 1934, courtesy of Anaconda AOH (hereafter cited as AOH).

16. Josephine Weiss Casey, interview by Alice Finnegan, 18 May 1989, AHS.

17. Maxine S. Seller, "Beyond the Stereotype: A New Look at the Immigrant Woman, 1880–1924," *Journal of Ethnic Studies* 3 (Spring 1975): 62; Diner, *Erin's Daughters*, 27.

18. Sweeney, McLean, and McCarthy interviews; Margaret Laughlin Kelly, interview by Alice Finnegan, 7 July 1987, MHSA. Bureau of the Census, *Fifteenth Census of the United States: Population* (1930), vol. 3, pt. 2, table 20, p. 34; *Sixteenth Census: Characteristics of the*

Population (1940), vol. 2, pt. 4, table 33, p. 110; *Seventeenth Census: Economic Characteristics of the Population* (1950), vol. 2, pt. 36, table 35, p. 264.

19. Diner, *Erin's Daughters*, 96. Sweeney and Tracy interviews.

20. Vaughan, McCarthy, and McLean interviews.

21. James H. Dorman, "Ethnic Groups and 'Ethnicity': Some Theoretical Considerations," *The Journal of Ethnic Studies* 7 (Winter 1980): 28; Nolan, *Ourselves Alone*, 3; McKeon and McCarthy interviews.

22. Vaughan and McCarthy interviews. For a discussion of why Gaelic was abandoned by Irish immigrants in Butte, see McCarthy, "From West Cork to Butte," 103–104.

23. Tracy interview.

24. Kelly interview.

25. Heaney and McLean interviews; Caithin "Kotch" Gallagher Francisco, interview by author, 20 March 1991, notes in possession of author.

26. McKeon interview.

27. Lucy McNelis quoted in McNelis interview; Bob Vine, *Anaconda Memories 1883–1983* (Butte: Artcraft Printers, 1983), 23. Mary Murphy discusses how wakes imposed a hardship on Irish widows in Butte, especially since the death of a male wage earner signified "hard scrambling for a wife," in "A Place of Greater Opportunity: Irish Women's Search for Home, Family, and Leisure in Butte, Montana," *Journal of the West* 31 (April 1992): 75–76.

28. Arthur A. "Tiny" Longfellow, interview by author, 2 October 1986, MHSA.

29. Howard Rosenleaf, interview, 29 July 1986, MHSA; Mike McNelis, Interview transcript, n.d., 2, courtesy of Alice Finnegan.

30. McNelis interview, 22 November 1982, MHSA; Sweeney interview. Tim Meagher contends that more Irish Americans suffered alcohol-related diseases than other ethnic groups well into the twentieth century. Meagher, *From Paddy to Studs*, 10.

31. The AOH was founded as a fraternal organization of Catholics of Irish birth in 1836 in New York City, but its roots began in Ireland in the seventeenth century. Michael F. Funchion, ed., *Irish American Voluntary Organizations* (Westport, Conn.: Greenwood Press, 1983), 50, 57; *Anaconda Standard*, 17 May 1896 and 18 March 1899.

32. For example, the Hibernians pledged support to families of rebels executed after the 1916 Easter Rebellion. AOH minutes, 10 May 1916. From the disbursements listed in the AOH account books, it is clear that Hibernian disability payments and widows' benefits represented critical contributions to Anaconda Irish women.

33. Catherine Dowling concludes that Butte Irish women "abandoned the traditions and memories of their homeland more readily" than did men in "Irish-American Nationalism in Butte, 1900–1916," *Montana The Magazine of Western History* 39 (Spring 1989): 59.

34. *Anaconda Standard*, 27 May 1896; AOH minutes, 12 January 1916. In later years, the men's and women's groups published a joint annual calendar, listing their joint and separately sponsored activities, including the Women's Saint Bridgette's (Ireland's patron saint) Day Observation and the Men's Annual Corned Beef Dinner. AOH Division Number One, Anaconda-Deer Lodge County, calendars 1982-1988, vertical files, AHS.

35. Anaconda AOH Records, account register of the AOH Ladies' Auxiliary, n.d. (c. 1900); AOH Ladies Auxiliary, financial records 1900–1908, 1 vol., Small Collection 1528, MHSA; AOH minutes, 10 March 1920 and 25 August 1920.

36. *Anaconda Standard*, 17 March 1902, 17 March 1903, and 18 March 1932; Francisco interview.

37. By 1920, Americans born of Irish parents outnumbered the Irish-born by more than three to one. Thernstrom, ed., *Harvard Encyclopedia*, 540. With fewer Irish-born, the Anaconda Hibernians extended membership to Irish Americans in the 1950s.

38. *Seventeenth Census* (1950), vol. 2, pt. 26, table 34a, pp. 26–40; Walter Mundstock, "Hibernians to Celebrate 100th Year," *Anaconda Leader*, 11 September 1985; Frank Quinn, "Anaconda Hibernians Steeped in History," *Montana Standard*, 15 March 1964.

39. Account book, 1922–1924, AOH Ladies' Auxiliary records, 1912–1928, courtesy of Caithin "Kotch" Gallagher Francisco.

40. Tracy and McNelis interviews.

41. Sweeney and Kelly interviews.

42. The conservative Catholic hierarchy supported ethnic parishes in the late nineteenth century to strengthen religious identification and combat the attractions of socialism. The Irish gained hegemony over the American Catholic Church by their knowledge of English and early appointments to important posts. Miller, *Emigrants and Exiles*, 526, 532; Meagher, *From Paddy to Studs*, 187; Thernstrom, ed., *Harvard Encyclopedia*, 535.

43. St. Paul's Catholic Church, "Nearly a Century of Service . . . St. Paul's Church, Anaconda, Montana, 1888–1980," (Anaconda: 1980), 3, "Churches" vertical file, AHS; "Birth of a Society," typescript (n.a., n.d.), "Churches" vertical file, AHS; Raymond A. Mohl, "The Immigrant Church in Gary, Indiana: Religious Adjustment and Cultural Defense," *Ethnicity* 8 (March 1981): 1–17.

44. *Anaconda Weekly Review*, 22 March 1888; *Anaconda Standard*, 3 May 1888 and 4 October 1906.

45. Meidl and Wellcome, *Anaconda, Montana*, 45.

46. R. L. Polk and Company, *Anaconda City Directory*, 1909, 1912, 1918, and 1925.

47. *Anaconda Standard*, 18 March 1902 and 18 March 1915. Some authors have perhaps exaggerated the power and influence of Irish American mothers, arguing that more than other ethnic women they dominated family life. See Andrew M. Greely, *The Irish Americans: The Rise to Money and Power* (New York: Harper & Row, 1981), 125; Marjorie R. Fallows, *Irish Americans: Identity and Assimilation* (Englewood Cliffs, N.J.: Prentice-Hall, 1979), 108. The evidence from Anaconda does, however, support Donna Gabaccia's contention that immigrant women experienced family life positively. Gabaccia argues that immigrant women often rejected individualistic society and found families as arenas of affirmation and support rather than as repressive institutions. Gabaccia, "Immigrant Women: Nowhere at Home?" *Journal of American Ethnic History* 10 (Summer 1991): 68–71.

48. *Anaconda Standard*, 22 June 1902.

49. Vaughan interview.

50. Kelly, Casey, Sweeney, and McCarthy interviews; St. Paul's Church, "Nearly a Century," 10.

51. In 1912, Bishop Carroll of Montana urged the AOH to ensure children's piety by encouraging the study of Irish history. Miller, *Emigrants and Exiles*, 533. AOH minutes, 1 February 1934 and 27 June 1934.

52. *Anaconda Standard*, 18 March 1926; Vaughan interview.

53. Tracy interview.

54. McCarthy, Vaughan, and Heaney interviews.

55. Sarah Deutsch, "Coming Together, Coming Apart—Women's History and the West," *Montana The Magazine of Western History* 41 (Spring 1991): 61. Micaela di Leonardo critiques the eastern "urban village" model that presupposes that "ethnic culture" determined European ethnic women's experiences in "The Myth of the Urban Village: Women, Work, and Family among Italian-Americans in Twentieth-Century California," in *The Women's West*, ed. Susan Armitage and Elizabeth Jameson (Norman: University of Oklahoma Press, 1987), 278–79. She argues that economics and the region where they settled played a much greater role in the lives of immigrant women.

56. Sweeney interview; Jerry Hansen, interview by author, 23 November 1982, MHSA.

57. Alice Finnegan, "History of the Anaconda AOH Auxiliary," in *Anaconda, Montana*, 27.

58. Tracy and Heaney interviews. Kerby Miller notes that the great majority of Irish immigrants never returned to Ireland but that for a significant minority, their homesickness shaped their American reality. Miller, *Emigrants and Exiles*, 512, 520. Mary Murphy emphasizes the choices Butte Irish women made in blending the best aspects of Irish and American culture in "A Place of Greater Opportunity," 73–78.

59. Ed Kemmick, "Anacondans Welcome Irish Consul," *Montana Standard*, n.d., vertical files, AHS; Kelly and Finnegan interviews.

60. Alice Finnegan, conversation with author, 21 March 1991, Anaconda, notes in possession of author. Ladies Ancient Order of Hibernians in America, *Official Constitution* (19 October 1985), in possession of Caithin "Kotch" Gallagher Francisco.

16.

Drag's a Life: Women, Gender, and Cross-Dressing in the Nineteenth-Century West

EVELYN A. SCHLATTER

In this article, Evelyn Schlatter suggests that women as well as men responded to Horace Greeley's famous exhortation to "go west, young man." Taking him literally, they went west dressed as men. Although sexual orientation doubtless motivated some cross-dressing women, Schlatter convincingly explores other reasons as well. As she suggests, cross-dressing could be a sensible choice. Opportunity in the West was gendered. Single women on their own in the West faced not only sexual hazards but a very limited number of occupational choices, mostly in low paid domestic work. Of course, successful cross-dressers went undetected, so we will never know how many women chose this option. Given the paucity of documentation, Schlatter's work is necessarily speculative, but she carefully explores the implications of the cases that exist in the public record. And she reminds us that Hollywood's "female westerns," which purport to show gender equality, remain Tinseltown fantasies, not accurate portraits of real cross-dressing women in the West.

[A] woman shall not wear anything that pertains to a man, nor shall a man put on a woman's garment.

—DEUTERONOMY 22:5

In *The Quick and the Dead* (1995), Sharon Stone breezes into a nineteenth-century southwestern town wearing men's clothing. Everybody knows she's a woman, and she doesn't try to disillusion them. She slings a mean gun, drinks in the saloon, and trades insults with every rummy, rough, rowdy man within city limits. She's a man's man without the masquerade; the male clothing identifies her not as a man but rather as an independent woman.

Madeline Stowe and Drew Barrymore adopt the same shape-shifting techniques in *Bad Girls* (1994). They ride the trails dressed as men, but everyone they meet knows they are women. They are multifaceted. They shift clothing and identities as needed. But neither they, their comrades, nor Stone's "Lady" ever abandon the primary social categorization in which they operate every day: their sex.

These examples of Hollywood's western women dress and do as they please. But in the "real" nineteenth-century West, clothes mattered. Like the East and the South, the West required adherence to older social and cultural rules. Among these rules were state-sanctioned expectations and stipulations that governed personal relationships, behaviors, and appearances. Had Sharon Stone or Drew Barrymore breezed into a real nineteenth-century western town wearing trousers, boots, and a man's hat, she would, at the very least, have been arrested. Her punishment might have been as lenient as a monetary fine or as harsh as a term in prison or an insane asylum.[1]

The nineteenth-century "imagined West" promised fortune and freedom to those who braved the journey. But it promised these things only to men who were presumably Anglo. The real West offered these opportunities to both men and women, but what either sex could wear and do was supported by social expectations and controlled by legal regulations.[2] So if one were born a woman, to go west required either compliance with gender norms or a certain amount of ingenuity.

What the real West most offered men was the most difficult for women to attain—independence. Even though it was legally acceptable for women to take land in their own names, most did not do so as lone, single women.[3] For a woman, setting out alone was extremely risky, usually because of unwanted male attentions. The West, even though it claimed to offer a taste of freedom for all, was a man's world. Some women, therefore, chose to adopt male garb and "pass" as men. They crossed the boundary between male and female not so much to stretch the limits of nineteenth-century roles but rather to escape the restrictions of womanhood and to seek opportunities available to westering men. The choices these women made and the strategy they employed make sense within the context of the economic and intimate crosscurrents of gender and the ways in which clothing marked and created that context in the late nineteenth century.

As a cultural phenomenon, dress signals personal identity both geographically and historically. It links an individual to a specific community and group, signals socioeconomic position, and can also indicate inclusion or exclusion in a variety of human communities.[4] In the mid- to late-nineteenth century, the largely anglocentric and middle-class Victorian civilities, social graces, and amenities emphasized male authority and female passivity.[5] The principles that publicly separated men from women, decreed women's subservience to men, and dictated gender roles and expectations as reflected in clothing hitched rides to the West in the cultural baggage of their human hosts and hostesses. Each day, whether you pulled on a pair of trousers or ratcheted yourself into a corset, you dressed your part. Some women challenged custom by using "split skirts" in order to ride horseback. Some adopted bloomers for daily life on the overland trail. And some challenged law by using conventions of dress to change their genders, thereby creating "opportunities" of their own definitions.[6]

The nineteenth-century West, for entirely practical and nonmystical reasons, proved an ideal destination for some female cross-dressers who wanted what a male world offered. They came west in search of personal independence, employment, or freedom from abusive male partners or family members. Some were in search of lost male lovers while others wished to live in peace with female lovers. Many came because of a combination of these factors. Whatever their individual reasons, cross-dressed women went west to find places for themselves, and they often gravitated to urban or urbanizing areas.

Certain western regions, because of their industrial and economic foundations, tended to attract a certain type of clientele. Growing urban centers and boomtowns in mining areas offered anonymity and opportunity to those who came to stay or simply passed through. Mining camps, especially, may have appealed to women cross-dressers because of the skewed sex ratios. A lone man in a mining camp or a quickly growing city was one of hundreds or even thousands. One more man among so many others garnered little scrutiny.

Demographic profiles of many nineteenth-century western mining regions and camps reveal a sex imbalance. The typical makeup of a mining camp was largely male, young, and ethnically and socially heterogeneous. The early years of western gold rushes, especially, could exhibit huge population disparities between men and women. In 1850, California's sex ratio was, in some places, 123 men to each woman. In places like Grass Valley, the ratio was 17 to 1. A decade later, during Colorado's gold rush years, the ratio of men to women in that state was 615 to 100.[7]

Likewise, western cities, with their conglomerations of humanity and frenetic activity, offered some anonymity to their residents. On the West Coast, the gold-rush years (1848–50) saw an extraordinary growth in San Francisco's population. With the thousands of single men pouring into the region came male impersonators. Papers chided a passing woman whose secret was unveiled during the 1850s. A "freak of fancy," trumpeted the editors. "Our municipal laws have affixed a penalty to this manner of deceiving the opposite sex. Our city laws have but little regard for the Bill of Rights adopted by the Women's Convention in the Atlantic States."[8]

Volatile boom-and-bust economies encouraged population mobility. In a largely homosocial (same-sex) environment, another scruffy young miner in old, baggy clothes was just another treasure hunter. So many different men raised few eyebrows. Those on the short or effeminate side were just a few more oddballs in a vast sea of men, all seeking work or fortunes. Male bartenders, storekeepers, and miners, when dealing with so many men all the time, had no reason to believe that a cross-dressed woman was anything other than the man she said she was.[9]

Westering women who dressed as men wanted to pass. It is difficult, therefore, to document them. Though we have access to a few biographies, autobiographies, legal documents, newspaper accounts, and semilurid magazine anecdotes, finding cross-dressers in the historical record is difficult. Those who passed successfully crossed the historical stage unnoticed and unremarked, the triumph of their deception ironically proving the researcher's loss. Women of color who chose to pass are nearly impossible to document accurately because of a double invisibility—class and race—rendered by political, economic, and social institutions that are both anglocentric and male-dominated. Many male impersonators may have slipped through the cracks of time because of these social categories; others adopted Anglo names, further cloaking their true identities and complicating the researcher's task of tracing them. Western folklore and journalism, however, tell us something about the boundaries women had to cross in order to attain male privilege and opportunities. Fortunately, these media lead us to real women who managed to breach the boundaries of sex and gender.

Newspaper correspondent Albert D. Richardson toured western mining regions between 1857 and 1867. He recorded his experiences and published them after his ten-year odyssey. One of his anecdotes described meeting a man who had advertised for "a young lad to bring water, black his boots and keep the sanctum in order." The caution he added to his advertisement was that "no young woman in disguise need apply." Richardson stated that such a stipulation "was needful in a mining country," because of his own knowledge of several male impersonators he himself had met, "each telling some romantic story of her past life." He dismissed them as being of "the wretched class against which society shuts its iron doors, bidding them hasten un-cared-for to destruction."[10]

Richardson's admonishments are part of a backlash against not only westering male impersonators but their predecessors. Westward women cross-dressers are part of a long romantic literary tradition in Euro-American history in which male impersonators enjoyed a bit of fame and perhaps a bit of infamy as well. Among the best-documented seventeenth- and eighteenth-century cross-dressers were soldiers and sailors who took on the guise of men in order to support themselves financially, act on patriotic impulses, escape abusive men, follow male lovers or relatives to battle or sea. Others wished to live in peace with female lovers. A few of these women who served admirably at sea or in battle prior to the nineteenth century revealed their secrets and published biographies, garnering friendly public attention. Some, even after "coming out" as women, were granted military pensions.[11] Their hard work and service to their countries as men made them novelties in the public eye, true, but heroic novelties nonetheless.

The American Revolution and the Civil War witnessed a flurry of male impersonation; a few cross-dressed women published accounts of their endeavors and scores more died on the battlefield.[12] In spite of the literary tradition, sharpened gender distinctions found expression in mid- to late-nineteenth-century commentary from people like correspondent Richardson. Western women cross-dressers increasingly suffered the burgeoning backlash.

Charlotte Arnold was one of these unfortunate women; she was arrested some twenty times for cross-dressing. Refusing to pay the fines, Arnold did jail time instead. Lillie Hitchcock Coit, who had a penchant for visiting San Francisco night spots in male attire, managed to avoid arrest, possibly because she was wealthy and city officials attributed her behavior to "eccentricity."[13] An Arizona woman, Mary Sawyer (aka Mollie Monroe), was not so fortunate and ended up in a Stockton, California, asylum in 1877. Sawyer spent Arizona's boom years mining, cross-dressing, drinking, and taking different men as sexual partners. The judge who finally sentenced her to the asylum could have done so on the basis of any of these behaviors, which were all "unwomanly" and subject to local regulation. Sawyer's alcoholism coupled with her cross-dressing and her refusal to settle down in a heterosexual monogamous union may have played most heavily in her sentence.[14]

In 1860, during Colorado's gold-rush years, a Denver woman in male attire attracted the attention of an eastern correspondent during an auction. He described her as dressed in "nicely fitting coat, vest, pants, boots, and beaver. . . . She frequently appears on horseback, and always astride the saddle." The letter writer further complained about what he perceived as evident moral decay. As the woman in male attire wandered the auction grounds, an immigrant man gambled with dice and the auctioneer solicited bids for the effects of a man who had died in a fire. "Is it surprising," the correspondent lamented, "that Christianity, in the midst of so much wickedness, should make but moderate progress?"[15]

Five years later, a Denver newspaper's editors reported a woman "perambulating" the city's streets in "bifurcated raiment." They suggested she had "best look out or she will be snatched."[16] The veiled warning was no idle threat for Colorado women. In 1887, Georgie Phillips, in and out of courts for ten years, served sixty days in jail. The policeman who arrested her stated that she "made a rather good looking 17 year old boy" but because of her history with the police, she could not fool him. Georgie was knock-kneed. Her crimes included charges of vagrancy and wearing men's clothes in public.[17]

Legal proscription of cross-dressing represents state and local attempts to control sexual behavior through the regulation of appearance.[18] Denver, like many American cities, included a lewd behavior statute in its ordinances. Cross-dressing in public fell under this designation. In 1875, anyone who appeared "in any public place within this city in a state of nudity, or in a dress not belonging to his or her sex, or in an indecent or lewd dress" was subject to pay "not less than ten dollars, nor more than one hundred dollars." Such acts were deemed "Offences against Good Morals and Decency."[19]

In spite of moral implications, Denver newspapers continued to print stories that involved women cross-dressers. In one 1889 issue of the *Denver Times*, several anecdotes that involved women wearing men's clothing appeared. Clearly, Denver officials were concerned about how far and for what reasons a woman pushed the bounds of propriety. If a cross-dressed woman was in the company of a man, then she seems to have avoided strict legal prosecution. Women who operated outside of heterosexual unions, on the other hand, were not so fortunate. Without male lovers or relatives to speak for them and with the presumption of sexual deviance hovering over them, cross-dressers who eschewed male companionship for whatever reasons received stricter punishment than their male-companioned counterparts.

The *Denver Times* details the following occurrences. Two men arrived in Cheyenne, Wyoming, looking for work. Both were printers. One, Jack Bennett, had a union card and soon obtained employment. His partner, "Jimmie," and he were inseparable during the week they spent in Cheyenne before deciding to go further west. The night before their scheduled departure, a saloon altercation with another group of printers resulted in the revelation of Jimmie's true identity—Jack's sister. The two departed Cheyenne hastily the next morning.[20] Jimmie may have been Jack's lover rather than sister; Jack made it a point to call her his sister, but the article's writer implies that Jack was merely claiming that she was. If Jimmie was actually Jack's lover, he may have claimed siblinghood in order to ensure that he could be a legal protector for her, especially if the two were not married.

In another incident, a Boston merchant disguised his mistress as a man, claiming she was his son, Arthur. They hobnobbed at a swanky hotel in Manitou Springs, an elegant spa near Colorado Springs. Arthur's true identity was soon discerned by private detectives the merchant's wife had hired. "Arthur" was arrested. The merchant paid the thousand-dollar bond only to be rebuffed; his mistress fled before the trial and his wife divorced him.[21]

A lighter occurrence in 1889 concerned two Denver men strolling downtown after dark. A police sergeant confronted the two, alert immediately to the fact that one was a woman. She was, in fact, her male companion's wife and had expressed an interest in seeing Denver's night life. Her husband had agreed to her request, loaned her one of his suits, and escorted her on their jaunt. The policeman, for his part, merely issued a warning and asked that the husband take his wife home.[22]

Because the cross-dresser had been in the company of her husband, and therefore within the sanctity of a heterosexual union with a proper guardian, the policeman let the two off with merely a warning. Georgie Phillips was a different matter. In 1887, the same issue of the *Times* reported, Georgie, dressed as a man, attempted to rent a room with a female companion in a Denver building. The proprietor, however, was a detective who had arrested her several times in the past, and Georgie and companion quickly left the premises before he could do so again.[23]

Women whose primary affective relationships involved other women were subject to greater public scrutiny than cross-dressers, as long as the latter had male lovers. A *Denver Times* account of two women in Colorado's Pitkin County demonstrates the growing public fear of homosexual relationships between women: "Society in this section of the county has been rent from center to circumference during the last six weeks over the sensational love affair between Miss Clara Dietrich, postmistress and general storekeeper at Emma [the town in question], and Miss Ora Chatfield . . . which culminated . . . in the elopement of the two ladies who are now supposed to be stopping at a hotel in Denver."[24]

The article then describes the two and plays upon fears of predatory women who draw younger, more innocent women into their clutches. Dietrich and Chatfield were cousins; Dietrich was the older of the two. The two lived together for a time, but Chatfield apparently succumbed to "nervous prostration" and an investigation (presumably family-initiated) revealed that she was madly in love with Dietrich. A warrant was issued for Dietrich's arrest in order to ascertain her sanity. Upon her arrest, the two women's correspondence was appropriated and turned over to the local sheriff. After an initial outcry, the two women then instigated a ruse; Dietrich left for Aspen under the auspices of marrying a man there and Chatfield claimed to be off to visit relatives. Neither did what they said; they instead fled the vicinity together, allegedly headed for Denver. One man commenting on the affair said that aside from the "unnatural affection for each other," the two women appeared to be "perfectly rational."[25]

By the late nineteenth century, scientific and public rhetoric about the dangers of homosexuality intertwined with male fears of women wresting political and economic clout from men. Women who cross-dressed—and, by extension, women who acted independently of men—were now conflated with those who expressed homosexual desires and, consequently, were construed to be "sick."[26]

Regardless of how public and legal opinion viewed them, male impersonators were as varied as the society within which they moved. Some married men or, like Mary Sawyer, had several male partners. Others maintained relationships with women. Still others may have had relationships with both men and women or with no one at all. Jeanne Bonnet, a Parisian transplant in San Jose, California, formed a gang of thieves in which her lover, Blanche Buneau, was also a member. Another San Jose gender-crosser, known as businessman Milton Matson, was engaged to Helen Fairweather, a San Francisco schoolteacher.[27]

In spite of rising public disapproval of their actions, some nineteenth-century women managed to find opportunities for better lives through cross-dressing. Male clothing offered them personal security, independence, and the chance to improve their economic positions without having to marry men. Others took to the road, wearing their new identities at first like stiff new boots, later like a favorite pair of trousers—comfortable and secretly familiar. Seeking new beginnings, some women gender-crossers headed for parts unknown where they might live as the men they projected. The West, as its mystique suggests, offered some of these cross-dressers the chance to begin anew.

In 1906, Gilbert Allen published a story he said he had heard from a Rocky Mountain prospector:

I was a scout for the government during the early frontier days. . . . This duty often carried me over the overland trail, and on several such occasions I had particularly noticed one pony rider who, when met with in his run by night or day, was wont to flit by me like a ghost. He rode the best of horses, was trim as a dandy in his dress of top boots, corduroy pants, velvet sack coat, neglige shirt and slouch hat. He was small, graceful and handsome enough for a girl, but he had a pluck nothing yet had daunted.[28]

The rider called himself Brown. He had endured confrontations with outlaws and Indians, he said, but he never spoke in detail of his past. When the prospector-scout discovered the rider's true sex, he agreed to keep the secret. Several months later, when he returned to the station where Brown habitually started her run, he discovered that she was gone, having suddenly given up her place as rider and headed back east.

Her stint as a man, it transpired, had begun when she followed a male lover who had fled to the West, accused of a crime Brown believed he hadn't committed. She had gone west to find him. One day, while traveling with the prospector-scout, she became involved in an altercation with a group of outlaws. She shot one only to discover that he was the lover she sought. As he lay dying, he told her that he had, indeed, committed the crime of which he was accused. It was at this juncture that the prospector-scout discovered Brown's true identity.[29]

Some women cross-dressers, like Brown, became Pony Express riders. Others turned to banditry. In New Mexico, a masked desperado with a beltful of guns held up a stage between Deming and Silver City. Upon closer examination, one of the stagehands discerned that the bandit was actually a woman. She robbed all present of their cash, taking a particularly large roll from "the heaviest fellow in the bunch." She then summarily dismissed her victims and took off her mask, pointing at the heavyset fellow. "This measly hound here," she allegedly announced, "was once my husband. I got a divorce from him up at Las Vegas and for a year I never could get a cent out of him for alimony." Therefore, she finished, "I've taken the law in my own hands as a high spirited woman should." And with that, the witness stated, she "swung her hat by way of farewell and disappeared in the chaparral bushes."[30]

Oklahoma's Tom King was legendary for her outlaw deeds. She escaped from an El Reno jail but was later captured in Kansas. Involved in various illicit practices, including horse theft, she had spent years on the run from federal marshals. In one incident, she passed herself off as a wealthy Texas ranchman, wearing "high heeled boots, ponderous spurs and the regulation sombrero." Rumor had it that she was not "altogether a white woman." It was said that she had been born in the Ozark Mountains in southwest Missouri, where her father (also Tom King) operated an illegal still and peddled contraband whiskey. One or both of her parents may have been either Native American or African American; regardless, known sources on King's ethnicity are silent, exemplifying once again the difficulty involved in finding women of color who cross-dressed.[31]

Not all women cross-dressers, when found out, ended up in asylums, courts, or jails. Some managed to win public support. Stockton, California,

Babe Bean. Stockton (California) *Evening Mail*, 9 October 1897.

provides a case in point. The city's favorite gender-crosser, known as Babe Bean, lived on a houseboat on nearby McLeod's Lake. Arrested in 1897 at age twenty for cross-dressing, she wrote out her story because she claimed to have lost her speech in an accident. As a man, she wrote, "I can travel freely, feel protected and find work."[32]

Though her neighbors called her "Jack," she noted that her real name was Babe Bean. She refused to discuss her family but claimed they were "one of the best in the land." Her mother, fearing for her tomboy daughter's future, had seen fit to consign her to a convent. At fifteen, Bean had married her brother's best friend in order to escape the convent and to see the world. She divorced him a few months later and wandered for four years through mountains, cities, and hobo camps. Bean often expressed regret that her "rough manner" may have offended her mother, whom she claimed to "love with all her heart."[33]

Intrigued by the young male impersonator and perhaps taking pity upon Bean because of her romantically tragic story, many Stockton residents began to treat her with affectionate curiosity. The local bachelor's club granted her an honorary membership and the Stockton *Evening Mail* hired her as a reporter, though some did not find Bean's social conduct amusing. A letter that appeared in the paper from the "Girls of Stockton" demanded to know "why Babe Bean should be allowed to dress that way, while if any of the rest of us wanted to walk out in that kind of costume for a change, we would be arrested quicker than quick. There used to be a law against females dressing like the male human being, but it seems not to apply to Babe Bean."[34]

Reasons for Bean's cross-dressing in full view of the public eye without further legal harassment remain obscure. She may simply have won local support through the force of her personality. The fact that she was mute (or claimed to be so) may have softened legislative hearts toward her. Or perhaps local governing officials saw no harm in allowing Bean to live as she chose, as long as she stayed out of real trouble. Besides, the explanation she offered—escaping from convent life—and her desire to protect her family identity may have garnered sympathy from Stockton residents.

With the outbreak of the Spanish-American War in 1898, Babe Bean disappeared both from local headlines and from Stockton, only to surface in the American forces as Lieutenant Jack Garland. After the war, Garland moved to San Francisco where she served as a male nurse during the earthquake and fire of 1906. She also provided emergency medical care for the homeless during these disasters. Garland stayed on in San Francisco for the next thirty years in various rooming houses and operated as a free-lance social worker for the homeless and hungry. In 1936, "Uncle Jack" collapsed and was summarily rushed to a hospital where she died. Hospital attendants, at first treating the death as routine, discovered not only the true sex of Jack Garland but her other two identities. It seems Babe Bean had been born Elvira Virginia Mugarrieta, daughter of José Marcos Mugarrieta, a Mexican military commander who, while in New Orleans, had met Bean's mother, Eliza Alice Denny Garland, the daughter of Rice Garland, Louisiana congressman and later Louisiana supreme court judge.[35]

Unlike Babe Bean, who managed to beat the system, most nineteenth-century women cross-dressers were in constant danger of exposure, arrest, or incarceration in jails or insane asylums. Some came west to seek the mother lodes of opportunity offered to their biological male counterparts who sometimes colluded with them. But the West, however seductive its promise of liberation, replicated many Euro-American social expectations and restrictions that dealt with sex and gender. Nevertheless, the rewards were worth the risks. Cross-dressing kept women off the public dole, protected them from sexual harassment, and enabled escape from abusive male partners or relatives. But it required the construction of a new self at the expense of the old in a social climate intent upon maintaining a woman's "proper place."

In 1992, TriStar Pictures released Maggie Greenwald's production of *The Ballad of Little Jo*, starring actress Suzy Amis as Jo Monaghan. Little Jo had gained notoriety upon her death around the turn of the century when her neighbors first discovered that the slightly built rancher was a woman. Greenwald's telling of Josephine Monaghan's story portrays a young woman who takes to male attire in order to escape family disgrace back east and to protect herself from unwanted, often violent male advances as she wends her way west to Idaho. Jo realizes that any opportunities for economic independence are much greater for her as a man than as a woman. She manages to save enough money to purchase a small ranch where she spends the rest of her life, mostly alone, jealously guarding the secret of her identity. Amis's Monaghan is desperately unapproachable and solitary. Beneath her prickly exterior, though, the audience senses a heavy sorrow and repressed guilt: Little Jo has left her son back east with her sister, who has told him his mother is dead, even though the two women correspond throughout Monaghan's life.

The Ballad of Little Jo is not an adventurous shoot-'em-up in which the bad guy gets his comeuppance and the good-girl-dressed-as-guy finds happiness in the arms of the leading man or at least happiness in a dress. The only respite Greenwald gives Monaghan is a brief relationship with a Chinese man whom Jo has saved from a lynching. When he dies after a long illness, Jo reverts to her secluded and detached existence. And so she remains until her death, as solitary and lonely as she was most of her life.[36]

The Ballad of Little Jo is not glamorous. As a result, as Greenwald learned, it did not do well at the box office. We can understand women dressing like men, as long as they still look like women, but we can't deal with women actually changing gender identities and passing as men. To do so threatens heterosexual constructions of gender and male authority. Amis's Jo Monaghan as the cross-dressed woman eschews all "feminine" characteristics and appearances and does not marry the handsome leading man. No one rides off into the sunset. No one wears a white hat. And the ending isn't happy. This is a true-to-life "western." Idaho gives Little Jo a new beginning, spectacular views, employment, personal liberty. But the price is enormous personal sacrifice.

The real Jo Monaghan, like so many other gender-crossers, at once subverted the nineteenth-century gender system and also affirmed it. By adopting the dress and mannerisms of the opposite sex, male impersonators became men. Their actions did not necessarily pave the way for feminism, though they proved threatening for many in the West, as reflected in the press and in popular fiction. For example, though many gender-crossers voted in western territories and states that had not yet granted women the vote, their actions went unremarked because they could not reveal their secret at risk of personal safety and livelihood. Ironically, the women who were discovered may have unwittingly created a feminist dialogue—however brief it seemed—in public discourse. By fooling men and gaining access to a male power structure, these women demonstrated that gender is not immutable, not biologically ordained— something far more threatening to a bipolar gender system than the simple act of appropriating male clothing.

However we imagine the "frontier" and the liberty it promised some people, the fact remains that it was and still is as much a creation of long-standing sociocultural desires as it was and is a historical process or a specific region. New beginnings in the West were actually reconstructions of old ways, but some women managed to prove that men, like women, are *made*, not necessarily *born*, which just goes to show that clothes could and did make the man.

Notes

Many thanks to Sue Armitage and Betsy Jameson for their attentive and gentle editing and continued guidance. Their comments and insights have proven both immensely helpful and often soothing.

1. Susan L. Johnson, "Sharing Bed and Board: Cohabitation and Cultural Difference in Central Arizona Mining Towns, 1863–1873," in *The Women's West*, ed. Susan Armitage and Elizabeth Jameson (Norman: University of Oklahoma Press, 1984), 84–86.

2. Mary Whisner, "Gender-Specific Clothing Regulation: A Study in Patriarchy," *Harvard Women's Law Journal* 5, no. 1 (Spring 1982): 76.

3. H. Elaine Lindgren, *Land in Her Own Name: Women as Homesteaders in North Dakota* (Fargo, N.D.: Institute for Regional Studies, 1991), 15, 24–25, 32–35. Lindgren also determined from her sample that most women who homesteaded were young (in their twenties) and single, but a few were older single women or widows with small children. Some were married but were caring for ill or incapacitated husbands (16). Lindgren charts a few women who homesteaded with other women. See also Elizabeth Jameson's introduction in *The Checkered Years: A Bonanza Farm Diary, 1884–1888*, by Mary Dodge Woodward (St. Paul: Minnesota Historical Society Press, 1989). Some women did decide to "go it alone." They often found kin or kinlike protection through ethnic networks upon arrival at their claims. See essays by Dee Garceau and Laurie Mercier, this volume.

4. Ruth Barnes and Joanne Eicher, eds., *Dress and Gender: Making and Meaning in Cultural Contexts* (New York: Berg, 1992), 1. See also Joanne B. Eicher and Mary Ellen Roach-Higgins, "Definition and Classification of Dress: Implications for Analysis of Gender Roles," in *Dress and Gender*, 8–29. Aileen Ribeira traces changes in clothing and social attitudes in western civilization over time from medieval Europe to the twentieth century. See *Dress and Morality* (New York: Holmes and Meier, 1986).

5. Historiographical debate about the applicability of so-called separate spheres abounds. Since Barbara Welter proposed "The Cult of True Womanhood" (*American Quarterly* 18[1966]:151–74), scholars have analyzed and reanalyzed the relations between men and women during the nineteenth century and on into the twentieth. The rhetoric of "separate spheres" did find expression on many sociopolitical levels, but its relevance to women who were not Anglo or middle class was most likely minimal, since basic human survival precluded the luxury of inactivity.

Robert L. Griswold, "Anglo Women and Domestic Ideology in the American West in the Nineteenth and Early Twentieth Centuries," notes that the domestic ideal existed as both formal ideology and imperfectly realized assumptions through which Anglo western women interpreted their reality. Griswold designates social expectations of women as "domestic ideology." Women's chief responsibilities were homemaking and child rearing, and women represented the moral foundation of not only the family but society. Griswold takes Welter to task when he notes that, at least in the West, domestic ideology was not a rigid set of assumptions about sex roles nor was it a well-defined "cult of true womanhood." It was more a way in which women made sense of their everyday lives. In *Western Women: Their Land, Their Lives*, ed. Lillian Schlissel, Vicki L. Ruiz, and Janice Monk (Albuquerque: University of New Mexico Press, 1988), 15–34.

6. The literature on Manifest Destiny and "frontier" is immense. Since Frederick Jackson Turner's 1893 essay, historians and laypersons alike have argued the nature of "frontier" and whether it actually existed or not. See Turner, "The Significance of the Frontier in American History," in *The Frontier in American History* (Tucson: University of Arizona Press, 1986). A

later generation of historians of women have expanded the literature to examine the ways in which women participated in the area dubbed "the West." For western women's history, see Armitage and Jameson's *The Women's West*. For trail accounts, see Lillian Schlissel's *Women's Diaries of the Westward Journey* (New York: Schocken Books, 1982, 1992). Other sources of western women's history include Schlissel, Ruiz, and Monk, eds., *Western Women*; Julie Roy Jeffrey, *Frontier Women: The Trans-Mississippi West, 1840–1880* (New York: Hill and Wang, 1979); Sarah Deutsch, *No Separate Refuge: Culture, Class, and Gender on an Anglo-Hispanic Frontier in the American Southwest 1880–1940* (New York: Oxford University Press, 1987); Peggy Pascoe, *Relations of Rescue: The Search for Female Moral Authority in the American West, 1874–1939* (New York: Oxford University Press, 1990); and Sandra Myres, *Westering Women and the Frontier Experience, 1800–1915* (Albuquerque: University of New Mexico Press, 1982).

7. Ralph E. Mann, *After the Gold Rush: Society in Grass Valley and Nevada City, 1849–1870* (Stanford, Calif.: Stanford University Press, 1982), 224, table 1. See also Elliott West, "Five Idaho Mining Towns: A Computerized Profile," *Pacific Northwest Quarterly* 73 (July 1982): 108–20; Duane A. Smith, "The San Juaner: A Computerized Portrait," *Colorado Magazine* 52 (Spring 1975): 137–52; Mary Murphy, "Women on the Line: Prostitution in Butte, Montana, 1878–1917," (master's thesis, University of North Carolina at Chapel Hill, 1983), 6. As gold fever cooled, the gap between numbers of men and women in some mining communities decreased. For example, in 1900 Butte, Montana, exhibited a population that was roughly 60 percent male and 40 percent female. About one-fourth of the total population was made up of children under sixteen. See Murphy, "Women on the Line."

8. Cited in the San Francisco Lesbian and Gay History Project (hereafter SFLGHP), " 'She Even Chewed Tobacco': A Pictorial Narrative of Passing Women in America," in *Hidden from History: Reclaiming the Gay and Lesbian Past*, ed. Martin Duberman, Martha Vicinus, and George Chauncey, Jr. (New York: Meridian Books, 1989), 187. This is an edited version of a slide-tape of the same title produced by Estelle Freedman and Liz Stevens. Allen Bérubé conducted the primary research. The slide-tape is available from Women Make Movies, 462 Broadway, New York, N.Y. 10013.

The women's convention to which the editors referred was the Seneca Falls Convention, the first women's rights conference in the United States. Organized by Elizabeth Cady Stanton and Lucretia Mott, the convention was held in 1848 in Seneca Falls, New York. The conference-goers hammered out a women's bill of rights using the framework of the American Declaration of Independence. See Carol Hymowitz and Michaele Weissman, *A History of Women in America* (New York: Bantam Books, 1978), chap. 7.

9. Historians have long documented the great numbers of men in western mining areas, especially those in the beginning throes of boom times. This is not to imply that women did not pass through, work, or settle in mining towns, though. See, for example, Jeffrey, *Frontier Women*, chap. 5. Elliott West's *The Saloon on the Rocky Mountain Mining Frontier* (Lincoln: University of Nebraska Press, 1979) is a fine analysis of male community in a predominantly male world and the prominence of the saloon in mining camps as a public institution. Robert V. Hine's *Community on the American Frontier—Separate but Not Alone* (Norman: University of Oklahoma Press, 1980) emphasizes the transience and mobility of mining-camp inhabitants. See also Duane Smith, *Rocky Mountain West: Colorado, Wyoming, and Montana 1859–1915* (Albuquerque: University of New Mexico Press, 1992), 28; Elliott West, "Women of the Rocky Mountain West," in *A Taste of the West: Essays in Honor of Robert G. Athearn*, ed. Duane A. Smith (Boulder, Colo.: Pruett, 1983), 148–74; Paula Petrik, *No Step Backward: Women and Family on the Rocky Mountain Mining Frontier, Helena, Montana, 1865–1900* (Helena: Montana Historical Society Press, 1987).

10. Albert D. Richardson, *Beyond the Mississippi: From the Great River to the Great Ocean 1857–1867* (Hartford, Conn.: American Publishing, 1867), 200.

11. Ireland's Christian Davies (1667–1739) became Christopher Welsh to follow a missing husband into the British army. She traveled extensively throughout Europe and earned a military

pension after her service. See C. J. S. Thompson, *The Mysteries of Sex: Women Who Posed as Men and Men Who Impersonated Women* (New York: Causeway Books, 1974; orig. pub. 1938), and Estelle Jelinek, "Disguise Autobiographies: Women Masquerading as Men," *Women's Studies International Forum* 10, no. 1 (1987): 53–62. Regarding Davies, see Jelinek, 54–55.

One of the best-known military cross-dressers was an Englishwoman, Hannah Snell (1723–92). Snell took the guise of a man and enlisted in the army in order to pursue an unfaithful husband. It took nine years of continuous lobbying before the English government grudgingly granted Snell her pension. See Jelinek, "Disguise Autobiographies," 55, and Julie Wheelwright, *Amazons and Military Maids: Women Who Dressed as Men in the Pursuit of Life, Liberty and Happiness* (Boston: Pandora Press, 1989). See also Snell's memoirs, *The Female Soldier, or the Surprising Life and Adventures of Hannah Snell* (London: R. Walker, 1750).

12. See Richard Hall, *Patriots in Disguise: Women Warriors of the Civil War* (New York: Marlowe and Company, 1993), xi, 107–32. Deborah Sampson (another spelling is "Samson") is one of the best-known male impersonators who fought in the Revolutionary War; two others are Margaret Corbin and Nancy Hart. Ibid., xi. A Cuban-born woman who successfully passed as a man in the Confederate ranks joined as Harry T. Buford. See Loreta Janeta Velazquez's autobiography, edited by C. J. Worthington, titled *The Woman in Battle: a Narrative of the Exploits, Adventures, and Travels of Madame Loreta Janeta Velazquez, Otherwise Known as Lieutenant Harry T. Buford, Confederate States Army* (Hartford, Conn.: Belknap, 1876).

Sarah Emma Edmonds served for the Union as Frank Thompson. Her autobiography is *Nurse and Spy in the Union Army: Comprising the Adventures and Experiences of a Woman in Hospitals, Camps, and Battlefields* (Hartford, Conn.: W. S. Williams, 1864). Charley (Charlotte) "Hatfield" also served in the Union Army for an Iowa regiment after an unsuccessful attempt to both strike it rich in the Pikes Peak gold rush and track down an errant paramour. The biographical, somewhat exaggerated tale of "Mountain Charley" is *The Adventures of Mrs. E. J. Guerin Who Was Thirteen Years in Male Attire as Mountain Charley* (Norman: University of Oklahoma Press, 1968) with introduction by Fred M. Mazzulla and William Kostka. The exploits and adventures of Charley entered western lore via an alleged confidant named George West, who began publishing excerpts from her life in 1885. See Hall, *Patriots in Disguise*, chap. 13.

13. SFLGHP, "'She Even Chewed Tobacco,'" 187.

14. Johnson, "Sharing Bed and Board," 84–86.

15. Libeus Barney, *Letters of the Pike's Peak Gold Rush: Early-Day Letters by Libeus Barney, Reprinted from the Bennington Banner, Vermont, 1859–1860* (San Jose, Calif.: The Talisman Press, 1959). This particular letter is dated 7 February 1860. The notation is Denver City, Jefferson Territory, Rocky Mountains.

16. *Rocky Mountain News* (Denver, Colo.), 20 September 1865.

17. *Denver Times*, 13 July 1889. The article is titled "Women Who Wear Trousers."

18. Whisner, "Gender-Specific Clothing," 97–98.

19. Section 3, Article I, *Denver City Ordinances*, Chapter VI. The same code and penalty was in effect in 1927. By 1950, the ordinance specified only men who appeared publicly in women's clothing. The presence of women in the workplace during World War II rendered the statute obsolete, since many women had to adopt trousers in order to work many wartime jobs. Cross-dressed men who appeared in public were continually arrested in Denver through the 1960s and on into the 1970s. It is my understanding that the ordinance finally went off the books in 1974.

20. *Denver Times*, 13 July 1889.

21. Ibid.

22. Ibid.

23. Ibid.

24. *Denver Times*, 6 July 1889. The headline and accompanying blurb is "Lovelorn Girls . . . Strange Infatuation of a Pair of Female Cousins. Vain Efforts to Check It . . . A Beautiful Aspen Girl Passionately in Love With Her Cousin, Who Reciprocates Her Affection With Masculine Ardor."

25. Ibid.

26. Julie Wheelwright argues that psychological redefinition of cross-dressing as deviant behavior swayed public opinion into viewing women who gender-crossed as "sick." See *Amazons and Military Maids*, 155. For primary documentation, see, for example, Richard von Krafft-Ebing, *Psychopathia Sexualis*, 1886. This book has several later editions. See also the works of Havelock Ellis, especially *The Psychology of Sex: A Manual for Students* (London: Heinemann, 1933) and *Sexual Inversion* (Philadelphia: F. A. Davis, 1915). Vern L. Bullough offers a recent survey of sexological research in *Science in the Bedroom: A History of Sex Research* (New York: Basic Books, 1994).

27. SFLGHP, " 'She Even Chewed Tobacco,' " 188–89.

28. Gilbert Allen, "The Woman Express Rider," *The Frontier* 4, no. 12 (June 1906): 14. Allen alleges that a prospector he met while traveling through the Rocky Mountains told this tale.

29. Ibid., 14–15.

30. "Frontier Sketches," *Denver Field and Farm*, 1387 (31 August 1912): 8. Author unknown.

31. "Frontier Tales," *Denver Field and Farm*, 452 (1 September 1894): 6. Author unknown.

32. SFLGHP, " 'She Even Chewed Tobacco,' " 187.

33. Ibid., 189–90.

34. Ibid., 190.

35. Louis Sullivan, *From Female to Male: The Life of Jack Bee Garland* (Boston: Alyson Publications, 1990), 154–56. The San Francisco Lesbian and Gay History Project lists Mugarrieta as founder of the Mexican consul[ate] in San Francisco (" 'She Even Chewed Tobacco,' " 191–92). Sullivan states that Mugarrieta was actually an appointee to the consulship in 1857. Mexican General Placido Vega removed him from his post in 1863. Because of his political ties and because of subsequent political disorganization in Mexico, Mugarrieta was unable to collect his military salaries, and he ended up trying to support his family as a Spanish teacher and translator in San Francisco. Sullivan, *From Female to Male*, 156–57.

36. I found a biography of Jo Monaghan in the 13 March 1904 *Rocky Mountain News Magazine*. The *News* is a Denver newspaper and the magazine insert started to appear on Sundays and holidays during the later years of the nineteenth century. Greenwald took some poetic license with Monaghan's story; the paper mentions the Chinese man who worked for a brief time on Jo's ranch but does not discuss any intimate relationship the two may have had. According to the newspaper, Monaghan was from Buffalo, New York, and was a member of an upper-crust family. Just prior to her societal debut shortly after the Civil War, she got involved with a man of whom her parents disapproved. When she became pregnant with his child, the man refused to marry her and her parents disowned her. She sought employment commensurate with her education but found it near impossible to support herself and her son. She did maintain contact with her sister, who asked Jo to move back into the family household following the deaths of both parents. Jo refused the offer, possibly trying to save her sister further embarrassment, and instead opted to head west. Leaving her infant son with her sister, Josephine Monaghan undertook the journey as Jo Monaghan. Eventually she settled in Idaho. Both Greenwald's version and the 1904 biography concur that Little Jo was extremely private and had no friends and few visitors but that she was "liked by all. He never did anyone any harm and bore no man ill-will." *Rocky Mountain News Magazine*, 13 March 1904.

PART FIVE

Seeking Empowerment

Conquests and migrations brought many people into unequal relationships with one another on common western ground. We have just begun to document the many ways these people responded to inequality, poverty, and discrimination. The articles in this section examine efforts to empower racial ethnic women from the 1890s through the 1930s. They highlight the different needs, values, assumptions, and options that defined what "equity," "power," and "opportunity" meant for women of different races and classes and also suggest new questions and frameworks for histories of social reform.

Many of the ways we have thought about reform have left out racial ethnic women. The first women's and ethnic histories emphasized political and legal change and focused, therefore, on suffrage campaigns, civil rights organizations, and public leadership. These works were path-breaking and important; they also helped us see the limits of older historical models. Their focus on public politics and organizations often emphasized the work of leaders. Histories of women's movements largely focused on white middle-class women, and histories of civil rights focused on racial ethnic men. The authors of an important African American women studies anthology summarized the problem in their title—All the Women Are White, All the Blacks Are Men, but Some of Us Are Brave.[1]

We need to examine the assumptions that have limited historical research on racial ethnic women's own activism. We must question histories that suggested that important changes occur only in the public arena, and thus that wealthy and socially powerful people, people with the leisure to devote to organizing, and male political leaders are the people who achieve significant change. In fact, many women have organized effectively through their daily activities. Tactics like consumer boycotts, for instance, are rooted in domestic work and informal networks. Histories of organizations often miss acts of resistance that originated in households and communities—women who scorched the shirts they ironed for abusive employers and spouses, the unorganized miners' wives who harassed strikebreakers, mothers who organized hot school lunches before the state accepted that responsibility, neighbors who sheltered battered women and children before there were battered women's shelters. We can document women's histories more fully by looking at local arenas, like church-based and neighborhood organizing or domestic and grassroots support for organized reform.

We must also question the cultural biases that have kept us from recognizing the full range of women's activism. Nationalist assumptions led us to focus on immigrants' efforts to become "American" and directed us away from political movements tied to struggles in their homelands. As a result, we missed anticolonial political activists like the Korean women discussed in Sucheng Chan's article in this section. We also believed too easily that traditional gender roles constrained women from seeking their own empowerment. Some historians, for instance, assumed that Mexican American women were home-bound traditionalists, restricted by deference to macho men from asserting their own needs. We were further limited by the assumption that women primarily sought equality as women, a perspective that excluded working-class organizing efforts and movements for racial equality from the range of women's politics. Another limiting misconception is the belief that feminism is a white middle-class movement and that women of color and working-class women do not have their own feminist histories. A mistaken corollary is that women of color organize for different reasons than white women or racial ethnic men—that if they organize, they do so for their families, their neighborhoods, their men, but not for "selfish" self-empowerment. Such assumptions do not encourage us to do the kind of digging necessary to document racial ethnic women's organizing.

The articles in this section challenge these assumptions. They examine some of the efforts of women of color to increase their own power, individually and collectively. In the process they demonstrate the importance of comparative frameworks for analyzing inequality and activism. Comparisons of class and race, for instance, illuminate the different assumptions of middle-class reformers and the working-class women of color they sought to help. As Vicki Ruiz shows in her article in this section, one way that racial ethnic women empowered themselves was through their selective use of the resources provided by well-intentioned white women. They might participate in literacy classes and use free kindergartens, for example, but not accept religious conversion or the desirability of cultural assimilation. The clients' constraints and their ranges of choice become important questions in these exchanges, as Lisa Emmerich emphasizes in her article on the campaign of BIA personnel to combat Indian infant mortality. Looking at organized reform as a two-way exchange between clients and reformers is one way to see power relationships more clearly. This interactive model includes the reformers, who sought to expand their own social authority and personal satisfaction by working to help others, and the clients, who chose, among limited options, the assistance that best met their own needs.

Further attention to race and class will help us compare women's activism in the contexts of specific power structures and inequalities. Middle-class women of color reformers, for instance, as Lynda Dickson demonstrates in her article on African American women's clubs, not only sought to help poorer racial ethnic women, as did their white counterparts. They also acted to change negative stereotypes of themselves as racial ethnic women. Race and gender produced particular conflicts for racial ethnic women's rights advocates, who encountered racism in the national women's rights movement and male privilege in movements for racial equality. Many Euro-American woman suffrage leaders made the racist argument that it was unfair to let immigrant and black men vote but not white women. The 1899 convention of the National American Woman Suffrage Association (NAWSA) defeated a resolution protesting the consequences of segregated transportation, "That colored women ought not to be compelled to ride in smoking cars, and that suitable accommodations should be provided for them." In 1913, NAWSA leaders asked Ida B. Wells-Barnett, president of a Chicago African American suffrage club, not to march with white Chicago women in a national suffrage parade. Their request, like the earlier failure to protest Jim Crow segregation on the railroads, had to do with region as well as race, particularly with the influence of white suffragists from the South. The suffrage leaders acceded to white southerners who objected to marching with racially integrated delegations. Wells-Barnett, however, announced that she would march with the Illinois delegation or not at all, rather than march with the segregated African American women's contingent. As the parade started, she simply joined the Illinois delegates, and two white Illinois women moved to march beside her.[2]

As they fought racism in the women's rights movement, women of color often had to fight men in movements for racial equality in order to have women's needs represented or to participate in making policy. Women struggled to establish their influence in middle-class civil rights organizations like the League of United Latin American Citizens (LULAC), which Cynthia Orozco addresses in her article in this section. Because women of color were restricted from top positions of public leadership, and because many histories of social movements focused on the actions and philosophies of male leaders, racial ethnic women's organizing was seldom visible. Their omission, however, distorted histories that missed the countless acts of daily resistance that achieved important change.

Consider one topic in the history of civil rights in America, the movement to integrate public transportation. For many Americans, that subject sparks an image of Martin Luther King, Jr., leading the Montgomery bus boycott of 1955. Fewer people think immediately of Rosa Parks, who started the boycott by refusing to relinquish her seat on a bus; even fewer see her realistically, as a community activist who made a conscious political choice. And very few of us, in all likelihood, think of

Charlotte Brown and Mary Ellen Pleasant, who challenged segregated public transportation in San Francisco almost a century earlier.

On 17 April 1863, Charlotte Brown was forced to get off a San Francisco streetcar because she was black. She filed suit against the Omnibus Company in county court, requesting $200 in damages. Although the judge reminded the jury that California law forbade excluding African Americans from streetcars, the jury awarded Brown only 5ᶜ, the price of her fare. Three days later, Charlotte Brown was again ejected from an Omnibus streetcar. This time she filed suit in Twelfth District Court and requested $3,000 in damages. On 17 January 1865, a jury awarded her $500. In a similar case the previous month, William Bowen won $3,199 in damages from another streetcar company, the North Beach and Mission Railroad Company. Subsequently, prominent African American business-woman Mary Ellen Pleasant filed two more streetcar segregation cases that were much more widely publicized. Removed from an Omnibus Railroad Company streetcar in October 1866, Pleasant charged racial discrimination. She withdrew her claim, however, when the company assured her that "negroes would hereafter be allowed to ride on the car." Two years later, she won a lawsuit against the North Beach and Mission Railroad Company that went to the California Supreme Court. The three plaintiffs, Charlotte Brown, William Bowen, and Mary Ellen Pleasant, shared a racial grievance that crossed class and gender lines. All three resisted segregation. Class mattered, however, in the publicity Pleasant won for their cause. Mary Ellen Pleasant's wealth and prominence helped her finally integrate public transportation for all African Americans in the city.[3]

Whether racial ethnic women organized to help other women of color, to build community institutions, to achieve social empowerment or political equity, or to support anticolonialist political movements, class and gender as well as race shaped their activism. Because they were often embattled in organizations led by white women or by men, women of color found their greatest support, developed their agendas, and articulated their particular needs in organizations and clubs they organized for themselves. Lynda Dickson emphasizes the importance of mutual support in her article on African American women's clubs in Denver.[4]

The articles in this section help us see how inequalities of race, wealth, and gender operated in resistance and in organized reform. In the process, they help us imagine a wider and more inclusive range of women's activism.

Notes

1. Gloria T. Hull, Patricia Bell Scott, and Barbara Smith, eds., *All the Women Are White, All the Blacks Are Men, but Some of Us Are Brave: Black Women's Studies* (Old Westbury, N.Y.: Feminist Press, 1982).

2. The parade was held in Washington, D.C., the day before Woodrow Wilson's inauguration as president. For both incidents, see Aileen S. Kraditor, *The Ideas of the Woman Suffrage*

Movement 1890–1929 (1965, Anchor Books; Garden City, N.Y.: Doubleday, 1971), 141–42, 166–67. See also Rosalyn Terborg-Penn, "Discrimination against Afro-American Women in the Woman's Movement, 1830–1920," in *The Afro-American Woman: Struggles and Images*, ed. Sharon Harley and Rosalyn Terborg-Penn (Port Washington, N.Y.: Kennikat, 1978), 17–27; and Rosalyn Terborg-Penn, "Discontented Black Feminists," in *Decades of Discontent: The Women's Movement, 1920–1940*, ed. Lois Scharf and Joan M. Jensen (Westport, Conn.: Greenwood Press, 1983).

3. See San Francisco *Daily Alta California*, 18 October 1866, and Lynn M. Hudson, "A New Look, or 'I'm Not Mammy to Everybody in California': Mary Ellen Pleasant, a Black Entrepreneur," *Journal of the West* 32, no. 13 (July 1993): 37. See also Robert J. Chandler, "Friends in Time of Need, Republican and Black Civil Rights in California during the Civil Rights Era," *Arizona and the West* 24, no. 4 (Winter 1982): 319–340, esp 332–34; and Albert Broussard, "The New Racial Frontier: San Francisco's Black Community: 1900–1940" (Ph.D. dissertation, Duke University, 1977), 26–27. We are grateful to Quintard Taylor for bringing these cases to our attention and for sharing his own research with us.

4. See also Marilyn Dell Brady, "Kansas Federation of Colored Women's Clubs, 1900–1930," *Kansas History* 9, no. 1 (Spring 1986): 19–30. The precursor of the KFCWC was the Ladies Refuge Aid Society of Lawrence, Kansas, which organized to provide food, clothing, money, and assistance for destitute ex-slaves.

17.

Dead Ends or Gold Mines? Using Missionary Records in Mexican American Women's History

VICKI L. RUIZ

In this article, first published in 1991, Vicki L. Ruiz uses a case study of the Rose Gregory Houchen Settlement House in El Paso to ask complex questions about the relationships between Anglo reformers and their Mexican clients. Ruiz begins with Houchen's records, which document an extraordinarily long-lived Progressive Era settlement house. But, as her title suggests, she questions whether selective and ethnocentric records can reveal the motives and choices of the women who used its services.

The title is deceptive, because it asks a question that has only two possible answers—missionary records are either dead ends that lead nowhere as sources for Mexican American women's history, or they are gold mines of as-yet-untapped historical ore. Ruiz rejects both answers and instead turns to the issue of methodology as she tries to reconstruct the clients' decisions and choices. To do that, she must, as she puts it, get "beneath the text." By juxtaposing the records with oral interviews, she demonstrates the selective use clients made of Houchen's services and the different assumptions staff and clients brought to their relationships. The result is a nuanced analysis of the decisions of Houchen staff and clients alike and of the sources of identity and community that influenced them. Ruiz produces not just a history of Houchen, but a case study of what she calls "cultural coalescence," or how people "pick, borrow, retain, and create distinctive cultural forms."

Ruiz thus goes far beyond the polarized formulations of dead ends or gold mines. The Houchen records become a point of departure for a much more interesting and complex history of relationships between missionaries and clients, settlement house and surrounding community, and methodology and theory. Focusing on the clients' side of the exchange, Ruiz demonstrates that we need to reevaluate both conventional archival sources and the questions we bring to them.

This essay addresses what is often ill perceived as the flip side of theory—that is, methodology. How do we use institutional records (for example, missionary reports, pamphlets, and newsletters) to illustrate the experiences and attitudes of women of color? How do we sift through the bias, the self-congratulation, and the hyperbole to gain insight into women's lives? What can these records tell us of women's agencies?

I am intrigued (actually, obsessed is a better word) with questions involving decision making, specifically with regard to acculturation. What have Mexican women chosen to accept or reject? How have the economic, social, and political environments influenced the acceptance or rejection of cultural messages that emanate from the Mexican community, from U.S. popular culture, from Americanization programs, and from a dynamic coalescence of differing and at times oppositional cultural forms? What were women's real choices? And, to borrow from Jürgen Habermas, how did they move "within the horizon of their lifeworld"?[1] Obviously, no set of institutional records can provide substantive answers, but by exploring these documents in the framework of these larger questions, we place Mexican women at the center of our study, not as victims of poverty and superstition (as they were so often depicted by missionaries) but as women who made choices for themselves and for their families.

Pushed by the economic and political chaos generated by the Mexican Revolution and lured by jobs in the U.S. agribusiness and industry, over 1 million Mexicans migrated northward between 1910 and 1930. When one thinks of Mexican immigration, one typically visualizes a single male or family group. However, women sometimes traveled as *solas* (single women). Mexicanos settled into the existing barrios and forged new communities in the Southwest and Midwest.[2] El Paso, Texas, was their Ellis Island, and many decided to stay in this bustling border city. In 1900, the Mexican community of El Paso numbered only 8,748 residents, but by 1930, its population had swelled to 68,476. Over the course of the twentieth century, Mexicans have composed over one-half of El Paso's total population.[3] Inheriting a legacy of colonialism wrought by Manifest Destiny, Mexicans, regardless of nativity, have been segmented into low-paying, low-status jobs. Perceived as cheap labor by Anglo business, they provided the human resources necessary for the city's industrial and commercial growth. Education and economic advancement proved illusory as segregation in housing, employment, and schools served as constant reminders of their second-class citizenship. To cite an example of stratification, from 1930 to 1960, only 1.8 percent of El Paso's Mexican workforce held high white-collar occupations.[4]

Segundo Barrio, or South El Paso, has served as the center of Mexican community life. Today, as in the past, wooden tenements and crumbling adobe structures house thousands of Mexicanos and Mexican Americans alike. For several decades, the only consistent source of social services in Segundo Barrio was the Rose Gregory Houchen Settlement House (named for a Michigan schoolteacher) and its adjacent health clinic and hospital. The records of Houchen Settlement form the core of this study.

Founded in 1912 on the corner of Tays and Fifth in the heart of the barrio, this Methodist settlement had two initial goals: (1) to provide a Christian rooming house for single Mexicana wage earners and (2) to open a kindergarten for area children. By 1918, Houchen offered a full schedule of Americanization programs—citizenship, cooking, carpentry, English instruction, Bible study, and Boy Scouts. The first Houchen staff included

three female Methodist missionaries and one "student helper," Ofilia
Chávez.[5] Living in the barrio made these women sensitive to the need for
low-cost, accessible health care. Infant mortality in Segundo Barrio was
alarmingly high. Historian Mario García related the following example:
"Of 121 deaths during July [1914], 52 were children under 5 years of age."[6]

In 1920, the Methodist Home Missionary Society responded (at last) to
Houchen appeals by assigning Effie Stoltz, a registered nurse, to the
settlement. Stoltz's work began in Houchen's bathroom, where she operated a first-aid station. More importantly, she persuaded a local physician
to visit the residence on a regular basis, and he, in turn, enlisted the
services of his colleagues. Within seven months of Stoltz's arrival, a small
adobe flat was converted into the Freeman Clinic. Run by volunteers, this
clinic provided prenatal exams, well-baby care, and pediatric services; in
1930, it opened a six-bed maternity ward. Seven years later, it would be
demolished to make way for the construction of a more modern clinic and
a new twenty-two-bed maternity facility—the Newark Methodist Maternity Hospital. Health care at Newark was a bargain. Prenatal classes,
pregnancy exams, and infant immunizations were free. Patients paid for
medicines at cost, and during the 1940s, thirty dollars covered the hospital
bill. Staff members would boast that for less than fifty dollars, payable in
installments, neighborhood women could give birth at "one of the best-
equipped maternity hospitals in the city."[7]

Houchen Settlement did not languish in the shadows of its adjacent
hospital; from 1920 to 1960, it coordinated an array of Americanization
activities. These included age- and gender-graded Bible studies, music
lessons, Camp Fire Girls, scouting, working girls' clubs, hygiene,
cooking, and citizenship classes. Staff members also opened a day nursery
to complement the kindergarten program. In terms of numbers, how
successful was Houchen? The records to which I had access gave little
indication of the extent of the settlement's client base. Fragmentary
evidence for the period from 1930 to 1950 suggests that perhaps as many
as 15,000 to 20,000 people per year (or approximately one-fourth to one-
third of El Paso's Mexican population) utilized its medical and/or educational services. Indeed, one Methodist cited in the 1930s pamphlet boasted
that the settlement "reaches nearly 15,000 people."[8]

As a functioning Progressive Era settlement, Houchen had amazing
longevity from 1912 to 1962. Several Methodist missionaries came to
Segundo Barrio as young women and stayed until their retirement.
Arriving in 1930, Millie Rickford would live at the settlement for thirty-
one years. Two years after her departure, the Rose Gregory Houchen
Settlement House would receive a new name, Houchen Community
Center. As a community center, it would become more of a secular agency
staffed by social workers and, at times, Chicano activists.[9] In 1991, the
buildings that covered a city block in South El Paso still furnished day-
care and recreational activities. Along with Bible study, there are classes
in ballet folklórico, karate, English, and aerobics. Unfortunately, the
Methodist Church, citing climbing insurance costs (among other reasons),

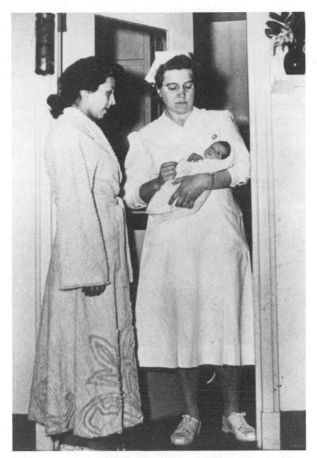

From 1937 to 1976, more than twelve thousand babies were born at Newark Hospital. (Courtesy Houchen Community Center.)

closed the hospital and clinic in December 1986 over the protests of local supporters and community members.[10]

From 1912 until the 1950s, Houchen workers placed Americanization and proselytization at the center of their efforts. Embracing the imagery and ideology of the melting pot, Methodist missionary Dorothy Little explained: "Houchen settlement stands as a sentinel of friendship . . . between the people of America and the people of Mexico. We assimilate the best of their culture, their art, their ideals and they in turn gladly accept the best America has to offer as they . . . become one with us. For right here within our four walls is begun much of the "Melting" process of our 'Melting Pot.' "[11]

To "become one with us" no doubt included a conversion to Methodism. It is important to remember that these missionaries were, indeed, missionaries, and they perceived themselves as harbingers of salvation. In "Our Work at Houchen," it was expressed this way: "Our Church is called El Buen Pastor . . . and that is what our church really is to the people—it is a Good Shepherd guiding our folks out of darkness and Catholocism [sic] into the good Christian life." Along similar lines, one Methodist pamphlet printed during the 1930s equated Catholicism (as practiced by Mexicans) with paganism and superstition. Settlement programs were couched in terms of "Christian Americanization," and these programs began early.[12]

Like the Franciscan missionaries who had trod the same ground three centuries before, the women of Houchen sought to win the hearts and minds of children. While preschool and kindergarten students spoke Spanish and sang Mexican songs, they also learned English, U.S. history, biblical verses—even etiquette à la Emily Post.[13] The settlement also offered a number of after-school activities for older children. These included "Little Homemakers," scouting, teen clubs, piano lessons, dance, Bible classes, and story hour. For many years, the most elaborate playground in South El Paso could be found within the outer courtyard of the settlement. Elsa Chávez, a lifelong resident of Segundo Barrio, remarked that her mother let her play there on the condition that she not accept any "cookies or Kool-Aid," the refreshments provided by Houchen staff. Other people remembered making similar bargains with their mothers. They could play on the swings and slide, but they could not go indoors.[14] How big a step was it to venture from the playground to story hour?

Settlement proselytizing did not escape the notice of barrio priests. Clearly troubled by Houchen, a few predicted dire consequences for those who participated in any Protestant-tinged activities. One priest went so far as to tell neighborhood children that it was a sin even to play on the playground equipment. Others, however, took a more realistic stance and did not chastise their parishioners for utilizing Methodist child-care and medical services. Perhaps as a response to both the Great Depression and suspected Protestant inroads, several area Catholic churches began distributing food baskets and establishing soup kitchens.[15]

Children were not the only people targeted by Houchen. Women, particularly expectant mothers, received special attention. Like the proponents of Americanization programs in California, settlement workers believed that women held a special guardianship over their families' welfare. As head nurse Millie Rickford explained, "If we can teach [the mother-to-be] the modern methods of cooking and preparing foods and simple hygiene habits for herself and her family, we have gained a stride."[16]

Houchen's "Christian Americanization" programs were not unique. Between 1910 and 1930, religious and state-organized Americanization projects aimed at the Mexican population proliferated throughout the Southwest. These efforts varied in scale from settlement houses to night classes, and the curriculum generally revolved around cooking, hygiene,

This dance recital captures the Eurocentric orientation advocated by Houchen residents. Settlement workers believed their students could "melt" into the "melting pot." (Courtesy Houchen Community Center.)

English, and civics. Music seemed a universal tool of instruction. One rural Arizona schoolteacher excitedly informed readers of the *Arizona Teacher and Home Journal* that, for the "cause of Americanization," her district had purchased a Victrola and several records, including two Spanish melodies, the· "'Star Spangled Banner,' 'The Red, White, and Blue,' 'Silent Night,' [and] 'Old Kentucky Home.'"[17] Houchen, of course, offered a variety of musical activities, beginning with the kindergarten rhythm band of 1927. During the 1940s and 1950s, missionaries offered flute, guitar, ballet, and tap lessons. For fifty cents per week, a youngster could take dance or music classes and perform in settlement recitals.[18] At these recitals, the youngsters were sometimes clothed in European peasant outfits. For instance, Alice Ruiz, Priscilla Molina, Edna Parra, Mira Gomez, and Aida Rivera, representing Houchen in a local Girl Scout festival held at the Shrine temple, modeled costumes from Sweden, England, France, Scotland, and Lithuania.[19] Some immigrant traditions were valorized more than others. Celebrating Mexican heritage did not figure into the Euro-American orientation pushed by Houchen residents.

Settlement workers held out unrealistic notions of the American dream, romantic constructions of American life. It is as if they endeavored to create a white middle-class environment for Mexican youngsters, complete with tutus and toe shoes. Cooking classes also became avenues for developing particular tastes. As Minerva Franco recalled, "I'll never forget the look on my mother's face when I first cooked 'Eggs Benedict' which I learned to prepare at Houchen."[20] The following passage taken from a report dated February 1942 outlines, in part, the perceived accomplishments of the settlement: "Sanitary conditions have been improving—more children go to school—more parents are becoming citizens, more are leaving Catholicism—more are entering business and public life—and more and more they are taking on the customs and standards of the Anglo people."[21]

There are numerous passages and photographs in the Houchen collection that provide fodder for sarcasm among contemporary scholars. As a Chicana historian, I am of two minds. I respect the settlement workers for their health and child-care services, but I cringe at their ethnocentrism and their romantic idealization of "American" life. Yet, before judging the maternal missionaries too harshly, it is important to keep in mind the social services they rendered over an extended period of time, as well as the environment in which they lived. For example, Houchen probably launched the first bilingual kindergarten program in El Paso, a program that eased the children's transition into an English-only first grade. Nor did Houchen residents denigrate the use of Spanish, and many became fluent Spanish-speakers themselves. The hospital and clinic, moreover, were important community institutions for over half a century.[22]

Furthermore, settlement workers could not always count on the encouragement or patronage of Anglo El Paso. In a virulently nativist tract, a local physician, C. S. Babbitt, condemned missionaries like the women of Houchen for working among Mexican and African Americans. In fact, Babbitt argued that religious workers were "seemingly conspiring with Satan to destroy the handiwork of God" because their energies were "wasted on beings . . . who are not in reality the objects of Christ's sacrifice."[23]

Perhaps more damaging than this extremist view was the apparent lack of financial support on the part of area Methodist churches. The records I examined revealed little in terms of local donations. The former Michigan schoolteacher for whom the settlement was named bequeathed one thousand dollars for the establishment of an El Paso settlement. The Women's Home Missionary Society of the Newark, New Jersey, Conference proved instrumental in raising funds for the construction of both the Freeman Clinic and the Newark Methodist Maternity Hospital. When the clinic first opened its doors in June 1921, all of the medical equipment—everything from sterilizers to baby scales—were gifts from Methodist groups across the nation. The Houchen Day Nursery, however, received consistent financial support from the El Paso Community Chest and, later, the United Way. In 1975, Houchen's board of directors conducted the first communitywide fund-raising drive. Volunteers sought to raise $375,000 to renovate existing structures and to build a modern day-care center. But the Houchen fund-raising slogan—"When people pay their own way, it's your affair . . . not welfare"—makes painfully clear the conservative attitudes toward social welfare harbored by affluent El Pasoans.[24]

The women of Houchen appeared undaunted by the lack of local support. For over fifty years, these missionaries coordinated a multifaceted Americanization campaign among the residents of Segundo Barrio.

But how did Mexican women perceive the settlement? What services did they utilize? And to what extent did they internalize the romantic notions of "Christian Americanization"?

Examining Mexican women's agency through institutional records is difficult; it involves getting beneath the text. Furthermore, one must take into account the selectivity of voices. In drafting settlement reports and publications, missionaries chose those voices that would publicize their "victories" among the Spanish-speaking. As a result, quotations abound that heap praise upon praise on Houchen and its staff. For example, in 1939, Soledad Burciaga emphatically declared, "There is not a person, no matter to which denomination they belong, who hasn't a kind word and a heart full of gratitude towards the Settlement House."[25] Obviously, these documents have their limits. Oral interviews and informal discussions with people who grew up in Segundo Barrio give a more balanced, less effusive perspective. Most viewed Houchen as a Protestant-run health-care and after-school activities center, rather than as the "light-house" in South El Paso.[26]

In 1949, the term "Friendship Square" was coined as a description for the settlement house, hospital, day nursery, and church. Missionaries hoped that children born at Newark would participate in preschool and afternoon programs and that eventually they and their families would join the church, El Buen Pastor. And a few did follow this pattern. One of the ministers assigned to El Buen Pastor, Fernando García, had himself been a Houchen kindergarten graduate. Emulating the settlement staff, some young women enrolled in Methodist missionary colleges or served as lay volunteers. Elizabeth Soto, for example, had attended Houchen programs throughout her childhood and adolescence. Upon graduation from Bowie High School, she entered Asbury College to train as a missionary and then returned to El Paso as a Houchen resident. After several years of service, she left settlement work to become the wife of a Mexican Methodist minister. The more common goal among Houchen teens was to graduate from high school and perhaps attend Texas Western, the local college. The first child born at Newark Hospital, Margaret Holguin, took part in settlement activities as a child and later became a registered nurse. According to her *comadre,* Lucy Lucero, Holguin's decision to pursue nursing was "perhaps due to the influence" of head nurse Millie Ricktord. Lucero noted, "The only contact I had with Anglos was with Anglo teachers. Then I met Miss Rickford and I felt, 'Hey, she's human. She's great.'" At a time when many (though certainly not all) elementary schoolteachers cared little about their Mexican students, Houchen residents offered warmth and encouragement.[27] On the basis of available data, one cannot make wholesale generalizations about Friendship Square's role in fostering mobility or even aspirations for mobility among the youth of Segundo Barrio. Yet, it is clear that the women of Houchen strove to build self-esteem and encouraged young people to pursue higher education.

Missionaries also envisioned a Protestant enclave in South El Paso, but, to their frustration, very few people responded. The settlement church,

El Buen Pastor, had a peak membership of 150 families. The church itself had an intermittent history. Shortly after its founding in 1897, El Buen Pastor disappeared; it was officially rededicated as part of Houchen in 1932. However, the construction of an actual church on settlement grounds did not begin until 1945. In 1968, the small rock chapel would be converted into a recreation room and thrift shop as the members of El Buen Pastor and El Mesias (another Mexican American church) were merged to form the congregation of the Emmanuel United Methodist Church in downtown El Paso. In 1991, a modern gymnasium occupied the ground where the chapel once stood.[28]

On the basis of selective case histories of converts, I suggest that many of those who joined El Buen Pastor were already Protestant. The Dominguez family offers an example. In the words of settlement worker Ruth Kern: "Reyna and Gabriel Dominguez are Latin Americans, even though both were born in the United States. Some members of the family do not even speak English. Reyna was born . . . in a Catholic home, but at the age of eleven years, she began attending The Methodist Church. Gabriel was born in Arizona. His mother was a Catholic, but she became a Protestant when . . . Gabriel was five years old."[29] The youth programs at Houchen brought Reyna and Gabriel together. After their marriage, the couple had six children, all born at Newark Hospital. The Dominguez family represented Friendship Square's typical success story. Many of the converts were children, and many had already embraced a Protestant faith. In the records I examined, I found only one instance of the conversion of a Catholic adult and one instance of the conversion of an entire Catholic family.[30] It seems that those most receptive to Houchen's religious messages were already predisposed in that direction.

The failure of proselytization cannot be examined solely within the confines of Friendship Square. It is not as if these Methodist women were good social workers but incompetent missionaries. Houchen staff member Clara Sarmiento wrote of the difficulty in building trust among the adults of Segundo Barrio: "Though it is easy for children to open up their hearts to us we do not find it so with the parents." She continued, "It is hard especially because we are Protestant, and most of the people we serve . . . come from Catholic heritage."[31] I would argue that the Mexican community played an instrumental role in thwarting conversion. In a land where the barrio could serve as a refuge from prejudice and discrimination, the threat of social isolation could certainly inhibit many residents from turning Protestant. During an oral interview, a woman who participated in Houchen activities for over fifty years, Estella Ibarra, described growing up Protestant in South El Paso: "We went through a lot of prejudice . . . sometimes my friends' mothers wouldn't let them play with us. . . . When the priest would go through the neighborhood, all the children would run to say hello and kiss his hand. My brothers and I would just stand by and look. The priest would usually come . . . and tell us how we were living in sin. Also, there were times when my brother and I were stoned by other students . . . and called bad names."[32]

When contacted by a Houchen resident, a Mrs. Espinosa admitted to being a closet Protestant. As she explained, "I am afraid of the Catholic sisters and [I] don't want my neighbors to know that I am not Catholic-minded." The fear of ostracism, while recorded by Houchen staff, did not figure into their understanding of Mexicano resistance to conversion. Instead, they blamed time and culture. As Dorothy Little succinctly related, "We can not eradicate in a few years what has been built up during ages.[33]

Although a Protestant enclave never materialized, settlement women remained steadfast in their goals of conversion and Americanization, goals that did not change until the mid-to-late fifties. Historians Sarah Deutsch and George Sánchez have noted that sporadic, poorly financed Americanization programs made little headway in Mexican communities. Ruth Crocker also described the Protestant settlements in Gary, Indiana, as having only a "superficial and temporary" influence.[34] Yet, even long-term sustained efforts, as in the case of Houchen, had limited appeal. This inability to mold consciousness or identity demonstrates not only the strength of community sanctions but, more significantly, the resiliency of Mexican culture and the astuteness of Mexicanos. Mexican women derived substantive services from Friendship Square in the form of health care and education; however, they refused to embrace the romantic idealizations of American life. Wage-earning mothers who placed their children in the day nursery no doubt encountered an Anglo world quite different from the one depicted by Methodist missionaries, and thus they were skeptical of the settlement's cultural ideations. Clara Sarmiento knew from experience that it was much easier to reach the children than their parents.[35]

How did children respond to the ideological undercurrents of Houchen programs? Did Mexican women feel empowered by their interaction with the settlement, or were Methodist missionaries invidious underminers of Mexican identity? In getting beneath the text, I found that the remarks of Minerva Franco that appeared in a 1975 issue of *Newark-Houchen News* posed a series of provocative questions: "Houchen provided . . . opportunities for learning and experiencing," Franco said. "At Houchen I was shown that I had worth and that I was an individual."[36] What did she mean by that statement? Did the settlement house heighten her self-esteem? Did she feel that she was not an individual within the context of her family and neighborhood?

Some young women imbibed Americanization so heavily that they rejected their own identity. In *No Separate Refuge*, Sarah Deutsch picked up on this theme as she quoted missionary Polita Padilla: "I am Mexican, born and brought up in New Mexico, but much of my life was spent in the Allison School where we had a different training so that the Mexican way of living now seems strange to me." Others, like Estella Ibarra and Rose Escheverría Mulligan, saw little incompatibility between Mexican traditions and Protestantism. Growing up in Los Angeles, Mulligan remembered her religion as reaffirming Mexican values. In her words,

"I was beginning to think that the Baptist Church was a little too Mexican. Too much restriction."[37]

Houchen documents reveal glimpses into the formation of identity, consciousness, and values. The Friendship Square calendar of 1949 explicitly stated that the medical care provided at Houchen "is a tool to develop sound minds in sound bodies; for thus it is easier to find peace with God and man. We want to help people develop a sense of values in life." In an era of bleaching creams, the privileging of color—with white as the pinnacle—was an early lesson. Relating the excitement of kindergarten graduation, day-nursery head Beatrice Fernandez included in her report a question asked by Margarita, one of the young graduates. "We are all wearing white, white dress, slip, socks and, Miss Fernandez, is it alright if our hair is black?"[38]

Houchen activities were synonymous with Americanization. A member of the settlement Brownie troop encouraged her friends "to become 'an American or Girl Scout' at Houchen." Scouting certainly served as a vehicle for Americanization. The all-Mexican Girl and Boy Scout troops of Alpine, Texas, enjoyed visiting El Paso and Ciudad Juárez in the company of Houchen scouts. In a thank-you note, the Alpine Girl Scouts wrote, "Now we can all say we have been to a foreign country."[39]

It is important to remember that Houchen provided a bilingual environment, not a bicultural one. Spanish was the means to communicate the message of Methodism and Christian Americanization. Whether dressing up children as pilgrims or European peasants, missionaries stressed "American" citizenship and values; yet, outside of conversion, definitions of those values or of "our American way" remained elusive. Indeed, some of the settlement lessons were not incongruous with Mexican mores. In December 1952, an Anglo settlement worker recorded in her journal the success of a Girl Scout dinner: "The girls learned a lot from it too. They were taught how to set the table, and how to serve the men. They learned also that they had to share, to cooperate, and to wait their turn."[40] The most striking theme is that of individualism. Missionaries emphasized the importance of individual decision making and individual accomplishment. In recounting her own conversion, Clara Sarmiento explained to a young client, "I chose my own religion because it was my own personal experience and . . . I was glad my religion was not chosen for me."[41]

The Latina missionaries of Houchen served as cultural brokers as they diligently strove to integrate themselves into the community. Until 1950, the Houchen staff usually included one Latina. During the 1950s, the number of Latina (predominately Mexican American) settlement workers rose to six. Mary Lou López, María Rico, Elizabeth Soto, Febe Bonilla, Clara Sarmiento, María Payan, and Beatrice Fernandez had participated in Methodist outreach activities as children (Soto at Houchen) and had decided to follow in the footsteps of their teachers. In addition, these women had the assistance of five full-time Mexican laypersons.[42] It is no coincidence that the decade of greatest change in Houchen policies occurred at a time when Latinas held a growing number of staff positions.

Friendship Square's greater sensitivity to neighborhood needs arose, in part, out of the influence exerted by Mexican clients in shaping the attitudes and actions of Mexican missionaries.

I will further suggest that although Mexican women utilized Houchen's social services, they did not, by and large, adopt its tenets of "Christian Americanization." Children who attended settlement programs enjoyed the activities, but Friendship Square did not always leave a lasting imprint. "My Mom had an open mind, so I participated in a lot of clubs. But I didn't become Protestant," remarked Lucy Lucero. "I had fun and I learned a lot, too." Because of the warm, supportive environment, Houchen settlement is remembered with fondness. However, one cannot equate pleasant memories with the acceptance of the settlement's cultural ideations.[43]

Settlement records bear out the Mexican women's selective use of Houchen's resources. The most complete set of figures I viewed was for the year 1944. During this period, 7,614 people visited the clinic and hospital. The settlement afternoon programs had an average monthly enrollment of 362, and 40 children attended kindergarten. Taken together, approximately 8,000 residents of Segundo Barrio utilized Friendship Square's medical and educational offerings. In contrast, the congregation of El Buen Pastor in 1944 included 160 people.[44] Although representing only a single year, these figures indicate the importance of Houchen's medical facilities and of Mexican women's selective utilization of resources.

Implemented by a growing Latina staff, client-initiated changes in Houchen policies brought a realistic recognition of the settlement as a social service agency rather than as a religious mission. During the 1950s, brochures describing the day nursery emphasized that, although children said grace at meals and sang Christian songs, they would not receive "in any way indoctrination" regarding Methodism. In fact, at the parents' request, Newark nurses summoned Catholic priests to the hospital to baptize premature infants. Client desire became the justification for allowing the presence of Catholic clergy, a policy that would have been unthinkable in the not-too-distant past.[45] Finally, in the new Houchen constitution of 1959, all mention of conversion was dropped. Instead, the document conveyed a more ecumenical, nondenominational spirit. For instance, the goal of Houchen Settlement was henceforth "to establish a Christian democratic framework for—individual development, family solidarity, and neighborhood welfare."[46]

Settlement activities also became more closely linked with the Mexican community. During the 1950s, Houchen was the home of two LULAC chapters—one for teenagers and one for adults: The League of United Latin American Citizens (LULAC) was the most visible and politically powerful civil rights organization in Texas.[47] Carpentry classes—once the preserve of males—opened their doors to young women, although on a gender-segregated basis. Houchen workers made veiled references to the "very dangerous business" of Juárez abortion clinics; however, it appears unclear whether or not the residents themselves offered any contraceptive counseling. But during the early 1960s, the settlement, in cooperation with Planned Parenthood, opened a birth control clinic for "married women." Indeed, a Houchen contraception success story was featured on the front page of a spring newsletter: "Mrs. G_____, after having her thirteenth and fourteenth children (twins), enrolled in our birth control clinic; now for one and one half years she has been a happy and non-pregnant mother."[48]

Certainly, Houchen had changed with the times. What factors accounted for the new directions in settlement work? The evidence on the baptism of premature babies seems fairly clear in terms of client pressure, but to what extent did other policies change as the result of Mexican women's input? The residents of Segundo Barrio may have felt more comfortable expressing their ideas, and Latina settlement workers may have exhibited a greater willingness to listen. Though it is a matter of pure speculation at this point, a working coalition of Mexican women that spanned the missionary-client boundary may have accounted for Houchen's more ecumenical tone and greater community involvement. In reviewing Houchen's history, I would argue that Mexican clients, not the missionaries, set the boundaries for interaction. For most women, Houchen was not a beacon of salvation but a medical and social service center run by Methodists. They consciously decided what resources they would utilize and consciously ignored or sidestepped the settlement's ideological premises. Like women of color in academia, they sought to take advantage of the system without buying into it.

Houchen provides a case study of what I term "cultural coalescence." Immigrants and their children pick, borrow, retain, and create distinctive cultural forms. There is not a single hermetic Mexican or Mexican American culture but rather permeable *cultures* rooted in generation, gender, region, class, and personal experience. Chicano scholars have divided Mexican experiences into three generational categories: Mexicano (first generation), Mexican American (second generation), and Chicano (third and beyond).[49] But this general typology tends to obscure the ways in which people navigate across cultural boundaries, as well as their conscious decision-making in the production of culture. Bear in mind too that people of color have not had unlimited choice. Racism, sexism, imperialism, persecution, and social, political, and economic segmentation have all constrained aspirations, expectations, and decision making. As an example, young women coming of age during the 1920s may have wanted to be like the flappers they saw on the silver screen or read about in magazines, but few would do more than adopt prevailing fashions. Strict parental supervision, including chaperonage, and the reality of poverty and prejudice served to blunt their ability to emulate the icons of a new consumer society. Young women encountered both the lure of Hollywood and the threat of deportation and walked between the familiarity of tradition and the excitement of experimentation.[50]

The ideations of Americanization were a mixed lot. Religious and secular Americanization programs, the elementary schools, movies, magazines, and radio bombarded the Mexican community with myriad models, most of which were idealized, stylized, unrealistic, and unattainable. Even the Spanish-language press promoted acculturation, especially in the realm of consumer culture. Aimed at women, advertisements promised status and affection if the proper bleaching cream, hair coloring, and cosmetics were purchased. SIGA LAS ESTRELLAS [FOLLOW THE STARS], beckoned one Max Factor advertisement.[51]

By looking through the lens of cultural coalescence, we can begin to discern the ways in which people select and create cultural forms. The fluidity of cultures offers exciting possibilities for research and discussion. Institutional records, like those of Houchen, are neither dead ends nor gold mines but points of departure. Creating the public space of the settlement, Methodist missionaries sought to alter the "lifeworld" of Mexican immigrants to reflect their own idealized versions of life in the United States. Settlement workers can be viewed as the narrators of lived experience. Houchen records reflect the cognitive construction of missionary aspirations and expectations. In other words, the documents revealed more about the women who wrote them than about those they served. At another level, one could interpret the cultural ideations of Americanization as indications of an attempt at what Jürgen Habermas has termed "inner colonization."[52]

Yet the failure of such projects illustrates the ways in which Mexican women appropriated desired resources, both material (infant immunizations) and psychological (self-esteem), while, in the main, rejecting the ideological messages behind them. The shift in Houchen policies during the 1950s meant more than a recognition of community needs; it represented a claiming of public space by Mexican women clients. Cultural coalescence encompasses both accommodation and resistance, and Mexican women acted, not reacted, to the settlement impulse. When standing at cultural crossroads, Mexican women blended their options and created their own paths.

Notes

This essay was first published in *Frontiers* 12, no. 1 (1991).

1. Steven Seidman, ed., *Jürgen Habermas on Society and Politics: A Reader* (Boston: Beacon Press, 1989), 171.

2. Mario T. García, *Desert Immigrants: The Mexicans of El Paso, 1880–1920* (New Haven, Conn.: Yale University Press, 1981), 144–45. On a national level, Mexicans formed the "third largest 'racial' group by 1930, outnumbered only by Anglos and African-Americans," according to T. Wilson Longmore and Homer L. Hitt, "A Demographic Analysis of First and Second Generation Mexican Population of the United States: 1930," *Southwestern Social Science Quarterly* 24 (September 1943): 140.

3. Oscar J. Martínez, *The Chicanos of El Paso: An Assessment of Progress* (El Paso: Texas Western Press, 1980), 17, 6.

4. Martínez, *Chicanos*, 29–33, 10. Mario García meticulously documents the economic and social stratification of Mexicans in El Paso; see García, *Desert Immigrants*. In 1960, the

proportion of Mexican workers with high white-collar jobs jumped to 3.4 percent, according to Martínez, *Chicanos*, 10.

5. "South El Paso's Oasis of Care," *paso del norte*, 1 (September 1982): 42–43; Thelma Hammond, "Friendship Square" (Houchen report, 1969), part of an uncataloged collection of documents housed at Houchen Community Center, El Paso, Texas [hereafter HF (Houchen Files)]; "Growing with the Century" (Houchen report, 1947), HF.

6. García, *Desert Immigrants*, 145; Effie Stoltz, "Freeman Clinic: A Resume of Four Years Work" (Houchen pamphlet, 1924), HF. It should be noted that Houchen Settlement sprang from the work of Methodist missionary Mary Tripp, who arrived in South El Paso in 1893. However, it was not until 1912 that an actual settlement was established, according to "South El Paso's Oasis of Care," 42.

7. Stoltz, "Freeman Clinic"; Hammond, "Friendship Square"; M. Dorothy Woodruff and Dorothy Little, "Friendship Square" (Houchen pamphlet, March 1949), HF; "Friendship Square" (Houchen report, circa 1940s), HF; "Health Center" (Houchen newsletter, 1943), HF; "Christian Health Service" (Houchen report, 1941), HF; *El Paso Times*, 20 October 1945.

8. "Settlement Worker's Report" (Houchen report, 1927), HF; letter from Bessie Brinson to Treva Ely, dated 14 September 1958, HF; Hammond, "Friendship Square"; Elmer T. Clark and Dorothy McConnell, "The Methodist Church and Latin Americans in the United States" (Board of Home Missions pamphlet, circa 1930s), HF. My very rough estimate is based on the documents and records to which I had access. I was not permitted to examine any materials then housed at Newark Hospital. The most complete statistics on utilization of services are for the year 1944 and are given in the letter from Dorothy Little to E. May Young, 10 May 1945, H.F. Because of the deportation and repatriation drives of the 1930s in which one-third of the Mexican population in the United States was either deported or repatriated, the number of Mexicans in El Paso dropped from 68,476 in 1930 to 55,000 in 1940; by 1960 it had risen to 63,796, according to Martínez, *Chicanos*, 6.

9. *El Paso Herald Post*, 7 and 12 March 1961; "Community Centers" (Women's Division of Christian Service pamphlet, May 1963), HF; "Funding Proposal for Youth Outreach and Referral Report Project" (30 April 1974), from the private files of Kenton J. Clymer, Ph.D.; *El Paso Herald Post*, 3 January 1983; *El Paso Times*, 8 August 1983.

10. Letter from Tom Houghteling, executive director, Houchen Community Center, to the author, dated 24 December 1990; Tom Houghteling, interview by author, 9 January 1991.

11. Dorothy Little, "Rose Gregory Houchen Settlement" (Houchen report, February 1942), HF.

12. Ibid.; "Our Work at Houchen" (Houchen report, circa 1940s), HF; Woodruff and Little, "Friendship Square"; Jennie C. Gilbert, "Settlements under the Women's Home Missionary Society" (pamphlet, circa 1920s), HF; Clark and McConnell, "Methodist Church."

13. Anita Hernandez, "The Kindergarten" (Houchen report, circa 1940s), HF; "A Right Glad New Year" (Houchen newsletter, circa 1940s), HF; Little, "Rose Gregory Houchen Settlement"; "Our Work at Houchen"; Woodruff and Little, "Friendship Square." For more information on the Franciscans, see Ramón Gutiérrez, *When Jesus Came, the Corn Mothers Went Away: Marriage, Sexuality, and Power in New Mexico, 1500–1846* (Stanford, Calif.: Stanford University Press, 1991).

14. "Settlement Worker's Report"; letter from Little to Young; letter from Brinson to Ely; Friendship Square calendar for 1949, HF; Lucy Lucero, interview by author, 8 October 1983; Elsa Chávez, interview by author, 19 April 1983; discussion following presentation on "Settlement Houses in El Paso," given by the author at the El Paso Conference on History and the Social Sciences, 24 August 1983, El Paso, Texas. (Tape of presentation and discussion is on file at the Institute of Oral History, University of Texas, El Paso.) Elsa Chávez is a pseudonym used at the person's request.

15. Discussion following "Settlement Houses in El Paso" presentation. The Catholic Church never established a competing settlement house. However, during the 1920s in Gary, Indiana, the Catholic diocese opened up the Gary-Alerding Settlement with the primary goal of Americanizing

Mexican immigrants. The bishop took such action to counteract suspected inroads made by two local Protestant settlement houses. See Ruth Hutchinson Crocker, "Gary Mexicans and 'Christian Americanization': A Study in Cultural Conflict," in *Forging Community: The Latino Experience in Northwest Indiana, 1919–1975*, ed. James B. Lane and Edward J. Escobar (Chicago: Cattails Press, 1987), 115–34.

16. "Christian Health Service"; "The Freeman Clinic and the Newark Conference Maternity Hospital" (Houchen report, 1940), HF; *El Paso Times*, 2 August 1961; *El Paso Herald Post*, 12 May 1961. For more information on Americanization programs in California, see George J. Sánchez, "'Go After the Women': Americanization and the Mexican Immigrant Women, 1915–1929," in *Unequal Sisters: A Multicultural Reader in U.S. Women's History*, ed. Ellen Carol DuBois and Vicki L. Ruiz (New York: Routledge, 1990), 250–63. The documents reveal a striking absence of adult Mexican male clients. The Mexican men who do appear are either Methodist ministers or lay volunteers.

17. Sánchez, "'Go After the Women,'" 250–283; Sarah Deutsch, *No Separate Refuge: Culture, Class, and Gender on an Anglo-Hispanic Frontier in the American Southwest, 1880–1940* (New York: Oxford University Press, 1987); "Americanization Notes," *Arizona Teacher and Home Journal* 11 (January 1923): 26. The Methodist and Presbyterian settlements in Gary, Indiana, also couched their programs in terms of "Christian Americanization," according to Hutchinson Crocker, "Gary Mexicans," 118–20.

18. "Settlement Worker's Report"; Friendship Square calendar for 1949; letter from Brinson to Ely; Chávez interview.

19. News clipping from the *El Paso Times* (circa 1950s), HF.

20. Sánchez, "'Go After the Women,'" 260; *Newark-Houchen News*, September 1975. I agree with George Sánchez that Americanization programs created an overly rosy picture of U.S. life. In his words, "Rather than providing Mexican immigrant women with an attainable picture of assimilation, Americanization programs could only offer these immigrants idealized versions of American life." Sánchez, "'Go After the Women,'" 260.

21. Little, "Rose Gregory Houchen Settlement."

22. "Settlement Worker's Report"; Hernandez, "Kindergarten"; "A Right Glad New Year"; Little, "Rose Gregory Houchen Settlement"; "Our Work at Houchen"; Woodruff and Little, "Friendship Square"; "South El Paso's Oasis of Care"; *El Paso Herald Post*, 7 and 12 March 1961, 12 May 1961.

23. C. S. Babbitt, *The Remedy for the Decadence of the Latin Race* (El Paso, Tex.: El Paso Printing Company), 55 (presented to the Pioneers Association of El Paso, Texas, 11 July 1909, by Mrs. Babbitt, widow of the author; pamphlet courtesy of Jack Redman).

24. "Account Book for Rose Gregory Houchen Settlement (1903–1913)," HF; Hammond, "Friendship Square"; "Growing With the Century"; *El Paso Times*, 5 September 1975; Stoltz, "Freeman Clinic"; Woodruff and Little, "Friendship Square"; *El Paso Times*, 3 October 1947; "Four Institutions. One Goal. The Christian Community" (Houchen pamphlet, circa early 1950s), HF; Houghteling interview; "A City Block of Service" (script of Houchen slide presentation, 1976), HF; *El Paso Times*, 19 January 1977; speech given by Kenton J. Clymer, Ph.D., June 1975 (Clymer Field Notes); *El Paso Times*, 23 May 1975; *Newark-Houchen News*, September 1975. It should be noted that in 1904 local Methodist congregations did contribute much of the money needed to purchase the property upon which the settlement was built. Local civic groups occasionally donated money or equipment and threw Christmas parties for Houchen children, according to "Account Book"; *El Paso Herald Post*, 14 December 1951; *El Paso Times*, 16 December 1951.

25. Vernon McCombs, "Victories in the Latin American Mission" (Board of Home Missions pamphlet, 1935), HF; "Brillante Historia de la Iglesia 'El Buen Pastor' El Paso" (Young Adult Fellowship newsletter, December 1946), HF; Soledad Burciaga, "Yesterday in 1923" (Houchen report, 1939), HF.

26. This study is based on a limited number of oral interviews (five, to be exact), but they represent a range of interaction with the settlement, from playing on the playground to serving

as the minister for El Buen Pastor. It is also informed by a public discussion of my work on Houchen held during an El Paso teachers' conference in 1983 (see note 14). Most of the educators who attended the talk had participated, to some extent, in Houchen activities and were eager to share their recollections. I am also indebted to students in my Mexican-American history classes at the University of Texas, El Paso, especially the reentry women, for their insight and knowledge.

27. Woodruff and Little, "Friendship Square"; Hammond, "Friendship Square"; "Greetings for 1946" (Houchen Christmas newsletter, 1946), HF; Little, "Rose Gregory Houchen Settlement"; Soledad Burciaga, "Today in 1939" (Houchen report, 1939), HF; "Our Work at Houchen"; "Christian Social Service" (Houchen report, circa 1940s), HF; Fernando García, interview by author, 21 September 1983; *El Paso Times*, 14 June 1951; Lucero interview; Vicki L. Ruiz, "Oral History and La Mujer: The Rosa Guerrero Story," in *Women on the U.S.-Mexico Border: Responses to Change*, ed. Vicki L. Ruiz and Susan Tiano (Boston: Allen and Unwin, 1987), 226–27; *Newark-Houchen News*, September 1975.

28. Spanish-American Methodist News Bulletin, April 1946, HF; Hammond, "Friendship Square"; McCombs, "Victories"; "El Metodismo en la Ciudad de El Paso," *Christian Herald*, July 1945 HF; "Brilliante Historia"; "The Door: An Informal Pamphlet on the Work of the Methodist Church among the Spanish-Speaking of El Paso, Texas" (Methodist pamphlet, 1940), HF; "A City Block of Service"; García interview; Houghteling interview. From 1932 to 1939, services for El Buen Pastor were held in a church located two blocks from the settlement.

29. A. Ruth Kern, "There Is No Segregation Here" (Methodist Youth Fund Bulletin, January-March 1953), 12, HF.

30. Ibid.; "The Torres Family" (Houchen report, circa 1940s), HF; Estella Ibarra, interview by Jesusita Ponce, 11 November 1982; Hazel Bulifant, "One Woman's Story" (Houchen report, 1950), HF; "Our Work at Houchen."

31. Clara Sarmiento, "Lupe" (Houchen report, circa 1950s), HF.

32. Ibarra interview.

33. Bulifant, "One Woman's Story"; letter from Little to Young.

34. Deutsch, *No Separate Refuge*, 64–66, 85–86; Sánchez, " 'Go After the Women,' " 259–61; Hutchinson Crocker, "Gary Mexicans," 121.

35. Sarmiento, "Lupe." In her study, Ruth Hutchinson Crocker also notes the propensity of Protestant missionaries to focus their energies on children and the selective uses of services by Mexican clients. As she explained, "Inevitably, many immigrants came to the settlement, took what they wanted of its services, and remained untouched by its message." Hutchinson Crocker, "Gary Mexicans," 122.

36. *Newark-Houchen News*, September 1975.

37. Deutsch, *No Separate Refuge*, 78–79; Ibarra interview; interview with Rose Escheverría Mulligan, vol. 27 of *Rosie the Riveter Revisited: Women and the World War II Work Experience*, ed. Sherna Berger Gluck (Long Beach: California State University at Long Beach Foundation, 1983), 24.

38. Friendship Square calendar for 1949; Beatrice Fernandez, "Day Nursery" (Houchen report, circa late 1950s), HF.

39. "Friendship Square" (Houchen pamphlet, circa 1950s), HF; letter to Houchen Girl Scouts from Troop 4, Latin American Community Center, Alpine, Texas, 18 May 1951, HF.

40. "A Right Glad New Year"; news clipping from the *El Paso Times* (circa 1950s); "Our Work at Houchen"; Little, "Rose Gregory Houchen Settlement"; Anglo settlement worker's journal, entry for December 1952, HF.

41. *Newark-Houchen News*, September 1975; Sarmiento, "Lupe."

42. Datebook for 1926, settlement worker's private journal, entry for Friday, 9 September 1926, HF; "Brillante Historia"; "Report and Directory of Association of Church Social Workers, 1940," HF: "May I Come In?" (Houchen brochure, circa 1950s), HF; "Friendship Square" (Houchen pamphlet, 1958), HF; Mary Lou López, "Kindergarten Report" (Houchen pamphlet, 1954), HF; *El Paso Times*, 14 June 1951; "Houchen Day Nursery" (Houchen pamphlet, circa 1950s), HF; *El Paso Times*, 12 September 1952. Methodist missionaries seem to have experienced

some mobility within the settlement hierarchy. In 1912, Ofilia Chávez served as a "student helper"; forty years later, Beatrice Fernandez would direct the preschool.

43. Chávez interview; Martha González, interview by author, 8 October 1983; Lucero interview; *Newark-Houchen News*, September 1974.

44. Letter from Little to Young; "The Door"; Woodruff and Little, "Friendship Square."

45. "Houchen Day Nursery"; "Life in a Glass House" (Houchen report, circa 1950s), HF.

46. Program for first annual meeting, Houchen Settlement and Day Nursery, Freeman Clinic and Newark Conference Maternity Hospital (8 January 1960), HF. It should be noted that thirty years later, there would be an apparent shift back to original settlement ideas. In the early '90s, Houchen Community again held regularly scheduled Bible studies, according to letter from Houghteling to the author.

47. Program for Houchen production of "Cinderella," HF; letter from Brinson to Ely. For more information on LULAC, see Mario T. García, *Mexican Americans: Leadership, Ideology, and Identity, 1930–1960* (New Haven, Conn.: Yale University Press, 1989), and essay by Cynthia Orozco in this volume.

48. Bulifant, "One Woman's Story"; "News from Friendship Square" (spring newsletter, circa early 1960s), HF.

49. As an example of this typology, see García, *Mexican Americans*, 13–22, 295–302. Richard Griswold del Castillo touches on the dynamic nature of Mexican culture in *La Familia: Chicano Families in the Urban Southwest, 1848 to the Present* (Notre Dame, Ind.: University of Notre Dame Press, 1984).

50. A more developed elaboration of these themes may be found in my essay, " 'Star Struck': Acculturation, Adolescence, and the Mexican American Woman, 1920–1940," in *Building with Our Hands: New Directions in Chicana Scholarship*, ed. Adela de la Torre and Beatríz Pesquera (Berkeley: University of California Press, 1993).

51. Ibid.; *La Opinion*, 5 June 1927 and 8 January 1938.

52. My understanding and application of the ideas of Jürgen Habermas have been informed by the following works: Jürgen Habermas, "Moral Consciousness and Communicative Action," trans. Christian Lenhardt and Sherry Weber Nicholsen, intro. Thomas McCarthy (Cambridge: MIT Press, 1990); Seidman, ed., *Jürgen Habermas*; Nancy Fraser, *Unruly Practices: Power, Discourse, and Gender in Contemporary Social Theory* (Minneapolis: University of Minnesota Press, 1989); and Seyla Benhabib and Drucilla Cornell, "Introduction: Beyond the Politics of Gender," in *Feminism as Critique*, ed. Seyla Benhabib and Drucilla Cornell (Minneapolis: University of Minnesota Press, 1987).

18.

Lifting as We Climb: African American Women's Clubs of Denver, 1880–1925

LYNDA F. DICKSON

In this article, which first appeared in 1992, Lynda Dickson turns our attention from middle-class white reformers, like the Houchen missionaries, to middle-class African American women who organized at least twenty-two women's clubs for themselves in Denver between 1900 and 1925. Seven of these clubs cooperated to found and support the Negro Women's Club Home, which, like Houchen, provided services for racial ethnic women—in this case, a clinic, rooms for single women, and a nursery for African American children.

The clubs might be seen as the reflection in the African American community of a national women's club movement that offered middle-class women opportunities to discuss books, art, and ideas, and to pursue self-improvement. When the African American women's clubs of Denver shifted their emphasis from self-improvement to reform, they followed the same course as the national General Federation of Women's Clubs. The General Federation changed under the leadership of a white Coloradoan, Sarah Platt Decker, who announced as she assumed the GFWC presidency in 1904, "Dante is dead. He has been dead for centuries, and I think it is time we dropped the study of the Inferno and turned the attention to our own."

Dickson does more, however, than simply document African American clubs as part of a larger women's club movement—she distinguishes how African American clubwomen operated from different organizational bases and different needs than white clubwomen and progressive reformers. The "Progressive" Era offered little progress for African Americans, for whom 1890 to 1920 marked a period of racist reaction, violence, and legalized segregation. Class itself meant different things for middle-class clubwomen of different races, as Dickson's careful reconstruction of African American clubwomen's families and jobs demonstrates. The "leisure" to engage in self-improvement and in community service meant very different things for Euro-American clubwomen who employed domestic servants and for African American clubwomen, some of whom were domestic servants. Their paid employment helped secure middle-class family incomes; their wages supported their clubs' impressive agendas. For women of all races, women's clubs offered social networks and self-fulfillment. But the African American clubwomen accepted a further mission to combat racism as well as sexism, to "lift" their black communities as they combated negative stereotypes of black women and improved their own lives.

The period of Reconstruction found black Americans generally optimistic about their future as full-fledged citizens—a condition, they believed, that would come about through the economic, political, and educational elevation of the race. For most of them, economic advancement—achieved through hard work, sobriety, and acquisition of wealth and property—was the key to full assimilation. Those who had already gained some degree of economic security stressed the attainment of political and civil rights. Yet, in spite of efforts in these areas, increasing racial prejudice and discrimination, especially in the South, was such that by the late nineteenth century, what few gains had been made had all but disappeared, and the 1890s marked the beginning of a period of decline in the status of black Americans that would continue through the 1920s.

By 1910 virtually all of the southern states had disenfranchised black citizens through amendments to state constitutions. In the North, while black political and civil rights still existed on paper, overt prejudice and discrimination were rapidly becoming the norm, so that by the early 1900s northern public opinion concerning African Americans mirrored that of the South on questions of racial inferiority, on denial of the franchise, and on justification of white domination.

Recognition of increasing racism and the very real social problems that were rapidly becoming a part of the black experience had a tremendous impact on African American thinking during this period. As early as the 1890s black optimism concerning full participation in mainstream society was gradually replaced by a sense of realism: Perhaps the focus should first be placed upon *preparation* for full participation. A change of tactics was called for. While achieving political and civil rights and full assimilation remained the long-range goal, emphasis now shifted to the belief that blacks must first accumulate wealth and develop the virtues of cleanliness, thrift, and high moral character. The assumption was that once wealth and morality were achieved—and largely through their own efforts—blacks would gain the respect of whites and thus be "worthy" of full citizenship. Thus self-help and racial solidarity became the dominant defensive philosophy.

In spite of the conflicts between radicals and conservatives within the black community, the major theme in African American thought on the race question from the last decade of the nineteenth century throughout the 1920s remained clear: The progress of the race could be achieved only through the united effort of the race itself. The emphasis on self-help and racial solidarity as defense reactions to white hostility and exclusion was manifest in all areas. Religious and educational institutions, business and professional associations, and cultural societies such as literary and study clubs—all adhered to this ideology. Especially prevalent during the period from 1890 to 1925 was the enthusiastic development of benevolent, social reform, and social welfare organizations within black urban communities. According to W. E. B. DuBois, these organizations represented "the efforts of the better classes of Negroes to rescue and uplift the unfortunate"; and a recent scholar claims that no single force better illustrated these efforts among blacks than the activities of women's clubs.[1]

During the late 1880s and early 1890s, Denver experienced rapid growth, and increasing numbers of blacks, along with other racial groups, came to the city in the hope of improving their lot. By 1890 a distinct black community had emerged.[2] Because of the (albeit limited) opportunities that existed—largely through providing services to this community—a prosperous, if small, middle class was soon established. It is from this class that the leaders of the club movement came. Many were recent arrivals from larger cities who had been exposed to and recognized the potential of women's clubs in helping the less fortunate within the race.

Elizabeth Piper Ensley was one such person. She had studied abroad during the 1870s and upon returning to the United States had established a circulating library in Boston, where she became a public schoolteacher. In 1882 she married Horwell N. Ensley and moved to the District of Columbia where they both served on the faculty at Howard University. They later moved to Mississippi where Elizabeth Ensley taught at Acorn University.[3] In the early 1890s the Ensleys moved to Denver, and Elizabeth quickly became active in club work. One of the founding members of the Woman's League of Denver, which was organized by black women around 1894, she served as Denver's correspondent to the *Woman's Era*, the official journal of the National Association of Colored Women.

In the 9 June 1894 issue of the *Woman's Era*, Ensley described the active role that black women had played in an election earlier that spring—the first time women in Colorado had been allowed to vote. She noted the "special part . . . colored women have taken in the election. Most of them have done admirable work in the interest of the Republican party. They also formed clubs on their own and heroically helped their brothers to elect a representative to the legislature, although the majority of those brothers voted against women's enfranchisement." This was not the first time that Denver's black women had organized to press for political and civil rights. A *Rocky Mountain News* article of 11 February 1885 offers evidence that at least one organization, the Colored Ladies Legal Rights Association, engaged in direct political action of the kind that informed post–Civil War strategies to gain civil rights. It was partly responsible, in fact, for a state civil rights bill, which provided penalties for denying equal rights in places of public accommodation.[4]

In 1904 Ensley founded the Colorado Association of Colored Women's Clubs—an idea that had begun to form as early as 1896, for Ida DePriest, another early club mover, had mentioned the possibility of such an organization to the National Association during that year. DePriest was also a member of the Woman's League of Denver, serving as corresponding secretary in 1895–96. She appears to have been most often linked with political activities, working through the Colored Women's Republican Club of Denver. This club, according to the *Denver Times*, had accomplished "more telling work in the last two campaigns than any other colored organization in the state."[5]

While they lasted, these late-nineteenth-century clubs represented broader, more politically active interests than those that were established after the turn of the century. Even their names serve to indicate this shift in interests—from the Colored Ladies Legal Rights Association and the Colored Women's Republican Club to the Taka Art and Literary Club, the Book Lovers Club, and the Carnation Art Club. Corresponding to broader ideological changes occurring among black intellectuals during the late nineteenth century, agitation by Denver's black clubwomen for equal political, economic, and social rights was gradually replaced with an emphasis on *preparation* for equal rights. Self-help, self-improvement, and racial unity became the dominant themes of the day, and the work of Denver clubwomen was no exception.

The new emphasis on self-improvement may also help explain why the most prevalent types of clubs came to be those directed toward the study of art, literature, music, and needlework. The Woman's League, one of the clubs formed prior to 1900, had complained to the National Association of Colored Women's Clubs in 1895 that the work of the league had been "crippled" by the loss of women who were insecure about their capabilities. Women who joined clubs devoted to art or needlework no doubt perceived them as less personally threatening than membership in a politically active club and could further justify their decisions by the prevalent ideology of self-improvement. This is not to suggest, however, that black clubwomen were unconcerned with the broader issues affecting the race as a whole—especially the goal of helping the less fortunate. In fact, the newer clubs used their skills in music, art, and needlework as major sources of fund-raising for that purpose. On the state level, for example, the clubs founded and supported the Colored Orphanage and Old Folks Home in Pueblo, a project that received continuing assistance through donations of money, food, and clothing.[6]

At least twenty-two federated clubs in Denver were organized between the years 1900 and 1925. Many of them lasted only a short time, then disbanded; others, as membership declined, merged with the stronger clubs. A few managed to withstand the test of time, and some still exist. Four currently existing clubs that were organized in the first quarter of the century are the focus of this study: the Pond Lily Art and Literary Club, the Taka Art and Literary Club, the Carnation Art Club, and the Self-Improvement Club.[7] All are members of city and state federations and of the National Association of Colored Women. In addition, they were—and still are—part of an association that established a day nursery in 1916, the maintenance of which has been a major factor in the success and survival of the clubs for more than eighty-five years.

Of the four clubs, the Pond Lily Art and Literary Club is the oldest. It was organized in the late summer of 1901 by Augustavia Young Stewart, who was then sixteen years old.[8] According to the club's historian, Young had become incensed over a local newspaper article that had made derogatory statements about black women. She decided to form a club composed of young women who could, through thought, word, and deed, help dispel negative stereotypes about women of color. She called upon other young women who were not yet out of high school, and they held their first meeting in City Park. During that meeting, they noticed the lilies floating in the pond and decided to call the club Pond Lily.

The immediate goal of the new organization was self-improvement. The members decided that they would develop their talents so that whether they were playing the piano in public, reciting their favorite poems, reading a paper, or reviewing a book, it would be done in a way that would help create a better opinion of colored people.

The club was officially organized in 1902, and its first president, Florence Walden, served in that capacity until 1908. The object of the club—very much in line with the prevailing conservative philosophy of racial betterment through moral uplift—was to "bring the women of Denver into communication for closer acquaintance, mutual helpfulness, and the promotion of higher social and moral conditions."[9] According to the State Federation of Colored Women's Clubs records, Pond Lily became a member in 1906.

Two of the other clubs under study were organized in 1903. The first, the Taka Art and Literary Club, was founded by Minnie Norman and Mary Chapman to promote mutual helpfulness.[10] The second, the Carnation Art, Literary, and Charity Club, was founded by Savilla Burnett to bring "Negro women closer together in friendship and love" and to make the community a better place in which to live. The object of the Carnation Club, according to its constitution, was to learn "how to educate our hands by doing needlework to beautify homes, broaden our minds, and bring us closer together in friendship and love."[11]

The last club under study, the Self-Improvement Club, was organized in 1906 to foster "improvement of self along all lines of literary, art, charitable and social activities." It had as its ultimate aim "to maintain a home for young women who might come to Denver and who lacked proper protection."[12] The Self-Improvement Club is credited as being the originator of the idea for the Negro Woman's Club Home, a girls home and day nursery, organized by the Negro Woman's Club Association in 1916.

Formal structure and rigid adherence to rules and regulations were important during the early life of the clubs. The number of officers to be elected, as well as the specific duties of each office, were clearly stated, as were the number of meetings to be held per month and the activities to be carried out within each meeting. The club year ran from October to June, ending with the state association convention, usually held during the first or second week in June. During this time, Taka Art met once a week on Wednesdays, the first Wednesday of the month being literary day while all others were devoted to art work. Carnation Art held its weekly meetings on Fridays, with the second Friday of the month being literary day. The Pond Lily and the Self-Improvement clubs met on every other Thursday.

Club members felt they could work best by limiting the size of their membership: The Pond Lily and Taka Art clubs held their membership to twenty; the Carnation Art and Self-Improvement clubs had a ceiling of thirty members. Further, all clubs worked through departments or committees, including ways and means, reciprocity, domestic science, rescue, and programming, with members either volunteering or being appointed to serve.

Requirements of members—including the wearing of club regalia, the number of pieces of artwork expected, the amount of dues, how often members were expected to act as hostess for meetings, and how they were to conduct themselves within and outside of club meetings—were clearly stated in the bylaws, as were the fines to be imposed for failure to fulfill these requirements. Judging from the number of fines imposed—which ranged from two cents for not being prepared with a quotation during roll call, to twenty-five cents for not attending a city federation meeting, to one dollar for not having a finished piece of artwork for the state association conference—clubs rigidly followed these bylaws.

Expulsion from the clubs could result from misconduct or overbearing behavior by club members or from spreading club news to outsiders. During a 1917 meeting of the Taka Art Club, for example, its president noted that "someone told her that some member of the club was talking club news to other than club members," and she would find out who it was if it was the last thing she did.[13]

During the early years, club meetings were held at members' homes, usually rotating alphabetically. But judging from the frequency with which certain names are mentioned, it appears that those members who had larger homes were called upon more often to act as hostess. In any event, after the Negro Woman's Club Home was established in 1916, clubs began holding all their meetings there.

The agenda for meetings was similar for all clubs. The president would call the meeting to order, and the club's chaplain would offer some form of devotional such as the Lord's Prayer or a scripture reading. Roll call generally followed, and members were required to respond with a biblical quotation which, at least in the case of Taka Art, they had to recall from memory to avoid a two-cent fine. For all meetings other than those on literary day, a work period of at least an hour ensued in which members worked on art pieces. In some cases, especially in the early years, an art teacher came to the club and worked with the women until they had developed the skills necessary to act as teachers themselves. After the work period, members concluded old business, took up new business, and paid dues (ten cents a week initially) before adjourning. After adjournment, the hostess would serve light refreshments.

In addition to similarities in purpose, structure, and format, these clubs had similar requirements for membership. Candidates had to have "willing hands," a "desire to help others," and an eagerness "to do something for the race—especially the children."[14] Furthermore, considering that a major aim of the clubs was to uplift the image of black womanhood, it is not surprising that the most common requirement was that the applicant have "high moral character." Aside from these expectations of membership, however, little may be found in the clubs' minute books and ledgers that paint an accurate portrait of Denver's black clubwomen—who they were, how they lived, and what motivated them to join. Nevertheless, a few remaining members who joined clubs prior to 1925—along with others no longer living whose stories could be reconstructed from the public record and interviews—shed some light on the lives of these women.

Florence Moore, one of the oldest surviving federated women in Denver when interviewed in 1982, had been an active member of the Carnation Art Club since 1917 and had rarely missed a meeting. Born in 1890 in San Marcos, Texas, she had come to Denver at the age of twenty-six to be with her husband, who was a railroad electrician, and had immediately joined the Carnation Club. She recalled that while most of the other members were married, they were also older than she, and while some of them were day workers, most were homemakers. Although she herself was not employed when she joined, her husband died in 1927 and she had worked from that time on. When asked about her educational background and that of other members, Moore indicated that she had completed eight years of school and that the other members had completed about the same number of years.[15]

Ora Harvey of the Pond Lily Art Club had similar recollections about other club members. Born in 1895 in Fort Smith, Arkansas, Harvey had spent her early years in Kansas City. She moved to Denver in 1920 and became a member of Pond Lily in 1925. At that time she was thirty years old, and she recalled that the ages of other members varied. Although single when she joined, she soon married a man who, like Moore's husband, worked for the railroad. Most of the other members were married, and about half of them had children. She was employed soon after moving to Denver by a "very rich white woman" as a live-in housekeeper and earned the then high salary of one hundred dollars per month. Most of the other members, she recalled, were also employed—some as domestics but others as hairdressers and seamstresses, and one as a schoolteacher. Harvey had a sixth-grade education when she joined Pond Lily; most of the others, she recalled, had at least a high school diploma.[16]

Reverend Susie Whitman was also a federated woman during the 1920s, though by the 1980s she was no longer active. She had joined the Taka Art Club shortly after moving to Denver in 1927; at the time she was thirty-three years old, married, and had one child. Other members, she recalled, were "mostly younger" than she but were also married and had children. Though she was not employed then, she recalled that other members were ministers' wives, teachers, or in some cases domestics. Reverend Whitman had completed four years of college, while most of the other members had achieved a high school education.[17]

All of these early club members indicated that their comembers were "Christian women" interested in "uplift work." A common church affiliation, however, was not the major determinant for membership in a given club, for members belonged to various churches. In fact, neither common church membership, mutual acquaintances, nor close residential proximity had much to do with a woman's decision to join a club. Florence Moore, for example, had only recently moved to Denver and knew no one there. But her husband, who played cards with Ada Webster (then president of the Carnation Art Club), mentioned to Webster that his wife was moving to Denver. Webster introduced Moore's name to the club, and she readily consented to become a member.[18] Ora Harvey had a similar experience with the Pond Lily Club. Her husband, who had lived in Denver for some time before she moved to the city, belonged to a card club with Corinne Lowry, who was a Pond Lily member. Harvey's husband introduced the two, and Lowry submitted her name to the club. Both Florence Moore and Ora Harvey indicated that they had never regretted their initial decision. As Harvey pointed out, she was a member of Pond Lily for over fifty years, and she stated, "I'll die a Pond Lily."[19]

For other members, however, it was necessary to go through a period of trial and error with clubs before they found the one that best suited them. Reverend Whitman indicated that she first joined Pond Lily but soon found that "the same person who invited me to join ended up working against me," so she left after only a few weeks. Later, Reverend Whitman joined the Taka Art Club, which she believed was "the cream of the crop."[20]

Gertie Ross, another member of the Taka Art Club, was particularly active in the early years. Born in Kansas in 1879, she moved with her family to Denver in 1881. She was an honor graduate of East High School, attended the Western Conservatory of Music, and did postgraduate work in New York. Returning to Denver, she taught music classes and was organist and musical director for the Shorter A. M. E. Church for twenty years. Ross was the first black woman employed by the United States Mint in Denver, where she served as a weigher.[21] In 1910 she married George Ross, an attorney, who also published the *Denver Star*, one of the earliest black newspapers in Denver.

Gertie Ross was a member of the Taka Art club from at least 1913 until her death in 1961, during which time she devoted her almost limitless energies to club work. Others described her as a "tireless worker" who had "a memory like an elephant" and who was always interested in furthering her education. According to Reverend Whitman, Ross knew something about everything and could "out-think anybody with a college degree"—in fact, she worked on her degree while a club member. Her interest in education no doubt contributed to her initiating the idea for an education fund, established in 1920 by the State Association of Colored Women's Clubs.[22] This fund, managed by a board of directors, gave scholarships to worthy young women, and Ross worked with this board throughout her career as a federated clubwoman.

While Ross's work with the state association, for which she served as president in 1918, is certainly worth mentioning, her continuous involvement with the local club provides the clearest picture of a truly committed clubwoman. Judging from Taka's minutes, Ross was the force that held the club together; she kept the members aware of parliamentary etiquette—of which she had considerable knowledge—and continually reminded members when they strayed from proper procedures. She not only contributed to writing and revising Taka's constitution and bylaws, but she would explain these in such a way that the members could easily understand them. The club's minutes suggest that she was a hard taskmaster: "Mrs. Ross," states one entry, "suggested a remedy for members' talking during the meeting." Another reads, "Mrs. Ross gave a splendid talk on conduct of members."[23] That her colleagues may have been ambivalent about Ross's "suggestions" for the improvement of the functioning of the club is indicated in her receiving the dubious honor of election as "club critic" in 1916.

Ross also kept before the club any charity cases in the community that had been brought to her attention. She encouraged the club to form a committee to survey the community to determine how many colored families needed help and to present this information to influential community leaders for their assistance.[24]

Perhaps because of her husband's contacts through the *Denver Star*, Ross was well informed on most issues and activities in the black community. In 1916, for example, she reported on a woman who wanted to adopt an eight-year-old girl and asked club members to let her know if they knew of such a child. She was especially aware of the need for clubwomen to participate in civil rights issues. When black community leaders organized to protest the showing of D. W. Griffith's *Birth of a Nation* in 1916, she strongly encouraged the club to send two representatives to the organizational meeting. She was also part of a committee appointed by the club to investigate a report that the Denver Dry Goods Company discriminated against its colored employees by forcing them to use specially designated restrooms.[25]

Finally, Ross kept the club informed of current works in the black intellectual community. During a program in 1915, she read from Booker T. Washington's "Exceptional Men" and, in the following year, read and reviewed the article "Are We Making Good?" by Margaret Washington. While there is less information on most of the other early clubwomen, Ross was not an exceptional case. Two other Taka members, Lillian Bondurant and Helen Gatewood, also provided direction to the club.

Bondurant was born and raised in Harrodsburg, Kentucky. In 1907, at twenty-five, she moved to Denver and in 1912 married Samuel Bondurant, who owned and operated the Bondurant Cleaners.[26] According to Taka's minutes, Bondurant visited the club in December 1914, but her name was not presented as an applicant until the next October. She was officially voted into the club on 13 October 1915.[27] From that time until her death in 1974 she worked tirelessly for the club. She was especially active in the Negro Woman's Club Home Association, established in 1916, chairing its board of directors for many years.

Helen Gatewood spent much of her adult life in Pueblo where she was active in both club and church work. When she moved to Denver in the early teens, she first focused on working with her church, New Hope Baptist, where she organized several youth groups. Her interest in young people carried over into her club work, for when she joined Taka in 1917, she devoted much of her time to working with the club home's day nursery and dormitory for young girls.[28] She served as the home's president for seven years. By the time of her death in 1945, she had donated a car to the home as well as the property at Twenty-eighth and Humboldt.[29]

One more example of a committed clubwoman is Ada Webster of the Carnation Art Club. Webster was serving as secretary to the club when it was asked to cooperate with other clubs in establishing a club home in 1916. Members were so split over the idea that all of the officers and most of the members resigned. Webster stayed and became president of the club. She encouraged the few remaining members to join with the other clubs in the project, and under her leadership the Carnation Club sponsored a chitterling dinner to raise its share of the money needed to open the home.[30]

For the most part, then, early clubwomen were generally married and had children, were high school graduates, and considered themselves Christian women. Well over half were employed as elocutionists, musicians, seamstresses, milliners, domestics, and laundresses. One major indication that many of the early members were employed (and in domestic and laundry work, at that) is the fact that meetings for all clubs were held on weekdays (domestics and laundresses rarely had Saturdays off).[31] But whether employed or not, all of the members felt a sense of obligation toward uplift efforts within their clubs, for they were actively involved in helping the less fortunate within the community. While some of the women may be considered exceptions, a major requirement of the early clubs was a commitment to hard work. Judging from the number of resignations, those who were not willing to contribute the amount of time and energy— not to mention money—needed by the clubs did not continue as members.

Interests and activities of the clubs varied so much that it would be difficult to place them into neat categories. However, they were generally focused on efforts to improve members' skills in arts and crafts, including music and literary and intellectual development; to help the poor and needy individually and through more formalized "giving," such as contributing to the Red Cross; to assist the community's attempt to combat discrimination; to work with children to encourage higher health and educational standards; and to sponsor mothers' meetings, girls' clubs, and fund-raising activities. All these activities required a tremendous amount of teamwork not only within but between clubs. To be a "federated woman" meant more than actively participating in one's own club; it meant living up to expectations of assisting other clubs in larger efforts and causes. In this, two types of activities were paramount: (1) assistance for the poor and needy and (2) the most important example of collective action between clubs, the Negro Woman's Club Home.

A primary objective of the clubs was to give direct assistance to cases of individual need that came to the attention of clubwomen. When members heard of someone who was impoverished, sick, or in trouble, they would report it to the club and the group would decide whether to provide outright assistance; to refer the case to the benevolent, charity, or rescue committees for investigation; or, in a few instances, to decline to provide help.

The Taka Art Club's minutes offer concrete examples of such help. In 1915, for example, one woman was given a pair of shoes and another a ton of coal—both of which cost the club $6.20. Further, states the minutes, "Mrs. Clay's little boy needs shoes" ($2.00 was allocated) and "Mrs. Jackson needs assistance" (her rent was paid for a month, and she was given a sack of flour).[32] In 1916 the club allotted a $1.00 for a prescription for a sick woman, $5.00 to purchase artificial limbs for a disabled man, $1.50 to help a woman secure a railroad ticket, and $2.00 to assist a destitute family.[33] In many instances, clothing, medicine, or food replaced direct cash contributions; in others, money was the only medium possible, as in 1920, when Taka Art members gave $5.00 to secure bond to release a woman from jail. Also during that year, the Taka Art Club received a letter from a mother in Colorado Springs whose son had recently been sentenced to the state prison in Cañon City. The club donated $10.00 to assist in his appeal.[34]

In spite of all this, Taka members did not give blindly. In fact one member, Georgia Contee, suggested in 1919 that Taka spend more time finding out whether the unfortunate "really needed help" before deciding to give it. Occasionally the relief committee visited a sick individual or family and reported that no help was needed. When Helen Gatewood presented the case of a woman with two children whose parents were about to put her out, the motion to pay part of her rent was denied.[35]

Not only did the club provide assistance to what it considered deserving individuals, it also made regular contributions to the YWCA, in the form of either money or materials. When Lillian Bondurant reported to the club on YMCA needs, members donated six sheets costing $3.00. The club also made regular contributions to the Red Cross and the Federated Charities, an organization for which the club raised $303 in 1921.[36] After the Community Chest was established in 1922, Taka members pledged regularly and paid off their contributions in weekly installments.

The Carnation Art Club provided similar kinds of individual and collective assistance, including carrying coal and wood to poor families, paying rent, assisting girls from the South to buy railroad tickets so that they could return home, giving shoes and clothing to needy families, and donating baskets of food at holidays like Thanksgiving and Christmas. Carnation members also established a "milk fund" for underprivileged children and made regular contributions to both the YMCA and the YWCA; Shorter, Zion, and Central Baptist churches; the Colored Blind Home; the Community Chest; and the Lincoln Orphanage in Pueblo.[37]

As is no doubt evident from this charity work, clubs needed to raise a considerable amount of money. Thus, a great deal of time and effort went into fund-raising through various activities. These included card parties, bake sales, rummage sales, home-cooked dinners, concerts, poetry readings, and plays. Fund-raising efforts were usually conducted under the auspices of the ways and means committee, but often members were asked to donate directly to a specific cause. Either these donations came out of pocket or the more creative (or less financially able) would hold their own entertainments (such as box suppers or card parties) and turn the proceeds over to the club. In 1918 Georgia Contee raised over thirty dollars through an entertainment benefit, and the Takas were so pleased that they sent the news to the *Denver Star*.[38] Other fund-raisers held by the Taka Art Club included an "entertainment" in 1914, a "guessing contest" in 1916, and a "Japanese entertainment" in 1918. They featured a play, *Wages of Sin*, in 1919 and hosted a Martha Washington tea party in 1920. The Carnation Art Club had similar types of fund-raisers as well as an annual Clown Dance, a chitterling dinner, and in 1918, an "Uncle Sambo and Aunt Dinah" entertainment.[39]

In order to encourage attendance at these events, the clubs would often give a small prize, such as a dress pattern or a middy waist, for either the first person in the door or the person bringing the most guests. All this, in any case, required a tremendous amount of cooperation among the members. While no doubt true of most club endeavors, it was particularly true in the fund-raising: The members worked as a team, and each member gave according to her ability or her means. When the clubs sponsored a bake sale, for example, it was rare that clubwomen donated whole products, such as a cake or a pie. Instead, they usually gave ingredients—sugar, eggs, or flour—and those members who were unable to contribute would volunteer to do the actual baking.[40]

Club membership thus involved a commitment to—and active participation in—a wide range of activities, including assisting the poor. While certain members may have shown more commitment than others, the successful functioning of the clubs called for considerable cooperation, and this extended well beyond the individual clubs. In fact, the most salient example of cooperative teamwork between clubs was the establishment and maintenance of the Negro Woman's Club Home.

The idea of a club home for which several clubs would be responsible was first suggested by the Self-Improvement Club, which recognized the need for a place where colored girls coming to Denver might stay. Since this was too ambitious an undertaking for one group, the Self-Improvement Club invited the presidents of the other clubs in Denver to consider supporting such a home. While the most logical organization to consider the proposition would have been the city federation, the only recorded action, according to Taka's minutes, was taken by the Self-Improvement Club.[41] The most reasonable explanation for this less-than-unanimous action is that some of the clubs in the city federation objected or were unwilling to take on such a responsibility, so the name of the city federation could not be placed on the home. In any event, seven clubs responded to the challenge—Taka Art, Pond Lily, Carnation Art, Self-Improvement, Progressive Art, Sojourner Truth, and Twentieth Century—and these became known as the Negro Woman's Club Home Association.

The decision to become a part of the Club Home Association was no doubt difficult for many of the clubs. In fact, as has been stated, the Carnation Art Club split over the issue to the point that all its officers resigned with the exception of Ada Webster, the club's secretary. Webster, along with six remaining members, kept the club alive. Under her leadership, Carnation joined the Club Home Association, raised the necessary funds for its share in getting the home started by throwing a large chitterling dinner, and ultimately became the second club to pay off its share of stock in the home—no small feat, given the club's small membership.

During late 1915 and early 1916, the association met regularly to make plans for the home. Each club submitted an idea for "the ideal club home," and Taka's suggestion was typical: "The home should take up all lines of charity, rescue, nursery, [and] employment. . . . A committee [should be established] to look into the matter of educational rights . . . a committee to look after Colored children who have been arrested to see that they are given a fair trial—[and] . . . anything else that might help humanity."[42] The Taka Art Club also suggested a fund-raising campaign, which began with a mass meeting held in July at Shorter Chapel.[43] Six months later, on 16 December 1916, the clubs moved into a modern, two-story brick structure at 2357 Clarkson Street. The home, which consisted of eight rooms, was incorporated for five thousand dollars, with each club buying equal shares of stock at ten dollars per share. The aim of the new home was the maintenance of a dormitory, while the lower floor housed the nursery.[44]

It is understandable that virtually all surviving club members, when asked, "What was the most important activity for you in your club?" responded without hesitation, "The running of the nursery." Not only was considerable time and effort devoted to raising money to purchase shares of stock, but the clubs were also responsible for soliciting sustaining members—either individuals or groups—who would pay a sustaining fee of twelve dollars, and associate members, who paid six dollars per year toward the maintenance of the home.

Not only was such a commitment ambitious, it is pertinent that the association—consisting of seven clubs—itself became a federated club and joined the city, state, and national associations. This meant that members in the individual clubs were required to pay weekly club dues, and the club in turn paid city, state, and national dues. But because the club was also part of the association, it had to contribute to the city, state, and national dues required of the association! When these dues were added to the numerous collections taken up during the meetings for one purpose or another regarding the home—combined with the collections made for charity cases, contributions to the YWCA, and other organizations to which the clubs were expected to contribute—it is little wonder why one irate member of the Carnation Art Club would suggest, "Why not raise the club dues rather than nickel-and-dimeing us to death?"[45] It is also understandable why all of the Denver clubs did not wholeheartedly embrace the idea of becoming part of the Club Home Association.

In addition to raising money for the home, the clubs also contributed whatever the home currently needed, ranging from dishes and other utensils, milk, bread, and even clothing for the children in the nursery, to the purchase of sheeting for the exterior of the building, screens for the windows, and rakes for the yard. Yet perhaps more important than any of these contributions was the amount of time spent in the home. Ora Harvey of the Pond Lily Club recalled that she "changed many a diaper" and "cooked many a meal" for the home. Other members recalled working toward keeping the facility clean and running smoothly. Some of the members devoted seemingly unlimited energies toward the home. Lillian Bondurant, who served as chair of the board of directors for the association, was known to make valuable suggestions for ways to cut corners, such as buying meat wholesale or contacting Oliver T. Jackson, head of the black agricultural colony at Dearfield, to solicit fresh vegetables for the home.[46]

Given the time and energy it took to get the home established and running smoothly, it is not surprising that the board of directors ran a tight ship. Every aspect of the home's functioning was taken seriously—from establishing the rules for the dormitory and nursery to hiring, and later firing, a yardman. The secretary maintained meticulous accounts of each transaction occurring in the home, and every action taken by the board was initiated by parliamentary motion, including insurance payments and the purchase of meat and staples.

By far the most important staff member in the home was the matron. She was responsible for endless tasks, especially those involved in the running of the dormitory. Young workingwomen could rent a room in the dormitory for $1.25 per week, including kitchen privileges. (The price was increased to $1.50 in 1920 and to $2.00 in 1924.)[47]

The "inmates"—as the residents were called—were governed by strict rules upheld by the matron: They were not allowed to bring furniture, boxes, trunks, or pictures into the home; lights were to be out by 10:30 P.M.; all washing and ironing were to be done in the laundryroom during specified days and hours, at a rate of twenty-five cents per person; and electric irons were prohibited in the building. Girls were responsible for making their own beds and keeping their portion of the room tidy, and they were "absolutely prohibited" from lounging on vacant beds. To use the kitchen, they had to make arrangements with the matron, and they were at all times to use the dining room for lunch hour, use club dishes, and leave the kitchen and dining room as found.[48]

The rules of the home clearly indicated the clubwomen's desire to provide proper training and instill morality in the girls. Specific requirements for washing dishes ("Must use pan instead of sink; must use soap when washing dishes"), personal grooming ("Arrangements of toilet, including the straightening of hair, must be done in one's room"), and entertainment of "company" ("Must use the parlor and matron must be present") were rigidly upheld.

The matron was responsible for assigning beds as well as bath times to the girls. Arrangements had to be made with her in order to use gas, water, and heat. She was also required to evict any person who was found destroying property or not following the rules. But the matron's duties did not end with the dormitory maintenance. She also opened the building at 7:00 A.M. and closed it at 6:00 P.M.; she was responsible for all cases of emergency; and she itemized weekly reports of transactions in the home. (Accounts for dormitory and nursery were to be kept separately.) She prepared the menus, collected fees for entertainments (or socials) in the home, and was responsible for the behavior of the children, including teaching them proper table manners. As if these duties were not enough, she was also admonished to "make the home comfortable and at all times take the place of mother for the girls entering the home." For all of these responsibilities, the matron's salary was forty dollars per month in 1920.[49]

In 1919 clubwomen of the association took up the question of allowing married women to stay in the dormitory. This issue was taken back to the individual clubs for a vote. While Taka approved the idea, most of the clubs did not, for the 13 June 1919 minutes of the association show that the board requested married women to move. In 1920 it recommended that the association rescind the earlier action concerning who could stay in the dormitory, but the motion lost.

Both the nursery and dormitory proved successful, and in 1921 the association's report to the State Board of Charities and Corrections indicated that the home had four paid officers—one man and three women—including a second matron. The nursery cared for thirty children, and the dormitory housed nine girls.[50] In addition to the dormitory and nursery, the home allowed various community organizations to rent its facilities for entertainments—stipulating that these could not be card parties, dancing parties, or political meetings. The women's clubs began holding their weekly meetings in the home, paying the nominal fee of fifty cents per meeting, while rent charged to other organizations was three dollars. In this way the association contributed to the home's income and became a community center in the process.

In spite of what was clearly an enormous undertaking to maintain the home, the association also sponsored yearly fund-raisers such as Harvest Home (a bazaar) and a charity ball. Although members of the association occasionally pointed out that as Christian women they should put on some form of entertainment other than a charity ball, this was nevertheless continued for a number of years. Another method of raising funds for the home was through raffles. In 1922, for example, a piece of lacework was given to the association by "a white man" and was raffled off at ten cents a chance.[51]

The association's concern with raising funds for the home led to soliciting help from the Denver Federation of Charities. When this organization became defunct in 1922, the clubs joined the Community Chest, where as members their responsibilities actually increased: They were required to participate in fund-raising drives, maintain additional records on the home, and publicize the Community Chest by providing reports of anything novel or newsworthy that occurred there.

In spite of the stipend received from the Community Chest, the association remained primarily responsible for maintaining the home and making improvements. In 1923 the board noted that, since the Community Chest would "give us nothing for a new building, and realizing if we expect to improve our home it must be through our own efforts, the Board recommends that the Association establish a building fund." Each of the seven clubs in the association was to put in one hundred dollars per year for two years, or until enough money was raised. On 2 October 1926, the Taka Art Club made its second installment of twenty-five dollars toward the building fund, and in 1927, as a result of such donations, a sun parlor was built on the home at a cost of twenty-seven hundred dollars cash.[52]

In addition to a continuing concern about money, the association maintained an interest in all of the details surrounding the functioning of the home. When the work of the yardman was found to be unsatisfactory, the board paid his monthly salary and dismissed him; when it learned that the first matron had been performing part of the second matron's work, it saw that she was paid an additional $5.33; when it learned that the mothers of children in the nursery were not as involved as they might be, it established "mothers' meetings."[53]

Another major activity, beginning in 1921, was the establishment of a health clinic in the home. The association had earlier recognized the need to relieve the congestion at the clinic located at Twenty-sixth and Lawrence, as well as the inconvenience this clinic posed to mothers who had to take their children such a distance. But it also knew that it must have the cooperation of the community if the clinic was to be successful. Thus, members of the board visited doctors in the area to determine whether or not they would be willing to cooperate, while other members visited the homes of mothers in the area to be assured that they would in fact use the clinic. After getting the support of both physicians and mothers, the association pursued the idea, and the clinic was officially opened in 1922.[54]

In other respects, too, as community needs changed, so did the home. When the YWCA sponsored the building of a dormitory for black women during the 1920s, the association found less use for its own dormitory. At the same time, however, there was a growing need to expand the nursery. Thus the dormitory was eliminated, and the association thereafter devoted most of its energies toward maintaining the nursery.

In addition to the seemingly endless tasks associated with the maintenance of the nursery, dormitory, and clinic, the association was, of course, also a federated club. This meant that, like other clubs, it was required to participate actively in city, state, and national functions as well as contribute to various fund-raisers, help with individual cases of charity, and generally assist in other community uplift efforts. In terms of assisting needy individuals, in 1921 alone the association gave assistance to a needy Denver family; investigated the well-being of a girl living in Denver whose concerned mother had called to inquire about her from Chicago; sent a large quantity of clothing to the poor and needy in Tulsa; and, after hearing of the sad plight of a girl in the Crittendon Home who was in dire need of shoes and clothing, readily provided these items.[55]

Monetary support was an ongoing necessity for the association. In 1922, when one of the residents in the home became ill, the association decided that since clubwomen were essentially providing her lodging, the clubs should also give fifty cents per week for her food. As the condition of the young woman worsened, the association discussed placing her in the hospital, and she was referred to the charity committee. The young woman's sister eventually arrived to help care for her, and the clubs were asked to support the two women.[56]

The association was also interested in cases of discrimination in Denver. In one instance, the chair of the house committee reported the arrest of one of the girls in the home, stating that the whole affair was "deplorable, in as much as the girl was innocent of the charge [and] was humiliated in having to ride in the patrol car and being roughly handled by the officers."[57] In 1923 a member of the board recommended that a letter be written to Governor Sweet commending him on his "splendid attitude" on the segregation of public schools in Denver. Also during 1923, a board member was appointed to investigate the report that the community lodging house had denied service to colored people. In cases where little could be done about discrimination, the association nevertheless expressed its concern, as in its report of a girl about to be hanged in Washington, D.C. Members were asked to pray for the commutation of her sentence, and the president urged all who could to attend a prayer meeting to be held in the club home.[58]

Each activity of the association—whether it was participating in Community Chest drives, assisting the YWCA, sponsoring fund-raisers for the club home, or hosting Christmas parties for the children in the nursery—required sincere commitment from each club. Their contributions ranged from buying stock, soliciting sustaining members, and making donations to the home, to devoting time and energy toward the home's maintenance.

As in most instances in which members of an organization must spend considerable time together, occasional conflicts arose. These stemmed from personality clashes as well as club differences. In 1920, for example, an oversight on the part of the secretary led to a reprimand by the association's president, Isabelle Stewart, who called on the other gathered members to ask what should be done with a secretary who neglected her duties. "That's what's wrong with the Association now," Stewart said, suggesting that members were leaving too many things undone. Then, evidently moved by anger, the president blamed the association for omitting her name from a newspaper story about the club home and ended by submitting her resignation. "My superiors won't insult me," she said, taking her seat, "[and] my inferiors can't insult me."[59]

This precipitated a later argument between the president and the chair of the social committee, Sarah Abernathy, on the question of who had initiated the idea for the club home. Stewart produced and read from what she claimed was the 1914 yearbook of the Self-Improvement Club, which proved, she stated, that that club was in fact the originator. Abernathy questioned the authenticity of the book, and an argument ensued during which Abernathy was told to "shut up" so the issue could be settled. The association members eventually credited the Self-Improvement Club with the idea for the home, and Abernathy resigned, as did the secretary who had been accused of neglecting her duties.[60]

In spite of these differences, clubwomen managed to stick together rather than let personal grudges and club allegiances destroy what they had worked so hard to accomplish. Three of the seven clubs eventually disbanded and in that way left the association, but the remaining clubs— Pond Lily, Self-Improvement, Carnation, and Taka Art—still compose the Negro Woman's Club Home Association. The name of the nursery was changed to George Washington Carver Day Nursery in 1946 and is now housed in a modern building in Denver.

Clearly, black women's clubs in Denver fulfilled important functions for the community, but equally important were the functions fulfilled for the women themselves. Sophonisba Breckenridge, in *Women in the Twentieth Century*, points out that women's organizations emerging during the early twentieth century served as places where members "could find refreshment, recreation, or culture, cultivate some intellectual or social interest or accomplish some public-spirited good."[61] In the matter of accomplishing "public-spirited good," according to some historians and sociologists, women's clubs were more effective in social, civic, and educational reform than were men's.

Notes

This essay was first published in *Essays in Colorado History* 13 (1992).

1. W. E. B. DuBois, *Some Efforts of American Negroes for Their Own Social Betterment*, Atlanta University Publications, No. 3 (1898), 5; Inabel Burns Lindsay, "The Participation of Negroes in the Establishment of Welfare Services, 1865–1900" (Ph.D. dissertation, University of Pittsburgh, 1952), 121–32.

While these clubs played a significant role within their communities, the general neglect or underestimation of their activities and achievements has been the rule rather than the exception. Furthermore, the exceptions have focused on the nation's major organization, the National Association of Colored Women, established in 1895, which maintained careful records of its activities. Considerably less is known about local club movements that formed during the same period and that later affiliated with the National Association. While initial clues may be found in early correspondence between the national, state, and city associations, the task remains to thoroughly investigate club activities on the local level and to place those clubs in the social and ideological context in which they functioned. The 1980s witnessed a number of attempts to fulfill this task, with several works on black women's club activities in Indianapolis, San Francisco, Cincinnati, Washington, D.C., and Kansas. See, for example, Earline Rae Ferguson, "The Women's Improvement Club of

Indianapolis: Black Women Pioneers in Tuberculosis Work, 1903–1938," *Indiana Magazine of History* 3 (1988): 237–61; Marilyn Dell Brady, "Organizing Afro-American Girls' Clubs in Kansas in the 1920's," *Frontiers* 9 (1987): 69–73; Marilyn Dell Brady, "Kansas Federation of Colored Women's Clubs, 1900–1930," *Kansas History* 9 no. 1 (Spring 1986): 19–30; Andrea Tuttle Kornbluh, "Woman's City Club: A Pioneer in Race Relations," *Queen City Heritage* 44 (1986): 21–38; Sharon Harley, "Beyond the Classroom: Organization Lives of Black Female Educators in the District of Columbia, 1890–1930," *Journal of Negro Education* 51 (1982): 254–65.

Undoubtedly one of the reasons for the renewed interest in the history of black women's club activities is the apparent reemergence of self-help advocates within black communities. It is also interesting to note the similarities in perceived problems today within black communities—unemployment, youth crime, unstable families, and conflicts between black men and women.

2. According to Gerda Lerner, there are three preconditions to club development among black women during the period 1890 to 1925: a sizable black population, educated women with leisure time (to provide the leadership), and unmet needs of the black poor. See Gerda Lerner, *Black Women in White America* (New York: Random House, 1973), 436–67.

3. "Milestones of the State Association of Colored Women's Clubs," undated scrapbook, Western History Department, Denver Public Library.

4. Group thesis, "Contributions by Blacks to Social Welfare History in the Early West" (master's thesis, University of Denver, 1974), 116.

5. National Association of Colored Women's Clubs, Inc., *A History of the Club Movement among the Colored Women of the United States of America* (Washington, D.C.: National Association of Colored Women's Clubs, 1902), 83; *Denver Times*, 28 March 1901.

6. State Federation of Colored Women's Clubs (hereafter CWC) minutes, 1904–20, 115, and CWC ledger, 1913, 33, both in Western History Department, Denver Public Library.

7. The research method for examining these clubs was as follows: The author contacted historians from each club and gained permission to examine all available materials, which included minute books (by far the best source of information), ledgers, scrapbooks, announcements of activities sponsored by the clubs, and numerous miscellaneous items. The condition of these materials depended upon a variety of factors, including the conscientiousness of the historians and the writing skills of the early secretaries and historians. Much of the information on the period in question has either been destroyed or misplaced over the years; thus the available sources are limited. In addition, the same type of information is not available for all clubs. Yet from the materials that are consistent for all clubs it appears that the clubs were so similar in purpose, structure, format, and activity that it is possible to provide a "picture," so to speak, of the typical club. In addition to examining available materials, the author interviewed the oldest living member of each club. These interviews were helpful in clarifying questions that emerged in reviewing written materials.

8. James T. Atkins Collection, box 48, file 2164, Colorado Historical Society, Denver.

9. Pond Lily Art and Literary Club constitution and bylaws, in possession of Ora V. Harvey, Denver, Colo.

10. Interview with Dorothy Reaves, 2 April 1981.

11. Carnation Art Club constitution and bylaws, in possession of Florence Moore, Denver, Colo.

12. Brochure for the State Federation of Colored Women's Clubs, 1928, Western History Department, Denver Public Library. This brochure contains brief sketches of clubwomen and clubs in the state federation.

13. Taka minutes, 7 February 1917, in possession of Dorothy Reaves, Denver, Colo.

14. Interviews with Florence Moore (Carnation), February 1982; Reverend Susie Rose Whitman (Taka), February 1982; and Ora Harvey (Pond Lily), January 1982.

15. Moore interview.

16. Harvey interview.

17. Whitman interview.

18. Moore interview.

19. Harvey interview.

20. Whitman interview

21. CWC minutes, 1904–10.

22. Taka minutes, 18 February 1914.

23. Ibid., 2 December 1914 and 7 February 1917.

24. Ibid., 1 December 1915.

25. Ibid.

26. Biographical notes on Lillian Bondurant are included in papers held by Dorothy Reaves, Denver, Colo.

27. Taka minutes, 13 October 1915. This point is made because most of the Taka information for later years refers to Bondurant as one of the earliest members. Some of the current members believed she was a charter member.

28. Ibid., 17 February 1917.

29. Notes maintained by Reaves.

30. Brief historical sketch of the Carnation Art Club, in possession of Florence Moore, Denver, Colo.

31. However, as members of the Coterie Club (the one nonfederated club the author examined that is not a part of this study) were quick to point out, theirs was the only club that always held meetings on Saturdays—clearly implying that there were no domestics or laundresses in the club. Coterie Club minutes, 1916, 1918, 1920; 1982 interview with Coterie historian Edith Hawkins, a club member since 1916.

32. Taka minutes, 12 May 1915 and 4 and 24 February 1915.

33. Ibid., 1 January 1916, 2 February 1916, 8 and 29 March 1916, and 19 July 1916.

34. Ibid., 12 March 1920 and 20 October 1920.

35. Ibid., 17 December 1919 and 16 Feburary 1921.

36. Ibid., 2 February 1921.

37. Carnation Art Club, "Summary of Past Contributions," undated, in possession of Moore.

38. Taka minutes, 1 September 1918.

39. Carnation minutes, 5 January 1917 and 4 December 1918, in possession of Florence Moore.

40. Taka minutes, 25 May 1920.

41. Ibid., 8 March 1915.

42. Ibid., 8 March 1916.

43. Carnation minutes, 3 December 1918.

44. Negro Woman's Club Home brochure, 1924, in possession of Reaves.

45. Carnation minutes, 3 December 1918.

46. Minutes of the Negro Woman's Club Home Association (hereafter NWCHA), 5 October 1920; minute book in possession of Reaves.

47. NWCHA minutes, 1 June 1920; 1924 brochure.

48. Ibid., 1 June 1919 ("Rules Governing Dormitory").

49. NWCHA minutes, 1 July 1919, 2 September 1919 ("Rules for Matron"), and 2 February 1920.

50. Annual report to the State Board of Charities and Corrections for the year ending 20 June 1921, in possession of Reaves.

51. NWCHA minutes, 15 December 1922.

52. NWCHA brochure, 1927.

53. NWCHA minutes, 4 April 1922.

54. Ibid., 7 February 1922.

55. Ibid., 6 September 1921, 5 July 1921, and 4 October 1921.

56. Ibid., 2 May 1922, 5 July 1922, and 3 October 1922.

57. Ibid., 4 October 1921.

58. Ibid., 5 October 1920 and 6 March 1923.

59. Ibid., 6 January 1920.

60. Ibid.

61. Sophonisba Breckenridge, *Women in the Twentieth Century* (New York: McGraw-Hill, 1933), 5.

19.
___

"Save the Babies!": American Indian Women, Assimilation Policy, and Scientific Motherhood, 1912–1918

LISA E. EMMERICH

In this article Lisa Emmerich explores the efforts of Bureau of Indian Affairs personnel to improve the health of Indian babies. Their laudable goal, however, was complicated by the white reformers' own cultural assumptions, which made it hard for them to analyze what caused the problems they sought to solve. Emmerich credits the good intentions of BIA personnel. She also "gets beneath" their words to probe underlying assumptions about assimilation and women's roles that guided their efforts to "save" Indian children and that ultimately limited their effectiveness.

Emmerich is less successful in documenting the Indian side of the story, a limitation she candidly acknowledges. The BIA records, like the Houchen records, reveal more about the values and preoccupations of policymakers and field staff than about the Indian women they sought to reach. Emmerich grounds her speculations about Indian women's decisions in a comparison of conflicting Euro-American and Native American understandings of gender, motherhood, and family. Her approach highlights how policymakers' commitments to the values of middle-class motherhood shaped government programs.

Emmerich's analysis is guided by her recognition that the Save the Babies campaign contained "two very different stories about American Indian women, their tribal cultures, and motherhood." Her sources, however, do not document the Indian women's decisions to seek BIA assistance or to resist its underlying messages. Emmerich carefully does not assume Indian mothers' actions from these secondary materials. She is scrupulous to recognize that there are voices she cannot record. Nonetheless, the fact that she recognizes which voices are silent and why leads Emmerich to a very different analysis than if she accepted the government records at their word and allowed them to tell both sides of the story.

In early November 1916, twenty-two Cocopah and Quechan women and their families traveled from across the Fort Yuma Indian Reservation to the local boarding school for a two-day fair. Sponsored by the Bureau of Indian Affairs (BIA), the event focused largely on the problems of rearing healthy Indian children. The centerpiece of the educational and social fair was the "baby show," a contest that pitted mother against mother and child against child as they vied for the coveted designation of "Best Baby."

Before the competition began, the excited Cocopah and Quechan women readied their offspring for evaluation in the school washroom. Soap and water, brushes and combs, and garments lovingly and expressly made for the occasion transformed twenty-seven children into picture-perfect contestants. Judges recruited from among the reservation Indian Service staff used a "scientific" numerical ranking system developed by the American Medical Association to evaluate each child on the basis of general health and physical and emotional development.[1]

The results of the 1916 Fort Yuma Baby Show were impressive. Five children outshone their peers to claim awards in their respective age groups. Competition was so fierce in three other categories that the judges selected second- and third-place winners too. Some contestants scored double victories. Josephine Acquinas, daughter of Mrs. Josephine Acquinas, won the award for "best" girl aged two to three years as well as the prize for the "best-dressed" girl under school age. Mrs. Marie Dewey's daughter, Geraldine, also won in two categories: first place as the "best-dressed" girl aged six months to one year and second place for the "best-dressed" girl under school age. In all, seven Indian boys and three Indian girls between six months and school age received prizes as the "best" babies, toddlers, and youngsters.

The Yuma *Morning Sun* reported the results of the Fort Yuma Baby Show to the surrounding nonnative community. The newspaper's correspondent proclaimed the baby show "one of the most interesting features of the fair."[2] And well it must have been for the Euro-American observers. The Fort Yuma Baby Show brought the most assimilated native women and their families, rather than the familiar "reservation Indians," into the public eye. Along with this measure of notoriety on and off the reservation, mothers of the winners also received prizes like washtubs, washboards, clothes baskets, hair brushes, tablecloths, and cutlery.[3]

Reporting to the Fort Yuma superintendent, field matron Mae Justus assessed the significance of the event she had helped organize. The baby show "arouse[d] ambition and thereby stimulate[d] effort [among native women]. The expressions of competition heard on every hand clearly denotes [*sic*] the spirit of rivalry engendered." Such were the benefits of the affair, she boasted, that Indian entrants might some day compete successfully alongside "white" babies. Moreover, the growing awareness of their parental responsibilities exhibited by the tribal women was something to be celebrated and encouraged. The Cocopah and Quechan women were, Justus proudly declared, "coming awake" to the individual and tribal importance of motherhood.[4]

Within the faded newspaper clippings and reports that compose the documentary record of the 1916 Fort Yuma Baby Show are two very different stories about American Indian women, their tribal cultures, and motherhood. One is, of course, the official BIA narrative recounted by

Mae Justus. Inchoate adults in this version, native women were slow to recognize and respond to their maternal obligations. The triumph of assimilation, exemplified by the success of the baby show, offered them freedom from traditions that had previously arrested their development as women and mothers. Thus, Justus's delight in their participation and progress was sincere. The maternal "great awakening" she envisioned at Fort Yuma promised the Cocopah and Quechan women, and their families, a bright future.

The official BIA story only hints at the second, tribal, version of the 1916 Fort Yuma Baby Show. For Mrs. Marie Dewey, Mrs. Josephine Acquinas, and the other Cocopah and Quechan women, the baby show and all its attendant hoopla underscored a family landscape that was changing in profound ways. Publicly, these changes meant participating in the systematic evaluation of infants and children that owed its standards of perfection to the Euro-American world. They meant accepting and acting on the principle that parental competition, individual rivalries, and consumer rewards were all elements of "civilized" child rearing. Privately, these changes meant accommodating an equally foreign set of standards for maternal behavior, family life, and health care that ultimately promoted the complete abandonment of traditional patterns.

This intense public scrutiny of Indian mothers and their children at Fort Yuma in 1916 was neither accidental nor localized. It was, rather, part of a national health campaign that focused exclusively on American Indian women in their roles as mothers. The Save the Babies campaign worked toward the wholesale redefinition of native family life according to Euro-American standards and models. Through their adoption of new strategies relating to the roles and responsibilities of mothers, the BIA hoped to enlist tribal women as allies in an all-out war against infant and child morbidity and mortality that seriously jeopardized American Indian survival. Between 1912 and 1918, the Save the Babies campaign worked to save some lives through the transformation of others.

As it emphasized the promotion of better Indian health care by undercutting traditional patterns of family life, the Save the Babies campaign reflected the most important themes in federal Indian affairs between the Civil War and World War I. Assimilation, as a process and as a goal, dominated Indian policy throughout the late nineteenth century. From the ground up, quite literally, no component of tribal life escaped the attention of the BIA and its allies, the self-styled "friends of the Indian." Reservations became "nurseries of civilization" where bureaucrats and reformers hoped to root out the last vestiges of traditionalism. The Major Crimes Act, passed in 1885, eroded tribal sovereignty and customary legal systems. After 1887, allotment disrupted social and political ties within communities as well as the metaphysical bonds connecting people to their lands. Private property and economic individualism thereafter competed against the tradition of communalism. Educational programs for tribal men, women, and children emphasized the importance of accommodation to this new world order of small homesteads, nuclear families, and Euro-American lifeways. Working in concert, these programs encouraged the timely Americanization of the remaining American Indians.

Time was not an ally for those anxious to witness the triumph of assimilation over traditionalism. In the Indian school system where coercion guaranteed compliance, de-Indianization continued at a steady, albeit slow, pace. Other areas proved more problematic. Many of the BIA's "civilization" programs had faltered by the end of the first decade of the twentieth century. Reformers and policymakers alike grossly underestimated the determination of tribal people to set their own pace and degree of acculturation. Stubborn resistance to the Euro-American gospels of private property, patriotic citizenship, and rugged individualism stymied federal efforts to lead American Indians down the "white man's road."[5]

Though troubling, this resistance was hardly the most serious problem confronting assimilationists in the early twentieth century. Belatedly, those living outside Indian country were realizing what others closer to tribal communities had known for years: The indigenous population base seemed on the verge of collapse. Though the decline of the native people of the Western Hemisphere began during the fifteenth century, the nineteenth century proved especially devastating for American Indians. The cumulative impact of ethnocide—wars, starvation, epidemics, and forced relocations—had reduced the American Indian population to approximately 228,000 by 1890. The rebound from this nadir point was painfully slow. In the native communities across the trans-Mississippi West where the decline was most dramatic, the "end" of the American Indian population seemed a real and immediate danger.[6]

This shocking situation was all the more poignant because the most visible victims of the health care crisis were native infants and children. Indian parents struggled to raise healthy families in communities where grinding poverty and a pervasive sense of cultural dislocation shaped daily life. Given those realities, it is hardly surprising that they often lost the battle, and with it their children. BIA field employees grimly notified increasingly alarmed policymakers of these family tragedies in reports that read like tribal obituaries: "visited Cora's [sick] babies; John Antelope['s] baby sick; Jessie Throwing Water her baby sick; went to see two babies and [?] they both die, in spite of all we can do."[7] Grief-stricken parents and frustrated Indian Service personnel watched helplessly as the deaths of infants and children became everyday calamities in Indian communities in the early twentieth century.

Responding to this emergency, Commissioner of Indian Affairs Robert G. Valentine ordered all BIA field employees in 1912 to "take immediate steps to greatly reduce infant mortality. Save the babies."[8] This dramatic rallying cry provided the impetus for a program that combined late-nineteenth-century Euro-American feminine ideals with the "science" of motherhood as understood by twentieth-century progressive reformers and public health specialists. Saving the babies provided the BIA and its reform allies with yet another opportunity to assimilate native women, this time through appeals to their maternal sensibilities. The doctrine of "scientific motherhood," a system of parenting that blended Euro-American gender ideology, family norms, and Westernized medical care, became the new tool to promote Americanization.

The belief that maternal attitudes and behaviors were of paramount importance in the lives of their children dominated the Save the Babies campaign from its creation. Here, the BIA's policy reflected a century of gradual change in middle-class Euro-American family life. The trans-formation of the family during the nineteenth century resulted in greater power for and emphasis on women within the sphere of motherhood. This visibility meant that they also bore more of the responsibility for the successful rearing and nurturing of their children. By the early twentieth century, their private duties as parents had grown beyond the boundaries of the individual family. Motherhood became a public activity that had a direct impact on the quality of community and, ultimately, national life.[9] Small wonder, then, that Indian reform activists and BIA policymakers made the popular axiom "The hand that rocks the cradle rules the world" one of the central tenets of the Save the Babies campaign.[10]

The BIA hoped that the hand rocking this globally important cradle would be that of an assimilated American Indian woman. That hope, of course, grew out of the assumption that only a fully Americanized native woman could understand the significance of her role as a parent. An "ignorant, coarse, [and] uncouth" Indian woman still trapped by archaic traditions could hardly appreciate, much less apply, the principles of scientific motherhood.[11] Only an assimilated mother would be ready to participate in what the BIA envisioned as "the rescue of a race."[12]

This blanket prejudice against Indian traditionalism hardly seems surprising, given the extraordinary efforts made by the U.S. government to eradicate every vestige of tribalism. But the addition of gender as a factor does invite a different reading of the BIA's characterization of native women who rejected assimilation. Indian women were captives in this version, trapped by a stereotype more than four centuries old. European and Euro-American transplants to the Western Hemisphere examined indigenous cultures for evidence of what they defined as "savagery" and believed they found it in the status of women. The "squaw drudge" stereotype emerged from their powerful blending of racial, cultural, and gender biases. Indian women were passive, mute, and ignorant household slaves in this rendering of native life. Supposedly relegated to lifelong degradation and servitude by virtue of their sex, they were tragic symbols to "civilized" observers.[13]

European and Euro-American ethnocentrism distorted the realities of tribal life like a warped telescope lens distorts the view of a starry night sky. American Indian women were vital members of tribal communities throughout North America in which survival depended upon the collab-orative efforts of all. Among matrilineal groups like the Navajo and Iroquois nations, women wielded substantial political, social, and eco-nomic power. Even in the more patrilineal tribes like the Lakota and the

Pawnee, their contributions to the welfare of the community earned them recognition, respect, and clout. Most Indian nations endorsed different spaces for men and women just as they acknowledged the complementary and reciprocal nature of their roles.[14] Native women, in short, were anything but degraded drudges.

Interaction with Europeans and Euro-Americans after "discovery" resulted in significant changes in the status of women in many tribal communities. One need only read the stories of Tsimshian, Creek, Seneca, or Maidu women to see how colonization transformed familiar worlds into entirely new cultural landscapes. Because Europeans and Euro-Americans privileged men as political and economic leaders, native women all too often faded into invisibility in tribal affairs. Even in those situations where their work as trade partners did support continued economic power, the concurrent destruction of tribal social and political networks frequently led to their subordination.[15]

Perhaps the one place where American Indian women were able to maintain their status in a rapidly changing tribal world was within the traditional realm of the family. As the loss of lands, resources, and autonomy shattered spirits, the familiar rhythms of family life became a refuge. Survival, more than ever, required the commitment of women to themselves, their families, and their communities. Food still had to be prepared for immediate consumption and preserved for an uncertain future; shelter still had to be provided for family members; clothing still had to be manufactured; and most importantly, children still had to be nurtured.

That Indian women carried within themselves the future of their nations was a power and a responsibility respected by all. The ability to bring life into the world and the capacity for rearing future generations meant that Indian women occupied special places within their communities. Accounts of native family life from across the United States commonly speak of the revered status of motherhood and the recognition of the demands that role entailed. Native authors like Kay Bennett (Navajo), Helen Sekaquaptewa (Hopi), Anna Moore Shaw (Pima), Lucy Thompson (Yurok), Beverly Hungry Wolf (Blackfoot), and Ella Deloria (Lakota) have written eloquently of the contributions women made to their communities through child rearing.[16] These authors, and others writing about tribal family life, make it clear that American Indian women took their maternal duties and responsibilities very seriously.

It was just this dedication and seriousness of purpose that the BIA hoped to harness through the Save the Babies campaign. Policymakers admitted that tribal women, whatever their inherent shortcomings, were devoted to their children. Commissioner of Indian Affairs Francis Leupp remarked on this very trait in 1910 when he candidly noted that the Indian woman "loves her babies with the same fervor as if she were cultured, and graceful, and white."[17] Cato Sells, his successor and the originator of the Save the Babies campaign, also acknowledged that "there is among the Indians [female] a marked and tender affection for their children."[18] That maternal fervor could not, however, protect native children from illness and death. Nor could that "marked and tender affection" ensure the survival of the American Indian population base.

To help native women address the demographic crisis facing their communities, the BIA needed field representatives who could move easily among them and their children. It needed advocates who could offer encouragement and support to tribal women as they learned the proper mix of maternalism and science. Above all, the agency needed independent, tireless workers who could energetically implement a practical, effective program on a shoestring budget. For all these reasons, the BIA turned to field matrons to lead the fight in the Save the Babies campaign.

One of the broad range of federal assimilation ventures instituted during the late nineteenth century, the field matron program had as its goal the transformation of American Indian women according to Euro-American standards of femininity and domesticity. Deeply influenced by contemporary Victorian reverence for domesticity and "woman's sphere," ethnocentric policymakers and reformers concluded that Indian home life exerted a powerful conservative force upon tribal peoples. To break this bond with the past, the BIA sent Euro-American women into Indian country after 1890 to teach their tribal counterparts "to respect and love and seek the ways of White women."[19]

Like most other BIA employees, field matrons did not have any special qualifications or training for their work nor were they required to. Because Euro-American society believed that "any good woman can teach every good woman what all good women should know" and, along with Florence Nightingale, that "every woman is a nurse," there was no need for any preparation beyond life experience. Conventional wisdom endowed middle-class Euro-American women with a unique, gender-based capacity for "civilizing" peoples and cultures sufficient to bridge the distance separating them from Indian women. Policymakers and Indian reform activists alike assumed that tribal women would welcome the field matrons and embrace them as allies. Thus, these common bonds of womanhood took on a special importance in the fight for healthy Indian infants and children.

From 1912 to 1918, the field matrons implemented the Save the Babies campaign on reservations and in Indian communities throughout the trans-Mississippi West. In doing so, they reinforced the standard assimilationist beliefs: Tribalism was a retrogressive force; traditional native family patterns and medical practices were antiquated and dangerous; and Indian women had to accept sole responsibility for the health and welfare of their children. The field matrons confronted tribal mothers with the message that a "good" woman uncritically accepted scientific motherhood as the only way to prevent infant and child morbidity and mortality.

The "science" of motherhood that the Save the Babies campaign promoted so vigorously was a by-product of the contemporary transformation of American medicine. The modernization of the American medical community after the Civil War brought about far-reaching changes in the ways Americans sought and received health care. The concurrent emergence of public health as an important national concern during the late nineteenth and early twentieth centuries resulted in an increased emphasis on the use of science, technology, and credentialed experts to fight pediatric morbidity and mortality.[20] Together, these movements gave birth to the philosophy of "scientific motherhood."

When the BIA superintendents, agents, physicians, and field matrons promoted scientific motherhood among American Indian women, they hoped to prompt a revolution in tribal family and community life. As native women saw evidence of the superiority of Western medicine and its practitioners, they would shun traditional tribal medical practices and practitioners. As they learned the benefits of "civilized" child rearing, they would reject time-honored models of motherhood and family life. As they became "scientific" mothers, native women would look to field matrons and physicians, not extended family networks, as sources of education and assistance. Assimilation and health care stood shoulder to shoulder under the banner of scientific motherhood.[21]

Thus, the Save the Babies campaign followed a model for saving the lives of Indian infants and children that combined individual instruction, group education, and community participation. The first strategy was familiar to both the field matrons and the Indian women. Home visits had long been considered one of the best ways to assist native women as they adopted Euro-American domestic practices. Field matrons routinely "dropped in" to native homes to monitor progress and offer help with any activity falling within the category of homemaking. With the Save the Babies campaign, these visits took on a new importance.

Field matrons used home instruction to handle both immediate medical issues as well as to offer more generalized advice on child care and family life. A common topic of discussion during these calls was "summer complaint," or weanling diarrhea. The most common nonepidemic cause of native infant and child morbidity and mortality, weanling diarrhea struck when mothers switched their children from breast milk to solid foods or prepared formulas.[22] Typically spread by contaminated water and food supplies as well as unsanitary waste disposal facilities, weanling diarrhea struck tribal communities hardest during the summer. Field matrons taught Indian women about the importance of hygienic food preparation and storage and helped them in building "sanitary privies" for family use. This work usually led to discussions of personal cleanliness and the adoption of "citizen's" dress in place of traditional clothing for adults and children.

Field matrons adopted a variety of strategies to make their home visits more successful and pleasant learning experiences for native women. To temper her rather stern lectures on diet and hygiene, Mabel E. Brown of the Sandia and Santa Ana Pueblos in New Mexico took along baby clothing and layette items to reward tribal women for their efforts in this area.[23] Mary V. Doyle distributed canned milk, malt, Castile soap, and baby blankets to the Tohono O'odham (Papago) women who followed the tenets of scientific motherhood.[24] Field matrons stationed in Anadarko, Oklahoma, notified the Indian Service superintendent there whenever a Kiowa mother made progress as a parent. He, in turn, wrote letters praising the women for their efforts. Leslie Ticeahkie received such a commendation for "the splendid way that you took care of your six year old daughter during her recent spell of typhoid fever." Mrs. Ticeahkie's behavior was encouraging, according to the superintendent, because "so many of our Indians are directly responsible for the deaths of their children."[25]

Group education and community participation, the other approaches utilized in the Save the Babies campaign, were direct products of the national "Better Baby" campaign. This was a contemporary movement supported by Julia Lathrop and the Children's Bureau, groups like the American Association for the Study and Prevention of Infant Mortality, and the influential periodical *Woman's Home Companion*. Here, federal Indian policy paralleled developments in Euro-American society as the health and welfare of rural and urban children became topics of concern for progressive politicians and public health activists.[26]

To accommodate the varied levels of assimilation within tribal communities, the Save the Babies campaign utilized a number of different educational strategies. Literate native women found themselves bombarded with the message of scientific motherhood. BIA personnel used boarding-school newsletters and newspapers to disseminate health care education. Copies of *The Carlisle Arrow* found their way onto reservations across the West, carried back by returning students who also brought with them firsthand training in scientific motherhood. In an article entitled "Save Your Baby," Carlisle students explained the importance of the public health venture in terms of tribal and national life. "Mothers!," read the conclusion, "do you realize that the health, strength, and goodness of your boys and girls are almost entirely in your hands? If your babies are brought up properly and from babyhood are taught the principles of health, truth, and honor, it will make us a Nation of healthy, clean men and women, with clean homes and honest hearts." Within the boundaries of the Save the Babies campaign, the relationship between "summer complaint," acculturation, and nationalism was explicit.[27]

Newspapers published at local boarding schools and agencies also added their voices to campaign for better Indian health. *The Indian School Journal*, a publication of the students at the Chilocco Indian School in Oklahoma, regularly addressed native health care issues. In a guest column, field matron supervisor Elsie E. Newton stressed the importance of assimilation and education for mothers. She reminded her readers that "unless Indian mothers learn more of the fundamentals of family and healthy living, we have not much hope. . . . [T]he children die, chiefly because of the ignorance of the simplest laws of health. The home must become the agent of prevention."[28] *The Nez Perce Indian* carried a similar message to those living in and around Lapwai, Idaho. In the article "Care of Your Baby during Hot Weather," Nez Percé women read (yet again) how their decisions determined the future of their children. The failure to observe "basic" (Euro-American) rules of child care could result in catastrophe, something that only a "scientific" mother could avoid.[29]

Pamphlets like *Indian Mothers: Save Your Babies*, published in 1914 and distributed nationally by the BIA, contained additional practical advice on dietary requirements, standards for personal and home sanitation, and discussions of health problems common to reservation communities. Photographs supplemented the text and reinforced its message. Pictures of smiling, well-dressed (in "citizen's" clothes) Indian women and their robust children in baby carriages contrasted sharply with the portrait of an unkempt Navajo child strapped to a cradleboard and left in the glaring sun. Such images, reminiscent of the BIA's "before and after" boarding-school portraits, required no editorial comment.

The Save the Babies campaign's relentless emphasis on Indian maternal responsibility for the welfare of infants and children became most explicit in the 1916 pamphlet *Indian Babies: How to Keep Them Well*. In the foreword to the publication, native mothers once again found themselves the culprits in the official explanation for the high morbidity and mortality rates among infants and children. According to Commissioner of Indian Affairs Cato Sells, "it is a pity . . . that so many Indian babies' lives have been lost because *their mothers did not know* how to keep them well. Almost every sickness your baby has could have been prevented." Lest any woman miss Sells's point about her duty to her children, the commissioner closed his remarks with the flat assertion that "it is because so many Indian mothers follow the wrong ideas in caring for their children that so many of them die."[30]

While publications like *Indian Mothers: Save Your Babies* and *Indian Babies: How to Keep Them Well* spoke to those native women literate in English, most Indian women heard the message of the Save the Babies campaign at a baby show. These social and educational events were first popularized by the *Woman's Home Companion*. In an atmosphere that detractors likened unfavorably to a livestock show, infants and children were judged according to a "scientific" standard that promoted race betterment.

Baby shows mustered community recognition and support for new child-rearing techniques by constructively focusing on family and tribal relationships and rivalries. Competition for material rewards like cash prizes, clothing patterns, and baby layettes linked Euro-American consumerism to scientific motherhood and offered tangible incentives to adopt new maternal models. The coveted designation of "Best Baby" went to the child judged "prettiest, cleanest, neatest, fattest, and best behaved." And, of course, the "Best Baby" was usually the child of an assimilated, "scientific" mother.

After 1913, baby shows became the BIA's preferred means of spreading the gospel of scientific motherhood. In reservation communities throughout the trans-Mississippi West, American Indian women gathered together to learn about health care and compete via their children. By 1916, the baby shows were the focal points of the campaign in most American Indian communities. Native women participated in contests designed to "center the attention of the Indian mothers upon the necessity for better care for their babies."[31] At the Kiowa Agency in Oklahoma, technology enhanced the learning environment for mothers and their children. In a specially erected tent, a lantern slide presentation with pictures of infants and children properly clothed in "citizen's" dress, mothers breast-feeding their babies, and youngsters sleeping peacefully in carefully screened bedrooms and prams entertained families. Members of the agency staff then lectured Kiowa mothers on "civilized" family life and health care.

The 1916 Kiowa Baby Fair was typical that year in Indian country. Judges evaluated fifty children according to the guidelines established by the Better Babies Bureau of the *Woman's Home Companion*.[32] Examiners and scorekeepers, all Euro-Americans, carefully evaluated the contestants using scorecards devised and distributed by the American Medical Association. After rating participants for everything from "flabby muscles" to "bad temper," they determined that eighteen-month-old Iris Ahl-sit-sinny was the "best" Kiowa baby.[33] The reward for this accomplishment? A bronze medal inscribed with the winner's name.[34]

The records of the 1916 Kiowa Baby Fair do not indicate how Iris Ahl-sit-sinny's mother regarded her daughter's victory. One can only assume that she was pleased by the public approbation that accompanied her own success at raising the "best" baby. Because few records from the tribal side survive to indicate how American Indian women regarded the campaign to save the lives of their children, a careful reading of the BIA documents generated during this program is all we have to gauge their responses. Sometimes the surviving records indicate that community support for the Save the Babies campaign ran high. In Kansas, a substantial number of Potawatomi women visited the 1916 Baby Fair headquarters where they saw two movies about child care, browsed through exhibits, and had their children evaluated by the local BIA physicians.[35] In Oklahoma in 1917, Cherokee women proudly brought more than one hundred "best" babies to the Tahlequah Baby Fair.[36] Over seventy-five Tohono O'odham (Papago) women at the San Xavier Reservation outside of Tucson attended Mary V. Doyle's week-long seminar in better health care that same year.[37]

Elsewhere, however, American Indian women expressed their feelings for the Save the Babies campaign and its unrelenting emphasis on their supposed failings by refusing to participate in house calls, public education, or the baby shows. At Fort Apache, Arizona, the problem was so extreme that the commissioner of Indian affairs himself lamented in 1916 that the agency field personnel could not "use coercive measures for the purposes of compelling the Indian women to adopt sanitary methods for caring for their children by detaining them under the personal supervision of a physician."[38]

The following year, the superintendent of the Southern Ute Agency in Colorado also acknowledged that the women of his community paid scant attention to the baby fair conducted on their behalf. Despite the best efforts of the agency field matron and other field service personnel, few Ute women attended and those who did were reluctant to have their children evaluated. The grand prize for the "best-kept baby" was ultimately divided among three children.[39]

Given the paucity of sources on the native reaction to the Save the Babies campaign, any attempt to determine why some women chose to become involved and others did not becomes an exercise in deduction and inference. Certainly, the ethnocentrism inherent within the program would have been enough to dissuade many tribal women from participation. Occasionally, field matrons understood this and deliberately muted the assimilationist emphasis of the campaign. Working with Kiowa women, Magdalena Becker let them select the level of Americanization they wished to adopt as mothers. She explained away her unusual sensitivity to the wishes of the tribal women by simply noting that "the women do not care to change to our way of dressing . . . so I do not insist on . . . [their adopting "citizen's"] dress] except for the younger children."[40] Becker was, however, the exception. All too often, American Indian women experienced the full force of the Save the Babies campaign's pressure to Americanize.

Another explanation for the lack of participation was the program's intentional use of contests and public evaluation to spread the gospel of scientific motherhood. When Mae Justus praised the Cocopah and Quechan women for their sharp rivalry at the 1916 Baby Fair, she expressed the typical Euro-American belief that competition is beneficial. However, for native people who believed that the health and well-being of tribal children reflected on the entire community, the notion that some children might be judged superior to others (who might be members of the same clan or religious society) on the basis of muscle tone or temperament must have seemed wholly inappropriate.

Perhaps the most likely reason for native women to resist involvement in the Save the Babies campaign pertains to what the program did *not* do. Because it did not accept the full range of Indian lifestyles, the campaign could not reach traditional women, those dismissed by Euro-Americans as "ignorant, coarse, [and] uncouth." Because it did not involve fathers or other extended family members, the program could not succeed in families where child rearing was still treasured as a communal responsibility. Because it did nothing to remedy the poverty and cultural instability that permeated the lives of most native families, the Save the Babies campaign was little more than an assimilationist Band-Aid. The program only "stuck" among those American Indian women who had already adopted Americanized lifestyles. Apparently, though, that was enough for federal policymakers who sought a quick resolution to this complicated problem.

In 1917, just five years after the campaign began, Commissioner Cato Sells reported that "the Indian is no longer a vanishing race."[41] Statistics gathered that year indicated that the mortality rate for Indian children under the age of three had declined by more than 50 percent from 1914 figures.[42] This was happy news for those BIA policymakers and reformers who had hoped that the Save the Babies campaign would bring about the "salvation of a race."[43]

Field matrons and American Indian women probably regarded this news with less credence and enthusiasm than did Commissioner Sells and the other BIA officials. Reports filed by the field matrons and other Indian Service personnel between 1912 and 1917 do suggest that progress was made toward improving the health of Indian infants and children. But few of these women would have agreed with Sells's assertion that five years of intervention had stabilized the American Indian population base. The field matrons knew only too well that "saving the babies" would require an ongoing commitment to Indian health care. And tribal women, who recognized how little their communities had changed in five years, understood that the battle for their children's health and survival would continue with or without newspaper coverage and bronze medals.

As it turned out, the official victory against infant and child morbidity and mortality was declared not a moment too soon. As the United States became increasingly involved in World War I, federal expenditures for military preparedness drew funds away from nonessential domestic programs. Wartime economy measures greatly reduced funding for the BIA's health program. The mobilization of more than half of the medical staff further eroded the federal government's ability to deal with Indian medical needs. This unrelieved state of neglect continued until the publication of *The Meriam Report* in 1928. Only then, when reformers pilloried the BIA, did the horrendous health problems facing American Indians receive anything more than cursory attention from federal policymakers.

Just how many Indian infants and children sickened and died after the BIA's self-declared "victory" over infant and child morbidity and mortality in 1917 has never been calculated. But one account, written after the end of the Save the Babies campaign, does provide some sense of the cumulative impact of the program. In 1923, field matron Alice May Ward recounted for readers of *Sunset* magazine a chilling and all-too-familiar scene. Called to the home of a seriously ill Cheyenne child, Ward pointedly asked the mother, "How many children have you had?" The reply was "nine." Ward then queried, "How many are living?" The mother indicated that the fading baby was the sole survivor. "You have had nine and soon you will have none," the field matron responded, asking the Indian woman to "trust your sick child to my care." Several days later, with the offer of assistance still open, Ward learned of the youngster's death.[44]

This "red tragedy," as the author entitled her story, reveals much about the effectiveness of the Save the Babies campaign. Clearly, Ward's account belied whatever claims the BIA may have made about the efficacy of the program. Six years after the campaign had ended in victory, a Cheyenne family had experienced the ultimate tragedy not once but nine times. Six years after Cato Sells declared that the race had been rescued, babies and children were still the most vulnerable members of native communities.

However much the Save the Babies campaign tried to make Euro-American and American Indian women partners in the venture to save lives, it did not lead to the replacement of traditional models of family life and motherhood. The Save the Babies campaign did live up to its name in those families and communities where tribal women were willing to adopt and follow the tenets of scientific motherhood. But it did not address any of the structural problems facing Indian parents as they tried to keep their families intact. Nor did the campaign offer any permanent solutions to the complex problems facing American Indian women as they struggled to save their babies on their own cultural terms.

Notes

I wish to acknowledge the financial assistance of the Graduate School of California State University, Chico, in completing the research for this essay. I am also indebted to Jacqueline Baker Barnhart and Dale Steiner for criticisms of an early draft.

1. American Medical Association, "Standard Scorecard for Babies," 1914, attached to Circular No. 1350, "Baby Shows," box 13, Records of the Hopi Reservation, Record Group 75, Records of the Bureau of Indian Affairs, National Archives—Pacific Southwest Region (hereafter cited as RG 75, BIA, NA—location).

2. Clipping from the Yuma *Morning Sun*, enclosed in Lonson L. Odle to Commissioner of Indian Affairs, 16 November 1916, Central Classified File 120474-1916-700, Records of the Fort Yuma Agency, RG 75, BIA, NA—Pacific Southwest Region.

3. Lonson L. Odle, Premium List, First Annual Yuma Indian Fair, 1915, box 9, Subject Files of Henry J. McQuigg, Record of the Sells Superintendency, RG 75, BIA, NA—Pacific Southwest Region.

4. Mae A. Justus to Superintendent Lonson L. Odle, 17 November 1916, Central Classified File 120474-1916-700, Records of the Fort Yuma Agency, RG 75, BIA, NA—Pacific Southwest Region.

5. For information on the de-Indianization campaign waged by the BIA in the nineteenth and twentieth centuries, see John F. Berens, "Old Campaigners, New Realities: Indian Political Reform in the Progressive Era, 1900-1912," *Mid-America* 59, no. 1 (January 1977): 51-64; Frederick Hoxie, *A Final Promise: The Campaign to Assimilate the Indians, 1880-1920* (Cambridge, Eng.: Cambridge University Press, 1989); Robert W. Mardock, *The Reformers and the American Indian* (Columbia: University of Missouri Press, 1981); Francis Paul Prucha, *American Indian Policy in Crisis: Christian Reformers and the American Indian, 1865-1900* (Lincoln: University of Nebraska Press, 1976), and Francis Paul Prucha, *The Great Father*, 2 vols. (Lincoln: University of Nebraska Press, 1984); Robert F. Trennert, *Alternative to Extinction: Federal Indian Policy and the Beginnings of the Reservation System, 1848-1851* (Philadelphia: Temple University Press, 1975); and Wilcomb Washburn, *The Assault on Tribalism: The General Allotment Law (Dawes Act) of 1887* (Philadelphia: Lippincott, 1975).

6. C. Matthew Snipp, *American Indians: The First of This Land* (New York: Russell Sage Foundation, 1991), 13, 63-65. The BIA did not systematically compile morbidity and mortality statistics until well into the twentieth century. While agents, superintendents, physicians, and field matrons were instructed to monitor morbidity and mortality rates for all American Indians, most readily conceded that illnesses, births, and deaths went underreported.

7. Weekly Report of Jane Gray, 13 April 1911, Field Matron Files, Records of the Cheyenne and Arapaho Agency, Oklahoma Historical Society, Oklahoma City (hereafter cited as OHS).

8. "Our Task," Education Circular No. 663, 29 April 1912, box 8, Subject Correspondence Files, 1903-1939, Records of the Crow Creek Agency, RG 75, BIA, NA—Rocky Mountain Region.

9. The scholarship on the role of women in the nineteenth-century family is voluminous. The following sources are among the most important as they pertain to this essay: Anna Davin, "Imperialism and Motherhood," *History Workshop* 5 (Spring 1978): 9-67; Nancy Schrom Dye and Daniel Blake Smith, "Mother Love and Infant Death, 1750-1920," *Journal of American History* 73, no. 2 (September 1986): 329-53; Mary Madeline Ladd-Taylor, "Mother-Work: Ideology, Public Policy, and the Mothers' Movement, 1890-1930" (Ph.D. dissertation, Yale University, 1986); Elizabeth M. R. Lomax, Jerome Kagan, and Barbara G. Rosenkrantz, *Science and Patterns of Child Care* (San Francisco: Free Press, 1978); and Steven Mintz and Susan Kellogg, *Domestic Revolutions* (New York: Free Press, 1988).

10. Commissioner of Indian Affairs Cato Sells reminded field employees of this in 1914. See "Supervision of Field Matron's Work," Education-Health Circular No. 865, 20 May 1914, National Archives Microfilm Publication M1121, reel 10.

11. Francis E. Leupp, *The Indian and His Problem* (New York: Scribner's, 1910), 134-35.

12. "Our Task."

13. See David Smits, "The 'Squaw Drudge': A Prime Index of Savagism," *Ethnohistory* 29, no. 2 (Fall 1982): 281-306, for an excellent discussion of this subject. See also Joan Jacobs Brumberg, "Zenanas and Girlless Villages: The Ethnology of American Evangelical Women, 1870-1900," *Journal of American History* 69, no. 2 (September 1982): 347-71.

14. There has been considerable debate about the social, political, and economic roles of American Indian women. The following sources, as well as those cited in note 15, offer a discussion of this subject: Paula Gunn Allen, *The Sacred Hoop: Recovering the Feminine in American Indian Tradition* (Boston: Beacon Press, 1986); Nancy Bonvillian, "Gender Relations in Native North America," *American Indian Culture and Research Journal* 13, no. 2 (1989): 1-28; Rayna Green, "Native American Women," *Signs* 6, no. 1 (Winter 1980): 248-67; Clara Sue Kidwell, "The Power of Women in Three American Indian Societies," *Journal of Ethnic Studies* 6, no. 3 (Spring 1979): 113-21; and Valerie Sherer Mathes, "A New Look at the Role of Women in American Indian Societies," *American Indian Quarterly* 2, no. 2 (Spring 1975): 131-39.

15. Sources on American Indian women and the impact of colonization include Patricia Albers, "Sioux Women in Transition: A Study of Their Changing Status in a Domestic and Capitalist Sector of Production," in *The Hidden Half: Studies of Plains Indian Women*, ed. Patricia Albers and Beatrice Medicine (Washington, D.C.: University Press of America, 1983), 175-236; Karen Anderson, "Commodity Exchange and Subordination: Montagnais-Naskapi and Huron Women, 1600-1650," *Signs* 11, no. 1 (Winter 1985): 48-62; Kathryn E. Holland Braund, "Guardians of Traditions and Handmaidens to Change: Women's Role in Creek Economic and Social Life during the Eighteenth Century," *American Indian Quarterly* 14, no. 3 (Winter 1990): 239-58; Priscilla K. Buffalohead, "Farmers, Warriors, Traders: A Fresh Look at Ojibway Women," *Minnesota History* 48 (Summer 1983): 230-45; Jo-Anne Fiske, "Colonization and the Decline of Women's Status: The Tsimshian Case," *Feminist Studies* 17, no. 3 (Fall 1991): 509-535; Robert S. Grumet, "Sunksquaws, Shamans, and Tradeswomen: Middle-Atlantic Coastal Algonkian Women during the 17th and 18th Centuries," in *Women and Colonization: Anthropological Perspectives*, ed. Mona Etienne and Eleanor Burke Leacock (New York: Praeger, 1980), 43-62; Diane Rothenberg, "The Mothers of the Nation: Seneca Resistance to Quaker Intervention," in *Women and Colonization*, 63-87; Michelle Rosaldo, "Women, Culture, and Society: Theoretical Overview," in *Women, Culture, and Society*, ed. Michelle Rosaldo and Louise Lamphere (Palo Alto, Calif.: Stanford University Press, 1974), 17-42; and Sylvia Van Kirk, *Many Tender Ties: Women in Fur-Trade Society, 1670-1870* (Norman: University of Oklahoma Press, 1980).

16. See Kay Bennett, *Kaibah: Recollections of a Navajo Girlhood* (Los Angeles: Western Lore Press, 1964); Helen Sekaquaptewa as told to Louise Udall, *Me and Mine* (Tucson: University of Arizona Press, 1985); Anna Moore Shaw, *A Pima Past* (Tucson: University of Arizona Press,

1974); Lucy Thompson, *To the American Indian: Reminiscences of a Yurok Woman* (Berkeley, Calif.: Heyday Press, 1992); Beverly Hungry Wolf, *The Ways of My Grandmothers* (New York: Quill, 1982); and Ella Deloria, *Waterlily* (Lincoln: University of Nebraska Press, 1990). See also Marla N. Powers, *Oglala Women: Myth, Ritual, and Reality* (Chicago: University of Chicago Press, 1986); Irene Stewart, *A Voice in Her Tribe: A Navajo Woman's Own Story* (Socorro, N.M.: Ballena Press, 1980); Nancy Oestriech Lurie, *Mountain Wolf Woman* (Ann Arbor: University of Michigan Press, 1974); and Carolyn Niethammer, *Daughters of the Earth* (New York: Collier Books, 1977).

17. Leupp, *The Indian and His Problem*, 145.

18. Save the Babies campaign flier, 29 January 1916, box 8, Administrative Correspondence Files, 1908–1922, Records of the Red Cliff Reservation, RG 75, BIA, NA.

19. For a full account of the field matron program, see Lisa E. Emmerich, " 'To Respect and Love and Seek the Ways of White Women': Field Matrons, the Office of Indian Affairs, and Civilization Policy, 1890–1938" (Ph.D. dissertation, University of Maryland, 1987).

20. See Paul Starr, *The Social Transformation of American Medicine* (New York: Basic Books, 1982), for a detailed account of this revolution in American health care.

21. See part 3 of Rima Apple's *Mothers and Medicine: A Social History of Infant Feeding, 1890–1950* (Madison: University of Wisconsin Press, 1987), for a superb general discussion of scientific motherhood.

22. Untitled circular draft, n.d., file 138107-1913-720, Elsie E. Newton, Special Agent Files, RG 75, BIA, NA.

23. Annual Reports, 9 August 1913, folder 052.2-1912-1917, box 14, Decimal Files, 1912–1938, Records of the Northern Pueblos Agency, RG 75, BIA, NA—Rocky Mountain Region.

24. List of Supplies, n.d., Mary V. Doyle, Field Matron Reports, 1916–1919, box 189, Records of the Sells Superintendency, RG 75, BIA, NA—Pacific Southwest Region.

25. C. V. Stinchecum to Mrs. Leslie Ticeahkie, 20 October 1916, Field Matron Files, Records of the Kiowa Agency, OHS.

26. Alisa Klaus of the University of California, Santa Cruz, explored this subject in her paper "Perfecting American Babyhood: Race Betterment and the Baby Health Contest," delivered at the 1990 annual meeting of the Organization of American Historians. I am indebted to her for sharing her research with me. See also Dye and Smith, "Mother Love," and Harvey Levenstein, " 'Best for Babies' or 'Preventable Infanticide?' The Controversy over Artificial Feeding of Infants in America, 1880–1920," *Journal of American History* 70, no. 1 (June 1983): 75–94.

27. "Save Your Baby," *The Carlisle Arrow*, 31 March 1916, Letterpress box 3, entry 106, box 14, Records of the Various Pueblos Agency, RG 75, BIA, NA—Rocky Mountain Region.

28. Elsie E. Newton, "What an Indian Girl Should Know," *The Indian School Journal*, March 1914, box 6, School Publications, Records of the Chilocco Indian School, RG 75, BIA, NA—Southwest Region.

29. *The Nez Perce Indian*, 1 September 1915, file 23918-1915-700, Central Classified Files, 1907–1939, RG 75, BIA, NA.

30. *Indian Babies: How to Keep Them Well*, Doctor's Files, Records of the Sac and Fox Agency, OHS. Emphasis in the original.

31. C. V. Stinchecum to "Farmers, Field Matrons, and Physicians," 21 February 1916, Field Matron Files, Records of the Kiowa Agency, OHS.

32. "How to Hold a Baby Health Conference," 1917, "Circulars from the Bureau of Indian Affairs, 1914–1918," box 8, Records of the Hopi Reservation, RG 75, BIA, NA—Pacific Southwest Region.

33. "Standard Scorecard for Babies," Sac and Fox Doctor's Files, Records of the Sac and Fox Agency, OHS.

34. C. V. Stinchecum to "Gentlemen," 5 April 1916, Doctor's Files, Records of the Kiowa Agency, OHS, and Annual Narrative Report of the Kiowa Agency, National Archives Microfilm Publication M1011, reel 14.

35. C. J. Bliss, M.D., to Supt. A. R. Snyder, 30 October 1916, enclosing "Additional Fair Notes," Mayetta Herald, n.d., File 81282-700-1916, Central Classified Files, 1907–1939, RG 75, BIA, NA.

36. "Indian Health Drive Meeting Fine Response," 15 October 1917, Tahlequah *Times-Democrat*, in "Clippings, Health Drive 1917," Records Relating to Health Correspondence Relating to Field Matrons, 1912–1917, Records of the Five Civilized Tribes, RG 75, BIA, NA—Southwest Region.

37. Report of Mary V. Doyle, 16 August 1917, File 98308-1916-700, Records of the San Xavier Agency, Central Classified Files, 1907–1938, RG 75, BIA, NA.

38. Cato Sells to Mr. M. W. Peterson, 27 April 1916, file 1038, Alphabetical Correspondence Files, 1914–1917, box 27, Records of the Fort Apache Agency, RG 75, BIA, NA—Pacific Southwest Region.

39. Superintendent to Honorable Commissioner of Indian Affairs, 9 May 1917, box 44013, Records of the Consolidated Ute Agency, RG 75, BIA, NA—Rocky Mountain Region.

40. Yearly Report of Magdalena Becker, 13 August 1913, Field Matron Files, Records of the Kiowa Agency, OHS.

41. *Annual Report of the Commissioner of Indian Affairs to the Secretary of the Interior for the Year 1917* (Washington, D.C.: U.S. Government Printing Office, 1918), 17.

42. For a more detailed analysis of American Indian morbidity and mortality rates during this period, see Diane T. Putney, "Fighting the Scourge: American Indian Morbidity and Federal Policy, 1897–1928," (Ph.D. dissertation, Marquette University, 1980), 176–79. Putney suggests that the BIA altered its statistical evidence of infant and child morbidity and mortality to produce this "victory" in 1917.

43. Education-Statistics Folder, "Deaths under Three Years of Age," 17, Records Concerning Reports and Statistical Information, 1911–1921, Records of the Statistical Division, RG 75, BIA, NA.

44. Alice May Ward, "Red Tragedies: The Experiences of a Field Matron on the Cheyenne Reservation in Montana," *Sunset* 50 (April 1923): 23.

20.

Introduction to *Quiet Odyssey:*
A Pioneer Korean Woman in America

SUCHENG CHAN

In 1990, in collaboration with Sucheng Chan, Mary Paik Lee published her autobiography, Quiet Odyssey: A Pioneer Korean Woman in America. *Eighty years earlier Lee, then five years old, had left Korea with her parents. She was one of fewer than two thousand Korean females to enter U.S. territory between 1902 and 1924, the year that a new immigration law slammed the door on all Asian immigrants.* Quiet Odyssey *is one of only a handful of Asian immigrant women's autobiographies to be published in English.*

This article is a shortened version of Sucheng Chan's introduction to Quiet Odyssey. *Chan attentively places Mary Paik Lee's rich life history in the international contexts that sparked Korean immigration. In so doing, Chan reminds us that all immigrants brought pressing cultural and political issues with them to the United States. Korean immigrants were originally recruited to Hawaii as strikebreakers to undermine organized Japanese sugarcane workers. Many Koreans had resisted Japanese colonial rule before they left, and, once in the United States, they remained deeply engaged in their nation's anticolonial struggle against Japan. Thus the common American practice of lumping all Asians together was doubly insulting to them. Part of the "insult" occurred when legislation to restrict Chinese and Japanese immigration included Koreans as well.*

Family responsibilities and political commitments exerted heavy demands on Korean women, who cared for their families and for Korean bachelors as well and whose wage work supported families and Korean nationalist organizations. Women also worked as volunteers to support Korean churches and secular women's organizations.

Chan reminds us that for many immigrants the political concerns of their homelands still mattered. For the first generation of Korean immigrants, their Christian churches and political organizations expressed deep desires for liberation and salvation. Chan also reminds us that ethnic identities changed from one generation to the next. Korean American children were less connected than their parents to Korean nationalist movements. Still, Chan says, they did not, like Chinese American and Japanese American youngsters, try hard to appear more "American." Perhaps, as she suggests, this was because Korean parents' nationalist politics demonstrated just how embattled and endangered their Korean identity really was.

Mary Paik Lee was born in Korea in 1905 and was baptized by an American Presbyterian missionary. When she was five years old, she emigrated with her family to Hawaii; a year and a half later, they moved to California. Her national origins, her religion, her minority status in the United States, and her gender have together defined her identity. A brief review of Korea's long tradition of fending off invaders, how it became a pawn in the struggle among imperialist powers, how Christianity served as a counterweight to Japanese colonialism, and how the lives of Korean women were changed by Christianity and the anti-Japanese struggle will elucidate why religion and politics—along with efforts to earn a living—absorbed so many Korean immigrants in the United States. This was as true of female immigrants as it was of male, because Korean women who settled in America made crucial contributions not only to the survival of their families but also to the nationalist struggle. Such responsibilities elevated their position in the immigrant community and transformed their consciousness. By discussing the major social and political forces that affected the lives of Korean immigrants in the early decades of this century, I hope to place Mary Paik Lee's life history in its global context.

Koreans, almost without exception, are extremely proud of their long history, which they claim dates back four millennia to a mythical ruler. The country's peninsular setting has shaped this history. Contiguous to the northeastern corner of China and surrounded by Russia, China, and Japan, Korea has served historically as a conduit for people, artifacts, and ideas, but it maintained ongoing intercourse with only one nation, China, until the nineteenth century. Its strategic location, however, has repeatedly subjected Korea to invasion by its neighbors. Toyotomi Hideyoshi, a Japanese feudal lord, invaded the country in 1592 with 150,000 men—an action that caused China to send troops to the peninsula to maintain its suzerainity there. After two years of fighting, both sides withdrew, but when a peace settlement was not reached by 1597, Japanese and Chinese troops fought again on Korean soil, devastating much of the south. A quarter century later, invading Manchu armies ravaged northwestern Korea. In response to these fearsome events, Korea sealed itself off from the outside world for the next two and a half centuries, which led Westerners to dub it the Hermit Kingdom.

Then, in 1876, the Japanese coerced Korea into signing the Treaty of Kanghwa, Korea's first modern treaty with a foreign nation. Japan established a permanent diplomatic mission in Korea in 1880, and thereafter its sway over the peninsula increased.

In 1882 the United States became the second nation to secure a treaty with Korea. Next came treaties with Great Britain and Germany (1883), Russia and Italy (1884), and France (1886). Each gave the signatory power the right to trade and to import goods into Korea at low tariff rates, to operate under conditions of extraterritoriality, and to enjoy most-favored-nation status. Upon the heels of the treaties came merchants, missionaries, and diplomats, all of whom not only vied with one another for power and influence but also quickly became involved in domestic Korean politics.

The entry of foreigners and the concessions they wrested led to intense factional struggles within Korea's ruling class. King Kojong, who had ascended the throne in 1864 at the tender age of twelve and who ruled until he was forced to abdicate in 1907, had to contend not only with palace factions but also with members of the Independence Club—reform-minded politicians who favored the Japanese path to modernity. The group attempted a coup on the evening of 4 December 1884. The conspirators placed King Kojong and his wife, the pro-Chinese Queen Min, under Japanese "protective custody" and proclaimed a new government, but it fell within three days, when the Chinese resident-general in Korea stormed the royal palace with fifteen hundred Chinese troops and restored Kojong and his ministers to power. During the next few years, the Chinese and Queen Min's faction were paramount in palace politics.

The outbreak of the Tonghak Rebellion gave China and Japan a pretext to renew their contest for the control of Korea. *Tonghak* (Eastern learning) was a syncretist religion that had first appeared in Korea in the 1860s. Even though the government had captured and executed its founder in 1864, the sect expanded greatly in the late 1880s, when poverty became widespread and disgruntled farmers joined its ranks. When the first uprising occurred in 1892, the government tried to suppress it, but that only caused the revolt to spread like wildfire. Unable to put down the rebellion with his own troops, King Kojong appealed to the Chinese for help in 1894. China eagerly sent troops to the peninsula. Japan reacted by sending an even larger contingent, though Korea had not requested its aid.

Open hostilities broke out between Chinese and Japanese troops stationed on Korean soil, marking the beginning of the Sino-Japanese War. The Japanese swiftly routed the Chinese, and while the war was still in progress, they forced Korea to sign agreements that opened all southern Korean ports to them and gave them many other rights. Dismayed by the unexpected turn of events, Tonghak leaders led hundreds of thousands of farmers in yet another uprising, this time against the Japanese, but the latter soon overpowered them. Japanese soldiers massacred Tonghak rebels everywhere. They also defeated the remaining Chinese forces, driving them completely out of Korea.

The war ended in April 1895 with the Treaty of Shimonoseki, which awarded to Japan some Chinese territory. Russia, France, and Germany, however, jointly protested the terms of the settlement and forced Japan to relinquish most of its gains. The three European nations then proceeded to acquire for themselves what they had denied to Japan. Cheated out of the fruits of its victory, Japan smoldered with resentment.

Meanwhile, Japan tightened its control over hapless Korea by promulgating new laws, changing the administrative and judicial systems, abolishing the old Korean class structure, building railroads and telegraph lines, and introducing capitalist features into the Korean economy. Foreigners scrambled to gain numerous concessions to exploit Korea's natural resources; to build roads, railroads, telegraph lines, power plants, and oil storage facilities; and to establish banks and process loans. When some of the investments did not prove particularly lucrative to their American and European investors, the Japanese bought them up as part of their efforts to exercise greater political and economic control over Korea. Viewing Queen Min as the chief obstacle to their plans, the Japanese instigated a clash between some soldiers and the palace guards to create a cover under which they forced their way into the royal chambers on the night of 8 October 1895. They wounded the queen, poured kerosene on her, and set her afire. King Kojong escaped, disguised as a female servant. The heavy-handed actions of the Japanese led to armed uprisings all over the country and led the king to accept Russian protection.

Kojong now issued decrees that disbanded the pro-Japanese government and installed a pro-Russian one in its place. Following Russian advice, he also changed his own title from "king" to "emperor" in 1897, in order to assert his equality with the rulers of China and Japan, who, as the Russians pointed out, were emperors and not kings.

Events in China soon brought Russian-Japanese rivalry to a head in Northeast Asia. In 1900, during the Boxer Rebellion, the Russians occupied Manchuria, from whence they refused to withdraw after the troubles in China proper were over. By 1903, they had moved into northern Korea, buying up land, cutting timber, and building roads. Japan demanded that the Russians withdraw from Manchuria. When the latter did not comply, Japanese warships struck the Russian fleet at Port Arthur without warning in February 1904.

This was the beginning of the Russo-Japanese War. Though Korea immediately declared its neutrality, Japanese troops landed at Inchon and marched to Seoul. They forced Emperor Kojong to let them traverse Korean territory unhindered. As Japan won one victory after another, it expropriated all the concessions Russia had gained in Korea. The war ended in July 1905 with the Treaty of Portsmouth. Japan took over all the Russian interests in Manchuria; Russia also ceded the southern half of Sakhalin Island to the victor. To ensure that the other powers would not interfere this time, Japanese Prime Minister Katsura Taro reached an understanding with U.S. Secretary of War William Howard Taft whereby the United States agreed to honor Japan's hegemony in the Korean peninsula in return for Japan's noninterference in American interests in the Philippines—a Spanish colony that the United States had acquired at the close of the Spanish-American War a few years earlier.

To signal to the world its newly won preeminence in Korea, Japan declared a protectorate over the country. Though Korea remained technically independent and Kojong continued to sit on his throne, the Japanese resident-general in Korea became the country's de facto ruler. Additional changes were made in the legal and monetary systems to facilitate Japanese land purchases and Japanese import-export trade. For the first time, Japanese began to settle in Korea in large numbers. Japan's farmers arrived as agricultural colonists; its businessmen bought up more firms, mines, and timberland; its fishermen laid claim to more and more fishing grounds; and its investors won concessions to build public works.

The new administration also disbanded the Korean army, restricted the number of weapons—including kitchen knives—that Koreans could possess, and limited the size of public gatherings. In 1907 the Japanese, with the aid of pro-Japanese members of the Korean cabinet, forced Emperor Kojong to abdicate and placed his son on the throne.

Thereafter the Japanese took over every aspect of internal administration. In 1910, they gave up all pretense and annexed Korea, which remained a Japanese colony until 1945. In the post-1910 period, countless Koreans lost their landholdings, lived in constant fear of the Japanese secret police, and seethed with repressed anger and resentment against their alien overlords. To undermine Korean culture and to suppress nationalism, Japan sent thousands of Japanese to replace Korean teachers and made the Japanese language the medium of instruction in Korean schools. The rules against public gatherings were further tightened so that assemblies of more than three persons became illegal. The Japanese also closed down newspapers and passed laws to control Buddhist temples and Christian churches, lest they become centers of resistance.

Such draconian measures notwithstanding, Koreans did resist, both inside and outside their colonized country. After forty centuries of sovereignty, they would not accept subjugation without protest. The most significant resistance was the March First (1919) Movement, also called the *Samil* (three-one, for the month and day it began) or the *Mansei* (ten thousand years, or "long live") Uprising. Koreans secretly planned massive, nonviolent demonstrations to call the world's attention to their colonial plight. The death of former Emperor Kojong in January 1919 gave them the occasion they needed. The date for his funeral was set for 3 March 1919. Planners of the national demonstration decided to proclaim Korea's independence on 1 March. Thirty-three individuals from all walks of life, sixteen (some accounts say fifteen) of them Christians, signed a document modeled after the U.S. Declaration of Independence. The organization then printed thousands of copies of this declaration and sewed thousands of (banned) Korean flags, which couriers distributed to towns and villages throughout the country. Christian leaders—such as the Reverend Hyun Soon, national superintendent of Methodist Sunday schools in Korea—under cover of their religious responsibilities, traveled far and wide to organize the event. Members of the *Chondogyo* (the name the Tonghaks had given their sect after their 1894 rebellion), who were deeply entrenched in the countryside, likewise played a crucial role in spreading the word and coordinating plans. The *Chondogyo* also bore the major financial burden for the undertaking. All the planning took place under such utter secrecy that the Japanese police, vigilant though they were, got no wind of it.

On that fateful day, masses of people streamed into Seoul for Kojong's funeral and gathered at Pagoda Park in front of one of the royal palaces. As a young man began to read the declaration of independence, the crowds thundered: *"Mansei! Mansei!"* (Long live Korea! Long live Korea!) The Japanese police, totally unprepared, gave no evidence of coordinated reaction. The second of March was a Sunday. The Christians insisted that the sabbath be observed, so no demonstrations took place. The next day, the third, was devoted to Kojong's funeral. But on 4 March large groups of people, including many schoolboys and schoolgirls, started marching through the streets again. This time, the police were ready. They fired into the crowds while mounted marines summoned to the scene charged into the throng, standing in their stirrups as they swung their sabers right and left, felling all those in their path. Such harsh reaction galvanized Koreans everywhere. By April, an estimated 1 million people—5 percent of the country's total population—were involved in the movement.

During March and April, demonstrators participated in more than eight hundred disturbances in over six hundred localities. The Japanese retaliated with brutality and seemed to single out Korean Christians for punishment. The police and the military searched neighborhoods, rounded up people, and killed many on sight. Even conservative Japanese sources have admitted that several thousand Koreans perished. Two hundred Japanese also died. Almost 20,000 persons, including some 500 women, were arrested. Some 10,000—186 women among them—were prosecuted. The captors inflicted incredible torture on their prisoners, while many who survived the torture were summarily executed. What outraged Koreans most of all was that women captives were often stripped and raped. In this manner, what began as a peaceful, nonviolent demonstration was crushed.

Though the movement failed, the fire of nationalism was not extinguished. It burned on, ever more fiercely. Korean expatriates formed a provisional government-in-exile in Shanghai at the end of April 1919 to carry on the struggle.

The fact that Christians played such a prominent role in the March First Movement was not a coincidence, because in Korea the spread of Christianity converged with the emergence of modern nationalism. Not only did missionary schools introduce the idea of democracy, but since one of Korea's *Asian* neighbors, Japan, rather than a European power, became its colonizer, Koreans did not equate Christianity with Western imperialism—a connection that hindered missionary efforts in other lands.

American missionaries were in every part of Korea to witness the events of 1919. This was because the Protestant proselytizers who had first entered Korea in 1884 had been enormously successful in their efforts—so much so that, for a century now, Korea has been called the best mission field in Asia and perhaps even in the world.

From the beginning, the Methodists and the Presbyterians competed with each other for influence. The Methodists set up the first schools, while the Presbyterians focused on providing medical services. It was the Presbyterians who brought the first women medical personnel to the country in the belief that a nurse or woman doctor might gain access to Queen Min, whose patronage would help them reach out to Korean women. In the end, both denominations received royal favor and made considerable headway in carrying out their mission. Quite apart from the useful services they provided, King Kojong had his own reasons for not hindering missionary efforts. To break free from Chinese control and to counter the growing Japanese influence, he had repeatedly requested American advisors, but the U.S. State Department never sent any. So Kojong began to rely on the American missionaries in Korea for informal advice, even on issues quite unrelated to their expertise.

Christian teachings appealed particularly to Korean women, who, to this day, remain the most stalwart church members, both within their country and abroad. Some scholars have argued that Korean women found Christianity emotionally appealing because it resonated with certain features of indigenous shamanistic beliefs and practices. But a social factor was also at work: Becoming Christians gave female converts a measure of freedom they had never known, and this, I think, helps to account for the fervor of female converts who, in turn, influenced their husbands and children.

During the Yi dynasty (1392–1910) Korean women led extremely secluded lives. By the late seventeenth century, the rulers had fully incorporated Confucian precepts into both their statecraft and the organization of society. Confucianism was most succinctly expressed in five sets of ideal social relationships, four of which were hierarchical: subjects, sons, younger brothers, and wives were to obey and serve their emperor, fathers, older brothers, and husbands, respectively, while the latter were to give the former benevolent protection. Only the fifth relationship—that between male peers—contained any hint of egalitarianism: Men of the same age and socioeconomic standing could be affectionate and comradely toward one another.

The family and society at large were structured according to patrilineal principles. Though females were included in genealogies, only the barest information about them was written down. From birth, girls were considered outsiders, reared only to be given away in marriage. Married women kept their own names, but they were cut off from contact with their natal families, having become members of their husbands' lineages. Women could not inherit property, while widows were forbidden to remarry. The unequal value accorded men and women was expressed in the saying, *Namjon; yobi* (Men are honored; women are abased).

The primary duties of married women were to serve their mothers-in-law and to bear sons for their husbands. Women who bore only daughters might as well have been childless—they had no social standing whatsoever. Men whose wives produced no male heirs took concubines; if the latter also failed to give birth to boys, the families resorted to adopting sons, because only men were allowed to perform the rituals of ancestor worship.

Even architectural design reflected the subordinate status of women. The ideal Korean house contained two el-shaped wings: The outer wing was reserved for men and the inner one for women. Poor peasants who lived in tiny thatched huts still kept an *anbang* (inner room) for their women. Men continued to sleep in the male quarters after they were married, visiting their wives only in the dark of night, and, in some cases, only with their parents' permission.

The filial daughter, the chaste woman, the obedient wife, and the devoted mother were the models of feminine virtue. Women were not allowed outdoors in the daytime: They could travel outside their gates, with heavy veils, only after the evening bell had tolled, signifying the beginning of a curfew for men. Slaves and outcasts who did housekeeping work, such as washing clothes by the river or by the village well, were the only women who could show their faces in public. Female shamans, known as *mudang*, who performed both divination and healing, and professional female entertainers, called *kisaeng*, also had greater freedom of movement, though the status of both was very low indeed. Paradoxically, *kisaeng* were the only women allowed some education, apart from a handful of *yangban* women taught by private tutors within the confines of their homes. Because *kisaeng* had to be witty and accomplished in order to amuse men, they learned to sing, to play musical instruments, and to compose and recite poetry and the classics.

Recent scholarship has shown that the status of Korean women had not always been so abject. Unlike the situation during the middle and late Yi dynasty, during the Silla (688–935), Koryo (935–1392), and early Yi dynasties women could inherit property—which was equally divided among all the children, regardless of sex, upon a father's death—could participate in ancestor worship, and could continue to relate to their natal families. Before the mid-seventeenth century, male adoption was rare. Widows could remarry, because the patrilineage was not then the basic unit of society. Therefore, what has been called the "traditional" status of Korean women was, in fact, a cultural borrowing, and a relatively late one at that.

War and the coming of missionaries greatly affected the lives of Korean women in the late nineteenth and early twentieth centuries. Invading armies, wherever they march in the world, have always abused women. The armies in Korea were no exception. Korean women who were raped—or worse, gang-raped—usually committed suicide. But the presence of would-be conquerors also allowed women to take part in resistance movements: They hid men with prices on their heads, acted as secret couriers, and succored their own troops by offering them food, washing and mending their clothes, making their sandals, and tending to the injured and the sick. It can be argued that, during such periods, Korean women fleetingly entered the public realm.

The changes introduced by the Protestant missionaries had an even more profound impact. Women missionaries and wives of male missionaries made the first efforts to educate and convert Korean women—not so much for the sake of liberating them, but because they thought women held the key to the conversion of Korean families. The women missionaries conducted Bible classes in their own homes, which more and more Korean women began to visit as time passed. The first three female converts were baptized in 1888. Because they had to overcome so many obstacles before they could adopt Christianity—a religion that directly challenged some of the fundamental tenets of Confucianism—those women who became Christians were ardent believers.

The women missionaries also provided new role models for their female converts, some of whom became "Bible women," who not only visited their neighbors but also on occasion traveled outside their hometowns or villages to proselytize the new faith—a hitherto unheard-of activity for Korean women. Many of the Bible women were widows from lower-class families who welcomed the wages they earned, meager though they were. Perhaps even more important, widows, who were accorded no rights whatsoever in Yi dynasty society, found Christianity appealing because it gave them a place in the new community of believers. Working within the church allowed formerly secluded women to learn to read, to get out of their household prisons, to organize themselves for good works, to travel in the cause of evangelism, and to become valued public persons.

The missionary schools produced the first women professionals and leaders in twentieth-century Korea. This was especially true of girls educated at Ewha Haktang. Esther Pak (née Kim Chomdong), a graduate of Ewha, was the first Korean woman to obtain a degree (in 1900) from an American medical school. Upon returning to her native land, she worked tirelessly for eleven years before dying at age thirty-three. Helen Kim, another graduate of Ewha, earned a doctorate from Columbia University—the first Korean woman to receive a Ph.D. anywhere—and became the first Korean president of Ewha Woman's University (which grew out of the girls' school). Louise Yim, a fighter for Korean independence, and Induk Pahk, an indefatigable "traveling secretary" for the World Student Christian Movement, were also graduates of Ewha. These four were but the most illustrious among many modern Korean Christian women leaders. According to Mary Paik Lee, her paternal grandmother, Sin Duk Bok, also dedicated her life to educating women after she had become a Christian.

The American presence also had an unintended consequence: Korean emigration to the Western Hemisphere. By the turn of the century, several hundred thousand Koreans lived abroad, the majority of them on the Asian mainland in the maritime provinces of Russia, in Manchuria, and in China proper, south of the Great Wall. These people had sought no government approval for their departure, having simply drifted across the boarder and settled wherever they found means of livelihood. In addition, a small number of Koreans had gone to Japan as students and workers. Then, between December 1902 and May 1905, more than seven thousand were recruited to work in the sugar plantations of Hawaii, while about one thousand were spirited out of Korea in May 1905 to labor in the henequen plantations of Mexico.

In 1902 the Hawaiian Sugar Planters Association became interested in recruiting Koreans because, by then, Japanese workers, who composed two-thirds of the total planation labor force in the islands, had become militant and were engaging in work stoppages and spontaneous strikes.

The planters wanted to import other ethnic groups to offset what they called the Japanese "labor monopoly."

Horace N. Allen, who had been the first American missionary to enter Korea (in 1884) and who became the American minister to Korea in 1897, helped the sugar planters by persuading Emperor Kojung that it would be desirable to allow his subjects to emigrate. Kojong agreed to set up an emigration bureau, partly because famine had stalked several northern provinces the year before, but also because Allen's argument—that the desire of American employers to hire Korean workers, at a time when they did not welcome Japanese, would give Korea international prestige—appealed to His Majesty. Allen then asked Kojong to grant the "emigration franchise" to his friend David Deshler.

Few Koreans responded to Deshler's recruitment efforts, however, until the American pastor of the Methodist Mission in Inchon persuaded members of his congregation that life for them as Christians would be more pleasant in Hawaii, a Christian land. About half of the first group to leave in December 1902 were members of this church. Other missionaries gave similar advice. As a result of the missionaries' role, an estimated 40 percent of the emigrants were Christian converts. Not all the missionaries encouraged emigration, however. Some, in fact, tried to prevent their followers from leaving, because each one who departed meant the loss of a convert.

Unlike Chinese and Japanese emigrants to America, who came from only a limited number of localities, Korean emigrants hailed from many places—particularly from the port cities of Inchon, Mokpo, Pusan, Masan, Wonsan, and Chinampo, as well as from the two largest cities in the country, Seoul and Pyongyang. As for their socioeconomic origins, according to Wayne Patterson and Hyung June Moon, most were laborers, former soldiers, artisans, or peasants—or from the ranks of the unemployed. There were also some students and professionals, however, such as Mary Paik Lee's father, who left for political reasons: Toward the close of the Russo-Japanese War, the Japanese had commandeered the Paik family's house, along with the houses of their neighbors, for quartering soldiers; uncertain of the future, the Paik family decided that some of their members should leave in order to ensure the survival of at least one branch of the family. One of the sons, Paik Sin Koo, and his nuclear family—including his daughter, Mary Paik Lee—were chosen to go.

The emigrants traveled on ships owned by Deshler to Kobe, Japan, where they were given medical exams before proceeding to Hawaii. The fact that almost 10 percent of the emigrants were women and about 8 percent were children indicates that quite a number intended to settle overseas. This is corroborated by the fact that only one-seventh of them eventually returned to Korea—a much lower percentage of return migrants than found among the Chinese and Japanese. Japan's ever-tightening grip over Korea no doubt also reduced the return migration rate. Between 1903 and 1907, more than a thousand of the Koreans in Hawaii sailed to the continental United States to join the several dozen *ginseng* merchants and students who had gone there directly.

Emigration ended suddenly in 1905 for two reasons. First, news drifted back to Korea that the workers who had gone to Mexico were being badly mistreated, so the Korean government halted emigration not only to that country but also to Hawaii. Second, Japan pressured Korea to close the emigration office in order to cut off the supply of Korean laborers to the islands, where the sugar plantation owners were using them as scabs against striking Japanese planation workers. The secondary migration from Hawaii to the mainland also ended when, on 14 March 1907, President Theodore Roosevelt issued Executive Order 589 to prohibit such movement. This was done to mollify anti-Japanese groups in California, which were demanding an end to Japanese immigration. Though Koreans were not the primary target of the curb, they were nevertheless affected by the order.

Under Japanese colonial rule, which lasted until 1945, the only Koreans allowed to leave legally for the United States were approximately one thousand picture brides. About five hundred students, many of them anti-Japanese activists, also managed to land in the United States without passports. After the passage of the 1924 Immigration Act, however, which greatly reduced the number of immigrants from eastern and southern Europe and barred virtually all Asian immigrants, Korean students were no longer allowed to remain in the United States after they had completed their studies.

Fewer than nine thousand Koreans landed on U.S. territory before the passage of the 1924 immigration law. Among the Koreans who entered before mid-1905 were some six hundred women. Between 1905 and 1910, another forty females came. Then from 1910 to 1924, more than a thousand "picture brides" arrived—women who had gone through marriage ceremonies in Korea (with the grooms absent) before sailing to join their husbands in Hawaii and on the Pacific Coast. Arranged marriages were the norm in most traditional Asian societies; what gave these transoceanic arrangements their nomenclature was that the match-makers showed photographs of the prospective partners to their interested families. Nine-tenths of the picture brides went to Hawaii and one-tenth to the continental United States. Though few in number, these women made possible a continuing Korean presence in Hawaii and the American West.

Almost all the Koreans who went to Hawaii initially worked on the sugar plantations, because that was what they had been recruited to do. Starting in 1835, when the first sugar planation was established, sugar production expanded until it became the very foundation of the Hawaiian economy. The 375 tons produced in 1850 increased to over 9,000 tons in 1870; almost 32,000 tons in 1880; 130,000 tons in 1890; 300,000 tons in 1900; and over half a million tons in 1910. In the latter year, some 44,000 workers labored in the fields, about 10 percent of them Koreans. But plantation labor was onerous, and as soon as some of the workers finished their terms, they moved to Honolulu to open small stores, bathhouses, or boardinghouses.

On the mainland, the early immigrants lived primarily in California, but small numbers were also found in other western states. In the beginning, most toiled in the fields, as they had done in Hawaii. This was not because, as was often assumed, they came from peasant societies and found agricultural work "natural," but because no other work was to be had.

As in Hawaii, income from agriculture became the basis of California's prosperity. Beginning in the 1870s, landowners in the state turned increasingly from cereal cultivation to the growth of specialty crops—fruits, nuts, and vegetables—which brought far larger returns but which required an enormous amount of "stoop-back" labor to cultivate, harvest, pack, and ship. Growers could not find enough white workers to toil at the wages they were willing to pay. Their solution was to import non-whites, who did not have the same rights as whites. Korean immigrants, including well-educated people like Mary Paik Lee's father, found seasonal farmwork to be one of the few available occupations. If they wished to remain in America, they had to accept such work to support themselves and their families. Virtually all of them, at one time or another, labored in the fields, orchards, and citrus groves of the western United States—sleeping on the floor in shacks and bunkhouses, cooking their meals over open fires, and moving from one harvest to another.

Only a small number managed to sustain themselves with nonagricultural work—mostly as domestic servants, cooks, common laborers, and railroad section hands. But these occupations, like farmwork, also required a migratory existence. Those who desired a more settled existence found only two avenues available: tenant farming in the countryside and selling fresh produce and ethnic merchandise in the towns and cities. The tenant farmers and merchants soon became the most-well-off members of the immigrant community, but the educated individuals and the political leaders received the most respect.

Like the Chinese and Japanese who had arrived before them, the Koreans engaged in three kinds of tenant farming: truck gardening, fruit growing, and cereal cultivation. Extant records in county offices in California indicate that Asian tenant farmers preferred to pay cash rent, although a small number did become sharecroppers. In a few instances, tenants not only paid a cash rent but also gave the landlords a share of the harvest. Farming is an uncertain source of income, since weather and market conditions are beyond the control of individual farmers. In spite of this, many an Asian immigrant family has been sustained by agriculture, even during very bleak years when others have starved, because they could grow most of the food they needed for family use—a form of insurance that urban dwellers did not possess.

Vegetables and small fruits were usually grown on family farms of ten to eighty acres. Family members generally preformed all the work, except during planting and harvesting seasons, when even very small farms had to hire temporary help. The best-known Korean fruit growers were

Charles Kim (Kim Ho) and Harry Kim (Kim Hyung-soon). In 1921 they established the Kim Brothers Company in Reedley in the San Joaquin Valley of California, where they managed six farms totaling five hundred acres. They developed several varieties of hybrid fruit, including a nectarine, with saplings they imported from Korea. They had their own packing sheds, where every harvest season they employed as many as two hundred workers. The tenant farmers leasing the largest acreages grew rice in Colusa, Glenn, Butte, Yuba, and Sutter Counties in the northern Sacramento Valley, from the mid-1910s to the early 1920s. Kim Chong-lim, who leased thousands of acres, was known as "the Korean Rice King."

The success enjoyed by Korean immigrant farmers was extraordinary in light of the laws enacted to hinder their efforts. In 1913 California passed an Alien Land Law to prevent persons "ineligible to [sic] citizenship" from buying agricultural land and from leasing it for more than three years. Chinese, Japanese, Korean, and Asian Indian immigrants, however, quickly learned to bypass this law by leasing land through their American-born children and relatives or through white friends. The Lees, for example, rented tracts in southern California in the name of Stanford Paik, Mrs. Lee's American-born younger brother. The law had little effect, partly because county and state officials did not enforce it strenuously and partly because landowners benefited from the good crops raised by Asian tenants. Then, too, the need for increased food production during World War I gave Asian tenant farmers a breathing spell.

After the war was over, however, farm prices declined, and efforts were renewed to eliminate or at least severely limit Asian competition. To plug the loopholes in the 1913 law, an initiative was placed on the ballot during the 1920 election. It passed by an overwhelming margin, denying "aliens ineligible to citizenship" any rights with respect to real property in California, other than those secured to them by "now existing" treaties between their country and the United States. Both the 1882 treaty between Korea and the United States and the 1911 treaty between Japan and the United States explicitly granted subjects of the signatories the right to acquire real estate for "domicile" and "business," but no mention was made of agriculture. Omission was thus interpreted as prohibition.

An amendment passed in 1923 made it illegal for Asian tenant farmers to enter into cropping contracts (though such agreements technically conferred no legal interest in the land itself), forbade any corporations in which they owned more than half of the stocks to engage in agriculture, and provided for the escheat of any holdings illegally acquired. The last condition was made retroactive to the date of acquisition, so that even though an original purchaser could bequeath a plot to someone else, the title received by the transferee was invalid.

Arizona in 1917, Washington and Louisiana in 1921, New Mexico in 1922, Idaho, Montana, and Oregon in 1923, and Kansas in 1925 passed similar laws. Two decades later, while World War II was in progress, Utah, Wyoming, and Arkansas also enacted such legislation, fearing that

Japanese released from the internment camps might reenter farming in a big way. Since, during this entire period, Koreans were colonial subjects of Japan, whatever obstacles were placed in the way of Japanese immigrants also affected them. But they managed to farm—as Mrs. Lee's family did—by resorting to oral agreements.

To take care of themselves in the new land, Korean immigrants quickly and effectively organized themselves. On the Hawaiian plantations, almost immediately upon their arrival, they formed *tong-hoe* (village councils) in each locality with ten or more Korean families. Every year, the adult males selected a *tong-jang* (head of the council), a sergeant-at-arms, and a few policemen to enforce the rules they had established for their own governance. Koreans in Honolulu created the *Sinmin-hoe* (New People Society) in 1903 to protest Japanese interference in their homeland. In 1907, the various *tong-hoe* united to form the *Hanin Hapsong Hyop-hoe* (United Korean Society), with headquarters in Honolulu. Two years later, that organization joined the *Kongnip Hyop-hoe* (Mutual Assistance Association) of San Francisco, which had been established in 1905, to become the *Taehan Kookmin-hoe* (Korean National Association, or KNA), which thereafter became the most important body representing Koreans throughout North America. The KNA even had chapters in Manchuria and Siberia. Its aims were to promote education, social welfare, and economic development among Koreans abroad, to train them to work together in equality and freedom, and to restore national independence. To disseminate these ideas, the KNA started publishing a weekly newspaper, the *Sinhan Minpo* (*New Korea*), in 1919.

Because so many of the immigrants were Christians who had left their homeland in the wake of Japanese encroachment, churches and political organizations best served their needs. Within half a year of their arrival in Hawaii, they held the first Korean-language church service and set up the Korean Evangelical Society. Although Presbyterians outnumbered Methodists in Korea, the latter denomination become more active among immigrants in the islands, mainly because George Heber Jones, who had encouraged members of his congregation to emigrate, was a Methodist. He had given some of the first emigrants letters of introduction to John Wadman, superintendent of Methodist missions in Hawaii, who helped the Koreans rent a house for their worship services. Other Korean Christians in the islands formed the Korean Episcopal Church in 1905, holding their dedication ceremony in the St. Andrew Episcopal Church in Honolulu, which rented a classroom in an elementary school for the group's use. A secessionist independent Korean Christian Church under the leadership of Syngman Rhee appeared in 1917. By 1918, there were thirty-three Korean Protestant churches in Hawaii.

On the mainland, Korean Christians started worshipping together at a mission school in Los Angeles in 1904; the following year, individuals in San Francisco established the Korean Methodist Church. The first Korean Presbyterian Church was founded in Los Angeles in 1906 and was supported by the Presbyterian Missionary Extension Board. This group （pagenum）424   Seeking Empowerment

worshipped in a rented house in the Bunker Hill district. The churches served more than religious needs; they were the centers of social life among Korean immigrants. People like Mrs. Lee and her husband financially supported the Korean Presbyterian Church in Los Angeles for years, even though, as farmers, they were always too busy on Sundays to attend services. Even non-Christians went to the functions held at the churches. Furthermore, since a number of the Korean pastors were vocal leaders in the nationalist struggle, some immigrant churches served as institutional bases for political activities.

Not only did the church dominate Korean immigrant life generally, being Christian also affected the way individual Korean immigrants responded to discrimination by white Americans. Paik Sin Koo, upon the family's arrival in San Francisco, urged his young daughter not to worry about the unfriendly reception shown the disembarking Asian passengers. He told her that the first missionaries in Korea had also been mistreated, but *they* had overcome the initial hostility, going on to achieve great things. So, said he, must she. It is likely that at least some of the other Christian immigrants shared Paik's attitude, perceiving Americans as potential benefactors rather than persecutors. Besides, they could not worry too much about discrimination when they had a far larger concern: freeing their homeland from colonial rule.

That homeland politics mattered more to Korean immigrants than did their treatment by American whites can be seen in what most aroused their ire. Because of their small numbers on the mainland, Koreans were never subjected to a separate, organized anti-Korean movement, like the movements against the Chinese and Japanese. Most of the time they were simply lumped together with the other Asians. After 1905, especially, whatever affected the Japanese also affected them. This fact made Koreans angrier than did anything else.

The so-called Hemet incident is a case in point. When Korean farm-workers were ousted from that small town in Riverside County in 1913, the southern California branch of the Japanese Association of America reported the incident to the Japanese consulate in San Francisco, which, in turn, informed the Japanese embassy in Washington, D.C. After instructing the acting consul general in San Francisco to investigate the occurrence, the Japanese ambassador filed a protest with the U.S. State Department. Even before he received the formal complaint, however, Secretary of State William Jennings Bryan had already asked the U.S. Department of Justice to make inquiries into the matter. But the concern shown by the Japanese infuriated the Koreans. The Reverend David Lee, who at that time was serving as president of the Korean National Association, sent a telegram to Bryan (the text of which was reprinted in the *Sinhom Minpo* of 4 July 1919), declaring, "We, the Koreans in America, are not Japanese subjects, . . . we will never submit to her as long as the sun remains in the heavens. The intervention of the Japanese Consulate-General in Korean matters is illegal, so I have the honor of requesting you to discontinue the discussion of this case with the Japanese government representatives. . . . We will settle it without Japanese interference." Bryan did not respond directly to the telegram, but he told the Associated Press that the investigation would be "discontinued" and that the United States would henceforth deal directly with the Korean National Association on all matters concerning Koreans.

Given their strong sense of nationalism, Korean immigrants founded many political organizations through which they made far larger financial contributions to the anti-Japanese movement than their numbers warranted. Though their wages were very low by American standards, they were still better off than were their compatriots at home or in Asian mainland settlements. Just as important, political activists in America could not be reached by the Japanese military police, whose agents operated not only in Korea but also on the Asian mainland.

The four best-known political leaders within the Korean immigrant community in the United States were So Chae-pil, more commonly known as Philip Jaisohn (1866–1951), Ahn Chang-ho (1878–1938), Park Yong-man (1881–1928), and Syngman Rhee (1875–1965). Each proposed a different strategy to achieve the common end they all desired: Korean independence.

Philip Jaisohn convened a Liberty Congress in Independence Hall in Philadelphia in April 1919 to publicize the March First Amendment, because, in his words, he wanted "America to realize that Korea is a victim of Japan." He carried out public relations work on behalf of Korean independence for many years.

Ahn Chang-ho came to San Francisco in 1899, where he set up the *Chinmok-hoe* (Friendship Society), the first social organization among Koreans in California. He believed that the Korean people had first to "regenerate" themselves before they could regain independence, so he encouraged his fellow immigrants to clean and beautify their homes—as an outward symbol of their moral rectitude—and to engage in honorable labor.

Park Yong-man, in yet another approach, thought that military means were necessary to liberate Korea. He established five military academies in Nebraska, California, Kansas, and Wyoming, as well as an airplane-pilot training program in Willows, California, this last endeavor being financed by Kim Chong lim, the Korean Rice King. In 1912, the different groups of cadets were consolidated into a single Korean National Brigade, with over three hundred members commanded by Park.

The most long-lived and controversial expatriate leader was Syngman Rhee. Rhee attended the Paechae Methodist School for Boys in Seoul for a number of years and was a member of the Independence Club. In 1898, when the government disbanded the club, Rhee took refuge in the American Methodist Hospital. One day, when he ventured outside, he was arrested. He spent the next seven years in prison. He read the Bible in jail, decided to become a Christian, and requested baptism after his release. He came to the United States in 1905, obtained a bachelor's degree from George Washington University in 1907, a master's degree from Harvard in 1908, and a doctorate from Princeton in 1910—the first Korean to hold a doctorate from an American university. His education was largely financed by contributions from Korean immigrants.

Rhee believed the best course to follow was to cultivate American public opinion and to influence the powerful nations to exert pressure on Japan. In 1919, he went to Washington, D.C., in an effort to obtain American recognition for the provisional government in Shanghai, but he failed in his mission. Then he journeyed to Shanghai in November of the same year to assume the post of "chief of executive" there. Rhee stayed in Shanghai only seventeen months. After his return to the United States in 1921, he started calling himself "president" of the provisional government.

When irreconcilable differences arose between Rhee and other leaders of the provisional government, however, Rhee put his energy into more personal instruments of power that he had established before he became "president." He had founded the Korean Christian Church, the *Tongji-hoe* (Comrade Society), and a magazine, the *Pacific Weekly*, in Hawaii to advance his own viewpoint in 1919; on these he now depended. He had many ardent supporters whose contributions kept him and his projects going for several decades. Rhee lobbied various American and European leaders whenever he could; he traveled to Geneva and to Moscow in 1932 to plead his country's cause. He gave lectures, published articles, and wrote two books to promote American sympathy for Korean independence. During most of this period he lived in Hawaii, but in 1939 he moved to Washington, D.C., to intensify his lobbying efforts when developments in east Asia signaled a change in the international balance of power. After World War II ended, he returned to Korea, where he won the 1948 elections to become the first president of the Republic of Korea. He held office until he was ousted by student demonstrators in 1960, whereupon he retired to Hawaii. He died there in 1965.

As charismatic leaders, men like Ahn, Park, and Rhee inspired strong loyalties. But conflict among them also led to intense factionalism within Korean immigrant communities in North America and, indeed, around the world. From the late 1920s until the end of World War II, the Korean nationalist movement survived in several settings. Leftists worked primarily within the Chinese Communist party. When the Communists set themselves up in northeastern China after 1936, Koreans in that part of the country, particularly those in Manchuria, gained prominence in the Korean nationalist movement. Then, as the Chinese Nationalists retreated inland to Chungking when the Japanese took over the eastern part of China, Kim Ku, chairman of the provisional government and founder of the right-wing Korean Independence Party, went to Chungking with them and set up the new headquarters of the Korean provisional government. A third faction operated underground in Seoul, while a fourth, a pro-American faction, existed under Rhee's leadership.

Not only did these political conflicts divide the Korean community in America, they also imposed heavy financial burdens on its members. Bong-Youn Choy has calculated that, for decades, virtually every Korean in America gave the equivalent of one month's wages every year to support the nationalist struggle, despite the fact that many immigrants were working themselves to utter exhaustion and living from hand to mouth through countless lean years. Yet they contributed willingly, because they felt a special responsibility to do so, living as they did in "freedom" away from their colonized homeland. Though the Japanese censored all news coming out of Korea, and though emigration to the United States had long ceased, the immigrants who were already here remained aware of the situation at home because, from time to time, a few refugee students did slip in. Their presence, along with the exhortations of expatriate leaders, helped to keep nationalism alive among the immigrants. Despite the political differences that existed, Koreans in North America had a true community. It was, by and large, endogamous. Sociologist Romanzo Adams found that as late as 1937 in Hawaii, only 104 Koreans had married non-Koreans. In Mary Paik Lee's family, the majority of her siblings who married had somehow found Korean spouses.

While all Koreans in America were weighed down with multiple responsibilities, women immigrants bore the heaviest burden of all. They not only did all the housework and bore and raised the children; nearly every one of them worked to help provide for their families and to raise funds for the nationalist cause. Their social adaptations were even more mind-boggling: Imagine the shock of moving from a world where women were confined to "inner rooms" and were forbidden to go outdoors during the day to a situation where, more often than not, only a piece of cloth separated the living quarters of married women from those occupied by dozens of rowdy young bachelors.

The women who came before 1910 and the picture brides who followed them between 1910 and 1924 lived strenuous lives. On the plantations of Hawaii and on the farms of the western United States, Korean women cooked, washed, and cleaned not only for their own families but also—for a fee—for bachelors or married men who had come without their wives. In many families, such supplemental earnings made the difference between starvation and survival. Those who fed unattached men had to arise several hours before dawn, often at 3 or 4 A.M., to cook breakfast for as many as forty persons and to pack an equal number of lunch boxes in primitive kitchens with no modern conveniences, not even running water. Those with children had to dress them for school. Others who worked in the fields for wages spent a full day under the sun, sometimes with babies strapped to their backs, before returning home to fix supper. In the evenings, they washed, ironed, and mended until midnight. Women who did laundry for a fee had to lug water from the well or the outdoor faucet, scrub the clothes on washboards, hang them out on lines to dry, and iron them with irons heated on stoves. For years on end, many of the immigrant women survived with no more than four hours of sleep a night. Those who bore children did all this work even while pregnant.

The life of Mary Paik Lee's mother was typical: Though Song Kuang Do did not work in the fields in Hawaii—as many other Korean and Japanese women did—after the Paik family arrived on the mainland, her cooking for thirty men sustained her family for the first four years they were in California. From the day she set foot on American soil until her old age, she worked day in and day out alongside her husband to eke out a living. Mary Paik Lee herself began helping out with chores at the age of six and obtained her first paying job through her own efforts when she was eleven. She did not stop working until she was eighty-five. Mrs. Lee, however, unlike many of the women who moved to urban settings, said in retrospect that she had preferred working with the clean earth to cleaning up other people's filth.

Given such a hard life on plantations and on farms, it is not surprising that many women exerted great pressure on their spouses to move to the cities. This was especially true among picture brides—many of whom were from more economically secure backgrounds and were better educated than their husbands. Those who did move opened bathhouses, boardinghouses, restaurants, small stores, and produce stands in Honolulu, San Francisco, Los Angeles, and other urban centers. Such work did not necessarily pay better, but it allowed them, through self-exploitation, to work without supervision and to accumulate some capital.

In spite of their arduous labor, some women found time to work for their churches and for secular women's associations. The percentage of Christians among Korean immigrant women increased after they settled in the United States, because those who had already accepted the faith before they left their homeland converted others. In time, women members exceeded men in numbers, though they still are not given leadership positions.

The first women's organization formed outside the church was the *Hankuk Puin-hoe* (Korean Women's Association), established in San Francisco in 1908. The *Taehanin Puin-hoe* (Great Korean Women's Association) was set up in Honolulu in 1913. In the wake of the March First Movement, the *Taehan Puin Kuje-hoe* (Korean Women's Relief Society) was organized, with branches in Hawaii and California, to support the Korean independence movement. To inaugurate their society, the members put on traditional Korean clothing and marched through the streets of downtown Honolulu, singing patriotic songs. They raised money by selling food and copies of the Korean Declaration of Independence, as well as by working overtime and scrimping at home. They sent the funds they raised to the provisional government in Shanghai, the Korean Commission in Washington, D.C., the Korean Independence Army in Manchuria and China, and to the family members of the thirty-three signers of the Korean Declaration of Independence who had been arrested, imprisoned, or killed. A second organization that grew out of the March First Movement was the *Taehan Yoja Aikuk-dan* (Korean Women's Patriotic Society), which had branches in California towns and cities with sizable Korean populations: Willows, Sacramento, San Francisco, Dinuba, Reedley, and Los Angeles. There were also two branches outside the United States—in Merida, Mexico, and in Havana, Cuba. These women's political organizations, like the ones formed by the men, became less active in the 1920s as a result of disunity in the Korean nationalist movement, but they revived after 1937 when Japan and China went to war. Women of Korean ancestry—immigrant and American-born alike— eagerly joined their Chinese sisters in America to protest the loading of scrap iron on ships destined for Japan, in an attempt to prevent American resources from benefiting Japan's armament industry.

The kind of life that Korean immigrant women and their American-born daughters led was a far cry from the secluded existence that had bound women in Korea. Even female Christians in the homeland did not have the same freedom of movement and the opportunities for social interaction that immigrant women found in America. To be sure, public exposure was thrust upon them by virtue of what they had to do to ensure family survival, but the fact is, they rose to the challenge and found meaning in so doing. Daughters like Mary Paik Lee had no choice but to help their mothers. In the process, they, too, learned to fend for themselves and to endure. And endurance mattered. Mrs. Lee, for example, admired the fact that her mother, her husband, and her youngest son—each of whom suffered bouts of ill health—"never complained."

Though Korean women in America could function in the public sphere, their lives were isolated in another sense: They seldom interacted with the larger society. Even their American-born children, who spoke English fluently and who went to public schools, lived in a world apart. Korean children did not have to attend segregated schools—as did Chinese children in San Francisco and in some other California localities—but they did not mix much with white children. Mary Paik Lee's first day at school in Riverside was frightening: The other children danced around her and "chopped" her head off. In Colusa in 1911, she and her older brother had to help their parents wash other people's laundry for meager pay; in addition, she found herself a job as a servant girl, working before and after school and on weekends. While her family lived in the mining town of Idria, she earned money cleaning the schoolhouse; during her first year in high school in Hollister, she earned her keep again as a live-in domestic. She obviously had no time for any social life. Even if she did, few white youngsters were willing to be her friend. In her entire auto- biography, she recalls only one white schoolmate who was nice to her.

Unlike their parents, for whom Christianity and nationalism were consuming passions—passions that inured them somewhat to the cruelties of life in America—the second generation felt keenly the sting of discrimination. Whereas the immigrant generation had no alternative but to cherish their churches and political organizations, because these served as the most visible symbols of their desire for personal salvation and national liberation, the American-born generation could not find solace in the same institutions. Paradoxically, however, Korean American young- sters like Mary Paik Lee seem not to have shared the desperate desire of Chinese American and Japanese American children—like Pardee Lowe, Jade Snow Wong, and Monica Sone—to "prove" how American they were. Perhaps this was so because their Korean heritage was an embattled

Mary Kuang Sun Paik Lee.
(Photo from author's collection.)

one—one that had to be kept alive and treasured, not resented or
discarded. Perhaps this enabled Mary Paik Lee to be a true Korean
American: She begins and ends her tale by citing Korean history, but in
between she shares with us what it was like to have grown up poor, Asian,
and female in the shadow of the American dream.

Note

"Introduction to *Quiet Odyssey: A Pioneer Korean Woman in America*" appears in *Quiet Odyssey*,
Mary Paik Lee's autobiography compiled in collaboration with Sucheng Chan and published
originally in 1990 by the University of Washington Press.

Bibliographic Essay

This is a highly edited version of the comprehensive bibliographic essay that Sucheng Chan
compiled for *Quiet Odyssey*. In this version, the volume editors emphasize works on Korean and
Korean American women. Readers are urged to consult the original essay for full references.

Accessible general histories of Korea include Takashi Hatada, *A History of Korea*, trans. and
ed. by Warren W. Smith, Jr., and Benjamin H. Hazard ((Santa Barbara, Calif.: ABC-Clio Press,
1969); Pow Key Sohn et al., *The History of Korea* (Seoul: Korean National Commission for
UNESCO, 1970); William H. Henthorn, *A History of Korea* (New York: Free Press, 1971); and

Woo-keun Han, *The History of Korea*, trans. Kyung-shik Lee and ed. Grafton K. Mintz (Honolulu: University of Hawaii Press, 1971).

On Korean cultural and social life, see Cornelius Osgood, *The Koreans and Their Culture* (New York: Ronald Press, 1951); Richard Rutt, *Korean Works and Days* (Tokyo: Charles E. Tuttle, 1964); Paul S. Crane, *Korean Patterns* (Seoul: Hollym Corp., 1967); Shin-Yong Chung, ed., *Folk Culture in Korea*, Korean Culture Series, no. 4 (Seoul: International Cultural Foundation, 1974); Eui-Young Yu and Earl H. Phillips, eds., *Religions in Korea: Beliefs and Cultural Values* (Los Angeles: Koryo Research Institute, Center for Korean and Korean-American Studies, California State University, Los Angeles, 1982); and Roger L. Janelli and Dawnhee Yim Janelli, *Ancestor Worship and Korean Society* (Stanford, Calif.: Stanford University Press, 1982).

Robert J. Moose, *Village Life in Korea* (Nashville, Tenn.: Publishing House of the Methodist Episcopal Church, South, 1911), is the earliest study in English of Korean villages. Rural life in twentieth-century Korea is described in Chungnim Choi Han, "Social Organization of Upper Han Hamlet in Korea" (Ph.D. dissertation, University of Michigan, 1949); Eugene Knez, "Sam Jong Dong: A South Korean Village" (Ph.D. dissertation, Syracuse University, 1959); John E. Mills, ed., *Ethno-Social Reports of Four Korean Villages* (San Francisco: United States Operations Mission to Korea, 1960); Vincent S. R. Brandt, *A Korean Village between Farm and Sea* (Cambridge, Mass.: Harvard University Press, 1971); Ki-hyuk Pak and Sidney D. Gamble, *The Changing Korean Village* (Seoul: Shin-hung, 1975); and Clark W. Sorensen, *Over the Mountains Are Mountains: Korean Peasant Households and Their Adaptations to Rapid Industrialization* (Seattle: University of Washington Press, 1988).

On the diplomatic history of Korea around the turn of the century, see Martina Deuchler, *Confucian Gentlemen and Barbarian Envoys: The Opening of Korea, 1876–1885* (Seattle: University of Washington Press, 1977); the introduction of Protestant Christianity is covered in Everett N. Hunt, Jr., *Protestant Pioneers in Korea* (Maryknoll, N.Y.: Orbis Books, 1980); and Martha Huntley, *Caring, Growing, Changing: A History of the Protestant Mission in Korea* (New York: Friendship Press, 1984).

Eyewitness accounts of the March First Movement (or Mansei Uprising) are quoted in Hugh Heung-wo Cynn, *The Rebirth of Korea: The Reawakening of the People, Its Causes, and the Outlook* (New York: Abingdon Press, 1920); and Peter Huyn, *Man Sei! The Making of a Korean American* (Honolulu: University of Hawaii Press, 1986).

Biographies of nationalist leaders who spent long years in the United States include Channing Liem, *America's Finest Gift to Korea: The Life of Philip Jaisohn* (New York: William-Frederick Press, 1952); Robert T. Oliver, *Syngman Rhee: The Man behind the Myth* (New York: Dodd, Mead, 1954); and Richard C. Allen, *Korea's Syngman Rhee: An Unauthorized Portrait* (Rutland, Vt.: Charles E. Tuttle, 1960).

Relatively little has been published about Korean women. The most complete study available in English is Yung-Chung Kim, ed. and trans., *Women of Korea: A History from Ancient Times to 1945* (Seoul: Ewha Woman's University Press, 1982), which is an abridged version of a three-volume study prepared by the Committee for the Compilation of the History of Korean Women at Ewha Woman's University, *Hanguk Yosongsa* [The History of Korean Women] (Seoul: Ewha Woman's University Press, 1972). The best short introduction to Korean women during the Yi dynasty is "Appendix B. Women and Family in Traditional Korea," in Youngsook Kim Harvey, *Six Korean Women: The Socialization of Shamans* (St. Paul, Minn.: West Publishing, 1979), 253–71. For a brief historical overview, see Hyon-ja Kim, "The Changing Role of Women in Korea," *Korea Journal* 11, no. 5 (1975): 21–24. Two feminist analyses are given in Tae-young Lee, "Elevation of Korean Women's Rights," *Korea Journal* 4, no. 2 (1964): 4–9, 43; and Hesung Chun Koh, "Yi Dynasty Women in the Public Domain: A New Perspective on Social Stratification," *Social Science Journal* (Korea) 3 (1975): 7–19. The only glimpse available of women's intellectual life during the Yi dynasty is in Dong-uk Kim, "Women's Literary Achievements," *Korea Journal* 3, no. 11 (1963): 33–36, 39. Stories about women are found in Frances Carpenter, *Tales of a Korean Grandmother* (Seoul: Royal Asiatic Society, Korea Branch, 1973); and Richard Rutt and

Chong Un Kim, trans., *Virtuous Women: Three Masterpieces of Traditional Korean Fiction* (Seoul: Royal Asiatic Society, Korea Branch, 1974).

Two anthologies, Sandra Martielli, ed., *Virtues in Conflict: Tradition and the Korean Woman Today* (Seoul: Royal Asiatic Society, Korea Branch, 1977); and Laurel Kendall and Mark Peterson, eds., *Korean Women: View from the Inner Room* (New Haven, Conn.: East Rock Press, 1983), contain several essays written from a feminist perspective.

Bae Kyung Sook, *Women and the Law in Korea* (Seoul: Korean League of Women Voters, 1973); In-ho Lee, "Women's Liberation in Korea," *Korea Journal* 17, no. 7 (1977): 4–11; and Uhn Cho and Hagen Koo, "Economic Development and Women's Work in a Newly Industrialized Country: The Case of Korea," *Development and Change* 14 (1983): 515–21, offer modern perspectives. Korean family life is analyzed in Doo-hun Kim, "Historical Review of Korean Family System," *Korea Journal* 3, no. 10 (1963): 4–9, 32; Chae-sok Choe, "Process of Change in Korean Family Life," *Korea Journal* 3, no. 10 (1963): 10–15; Hang-nyung Lee, "Civil Law and Korean Family System," *Korea Journal* 3, no. 10 (1963): 20–21, 32; Seong-hi Yim, "Changing Patterns in Korean Family Structure," *Korea Journal* 6, no. 8 (1966): 4–9; Hae Yong Lee, "Modernization of the Family Structure in an Urban Setting—with Special Reference to Marriage Relations," in *Aspects of Social Change in Korea*, ed. E. Kim and C. Chee (Kalamazoo, Mich.: Korea Research and Publications, 1969), 44–69; Chang Shub Roh, "Family Life in Korea and Japan," *Silliman Journal* (Philippines) 16 (1969): 200–215; Un Sun Song, "Marriage and the Family in Korea," in *Marriage and Family in the Modern World: A Book of Readings*, ed. Ruth Shonle Cavan (New York: Thomas Y. Crowell, 1969), 92–98; Tae-hung Ha, *Folk Customs and Family Life* (Seoul: Yonsei University Press, 1972); Hyo-chai Lee, "Changing Korean Family and the Old," *Korea Journal* 13, no. 6 (1973): 20–25; and Cha-whan Chung, "Change and Continuity in an Urbanizing Society: Family and Kinship in Urban Korea" (Ph.D. dissertation, University of Hawaii, 1977).

The most detailed study of early Korean emigration is Wayne K. Patterson, *The Korean Frontier in America: Immigration to Hawaii, 1896–1910* (Honolulu: University of Hawaii Press, 1988). Korean emigration is also discussed in Yo-jun Yun, "Early History of Korean Emigration to America," pt. 1, *Korea Journal* 14, no. 6 (1974): 21–26, and pt. 2, *Korea Journal* 14, no. 7 (1974): 40–45; Wayne K. Patterson, "Sugar-Coated Diplomacy: Horace Allen and Korean Immigration to Hawaii, 1902–1906," *Diplomatic History* 3 (1979): 29–38; and Linda Pomerantz, "The Background of Korean Emigration" in *Labor Immigration under Capitalism: Asian Workers in the United States before World War II*, ed. Lucie Cheng and Edna Bonacich (Berkeley: University of California Press, 1984), 277–315.

The only available general histories of Korean Americans are Bong-Youn Choy, *Koreans in America* (Chicago: Nelson-Hall, 1979), and Herbert Barringer and Sung-nam Cho, *Koreans in the United States: A Fact Book* (Honolulu: University of Hawaii, Center for Korean Studies, 1989), while Hyung June Moon, "The Korean Immigrants in America: The Quest for Identity in the Formative Years, 1903–1918" (Ph.D. dissertation, University of Nevada, Reno, 1977), has details not found elsewhere. Useful overviews, especially for classroom use, are Lee Houchins and Chang-su Houchins, "The Korean Experience in America, 1903–1924," *Pacific Historical Review* 18 (1974): 548–72 [reprinted in *The Asian American: The Historical Experience*, ed. Norris Hundley, Jr. (Santa Barbara, Calif.: ABC-Clio Press, 1976), 129–56]; H. Brett Melendy, *Asians in America: Filipinos, Koreans, and East Indians* (Boston: Twayne Publishers, 1977), 111–72; Eui-Young Yu, "Koreans in America: An Emerging Ethnic Minority," *Amerasia Journal* 4, no. 1 (1977): 117–32; Eui-Young Yu, "Korean Communities in America: Past, Present, and Future," *Amerasia Journal* 10, no. 2 (1983): 23–52.

Articles (which will not be cited individually here) in several anthologies provide valuable insights into various aspects of immigrant life: Hyung-chan Kim, ed., *The Korean Diaspora: Historical and Sociological Studies of Korean Immigration and Assimilation in North America* (Santa Barbara, Calif.: ABC-Clio Press, 1977); Byong-suh Kim and Sang Hyun Lee, eds., *The Korean Immigrant in America* (Montclair, N.J.: Association of Korean Christian Scholars in North America, 1980); and Eui-Young Yu et al., eds., *Koreans in Los Angeles: Prospects and*

Promises (Los Angeles: Koryo Research Institute, Center for Korean and Korean-American Studies, California State University, Los Angeles, 1982).

For regional studies of Koreans in the western United States, see Helen Lewis Givens, *The Korean Community in Los Angeles County* (1939; repr. San Francisco: R and E Research Associates, 1974); Dale White, "Koreans in Montana," *Asia and the Asians* 17 (1945): 156; Kyung Sook Cho Gregor, "Korean Immigrants in Gresham, Oregon: Community Life and Social Adjustment" (master's thesis, University of Oregon, 1963); Jay Kun Yoo, *The Koreans in Seattle*, Philip Jaisohn Memorial Papers, no. 4 (Elkins Park, Penn.: Philip Jaisohn Memorial Foundation, 1979); and Samuel S. O. Lee et al., eds., *75th Anniversary of Korean Immigration to Hawaii, 1903–1978* (Honolulu: 75th Anniversary of Korean Immigration to Hawaii Committee, 1978).

Korean immigrant communities in the early decades of their existence were torn by factional political struggles. Warren Y. [Won Yong] Kim, *Koreans in America* (Seoul: Po Chin Chai, 1971), which is an abbreviation in English of his larger work, *Chaemi Hanin Osimnyonsa [A Fifty-Year History of the Koreans in the United States]* (Reedley, Calif.: Charles Ho Kim, 1959), is definitive but hard to obtain. A more readily accessible source on Korean expatriate politics is Kinsley K. Lyu, "Korean Nationalist Activities in Hawaii and the Continental United States, 1900–1945," pt. 1 (1900–1919), *Amerasia Journal* 4, no. 1 (1977): 23–90; and pt. 2 (1919–1945), *Amerasia Journal* 4, no. 2 (1977): 53–100.

Though Korean immigrants have been similar in many ways to newcomers from other Asian countries, they differ in one significant aspect: An unusually large proportion of them are Protestant Christians, partly as a result of the active involvement of missionaries in the original exodus. For that reason, churches have played a crucial role in Korean immigrant communities. Studies of the religious life of Korean American Christians include Sangho Joseph Kim, *A Study of the Korean Church and Her People in Chicago, Illinois* (San Francisco: R and E Research Associates, 1975); Illsoo Kim, "Problems of Immigrant Society and the Role of the Church with Reference to the Korean Immigrant Community in America," *Korean Observer* 7 (1976): 398–431; Steve S. Shim, *Korean Immigrant Churches in Southern California Today* (San Francisco: R and E Research Associates, 1977); and Illsoo Kim, "Organizational Patterns of Korean-American Methodist Churches: Denominationalism and Personal Commitment" in *Rethinking Methodist History*, ed. Russell Richey and Kenneth E. Rowe (Nashville, Tenn.: United Methodist Publishing House, 1985), 228–37. See also the articles on Korean churches in America in the anthologies edited by Hyung-chan Kim, Byong-suh Kim and Sang Hyun Lee, and by Eui-Young Yu et al.

The assimilation and acculturation of Koreans in America are explored in Hyung-chan Kim, "Some Aspects of Social Demography of Korean Americans," *International Migration Review* 8 (1974): 23–42; Marn J. Cha, "Ethnic Political Orientation as Function of Assimilation: With Reference to Koreans in Los Angeles," *Journal of Korean Affairs* 5 (1975): 14–25; Won Moo Hurh, *Assimilation of the Korean Minority in the United States*, Philip Jaisohn Memorial Papers, no. 1 (Elkins Park, Penn.: Philip Jaisohn Memorial Foundation, 1977); Bok-Lim C. Kim, *The Asian Americans: Changing Patterns, Changing Needs* (Montclair, N.J.: Association of Korean Christian Scholars in North America, 1978), 177–211; Won Moo Hurh, "Towards a Korean American Ethnicity: Some Theoretical Models," *Ethnic and Racial Studies* 4 (1980): 444–63; Kwang Chung Kim and Won Moo Hurh, "Korean Americans and the 'Success' Image: A Critique," *Amerasia Journal* 10, no. 2 (1983): 3–22; David M. Oh, *An Analysis of the Korean Community in the Mid-Wilshire Area*, pts. 1 and 2 (Los Angeles: Mid-Wilshire Community Research Center Corp., 1983), 3–21; Peter Hyun, *In the New World: The Making of a Korean American* (Honolulu: University of Hawaii Press, 1991); and Connie Kang, *Home Was the Land of Morning Calm: A Saga of a Korean-American Family* (Redding, Mass.: Addison-Wesley, 1995).

For two overviews on Korean women in America during the pioneer period, see Eun Sik Yang, "Korean Women of America: From Subordination to Partnership, 1903–1930," *Amerasia Journal* 11, no. 2 (1984): 1–28; and Alice Y. Chai, "Korean Women in Hawaii, 1903–1945," in *Asian and Pacific American Experiences: Women's Perspectives*, ed. Nobuya Tsuchida (Minneapolis: Asian/Pacific American Learning Resource Center, University of Minnesota, 1982) 75–87. Alice Y. Chai, "The Life History of an Early Korean Immigrant Women in Hawaii," *University of*

Hawaii Women's Studies Program Working Papers Series 1 (1978): 50–59; Harold Hakwon Sunoo and Sonia Shinn Sunoo, "The Heritage of the First Korean Women Immigrants in the United States: 1903–1924," *Korean Christian Scholars Journal* 2 (1977): 142–71; Sonia S. Sunoo, "Korean Women Pioneers of the Pacific Northwest," *Oregon Historical Quarterly* 79 (1978): 51–63; and Sonia Shinn Sunoo, ed., *Korean Kaleidoscope* (Davis, Calif.: Korean Oral History Project, Sierra Mission Area, United Presbyterian Church, U.S.A., 1982), based on oral history transcriptions, offer glimpses of individual women, most of them picture brides. Bong-Youn Choy, *Koreans in America*, 308–324, also contains biographical sketches of three women.

Harold Hakwon Sunoo and Dong Soo Kim, eds., *Korean Women in a Struggle for Humanization* (Memphis, Tenn.: Association of Korean Christian Scholars in North America, 1978); and Eui-Young Yu and Earl H. Phillips, eds., *Korean Women in Transition at Home and Abroad* (Los Angeles: Koryo Research Institute, Center for Korean and Korean-American Studies, California State University, Los Angeles, 1987), contain essays on women in Korea as well as in the United States.

21.

Alice Dickerson Montemayor:
Feminism and Mexican American Politics
in the 1930s

CYNTHIA E. OROZCO

In this article Cynthia E. Orozco offers an example of what happens when historians question limiting assumptions about women of color. Although, as Orozco tells us, there was no organized Mexican American feminist movement before the 1970s, and the first national Chicana gathering did not occur until 1971, still it is wrong to assume that before then Mexican-origin women were traditionalists who accepted male authority and who therefore did not organize for social change. By examining the records and publications of the League of United Latin American Citizens (LULAC), the oldest Mexican American civil rights organization, Orozco located many women who participated in the separate Ladies LULAC chapters. She combines these sources with oral histories to fill in the blanks of Mexican American women's activism.

Contrary to the assumptions of many male LULAC members, and many historians as well, that if women participated at all, they did so to support their husbands, Orozco finds that many LULAC women were single. Many who were married participated independently of their husbands. Orozco examines the activist career of one such woman, Alice Dickerson Montemayor, who challenged male authority within the national LULAC leadership. She thus provides an important case study of gender politics within the most important Mexican American civil rights organization in the 1930s. Orozco also demonstrates that feminism and activism take many historical forms. If we look for Mexican American women in national women's rights organizations before 1940, we will not find very many. But we cannot therefore conclude that Mexican-origin women did not organize for their rights or have their own feminist histories. Montemayor was clearly a pathbreaker within LULAC. She and other women members of Ladies LULAC are part of the history of Mexican American civil rights movements. Their earlier efforts to establish women's authority within the civil rights movement paved the way for the later emergence of a Chicana movement.

The history of Mexican-origin women in voluntary organizations is a history largely untold.[1] Women's historians have studied women's organizations (where most women have historically organized) but have given little attention to organizations composed of both women and men and those

435

composed of Mexican-origin women.[2] In her recent book, *The Grounding of Modern Feminism*, historian Nancy Cott refers to those activities outside of electoral politics in which women participated as "voluntarist politics."[3] Cott's analysis has little relevance for Mexican-origin women who belonged to no national women's organizations until the early 1970s. In fact, the first national Chicana gathering occurred in 1971, although women had opportunities to congregate before then at national meetings and conventions of mutual aid, civil rights, and labor associations.[4]

Chicano studies scholars have rarely addressed women in organizations.[5] In particular, historians of Chicanos have yet to fully study women's participation in the League of United Latin American Citizens (LULAC). LULAC is the oldest Mexican American civil rights organization in the United States.[6] Founded in 1929 in Corpus Christi, Texas, by Mexican American men, the League quickly evolved into a statewide and then a national organization.[7] By 1940, LULAC had reached into New Mexico, Colorado, California, Arizona and Washington, D.C.

LULAC can be compared with the National Association for the Advancement of Colored People (NAACP). It is a middle-class organization that has diligently protected the civil rights of Mexican-descent people in the United States. In the 1930s, LULAC men filed the first class-action lawsuit against segregated public schools. They were also responsible for changing the classification of La Raza from "Mexican" to "white" in the 1940 U.S. census. LULAC also moved the Federal Employment Practices Commission (the first federal civil rights agency) to protect La Raza from employment discrimination. At the local level, LULAC desegregated schools, pools, theaters, housing, and real estate.[8]

In 1933, LULAC extended full membership privileges to women through gender-segregated chapters (or councils) called "Ladies LULAC," and women typically organized only with women until the 1960s.[9] Ladies LULAC became particularly important in Texas and New Mexico. The first Ladies Council was formed in 1933 in Alice, Texas, and in 1934 LULAC created the office of ladies organizer general (LOG) to organize women's chapters. By 1940 these chapters numbered twenty-six while men's totaled one hundred. In the 1990s, women constitute over 50 percent of LULAC's membership, and they helped elect the first female national president in 1994.

This essay analyzes gender politics in LULAC in the 1930s, assessing LULAC's ideology as it related to the family and addressing women's participation in LULAC. It focuses on LULAC feminist Alice Dickerson Montemayor, a member of Laredo's Ladies LULAC. I will discuss her activism and analyze her essays, which challenged the entrenched patriarchal nature of LULAC and of Mexican American society in the 1930s. At the time of her activism she was a wife, mother, worker, businesswoman, and middle-class woman. She was also a free-thinking, assertive, independent feminist who belonged to LULAC when patriarchal ideology was especially strong. It is important to note that her husband, Francisco Montemayor, Sr., was not a member of LULAC.[10]

Many view LULAC as a men's organization because its leadership has been overwhelming male.[11] Others believe that all women in LULAC were in ladies' auxiliaries.[12] In 1983 historian Marta Cotera argued that women took "a more subdued club woman reformist approach channeled through female auxiliary groups."[13] These auxiliaries were thought to be composed of wives. Still others believe all women participated in a sex-segregated Ladies LULAC. Others contend that for women, LULAC was "a social gathering for women to go drink coffee and get together."[14]

In sum, historians have hardly addressed Ladies LULAC. For instance, Julia Kirk Blackwelder's study of the depression in San Antonio, Texas, mentioned middle-class women's volunteerism but did not cite any Mexican-origin women's voluntary organizations other than Beneficiencia Mexicana.[15] Ladies LULAC, perhaps the largest Mexican American women's organization in the city (outside of unions), went unmentioned.[16] Richard A. García's *The Rise of the Mexican American Middle Class*, which addressed San Antonio and LULAC in the 1930s, overlooked the San Antonio Ladies LULAC, which had the largest membership in the state. He addressed LULAC as a male institution, discussing women only as wives and family members.[17] Arnoldo De León's brief treatment of Ladies LULAC in Houston in the 1950s should be praised.[18]

Mario T. García devoted a chapter to the League in *Mexican Americans: Leadership, Ideology, and Identity*, a book on Mexican American civil rights activism. He briefly addressed women as a group and identified several leaders. He emphasized the work of Ester Machuca, a ladies organizer general (LOG) in the 1930s; he mistakenly believed she was the first such organizer; in actuality, Estefana Valdez of Mission held that honor. García mentioned Dickerson Montemayor, but he did not explain her significance.[19]

Benjamin Márquez's *LULAC, The Evolution of a Mexican American Political Organization*, the only book-length survey of LULAC, offers several paragraphs on women. Though Márquez noted that women constituted 50 percent of the membership, he did not analyze women's historical participation.[20] Yet among those who built LULAC were women from every locale where the League existed. These women constituted a diverse group. Not all had a familial or sexual tie to a man in LULAC. Many participated in the League as single women, as married women whose husbands had no connection to LULAC, or as lesbians. Historically, the majority never participated in the ladies' auxiliaries; rather, they belonged to Ladies LULAC and, after 1960, to councils composed of women and men.

Among the ranks of LULAC were independent women, a few, like Alice Dickerson Montemayor, with feminist inclinations. Mexican American women had a distinctive feminist heritage that countered a virulent patriarchal heritage. In the 1930s ideologies about the family were typically patriarchal in the United States, in Mexico, and in Chicano society; LULAC reflected these three influences. The organization first revealed its patriarchal tendency when it excluded women in 1929, and its patriarchal ideology was clearly conveyed in *LULAC News*. Member J. Reynolds Flores expressed the typical sentiment about women's place in his 1932 essay, "How to Educate Our Girls," writing, "The foundation of society rests on the homes. The success of our homes rests on the wives. Therefore, first of all, teach our girls how to be successful wives. . . . Train them to do small things well and to delight in helping others, and instill constantly into their minds the necessity for sacrifice for others' pleasure as a means of soul development."[21]

Another LULAC publication, *Alma Latina*, a short-lived magazine for parents, included an essay titled "La Mujer." The author viewed women "como madres, como esposas, como hijas o como hermanas" (as mothers, as wives, as daughters, or as sisters), basing this description on Catholic doctrine, especially on the story of Adam and Eve where Adam represented *fuerza* (strength) and Eve *amor* (love).[22]

LULAC men generally placed women on a pedestal. In 1938 Leo Durán of the Corpus Christi men's council idealized "all mothers of Lulackers as the ones responsible and ever watchful of all Lulackers and the teachers of future generation that LULAC might start in all Latin homes."[23] A 1934 LULAC song, "To Our Ladies Councils," noted that "Ladies councils are our inspiration head and soul of our splendid LULAC."[24] But men made little effort to mobilize women into chapters.

One LULAC member provided a progressive stance on men's familial responsibility. An article entitled "Parents Are Fathers" in *Alma Latina* stated, "Fathers often leave all of the raising of the small child to the mothers. This isn't fair to any one concerned. It gives the mother too much to do, robs the child of father's influence, and leaves the father, in a sense childless."[25] It is unclear if the author was male or female. The article, however, was atypical of LULAC members' ideology.

LULAC men's gender ideology reflected the thought of México Texanos and other Chicanos, a borderlands people whose thought reflected a blend of U.S. and Mexican thought. Women in the United States obtained the vote in 1920, and Mexico offered them the vote in 1958. México Texanos, a product of two cultures and two nations, offered women full membership in LULAC (and thus the vote) in 1933. LULAC men were influenced by events in Mexico as reported by the Mexican and México Texano press. In 1929 *El Paladin*, another official LULAC organ, editorialized, "Es justa la aspiración de la mujer de nuestro Pais," favoring women's right to vote in Mexico and betraying the fact that the author still considered Mexico his country.[26] The essay suggests that LULAC men were influenced by women's suffrage in Mexico. But they were also influenced by patriarchal ideology in Spanish- and English-language newspapers in the United States. *La Prensa*, the only statewide Spanish-language newspaper, espoused this patriarchal ideology. Feminist writers were few.

In the 1930s few LULAC women espoused feminism. Besides Alice Dickerson Montemayor, only one other woman penned a feminist essay in *LULAC News* in the 1930s. Adela Sloss of San Juan, Texas, a high school graduate in 1927, was a member of one of several ladies auxiliaries that existed only briefly before Ladies LULAC was formed. In 1934 she wrote an essay entitled "Por Que en Muchos Hogares Latinos no Existe Verdadera Felicidad" (Why Most Homes are Unhappy). For Sloss, *la mujer* was heterosexual and married to a member of La Raza. Sloss challenged sexism in the home and male privilege. She wrote, "A la mujer Latina desde nina se le aprisiona" (Since childhood, Latinas are imprisoned) and "El hombre Latino tiene todos los privilegios y derechos" (Latino men have all the privileges and rights). She argued that there was happiness in European American homes because in the home "ella es la compañera del esposo y no la esclava" (she is the husband's companion and not a slave).[27] Too, through her life she championed civil rights as an orator, organizer, and newspaper essayist in the lower Rio Grande Valley in Texas. She continued to challenge patriarchal family ideology when she married. She raised children and reorganized traditional family life by using day care and involving her children in her political activities. Sloss was no prisoner of her home or marriage, though she found no support for her vision of family life in LULAC.[28]

Alice Dickerson Montemayor followed Sloss as a critic of LULAC's family ideology. A committed member, Montemayor was a woman of many "firsts." In 1937 she was the first woman elected to a national office not specifically designated for a woman, the position of second vice-president general; it was the third-highest post in the organization.[29] She was also the first woman to serve as an associate editor of *LULAC News* and the first person to write a charter to sponsor a Junior LULAC (youth) chapter. She was an ardent advocate for the inclusion of youth, including girls. Moreover, she was an avid supporter of more Ladies LULAC chapters. In short, Montemayor promoted the interests of middle-class Mexican American women, girls, and youth during her tenure in LULAC from 1936 to around 1940.

Born on 6 August 1902 in Laredo, Texas, Alice Dickerson (known as Alicia) was a woman of mixed heritage. She was born an only child to Manuela Barrera of Laredo and Irishman John Randolph Dickerson, a native of New Orleans. She was a descendant of one of the first twenty-eight families who settled Laredo in the 1750s; her grandmother was Juana Inez de la Cruz. John R. Dickerson had moved from New Orleans to San Antonio where he worked as a railroad engineer for the International and Great Northern Railway Company (now the Missouri Pacific). As an engineer, he helped build the railroad from Austin to San Antonio and brought the first passenger train from San Antonio to Laredo. Alicia's mother had worked as a seamstress out of her home before she married Dickerson.[30]

Because she was born and raised in Laredo on the Texas-Mexico border, Alicia grew up with a México Texano identity. She also claimed her indigenous and Irish heritage. Because she was part Irish, La Raza sometimes called her "gringa," although her brown color made her look like a mestiza (of Spanish and Indian descent). Unlike most of La Raza in the early twentieth century, she grew up in a bilingual home. Her command of English gave her an advantage over other México Texanos, while her mixed heritage also privileged her. Her middle-class status also distinguished her from most of La Raza in Laredo.[31]

What life experiences help explain Montemayor's feminism and her rise in LULAC? Her education and extracurricular activities prepared her for an active, meaningful adult life. She attended the private Catholic school, Colegio de Guadalupe (Guadalupe College, later called the Ursuline Academy). As a girl she constantly got in trouble because of her admittedly clownish behavior. At Laredo High School (now Martin High) she participated in the Glee Club, the Nike Literary Club, and the Science Club, and she was on the debating team. She joined the Library Club and served as an assistant librarian. During her junior and senior years, she wrote editorials for the *Laredo High School Journal*, contributed to the humor column, and reported girls' athletic activities. She also served as editor and columnist for *The Live Wire*, the student newspaper.[32]

Besides her intellectual preparation, Dickerson developed her physical abilities. She made the girls' volleyball, tennis, and basketball teams, serving as captain of the basketball team her junior and senior years. For four years the school selected her as "best girl athlete." These physical activities convinced her of girls' and women's capabilities.[33]

Dickerson's education made her an exception in the Mexican-origin community in Texas, especially for women. She graduated from high school in 1924 and attended night school at Laredo Business College for a year.[34] A high school education was rare for the working class and Mexican Americans in the 1920s. In the 1910s, compulsory education brought more children of Mexican descent into Texas schools, although often in separate schools. Those attending college were few; in 1930, 250 persons of Mexican origin were in college, most of them men.[35]

Barriers created by race and gender limited Dickerson's schooling, despite her desire for higher education. Southwest Teachers College in San Marcos accepted her but she was unable to leave home,[36] and Laredo had no college in the 1920s. (Later, when Laredo Junior College opened its doors in 1947, she registered for night school and attended for two years.[37]) Few of her intellectual influences are known; she read George Eliot and William H. Allen, author of "Women's Part in Government." Her role models through life would include Marie Curie, Amelia Earhart, Carry Nation, Frances Perkins, Eleanor Roosevelt, Helen Hayes, and Irene Dunne. Her Méxicana role model was Sor Juana Inez de la Cruz, the feminist nun and intellectual.[38]

After graduation, Dickerson considered four careers—lawyer, actress, author, and artist.[39] She first contemplated college and law school but two days before her high school graduation her father died, and she was "forced to earn her livelihood in order to support herself and her mother."[40] And she gave up thoughts of acting because, although she had belonged to the high school drama club, her mother believed that women on stage were not members of "decent society." She achieved her dreams of writing in the articles she produced for *LULAC News* in the 1930s— articles through which her legacy is known—but she published no books of poetry or prose during her lifetime. She realized her talent for art much later in life. In 1973, with an ill husband at home and at the urging of her son, she finally picked up a paintbrush. By 1980, she was an acclaimed folk artist in Texas known to her admirers as ADMonty, and she became the subject of a chapter in *Folk Art in Texas*. Chicana and Chicano artists embraced her as their own.[41] Though she never worked for pay as an artist, lawyer, actress, or author, she nonetheless left an imprint on the local community of Laredo.[42] Moreover, because of her work in LULAC, she impacted Texas and beyond.

Dickerson had been born into the middle class and her education provided employment in that sector. She worked at a local dry goods store while she attended Laredo Business College. Western Union employed her as desk clerk from 1924 to 1927, her first full-time job. After a short time at Western Union, she was made the supervisor of the messenger boys. On the job she met Francisco Montemayor of Nuevo Laredo, a book-keeper at Banco Longoria, and they married in 1927 when Dickerson was twenty-two. With her marriage, she quit her job and shortly after, in 1927, bore her first son, Francisco, Jr. Then, around 1930, she returned briefly to Western Union before taking on a supervisory job at Kress Restaurant.[43] Her employment patterns typified those of the Mexican-origin female middle class, whose occupations included teachers and clerks.[44]

In 1933 she became a social worker, a position that broadened her horizons. Traveling beyond Laredo, she encountered race discrimination. After taking a merit exam in Austin, she qualified as a caseworker for the Department of Public Welfare. During the depression, she worked in Laredo, in broader Webb County, and in Cotulla in adjacent La Salle County. When she arrived in Cotulla, the European American county judge refused to give her a key to her county courthouse office, and she worked under a tree for two weeks until he finally conceded. Even her clients discriminated against her; poor whites refused to reveal their financial circumstances to a "Meskin," and she was protected by a bodyguard. Still, in Cotulla she placed an estimated four hundred to five hundred Mexican Americans on the welfare rolls.[45]

During her fifteen-month stay in Cotulla, Montemayor challenged white privilege. She helped desegregate the county courthouse, which prohibited "Mexicans" on the second floor, personally escorting the first group to her upstairs office. While in Cotulla, she also questioned the practice of segregated masses at the Catholic Church, which had a 7 A.M. mass for "Mexicans" and a 9 A.M. mass for "whites."[46] Reminiscing in 1986, Montemayor expressed the greatest job satisfaction with her Cotulla job; there, she said she had "had to fight."[47]

In 1936 she opened Monty's Fashion Shop, a dress store in Laredo, a business that typified the kind a Mexican-origin woman might own, a small business in the service sector with a female clientele who purchased goods for themselves, the family, or the household. But apparently the dress store failed, and by September of 1936, she was heading the business office of the fashion department of the Montgomery Ward in Laredo.[48]

Alice Dickerson Montemayor as she appeared in the September 1937 issue of *LULAC News* as second vice-president general. (Courtesy Aurelio Montemayor, San Antonio, Texas.)

Several anecdotes about her personal life reveal a rebellious Alicia. Despite Dickerson's active life as a student, her mother wielded control over her, treating her like a "little princess." Beyond that, Catholic doctrine and family ideology mandated the "protection" of females, and young women were not to work outside of the home or to travel unaccompanied by a man. Thus Dickerson was prohibited from going out and visiting with others; and even during her courtship with Francisco Montemayor, a female cousin chaperoned her on a regular basis.[49] Perhaps these societal restrictions made Dickerson rebel.

In any event, she began to break from expectations. Although Francisco Montemayor's mother had asked her to wear the traditional white long wedding gown, the practical and rebellious Alice wore a suit appropriate for her California honeymoon. She also defied her mother-in-law's belief that a mixed marriage would not work. She challenged the idea that because she was part Irish, the marriage would result in divorce. Even so, the new bride told her mother-in-law, "I'm not guaranteeing I won't get a divorce if my husband doesn't treat me right."[50]

Montemayor joined civic life around 1937 when her then only child, Francisco, Jr., was in school. Her participation in public life paralleled many heterosexual women's traditional life cycle, which revolved around patterns of childbearing and child rearing. In 1936, Ladies Organizer

General Ester Machuca, a member of Ladies LULAC in El Paso, contacted Montemayor. Along with Minnie Zamora, Juanita Villarreal, Adelina Dominguez, Mrs. O. N. Lightner, and Mrs. A. R. Marulanda, Montemayor helped charter a council in Laredo. Husbands Arnulfo Zamora, J. G. Villarreal, and Fred O. Dominguez belonged to the local LULAC men's council, which had existed there since 1929.[51]

Membership was limited, fluctuating between seventeen and thirty-four, and excluded of working-class women. Members had to be recommended, and most had a high school education. Most were married homemakers, while others worked as secretaries for the city and county. Among those who were unmarried were Lucinda Coronado, Emma Hernández, Elvira García, Esperanza E. Treviño, and Elena Leal, probably all recent high school graduates.[52]

In the 1930s, Laredo Ladies LULAC was one of the most active councils. *LULAC News* noted, "What council in the League has shown the most activity since the beginning of the present fiscal year and has obtained results? Without hesitation we answer the Laredo Ladies Council No. 15."[53] The chapter encouraged women to vote, held citizenship classes, and urged members "to have aspirations to work away from home." Members helped Cotulla, Texas, women organize a chapter, no doubt through Montemayor's contacts there. The educational committee helped the mother of second-grader Roberto Moreno obtain justice for her son, whom teacher Joyce Williams had "severely whipped." The council also sponsored benefits for the Laredo orphanage, raised $250 for flood survivors, bought school supplies for poor Mexican-origin children, sponsored a column in Laredo's major newspaper, and published an edition of *LULAC News*. Delegates traveled to LULAC's annual national conventions out of town and sponsored Junior LULAC. Class defined their activism; there was no direct assistance to the working class and labor during these depression years.[54]

LULAC News reports indicate that Ladies LULAC largely worked independently of the Laredo men's council. It was definitely not an auxiliary. In a 1984 interview, Montemayor said, "[M]en's LULAC had nothing to do with us."[55] On two occasions when the two councils cosponsored events, the division of labor fell along gender lines. For instance, when the national president general visited from New Mexico in 1939, Montemayor chaired the banquet decoration committee to which only women belonged. Men were in charge of arrangements and guests, many of whom were political officials. On another occasion at a jointly sponsored ceremony in 1938, both councils "enjoyed refreshments served by the different committees of Ladies."[56]

The group also functioned as a social club. The chapter met on Friday nights (probably over dinner) and for a time met at a room in the Hamilton Hotel at 8 P.M. They held "just Lulac parties for good Lulac members," some of which were benefits. In March 1937 members entertained husbands with a dinner party, although not all were married and not all of the members' husbands were LULAC members.[57]

Montemayor was the first secretary of the Laredo council and was president from 1938 to 1939.[58] As secretary, she reported the chapter's activities to the *LULAC News* column "Around the Shield," which focused on local councils. She wrote, "We have always said and we still maintain that at the back of progress and success the ladies take a leading hand."[59] Because she was so diligent about sending in news, *LULAC News* staff member J. C. Machuca (the husband of Ester) took notice. Moreover, Fred O. Dominguez, who was from her hometown and could speak in her favor, served as an associate editor. Consequently, in June 1937 the *News* named Laredo Ladies LULAC as one of two outstanding LULAC chapters. This should be attributed to the council's activism, Montemayor's reports, and probably to the fact that the chapter sold ads for the *News* and increased the magazine's circulation.[60]

Montemayor soon garnered national attention. She was one of two Laredo Ladies council delegates to the national 1937 Houston and 1938 El Paso conventions. At Houston she was the only woman on the five-member finance committee. In 1937 the nominating committee, which consisted of one delegate from each council and was overwhelmingly male, named her to a national post. Albert Redwine of the El Paso's men's council nominated her. Montemayor was a member of the nominating committee but recalled being out of the room when the appointment by acclamation occurred; it took her by complete surprise. The news of her sudden rise in LULAC began to spread.[61]

Between 1937 and 1940, Montemayor held three national positions—second national vice-president general; associate editor of *LULAC News*, and director general of Junior LULAC.[62] The position of second vice-president was not gendered; indeed, the first person to fill the position was a man, Fidencio Guerra of McAllen, Texas. But from the time of Montemayor's ascension to that office in 1937 until the office was abolished in 1970 women continued to hold this post. Apparently, the position became defined by gender only after a woman held it. There is no evidence that women defined this position as their own.

Montemayor used her three positions to advocate for women and youth. As second vice-president she promoted the establishment of more ladies' councils in her columns, speeches, and letters.[63] As associate editor of *LULAC News*, she also advocated for women, penning a stinging, unsigned editorial titled "Son Muy Hombres(?)."[64] Two sexist incidents moved her to do so. An unidentified male LULACker had written a national officer, "I hope that President Ramón Longoria will get well soon. There are those of us who hate to be under a woman," a clear expression of fear that Montemayor would became national president. The second incident also involved a national officer, presumably President Ramón Longoria of Harlingen, who ignored three letters from El Paso Ladies LULAC, eventually prompting the group to withdraw from the League "rather than create trouble and friction." (The chapter later reorganized.) According to Montemayor, the inaction of the national office could be attributed to men who "are cowardly and unfair, ignorant and narrow minded." In her written critique of the incident, she appealed to the LULAC and United States constitutions. She concluded her essay by asking any member to step forward and write an article favoring the suppression of ladies' councils and their denial of equal rights.[65]

The third national position held by Montemayor was the position of director general, Junior LULAC. In 1937 Mrs. Charles Ramirez of San Antonio's Ladies LULAC developed the idea for Junior LULACs and sponsored a resolution to create the youth chapters. Ramirez and Mrs. Santos Herrera organized the first Junior LULAC, but Montemayor was the primary force behind the youth chapters. In August 1938 Montemayor began writing a series of essays in *LULAC News* encouraging senior councils to organize youth. Besides serving as a local sponsor, she penned several essays to foster their organization after she was no longer an associate editor or an official youth organizer, and she wrote the first charter for a youth chapter.[66]

Around March 1937 Montemayor organized the second Junior council at her house, and it proved the most active chapter. Its first president was Ezequiel D. Salinas whose father was a LULAC member. In March 1938 officers included Perfecto Solis, president; Delia Davila, vice-president; Fernando Salinas, secretary; Gloria E. Benavides, assistant secretary; and Francisco I. Montemayor Jr. (Montemayor's son), assistant treasurer. Most of the twenty-two members were children of LULAC members. Their ages ranged between nine and fifteen. These Junior LULACkers wrote articles for *LULAC News* and worked on raising funds for a drum and bugle corps.[67]

Montemayor recruited both girls and boys for Junior LULAC. She believed this necessary so "by the time they are ready to join the Senior Councils they will abandon the egotism and petty jealousies so common today among our Ladies' and Men's councils." Her son Francisco echoed his mother's sentiments, writing for the *LULAC News*, "We have heard that there is a Junior Council of 'just girls.' Heck, we don't like that. We [would] rather have a mixed group like we have in Laredo, because we feel like there is nothing like our SISTERS." He warned against a majority of girls and rallied the boys to prevent this.[68]

Montemayor believed that leadership training was necessary to the formation of good citizens and future LULAC senior members. From Junior LULAC would come "good Americans" who would be capable public servants, skillful debaters, knowledgeable citizens, and literate, independent thinkers. Montemayor taught the Juniors debate and acting skills every Sunday. She also took five Junior officers to the El Paso national convention.[69]

Montemayor's feminism even affected the youth group. In 1938 Laredo Junior LULAC member Leonor Montes rallied for a girl president. She wrote, "Now that the publicity chairman is of the "nervier" sex but HOW ABOUT A GIRL PRESIDENT this coming term? We want a girl president! We want a girl president! RAH! RAH! RAH! BOOM!" Montemayor's son called Montes "the little Monty of the Juniors" for "she

Laredo Junior LULAC Council No. 1 (1939). Alice Dickerson Montemayor, supervisor, back row, fifth from left; Francisco I. Montemayor, Jr., second row, first on left; and Leonor Montes, second row, sixth from left. (Courtesy Aurelio Montemayor, San Antonio, Texas.)

too is always wanting for the girls to outshine the boys." He warned her this could not be done "aunque somos pollos, pero nosotros mandamos" (although we are young, we are still in charge).[70]

The organization of the youth also suggested women's primary responsibility. In 1943 when George Garza of Laredo reorganized the Juniors, he changed the focus from preteens to teenagers, and thereby removed the "babysitting" aspect of the work. Nevertheless, most of the Junior LULAC sponsors continued to be ladies' councils. Men's councils, on the other hand, typically sponsored Boy Scout troops, which coexisted with the Junior councils.[71]

Besides challenging the patriarchal nature of LULAC's method of political mobilization by including women and children, Alice Montemayor also challenged patriarchal ideology through her essays. She wrote more articles for the *News* than any other woman in the history of LULAC, typically signing her name Mrs. F. I. Montemayor. She also penned several essays without signing her name.[72]

Among youth and adults, Montemayor stressed independent thinking. She wrote, "Having the ability to think for oneself and forming an opinion of your own is a necessity in our organization." She asked LULAC to recall the 1938 national LULAC election and asked, "Did we not have a hard time to think for ourselves about the candidates? Did not some of us have the desire to influence our fellow members to vote our own way?"[73]

"We Need More Ladies Councils" was her first essay. In it she pointed to many inactive LULAC councils and asked women to come to the rescue. "Sister LULACS," she wrote, "our brothers need a good big dose of competition." She noted that there were seventy-one men's and fifteen women's chapters but only twenty-six and four, respectively, had been represented at the annual convention. Competition with men became a rallying point for Montemayor: "Now that our brothers have given the women a chance to show them what we can do, let all the Ladies Councils that are active now try and revive the Dormant Ladies Councils, and the Ladies Organizers and Governors try and get more Ladies Council [sic] to join our League so that we may prove to our brothers that we can accomplish more than they can."[74] She believed men engendered this competition because of their allegations that they were superior to women.

But Montemayor also believed in the fundamental superiority of women. In "A Message from Our Second Vice-President General," she asked women to join the "LULAC family." Women, she believed, had intuition. "Women wish to mother men just because it is their natural instinct and because they see into the men's helplessness." Women also had common sense and were "able to see at a glance and penetrate into in a second what most men would not see with a searchlight or a telescope in an eternity." She added, "Women are the possessors of a super logic. They hang to the truth and work with more tenacity than our brothers." She concluded that LULAC would not flourish until the women got involved to help the men.[75]

Montemayor also penned "Women's Opportunity in LULAC," which proclaimed, "The idea that 'the women's place is in the home' passed out of the picture with hoop skirts and bustles, and now it is recognized that women hold as high a position in all walks of life as do the men." She noted that among the Greeks and Romans "the girl was not trained for public life, as that was left for the boys and men. She occupied no place in the activities of her country." She added that "no thought was given to the girls in anything other than the keeping of the homes." Rejecting woman's place as "entirely in the home," she defined women's place to be "in that position where she can do the most for the furthering of her fellow women." She called on "women LULAC" to "realize that it is now time to get into our League, and stay in it."[76]

The editorial "Son Muy Hombres (?)" appeared in March 1938. Despite the question mark, Montemayor did not doubt that machismo was prevalent in LULAC, but she had faith in men's ability to change. She noted there "has been some talk about suppressing the Ladies Councils of our League or at least to relegate them to the category of auxiliaries." She attributed this reaction to the "aggressive attitude which some of our women members have adopted." She noted that men "fear that our women will take a leading role in the evolution of our League; that our women might make a name for themselves in their activities; that our MUY HOMBRES (?) might be shouldered from their position as arbiters of our League."[77]

Montemayor also noticed that gender lines were drawn on these issues. She noted, "What surprises us mostly is the attitude assumed by some of our General Officers and members. While some of them may not be in complete accord with the move, at least they countenance it. Others are noncommittal and remain painfully silent."[78] Male bonding and collusion were in effect, and *LULAC News* includes no articles written in support of Montemayor.

"When . . . and Then Only," another of Montemayor's articles, emphasized the necessity of organizing women and youth. She noted that "God gave Eve to Adam, because Adam was lonesome and needed a mate." "Back of the success of any man, there is a woman," she said, and "women are God's MOST PRECIOUS GIFT to MEN, therefore let's organize more Ladies Councils. Ladies, let's organize more Junior LULAC Councils, let's train our children." For Montemayor, heterosexuality was commanded by God, women were to assist their mates, and bear and raise children.[79]

Competition and conflict could sometimes characterize relations between men's and women's councils. The February 1937 *News* hinted at a conflict in Laredo when it mentioned that the chapter had "weathered a storm" of local character, but the article did not detail the nature of the storm "since such things happen in the best regulated families."[80] In a 1984 interview, Montemayor recalled that the Laredo LULAC men "had no use for us . . . they didn't want us." In fact, according to Montemayor, the men "just hated" her, especially Ezequiel Salinas of Laredo, the national president from 1939 to 1940; the men, she claimed, refused to vote for her at the national conventions.[81]

Still, Montemayor believed that she had the respect of some men's councils.[82] Indeed, she must have had their support because in 1937 she participated in the Corpus Christi ceremony honoring the deceased Ben Garza, LULAC's first president. And she optimistically believed she had the support of men throughout Texas. She could count among her allies J. C. Machuca, San Antonio attorney Alonso S. Perales, Brownsville attorney J. T. Canales, and Austin educator Dr. Carlos Castañeda. She also corresponded with San Antonio attorney Gus García. All of these supporters, however, were atypical LULAC members, all college graduates and well traveled.[83] LULAC's dismal record of gender politics suggests that Laredo men's attitude was the typical male sentiment.

After April 1940, Montemayor's name is absent from *LULAC News*, perhaps because of the temporary decline of LULAC, perhaps because of repression from macho LULACkers, or perhaps because of changes in Montemayor's family life. The league witnessed growth and expansion in the 1930s, but World War II proved disruptive to organizing efforts. Like men's councils, Ladies LULAC declined. National LULAC reorganized in 1945; ten men's councils attended the annual convention that year but only Albuquerque represented women.[84]

In 1943 the Montemayors adopted a son, Aurelio, adding new familial responsibilities. And in the mid-forties Francisco Montemayor, Jr., who was attending Texas A&M University, died in an accident.[85] For the next forty years Alice Dickerson Montemayor gave her energies to community activities in Laredo, dying there in 1989.[86]

Without a doubt, Alice Montemayor left her mark. As early as June 1937 *LULAC News* wrote, "No wonder she has been cussed and discussed, talked about, lied about, lied to, boycotted, and almost hung, but she claims she has stayed in there, first because she is a LULACker, and next because she wanted to see what the heck would happen next."[87] A Junior LULACker noted that she seemed like a "hard-boiled supervisor" but was really "the swellest dame."[88]

LULAC's method of political mobilization, its theory of political empowerment, and its familial ideology were patriarchal. Montemayor's activism and ideology challenged male privilege. She argued that women and children be mobilized by LULAC to empower La Raza. She defined women's place as extending outside the home and helping other women.

Her radical voice, however, proved a lonely one, and her local chapter did not promote her vision as a collective body, refusing directly to challenge male privilege or battle gender segregation. Montemayor may have influenced Laredo women and women in the national organization, but there is no evidence she attempted to garner their support for a united front. According to her son Aurelio, she was highly individualistic. By her own report, she was "very independent. Nobody tells me what to do. [But] I can take always advice from people I think are intelligent."[89]

What were the limitations of Montemayor's vision? She attacked male privilege and power but did not question the family, marriage, or religion as oppressive institutions. Nor did she question separate councils for men and women in LULAC, although she insisted on integrated youth councils. Segregated councils allowed her—and other women—to thrive in a distinctive women's political culture where they learned to organize, dealt with issues they deemed important, and socialized with other women in a safe, nonsexist environment.

Montemayor did not challenge the division of labor within the home, viewing women largely as heterosexuals and mothers. According to one of her supporters, "Her hobby is housekeeping, making that 'tenable' husband of hers, as well as her sonnyboy as comfortable and happy as possible."[90] The rearing of children she saw as women's responsibilities, a view she extended to the public domain through Junior LULAC.

Montemayor believed women superior to men and, an optimist, believed men could change their errant ways. She believed women should not quit LULAC when sexism surfaced. She believed in cooperation and flatly rejected notions of male superiority: "I think a woman can do a better job than a man in many instances," she said.[91]

How did Montemayor view LULAC and her place in the orgainization? She was a staunch advocate of the League, arguing that it could "educate our race and make better American citizens out of every Latin American." It was "as much a vital organ to the Latin American women, as it is to the Latin American men," she said, and to the end, she considered LULAC the most important organization in which she had ever been involved.[92] About her role in LULAC, she reminisced, "I was a very controversial person. Many men didn't want any ladies involved in LULAC."[93] She said, "The men just hated me . . . I guess men don't think women can do anything."[94]

As seen through articles in *LULAC News*, Alice Dickerson Montemayor introduced progressive ideas to LULAC, decrying women's oppression decades before the Chicana feminist movement. She challenged the notion of women's place as the home and by example showed the diligent work women were capable of in public and political life. She questioned the myth of male superiority and argued that women were as competent as men, if not superior. She identified machismo in action and fought to eradicate it through informed feminist reasoning. While she exhibited a feminist consciousness, she also embodied a female consciousness in her concern for children and family.

By example, Montemayor disproves assumptions about women in LULAC, about wives, and about members of Ladies LULAC councils. Nevertheless, she was an anomaly in the history of LULAC. She was unusual in that she was openly feminist long before other Chicana feminists.

Notes

I would like to thank Norma Cantú for conducting an interview for me and Aurelio Montemayor for clarifying several issues. The Rare Books staff at the Nettie Lee Benson Latin American Collection at the University of Texas at Austin should also be thanked. A version of this paper was presented at the Texas Women's History Conference sponsored by the Texas State Historical Association in Austin, Texas, on 5 October 1990.

1. Studies focusing on women include Christine Marin, "La Asociación Hispano-Americana de Madres y Esposas," *Renato Rosaldo Lecture Series Monograph* 7, 1989–1990 (Tucson: Mexican American Studies and Research Center, 1985), 5–18; Thomas E. Kreneck, "The Letter from Club Chapultepec," *The Houston Review* 3, no. 2 (Summer 1981): 268–71; Mary Pardo, "Mexican American Grassroots Community Activists, Mothers of East Los Angeles," in this volume; Emma M. Pérez, "'A La Mujer': A Critique of the Partido Liberal Mexicano's Gender Ideology" in *Between Borders: Chicana/Mexicana History*, ed. Adelaída del Castillo (Encino, Calif.: Floricanto Press, 1990), 459–82; María Linda Apodaca, "They Kept the Home Fires Burning: Mexican American Women and Social Change" (Ph.D. dissertation, University of California at Irvine, 1994); Margaret Rose, "Gender and Civic Activism in Mexican American Barrios in California: The CSO from 1948–1962," in *Not June Cleaver* (Philadelphia: Temple University Press, 1994). See also Cynthia E. Orozco, "Beyond Machismo, La Familia, and Ladies Auxiliaries: A Historiography of Mexican-Origin Women in Voluntary Associations and Politics in the United States, 1870–1990," *Renato Rosaldo Lecture Series Monograph* 10 1992–1993 (Tucson: Mexican American Studies and Research Center, 1995), 37–78.

2. Karen J. Blair failed to list Chicana organizations in her recent bibliography of women's organizations. Karen J. Blair, *The History of American Women's Voluntary Organizations, 1810–1960: A Guide to Sources* (Boston: G. K. Hall, 1989).

3. Nancy Cott, *The Grounding of Modern Feminism* (New Haven, Conn.: Yale University Press, 1989).

4. Marta P. Cotera, *Diosa y Hembra: The History and Heritage of Chicanas* (Austin, Tex.: Information Systems Development, 1976).

5. Key studies, all of which are male-centered, include Kaye Lynn Briegel, "Alianza Hispano Americano, 1894–1965: The Mexican-American Fraternal Insurance Society" (Ph.D. dissertation, University of Southern California, 1974); Juan Gómez Quiñones, *Sembradores, Ricardo Flores Magón y El Partido Liberal Mexicano: A Eulogy and Critique* (Los Angeles: Aztlán Publications, Chicano Studies Center, University of California, Los Angeles, 1973); José E. Limón, "El Primer Congreso Mexicanista de 1911: A Precursor to Contemporary Chicanismo," *Aztlán* 5, no. 1–2 (1974): 85–118; José Hernández, *Mutual Aid for Survival: The Case of the Mexican American* (Malabar, Fla: Krieger, 1983); Julie Lenninger Pycior, "La Raza Organizes: Mutual Aid Societies in San Antonio, 1915–1930" (Ph.D. dissertation, University of Notre Dame, 1979); Richard A. García, *The Rise of the Mexican American Middle Class* (College Station: Texas A&M Press, 1991); Mario T. García, *Mexican Americans: Leadership, Ideology, and Identity* (New Haven, Conn.: Yale University Press, 1989); Carl Allsup, *The American G.I. Forum: Origins and Evolution* (Austin: Center for Mexican American Studies, University of Texas at Austin, 1982); Henry A. J. Ramos, *A People Forgotten, A Dream Pursued: The History of the American G.I. Forum, 1948–72* (n.p.: American G.I. Forum of the U.S., 1982?); Liliana Urrutia, "An Offspring of Discontent: The Asociación Nacional México-Americana, 1949–1954," *Aztlán* 15, no. 2 (Spring 1984): 177–84; Kaye Briegel, "Alianza Hispano Americano and Some Civil Rights Cases in the 1950s" in *An Awakened Minority: The Mexican Americans*, ed. Manuel Servín (Beverly Hills, Calif.: Glencoe Press, 1970), 174–87; Ricardo Romo, "George I. Sánchez and the Civil Rights Movement: 1940–1960," *La Raza Law Journal* 1, no 3 (Fall 1986): 342–69; Guadalupe San Miguel, Jr., *"Let All of Them Take Heed," Mexican Americans and the Campaign for Educational Equality in Texas, 1910–1981* (Austin: University of Texas Press, 1987); Ignacio M. García, *United We Win: The Rise and Fall of La Raza Unida Party* (Tucson: Mexican American Studies & Research Center, University of Arizona, 1989); and Ricardo Romo, "Southern California and the Origins of Latino Civil Rights Activism," *Western Legal History* 3, no. 2 (Summer-Fall 1990).

6. On LULAC, see Oliver Douglas Weeks, "The League of United Latin American Citizens: A Texas-Mexican Civic Organization," *Southwestern Political and Social Science Quarterly* 10, no. 3 (December 1929): 257–78; Edward Garza, "LULAC: League of United Latin American Citizens" (master's thesis, Southwest Texas State Teachers College, 1951); Moisés Sandoval, *Our Legacy: The First Fifty Years* (Washington D.C.: LULAC, 1979); San Miguel, *"Let All of Them"*; Arnoldo De León, *Ethnicity in the Sunbelt: A History of Mexican Americans in Houston* (Houston: Mexican American Studies, University of Houston, 1989); Mario T. García, *Mexican Americans*; Richard A. García, *Rise of the Mexican American Middle Class*; Benjamin Márquez, *LULAC, The Evolution of a Mexican American Political Organization* (Austin: University of Texas Press, 1993).

7. LULAC was organized in 1929 with a national vision. When it expanded outside of Texas, members considered LULAC a national association. The 1939 constitution referred to the organization as a national entity and in the early 1940s the U.S. government recognized LULAC as a voice for the Mexican and Mexican American population in the United States. See "The Constitution of the League of United Latin American Citizens," *LULAC News*, July 1939, George I. Sánchez Papers, Nettie Lee Benson Latin American Collection, University of Texas at Austin (hereafter BLAC). See also "Showdown Expected This Week in Shell Walkout Threat," *Houston Press*, 23 April 1945, folder: Adequacy of Housing, box 454 (Tension Files), Federal Employment Practices Commission, National Archives. Most of the *LULAC News* can be found in the LULAC Archive at BLAC.

8. Cynthia E. Orozco, "The Origins of the League of United Latin American Citizens (LULAC) and the Mexican American Civil Rights Movement in Texas with an Analysis of Women's Political Participation in a Gendered Context, 1910–1929" (Ph.D. dissertation, University of California at Los Angeles, 1992). See Mario T. García, "Mexican Americans and the Politics of Citizenship: The Case of El Paso, 1936," *New Mexico Historical Review* 59 (April 1984): 187–204; Emilio Zamora, "The Failed Promise of Wartime Opportunity for Mexicans in the Texas Oil Industry," *Southwestern Historical Quarterly* 95 (January 1992): 323–50; Márquez, *LULAC*; and San Miguel, *"Let All of Them."*

9. According to Sandoval, "In the beginning, LULAC was a man's organization. The persons who gathered to found the League were all men." Sandoval, *Our Legacy*, 70. But women and girls attended the constitutional convention (considered the first annual convention) on 18–19 May 1929. Their names are available in a translated typescript of "The Convention Held in This Port on the 18th and 19th of This Month Was a Tremendous Success," *El Paladin*, 24 May 1929, Oliver Douglas Weeks Papers, BLAC.

10. LULAC recognized Montemayor twice in the late 1930s with a *News* cover page and articles about her. See "Our Second Vice-President General," *LULAC News*, September 1937, and the special women's issue in May 1939, especially the article by Esperanza E. Treviño, "Mrs. F. I. Montemayor." See also Cynthia E. Orozco, "Alice Dickerson Montemayor," in *New Handbook of Texas* (Austin: Texas State Historical Association, 1996).

According to the Montemayors' son, Aurelio Montemayor, his father was not politically disposed to joining LULAC. Moreover, as resident alien, Franscisco Montemayor, Sr., was not officially qualified to join the orgainization, even though some Mexican citizens did. Phone conversation with Aurelio Montemayor, 29 August 1995, San Antonio, Texas.

11. Lillian Gutiérrez, "LULAC—A Vehicle for Meeting the Political Challenge," *Intercambios Femeniles* 2, no. 3 (Autumn 1984): 9–10.

12. For instance, see María Berta Guerra, "The Study of LULAC" in which she refers to McAllen Ladies LULAC council as a women's council and as an auxiliary. Undergraduate paper, 1979, Río Grande Valley Collection, University of Texas-Pan American. Ladies' auxiliaries were only one form of women's historical participation in LULAC; the auxiliaries existed primarily from 1932 to 1933.

13. Marta Cotera, "Brief Analysis of the Political Role of Hispanas in the United States," paper presented for the Women of Color Institute, Washington D.C., November 1983, BLAC; Marta Cotera, "Hispana Political Tradition," *Intercambios Femeniles* 2, no. 3 (Autumn 1984): 9.

14. Oral History Transcript, José A. Estrada interview with Belen B. Robles, 26–27 April 1976, 9, Institute of Oral History, University of Texas at El Paso.

15. Julia Kirk Blackwelder, *Women of the Depression: Caste and Culture in San Antonio, 1929–1939* (College Station: Texas A&M Press, 1984). Blackwelder made little use of *La Prensa*, the most important Spanish-language newspaper in San Antonio and the state of Texas, or of *LULAC News*.

16. See Cynthia E. Orozco, "League of United Latin American Citizens," "Ladies LULAC," in *New Handbook of Texas*, and Cynthia E. Orozco, "League of United Latin American Citizens," in *Reader's Companion to U.S. Women's History*, ed. Wilma Mankiller, Gwendolyn Mink, Marysa Navarro, Barbara Smith, and Gloria Steinem (Boston: Houghton Mifflin, forthcoming).

17. Richard A. García, *Rise of the Mexican American*, xvi. Unfortunately, Richard García did not integrate his research on women into his book. See also Richard A. García, "The Making of the Mexican American Mind, San Antonio, Texas, 1929–1941: A Social and Intellectual History of an Ethnic Community" (Ph.D. dissertation, University of California at Irvine, 1980); Richard A. García, "Class, Consciousness, and Ideology: The Mexican Community of San Antonio," *Aztlán* 9 (Fall 1978): 23–70; Richard A. García, "The Mexican American Mind: The Product of the 1930s," in *History, Culture, and Society in the 1980s*, ed. Mario T. García, et. al. (Ypsilanti, Mich.: Bilingual Review Press, 1983), 67–94; Richard García, "Mexican Women in San Antonio, Texas: A View of Three Worlds," paper delivered at the Pacific Historical Branch of the American Historical Association, 1980, Los Angeles; "Around the LULAC Shield" *LULAC News*, March 1938.

18. Arnoldo De León, *Ethnicity in the City: A History of Mexican Americans in Houston* (Houston: Mexican American Studies, University of Houston, 1989).

19. Mario T. García, *Mexican Americans*. García emphasized the role of Machuca because LULAC itself has mistakenly recognized her as the first ladies organizer general and a more significant figure than Montemayor. Moreover, he conducted much of his research in El Paso, and both the subject and author are natives of that community. See "First Ladies Organizer General," *LULAC*, March 1979 (*LULAC* was a new title for *LULAC News*.) This special issue on women,

the second such issue in LULAC history, featured Machuca on the cover. See also Cynthia E. Orozco, "Ester Machuca," in *New Handbook of Texas*.

20. Marquez, *LULAC*, 93.

21. J. Reynolds Flores, "How to Educate Our Girls," *LULAC News*, December 1931.

22. "La Mujer," *Alma Latina*, 1, no. 3 (April 1932), Paul S. Taylor Collection, Bancroft Library, University of California at Berkeley (hereafter PSTC, BL).

23. "Around the LULAC Shield," *LULAC News*, February 1938.

24. "To Our Ladies Councils," *LULAC News*, May 1934.

25. "Parents Are Fathers," *Alma Latina* 1, no. 3 (April 1932), PSTC, BL. "N. Aguilar and Son" of San Antonio served as editors and publishers of *Alma Latina*.

26. "Es Justa la Aspiración de la Mujer de Nuestro Pais," *El Paladin*, 25 October 1929, Chicano Studies Research Center, UCLA.

27. Adela Sloss, "Por Que en Muchos Hogares Latinos No Existe Verdadera Felicidad," *LULAC News*, March 1934, PSTC, BL.

28. See also Adela Sloss Vento, *Alonso S. Perales, His Struggle for the Rights of Mexican Americans* (San Antonio, Tex.: Artes Graficas, 1979); and Cynthia E. Orozco, "Adela Sloss Vento," unpublished manuscript.

29. *LULAC News*, March 1937. Fidencio Guerra of McAllen held the position from 1936 to 1937. On the Guerra family, see Evan Anders, *Boss Rule in South Texas* (Austin: University of Texas Press, 1982).

30. Norma Cantú videotaped interview with Alice Dickerson Montemayor, 26 January 1986, Laredo, Texas; "Our Second Vice-President General," *LULAC News*, September, 1937; Andre Guererro interview with Alice Dickerson Montemayor, January 1983, Alice Dickerson Montemayor Collection (hereafter ADMC), BLAC; Norma Cantú interview with Alice Dickerson Montemayor, with questions prepared by Cynthia E. Orozco, 24 January 1984. Manuela Barrera was the granddaughter of Don Desiderio de la Cruz and Doña Apolonia Reyes, who helped found Laredo. "Our Second Vice-President General." Montemayor referred to her mother as a "clothes designer."

31. "Alicia D. Montemayor: Young at 82," *Laredo Morning Times*, 15 July 1984, ADMC, BLAC; Phone conversation by author with Aurelio Montemayor, 15 June 1989, San Antonio, Texas; Guerrero interview.

32. "Our Second Vice-President General"; Cantú interview, 24 January 1984; Guerrero interview.

33. "Our Second Vice-President General"; Cantú interview, 24 January 1984.

34. Guerrero interview.

35. See San Miguel, "Let All of Them Take Heed"; H. T. Manuel, *The Education of Mexican and Spanish-Speaking Children in Texas* (Austin, Tex.: Fund for Research in the Social Sciences, 1930), p. 106

36. Cantú videotaped interview, 26 January 1986.

37. Ibid.; Kathy Ariana Vincent, "'Monty' Montemayor: Portrait of an Artist," *Arriba*, 1980. *Arriba* is a Chicano arts and business newspaper in Austin, Texas.

38. Mrs. F. I. Montemayor, "Women's Opportunity in LULAC," *LULAC News*, December 1937; Mrs. F. I. Montemayor, "Let's Organize Junior Councils," *LULAC News*, August 1938; phone conversation by author with Aurelio Montemayor, 29 August 1995, San Antonio. In 1937 *LULAC News* reported that she read educational books in her spare time and directed "all her efforts towards giving her son the advantages of an education." "Our Second Vice-President General."

39. "Alicia D. Montemayor," *San Antonio Express News*, 28 October 1979, Vertical Files, Institute of Texas Cultures Library, San Antonio.

40. Montemayor told Andre Guerrero that her mother prohibited her from leaving Laredo to go to college. "Our Second Vice-President General"; Veronica Salazar, "Alicia D. Montemayor," *San Antonio Express News*, 28 October 1979; Cantú videotaped interview, 26 January 1986.

41. *San Antonio Express News*, 28 October 1979; *Laredo Morning Times*, 15 July 1984; Agueta Canales and Lauro Canales, "A Tribute to Admonty," ca. 1979; Amy Dawes, "Vibrant Artist,

Vibrant Works," *Laredo Morning Times*, ca. 1988, ADMC, BLAC. Montemayor's son Aurelio gave her paint for Mother's Day in 1976. Vincent, "Monty Montemayor"; Sandra Jordan, "Alice Dickerson Montemayor," in *Folk Artists of Texas*, ed. Francis Edward Abernethy (Dallas: Southern Methodist University Press, 1985), 184–87. Montemayor was considered a Chicana folk artist and the inventory to her collection at the Benson refers to her as "Chicana Folk Artist." She expressed discomfort with the term "Chicana" but looked favorably on the Chicano movement. "Materials Related to the Paintings and Art of Alice Dickerson Montemayor, Chicana Folk Artist of Laredo Texas"; Guerrero interview.

42. Montemayor's greatest imprint on Laredo was not her work in LULAC or in art, but as a local community builder. She worked as the school registrar at Christian Junior High School for sixteen years, from 1956 to 1972. She was also active in her parish, Our Lady of Guadalupe, where she played the organ, organized the first choir, trained altar boys, taught catechism classes, and helped at church jamaicas. Salazar, "Alicia D. Montemayor."

43. "Our Second Vice-President General"; *San Antonio Express News*, 28 October 1979. This article reports her first (presumably full-time) job with Western Union.

44. Vicki L. Ruiz, "Working for Wages: Mexican Women in the Southwest, 1930–1980," Working Paper #19 (Tucson, Ariz.: Southwest Institute for Research on Women, 1984).

45. Cantú videotaped interview, 26 January 1986; *San Antonio Express News*, 28 October 1979. Montemayor set up three apple crates under a tree to conduct her work. The San Antonio newspaper noted that two other Mexican Americans had been sent to Cotulla "but were not accepted because they were Mexican-Americans."

46. Phone conversation by author with Aurelio Montemayor, 15 June 1989.

47. Cantú videotaped interview, 26 January 1986.

48. "Around the LULAC Shield, Laredo Ladies Council No. 15," *LULAC News*, December 1936; J. T. Canales Collection, John Conner Museum, Texas A&I University, Kingsville; "Around the Shield, Laredo, Ladies Council No. 15," *LULAC News*, February 1937.

49. "Our Second Vice-President General"; Guerrero interview; Cantú videotaped interview, 26 January 1986.

50. *Laredo Morning Times*, 15 July 1984.

51. "Outstanding Councils of the League, Laredo Ladies Council No. 15," *LULAC News*, June 1937; "Around the LULAC Shield, Laredo Ladies Council No. 15," *LULAC News* July 1937; "Our Second Vice-President General." The first names of some of these women were not readily available.

52. Cantú interview, 24 January 1984; "Around the LULAC Shield, Laredo Ladies Council No. 15," *LULAC News*, December 1936.

53. "Around the LULAC Shield, Laredo Ladies Council No. 15," *LULAC News*, December 1936.

54. Montemayor did not vote on a Democratic or Republican ticket; she was an independent. Cantú interview, 24 January 1984; "Outstanding Councils of the League, Laredo Ladies Council No. 15," *LULAC News*, June 1937.

55. Cantú interview, 24 January 1984.

56. "President General and the Three Laredo Councils," *LULAC News*, December 1938; "Around the LULAC Shield, Laredo Ladies LULAC No. 15," *LULAC News*, February 1937 and August 1938.

57. Cantú interview, 24 January 1984; "Around the LULAC Shield," *LULAC News*, March 1937, December 1936, February 1937, and July 1937.

58. "Around the Shield, Laredo, Ladies Council No. 15," *LULAC News*, February 1937. According to the July 1937 *LULAC News* issue, Miss Elena Leal had replaced Montemayor as secretary for 1937–38. See "Around the LULAC Shield, Laredo Ladies Council No. 15," *LULAC News*, July 1937 and August 1938.

59. "Around the LULAC Shield, Laredo Ladies Council No. 15," *LULAC News*, March 1937.

60. "Outstanding Councils of the League, Laredo Ladies Council No. 15," *LULAC News*, June 1937 and March 1937.

61. "Outstanding Councils of the League, Laredo Ladies Council No. 15," *LULAC News*, June 1937; "Minutes of the Tenth Annual Convention of the League of Latin American Citizens," *LULAC News*, July 1938; "Convention Proceedings, Minutes of the Ninth Annual General Convention of the LULAC held in Houston, Texas, June 5th & 6th 1937," *LULAC News*, July 1937; Cantú videotaped interview, 26 January 1986. A nominating committee, not a general election, selected officers. See "Convention Proceedings," *LULAC News*, July 1937, and "Our Second Vice-President General."

62. No title (list of officers, 1939–40), *LULAC News*, July 1939.

63. "We Need More Ladies Councils," *LULAC News*, July 1937. The article is unsigned but written by Montemayor. See also Mrs. F. I. Montemayor, "A Message from Our Second Vice-President General," *LULAC News*, September 1937, and Mrs. F. I. Montemayor, "Echoes of the Installation of Officers of Council No. 1, Corpus Christi, Texas," *LULAC News*, December 1937.

64. "Son Muy Hombres (?)" (editorial), *LULAC News*, March 1938.

65. Ibid.

66. Garza, "LULAC," 24; "Special Convention Minutes, Minutes of the Special Convention Held in Laredo, Texas, February 20, 1938," *LULAC News*, December 1937; "Around the LULAC Shield, Laredo Junior Council No. 1," *LULAC News*, February 1938; Francisco I. Montemayor, Jr., "The Laredo Junior Council," *LULAC News*, December 1938. Mrs. Charles Ramirez became the ladies organizer general for Junior LULAC from 1937 to 1938. Montemayor served from 1939 to 1940. M. C. Gonzáles, a man, replaced her in 1940–41. The first two official field organizers of youth councils were Sergio González, Jr., a lawyer from Del Rio, and Fidencio M. Guerra of McAllen, but the men did not offer assistance until December 1938 when a Junior LULACker noted that now the groups would not only have MAMAS but PAPAS as well.

67. Francisco I. Montemayor, Jr., The Laredo Junior Council"; "Around the LULAC Shield, Laredo LULAC Council, No. 15," *LULAC News*, October 1937; Esperanza E. Treviño, "Mrs. F. I. Montemayor," *LULAC News*, May 1939; "Laredo Junior LULAC Council," *LULAC News*, March 1938; Cantú interview, 24 January 1984; "Around the LULAC Shield, Laredo Junior Council No. 2," *LULAC News*, December 1937; Perfecto Solis, Jr. "Laredo Junior LULAC Council," August 1938; Leonor Montes, "Who Is Who in Laredo Junior Council," *LULAC News*, October 1938; and Fernando Salinas, "My Junior LULAC Activities," *LULAC News*, August 1938. Though Laredo Juniors ranged from nine to fifteen, the organization was open to young people between the ages of eight and eighteen.

68. Mrs F. I. Montemayor, "Let's Organize Junior Councils," *LULAC News*, August 1938; "Around the LULAC Shield, The Laredo Junior Council," *LULAC News*, December 1938.

69. Cantú videotaped interview, 26 January 1986; Cantú interview, 24 January 1984.

70. Montes, "Who Is Who"; Francisco Montemayor, Jr., "Laredo Junior Council."

71. "The Junior LULAC Council, Laredo, Texas," *LULAC News*, July 1945. As early as 1934 the national LULAC recognized a "director of Boy Scout activities."

72. See Mrs. F. I. Montemayor, "A Message from Our Second Vice-President General"; "Take Stock of Yourself," *LULAC News*, September 1937; Mrs. F. I. Montemayor, "Women's Opportunity in LULAC," *LULAC News*, October 1937; "Son Muy Hombres (?)"; Mrs. F. I. Montemayor, "Echoes of the Installation of Officers of Council No. 1," *LULAC News* February 1938; Mrs. F. I. Montemayor, "Let's Organize Junior Councils"; Mrs. F. I. Montemayor, "President General and Three Laredo Councils"; Mrs. F. I. Montemayor, "When . . . and Then Only," *LULAC News*, March 1939; Mrs. F. I. Montemayor, "Our Ladies Organizer General," *LULAC News*, May 1939; Mrs. F. I. Montemayor, "Why and How More Junior Councils," *LULAC News*, April 1940. See also "Our Second Vice-President General."

73. Mrs. F. I. Montemayor, "Let's Organize Junior Councils."

74. "We Need More Ladies Councils," *LULAC News*, July 1937.

75. Mrs. F. I. Montemayor, "A Message."

76. Mrs. F. I. Montemayor, "Women's Opportunity in LULAC."

77. "Son Muy Hombres (?)."

78. Ibid.

79. Mrs. F. I. Montemayor, "When . . . and Then Only"; Mrs. F. I. Montemayor, "Let's Organize Junior Councils."

80. "Around the Shield, Laredo, Ladies Council No. 15," *LULAC News*, February 1937.

81. Cantú interview, 24 January 1984, and Cantú videotaped interview, 26 January 1986. Carmen Cortés of Houston Ladies LULAC 14, a member in the '30s, also mentioned Laredo men's opposition to Montemayor in an interview. Thomas Kreneck and Cynthia E. Orozco interview with Carmen Cortés, 16 December 1983, Houston, Texas.

82. Norma Cantú interview, 24 January 1984.

83. Mrs. F. I. Montemayor, "Echoes of the Installation of Officers," "Dedicatoria del Nuevo Parque Ben Garza," *El Paladin*, 3 March 1939; Cantú videotaped interview, 26 January 1986 (here Montemayor named a "Dr. Canales" among her male supporters, but I assume she was referring to Dr. Carlos Castañeda *and* J. T. Canales); Cantú interview, 24 January 1984.

84. *LULAC News*, July 1945.

85. Phone conversation with Aurelio Montemayor, 15 June 1989; "Alice D. Montemayor: Young at 82," *Laredo Times*, 15 July 1984; Guerrero interview.

86. See "Alice D. Montemayor," *Austin American-Statesman*, 16 May 1989.

87. "Outstanding Councils of the League."

88. Salinas, "My Junior LULAC Activities."

89. Phone conversation with Aurelio Montemayor, 15 June 1989; Guerrero interview.

90. Montemayor told Andre Guerrero that "A girl's most beautiful day is graduation day. Then when she gets married. Then when she has a baby. Or have you a career." Guerrero interview.

91. Cantú videotaped interview, 26 January 1986.

92. "We Need More Ladies Councils"; "Women's Opportunity in LULAC."

93. *Laredo Morning Times*, 15 July 1984.

94. Cantú interview, 26 January 1986.

PART SIX

Cultures and Identities

We said in the Editors' Introduction that cultures are not rigid molds but complex and changing systems. One of the most intricate areas of that broad thing we call "culture" involves the ways people understand cultural symbols and practices and internalize them in personal identities—and the ways individual identities, in turn, are connected to our sense of belonging to groups. We all internalize who we are and imagine new self-images from mental reservoirs of behaviors, symbols, values, and practices. We watch adults, absorb how we are treated by others, and come to expect particular treatment because of our race, our sex, our religion. Little boys learn to open doors for girls; girls learn to wait at closed doors and to defer to males in conversations. Similarly, African American and Mexican American children once learned that they could not swim in municipal swimming pools, always to go to the bathroom before they went downtown, and not to throw a fit in public because they could not use "public" facilities.

We learn, too, to expect different treatment from different people—to experience belonging in some circumstances, estrangement and discrimination in others. We learn when and with whom we can discuss sex, childbirth, menstruation, or racial insults. We learn who will laugh at jokes that make fun of white people or have Yiddish punchlines. We learn when to defer to more powerful people and when we can make fun of them for thinking we are stupid.

We also imagine our possibilities through popular media—television, books, songs, movies, magazines, and advertisements. Are people like "us" a significant part of the symbolic landscape that surrounds us? What images do we absorb daily of who we are and what we can be? Until the civil rights movements of the 1950s and 1960s alerted many Americans to the question of cultural exclusion, many white people had never thought about the symbolic representation of diverse Americans in textbooks or in popular culture. As the reform movements discussed in the previous sections demonstrate, Euro-Americans most often assumed their own cultural superiority and sought to help newcomers "assimilate" by learning English, converting to Christianity, and adopting middle-class practices of courtship, marriage, and gender-appropriate behavior. For some immigrants, adopting "Americanized" behavior did lead, over time, to greater social and cultural inclusion, often accompanied by conflicted feelings about social gain and cultural loss. For other groups, particularly for people of color, no amount of cultural adaptability could overcome racist exclusion and stereotyping.

Adopting new cultural practices often created tensions between generations. Immigrant children learned English in school and met children of other racial ethnic heritages. Their parents, and particularly their mothers, remained more isolated at home. Children thus had different cultural reservoirs from which to choose than their parents did. Parents saw children they named Jesús and Rivka become "Jesse" and "Becky" to their schoolmates. Indian children returned from government boarding schools speaking English and celebrating Christian holidays, shorn not only of their hair but often of languages and cultural practices that connected their identities with their parents'. Jewish children began to eat pork and work on Saturday like their Christian bosses and customers. New practices, adopted through choice or coercion, brought conflicts about adopting new foods, names, marriage customs, dress, or business practices that made it easier to "fit in," and about choices like intermarriage and conversion to other religions that threatened racial ethnic cultures. The tensions about these choices mirrored the suspicions with which people of different religions and races and ethnic heritages viewed one another and the unequal power relationships among them.[1]

We have only recently begun to learn how deeply cultural stereotypes and images affect people's self-images. The landmark 1954 Brown v. Board of Education *Supreme Court decision that outlawed segregation in public schools was based in part on psychological and sociological evidence about the symbolic power of inclusion or exclusion. Psychologist Kenneth Clark testified about his research that demonstrated that African American children learned their own inferiority very early from a culture that separated them from white children and that offered few positive images of black youngsters. Similar research demonstrated that female figures—or their absence—in textbooks, movies, songs, cartoons, and other cultural media affected girls' senses of themselves, of what they could be and do. If Dick and Jane are always white, if only Dick has adventures, if only men's sports are televised, then whiteness and maleness become "normal" and valued. If all the white women in movies are dumb blondes, and all the Mexican American women are sexy barmaids, and all the African American women are maids, then little girls learn different demeaning images of how to be pretty, sexy, manipulative, and/or subservient to get what they want. If all the U.S. presidents are white men, then girls and children of color do not really believe, at a deep level, that anyone can grow up to be president.*[2]

Still, as with middle-class reforms, this process of creating identity is not a one-way exchange. Assimilation theory assumed that newcomers would want to assimilate. Instead, as we have seen, racial ethnic people were selective about what practices they adopted, and drew from their own communities and cultures competing symbols of selfhood and empowerment. Identity was not a simple matter of learning new and better self-images, particularly since popular images continued to project demeaning stereotypes.

In the West, as elsewhere, racial ethnic women forged their identities from competing cultural reservoirs. The result, in the words Gail Nomura chose for the title of her article in this section, was often "a grafting" of new customs and habits on older roots, as women reshaped their self-images using the cultural resources they inherited as well as new images they encountered in popular culture. As the authors in this section demonstrate, culture is a two-way street. Racial ethnic women found new sources of identity, and in turn new images of racial ethnic women entered the popular culture. That particularly western medium, motion pictures, developed its own set of stock stereotypes for women of color—the "mammies," "hot tamales," and "China dolls" who entered the cultural mainstream, reinforced racist and sexist perceptions, and "justified" exploitation. For second-generation daughters, these demeaning stereotypes, coupled with the attractions of "mainstream" gender roles and opportunities, led some to choose new identities they created using borrowed cultural forms, like advice columns, fashion magazines, and the images they saw on the silver screen.

Identity, like culture, is not a single simple thing. Many of us are "multicultural" in the sense that we behave differently and establish connections with other people differently depending on circumstances. Racial, ethnic, gender, and religious identities might remain meaningful at home, in racial ethnic communities, in churches and synagogues, while other forms of behavior and identity function better in "mixed" settings, like work or school. People who adopted "mainstream" English, makeup, and fashion could still speak Spanish or Italian at home, eat fry bread or tortillas or matzo balls, and observe life-cycle ceremonies like first communions, bat mitzvahs, and kinaaldas.[3]

For some women, familiar cultural practices remained positive sources of identity and power. When Mexican American women assembled home altars, Issei women wrote poetry, or Jewish women lit the Sabbath candles, they affirmed sources of identity that remained meaningful in new circumstances. Special foods, holidays, and celebrations depended on women to do what anthropologist Micaela di Leonardo called "kinwork," which maintained family ties and traditions.[4] *Home-centered family observances continued racial ethnic ties as well. Women's domestic and family roles made them responsible for preserving private domestic traditions that maintained racial ethnic identities. The same familiar practices could be a form of daily resistance to the power of a popular "mainstream" culture.*

As these articles demonstrate, the private practice of cultural identity was not always an equal match for public popular culture, which often exploited the images of "exotic" women of color for a mass audience. "Culture" in this sense is not an unqualified benefit but a medium that records and teaches relationships of subservience and power. For women of color, negotiating a new culture was a contradictory process of establishing self-validating and empowering identities in a broader cultural context that denied their traditions and distorted their lives.

Notes

1. For examples, see Akemi Kikumura, *Through Harsh Winters: The Life of a Japanese Immigrant Woman* (Novato, Calif.: Chandler & Sharp, 1881); Maxine Hong Kingston, *The Woman Warrior: Memoirs of a Girlhood among Ghosts* (New York: Knopf, 1975); Polingaysi Qoyowayma, *No Turning Back: A True Account of a Hopi Indian Girl's Struggle to Bridge the Gap between the World of Her People and the World of the White Man*, with Vada F. Carlson (Albuquerque: University of New Mexico Press, 1964); Sophie Trupin, *Dakota Diaspora: Memoirs of a Jewish Homesteader* (Lincoln: University of Nebraska Press, 1984); and J. Sanford Rikoon, ed., *Rachel Calof's Story: A Jewish Homesteader on the Northern Plains* (Bloomington: University of Indiana Press, 1995).

2. See Kenneth B. Clark, *Prejudice and Your Child* (Boston: Beacon Press, 1963); and Women on Words & Images, *Dick and Jane as Victims: Sex Stereotyping in Children's Readers: An Analysis* (Princeton, N.J.: Women on Words & Images, 1975). For recent works that revisit these issues, see Kenneth B. Clark, "Unfinished Business: The Toll of Psychic Violence," *Newsweek*, 11 January 1993, 38; Kenneth B. Clark and Michael Meyers, "Separate Is Never Equal," *New York Times*, 1 April 1995; and Piper Purcell and Lara Stewart, "Dick and Jane in 1989," *Sex Roles: A Journal of Research* 22, no. 3–4 (February 1990): 177–86.

3. Bat mitzvah and kinaalda are, respectively, Jewish and Navajo girls' life-cycle ceremonies. While the kinaalda is a long-standing Navajo observance of a girl's first menstruation, the bat mitzvah is a much newer practice that reflects the influence of feminism on Judaism. The bat mitzvah enables girls to participate in a ceremony previously restricted to boys—bar mitzvah— when they read the Torah and become adult members of the religious community on their thirteenth birthdays.

4. Micaela di Leonardo, "The Female World of Cards and Holidays," *Signs* 12, no. 3 (Spring 1987): 440–53. See also Micaela di Leonardo, *The Varieties of Ethnic Experience: Kinship, Class, and Gender among California Italian-Americans* (Ithaca, N.Y.: Cornell University Press, 1984), 194–205, 208–18, 228, 233.

22.

Desperately Seeking "Deirdre": Gender Roles, Multicultural Relations, and Nisei Women Writers of the 1930s

VALERIE MATSUMOTO

How do immigrants' children forge ethnic identities? What do they draw from their parents, what from the surrounding culture? Most children do not accept their parents' values, options, and behaviors as road maps for their own lives. If they did, cultures would be static and we would not need to chart historical changes. The question of generational change, however, becomes more intricate in the contexts of the competing cultural systems of immigrant parents and a discriminatory "mainstream" culture. In an article originally published in 1991, Valerie Matsumoto probes this issue of ethnic identity for second generation Japanese Americans (Nisei) in the 1930s. She uses as her source the advice columns of Deirdre (Mary Oyama Mittwer), a Nisei "Dear Abby," and the literature produced by 1930s Japanese American literati, both of which record some recurrent Nisei concerns. Deirdre is particularly interesting because her task was more complex than prescribing appropriate behavior. For Japanese American young people in the 1930s, older Nisei like Deirdre became guides to the competing worlds of their parents and "mainstream" America.

Advice and etiquette columns, as Matsumoto notes, have been an American staple since the Victorian era. Women of color historians correctly reminded us that we could not assume that the behavior they prescribed for a white elite applied to all classes and races.[1] Deirdre might use the same form as Ann Landers and her literary forebears, but her readers asked different questions as they struggled with possibilities like interracial dating and romance versus arranged marriage. Deirdre's dialogues with her readers do not reveal "cookie-cutter" prescriptions for proper behavior, but they tell us a lot about the cultural pulls the Nisei experienced and the resources they had from which to choose and to build their identities. Matsumoto uses prescriptive literature, fiction, poetry, and other products of Nisei "high culture" to raise questions about changes in gender and ethnic identities and how these pulled people across cultures and generations. Her emphasis on what advice people sought rather than on Deirdre's answers is an approach that might fruitfully be applied to advice literature in general.

In July 1941, as wartime tensions rose in the United States, a second-generation Japanese American woman poet, Toyo Suyemoto, wrote:

> Out of the anguish of my heart
>   There must come gentle peace.
> That will bid wayward grief
>   And troubled thoughts to cease.
>
> When one by one, old sorrows pass
>   And I know my own will,
> Let not the spirit fear again
>   Or let my songs grow still.[2]

The World War II internment of the Japanese Americans in concentration camps would swallow up many of the "songs" pouring forth from the second-generation, or Nisei, women writers of the 1930s like Suyemoto. Indeed, the postwar silence of the hardscrabble resettlement years of the 1940s and the cold war era's discouragement of celebrating ethnicity have obscured the vitality and creative ferment of the prewar Japanese American literati. Their writings provide many windows onto the cultural diversity of life on the West Coast. Viewed through the lens of Nisei efforts to shape ethnic culture, the dynamics of interracial/interethnic relations and gender roles come into provocative focus.

Until recently, very little attention—scholarly or otherwise—has been paid to this prewar literature.[3] I first became aware of the flood of poetry, fiction, articles, and essays by the Nisei in the vernacular press (as they called it) when, a few years ago, Nisei activist Chizu Iiyama drew my attention to the lovelorn and etiquette-advice columns written by "Deirdre"—a Japanese American "Dear Abby" of the 1930s—for a San Francisco Japanese American newspaper, the *New World-Sun*. The more I delved into the background of the witty and opinionated "Deirdre," the more aware I became of the active network of Japanese American women and men writers and the breadth of the cultural and social issues they tackled. Like a gumshoe of the 1930s detective thrillers, I became enmeshed in a seemingly endless search for clues and leads, running into the classic dead ends of memory loss, the destruction of personal papers, and the disappearance of potential informants through death or change of name. I am still in the thick of doing basic "first-stage women's history" in recovering information about Deirdre and her literary sisters. And, like a detective, I am finding that the primary research brings to light a host of intriguing theoretical questions.

In this essay, I will draw on the work of a number of these writers—on Deirdre's, in particular—as a way to discuss some of the interpretive issues that emerge as one does documentary research. What I have found is suggestive rather than conclusive, but even at this early stage, it raises speculations regarding the attempt to create and promote ethnic culture, the search for role models, and the tension of women's dreams caught between gender-role expectations and the economic realities of a racially discriminatory society.

Throughout the nineteenth and twentieth centuries U.S. women have looked to advice literature for moral guidance and etiquette, from the Victorian arbiters like *Godey's Lady's Book* to the modern-day columns and manuals of Abigail Van Buren, Ann Landers, Miss Manners, the Mayflower Madam, and others. It was within this long tradition that Deirdre addressed the social problems facing the Nisei, stating that she would be "happy to answer any question put her concerning family affairs, love and other sex problems, social etiquette and other personal questions."[4]

However, Deirdre's situation, as advice columnist of the *New World-Sun* from 1935 to 1941, was far more complex than that of mainstream etiquette mavens. Her task was to provide the Nisei with guidelines to proper behavior that would enable them to navigate safely the social conventions of the white world as well as to meet the standards of their parents and the Japanese American community. She also had to tailor her advice to racial ethnic readers grappling with complex issues such as interracial relations and dating, whether to resist arranged marriage in favor of love matches, and how to reconcile conflicts between marriage and career. With considerable panache, Deirdre briefed her readers on dinner place settings and the mechanics of a proper bow, mediated lengthy pen battles between readers with opposing views, and dispensed brisk advice to the shy, lovelorn, and confused.

Who was Deirdre? Some sleuthing by Nisei activist and writer Nikki Sawada Bridges revealed that her real name was Mary ("Mollie") Oyama Mittwer. At the time of her death in 1995, she was living with her daughter in southern California. From talking with Vicki Mittwer Littman, her daughter, and other Nisei journalists, I learned that Mary Oyama Mittwer did more than pen advice columns: As one of the most prolific and energetic Nisei writers, she contributed articles, interviews, poetry, and regular columns to nearly all of the major Japanese American newspapers as well as to the Nisei magazine *Current Life* and to *Common Ground*, a liberal journal that provided a rare forum open to ethnic voices.

Mary Oyama was born in 1907, in Petaluma, California, the oldest daughter in a family of six children. According to her brother Joe and daughter Vicki, the warm encouragement she received from European American teachers nurtured her confidence and writing skills. She graduated from Sacramento High School in 1925 and from the San Francisco National Training School (a Methodist school for training missionaries) in 1928. After a short stint of studying journalism at the University of Southern California around 1931, Oyama moved briefly to Spokane, Washington, and then returned to Los Angeles. There she developed as a prolific writer for a host of papers, including the *Kashu Mainichi* and the *Rafu Shimpo* in Los Angeles and the *Nichibei* and the *Shin-Sekai* in San Francisco.

Pursuing the thread of Mary Oyama's career revealed not only the energy of the Nisei writers but also how many of them were women. A

Mary Oyama upon gradua-
tion from the San Francisco
National Training School for
missionaries in 1928. (Courtesy Vicki Littman.)

1940 article in *Current Life* on "Who's Who in the Nisei Literary World"
profiled fifteen men and women, including Mary Oyama, who was
described as "earnestly interested in promoting better race understanding"
and as "an affectionate young matron—poised, neat, with a tranquil charm
all her own."[5] These columnists, poets, fiction authors, and fashion
editors published energetically in the vernacular press, experimenting
with form and style in the process of developing their own voices. Many
adopted a flippant and brash jazz style; Hisaye Yamamoto poked fun at
lyric convention in humorous poems with Latin titles, and Toyo Suyemoto
limned her subjects in powerful austere rhymes, stating:

> . . . all that I can give to you
> Is simple speech of everyday . . .
> Words stripped and stark like life and death
> Wherein you stand midway.[6]

These writers explored a range of sensitive and timely subjects as well
as styles. Interracial relations, interethnic prejudice, and women's roles in
the Japanese American family provided grist for their mills. Mary Oyama,

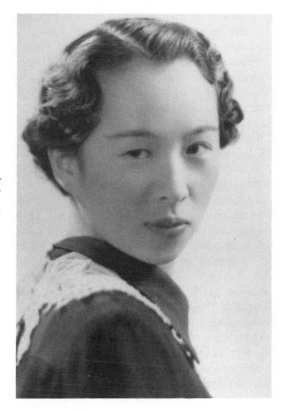

Mary Oyama in 1937 as her "I'm Telling you, Deirdre" column gained popularity. (Courtesy Vicki Littman.)

in the guise of Deirdre, pushed especially hard for more political involvement by "Alice Nisei," as well as for harmonious interracial relations and women's pursuit of independence and personal goals. In many ways, such "New Woman" sentiments were embodied in Oyama's own life: She pieced together a full-time journalism job by writing for many papers in a range of different formats. Leaving in her wake a string of beaus, she married at the age of thirty, late for a Nisei. Her husband, Frederick Mittwer, a handsome linotypist for the *Rafu Shimpo* newspaper, was a Japan-born man of European and Japanese parentage.

Oyama's writings and her life illustrate the tensions confronting Nisei women who dreamed of careers as well as marriage. Though Deirdre encouraged ambitious readers, in 1990s terms, "to do it all," she also permitted herself to grumble that "housewives have no spare time" in a 1939 column. Her complaint presaged the discontent Betty Friedan would later examine in *The Feminine Mystique*. "Domesticity," Oyama found, "seems to allow less time for self-improvement . . . than regular routine work outside. . . . As hard as I'm toiling around the house, my folks complain and think that I'm not doing enough. It's aggravating, really."[7]

Gender-role expectations were not the only hurdle Nisei women faced. Of the many Japanese American young women energetically penning articles, stories, and poems for the vernacular press, few ever made inroads into the mainstream media. Mary Oyama, writing for *Common Ground*, and Hisaye Yamamoto, whose fiction later appeared in *Harper's Bazaar* and *Martha Foley's Best American Short Stories*, were among the exceptions. In this sense, the writer's situation mirrored that of Nisei and other ethnic women who found it difficult to obtain work outside the ethnic community. In addition, their careers met the devastating roadblock of World War II internment, the painful net of many dreams.

The concerns aired in Deirdre's column, as well as the themes elaborated by the literati, suggest that for the Nisei, cultural crossroads were the inescapable locations of daily life. Although the Japanese American community monitored their behavior as modest, industrious *musuko* (sons) and *musume* (daughters), public schooling provided another arena of interaction with non-Asian American teachers and classmates. The daily routine of most Nisei children—the majority of whom were born between 1910 and 1940—revolved around work and education. Many worked in the fields or the family business before school, attended Japanese language class after public school finished, and then returned home where further chores awaited. Whether urban or rural, they often acted as intermediaries between their immigrant parents and the dominant society, being called upon to develop translation skills early on. And the younger members of the second generation looked to older Nisei like Deirdre for guidance in negotiating the demands of immigrant parents and the surrounding society.

The offerings of the Japanese American press during the 1930s and on into the early 1940s evidence the rich diversity of cultural influences permeating the lives of the Nisei. The second generation, most of them able to speak but not read Japanese, pored over growing English sections in the vernacular newspapers. A young reader might follow the comic strip adventures of "Tarzan and the Golden Lion" as well as the exploits of local Nisei baseball and basketball teams, or join a Nisei pen-pal club. For older readers, the sections included Buddhist and Christian church news, U.S.-Japan relations, and articles on women's status and concerns in the United States. Women as well as men enthusiastically submitted poetry and fiction, and they sought advice from the outspoken Deirdre.

The photographs of movie stars and the fashion columns particularly reflected the impact of mainstream society. Like other U.S. women, the Nisei might try to determine what "Hollywood type" they were and then attempt to enhance their best features accordingly. As one fashion columnist advised, "If you have broad Garboesque shoulders—softly tailored lines will streamline your size. . . . If you are small with a Constance Bennett chin—tall hats give you a lift with a lean look."[8] Incidentally, the fashion page in the Nisei magazine, *Current Life*, always featured Japanese American models wearing the latest styles, usually available at "Kiyo's Dress Shop."

The English section of the newspapers also reflected the culinary diversity for which California is famous. Women readers shared a variety of recipes, ranging from sukiyaki and *kuromame* (back beans) to *bok choy chow yuk*, fruitcake, and cream puffs. Mothers might glean helpful hints like adding pizzazz to *kanten*, a Japanese gelatin, by putting in bits of canned pineapple or giving their children a healthy snack of Wheaties.

In addition, Nisei fiction writers charted the multicultural landscape of their generation. For example, issues of gender and race permeate the short stories of Hisaye Yamamoto, one of the most widely acclaimed Japanese American writers. Born in southern California in 1921, Yamamoto began writing as a teenager, submitting poems and essays— under the pseudonym "Napoleon"—to the ethnic press in the 1930s and 1940s. During her World War II internment in Arizona, she wrote for the Poston *Chronicle*, the concentration camp newspaper. Her fiction found receptive mainstream and Japanese American audiences in the postwar years.[9] These short stories delineate the multicultural flavor of prewar life in both city and country: The repertoire of treats to be enjoyed in Little Tokyo in Los Angeles included Eskimo Pies purchased on the street and popular *China-meshi* (Chinese food) as well as sushi and Japanese confections. Interethnic relations weave through the stories, whether in the form of remedies sold by a Korean herbalist, an affair between a Filipino hired hand and an Issei woman, or a Nisei teenager's first kiss from a Chicano schoolmate and harvest worker. For Yamamoto's characters, as for Deirdre's readers, the dynamics of romantic relations exposed the interethnic/interracial and gender-role tensions faced by the Nisei.

Marriage was a recurrent theme in Deirdre's column.[10] Nisei readers engaged in spirited discourse over the merits of mainstream "love marriage" versus the arranged matches expected by many Issei parents, and they debated the ramifications of marrying a farmer, especially for urban women. Both men and women—protected by the anonymity of pseudonyms like "Voice of the Rockies," "Modern Miss," and "Farmer Bob"— set forth the attributes they hoped to find in a mate. Their letters evidence the influence of mainstream ideals of romantic affection and companionate marriage, which deviated considerably from the Issei's marital expectations. As Deirdre and one female correspondent agreed, "This marriage business comes to 'a question of loving someone.'"[11] The later findings of anthropologist Sylvia Yanagisako have documented the development of Nisei marriage as a compromise between Japanese and American ideals, valorizing love and affection but not at the expense of duty and commitment.[12]

Tensions surrounding the issues of courtship and marriage were compounded when the factor of race entered the picture. The dominant society's opposition to interracial marriage made the unions of Asian Americans or African Americans with whites illegal under California's miscegenation laws until 1948.[13] Given this prohibition and the Japanese American community's own disapproval of intermarriage, it is not surprising that the topic was a sensitive one for the Nisei. In such a context, the Nisei's discussion of interracial/interethnic dating and relationships reveals complicated junctures of race, gender, and class. Short stories, articles, and Deirdre's column shed light on Japanese American perceptions of ethnicity and identity as well as ambivalence about mainstream and ethnic cultural norms regarding male and female standards.

The white population might have lumped all Asian Americans into one category, regardless of cultural differences and historic enmities, but they themselves drew distinctions. Nisei critiques of Japanese American prejudices indicate the prevalence of such attitudes. In this vein, one Nisei wrote to ask Deirdre's opinion of Japanese Americans who dated Chinese or "young people of other nationalities." The irate author was prompted to write after overhearing his sister stigmatized for dating a Chinese American, "as if that were a great social crime."[14] He criticized the Japanese American community for narrow-mindedness and intolerance and defended his sister's friend as a well-educated, widely traveled third-generation U.S. citizen. At the same time, he was quick to mention that his sister's date was "perfectly platonic," thereby skirting the issue of interethnic sexual relations while claiming the right of association. Less ambiguously, Jeanne Nishimori's short story titled "I Cannot Marry Thee" bitingly indicted the prejudice of a male protagonist—presumably Nisei—who felt attracted to a woman he met on the bus until he learned that she was a Chinese American.[15]

Although Deirdre, who supported interracial dating, may not have been representative of Japanese Americans, her writing on this subject revealed the social matrix of the issue. In 1935, she wrote in a positive tone about a Nisei woman's dating a white male whom the columnist described as "well-educated, charming and extremely nice-looking."[16] His "utter lack of prejudice" she attributed to the fact that he came from a less prejudiced state than California. Like the Nisei man who defended his sister's right to date a Chinese American, Deirdre sought to remove the issue from the troubling realm of erotic attraction to the less threatening ground of casual camaraderie. The columnist was quick to establish that, although he was a "nice chap," the Nisei woman was not in love with him but regarded him as a "pal." Indeed, the woman said that she considered herself "too young to be thinking about such things"—although clearly this did not stop her, Deirdre, or Deirdre's readers from doing so. The woman also said she supposed that her Japanese American friends considered her "eccentric" for dating a European American but declared, "It's about time we Nisei and we Japanese got over our prejudices. You must admit that a lot of us have them, too." Again, careful ambiguity and mixed messages like the endorsement of nonromantic friendship in conjunction with the mention of the "charm" of the attractive interracial couple suggest the tensions within and outside the ethnic community in regard to such relations. We are reminded simultaneously of the strength of prevailing norms and the presence of a small minority who pushed against sociocultural boundaries, both ethnic and mainstream.

Although the dominant society might regard racial ethnic people as inferior—the cornerstone of the argument against interracial unions—this did not always translate into minority acceptance of such views. Neither did their being subject to racial discrimination necessarily prevent them from holding their own prejudices, as Deirdre's subject asserted. Contrary to mainstream eugenic objections to intermarriage, Japanese Americans did not accept notions of their presumed physiological deficiency. As Charles Kikuchi said, "In regard to intermarriage, most of the Nisei oppose it on sociological and economic lines, but not on biological lines." Rather, he stated, "they are proud of their ancestry and do not consider themselves as products of an inferior race."[17] However, the terminology of ethnicity evidenced the unequal sense of entitlement in U.S. society: While the Japanese Americans referred to themselves as "Nisei" or "Japanese," the term "American" was usually synonymous with "white." European Americans were also occasionally called *hakujin* (literally, white person).

The Nisei's integration of popular cultural beliefs with the values of the Issei did not always proceed smoothly. At least one epistolary debate in Deirdre's column suggested the cultural conflict faced by Nisei seeking to reconcile two sets of sometimes incompatible norms. In this case, friction over standards of appropriate female behavior became cast in ethnic terms. Through the forum of Deirdre's column, a reader calling himself "Bachelor Bob" castigated Nisei women as "dead and uninteresting in comparison to American girls." "Matsu-chan," a rural teenager, responded by asking, "Don't you think the 'hakujin' girls are a little too talkative and lively? . . . What would our parents think of us if we suddenly became like the 'hakujins'—running wild, etc.?" She added, perhaps to get Bachelor Bob's goat, "The Nisei boys, too, seem dead to me." This exchange, though brief, exemplifies the linkage of issues of gender and ethnicity.[18]

The lively English section of the vernacular newspapers and Nisei fiction allow us to glimpse the diversity surrounding the Nisei and the complex themes of race and gender with which they grappled. A small but active network of writers energetically sought to create and promote a distinctive Japanese American culture. Growing up in the U.S. West exposed them to many cultural influences and, I think, spurred the literati to experiment with form and content as they tried to define themselves and their role in U.S. society.

The Nisei literati had a strong consciousness of themselves as a generation, and the subject of "the Nisei problem" figured largely in many of their articles and editorials. The "Nisei problem" was a catchall term encompassing the social and economic limitations the Japanese Americans faced. A 1935 editorial in the *Hokubei Asahi* newspaper noted that, despite the fact that the Nisei were in essence no different from other second-generation ethnic people in the United States, "the welter of dilemmas such as whether or not they should be Americans or Japanese, and whether they should seek a career in Japan or America, have proved somewhat of a handicap, not typical to other immigrants."[19] Such editorials and letters to the newspapers gave the Nisei an outlet to vent their frustrations at being perceived as foreigners and treated like second-class citizens.

Many of the literati strongly critiqued racism as the main obstacle to their full participation and acceptance in the larger society. When an Englishman wrote to "Dear Deirdre" to discuss whether the Nisei could be assimilated into U.S. life, she responded: "One of our Nisei boys said frankly, 'you see, it isn't a question of: "Can the Nisei become assimilated" for we already are quite thoroughly Americanized and we have learned quickly and readily how to adapt ourselves to American life; rather it is a question of: "How far are the Americans willing to LET US BECOME ASSIMILATED." ' "[20] Another Nisei added, "The Americans sometimes accuse us of not becoming thoroughly assimilated, little realizing that they themselves have set up certain restrictions which limit our capacity for assimilating. Take, for instance, the law which prohibits marriages between the Occidentals and Orientals."[21] Deirdre also cited the barring of Japanese Americans from certain restaurants, public swimming pools, and other facilities.

Although the Nisei writers maintained a critique of U.S. racism, they also believed that part of the answer to the "Nisei problem" lay in their own hands. As the *Hokubei Asahi* editor concluded, "Something new must be created by the Nisei—and by only them."[22] Somewhat like the writers of the Harlem Renaissance of the 1920s, the Japanese American literati sought to shape and promote their own culture, exhorting each other to "find a way of their own." Mary Oyama was one of the cofounders of the League of Nisei Artists and Writers, a group that met weekly at her house to foster this creative effort, organizing themselves like the League of American Writers.

What heroes and models inspired the Nisei? Pursuit of this question yields additional evidence of the cultural diversity of the West Coast as well as clues about how the Japanese Americans thought about themselves as racial ethnic Americans. Examining this issue also raises even more questions about how racial ethnic and/or ethnic groups perceive each other. The Nisei, in their attempt to create something new, cast about for role models. Mary Oyama, in a series of interviews for *Current Life* magazine, presented other ethnic Americans and the children of immigrants to stimulate her readers. One such potential role model was Leon Surmelian, a writer Oyama described as an "Armenian Nisei," whose articles about the "second-generation problem" of the Armenian Americans reminded her of the "Nisei problem." Upon learning that Surmelian lived in Hollywood, Oyama promptly invited him and several Japanese Americans to her house for a bull session. "Over the tea-cups and rice-cookies," as she put it, "everything under the sun was discussed: Buddhism, Christianity, . . . the Nisei, interracial marriage, racial background of the Japanese people, Protestantism, Catholicism." Oyama relayed Surmelian's sympathy with the Japanese Americans and the "Nisei problems," which she viewed as "really the common problems of all racial minority groups here in the United States."[23]

Oyama's writing reflected her strong concerns regarding multicultural relations. She never tired of trying to push her readers to "mix" socially with non-Japanese and to politicize her readers—as racial minority people and as citizens. For example, in July 1941, she interviewed the Italian American writer John Fante, whom she called "a Nisei like the rest of us, as he was born in the United States."[24] Oyama, in her breezy prose, deftly drew attention to another interethnic issue by focusing the article on a story by Fante that had appeared in the *Saturday Evening Post*. The story, centering around a Filipino man, had met with strong criticism from the Filipino American intelligentsia. Fante sheepishly admitted to Oyama that he had, indeed, learned more about Filipinos *after* he wrote the story.

William Saroyan held particular appeal for Nisei writers, who mentioned him frequently. They drew encouragement from his assurance that "each of us is a Nisei" as well as from his exhortation to write. "The life of the Japanese in California is rich and full of American fables that need to be told to other Americans," he urged; "they must be written by those who lived them in order to become a part of the whole American life."[25] Words of support from such an acclaimed ethnic author must have meant a great deal to the Nisei, struggling to develop a voice and to reach a wider audience.

The Nisei literati's choice of role models raises further speculations. They were clearly drawn to ethnic individuals like the Italian American Fante and the Armenian American William Saroyan. But what about African American authors and artists? Why the Armenian Americans and Italian Americans? Perhaps regional visibility was a factor since many Armenian and Italian immigrants had settled in California at the turn of the century when the majority of the Japanese arrived. For a brief period, the Armenians had shared the legal kinship of being categorized as "Orientals" in California. Fante, Saroyan, and Surmelian were also the children of immigrants, like the Nisei. There were far fewer African Americans in the West, and the Harlem Renaissance (in the pretelevision era) had been a dazzling eastern regional development. Also, prejudice against African Americans may have prevented some Japanese Americans from viewing them as models to emulate. The choice of role models certainly poses further questions regarding interethnic relations and perceptions. Nonetheless, it is clear that Nisei writers looked both into their own community and out into the large society for inspiration in grappling with the articulation of a distinctive American ethnic identity.

By 1940, however, the lively discussion of literary aspirations, gender roles, and intergenerational dynamics that filled the columns of the 1930s had dwindled as impending war between the United States and Japan intensified the "Nisei problem." Political concerns overshadowed other issues. Tones of insecurity and vulnerability infused the writings of the

Toyo Suyemoto sent this picture of herself, taken in Sacramento, California, during the 1930s, to "Molly" Oyama. (Courtesy Vicki Littman.)

Nisei, reflecting their position. Toyo Suyemoto's metaphors took on larger meaning in this uncertain time:

> I know I must learn to accept,
>   Not question overmuch
> Lest I forget myself
>   And try to clutch
> At beauty never meant for me,
>   Till slipping fingers seize
> A blade of grass or two
>   And find some ease
> In nearness of familiar things—
>   But even these betray
> The heart at length, for they
>   Will pass away.[26]

The Japanese Americans left familiar things far behind them when they were sent to the concentration camps. World War II has been the focus of Japanese American history, encompassing a lion's share of the scholarship—a focus that, while important, has obscured the richness of prewar creativity. Examining the work of Mary Oyama and her literary sisters not only brings to light the talents and concerns of the Nisei but also opens up critical questions regarding relations among racial ethnic groups, the impact of regional influences on ethnic culture, and the challenges faced by women seeking their niche in both mainstream U.S. society and the ethnic community.

Notes

This essay first appeared in *Frontiers* 12, no. 1 (1991).

I am grateful to Vicki Littman, Mary Oyama Mittwer, Lily and Yasuo Sasaki, Joe and Clem Oyama, Nikki Sawada Bridges, Chizu Iiyama, Hisaye Yamamoto, and Seizo Oka for generously sharing their history. For their valuable insights, I wish to thank Peggy Pascoe, Vicki Ruiz, Glenn Omatsu, Elaine Kim, Evelyn Nakano Glenn, Moira Roth, and Stan Yogi. I am also indebted to the Humanities Institute and the Women's Studies Program at the University of California, Davis, for their support of my research.

1. The classic work based in Euro-American prescriptive literature is Barbara Welter, "The Cult of True Womanhood: 1820–1860," *American Quarterly* 18, no. 2 (Summer 1966): 151–74. For a work that raises critical questions from the perspectives of racial ethnic women, see Rosalinda Méndez González, "Distinctions in Western Women's Experience: Ethnicity, Class, and Social Change," in *The Women's West*, ed. Susan Armitage and Elizabeth Jameson (Norman: University of Oklahoma Press, 1987), 237–52.

2. Toyo Suyemoto, "Afterwards," *Current Life, The Magazine for the American Born Japanese*, July 1941, 6. For a thoughtful examination of Suyemoto's wartime poetry, see Susan Schweik, "The Pre-Poetics' of Internment: The Example of Toyo Suyemoto," *American Literary History*, Spring 1989: 89–109.

3. Literary scholar Stan Yogi and poet Yasuo Sasaki are currently compiling a collection of writings by Nisei literati, with bibliographic profiles. Historian Yuji Ichioka is writing a book about the Nisei from the 1920s to World War II, with considerable attention to the journalists. A collection of Hisaye Yamamoto's fiction, *Seventeen Syllables and Other Stories*, was published in 1988 by Kitchen Table/Women of Color Press, Latham, N.Y.

4. *Hokubei Asahi*, 5 January 1935.

5. Kenny Murase, "Who's Who in the Nisei Literary World," *Current Life*, October 1940, 8.

6. Toyo Suyemoto, "Praise," *New World-Sun*, 23 June 1941.

7. *New World-Sun*, 12 January 1939.

8. *Current Life*, January 1941, 11. (In November 1941, the magazine changed its subtitle from *The Magazine for the American Born Japanese* to *The Only National Nisei Magazine*.)

9. For more information about Hisaye Yamamoto, see King-Kok Cheung's insightful biography and critical introduction to Yamamoto's fiction collection, *Seventeen Syllables and Other Stories*, xi–xxv.

10. I have discussed Nisei ideas regarding marriage at greater length in a paper entitled "Redefining Expectations: Nisei Women in the 1930s," *California History* 73, no. 1 (Spring 1994): 44–53, 88.

11. *New World-Sun*, 11 February 1937.

12. Sylvia Yanagisako, *Transforming the Past: Tradition and Kinship among Japanese Americans* (Stanford, Calif.: Stanford University Press, 1985), 107–108.

13. For a detailed examination of antimiscegenation laws and their application to Asian Americans, see Megumi Dick Osumi, "Asians and California's Anti-Miscegenation Laws" in *Asian and Pacific American Experiences: Women's Perspectives*, ed. John Nobuya Tsuchida (Minneapolis: Asian/Pacific American Learning Resource Center and General College, University of Minnesota, 1982), 1–37.

14. *New World-Sun*, 10 October 1935.
15. *Current Life*, March 1941, 12.
16. *New World-Sun*, 3 October 1935.
17. Charles Kikuchi, "The Nisei and Marriage," *Current Life*, August 1941, 8.
18. *New World-Sun*, 25 October 1935.
19. *Hokubei Asahi*, 1 January 1935.
20. Ibid., 23 October 1936.
21. Ibid.
22. Ibid., 1 January 1935.
23. *Current Life*, April 1941, 10.
24. Ibid., July 1941, 13.
25. Ibid., May 1941, 8.
26. Toyo Suyemoto, "Ilae Quoque," *Current Life*, August 1941, 10.

23.

Dolores Del Rio and Lupe Velez:
Images on and off the Screen, 1925–1944

ALICIA I. RODRÍQUEZ-ESTRADA

In this fascinating double biography of Dolores Del Rio and Lupe Velez, Alicia Rodríquez-Estrada introduces us to the complexities of sexuality, ethnicity, and identity in American films. Hollywood elevated both Mexican women to stardom in the 1920s and 1930s but portrayed them very differently: Del Rio as a sophisticated upper-class European, Velez as a lower-class "Mexican Spitfire." The differences reflected the women's own class backgrounds and the choices they made within the severely limited range of images offered by Hollywood. Del Rio escaped the negative ethnic stereotyping of Mexicans but was still portrayed as "foreign." She eventually left Hollywood for the more congenial Mexican film industry. In contrast, Velez apparently cooperated with her image as a "hot tamale," both on and off screen, but her biography is both tumultuous and tragic. Rodríquez-Estrada shows us how female sexuality, always a major topic in films, was dramatically affected by Hollywood's use of ethnic stereotypes. But she also emphasizes that neither woman was a passive victim. Within the range of available options, they chose their images.

Cinema historians consider the two decades prior to World War II the Golden Age of Hollywood.[1] Screen legends like Clara Bow, Marlene Dietrich, Clark Gable, Gary Cooper, and numerous others are often remembered for their personalities as well as their on-screen performances. This is also true for "ethnic" stars.[2] Historians of ethnic representation need to pay particular attention to this, for study of ethnic stars' experiences can illuminate the way in which real and imagined identities were reflected within shifting cultural contexts. Hollywood, in fact, did have Mexican movie stars: Ramon Navarro, Gilbert Roland, and Leo Carrillo stood out during Hollywood's Golden Age. This article focuses on two of those stars: Dolores Del Rio and Lupe Velez, two women whose careers as actresses and personalities raise some important questions for scholars of Mexican and Mexican American women and of racial ethnic women in general.[3]

Just as Clara Bow and Marlene Dietrich created memorable styles, so did Dolores Del Rio and Lupe Velez. Each woman fashioned her own persona and craft very differently. In her eighteen-year career in Hollywood, Velez consciously chose and groomed her image as "Whoopee

Lupe," the "Hot Tamale," and "Hot Pepper." With her proclamation, "I am not wild. I am just Lupe," Velez developed a public reputation as the "Hot Baby" of Hollywood and found herself in roles portraying "half-castes" and "exotic" characters (Asians, Latins, and Indians).[4] In contrast, magazines, newspapers, and gossip columnists placed Dolores Del Rio upon a pedestal, extolling her beauty and character. Because of her elite background and the patronage of an influential Hollywood director, Del Rio was regal on and off the screen, perceived by audiences and critics alike as a sophisticated movie star.

Del Rio and Velez began their careers in 1925 and 1927, respectively, near the end of the silent era of Hollywood when Gloria Swanson and Clara Bow dominated the screen. They reached the height of their careers in the early 1930s when two other "foreign" women, Greta Garbo and Marlene Dietrich, claimed star status.

By examining Dolores Del Rio's and Lupe Velez's careers, I hope to understand the manufacturing of images as well as to gain a clearer understanding of why these two did not attain the status attained by Garbo and Dietrich. The roles of ethnic stars and their audiences are insufficiently studied in mainstream scholarship. The few scholarly accounts of Velez and Del Rio only begin to explore their rich and complex lives, although they have appeared in several popular sources.[5] Del Rio's and Velez's lives need to be seen in the social constructs of race, class, and gender in the Hollywood culture of their time.

I examine the careers and private lives of Del Rio and Velez by looking at the interactions between role *playing* and role *making* and the differing perceptions of Anglo and Mexican audiences as indicated by the English-language movie magazine *Photoplay* and the Spanish-language newspaper *La Opinión*. These two media provide a window to understanding how Hollywood and audiences constructed and perceived their images. Just as one can argue that films create ethnic identities, so too do movie magazines. Established in 1911, *Photoplay* represented the growing fascination of moviegoers with Hollywood and the movies. Written for Anglo audiences, fan magazines such as *Photoplay* provided an avenue (and still do today) for readers to fantasize about their favorite movie stars and allowed them to feel that they knew them intimately.[6] *Photoplay's* inclusion of ethnic movie stars such as Del Rio and Velez reinforced preconceived images fostered by Hollywood films.

The other source, *La Opinión*, is not a movie magazine but a Spanish-language newspaper established in 1926 that served the large Spanish-speaking population of Los Angeles. While *La Opinión* should not be considered the single voice of the Mexican community in Los Angeles, it, too, helped feed the fascination of Mexican audiences with Hollywood and the movies. Its section "La Sociedad" represented the Latino version of *Photoplay*, publishing stories and gossip about both Anglo and Mexican movie stars. *La Opinión* regularly featured stories on Ramon Navarro, Gilbert Roland, Dolores Del Rio, and Lupe Velez as well as Clark Gable, Greta Garbo, and other stars. Whether announcing their latest films, marriages, divorces, illnesses, or awards, La Opinión followed and commented upon the careers of Mexican movie stars. The knowledge that Mexican movies stars existed inspired Mexican readers to dream of stardom.[7] Furthermore, La Opinión's often critical coverage of Del Rio and Velez shows that these two women did not exist in a vacuum, passively accepting the stereotypes of Mexicans that had been developed by Anglos.[8]

Born into an elite family in Durango, Mexico, in 1905 and married at the age of fifteen to Jaime Martínez del Río, Dolores enjoyed the privileges of an upper-class Mexican woman. When the director Edwin Carewe journeyed to Mexico City on his honeymoon, he met Jaime and his wife. He inquired if Dolores would like to come to Hollywood and become an actress. As her Svengali, Carewe cast Del Rio in European peasant roles—What Price Glory? (1926), Resurrection (1927), and Evangeline (1929). After Del Rio's marriage failed, Carewe, himself newly divorced, assumed she would marry him. But instead, she broke off their personal and professional relationship and married the head art director for MGM, Cedric Gibbons, seven months later. In films like Flying Down to Rio (1932), Madame Dubarry (1934), The Widow from Monte Carlo (1935), and International Settlement (1938), Del Rio portrayed femmes fatales and sophisticated upper-class European and Latin women. After making Journey into Fear (1943), she returned to Mexico, where she became that country's leading movie star.[9]

The daughter of a military colonel and an opera singer, Lupe Velez attended a Catholic girls' school in Texas. Her father's abandonment forced her to return to Mexico to find work as a salesclerk and dancer. Popular on the Mexican stage, she journeyed to Hollywood to seek stardom. She was cast as an extra in several films before her big break came as Douglas Fairbanks's girlfriend in the film, The Gaucho (1928). Her aggressive personality and sexuality meshed with her ethnicity, as producers gave her exotic and half-caste parts in films such as Wolf Song (1928), East Is West (1930), Cuban Love Song (1931), and The Broken Wing (1932). Her marriage to and subsequent separations from Johnny "Tarzan" Weissmuller kept her in the spotlight, though she found herself relegated to B movies—The Half Naked Truth (1932), Hot Pepper (1933), Hollywood Party (1934), and La Zandunga (1938). From 1939 to 1943, Velez portrayed Carmelita Woods in the "Mexican Spitfire" series. She was scheduled to do a play in New York and a film in Mexico when, five months pregnant, she committed suicide in December of 1944.[10]

The careers of these two women preceded the introduction of a non-identifying "Spanish" beauty in Hollywood, Rita Hayworth.[11] Their careers raise many questions about how Del Rio and Velez interacted with Hollywood and its culture. What leeway did these two women have in choosing roles? Did they accept a stereotyped portrayal of Mexican people? And if so, does this mean that they assimilated into Anglo-American culture? How did Anglo-American and Mexican audiences perceive them? How did they manage to attain stardom during a time of limited opportunities for Mexicans?[12] And finally, how did they negotiate the images of sexuality and ethnicity with Hollywood, the creator of images?

Dolores Del Rio and Lupe Velez played a part in developing their own images of sexuality on and off the screen. Their social class, beauty, and images of sexuality affected both women's careers, but in very disparate ways. Yes, Hollywood attempted to act as a "cultural ethnographer" (as it still does today), manipulating and distorting the images of Mexican characters as well as the images of Latino and Latina actors. However, both Del Rio and Velez demonstrated that they negotiated for space within a structured culture and therefore helped to create their own destiny.

Before Del Rio arrived in Hollywood in 1925, she lived a relatively sheltered life. Born Lolita Dolores Asúnsolo y López Negrete on 3 August 1905, in Durango, Mexico, she was the only child of Antonia López Negrete de Asúnsolo and Jésus L. Asúnsolo. Señor Asúnsolo was president of the Durango Bank and a large landowner. In 1910, at the age of five, young Dolores and her family fled to Mexico City to be with relatives and to avoid Pancho Villa, whose forces seized their home and bank. They never returned to Durango.[13]

As dictated by her class and culture, Dolores's parents arranged her marriage. In 1920, shortly before her sixteenth birthday, Dolores married Jaime Martínez del Río, descendant of one of the oldest families in Mexico and eighteen years her senior. They spent their honeymoon in Europe, traveling for two years, before returning to his family's ranch and subsequently settling in Mexico City. In 1925, while on his honeymoon, the director Edwin Carewe and his wife, Mary Aikins, met the del Ríos. Since Dolores could not speak English, Jaime translated the entire conversation for her. Carewe, fascinated by her beauty, inquired if she would like to come to Hollywood and become an actress. Both Dolores's and Jaime's families absolutely forbade it, but as her husband, it was Jaime's decision as to whether or not his wife would try Hollywood, and he had aspirations of his own to become a screenwriter.[14]

Under the direction of Carewe, Del Rio soon became a star. With such films as *What Price Glory?* (1926), *Resurrection* (1927), *The Loves of Carmen* (1927), *Ramona* (1928) and *Evangeline* (1929), Del Rio's success was assured.[15]

During this time, besides printing her publicity photos, *Photoplay* began doing articles on Del Rio. An article entitled "A Daughter of the Dons" in the June 1927 issue extolled Del Rio as a "flower of that ancient and aristocratic and enormously rich family whose name is part of Mexico's history."[16] In the wake of her success, Del Rio's marriage failed. Articles speculated that Edwin Carewe had come between Del Rio and her husband. After Jaime moved to New York, Del Rio filed for divorce on April 21, 1928. Jaime eventually left for Europe, where he died in late December of 1928. Biographers and gossip columnists speculated that he died of a broken heart.[17]

Dolores Del Rio. (Courtesy the Academy of Motion Picture Arts and Sciences.)

Del Rio made *Evangeline* (1929), her last film with Carewe, before cutting her ties with him in early 1930. Gossip columnists had speculated she would marry him, since his wife, Mary Aikins, had already divorced him.[18] Seven months after breaking with Carewe, however, Del Rio met Cedric Gibbons, art director for MGM studios, and they were married at the mission in Santa Barbara on 6 August 1930. Soon after, Del Rio became ill and rumors claimed she had suffered a nervous breakdown, spurred by Jaime's death and her break with Carewe. Del Rio was set to film *The Dove* for United Artists under a contract that stated that if she was away from the studio for more than a month, she could be released. When doctors recommended she not return to work, United Artists terminated her contract. Sick for over a year, Del Rio made no movies in 1931, and many considered her career over.[19]

Photoplay responded to these rumors by publishing an interview with Del Rio soon after she recovered. "Dolores vs. the Jinx" appeared in the August 1931 issue of *Photoplay*. Treating her with gracious diplomacy, the article depicted Del Rio as blameless, suffering from unhappiness and misfortune: "it was circumstances and not Dolores who caused [the illness]."[20]

Del Rio also did an interview with Gabriel Navarro of *La Opinión*. Featured in four consecutive Sunday editions in July of 1931, Del Rio talked about her childhood, marriage to Jaime Martínez del Río, Hollywood, Edwin Carewe, and her health. She stated that she had never loved Jaime and that neither one of them was to blame for the failure of their marriage. She understood that her refusal to talk to the press earlier had made her look guilty of causing Jaime's death. Only now could she give this interview and begin her new life with Cedric Gibbons.[21]

By the end of 1931, her health better, Del Rio contracted with RKO. The film, *The Dove*, which United Artists had planned to make with her, had been bought by RKO and was now made into *Girl of the Rio*. Featured as "the Dove" in a Mexican cantina, Del Rio's character falls in love with an American, who is framed by the evil Señor Tostada (Leo Carrillo). Such blatant stereotypes of Mexican people abounded in this film that the Mexican government made a formal protest.[22]

La Opinión also reprimanded Del Rio for accepting the role in the film under a caption reading "We Have Lost Dolores Del Rio!" Del Rio defended her decision to take the part: "I accepted the part," she said, "because they permitted me to modify the argument, and the development of the scenes, in such a manner that did not damage our (Mexican) reputation at all."[23]

Photoplay readers knew nothing of the conflict between Del Rio and Mexican viewers. Instead, *Photoplay* focused on Del Rio's sense of fashion. In an October 1933 *Photoplay* article entitled "How Many Lives Has Del Rio," the actress spoke in great detail of clothes and her image. She pointed out that she had always possessed a good sense of fashion but previously had not been allowed to choose her garments. Such movies as *What Price Glory?, Resurrection, Evangeline,* and *Ramona* displayed her in simple clothing. No longer accepting this model and with the Hollywood clout to shape her image, Del Rio emphasized how she wanted clothes to fit within her acting career, stating, "I do not want to wear exotic clothes. I want to be *very, very* fashionable. I want to show *fashion* through architectural lines."[24]

Three years later this modern image was further demonstrated in a *Photoplay* article entitled "Luncheon at Dolores Del Rio's: Hostess in the Modern Manner." According to *Photoplay*, Del Rio's homemaking reflected sophistication and the modern woman. Her husband, Cedric Gibbons, had designed the house himself to reflect their personalities—he the master and she his decoration. The article's author claimed that "Every line, every detail, every stick of furnishing were worked out in the brain of that ace interior decorator and master of the household, Cedric Gibbons, as the perfect background for his exotic and darkly lovely wife."[25]

Thoroughly modern in fashion, marriage, and home, Dolores Del Rio wanted to reflect that in her career. However, in the next eight years fewer roles came her way. As her career faltered, so did her marriage to Gibbons, and in March of 1940 they separated. Granted a divorce in

January of 1941 on the grounds that Gibbons "was cold and indifferent," Del Rio was soon involved with the twenty-six-year-old Orson Welles. The romance didn't last long and the actress decided to return to Mexico, stating, "I wish to choose my own stories, my own director, and camera-man. I can accomplish this better in Mexico."[26]

And this she did, making over nineteen films and enjoying a career that lasted until her death in 1983. Additionally, she returned to the United States several times and made films in Argentina, Italy, and Spain. She won four Ariels (Mexico's Oscar) and one Quixote (Spain's).[27]

Del Rio's early movies demonstrate that she could have developed a sensual and sexual image similar to Velez's "sex kitten" image. Instead, she managed to steer clear of the "Mexican Spitfire" stereotype with the help of her elite background, director Edwin Carewe, and certain choices she made for herself during her tenure in Hollywood.

An analysis of Del Rio's roles shows us that Hollywood studios did not exclusively identify her as a Latina character. Ana M. López argues that Hollywood identified Del Rio's style as "a vague upper-class exoticism articulated within a general category of 'foreign/other' tragic sensuality."[28] This translated into a sexual rather than ethnic identity for Del Rio. She garnered and cultivated an image of respectability in Hollywood, but she had limited options. Because of her class background and her light complexion, Hollywood studios allowed her to play only European nobility, adorable waifs, and high-class exotic characters.

In contrast, Lupe Velez did not have the advantages of Del Rio. Although the daughter of a colonel and an opera singer, Jacobo Villalobos and Josefina Velez, Velez was brought up quite differently from Del Rio. Born on 18 July 1909, in San Luis Potosí, she was named Maria Guadalupe Villalobos. For a few years, she attended a Catholic girls' school in Texas, but her father's abandonment forced her to return to Mexico and find work, first in a department store and then as a chorus girl. Her discovery by an American agent led her to Hollywood, where she worked in a musical that garnered her the attention of film producer Hal Roach in 1926.[29]

In 1928 Douglas Fairbanks sought Velez out to portray a wild mountain girl opposite him in the film, *The Gaucho* (1928). The positive reviews Velez received for *The Gaucho* led United Artists to offer her a five-year contract, and her strong sexual presence and personality would be emphasized in every film she made thereafter.[30]

Through the years, Velez invariably found herself in half-caste roles. Paramount's *Wolf Song* (1929) brought her into contact with Gary Cooper. The success of that film was attributed to Cooper's and Velez's off-screen romance. The studios approved and publicized the romance for all it was worth.[31]

Just as Del Rio sought to reflect the modern woman, so did Lupe Velez—but without Del Rio's success. A 1929 *Photoplay* article entitled, "Lupe—No Change!"—with the smaller caption reading "The voluble Velez here spikes rumor that she's turned tame—she's a little smarter,

Lupe Velez. (Courtesy the Academy of Motion Picture Arts and Sciences.)

that's all!"—dealt with the reporter's astonishment at the notion that Velez aspired to become a "lady":

Outwardly, Lupe has changed. She curbs her tongue with people she doesn't know. To interviewers she talks in a dignified manner of her home, which she really loves, her dogs and her work. She dresses better. Gone are the little short pleated skirts and blouses cut almost to her waist. In her wardrobe hang gowns that any Park Avenue lady would be delighted to own. In them, of course, Lupe does not look like a Park Avenue lady, merely because she is too striking a type.[32]

Using the justification that Velez was "too striking a type," *Photoplay* infers that Velez's ethnicity prevents her from identifying with upper-class society.

La Opinión also had standards that they expected Velez to consider. On 23 January 1929, an interview of Velez by an Anglo reporter appeared. The caption of the article read, "I Am Free; Free! Shouts Lupe Velez." In the interview, Velez discussed and compared the customs of Mexico and the United States. She also touched on topics related to femininity, marriage, and smoking, stating, "I believe that they are lying to the girls in Mexico, but what else can I do? One is not able to laugh, speak, say what you think. All you can say is yes, sir. He can say what he wants. Here I laugh and do what I want, because the American boys understand well."[33]

Here Velez expressed what she felt to be the strict and rigid codes of conduct for women in Mexico. The Mexican community was apparently outraged at this interview, because one week later, on 31 January 1929, another article appeared in *La Opinión*, which contained a letter of apology written by Velez and was entitled "Lupe Velez Says That She Loves Mexico and Mexicans." Velez explained that the interviewer misinterpreted her answer in English: "I wish to explain that when I spoke about the liberties enjoyed in America, compared with what young women in Mexico enjoy, I only commented on the peculiar customs of our country in general, without referring to them negatively, one or the other, and certainly this is not my personal opinion about this topic."[34] The article ended with the comment that the Mexican government had started procedures to boycott all future films made by Velez, but the Mexican community itself apparently forgave her, because she continued to appear in the paper's columns.

With the debut of her film *Cuban Love Song* (1931), Velez's relationship with Gary Cooper ended. While promoting the film in New York, Velez met Johnny Weissmuller, who was promoting his own film, *Tarzan the Ape Man* (1932). MGM viewed Weissmuller as its newest star and encouraged the romance between him and Velez.[35]

In the meantime, RKO continued to relegate Velez to stereotypical parts. In *The Half-Naked Truth* (1932), she portrayed "Princess Exotica, a publicity hungry actress posing as an escaped harem beauty." Velez's character, Princess Exotica, displayed aggressive sexual behavior and the ability to promote herself, a parody of Velez's own off-screen abilities.[36] This film became the basis for her Mexican Spitfire series later. Through it all, reports of Velez's relationship with Weissmuller remained in the forefront of *Photoplay* gossip. The magazine's announcement of their marriage on 8 October 1933, at 4:15 in the morning, made good press.[37]

Although Velez was a popular actress, RKO did not renew her contract in 1934.[38] Over the next few years, Velez traveled from studio to studio; she also spent two years in England making films.[39] Her roles grew increasingly more stereotypical, and her marriage began to fail. Art and life intertwined when *Photoplay* discussed Velez's matrimonial and domestic skills. The article entitled "Lupe and Johnny Were Lovers," with a smaller caption reading, "They done each other wrong! But Lupe relented. Now peace and Johnny reign," portrayed Velez and Weissmuller's relationship as one big battle of control that Johnny had finally won:

And now, all those gorgeous battles are over. And Lupe has become a "yes woman" and as model a housewife as ever wifed a house. You wouldn't, you just couldn't believe it. To think that Lupe, the spitfire of Hollywood, is now worrying over whether Johnny wants his chicken with spaghetti or without. And Lupe, with her own little bediamonded hands, cooks it all for Johnny herself. No going out to restaurants at night for Johnny. Lupe, with no cook but herself, does it all.[40]

As noted by Vicki L. Ruiz, the article's author downplayed or ignored the obvious insinuations of domestic violence in the Weissmuller and Velez home. Instead, her reputation as a "Spitfire" prompted disbelief on the part of the author that Velez could ever become domestically inclined. As her movies personified the need for her to be conquered, so did the imagery in her personal life. From 1934 to 1939, Velez and Weissmuller separated three times; their divorce was finalized in August of 1939, on the grounds of cruelty and physical and mental violence.[41]

In 1938, before her divorce became final, Velez returned to Mexico after an eleven-year absence. She was greeted by ten thousand fans in Mexico City. Her spirits soared. Her first Mexican film, *La Zandunga* (1938), costarred Arturo del Cordova. Mexican critics and audiences loved this comic love story, and Velez planned to make four more films.[42] But instead she returned to RKO. *Girl from Mexico* (1938) turned out to be a financial hit, and the Spitfire series was launched. A redhead "Spitfire," Velez played Carmelita, a singer hired by an American ad executive named Dennis, played by actor Donald Woods, who falls for her, much to the dismay of his aunt. In the second film of the series, *Mexican Spitfire* (1939), Carmelita marries Dennis, countering the Hollywood stereotype of the Latin woman who loses the Anglo man to an Anglo woman. Yet through all these films, other stereotypes abound, including Carmelita's lack of breeding, her social unacceptability, her refusal to put her show business career aside, her lack of desire to have children, and her failure to promote Dennis's career. In each film Dennis's aunt questions Carmelita's background and implores Dennis to divorce her and marry his ex-fiancée, Elizabeth (Linda Hayes). *Mexican Spitfire's Blessed Event* (1943) was the eighth and final movie of the series, for by that time the novelty had worn off.[43]

With the end of the Spitfire series, Velez returned to Mexico to make the film *Nana* (1944). While she waited for a Hollywood release of the film, she made plans for a new play in New York. She also announced her engagement to Harald Ramond, an unknown actor, on 27 November 1944. The newspapers that carried the announcement did not reveal that Velez was four months pregnant. Two weeks later, Louella Parsons announced that Velez's engagement to Ramond was off. Only days later, on the evening of 13 December 1944, Lupe Velez committed suicide.[44]

From the moment Velez was introduced to Hollywood audiences, her sexuality was attributed to her ethnicity. Her image and her behavior transgressed "traditional" boundaries of accepted Anglo standards.[45] Yet Hollywood, the studios and movie magazines such as *Photoplay*, promoted this image. Although Del Rio could not be identified ethnically, Velez's sexual personification was distinctly meshed with her ethnicity.[46] Those who have argued that Velez internalized her image as a "Mexican Spitfire" need to reconcile the fact that there is evidence that Velez knew and understood what she portrayed.[47]

Clearly the chasm of class influenced Hollywood's perceptions of these two Mexican women. Del Rio's background had a profound effect on her image. *Photoplay* always depicted her elite origins, and although Del Rio insisted upon being referred to as Mexican, Carewe and studios promoted her as Spanish.[48] On the other hand, from the moment of Velez's introduction to Hollywood until her death, she was Mexican.

The dichotomy between "good" Spanish and "bad" Mexican images has roots in American history. Historian Antonia Castañeda has argued that Anglo perceptions of Spanish and Mexican women in nineteenth-century California were based upon sex and race—and class as well: "Both stereotypes revolved around sexual definitions of women's virtue and morality," Castañeda has written. "Both dealt with race but with a crucial difference. The elite Californianas were deemed European and superior while the mass of Mexican women were viewed as Indian and inferior." Anglos already perceived Mexicans as racially inferior but exempted some Californiana women who possessed land and who intermarried with Anglo men. These women were depicted in a positive manner. With their aristocratic and virtuous qualities, these elite Californianas epitomized "good" women, but at the price of "denying their racial identity, and [being treated] as racially superior to Californiano males and the rest of their people."[49]

Later, these same ethnic images transferred onto the screen.[50] In the 1920s Latino movie stars portrayed other ethnicities to avoid playing the stereotypical "greasers," though a few actors like Ramon Navarro and Dolores Del Rio portrayed "romantic and erotic" images of Latins.[51] These romantic images moved from the screen to images in Del Rio's personal life, as coverage in *Photoplay* illustrates.[52]

The opposite occurred for Velez. Just as "good" and "bad" Mexican women emerged in nineteenth-century California, negative images of the "Latin-lover" type transformed into images of the "Latino gigolo and Latina vamp." This can be seen in *Photoplay's* reference to Velez as Mexican; such titles as "Mexican wild kitten" and "Mexico's IT girl" refer to Velez's ethnicity.[53] Velez's stardom manifested an image that focused upon her sexuality and aggressive personality, an image that seems to have been consciously negotiated. In her *Photoplay* article, "The Best Showman in Town," Ruth Biery stated, "There is never a moment when [Velez] is not emoting—putting on a show as definitely as a vaudeville performer before a filled house." Velez's whole personality was tied to her screen image.[54]

In contrast, *Photoplay* did not focus on Del Rio's sexuality but rather on her personal sense of fashion and her home decorating abilities. These stories clearly indicate that Del Rio understood that her sense of style—how she presented herself—could influence the kind of roles she sought. Del Rio's stardom did not cause her to deny her Mexican heritage, but she chose to reflect the modern 1930s woman in the manner Vicki L. Ruiz has termed "cultural coalescence."[55] Although Del Rio took on modern fashions, she had pride in her ethnic identity, as indicated by her insistence upon being identified as Mexican and not Spanish. Another indication was a 1931 article in *La Opinión*. Its title, "Dolores Del Rio Has Refused a

Defaming Film," indicated both ethnic pride on her part and the obvious approval of the newspaper and community.[56] Lupe Velez subsequently accepted the same "defaming" script.

Although both women sought to control and further their own careers, Del Rio appears to be the one who had mobility. Once she was settled in Hollywood with Carewe's help, her beauty established her as one of the most talented women there. Velez did not have that guidance, and she could only rely on her own instincts. Hollywood studios dictated the image and roles they felt suited an actor or actress, but Del Rio broke repeatedly with the studios, indicating her desire to find roles she felt suited her image. Once these characters and films proved useless to Del Rio, she moved back to Mexico and to more appropriate roles. Velez apparently planned a similar move in 1944, but she was overwhelmed by the difficulties of her personal life.[57]

From *Photoplay's* perspective, the characters each woman portrayed on the screen personified their own lives off the screen. However, the reality was much more complicated. How did Del Rio's and Velez's images in real life differ from their movie characters? Except for the *Gateway of the Moon* (1928), *The Trail of '98* (1928), and *Ramona* (1928), Del Rio's characters were European ethnic women. Always exotic or ethnic, Del Rio was never given the standard flapper role. In several of her movies, her character did the honorable thing and let the man she loved go. In *What Price Glory?* (1926), she watched the soldier she loved go off to battle when she knew he would not return. In her later films, Del Rio continued to portray women of other ethnicities, but with altered class status. With her beauty and elegance, Hollywood placed her in lavish and expensive movies: *Bird of Paradise* (1932), *Flying Down to Rio* (1933), *Madame Dubarry* (1934), and *The Widow from Monte Carlo* (1935) are a few examples. Del Rio portrayed ethnic heroines who either sought male help or fell in love, or both.[58]

Although Del Rio could not be identified ethnically on the screen, this was not the case with Velez. Her sexual personification was distinctly meshed with her ethnicity. As did Del Rio, Velez appeared both on and off the screen with European and Euro-American men. However, Velez's sexuality and ethnicity posed a threat to these men. Within her movies, misunderstanding and confusion abounded (e.g., the Spitfire series). Harmony could only be restored by submission to male domination. In her personal life, Weissmuller assumed the role of the dominant partner in their marriage. Mirroring her personal life, the movies of Lupe Velez often demonstrated the superiority of Anglo men over their Mexican peers. In *Broken Wings* (1931), Velez's character, a "cantina girl," dumps a "Mexican bandit" for an Anglo pilot.[59]

Does this indicate that Velez internalized and epitomized the "tragic prototype of the Latin spitfire stereotype"?[60] She had a number of affairs with men (John Gilbert, Gary Cooper, and Johnny Weissmuller) and did not follow traditional cultural rules. Yet she chose suicide over the "stigma" of either having a child out of wedlock or having an abortion.[61]

In both Mexican and Anglo culture in 1944, a child out of wedlock seemed unthinkable for a public figure.[62] In her suicide note, Velez wrote,

To Harald
May God forgive you and forgive me, too but I prefer to take my life away and our baby's before I bring him with shame or [kill] him. How could you[,] Harald, fake such a great love for me and our baby when all the time you didn't want us? I see no other way out for me, so good-by and good luck to you. Love Lupe[63]

Her note clearly indicated that she could not live with herself if she bore this child. Velez's flamboyant personality and aggressive sexuality were permissible, but at her age and with limited career opportunities, death seemed preferable to life as an unwed mother and a "has-been."

Both Del Rio and Velez made choices that could be construed as attempts to assimilate themselves into Anglo culture. Yet they both actively kept their ties with the Mexican community. Even so, *La Opinión* saw Del Rio and Velez as two distinct women, perceiving differences in the characters they portrayed and commenting on these differences. While *La Opinión* placed *both* women on a pedestal, the paper protested their appearance in films considered derogatory toward Mexican people, conveying images of Mexican men as lazy, evil, and scheming.[64]

Consequently, just as Del Rio and Velez struggled to create their own images in a culture such as Hollywood, they had to struggle with opinions within their own culture and community. Neither woman allowed *La Opinión* or the Mexican community to influence her decisions as to the roles she chose. For whatever reasons, Del Rio chose not to make Spanish-language films in Hollywood, and she felt she made the right choice in accepting the role for *Girl of the Rio* (1932). Velez's decision to be stereotyped as a "Mexican Spitfire" brought her fame, a decision consistent with talent for self-promotion.

This study of Dolores Del Rio and Lupe Velez demonstrates how both women created and responded to the images they cultivated. After Lupe Velez's introduction into Hollywood in 1927, sexual innuendoes and representations abounded in her films and in her magazine interviews. Relegated to B movies, she had a dubious reputation at best. Her Mexican Spitfire series represented the culmination of her sexual personification. Historians and amateur film buffs have speculated as to whether or not she internalized this image of the hot-tempered, passionate woman. The evidence suggests that she did indeed cultivate this persona. In contrast, because of her marriage and upbringing, Hollywood assumed Dolores Del Rio to be a woman of "'unhuman' loveliness," thus creating an almost untouchable image, which often made it hard for her to find work.[65] But with this image came respectability. Once she could no longer find roles that reflected positive images of Mexican people, Del Rio made the decision to leave Hollywood and return to Mexico, becoming the doña of Mexican cinema. It is possible that once Del Rio could no longer use her image to her advantage in Hollywood, she decided to return to Mexico, where her beauty and talent would be best utilized. It can then be argued that each woman played a part in shaping her own destiny. Hollywood's expectations collided, influencing each woman and in turn, Del Rio and Velez, acting on cue, created their own personas.

Notes

This article is dedicated to "The Sisterhood": Kathy Cairns, Yolanda Calderón-Wallace, Margaret Jacobs, Olivia Martínez-Krippner, Annette Reed-Crum, and Vicki L. Ruiz. I am indebted to Matthew Lasar and Michael J. González for their thorough readings, and I thank Robert Dawidoff for his insightful comments, criticisms, and required readings. Lastly and most importantly, I thank Vicki L. Ruiz, my mentor and friend. In addition to reading numerous drafts, she introduced me to Dolores Del Rio and Lupe Velez and showed me that I could incorporate my love of movies with the history of Mexican women.

1. Thomas Schatz, *The Genius of the System: Hollywood Filmmaking in the Studio Era* (New York: Pantheon Books, 1988).

2. For the purpose of this paper, "ethnic" stars refers to groups of people (i.e., Mexican, Asian, African American, and Native American) who have been historically misrepresented or underrepresented on the screen.

3. Two other Latina actresses appeared before Del Rio and Velez. Beatríz Michelena (1890–1942) and Myrtle Gonzalez (1891–1918) were among the first Latina "leading ladies of the silent screen" as Antonio Ríos-Bustamante has described in his book, *Latinos in Hollywood: A Pictorial History of Latinos in the Film Industry, 1911–1945* (Encino, Calif.: Floricanto Press, 1992). See also Antonio Ríos-Bustamante, "Latino Participation in the Hollywood Film Industry," in *Chicanos and Film: Essays on Chicano Representation and Resistance*, ed. Chon A. Noriega (New York: Garland Publishing, 1992), 21–32. Michelena appeared in fourteen films between 1914 and 1919. Gonzalez appeared in more than forty Vitagraph and Universal Picture films. As Ríos-Bustamante has noted, these two women's careers are noteworthy because they opened the door for other Latino/a actors in the film industry.

4. Robert Parish and T. Allen Taylor, eds., *The RKO Gals* (New York: Arlington House, 1974), 598.

5. Carlos E. Cortés, "Chicanas in Film: History of an Image," in *Chicano Cinema: Research, Reviews and Resources*, ed., Gary Keller (Binghamton, N.Y.: Bilingual Reviews, 1985), 94–108; Gustavo Lamanna, "Images of Latinas in Hollywood: A historical perspective," *La Gente de Aztlán* 19, no. 3 (February 1989): 7, 15, 23; Antonio Ríos-Bustamante, "Latinos and the Hollywood Film Industry, 1920s–1950s," *Américas 2001* 1, no. 4 (January 1988): 6–12; Allen L. Woll, *The Latin Image in American Film* (Los Angeles: University of California Latin American Center Publication, 1980), and Allen L. Woll, "Bandits and Lovers: Hispanic Images in American Film," in *The Kaleidoscopic Lens: How Hollywood Views Ethnic Groups*, ed. Randall M. Miller (Englewood, N.J.: Jerome S. Ozer, 1980), 54–72. For popular accounts of Lupe Velez, see Kenneth Anger, *Hollywood Babylon* (New York: Dell, 1975), 327–42; and Parish and Taylor, *RKO Gals*, 591–641. For Del Rio, see Larry Carr, *More Fabulous Faces* (New York: Doubleday, 1979), 1–51; De Witt Bodeen, *More from Hollywood: The Careers of 15 Great American Stars* (New York: A. S. Barnes, 1976), 281–89; and Robert Parish, Gregory W. Mank, and Don E. Stank, *Hollywood Beauties* (New York: Arlington House, 1978), 13–62. For both women, see George Hadley-Garcia, *Hispanic Hollywood: The Latins in Motion Pictures* (New York: Carol Publishing, 1990).

6. Jib Fowles, *Star Struck* (Washington: Smithsonian Institution Press, 1992), 121.

7. An example of *La Opinión* capitalizing on these aspirations occurred when the paper sponsored a contest in conjunction with Metro-Goldwyn-Mayer, offering the winner a screen test with MGM. See Vicki L. Ruiz, "'Star Struck': Acculturation, Adolescence, and the Mexican American Woman, 1920–1950," in *Building with Our Hands: New Directions in Chicana Studies*

eds. Adela de la Torre and Beatríz M. Pesquera (Berkeley: University of California Press, 1993), 113.

8. Ríos-Bustamante, "Latino Participation in the Hollywood Film Industry," 24. Ríos-Bustamante argued that Del Rio resisted stereotyping; he did not mention Velez.

9. Carewe first shortened Dolores's name to Dolores del Rio. Later the lowercased "d" would be changed to an uppercased "D" for audience appeal. See Bodeen, *More from Hollywood*, 288. See also Carr, *More Fabulous Faces*, 3–4; De Witt Bodeen, "Dolores Del Rio Was the First of Family to Act in Hollywood," *Films in Review* 17, no. 5 (March 1967): 266–83; José Gómez-Sicre, "Dolores Del Rio," *Américas* 19, no. 11 (November 1967): 8–17; and the chapter entitled "Dolores Del Rio," in Parish, Mank, and Stank, *Hollywood Beauties*, 13–62.

10. Parish and Taylor, *RKO Gals*, 592–623. See also Alfonso Pinto, "Lupe Velez, 1909–1944," in *Films in Review* 28, no. 9 (November 1977): 513–24.

11. Hadley-Garcia, *Hispanic Hollywood*, 58, and John Koball, *Rita Hayworth: The Time, the Place and the Woman* (New York: W. W. North, 1971), 44–70. Born Margarita Carmen Cansino to Volga Haworth and Eduardo Cansino, Hayworth began her dancing career in Tijuana, Mexico. Only when she underwent electrolysis, dyed her hair red, and changed her name to Rita Hayworth did she attain stardom. Her career calls into question whether Latinas must deny their ethnicity to achieve stardom in the film industry.

12. Rodolfo Acuña, *Occupied America: The Chicano's Struggle toward Liberation*, 3d ed. (New York: HarperCollins, 1988), 202–203. These two women were Hollywood movie stars when the U.S. government was deporting or repatriating 500,000 Mexican people, one-third of the Mexican population in the United States, back to Mexico.

13. Carr, *More Fabulous Faces*, 3; Bodeen, "Dolores Del Rio," 266; and Gómez-Sicre, "Dolores Del Rio," 9.

14. Bodeen, "Dolores Del Rio," 266–67.

15. Carr, *More Fabulous Faces*, 4–5; Parish, Mank, and Stank, *Hollywood Beauties*, 18. Del Rio was also chosen as one of the "Wampa Baby" stars of Hollywood in 1926. A Wampa Baby became a genuine Hollywood starlet who could expect a bright future in the studio system. The Western Association of Motion Picture Advertisers (WAMPA) for twelve years picked thirteen women whom they saw as star material; 1926 proved to be a banner year for Wampa Babies. That year, Joan Crawford, Mary Astor, Fay Wray, and Janet Gaynor joined Del Rio as Wampa Babies.

16. Ivan St. Johns, "A Daughter of the Dons," *Photoplay*, June 1927, 67.

17. Ibid., 20; newspaper clipping, 8 December 1928, found in Academy of Motion Picture Arts and Sciences (AMPAS) Library, Beverly Hills, Calif. See also Ruth Waterbury, "Going Hollywood," *Photoplay*, February 1929, 30. This article very dramatically detailed the last moments of Jaime's life and Dolores's last attempt to let him know "how much she truly loved him."

18. Newspaper clipping, 6 August 1930, found in AMPAS Library. Carewe's career plummeted after Del Rio broke her ties with him. He remade *Resurrection* with Lupe Velez in 1931, and he remarried Mary Aikins, but his career ended with the film *Are We Civilized?* (1934). He committed suicide on 20 January 1940.

19. Bodeen, *More from Hollywood*, 271. Though the illness was later described as a nervous breakdown, Del Rio denied this. *Photoplay* only referred to Del Rio's illness twice: Katherine Albert, "Dolores vs. the Jinx," *Photoplay*, August 1931, 69, and "What Price Stardom," *Photoplay*, September 1932, 58. The second article described Del Rio's illness as resulting from a kidney ailment.

20. Albert, "Dolores vs. the Jinx," 69, 102.

21. *La Opinión*, 5, 12, 19, and 26 July 1931.

22. Woll, *Latin Image in American Film*, 33, and "Bandits and Lovers," 57–58.

23. *La Opinión*, 15 and 22 May 1932.

24. Ruth Biery, "How Many Lives Has Del Rio?" *Photoplay*, October 1933, 60, 89–91.

25. "Luncheon at Dolores Del Rio's: Hostess in the Modern Manner," *Photoplay*, February 1936, 75.

26. Parish, Mank, and Stank, *Hollywood Beauties*, 41. See also Barbara Leaming, *Orson Welles* (New York: Viking Penguin, 1985), 207. Welles married Rita Hayworth soon after his break with Del Rio.

27. Bodeen, "Dolores Del Rio," 274–83.

28. Ana M. López, "Are All Latins from Manhattan? Hollywood, Ethnography, and Cultural Colonialism," in *Unspeakable Images: Ethnicity and the American Cinema*, ed. Lester D. Friedman (Chicago: University of Illinois Press, 1991), 410. López's argument is based on the period of the Good Neighbor Policy and specifically employs films from that period, but that same argument can be made about almost all Del Rio's films during her tenure in Hollywood.

29. Parish and Taylor, *RKO Gals*, 592; and Pinto, "Lupe Velez," 513. Gabriel Ramírez has written a biography, *Lupe Velez: la mexicana que escupía fuego* (Mexico City: Cineteca National, 1986). Unlike Del Rio, Velez was not an only child. She had two sisters and one brother: Mercedes, Josephina, and Emigdio.

30. Parish and Taylor, *RKO Gals*, 595. The authors described Velez's abilities as "striking good looks, energetic behavior (particularly in dancing and cavorting about), a strong sense of comedy timing, and her most marketable screen trait—her ability to enact a prime termagant, a girl quickly fired to anger, who unleashes her pent-up emotions in a barrage of physical assault on her male target." In 1928, the year *The Gaucho* was made, Velez was chosen as a Wampa Baby.

31. Parish, and Taylor, 597–98; *RKO Gals*, Pinto, "Lupe Velez," 514.

32. Barbara Lawton, "Lupe—No Change!" *Photoplay*, December 1930, 74 and 135. Part of this "change" included enhancing her accent in films and in public, even though she spoke correct English.

33. *La Opinión*, 23 January 1929.

34. *La Opinión*, 31 January 1929.

35. Parish and Taylor, *RKO Gals*, 603.

36. Ibid., 605; Pinto, "Lupe Velez," 516–17.

37. Parish and Taylor, *RKO Gals*, 607; Pinto, "Lupe Velez," 517. The press officially announced their marriage on 28 October 1933.

38. Pinto, "Lupe Velez," 517. Unlike Del Rio, Velez made Spanish-language films in Hollywood: *Oriente es Occidente* (Universal, 1930), *Resurección* (Universal, 1931), and *Hombres en mi vida* (Universal, 1932).

39. Parish and Taylor, *RKO Gals*, 611. These films included *The Morals of Marcus* (Gaumont-British, 1935), *Gypsy Melody* (Associated British-Pathé, 1936), and *Mad about Money* (British Lion, 1938).

40. Jane Hampton, "Lupe and Johnny Were Lovers," *Photoplay*, June 1934, 58, 98–100.

41. Vicki L. Ruiz, "La Malinche Tortilla Factory: Negotiating the Iconography of Americanization, 1920–1950," 12, 13. Paper presented at the American Studies Annual Meeting, Costa Mesa, California (5–8 November 1992). Permission of author to quote. Hampton detailed Velez's and Weissmuller's fights with battle images. "But the dog-fight was really the climax of the whole uncivil war. . . . What a battle that was! The cannons roared and the bayonets flashed, while the servants, wearing steel helmets and gas masks, went right on making the beds and fixing the spaghetti. They were veterans of wars at their bloodiest." Hampton, "Lupe and Johnny," 99; Parish and Taylor, *RKO Gals*; 610–13. Each time they separated, Velez filed divorce proceedings. She filed on 24 January 1934, but rescinded on 20 July 1934. She filed again on 2 January 1935, and later rescinded the decree. She filed again in early 1938, and the divorce was finalized on 16 August 1939. In each filing Velez accused Weissmuller of cruelty and physical and mental violence.

42. Parish and Taylor, *RKO Gals*, 614; Pinto, "Lupe Velez," 518. Cordova himself went to Hollywood in the early 1940s as a "Latin-lover" type.

43. The Spitfire titles include *Girl from Mexico* (1938), *Mexican Spitfire* (1939), *Mexican Spitfire Out West* (1940), *Mexican Spitfire's Baby* (1941), *Mexican Spitfire at Sea* (1942), *Mexican Spitfire Sees a Ghost* (1942), *Mexican Spitfire's Elephant* (1942) and *Mexican Spitfire's Blessed Event* (1943). The Good Neighbor policy affected RKO's decision to continue the series. See

Allen Woll's article, "Good Neighbor Policy: The Latin Image in American Film, 1939–1946," *Journal of Popular Film* 3 (Fall 1974): 278–93. See also Ana M. López's article, "Are All Latins from Manhattan?" which talks about how RKO interpreted the Good Neighbor policy.

44. Parish and Taylor, *RKO Gals*, 623–624. See also *Los Angeles Times*, 15 December 1944. In an article in that issue, Ramond admitted to knowing about the baby. Velez's agents, Bo Roos and Charles Tresona, revealed that Ramond planned to have the marriage annulled once the baby was born. Other sources indicated that Velez broke off the engagement when she heard of Ramond's plan.

45. Although the 1920s were known for flappers and their transcendence of sexual norms (at least in theory), by the 1930s, the way women dressed and behaved had reverted to more traditional behavior. Hollywood produced films presenting women in nontraditional jobs (e.g., reporters), but these women worked only until they found a husband. Velez transcended "traditional" boundaries by flaunting her sexuality. She did not display the ladylike qualities of elegance, decorum, and reserve. Her ethnicity and her embellished Spanish accent added to an aggressive style of personality that permitted yelling and physical contact, behavior not displayed by Anglo women. For more information on the 1930s genre, see Molly Haskall, *From Reverence to Rape: The Treatment of Women in the Movies* (New York: Penguin Books, 1973), 90–152; and Marjorie Rosen, *Popcorn Venus: Women, Movies and the American Dream* (New York: Coward, McCann & Geoghegan, 1973), 133–185.

46. López, "Are All Latins from Manhattan," 410. Del Rio did identify as a Mexican character in *Girl of the Rio* (1933). The most obvious role to substantiate López's argument that Del Rio was categorized as "foreign/other" is her character in the film *In Caliente* (1935), where she portrayed "the world's most famous dancer" and not a "Mexican beauty."

47. Antonio Ríos-Bustamante made this argument in his article, "Lupe Velez: Tragic Prototype of the Latin Spitfire Stereotype," *Américas 2001* 1:4 (January 1988): 24–25. For an example of Velez's conscious promotion of herself, see Ruth Biery, "The Best Showman in Town," *Photoplay*, November 1931, 73.

48. Ríos-Bustamante, *Latinos in Hollywood*, 4.

49. Antonia Castañeda, "The Political Economy of Nineteenth Century Stereotypes of Californianas," in *Between Borders: Essays on Mexicana/Chicana History*, ed. Adelaida R. del Castillo (Encino, Calif.: Floricanto Press, 1990), 213–36; quotes, 225, 224.

50. Ibid., 225.

51. Ríos-Bustamante, "Latino Participation," 24. For a full description of the "greaser" in films, see Arthur G. Pettit, *Images of the Mexican American in Fiction and Film* (College Station: Texas A&M University Press, 1980). Not all male Latin movie stars were able to avoid "greaser" stereotyping; Leo Carrillo and Julian Rivero were allowed to play only these kinds of roles. Male stars like Antonio Moreno and Ramon Navarro were designated the "Latin-lover" type and avoided stereotypical "greaser" roles. For a description of the "Latin-lover" image, see Woll's *Latin Image in American Film*.

52. St. Johns, "Daughter of the Dons," 67. See also Katherine Franklin, "Dolores Extols Passive Love," *Photoplay*, April 1934, 39, 106–107.

53. "Mexican Wild Kitten," *Photoplay*, February 1928, 33; "Mexico's IT Girl," *Photoplay*, April 1928, 62; and Marquis Busby, "Lookee Lupe Whoopee!" *Photoplay*, March 1930, 45.

54. Biery, "Best Showman In Town," 73, 106–107. See also Katherine Albert, "The Hot Baby of Hollywood: Otherwise Lupe Velez," *Photoplay*, February 1929, 36–37, 141–44; Mary Anderson, "The Sex-Jinx on Stardom," *Photoplay*, August 1935, 28–29, 103–104.

55. Just as Anglo women became influenced by the clothes and fashions they saw on the screen, so too were Mexican women. See Vicki L. Ruiz's article, "Dead Ends or Gold Mines? Using Missionary Records in Mexican-American Women's History," in this book. Ruiz argues for "cultural coalescence," stating, "There is not a single hermetic Mexican or Mexican-American culture but rather permeable *cultures* rooted in generation, gender, region, class, and personal experience." Just as Ruiz argued that material acculturation did not overshadow the Mexican women's identity, I argue that Del Rio did not deny her own heritage.

56. *La Opinión*, 24 May 1931.

57. Just as Anglo actresses like Mary Pickford, Marion Davies, and Gloria Swanson promoted their own careers, Del Rio and Velez did the same. See Lary May, *Screening Out the Past: The Birth of Mass Culture and the Motion Picture Industry* (New York: Oxford University Press, 1980), for a discussion of Mary Pickford. See also Rosen, *Popcorn Venus*. Studio and producer power should not be underestimated. The Hollywood studio system was a complex, hierarchical system. For a more complete understanding, see Thomas Schatz, *The Genius of the System: Hollywood Filmmaking in the Studio Era*, (New York: Pantheon Books, 1988). See also Ethan Mordan, *The Hollywood Studios: House Style and the Golden Age of the Movies* (New York: Simon & Schuster, 1988). See also Neal Gabler, *An Empire of Their Own: How the Jews Invented Hollywood* (New York: Doubleday, 1988).

When Del Rio broke with Carewe, she signed on with United Artists at a salary of nine thousand dollars a week. In 1933, she signed on with Warner Bros. to make five films for them. She then signed a contract with Columbia, filming *The Devil's Playground* (1937), and later signed with Darryl F. Zanuck and Twentieth Century Fox for whom she portrayed the femme fatale in *Lancer's Spy* (1937) and *International Settlement* (1938). She did no movies for two years, but in 1940, she accepted the female lead for MGM's *The Man from Dakota*.

58. In *Resurrection* (1927) Del Rio sends Prince Dimitri back while she stoically marches off to a life of exile in Siberia. For a discussion of movies that differentiated Latinos on the basis of "coloredness" and "whiteness," see Carlos E. Cortés, "Who Is Maria? What Is Juan? Dilemmas of Analyzing the Chicano Image in U.S. Feature Films," in *Chicanos and Film: Essays on Chicano Representation and Resistance*, ed. Chon Noriega (New York: Garland Publishing, 1992), 83–104.

59. Hampton, "Lupe and Johnny," 100; Ruth Biery, "Inside Politics of the Studios," *Photoplay*, August 1931, 48–49, 106–108; Ríos-Bustamante, "Latinos and the Hollywood Film Industry," Velez did have an affair with Gilbert Roland (Luis Antonio Dámaso de Alonso), but all her other major love affairs were with white/Anglo men. It should be noted that the father of Velez's baby, Harald Ramond, was a French citizen. It should also be noted that Velez had the ability to "work with difficult directors." Several of Del Rio's films also depicted male Anglo superiority over Latin males. In *Flying Down to Rio* (1933), Del Rio's character ends up with Gene Raymond rather than with her Brazilian fiancé, Raul (Julio Rubiero). In *I Live for Love* (1935), Del Rio's character, Donna Alvarez, falls out of love with Rico (Don Alvarado) and in love with Roger Kerry (Everett Marshall).

60. This phrasing is taken from Antonio Ríos-Bustamante's article, "Lupe Velez."

61. Anger, *Hollywood Babylon*, 332; Parish and Taylor, *RKO Gals*, 623; Pinto, "Lupe Velez," 520; and Ríos-Bustamante, "Lupe Velez," 23. According to Anger, Parish and Taylor, Pinto, and Ríos-Bustamante, because Velez was Catholic an abortion was not possible.

62. Less then ten years later, the actress Ingrid Bergman was blackballed from Hollywood when she left her husband and daughter for the director Roberto Rossellini. She became pregnant before her divorce was final. See Ingrid Bergman and Allan Burgess, *Ingrid Bergman: My Story* (New York: Delacorte Press, 1972).

63. *Los Angeles Times*, 15 December 1944. See also Anger, *Hollywood Babylon*, 336–37.

64. *La Opinión*, 24 May 1931.

65. The phrase " 'unhuman' loveliness" was coined in Julie Lang Hunt's article, "The Beauty Who Sits Alone," in *Photoplay*, December 1935, 119.

24.

Tsugiki, A Grafting: A History of a Japanese Pioneer Woman in Washington State

GAIL M. NOMURA

For this biography of Teiko Tomita, Gail Nomura draws on a special source, Tomita's own poems. Tomita, like many other Japanese immigrants, recorded her new life in the short poetry form known as "tanka." The poems express a wide range of Tomita's feelings over the years, giving us a rare glimpse into the ways in which she incorporated new experience into her own sense of personal identity. We share with Tomita the sadness of her youthful parting with her parents in Japan, her years farming and raising a family in Washington State, her experience of internment in 1941–45, the cross-cultural friendships she found as a garment worker in Seattle, and finally her hopes for her children. This study shows the complex ways in which Tomita and other Issei women drew on old tradition and new circumstance to make a home in a new place. And Gail Nomura offers a powerful image, drawn from Tomita's poetry, to express that experience—tsugiki, a grafting, a simultaneous symbol of rootedness and newness.

In the imagination of many, the pioneer woman is represented by a sunbonneted Caucasian traveling westward on the U.S. landscape. Few are aware of the pioneer women who crossed the Pacific Ocean east to the United States from Japan. Among these Japanese pioneer women were some whose destinies lay in the Pacific Northwest.

In Washington State, pioneer women from Japan, the *Issei*—or first (immigrant) generation—and their *Nisei*—second generation, or U.S.-born daughters—made up the largest group of nonwhite ethnic women in the state for most of the first half of the twentieth century.[1] These Issei women contributed their labor in agriculture and small businesses to help develop the state's economy. Moreover, they were essential to the establishment of a viable Japanese American community in Washington. Yet little is known of the history of these women.[2] This essay examines the life of one Japanese pioneer woman, Teiko Tomita, as a method of exploring the historical experience of Japanese pioneer women in Washington State.

Through interviewing Teiko Tomita, I have been able to gather certain facts about her life. But beyond this oral history, Tomita's experience is illumined by the rich written legacy of tanka poems she began writing when she was a high school girl in Japan. The tanka written by Tomita served as a form of journal for her, a way of expressing her innermost thoughts as she became part of the United States. Tomita's poems give us insight into how she viewed her life in the new country and capture the essence of the Japanese pioneer woman's experience in Washington State. Indeed, *tsugiki*, the title Tomita gave to her section of a poetry anthology, meaning a grafting or a grafted tree, reflects her vision of a Japanese American grafted community rooting itself in Washington State through the pioneering experiences of women like herself.

The tanka provided a natural and common vehicle of expression for Japanese immigrants like Tomita. Coming from a country that had instituted compulsory education in the late nineteenth century, Issei were often highly literate. But one did not have to be highly educated or uniquely gifted to compose tanka. Although the haiku, which is the Japanese short poem of seventeen syllables arranged in three lines of five, seven, and five syllables, is better known in the United States, the tanka is the more traditional poetic form. The tanka is a Japanese short poem consisting of thirty-one syllables arranged in five lines of five, seven, five, seven, and seven syllables successively. Japanese have from ancient times used the tanka to express their deepest emotions. Lyrical verse of the earliest collections of Japanese poetry used the brevity of the tanka form to speak of life, love, and grief of separation. Commoners as well as aristocrats wrote tanka, which for centuries remained the most popular means of poetic expression for men and women of all classes. Concentration and compression are the essence of the tanka, and in its brief thirty-one syllables Japanese were able to convey what might otherwise have required many pages, or even volumes.

Japanese immigrants like Tomita brought this poetic form with them to the United States and recorded their new lives through it. Issei-composed tanka reflected the imagery, feelings, and sensibilities of an immigrant generation taking root in a new land. Teiko Tomita used a traditional Japanese image, the cherry tree, in many of her *tsugiki* tanka to speak metaphorically of the grafting process of the Japanese immigrants to the root stock of America. Thus using the traditional poetic form and traditional metaphors, Tomita created new meanings expressing the Issei immigrant experience. In writing of this immigrant experience so different from life in Japan, Issei poets also created new metaphors and images and added new vocabulary. Tomita's early tanka in eastern Washington mention sagebrush and deserts unknown in Japan, and some of her tanka contain English words. The Issei-written tanka was itself adapted to the new land, the poet adapting its content and language while maintaining its ancient form. Together with oral histories and other prose accounts, the tanka poems of Tomita give us a better understanding of the Japanese immigrant woman's experience in Washington State.

In an interview, Tomita recounted that she was born 1 December 1896 in Osaka Prefecture, Japan, the second of nine children born in the Matsui family.[3] She graduated from a girls' high school, and while there learned to write tanka. Her teacher gave her the pen name "Yukari," which she used even in the United States. She went on to take a one and a half years' course at a normal school, which earned her a certificate to teach at the elementary school level. She taught until her marriage in 1920.

Most women in Japan at that time married before they were twenty-five, and as Tomita approached her mid-twenties she was urged to marry. Family-arranged marriages were the norm in Japan, rather than love marriages, since marriages were more of a contract between families than between individuals. Through a go-between, she was matched with her husband, Masakazu Tomita, who was farming near Wapato, Washington. She was shown his picture and told of his background and character. She met with his family in the neighboring prefecture in Japan and was impressed by them. Tomita and her husband-to-be exchanged letters over a two-year get-acquainted period before their marriage. In late 1920, Masakazu Tomita came back to Japan for a couple of months before returning with his bride to Wapato, in February 1921, to farm on the Yakima Indian Reservation.

Tomita's husband had promised her grandparents, who headed the extended family, that they would return in three years, and the grandparents consented, expecting her to work in the United States for three to five years at most. No one knew that the three-year stay would turn into almost seven decades, though Tomita said that when she got to Washington and saw the poor conditions there, she knew they would not be able to return to Japan in so short a time. Indeed she would never again see her parents.

Tomita's poems indicate the feelings of Issei women toward the families and life they left behind in Japan. Although starting a new life abroad, the women still had solid roots in their homeland. Ties with their families were strong. In one poem Tomita recalled the parting words of their parents:

> "Live happily,"
> Said my parents
> Holding my hands,
> Their touch
> Even now in my hands[4]

Tomita always remembered her parents' words of hope for her happiness in the new land. The warmth of her parents' love as expressed in their parting words and touch would sustain her through the years of separation. Tomita herself would pass this hope of happiness on to her own children.

Separation from her family gave Tomita new insights into the depths of family ties. This is apparent in a poem about her father that grew out of an incident that Tomita liked to recount over and over again. Marriage meant for her that her husband and children became the focus of her life and thoughts and that work left little time to feel any longing to return home. She claimed that she had no thoughts of returning to Japan, no sadness over her life in the United States. But her husband once saw her in the fields, shedding tears. He thought that she had become homesick after receiving a letter from her father. At dinner that night, he sympathized with her, saying he understood that she longed for her home, far away from the harsh land of the Yakima Valley. To his surprise, Tomita replied that she had no thoughts of returning to Japan. Rather, she had cried upon reading the letter, because it revealed a gentle, caring father she had not understood:

> The father I thought so strict
> Where did he conceal
> Such tender feelings
> Revealed in those gentle letters
> Many days I cried[5]

"Those gentle letters" inquired after her well-being and happiness in the new land. Tomita came to have a fuller picture of her father than the severe figure of her childhood. She came to understand the love of father for child. The tears were tears of understanding.

The strength of ties with family and homeland over the thousands of miles separating them is apparent in another tanka by Tomita, encapsulating her emotions upon receiving a package from her family:

> When I think
> It is from Japan
> Even wrapping paper
> Seems so close to me
> It's hard to throw it away[6]

Issei women had settled in the Yakima Valley since the 1890s, but even in 1921, when Tomita came to Wapato, the valley was still a raw frontier. Instead of moving from Japan to a richer life, Tomita embarked on a primitive pioneer life. In Kazuo Ito's book *Issei: A History of Japanese Immigrants in North America*, Tomita noted that her Wapato house "was only a little better than a shack, being a two-room cabin hastily put together." Although everyone she knew in Japan had electricity, in Wapato "there was no electric light, so I had to polish oil lamps every morning. We had one small stove in there which took wood or coal, and from time to time I picked up roots of sagebrush and used it as fuel, too." There was no running water. Water had to be drawn from the well outside. The weather, too, was not gentle. Tomita recalled that in deepest winter it was so cold in the house that "you could hear the eggs in the cupboard in the kitchen cracking" and "the place where the sheet was turned down under our chins at night got covered with frost from our breath." When summer came roaring in, "it was scorching hot with a temperature of more than 100 degrees," and at night the Tomitas would have to "spread a blanket under the peach tree" to sleep on.[7]

Tomita helped her husband with the farming on the Yakima Indian Reservation, where he had leased land to grow hay. But in 1921, the year she arrived, and again in 1923, Washington passed stricter alien land laws, which anti-Japanese agitators pressured the Department of Interior to apply to the Yakima Indian Reservation. The Yakima Indian Agency was thus forced to stop issuing leases to Japanese Issei, since the new alien land laws prohibited not only the ownership of land but the renting, share-cropping, and issuance of leases to those who had not in good faith registered their intent to become citizens. Inasmuch as the Japanese were denied naturalization rights by U.S. law strictly on a racial basis, they could not in good faith register their intent to become citizens. Thus they were ineligible to lease land either in Washington or on the reservation, and the Tomitas lost their lease rights to their farm on the Yakima Indian Reservation.

Luckily, Tomita's husband was an accomplished agriculturist, and a white nursery owner quickly hired him as a foreman for his nursery in Satus. Tomita served as cook for the laborers working under her husband. She remembered having to cook in shifts in her small house, first serving the work crew, then her own family. It was in Satus that her first child was born.

For Tomita, Satus was an even more remote, isolated area of Washington than Wapato had been. She had to walk five miles to see another Japanese face. Isolated as she was, she took solace by writing tanka for herself, recording her life and thoughts. She conveyed in one poem the loneliness and monotony of her life, in which the only way to distinguish one day from another might be the sun's rising and setting:

> Neighbors are five miles far away
> Many days without seeing anyone
> Today, too, without seeing anyone
> The sun sets[8]

This isolated life was common to most pioneer women of the West, as was exposure to the harshness of nature. The houses built by the pioneers with their own hands were not proof against the elements. Tomita's poems speak eloquently of this ceaseless intrusion of nature:

> Yakima Valley
> The spring storm raging
> Even in the house
> A cloud of sand
> Sifts in[9]

The Yakima Valley was a desert that with water and sweat could be made to bloom. The Issei worked the land, transforming desert and sagebrush into fertile fields of alfalfa, onions, tomatoes, beans, and melons. But hard work did not ensure success. In another poem, Tomita expressed her realistic assessment of the immigrants' struggle to cultivate the land:

> Sagebrush desert to fertile plain
> A transformation, I hear,
> But when the windy season comes
> There's no transforming the sandstorm[10]

The persistent sand was a constant reminder of the desert that could reclaim the newly fertile land at any moment and of the tenuous hold on success that the Japanese as aliens had on the leased land. At any moment a whirling sandstorm could engulf them and return the fertile plain to sagebrush desert.

Tomita's poems evoke not only the grit of the desert sand in the newly developed Yakima Valley, but also the severe desert heat:

> As we busily pick beans
> Even the breeze stirring
> The weeds at our feet
> Feels hot[11]

Perseverance in the face of adversity characterized the early Issei women. This same spirit was imbued in the children, who worked in the fields with their parents. Tomita wrote:

> "Soon the heat will be gone"
> While picking beans
> I encourage my children
> And myself[12]

In encouraging her children to persevere in adversity, Tomita strengthened herself to persevere for her children.

Tomita's poems offer a key to her motivation for enduring, for continuing to cultivate the burning frontier. Her use of the symbolism of grafted cherry trees makes particularly clear the way she viewed her place in this new land:

> Carefully grafting
> Young cherry trees
> I believe in the certainty
> They will bud
> In the coming spring[13]

The cherry blossom is a Japanese symbol not only of spring but of Japan and of the Japanese people themselves. In the grafting of cherry trees, Tomita saw the grafting of the Japanese immigrant onto the root stock of the United States, where the graft would continue to grow and become a permanent part of the stock. The importance of this symbolism is again underscored in her choice of the title "Tsugiki" for her section of the Issei poetry anthology *Renia no yuki*. She viewed not only her past work in the nursery as grafting but perhaps also her own self.

In the poem above she expressed her belief in a coming spring when the grafted tree would bud and grow, just as the hopes and dreams of the immigrant Japanese would be fulfilled. The centrality of this hope of a coming spring is expressed in another poem:

> Whirls of storming winter
> I tolerate
> Believing in spring
> To come again[14]

By believing in the certainty that the grafted tree would bloom in its new environment, one could endure the winter of travails. Perhaps, though, the blossoms would be the next generation, not Tomita's own. Meanwhile, the grafting process was an arduous one, as another poem indicates:

> Grafting cherry saplings
> Along long furrows
> The August sun
> Burns on our back[15]

In 1929 the Tomitas moved to Sunnydale, near Seattle, where Seattle-Tacoma International Airport (Sea-Tac) now sprawls. There they started their own nursery. Moving to more populous Sunnydale meant that Tomita was able to have many Japanese families as neighbors for the first time in the United States. It also meant the further development of her poetry, for she heard of a tanka club in Seattle and joined the group in 1939. Although she was not able to attend the monthly meetings, she would each month send new poems for criticism. Many of her poems were sent on to Japan for publication. But in Sunnydale, misfortunes and hardships continued, with the loss of the youngest daughter of the Tomitas' five children and the impact of the Great Depression. Tomita became a Christian during the Sunnydale years, and many of her later poems reflect her new faith.

The small economic gains made by the Tomitas were wiped out by the outbreak of war between the motherland and the adopted land in December 1941. Since they were denied naturalization rights, all Japanese immigrants were aliens, now enemy aliens. Furthermore, even their U.S.-born children were considered suspect. The old anti-Japanese agitation was rekindled, and this time succeeded in perpetrating one of the most massive violations of civil rights in U.S. legal history. With no formal charges of any wrongdoing, more than 110,000 Issei and their U.S. citizen–children were removed from their homes on the West Coast to incarceration in concentration camps. They were not to be allowed to return to their homes until 1945. Although most Seattle Japanese were interned at Minidoka in

Idaho, those in the outlying area of Seattle, like the Tomitas, were interned at Tule Lake, California, in 1942. In late 1943 they were moved to Heart Mountain in Wyoming, where ironically, Tomita was reunited with Japanese from the Yakima Valley, her first home in the United States.[16]

Immediately after the bombing of Pearl Harbor, many rumors circulated in the Japanese community that military men were searching all Japanese homes for any incriminating evidence that would link them with Japan. Later, there was talk about something fearsome called "camp." Under this pressure, Tomita gathered up her precious poetry manuscripts, took them to the fields, and burned them all, fearing that the private thoughts recorded in her tanka might be twisted into something harmful to her family. Being forced to burn her poems remained one of the most painful memories of the war for Tomita. Much of the poetic record of her life was wiped out.

But despite the destruction of the manuscripts, not all the poems were lost. Many of the burned tanka remained etched in Tomita's mind, to be recalled in later years. Easily committed to memory, poetry has often been the device of oral tradition's preservation of preliterate history, passed on from one generation to the next.

When war broke out between Japan and the United States in December 1941, it looked as though spring would not come, even for the next generation. The war years were difficult ones for the Issei women. After years of struggling, the little they had gained was wrenched from them overnight. Forced by the government to leave the land they had pioneered, they were imprisoned in even more isolated and desolate regions of the United States than they could ever have imagined. The internment camps were located in remote desert lands. Yet even here, surrounded by barbed wire, the creative spirit of the Issei inmates persisted. The creative arts in the camps found expression in forms ranging from polished sagebrush roots to accomplished poetry. Many Issei learned to write Japanese poetry for the first time in camp, and they continued to write even after they had left the camps.[17]

At Heart Mountain, Tomita, with other Issei, attended lectures and classes in poetry to while away the seemingly endless years of internment. Tomita began to keep a journal of her class lectures, as well as of her poems—a fresh book to replace the volumes she had burned. Her book of poems shows the changes she made from one draft to another to final form. In poetry many Issei found the solace Tomita noted in a poem written in 1943 at the Tule Lake internment camp:

> Within the iron stockade
> Always composing poems
> From the sorrows of war
> A little consolation[18]

As she had done in the desert of the Yakima Valley, Tomita turned to poetry to comfort herself in her troubles. But, as always, her poems also reflected hope. In the midst of the sorrow and uncertainty of imprisonment at Tule Lake, in January 1943 she could still write:

> In the war concentration camp
> The New Year's Day's sun rises
> Look up at the light
> Which breaks up the darkness of night[19]

New Year's Day meant the hope of a new start, the hope that the darkness of the past year might be pierced by the light of freedom. But freedom did not come quickly. The war continued. Tomita's poems written in 1944 reflect the inner turmoil experienced by the Issei caught by a war between the country of birth and the adopted country that had not accepted them as its own:

> I read the war news
> Today again
> My heart clouds
> And my thoughts are frozen[20]

When the war finally ended in 1945, the Tomitas were living in Minnesota, having secured a work release earlier in the year. The war that had torn them from their homes and made prisoners of them had ended, but the war's end was bittersweet news:

> Among whites jubilantly shouting
> "The war is over"
> My husband and I
> Cried throughout the night[21]

Horrifying atomic bombs had been dropped and Japan was defeated, but Japanese Americans had at last been released from the camps in which they had been held for years without any justification. Joy and relief at the end of the grief and hardships of the war combined with the sadness of war's aftermath and the uncertain future. Tomita worried over the fate of her family in Japan and their inevitable concern over her fate in America:

> For the first time in five years
> Letters are permitted to the home country
> Today I only write
> "We're safe"[22]

The link with family in the home country was reestablished. The silence brought by war ended with the simple message, "We're safe."

They were safe. They had survived another hardship, but now they once again had to start from scratch. Tomita wrote:

> Returning home from the iron stockade
> Five years ago
> Reconstructing our lives
> Is no small thing even now[23]

Her poem reflects the cold reality for Japanese Americans that even after returning from the concentration camps they still faced a long struggle to rebuild their lives. But although it was indeed "no small thing," Tomita did reconstruct her life. Because of the internment, the Tomitas had not only lost their nursery business but had no capital to invest in another venture. Tomita took the only wage job available to her. She became a garment worker in Seattle. This job opened new worlds for her.

Sewing alongside other immigrant women in Seattle, Tomita gained closer contact and better understanding of women from other ethnic groups. The poems written while she was a seamstress reflect a growing awareness of the commonality of experience and emotions she shared with her coworkers. In one poem she wrote:

> A German woman and I
> Sewing together
> Sharing the same feelings
> Speaking of the war destruction
> In each of our home countries[24]

Although they came from two countries separated by thousands of miles and by different cultural traditions, here in the workplace the two women shared their wartime experiences and became one.

While her prewar poems dealt mainly with herself or her family, Tomita's poems were now enlivened with observations of other people. In contrast to the isolation of her former rural life, her urban workplace offered a microcosm of the multiethnic, multicultural U.S. society of which she was a part. In a series of more narrative poems, Tomita observed some conflict between white and black workers, but in general her poems suggest a sisterhood among the women workers that cut across ethnic lines.

Tomita's poems bring to life the variety of women she worked with, among them a black woman who had such a fine voice that when she sang, her voice rose clear and strong above the roar of the sewing machines, and a Filipino woman who seemed very cheerful and carefree and who had learned a little Japanese that helped her communicate with Tomita. Tomita savored and valued these experiences:

> For many years
> Mixed among the workers of different races
> I sew
> I'm used to it
> Such life is enjoyable[25]

Tomita's growing appreciation of interaction with other ethnic groups is further demonstrated in a series of poems about her Italian neighbors. The first in the series notes the presence in her neighborhood of many Italians, most of them farmers who worked very diligently. She admired their industry, which made her feel an affinity with them. In the second poem of the series she again took up this theme:

> In their hard work
> Italians are like we Japanese
> Daughters and wives, too
> Work all day in the fields[26]

It was in their shared history of the hard work of farming that Tomita found a commonality of experience with these European immigrants. And the feelings were mutual, it seems, for in the next poems we see that at least one of the Italian neighbors had become a friend. Beyond sharing hard work and vegetables with his Japanese neighbors, he shared the immigrant experience of separation from the land of one's birth:

> Mutual shared feelings
> This Italian
> Speaking fervently about
> His homeland[27]

In the postwar period we see Tomita's poems reflecting not only a more urban, multiethnic awareness but also a more global viewpoint. Fully understanding the terrible costs of war, Tomita was well aware of the world events that might lead to a war for which her children would have to pay the high price:

> My son is still young
> I daily pray
> For eternal peace
> In this violent world[28]

In particular, she had become ardently opposed to the nuclear arms race, and she devoted a whole series of poems to this subject. News of the Bikini Island nuclear test victims moved her to write:

> Reading of the condition
> Of Bikini patients
> Incurable disease
> The power of science
> Is rather a curse[29]

She noted that Japan was a leader in the nuclear disarmament movement:

A country that experienced
The death ash
Japan's accusing voice
Voice of desperation[30]

In another poem in the series, Tomita observed that a ban on nuclear bombs had already been written with the blood of Japan, the only country to suffer an atomic bombing. But, she noted sadly,:

Regardless of the earnest prayers
Of the suffering country
Nuclear bombs
Are steadily produced[31]

After decades of hard work, Tomita was finally able to realize her dream of owning a home. Her joy in the fulfillment of the dream was recorded in a series of poems:

I enjoyed drawing pictures
Of my desired house
The long held dream
Became a reality[32]

The dream became a reality just when she and her husband had virtually given up hope of achieving it in their generation:

The dream I passed
On to my children
How many years!
The house is finished[33]

But this joy at a dream finally fulfilled in America was also to be dashed. Her Sunnydale home was directly north of Seattle-Tacoma International Airport. Soon the roar of the airplanes shook her house: ·

The runways are to be expanded,
I hear,
The roaring sound
Is drawing closer to me[34]

The airport expanded, she wrote, despite the complaints and puzzlement of the surrounding people. Its expansion changed the environment:

Farms and houses, too
Before I'm aware
I see their shadows no more
The runways are being built expansively[35]

As houses and farms disappeared, the people disappeared. The Port of Seattle responded to the complaints of noise and low-flying jets by removing the people who complained. It acquired by eminent domain the property of people like Tomita to form a buffer zone around Seattle-Tacoma International. In 1967, Tomita was once again forced to relocate. More fortunate than some, she and her husband were able to move in with her daughter's family in Seattle.

The realization of the passing of time is very much part of the later writings of Tomita. Reflecting on the decades of pioneering that had flown past, she wrote:

> Long ago are the days
> I helped my husband
> Cultivate the raw land
> And raised our children
> We two have grown old[36]

Another poem continued the theme of old age:

> My husband
> Reading with bifocals
> So many decades of struggles
> Engraved deeply
> In the wrinkles on his face[37]

Thoughts rose of the unfulfilled aspirations of youth. For Tomita those memories were of dashed hopes of continuing her studies. In a series of poems she recalled these hopes of scholarship, symbolized in a treasured box given to her as a graduation prize:

> As a lifetime memory
> Placed in a suitcase with love and care
> For thirty years
> A lacquer calligraphy box[38]

She remembered the words that accompanied the prize- words admonishing her to continue to train her mind and soul. But since coming to the United States,

> Too busy were
> Thirty years of life
> In a foreign country
> Never used the brush and ink[39]

There had never been time for her formal studies. She had written her tanka in isolation in the fields of the Yakima Valley. Even after moving to the Seattle area, though she had been able to join a tanka club, she had not been able to attend the monthly meetings because the nursery had required her constant care.

Her life, she said in an interview, could be summed up in one word, *isogashii*—busy, a life filled always with things she had to do.[40] As for thoughts of the luxury of studies,

> Never to return are the days
> When I put my heart and soul
> In my studies only
> I grow old in a foreign country[41]

Although her aspirations may have had to be set aside in the grafting process of settling in the United States, there was always the belief in the fulfillment of dreams for the next generation, when the grafted tree would bloom and bear fruit. The struggles were well worth the pain for Tomita, if her children could fulfill their own dreams and aspirations. Tomita reveled in the fact that her children had not been adversely affected by the family's hard life:

> My daughter has
> A rainbow-like dream
> Cheerful as she is
> The poverty of me her mother
> Hasn't stained her life.[42]

Memories of the poverty of much of her life in the United States, with repeated setbacks, led her to write:

> When winter comes
> I wonder what it was
> That enabled me to endure
> Heartrending sorrows[43]

It was for her children that she had worked, and it was the hope of their spring that sustained her through her winter of struggles and sorrows. In her poems, she celebrated the triumphs of her children as they went off to college, got married, and started new, exciting jobs. Her poems reveal a conviction on her part that her children would not suffer the trials and tribulations she had endured:

> My son's start in life
> Like a clear morning
> Without a single cloud
> Limitless blue sky of hope[44]

Her struggles had not adversely affected the lives of her children but rather seemed to have ensured their future. She could write hopefully in 1968:

> The centennial of
> The Japanese immigrants in America
> Our next generation
> With a great future before them[45]

Fifteen years later Tomita looked back on her more than six decades of life experiences in America and concluded:

> The bitter ordeals I have suffered
> One after another
> As I remember
> Now without sorrow
> Filled with grace[46]

Tomita's later poems reflect a continuation of her thanksgiving that her grandchildren, too, were enjoying the spring that had come out of the travails of her winters. In a series of poems in the summer of 1983 she wrote of her trip to the East Coast to attend her granddaughter's graduation from Sarah Lawrence. With this commencement came a new flowering for the third-generation *tsugiki*, and a celebration uniting the generations. The ties that bound the generations together appeared strong, as her grandchildren made efforts to communicate with their grandmother in Japanese:

> From my granddaughter in New York
> A letter in Japanese
> As I read it
> Tears of joy overflow[47]

Whatever their literary merits, the poems presented in this essay provide valuable information and insight into the life of Teiko Tomita. Each poem is a diary entry relating a significant event or thought in her life. Often a series of poems gives a full account of a particular incident in her life. Even more than a diary, the poems reveal the inner thoughts and emotions of the author. Tanka critic Hideko Matsui, in an article in *Cho-on*, the Japanese poetry magazine to which the Seattle tanka club sent their selected poetry for publication, asserted that although poems such as Tomita's in *Renia no yuki* have a simple, classical moving quality about them, their importance is mainly that they relate the immigrants' history in the traditional form of the Japanese tanka. In fact, both the historical value and the literary merit of Issei poetry deserve a great deal of further discussion.[48]

Recognition of the value of Issei poetry as a vehicle for understanding the Japanese American experience in the United States has led to the publication of anthologies of translated poems written by the Issei. One such anthology is *Poets behind Barbed Wire*, which contains Japanese short poems, haiku and tanka, written by Hawaii Issei interned during World

War II. The editors of the anthology note that "in view of the scarcity of writing paper, these short poems, being less cumbersome than long diaries, were ideal forms for the internees' expression of their pent-up emotions." They further point out that "it also perpetuates the Japanese tradition of expressing their innermost emotions through short poems instead of prose." The editors believe that the short poems express the Issei internment experience far better and more explicitly than prose written on the experience. Indeed, one of these poets behind barbed wire scribbled hundreds of poems on the only two sheets of paper he was able to take with him from detention to internment camps.[49]

For Tomita and a great many Issei, poetry was a means of recording their lives for posterity as well as an artistic release of their emotions. They wrote their tanka as poetic expressions of their lives and thoughts. In writing their tanka they were conscious of their role in recording their history—a history they believed would not be included in general histories about American immigrants. Another Issei woman poet, Keiko Teshirogi, wrote:

> Not recorded in immigrant history
> Your struggles are inscribed
> In the depths of my heart alone[50]

As it was for Tomita, the cherry tree was a common Issei symbol of Japan and the Japanese. Teshirogi also composed a tanka similar to those of Tomita, speaking of the Issei as cherry trees making the adaptation to the American continent from their roots in the island environment of Japan:

> A cherry tree
> That cannot adapt itself to a continent
> Is small
> And without taking on autumn colors
> Its leaves fall[51]

Despite great hardships, the Issei immigrants did indeed adapt to their new environment. For some, like Tomita, poetic expression helped to make that adaptation more endurable. Their poetry, in turn, helps us grasp the history of that adaptation and survival.

Teiko Tomita's life as presented in this essay provides an outline generally representative of the Issei woman's rather harsh life in Washington State. Although the early Japanese immigrants to Washington were predominantly young single men, women began to enter the state in large numbers after the so-called Gentlemen's Agreement in 1907–08 that restricted the further immigration of Japanese male laborers to the United States. Like Tomita, most women who came were wives of settled immigrants. Many were "picture brides" whose marriages had been arranged by their families through the exchange of pictures with Japanese male immigrants living in Washington. After 1921, because the Japanese government did not issue passports to picture brides, most grooms, like Tomita's husband, traveled to Japan to marry and brought their wives back with them. In 1924, Congress passed a new immigration and naturalization act that prohibited the immigration of "aliens ineligible to citizenship," a category the U.S. Supreme Court had created in its 1922 *Ozawa* decision and 1923 *Thind* decision, ruling that Mongolians as a racial group and people from India were not eligible for naturalization. Thus no new immigrants from Japan, male or female, arrived after 1924. Still, because the Japanese males had been able to send for wives from 1908 to 1924, there occurred a dramatic increase in the numbers of women of Japanese ethnicity in Washington.[52]

The Japanese women who came between 1910 and 1924 played a crucial role in the growth of a Japanese American community in Washington. The summoning of wives like Teiko Tomita reinforced the commitment to permanent residency in America more than did economic stakes in farms and businesses. There was a settled family life with the coming of wives, and an emergence of Japanese American family units with the dramatic increase in American-born children between 1900 and 1930. With the birth of the second generation, there was a transformation from immigrant society to permanent settlers, as Issei began to focus and identify their own futures in terms of the future of their children in America. Entry of women into Japanese immigrant society was an integral part of the process by which that society sent its roots into U.S. soil. The arrival of women guaranteed that a community with a family life could be established in the United States. The Japanese community developed a family orientation around schools, churches, clubs, and associations. The women brought both community and Japanese culture with them. Often highly educated, like Tomita, they preserved such values as love of learning and an appreciation of the arts.

Tomita's lifetime of work in the Yakima Valley, Sunnydale, and Seattle underscores the fact that Japanese pioneer women were not only wives and mothers but also workers. Their labor was indispensable in the operation of farms, small businesses, and labor camps, as well as in family enterprises such as small shops and tiny farms. Japanese women played a vital economic role in the new land.

The majority of Japanese women initially lived in rural areas, helping their husbands till the soil as farmers. Japanese agriculturalists were especially prominent in Washington. In urban areas, women entered small businesses operated by their husbands, such as laundries, markets, restaurants, and boardinghouses, or they became domestic servants, seamstresses, and cannery workers. Labor camps that provided laborers for railroads, lumber camps, and mills were often run by Issei men. Many Issei women worked in these labor camps. As Tomita did in her Yakima years, the women cooked for large groups of workers employed by their husbands.

Japanese women performed tasks essential to the maintenance of the family by earning income, rearing children, preparing meals, shopping, and tending the sick. Because of their essential role in running the family and their valuable economic role, the women enjoyed greater power in decision making for the family than did their counterparts in Japan. Moreover, in the pioneer setting the Issei women were free of the traditional control of the mother-in-law, another factor that greatly enlarged their influence in the family.

In the 1930s the power of Issei wives in the family increased as the men aged. Many of the Issei men in the 1930s were over fifty-five. As the men aged, their wives—on the average, ten years younger—took on increased economic responsibilities and made more of the important decisions. The women thus became increasingly the focal point of the Japanese American family.

Issei women did not have an easy time making a home in Washington. The most sustained and serious difficulty they faced was anti-Japanese sentiment. As we have seen, Japanese were denied naturalization on the basis of race, and so were condemned to remain aliens in their adopted land. In Washington, their status as "aliens ineligible to citizenship" made it possible to restrict their economic opportunities severely through a series of antialien land laws. The culmination of these anti-Japanese policies came with World War II, when thousands of Washington Japanese—aliens and U.S. citizens alike—were removed to concentration camps.

After the war, the Issei pioneers, now nearing retirement age, had to begin their lives over again. Like Tomita, many Issei women, whose assets and capital had been taken from them by the internment, went to work in garment factories or into domestic service. Tomita's postwar urban life also reflects a general shift of Japanese Americans after the war to urban residences and occupations.

In the postwar years, hard work once more bore fruit—though not as great a harvest as might have been possible, given more hospitable conditions. The children of the pioneers, the Nisei, married and had children of their own. A third generation was born. The Issei women looked back on their years of struggle, and saw in their grandchildren the fulfillment of hopes they held when they first came to the United States. They believed the *tsugiki* to be strong and firmly rooted in its adopted land. The children and the grandchildren, the second- and third-generation branches of the *tsugiki*, bloomed in the spring that finally came. Tomita could write in May 1983:

> The seeds I planted
> Sprout and grow up
> Even in this very old body
> Joy overflows[53]

Through the struggles of Tomita and other Issei pioneer women, the history of Washington State has been enriched.

Notes

An earlier version of this essay appeared in *Women in Pacific Northwest History*, edited by Karen Blair (Seattle: University of Washington Press, 1988).

I would like to thank Stephen H. Sumida, Sachiko Honda, Karen Blair, and Sue Armitage for their assistance with this article.

1. In the 1920, 1930, and 1940 censuses, women of Japanese ethnicity were the most numerous nonwhite women in Washington State, making up almost half of the nonwhite female population, including Native American women. See U.S. Bureau of Census, *Sixteenth Census of the United States (1940), vol. 2: Population 2: Characteristics of the Population* (Washington, D.C.: U.S. Government Printing Office, 1943), pt. 7, Utah-Wyoming, 304.

2. The best English source of information on Issei women in Washington is Kazuo Ito, *Issei: A History of Japanese Immigrants in North America*, trans. Shinichiro Nakamura and Jean S. Gerard (Seattle: Executive Committee for Publication, Japanese Community Service, 1973). This is a translation of Ito's *Hokubei hyakunen zakura* (North American Hundred Years Cherries) (Tokyo: Hokubei hyakunen zakura jikko iinkai, 1969), which contains written statements and poetry by Issei women recalling their lives in the Pacific Northwest.

3. The biographical information is drawn from an interview with Teiko Tomita, Seattle, Washington, 26 July 1983.

4. Mihara Senryu et al., *Renia no yuki* (Snow of Rainier) (Kamakura, Japan: Cho-onsha, 1956), 249. This anthology contains the best published collection of Tomita's poems. Some of the earlier poems have annotations that give the date of writing. Other poems can be dated by their content, since Tomita wrote her poems contemporaneously with the events about which she wrote. The best source of her more recent poems is the Seattle newspaper *Hokubei Hochi*, in which her poems appeared monthly. The English translations of Tomita's tanka that appear in this chapter do not fully convey, of course, the poetic beauty, rhythm, and nuances of the original. I have made an attempt to remain as close to the original Japanese meaning of the tanka as possible, though I was not able at this time to render the translation into an English poetic equivalent, if that is ever possible. It is hoped that in the near future better translations will be forthcoming to allow the reader to understand and appreciate more fully the poetic beauty of these poems.

5. Ito, *Hokubei hyakunen zakura*, 325.

6. Ibid., 490

7. Ito, *Issei*, 428-29.

8. Ito, *Hokubei hyakunen zakura*, 519.

9. Ibid.

10. Ibid,

11. Ibid., 539.

12. Ibid.

13. Ibid.

14. Ibid.

15. Mihara, *Renia no yuki*, 248.

16. See Frank F. Chuman, *The Bamboo People: The Law and Japanese Americans* (Del Mar, Calif.: Publisher's Inc., 1976), for information on restrictive laws. For information on the internment of Japanese Americans, see such works as Commission on Wartime Relocation and Internment of Civilians, *Personal Justice Denied* (Washington, D.C., 1983); Roger Daniels, *Concentration Camps: North America* (Malabar, Fla.: Robert E. Krieger, 1981); Peter Irons, *Justice at War* (New York: Oxford University Press, 1983); and Michi Weglyn, *Years of Infamy* (New York: William Morrow, 1976).

17. Interview with Toshiko Toku, Seattle, Washington, 25 July 1983. Toku learned to write *senryu*, Japanese satirical poems, in an internment camp during World War II and continued to write in the postwar years.

18. Mihara, *Renia no yuki*, 243.

19. Ibid.
20. Ibid.
21. Ibid.
22. Ibid.
23. Ibid., 244.
24. Ibid., 243.
25. Ibid., 245.
26. Ibid., 246.
27. Ibid., 247.
28. Ibid., 250.
29. Ibid., 251.
30. Ibid., 252.
31. Ibid.
32. Ibid., 249.
33. Ibid.
34. Ibid., 245.
35. Ibid., 246.
36. Ibid., 251.
37. Ibid.
38. Ibid., 247.
39. Ibid.
40. Interview with Tomita.
41. Mihara, *Renia no yuki*, 247.
42. Ibid., 246.
43. Ito, *Hokubei hyakunen zakura*, 173.
44. Mihara, *Renia no yuki*, 250.
45. Kazuo Ito, *Zoku hokubei hyakunen zakura* (North American Hundred Years Cherries, Supplement) (Tokyo: Hokubei hyakunen zakura jikko iinkai, 1972).
46. "Shiatoru tankakai," *Hokubei Hochi* (Seattle), 25 May 1983.
47. Ibid., 12 October 1983.
48. Hideko Matsui, "Renia no yuki no igi" (Significance of *Renia no yuki*) *Cho-on* 42, no. 6 (1956): 27-28. For a discussion of how local U.S. settings, history, and culture have affected the creation of an Issei poetry, see Stephen H. Sumida, "Localism in Asian American Literature and Culture of Hawaii and the West Coast," *Hawaii Literary Arts Council Newsletter* 71 (August-September 1983): n.p. Sumida's essay was originally presented at the Asian Studies on the Pacific Coast Conference, University of Alaska at Fairbanks, June 1983. Issei poetry calls for literary evaluation in terms of the poetry's Issei contexts.
49. Keiho Soga, Taisanboku Mori, Sojin Takei, and Muin Ozaki, *Poets behind Barbed Wire*, ed. and trans. Jiro Nakano and Kay Nakano (Honolulu: Bamboo Ridge Press, 1983); quotes, vii.
50. Mihara, *Renia no yuki*, 239.
51. Ibid., 240.
52. *U.S. Census (1940)*, 304. In 1900 there were 185 Japanese women in Washington, including 21 born in the United States; in 1910 there were 1,688, with 347 being U.S.-born. But in 1920, after a decade of immigration of wives and picture brides, there were 6,065 women of Japanese ethnicity, with 2,117 U.S.-born. From 1920 until 1940, women of Japanese ethnicity composed the largest group of nonwhite women in Washington State. In 1920, women of Japanese ethnicity numbered 6,065 out of 13,836 nonwhite women in Washington. In 1930, out of 16,744 nonwhite women in Washington, 7,637 were women of Japanese ethnicity, including 4,308 U.S.-born. And in 1940, out of 15,975 nonwhite women, 6,532 women were of Japanese ethnicity, including 4,234 U.S.-born. The numbers of Issei women actually fell between 1920 and 1940 because of increasing legal restrictions, which greatly limited the Issei's economic opportunities, forcing them to seek better opportunities in other states.
53. "Shiatoru tankakai," *Hokubei Hochi*, 8 June 1983.

We began this book with the colonial frontiers that shaped relationships among women and men of all races throughout the West. In this final section we turn to "frontiers" of a different sort in the urban West, where again different peoples met and wove new relationships of race and gender among themselves. Three major kinds of migrations brought racial ethnic women to the workplaces and communities of the twentieth-century West. Jobs in western cities attracted people from the rural West, among them American Indian women from rural reservations. An enormous twentieth-century westward movement from other regions brought, among others, the largest African American migration to the West. And international migrations brought new immigrants from Latin America, Southeast Asia, and elsewhere who added new layers to already complex regional racial ethnic rankings.

These new westerners met on predominantly urban "frontiers." Cities had long provided more wage work for women than they could find in the rural West. Further, just as colonial encounters rippled to affect far-distant peoples, western urbanization and industry changed rural western life and what it seemed to offer compared with urban options. Racial ethnic women throughout the West faced the dilemma of sustaining families, communities, and cultural identities in economies that increasingly separated home from work and in places geographically removed from their cultural homelands.

World War II is generally seen as a turning point in western history because it transformed western economies and stimulated enormous population growth throughout the region. For the West as a whole, the war brought increased military construction, new jobs on army and navy bases, and civilian employment in shipyards, aviation factories, and other war-related industries. Defense jobs drew many women west during the war, including African American women who, for the first time, had access to industrial jobs and paychecks, as well as women from western farms and reservations. Women's employment skyrocketed as new war plants like shipyards and airplane factories opened up jobs for them. At the war's height, for instance, one Los Angeles woman in ten worked in the aviation industry.[1]

The war plants created new opportunities, which in turn brought new inequalities among westerners. "Okies" who migrated to California during the 1930s dust-bowl years entered the war plants and factories. The federal government recruited workers from Mexico to take their places in the "less desirable," and less-well-paid, migrant agricultural workforce. Mexicano/as and Mexican Americans had been deported to Mexico during the hard times of the 1930s depression to make room for Anglos in the agricultural workforce. They were now pulled back into the lower rungs of the U.S. economy as agricultural and service workers.

The war brought, too, the legacy of the atom bomb, in new towns like Los Alamos, New Mexico, where the bomb was born; in new scientific laboratories that sparked western economies; and in the environmental legacies of desert test sites and nuclear production plants like Rocky Flats, Colorado, and Hanford, Washington. The women of these nuclear towns had limited work options in industries dominated by scientific and technical expertise. As in nineteenth-century mining, lumber, and cattle towns, women provided domestic labor and a variety of service work. The hazards of nuclear development also affected them as mothers, as miscarriage rates and birth anomalies occurred with disproportionate frequency around the new atomic sites.[2]

The military buildup changed what the West offered racial ethnic women. For many, the changes were positive in terms of better jobs and wages. For Japanese American women, however, as Teiko Tomita so eloquently testified, the reaction to Pearl Harbor began a nightmare of suspicion and loss. In February 1942, President Roosevelt issued Executive Order No. 9066, which established "military areas" from which any or all people could be barred. In May 1942, 112,000 Japanese Americans were ordered to leave the West Coast in a matter of days. Most lost their homes, farmland, and personal property and were interned for much of the war in ten "relocation camps." Internment, it should be noted, applied particularly to persons of Japanese ancestry, including native-born U.S. citizens, but not, for instance, to persons of German or Italian ancestry.[3]

Japanese American women and men shared economic loss, shame, and imprisonment. At the same time, the conditions of life in the camps profoundly changed gender roles and family relations. Large communal mess halls replaced private family meals. Collective meals and limited housing meant that women spent less time on domestic duties. As people spent more time with peer groups based on age and gender, parental authority declined. Within the larger negative contexts of racist policies and camp life, there were also lesser benefits of increased leisure, equal (low) pay with men at the jobs required of everyone in the camps, and new opportunities for younger women who were relocated from the camps to work or to attend school. These new options and the increased time spent with peers accelerated the disintegration of traditional arranged marriages among the Nisei (second-generation), who based their marital choices increasingly on romantic love.[4]

For Japanese American women, as for other racial ethnic women, the wartime labor shortage opened doors to industrial, clerical, and managerial work from which they were previously excluded. When the war plants closed in 1945 and 1946, women and people of color were pushed back out of industrial jobs. Their options changed with the development of new regional industries, but generally women of color were offered the lowest-paid jobs in the region's service sector, in tourism, in new industries like electronics and garment manufacturing, and in the agricultural workforce. These new jobs, while generally less lucrative than wartime employment, were still a significant shift from prewar job opportunities. For Japanese American women, as for most women of color, the most common prewar employment was domestic service. By 1950, 47 percent of employed Japanese American women were clerical and sales workers and operatives; only 10 percent worked as domestics.[5] *Thus, for Japanese American women, World War II brought both the racist relocation policies targeted specifically at Japanese Americans and the changes in women's work and family roles that affected other racial ethnic women in the postwar West.*

Like women of other regions, western women experienced new demands for their labor during the war. And like women throughout postwar America, more and more western women worked for pay outside their homes to support themselves and their families. If all American women experienced these changes, then what difference did it make that they lived in the West or belonged to particular racial ethnic groups? At least part of the answer lies in the particular economies and racial patterns of the postwar West. During the war and after, women found new job possibilities in western economies increasingly devoted to defense industries and to tourism. Their jobs depended in part on how western labor markets assigned work by the West's distinctive racial, ethnic, and gender rankings. Thus, for instance, during World War II, Mexican immigrant women might work as migrant farmworkers, African American women as tack welders in Oregon shipyards or as riveters in Los Angeles aviation factories, Anglo men as supervisors and foremen in the same war industries. During the 1970s and 1980s, as American businesses expanded internationally and sought cheaper labor, racial ethnic women along the U.S.-Mexican border and throughout the West were hired to work in textile, high-technology, and other expanding "sunbelt" industries.[6]

Both family needs and the jobs that were available affected women's decisions to enter the paid workforce, as they did in increasing numbers. The stresses of managing families and jobs, increasingly common for all women, were intensified for racial ethnic women whose jobs often carried low wages and poor benefits.

The particular circumstances of urban life moved women to organize for better conditions. Racial ethnic women organized through community-based alliances, through civil rights and feminist movements, and in new labor unions that worked to organize industries in which racial ethnic women and men were concentrated, like textiles, agricultural labor, and service work. They participated in these movements as leaders and as grassroots activists, responding to racial and gender discrimination in the workplace, to the conditions of life in urban racial ethnic communities, and to rural poverty on reservations and in the agricultural workforce. As with earlier reform efforts, the social change movements of the 1950s, '60s and '70s involved alliances across class and gender lines. Now, however, poor and working-class women increasingly prevailed to participate in shaping policies and strategies. We see in this section their efforts to achieve economic and social advancement. We see, too, a wrenching dilemma for many racial ethnic mothers—their efforts to achieve better chances for their children prepared the children to leave, to seek educations, jobs, and relationships apart from their parents.

In the postwar years as before, daily choices and daily acts forged new relationships among the diverse people of the West. Those ever-changing and never-equal relationships of race, gender, class, and generations remain our common creation, our common legacy, and the starting point for any inclusive future.

Notes

1. Michael Schaller, Virginia Scharff, and Robert D. Schulzinger, *Present Tense: The United States since 1945* (Boston: Houghton Mifflin, 1992), 29.

2. On women in wartime Los Alamos, see Kathleen E. B. Manley, "Women of Los Alamos during World War II: Some of Their Views," *New Mexico Historical Review* 65, no. 2 (April 1990): 251–66; on the hazards of nuclear sites, see, for instance, Michele Gerber, *On the Home Front: The Cold War Legacy of the Hanford Nuclear Site* (Lincoln: University of Nebraska Press, 1992).

3. Eight of the ten camps were in isolated sites throughout the West. The ten camps were located in Topaz, Utah; Poston and Gila River, Arizona; Amache, Colorado; Manzanar and Tule Lake, California; Heart Mountain, Wyoming; Minidoka, Idaho; and Denson and Rohwer, Arkansas. Some Italian Americans were removed from their homes, but they were not interned. For Italian Americans, see Stephen Fox, *The Unknown Internment: An Oral History of the Relocation of Italian Americans during World War II* (Boston: Twayne Publishers, 1990).

4. A third of the first college students relocated from the camps were young women; some 40 percent overall were female. This portrait of gender in the camps is drawn from Valerie Matsumoto, "Japanese American Women during World War II," *Frontiers* 8, no. 1 (1984): 6–14.

5. Ibid., 11. See also Evelyn Nakano Glenn, "The Dialectics of Wage Work: Japanese-American Women and Domestic Service, 1905–1940," *Feminist Studies* 6, no. 3 (Fall 1980): 432–71.

6. See Vicki L. Ruiz and Susan Tiano, eds., *Women on the United States–Mexican Border: Responses to Change* (Westminster, Mass.: Allen and Unwin, 1987); Louise Lamphere, Patricia Zavella, Felipe Gonzáles, with Peter Evans, *Sunbelt Working Mothers: Reconciling Family and Factory* (Ithaca, N.Y.: Cornell University Press, 1993).

25.

"Not in Somebody's Kitchen": African American Women Workers in Richmond, California, and the Impact of World War II

SHIRLEY ANN WILSON MOORE

Studies of African American women in the West are still rare. That makes this essay by Shirley Ann Moore, drawn from her book-length study, doubly welcome, for the story she has to tell of women's activities in World War II California is fascinating.[1] A good job in wartime industries was the magnet that drew many African Americans to the West Coast in 1940–45. This migration, up to that time the largest movement of African Americans to the West, created a number of sizable black communities—Richmond, California, among them. Unlike the transient communities so typical of nineteenth-century mining booms, these were permanent settlements. The establishment of these wartime communities marked a turning point for blacks in the West: Since then, African Americans have been major players in regional politics and in racial ethnic coalitions and rivalries.

Although they still faced blatant discrimination, African Americans found the jobs at the Kaiser shipyards in Richmond a significant step upward. For black women, wartime jobs were an important turning point because they offered, for the first time, alternatives to domestic service in "some white woman's kitchen." Important as is this story of the demolition of racial and gender barriers in employment, Moore documents something else of equal importance. African American women who owned Richmond's wartime jazz and blues clubs made money by entertaining the men at the nearby military bases. Because what they offered was black music and black entertainment, they not only made a profit but helped to build black cultural institutions.[2]

Finally, Moore's study makes an even more general point. By showing us the ways in which African American migrant women made significant breakthroughs both in the labor market and in cultural life, Moore gives us insight into precisely how migrants of all races and ethnicities built today's multicultural West.

Before World War II, Richmond was hardly more than a dot on the California map. Lying along the east side of the San Francisco Bay with a total population of twenty-three thousand in 1940, Richmond had a mild climate, a deep harbor, and vast tracts of unused land that led city founders to pursue a dream of becoming the industrial center of the Pacific Coast. Within a decade of its incorporation in 1905, major industries, including

Standard Oil, the Santa Fe Railroad, and the Pullman Coach Company, had been wooed and won by developers and city boosters who dreamed of making Richmond the "Pittsburgh of the West." City founders liked to boast that Richmond had a stable, deferential workforce who were content to let the native-born white elite run civic and political affairs.[3]

Prior to the war, black Richmondites were relegated to the economic and social margins, but World War II and the coming of the Kaiser shipyards to Richmond opened up new possibilities for black women and men in the city and throughout the Bay Area. For a small number of black female entrepreneurs who ran the blues clubs and after-hours establishments in the city, Richmond's war boom provided an opportunity to achieve an economic and social shift upward through culturally based enterprises that catered to the social, culinary, and cultural preferences of the thousands of southern black migrants who poured into the city during the 1940s and 1950s. While World War II transformed the lives of all African Americans, wartime changes were particularly liberating for some working-class African American women who were able to loosen the restrictions that race, class, and gender had imposed on them.

In 1940 Richmond's black population numbered 270 out of a total of 23,000 people. African American residents had lived in Richmond since its founding and worked and lived in a multiethnic environment that included residents of European, Asian, Mexican, and Native American descent. Black people living in larger, more cosmopolitan Oakland and San Francisco tended to look down on the African American community in Richmond as a social and cultural backwater, lacking in a real middle or professional class. Unlike the thriving black middle class and professional class in Oakland and San Francisco, Richmond's black middle and professional class did not emerge until the war and postwar period. African Americans in the larger Bay Area cities considered themselves more sophisticated and urbane than black Richmondites. Thus, Richmond residency connoted undesirability and lower-class status. For example, when Ivy Reid Lewis's family moved from Oakland to Richmond in the late 1930s to escape what her father considered to be the artificiality of middle-class society in Oakland, her Oakland relatives were outspoken in their disapproval: "When we moved to Richmond," Lewis recalled, "I know my aunt would come and say she thought it was a shame [my father] moved us back there in Richmond with all those backwards, backwoods people. She was always mad about it and my grandmother didn't like it either."[4]

However reluctant other African Americans might be to live in Richmond, many sought employment there. The opportunity for work in Richmond's numerous industries, factories, and foundries attracted black workers to the city, but they encountered racial discrimination and segregation in the hiring process and in the workplace that confined them to the lowest rungs of the employment ladder. Indeed, a number of Richmond industries, including Standard Oil, the city's largest employer, and the massive Filice and Perrelli cannery, did not employ black people at all or employed only a handful prior to World War II. Where blacks were employed, they were relegated to the hardest, most menial jobs. Irene Batchan, who came to Richmond from Louisiana in 1926, explained the prewar employment situation in Richmond for most black men: "You see, if you were just brute strength, they would hire you for lifting pieces of steel, but if you had a little bit of education, they would not hire you."[5]

The situation was little better for African American women. Compelled by economic necessity to enter the workforce, they were, like their male counterparts, relegated to low-paying, menial labor. Some found work in the produce and fish canneries in and around the city that relied on a seasonal, female workforce that included Filipina, Mexican, Italian, and Portuguese women. However, the majority of black women in prewar Richmond's labor force worked as domestics or "day workers." Irene Batchan noted that prewar black women who "weren't too old . . . were working cleaning up white folks' kitchens, cleaning [and] cooking." Black female domestic workers earned an average of two to five dollars a week in boarding and rooming houses that proliferated in Richmond and in the homes of affluent whites living in Richmond, Berkeley, San Francisco, and the surrounding East Bay suburbs. The 1910 census, for example, notes that Orilla Varlick, a thirty-four-year-old married black woman from Mississippi, was employed as a "servant" in a Richmond boarding-house that served an all-white clientele. In 1915 Jessie Freeman worked as a cook for a white family in San Francisco and came home to Richmond only on weekends. Mattie Hudson, who arrived with her sister Mildred in 1939, became the family's biggest breadwinner, "working for the whites mostly in the outer areas, in towns like Orinda and over in the Oakland hills doing housework."[6]

African American women in prewar Richmond, like their counterparts around the country, were more able to obtain stable employment than were African American men, who frequently had to settle for seasonal or "occasional" work. Domestic work, though low-paying and arduous, was at least steady and it brought black women into contact with the white world on a regular basis. Therefore, prewar black women often served as liaisons between the two worlds, demystifying and interpreting white society for the rest of their community. For instance, Jessie Freeman's cooking job in a doctor's household afforded her the opportunity to acquire "lots of good medical sense" that she took home to "doctor" her family when they were ill. In another case, Ida and George Johnson, who arrived in the Bay Area in 1918 from Pennsylvania, found employment as maid and chauffeur in the home of a wealthy East Bay banker. George Johnson recalled that the banker taught "Ida about the stock market," warning her of the impending crash of 1929, but "it didn't matter since we didn't have any money to invest anyway."[7]

African American women domestics sometimes served as "employment ambassadors" for black men in the workplace. One resident, Irene Batchan, noted: "If they [white people] liked the way the women would work in their homes or did ironing, they might throw some work to your husband or son or something from time to time." Thus, low-paying female domestic employment provided a substantial portion of the economic foundation upon which the prewar black community in Richmond rested. Even so, it appears that many of these women labored under a triple yoke of oppression—confined by racism to the employment margins, stigmatized by a class bias imposed by their residency in Richmond, and constrained by male notions of a "woman's place." "If you were married and your husband had a steady job, you might stay at home," Batchan remembered. "You did that. But most had to work and the men seemed to think that only day work, or housework was suited to a black woman."[8]

Everything changed, however, when Richmond developers and city boosters persuaded industrialist Henry Kaiser to locate four shipyards in Richmond in 1940. As the United States geared up to become the "arsenal of democracy," it seemed that Richmond had at last achieved its dream of becoming an industrial force on the West Coast. The city was transformed from a "sleepy little backwater" to a wartime boomtown virtually overnight. By 1943 Richmond's population had soared to over one hundred thousand and the black population increased some 5,000 percent. The Kaiser shipyards dominated the life of the city. By January 1941, four shipyards covered almost nine hundred acres and operated twenty-four hours a day, churning out Liberty Ships at an astounding rate. By 1943 the yards employed almost one hundred thousand workers.[9]

Eager for an economic shift upward via shipyard work as welders, burners, riggers, or general laborers in the highly mechanized Kaiser shipyards, African Americans joined their white counterparts flooding into Richmond. The black migrants came primarily from Texas, Arkansas, Louisiana, Oklahoma, and Mississippi and composed 13 to 25 percent of the Kaiser shipyard workforce. In contrast to the Great Migration of World War I, women made up the majority of black migrants to the Bay Area during this period by a ratio of 53 to 47 percent. Black Bay Area migrants were younger than World War II migrants to other parts of the country (23.13 years on average) and most were married. Contemporary observers speculated that the higher number of black women migrants settling in the Bay Area during World War II resulted from the large number of men in that age group who migrated to the region and were subsequently drafted into military service while their spouses settled in the area to work and await their loved ones' return.

The women benefited from the chronic labor shortages that plagued Bay Area defense industries. Despite their high hopes for economic and social freedom in California, however, black workers encountered blatant discrimination in the shipyards from powerful shipyard unions. The Boilermakers' Union's exclusionary practices were among the most egregious. Although union membership was a prerequisite for shipyard employment, the Boilermakers' Union did not accept black members and eventually established segregated "auxiliary unions" for black workers. However, a black woman managed to put a dent in this practice in the Richmond shipyards. In 1942 Frances Mary Albrier, a longtime Bay Area resident and civil rights activist, passed the welders test "with flying colors" but had her welder's application refused at Kaiser's Shipyard Number Two because the company "had not yet set up an auxiliary to take in Negroes." Undeterred, Mrs. Albrier threatened to sue Kaiser if she was not permitted to join Local 513, the "all-white" union. Mrs. Albrier was permitted to pay her dues in Richmond, but white union officials sent them to the "auxiliary" at Moore Dry Dock in Oakland. Thus the Kaiser shipyards technically maintained union segregation until "auxiliary" Local A-36 could be established in Richmond. In this way, black shipyard workers in Richmond, male and female, routinely were assigned to the lower-paying unskilled job categories and tended to remain there. While white workers generally made an hourly wage of $1.25 per eight-hour shift, black workers earned about 90 cents an hour for an eight-hour shift.[10]

Nevertheless, shipyard work represented a significant shift upward for the overwhelming majority of black workers. A new culture of expectation began to emerge among African Americans in Richmond. For women particularly, the experience of migration and entry into the urban industrial labor force via shipyard work helped shatter the deferential and stereotypical racial and gender roles that had confined them. A Marshall, Texas, migrant explained, "I'll tell you. You see, I am a colored woman and I am forty-two years old. Now, you know that colored women don't have a chance for any kind of job back there [Texas] except in somebody's kitchen working for two or three dollars a week. I have an old mother and a crippled aunt to take care of. . . . I went to work for Kaiser and saved enough money to bring my aunt and mother out here."[11]

African American women not only took the initiative in migrating, in many cases they supplied the impetus for migration. For example, Arkansas native Margaret Starks, who had worked as a cook in Pine Bluff, recalled that after seeing a Kaiser shipyard recruiting advertisement in her hometown newspaper, she demanded that her husband "go to California and get a job [then] send for me later." Upon her arrival in Richmond, Mrs. Starks obtained a job in the Kaiser shipyards as a laborer. However, she subsequently discovered that she was pregnant and that her husband was "playing around on me." She decided to take matters into her own hands because "I knew I couldn't go back to Pine Bluff [so] I had an abortion, divorced him and with the money I earned from the shipyards I started a life of my own."[12]

Many African American women now saw an alternative to the cycle of low-paying, low-status factory or domestic work. As a result, the presence of the shipyards had a great impact on the city's other employers. For instance, the canneries that had relied heavily on black female labor before the war now saw most of their workers quit for shipyard work. In an effort to retain its dwindling workforce, Richmond's Red Rock Fish Cannery provided virtual door-to-door bus transportation for its female workers who lived in predominantly black North Richmond. This was an extraordinary measure at a time when wartime transportation problems plagued Richmond and other cities throughout the nation. The Santa Fe Railroad experienced similar high turnover rates and shortages as employees left for the shipyards and other higher-paying war work.[13]

When Mildred Slocum quit her cook's job at Santa Fe her employers begged her to come back, offering her a substantial raise in pay. On the other hand, Marguerite Williams preferred to remain at Santa Fe cleaning troop cars rather than go over to the shipyards where "the women had to work like men." Williams explained that "it was too hard. It was what you call slave labor. I never could do that kind of work." Nevertheless, the shipyard option made "good help hard to find" in white homes and even those women who continued with domestic work gained a powerful bargaining chip with which to negotiate better wages and working conditions. Black women discovered that their domestic services had become precious commodities in the marketplace. Mildred Slocum, whose sister Mattie had supported the family as a live-in maid in suburban Orinda before the war, recalled that black women were "quick to let" prospective employers "know that they didn't have to take just whatever white folks wanted to give you anymore." While economic necessity ensured that African American women would remain in the workforce, the coming of Kaiser shipyards to Richmond opened up their employment opportunities beyond "somebody's kitchen."[14]

Despite the economic shift upward shipyard work represented for most African American women, some found the choice between the shipyards or "somebody's kitchen" still too limited. Unlike their male counterparts, black women were constrained by a double standard that appealed to their patriotism and to their "domestic obligations." Black women were expected to do their part for the war effort by laboring in the shipyards, but at the same time, many felt pressure from spouses, children, and society to fulfill their "real womanly duties." Margaret Starks referred to this as "doing double duty, sometimes triple duty." Another black female shipyard worker recalled, "you'd be so tired when you got home you just didn't want to do anything else and then you had to get up and start all over again."[15]

Therefore, some enterprising black women sought other avenues of independence. Utilizing their shipyard earnings and employing skills traditionally considered "women's work," a handful of African American women established or ran some of the blues clubs that flourished in North Richmond during the 1940s and 1950s. With names like Tappers Inn, Savoy Club, and Minnie Lues, these clubs provided the channels through which some African American women were able to carve out a degree of economic and personal autonomy. Minnie Lue Nichols, a Georgia native who came to Richmond after living in New York, explained that this was a natural progression for black women: "It was just easier to take care of a club, give them music in a club, than it was to work all day and night in the yards, then turn around and work at home taking care of babies. Besides, if women were going to cook, they could make some real money off it."[16]

The blues clubs that sprang up in North Richmond during the 1940s and 1950s were owned and/or operated by women who understood the profitability of catering to African American cultural preferences. African American migrants who came to California from the South during the war years brought with them not only an expectation of economic and social mobility, but a desire for cultural continuity that included southern cuisine and blues music. Ironically, the large and rapid influx of African Americans to California tended to undermine the state's color bar in some areas. For instance, in many of the night clubs throughout the state blacks and whites mingled on an equal basis. Neither housing nor recreational facilities could be built quickly enough to accommodate the state's unwritten code of racial separation.

While housing posed the more pressing problem, blacks and whites often sought out the same recreational outlets. The more sophisticated supper clubs and lounges that dotted Seventh Street, Oakland's bustling black commercial and entertainment corridor, often attracted a racially mixed clientele who listened to more "subdued" musical offerings. In contrast, the blues clubs that proliferated in North Richmond catered to black working-class men and women who demanded music, cuisine, and entertainment that was closer to their rural southern roots. Although some of North Richmond's blues establishments attracted white patrons and those from the black middle class, they had a decidedly black southern working-class character. They gained the reputation as "rough places that catered to a hard-drinking, fast-living black clientele." Some black people referred to the North Richmond clubs as "honky tonks," "juke joints," or "buckets of blood." One black Richmondite recalled: "If someone of some kind of stature went out there, they'd generally have to sneak to go out there." Nevertheless, many middle-class blacks frequented the Richmond clubs because, as Ivy Reid Lewis noted, "that's where you went if you wanted to hear good music." [17]

The often illicit and transitory nature of some of the clubs in North Richmond makes it difficult to know the precise number of female-owned and/or -managed establishments. Perhaps three or four blues clubs were owned or operated by women. The more numerous "after-hours" clubs, which usually operated from private homes, were more transient, clandestine, and thus harder to get a fix on. It appears that many after-hours clubs were also run by women. Information on the women club owners or operators is even more difficult to ascertain, but the best-known women blues club entrepreneurs seem to have had similar backgrounds. All were migrants from the South during the war or immediate postwar period, coming from Texas, Arkansas, or Georgia. All of the women had been employed in traditional domestic or service work in their home states before coming to Richmond. Some had worked in the Richmond shipyards prior to starting the clubs, and most were or had been married while operating their clubs. At least one, Billye Strickland, married into a black family that had resided in Richmond since before World War I.

Willie Mae ("Granny") Johnson, an Arkansas migrant and sister-in-law of blues pianist and singer, Jimmy McCracklin, opened the popular Savoy Club in North Richmond during the war years. The Savoy hosted blues greats like Lowell Fulson, L. C. ("Good Rocking") Robinson, and Jimmy McCracklin. Patrons recall that its decor resembled an "old road house" with "oilcloth tablecloths" on wooden tables. The room-length bar sold beer and wine and Johnson cooked and served meals of "greens," ribs, chicken, and other southern delicacies. She controlled all the hiring, firing, and bookkeeping in the club. Her husband, Deacon, worked a "day job . . . and didn't have anything to do with it." While patrons played the slot machines and dice and card games, others danced to live music on a dance floor out front. Jimmy McCracklin paid homage to the Savoy Club in a popular 1950s recording:

> Now Richmond, California, is a great little town
> and I live there and Jack, I gets around.
> If you ever go there and you want to jump for joy,
> I'll tell you where to go. That's the Club Savoy.

Another woman-operated North Richmond nightspot was the B and L Club. It was owned by the husband-and-wife team of Lawrence and Billye Strickland. The Stricklands built the club themselves, finishing it in knotty pine, and operated a trailer camp that could accommodate twenty trailers in back. The couple also operated a fourteen-room motel next to the club that advertised a "spacious rumpus room at the disposal" of their customers. When Lawrence was drafted, Billye took over as sole proprietor of all the operations.[18]

Tappers Inn was the most popular night spot in North Richmond from its opening in 1941 until its demise in the mid-1950s. It offered a variety of services, including round-the-clock barber and beauty shops and a service station. It was owned by East Indian entrepreneur George Bally, whom many black residents called "the Hindu." Arkansas migrant Margaret Starks became the manager of the club and handled all the business and talent booking for Tappers and other night clubs in North Richmond. As a "peacekeeper" or bouncer at Tappers, Starks was rarely without her .38 revolver as she went about her duties. Tappers was a "very lavish place" that sometimes hosted six hundred people. Margaret Starks recalled that "it got so crowded on weekends that we had to take the bar stools out and the people just stood three and four deep at the bar." While patrons jitterbugged or "slow-dragged" out on the dance floor to a band or the jukebox, others engaged in illegal gambling or played the slot machines that operated night and day in the back of the building.[19]

Minnie Lue Nichols's club, "Minnie Lues," became a blues staple in North Richmond. A native of Atlanta, Georgia, Nichols served a period of apprenticeship cooking in restaurants and clubs in New York State where she moved before coming to Richmond to join her cousin in 1948. With little formal education, Minnie Lue Nichols nevertheless proved to be an astute businesswoman. After sampling uninspired cooking in local Richmond restaurants, Nichols approached a Mr. Brown, the proprietor of a North Richmond club, for a job as a cook. Instead, he offered to lease her his sagging business for ninety dollars a month. Lacking the funds to lease, she struck a deal, promising to cook in the restaurant for three days and improve business. In return she would gain the lease. Nichols explained, "I didn't have any money to start with and I didn't have anything to lose." Before long, her cooking skills and outgoing personality filled the restaurant with "customers [who] kept the juke box going day and night." In three days the jukebox brought in sixty dollars, an amount that represented more than the owner had "collected from that box in a month previously." Brown was "so enthused over the amount of money she had made in three days that he did not hesitate to let her have $40.00 to buy the food she needed" to continue operating the restaurant.[20]

Nichols opened her own place shortly after, and it was an immediate hit with black Bay Area residents. Aside from offering home cooking, Minnie Lues was the first black establishment to obtain a full liquor license, and it showcased local blues musicians and national celebrities like B. B. King, Bobby "Blue" Bland, Sugar Pie DeSanto, Charles Brown, Jimmy McCracklin, Ray Charles, and Dinah Washington. African Americans came from around the Bay Area to partake of the food and the cultural solidarity found in the blues music. Minnie Lue Nichols described the atmosphere in her club: "Well, if you've never felt the blues, I can't hardly explain. You know how it *feels!* It was a blues crowd, a beautiful crowd. When the house is full and they're rocking with members of the band, you just enjoy it!"[21]

Club patrons were grateful for an oasis where, in contrast to the outside world, the rules were straightforward and consistent. Club patrons tended to subscribe to if not always honor the "etiquette" of the blues club that stressed equality of treatment above all. Margaret Starks explained the blues-club etiquette: "It didn't matter what you did outside on your job or who you were. If you acted right, nobody was better than anybody else." The blues clubs of North Richmond provided black newcomers with a welcome refuge from the racial hostility that permeated the world in which they earned their livelihood. Moreover, North Richmond's clubs also blunted some of the intraracial class conflict that pitted black newcomers against longtime black residents. The latter often characterized the black newcomers as unsophisticated, uncouth, troublemakers. Even though the rough-and-tumble atmosphere of the blues clubs implied lower-class status, club etiquette demanded that patrons discard their pretensions and distinctions upon entering. Thus, North Richmond's blues clubs tended to erode intraracial class conflict and provided working-class black people an escape from some of the harshness of urban industrial life. As Margaret Starks noted, "Those people didn't have too much, so they weren't about to let go of the music and good times they were used to. It made them feel better. I remember one lady from Louisiana, had gold all in her mouth, told me that she loved to hear that music because

Opening night at Minnie Lues, North Richmond, circa 1950. Minnie Lue Nichols on left behind counter. (Photo from author's collection.)

[it] made her forget all that stuff in the shipyards. She always felt better when she left."[22]

The clubs also served another purpose for the community. Like the urban saloons that catered to European immigrants who poured into the United States in the nineteenth and early twentieth centuries, Richmond's blues clubs helped orient African American newcomers to the urban industrial workplace during World War II. Female club owners and operators often served as information and power brokers in their communities. For example, Margaret Starks earned the title of "mayor of North Richmond" because of her numerous community and entrepreneurial activities. She not only acted as a talent-booking agent for several of the clubs but published Richmond's first black newspaper in the back room of one of the clubs. The weekly *Richmond Guide* was distributed throughout the wartime housing projects where most black shipyard workers lived. The paper focused on local and national civil rights and employment issues and kept readers up to date on social and community activities. As secretary of the newly established Richmond NAACP in 1944, Starks conducted much of that organization's business from offices located in the clubs. Thus, many black newcomers were introduced to their first political activism through North Richmond's blues clubs. A number of the NAACP-led desegregation campaigns of the late 1940s and 1950s that targeted segregated downtown hotels, restaurants, and supermarkets were organized in club offices. Margaret Starks explained that "everyone knew where to find me if they needed something or had something to tell me. Everyone came through those clubs. We plotted many strategies there."[23]

Blues clubs in North Richmond, catering to newcomers' cultural tastes, had a substantial economic impact on the larger African American community as well. Club owners served as employers and informal employment agents for black Richmondites and blacks residing elsewhere the Bay Area. Their clubs provided employment for a cross-section of black workers, including musicians, bartenders, cooks, bookkeepers, custodians, "peacekeepers," and private security guards. This function became particularly critical after the shipyards shut down in 1946 and African Americans were once again thrown out of work in disproportionate numbers.

Female club owners and operators who had to contend with obtaining liquor licenses, building permits, and bank loans acquired a considerable amount of expertise in dealing with Richmond's business and financial establishment and gained access to the larger white community. These African American women frequently were called upon to negotiate financial and local government bureaucracies not only for themselves but for the inexperienced and less-well-connected members of their community. Therefore, these African American women managed to attain influence and power beyond their immediate communities. They were able to step outside the traditional economic and social spheres to which racism, class divisions, and sexism confined most of their sisters.[24]

North Richmond's blues club scene was an area in which some black women could exercise power over their lives and the economic life of their community by regulating white access. Illegal high-demand services such as prostitution and gambling flourished in the boomtown atmosphere of World War II Richmond, and the blues clubs attracted a significant white clientele who were eager to participate in these activities. African American women who owned and/or operated the clubs established the rules by which whites could gain entry into their world. Margaret Starks explained the rules governing white club patrons: "Well, the whites were scared to come out here. The blacks didn't allow them just to come out here anytime. If they came out, they said they were Mexicans. A taxi couldn't bring them. I didn't allow a white taxi cab company out here because they [the cab companies] were prejudiced. . . . When whites came, I told them to come 'round through the back."[25]

Capitalizing on the exoticism that North Richmond represented for many whites, some black women entrepreneurs catered to black and white clientele in the after-hours clubs that flourished in the 1940s and 1950s. Such clubs featured blues "jams," with musicians coming from all over the Bay Area and the United States. Club patrons could purchase home-cooked meals and liquor. Although most of the clubs served a racially mixed clientele, some catered to whites only. White men from some of the Bay Area's most prominent families were able to indulge in sexual liaisons with prostitutes of many races in these after-hours clubs. Margaret Starks visited one such club where some of the white patrons belonged to a social organization comprised of World War I veterans that was called the Last Man Club: "It was nice," Starks recalled. "Nice little furniture and everything. It had a bar and one of these Magnavox things. They'd come there and party. Sometimes they had live music. I was there one time and I saw all these Last Men, all these married men, lawyers and doctors."[26]

Thus, the working-class, culturally based blues clubs of North Richmond afforded African American women the opportunity to achieve some measure of economic mobility and personal autonomy. These female-owned and -operated enterprises, anchored firmly in black working-class culture, helped undermine the racial, gender, and sexual proscriptions that kept most black women at the bottom of the socio-economic hierarchy. Not only did the clubs provide a cultural and economic bridge that facilitated African Americans' transition from rural agrarian workers to urban industrial workers, they provided some black women a path to a measure of personal economic independence and enabled them to achieve a degree of power and influence at a time when most black working-class women had little access to either.

The postwar shutdown of the shipyards, however, made it difficult for most African Americans in Richmond to sustain the economic shift upward that the wartime boom had begun. Some one thousand people a day were thrown out of work at the yards. Black workers were hit dispro-portionately hard and were unable to find comparable work in the civilian sector. At the close of the war, Richmond's white political and civic leaders hoped that most black residents would "go back where they came from." This did not happen, however, and the postwar years saw African Americans in Richmond grow to represent almost 40 percent of the city's population. Working-class black newcomers and their cultural expressions became fixed in the social and political fabric of the city. Whites began to move out of the city to newly constructed, segregated housing develop-ments that began to proliferate in the Bay Area. Blacks had no such options, and the black population in the city increased, going from almost thirteen thousand in 1950 to almost fifteen thousand in 1960. The white population declined from eighty-five thousand to almost seventy-two thousand during the same period.[27]

Although some workers transferred to shipyards at Hunter's Point in San Francisco or Mare Island in Vallejo or obtained jobs at the Ford Motor Company, which had located in Richmond in 1931, the majority of black workers were forced once again to settle for a cycle of low-paying domestic, seasonal, factory, and cannery employment. African American women, who remained in the workforce in numbers higher than white women in the postwar period, now found themselves in competition with white men, white women, and black men. In addition to racial discrimination, it appears that African American women in postwar Richmond were faced with hostility from some of their male counterparts who feared that black women, whom they considered docile and willing to work for lower wages, would be given higher priority for the scarce postwar, nontraditional jobs that remained open to blacks. Columnist Lewis Campbell, writing for the Oakland-based black newspaper, the *California Voice*, warned that when the shipyards pulled out, the "good jobs" would be filled with "women and Chinese boys."[28]

The postwar employment reality for African Americans, both men and women, however, was different. They were once again relegated to the lowest rungs of the employment ladder. As a result, black newcomers and longtime residents in Richmond began to forge a postwar civil rights and political coalition that concentrated on dismantling the city's policies and traditions of segregation in employment and housing. Richmond's NAACP, growing out of a coalition of black shipyard workers fighting shipyard discrimination in 1944, became the fastest-growing and most active branch in the nation. African American women were in the forefront of the organization. From 1946 onward, the NAACP worked with African American women's clubs and interracial coalitions in Richmond and the Bay Area, civil rights activists from the University of California, and the Communist Party to successfully desegregate a number of downtown supermarkets and businesses.

Although black women who owned or operated blues or after-hours clubs represented only a small minority of the black female workforce in Richmond, their mere presence attests to the profound transformation black women were undergoing as a result of migration and World War II. The transformation thrust black women more firmly into the public sphere as they joined their male counterparts in dismantling racial barriers. The changes brought about by the war provided them the opportunity to wage their own personal battles against racial, gender, and class oppression. Some black women in Richmond were able to utilize the experience and money that they had gained as blues club operators to achieve "middle-class respectability" in a community that did not have a black doctor or lawyer until the mid-1950s. For example, one woman who worked as manager and bookkeeper for an after-hours club and a chain of brothels that operated in California and the Pacific Northwest translated that experience into building her own "legitimate bookkeeping service and made a good living." Similarly, a mother and daughter team who had operated an after-hours club in North Richmond during the war, put themselves through nursing school on their club earnings and became registered nurses. "They're good nurses, some of the best Contra Costa [County] ever had too," Irene Batchan claimed, "and their husbands didn't have a a word to say about it."[29]

Though African Americans in postwar Richmond had their economic shift upward thwarted by the dismantling of the Kaiser shipyards, their participation in the urban industrial workforce created a strong culture of expectation that could not be dismantled. African American women in

Richmond, working against a triple burden of oppression, were crucial in creating, nurturing, and realizing those expectations in the postwar period. Margaret Starks, whose own life as a shipyard worker, nightclub manager, newspaper publisher, and NAACP activist embodied these struggles, explained that African American women were so actively involved in Richmond's wartime and postwar civil rights struggles because "They said they weren't going into some white woman's kitchen and make five dollars a week again. They said they did that back home in the South and they weren't going to do that out here."[30]

Thus during the war and postwar period working-class black women in Richmond drew on African American cultural forms and traditions to expand their options and subvert the racial, sexual, and class barriers that had for decades denied them full and equal access to America's economic and social resources. In this respect they joined other black women and men throughout the United States in ushering in the civil rights movement that transformed the nation.

Notes

Many people have helped me with this essay, which represents a small portion of a book on the African American community forthcoming from the University of California Press. Thanks to Lawrence Levine, Earl Lewis, Joe William Trotter, Jr., and Olly Wilson, whose knowledge of African American urbanization, migration, and culture helped my understanding of the impact of migration and urbanization on black Richmondites and sharpened my analysis of the role of blues music and blues clubs in North Richmond. Thanks also to Lee Hildebrand for putting me in touch with blues legend Lowell Fulson. I am grateful to Joe Louis Moore for his photographic expertise. I am indebted to the following for their invaluable assistance: Emma Clark, Linda Holmes, and staff at the Richmond Public Library; the staff at the Oakland Public Library; Kathleen Rupley and staff at the Richmond Museum; and the staff at the Doe and Bancroft Libraries at UC Berkeley. Finally, I am indebted to the women and men who lived and worked in Richmond, California, and allowed me into their homes and lives.

1. Shirley Ann Wilson Moore, *To Place Our Deeds: The Black Community in Richmond, California* (forthcoming, Berkeley, Calif.: University of California Press).

2. A similar and concurrent cultural movement, the building of gay cultures in the shadow of the military, is examined in Allan Berube's *Coming Out under Fire. The History of Gay Men and Women in World War II* (New York: Free Press, 1990).

3. Joseph C. Whitnah, *A History of Richmond, California: The City That Grew from a Rancho* (Richmond: Chamber of Commerce 1944), 8, 18–31, 46–48, 78; Eleanor Mason Ramsey, "Richmond, California, between 1850–1940: An Ethnohistorical Reconstruction," unpublished monograph (San Francisco; California Archeological Consultants, 1980), 7–15; Susan D. Coles, *Richmond: Windows to the Past* (Richmond, Calif.: Wildcat Canyon Books, 1980), 51–52; *The Richmond Independent Newspaper, The Woman's Edition* (Richmond Historical Association, 1910), 8, 15, 17, 21; "Burg Brothers Real Estate Agents," pamphlet, 1910; F. J. Hulaniski, ed., *History of Contra Costa County, California* (Berkeley: Elms Publishing Company, 1917), 35, 336; Hubert Owen Brown, "The Impact of War Worker Migration on the Public School System of Richmond, California, from 1940 to 1945" (Ph.D. dissertation, Stanford University, 1973), 18.

4. Ivy Reid Lewis, Richmond resident since the 1930s, interview by author, 29 July 1987.

5. Irene Malbrough Batchan, interview by author, 14 September 1985; Wilbur and Vesper Wheat, Richmond residents since 1942, interview by author, 24 January 1987.

6. Batchan interview, 14 September 1985; U.S. Department of Commerce, Bureau of the Census, *Thirteenth Census of the United States (1910)* (Washington, D.C.: U.S. Government Printing Office, 1910); Walter Freeman, Jr., Jessie Freeman's son and Richmond resident since 1915, interview by author, 28 November 1987; Mildred Hudson Slocum, interview by author, 17 November 1987.

7. For an overview of domestic service in general and especially black domestic workers, see David M. Katzman, *Seven Days a Week: Women and Domestic Service in Industrializing America* (Urbana: University of Illinois Press, 1981), 24–26, 46, 55, 65–94, 221–22, 266–79; and James Borchert, *Alley Life in Washington: Family, Community, Religion and Folk Life in the City, 1850–1970* (Urbana: University of Illinois Press, 1980), 168–95. Quotes from Walter Freeman, Jr., interview; George Johnson, interview by author, 13 August 1985.

8. Irene Malbrough Batchan, interview by author, 18 August 1985.

9. Shirley Ann Moore, "Getting There, Being There: African-American Migration to Richmond, California, 1910–1945," in *The Great Migration in Historical Perspective: New Dimensions of Race, Class, and Gender*, ed. Joe William Trotter, Jr. (Bloomington: Indiana University Press, 1991), 112.

10. Charles S. Johnson, *The Negro War Worker in San Francisco* (San Francisco: n.p., 1944), 5–8; Moore, "Getting There," 112, 118–20.

11. Moore, "Getting There," 115.

12. Margaret Starks, interview by author, 2 April 1988.

13. For turnover rates, see Sam Kagel to Edward Rutledge, letter, 9 June 1944, and attached statistical report, "An Analysis of Non-White Employment in Richmond, California, May 1, 1944," and "Employment Figures Taken from Richmond ES-270 Reports," May 1944, all in President's Committee on Fair Employment Practice, National Archives Pacific Sierra Region Collection, Record Group 228, entry no. 68, box 11, hereafter FEPC Records.

14. Slocum interview; Harry and Marguerite Williams, "Reflections of a Longtime Black Family in Richmond," an oral history conducted in 1985 by Judith K. Dunning, Regional Oral History Office, the Bancroft Library, University of California, 1990, 109–110, hereafter cited as Williams, "Reflections"; Lewis interview.

15. Starks interview, 2 April 1988; Vesper Wheat interview.

16. Minnie Lue Nichols, interview by author, August 1981.

17. Lee Hildebrand, "Oakland Blues," *East Bay Express*, n.d.; Lee Hildebrand, "North Richmond Blues," *East Bay Express*, 9 February 1979; Bill Thurston, Mississippi migrant to Richmond in 1944, interview by author, 8 September 1983; Margaret Starks, interview by author, 29 June 1988; Lewis, interview.

18. Hildebrand, "North Richmond Blues;" Thurston, interview; Lowell Fulson, telephone interview by author, 21 January 1993; "Club Savoy," quoted in Hildebrand, "North Richmond Blues"; Starks interview, 29 June 1988; *We Also Serve* (Berkeley: Tilghman Press, 1945), 59, 61, 66; *We Also Serve: Armed Forces Edition* (Berkeley: 1945), 38; Joseph Malbrough, interview by author, 18 August 1985.

19. Malbrough interview; Starks interview, 29 June 1988; *We Also Serve: Armed Forces Edition*, 38.

20. Hildebrand, "North Richmond Blues"; Minnie Lue Nichols, interview by author, 6 January 1980; Eldreadge Wright, "An Interview with Minnie Lue," unpublished manuscript, 24 March 1972, in the personal collection of Minnie Lue Nichols.

21. Nichols interview, 6 January 1980.

22. Starks interview, 2 April 1988.

23. Ibid.

24. Nichols interview, August 1981; Malbrough interview; Starks interview, 2 April 1988.

25. Starks interview, 2 April 1988.

26. Ibid.

27. See letter from Walter White, Executive Secretary, NAACP to Noah W. Griffin, West Coast Regional Director, NAACP, 16 July 1945, in collected papers of the West Coast Regional

Office of the National Association for the Advancement of Colored People (NAACP), carton 16, Miscellaneous papers, 4 folders (1944–59), University of California, Berkeley, Bancroft Library collection. See also U.S. *Census of Housing and Population, 1950, 1960,* "Total Population, Ethnic, Sex and Age Distribution of Richmond."

28. *California Voice,* 1 August 1941.
29. Batchan interview, 14 September 1985.
30. Starks interview, 2 April 1988.

26.

Changing Woman Meets Madonna:
Navajo Women's Networks and
Sex-Gender Values in Transition

CHRISTINE CONTE

Our images of women's war work frequently evoke the white "Rosie the Riveter" of the famous World War II poster, her hair tied up in a red bandana, biceps flexed and fist upraised, telling a war-torn America, "We Can Do It!" In reality, the wartime economy created new jobs for women of color, many of them in new war plants throughout the West. In this article, anthropologist Christine Conte looks at Navajo women who were drawn from their reservation to jobs at the aptly named Navajo Army Depot near Flagstaff, Arizona. Anthropologists' methods differ from historians' in that their primary sources are the people they study. Conte uses interviews with forty Navajo women to describe how this first wartime movement into urban wage work later drew other Navajo women from the reservation to Flagstaff. The forty individual case studies help her identify some basic patterns in urban Navajo women's experiences. Urban life, she finds, could offer very different possibilities, depending on women's support systems in Flagstaff and on the reservation, on how they combined their families and their work, and on their access to an urban Navajo community. We are able to see, within the contours of larger regional changes that brought women from the reservation, the individual consequences of their options and choices. And, by examining kinship, work, and culture, Conte creates some order and explanation for these different experiences as well.

When I was growing up on the Reservation, when I'd ask my dad if I could go somewhere he'd always say, "O.K., but you have to ask your mom." With money matters, even my father's paycheck, my mother always had the last word. . . . My mother holds the grazing permit for the whole family—aunts and uncles too—so if anyone wants to sell any livestock they have to get her O.K. on it. . . . Here the man and the woman are all the time discussing decisions but here, the women don't get the last word as much.

—LOUISE BIGHORSE
NAVAJO MIGRANT TO FLAGSTAFF, ARIZONA

Why don't women like Louise Bighorse "get the last word as much" in Flagstaff, and how do they perceive, and cope with, conflicting ideologies about gender?[1]

As for poor and working-class people of other cultures, women-centered networks are important for the Navajo. In cases as diverse as those of working-class women in London, African American welfare mothers in a midwestern city, Chicana cannery workers in northern California, Italian and Jewish immigrants in the same city, and Native American women of the Plains, dense—and often enduring—connections to female relatives and friends support a flow of crucial resources and mediate tensions between the home and the workplace.[2] Women-centered networks can also encourage the development of a positive self-image in girlhood that will later translate into positive maternal behaviors. Navajo urban mothers first experienced the negative impacts of the loss of such networks as children when they were involuntarily separated from their families on the reservation to attend Bureau of Indian Affairs boarding schools.[3]

Drawing upon interviews with forty Navajo women living in the reservation border town of Flagstaff, Arizona, conducted in 1981 and 1982, I discuss here the unique but related experiences and strategies of these Native American women. Like those of the poor and working-class women of other ethnic groups, the women-centered networks of Navajo women migrants cushion the pressures of migration, though the networks may themselves be transformed or destroyed in the process.

Unlike many other groups, however, the Navajo cultural tradition shows maternal biases both linguistically and in the structure of kinship relations. Although the nuclear family is the basic unit of Navajo social organization, the mother-child relationship is considered the most important relationship within that social unit. In contrast to the dominant Western view of parentage that gives equal weight to the procreative roles of mothers and fathers, the Navajo view selectively emphasizes the greater significance of the maternal acts of giving sustenance both before and after birth. Therefore, the Navajo term for "mother" (shimá) refers to a number of female persons, or even such objects as sheep and corn, which also give and sustain life.[4]

The experiences of Navajo women migrants also differ from those of other ethnic groups whose urban network strategies have been described. For many women on the reservation, the workplace and the household are the same. Women who do not work for wages raise cattle and sheep, tend gardens, weave, and produce other crafts and thus provide goods for their household or for exchange for cash, goods, or services. For these women, migrating to the city means an abrupt separation of workplace and home life.

Particularly for those women who leave their reservation homelands seeking autonomy from the authority of female elders over their labor, cash, and lifestyle, migration implies a cruel paradox. In Flagstaff they are more vulnerable to claims on their cash and commodities from a wider range of kin and nonkin and are exposed to patriarchal values about family life espoused by evangelical Christian and Mormon missionaries.

For a better understanding of their experience, especially of the effects of migration on their women-centered networks and gender values, further

Women working at the Navajo Army Depot, 26 May 1944. (Navajo Army Depot Collection, courtesy of Cline Library, Special Collections and Archives, Northern Arizona University, no. 1402.)

cultural and historical background is needed. Navajo women's home and work lives and connections between the two have undergone profound changes in recent decades. Political and economic development has influenced the level and extent to which the women have been drawn into wage labor or excluded from the labor market. As many scholars have pointed out, the reservation's transfers of value and economy and certain features of underdevelopment are similar to those of the third world. In regional terms, a few reservation border towns have historically dominated commerce and drained the reservation hinterlands of natural resources, population, and purchasing power.[5] As a result, traditional subsistence production on the reservation has been progressively undermined; unemployment and dependence on various forms of federal, state, and tribal welfare have become widespread on the reservation; and migration to the border towns and to more distant urban centers has increased steadily since World War II.

Situated in the ponderosa pine forests of northern Arizona, Flagstaff, the third-largest city in the state, is only thirty miles from the southwestern border of the Navajo Reservation. During World War II, Navajos were actively recruited to provide unskilled manual labor at an army installation about ten miles west of the city. Aptly named the Navajo Army Depot, the facility became a "town" for its civilian recruits and their families.

Before World War II, Navajo relocation to Flagstaff was predominantly restricted to men seeking seasonal railroad work. The army ordnance

Hogans at Navajo Army Depot. (Navajo Army Depot Collection, courtesy of Cline
Library, Special Collections and Archives, Northern Arizona University.)

depot records, however, reveal that the number of Native American female
employees rose abruptly from zero to eighty between the months of
January and March of 1943 alone. According to Navajo women and men
I interviewed who worked at the facility during this period, Native
American women worked alongside men in assembling and shipping
munitions, as well as in the more sex-segregated areas of cleaning and
clerical work.

The end of the war curtailed employment in war-related industries
nationwide, and the Navajo Army Depot was no exception. A few Navajo
men and even fewer Navajo women (mainly clerical workers) found stable
employment at the facility after the war, but most lost their jobs and either
returned to the reservation or sought other wage work in Flagstaff. By
1950 most Navajos who had relocated to Flagstaff during the previous
three-year period were ex-employees of the army depot. They entered the
lowest occupational levels of the labor force, working as gardeners,
domestics, janitors, kitchen help, interpreters, and dormitory aides in the
local Bureau of Indian Affairs school.[6] These individuals became the
touchstones for succeeding generations of their kin who have since emigrated from the reservation, including many of the women I interviewed.

In 1981, approximately two thousand of Flagstaff's more than thirty-four
thousand residents were Navajo.[7] Adult Navajos living in Flagstaff were
younger and had more formal education than their reservation counterparts. The average age of the women I interviewed was about twenty-eight.
(Demographically the population drain of young adults from the reservation is reflected in the disproportionately high representation of nineteen-
to thirty-four-year-olds among Flagstaff Navajos as compared with the
reservation.[8]) All forty interviewees were bilingual in Navajo and English.

Table 26.1. Occupation of Flagstaff Navajo Women in Sample

Occupation	Number	Percent
Professional	7	17.5
Clerical/sales	10	25.0
Service	8	20.0

Nonwage
  Crafts
  Babysitting
  Small business
	6	15.0

Nonwage
  Homemakers
  Students
  Retirees
	9	22.5

Most had completed high school; the women had lived in Flagstaff for an average of about ten years. These women typify the Navajo population of Flagstaff in that they are a relatively stable, rather than a transient, population. Only two of the forty women were born and raised in town; the majority came from the Western Navajo Reservation in Arizona.

Wage labor is the dominant means of livelihood for Flagstaff Navajos. Most of the women I interviewed were employed, and all had some wage labor experience. Some were professionals—teachers, counselors, and social workers. Some described themselves as unemployed, as retired, or as homemakers. The majority, like women of all ethnic groups in the national labor force, worked in the clerical and services sector of the economy including such occupations as motel maid, kitchen helper, and beautician. Table 26.1 summarizes the distribution of occupations for the sample. Annual household income ranged from two thousand dollars to over thirty thousand dollars, with a median of about fourteen thousand dollars. Secondary sources of income included pensions, social security, and college scholarships. Several women were self-employed and produced kachina dolls, beadwork, silver jewelry, or traditional tapestries in their homes to supplement the family income. In two cases, craft production brought income that equaled that from wages and scholarships, but in only one instance were crafts the sole means of support for the household.

Whether they worked outside the home or not, most Navajo women in Flagstaff, like their reservation counterparts, retained primary responsibility for child care and housework. Very few received substantial assistance from their husbands or other male household members with these tasks. This "double day" for women is prescribed not only by gender roles, but also by the frequent, sometimes prolonged absences of

male household members who work on construction or highway maintenance crews throughout the state. This situation also typifies those of
other Native American groups who, like Navajos, suffer from a lack of
employment opportunities on their reservation homelands.

For Navajos on the reservation and in town alike, kinship plays a
central role in the organization of work relations and in the allocation of
resources. Kinship relationships also govern the intensity of affective ties
between individuals and their expectations of emotional support. The
centrality of kinship in Navajo life has long been emphasized in the
ethnographic literature as well as in biographical and autobiographical
accounts.[9] Navajos still customarily identify themselves by their maternal
clan when making an acquaintance, and one of the worst things a Navajo
can say about someone is that they act as if they have no relatives.

On the reservation, the importance of kin, particularly maternal kin, in
Navajo life is expressed in the prevalence of matrilocal postnuptial
residence (where the husband moves into his wife's household or land-
use area) and in the practice of reckoning land tenure rights mainly
through the female line. In the hinterlands, settlement typically consists
of clusters of dwellings (usually from two to as many as eight) called
"camps," dispersed across the countryside. Junior households of younger
kin fission off to establish new camps within the land-use area of the
parent camp. Thus the distribution of tasks and decision-making authority
among women varies with their position in the developmental cycle of the
domestic group. Senior women, whose age commands the respect of their
juniors and whose resource networks are expanded through their satellite
households, are at the fulcrum of production, consumption, and distribution. Although women's participation in the labor force has increased
dramatically on the reservation in recent decades (especially in the
burgeoning administrative centers), livestock raising, gardening, and, to
a certain extent, gathering wild foods for household use and for sale
remain their principal occupations.

Most of the Flagstaff women I interviewed were raised on the reservation. Most of their close female kin—mothers, sisters, daughters, sister's
daughters, and sometimes, daughters- and mothers-in-law—still lived
there in a context of intense cooperation characterized by sharing of labor,
subsistence products, transportation, information, capital, and commodities. By pooling resources they minimized discrepancies in wealth
among them and their households.

At the same time, differences in the strength and vitality of women's
close kin networks also means that some women have distinct advantages
over their neighbors in terms of power, authority, and wealth. Women who
have maintained relations of reciprocity with kin who have emigrated to
urban centers, for example, can use these connections to tap into innovations in production techniques and to learn how to manipulate the external
jurido-political system to claim and sustain land-use rights.[10]

Navajo women's kin-based resource networks in Flagstaff differ in some
fundamental ways from those of their reservation counterparts. First, in

Flagstaff, relations of consumption and distribution are largely separate from those of production. In other words, people who work for wages do not own or control what they produce and hence cannot exchange what they produce as women do on the reservation. Instead, women in Flagstaff are likely to enter exchange relations with female kin outside the workplace and to borrow, take, lend, or give cash, cars, and other commodities. Child care, cooking, transportation, and other labor essential to the household are also shared and coordinated mainly through women's kin-based networks.

One case I observed will illustrate how creative and competitive this process can be as women marshal their kin networks to obtain and keep resources. Late one afternoon I was sitting in a cafe with Jessie Benali, a working mother in her early twenties. Jessie had just finished explaining how her uncle (her mother's brother) had given her his pickup truck when he was laid off from his job because he couldn't keep up the payments, when the uncle's wife, Alice, strode into the cafe and headed straight for our booth. With an outstretched hand Alice demanded the keys to her husband's pickup, claiming that he had found work in Wyoming and had written to tell her to get the pickup back. Jessie countered that she was not about to give the truck back unless Alice reimbursed her for the payments she had made and the parts she had put into it. As Jessie was fishing in her purse to present the payment receipts as evidence, Alice stormed out with the parting threat that she had better see the pickup back at her place before she left for the reservation on Sunday. Jessie leaned over the table, calmly told me that her uncle would never have asked Alice to take the car without paying her back, and with a flip of her bangs changed the subject.

But Jessie was by no means finished with Alice and the pickup. While she and I continued our conversation in the cafe, Alice was at Jessie's, hot-wiring the vehicle and making her escape. When Jessie discovered what had happened, she rapidly deduced which of Alice's kin might have agreed to hide the pickup for her, walked to her mother's to borrow a pickup and leave her young son for the evening, and took off with her husband and his friend to search for the vehicle. Following Jessie's list of "suspects," they located it quickly and, making sure no one was home, proceeded to remove all of the parts that Jessie had put into it. The last time I saw her, Jessie told me that she had sold the parts and had made a deal directly with her uncle for the reimbursement of the payments she had made.

Households in Flagstaff, at the heart of distribution and consumption activities, also differ from those on the reservation in composition and, consequently, in the allocation of power and authority within them. Nuclear households are more common in Flagstaff and the urban Navajo households are less likely to be multigenerational than their reservation counterparts. Comparison of the household types of the two sample populations (see Table 26.2) highlights the prevalence of "joint" households formed by adult kin of the same generation, as opposed to the "stem" type of multigenerational households that predominate in the reservation population.

Table 26.2. Comparison of Household Types of Two Populations

Household Type	Flagstaff Navajo Women in Sample		Reservation Women Sampled	
	Number	Percent	Number	Percent
Nuclear				
Conjugal pair	3	6.5	4	10.3
Conjugal pair with children	29	63.0	2	30.8
Conjugal pair with children and a single adult	1	2.2	2	5.1
Total nuclear	27	71.7	8	46.2
Remnant				
Woman with own children and/or grandchildren	3	6.5	9	23.1
Total remnant	3	6.5	9	23.1
Multiple				
Joint*	7	15.2	2	5.1
Stem†	0	0	10	25.6
Extended‡	3	6.5	0	0
Total multiple	10	21.7	12	30.7
Total	40	99.9	29	100.0

* Joint composition is defined as sisters and brothers and/or cousins with or without spouses and children.

† Stem composition is defined as a parent couple with one married offspring with or without children. It may also include the senior couple's unmarried children.

‡ Extended composition is defined as a senior couple with at least two married offspring and at least one junior couple having children; i.e., three generations.

Most dramatic is the absence of senior kin living in town. Several women in the Flagstaff group cited their eagerness to be free of the control of senior relatives over their labor, income, and lifestyle as primary reasons for moving to town. According to Grace Joe, "Seems like my sisters that stayed there have to run to my mom before they can do anything even though they've got kids of their own. Here, I run the whole show. My parents sees [sic] it that way too. They just don't fight it."

Sisters or cousins (with or without husbands and/or children) may rent a mobile home or apartment together and provide each other with financial and emotional support. Often a younger sister, cousin, or niece will be recruited from the reservation to help with child care and housekeeping in exchange for room and board, a little spending money, and the opportunity to experience town life. Such sponsorship is perceived by most women as an obligation, but it is also seen as a welcome means to escape social isolation. Thus, although Navajo women may migrate to distance themselves from social obligations to senior female relatives, they also recognize, and replicate in the urban environment, their parents' woman-centered households.

Joint households made up of siblings and/or cousins with or without spouses and children were considered temporary arrangements by both the Flagstaff and the reservation women. Women commonly expressed the belief that a mother and her child, and especially a nuclear family, should move out and "get a place of their own" as soon as they become financially able. This belief was maintained in Flagstaff, despite the fact that households merged and separated periodically because of the loss of a job or the departure of a wage earner through death or divorce. Once a woman established a separate residence, she would in turn accept the responsibility for sponsoring other immigrant kin. In one case, two employed Flagstaff sisters living a few miles apart shifted their two younger sisters back and forth every few months. This strategy enabled them to equalize the financial burden of sponsorship while, at the same time, retaining access to the housekeeping and child-care services of their younger kinswomen.

The persistence of female-centered values and resource networks in urban Navajo households is abundantly illustrated in women's accounts of their move from the reservation and the early months of adjustment to life in Flagstaff. Of the married women, only a small minority cited their husbands' jobs or schooling as the primary reason for the move. Financial independence, educational opportunities for themselves and their children, and the desire to "start a new life" following the death of a spouse or divorce were more typical motivations. Whether married or single, women tend to rely on other women for aid in relocation.

The case of Violet James is illustrative. Violet spent her early childhood in Flagstaff where her father was employed at the Navajo Army Depot. When he lost his job after the war, Violet's parents and her siblings moved back to the reservation while her mother's sister, Ethel, found work and decided to stay in town. As a teenager, Violet would spend the summers with her aunt in Flagstaff, babysitting her niece, Ella Mae, in exchange for room and board. According to Violet, "I always liked Flagstaff, so when I graduated from high school I just came back and stayed with Ethel and Ella Mae. I didn't pay anything for food or rent until I got a job as a hairdresser."

When Violet got married, her husband didn't want her to work outside the home. At his urging, they moved outside town and Violet quit her job. As Violet expressed it, "I *tried* to quit my job . . . but I didn't like living way out there and staying home alone." She convinced her husband to move back into town within a few blocks of her aunt's house, and she went back to her old job. Within a year the marriage fell apart and Violet and her young daughter moved next door to her Aunt Ethel and niece Ella Mae.

Experiences like Violet James's show that changes in household structure are at least partially explained by women's management of domestic affairs to accommodate their own wage labor. The often-repeated witticism that every Navajo household on the reservation contains at least one "resident anthropologist" might better be rephrased with respect to Flagstaff to include "one resident babysitter."

Furthermore, fluctuations in household composition are the consequence of overlapping strategies of *both* women in Flagstaff and their female kin on the reservation. One teenage mother, for example, received room and board from her older married sister who attended university classes and worked part-time on campus. The younger sister also earned spending money by babysitting for other students and through the sale of tapestries she wove on a traditional loom set up in a corner of her sister's apartment. With the approach of the lambing season in the early spring, however, her mother, left home alone on the reservation, required the younger daughter's assistance. The older sister was forced to recruit a young sister-in-law from the reservation as a replacement babysitter. Thus, residence patterns in Flagstaff reflected accommodations between senior kinswomen on the reservation who managed what remains of a subsistence economy and their junior wage-earning kinswomen in Flagstaff. Examples like this illustrate how women's kin-based urban networks are linked with those of the reservation.

Unlike the younger women in Flagstaff and the older women on the reservation, the six most senior women interviewed in Flagstaff had no kin of their same generation living in town. Their resource network was circumscribed, consisting mainly of their children, grandchildren, and their children's spouses. In every case, the senior woman gave more cash and services to her satellite household members than she received from them. These women consoled themselves with the belief that when they became "really" old the kids would take care of them both financially and physically.

In Flagstaff, the range of network structures through which resources were extended was more varied than it was among the reservation group. The urban women relied more on in-laws, friends, coworkers, and urban institutions for supplementary aid. They differed from one another in the degree to which they maintained cooperative ties with reservation kin. Most visited their kin on the reservation about once a month. A few of the Flagstaff women were totally estranged from their reservation kin, while others visited them nearly every weekend and regularly exchanged cash, goods, and services with them.

The institutions most often cited as an important source of aid in Flagstaff were the Mormon and other Christian churches. This was especially true for women who had few kin in town and for those senior women who said they were usually the source, rather than the recipient, of assistance for their junior kinswomen. For these women, the church mediated the exchange of cash, services, and commodities with nonkin, including Navajos, other working-class or lower-middle-class Native Americans, Anglos, African Americans, and Mexican Americans. Several Christian converts referred to their coreligionists as "family" or "just like a family" when describing the economic and spiritual benefits they derived from their church-based social relationships. When she first moved to Flagstaff, one of these women said, she had received a month's rent and groceries from the Mormon Church, with which she had become affiliated while still living on the reservation. Others relied on their female coreligionists for occasional babysitting, small cash loans, or family counseling and moral guidance.

In a context in which values, sources of livelihood, and the content of social relations are in flux, such extrakin social ties seemed to enable some Flagstaff Navajo women to extricate themselves from kin-dominated networks that they perceive as financially draining. At the same time, they provided a moral rationale for doing so. Of the twenty-two Christian women in the sample, five cited Christian doctrine as the basis for rejecting the traditionally central role of their kinswomen in mediating the affairs of the nuclear family. For them, the meaning of the term "family" had been transformed from a web of kinship, and the reciprocal obligations these relationships entail, to an autonomous social unit with ultimate authority vested in the male spouse. Within this context, "motherhood" emerges as a moral imperative rooted in biology in contrast to the traditional Navajo view that emphasizes the pragmatic aspects of providing sustenance and sustaining life.

The conscious constriction of kin-based social networks among the Flagstaff Christian women also presented them with a moral dilemma that they struggled to reconcile. When the meaning of "motherhood" shifts from the arena of social action to that of biological imperative, the acceptability of "alternative mothers" is called into question. Women who had to rely on others to care for their children while they were working expressed an emotional conflict with their belief that the biological mother should care for her own children. They saw themselves and other women as either "housewives" or "career women," a dichotomy virtually nonexistent on the reservation.

In sum, Navajo women migrants to Flagstaff were faced with the challenge of gaining autonomy from senior kinswomen while simultaneously maintaining a support network for domestic services. The establishment of joint households by maternal kinswomen and cooperative links with more distant kin and nonkin were some of the strategies women employed to meet this challenge. However, there was also a great deal of variability in women's network structures and in the degree to which women adopted non-Navajo patriarchal values in the urban context.

Flagstaff women's resource networks influenced their values about gender. Particular types of exchange networks and the constellations of cash, commodities, and services marshaled through them affected the way they viewed themselves as women. In this study I focused on the different types of social networks Navajo women employed in Flagstaff, looking at the mutuality, redundancy, or incompatibility of resources within these systems and exploring the interplay with the social relations of the wage-labor workplace.

Table 26.3. Structural Types of Flagstaff Women's Resource Networks

Network Type		Number	Percent
Most vital	1	17	42.5
	2	7	17.5
	3	2	5.0
Least vital	4	14	35.0
TOTAL		40	100.0

The strength of women's resource networks, or resource vitality, was measured in the areas of subsistence production, consumption (including both domestic labor and the affective ties among women), and the distribution of cash and commodities. The most vital networks included greater-than-average numbers of individuals and a higher frequency of exchange among them. Vital networks were also more likely to include both nonkin and kin and to contain more multiplex relationships, those in which a woman exchanges many different kinds of resources with another woman.[11] These criteria were employed in developing a four-point scale of network vitality. See Table 26.3 for a summary of the number and frequency of the network types in my sample.

The first case described below is that of a woman I will call Margaret Tsosie. Her resource network represents the most vital type of resource network. Women with resource networks like Margaret's (Type 1) exhibited the most matriarchal values. Their occupations usually involved dealing with Navajo coworkers, clients, customers, or students. Second, the case of a women I will call Sally Nez illustrates a somewhat less vital resource network (Type 2) and a mixed or more egalitarian gender ideology. Finally, at the other end of the spectrum a woman I will call Doris Littlesinger represents the group whose brittle resource network (Type 4) had left her vulnerable to extremely patriarchal values. In addition to the strength of their resource networks, women's gender values were secondarily related to the length of time they had lived in town, the number of close kin residing in town, and the geographical distance from close kin on the reservation or in other off-reservation towns.

A TYPE 1 RESOURCE NETWORK: MARGARET TSOSIE

Margaret Tsosie worked in a Navajo-staffed and -oriented social service program. Her office was devoted to families recently relocated to Flagstaff from the reservation under the terms of the federal Navajo-Hopi land dispute settlement. Despite the physical separation of home and wage workplaces, for Margaret Tsosie there was congruence in the social-labor processes and in the dominant values surrounding cultural identity and gender roles.

Margaret's job involved a great deal of face-to-face contact with staff and clients alike. These interactions were fostered by a relatively informal, unpartitioned office space and Margaret's commitment to incorporating the traditional Navajo practice of consensual decision making among her staff in contrast to the more hierarchical and authoritarian style of the dominant society. Her participation in programs that addressed the needs of Navajo relocatees made her acutely aware of the ways in which kin-based resource networks and traditional value systems intersect with the exigencies of urban life. Thus her job encouraged her to draw upon her personal experiences in integrating the norms and values of the dominant society with those of her Navajo heritage and, in turn, to redefine her identity as a Navajo woman.

Margaret had decided to get a job to supplement her husband's earnings soon after the birth of her third child and the completion of her B.A. degree. As she explained, "I wanted to do something worthwhile. I mean, it had to pay enough to make it worth having to be away from my kids all day. . . . When I wasn't working I was always borrowing money from my sister. I wanted to pay her back and help my parents too. I needed my own money to help out my family."

Margaret's husband continued to contribute most of his wages to meet the daily subsistence of the household, leaving Margaret to reinvest most of hers in property outside of town, where she hoped someday to raise cattle. She gave cash and commodities to her parents and siblings and loaned cash to a maternal aunt and several cousins residing in Flagstaff. Occasionally, she also made smaller cash loans to coworkers and other Navajo friends from school. With her siblings and parents, Margaret used her job skills to revitalize their subsistence production on the reservation. For Margaret, wage labor was a means to realize traditional Navajo goals and values and to support her ideal of cultural identity.

Margaret's ideals were shared by her father, who, upon his retirement from the Navajo Army Depot, had cashed in his retirement funds and purchased cattle. Margaret's parents had then moved back to her mother's maternal land-use area with their cattle and established a new camp. They did this despite the objections of Margaret's mother's resident kin who demanded, but did not receive, payment for infringement on the lands they were grazing.

Margaret played a direct role in introducing innovations from the dominant market economy and society into the reservation subsistence sector. Using financial planning skills she had learned at college and on the job, Margaret, with her father's consent, set up what we describe as a "legal corporation" and management system for the livestock and the income generated by their sale. According to this plan, Margaret and her younger siblings, several of whom also worked in town, each paid monthly dues into a special savings account to maintain their joint ownership of the livestock. Margaret was also the initiator and organizer of what she described as "quarterly meetings" on the reservation where she, her siblings, and parents planned production, consumption, and distribution strategies for the "corporation." These meetings even decided which of the grandchildren would spend their summer vacation on the reservation while their parents worked in town.

The economic relationship among members of the "corporation" also colored their affective ties. For example, funds from the livestock account were allocated for Native American Church ceremonies to mediate discord between its members and their spouses. For Margaret, the intersection of the dominant wage-labor economy with the social relations of her domestic, kin-based network was striking. While on the one hand she extolled and practiced the Navajo tradition of giving generously to close kin with no expectation of immediate reciprocity, she also admitted to keeping precise records and receipts for all such expenditures in order to claim them as tax deductions.

In a workplace environment where "Navajoness" as a corporate ethnic identity is highly valued, Margaret's activities within her domestic network were relevant. Reinvesting wages into land and livestock, traditional symbols of wealth and prestige, also confers prestige in the workplace. Paradoxically, these appeals to "traditionalism" also facilitate and justify innovation. The innovations she introduced into the reservation subsistence sector transformed the very traditions Margaret sought to practice.

Margaret's socioeconomic status in the marketplace conferred distinct advantages that enabled her to adapt the structure and relationships of her kin-based resource network. A combination of circumstances promoted her network vitality:

1. Relatively high wage income with both husband and wife fully employed left capital to reinvest in cultural and kin-oriented activities.

2. Because close kin were in a similar socioeconomic situation, they did not drain Margaret's personal resources.

3. Social and technical skills practiced in her workplace were relevant to those of the domestic arena.

4. The social and economic benefits of her job provided a rationale for Margaret to leave home and entrust the care of her children to a commercial day-care facility.

Women with professional occupations that pay relatively well represented the majority of the vital resource network group, but vital resource networks were not limited to these occupations. Another woman in the vital resource network category, for example, worked as a part-time cleaner along with her three sisters-in-law.

A TYPE 2 RESOURCE NETWORK: SALLY NEZ

Sally Nez, an exceptionally energetic and gregarious person, was a self-employed beadworker and tailor. Other than occasional help from a clan-related tailor, Sally did all the beadwork and sewing herself in the mobile home that she shared with her unemployed husband and four young children. With the recommendation of a female clan relative from her community on the reservation who worked at the local Indian Center, Sally had been able to create a lively market for her crafts among the mostly Navajo staff and clientele.

A skilled and imaginative artist, Sally had found that she could increase her production efficiency by limiting the number of different items and the variety of designs she produced. This method also allowed her to carry on social relations with kin, friends, and customers. For Sally, the telephone helped break the social isolation of working at home; the phone also allowed her to solicit business and still meet self-imposed production levels. As she quipped, "My husband always tells me my mouth goes a hundred mile [*sic*] an hour when I do my beadwork and talk on the telephone. I get business call [*sic*] and talk to friends—Navajo, black, white, all kinds."

As her own boss, Sally maintained a flexible work schedule, enabling her to integrate social relations of home into those of her business. She earned more money than in any of her previous jobs as a cashier, motel cleaner, and sewer in a local textile mill. For example, if one of her Navajo neighbors stopped by to request a ride to Tuba City in return for gas money, Sally would willingly oblige, seizing the opportunity for subsidized transportation to market her wares in the government offices. During her regular business/social calls to the Indian Center, she would scan the employment listings of the center's Job Services office for her husband. On occasion, she had even submitted job applications in his name when he failed to take the initiative.

The financial success of Sally's enterprise required her husband to contribute some cash and domestic labor. As a union construction worker, his prospects for employment fluctuated seasonally and with larger economic trends in the building industry. He was typically unemployed for a few months every fall and winter. Sally would take advantage of his child-care services during this period to prepare her wares for the busy Christmas and summer tourist seasons. During summer vacation, when her husband was often out of town on a work crew, she would either bring her children along with her on marketing trips or leave them with close kin on the reservation. When the children were with her, the two eldest would care for their younger siblings and lend a hand with their mother's marketing enterprises. Thus, for Sally, the linkages between the work of home and the marketplace were more integrated than they were for many women wage workers in Flagstaff.

Unlike Margaret Tsosie, however, Sally's reservation kin and her husband depended on her for cash, at least seasonally. She had no livestock on the reservation, no close kin in town, and received little in the way of services from her reservation kin. Sally's income was also substantially less than Margaret's and was less stable. Finally, while Sally's network was almost as extensive as Margaret's, it consisted of more opportunistic relationships with customers, neighbors, and other acquaintances. For these reasons, the independence she sought in the urban context carried with it a heavier burden than it did for Margaret.

Sally's interview highlighted her struggle to shift some of that burden to her husband, Al. She voiced some conflicting views about gender-based power and authority that emerged from the Flagstaff study at both ends of the matriarchal-to-patriarchal values spectrum. In Sally's words: "I *try* to put Al there making the decisions for us sometimes. I think the man should have the responsibility for that and learn how to plan. I try to do everything with Al—to put him there so he can be somebody. I want him to manage our money and make all kinds of decisions and give advice. Now I manage our money, but I'm trying to put him there."

Based on this excerpt alone, Sally seems to fit with the group of women who support a patriarchal system of values about power and authority in the household. But in other situations, she had resisted her husband's control over her property, and her views were more similar to those of reservation women and Flagstaff women like Margaret Tsosie. As Sally said, "I *try* to go through him [Al] for decisions like when I want to buy a new pickup and give the old one to my dad. I ask [*sic*] him about it and he didn't agree with that." When the interviewer asked what she did then, she replied: "Well to me, I already planned it so I realize I should go ahead. . . . Dad pitched in some for my new pickup so I just let him have the old one."

A TYPE 3 RESOURCE NETWORK:
DORIS LITTLESINGER

Doris Littlesinger represents the group of migrants whose brittle resource networks left them vulnerable to evangelical Christian gender values. For Doris, little integration existed between the social relations of her wage-labor workplace and those of her home life. For over twenty of her forty-nine years, Doris had held a variety of jobs in the service sector of the labor force, both in Flagstaff and in another reservation border town. At the time of our interviews, she was working part-time as a preschool teacher's aide through CETA, a federal program to provide temporary jobs for people with limited formal education and employment skills.

Because Doris was the only Navajo employed in a Catholic school, her workplace did not function as a springboard for developing a dynamic perspective of her cultural identity nor for actualizing her values on the job. Her temporary and part-time status, coupled with a hierarchical and authoritarian management style, furthered her social isolation.

Doris, a single mother of four teenagers, struggled to support her family on her meager salary and monthly food-stamp allotment. She had no kin living in town and her relationship with her siblings on the reservation, none of whom are employed, was estranged. Doris explained the estrangement from her reservation kin as stemming from her own inability, and increasing unwillingness, to meet their requests for gifts of cash and commodities. She particularly objected to their continued expectations that she contribute to their traditional Navajo ceremonies, since these ceremonies were unfavorably regarded by her newly adopted Baptist religion.

Doris's kin-based resource network deteriorated still further when, in acute financial need, she cut off remittances of cash to her sisters on the reservation, cash they used to purchase seeds, fertilizer, and hay and feed for the livestock. Doris's sisters responded by appropriating the small flock of sheep and goats she had left in their care. Doris's social network in town, in turn, was limited to an Anglo woman from her church and a Navajo woman instructor in the Indian Center's continuing education program where she was pursuing a high school equivalency diploma. These women sometimes provided transportation, small cash loans, and emotional support.

Doris's experience offers a poignant example of the social alienation and emotional conflict that confront some Flagstaff Navajo women and impels them to adopt evangelical Christian or Mormon doctrine as a new model for gender values. As Doris said of her failed marriage to an Anglo: "Back then if I really wanted something that's when I didn't ask him or listen to what he tells me to do. He said my biggest problem is not to listen to him. It's like that in the Christian way too. Now he's gone I finally admitted he was right. Maybe the whole thing was my fault."

CONCLUSION

The structure and dynamic of Navajo women's resource networks affect how Navajo women migrants to Flagstaff perceive, and cope with, conflicting gender ideologies. My research revealed that gender ideologies about decision-making authority and the division of labor ranged widely between the matriarchal and patriarchal extremes. Navajo women who identified themselves as Christian tended to hold the most extreme patriarchal beliefs and to exhibit the most brittle women-centered resource networks. Why should women with an economic and cultural tradition of female power and authority reject that tradition in favor of one that places them in a vulnerable and dependent position? Contact with these belief systems alone cannot account for the acceptance of these values by some women. Two important and interrelated sets of factors seem to create this variability.

First, the receptivity of Navajo women migrants to patriarchal values is conditioned by the social and economic status of a woman's kin on the reservation. The reservation is not an unchanging bastion of tradition, a uniform cultural backdrop. Economic development on the reservation is uneven and is intimately tied to the regional economy revolving around border towns like Flagstaff. Differences in social and economic status on the reservation promote the kin-based networks of some women over others. As Margaret Tsosie's story demonstrates, livestock and the cash they generate for her family depend on reciprocal relationships. Margaret, the urban migrant, remits cash and occasional labor. In exchange, she receives care of her livestock on the reservation, domestic services such as child care, and the maintenance of her land-use rights. Equally important, the reservation women provide the migrant with a positive female role model that she is more likely to re-create in the urban context than to abandon. In situations like these, urban nonkin ties tend to supplement, but not supplant, ties to reservation kin.

In contrast, Doris Littlesinger's experience shows us how the poverty of senior women on the reservation pressures a wage-earning migrant to deplete her cash resources if she does not distance herself from them. Switching her allegiance from kin to church is one strategy women use to accomplish this while ensuring a new source of assistance for themselves. The church becomes the center of exchange for cash and services. However, women's resource networks also provide such intangibles as friendship, emotional support, and gender values.

The transformation of a woman's economic power base from a women-centered kin network to one in which nonkin, and predominantly non-Navajo, religious institutions play a major role makes Navajo women more emotionally and economically dependent upon men. It leaves them vulnerable to authoritarian and patriarchal ideologies that further isolate them in male-headed nuclear families. When male participation in the labor force is marginal and unstable—but the traditional concept of the family places central importance on the mother-child bond rather than on relationships between fathers and children or husbands and wives— "putting him there" as head of the household may be a futile task. Migrant women who resist the control of their female elders on the reservation over their labor and cash may find themselves between the proverbial rock and a hard place in Flagstaff. If their mothers drained their resources on the reservation, at least they themselves might expect to accede to a position of power and authority in their old age. Instead, in Flagstaff, women like Doris Littlesinger find themselves virtually alone.

Second, the range and diversity in Navajo women's experiences illustrate how the social relations of different types of workplaces in Flagstaff can influence values about gender. Work among, and oriented toward, other Navajos, whatever the occupational category, permits social relations and values practiced at home to be practiced at work as well.

The complex relationship between the social relations of the workplace and those of the household enables some women, an elite minority, to meet their needs better than others. There is evidence for the truth of the homily that the rich get rich and the poor get poorer. These women's experiences also show that the particular *mix* of resources—cash, commodities, and services—as well as the amount of resources determines domestic network structure. The conditions favoring women-centered values and cooperative ties are most likely to be found in professions such as teaching or counseling in programs oriented toward Native Americans. The Navajo women I interviewed in these professions were more likely to reject the model of the autonomous nuclear family with ultimate authority vested in the husband. However, my research sample included a greater proportion of women from these types of occupations than are represented in the Flagstaff population as a whole. The relationship between workplace and household is not typically as congenial as Margaret Tsosie's.

Even women like Margaret who have retained a measure of authority in their own households agree with Louise Bighorse that, compared with their mothers and grandmothers on the reservation, Navajo women in Flagstaff "don't get the last word as much."

Notes

Field research on the Western Navajo Reservation and in Flagstaff, Arizona, during 1981–82 was supported by grants from the National Science Foundation and the Wenner-Gren Foundation for Anthropological Research. Their support is very gratefully acknowledged. I also thank Louise Lamphere, Rayna Rapp, and Jan Hogel for their editorial assistance on an earlier draft of this paper. All names in this essay, except that of the city of Flagstaff, are fictitious to protect the anonymity of the Navajo women I interviewed. May they walk in beauty.

1. Gayle Rubin, "The Traffic in Women," in *Toward an Anthropology of Women*, ed. Rayna Rapp Reiter (New York: Monthly Review Press, 1975).

2. Elizabeth Bott, *Family and Social Network: Roles, Norms and External Relationships in Ordinary Urban Families* (London: Tavistock Publishing, 1957); Carol B. Stack, "All Our Kin: Strategies, Cooperation and Conflict among Women in Domestic Groups," in *Women in Culture and Society*, eds. Michele Zimblast Rosaldo and Louise Lamphere (Stanford, Calif.: Stanford University Press, 1974); Patricia Zavella, *Women's Work and Chicano Families: Cannery Workers of the Santa Clara Valley* (Ithaca, N.Y.: Cornell University Press, 1987); Louise Lamphere, *From Working Daughters to Working Mothers: Immigrant Women in a New England Industrial Community* (Ithaca, N.Y.: Cornell University Press, 1987); Judith E. Smith, "Our Own Kind: Family and Community Networks in Providence," *Radical History Review* 17 (Spring, 1978): 99–120; Judith E. Smith, *Family Connections: A History of Italian and Jewish Immigrant Lives in Providence, Rhode Island, 1900–1940* (Albany, N.Y.: SUNY Press, 1985); Patricia Albers and Beatrice Medicine, eds., *The Hidden Half: Studies of Plains Indian Women* (Washington, D.C.: University Press of America, 1983); Marla Powers, *Oglala Women: Myth, Ritual, and Reality* (Chicago: University of Chicago Press, 1986).

3. Ann Metcalf, "The Effects of Boarding School on Navajo Self-Image and Maternal Behavior" (Ph.D. dissertation, Stanford University, 1974).

4. Gary Witherspoon, *Navajo Kinship and Marriage* (Chicago: University of Chicago Press, 1975).

5. For an extended treatment of this subject, see Klara Bonsack Kelley, "Commercial Networks in the Navajo-Hopi-Zuni Region" (Ph.D. dissertation, University of New Mexico, 1977).

6. John C. McPhee et al., *Indians in Non-Indian Communities: A Survey of Living Conditions among Navajo and Hopi Indians Residing in Gallup, New Mexico; Cortez, Colorado; Winslow, Arizona; Farmington, New Mexico; Flagstaff, Arizona; Holbrook, New Mexico* (Window Rock, Ariz.: U.S. Indian Service Welfare, Placement Branch, 1953), 37.

7. U.S. Department of Commerce, Bureau of the Census, *U.S. 1980 Census of the Population, Characteristics of the Population, General Social and Economic Characteristics*; pt 4, Arizona (Washington, D.C.: U.S. Government Printing Office, 1980).

8. Stephen J. Kunitz, Jerrold Levy, Paul Bellet, and Tom Collins, "A One-Year Follow-up of Navajo Migrants to Flagstaff, Arizona," *Plateau* 59, no. 1 (1970): 101–110.

9. The literature on Navajo kinship and social organization is vast. The following references are examples of those works that focus particularly on Navajo women or on gender constructs: Laila Shukry Hamamsey, "The Roles of Navajo Women in a Changing Navajo Society," *American Anthropologist* 59, no. 1 (1957): 101–110; Ruth Roessel, *Women in Navajo Society*, (Rough Rock, Ariz.: Navajo Resource Center, 1981); and Witherspoon, *Navajo Kinship*.

10. For a more extensive treatment of Navajo women's resource networks in the reservation hinterlands, see Christine Conte, "Ladies, Livestock, Land and Lucre: Navajo Women's Resource Networks on the Western Navajo Reservation," *American Indian Quarterly* 1 and 2 (1982):

105–24; and Christine Conte, "The Navajo Sex-Gender System: The Impact of Economic Development in Two Northern Arizona Communities" (Ph.D. dissertation, New School for Social Research, 1985).

11. For a definition of network multiplexity, including techniques of measurement and its relevance as an index of the strength of a dyadic tie, see Bruce Kapferer, "Norms and the Manipulation of Relationships in a Work Context," in *Social Networks in Urban Situations*, ed. J. Clyde Mitchell (Manchester, Eng.: Manchester University Press, 1969).

27.

Mexican American Women
Grassroots Community Activists:
"Mothers of East Los Angeles"

MARY PARDO

This article on the activism of the "Mothers of East Los Angeles" concerning quality-of-life issues underlines a point made repeatedly throughout this volume: We don't see women's activities because we don't ask the right questions. Mary Pardo asked the right questions when she interviewed Mexican American women in East Los Angeles and became a participant-observer in their activities. "It started when my kids went to school," Juana Gutiérrez says. Pardo's deceptively simple story of the way a powerful community coalition developed naturally from maternal concerns is at the same time a thorough critique of conventional political science beliefs about political participation. Family, long believed by political scientists to lock women into political passivity, is in fact their spur toward activism in the face of environmental threats to their communities. Pardo shows us that around the world, women are mobilizing to link family and community on behalf of environmental justice. Like the proverbial small cloud on the horizon, such "nontraditional" worldwide political movements are a portent of things to come. Thanks to Mary Pardo's careful analysis, we understand the issues in Los Angeles, in other parts of the West, and around the world that make environmental justice a powerful women's cause.

The relatively few studies of Chicana political activism show a bias in the way political activism is conceptualized by social scientists, who often use a narrow definition confined to electoral politics.[1] Most feminist research uses an expanded definition that moves across the boundaries between public, electoral politics and private, family politics; but feminist research generally focuses on women mobilized around gender-specific issues.[2] For some feminists, adherence to "tradition" constitutes conservatism and submission to patriarchy. Both approaches exclude the contributions of working-class women, particularly those of African American women and Latinas, thus failing to capture the full dynamic of social change.[3]

The following case study of Mexican American women activists in the organization called Mothers of East Los Angeles (MELA) contributes another dimension to the conception of grassroots politics. It illustrates how these Mexican American women have transformed "traditional" networks and resources based on family and culture into political assets

to defend the quality of urban life. Far from unique, these patterns of
activism are repeated in Latin America and elsewhere. Here, as in other
times and places, the women's activism arises out of seemingly "traditional" roles, addresses wider social and political issues, and capitalizes
on informal associations sanctioned by the community.[4] Religion, commonly viewed as a conservative force, is intertwined with politics.[5] Often,
women speak of their communities and their activism as extensions of
their family and household responsibility. The central role of women in
grassroots struggles around quality of life, in the third world and in the
United States, challenges conventional assumptions about the powerlessness of women and static definitions of culture and tradition.

In general, the women in MELA are longtime residents of East Los
Angeles; some are bilingual and native-born, others Mexican-born and
Spanish-dominant. All the core activists are bilingual and have lived in the
community over thirty years. All have been active in parish-sponsored
groups and activities; some have had experience working in community-
based groups arising from schools, neighborhood watch associations, and
labor support groups. To gain an appreciation of the group and the core
activists, I used ethnographic field methods. I interviewed six women,
using a life history approach focused on their first community activities,
current activism, household and family responsibilities, and perceptions
of community issues.[6] Also, from December 1987 through October 1989,
I attended hearings on the two projects of contention—a proposed state
prison and a toxic waste incinerator—and participated in community and
organizational meetings and demonstrations. The following discussion
briefly chronicles an intense and significant five-year segment (1985–90)
of community history from which emerged MELA and the women's
transformation of "traditional" resources and experiences into political
assets for community mobilization.[7]

THE COMMUNITY CONTEXT:
EAST LOS ANGELES RESISTING SIEGE

Political science theory often guides the political strategies used by local
government to select the sites for undesirable projects. In 1984, the State
of California commissioned a public relations firm to assess the political
difficulties facing the construction of energy-producing waste incinerators. The report provided a "personality profile" of those residents most
likely to organize effective opposition to projects: "[M]iddle and upper
socioeconomic strata possess better resources to effectuate their opposition. Middle and higher socioeconomic strata neighborhoods should not
fall within the one-mile and five-mile radii of the proposed site. Con-
versely, older people, people with a high school education or less are least
likely to oppose a facility."[8]

The state accordingly placed the plant in Commerce, a predominantly
Mexican American, low-income community. This pattern holds throughout the state and the country: Three out of five African Americans and

Latinos live near toxic waste sites, and three of the five largest hazardous waste landfills are in communities with at least 80 percent minority populations.[9]

Similarly, in March 1985, when the state sought a site for the first state prison in Los Angeles County, Governor Deukmejian resolved to place the seventeen-hundred-inmate institution in East Los Angeles, within a mile of the long-established Boyle Heights neighborhood and within two miles of thirty-four schools. Furthermore, violating convention, the state bid on the expensive parcel of industrially zoned land without compiling an environmental impact report or providing a public community hearing. According to James Vigil, Jr., a field representative for Assemblywoman Gloria Molina, shortly after the state announced the site selection, Molina's office began informing the community and gauging residents' sentiments about it through direct mailings and calls to leaders of organizations and business groups.

In spring of 1986, after much pressure from the Fifty-sixth Assembly District office and the community, the Department of Corrections agreed to hold a public information meeting, which was attended by over seven hundred Boyle Heights residents. From this moment on, Vigil observed, "the tables turned, the community mobilized, and the residents began calling the political representatives and requesting their presence at hearings and meetings."[10] By summer 1986, the community was well aware of the prison site proposal. Over two thousand people, carrying placards proclaiming "No Prison in ELA," marched from Resurrection Church in Boyle Heights to the Olympic Boulevard bridge linking East Los Angeles with the rapidly expanding downtown Los Angeles.[11] This march marked the beginning of one of the largest coalitions to emerge from the Latino community in the last decade.

Prominent among the coalition's groups is Mothers of East Los Angeles, a loosely knit group of over four hundred Mexican American women.[12] MELA initially coalesced to oppose the state prison construction but has since organized opposition to several other projects detrimental to the quality of life in the central city.[13] Its second large target was a toxic waste incinerator proposed for Vernon, a small city adjacent to East Los Angeles. This incinerator would worsen the already debilitating air quality of the entire county and set a precedent dangerous for other communities throughout California.[14]

When MELA took up the fight against the toxic waste incinerator, it became more than a single-issue group and began working with environmental groups around the state.[15] As a result of the community struggle, AB58 (Roybal-Allard), providing all Californians with the minimum protection of an environmental impact report before the construction of hazardous waste incinerators, was signed into law. But the law's effectiveness relies on a watchful community network. Since its emergence, Mothers of East Los Angeles has become centrally important to just such a network of grassroots activists, including a select number of Catholic priests and two Mexican American political representatives.

Mothers of East Los Angeles on the march.   (Photo from author's collection.)

Furthermore, the group's very formation, and its continued spirit and
activism, fly in the face of the conventional political science beliefs
regarding political participation.

"Experts" attribute the low formal political participation (i.e., voting) of
Mexican American people in the United States to a set of cultural
"retardants," including primary kinship systems, fatalism, religious
traditionalism, traditional cultural values, and mother country attachment.[16]
The core activists in MELA may appear to fit this description, as well as
the state-commissioned profile of residents least likely to oppose toxic waste
incinerator projects. All the women live in a low-income community.
Furthermore, they identify themselves as active and committed participants
in the Catholic Church; they claim an ethnic identity—Mexican American;
their ages range from forty to sixty; and they have attained at most high
school educations. However, these women fail to exhibit the predicted
political apathy. Instead, they have transformed social identity—ethnic
identity, class identity, and gender identity—into an impetus as well as basis
for activism. And, in transforming their existing social networks into
grassroots political networks, they have also transformed themselves.

TRANSFORMATION AS A DOMINANT THEME

From the life histories of the group's core activists and from my own field
notes, I have selected excerpts that illustrate not only the events that led

to community mobilization in East Los Angeles but also a story of transformation, the process of creating new and better relationships that empower people to unite and achieve common goals.[17]

First, women have transformed organizing experiences and social networks arising from gender-related responsibilities into political resources.[18] When I asked the women about the first community, not necessarily "political," involvement they could recall, they discussed experiences that predated the formation of MELA. Juana Gutiérrez explained:

Well, it didn't start with the prison, you know. It started when my kids went to school. I started by joining the Parents Club and we worked on different problems here in the area. Like the people who come to the parks to sell drugs to the kids. I got the neighbors to have meetings. I would go knock at the doors, house to house. And I told them that we should stick together with the Neighborhood Watch for the community and for the kids.[19]

Erlinda Robles similarly recalled:

I wanted my kids to go to Catholic school and from the time my oldest one went there, I was there every day. I used to take my two little ones with me and I helped one way or another. I used to question things they did. And the other mothers would just watch me. Later, they would ask me, "Why do you do that? They are going to take it out on your kids." I'd say, "They better not." And before you knew it, we had a big group of mothers that were very involved.[20]

Part of a mother's "traditional" responsibility includes overseeing her child's progress in school, interacting with school staff, and supporting school activities. In these processes, women meet other mothers and begin developing a network of acquaintanceships and friendships based on mutual concern for the welfare of their children.

Although the women in MELA carried the greatest burden of participating in school activities, Erlinda Robles also spoke of strategies they used to draw men into the enterprise and into the networks:[21]

At the beginning, the priests used to say who the president of the mothers guild would be; they used to pick 'em. But, we wanted elections, so we got elections. Then we wanted the fathers to be involved, and the nuns suggested that a father should be president and a mother would be secretary or be involved there [at the school site].[22]

Of course, this comment piqued my curiosity, so I asked how the mothers agreed on the nuns' suggestion. The answer was simple and instructive:

At the time we thought it was a "natural" way to get the fathers involved because they weren't involved; it was just the mothers. Everybody [the women] agreed on them [the fathers] being president because they worked all day and they couldn't be involved in a lot of daily activities like food sales and whatever. During the week, a steering committee of mothers planned the group's activities. But now that I think about it, a woman could have done the job just as well![23]

So women got men into the group by giving them a position they could manage. The men may have held the title of president, but they were not making day-to-day decisions about work nor were they dictating the direction of the group. Erlinda Robles laughed as she recalled an occasion when the president insisted, against the wishes of the women, on scheduling a parents' group fund-raiser—a breakfast—on Mother's Day. On that morning, only the president and his wife were present to prepare breakfast. This should alert researchers against measuring power and influence by looking solely at who holds titles.

Each of MELA's cofounders had a history of working with groups arising out of the responsibilities usually assumed by mothers—the education of children and the safety of the surrounding community. From these groups, they gained valuable experiences and networks that facilitated the formation of Mothers of East Los Angeles. Juana Gutiérrez explained how preexisting networks progressively expanded community support:

You know nobody knew about the plan to build a prison in this community until Assemblywoman Gloria Molina told me. Martha Molina called me and said, "You know what is happening in your area? The governor wants to put a prison in Boyle Heights!" So, I called a Neighborhood Watch meeting at my house and we got fifteen people together. Then, Father John [Moretta] started informing his people at the Church and that is when the group of two to three hundred started showing up for every march on the bridge.[24]

MELA effectively linked preexisting networks into a viable grassroots coalition.

Second, the process of activism also transformed previously "invisible" women, making them not only visible but the center of public attention. From a conventional perspective, political activism assumes a kind of gender neutrality. This means that anyone can participate, but men are expected to be the key actors. In accordance with this pattern, in winter 1986 an informal group of concerned businessmen in the community began lobbying and testifying against the prison at hearings in Sacramento. Working in conjunction with Assemblywoman Molina, they made many trips to Sacramento at their own expense. Residents who did not have the income to travel were unable to join them. Finally, Molina, commonly recognized as a forceful advocate for Latinas and the community, asked Frank Villalobos, an urban planner in the group, why there were no women coming up to speak in Sacramento against the prison. As he phrased it, "I was getting some heat from her because no women were going up there."[25]

In response to Molina's inquiry, Villalobos invited Veronica Gutiérrez, a law student who lived in the community, to accompany him on the next trip to Sacramento.[26] He also mentioned Molina's comment to Father John Moretta at Resurrection Catholic Church. Meanwhile, representatives of the business sector of the community and of the Fifty-sixth Assembly District office were continuing to compile arguments and supportive data against the East Los Angeles prison site. Frank Villalobos stated one of the pressing problems:

We felt that the Senators whom we prepared all this for didn't even acknowledge that we existed. They kept calling it the "downtown" site, and they argued that there was no opposition in the community. So, I told Father Moretta, what we have to do is demonstrate that there is a link [proximity] between the Boyle Heights community and the prison.[27]

The next incident illustrates how perceptions of gender-specific behavior set in motion a sequence of events that brought women into the political limelight. Father Moretta decided to ask all the women to meet after mass. He told them about the prison site and called for their support. When I asked him about his rationale for selecting the women, he replied:

I felt so strongly about the issue, and I knew in my heart what a terrible offense this was to the people. So, I was afraid that once we got into a demonstration situation we had to be very careful. I thought the women would be cooler and calmer than the men. The bottom line is that the men came anyway. The first times out the majority were women. Then they began to invite their husbands and their children, but originally it was just women.[28]

Father Moretta also named the group. Quite moved by a film, *The Official Story*, about the courageous Argentine women who demonstrated for the return of their children who had disappeared during a repressive right-wing military dictatorship, Moretta transformed the name used by the Argentine women, "Las Madres de la Plaza de Mayo," into "Mothers of East Los Angeles."[29]

However, Aurora Castillo, one of the cofounders of the group modified my emphasis on the predominance of women: "Of course, the fathers work," she said. "We also have many, many grandmothers. And all this *is* with the support of the fathers. They make the placards and the posters; they do the security and carry the signs; and they come to the marches when they can."[30] Thus, although women played a key role in the mobilization, they emphasized the group's broad base of active supporters as well as the other organizations in the Coalition against the Prison. The women's intent was to counter any notion that MELA was composed exclusively of women or mothers and to stress the inclusiveness of the group. All the women who assumed lead roles in the group had long histories of volunteer work in the Boyle Heights community, but formation of the group brought them out of the private margins and into public light.

Third, the women in Mothers of East L.A. have transformed the definition of "mother" to include militant political opposition to state-proposed projects seen as adverse to the quality of life in the community. Explaining how she became aware of the issue, Aurora Castillo said:

You know if one of your children's safety is jeopardized, the mother turns into a lioness. That's why Father John got the mothers. We have to have a well-organized, strong group of mothers to protect the community and oppose things that are detrimental to us. You know the governor is in the wrong and the mothers are in the right. After all, the mothers have to be right. Mothers are for the children's interest, not for self-interest; the governor is for his own political interest.[31]

The women also expanded the boundaries of "motherhood" to include social and political community activism and redefined the word to include women who are not biological mothers. At one meeting a young Latina expressed her solidarity with the group and, almost apologetically, qualified herself as a "resident," not a "mother," of East Los Angeles. Erlinda Robles replied, "When you are fighting for a better life for children and 'doing' for them, isn't that what mothers do? So we're all mothers. You don't have to have children to be a 'mother.' "[32]

At critical points, grassroots community activism requires attending many meetings, making many phone calls, and convassing door-to-door—all very labor-intensive work. In order to keep harmony in the domestic sphere, the core activists must creatively integrate family members into their community activities. I asked Erlinda Robles how her husband felt about her activism, and she replied quite openly:

My husband doesn't like getting involved, but he takes me because he knows I like it. Sometimes we would have two or three meetings a week. And my husband would say, "Why are you doing so much? It is really getting out of hand." But he is very supportive. Once he gets there, he enjoys it and he starts in arguing too! See, it's just that he is not used to it. He couldn't believe things happened the way that they do. He was in the Navy twenty years and they brainwashed him that none of the politicians could do wrong. So he has come a long way. Now he comes home and parks the car out front and asks me, "Well, where are we going tonight?"[33]

When the women explained their activism, they linked family and community as one entity. Juana Gutiérrez, a woman with extensive experiences working on community and neighborhood issues, stated:

Yo como madre de familia, y como residente del Este de Los Angeles, seguiré luchando sin descanso por que se nos respete. Y yo lo hago con bastante cariño hacia mi communidad. Digo "mi comunidad" porque me siento parte de ella, quiero a mi raza como parte de mi familia, y si Dios me permite seguiré luchando contra todos los gobernadores que quieran abusar de nosotros.

As a mother and a resident of East L.A., I shall continue fighting tirelessly so we will be respected. And I will do this with much affection for my community. I say "my community" because I am part of it. I love my people as part of my family; and if God allows, I will keep on fighting against all the governors that want to take advantage of us.[34]

Like the other activists, Gutiérrez expanded her responsibilities and legitimated militant opposition to abuse of the community by representatives of the state.

Working-class women activists seldom opt to separate themselves from men and their families. In this particular struggle for community quality of life, they are fighting for the family unit and thus are not competitive with men.[35] Of course, this fact does not preclude different alignments in other contexts and situations.[36]

Fourth, the story of MELA also shows the transformation of class and ethnic identity. Aurora Castillo told of an incident that illustrated her growing knowledge of the relationship of East Los Angeles to other communities and the basis necessary for coalition building:

And do you know we have been approached by other groups? [She lowers her voice in emphasis.] You know that Pacific Palisades group asked for our backing. But what they did, they sent their powerful lobbyist that they pay thousands of dollars to get our support against the drilling in Pacific Palisades. So what we did was tell them to send their grassroots people, not their lobbyist. We're suspicious. We don't want to talk to a high-salaried lobbyist; we are humble people. We did our own lobbying. In one week we went to Sacramento twice.[37]

The contrast between the often tedious and labor-intensive work of mobilizing people at the grassroots level and the paid work of a "high salaried lobbyist" represents a point of pride and integrity, not a deficiency or a source of shame. If the two groups were to construct a coalition, they had to communicate on equal terms.

The women of MELA combine a willingness to assert opposition with a critical assessment of their own weaknesses. At one community meeting, for example, representatives of several oil companies attempted to gain support for placement of an oil pipeline through the center of East Los Angeles. The exchange between the women in the audience and the oil representatives was heated, as women alternated asking questions about the chosen route for the pipeline:

"Is it going through Cielito Lindo [Reagan's ranch]?" The oil representative answered, "No." Another woman stood up and asked, "Why not place it along the coastline?" Without thinking of the implications, the representative responded, "Oh, no! If it burst it would endanger the marine life." The woman retorted, "You value the marine life more than human beings?" His face reddened with anger and the hearing disintegrated into angry chanting.[38]

The proposal was quickly defeated. But Aurora Castillo acknowledged that it was not solely their opposition that brought about the defeat:

We won because the Westside was opposed to it, so we united with them. You know there are a lot of attorneys who live there and they also questioned the representative. Believe me, no way is justice blind. . . . We just don't want all this garbage thrown at us because we are low-income and Mexican American. We are lucky now that we have good representatives, which we didn't have before.[39]

Throughout their interviews, the women referred to the disruptive effects of land-use decisions made in the 1950s. As longtime residents, all but one share the experience of losing a home and relocating to make way for a freeway. Juana Gutiérrez referred to the community response at that time:

Una de las cosas que me caen muy mal es la injusticia y en nuestra comunidad hemos visto mucho de eso. Sobre todo antes, porque creo que nuestra gente estaba mas dormida; nos atrevíamos menos. En los cincuentas hicieron los freeways y así, sin más, nos dieron la noticia de que nos teníamos que mudar. Y eso pasó dos veces. La gente se conformaba porque lo ordeno el gobierno. Recuerdo que yo me enojaba y quería que los demás me secundaran, pero nadio quería hacer nada.

One of the things that really upsets me is the injustice that we see so much in our community. Above everything else, I believe that our people were less aware; we were less challenging. In the 1950s they made the freeways and just like that they gave us a notice that we had to move. That happened twice. The people accepted it because the government ordered it. I remember that I was angry and wanted the others to back me but nobody else wanted to do anything.[40]

The freeways that cut through communities and disrupted neighborhoods are now a concrete reminder of shared injustice, of the vulnerability of the community in the 1950s. The community's social and political history thus informs perceptions of its current predicament; however, today's activists emphasize not the powerlessness of the community but the change in status and their progression toward political empowerment.

Fifth, the core activists typically told stories illustrating personal change and a new sense of entitlement to speak for the community. They have transformed the unspoken sentiments of individuals into a collective community voice. Lucy Ramos related her initial apprehensions:

I was afraid to get involved. I didn't know what was going to come out of this and I hesitated at first. Right after we started, Father John came up to me and told me, "I want you to be a spokesperson." I said, "Oh no, I don't know what I am going to say." I was nervous. I am surprised I didn't have a nervous breakdown then. Every time we used to get in front of the TV cameras and even interviews like this, I used to sit there and I could feel myself shaking. But as time went on, I started getting used to it.

And this is what I have noticed with a lot of them. They were afraid to speak up and say anything. Now, with this prison issue, a lot of them have come out and come forward and given their opinions. Everybody used to be real "quietlike."[41]

Ramos also related a situation that brought all her fears to a climax, which she confronted and resolved as follows:

When I first started working with the coalition, Channel 13 called me up and said they wanted to interview me and I said OK. Then I started getting nervous. So I called Father John and told him, "You better get over here right away." He said, "Don't worry, don't worry, you can handle it by yourself." Then Channel 13 called me back and said they were gong to interview another person, someone I had never heard of, and asked if it was OK if he came to my house. And I said OK again. Then I began thinking, what if this guy is for the prison? What am I going to do? And I was so nervous and I thought, I know what I am going to do!

Since the meeting was taking place in her home, she reasoned that she was entitled to order any troublemakers out of her domain:

If this man tells me anything, I am just going to chase him out of my house. That is what I am going to do! All these thoughts were going through my head. Then Channel 13 walked into my house followed by six men I had never met. And I thought, Oh, my God, what did I get myself into? I kept saying to myself, if they get smart with me I am throwing them *all* out.[42]

At this point in the interview her tone expressed resolve. In fact, the situation turned out to be neither confrontational nor threatening, as the "six men" were also members of the coalition. This woman confronted an anxiety-laden situation by relying on her sense of control within her home and family—a quite traditional source of authority for women—and transforming that control into the courage to express a political position before a potential audience all over one of the largest metropolitan areas in the nation.

People living in third world countries as well as in minority communities in the United States face an increasingly degraded environment.[43] Recognizing the threat to the well-being of their families, residents have mobilized at the neighborhood level to fight for quality-of-life issues. The common notion that environmental well-being is of concern solely to white middle-class and upper-class residents ignores the specific way working-class neighborhoods suffer from the fallout of urban "growth machines" geared for profit.[44]

In Los Angeles, the culmination of postwar urban renewal policies, the growing Pacific Rim trade surplus and investments, and low-wage international labor migration from third world countries have combined to create potentially volatile conditions. Literally palatial financial buildings swallow up the space previously occupied by modest low-cost housing. Increasingly, density and development not matched by investment in social programs, services, and infrastructure erode the quality of life, beginning in the core of the city.[45] Latinos, the majority of whom live close to the center of the city, must confront the distilled social consequences of development focused solely on profit. The Mexican American community of East Los Angeles, much like other minority working-class communities, has been a repository for prisons instead of new schools, hazardous industries instead of safe work sites, and one of the largest concentrations of freeway interchanges in the country, which transports much wealth past the community. And the concerns of residents in East Los Angeles may provide lessons for other minority as well as middle-class communities. Increasing environmental pollution resulting from inadequate waste disposal plans and an out-of-control need for penal institutions to contain the casualties created by the growing bipolar distribution of wages may not be limited to the Southwest.[46]

These conditions set the stage for new conflicts. But they also provide new opportunities to transform old relationships into coalitions that can challenge state agendas and create new community visions.[47]

Mexican American women living east of downtown Los Angeles exemplify the tendency of women to enter into environmental struggles in defense of their community. Women have a rich historical legacy of community activism, partly reconstructed over the last two decades in social histories of women who contested other quality-of-life issues, from the price of bread to the evils of "demon rum" (often representing domestic violence).[48]

But something new is also happening. The issues traditionally addressed by women—health, housing, sanitation, and the urban environment—have moved to center stage as capitalist urbanization progresses. Environmental issues now fuel the fires of many political campaigns and drive citizens beyond the rather restricted, perfunctory political act of voting. Instances of political mobilization at the grassroots level, where women often play a central role, allow us to see abstract concepts like participatory democracy and social change as dynamic processes.

The existence and the activities of Mothers of East Los Angeles attest to the dynamic nature of participatory democracy as well as to the dynamic nature of our gender, class, and ethnic identity. The story of MELA reveals, on the one hand, how individuals and groups can transform a seemingly traditional role such as that of "mother." On the other hand, it illustrates how such a role may also be a social agent drawing members of the community into the political arena. Studying women's contributions as well as men's will shed greater light on the network dynamics of grassroots movements.[49]

The work Mothers of East Los Angeles does to mobilize the community demonstrates that people's political involvement cannot be predicted by their cultural characteristics. These women have defied stereotypes of apathy and used ethnic, gender, and class identity as an impetus, a strength, a vehicle for political activism. They have expanded their—and our—understanding of the complexities of a political system, and they have reaffirmed the possibility of "doing something."

They also generously shared the lessons they have learned. One of the women in Mothers of East Los Angeles told me, as I hesitated to set up an interview with another woman I hadn't yet met in person, "You know, nothing ventured, nothing lost. You should have seen how timid we were the first time we went to a public hearing. Now forget it. I walk right up and make myself heard and that's what you have to do."[50]

Notes

This essay first appeared in *Frontiers* 11, no. 1 (1990).

1. See Vicky Randall, *Women and Politics, An International Perspective* (Chicago: University of Chicago Press, 1987), for a review of the central themes and debates in the literature. For two of the few books on Chicanas, work, and family, see Vicki L. Ruiz, *Cannery Women, Cannery*

Lives: Mexican Women, Unionization, and the California Food Processing Industry, 1930–1950 (Albuquerque: University of New Mexico Press, 1987), and Patricia Zavella, *Women's Work and Chicano Families* (Ithaca, N.Y.: Cornell University Press, 1987).

2. For recent exceptions to this approach, see Anne Witte Garland, *Women Activists: Challenging the Abuse of Power* (New York: Feminist Press, 1988); Ann Bookman and Sandra Morgen, eds., *Women and the Politics of Empowerment* (Philadelphia: Temple University Press, 1987); Karen Sacks, *Caring by the Hour* (Chicago: University of Illinois Press, 1988). For a sociological analysis of community activism among African American women, see Cheryl Townsend Gilkes, "Holding Back the Ocean with a Broom," *The Black Woman*, ed. La Frances Rogers-Rose (Beverly Hills, Calif.: Sage Publications, 1980).

3. For two exceptions to this criticism, see Sara Evans, *Born for Liberty: A History of Women in America* (New York: Free Press, 1989), and Bettina Aptheker, *Tapestries of Life, Women's Work, Women's Consciousness, and the Meaning of Daily Experience* (Amherst: University of Massachusetts Press, 1989). For a critique, see Maxine Baca Zinn, Lynn Weber Cannon, Elizabeth Higginbotham, and Bonnie Thornton Dill, "The Costs of Exclusionary Practices in Women's Studies," *Signs* 11, no. 2 (Winter 1986), 290–303.

4. For cases of grassroots activism among women in Latin America, see Sally W. Yudelman, *Hopeful Openings, A Study of Five Women's Development Organizations in Latin American and the Caribbean* (West Hartford, Conn.: Kumarian Press, 1987). For an excellent case analysis of how informal associations enlarge and empower women's world in third world countries, see Kathryn S. March and Rachelle L. Taqqu, *Women's Informal Associations in Developing Countries: Catalysts for Change?* (Boulder, Colo.: Westview Press, 1986). Also see Carmen Feijoó, "Women in Neighbourhoods: From Local Issues to Gender Problems," *Canadian Woman Studies* 6, no. 1 (Fall 1984): 86–89, for a concise overview of the patterns of activism.

5. The relationship between Catholicism and political activism is varied and not unitary. In some Mexican American communities, grassroots activism relies on parish networks. See Isidro D. Ortiz, "Chicano Urban Politics and the Politics of Reform in the Seventies," *The Western Political Quarterly* 37, no. 4 (December 1984): 565–77. Also see Joseph D. Sekul, "Communities Organized for Public Service: Citizen Power and Public Power in San Antonio," in *Latinos and the Political System*, ed. F. Chris Garcia (Notre Dame, Ind.: University of Notre Dame Press, 1988). Sekul tells how COPS members challenged prevailing patterns of power by working for the well-being of families and cites four former presidents who were Mexican American women, but he makes no special point of gender.

6. I also interviewed other members of the Coalition against the Prison and local political office representatives. For a general reference, see James P. Spradley, *The Ethnographic Interview* (New York: Holt, Rinehart and Winston, 1979). For a review essay focused on the relevancy of the method for examining the diversity of women's experiences, see Susan N. G. Geiger, "Women's Life Histories: Method and Content," *Signs* 11, no. 2 (Winter 1986): 334–51.

7. During the five years from 1985 to 1990, over three hundred newspaper articles appeared on the issue. Frank Villalobos generously shared his extensive newspaper archives with me. See Leo C. Wolinsky, "L.A. Prison Bill 'Locked Up' in New Clash," *Los Angeles Times*, 16 July 1987; Rudy Acuña, "The Fate of East L.A.: One Big Jail," *Los Angeles Herald Examiner*, 28 April 1989; Carolina Serna, "Eastside Residents Oppose Prison," *La Gente UCLA Student Newspaper* 17, no. 1 (October 1986): 5; Daniel M. Weintraub, "$10,000 Fee Paid to Lawmaker Who Left Sickbed to Cast Vote," *Los Angeles Times*, 13 March 1988.

8. Cerrell Associates, Inc., "Political Difficulties Facing Waste-to-Energy Conversion Plant Siting," Report Prepared for California Waste Management Board, State of California, Los Angeles, 1984, 43.

9. Jesus Sanchez, "The Environment: Whose Movement?" *California Tomorrow* 3, n. 3 and 4 (Fall 1988): 13. Also see Rudy Acuña, *A Community under Siege* (Los Angeles: Chicano Studies Research Center Publications, UCLA, 1984). The book and its title capture the sentiments and the history of a community that bears an unfair burden of city projects deemed undesirable by all residents.

10. James Vigil, Jr., field representative for Assemblywoman Gloria Molina, 1984–86, interview by author, Whittier, Calif., 27 September 1989. Vigil stated that the Department of Corrections used a threefold strategy: political pressure in the legislature, the promise of jobs for residents, and contracts for local businesses.

11. Edward J. Boyer and Marita Hernandez, "Eastside Seethes over Prison Plan," *Los Angeles Times*, 13 August 1986.

12. Martha Molina-Aviles, former administrative assistant for Assemblywoman Lucille Roybal-Allard, Fifty-sixth Assembly District, and former field representative for Gloria Molina when she held this assembly seat, interview by author, Los Angeles, 5 June 1989. Molina-Aviles, who grew up in East Los Angeles, used her experiences and insights to help forge strong links among the women in MELA, other members of the coalition, and the assembly office.

13. MELA also opposed the expansion of a county prison across the street from William Mead Housing Projects, home to two thousand Latinos, Asians, and African Americans, and the construction of a chemical treatment plant for toxic wastes.

14. The first of its kind in a metropolitan area, the incinerator would have burned 125,000 pounds per day of hazardous wastes. For an excellent article that links struggles against hazardous waste dumps and incinerators in minority communities and features women in MELA, see Dick Russell, "Environmental Racism: Minority Communities and Their Battle against Toxics," *The Amicus Journal* 11, no. 2 (Spring 1989): 22–32.

15. Miguel G. Mendívil, field representative for Assemblywoman Lucille Roybal-Allard, Fifty-sixth Assembly District, interview by author, Los Angeles, 25 April 1989.

16. John Garcia and Rudolfo de la Garza, "Mobilizing the Mexican Immigrant: The Role of Mexican American Organizations," *The Western Political Quarterly* 38, no. 4 (December 1985): 551–64.

17. This concept is discussed in relation to Latino communities in David T. Abaolos, *Latinos in the U.S.: The Sacred and the Political* (Notre Dame, Ind.: University of Notre Dame Press, 1986). The notion of transformation of traditional culture in struggles against oppression is certainly not a new one. For a brief essay on a longer work, see Frantz Fanon, "Algeria Unveiled," in *The New Left Reader*, ed. Carl Oglesby (New York: Grove Press, 1969): 161–85.

18. Sacks, *Caring by the Hour*.

19. Juana Gutiérrez, interview by author, Boyle Heights, East Los Angeles, 15 January 1988.

20. Erlinda Robles, interview by author, Boyle Heights, Los Angeles, 14 September 1989.

21. For theory behind such strategizing, see Mina Davis Caulfield, "Imperialism, the Family, and Cultures of Resistance," *Socialist Revolution* 29 (1974): 67–85.

22. Robles interview.

23. Ibid.

24. Gutiérrez interview.

25. Frank Villalobos, architect and urban planner, interview by author, Los Angeles, 2 May 1989.

26. The law student, Veronica Gutiérrez, is the daughter of Juana Gutiérrez, one of the cofounders of MELA. Martín Gutiérrez, one of her sons, was a field representative for Assemblywoman Lucille Roybal-Allard and also central to community mobilization. Ricardo Gutiérrez, Juana's husband, and almost all the other family members are community activists. They are a microcosm of the family networks that strengthened community mobilization and the Coalition against the Prison. See Raymundo Reynoso, "Juana Beatrice Gutiérrez: La incansable lucha de una activista comunitaria," *La Opinión*, 6 Agosto de 1989, Acceso, 1; and Louis Sahagun, "The Mothers of East L.A. Transform Themselves and Their Community," *Los Angeles Times*, 13 August 1989.

27. Villalobos interview.

28. Father John Moretta, Resurrection Parish, interview by author, Boyle Heights, Los Angeles, 24 May 1989.

29. The Plaza de Mayo mothers organized spontaneously to demand the return of their missing children, in open defiance of the Argentine military dictatorship. For a brief overview of the group

and its relationship to other women's organizations in Argentina, and a synopsis of the criticism of the mothers that reveals ideological camps, see Gloria Bonder, "Women's Organizations in Argentina's Transition to Democracy," in *Women and Counter Power*, ed. Yolanda Cohen (New York: Black Rose Books, 1989), 65–85. There is no direct relationship between this group and MELA.

30. Aurora Castillo, interview by author, Boyle Heights, Los Angeles, 15 January 1988.

31. Ibid.

32. Robles interview.

33. Ibid.

34. Reynoso, "Juana Beatrice Gutiérrez."

35. For historical examples, see Chris Marin, "La Asociación Hispano-Americano de Madres Y Esposas: Tucson's Mexican American Women in World War II," *Renta Rosaldo Lecture Series 1: 1983–1984* (Tuscon: Mexican American Studies Center, University of Arizona, Tucson, 1985); and Judy Aulette and Trudy Mills, "Something Old, Something New: Auxiliary Work in the 1983–1986 Copper Strike," *Feminist Studies* 14, no. 2 (Summer 1988): 251–69.

36. Caulfield, "Imperialism, the Family and Cultures of Resistance."

37. Castillo interview.

38. As reconstructed by Juana Gutiérrez, Ricardo Gutiérrez, and Aurora Castillo.

39. Castillo interview.

40. Gutiérrez interview.

41. Lucy Ramos, interview by author, Boyle Heights, Los Angeles, 3 May 1989.

42. Ibid.

43. For an overview of contemporary third-world struggles against environmental degradation, see Alan B. Durning, "Saving the Planet," *The Progressive* 53, no. 4 (April 1989): 35–59.

44. John Logan and Harvey Molotch, *Urban Fortunes* (Berkeley: University of California Press, 1988). Logan and Molotch use the term "growth machines" in reference to a coalition of businesspeople, local politicians, and the media.

45. Mike Davis, "Chinatown, Part Two? The Internationalization of Downtown Los Angeles," *New Left Review* no. 164 (July/August 1987): 64–86.

46. Paul Ong, *The Widening Divide: Income Inequality and Poverty in Los Angeles* (Los Angeles: The Research Group on the Los Angeles Economy, 1989). This UCLA-based study documents the growing gap between "haves" and "have nots" in the midst of the economic boom in Los Angeles. According to economists, the study mirrors a national trend in which rising employment levels are failing to lift the poor out of poverty or to boost the middle class; see Jill Steward, "Two-Tiered Economy Feared as Dead End of Unskilled," *Los Angeles Times*, 25 June 1989. At the same time, the California prison population has grown to twice its designed capacity. See Carl Ingram, "New Forecast Sees a Worse Jam in Prisons," *Los Angeles Times*, 27 June 1989.

47. The point that urban land-use policies are the products of class struggle—both cause and consequence—is made by Don Parson, "The Development of Redevelopment: Public Housing and Urban Renewal in Los Angeles," *International Journal of Urban and Regional Research* 6, no. 4 (December 1984): 392–413. Parson provides an excellent discussion of the working-class struggle for housing in the 1930s, the counterinitiative of urban renewal in the 1950s, and the inner-city revolts of the 1960s.

48. Louise Tilly, "Paths of Proletarianization: Organization of Production, Sexual Division of Labor, and Women's Collective Action," *Signs* 7, no. 2 (1981): 400–417; Alice Kessler-Harris, "Women's Social Mission," in *Women Have Always Worked* (Old Westbury, N.Y.: Feminist Press, 1981), 102–35. For a literature review of women's activism during the Progressive Era, see Marilyn Gittell and Teresa Shtob, "Changing Women's Roles in Political Volunteerism and Reform of the City," in *Women and the American City*, ed. Catharine Stimpson et al. (Chicago: University of Chicago Press, 1981), 64–75.

49. Sacks, *Caring by the Hour*, argues that often the significance of women's contributions is not "seen" because they are accomplished in networks.

50. Castillo interview. In the years since my interview with Castillo, MELA, after defeating the proposed state prison construction, split into two separate groups, somewhat along parish lines. The split occurred when some of the women, and some men, began questioning the group's decision-making process. They questioned the community issues to be addressed and the relationship of the pastor to the organization. One group continues to work with Resurrection Parish and Father Moretta. The other, which calls itself MELASI—Madres del Este de Los Angeles, Santa Isabel Parish—was formed by Juana Gutiérrez, a core member of the original MELA. The women in MELASI keep their pastor informed, but he supports rather than directs their activities. This group has developed a water conservation program that employs residents; it also provides scholarships for college students. MELA and MELASI, though working independently of one another today, still engage in common struggles.

28.

Southeast Asian Refugee Women, War, and Resettlement

TERRI BRYAN

Terri Bryan's article on Southeast Asian refugee women reminds us, first, what the commonplace phrase "culture shock" can mean in the lives of real people. Few immigrants to the U.S. West experienced such an overwhelming combination of war, refugee camp, and disorienting resettlement as did Southeast Asian women in the 1970s and 1980s. Still, the immediacy of their painful adjustment ought to help us better appreciate the full impact of the many shocks of coming to terms with a new culture that all immigrants to the U.S. West have faced.

Another important aspect of this article is its emphasis on the government's specially designed programs for helping Southeast Asian families. These programs, like the earnest efforts of women reformers mentioned in earlier sections, sometimes produced unintended results. Perhaps, in both cases, this happened because the programs were designed for rather than with the recipients. Throughout the article, Bryan shows us a number of ways in which Southeast Asian women exercised choice in the options available to them.

Finally, the author's comparison of the urban situations for Southeast Asian immigrants in Seattle, San Diego, Denver, Dallas, and Albuquerque underlines the fact that there have always been many Wests. Indeed, the historical study of "the West," as the many and varied stories of the racial ethnic women in this volume make clear, can only really begin when the existence of these many Wests is fully acknowledged.

Immigrants from Southeast Asia, displaced by the Vietnam War, represent the vast majority of refugees admitted into the United States from 1975 to 1987. Well over a million arrived in the twelve years after the fall of Saigon and America's client governments in Laos and Cambodia in 1975. They fled persecution from communist regimes in Vietnam and Laos and from the genocidal policies of Pol Pot in Cambodia. Thirty-eight percent of the refugees, about 90 percent of whom were from Vietnam, arrived with the first wave from 1975 to 1980 under "special parole programs." Many entered with connections to the American government, came from educated middle- to upper-class families, and were certainly more urban and Catholic than the "boat people" who began arriving in 1980. No complete enumeration of the refugee population has been carried out since

1981, but 29 percent of the Southeast Asians were second-wave boat people who arrived in the United States during the peak emigration years of 1980 and 1981. Vietnamese remained proportionately the largest group, but as second-wave Cambodians and Laotians arrived, the refugees were increasingly less educated, more rural, impoverished, and non-English-speaking.[1]

The federal government and welfare agencies dispersed the first refugees throughout the United States so they wouldn't place a burden on any one state. But as refugees themselves sought larger ethnic communities, better social welfare programs, and familiar climates, secondary migration led a majority to the West. Between 1983 and 1992, over 40 percent of Southeast Asians resettled in California, Texas, and Washington. California alone claimed 31 percent during that period.[2]

This essay explores resettlement issues between men and women and between parents and children in communities of Vietnamese, Cambodians, and Laotians in Seattle, San Diego, Albuquerque, Dallas, and Denver. It is a preliminary survey of the factors affecting Southeast Asian women and their families in these cities. Much of this survey derives from primary sources, including interviews with refugee families, government policymakers, municipal agents, and leaders of refugee organizations; other sources include *Reports to Congress* compiled by the Department of Health and Human Services's Office of Refugee Resettlement and municipal statistical documentation.

Prior culture, class, religion, period of immigration, generation, regional ethnic communities, and economies all affected Southeast Asian women's particular adjustments and choices in the United States. All of these factors invite further research as we explore the changing gender options of some of the West's most recent newcomers. As with earlier immigrants, region mattered in shaping the women's options. And, just as clearly, the women were active agents who made their own choices within the limits of their unique needs and circumstances.

THE WAR AND MIDDLE PASSAGE

Compared with previous immigrants, Southeast Asian refugees were unusual because they and Americans first met not in the United States but in Southeast Asia during the Vietnam War. In 1990, the U.S. government implemented the Amerasian Homecoming Act, and 22,392 Amerasians migrated to the United States.[3] These were children who embodied the interactions of Southeast Asian women and American men in Asia. Hence, for some women, especially those who were single and newly urbanized, their prior concepts of work, sex, and values had begun to change during the war.

Most Southeast Asians were rural peoples.[4] Because Laos is remote and mountainous, Laotian women experienced less cultural transformation during the war than did Cambodians and Vietnamese. French colonizers influenced first-wave Cambodians through government employment and education. Urban Cambodians typically sought education and economic advancement. But these Western influences did not penetrate Cambodia's rural regions, which generated the largest group of Cambodians to emigrate. In Vietnam, the defeat of the French in 1954 at Dien Bien Phu sparked an American war economy on which the Vietnamese came to depend, and which affected women's concepts of family and their means of subsistence. The greatest cultural change came with the arrival of large numbers of American forces in Vietnam in the 1960s.[5]

Single Vietnamese women, uprooted during the war from their native rural communities, were forced to migrate to the South Vietnamese capital of Saigon and to participate in the developing urban war economy. Saigon, designed by the French to accommodate 300,000 people, swelled as over three million Vietnamese migrants crowded into a twenty-one-square-mile area. These migrants joined thousands of American military, government, and war-related personnel. The economy for Vietnamese women was a service economy for the Americans, a money-based economy completely foreign to their rural agricultural lifestyle.[6]

Journalist Ann Froines reported in 1972 on the cultural changes that she observed in Saigon. She described a beach of white sand, covered with barbecue grills. Women with long dark hair watched a water skier. "California? No, Vietnam," Froines wrote. The women were Vietnamese and the men were American. The beach was littered with Budweiser bottles, Coke cans, and Pall Mall packs. On the back of a Honda motorcycle was a poster displaying a woman, half "go-go girl" and half stripper, and the English word "sexy." The values of the village had been replaced by consumer-oriented values.[7] Later, one American first-wave sponsor noted, "[The immigrant Vietnamese's] image of America is how rich we are. . . .[T]hey saw in Vietnam easily obtained jeeps, weapons, cigarettes, and liquor."[8]

After America withdrew from Vietnam in 1975, pro-Western families did whatever they could to escape the reeducation camps and persecution in postwar Vietnam, the ruthless policies of Pol Pot in Cambodia, and oppression under the Communist Pathet Lao in Laos. They chanced daring escapes across the Gulf of Thailand as they headed for overseas asylums in countries like Thailand, Singapore, Malaysia, Hong Kong, and the Philippines. In fact, fewer than 60 percent of the boat people survived the trip across the gulf in 1981, a peak year of migration. In 1985, Thai pirates attacked one-third of the boats, killing thirty-seven people and raping sixty-eight women.[9]

This first stage of migration was the refugees' purgatory—sailing in rickety boats across the gulf, only to arrive at internment camps in countries of asylum. Overseas asylums presented refugee women with some of their greatest challenges. The danger they found in the camps, combined with the emotional effects of migration itself, created an important setting for the initial reformulation of gender and family roles. In the camps, class, region, education, and age did not matter. All refugee women were vulnerable.

Women and children had little physical protection from violence occurring within the camps. Moreover, the camps heightened problems unique to women. Domestic violence increased with the psychological strain placed on refugee men, resulting in male aggression toward wives and children. Prostitution in the camps was often women's only means of survival. Malnourishment also became a problem for women who could not feed themselves or their children. Cultural practices intersected with poor food distribution because men were fed first. Basic necessities such as cooking utensils, shelter, and clothing were often unavailable. Further complications for women resulted from inadequate gynecological services, lack of midwife training, unsanitary conditions, and infection from sexually transmitted diseases through rape and prostitution. Thus, social structures in place prior to a woman's flight were fragmented or destroyed through displacement and the camp stays.[10] The United Nations High Commission for Refugees (UNHCR), which ran the notoriously corrupt, crime-ridden, and filthy camps, largely ignored sexual abuse, exploitation, and sexual discrimination.

Refugees often took matters into their own hands, redefining their spatial boundaries and concepts of family. The story of first-wave refugee Thai Tieng Lim and his family mirrored the experiences of many refugees stranded in the asylums. Thai Tieng Lim explained that refugees had to be very clever to survive in the camps. "Robbers" searched the migrant families for any gold, money, or food. Most refugees were abused, raped, abducted, or forced to pay for protection and documents or to exchange sexual favors for assistance.[11] Because the robbers commonly abducted young refugee girls, Thai Tieng Lim secretly dug a hole ten meters from the family tent, under the camp latrine, in which his daughters hid. For Thai Tieng Lim's daughters, the isolation of living in the secret hole was better than the harm that would have otherwise come to them.[12]

RESETTLEMENT IN THE UNITED STATES

Once families reached the United States, after sometimes waiting six years to receive clearance out of the camps, changes depended on the inter-relationships of work, family, and government policy. Once in America, many first-generation women were forced to find jobs in the wage economy. The regional economy and local and federal government policies strongly influenced work choices for refugee women. Although special employment training projects were provided to meet the special cultural needs of the Southeast Asian women and their families, women's new work roles and the inevitable Americanization of their children diminished the father's control over the family.[13]

This is a familiar immigrant story. What is unique to this immigrant population is the direct role government played in the Southeast Asian family's adaptation. The Indochinese represented the first immigrant group that the federal government actively and financially resettled. While the urban "boss" selectively helped resettle Irish immigrants in the late nineteenth century, and the government and moralistic reformers made attempts to resettle Native Americans in the nineteenth and early twentieth centuries, formal adaptation programs intended for Southeast Asians often incorporated a cultural sensitivity that had not existed for earlier immigrant groups. Whether government agents in the 1980s and early 1990s ever fully appreciated the distinctions among Southeast Asians and the unique circumstances of their migration invites further discussion. Nevertheless, with Southeast Asians, for the first time the American government allocated funding and set up formal programs to help the refugees become self-sufficient within the confines of cultural and family needs.

The fall of Saigon in 1975 prompted unusual support for unprecedented government efforts on behalf of the Indochinese. Social workers wrote adaptation policies that incorporated the particular needs of the extended Southeast Asian families, including programs to set up familiar craft-related cottage industries and small farms. In turn, these policies set the model for subsequent immigrant adaptation programs for refugees from Afghanistan, Somalia, Haiti, and, most recently, Bosnia. These are unexpected cultural legacies of American responsibility for the Vietnam War.[14]

WOMEN AND RESETTLEMENT

Despite this novel governmental cultural sensitivity, Southeast Asian women were at first marginalized in American society. Unlike men, it was difficult for women to earn money or to become educated. Government resettlement and ethnic mutual assistance association programs did not initially incorporate women's needs in employment training. Government policies reflected inadequate understanding of the significant economic roles women played in rural Asian economies, because their former work had not been part of a wage or market economy. Women contributed greatly in the subsistence economy, food distribution, health maintenance, and other nonpaid family work, but these roles didn't translate into the American market economy. Additionally, women failed to seek English-language training—and, thus, employment—because of their fear of the new urban environment or because of family needs. In fact, most refugees claimed that family needs and a lack of education most prevented them from seeking employment.[15]

In 1988, Chhorm Chhin, a second-wave Cambodian refugee, spoke for his family, relocated in San Diego, stating that neither he nor his wife spoke English. His wife, introduced by his name, was homebound for fear of going out. Chhorm Chhin had found work as a gardener in suburban La Jolla but had quit because it was too far from home and his wife and seven children "needed his attention." Above all else, family came first, and this first-generation Cambodian man and woman remained relatively isolated at home. As Chhorm Chhin said, "Our home is where my wife stays. She's shy, and I want our home to be nice for the kids. It's very colorful and we have a TV, stereo, and VCR. My wife can't work. We have too many kids."[16]

Nevertheless, the high cost of urban living compelled most refugee women to enter the workforce. Regardless of earlier class distinctions among them, in the United States first- and second-wave women typically found employment as seamstresses, factory operatives, janitors, cashiers, and hospital workers.[17] At the same time, the pushes and pulls of family needs still kept some women at home, suggesting the persistence of prior cultural values. Whether government policy and the cost of urban living eventually outweighed those values depended on individual circumstances.

Indeed, certain niches of the refugee communities were initially untouched by the wage economy and government policy. Many early arrivals, for instance, continued to lack the basic language and vocational skills to function independently outside of the home. Elderly women were also marginalized because families didn't encourage elderly members to work, nor did government policymakers who largely ignored this segment of the refugee population. Finally, the structure of the traditional extended family led refugees to pool their incomes, which allowed certain members, like elderly women, to stay home.

Older understandings of social roles and family needs, then, remained influential during resettlement, especially from 1975 to 1980, prior to the second-wave influx. But the economic challenges of adjustment began placing greater pressure on women's work roles in the early 1980s with the immigration of boat people. At that point, the combined impacts of family, government, and employment shaped resettlement. In cities like San Diego, with large refugee communities, local government agents and ethnic-community leaders noticed that the Southeast Asian poverty rate remained as high as 66 percent compared with 12 percent for the general population. Once resettled, first wave entrepreneurs weren't employing a significant number of newer arrivals. The welfare dependency rate continued to hover around 20 percent.[18] In the early 1980s, for fear the refugee families would never become self-sufficient, federal policymakers, mutual assistance associations, and refugees took steps to overcome refugee economic and social alienation. Paradoxically, while Reagan-era budget cuts targeted departments like Health and Human Services, which included the Office of Refugee Resettlement, the government actually increased its responsibility for resettlement by designing policy to deal with unemployed refugees.

By 1984, more culturally sensitive outreach programs were targeting the needs of women and their families, including transportation services, child care, family planning, personal counseling, and home employment. The government also designed job training for women's education and employment that would accommodate traditional roles. These projects were culturally suitable, and, in the mid-1980s, first-generation women began changing their employment status.[19] Many sewed out of their home, formed refugee child-care agencies, and worked as resettlement agents for newer arrivals. Thus the local economy, government, and native culture intertwined to produce the change women experienced as wage workers.

Even women of the Hmongs, a group notable for a rigid maintenance of native customs, early marriages, high fertility rates, preliteracy, and self-segregation, changed with the dictates of the American economy. Many of these tribal people adapted to their new environments by participating in a prosperous cottage industry that promoted traditional crafts and heritage.[20] Art centers throughout the West began displaying Hmong crafts. In Denver, Hmong women generated great publicity over their cottage needlework businesses. Native culture facilitated their entrance into the American cash economy, and the art itself became a reminder of a lost way of life.

WOMEN AND THE CHANGING FAMILY STRUCTURE

There is an old Vietnamese proverb that says, "The father's merit is as high as the great mountain; the mother's merit is as everlasting as the water gushing from the mountain spring."[21] Women traditionally commanded authority over the children, yet in the United States their influence dwindled as they began working outside rather than inside the home. Another great change for women has been their newfound dependence on children for survival in strange new cities, reversing centuries of filial piety and a sense of traditional deference to living parents and ancestors.[22] This is significant since women in Vietnamese, Laotian, and Cambodian societies were young children's primary role models, but in the United States, they became dependent on these children for translation and other interactions with American officials and the wider society.[23]

Fertility rates also declined when first-generation wage earners lacked the time and money to have more children and second-generation Southeast Asian women began delaying marriage and childbearing until they finished school. Schools and other American institutions began playing greater roles in refugee children's lives, and permissiveness replaced stricter parental authority. Children were more mobile. For the first time, they rented their own apartments rather than live with their extended families as in Southeast Asia. The result was less social interaction with kin and greater freedom for self-expression. Looser family structures surfaced with the second wave in the mid-1980s.[24]

Familial role change and dysfunction challenged the refugees' traditional value system. The government imposed additional strain on families when it mandated economic independence but cut the necessary vocational training to secure jobs. Moreover, like many native-born Americans, refugees couldn't afford to get off welfare since health benefits and food stamps would not accompany a low-wage job. This kind of welfare entrapment plagued many families after Reagan-era budget cuts. Refugees, in particular, found themselves in a quandary, searching for their identity while trying to make ends meet. Some second-generation children turned to gangs, adopted American dress, and pursued their schooling in search of an identity. Meanwhile, first- and second-wave parents tried to hold onto a sense of rootedness through traditional culture and family roles.

In America, refugee parents, especially fathers, struggled with their children's newfound independence, lack of respect for the family, and acceptance of looser social mores. At the same time, government social workers—Southeast Asian and native-born American alike—tried to impose new parenting methods on refugee parents, which included teachings about the inappropriateness of spanking or hitting children. The end result was frustrated refugee fathers who sensed a loss of control over their families. As Dr. Kry Trang, director of the San Diego Indochinese Mutual Assistance Association, has said, "The parents are so upset. They don't know what to do about their children or how to discipline them. They don't understand why they can't spank their children. So they just sit by and watch their children do whatever they want. They also have to rely on their children to take them around the city. They don't know where they fit in. Their whole world has changed."[25]

Domestic violence was a dramatic manifestation of refugee dependence on children and changing family roles. Some refugee fathers clearly took their frustrations out on their families when they lost their self-esteem and economic independence, saw their wives integrating into the wage economy, and witnessed their children drifting from the extended family into a more integrated peer culture. Women filled the gaps when prior male authority declined, and female authority gradually increased. Southeast Asian women faced family dysfunction, disruptiveness, uprootedness, migration, and entrance into a foreign society—all at the same time.[26]

GOVERNMENTAL INFLUENCES

By 1985, the government had stepped into these private family struggles to try to generate financial independence for the former patriarchs. Mutual assistance associations, usually run by more acculturated first-wave ethnic leaders trying to carve out political niches for themselves, played an active role in curbing domestic violence. Policymakers like Kry Trang of the Indochinese Mutual Assistance Association in San Diego and Southeast Asian social workers at the East Dallas Counseling Center and the Asian Pacific Development Center in Denver counseled troubled families in which mothers and fathers fought to understand the changes in their children's behavior. Refugees tried to maintain their traditional parental roles, yet the onslaught of government agents, combined with second-generation mobility, made it impossible.[27]

With concern for welfare dependency paramount, policymakers increasingly sought ways to encourage self-sufficiency and social activity away from the home. Counseling centers sprang up in refugee communities to facilitate family resettlement, to address issues of domestic violence, and to teach refugees vocational skills. The refugees' social and economic lives became greatly influenced by government policies and remained that way as long as refugees received public cash assistance.

Moreover, many refugees showed a high incidence of infectious diseases and general illnesses; 72 percent of the new arrivals needed immediate medical attention. Since more than 50 percent of the refugees depended on cash assistance, they were automatically wed to federal Medicaid programs.[28] Slowly, government policymakers, social workers, and medical officials realized the persistence of traditional Southeast Asian healing methods—the use of shamans, holistic practices, coining (*cao gio*), and midwifery—and began, in major western cities, to try to integrate native practices into hospital programs. Large county hospitals in San Diego, Denver, and Seattle began maximizing their services by offering traditional folk healing, by providing adequate translation and phone services, and by employing Southeast Asian doctors.[29] City streets in Southeast Asian neighborhoods in the West became dotted with prenatal care centers and clinics offering the services of gynecologists, pediatricians, dentists, and optometrists, all targeted to the refugee communities. Mental health care brought greater adjustments through Western medicine and government-funded clinics.

At least 50 percent of the refugees suffered from stress disorders, and social workers clamored to open centers to treat family members for post-traumatic stress disorder (PTSD), domestic violence, and adaptation to new roles and loss of status.[30] Meanwhile, policymakers wrestled with the issue of cultural sensitivity, trying to respect folk healing such as the Vietnamese curing practice of "coining." But, overtly battered, starved, or burned children eventually led refugees to seek western mental and medical health care. Refugees, and specifically women, the traditional providers, were influenced by Western medicine, psychological counseling, American hospitals, and the overwhelming Medicaid bureaucracy. Inevitably, their roles as the traditional medical providers for their families declined.

REGIONAL FACTORS

Regional variables influenced the lives of refugee families. Large refugee communities like those found in San Diego and Seattle, with forty thousand and thirty thousand Southeast Asians, respectively, allowed ethnic clustering: voluntarily segregated communities that did not interact much with the larger Anglo society. These ethnic clusters also attracted secondary migration from less-populated states, which is one reason why the largest proportion of refugees resettled in California. The West appealed to refugees because of its ethnic communities, but also for its climate; proximity to the Pacific Rim; and employment opportunities in government, service, and small-scale industrial jobs. Ethnic clusters provided jobs for newer arrivals created by first-wave entrepreneurs who also generated crucial social support networks. Therefore, in some ways, refugees experienced less change in larger ethnic communities than they did in smaller ones like those of Albuquerque and Denver. Populous ethnic communities allowed self-segregation, while immigrants in areas with smaller numbers of refugees were forced to integrate into the larger population and, hence, to acculturate more rapidly.

Ethnic enclaves were partly the result of local government policy. Many refugees migrated to California and Washington because these two states offered relatively generous social welfare programs. California's cash assistance grants, for instance, were 65 percent higher than the national average. Moreover, MediCal's health care benefits exceeded those of any other state. Generally only able to find low-wage employment, new arrivals couldn't afford to get off government assistance and the additional health care and food stamp benefits that went with it.[31]

Local economies did not influence the variety of work available to women to a great degree. Whether in Albuquerque, Denver, Dallas, Seattle, or San Diego, refugee women commonly located "last-hired, first-fired" low-wage employment in the service sector. Tourism in the West, for example, created employment in restaurants, hotels, and transportation facilities. Additional employment developed in defense-related industries as soon as Southeast Asian men and women received training as operatives. In each of the five western cities, jewelry making employed a significant number of women. Such small-scale factory employment required little English, and these small business operators welcomed the low-wage employees who had little choice regarding their first American jobs.

Larger cities, with vibrant ethnic communities, offered many low-wage service jobs in small Southeast Asian businesses, restaurants, clinics, and resettlement agencies, but these first-wave efforts to employ newer arrivals had one unexpected result. In larger communities, clusters of refugees were more noticeable to local officials. The attention they drew generated additional government-inspired services such as mental health care, mutual assistance programs, and employment training. Clusters also attracted the attention of the Department of Health and Human Services, hence more government assistance to disperse these communities, and consequently changes from prior work and social relations to daily interaction with federal policymakers. Ironically, then, refugees who were self-segregated in larger enclaves attracted more government interference in their lives and in their adaptation processes.

Finally, urban ethnic and racial hierarchies have also influenced regional adjustment patterns, which in turn determined the ethnic communities' politicization and interaction with the larger population. Seattle is a city rich in Asian American history. At least 119,000 Asian and Pacific Islanders were living in this metropolis by 1992.[32] Seattle featured more Asian business clusters and urban cultural centers, like the Wing Luke Museum, than any of the five areas researched for this study, but these were not built without a struggle. Historically, in response to nativism, Seattle's Asian American community became highly politicized and mobilized a powerful voting block. With a history of ethnic empowerment, in a city where minorities were predominately Asian American, Southeast Asian refugees didn't seem so "foreign" to the larger native-born community, although alliances and disparities existed among Asian Americans.

On the other hand, in Albuquerque, Southeast Asians left as quickly as they entered the "Land of Enchantment." In a tricultural state with predominant Hispanic, Native American, and Anglo interests, Asian Americans fell through the cracks. Refugees claimed that Dallas provided them with better opportunities to become self-sufficient and, thus, to regain self-confidence. In Texas, a state with no General Cash Assistance programs, refugees were forced to move quickly into the larger social and economic community and failed to develop a viable ethnic neighborhood for support. As a result, refugees melded into the general population but lacked a sense of minority empowerment. Intraethnic tension arose in Dallas where first-wave Vietnamese women moved into affluent white suburbs like Plano, drove second-generation children to swim team practice in Jeep Cherokees, and played Bunko with their upper-middle-class neighbors. Refugees were obviously adjusting in Dallas, but they failed to support second-wave refugees. One first-wave woman, Janet Teng, commented, "Mo, I don't go down there [to East Dallas where new arrivals typically settle]. I have my kids and my [native-born American] husband. I don't have time. My kids have swimming lessons, sports, dance lessons. We live up here away from all that. No, I don't need to shop there either. I would like to help, if I had time."[33]

Affluent first-wave refugee Janet Teng represents one example of assimilationist adjustment. However, large refugee clusters in cities like San Diego have maintained a sense of cultural identity through self-segregation, allowing the development of Southeast Asian political mobilization. Anything was up for grabs in California, a diverse state accustomed to various ethnic voices. San Diego's size, however, also camouflaged many women who were marginalized and impoverished in the city's refugee neighborhoods. With its crowded and unfamiliar freeways, lack of public transport, and government red tape, California cities like San Diego presented refugees with unique challenges.

Denver offered still another option for refugee women. Denver's Southeast Asian population was large enough to provide ethnic support but not so large as to be isolating. With Colorado's sizable military presence, many first-wave Vietnamese who immigrated to Denver with significant ties to the American government had a head start in the adjustment process. This was the case for many first-wave refugees who relocated in similar defense industry areas. However, that kind of proximity to government assistance didn't translate into long-term adjustment for refugees near bases like Fort Chaffee, Arkansas, or even Kirtland Air Force Base in Albuquerque. Refugees who first settled in Arkansas and New Mexico often migrated a second time to live closer to fellow Southeast Asians in California. In general, then, initial government dispersal efforts were a failure. Some degree of ethnic clustering was essential to the refugees themselves. Adaptation is a complex process, as the second-generation experience attests.

THE SECOND GENERATION

Young Cambodian, Vietnamese, and Laotian women redefined their traditional upbringing as they were increasingly exposed to American mores, media, and popular culture. Asian American women's magazines portrayed female role models adorned in Western clothing, makeup, and jewelry.[34] Even a local nationalist, politically oriented Vietnamese newspaper featured photos of scantily clad Anglo models, emphasizing sexuality, physical beauty, and American values commonly found on the pages of *Vogue* or *Harper's Bazaar*.[35] Larger western cities became inundated with Vietnamese video stores, examples of first-wave entrepreneurial businesses that reflected a certain degree of acculturation. Many popular Vietnamese videos resembling Arnold Schwarzenegger, James Bond, and Gidget movies displayed cover pictures with suave Asian businessmen surrounded by beautiful, adoring women. Additionally, urban ethnic enclaves became more fluid as Vietnamese restaurateurs, responding to American gastronomic trends, cultivated the appetites of American tourists who ventured into "Little Saigons" for exotic food. A quick drive down Federal Boulevard in Denver, El Cajon Boulevard in San Diego, or through the International District in Seattle revealed numerous such small businesses.

These forms of adaptation, sensitive to the dictates of the American cultural and economic environment, presented special challenges to young Southeast Asian women. Second-generation women adapted by pursuing Western educations and dress, yet they were conflicted in various ways. American media attention focused on some troubled second-generation children who, lacking a sense of family and stability, turned to local gangs for a sense of camaraderie, community, and direction. These children inhabited a precarious place between their parents' ethnic orientation and the temptations of a looser American culture. Some second-wave young women became "gangster girls" in larger communities like Dallas, San Diego, and Seattle. With a loss of family support, compounded by ethnic prejudice at school, girls, like boys, quickly formed gangs for social support.[36] These young women wore special clothing, used gang jargon, and painted graffiti around the city, staking out their territory.

Gangster girls formed gangs for social support, but young refugee men generally shunned them. Although members of gangs themselves, young men said they preferred "home girls" who excelled in school, stayed at home, and respected their parents' mores. In Dallas, a young second-wave Vietnamese boy said, "Me, no, I don't like gangster girls. I like 'home' girls that stay at home. They don't mess around. That's the kind of girl I want to marry." Gangster girls, grappling to define themselves, discovered that they had become peripheral to both their own communities and larger American ones.[37]

On the other hand, many second-generation Vietnamese, Laotian, and Cambodian young adults exhibited extraordinary educational achievement. Such achievement required enormous work and motivation, yet Southeast Asian youths generally earned the highest GPAs of any ethnic group in their public schools. This was true even for the Hmong, a particularly surprising statistic since the Hmong didn't have a written language until the late 1950s.[38]

These educational considerations suggest two things regarding young refugee women and their work roles. A combination of cultural resilience and family support has led to behaviors consistent with both Confucian and Protestant ethics. For many first-wave Vietnamese, in particular, American education provided channels for their sense of social order, ambition, industry, and hard work. In the United States these values steered them toward different work options than were available in Southeast Asia.

Second-generation refugee women acculturated more completely than their parents to American roles and values, enjoying high rates of college participation, integration into the larger American society, intracity mobility, and less interaction with government resettlement agents than their parents. These factors created more options for second-generation women than for their mothers.[39] Indeed, generational distinctions came to differentiate refugee women more than did previous class and regional differences. A Hmong farmer resettled in Dallas, Vang Tily Thao, expressed such a generational distinction. An illiterate man who wasn't even aware of his own age, Vang Tily Thao decided that his daughter must pursue her education for "this is the only way she'll get a job in the United States. Then she may marry." At the time, Thao's daughter was a student at New York University. He proudly emphasized that this wasn't the way the Hmong lived in the isolated highlands of Laos.[40]

Indeed, youth and Americanization appeared more important than class, native ethnicity, and times of arrival. First-wave, second generation Sindy Nguyen, a young Vietnamese graduate of the University of Washington, illustrated the point. Dressed in a chic Ann Taylor black linen dress and stylish sandals, wearing makeup, and sporting an expensive haircut, Nguyen described her politicization as an active Asian American student. She explained that initially younger, second-generation children of first-wave parents didn't want to associate with later arrivals because their lack of westernization was embarrassing.[41] Echoing this point, young Chris Nguyen of Denver, first-wave and second-generation Vietnamese, claimed, "No, I don't hang out with new arrivals who don't have families here and stuff. They're all at a disadvantage until the kids go through the school system. Then we might all be hanging out together at the American clubs. That's where we go."[42]

Once second-wave children became more acculturated through high school and gained a sense of confidence, they typically proceeded through college and began living a lifestyle similar to that of first-wave children. Generational characteristics and experiences outweighed prior class constraints that continued to distinguish first- from second-wave parents.[43]

CONCLUSION

This essay represents an initial contribution to the research and analysis needed for the Vietnamese, Cambodian, and Laotian communities in the West. Diverse urban environments influenced cultural change among America's recent emigrés but Southeast Asian traditions and values remained historically dynamic. Ultimately, Southeast Asian women's experiences and gender change were the products of prior culture and history; period of migration; wartime experience; and, once they got here, regional economy, government policy, and generational access to education and jobs. The new element to this immigrant story is the extent of government involvement in the lives of Southeast Asian families. From the initial settlement and adjustment programs to later employment training, health programs, and family counseling, government support for Southeast Asian resettlement far exceeded that offered any earlier immigrant groups. Compared with earlier immigrants, Southeast Asian women received generous financial support and programs designed to be culturally sensitive to their special needs. Even so, it is clear from this brief survey that government programs often produced unintended results, apparently because even the most "culturally sensitive" programs persisted in viewing refugees as passive clients rather than active participants. This is a topic that deserves further study.

What is clear is that even when faced with the overwhelming shock of war, escape, internment, and resettlement in a foreign culture, Southeast Asian women survived and persisted. It is no surprise that the experiences of Southeast Asian women were as varied as their rich cultural traditions, histories, and regions would suggest. At the same time, it should be no surprise that there were many "Wests" for Southeast Asian women and that subregionalism continued to play a great role in the evolution of the U.S. West.

Notes

I'd like to thank the many service agents, government policymakers, and refugee families who were willing to be interviewed. My dissertation research in Seattle, San Diego, Dallas, Denver, and Albuquerque was a pleasure. Thanks also to Howard Rabinowitz. As chair of my doctoral work at the University of New Mexico, Howard sparked my interest in urban race relations and told me about the need for research on Vietnamese refugee adaptation in American cities.

1. U.S. Department of Health and Human Services, *Report to Congress*, Office of Refugee Resettlement, 31 January 1993, 5, 49.

2. Several publications began discussing backlash against immigrants, especially in California, in the early 1990s. *Report to Congress*, 1993, 62. Numerous popular media reports suggest that this attitude harkened back to the 1840s, 1920s, and 1950s; see Tony Emerson with Robin Gibb and Donna Foote, "Boat People, Go Home," *Newsweek*, 1 January 1990, 11; "U.S. Ethnics Caught in Backlash against New Immigrants," *Chicago Tribune*, 1 August 1993; "The New Face of America," *Time*, Fall 1993 (special issue); and "1994 May Be Watershed Year in Immigration Debate," *Dallas Morning News*, 16 January 1994.

3. *Report to Congress*, 1991, 6.

4. *Report to Congress*, 1986, 103.

5. For cultural information on the Southeast Asians, a useful source written by Southeast Asians is Sun-Him Chhim, Khamchong Luangpraseut, and Huynh Dinh Te, *Introduction to Cambodian Culture; Laos Culturally Speaking; Introduction to Vietnamese Culture* (San Diego: Multifunctional Service Center, 1982).

6. Ann Froines, "What We'll Leave Behind," *Women's Press*, 2, no. 3 (May 1972): 13.

7. For the economic and cultural effects of the war, see Marilyn Young, *The Vietnam Wars: 1945–1990* (New York: HarperCollins, 1991); George Herring, *America's Longest War: The United States and Vietnam, 1950 to 1975* (New York: Alfred A. Knopf, 1979); Stanley Karnow, *Vietnam, A History* (New York: Penguin, 1983); and Thomas Patterson, *On Every Front: The Making of a Cold War* (New York: W. W. Norton, 1979).

8. Ellen Matthews, *Culture Clash* (Chicago: Intercultural Press, 1982), 9.

9. Tricia Knoll, *Becoming Americans: Asian Sojourners, Immigrants, and Refugees in the Western United States* (Portland, Ore.: Coast to Coast Books, 1982), 266; Bien Quang Do, "Parent-Child Relations among Vietnamese Catholic Refugees in San Diego County: A Study of Cultural Adjustment" (master's thesis, San Diego State University, 1987), 9.

10. Susan Forbes Martin, *Issues in Refugee Displaced Women and Children* (Washington, D.C.: Refugee Policy Group, June 1990). Forbes Martin is a leading government policymaker on behalf of refugee resettlement, which falls under the authority of the Department of Health and Human Services.

11. Ibid., 4.

12. Thai Tieng Lim and family, Vietnamese refugees, interview by author, Albuquerque, New Mexico, 27 April 1988.

13. Forbes Martin, *Issues*, 29.

14. See *The Congressional Record*, April-December 1975; *Reports to Congress*, 1981–93; and David Butler, *The Fall of Saigon* (New York: Simon and Schuster, 1985).

15. Forbes Martin, *Issues*, 2; Susan Forbes Martin and Emily Copeland, *Making Ends Meet?: Refugee Women and Income Generation*, (Washington, D.C.: Refugee Policy Group, May 1988), 8; *Report to Congress*, 1991, 92.

16. Chhorm Chhin and family, Cambodian refugees, interview by author, San Diego, Calif., January 1989.

17. "Refugee Employment Services Plan," County of San Diego Department of Social Services, July 1992, 32. There is no statistical enumeration comparing women's prior work roles and their American occupations. However, Southeast Asians, especially those in the first wave, experienced significant downward mobility. Thirty-nine percent of the refugees had held white-collar jobs (managerial or professional employment) at home, but that figure dropped to 16 percent in the United States. By the same token, 20 percent of the refugees had held blue-collar jobs in Southeast Asia; 61 percent entered such occupations in the United States. The number of white-collar refugees declined in the early 1980s when the second-wave boat people entered the country. See *Reports to Congress*, 1986–93.

18. Department of Social Services, *Plan for Provision of Targeted Assistance Funded Support Services to Refugees*, TA I-IV (County of San Diego, 1983–88); and Dr. Kry Trang, executive director, Indochinese Mutual Assistance Association, interview by author, San Diego, Calif., August 1988 and November 1992.

19. Lola Garona, refugee coordinator, Department of Social Services, interview by author, San Diego, Calif., November 1992; Linda Wong-Kerberg, Union of Pan-Asian Communities, San Diego, California, interview by author, San Diego, Calif., November 1992; Sharon Hoskins, administrator, Catholic Charities, Migration and Refugee Services, interview by author, Dallas, Tex., August 1993; and Laurie Bagen, state refugee coordinator, Department of Social Services, Colorado Refugee Service Program, interview by author, Denver, Colo., March 1993.

20. Janet Wiscombe, "Laotian Refugees Continue Hmong Heritage," *Denver Post*, 1 April 1981; and see "Refugee Honored at Annual Fair," *Southern Cross*, 15 July 1988.

21. Quang Do, "Parent-Child Relations," 11.

22. See Arthur Waley, *The Analects of Confucius* (New York: Vintage Books, 1938); of related interest, see William Wei, *The Asian American Movement* (Philadelphia: Temple University Press, 1993).

23. Chhim, Luangpraseut, and Te, *Introduction to Culture*, 20.

24. See Meredith McGuire, *Religion: The Social Context* (Belmont, Calif.: Wadsworth Publishing, 1992).

25. Trang interview, November 1992.

26. Quang Do, "Parent-Child Relations," 14–40; Wong-Kerberg interview; Trang interview, Chris Nguyen, Vietnamese refugee and translator, CRISP Health Screening, interview by author, Denver, Colo., 16 March 1993; Thao Phia Xaykao, executive director, Hmong American Planning and Development Center, Grand Prairie, Texas, interview by author, 17 August 1993, See also David Haines, "Southeast Asian Refugees in the U.S.: The Interaction of Kinship and Public Policy," *Anthropological Quarterly* 55, no. 3 (July 1982): 170–81; Frederick Ahearn and Jean Athey, eds., *Refugee Children: Theory, Research, and Services* (Baltimore: Johns Hopkins Press, 1991); and Chhim, Luangpraseut, and Te, *Introduction to Culture.*

27. Trang interview, November 1992, Bob Hovey, Gang Unit detective, San Diego Police Department, interview by author, San Diego, Calif., November 1993; Ron Cowart, East Dallas Precinct, Dallas Police Department, interview by author, Dallas, Tex., August 1993; Maxine Chan, Family Violence Unit, Seattle Police Department, interview by author, Seattle, Wash., July 1993; Quang Do, "Parent-Child Relations," and Forbes Martin *Issues.*

28. *Reports to Congress,* 1982–93.

29. David E. Berman and Susan Forbes, *The Potential for Enrolling Refugees in Health Maintenance Organizations* (Washington, D.C.: Refugee Policy Group, July 1983), 7.

30. David Kinzie, M.D., R. H. Frederickson, M.D., Ben Rath, Jenelle Frock, and William Karls, "Post-Traumatic-Stress-Disorder among Survivors of Cambodian Concentration Camps," *American Journal of Psychiatry* 141, no. 5 (May 1984): 9; Ruben Rumbaut, *Migrant Health Care* (Washington, D.C.: Office of Refugee Resettlement, 1985). Clinics include the Union of Pan Asian Communities Center in San Diego, the East Dallas Counseling Center, and the Asian Pacific Mental Health Center in Denver.

31. Department of Social Services, San Diego, California; *Reports to Congress,* 1982–93; and Dr. Thuy Vu, director, Department of Social and Health Services, Division of Refugee Assistance, Olympia, Washington, interview by author, July 1993.

32. *1991 Population Trends for Washington State,* Office of Financial Management, 61.

33. Janet Teng, Vietnamese refugee, Plano, Texas, phone interview by author, Dallas, Tex., August 1993.

34. Shi Kagy, ed., *Face* (Malibu, Calif.: Transpacific Media, November/December 1992); *Transpacific* (Malibu, Calif.: Transpacific Media, March 1994); and *The Asian American Quarterly Magazine* 1, no. 3. Teachers also comment on these pop cultural changes among refugee girls, as evidenced in interview with Howard Jenkins, Highland High School, Albuquerque, N.M., April 1988.

35. *Nguoi Viet,* Ngay 16 Thang Tu 1994, So 450, San Diego, Calif., 21, 39, 59.

36. Hovey interview; Cowart interview; Mike McElroy, Seattle Police Department, Inter-Asian Gang Division, interview by author, Seattle, July 1993.

37. Many young men confirmed this attitude as did local Indochinese precinct police officers. Chris Nguyen interview and Phia Xaykao interview. Also personal attendance at Ron Cowart's Dallas Storefront Scout's group meeting, Dallas, Tex., August 1993. This young extracurricular group strives to clean up East Dallas and acts as a liaison between Dallas police and the second-wave, newly arriving Southeast Asian community.

38. Ruben Rumbaut and Kenji Ima comment on this issue in *The Adaptation of Southeast Asian Refugee Youth, A Comparative Study: Final Report to the Office of Refugee Resettlement* (San Diego: San Diego State University, 1986–87). Also see San Diego City Schools, *Requirements and Services for Limited English Proficient Students: Elementary Administration Handbook* (San Diego: Second Language Department, October 1987); Mary Larson, ESL teacher, Wilson Middle School, interview by author, Albuquerque, N.M., April 1988.

39. Rumbaut and Ima, *Adaptation of Southeast Asian Refugee Youth,* 2.

40. Vang Tily Thao, Hmong refugee, interview by author, Dallas, Tex., August 1993.

41. Sindy Nguyen, Vietnamese refugee, interview by author, Seattle, Wash., 23 July 1993.

42. Chris Nguyen interview.

43. Chhin interview.

29.

"My Mother Was a Mover":
African American Seminole Women
in Brackettville, Texas, 1914–1964

B. ANN RODGERS AND LINDA SCHOTT

Most histories of cross-cultural contact have focused on relationships between people of color and white Europeans or Americans. This article provides a fascinating exception to that rule, as B. Ann Rodgers and Linda Schott examine the Brackettville Seminoles, a tribe descended from African American runaway slaves and Seminole Indians. The Brackettville Seminoles claim a unique history and identity based in the men's service as U.S. Army scouts. Rodgers and Schott examine how the particularities of their history led to the local public leadership of three women, Rebecca July Wilson and her two daughters, Dorothy and Charles Wilson. Based largely on Annie Rodgers's interviews with Charles Wilson, the history of the Brackettville Seminoles is, as Rodgers and Schott tell us, "a cautionary tale" against any simple historical narrative of racial or gender relationships. The intricacies of both race and gender emerge in this fascinating study of how three women came to represent the descendants of warrior scouts. The ironies compound as we explore the consequences of the Wilson women's commitments to preserving their heritage and ensuring their children's futures. Their devotion to education, coupled with increased opportunities achieved by the African American civil rights movement, helped many Brackettville Seminole young people get better educations and jobs. But ironically, the younger generation's best opportunities lay not in rural Brackettville but in cities. Outside Brackettville, they were seen as African Americans, and their unique Brackettville Seminole identity was difficult to maintain.

Rodgers and Schott emphasize several important points that underlie much of this volume. They highlight the importance of racial ethnic women in maintaining cultural identities and in local community organizing. They remind us again that racial and gender identities are historical constructs and that they are enormously varied and changeable. And this history underscores the importance of writing multicultural histories from inclusive perspectives, rather than looking only at how racial ethnic people interacted with whites. That limited perspective would exclude the Brackettville Seminoles altogether. It would also exclude the many racial ethnic women who worked largely within their own communities and other peoples who, like the Brackettville Seminoles, bore witness to the intimate frontiers of western history.

Some 130 miles southwest of San Antonio the village of Brackettville rests
nestled in the last southward stretch of the Texas hill country. Surrounded
by a flat brushland savanna of catclaw and *cenizo*, Brackettville is strikingly different—a dark-green anomaly of live oak, spring water, and cool
blue hills. Starting in the late nineteenth century, between the restful shade
along Los Moras Creek and the blistering sun-drenched pastures that surround it, a little known but highly dramatic collision of cultures and
ideologies played itself out between a wandering tribe of African
American Seminoles and a settlement of German American and Hispanic
ranchers and Hispanic laborers. There two minorities, Hispanic and
African American Seminole, would maneuver separately for survival
within an increasingly powerful white community. This is the story of the
African American Seminole effort. What this story offers beyond its
relevance to the regional history of south Texas is a cautionary tale of how
mercurial gender, racial, and class relationships can be, not only within
minority groups but between minorities and majority populations, and
how quickly these relationships can change. It is a tale of ironies and it
is told as an argument for the careful consideration of all racial, class, and
gender categories of analysis within any given population.

The African American Seminoles were the descendants of runaway slaves
who were given sanctuary by the Seminole Indians of southern Florida. At
first the two groups lived as economic partners, the blacks functioning as
well-treated serfs in the Seminole economy. As time passed and Euro-
American encroachment increased during the late 1700s through the early
1800s, blacks took on an increasingly coequal status, fighting alongside the
Seminole Indians in their long war against Euro-American domination.
Intermarriage between African and Indian was not rare. Over time the
African American Seminoles came to perceive themselves not as Africans
or Indians but as a tribe of African Indians who were continuing African
tribal traditions while learning and incorporating new traditions—not from
Euro-American culture like most other blacks in the United States before
the Civil War, but from the Seminole culture. Though African American
Seminoles would eventually find themselves forced into close contact with
Euro-American culture and take on many of its traditions, the fact that they
lived not as slaves but with the Native Americans actively fighting
domination gave their descendants their special identity.[1]

In 1835, when the U.S. government removed several Seminole Indian
groups from Florida, many African American Seminoles went to Indian
Territory (now Oklahoma) with them. But once in Indian Territory, the
African American Seminoles were in constant danger of being recaptured
by white slave traders. Thus many African American Seminoles chose a
perilous flight across Texas to Mexico, where with some of their Seminole
Indian allies, they finally settled in Nacimiento, Coahuila. For various
reasons, all the Seminole Indians had returned to Indian Territory by 1861.
The harsh climate and hardscrabble soil of Nacimiento ultimately inspired
about half the African American Seminoles (some 300 to 350 in number,
hereafter called the Brackettville Seminoles) to move to Fort Clark near

the village of Brackettville, Texas, where the U.S. Army offered to settle them permanently on the fertile soil along Los Moras Creek in exchange for the scouting services of their able-bodied men.[2] The Brackettville Seminoles served as scouts in campaigns against various hostile Native Americans and then against enterprising outlaws who thrived in the trackless wastes of the Chihuahua Desert. Having suffered greatly from attacks by the same Indians at Nacimiento, the Seminole Negro Indian Scouts of Fort Clark felt no conflict of interest in being paid to fight them in the United States.

The heroic history of the scouts and their tribal traditions is today the glue of cultural identity that holds the Brackettville Seminoles together. Unifying activities in this small community focus on the maintenance of the Seminole Negro Indian Scout Cemetery with its four Medal of Honor recipients who won their honors in campaigns against the Apache from 1873 to 1881.[3] The defining feature of Brackettville Seminole culture is its warrior identification that revels in a history of self-emancipation. As Charles Wilson, tribal historian, explained, celebration of "Juneteenth," (June 19 was the day the Emancipation Proclamation was officially read in Texas) was to show solidarity with "our brother and sister who were slaves . . . but we were always free."[4] The final irony is that after long struggles to survive, the tribe was dispersed not by adversity but by laws passed to aid all African Americans.

The most compelling evidence of the African connection among the Brackettville Seminoles is their use of Gullah. Gullah, an African-English creole (a mix of two or more languages), was first developed on the west coast of Africa some four hundred years ago for trade purposes. Until the early twentieth century, it was the dominant language used among the Brackettville Seminoles. Though only a few people can speak more than a few words of Gullah in the 1990s, it was viable enough in Brackettville in the late 1950s finally to be recorded and for a written syntax to be formulated.[5] The Seminole influence is now harder to trace in the south Texas community, but photographs of the tribal village on Los Moras Creek prior to 1914 clearly show Native American river-cane building methods being practiced. Interestingly, Charles Wilson referred to "the Indian in us" whenever pointing out positive traits in her own family or in other tribal members.[6]

While the political, linguistic, and military history of the Brackettville Seminoles has been documented prior to 1914, the social-cultural history of this group prior to 1914 has not.[7] The data to reconstruct this picture are unlikely to be recovered since those who lived the tribal life are dead. This article picks up the story of the Brackettville Seminoles in 1914 at one of the most pivotal moments in their history, when the U.S. Army decided, over the vociferous protest of the Fort Clark command, to fire the Seminole Negro Indian Scouts and not to honor the land agreements the army had made with them. Fired after fifty years of exemplary service, the Seminole scouts and their families were evicted from the fort, and the Brackettville Seminoles suddenly found themselves having to find wage work in and around the village. Brackettville was a very small settlement of a few hundred people at its height, and wage work in town was limited. This change had subtle but measurable effects on the balance of power within the tribal leadership, especially in how the tribe related to the outside world.

With no land to continue their traditional lifestyle and no dependable source of supplies for scouting duties, the tribe went overnight from relative comfort to penury. Forced to rent housing, the tribe dispersed throughout the village; suddenly forced to pay for food with wages, the people were pushed into a social crisis that was exemplified in a split within their tribal church. At the heart of the schism was how best to survive as a people. Some wished for total isolation. They wanted to rent available land and quickly reestablish a tribal existence. They also wanted to keep their social organizations, especially their church, separated from any outside influences, and particularly from the use of English. Some of this group simply went back to Nacimiento. Others, under the leadership of a former scout, Sampson July, opted for a more integrated approach.[8] The July family led the fight to unite the church with the black Baptist church associations in the state; they advocated private land ownership and supported public school education for the tribe, which would increase the use of English. July and his followers were not interested in becoming "white" but in having enough economic clout to secure the tribe's financial and cultural integrity against the fickle Euro-American political system.

In the end, the congregation split into two churches, the "moderns" and the "elderlies."[9] The "moderns" were the larger group, and after July's death, its leadership passed to Sampson July's only daughter, Rebecca July Wilson. Thus, in this particular story, a warrior, male-centered culture came to be represented publicly primarily by a family of three women: Rebecca July Wilson and her two daughters, Dorothy and Charles, all descendants of Sampson July.

It is through the personal story of the Wilson women, recorded through oral interviews with the surviving daughter, Charles Wilson, and other community women and augmented by official documents, that this article explores the importance of gender and class analysis even within a small population. Such a limited case study cannot prove general principles of analysis nor totally capture the whole social history of the Brackettville Seminoles, especially during the period when they lived in river-cane homes and received from the army, in return for their scouting duties, food and other supplies to supplement their small farms. But it does suggest methods for viewing other studies as it recaptures what is left of a compelling historical narrative that time is quickly eradicating with the death of each storyteller. Whatever details are lost in this primarily oral history are less important than the mythological qualities of the stories of the Wilson family and their importance in transmitting personal and group identity. Through these stories we are shown the interracial relationships and boundaries of power as they existed in Brackettville from 1914 to 1964, as the people who lived there understood them.

According to Charles Wilson, her mother's rise into a position of leadership was definitely aided by her descent from Sampson July. But more important was the fact that the Seminole men were widely scattered about the local ranches, looking for work, and were gone for days and weeks at a time, whereas the Seminole women tended to stay in Brackettville and do domestic wage work, often in their own homes, for the troops and the local citizenry. Therefore, it was the Seminole women who became the counterpart of the white "old-boy network" for news and information about what was going on in town. For the same reasons, they were the ones who could best respond to changing situations in the community. It would be the Seminole women who would form the connections with other ethnic groups in the village and who would know how the power structure operated.

Rebecca July Wilson was reportedly a charismatic individual who had a way of "just convincing" people.[10] Not only was she leader of the "moderns," she was the founder and president of the Mothers' Club (PTA), which raised money for all supplies the black segregated school received for most of its history, from the early nineteen teens until it was closed in 1965. "My mother was a mover," Charles Wilson remembered, "She got herself into everything."[11] Charles Wilson believed that within the tribe, the roles of women and men were "equal. They didn't do anything without discussion. That was part of the culture."[12] Even though public leadership had always been male, "Mother was a very good leader, and if they thought she was right they would follow her."[13]

The tensions that Rebecca Wilson had to deal with as de facto leader, her daughter explained, were the unresolved issues between the "moderns" and the "elderlies" within the tribe and the racial tensions between the tribe and the Euro-American and Hispanic communities. Though not held without friction, Rebecca Wilson's authority within the tribe was secured by her ancestry as July's daughter, the tribal tradition of gender equity in decision making, and the extreme limitations imposed on the tribe by the Euro-American and Hispanic power structure in Brackettville. Within the tribe Rebecca Wilson's gender was less an issue than her "modern" strategies for coexistence. In dealing with non-Seminoles, her race and her class were more an issue than her gender, while at the same time it was her traditional woman's work as cook and midwife that led her to be the businesswoman the non-Seminoles came to respect. While Brackettville was very socially segregated, commerce and voting were unusually integrated for that region and that time.[14] Charles Wilson, born about 1910, could not remember ever not being able to vote.

The following story serves to illustrate several points about Rebecca Wilson and her place in the Brackettville community. By the 1940s Rebecca Wilson owned the best restaurant in town. She was a renowned chef who had worked for several commandants at Fort Clark, where her reputation was first established. Almost everyone in Kinney County, of all races, ate at Wilson's place. During World War II, large regiments of African American troops were stationed at Fort Clark, and at first the more relaxed forms of segregation in Brackettville caught the soldiers off guard. One day shortly after the troops arrived, there was a knock on the back door of the restaurant. Rebecca Wilson went to the screen and found three Euro-American secretaries who were regular customers standing outside. She asked the young women (all of whom she had delivered into the world) what they were doing at the back door. They were there because the black solders wouldn't let them in the restaurant, they said. Rebecca Wilson then told them to go on back to the front door and she would see to the problem. Charles Wilson, who was there helping out in the kitchen, remembered the scene clearly. "My mother was not a violent person, but she grabbed that old butcher knife," Wilson said, and walking out into the dining room, she strolled to the table where the African American soldiers were settling in. When she asked them what they thought they were doing, the soldiers explained that since white people were always telling black people where they were and were not wanted, they didn't see why they couldn't have this place to themselves. Charles Wilson remembered that her mother, never raising her voice (or the knife), told the soldiers: "Now look, they are coming in here, [and] you can go or stay but they are coming in to eat. Now you are welcome to stay if you want to but you're not starting anything in here." When one soldier complained, "Well, we don't want them in here," Rebecca Wilson replied, "Well, this isn't your place. Now, soldier, you are welcome to come back but right here I don't have segregation."

The secretaries filed in, the soldiers sat down, and all parties ate lunch with no further incident, then or later. Clearly Rebecca Wilson was a highly charismatic and forceful person. But it is fair to assume that she also had status in the community at large, status that rested on her midwifery and entrepreneurial skills and that allowed for such confident and confrontational action. The secretaries went directly to her for a resolution to the conflict; they did not simply go away. Nor did Rebecca Wilson's husband, Billy Wilson, who witnessed the entire scene, feel compelled to interfere or aid his wife.[15]

But Rebecca Wilson wanted her daughters to have more than she had. She had only a grade school education; she wanted her daughters to go to college. "I guess that was an Indian trait too, she wanted us to have an education, she wanted the finer things . . . [so] we worked hard," Charles Wilson recalled.[16] Over the objections of their father, both girls were sent off to high school in Giddings and Elgin, Texas, because the Brackettville district maintained only an elementary school for the Brackettville Seminoles before 1942, when the U.S. Army moved the first large group of African Americans into the area. The sisters then went to college in Austin, where they both earned degrees in education at Huston-Tillotson (an African American college).

The girls' departure for Austin met with tribal disapproval. Some of the tribe even "hated us for it, [said] we were uppity," Charles Wilson recalled. "[T]hey [didn't] see the need." Before integration, most Brackett-ville Seminoles believed that there was no point in separating the family for a better education in light of the fact that "you would never get a [better] job [anyway]!" Even their father, Billy Wilson, who prized family unity above all things, had his doubts about allowing his daughters to go away to school. As it turned out, despite her college education, Charles Wilson, who did not want to teach at the Brackettville Seminole school, was left with the only other job open to her—domestic work—when she first came back from Austin.[17]

Yet Billy's Wilson's greatest fear, that his daughters would never return, turned out to be unfounded. Both Dorothy and then Charles Wilson returned to Brackettville because, despite the fact that the black college was a "haven," for them, racism in Austin and other parts of the state was "much worse" than it was in Brackettville. More importantly, both women still felt a strong commitment to the tribe. Neither would marry, and both would devote the rest of their lives to the education and historical preservation of the Brackettville Seminole tribe. "We didn't have time to get married!" Charles Wilson explained. "There was always another meeting. We did something [with the students and parents] just about every Friday night."[18] Every evening Dorothy Wilson, as a volunteer, coached baseball or basketball.

It is also true that marriage for the Wilson sisters in any event would have been problematic. Their college degrees made them anomalies. More educated than the vast majority of whites and all the rest of the Brackettville Seminoles, they were also isolated by race from similarly educated white people. Their own fierce allegiance to their heritage and identity further isolated them from the very few African American men who passed through Fort Clark or who taught at Carver Elementary, the Brackettville Seminole school.

When Dorothy Wilson was hired in 1941 to teach at Carver Elementary, she was the first Brackettville Seminole to hold such a post. All other teachers at the school had been African Americans hired from other areas. By 1945, Dorothy Wilson was the principal at Carver, and the Brackettville school district was providing a full first-through-twelfth-grade education for black students.[19] By all accounts, Dorothy Wilson, who in 1944 was finally able to cajole her reluctant sister into joining the staff at Carver, was as tenacious and intrepid as her mother in getting what she wanted.[20] She was often more successful at wheedling concessions, such as the use of buses for Carver, from the white school board than the previous African American principals had been. She seems also to have received the same principal's salary as was paid the African American male principals before her.[21] Though the salaries paid the principals at Carver were much lower than those paid the principals at the white school, the equity within Carver is worth noting since at the same time, a German American woman, Else Sauer, the first white woman to be appointed principal of the white elementary school, was not paid a full principal's salary.[22]

The Wilson sisters would use their positions in the school to build upon their mother's work to move the tribe into the mainstream economy

Carver Elementary School, circa 1920s. (Photo from personal collection of Annie Rodgers.)

through education. "Mother led the pack; she had the 'calling'—then Dorothy," Charles Wilson said, "It just ran through the family."[23] Other than allotting almost no funds for the black school (a major impediment to be sure), the white school board and the superintendents did little to impede the Wilson sisters' activities, as the following story demonstrates.

When the sisters took over the school in the 1940s, they came face to face with the unresolved issues within the tribe between the "moderns" and the "elderlies." Many of the "elderlies" did not want their children to attend school at all, especially since most were migrant workers and needed their children's labor to survive. But as Charles Wilson recalled, "[T]he children didn't have anything to do. [And] they loved sports."[24] So with boredom as an ally, the Wilson sisters spent many hours berating and cajoling parents. They also bent registration deadlines to match the pecan season in order to increase school attendance. The cumulative result of the Wilsons' tactics caught some very unexpected attention at the state level.

The day the state inspector came stands out very clearly in Charles Wilson's mind. By this time she was principal of Carver, having assumed the post in 1962 after her sister's death. Wilson had to drop everything she was doing to spend the day accompanying the inspector from one student's home to another as he tried diligently to prove that she was padding the attendance records. She acknowledged that she knew of many black schools in Texas at that time that did pad their records by not recording all their absentees, a practice that allowed them to stay open because their meager state funding was based on student attendance. But Wilson did not pad: "I was too afraid of going to jail" to do such a thing, she joked.

Besides, subterfuge at Carver was hardly necessary since Charles and Dorothy Wilson had managed through herculean efforts to get most of the Brackettville Seminole community to send their children to school on a regular basis.[25]

Ironically, it was the good attendance at Carver that caused the problem. The attendance was "too good" for a black school, according to the state inspector, but as the day wore on, it became abundantly apparent that Wilson's records were impeccably legitimate. Finally, the inspector drove to the white campus in a huff. The superintendent, Marion Wills, was outside the white school as the inspector and Wilson drove up. Seeing Charles Wilson in the state inspector's car, Wills asked her what she was doing. "Oh, just going for a ride," she responded. Wills, of course, knew why the inspector was in town. Yet he just smiled at Wilson and wandered on his way across campus, never questioning her rather flippant answer nor bothering to acknowledge the inspector's existence. The scene was not lost on the poor fellow, who "softened a bit . . . " at what clearly amounted to a vote of confidence in Wilson by the superintendent. "I wouldn't say he apologized," Charles Wilson said, "but then he also never came back."[26]

As school attendance demonstrated, the Wilson women clearly had an effect on the dynamic of the tribe. One needs to be careful, however, about describing their power within the white community. Until the U.S. Army forced the Brackettville school district to build a full twelve-year school in 1942 for the children of its African American troops, no amount of pressure from the Brackettville Seminoles for such a school had worked. So there were very real limits to the Wilsons' influence. At the same time, their more middle-class status, Rebecca Wilson's highly successful entrepreneurship, and the sisters' college degrees all brought the Wilson women in closer contact with the white power elites. Of all the tribe, they knew how the power structure operated. This knowledge did not always merit tribal respect. "We never got above our heritage," Charles Wilson mused, "but [the tribe] thought we did."[27]

The fact remains that because the Wilsons knew how to access power, the tribe continued to look to them. It was likely that the non-Seminole community also felt more comfortable dealing with the Wilson women, who in occupation and in speech were more like themselves than were other tribal members.

Rebecca and Dorothy Wilson both died of tuberculosis in 1962, and the mantle of leadership fell to a reluctant Charles Wilson. A shier, more withdrawn woman than either her mother or sister, Charles Wilson had always felt a bit overwhelmed by their confidence. "My mother was a mover. . . . I guess it was in me somewhere, too; I was just pampered," she admitted.[28] Nonetheless, she had learned their methods well, as the following story shows.

As in most African American communities in Texas, the Brackettville Seminole school was an important community center prior to integration. As in other black communities, Carver School was bigger and more

Miss Charles Wilson in old
school. (Photo from personal
collection of Annie Rodgers.)

neutral than the various church buildings. Though the school had been
erected in 1942 by the local school district, the Brackettville Seminole
community had been the only one to use it, and they, not the school
district, provided for most of its upkeep. Over the years the Mothers' Club
had raised money to invest in repairs and just before the schools
integrated, the club purchased fifty new folding chairs for their school.
Therefore, it came as a shock in the summer of 1963 when school
maintenance trucks pulled up to the door of Carver School and men
started to clean out the building in preparation for selling it. The men
loaded the new chairs the Mothers' Club had just purchased and drove off
with them.

Now, all of this happened without any word from the school board to
anyone in the Brackettville Seminole community. Charles Wilson had just
arrived home from a trip to California when a cousin called in a state of
panic to tell her what was happening at the school. Wilson lost no time
in organizing a committee of people whom she "could depend on" to
approach the school board with a proposal to buy the building from the
district.[29] Wilson stayed in the background, talking to the most sympathetic board members in private. "I wanted them to know the people

wanted to keep it—not just Charles Wilson," she explained. It took some time, but the board finally relented. Wilson then coached a committee on how to approach the bank for the money they needed to buy the building. Indeed, they were able to get a loan in the name of the Seminole Negro Scout Cemetery Association. Even so, the committee had to go back to the school board after purchasing the building to get their chairs back. "We always had to talk a bit more," Wilson mused.[30]

Though the tribal organizations were still strong, and attendance at annual celebrations was swelled by the return of expatriated Brackettville Seminoles, it was clear by the 1990s that the tribe was fading from existence. There were fewer than one hundred resident members in a town of about seventeen hundred.[31] The breakup, according to Charles Wilson, came in two stages. It had begun much earlier with the arrival of African American troops at Fort Clark during World War II. At first the Brackettville Seminoles were as frightened by this invasion of foreigners as was the non-Seminole community: "We were afraid of one another. We had never seen so many Blacks!" Charles Wilson recalled. But over time the African American troops "opened the eyes" of the Brackettville Seminoles to the much larger world outside of south Texas.[32] When the troops left, so did many Brackettville Seminoles. This process was greatly accelerated, Wilson noted, with the integration of the schools in the '60s. That, she felt, had more to do with the breakup of the tribe than anything else.

There is an irony here that was not lost on Wilson. The Brackettville Seminoles were able to take advantage of integration in 1964 because of the efforts of the Wilsons to get so many of them in school to begin with. "Parents were afraid. I think that was the problem, but then they [grew] out of it. That was what split the group, the church and us. See, one was for progress, the other just wanted to stay with the old ways, and we went through a lot. I enjoyed it and they wondered why I stayed." But integration led to outside economic opportunity and "so many kids were denying [their Creole traditions] because they didn't want to stay here. They wanted to go to California. Integration [made] it easier to move away."[33]

An unintended result of education was that it began to scatter the tribe to the four winds. In true July-Wilson tradition, Charles Wilson set about doing what she could to save the memory of her people. She has worked with several scholars and granted numerous interviews to writers of the popular press.[34] She was also invited to lead a delegation of the tribe to the Smithsonian 1992 Festival of American Folklife held on the mall in Washington, D.C. To preserve her peoples' story, she has actively promoted the glorious tales of warriors and the Wild West that are so important to the public mythology that Brackettville now packages and sells to its burgeoning tourist and movie industry.[35] All her interviews to date, except the ones on which this article is based, have been focused on the Seminole Negro Indian Scouts and couched in the heroic language that fits the inexhaustible fascination with the "wild and woolly West" that is a part of the public cultural mythology.

But even the simple task of preserving the Seminole Negro Indian Scouts' legitimate place in the tale of western heroism has met with covert opposition from the white community in Brackettville. Whites in the community, while deferential to Charles Wilson and careful to invite her to civic functions to which few other Brackettville Seminoles are ever invited, would confide privately that they could not understand what the fuss was about: "After all, they [the Brackettville Seminoles] didn't look like Indians." Intermarriage with Indians was very rare after 1861 when the Seminoles left Nacimiento for Oklahoma, though some Brackettville Seminoles occasionally married Apaches. In the intervening years, African features became dominant. Charles Wilson described both her mother and her sister as having light, red-brown skin and hair, features considered by the tribe to be very beautiful; Charles herself is dark and has African features. But racial characteristics were never the central focus of tribal identity for the Brackettville Seminole. Rather, it was their long history of self-emancipation.

The white community has never been comfortable with the tribe's African quality nor with their claims to western heroism. The whites prefer to evoke a more sterile western romanticism and have actively worked to refocus the depiction of Bracketville Seminole history. Some of the local tourist pamphlets show a Plains Indian in buckskin next to the paragraph on the Seminole Indian Scouts. While it is true that some Apaches served with the scouts, the vast majority were very-African-looking men who wore standard military uniforms.[36] The state historical marker that identifies the scout cemetery has the word "Negro" carefully edited out to read simply "Seminole Indian Scouts Cemetery." Nor in the text that follows is there any indication that the scouts were anything but Native Americans. When asked recently if the local school taught about the scouts' role in Brackettville's history, Superintendent Steve Mills explained that he didn't "believe it's the job of the local schools to encourage Seminole Negro children to remain interested in their ancestry. . . . I myself am a Baptist, and it's my responsibility as a parent to raise my children up dedicated to that. . . . [T]he school can't do everything."[37]

Maybe so, but then the Baptist Church did not prevent the annihilation of Brackettville by hostile and highly skilled Native American warriors or lawless gangs of thieves. The Seminole Negro Indian Scouts did. It is not hard to see why many young Brackettville Seminoles have never attended the special ceremonies held in honor of the scouts. As fourteen-year-old Windy Goodlow explained, she had never been to the ceremony. "I don't think any of my friends have either," she concluded.[38] Perhaps Charles Wilson understands, though she complained that "[T]he kids don't want to learn about where they came from, they want to watch television."[39]

There is little to gain in Brackettville today for a black of any identity, African American or Brackettville Seminole. Outside Brackettville, no one recognizes the Brackettville Seminole identity nor sees Brackettville Seminoles as anything other than African Americans. Since the non-

Seminole Brackettville community does not want to acknowledge the special quality of its black citizens, it is unlikely the young will stay. There are simply not enough service jobs to go around. At least there are jobs in California—and a larger African American community with which to identify. In time, nothing but articles and books on the Brackettville Seminole culture will remain. Like the façade of the Alamo constructed a few miles outside of town, which one can see from the luxury of an air-conditioned car, Brackettville will substitute a comfortable illusion for a troubled past, an illusion that can be peddled to the unsuspecting East Coast retirees who now live on Los Moras Creek in multimillion-dollar homes.

The story of the Brackettville men and women became very different, once they were forced into a wage-market economy. Public representation shifted from that of military warrior to that of women descended from warriors. This shift was made necessary by changes in the economy, but it was also made possible by the tribal tradition of shared decision making and by the gendered structure of work in the regional economy. This too is rapidly changing as the whole tribe disappears into the general population.[40] The lesson here is that gender relations within groups are neither static nor the same as those of other populations in the same region or at the same time. Obviously, gender was not the only factor in this story. The Wilson women's gender was not as important in their service as tribal leaders as were their heritage and their education. Gender was also less an issue with the other populations with which the Wilson women had to deal. Rather, race limited their field, while at the same time skill, entrepreneurship, and education expanded the control they had over their lives and their ability to act on the behalf of others. It should be noted, however, that Rebecca July Wilson's entrepreneurial ties were rooted in the gender-specific skills that she could market in Brackettville. But as her determination to improve her daughters' options demonstrated, the Brackettville Seminole minority culture continued to change. This fact suggests the importance of generational change in histories of racial and ethnic groups.

Sadly, the youngest generation finds little to inspire them to cling to their special Brackettville Seminole identity. The limited economic choices that were set by the dominant white culture at first segregated the tribe into a unified people and now integrates them into the general population of other cities. Such integration into the dominant culture was never advocated by Rebecca July Wilson or her daughters, Dorothy and Charles Wilson; it resulted from larger social, economic, and cultural forces that buffeted the Brackettville Seminoles once they were evicted from Fort Clark. In opposition to these forces pushing toward integration, however, is a strong effort to preserve the heritage of the Brackettville Seminoles. For Charles Wilson in particular, knowledge of her ancestors provided a well of inspiration. Her work to preserve that knowledge helps ensure that it will inspire other generations as well.

The Wilson women provided leadership to the Brackettville Seminoles throughout the twentieth century. They facilitated their transition from a warrior culture to a wage market economy, negotiated conflicts with the dominant culture, and worked to maintain their cultural heritage. As Texas Ranger Lee Roy Young, Jr., a descendant of Seminole Negro Indian Scouts and the first black to join the Rangers, proclaimed "It's just the type of people they were. . . . If the scouts had a job to do or a duty to accomplish, they would go out and do whatever was necessary."[41] This seems a fitting description of the Wilson women as well.

Notes

1. Scott Thybony, "Against All Odds, Black Seminole Won Their Freedom," *Smithsonian*, August 1991, 90.

2. Kevin Mulroy, *Freedom on the Border: The Seminole Maroons in Florida, the Indian Territory, Coahuila, and Texas* (Lubbock: Texas Tech University Press 1993), 180.

3. Ibid., 90: "[W]ithin an eight-year period of active campaigns against the Indians . . ., Black Seminole Scouts fought in 25 actions without a man killed or seriously wounded."

4. Ibid., 101. The title of "tribal historian" is unofficial but is widely recognized within the community of Brackettville as legitimate, owing to Wilson's thirty years of work with scholars and writers of the popular press to preserve the Brackettville Seminole story. Charles Emily Wilson, interview by B. Ann Rodgers, Brackettville, Tex., 31 August 1992.

5. Ian F. Hancock, *The Texas Seminoles and Their Language* (Austin: University of Texas Press, 1980).

6. Wilson interview, 31 August 1992. Wilson noted that the tribe still "had a lot of African culture," seen not only in the language but in wakes that "were all night long . . . with shouting and singing." (Before cold storage and cars were common, ice would be put in the coffin until everybody had the chance to gather from the surrounding ranches where they worked.) See also Mulroy, *Freedom on the Border*, 176, where he notes, "[T]he Texas group . . . continued to practice a syncretic religion, traceable to Florida . . . [combining] elements of Africanisms and Seminole ceremonials with Prebyterianism, Southern Baptism, and Roman Catholicism."

7. Mulroy's *Freedom on the Border* is the most recent example of a political and military history of the Brackettville Seminole.

8. Ibid. See 163–65 for Sampson July's role as "patriarch of the tribe."

9. The term "elderlies" is what Charles Wilson used to refer to the more traditional people of the tribe; the term does not indicate a person's age. The term "moderns" is the authors' invention of convenience, as Wilson tended to use longer terms for this faction—terms like "those who wanted more" that were too awkward for use in this short article.

10. Charles Emily Wilson, interview by B. Ann Rodgers, Brackettville, Tex., 24 February 1992.

11. Ibid.

12. Wilson interview, 31 August 1992.

13. Wilson interview, 24 February 1992.

14. See Kinney County, Brackettville (Texas) Certified List of Voters Qualified 1932, Precinct #1 to 7, and 1939, Precinct #1. All show that Brackettville Seminoles, both men and women, were registered to vote and markings on some lists appear to indicate voting activity.

15. Wilson interview, 24 February 1992.

16. Ibid.

17. Charles Emily Wilson, interview by B. Ann Rodgers, Brackettville, Tex., 13 April 1992.

18. Wilson interview, 24 February 1992.

19. As longtime resident and officeholder, Emma Castro Swain, explained, in 1941 the U.S. government ordered the school district to build a full twelve-year black school and supply it with

new textbooks because the army was going to station twelve thousand black servicemen and many of their families at Fort Clark. Though the district complied only when protests by rich white ranchers to Washington, D.C., failed, it maintained the school with new textbooks from that point until the school was closed by integration in 1965. Emma Castro Swain, interview by B. Ann Rodgers, Brackettville, Tex., 11 August 1992. See also Brackettville, Texas, Independent School District, minutes of the Meeting of the School Board 29 August 1941.

20. Brackettvile, Texas, Independent School District, minutes of meeting of the school board of 18 April 1944.

21. Brackettville, Texas, Independent School District, minutes of the meeting of the school board of 22 June 1943, compared with Brackettville, Texas, Independent School District, cash records of 1955, 30 September 1955.

22. Brackettville, Texas, Independent School District, minutes of the meeting of the school board of 9 October 1945; Brackettville, Texas, Independent School District, minutes of the meeting of the school board of 1 July 1946; Brackettville, Texas, Independent School District, cash records of 19 September 1943–May 1944.

23. Wilson interview, 31 August 1992.

24. Wilson interview, 24 February 1992.

25. Ibid.

26. Ibid.

27. Ibid.

28. Ibid.

29. Ibid.

30. Wilson interview, 31 August 1992.

31. "Seminole Negro Heritage Fading in Border Town," Jeff Guinn, *San Antonio Express-News*, 18 September 1994.

32. Wilson interview, 24 February 1992.

33. Wilson interview, 31 August 1992

34. Charles Wilson was used as a major source in the following publications: Hancock, *Texas Seminoles*; Doug Sivad, *The Black Seminole Indians of Texas*, 2d ed. (The Sivad Group Co-Sponsored by The Texas Association for the Studies of Afro-American Life and History, 1986); Mulroy, *Freedom on the Border*; C. Kevin Swisher, "Frontier Heroes," *Texas Highways*, July 1992; Thybony, "Against All Odds." Charles Wilson was also the subject or the source of many newspaper articles.

35. *The Alamo*, starring John Wayne, would be only the first of many western movies filmed in the area. Alamo village is a major tourist attraction for Brackettville, as is hunting in the fall.

36. See photos in Thybony's article, "Against All Odds."

37. Guinn, "Seminole Negro Heritage."

38. Ibid.

39. Ibid

40. In *Freedom on the Border*, Kevin Mulroy notes, "There are now only some 100 to 150 Seminole Blacks in West Texas, with the same number living in or around Nacimiento," 181. Why Mulroy calls Brackettville "west" is unclear.

41. Guinn, "Seminole Negro Heritage."

Selected Bibliographies

COMPILED BY DEDRA S. MCDONALD,
EVELYN A. SCHLATTER, AND JUNEAL LEVERSEE

GENERAL BIBLIOGRAPHY

Anderson, Karen. *Changing Woman: A History of Racial Ethnic Women in Modern America*. New York: Oxford University Press, 1996.

Anzaldúa, Gloria. *Borderlands/La Frontera*. San Francisco: Spinster/Aunt Lute Book Company, 1987.

———. *Making Face, Making Soul/Haciendo Caras*. San Francisco: An Aunt Lute Foundation Book, 1990.

Anzaldúa, Gloria, and Cherríe Moraga, eds. *This Bridge Called My Back: Writings by Radical Women of Color*. New York: Kitchen Table/Women of Color Press, 1981, 1983.

Armitage, Susan. "Women and the New Western History." *OAH Magazine of Hsitory* 9, no. 1 (Fall 1994): 22–27.

Armitage, Susan, and Elizabeth Jameson, eds. *The Women's West*. Norman: University of Oklahoma Press, 1987.

Benson, Bjorn, Elizabeth Hampsten, and Kathryn Sweeney. *Day In, Day Out: Women's Lives in North Dakota*. Grand Forks: University of North Dakota Press, 1988.

Blackburn, George M., and Sherman L. Ricards. "The Prostitutes and Gamblers of Virginia City, Nevada, 1870." *Pacific Historical Review* 48 (May 1979): 239–58.

Blair, Karen J., ed. *Women in Pacific Northwest History: An Anthology*. Seattle: University of Washington Press, 1988, 1990.

Castañeda, Antonia I. "Women of Color and the Rewriting of Western History: The Discourse, Politics, and Decolonization of History." *Pacific Historical Review* 61 (November 1992): 501–533.

Chan, Sucheng, Douglas Henry Daniels, Mario T. García, and Terry P. Wilson. *Peoples of Color in the American West*. Lexington, Mass.: D. C. Heath, 1994.

Croxdale, Richard, and Melissa Hield, eds. *Women in the Texas Workforce: Yesterday and Today*. Austin: People's History in Texas, 1979.

Deutsch, Sarah, et al. "The History of Women in the West: A Search for Understanding amid Diversity." *Montana The Magazine of Western History* 41 (Spring 1991): 58–61.

DuBois, Ellen Carol, and Vicki L. Ruiz, eds. *Unequal Sisters: A Multicultural Reader in U.S. Women's History*. New York: Routledge, 1990, 1994.

Hull, Gloria T., Patricia Bell Scott, and Barbara Smith, eds. *All the Women Are White, All the Blacks Are Men, but Some of Us Are Brave: Black Women's Studies*. Old Westbury, N.Y.: Feminist Press, 1982.

Hurtado, Aída. "Relating to Privilege: Seduction and Rejection in the Subordination of White Women and Women of Color." *Signs* 14, no. 4 (1988): 833–55.

Jameson, Elizabeth. "Toward a Multicultural History of Women in the Western United States." *Signs* 13 (Summer 1988): 761–91.

Jensen, Joan. *One Foot on the Rockies: Women and Creativity in the Modern American West.* Albuquerque: University of New Mexico Press, 1995.

Jensen, Joan, and Gloria Ricci Lothrop. *California Women: A History.* San Francisco: Boyd & Fraser, 1987.

Jensen, Joan, and Darlis Miller. "The Gentle Tamers Revisited: New Approaches to the History of Women in the American West." *Pacific Historical Review* 49 (May 1980): 173–213.

———, eds. *New Mexico Women: Intercultural Perspectives.* Albuquerque: University of New Mexico Press, 1986.

Malone, Ann Patton. *Women on the Texas Frontier: A Cross-Cultural Perspective.* El Paso: Texas Western Press, University of Texas at El Paso, 1983.

Myres, Sandra L. *Westering Women and the Frontier Experience, 1800–1915.* Albuquerque: University of New Mexico Press, 1982.

Pacific Historical Review 61 (November 1992). Theme issue, Western Women's History Revisited.

Pascoe, Peggy. *Relations of Rescue: The Search for Female Moral Authority in the American West, 1874–1939.* New York: Oxford University Press, 1990.

Patterson-Black, Sheryll. *Ethnic Life, Agriculture, and the North Platte Valley.* Crawford, Neb.: Cottonwood Press, 1984.

Riley, Glenda. *Women and Indians on the Frontier, 1825–1915.* Albuquerque: University of New Mexico Press, 1984.

Root, Maria P. P., ed. *Racially Mixed People in America.* Newbury Park, Calif.: Sage Publications, 1992.

Rothschild, Mary Aiken, and Pamela Claire Hronek. *Doing What the Day Brought: An Oral History of Arizona Women.* Tucson, University of Arizona Press, 1992.

Schlissel, Lillian, Vicki L. Ruiz, and Janice Monk, eds. *Western Women: Their Land, Their Lives.* Albuquerque: University of New Mexico Press, 1988.

Taylor, Quintard. "Blacks and Asians in a White City: Japanese Americans and African Americans in Seattle, 1890–1940." *Western Historical Quarterly* 22 (November 1991): 401–29.

Utah Historical Quarterly 59 (Winter 1991). Theme issue on women.

Winegarten, Ruth. *Texas Women's History Project Bibliography.* Austin: Texas Foundation for Women's Resources, 1980.

Zinn, Maxine Baca, and Bonnie Thornton Dill. *Women of Color in U.S. Society.* Philadelphia: Temple University Press, 1994.

AFRICAN AMERICAN WOMEN

Abajian, James de T. *Blacks and Their Contributions to the American West: A Bibliography.* Boston: G. K. Hall, 1974.

———. comp. *Blacks in Selected Newspapers, Censuses and Other Sources: An Index to Names and Subjects.* 3 vols. Boston: G. K. Hall, 1977.

Alpha Kappa Alpha Sorority, Inc. Alpha Tau Omega Chapter. *Historical Review: Sixty Years of Gems, 1930–1990.* San Antonio: Alpha Kappa Alpha, 1990.

Anderson, Larry. "We Need Acceptance Where We Are: A Central Area Negro Leader Gives Her Views." *Seattle Times Magazine*, 18 September 1966.

Armitage, Susan, Theresa Banfield, and Sarah Jacobus. "Black Women and Their Communities in Colorado." *Frontiers* 2 (Summer 1977): 45–51.

Armitage, Susan, and Deborah G. Wilbert. "Black Women in the Pacific Northwest: A Survey and Research Prospectus." In *Women in Pacific Northwest History*, edited by Karen Blair. Seattle: University of Washington Press, 1988.

Barr, Alwyn. *Black Texans: A History of Negroes in Texas, 1528–1971*. Austin: Jenkins Publishing, 1973.

Barr, Alwyn, and Robert A. Calvert, eds. *Black Leaders: Texans for Their Times*. Austin: Texas State Historical Association, 1981.

Beasley, Delilah L. *The Negro Trail Blazers of California*. Los Angeles, 1919; reprint San Francisco: R & E Associates, 1969.

Berwanger, Eugene H. *The Frontier against Slavery: Western Anti-Negro Prejudice and the Slavery Extension Controversy*. Urbana: University of Illinois Press, 1967.

"Black Women in Colorado: Two Early Portraits." *Frontiers* 7 (1984), 21.

Blackwelder, Julia Kirk. "Women in the Work Force: Atlanta, New Orleans, and San Antonio, 1930 to 1940." *Journal of Urban History* 4 (May 1978): 331–58.

———. *Women of the Depression: Caste and Culture in San Antonio, 1929–1939*. College Station: Texas A&M University Press, 1984.

Blood, Kathryn. *Negro Women War Workers*. Bull. 205. Washington, D.C.: U.S. Department of Labor, Women's Bureau, 1945.

Brandenstein, Sherilyn Ruth. "Prominent Roles and Themes of Black Womanhood in *Sepia Record*, 1952–1954." Master's thesis, University of Texas at Austin, 1989.

———. "*Sepia Record* as a Forum for Negotiating Women's Roles." In *Women and Texas History: Selected Essays*, edited by Fane Downs and Nancy Baker Jones. Austin: Texas State Historical Association, 1993.

Broussard, Albert S. *Black San Francisco: The Struggle for Racial Equality in the West, 1900–1954*. Lawrence: University Press of Kansas, 1993.

Brown, Jean. *The Negro Woman Worker*. Bull. 165. Washington D.C.: U.S. Department of Labor, Women's Bureau, 1938.

Bruyn, Kathleen. *"Aunt" Clara Brown: Story of a Black Pioneer*. Boulder, Colo.: Pruett Publishing, 1970.

Bryant, Ira B. *Barbara Charline Jordan: From the Ghetto to the Capitol*. Houston: D. Armstrong, 1977.

Butler, Anne M. "Still in Chains: Black Women in Western Prisons, 1865–1910." *Western Historical Quarterly* 20 (February 1989): 19–36.

Chaudhuri, Nupur. " 'We All Seem Like Brothers and Sisters': The African-American Community in Manhattan, Kansas, 1865–1940." *Kansas History* 14 (Winter 1991–92): 270–88.

Cloyd, Iris, ed. *Who's Who among Black Americans, 1990–91*. 6th ed. Detroit: Gale Research, 1990.

Crowell, Evelyn. "Twentieth Century Black Women in Oregon." *Northwest Journal of African and Black American Studies* 1 (Summer 1973): 13–15.

Crouchett, Lawrence P., Lonnie G. Bunch III, and Martha Kendall Winnacker. *The History of the East Bay Afro-American Community, 1851–1977*. Oakland: Northern California Center for Afro-American History and Life, 1989.

Daniels, Henry Douglas. *Pioneer Urbanites: A Social and Cultural History of Black San Francisco.* Philadelphia: Temple University Press, 1980; reprint, Berkeley: University of California Press, 1990.

Davis, Angela. *An Autobiography.* New York: Random House, 1974.

Davis, Elizabeth Lindsay. *Lifting as They Climb.* Chicago: National Association of Colored Women, 1933.

Davis, Lenwood G. *The Black Woman in American Society: A Selected Annotated Bibliography.* Boston: G. K. Hall, 1975.

———. *Blacks in the American West: A Working Bibliography.* Exchange Bibliography 582. Monticello, Ill.: Council of Planning Librarians, 1974.

———. *Blacks in the Pacific Northwest, 1788–1972.* Exchange Bibliography 355. Monticello, Ill.: Council of Planning Librarians, 1972.

———. *Blacks in the State of Oregon, 1788–1974.* Exchange Bibliography 616. Monticello, Ill.: Council of Planning Librarians, 1974.

———, "Sources for History of Blacks in Oregon." *Oregon Historical Society* 73 (September 1972): 196–211.

———. "Sources for History of Blacks in Washington State." *Western Journal of Black Studies* 2 (March 1978): 60–64.

De Graaf, Lawrence B. "Race, Sex and Region: Black Women in the American West, 1850–1920." *Pacific Historical Review* 49 (May 1980): 285–313.

Delta Sigma Theta Sorority, Inc., Austin Alumnae Chapter. *Pictorial History of Austin, Travis County, Texas' Black Community, 1839–1920.* Austin: Delta Sigma Theta, ca. 1972.

Dickson, Lynda Fae. "The Early Club Movement among Black Women in Denver, 1890–1925." Ph.D. dissertation, University of Colorado, 1982.

Duren, Almetris March, and Louise Iscoe. *Overcoming: A History of Black Integration at the University of Texas at Austin.* Austin: University of Texas Press, 1979.

Enstam, Elizabeth. "The Frontier Woman as City Worker: Women's Occupations in Dallas, 1856–1880." *East Texas Historical Journal* 18 (1980): 12–28.

Gee, Sadye, comp., and Darnell Williams, ed. *Black Presence in Dallas, Historic Black Dallasites.* Dallas: Museum of African-American Life and Culture, 1986.

Giddings, Paula. *In Search of Sisterhood: Delta Sigma Theta and the Challenge of the Black Sorority Movement.* New York: William Morrow, 1988.

———. *When and Where I Enter: The Impact of Black Women on Race and Sex in America.* New York: Bantam Books, 1985.

Goode, Kenneth B. *California's Black Pioneers: A Brief Historical Survey.* Santa Barbara: McNally and Loftin, 1974.

Hayden, Dolores. "Biddy Mason's Los Angeles, 1856–1891." *California History* 68 (Fall 1989): 86–99.

Hayes, Elizabeth Ross. "Negroes in Domestic Service in the United States." *Journal of Negro History* 8 (October 1923): 384–442.

Herzog, June. "A Study of the Negro Defense Worker in the Portland-Vancouver Area." Bachelor's thesis, Reed College, Portland, Oregon, 1944.

Hill, Mozell C. "The All-Negro Communities of Oklahoma: The Natural History of a Social Movement." *Journal of Negro History* 31 (1946): 254–68.

Hill, Ruth Edmonds, ed. *Women of Courage: An Exhibition of Photographs by Judith Sedwick.* Cambridge, Mass.: Radcliffe College, 1984.

———. *Black Women in White: Racial Conflict and Cooperation in the Nursing Profession, 1890–1950.* Bloomington: Indiana University Press, 1989.

———. "Voices of Experience: Black Women Chronicle Their Communities." *Organization of American Historians Newsletter* 12, no. 3 (1984): 2–5.

———, ed. *Black Women in America: An Historical Encyclopedia.* 2 vols. Brooklyn: Carlson Publishing, 1991.

Hull, Gloria T., Patricia Bell Scott, and Barbara Smith, eds. *All the Women Are White, All the Blacks Are Men, but Some of Us Are Brave: Black Women's Studies.* Old Westbury, N.Y.: Feminist Press, 1982.

Institute of Texan Cultures, Melvin M. Sance, Jr., principal researcher. *The Afro-American Texans.* San Antonio: University of Texas at San Antonio, 1975.

Irwin, Dona L. *The Unsung Heart of Black America: A Middle Class Church at Midcentury.* Columbia: University of Missouri Press, 1992.

Jackson, Charles Christopher. "A Southern Black Community Comes of Age: Black San Antonio in the Great Depression, 1930–1941." Master's thesis, Texas A&M University, 1989.

Janes, Daryl, ed. *No Apologies: Texas Radicals Celebrate the '60s.* Austin: Eakin Press, 1992.

Jones, Howard. *The Red Diary: A Chronological History of Black Americans in Houston and Some Neighboring Harris County Communities—122 Years Later.* Austin: Nortex Press, 1991.

Jordan, Barbara, and Shelby Hearon. *Barbara Jordan, A Self-Portrait.* Garden City, N.Y.: Doubleday, 1979.

Jordan, Julia K. Gibson, in collaboration with Charlie Mae Brown Smith. *Beauty and the Best: Frederica Chase Dodd, the Story of a Life of Love and Dedication.* Dallas: Delta Sigma Theta Sorority, Dallas Alumnae Chapter, 1985.

Katz, William Loren. *The Black West.* New York: Doubleday, 1971; Seattle: Ethrac Publications, 1987.

Lanker, Brian, photographer, and Barbara Summers, ed. *I Dream a World: Portraits of Black Women Who Changed America.* New York: Stewart, Tabori, and Chang, 1989.

Lapp, Rudolph M. *Blacks in Gold Rush California.* New Haven, Conn.: Yale University Press, 1977; San Francisco: Boyd & Fraser Publishing, 1987.

Ledé, Naomi W. *Precious Memories of a Black Socialite: A Narrative of the Life and Times of Constance Houston Thompson.* Houston: D. Armstrong, 1991.

Lemke-Santangelo, Gretchen. *Abiding Courage: African American Migrant Women and the East Bay Community.* Chapel Hill, N.C.: University of North Carolina Press.

Littlefield, Mary Ann, and Daniel F. Littlefield. "The Beams Family: Free Blacks in Indian Territory." *Journal of Negro History* 6 (1976): 16–35.

Loewenberg, Bert James, and Ruth Bogin, eds. *Black Women in Nineteenth-Century American Life: Their Words, Their Thoughts, Their Feelings.* University Park: Pennsylvania State University Press, 1976.

Lortie, Francis. *San Francisco's Black Community, 1870–1890.* San Francisco: R & E Associates, 1973.

Martinello, Marian L., and Melvin M. Sance. *A Personal History: The Afro-American Texans.* San Antonio: Institute of Texan Cultures, 1982.

McKnight, Mamie L., ed. *First African-American Families of Dallas: Creative Survival.* Vol. 1. Dallas: Black Dallas Remembered, 1987.

McKnight, Mamie L., and BDR Editorial Board, eds. *African-American Families and Settlements of Dallas: On the Inside Looking Out.* 2 vols. Dallas: Black Dallas Remembered, 1990.

McLagan, Elizabeth. *A Peculiar Paradise: A History of Blacks in Oregon, 1788–1940.* Portland: Georgian Press, 1980.

Miles, Merle Yvonne. "'Born and Bred' in Texas: Three Generations of Black Females: A Critique of Social Science Perceptions on the Black Female." Ph.D. dissertation, University of Texas at Austin, 1986.

Mills, Hazel E., and Nancy B. Pryor. *The Negro in the State of Washington: 1788–1969.* Olympia: Washington State Library, 1970.

Mock, Charlotte. *Bridges: New Mexican Black Women, 1900–1950.* Albuquerque: New Mexico Commission on the Study of Women, 1985.

Moore, Shirley Ann. *To Place Our Deeds: The Black Community in Richmond, California, 1910–1963.* Berkeley: University of California Press, forthcoming.

Mumford, Esther Hall. *Seattle's Black Victorians, 1852–1901.* Seattle: Ananse Press, 1980.

Mungen, Donna. *Life and Times of Biddy Mason: From Slavery to Wealthy California Laundress.* N.p., 1976.

Museum of African-American Life and Culture. *They Showed the Way: An Exhibit of Black Texas Women, 1836–1986.* Dallas: Museum of African-American Life and Culture, 1986.

Northwood, Lawrence K., and Ernest A. Barth. *Urban Desegregation: Negro Pioneers and Their White Neighbors.* Seattle: University of Washington Press, 1965.

Painter, Nell Irvin. *Exodusters: Black Migration to Kansas after Reconstruction.* New York: Alfred A. Knopf, 1977.

Parker, Marjorie H. *Alpha Kappa Alpha through the Years, 1908–1988.* Rev. edition. Chicago: AKA, 1990.

Pruett, Jakie L., and Everett B. Cole. *As We Lived: Stories by Black Story Tellers.* Burnet, Tex.: Eakin Press, 1982.

Ray, Emma P. *Twice Sold, Twice Ransomed: Autobiography of Mr. and Mrs. L. O. Ray.* Chicago: n.p., 1926.

Rich, Doris L. *Queen Bess: Daredevil Aviator.* Washington, D.C.: Smithsonian Institution Press, 1993.

Riley, Glenda. "American Daughters: Black Women in the West." *Montana The Magazine of Western History* 39 (1988): 14–27.

Robinson, Dorothy. *The Bell Rings at Four: A Black Teacher's Chronicle of Change.* Austin, Tex.: Madrona Press, 1978.

Rusco, Elmer F. *"Good Time Coming?" Black Nevadans in the Nineteenth Century.* Westport, Conn.: Greenwood Press, 1975.

Savage, W. Sherman. *Blacks in the West.* Westport, Conn.: Greenwood Press, 1976.

Schaffer, Ruth C. "The Health and Social Functions of Black Midwives on the Texas Brazos Bottom, 1920–1985." *Rural Sociology* 56 (Spring 1991): 89–105.

Schwendermann, Glen. "Nicodemus: Negro Haven on the Solomon." *Kansas Historical Quarterly* 34 (1968): 10–31.

Second Baptist Church of San Antonio. *100 Years: A Century of Progress, 1879–1979.* San Antonio: n.p., 1979.

Shaw, Stephanie J. "Black Club Women and the Creation of the National Association of Colored Women." *Journal of Women's History* 3 (Fall 1991): 10–25.

Sims, Janet L. *The Progress of Afro-American Women: A Selected Bibliography and Resource Guide.* Westport, Conn.: Greenwood Press, 1980.

Smallwood, James M. *The Struggle for Equality: Blacks in Texas*. Boston: American Press, 1983.

Spokane Bethel African Methodist Episcopal Church. *50 Years of Progress*. N.P., 1940.

Spurlin, Virginia Lee. "The Conners of Waco: Black Professionals in Twentieth Century Texas." Ph.D. dissertation, Texas Tech University, 1991.

Sterling, Dorothy. *We Are Your Sisters: Black Women in the Nineteenth Century*. New York: W. W. Norton, 1984.

Sullivan, Mary Loretta, and Bertha Blair. *Women in Texas Industries: Hours, Wages, Working Conditions, and Home Work*. Women's Bureau Bulletin No. 126. Washington, D.C.: U.S. Department of Labor, 1936.

Taylor, Quintard. "Blacks in the West: An Overview." *Western Journal of Black Studies* 1 (March 1977): 4–10.

———. "The Emergence of Black Communities in the Pacific Northwest, 1864–1910." *Journal of Negro History* 64 (Fall 1979): 346–51.

———. *The Forging of a Black Community: A History of Seattle's Central District, 1870 through the Civil Rights Era*. Seattle: University of Washington Press, 1994.

———. "Migration of Blacks and Resulting Discriminatory Practices in Washington State between 1940 and 1950." *Western Journal of Black Studies* 2 (March 1978): 65–71.

Thomas, Jesse O. *A Study of the Social Welfare Status of the Negroes in Houston, Texas*. Houston: National Urban League, 1929.

Thompson, Era Bell. *American Daughter*. Chicago: University of Chicago Press, 1946; reprint, St. Paul: Minnesota Historical Society, 1986.

Thurman, Sue Bailey. *Pioneers of Negro Origin in California*. San Francisco: Acme Publishing, 1949; reprint, San Francisco: R & E Associates, 1971.

Tolson, Arthur L. *The Black Oklahomans: A History, 1541–1972*. New Orleans: Edwards Print, 1972.

Trammell, Camilla Davis. *Seven Pines, Its Occupants and Their Letters, 1825–1872*. Houston: privately published, distributed by Southern Methodist University Press, 1986.

U.S. Department of Commerce, Bureau of the Census. *Negroes in the United States, 1920–1932, 1935*.

U.S. Department of Labor. *Negro Women in Industry*. Bulletin 20. Washington, D.C.: U.S Government Printing Office, 1922.

———. *Negro Women in the Population and the Labor Force*. Item 782. Washington, D.C.: U.S. Government Printing Office, 1968.

———. *Negro Women Workers in 1960*. Bureau Publication 287. Washington, D.C.: U.S. Government Printing Office, 1963.

———. *A Survey of Laundries and Their Women Workers in 23 Cities*. Bulletin 78. Washington, D.C.: U.S. Government Printing Office, 1930.

———. Women's Bureau. *Guide to Sources of Data on Women Workers for the United States and for Regions, States, and Local Areas*. Washington, D.C.: U.S. Government Printing Office, 1972.

Wayne, George H. "Negro Migration and Colonization in Colorado, 1870–1930." *Journal of the West* 15 (1976): 102–20.

Wells[-Barnett], Ida B. *Crusade for Justice: The Autobiography of Ida B. Wells*. Edited by Alfreda M. Duster. Chicago: University of Chicago Press, 1970.

Who's Who in Colored America. 7th ed. New York: Christian E. Burkel, 1950.

Winegarten, Ruthe. *Black Texas Women: 150 Years of Trial and Triumph.* Austin: University of Texas Press, 1995.

————. *I Am Annie Mae [Hunt]: The Personal Story of a Black Texas Woman.* Austin: Rosegarden Press, 1983.

Women of Texas: A Brochure Honoring Miss Ellie Alma Walls, First Woman President of the Colored Teachers Association of Texas. 65th Annual Convention, 24–26 November 1949, Houston.

ASIAN AMERICAN WOMEN

Abbott, Elizabeth Lee, and Kenneth Abbott. "Chinese Pilgrims and Presbyterians in the United States, 1850–1977." *Journal of Presbyterian History* 55 (Summer 1977): 125–44.

Abelmann, Nancy, and John Lie. *Blue Dreams: Korean Americans and the Los Angeles Riots.* Cambridge, Mass.: Harvard University Press, 1995.

Aguino, Belinda A. "A History of Filipino Women in Hawaii." *Bridge* 7 (Spring 1979): 17–21.

Almirol, Edwin B. *Ethnic Identity and Social Negotiation: A Study of a Filipino Community in California.* New York: AMS Press, 1985.

Amerasia Journal 19, no. 1 (1993). Commemorative issue: Japanese American Internment, Fiftieth Anniversary.

Anderson, Robert N., Richard Collier, and Rebecca F. Pestano. *Filipinos in Rural Hawaii.* Honolulu: University of Hawaii Press, 1984.

Asian Women United of California, eds. *Making Waves: An Anthology of Writings by and about Asian Women.* Boston: Beacon Press, 1989.

Azuma, Eiichiro. "A History of Oregon's Issei, 1880–1952." *Oregon Historical Quarterly* 94 (Winter 1993–94): 315–67.

Barringer, Herbert, and Sung-nam Cho. *Koreans in the United States: A Fact Book.* Honolulu: University of Hawaii, Center for Korean Studies, 1989.

Beesley, David. "From Chinese to Chinese American: Chinese Women and Families in a Sierra Nevada Town." *California History* 67 (September 1988): 168–79.

Bonacich, Edna, and Ivan Light. *Immigrant Entrepreneurs: Koreans in Los Angeles.* Berkeley: University of California Press, 1988.

Broom, Leonard, and John I. Kituse. *The Managed Casualty: The Japanese-American Family in World War II.* Berkeley: University of California Press, 1973.

Chai, Alice Y. "Korean Women in Hawaii, 1903–1945." In *Asian and Pacific American Experiences: Women's Perspectives,* edited by John Nobuya Tsuchida. Minneapolis: Asian/Pacific American Learning Resource Center, University of Minnesota, 1982.

————. "The Life History of an Early Korean Immigrant Woman in Hawaii." *University of Hawaii Women's Studies Program Working Papers,* Series 1 (1978): 50–59.

Chan, Sucheng. *Entry Denied: Exclusion and the Chinese Community in America, 1882–1943.* Philadelphia: Temple University Press, 1991.

————. *This Bittersweet Soil: The Chinese in California Agriculture, 1860–1910.* Berkeley: University of California Press, 1986.

Cheng, Lucie, and Edna Bonacich. *Labor Immigration under Capitalism: Asian Workers in the United States before World War II.* Berkeley: University of California Press, 1984.

Chinn, Sherry Lee. "Plum Blossoms in Winter: The Odyssey of Emancipation of Chinese Immigrant Women in the American West, 1848-1948." Master's thesis, University of Oregon, 1989.

Chinn, Thomas W. *Bridging the Pacific: San Francisco Chinatown and Its People.* San Francisco: Chinese Historical Society of America, 1989.

Cole, Cheryl L. *A History of the Japanese Community in Sacramento, 1883-1972: Organizations, Businesses, and General Response to Majority Domination and Stereotypes.* San Francisco: R & E Research Associates, 1974.

Connor, John W. "Family Bonds, Maternal Closeness, and the Suppression of Sexuality in Three Generations of Japanese Americans." *Ethos* 4 (Summer 1976): 189-222.

Daniels, Roger. *Concentration Camps, North America: Japanese in the United States and Canada in World War II.* Malabar, Fla.: Robert E. Krieger, 1981.

Daniels, Roger, et al., eds. *Japanese Americans: From Relocation to Redress.* Salt Lake City: University of Utah Press, 1986.

Friday, Chris. *Organizing Asian American Workers: The Pacific Coast Canned-Salmon Industry, 1870-1942.* Philadelphia: Temple University Press, 1994.

Fugita, Stephen S., and David J. O'Brien. *Japanese American Ethnicity: The Persistence of a Community.* Seattle: University of Washington Press, 1991.

Gee, Emma, ed. *Counterpoint: Perspective of Asian America.* Los Angeles: Asian American Studies Center, University of California, 1976.

Gesensway, Deborah, and Mindy Roseman. *Beyond Words: Images from America's Concentration Camps.* Ithaca, N.Y.: Cornell University Press, 1987.

Gillenkirk, Jeff, and James Motlow. *Bitter Melon: Stories from the Last Rural Chinese Town in America.* Seattle: University of Washington Press, 1987.

Givens, Helen Lewis. *The Korean Community in Los Angeles County.* 1939; reprint, San Francisco: R & E Research Associates, 1974.

Glenn, Evelyn Nakano. "The Dialectics of Wage Work: Japanese-American Women as Domestic Servants, 1905-1940." *Feminist Studies* 6 (Fall 1980): 432-71.

———. *Issei, Nisei, War Bride: Three Generations of Japanese American Women in Domestic Service.* Philadelphia: Temple University Press, 1986.

———. "Split Household, Small Producer, and Dual Wage Earner: An Analysis of Chinese American Family Strategies." *Journal of Marriage and the Family* 45 (February 1983): 35-46.

Glick, Clarence E. *Sojourners and Settlers: Chinese Migrants in Hawaii.* Honolulu: University of Hawaii Press, 1980.

Gregor, Kyung Sook Cho. "Korean Immigrants in Gresham, Oregon: Comunity Life and Social Adjustment." Master's thesis, University of Oregon, 1963.

Hanawa, Yukiko. "The Several Worlds of Issei Women." Master's thesis, California State University at Long Beach, 1982.

Hirata, Lucie Cheng. "Chinese Immigrant Women in Nineteenth Century California." In *Women of America: A History,* edited by Carol Berkin and Mary Beth Norton. Boston: Houghton Mifflin, 1979.

———. "Free, Indentured, Enslaved: Chinese Prostitutes in Nineteenth-Century America." *Signs* 5 (Autumn 1979): 3-29.

Hom, Marlon K. *Songs of Gold Mountain: Cantonese Rhymes from San Francisco Chinatown*. Berkeley: University of California Press, 1987.

Houston, Jeanne Wakatsuki, and James D. Houston. *Farewell to Manzanar*. Boston: Houghton Mifflin, 1973.

Hyung-Chan, Kim, and Wayne Patterson. *The Koreans in America, 1882–1974: A Chronology and Fact Book*. Dobbs Ferry, N.Y.: Oceana Publications, 1974.

Ichioka, Yuji. "*Amerika Nadeshiko*: Japanese Immigrant Women in the United States, 1900–1924." *Pacific Historical Review* 49 (May 1980): 339–57.

————. "Ameyuki-San: Japanese Prostitutes in Nineteenth-Century America." *Amerasia Journal* 4 (1977): 1–21.

————. *The Issei: The World of the First Generation Japanese Immigrants, 1885–1924*. New York: Free Press, 1988.

Ishigo, Estelle. *Lone Heart Mountain*. Los Angeles: Anderson, Ritchie & Simon, 1972.

Kang, Connie K. *Home Was the Land of the Morning Calm: A Saga of a Korean-American Family*. Reading, Mass.: Addison-Wesley, 1995.

Kessler, Lauren. *Stubborn Twig: Three Generations in the Life of a Japanese-American Family*. New York: Random House, 1993.

Kikumura, Akemi. *Through Harsh Winters: The Life of a Japanese Immigrant Woman*. Novato, Calif.: Chandler and Sharp, 1981.

Lai, Mark H., Genny Lim, and Judy Yung. *Island: Poetry and History of Chinese Immigrants on Angel Island, 1910–1940*. Seattle: University of Washington Press, 1991.

Laing, Michiyo, Carl Laing, Heihachiro Takarabe, Takuno Asako, and Stanley Umeda, eds. *Issei Christians: Selected Interviews from the Issei Oral History Project*. Sacramento, Calif.: The Issei Oral History Project, 1977.

Lee, Mary Paik. *Quiet Odyssey: A Pioneer Korean Woman in America*. Edited by Sucheng Chan. Seattle: University of Washington Press, 1990.

Levine, Gene N., and Colbert Rhodes. *The Japanese American Community: A Three-Generation Study*. New York: Praeger, 1981.

Lim, Shirley Genny, ed. *The Chinese American Experience: Papers from the Second National Conference on Chinese American Studies*. San Francisco: Chinese Historical Society of America and the Chinese Culture Foundation of San Francisco, 1984.

Lim, Geok-lin, Mayumi Tsutakawa, and Margarita Donnelly, eds. *The Forbidden Stitch: An Asian American Women's Anthology*. Corvallis, Ore.: Calyx Books, 1989.

Ling, Huping. "Surviving on Gold Mountain: Chinese-American Women and Their Lives." Ph.D. dissertation, Miami University, 1991.

Linking Our Lives: Chinese American Women of Los Angeles: A Joint Project of the Asian American Studies Center, University of California, Los Angeles, and the Chinese Historical Society of Southern California. Los Angeles: Chinese Historical Society of Southern California, 1984.

Loo, Chalsa M. *Chinatown: Most Time, Hard Time*. New York: Praeger, 1991.

Low, Victor. *The Unimpressible Race: A Century of Educational Struggle by the Chinese in San Francisco*. San Francisco: East/West, 1982.

Lukes, Timothy J., and Gary Y. Okihiro. *Japanese Legacy: Farming and Community Life in California's Santa Clara Valley*. Local History Studies, vol. 31. Cupertino: California History Center, 1985.

Lydon, Sandy. *Chinese Gold: The Chinese in the Monterey Bay Region*. Santa Cruz, Calif.: Capitola Book Co., 1985.

Lyman, Stanford M. "Marriage and Family among Chinese Immigrants to America, 1850–1860." *Phylon* 29 (Winter 1968): 321–60.

Magnaghi, Russell M. "Virginia City's Chinese Community, 1860–1880." *Nevada Historical Society Quarterly* 24 (1981): 130–57.

Masakazu, Iwata. *Planted in Good Soil: A History of the Issei in United States Agriculture*. New York: Peter Lang, 1992.

Matsumoto, David Mas. *Country Voices: The Oral History of a Japanese American Family Farm Community*. Del Rey, Calif.: Inaka Countryside Publications, 1987.

Matsumoto, Valerie. *Farming the Home Place: A Japanese American Community in California, 1919–1982*. Ithaca, N.Y.: Cornell University Press, 1993.

———. "Japanese American Women during World War II." *Frontiers* 8 (1984): 6–14.

———. "Redefining Expectations: Nisei Women in the 1930s." *California History* 73, no. 1 (Spring 1994): 44–53, 88.

McCunn, Ruthanne Lum. *Chinese American Portraits: Personal Histories, 1828–1988*. San Francisco: Chronicle Books, 1988.

———. *A Thousand Pieces of Gold: A Biographical Novel*. New York: Dell, 1983.

Melendy, H. Brett. *Asians in America: Filipinos, Koreans, and East Indians*. Boston: Twayne, 1977.

Minnick, Sylvia Sun. *Samfow: The San Joaquin Chinese Legacy*. Fresno, Calif.: Panorama West, 1988.

Miyamoto, S. Frank. *Social Solidarity among the Japanese in Seattle*. Seattle: University of Washington Press, 1984.

Modell, John. *The Economics and Politics of Racial Accommodation: The Japanese of Los Angeles, 1900–1942*. Chicago: University of Illinois Press, 1977.

———. "Japanese American Family: A Perspective for Future Investigations." *Pacific Historical Review* 37 (February 1968): 67–81.

Montero, Darrel. *Japanese Americans: Changing Patterns of Ethnic Affiliation over Three Generations*. Boulder, Colo.: Westview, 1980.

Moon, Hyung Jun. "The Korean Immigrants in America: The Quest for Identity in the Formative Years, 1903–1918." Ph.D. dissertation, University of Nevada at Reno, 1977.

Naka, Kaizo. *Social and Economic Conditions among Japanese Farmers in California*. San Francisco: R & E Research Associates, 1974.

Nakane, Kazuko. *Nothing Left in My Hands: An Early Japanese Community in California's Pajaro Valley*. Seattle: Young Pine Press, 1985.

Nakano, Mei. *Japanese American Women: Three Generations, 1890–1990*. Berkeley: Mina Press; San Francisco: National Japanese American Historical Society, 1990.

Nee, Victor, and Brett DeBary Nee. *Longtime Californ': A Documentary Study of an American Chinatown*. New York: Pantheon, 1973.

Ng, Wendy Lee. "Collective Memory, Social Networks, and Generations: The Japanese-American Community in Hood River, Oregon." Ph.D. dissertation, University of Oregon, 1989.

Noda, Kesa. *Yamato Colony, 1906–1960: Livingston, California*. Livingston, Calif.: Japanese American Citizens League, 1981.

Nomura, Gail, Russell Endo, Stephen Sumida, and Russell C. Leong, eds. *Frontiers of Asian American Studies: Writing, Research, and Commentary*. Pullman: Washington State University Press, 1989.

O'Brien, Robert. *The College Nisei*. Palo Alto, Calif.: Pacific Books, 1949.

Odo, Franklin, and Sinoto Kazuko. *A Pictorial History of the Japanese in Hawaii, 1885-1924*. Honolulu: Hawai'i Immigrant Heritage Preservation Center, Department of Anthropology, Bernice Pauahi Bishop Museum, 1985.

Okihiro, Gary. *Cane Fires: The Anti-Japanese Movement in Hawaii, 1865-1945*. Philadelphia: Temple University Press, 1991.

————. *Japanese Legacy: Farming and Community Life in California's Santa Clara Valley*. Cupertino: California History Center, 1985.

Pacific Northwest Forum 6 (Winter–Spring 1993). Theme issue, The Chinese in the Frontier Northwest.

Patterson, Wayne K. *The Korean Frontier in America: Immigration to Hawaii, 1896-1910*. Honolulu: University of Hawaii Press, 1988.

Peffer, George Anthony. "Forbidden Families: Emigration Experiences of Chinese Women under the Page Law, 1875-1882." *Journal of Ethnic History* 6 (Fall 1986): 28-46.

Rhoads, Edward J. M. "The Chinese in Texas." *Southwestern Historical Quarterly* 81 (July 1977): 1-36.

Sarasohn, Eileen Sunada, ed. *The Issei: Portrait of a Pioneer: An Oral History*. Palo Alto, Calif.: Pacific Books, 1983.

Sone, Monica. *Nisei Daughter*. Seattle: University of Washington Press, 1979.

Sung, Betty Lee. *An Album of Chinese Americans*. New York: F. Watts, 1977.

Sunoo, Harold Hakwon, and Sonia Shinn Sunoo. "The Heritage of the First Korean Women Immigrants in the United States, 1903-1924." *Korean Christian Scholars Journal* 2 (1977): 142-71.

Sunoo, Sonia Shinn. "Korean Women Pioneers of the Pacific Northwest." *Oregon Historical Quarterly* 79 (1978): 51-63.

Takaki, Ronald. *In the Heart of Filipino America: Immigrants from the Pacific Isles*. New York: Chelsea House, 1995.

Tamura, Linda. *The Hood River Issei: An Oral History of Japanese Settlers in Oregon's Hood River Valley*. Urbana: University of Illinois Press, 1993.

Tong, Benson. *Unsubmissive Women: Chinese Prostitutes in Nineteenth-Century San Francisco*. Norman: University of Oklahoma Press, 1994.

Tsuchida, John Nobuya, ed. *Reflections: Memoirs of Japanese American Women in Minnesota*. Covina, Calif.: Pacific Asia Press, 1994.

————. *Asian and Pacific American Experiences: Women's Perspectives*. Minneapolis: Asian/Pacific American Learning Resource Center and General College, University of Minnesota, 1982.

Uchida, Yoshiko. *Desert Exile: The Uprooting of a Japanese American Family*. Seattle: University of Washington Press, 1982.

Weglyn, Michi. *Years of Infamy: The Untold Story of America's Concentration Camps*. New York: Morrow, 1976.

White, Dale. "Koreans in Montana." *Asia and the Asians* 17 (1945): 156.

White-Parks, Annette. *Sui Sin Far*. Urbana: University of Illinois Press, 1995.

Wong, Jade Snow. *Fifth Chinese Daughter*. New York: Harper & Row, 1945; reprint, Seattle: University of Washington Press, 1989.

Wong, Joyce Mende. "Prostitution: San Francisco Chinatown, Mid- and Late-Nineteenth Century." *Bridge* 6 (Winter 1978–79): 23–28.

Woo, Wesley. "Protestant Work among the Chinese in the San Francisco Bay Area, 1850–1920." Ph.D. dissertation, Graduate Theological Union, 1983.

Wunder, John R. "The Chinese and the Courts in the Pacific Northwest: Justice Denied?" *Pacific Historical Review* 52 (1983): 191–211.

———. "The Courts and the Chinese in Frontier Idaho." *Idaho Yesterdays* 25 (1981): 23–32.

———. "Law and Chinese in Frontier Montana." *Montana The Magazine of Western History* 30 (1980): 18–31.

Yanagisako, Sylvia Junko. *Transforming the Past: Tradition and Kinship among Japanese Americans.* Stanford, Calif.: Stanford University Press, 1985.

Yang, Eun Sik. "Korean Women of America: From Subordination to Partnership, 1903–1930." *Amerasia Journal* 11, no. 2 (1984): 1–28.

Yo, Eui-Young. "Korean Communities in America: Past, Present, and Future." *Amerasia Journal* 10, no. 2 (1983): 23–52.

Yung, Judy. "'A Bowlful of Tears': Chinese Women Immigrants on Angel Island." *Frontiers* 2, no. 2 (Summer 1977): 52–55.

———. *Chinese Women of America: A Pictorial History.* Seattle: University of Washington Press for the Chinese Culture Foundation of San Francisco, 1986.

———. "The Social Awakening of Chinese American Women as Reported in *Chung Sai Yat Po,* 1900–1911." In *Unequal Sisters,* edited by Vicki L. Ruiz and Ellen Carol DuBois. 2d ed. New York: Routledge, 1994.

———. *Unbound Feet: A Social History of Chinese Women in San Francisco.* Berkeley, CA: University of California Press, 1995.

EURO-AMERICAN ETHNIC WOMEN

Aylesworth, Elva. "Basque Sheepherders." *Northwestern Nevada Historical Society Quarterly* 4 (1994).

Barton, Arnold H. "Scandinavian Immigrant Women's Encounter with America." *Swedish Pioneer History Quarterly* 25 (1974).

Beecher, Maureen Ursenbach. "Women's Work on the Mormon Frontier." *Utah Historical Quarterly* 49, no. 3 (1981): 276–90.

Beecher, Maureen Ursenbach, and Lavina Fielding Anderson. *Sisters in Spirit: Mormon Women in Historical Perspective.* Urbana: University of Illinois Press, 1987.

Belfiglio, Valentine J. "The Italians of Bexar County, Texas: Tradition, Change, and Intraethnic Differences." *East Texas Historical Journal* 30 (Fall 1992).

Biesanz, Mavis Hiltunen. *Helmi Mavis: A Finnish American Girlhood.* St. Cloud, Minn.: North Star Press of St. Cloud, 1989.

Blegen, Theodore. "Immigrant Women and the American Frontier." *Norwegian-American Studies and Records* 5 (1930): 26–29.

———. *Land of Their Choice: The Immigrants Write Home.* Minneapolis: University of Minnesota Press, 1955.

Bohman, Lisa Bryner. "A Fresh Perspective: The Woman Suffrage Associations of Beaver and Farmington, Utah." *Utah Historical Quarterly* 59, no. 1 (1991): 4–21.

Bushman, Claudia L. *Mormon Sisters: Women in Early Utah.* Cambridge, Mass.: Emmeline Press, 1976.

Byrne, Patricia. "Sisters of St. Joseph: The Americanization of a French Tradition." *U.S. Catholic Historian* 5, no. 3–4 (1986): 241–72.

Calof, Rachel, and J. Sanford Rikoon. *Rachel Calof's Story: Jewish Homesteader on the Northern Plains.* Bloomington: Indiana University Press, 1995.

Clar, Reva, and William M. Kramer. "The Girl Rabbi of the Golden West, Part I." *Western States Jewish History* 18, no. 2 (1986): 99–111.

Coburn, Carol K. "Learning to Serve: Education and Change in the Lives of Rural Domestics in the Twentieth Century." *Journal of Social History* 25, no. 1 (1991): 109–22.

Costa, Janeen Arnold. "A Struggle for Survival and Identity: Families in the Aftermath of the Castle Gate Mine Disaster." *Utah Historical Quarterly* 56, no. 3 (1988): 278–92.

Crawford, Charlotte. "The Position of Women in a Basque Fishing Community." In *Anglo-American Contributions to Basque Studies: Essays in Honor of Jon Bilbao,* edited by William A. Douglass, Richard W. Etulain, and William H. Jacobsen, Jr. Reno: Desert Research Institute, 1977.

DeCroos, Jean. *The Long Journey: Social Integration and Ethnicity among Urban Basques in the San Francisco Bay Region.* Reno, Nev.: Associated Faculty Press and Basque Studies Program, 1983.

di Leonardo, Micaela. "The Myth of the Urban Village: Women, Work, and Family among Italian-Americans in Twentieth Century California." In *The Women's West,* edited by Susan Armitage and Elizabeth Jameson. Norman: University of Oklahoma Press, 1987.

———. *The Varieties of Ethnic Experience: Kinship, Class, and Gender among California Italian-Americans.* Ithaca, N.Y.: Cornell University Press, 1984.

Echeverria, Jeronima. "*California-ko ostatuak*: A History of California's Basque Hotels." Ph.D. dissertation, University of North Texas, 1988.

Embry, Jessie L. "Effects of Polygamy on Mormon Women." *Frontiers* 7, no. 3 (1984): 56–61.

———. *Mormon Polygamous Families: Life in the Principle.* Salt Lake City: University of Utah Press, 1987.

———. "Mothers and Daughters in Polygamy." *Dialogue* 18, no. 3 (1985): 98–107.

Ewens, Mary, O.P. "Catholic Sisterhoods in North Dakota." In *Day In, Day Out: Women's Lives in North Dakota,* edited by Bjorn Benson, Elizabeth Hampsten, and Kathryn Sweeney. Grand Forks: University of North Dakota, 1988.

"First Jewish Lady Architect of the West: A Picture Story." *Western States Jewish History* 17, no. 1 (1984): 19–25.

Frank, Roslyn. "The Religious Role of Women in Basque Culture." In *Anglo-American Contributions to Basque Studies: Essays in Honor of Jon Bilbao,* edited by William A. Douglass, Richard W. Etulain, and William H. Jacobsen, Jr. Reno: Desert Research Institute, 1977.

Friedlander, Alice G. "A Portland Girl on Women's Rights—1893." *Western States Jewish Historical Quarterly* 10 (1978): 146–50.

Garroni, Maria Susanna. "Coal Mine, Farm and Quarry Frontiers: The Different Americas of Italian Immigrant Women." *Storia Nordamericana* [Italy] 5, no. 2 (1988): 115–36.

Gehrki, Barbara A., O.S.B. "Sister Boniface Timmins." In *Day In, Day Out: Women's Lives in North Dakota*, edited by Bjorn Benson, Elizabeth Hampsten, and Kathryn Sweeney. Grand Forks: University of North Dakota, 1988.

Godfrey, Kenneth W., Audrey Godfrey, and Jill Mulvay Derr. *Women's Voices: An Untold History of the Latter-day Saints, 1830–1900*. Salt Lake City, Utah: Deseret Book Co., 1982.

Hendrickson, Gordon Olaf, ed. *Peopling the High Plains: Wyoming's European Heritage*. Cheyenne: Wyoming State Archives and History Department, 1977.

Hoerig, Karl A. "The Relationships between German Immigrants and the Native Peoples in Western Texas." *Southwestern Historical Quarterly* 97 (January 1994): 423–51.

Holloway, Marcella M. "The Sisters of St. Joseph of Carondelet: 150 Years of Good Works in America." *Gateway Heritage* 7, no. 2 (1986): 24–31.

Iseminger, Gordon L., "Are We Germans, or Russians, or Americans? The McIntosh County German-Russians during World War I." *North Dakota History* 59 (Spring 1992): 2–16.

Johnson, Niel M. "Swedes in Kansas City: Selected Highlights of Their History." *Swedish-American Historical Quarterly* 43 (January 1992): 19–40.

Johnson, Ruth, and Elna Peterson, "The Swedish Women's Chorus of Seattle." *Swedish-American Historical Quarterly* 34, no. 4 (1983): 294–305.

Journal of the West 31 (April 1992). Issue devoted to the Irish in the West.

Kattner, Lauren Ann. "Growing Up Female in New Braunfels: Social and Cultural Adaptation in a German-Texan Town." *Journal of American Ethnic History* 9, no. 2 (1990): 49–72.

Kilpinen, Jon T. "Finnish Cultural Landscapes in the Pacific Northwest." *Pacific Northwest Quarterly* 86 (Winter 1994/95): 25–34.

Lagerquist, De Ane L. "As Sister, Wife, and Mother: Education for Young Norwegian-American Lutheran Women." *Norwegian-American Studies* 33 (1992): 99–138.

Lawson, Michael L. "Flora Langermann Spiegelberg: Grand Lady of Santa Fe." *Western State Jewish Historical Quarterly* 8 (1976): 291–308.

Lindgren, H. Elaine. "Ethnic Women Homesteading on the Plains of North Dakota." *Great Plains Quarterly* 9, no. 3 (1989): 157–73.

Lintelman, Joy K. "'America Is the Woman's Promised Land': Swedish Immigrant Women and American Domestic Service." *Journal of American Ethnic History* 8, no. 2 (1989): 9–23.

———. "'Our Serving Sisters': Swedish-American Domestic Servants and Their Ethnic Community." *Social Science History* 15, no. 3 (1991): 381–95.

Luebke, Frederick C. "Ethnic Group Settlement on the Great Plains." *Western Historical Quarterly* 8 (1977): 405–30.

Merrow, Eleanor. "Grey Nuns." In *Day In, Day Out: Women's Lives in North Dakota*, edited by Bjorn Benson, Elizabeth Hampsten, and Kathryn Sweeney. Grand Forks: University of North Dakota, 1988.

Murphy, David. "*Jejich Antonie*: Czechs, the Land, Cather, and the Pavelka Farmstead." *Great Plains Quarterly* 14 (Spring 1994): 85–106.

Murphy, Mary. "A Place of Greater Opportunity: Irish Women's Search for Home, Family, and Leisure in Butte, Montana." *Journal of the West* 31, no. 2 (1992): 73–78.

Nebraska History 74 (Fall/Winter 1993). Theme issue, The Czech-American Experience.

Olseth, Olaf H. *Mama Came from Norway.* New York: Vantage Press, 1955.

Papanikolas, Helen. *Emily-George.* Salt Lake City: University of Utah Press, 1987.

———. "Greek Immigrant Women in the Intermountain West." *Journal of the Hellenic Diaspora* 16, no. 1–4 (1989): 17–35.

———. "Magerou, the Greek Midwife." *Utah Historical Quarterly* 38 (1970): 50–60.

Paquette, Mary Grace. *Basques to Bakersfield.* Bakersfield, Calif.: Kern County Historical Society, 1982.

Ragsdale, Crystal Sasse. *The Golden Free Land: The Reminiscences and Letters of Women on an American Frontier.* Austin, Tex.: Landmark, 1976.

Reis, Elizabeth. "Cannery Row: The AFL, the IWW and Bay Area Cannery Workers." *California History* 64, no. 3 (1985): 174–91.

Richter, Anthony H. "A Heritage of Faith: Religion and the German Settlers of South Dakota." *South Dakota History* 21 (Summer 1991): 155–72.

Ross, Carl, and K. Marianne Wargelin Brown, eds. *Women Who Dared: The History of Finnish-American Women.* St. Paul: University of Minnesota, Immigration History Resource Center, 1986.

Sannes, Erling N. " 'Free Land for All': A Young Norwegian Woman Homesteads in North Dakota." *North Dakota History* 60 (Spring 1993): 24–28.

Schloff, Linda Mack. *"And Prairie Dogs Weren't Kosher": Jewish Women in the Upper Midwest since 1855.* St. Paul: Minnesota Historical Society Press, 1996.

Schow, H. Wayne. "The Scandinavians in Idaho." *Idaho Yesterdays* 36 (Winter 1993): 2–13.

Sidell, Lorraine. "Sephardic Jews of Seattle." *Western States Jewish History* 24 (April 1992): 201–13.

Sweetnam, Susan H. "Turning to the Mothers: Mormon Women's Biographies of Their Female Forebears and the Mormon Church's Expectations for Women." *Frontiers* 10, no. 1 (1988): 1–6.

Tanner, Annie Clark. *A Mormon Mother: An Autobiography.* Salt Lake City: Tanner Trust Fund, University of Utah, 1976.

Toll, William. "Jewish Families and the Intergenerational Transition in the American Hinterland." *Journal of American Ethnic History* 12, no. 2 (1993): 3–34.

Trupin, Sophie. *Dakota Diaspora: Memoirs of a Jewish Homesteader.* Lincoln: University of Nebraska Press, 1984.

Wagner, Jonathan F., "In Pursuit of *Gesundheit*: Changing Health Practices among North Dakota's German-Russians, 1890–1930." *North Dakota History* 58 (Summer 1991): 2–15.

Webster, Janet Reiff. "Domestication and Americanization: Scandinavian Women in Seattle, 1888–1900." *Journal of Urban History* 4 (1978): 275–90.

Williamson, Erik Luther. " 'Doing What Had to Be Done': Norwegian Lutheran Ladies Aid Societies of North Dakota." *North Dakota History* 57, no. 2 (1990): 2–13.

Zellick, Anna. " 'We All Intermingled': The Childhood Memories of South Slavic Immigrants in Red Lodge and Bearcreek, Montana, 1904–1943." *Montana The Magazine of Western History* 44 (Summer 1994): 34–45.

NATIVE AMERICAN WOMEN

Ackerman, Lillian. "Sexual Equality in the Plateau Culture Area." Ph.D. dissertation, Department of Anthropology, Washington State University, Pullman, 1982.

Agonito, Rosemary, and Joseph Agonito. "Resurrecting History's Forgotten Women: A Case Study from the Cheyenne Indians." *Frontiers* 6, no. 3 (Fall 1981): 8–16.

Albers, Patricia, and Beatrice Medicine. *The Hidden Half: Studies of Plains Indian Women*. Washington, D.C.: University Press of America, 1983.

Allen, Elsie. *Pomo Basketmaking: A Supreme Art for the Weaver*. Happy Camp, Calif.: Naturegraph, 1988.

Allen, Paula Gunn. *The Sacred Hoop: Recovering the Feminine in American Indian Traditions*. Boston: Beacon Press, 1986.

Arnold, Mary Ellicott. *In the Land of the Grasshopper Song: Two Women in the Klamath River Indian Country, 1908–09*. Lincoln: University of Nebraska Press, 1980.

Barrett, S. A. "Pomo Indian Basketry." *University of California Publications in American Archeology and Ethnology* 7 (1908): 133–276.

Bataille, Gretchen M., and Kathleen Mullen Sands, eds. *American Indian Women: A Guide to Research*. New York: Garland, 1991.

———, eds. *American Indian Women: Telling Their Lives*. Lincoln: University of Nebraska Press, 1984.

Bernstein, Alison R. "Outgrowing Pocahontas: Toward a New History of Indian Women." *Minority Notes* (Spring/Summer 1971): 3–8.

Berry, Carolyn. "Comenha." *Frontiers* 6, no. 3 (Fall 1981): 17–19.

Blackman, Margaret. *During My Time: Florence Edenshaw Davidson, A Haida Woman*. 2d ed. Seattle: University of Washington Press, 1992.

———. *Sadie Brower Neakok, An I'nupiaq Woman*. Seattle: University of Washington Press, 1989.

Blackwood, Evelyn. "Sexuality and Gender in Certain American Indian Tribes: The Case of Cross-Gender Females." *Signs* 10, no. 1 (1984): 27–42.

Boyer, Ruth M., and D. Gayton Narcissus. *Apache Mothers and Daughters: Four Generations of a Family*. Norman: University of Oklahoma Press, 1995.

Brave Bird, Mary, and Richard Erdoes. *Ohitika Woman*. New York: Grove Press, 1995.

Brooks, Maria. "Remembering the Reindeer Queen." *Frontiers* 6, no. 3 (Fall 1981): 59–61.

Brown, Jennifer S. H. "Métis, Halfbreeds, and Other Real People: Challenging Cultures and Categories." *History Teacher* 27, no. 1 (1993): 19–26.

———. *Strangers in Blood: Fur Trade Company Families in Indian Country*. Vancouver: University of British Columbia Press, 1980.

Colson, Elizabeth. *Autobiographies of Three Pomo Women*. Berkeley: Archaeological Research Facility, Department of Anthropology, University of California, 1974.

Croonenberghs, Lise. "Métis Women at Turtle Mountain." In *Day In, Day Out: Women's Lives in North Dakota*, edited by Bjorn Benson, Elizabeth Hampsten, and Kathryn Sweeney. Grand Forks: University of North Dakota, 1988.

Crow Dog, Mary, and Richard Erdoes. *Lakota Woman*. New York: Harper Perennial, 1991.

Cruickshank, Julie, Angela Sidney, Kitty Smith, and Annie Ned. *Life Lived like a Story: Life Stories of Three Yukon Native Elders*. Lincoln: University of Nebraska Press, 1991.

Frontiers 6, no. 3 (Fall 1981). Theme issue on Native American women.

Gray, John S. "The Story of Mrs. Picotte-Galpin, a Sioux Heroine: Eagle Woman Learns about White Ways and Racial Conflict, 1820–1868." *Montana The Magazine of Western History* 36, no. 2 (Spring 1986): 2–21.

Green, Rayna. *Native American Women: A Contextual Bibliography.* Bloomington: Indiana University Press, 1983.

———. "The Pocahontas Perplex." *Massachusetts Review* 16 (Autumn 1976): 698–714.

Hale, Janet Campbell. *Bloodlines: Odyssey of a Native Daughter.* New York: Random House, 1993.

Hogan, Linda. "Native American Women: Our Voice, the Air." *Frontiers* 6, no. 3 (Fall 1981): 1–4.

Hungry Wolf, Beverly. *The Ways of My Grandmothers.* New York: Morrow, 1980.

Hurtado, Albert L. " 'Hardly a Farm House—A Kitchen without Them': Indian and White Households on the California Borderland Frontier in 1860." *Western Historical Quarterly* 13, no. 3 (1982): 245–70.

Hussey, John A. "The Women of Fort Vancouver." *Oregon Historical Quarterly* 92, no. 3 (Fall 1991): 265–308.

Kidwell, Clara Sue. "Indian Women as Cultural Mediators." *Ethnohistory* 39 (Spring 1992): 97–107.

Klein, Laura F., and Lillian Ackerman, eds. *Women and Power in Native North America.* Norman: University of Oklahoma Press, 1995.

Koehler, Lyle. "Native Women of the Americas: A Bibliography." *Frontiers* 6, no. 3 (Fall 1981): 73–101.

Kroeber, Alfred L. "California Basketry and the Pomo." *American Anthropologist* 11, no. 2 (1909): 233–49.

LaCroix, Debbie. "Indian Boarding School Daughters Coming Home: Survival Stories as Oral Histories of Native American Women." Ph.D. dissertation, University of Oregon, 1993.

Lewis, Oscar. "Manly-Hearted Women among the North Piegan." *American Anthropologist* 43, no. 2 (1941): 173–87.

Liberty, Margot. "Hell Came with Horses: Plains Indian Women in the Equestrian Era." *Montana The Magazine of Western History* 32 (Summer 1982): 10–17.

Linderman, Frank B. *Pretty-Shield: Medicine Woman of the Crows.* New York: John Day, 1972, originally published as *Red Mother,* 1932.

Linnekin, Jocelyn. *Sacred Queens and Women of Consequence: Rank, Gender, and Colonialism in the Hawaiian Islands.* Ann Arbor: University of Michigan Press, 1990.

Lowmawaima, K. Tsianina. *They Called It Prairie Light: The Story of the Chilocco Indian School.* Lawrence: University Press of Kansas, 1994.

Lurie, Nancy O. *Mountain Wolf Woman.* Ann Arbor: University of Michigan Press, 1961.

Mankiller, Wilma, and Michael Wallis. *Mankiller: A Chief and Her People.* New York: St. Martin's, 1993.

Mathes, Valerie S. "Native American Women in Medicine and the Military." *Journal of the West* 31 (April 1982): 41–47.

Matthiasson, C. J., ed. *Many Sisters: Women in Cross-Cultural Perspective.* New York: Free Press, 1974.

McBeth, Sally. "Collaboration." In *Day In, Day Out: Women's Lives in North Dakota,* edited by Bjorn Benson, Elizabeth Hampsten, and Kathryn Sweeney. Grand Forks: University of North Dakota, 1988.

McLendon, Sally, and Brenda Shears Holland. "The Basketmaker: The Pomans of California." In *The Ancestors: Native Artisans of the Americas*, edited by Anna Curtenius Roosevelt and James G. E. Smith. New York: Museum of the American Indian, 1979.

Medicine, Beatrice. "Contemporary Literature on Indian Women: A Review Essay." *Frontiers* 6, no. 3 (Fall 1981): 122–25.

Mihesuah, Devon. *Cultivating the Rosebuds: The Education of Women at the Cherokee Female Seminary, 1851–1909*. Urbana: University of Illinois Press, 1994.

Miller, Jay, ed. *Mourning Dove: A Salishan Autobiography*. Lincoln: University of Nebraska Press, 1990.

Moore, Kimberly Beth. "'Braver Than Most and Cunning in Strategy': Historical Perspectives on Apache and Other Native American Women Warriors." Ph.D. dissertation, Texas Tech University, 1984.

Mourning Dove. *Cogewea, the Half-Blood: A Depiction of the Great Montana Cattle Range*. Lincoln: University of Nebraska Press, 1981; reprint of 1927 edition.

Murphy, Justin D. "Wheelock Female Seminary." *Chronicles of Oklahoma* (Spring 1991): 48–61.

Niethammer, Carolyn. *Daughters of the Earth: The Lives and Legends of American Indian Women*. New York: Collier, 1977.

Osburn, Katherine. "'And as the Squaws Are a Secondary Consideration': Southern Ute Women under Directed Culture Change, 1887–1934." Ph.D. dissertation, University of Denver, 1993.

Oshana, Maryann. "Native American Women in Westerns: Reality and Myth." *Frontiers* 6, no. 3 (Fall 1981): 46–50.

Parezo, Nancy J., Kelley A. Hays, and Barbara F. Slivac. "The Mind's Road: Southwestern Indian Women's Art." In *The Desert Is No Lady: Southwestern Landscapes in Women's Writing and Art*, edited by Vera Norwood and Janice Monk. New Haven, Conn.: Yale University Press, 1987.

Parsons, Elsie W. Clews, and Barbara A. Babcock, eds. *Pueblo Mothers and Children: Essays*. Santa Fe, N.M.: Ancient City Press, 1991.

Patterson, Victoria D. "Indian Life in the City: A Glimpse of Pomo Women in the 1930s." *California History* 71, no. 3 (Fall 1992): 402.

Perdue, Theda. "Cherokee Women and the Trail of Tears." *Journal of Women's History* 1 (Spring 1989): 14–30.

Peters, Virginia Bergman. *Women of the Earth Lodges: Tribal Life on the Plains*. North Haven, Conn.: Archon Books, 1995.

Peterson, Jacqueline, and Jennifer S. H. Brown, eds. *The New Peoples: Being and Becoming Métis in North America*. Lincoln: University of Nebraska Press, 1985.

Plummer, Stephen, and Suzanne Julin. "Lucy Swan, Sioux Woman: An Oral History." *Frontiers* 6, no. 3 (Fall 1981): 29–32.

Powers, Marla N. *Oglala Women: Myth, Ritual, and Reality*. Chicago: University of Chicago Press, 1986.

Ridington, Robin. *Trail to Heaven: Knowledge and Narrative in a Northern Native Community*. Iowa City: University of Iowa Press, 1988.

Shoemaker, Nancy, ed. *Negotiators of Change: Historical Perspectives on Native American Women*. New York: Routledge, 1995.

Smith, Patricia Clark, with Paula Gunn Allen. "Earthy Relations, Carnal Knowledge: Southwestern American Indian Women Writers and Landscape." In *The*

Desert Is No Lady: Southwestern Landscapes in Women's Writing and Art, edited by Vera Norwood and Janice Monk. New Haven, Conn.: Yale University Press, 1987.

Smith, Sherry L. "Beyond Princess and Squaw: Army Officers' Perceptions of Indian Women." In *The Women's West*, edited by Susan Armitage and Elizabeth Jameson. Norman: University of Oklahoma Press, 1987.

————. "A Window on Themselves: Perceptions of Indians by Military Officers and Their Wives." *New Mexico Historical Review* 64, no. 4 (October 1989): 447–61.

Smith-Ferri, Sherrie. "Basket Weavers, Basket Collectors, and the Market: A Case Study of Joseppa Dick." *Museum Anthropology* 17, no. 2 (1993): 61–66.

Sneed, Roseanna. "Two Cherokee Women." *Frontiers* 6, no. 3 (Fall 1981): 35–38.

Spector, Janet. *What This Awl Means: Feminist Archeology at a Wahpeton Dakota Village*. St. Paul: Minnesota Historical Society Press, 1993.

Stewart, Irene. *A Voice in Her Tribe: A Navajo Woman's Own Story*. Socorro, N.M.: Ballena Press, 1980.

Sutter, Virginia. "Today's Strength from Yesterday's Tradition—The Continuity of the American Indian Woman." *Frontiers* 6, no. 3 (Fall 1981): 53–57.

Thompson, Lucy [Che-na-wah Weitch-ah-wah]. *To the American Indian: Reminiscences of a Yurok Woman*. Berkeley, Calif.: Heyday Books, 1991; reprint of 1916 edition.

Trask, Huanani-Kay. *From a Native Daughter: Colonialism and Sovereignty in Hawai'i*. Monroe, Maine: Common Courage Press, 1993.

Trennert, Robert A. "Educating Indian Girls at Nonreservation Boarding Schools, 1878–1920." *Western Historical Quarterly* 13 (July 1982): 271–90.

Tsosie, Rebecca. "Changing Women: The Crosscurrents of American Indian Feminine Identity." *American Indian Culture and Research Journal* 12, no. 1 (1988): 1–37.

Underhill, Ruth, ed. *Papago Woman*. Menasha, Wisc.: The American Anthropological Association, 1936.

Van Kirk, Sylvia. *Many Tender Ties: Women in Fur-Trade Society, 1670–1870*. Norman: University of Oklahoma Press, 1983.

Vogt, Fred W., and Mary K. Mee. *They Call Me Agnes: A Crow Narrative Based on the Life of Agnes Yellowtail Deernose*. Norman: University of Oklahoma Press, 1995.

White, Gilbert. *Buffalo Bird Woman's Garden*. 1917. Reprint, St. Paul: Minnesota Historical Society Press, 1987.

Whitehead, Harriet. "The Bow and the Burden Strap: A New Look at Institutionalized Homosexuality in Native North America." In *Sexual Meanings: The Cultural Construction of Gender and Sexuality*, edited by Sherry B. Ortner and Harriet Whitehead. Cambridge, Eng.: Cambridge University Press, 1981.

Williams, Walter L. *The Spirit and the Flesh: Sexual Diversity in American Indian Culture*. Boston: Beacon Press, 1986.

Winther, Barbara. "Pomo Banded Baskets and Their Dau Marks." *American Indian Art Magazine* 10, no. 4 (1985): 50–57.

Witt, Shirley Hill. "An Interview with Dr. Annie Dodge Wauneka." *Frontiers* 6, no. 3 (Fall 1981): 64–67.

Wolcott, Harry. F. *A Kwakiutl Village and School*. Prospect Heights, Ill.: Waveland Press, 1967, 1989.

Wright, Mary C. "Economic Development and Native American Women in the Early Nineteenth Century." *American Quarterly* 33 (Winter 1981): 525–36.

LATINAS/HISPANAS

Acuña, Rudolfo A. "The Struggle of Class and Gender: Current Research in Chicano Studies." *Journal of American Ethnic History* 8, no. 2 (1989): 134–38.

Ahlborn, Richard Eighme. "The Will of a New Mexico Woman in 1762." *New Mexico Historical Review* 65, no. 3 (July 1990): 319–55.

Alarcón, Norma, Ana Castillo, and Cherríe Moraga, eds. "The Sexuality of Latinas." Special issue of *Third Woman* 4 (1989).

Alvarez, Robert, Jr. *Familia: Migration and Adaptation in Baja and Alta California, 1880–1975.* Berkeley: University of California Press, 1987.

Apodaca, María Linda. "They Kept the Home Fires Burning: Mexican-American Women and Social Change." Ph.D. dissertation, University of California at Irvine, 1994.

Aragon de Valdez, Theresa, "Organizing as a Political Tool for the Chicana." *Frontiers* 5, no. 2 (1984): 1–6.

Babcock, Barbara. " 'A New Mexican Rebecca': Imaging Pueblo Women." *Journal of the Southwest* 32, no. 4 (1990): 400–437.

Baer, Barbara, and Glenna Matthews, "The Women of the Boycott." In *America's Working Women: A Documentary History—1600 to the Present*, edited by Rosalyn Baxandall, Linda Gordon, and Susan Reverby. New York: Vintage Books, 1976.

Blackwelder, Julia Kirk. *Women of the Depression: Caste and Culture in San Antonio, 1929–1939.* College Station: Texas A&M University Press, 1984.

Blea, Irene I. "Bessemer: A Sociological Perspective of a Chicano Barrio." Ph.D. dissertation, University of Colorado, Boulder, 1980.

———. *La Chicana and the Intersection of Race, Class, and Gender.* New York: Praeger, 1992.

Broyles-González, Yolanda. "The Living Legacy of Chicana Performers: Preserving History through Oral Testimony." *Frontiers* 11, no. 1 (1990): 46–52.

———. "Toward a Re-Vision of Chicano Theatre History: The Women of El Teatro Campesino." In *Making a Spectacle: Feminist Essays on Contemporary Women's Theatre*, edited by Lynda Hart. Ann Arbor: University of Michigan Press, 1989.

Buss, Fran Leeper. *La Partera: Story of a Midwife.* Ann Arbor: University of Michigan Press, 1980.

Buss, Fran Leeper, ed. *Forged under the Sun/Forjada bajo el sol: The Life of María Elena Lucas.* Ann Arbor: University of Michigan Press, 1993.

Camarillo, Albert. *Chicanos in California.* San Francisco: Boyd and Fraser, 1984.

Campbell, Julie A. "*Madres y Esposas*: Tucson's Spanish-American Mothers and Wives Association." *Journal of Arizona History* 31, no. 2 (1990): 161–182.

Candelaria, Cordelia. "La Malinche, Feminist Prototype." *Frontiers* 5, no. 2 (1984): 1–6.

Cantarow, Ellen. "Jessie López de la Cruz." In *Moving the Mountain: Women Working for Social Change*, edited by Ellen Catarow. Old Westbury, N.Y.: Feminist Press, 1980.

Carillo, Loretta, and Thomas A. Lyson. "The Fotonovela as a Cultural Bridge of Hispanic Women in the United States." *Journal of Popular Culture* 17, no. 3 (1983): 59–64.

Carr, Irene Campos. "A Survey of Selected Literature on La Chicana." *NWSA Journal* 1, no. 2 (1988–89): 253–73.

Castañeda, Antonia I. "Gender, Race and Culture: Spanish-Mexican Women in the Historiography of Frontier California." *Frontiers* 11, no. 1 (1990): 8–20.

———. "The Political Economy of Nineteenth Century Stereotypes of Californians." In *Between the Conquests*, edited by Michael R. Orñelas. Dubuque, Iowa: Kendall Hunt Publishing, 1991.

———. "Presidarias y Pobladoras: Spanish-Mexican Women in Frontier Monterey, Alta California, 1770–1821." Ph.D. dissertation, Stanford University, 1990.

———. "Sexual Violence in the Politics and Policies of Conquest: Amerindian Women and the Spanish Conquest of California." In *Building with Our Hands: New Directions in Chicana Studies*, edited by Adela de la Torre and Beatríz M. Pesquera. Berkeley: University of California Press, 1993.

———. "Spanish and English Speaking Women on Worldwide Frontiers: A Discussion of the Migration of Women to Alta California and New Zealand." In *Western Women: Their Land, Their Lives*, edited by Lillian Schlissel, Vicki L. Ruiz, and Janice Monk. Albuquerque: University of New Mexico Press, 1988.

Castillo Crimm, Ana Carolina. "Success in Adversity: The Mexican Americans of Victoria County, Texas, 1800–1880." Ph.D. dissertation, University of Texas at Austin, 1994.

Castillo-Speed, Lillian. "Chicana Studies: A Selected List of Materials since 1980." *Frontiers* 11, no. 1 (1990): 66–84.

Castro, Rafaela. "Mexican Women's Sexual Jokes." *Aztlán* 13, no. 1–2 (1982): 275–93.

Chabram-Dernersesian, Angie. "I Throw Punches for My Race, but I Don't Want to Be a Man: Writing Us—Chica-nos (Girl, Us)/Chicanas—into the Movement Script." In *Cultural Studies*, edited by Lawrence Grossberg, Cary Nelson, and Paula Treichler. New York: Routledge, 1992.

Chávez, Carmen. "Coming of Age during the War: Reminiscences of an Albuquerque Hispana." *New Mexico Historical Review* 70, no. 4 (October 1995): 383–97.

Chávez, Ernesto. "Creating Aztlán: The Chicano Movement in Los Angeles, 1966–1978." Ph.D. dissertation, University of California at Los Angeles, 1994.

Cook, Annabel Kirschner. "Diversity among Northwest Hispanics." *Social Science Journal* 23, no. 2 (1986): 205–16.

Cortera, Marta. *The Chicana Feminist.* Austin, Tex.: Information Systems Development, 1977.

———. *Diosa y Hembra: The History and Heritage of Chicanas in the U.S.* Austin, Tex.: Information Systems Development, 1976.

Cota-Cárdena, Margarita. "The Faith of Activisits: Barrios, Cities, and the Chicana Feminist Response." *Frontiers* 14, no. 2 (1993): 51–80.

Craver, Rebecca McDowell. *The Impact of Intimacy: Mexican-Anglo Intermarriage in New Mexico, 1821–1846.* El Paso: Texas Western Press, 1982.

Cuádraz, Gloria Holguin. "Meritocracy (Un)Challenged: The Making of a Chicano and Chicana Professoriate and Professional Class." Ph.D. dissertation, University of California at Berkeley, 1993.

Davis, Marilyn. *Mexican Voices/American Dreams: An Oral History of Mexican Immigration to the United States.* New York: Henry Holt, 1990.

de la Torre, Adela, and Beatríz Pesquera. *Building with Our Hands: New Directions in Chicana Studies.* Berkeley: University of California Press, 1993.

del Castillo, Adelaída, ed. *Between Borders.* Los Angeles: Floricanto Press, 1989.

Deutsch, Sarah. "Gender, Labor History, and Chicano/a Ethnic Identity." *Frontiers* 14, no. 2 (1993): 1–22.

———. *No Separate Refuge: Culture, Class, and Gender on an Anglo-Hispanic Frontier in the American Southwest, 1880–1940.* New York: Oxford University Press, 1987.

———. "Women and Intercultural Relations: The Case of Hispanic New Mexico and Colorado." *Signs* 12, no. 4 (1987): 719–39.

Dolan, Jay, and Gilberto M. Hinojosa. *Mexican Americans and the Catholic Church, 1900–1965.* Notre Dame, Ind.: University of Notre Dame Press, 1994.

Downs, Fane. "'Travels and Trubbles': Women in Early Nineteenth Century Texas." *Southwestern Historical Quarterly* 90, no. 1 (1986): 35–56.

Durón, Clementina. "Mexican Women and Labor Conflict in Los Angeles: The ILGWU Dressmakers' Strike of 1933." *Aztlán* 15 (Spring 1989): 145–62.

Dysart, Jane. "Mexican Women in San Antonio, 1830–1860: The Assimilation Process." *Western Historical Quarterly* 6, no. 4 (October 1976): 365–75.

Elasasser, Nan, Kyle MacKenzie, and Yvonne Tixier y Vigil. *Las Mujeres: Conversations with the Hispanic Community.* Old Westbury, N.Y.: Feminist Press, 1980.

Fernández, Roberta. "*Abriendo caminos* in the Brotherland: Chicana Writers Respond to the Ideology of Literary Nationalism." *Frontiers* 14, no. 2 (1993): 23–50.

Franzen, Trisha. "Differences and Identities: Feminism and the Albuquerque Lesbian Community." *Signs* 18, no. 4 (Summer 1993): 891–906.

García, Alma M. "The Development of Chicana Feminist Discourse, 1970–1980." *Gender and Society* 3 (1989): 217–38.

García, Mario T. "The Chicana in American History: The Mexican Women of El Paso, 1880–1920: A Case Study." *Pacific Historical Review* 49, no. 2 (May 1980): 315–37.

———. *Desert Immigrants: The Mexicans of El Paso, 1890–1920.* New Haven, Conn.: Yale University Press, 1981.

García, Richard A. "Dolores Huerta: Woman, Organizer, and Symbol." *California History* 72, no. 1 (1993): 56–71.

Gaspar de Alba, Alicia. "*Tortillerismo*: Work by Chicana Lesbians." *Signs* 18, no. 4 (Summer 1993): 956–63.

Gilbert, Fabiola Cabeza de Baca. *We Fed Them Cactus.* Reprint. Albuquerque: University of New Mexico Press, 1994.

Goldsmith, Raquel Rubio. "Shipwrecked in the Desert: A Short History of the Mexican Sisters of the House of the Providence in Douglas, Arizona, 1927–1949." In *Women on the U.S.-Mexico Border: Responses to Change,* edited by Vicki L. Ruiz and Susan Tiano. Westminster, Mass.: Allen and Unwin, 1987; reprint Westview Press, 1991.

Gómez-Quiñones, Juan. *Roots of Chicano Politics, 1600–1940.* Albuquerque: University of New Mexico Press, 1994.

González, Deena J. *Refusing the Favor: Spanish-Mexican Women of Santa Fé, 1820–1880.* New York: Oxford University Press, forthcoming.

————. "La Tules of Image and Reality: Euro-American Attitudes and Legend Formation on a Spanish-Mexican Frontier." In *Building with Our Hands: Directions in Chicana Scholarship*, edited by Adela de la Torre and Beatríz M. Pesquera. Berkeley: University of California Press, 1993.

————. "The Widowed Women of Santa Fe: Assessments on the Lives of an Unmarried Population, 1850–1880." In *On Their Own: Widows and Widowhood in the American Southwest, 1848–1939*, edited by Arlene Scadron. Urbana: University of Illinois Press, 1988.

González, Michael J. "Searching for the Feathered Serpent: Exploring the Origins of Mexican Culture in Los Angeles, 1830–1850." Ph.D. dissertation, University of California at Berkeley, 1993.

González, Rosalinda M. "Chicanas and Mexican Immigrant Families, 1920–1940: Women's Subordination and Family Exploitation." In *Decades of Discontent: The Women's Movement, 1920–1940*, edited by Lois Scharf and Joan Jensen. Westport, Conn.: Greenwood Press, 1983.

————. "Distinctions in Western Women's Experience: Ethnicity, Class, and Social Change." In *The Women's West*, edited by Susan Armitage and Elizabeth Jameson. Norman: University of Oklahoma Press, 1987.

Griswold del Castillo, Richard. *La Familia: The Mexican-American Family in the Urban Southwest*. Notre Dame, Ind.: University of Notre Dame Press, 1984.

Guerín-González, Camille. *Mexican Workers and American Dreams: Immigration, Repatriation, and California Farm Labor, 1900–1939*. New Brunswick, N.J.: Rutgers University Press, 1996.

Gutiérrez, Ramón A. "Community, Patriarchy, and Individualism: The Politics of Chicano History and the Dream of Equality." *American Quarterly* 45, no. 1 (March 1993): 44–72.

————. "Ethnic and Class Boundaries in America's Hispanic Past." In *Social and Gender Boundaries in the U.S.*, edited by Sucheng Chan. Lewiston: Edwin Mellon Press, 1989.

————. "Honor, Ideology, Marriage Negotiation and Class-Gender Domination in New Mexico, 1690–1846." *Latin American Perspectives* 12, no. 1 (Winter 1985) 81–104.

————. "Marriage and Seduction in Colonial New Mexico." In *Between Borders*, edited by Adelaída del Castillo. Encino, Calif.: Floricanto Press, 1990.

————. *When Jesus Came, the Corn Mothers Went Away: Marriage, Sexuality, and Power in New Mexico, 1500–1846*. Stanford, Calif.: Stanford University Press, 1990.

Gutiérrez, Ramón and Genaro Padilla. *Recovering the U.S. Hispanic Literary Heritage*. Houston: Arte Publico Press, 1993.

Harris, Mary Ginzel. "Mexican-American Girls and Gangs: A Social Psychological View." Ph.D. dissertation, University of Southern California, 1983.

Hernández, Inés. "Sara Estela Ramírez." *Legacies* (1989): 13–26.

————. "The U.S. Southwest: Female Participation in Official Spanish Settlement Expeditions: Specific Case Studies in the Sixteenth, Seventeenth, and Eighteenth Centuries." Ph.D. dissertation, University of New Mexico, 1987.

Hernández, Salomé. "No Settlement without Women: Three Spanish California Settlement Schemes, 1790–1800." *Southern California Quarterly* 72, no. 3 (Fall 1990): 203–33.

————. "Nuevas Mexicanas as Refugees and Reconquest Settlers, 1680–1696." In *New Mexico Women: Intercultural Perspectives*, edited by Joan Jensen and Darlis Miller. Albuquerque: University of New Mexico Press, 1986.

Herrera-Sobek, María. "The Discourse of Love and Despecho: Representations of Women in the Chicano Décima." *Aztlán* 18, no. 1 (1987): 69–82.

Hondagneu-Sotelo, Pierrette. *Gendered Transitions: Mexican Experiences of Immigration.* Berkeley: University of California Press, 1994.

————. "New Perspectives on Latina Women." *Feminist Studies* 19, no. 1 (1993): 193–205.

Huaco-Nozum, Carmen Juana. "Mestiza Subjectivity: Representation and Spectatorship in Mexican and Hollywood Films." Ph.D. dissertation, University of California at Santa Cruz, 1993.

Jensen, Joan M. "Crossing Ethnic Barriers in the Southwest: Women's Agricultural Extension Education, 1914–1940." *Agricultural History* 60, no. 2: 169–81.

————. " 'Disfranchisement Is a Disgrace': Women and Politics in New Mexico, 1900–1940." *New Mexico Historical Review* 56, no. 1 (1981): 5–35.

Jones, Pamela. " 'There Was a Woman': La Llorona in Oregon." *Western Folklore* 47, no. 3 (1988): 195–211.

Kaminsky, Amy. "Gender, Race, Raza." *Feminist Studies* 20, no. 1 (Spring 1994): 7–31.

Karnig, Albert K., Susan Welch, and Richard A. Eribes. "Employment of Women by Cities in the Southwest." *Social Science Quarterly* 21, no. 4 (1984): 41–48.

Kingsolver, Barbara. *Holding the Line: Women in the Great Arizona Mine Strike of 1983.* Ithaca, N.Y.: ILR Press, 1989.

Lamphere, Louise, Patricia Zavella, and Felipe Gonzales, with Peter Evans. *Sunbelt Working Mothers: Reconciling Family and Factory.* Ithaca, N.Y.: Cornell University Press, 1993.

Laslett, John H. M. "Gender, Class, or Ethnic-Cultural Struggle? The Problematic Relationship between Rose Pesotta and the Los Angeles ILGWU." *California History* 72, no. 1 (1993): 20–39.

Lecompte, Janet. "The Independent Women of Hispanic New Mexico, 1821–1846." *Western Historical Quarterly* 12, no. 1 (1981): 17–35.

Ledesma, Irene. "Texas Newspapers and Chicana Workers' Activism, 1919–1974." *Western Historical Quarterly* 26, no. 3 (Autumn 1995): 309–31.

————. "Unlikely Strikers: Mexican-American Women in Strike Activity in Texas, 1919–1974." Ph.D. dissertation, Ohio State University, 1992.

Leonard, Karen Isaksen. *Making Ethnic Choices: California's Punjabi Mexican Americans.* Philadelphia: Temple University Press, 1992.

Loeb, Catherine. "La Chicana: A Bibliographic Survey." *Frontiers* 5, no. 2 (1984): 59–74.

Lothrop, Gloria Ricci. "Rancheras on the Land: Women and Property Rights in Hispanic California." *Southern California Quarterly* 76, no. 1 (Spring 1994): 59–84.

Malone, Ann Patton. *Women on the Texas Frontier: A Cross-Cultural Perspective.* Southwestern Studies Monograph. El Paso: Texas Western Press, 1983.

Martin, Patricia Preciado. *Songs My Mother Sang To Me: An Oral History of Mexican American Women.* Tucson: University of Arizona Press, 1992.

Martin, Patricia Preciado, and Luis Bernal. *Images and Conversations: Mexican-Americans Recall a Southwestern Past.* Tucson: University of Arizona Press, 1983.

Martínez, Elizabeth. *500 Years of Chicano History in Pictures*. Albuquerque: Southwest Organizing Project, 1991.

Martínez, Oscar J. *Border People: Life and Society in the U.S.–Mexico Borderlands*. Tucson: University of Arizona Press, 1994.

Martínez-Saldaña, Jesus. "At the Periphery of Democracy: The National Politics of Mexican Immigrants in Silicon Valley." Ph.D. dissertation, University of California at Berkeley, 1993.

McCaughan, Ed. "Chicanas and Mexicanas within a Transnational Working Class: Theoretical Perspectives." *Review* (Fernand Braudel Center) 7, no. 1 (1983): 109–50.

McDonald, Dedra S. "'The Labor Movement Was the Way': Mexican-American Women's Solidarity and Political Power in Depression-Era San Antonio." Master's thesis, University of Wisconsin, Madison, 1993.

McEwen, Bonnie G. "The Archaeology of Women in the Spanish New World." *Historical Archaeology* 25, no. 4 (1991): 33–41.

Melville, Margarita B., ed. *Mexicanas at Work in the United States*. Houston: Mexican American Studies Center, University of Houston, 1988.

———. ed. *Twice a Minority: Mexican-American Women*. St Louis: C. V. Mosby, 1980.

Miller, Darlis. "Cross-Cultural Marriages in the Southwest: The New Mexico Experience, 1846–1900." *New Mexico Historical Review* 57 (1982): 335–59.

Miranda, Gloria E. "Gente de Razón Marriage Patterns in Spanish and Mexican California: A Case Study of Santa Barbara and Los Angeles." *Southern California Quarterly* 63, no. 1 (Spring 1981): 1–21.

———. "Hispano-Mexican Childrearing Practices in Pre-American Santa Barbara." *Southern California Historical Quarterly* 65, no. 4 (Winter 1983): 307–320.

Mirandé, Alfredo, and Evangelina Enríquez. *La Chicana: The Mexican-American Woman*. Chicago: University of Chicago Press, 1979.

Monroy, Douglas. *Thrown among Strangers: The Making of Mexican Culture in Frontier California*. Berkeley: University of California Press, 1990.

Montoya, María Elaine. "Dispossessed People: Settler Resistance on the Maxwell Land Grant, 1860–1901." Ph.D. dissertation, Yale University, 1993.

Mora, Magdalena, and Adelaída del Castillo, eds. *Mexican Women in the United States: Struggles Past and Present*. Los Angeles: University of California, Chicano Studies Publications, 1980.

National Association for Chicano Studies. *Chicana Voices: Intersections of Class, Race, and Gender*. Colorado Springs, Colo.: NACS, 1990.

———. *Voces de la Mujer*. Austin: University of Texas Mexican American Studies Center, 1986.

Nelson, Kathryn J. "Excerpts from *Los Testamentos*: Hispanic Women Folk Artists of the San Luis Valley, Colorado: Oral History from Eppie Archuleta." *Frontiers* 5, no. 3 (1980): 34–43.

Orozco, Cynthia E. "The Origins of the League of United Latin American Citizens (LULAC) and the Mexican American Civil Rights Movement in Texas with an Analysis of Women's Political Participation in a Gendered Context, 1910–1929." Ph.D. dissertation, University of California at Los Angeles, 1992.

Ortiz, Flora Ida. "Hispanic American Women in Higher Education: A Consideration of the Socialization Process." *Aztlán* 17, no. 2 (1986): 125–52.

Ortiz González, Victor Manuel, "Market Identity: 'Hispanic' Entrepreneurship and Global Economic Integration in El Paso, Texas," Ph.D. dissertation, Stanford University, 1993.

Pesquera, Beatríz, "Work and Family: A Comparative Analysis of Professional, Clerical and Blue Collar Chicana Workers." Ph.D. dissertation, University of California at Berkeley, 1985.

Ponce, Mary Helen. *Hoyt Street: An Autobiography.* Albuquerque: University of New Mexico Press, 1993.

Poyo, Gerald, and Gilberto Hinojosa, eds. *Tejano Origins in Eighteenth Century San Antonio.* Austin: University of Texas Press, 1991.

Ramírez, Elizabeth C. "Hispanic and Mexican American Women on the Texas Stage, 1875-1990." In *Women and Texas History: Selected Essays*, edited by Fane Downs and Nancy Baker Jones. Austin: Texas State Historical Association, 1993.

Rebolledo, Tey Diana. *Nuestras Mujeres: Hispanas of New Mexico: Their Images and Their Lives, 1582-1992.* Albuquerque: El Norte Publications/Academia, 1992.

———. "Tradition and Mythology: Signatures of Landscape in Chicana Literature." In *The Desert Is No Lady: Southwestern Landscapes in Women's Writing and Art*, edited by Vera Norwood and Janice Monk. New Haven, Conn.: Yale University Press, 1987.

———. *Women Singing in the Snow: A Cultural Analysis of Chicana Literature.* Tucson: University of Arizona Press, 1995.

———. "*Y Dónde Estaban Las Mujeres?*: In Pursuit of an Hispana Literary and Historical Heritage in Colonial New Mexico, 1580-1840." In *Reconstructing a Chicano/a Literary Heritage*, edited by Maria Herrera-Sobek. Tucson: University of Arizona Press, 1993.

Rebolledo, Tey Diana, Erlinda Gonzáles-Berry, and Teresa Márquez. *Las Mujeres Hablan: An Anthology of Nueva Mexicana Writers.* Albuquerque: El Norte Publications, 1988.

Rebolledo, Tey Diana, and Eliana S. Rivera. *Infinite Divisions: An Anthology of Chicana Literature.* Tucson: University of Arizona Press, 1993.

Rock, Rosalind. "*Mujeres de Substancia*: Case Studies of Women of Property in Northern New Spain." *Colonial Latin American Historical Review* 2, no. 4 (Fall 1993): 425-40.

———. "'*Pido y Suplico*': Women and the Law in Spanish New Mexico, 1697-1763." *New Mexico Historical Review* 65, no. 2 (April 1990): 145-59.

Rodríguez, Gregorita. *Singing for My Echo: Memories of a Native Healer of Santa Fe.* Santa Fe: Ocean Tree Books, 1988.

Rodríguez, Maria Elena. "Roman Catholicism, Folk Medicine, and Medical Institutions." *Purview Southwest* (1991): 15-20.

Romero-Cachinero, M. Carmen. "Hispanic Women in Canada: A Framework for Analysis." *Resources for Feminist Research* [Canada] 16, no. 1 (1987): 19-20.

Rose, Margaret. "From the Fields to the Picket Line: Huelga Women and the Boycott, 1965-1975." *Labor History* 31, no. 3 (1990): 271-93.

———. "Traditional and Nontraditional Patterns of Female Activism in the United Farm Workers of America, 1962 to 1980." *Frontiers* 11, no. 1 (1990): 26-32.

———. "Women in the United Farm Workers: A Study of Chicana and Mexicana Participation in a Labor Union, 1950-1980." Ph.D. dissertation, University of California at Los Angeles, 1988.

Rozek, Barbara J. "The Entry of Mexican Women into Urban Based Industries: Experiences in Texas during the Twentieth Century." In *Women and Texas History: Selected Essays*, edited by Fane Downs and Nancy Baker Jones. Austin: Texas State Historical Association, 1993.

Ruiz, Vicki L. *Cannery Women, Cannery Lives: Mexican Women, Unionization, and the California Food Processing Industry, 1939–1950.* Albuquerque: University of New Mexico Press, 1987.

——. "The Flapper and the Chaperone: Historical Memory among Mexican American Women." In *Seeking Common Ground: Multidisciplinary Studies of Immigrant Women in the United States*, edited by Donna Gabaccia. Westport, Conn.: Greenwood Press, 1992.

——. "A Promise Fulfilled: Mexican Cannery Workers in Southern California." *Pacific Historian* 30, no. 2 (1986): 50–61.

——. "Texture, Text, and Context: New Approaches in Chicano Historiography." *Mexican Studies/Estudios Mexicanos* 2, no. 1 (1986): 145–52.

Ruiz, Vicki L., ed. "Las Obreras: The Politics of Work and Family." Special double issue of *Aztlán* 20, no. 1–2 (1993).

Ruiz, Vicki L., and Susan Tiano, eds. *Women on the United States–Mexico Border: Responses to Change.* Westminster, Mass.: Allen and Unwin, 1987; reprint ed. Westview Press, 1991.

Sabagh, Georges, and David Lopez. "Religiosity and Fertility: The Case of Chicanas." *Social Forces* 59, no. 2 (1980): 431–39.

Salas, Elizabeth. "Ethnicity, Gender, and Divorce: Issues in the 1922 Campaign by Adelina Otero-Warren for the U.S. House of Representatives." *New Mexico Historical Review* 70, no. 4 (October 1995): 367–82.

Sánchez, George J. *Becoming Mexican-American: Ethnicity, Culture, and Identity in Chicano Los Angeles, 1900–1945.* New York: Oxford University Press, 1993.

——. "'Go After the Women': Americanization and the Mexican Immigrant Woman, 1915–1929." Stanford University Center for Chicano Research Working Papers Series 6, 1984.

Sánchez, Rosaura, and Rosa Martínez Cruz, eds. *Essays on La Mujer.* Los Angeles: University of California Chicano Studies Publications, 1977.

Sánchez-Walker, Marjorie. "Woven within My Grandmother's Braid: The Biography of a Mexican Immigrant Woman, 1898–1982." Master's thesis, Washington State University, 1993.

Schuele, Donna C. "Community Property Law and the Politics of Married Women's Rights in 19th-Century California." *Western Legal History* 7 (Summer/Fall 1994): 245–87.

Schuerman, L. A. "Migration from Latin American Countries to the United States: The Economic, Social and Reproductive Lives of Hispanic Female Immigrants, 1980." *International Migration* [Switzerland] 29, no. 4 (1991): 573–99.

Segura, Denise. "Chicana and Mexican Immigrant Women at Work: The Impact of Class, Race, and Gender on Occupational Mobility." *Gender and Society* 3, no. 1 (March 1989): 37–52.

——. "Chicana and Mexican Immigrant Women in the Labor Market: A Study of Occupational Mobility and Stratification." Ph.D. dissertation, University of California at Berkeley, 1986.

———. "Chicanas in White-Collar Jobs: 'You Have to Prove Yourself More.'" *Sociological Perspectives* 35, no. 1 (1992): 163–82.

Segura, Denise, and Beatríz Pesquera. "Beyond Indifference and Apathy: The Chicana Movement and Chicana Feminist Discourse." *Aztlán* 19, no. 2 (Fall 1988–1990): 69–92.

Sheridan, Thomas. *Los Tucsonenses*. Tucson: University of Arizona Press, 1986.

Sosa Riddell, Adaljiza. "Chicanas and El Movimiento." *Aztlán* 5, no. 2 (Spring and Fall 1974): 155–65.

Stephen, Elizabeth Hervey, and Frank D. Bean. "Assimilation, Disruption and the Fertility of Mexican-Origin Women in the United States." *International Migration Review* 26, no. 1 (1992): 67–88.

Stoller, Marianne. "The Hispanic Women Artists of New Mexico: Present and Past." *El Palacio* 92, no. 1 (1986): 21–25.

———. "'Pergrinas' with Many Visions: Hispanic Women Artists of New Mexico, Southern Colorado, and Texas." In *The Desert Is No Lady: Southwestern Landscapes in Women's Writing and Art*, edited by Vera Norwood and Janice Monk. New Haven, Conn.: Yale University Press, 1987.

Strachwitz, Chris, with James Nicolopulos, eds. *Lydia Mendoza: A Family Autobiography*. Houston: Arte Público Press, 1993.

Tiano, Susan. *Patriarchy on the Line: Labor, Gender, and Ideology in the Mexican Maquila Industry*. Philadelphia: Temple University Press, 1995.

Tigges, Linda. "Santa Fe Landownership in the 1880s." *New Mexico Historical Review* 68, no. 2 (April 1993): 153–80.

Treviño, Roberto R. "*La Fe*: Catholicism and Mexican Americans in Houston, 1911–1972." Ph.D. dissertation, Stanford University, 1993.

Trotter, Robert T., and Juan Antonio Chavira. *Curanderismo*. Athens: Unversity of Georgia Press, 1981.

Trujillo, Armando L. "Community Empowerment and Bilingual/Bicultural Education: A Study of the *Movimiento* in a South Texas Community." Ph.D. dissertation, University of Texas at Austin, 1993.

Trujillo, Carla, ed. *Chicana Lesbians: The Girls Our Mothers Warned Us About*. Berkeley, Calif.: Third Woman Press, 1991.

Velez, María Luisa. "The Pilgrimage of Hispanics in the Sisters of Charity of the Incarnate Word." *U.S. Catholic Historian* 9, no. 1–2 (1990): 181–94.

Weber, Devra Anne. "*Raiz Fuerte*: Oral History and Mexicana Farmworkers." *Oral History Review* 17, no. 2 (Fall 1989): 47–62.

Wiersema, Joy. "Patriotism, Pragmatism, and Prostitution: Interplay of Class, Political, Gender, and Medical Issues in the Borderlands." *New Mexico Historical Review* 70, no. 4 (October 1995): 399–416.

Williams, Linda. "Type and Stereotype: Chicano Images in Film." *Frontiers* 5, no. 2 (1984): 14–17.

Williams, Norma. *The Mexican American Family: Tradition and Change*. Boston: G. K. Hall, 1990.

Ybarra, Lea. "When Wives Work: The Impact on the Chicano Family." *Journal of Marriage and the Family* 44, no. 1 (February 1982): 169–78.

Yohn, Susan M. "An Education in the Validity of Pluralism: The Meeting between Presbyterian Mission Teachers and Hispanic Catholics in New Mexico, 1870–1912." *History of Education Quarterly* 31, no. 3 (1991): 343–64.

————. *A Contest of Faiths: Missionary Women and Pluralism in the American Southwest*. Ithaca, N.Y.: Cornell University Press, 1996.

Zavella, Patricia. " 'Abnormal Intimacy': The Varying Work Networks of Chicana Cannery Workers." *Feminist Studies* 11, no. 3 (Fall 1985): 541–57.

————. "The Impact of 'Sun Belt Industrialization' on Chicanas." *Frontiers* 8, no. 1 (1984): 21–27.

————. "Reflections on Diversity among Chicanas." *Frontiers* 12, no. 2 (1991): 763–85.

————. *Women's Work and Chicano Families: Cannery Workers of the Santa Clara Valley*. Ithaca, N.Y.: Cornell University Press, 1987.

Zinn, Maxine Baca. "Gender and Ethnic Identity among Chicanos." *Frontiers* 5, no. 2 (1984): 14–18.

————. "Mexican-American Women in the Social Sciences." *Signs* 8, no. 2 (1982): 259–72.

Contributors

ELIZABETH JAMESON is a coeditor of *The Women's West* (1987). She is associate professor of history at the University of New Mexico.

SUSAN ARMITAGE is a coeditor of *The Women's West* (1987). She is professor of history at Washington State University and editor of *Frontiers: A Journal of Women Studies*.

JAMES F. BROOKS is assistant professor of history at the University of Maryland, College Park. He took his B.A. in history and anthropology at the University of Colorado, Boulder, and his Ph.D. at the University of California, Davis. His dissertation, "Captives and Cousins. Violence, Kinship, and Community in the New Mexico Borderlands, 1680–1880," investigates the historical construction of slavery, identity, and community in the American West.

TERRI BRYAN is a Ph.D. candidate at the University of New Mexico. She has taught at UNM and at the Technical Vocational Institute (TVI) in Albuquerque. As she completes her dissertation, she's raising a precocious three-year-old and acts as director of marketing communications for a Reuters venture in educational software.

SUCHENG CHAN is Professor and Chair of the Department of Asian American Studies at the University of California, Santa Barbara. She has written and edited ten books and has received seven prizes for her scholarly writing.

CHRISTINE CONTE is director of communications for the Arizona chapter of the Nature Conservancy. Before joining that organization, she was director of the Old Pueblo Museum in Tucson. Conte holds master's degrees in anthropology and museum studies from the University of Arizona and a Ph.D. in cultural anthropology from The New School for Social Research. In addition to her work among the Navajo, she has researched women's traditional arts in West Africa, developing a collection for the Smithsonian Institution. Conte lives in Tucson with her husband and son.

LYNDA F. DICKSON is associate professor and chair of sociology at the University of Colorado, Colorado Springs. Her teaching and research areas include the sociology of family, race, and ethnic relations and poverty. In addition to her article in this volume, she has published "The Colored Women's Club Home Association" and "Black Clubwomen in Denver," both in *Black Women in America* (1993).

JERONIMA (JERI) ECHEVERRIA is professor and chair of history at California State University, Fresno. Among her earliest and fondest memories are those of the southern

California sheep ranch where she grew up, the Spanish Basque parents who raised her there, and the ethnic boardinghouse she visited with her family on Sundays and special occasions. In these settings, she developed an early appreciation of and curiosity about Basques and their immigration to America. Echeverria earned her M.A. and Ph.D. in history at the University of North Texas. Her history of Basque boardinghouses in the American West is forthcoming from the University of Nevada Press, and she is coediting an anthology on Basques in the history of the Western Hemisphere with Richard Etulain.

LISA E. EMMERICH is associate professor of history and American Indian studies at the California State University, Chico. Her research concentrates on American Indian women and federal efforts to assimilate them in the late nineteenth and early twentieth centuries. She is the author of three articles dealing with the field matron program.

RAMONA FORD is professor of sociology at Southwest Texas State University. Her degrees are from Baker University, Indiana University, The New School for Social Research, and Southern Illinois University. She teaches and publishes in the area of ethnic relations, gender studies, and industrial sociology. Her current research is on Native American women of the past and present.

DEE GARCEAU earned a Ph.D. in American civilization from Brown University. She founded the Desert Writers' Workshop, sponsored annually in Moab, Utah, by Canyonlands Field Institute and the Utah Endowment for the Humanities. She has served on the history faculty at the University of Montana and as research editor for several multimedia productions. Currently she teaches American women's history and Native American history at Rhodes College in Memphis, Tennessee. Her research interests center on issues of gender and bicultural identity.

ALBERT L. HURTADO is associate professor and director of graduate studies in the Arizona State University Department of History. He has published widely in the fields of western and American Indian history. His books include *Indian Survival on the California Frontier* (1988) and, as editor with Peter Iverson, *Major Problems in American Indian History* (1994).

MARGARET D. JACOBS received her Ph.D. in American history from the University of California, Davis, in 1996. Her interests lie in the history of the West, of women, and of Native Americans. Her dissertation concerns how changes in white women's notions of gender and sexuality at the turn of the century transformed their views of and interactions with Pueblo Indians.

ROBERT H. KELLER, JR., is a graduate of the University of Chicago, author of *American Protestantism and U.S. Indian Policy* (1983) and contributor to a book in honor of Wallace Stegner from the University of New Mexico Press. He is currently finishing a book on national parks and Indian policy. Since retiring from Fairhaven College, Bellingham, Washington, he has worked with the Whatcom County Land Trust.

JUNEAL LEVERSEE is an editor with ABC-Clio in Santa Barbara, working with the *America: History and Life* reference series. She holds an M.A. in history from the

University of Oregon and has completed course work toward a Ph.D. in the Department of History at the University of New Mexico.

YOLANDA CHÁVEZ LEYVA is a Ph.D. candidate in history at the University of Arizona. She received her M.A. in border history at the University of Texas at El Paso. Her research and publications focus on the interplay of ethnicity, gender, and sexuality in the lives of Mexicanas and Chicanas. Growing up on *la frontera*, she learned early on the challenges and the lessons of living on the margins. She continues to incorporate these lessons in her research, her writing, and her teaching.

DEDRA S. McDONALD is a doctoral student in the Department of History at the University of New Mexico. Her research interests include western women, the American West, and women in colonial Latin America. She is the compiler of *Guide to the Spanish and Mexican Manuscript Collection at the Catholic Archives of Texas* (1994).

VALERIE MATSUMOTO is an associate professor of history and Asian American studies at the University of California at Los Angeles. She is the author of *Farming the Home Place: A Japanese American Community in California, 1919–1982* (1993). Presently she is researching Nisei women writers and artists in the 1930s.

LAURIE MERCIER received her Ph.D. in history from the University of Oregon and is currently assistant professor of history at Washington State University-Vancouver and program director of the Center for Columbia River History. Her article in this volume, originally published in *Montana The Magazine of Western History*, is part of her larger dissertation study on labor, gender, and cultural politics in Anaconda between 1934 and 1980. She is author of several essays on oral history and Montana women's history.

DARLIS A. MILLER, professor of history, teaches western history at New Mexico State University. She coauthored with Joan Jensen the award-winning essay "The Gentle Tamers Revisited: New Approaches to the History of Women in the West." She also coedited with Jensen *New Mexico Women: Intercultural Perspectives* (1986). She has published three other books on the American West and is currently researching the life of western illustrator and writer Mary Hallock Foote.

SHIRLEY ANN WILSON MOORE received her Ph.D. in U.S. history from the University of California at Berkeley in 1989 and is associate professor of history at California State University, Sacramento. Her areas of specialty are African American western, urban, and migrational history. She is completing her first book, *To Place Our Deeds: The Black Community in Richmond, California, 1910–1963*. Moore is also a singer and songwriter and has performed her one-woman show, "Women's Lives in Song: Workers, Wives, Mothers, Daughters, Lovers and Wild Women," for audiences around California.

GAIL M. NOMURA is director of the Asian/Pacific American Studies Program and faculty member of the Program in American Culture and of the Residential College at the University of Michigan. She is president of the Association for Asian American Studies for 1995–97. She has coedited two anthologies, *Frontiers of Asian American Studies* and *Bearing Dreams, Shaping Visions: Asian Pacific American Perspectives*, and has published numerous chapters and articles on the history of Asian Americans, particularly in Hawaii and the Pacific Northwest, and on Asian American women. She is completing a book, *Contested Terrain: Asian Americans on the Yakima Indian Reservation.*

CYNTHIA E. OROZCO is currently a postdoctoral fellow at the Center for Regional Studies at the University of New Mexico. She held a Ford Foundation postdoctoral fellowship at the University of Texas at Austin, is a past visiting professor of history at the University of Texas at San Antonio, and was a research associate at the Texas State Historical Association, where she wrote over seventy-five encyclopedic entries about Tejana and Tejano history for the *New Handbook of Texas.* She is the author of the forthcoming book, *No Mexicans Allowed: The Rise of the Mexican American Civil Rights Movement.*

GENARO PADILLA is associate professor of English and vice chancellor for under-graduate affairs at the University of California at Berkeley. His publications include *My History, not Yours: The Formation of Mexican American Autobiography* (1993) and *The Recovery of the U.S. Hispanic Literary Tradition,* coedited with Ramón Gutiérrez (1993).

MARY PARDO, who received her Ph.D. in sociology from the University of California at Los Angeles in 1990, teaches in the Department of Chicano Studies at California State University, Northridge. She is currently at work on a book-length study of the grassroots activism of Mexican American women.

PEGGY PASCOE is Beekman Professor of Western History at the University of Oregon. She is the author of *Relations of Rescue: The Search for Female Moral Authority in the American West, 1874–1939* (1990) and is currently at work on a history of miscegenation law, tentatively entitled *What Comes Naturally: Race, Sex, and Marriage Law in the United States, 1870 to the Present.*

MARIAN PERALES is a Ph.D. candidate at The Claremont Graduate School. Her research interests are in nineteenth-century intellectual and cultural history, Chicano/a history, and women and religion. She is currently completing research on her dissertation on late-nineteenth-century Mexican healing.

B. ANN RODGERS is a fourth-generation Texan and schoolmarm. She received her B.A. in history at Angelo State University in 1980, taught high school world history for ten years, received her M.A. in American history in 1992 from the University of Texas at San Antonio, and is currently working on a Ph.D. in women and gender history at the University of New Mexico.

ALICIA I. RODRÍQUEZ-ESTRADA, a native Californian, received her B.A. and M.A. in American history from the University of California, Davis. She is a Ph.D. candidate in American history/American studies at The Claremont Graduate School and is currently completing her dissertation, entitled "Playing the Part: Gender, Race, and Representation in U.S. Cinema, 1926–1964."

VICKI L. RUIZ is professor of history and women's studies at Arizona State University. She is the author of *Cannery Women, Cannery Lives* (1987); co-editor of

Unequal Sisters (1990, 1994); *Western Women: Their Land, Their Lives* (1988); and *Women on the U.S.-Mexican Border.* Her book *From Out of the Shadows: A History of Mexicans in the United States, 1900–1995* is forthcoming. Ruiz formerly held an endowed chair at The Claremont Graduate School.

EVELYN A. SCHLATTER earned her M.A. in anthropology at the University of Denver. She is currently a Ph.D. candidate in the Department of History at the University of New Mexico.

LINDA SCHOTT grew up on a cattle ranch in the Texas hill country. She attended college at Baylor University, earning a B.A. in history and German in 1979. She then attended Stanford University, where she earned an M.A. in history in 1982 and a Ph.D. in history and humanities in 1986. She is currently associate professor of history at the University of Texas at San Antonio and the director of the Center for the Study of Women and Gender. She is the author of *Reconstructing Women's Thoughts: The Ideas of the Women's International League for Peace and Freedom before World War II* (1996).

COLL-PETER THRUSH is a graduate of the Law and Diversity Program at Fairhaven College, the interdisciplinary wing of Western Washington University in Bellingham. Among other things, he has been a cave guide, ethnohistorian, gay rights activist, forest ranger, and university administrator. His articles on Pacific Northwest history have appeared in the *Western Historical Quarterly and Pacific Northwest Forum.* Thrush is currently a graduate student and Smith Fellow in the Department of History at the University of Washington. He lives in Seattle with his partner, Simon Martin.

WENDY L. WALL is a visiting assistant professor at Duke University. She is completing her dissertation at Stanford University on competing efforts to construct an American nationalism against the backdrop of World War II and the cold war.

ANNETTE WHITE-PARKS is an associate professor of English at the University of Wisconsin–La Crosse. Her research and teaching specialty is multicultural literature. She is author of *Sui Sin Far/Edith Maude Eaton: A Literary Biography*, winner of the 1995 Association for Asian American Studies Book Award for Cultural Studies, and coeditor of *Mrs. Spring Fragrance and Other Stories* by Sui Sin Far.

Index